The Oxford Handbook of Cross-Cultural Organizational Behavior

OXFORD LIBRARY OF PSYCHOLOGY
AREA EDITORS

Clinical Psychology
David H. Barlow

Cognitive Neuroscience
Kevin N. Ochsner and Stephen M. Kosslyn

Cognitive Psychology
Daniel Reisberg

Counseling Psychology
Elizabeth M. Altmaier and Jo-Ida C. Hansen

Developmental Psychology
Philip David Zelazo

Health Psychology
Howard S. Friedman

History of Psychology
David B. Baker

Methods and Measurement
Todd D. Little

Neuropsychology
Kenneth M. Adams

Organizational Psychology
Steve W. J. Kozlowski

Personality and Social Psychology
Kay Deaux and Mark Snyder

The Oxford Handbook of Cross-Cultural Organizational Behavior
Michele J. Gelfand and Miriam Erez

OXFORD LIBRARY OF PSYCHOLOGY

The Oxford Handbook of Cross-Cultural Organizational Behavior

Edited by

Michele J. Gelfand

Miriam Erez

OXFORD
UNIVERSITY PRESS

OXFORD
UNIVERSITY PRESS

Oxford University Press is a department of the University of Oxford. It furthers the University's objective of excellence in research, scholarship, and education by publishing worldwide. Oxford is a registered trade mark of Oxford University Press in the UK and certain other countries.

Published in the United States of America by Oxford University Press
198 Madison Avenue, New York, NY 10016, United States of America.

CIP data is on file at the Library of Congress

ISBN 978–0–19–008538–4

DOI: 10.1093/oxfordhb/9780190085384.001.0001

Printed by Integrated Books International, United States of America

MIX
Paper
FSC FSC® C183721

CONTENTS

ABOUT THE EDITORS

Michele J. Gelfand is the John H. Scully Professor of Cross-Cultural Management and Professor of Organizational Behavior at the Stanford Graduate School of Business School and Professor of Psychology by Courtesy. Gelfand uses field, experimental, computational, and neuroscience methods to understand the evolution of culture and its multilevel consequences. She has won numerous awards for her scholarship and been published in outlets such as *Science*, the *Proceedings of the National Academy of Sciences*, and the *Journal of Personality and Social Psychology*, among others. Gelfand is the founding co-editor of the *Advances in Culture and Psychology* series and the author of *Rule Makers, Rule Breakers: How Tight and Loose Cultures Wire the World.* She is a member of the National Academy of Sciences, American Academy of Arts and Sciences and the Council on Foreign Relations.

Miriam Erez is a Professor Emeritus in Organizational Psychology and Management, at Faculty of Data and Decision Sciences (former Faculty of Industrial Engineering and Management), Technion, Israel Institute of Technology. She is the Vice Dean of the MBA program and Founder, and Chair of the Knowledge Center for Innovation, Technion. Erez's research areas are innovation and entrepreneurship, cross-cultural, global organizational behavior, and work motivation. She has authored two books, co-edited four books, and published over 100 journal papers and book chapters. She serves as the Vice-Dean of the Academy of Management Fellows Group. Erez is the recipient of the Israel Prize, 2005, The distinguished Scientific Contributions Award, by the International Association of Applied Psychology 2002, and SIOP Distinguished Scientific Contirbutions Award, 2023.

CONTRIBUTORS

Soon Ang
Distinguished University Professor and Professor of Management, Nanyang Technological University, Singapore

Zeynep Aycan
Koç Holding Chair of Management and Strategy, Koç University, Turkey

Jeanne M. Brett
DeWitt W. Buchanan, Jr. Professor Emerita of Dispute Resolution and Organizations, Northwestern University, USA

Alexander I. Butler
Graduate Student in Psychology, University of Maryland, USA

Wayne F. Cascio
Distinguished University Professor of Management Emeritus, University of Colorado, Denver, USA

Gilad Chen
Robert H. Smith Chair in Organizational Behavior, University of Maryland, USA

Terence Chia
Research Associate, University of Western Australia, Australia

Callen C. Clegg
Business Manager, Hiscox, Germany

David G. Collings
Chair of Sustainable Business, Trinity College, Dublin, Ireland

Ilya R. P. Cuypers
Associate Professor of Strategy, Singapore Management University, Singapore

Youtha Cuypers
Assistant Professor in Strategy, Universidade NOVA de Lisboa, Portugal

Mary Sully de Luque
Professor of Global Management and Leadership, Arizona State University, USA

Elif Gizem Demirag Burak
Ph.D. Candidate, Koç University, Turkey

Emmy Denison
CORE Technology Associate, Comcast, USA

Eva Derous
Professor of Personnel Psychology, Ghent University, Belgium

Julie V. Dinh
Assistant Professor of Organizational Behavior & Human Resource Management, University of Houston, USA

Selin Eser Erdil
Assistant Professor, Social Sciences University of Ankara, Turkey

Miriam Erez
Professor Emeritus, Vice Dean MBA program, Faculty of Data and Decision Sciences, Technion, Israel

Weiqiao Fan
Chair Professor of Applied Psychology, Shanghai Normal University, China

Yanran Fang
Assistant Professor of Leadership and Organization Management, Zhejiang University, China

Matthew Farrell,
Assistant Professor of Management and Marketing, Austin Peay State University, Tennessee, USA

Maria Cristina Ferreira
Professor of Psychology, Salgado de Oliveira University, Brazil

Donald L. Ferrin
Professor of Organizational Behavior & Human Resources, Singapore Management University, Singapore

Ronald Fischer
Professor of Psychology, Victoria University of Wellington, New Zealand

Emily E. Forgo
Graduate Student in Psychology, University of Maryland, College Park, USA

C. Ashley Fulmer
Assistant Professor of Management, Georgia State University, USA

Michele J. Gelfand
John H. Scully Professor of Cross-Cultural Management and Professor of Organizational Behavior and Psychology (by courtesy), Stanford University, USA

Cristina B. Gibson
University Professor and Dean's Distinguished Professor of Management, Pepperdine University, USA

Nicole Gillespie
KPMG Chair in Organizational Trust and Professor of Management, University of Queensland, Australia

Paul J. Hanges
Professor of Industrial/ Organizational Psychology, University of Maryland, USA

William Q. Judge
E. V. Williams Endowed Chair of Strategic Leadership, Old Dominion University, Virginia, USA

Bradley L. Kirkman
General (Retired) H. Hugh Shelton Distinguished Professor of Leadership, North Carolina State University, USA

Mila B. Lazarova,
Canada Research Chair in Global Workforce Management, Simon Fraser University, Canada

Frederick T. L. Leong
Retired Professor of Psychology, Michigan State University, USA

Mengting Li
Assistant Professor, Renmin University, China

Leigh Anne Liu
Professor and Director of the Institute of International Business, Georgia State University, USA

Ella Miron-Spektor
Associate Professor of Organizational Behavior, INSEAD, France

Christof Miska
Associate Professor of Global Business and Trade, Vienna University of Business and Economics, (WU, Vienna) Austria

Aiden Norouzi
Professor of Economics and Finance, Virginia Wesleyan University, Virginia, USA

Shaul Oreg
: Professor of Organizational Behavior, The Hebrew University of Jerusalem, Israel

Susannah B. F. Paletz
: Associate Professor College of Information Systems, University of Maryland, USA

Niti Pandey
: Dean of the School of Education and Professional Studies, Eastern Connecticut State University, USA

Dorota Piaskowska
: Associate Professor of Strategy and International Business, University College, Dublin, Ireland

Jana L. Raver
: E. Marie Shantz Professor of Organizational Behaviour, Queen's University, Canada

B. Sebastian Reiche
: Professor of the Department of Managing People in Organizations and Associate Director of Faculty, University of Navarra, Spain

Thomas Rockstuhl
: Associate Professor, Leadership, Management and Organisation, Nanyang Technological University, Singapore

Maria A. Rodas
: Assistant Professor of Business Administration and Shebik Centennial Fellow, University of Illinois at Urbana-Champaign, USA

Deborah E. Rupp
: Professor of Psychology, George Mason University, USA

Ann Marie Ryan
: Professor of Organizational Psychology, Michigan State University, USA

Lise Saari
: Adjunct Professor of Industrial/Organizational Psychology, Baruch College and New York University, USA

Eduardo Salas
: Professor and Chair of the Department of Psychological Sciences, Rice University, USA

Suraj Sharma
: Postdoctoral Fellow, California State University, Northridge, USA

Jie (Doreen) Shen
: Data Scientist, Meta, USA

Winny Shen
: Associate Professor of Organizational Studies, York University, Canada

Kristen M. Shockley
: Associate Professor of Psychology, University of Georgia, USA

Rukman Singh
: Associate Professor of Law and Practice, Pepperdine University, USA

Paul E. Spector
: Adjunct Distinguished Professor, University of South Florida, USA

Günter K. Stahl
: Professor of International Management and Director of the Centre for Sustainability Transformation and Responsibility (STaR), Vienna University of Business and Economics (WU Vienna), Austria

Noga Sverdlik
: Senior Lecturer in Psychology, Ben-Gurion University of the Negev, Israel

Carlos J. Torelli
: Anthony J. Petullo Professor of Business Administration, University of Illinois at Urbana-Champaign, USA

Mo Wang
University Distinguished Professor, University of Florida, USA

Ting Wang
Master of Higher Education Science, Shanghai Normal University, China

S. Arzu Wasti
Professor of Management and Organization Studies, Sabancı University, Turkey

PART I

Fundamental Theoretical and Methodological Issues in Cross-Cultural Organizational Behavior Research

CHAPTER 1

Frontiers of Cross-Cultural Organizational Behavior: An Introduction to the Volume

Michele J. Gelfand *and* Miriam Erez

Abstract

The quest to understand work behavior has been a global concern since antiquity. Yet, global perspectives in organizational behavior (OB) have only recently become a theoretical and empirical force within the field. Joining this intellectual momentum, contributors to this volume have collectively paved the way for a new global revolution in the field of organizational behavior. This chapter highlights common themes across all the Handbook chapters, including the call to (1) increase the global scope in the questions we ask and the contexts we study; (2) broaden our cultural toolkit to unpack the proximal and distal factors that explain cultural differences; (3) understand the complexity of the global context and the duality of global integration with local responsiveness; (4) focus on the dynamics of culture across levels of analysis; (5) cross-fertilize research in cross-cultural OB; and (6) build bridges between theory and practice.

Key Words: cross-cultural organizational behavior, multilevel theory, globalization, cultural values, norms

Cross-cultural organizational behavior (CCOB) has a long past and a short history. Although the scientific study of organizational behavior began in the twentieth century, interest in human behavior at work can be traced back thousands of years. The Greek philosophers discussed the importance of matching individuals to their abilities (e.g., Plato's *The Republic*; Williamson, 2008), and the first systematic employee selection system (i.e., the "imperial examination") was developed in China as early as the Han Dynasty. Questions of what constitutes fairness and effective leadership are found in the Old Testament (Wright & Goodstein, 2007), the Qur'an (Mukred Mohsen, 2007), and other ancient texts. Predating *Getting to Yes* by centuries, negotiation principles can be found in Sun Tzu's *The Art of War* (Ko, 2003). Even discussions of "mergers" between people of different cultures were discussed as early as Herodotus in 550 BC in *The Histories,* and were well documented in Marco Polo's travels along the Silk Road between 1271 and 1295.

Clearly, the quest to understand work behavior has been a global concern since antiquity. Yet, even though questions regarding work transcend time and space, global perspectives in organizational behavior (OB) have only recently become a theoretical and empirical force within the field. With increasing global interdependence and mobility, virtually all areas in OB have begun to broaden their global scope with increasing theoretical and methodological sophistication (Gelfand et al., 2017).

Joining this intellectual momentum, contributors to this volume have collectively paved the way for a new global revolution in the field of organizational behavior. The *Oxford Handbook of Cross-Cultural Organizational Behavior* consists of 28 chapters organized in six sections that span multiple levels of analysis. Micro, meso, and macro scholars provide the most recent and compelling evidence for the proposition that global perspectives are essential to understanding organizational behavior. *Part I* of the *Handbook* begins with a discussion of *Fundamental Theoretical and Methodological Issues in Cross-Cultural OB Research. Part II* focuses on *Culture and Organizational Entry*, including culture and recruitment and selection, training and development, appraisal and management of performance, and careers across the lifespan. *Part III* turns to *Culture and Individual Behavior in Organizations*, focusing on cultural influences on motivation, job attitudes, justice, creativity, deviance, and stress and well-being. *Part IV* moves to *Culture and Social Dynamics in Organizations*, with chapters on cultural influences on trust, leadership, teams, communication, and conflict and negotiation. *Part V* examines *Culture at the Organizational Level*, including culture and social networks, strategic management, and organizational change. *Part VI turns* to the *Cross-Cultural Organization Interfaces*, including culture and work–family dynamics, culture and consumer behavior, global mobility, joint ventures and alliances, multinational enterprises and Global HRM (human resource management), cultural intelligence and global identity, and corporate social responsibility and sustainability. The final chapter analyzes the research–practice interface and gaps within cross-cultural OB.

In each chapter, the authors reflect on seminal theories and empirical discoveries that we have achieved, and then they provide a thoughtful window into the future of research in cross-cultural OB. With a science–practitioner model in mind, they also identify key practical insights for managers operating in this brave new globalized world. In addition to looking back on past discoveries and forecasting exciting future opportunities, the chapters draw attention to a much deeper concern with the philosophy of science on which the field of OB is based. It is a historical accident that OB and related fields started in the West. Thus, we must ask: What if the field had started in Africa, the Middle East, or Asia? How would our constructs, theories, and even the questions we ask be similar and different? To date, much of the work in the field still implicitly assumes that the phenomena we study are *etic*, or universal, and

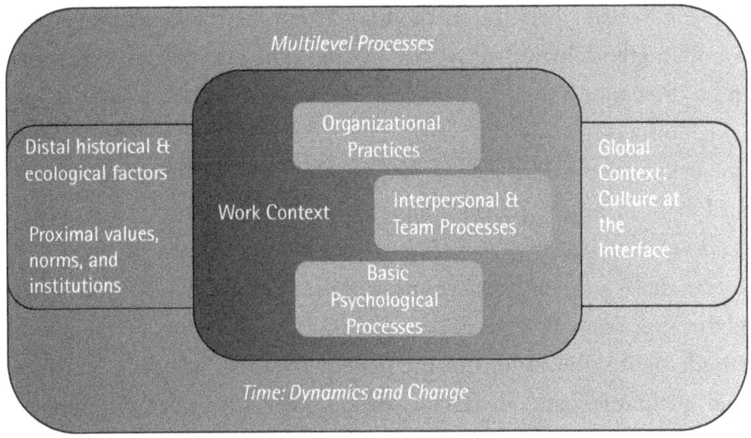

Figure 1.1 Cross-Cultural Organizational Behavior

that human beings share an underlying common "true" nature. The chapters remind us to challenge this Western hegemony and to incorporate global voices across all areas of CCOB.

We are thrilled to feature this diverse territory in cross-cultural organizational behavior (CCOB) under one intellectual roof (Figure 1.1). This framework illustrates that the field is truly multilevel—spanning from the individual to group to organization—which are all situated in specific work contexts. In turn, all these processes are embedded in cultures with their own proximal values, norms, and institutions, and more distal ecological and historical pressures. Moreover, all of these processes can change over time, making the study of CCOB truly dynamic. The field also captures the *cultural interface*, as people, teams, and organizations all interact in the global ecosystem. In this respect, the field of CCOB not only seeks to truly globalize the largely Western-based theory traditions that dominate our scholarship, but also has a keen eye toward solving real problems—from managing organizational change, expatriation and repatriation to virtual global team interactions, mergers and acquisitions, corporate responsibility, and beyond.

Road Map of the Book

The *Handbook of Cross-Cultural Organizational Behavior* is designed to provide a comprehensive view of culture and organizational behavior that should be of broad interest to scholars, practitioners, and laypeople alike. Here we provide a glimpse into each chapter and end with a summary of the collective wisdom they provide for the road ahead.

Part I explores *Fundamental Theoretical and Methodological Issues in Cross-Cultural OB Research*. In their chapter, "Culture and Organizations: Theoretical and Methodological

Perspectives," Fischer and Ferreira set the foundation for the book by reviewing recent theoretical and methodological advances in the study of culture and organizations. They begin by discussing values frameworks used to study culture in the organizational literature, including Hofstede, Schwartz, and the GLOBE (Global Leadership and Organizational Behavior Effectiveness) project, along with more recent work on social norms, social axioms, honor and face logics, and cultural archetype models. They also highlight *emic* (culture-specific) constructs, including Brazilian *jeitinho brasileiro* and Chinese *guanxi,* among others. Fischer and Ferreira then cover recent advances in evolutionary and dynamic approaches to understanding cultural dynamics. Finally, they discuss several methodological innovations in the field of CCOB, including multilevel models, big data, and qualitative data, as well as methodological transparency, replicability, and validity of measures across cultures. They conclude with a discussion of ongoing challenges, including the need for greater nuance beyond simple culture-fit arguments and the need to adopt frameworks, such as polyculturalism, to understand the increasing complexity of modern societies.

Part II focuses on *Culture and Organizational Entry.* In Chapter 3, "Recruiting and Selecting with Culture in Mind: Insights and Emerging Issues," Ann Marie Ryan and Eva Derous discuss classic research on cultural variation recruiting and selection practices across cultures. They highlight areas where culture may have both a direct and moderating impact on the selection process. They then turn to the intercultural interface of recruitment and selection, exploring how best to select for cultural competence in expatriate assignments. Next, the authors discuss how culture interacts with technological changes in recruitment and assessment methods. For example, social media may interact with traditional cultural forms of networking to influence the referral process and candidates' information-gathering on companies. Technology may also interact with culture in the form of algorithms that are becoming more prominent in the recruitment–selection process. Algorithms that do not take culture into account may introduce unintended bias into the process. Ryan and Derous suggest that rather than studying the methodological advances afforded by technology, future research should focus on reactions to technological changes that may be most influenced by culture.

In Chapter 4, "Cross-Cultural Studies of Career Theories," Frederick Leong, Weiqiao Fan, Mengting Li, and Ting Wang review cross-cultural work-related career trajectories. After a brief overview of cultural validity (i.e., whether theories and models are valid and predictive across cultures) and cultural specificity (i.e., how concepts and models specific to cultures explain and predict behavior), the authors review whether key career theories are generalizable to other cultures. Specifically, they examine cross-cultural comparisons of Super and colleagues' career-development theory, trait and factor theories of vocational interests (e.g., Holland's hexagonal model), and social cognitive career theories (Lent et al., 1994) before discussing cross-cultural studies of career indecision theories. They note that most studies still use and generalize findings from Western samples, with a paucity of studies examining the predictive validity of career theories across cultures. They call for making the examination of culture-specific aspects of vocational psychology a priority.

Next, in Chapter 5, "Culture and Learning, Training, and Development," Julie Dinh and Eduardo Salas examine the impact of culture across all stages of the training process. They first discuss how culture affects *training analysis*—when data is gathered on the needs of the organization, task, and participants. Next, they discuss *training design* and the importance of matching training design strategies to cultural needs. The next stages, *training development* and *training implementation,* involve building, pilot testing, and deploying training programs, and the authors highlight the importance of how the trainee–trainer match affects training outcomes. For *training evaluation,* the authors recommend that trainers measure multiple outcomes (e.g., satisfaction, knowledge, attitudes) using a variety of methods, given that simple self-report measures may not accurately gauge training outcomes. In the final stage, *training transfer,* Dinh and Salas note that to maximize continued on-the-job learning, managers should consider both national and organizational culture when designing opportunities for practice and feedback.

In Chapter 6, "Culture and Performance Management at Individual and Team Levels," Zeynep Aycan and Elif Burak synthesize research on the role of culture in three stages of performance management (PM): goal setting, performance appraisal, and rewards and reinforcements. They first describe research showing that the meaning and preference for goal-setting methods differ across cultures, and then they note that specific cultural practices (e.g., *guanxi, wasta*) may make it difficult to implement Western performance-management systems in other cultures. Next, they review cultural differences in desired performance-appraisal systems, as well as in preferences for giving and receiving positive and negative feedback. Finally, the authors discuss ways in which culture influences preferences for rewards: preferred type of reward (i.e., financial, and social incentives), method of distribution (i.e., equality, equity, or need), and criteria (i.e., merit vs. seniority and individual vs. team). In all, they illustrate that culture can moderate the relationship between PM practices and outcomes. A key to managing performance across cultures, they suggest, is to balance standardization and localization by either slowly introducing practices that may not align with cultural values or "regionalizing" practices to blend global and local values.

Part III explores *Culture and Individual Behavior in Organizations.* In Chapter 7, "The Study of Work Motivation across Cultures: A Review and Directions for Future Research," Gilad Chen and Bradley Kirkman review work motivation research, including the concepts of goal choice and goal striving, as well as integrative models and antecedents of goal processes across cultures. At the individual level, the authors discuss the effects of culture on preferences for prosocial, supervisory-set, and/or pursuing multiple goals that involve risk, as well as the impact of group-focused motivational interventions over individual involvement across cultures. At the collective level, the authors highlight various findings demonstrating both the direct and indirect effects of culture on group performance. Noting that most research has focused on one cultural value and motivational outcome at a time, they encourage researchers to better integrate national cultural differences with more comprehensive models of motivation. The authors also suggest that managers of multicultural teams should carefully assess their employees' cultural values to adopt motivational techniques matched to their unique team.

In Chapter 8, "Culture and Job Attitudes," S. Arzu Wasti and Selin Erdil review cross-cultural differences in the antecedents and consequences of job attitudes. They first discuss cross-cultural work on job conditions (job demands and resources), leadership, organizational practices, and the economic context, noting both the direct and moderating effects of culture on job attitudes. Next, they review findings on the consequences of job attitudes across cultures, including the outcomes of turnover intentions, the effect of perceived organizational support (POS) on organizational citizenship behavior (OCB), and the outcomes of job embeddedness. They recommend that research integrate cultural and structural perspectives, and they test organizational- and individual-level mediators and moderators. Moreover, they discuss how understanding the relationship between culture and job attitudes can help managers navigate culture change, retain immigrant employees, and manage talent and new work arrangements.

In Chapter 9, "Reconsidering Assumptions about Organizational Justice through the Lens of Culture and Moral Philosophy," Niti Pandey and Deborah Rupp review research on justice across cultures. Beginning at the individual level of analysis, they detail cultural universals and specificity in notions of distributive, procedural, and interactional justice, as well as important moderators of these effects. Next, they synthesize research on culture and employment practices, including ethical and abusive supervision/leadership, human resource management strategies, and organizational justice climates. Finally, they introduce several schools of moral philosophy—namely, Rawls's theory of justice, Kantian deontology, utilitarianism, natural law, feminist traditions, Hinduism, Confucianism, and Buddhism—and they integrate them with distinct aspects of culture. Given the growing momentum of social justice movements across the globe, they conclude by stressing the importance of organizational justice for employee well-being, and they urge the field to move beyond typically Western philosophical conceptions of justice.

In Chapter 10, "Culture and Creativity in Organizations: New Directions and Discoveries," Ella Miron-Spektor and Susannah Paletz synthesize research on creativity in individuals and teams across cultures. They begin by examining different approaches to the study of culture and creativity, including cultural values, tightness–looseness, logics, and implicit theories. They note that researchers also have begun to use "cultural bundles" (Yong et al., 2020), which consider cultural values along with cultural tightness, and to examine within- and between-cultural variance and the impact of context on the connection between culture and creativity. Next, the authors focus on findings specific to creativity, multicultural experiences, and cross-cultural teams. Multicultural experiences are generally associated with higher levels of creativity, and while multicultural teams have historically been found to be more creative, the authors highlight the importance of considering the specific types of heterogeneity found in teams to accurately predict their creativity. Finally, they discuss the need to focus on specific cultural configurations of teams, use different creativity tasks, consider different conceptions of culture, examine the psychological processes that underlie creativity in different cultures, and test whether current findings hold in extreme conditions, such as times of crisis.

Next, in Chapter 11, "Culture and Workplace Deviance," Jana Raver synthesizes the current literature on culture and workplace deviance, defined as any voluntary behavior by a member of an organization that violates organizational norms and threatens the well-being of the organization and/or its members, including bullying, aggression, counterproductive work behavior, harassment, incivility, and abusive supervision. After mapping this conceptual space, she discusses the nature and comparability of deviance across cultures, including whether scales that assess deviance have equivalence across cultures. Next, she reviews how culture influences the overall prevalence of workplace deviance from both a proximal cultural-values perspective and a distal climate–economic perspective. She then examines the moderating role of culture in the relationship between workplace deviance and negative outcomes for targets. Lastly, she reviews the literature on culture and enacting deviance. She calls for increasing methodological sophistication (e.g., moving beyond country-as-culture assumptions, conducting large-scale studies across multiple countries rather than just two) and examining additional dimensions of culture beyond Hofstede and/or GLOBE cultural values.

In Chapter 12, "Occupational Stress in the Global World," Paul Spector synthesizes global research on occupational stress. He first reviews the differences between cross-cultural (CC) studies, which examine an aspect of culture that might vary at the individual, group, or country level, and cross-national (CN) studies, which examine differences between countries without considering any specific cultural elements. He also provides an overview of the types of approaches used in CC/CN research, including single-country studies, two-country studies, multicountry studies that analyze data at the country level, and multilevel studies that analyze data at both the person and country level. He then reviews scale-development studies and whether they illustrate measurement equivalence/invariance to support comparisons across cultures. Next, Spector examines cross-national studies that compare two or more cultures without specifically considering cultural dimensions, work examining cross-national differences in occupational stressors, and CC/CN studies of emotional labor. Lastly, Spector reviews work on the role of specific cultural values (typically individualism–collectivism) in differences in occupational stress. Spector ultimately calls for research on how culture contributes to differences in stressors and strains, moderators of stressor-strain relationships, and whether they differ across cultures.

Part IV examines *Culture and Social Dynamics in Organizations.* In Chapter 13 "Culture and Trust in Organizational Contexts," C. Ashley Fulmer, Donald Ferrin, Emily Denison, and Nicole Gillespie review work on the interplay between trust and culture in organizations. Their review highlights that cultural values directly shape how trust is conceptualized and how it moderates the effects of trust on other organizational outcomes, such as creativity, initiative-taking, and knowledge transfer. They first examine culture at the regional and individual level. Next, they review research on trust in intercultural relationships, such as strategic alliances, expatriate assignments, and multicultural virtual teams. Finally, the authors review research that conceptualizes trust as culture. Specifically, these studies tend to consider generalized trust as a cultural dimension shared by members of a society that affects various organizational outcomes, both directly and as a moderator. They conclude by calling for more systematic research on neglected topics, such as distrust, trust calibration, and motivation to trust, and promising methodologies, including agent-based modeling, actor–partner interdependence models, and network models.

In Chapter 14, "Leaders, Followers, and Culture: The Entangled Triangle," Paul Hanges, Emily Fargo, and Alexander Butler review literature on leadership and culture. They begin by defining leadership as "a dyadic or group level emergent phenomenon resulting from the dynamic, asymmetric influence process actively co-created by both leaders and followers over time." Next, they integrate DeRue's (2011) dynamic model of adaptive leadership, which frames leadership in terms of a "double interact" between leaders and followers that varies on two dimensions: magnitude of leading/following (i.e., the frequency of leading/following double interacts in a group) and dispersion of leadership (i.e., whether the leadership role is usually enacted by one group member or shared by members over time). The authors hypothesize that culture influences the dispersion and magnitude of double-interaction patterns and review extant research that supports this perspective. For example, they predict that groups from cultures higher in power distance would show lower levels of dispersion (one person is likely to consistently act as the leader) and higher levels of magnitude (followers expect frequent direction from leaders) in the double-interact method. Their new dynamic perspective of leaders and followers challenges the way we study leadership across cultures and expands both theory and practice.

In Chapter 15, "The Technology-Enabled, Task-Specific, and Time-Variant Role of Culture in Teams," Cristina Gibson, Terence Chia, and Rukman Singh explore research from the past decade on the role of culture in three specific team features: technology, task, and time. After reviewing seminal studies in this area, which generally examine the main effects of culture on teams, they focus on more complex interactions of culture and the team context. First, reviewing research on the interplay of culture and technology in teams, they find that some work suggests that technology mitigates the effects of culture, while other studies suggest that technology exacerbates the effects of culture in teams. Second, they review research investigating whether the role of culture in teams depends on the task being conducted or the type of team. They summarize both conceptual and empirical work with varying definitions of culture (e.g., diversity, language, country, cultural dimensions, organizational culture), each noting a unique and often moderating relationship between team tasks, culture, and various outcomes, most notably on innovation. Third, they illustrate how the effects of culture in teams may change over time depending on the situational context. In all, they present a dynamic view of culture in teams that promises to open new directions in the field.

Next, in Chapter 16, "Culture and Communication," Suraj Sharma and Leigh Anne Liu focus on the mutual constitution of culture and communication. They discuss early research that focused on stable and static influences of culture on communication, generally regarding cultural differences as negative barriers to be overcome. For example, cultural differences in perceptions of time and space, thinking styles (holistic vs. analytic), and communication styles (high- vs. low-context) were regarded as sources of miscommunication. Later work has shifted to studying culture as a dynamic process in communication, focusing on how norms, motivations, and mental models affect communication across situational contexts. Sharma and Liu then examine three key avenues through which communication interacts with and shapes culture: (1) language, (2) nonverbal communication and emotions, and (3) music. In all, they illustrate the need to take a more holistic and dynamic approach to culture and communication that focuses on temporal, spatial/contextual, inter- and intrapersonal, and inter- and intracultural influences.

In Chapter 17, "Culture and Conflict and Negotiation Strategy," Jeanne Brett summarizes research on cultural differences in the use of negotiation strategy in two specific domains: deal making and conflict management. She begins with cultural differences in the use of value-claiming versus value-creating strategies that are predicted by the interplay of cultural trust and tightness–looseness. In contrast to research from Western cultures, value-claiming strategies are not found to be as detrimental in non-Western cultures, as they require negotiators to reveal less information directly while offering insight into their priorities based on when they concede versus hold firm on an issue. As a result, value-claiming strategies may be particularly beneficial in low-trust contexts. Turning next to culture and conflict management, Brett reviews new research on how honor, dignity, and face cultures differ in their emotional responses to conflict, confrontations of conflict, and use of third parties. She concludes with insights into the future of intercultural negotiation research with an eye toward leveraging AI technology.

Part V showcases research on *Culture at the Organizational Level.* In Chapter 18, "Culture and Social Networks," Mo Wang and Yanran Fang synthesize research on culture and social networks. They argue that both culture and social networks function at multiple levels (e.g., individual, group, organizational, national) and evolve dynamically over time. They then summarize the effects of different levels of culture on social networks, including how macro-level culture shapes the structure, density, interconnectedness, and complexity of social networks; how meso-level organizational and team-level culture impact network structure and the relationships employees form with each other; and how micro-level factors, such as cultural identification, influence personal social networks. Next, they discuss the role of social networks in shaping culture and acculturation processes. They argue that sociocentric networks shape culture at the macro and meso levels, in that people in a given cluster have been shown to develop more homogeneous beliefs over time as they interact. Additionally, at the organizational level, interorganizational network structure and dynamics have been found to influence industry culture over time. Finally, at the micro level, egocentric social networks have been found to play a strong role in the acculturation process for expatriates and immigrants, particularly in terms of reducing the stress of resettlement and shaping personal perceptions of cultural identity. In all, they provide a much-needed perspective on a microstructural approach to cultural differences.

Next, in Chapter 19, "National Culture and Strategic Management," William Judge, Aiden Norouzi, and Matthew Farrell review research on the influence of national culture on strategic management, focusing on two sub-branches of the field of strategy: *strategy content*, which focuses on how firms determine which strategies work best, and *strategy process*, which aims to understand the strategy-formation process. With respect to strategy content, they review research on cultural values and cultural distance, along with institutional factors related to the risk of the entry mode strategy and merger and acquisition (M&A) strategies across time, along with culture and financial and risk management strategy, foreign direct investment and diversification strategy, and strategy regarding operations, entrepreneurial orientation, and innovation management. Next, they focus on culture and strategy processes, including corporate governance processes, organizational trust processes, and knowledge transfer within multinational firms, along with culture and corporate control processes, innovation processes, entry mode processes, alliance formation processes, organizational learning processes, strategic renewal processes, and strategic decision processes, among others. The authors expand the dominant paradigms in strategic management to incorporate key aspects of culture.

In Chapter 20, "National Culture and Organizational Change," Noga Sverdlik and Shaul Oreg discuss how best to manage organizational change across cultures. They begin by synthesizing research on how national culture affects both the content of organizational change and the process by which changes are made (i.e., how they are communicated, level of employee participation). They also note that culture affects individual members' responses to change, such as their dispositional resistance and commitment to change, and moderates the relationship between change management and members' responses to change. They then introduce a taxonomy of cultural change with three distinct cultural dimensions: cultural rigidity, affective reactance, and routine seeking. Empirically, they show which aspects of culture are relevant to each dimension and how these dimensions are correlated with other societal indices, including economic and technological development and national well-being. They also highlight how national culture relates to organizational change by considering how each dimension theoretically relates to the initiation of change, the nature of change, and the process through which change is introduced and managed.

Part VI focuses on the *Cross-Cultural Organization Interfaces*. In Chapter 21, "Culture and Work–Family Dynamics," Winny Shen and Kristen Shockley synthesize cross-cultural work–family research, including work-interference-with-family (WIF; when work intrudes upon the family domain), and family-interference-with work (FIW; when family intrudes upon the work domain). Specifically, culture often moderates the relationships between work–family conflict and its correlates. For example, they note that WIF and FIW are more strongly related to outcomes in individualistic cultures than in collectivistic ones. They emphasize that while new approaches to examining culture are emerging, most research on work–family conflict and culture still uses the country as a proxy for culture and ignores large areas of the world, such as Africa, the Middle East, and South Asia. Studies also tend to ignore work–family enrichment and balance. They end their chapter with a call for new theoretical and methodological innovations in the field.

Next, in Chapter 22, "Culture and Consumer Behavior: A Review and Agenda for Future Research," Carlos Torelli, Jie (Doreen) Shen, and Maria Rodas review the influence of culture on consumer behavior through three distinct approaches: the dimensional approach, the dynamic-constructivist approach, and the consumer theory of marketplace cultures. The dimensional approach breaks culture down into a handful of dimensions that have been used to predict how consumers attend to and process information in order to develop persuasive ads. The dynamic-constructivist approach argues that culture is not a general underlying process that continually influences a person's thoughts and actions but rather a set of implicit theories and values that can be activated by environmental stimuli. The authors note that this approach has been used to identify the specific contexts that make culture salient and important to consumer behavior, especially among bicultural individuals. The third approach, consumer culture theory, explores how consumers develop collective identities around brands and bestow them with cultural meaning. They also pay special attention to multiculturalism, or culture mixing, in products and brands, and the multilevel factors that affect evaluations of such products.

In Chapter 23, "Shifts in Research on Global Mobility," Mila Lazarova, B. Sebastian Reiche, and Callen Clegg identify seven key shifts in the literature on expatriation. The first shift is the move to distinguish traditional corporate expatriates, who are sent abroad and are financially supported by their employers, from self-initiated expatriates. Second, organizations now use a variety of strategies to manage global mobility, including permanent transfers to other countries, various types of "flexpatriation" that leverage the ease of travel, and "global domestics," whose jobs are simultaneously global and completely virtual. Third, expatriate research has broadened its focus to other stakeholders beyond expatriates to consider family members, host country nationals, the local community, and the wider organization. Fourth, definitions of expatriate success have broadened to include career advancement, employability, and work–life balance. Fifth, the field is beginning to acknowledge that repatriation is not merely a set period of time when employees transition back to their previous job, but rather a process that involves reconciling substantial changes in the individuals themselves, their work roles, and the broader social context. Sixth, global mobility research has grown in its theoretical orientation, leading to growing theoretical fragmentation and a need for theoretical integration. Finally, the field is experiencing increasing methodological sophistication, which holds promise for the questions being asked about global mobility.

In Chapter 24, "National Culture and Alliances," Youtha Cuypers, Dorota Piaskowska, and Ilya Cuypers synthesize the literature on the effects of culture and cultural distance on cross-border alliances, which are "voluntary arrangements between two or more independent firms (from different home countries) made with the intention to share, exchange and/or jointly develop resources, products, or services." First, they systematically review what is known about the influences of culture and cultural distance on partner identification and selection, alliance negotiations, and alliance design and governance choices. Thereafter, they focus on postformation alliance management, including communication, trust, conflict, and cooperative learning. Lastly, they focus on the impact of culture on the financial performance of the alliance or the parent firm, alliance longevity, stability of the governance structure, and perceptual outcomes, such as satisfaction with the alliance. They call for exploration of the mechanisms underlying the impact of cultural distance and cultural traits on alliances, consideration of the positive effects of culture on alliances, better integration of research across different alliance stages, and examination of other culture-related concepts beyond cultural distance and cultural traits.

In Chapter 25, "Multinational Enterprises and Global Human Resource Management," Wayne Cascio and David Collings review the literature on international human resource management (IHRM) in multinational enterprises (MNEs). After detailing how IHRM differs from domestic HRM, in terms of scope, risk, and tensions to find a strategic balance between global and local practices, they next discuss how MNEs employ strategic IHRM. They summarize four key influences that shape IHRM strategies: country-of-origin effects, host country effects, dominance effects (which refers to the assumption that economies that are more "dominant" in the international capitalist system must have developed better HRM practices), and international integration (which focuses on linking units of MNEs across borders). They also discuss several controversies that have arisen in global HRM research, such as whether globalization only benefits large corporations and is contributing to stagnating wages, and whether global HRM practices are converging or diverging. They highlight several boundary conditions on global HRM practices and key questions for the field to examine in the next decade.

In Chapter 26, "Cultural Intelligence and Global Identity: Complementarity in Global Leadership," Soon Ang, Thomas Rockstuhl, and Miriam Erez review the burgeoning literature on cultural intelligence (CQ) and global identity (GI) across different levels of analysis. They begin with a discussion of the ways in which CQ is distinct from cultural competence, personality, international experience, and other types of intelligence (e.g., IQ, EQ), and related to outcomes such as well-being, decision making, and job and leadership performance. Next, they review research on GI, which is distinct from constructs such as cosmopolitanism and bicultural and multicultural identities, and they show its connection to multicultural team success and global leadership effectiveness. They view global identity and cultural intelligence as a person's global capital, strengthened by their accumulated global experiences. A combination of CQ and GI can help global leaders achieve three goals at the firm level: (1) internationalizing local firms; (2) sustaining their global competitive advantage; and (3) resolving global-local conflict, mostly by balancing global and local identity. Ang et al. also discuss the potential "dark sides" of CQ and global identity.

In Chapter 27, "Culture and Corporate Social Responsibility and Sustainability," Günter Stahl, Mary Sully de Luque, and Christof Miska discuss emerging research on culture and corporate social responsibility and sustainability (CSR/CS). CSR is defined as a "firm's consideration of, and response to, issues beyond the narrow economic, technical, and legal requirements of the firm" (Davis, 1973, p. 312) and CS as "a development that meets the needs of the present without compromising the ability of future generations to meet their own needs" (WCED, 1987, p. 43). They review the extant literature by separating comparative and intercultural/multicultural perspectives as well as distinguishing between responsible/sustainable (i.e., "doing good") and irresponsible/unsustainable practices (i.e., "avoiding harm"). They describe research showing which cultural dimensions are implicated in the propensity for both behaviors before discussing three prototypical approaches to transnational CSR/CS issues: cultural dominance, cultural accommodation, and cultural synergy in promoting responsible behaviors. They conclude with numerous CSR/CS-related challenges that need to be leveraged against local and global norms: diversity and inclusion, ethics, sustainability, and human rights. The chapter offers a clear agenda for assessing the connection between cultural practices, values, and strategies to handle CSR/CS.

Finally, in Chapter 28, "The Research-Practice Gap in Cross-Cultural Organizational Psychology and Behavior: Practitioners' Perspectives," Lise Saari closes the handbook with a discussion of the gaps between research and practice in CCOB. The chapter draws on the cross-cultural literature, with a special emphasis on practitioner-oriented publications and on interviews conducted with organizational psychologists with years of experience working with international companies. Saari begins with a discussion of the major cross-cultural theories that practitioners have used in practice. She then discusses key lessons that practitioners embrace, that are not widely featured in the literature. These lessons include using global teams to design and implement projects to maximize cross-cultural effectiveness; considering how local labor and privacy laws differ between countries when developing programs; knowing the importance of thorough translations; and being cautious when comparing ratings across countries. Saari concludes by outlining ongoing gaps between research and practice and offering key takeaways and future directions for both theory/research and practitioners.

Cross-Cultural Perspectives in Organizational Behavior: The Road Ahead

Research in this volume illustrates that we are entering an era in which global perspectives are beginning to infiltrate all topics in organizational behavior. Once a field that was largely *culture-bound* (i.e., tested its theories only on American samples) and *culture blind* (i.e., did not consider culture as an important factor in organizational research) (Bond & Smith, 1996), OB is increasingly encompassing cross-cultural perspectives in all areas of scholarly inquiry, ranging from micro studies of culture and motivation, attitudes, stress, creativity, and deviance, to meso topics such as leadership, conflict, negotiation, communication, and teams, to macro topics, including social networks, HRM practices, strategy, global mobility, and joint ventures. The field is beginning to broaden both its theoretical scope to incorporate different aspects of culture and its methodological toolbox to include sophisticated ways of establishing equivalence before testing hypotheses, testing multilevel models, and using meta-analyses to examine trends across diverse research domains. At a meta-theoretical level, the field is increasingly questioning the Western hegemony of our constructs, measures, and theories. Authors across the volume provide a much-needed critical evaluation of many theories in the field that were assumed to be universal but now require expansion and/or modification in other areas of the globe. From theories about the role of voice in justice, the effect of participation in goal setting, what constitutes effective performance, or how organizational change is managed, the authors make clear that findings from the West often need to be challenged, revised, and expanded when considering the global context of OB.

The authors provide much collective wisdom about how the science of cross-cultural OB can be radically improved in the coming decades. A number of common themes can be distilled across all the chapters, including the need to (1) increase the global scope in the questions we ask and the contexts we study; (2) broaden our cultural toolkit to unpack the proximal and distal factors that explain cultural differences; (3) understand the complexity of the global context and recognize the duality of global integration with local responsiveness; (4) focus on the dynamics of culture across levels of analysis, (5) cross-fertilize research in cross-cultural OB that has been siloed; and (6) build bridges between theory and practice. Next, we briefly highlight their hopes and visions for the future of the field.

Expanding Our Global Scope. While cross-cultural perspectives are becoming more common in OB, the authors show that the field is still very narrow in scope. Overall, attention to cross-cultural perspectives in our journal space is still remarkably low. Top journals, such as the *Journal of Applied Psychology,* have featured culture in approximately 2% of their articles over the last 100 years (Gelfand et al., 2017). Even within cross-cultural OB, the scope of our work is highly limited, with the vast majority of samples drawn from the East and West, and samples from Africa, Latin America, and the Middle East largely excluded. While there has been a gradual global shift in the field, it can be characterized as reflecting small but steady incremental changes that are still the exception rather than the norm.

Many also question whether the questions being asked in cross-cultural organizational OB, as well as the constructs, theories, and measures, are fundamentally infused with Western values and assumptions (Gelfand et al., 2008). "Modern science emerged within a particular sociohistorical context [in which] the values of liberalism, individualism, and capitalism, [are] primary," Sampson noted (1978, 1334). These values are often invisible in our science, and yet they affect the questions we find worthy of study and those we do not. CCOB research is no exception; it has largely been pioneered in the West and may be laden with culture-specific values and norms (e.g., freedom of choice, the pursuit of happiness, personal satisfaction) and sociopolitical realities (e.g., affluence, relative social tranquility) that risk being exported to cultures where other values and norms (interdependence, religiosity) and concerns with corruption, poverty, job insecurity, and violence loom larger (Gelfand et al., 2008). Moreover, we may be missing important aspects of culture that are important in other cultures across the globe. Indeed, many of the contributors throughout the volume call for more work on emic constructs, such as paternalistic leadership, the evil eye, *guanxi, wasta, jeitinho, moqi,* and core concepts from Hinduism, Confucianism, and Buddhism to shed new light on OB phenomena around the world. The authors also note that expanding our constructs and questions deemed worthy of study are not only critical for capturing neglected global voices; they also identify neglected dimensions that may be relevant in Western contexts. For example, Ramesh and Gelfand (2010) showed that *family embeddedness*—a construct critical for predicting actual turnover in India—is also a predictor of turnover in the United States. Ultimately, by gaining knowledge of emic constructs, we can begin to build a global science of OB.

Broadening our multilevel cultural toolkit. This handbook indicates that scholars are increasingly expanding their toolkits to "unpackage" cultural influences on OB phenomena. Yet, they also show that the field still largely relies on a narrow set of values at the national level (e.g., Hofstede) to the neglect of other values, norms, sociostructural factors (e.g., networks), and power relations. Moreover, a number of authors question whether national boundaries, some of which are admittedly arbitrary, may not always offer the most appropriate unit of analysis to study culture. Accordingly, they call for greater attention to culture at different levels of analysis in cross-cultural OB. Research is indeed increasingly showing cultural differences across class, profession, religion, ethnicity, age, and region within countries (e.g., Chua et al., 2019; Harrington & Gelfand, 2014; Luiz, 2015; Markus & Conner, 2014; Ronen & Shenkar, 2013; Taras et al., 2010). The authors encourage us to develop more complex models that simultaneously examine how multiple levels of culture, such as global, national, regional, state, community, industry, organizational, and team levels, affect behavior in organizations.

The authors also call for a focus on *context* at multiple levels. For example, they highlight the need to understand how national culture dynamically interacts with global, industry, work, and technological contexts, along with demographic and personality attributes (e.g., socioeconomic status, gender, age), to affect work behavior. More generally, with the advent of multilevel modeling techniques, we can examine many different models of cultural influence, ranging from *single-level models* to *cross-level direct* and *cross-level moderated* models of culture. We can also model the simultaneous influence of different sources of culture on units, teams, and individuals (e.g., *mixed-determinant* models) (Klein & Kozlowski, 2000; see also Gelfand et al., 2008). In the quest to model cultural influences in OB, the authors also advise controlling for noncultural factors (regulatory, political, and economic, among others) that tend to be the focus in sociology, industrial relations, and political science. Numerous authors also highlight the need to understand *reciprocal causal relationships* between culture and OB phenomenon. For example, while culture affects the nature of social network structures, in turn, social network structures reinforce certain cultural norms and values (see Chapter 18). Similarly, culture affects communication, but communication is also a vehicle through which culture is reproduced, contested, and changed (see Chapter 16; see also Chapters 13 and 14 for mutual relations among culture and trust and leadership, respectively). Finally, the authors call for expanding our explanatory toolkit beyond proximal predictors to include broader ecological and historical factors (e.g., climate, economic instability, conflict) that may be important drivers of the macro-evolution of organizational behavior around the globe (see Chapter 2).

Focusing on the Macro Level of the Global Context. The recent COVID-19 pandemic has shown that we all belong to the same global system. The virus spread across the globe, ignoring geographical, political, and cultural borders. To avoid contamination, people worldwide had to stay isolated and wear masks. Thanks to the internet, many employees were able to work from home, and e-commerce accelerated worldwide. We also witnessed a new global wave of resignation. These significant changes and their effects on organizational and work behaviors underscore the global context as the most macro-level culture (Erez & Gati, 2004). Future research should further study the interplay between the global work culture and the meso and micro levels of organizational behaviors.

Focusing on Cultural Dynamics across Time. As highlighted in this volume, cross-cultural OB culture research needs to capture *cultural dynamics* (i.e., change and interaction) at all levels of analysis, including cultural frame shifting within individuals, dynamics of intercultural negotiations and virtual teams, cross-cultural mergers and acquisitions, and large-scale cultural changes resulting from ecological, demographic, and market forces. A shift to cultural dynamics will necessitate theories of culture and time that examine when, how, and why cultural factors affect interactions in organizations. This perspective also invites us to examine processes of cultural change—how aspects of culture are negotiated, contested, and challenged through both bottom-up and top-down processes (Kashima et al., 2019). And as Zellmer-Bruhn and Gibson (2014) note, since cross-cultural interactions tend to be more "frequent, horizontal, unstructured, temporary, sporadic, and across global locations" (p. 3), we need to shift from theorizing about static cultural differences to dynamic cultural interfaces. Methodologically, longitudinal methods—both qualitative and quantitative—will be needed to adequately capture such temporal shifts.

Cross-fertilizing Research in Cross-cultural OB. This volume provides insight into exciting findings across the multilevel field of OB; yet it also illustrates that this knowledge is largely siloed. Insights on individual- and meso-level processes are rarely integrated with macro research, and vice versa. For example, micro negotiation and culture research is thriving (Chapter 17), as is research on negotiation in joint ventures (Chapter 24), yet they remain isolated. Considerable synergy can be gained by cross-fertilizing these separate research streams. Likewise, the authors noted the potential intellectual integration of research on work–family dynamics and expatriation (Chapters 21 and 23), social networks and global mobility (Chapters 18 and 23), as well as cultural intelligence, global identity, and the building of high-quality social networks and effective M&As (Chapters 26, 18, and 24). Cross-cultural OB research also remains separate from other disciplines, including research in anthropology, artificial intelligence, computational linguistics, economics, evolutionary biology, machine learning, and neuroscience. These fields not only offer new theories on culture, but also new methods (for examples, see Choi et al., 2022, for new linguistic dictionaries that assess culture; Varnum & Grossman, 2021, and Pan et al., 2021, for computational approaches to culture; Kirmayer et al., 2020, for insights from cultural neuroscience; and Nunn, 2022, for insights from the emerging field of cultural economics). As Karl Popper (1963) so cogently argued, "we are not students of some subject matter, but students of problems . . . and problems may cut right across the borders of any subject matter or discipline" (p. 88). The future of cross-cultural OB will benefit greatly from these interdisciplinary synergies.

Creating Bridges between Theory and Practice. In the spirit of Kurt Lewin, who argued that "there is nothing as practical as a good theory" (Lewin, 1943, p. 118), the authors in this volume were charged with distilling five theoretical and five practical insights from their reviews. Yet, a large gap between research and practice in CCOB remains. All too often, novel theoretical and empirical research published in academic journals does not reach practitioners. Likewise, practitioners' new insights into critical needs and constraints on the ground are not communicated to scholars. To be sure, cultural values, norms, and time pressures are highly divergent among scholars and practitioners; thus, cultural differences between them will need to be bridged to synergize insights from theory and practice. Academic–practitioner international teams that have dialogues in conferences, journals, and the popular press would go a long way toward rectifying these gaps. Other forms of institution building, such as open science platforms that hold translations of scales, data, and code in cross-cultural OB research, will foster collaboration across academics and practitioners.

In closing, we would like to thank all of the authors for their insights into the past, present, and future of cross-cultural OB. We also thank Abby Gross at Oxford University Press and Steve Kozlowski for their vision of this handbook and our families for their support of our work over many decades. Finally, we dedicate this handbook to our intellectual hero, Harry C. Triandis, one of the founders of cross-cultural psychology, for whom we have immense gratitude.

References

Bond, H. M., & Smith, B. P. (1996). Cross cultural social and organizational psychology. *Annual Review of Psychology, 47*, 205–35.

Choi, V. K., Shrestha, S., Pan, X., & Gelfand, M. J. (2022). When danger strikes: A linguistic tool for tracking America's collective response to threats. *Proceedings of the National Academy of Sciences, 119*(4), e2113891119.

Chua, R. Y., Huang, K. G., & Jin, M. (2019). Mapping cultural tightness and its links to innovation, urbanization, and happiness across 31 provinces in China. *Proceedings of the National Academy of Sciences, 116*(14), 6720–6725.

Davis, K. (1973). The case for and against business assumption of social responsibilities. *Academy of Management Journal, 16*(2), 312–322.

DeRue, D. S. (2011). Adaptive leadership theory: Leading and following as a complex adaptive process. *Research in Organizational Behavior, 31*, 125–150.

Erez, M., & Gati, E. (2004). A dynamic, multi-level model of culture: From the micro level of the individual to the macro level of a global culture. *Applied Psychology, 53*(4), 583–598.

Gelfand, M. J., Aycan, Z., Erez, M., & Leung, K. (2017). Cross-cultural industrial organizational psychology and organizational behavior: A hundred-year journey. *Journal of Applied Psychology, 102*(3), 514.

Gelfand, M. J., Leslie, L. M., & Fehr, R. (2008). To prosper, organizational psychology should adopt a global perspective. *Journal of Organizational Behavior: The International Journal of Industrial, Occupational and Organizational Psychology and Behavior, 29*(4), 493–517.

Harrington, J. R., & Gelfand, M. J. (2014). Tightness–looseness across the 50 United States. *Proceedings of the National Academy of Sciences, 111*(22), 7990–7995.

Kashima, Y., Bain, P. G., & Perfors, A. (2019). The psychology of cultural dynamics: What is it, what do we know, and what is yet to be known? *Annual Review of Psychology, 70*, 499–529.

Kirmayer, L. J., Worthman, C. M., Kitayama, S., Lemelson, R., & Cummings, C. A. (Eds.). (2020). *Culture, mind, and brain: Emerging concepts, models, and applications.* New York: Cambridge University Press.

Klein, K. J., & Kozlowski, S. W. (2000). *Multilevel theory, research, and methods in organizations: Foundations, extensions, and new directions.* San Francisco: Jossey-Bass.

Ko, A. S. O. (2003). Can principles from Sun Tzu's *Art of War* be used to address the problems of consensus-seeking organizations? *Corporate Communications: An International Journal, 8*(3), 208–212.

Lent, R. W., Brown, S. D., & Hackett, G. (1994). Toward a unifying social cognitive theory of career and academic interest, choice, and performance. *Journal of vocational behavior, 45*, 79–122.

Lewin, K. (1943). Psychology and the process of group living. *Journal of Social Psychology, 17*(1), 113–131.

Luiz, J. (2015). The impact of ethno-linguistic fractionalization on cultural measures: Dynamics, endogeneity and modernization. *Journal of International Business Studies, 46*(9), 1080–1098.

Markus, H. R., & Conner, A. (2014). *Clash!: How to thrive in a multicultural world.* New York: Penguin.

Mukred Mohsen, N. R. (2007). *Leadership from the Qur'an relationship between Taqwa, Trust and business leadership effectiveness* (Doctoral dissertation, Universiti Sains Malaysia).

Nunn, N. (2022). On the causes and consequences of cross-cultural differences. *Handbook of Advances in Culture and Psychology: Volume 9*, p. 125.

Pan, X., Gelfand, M., & Nau, D. (2021). Integrating evolutionary game theory and cross-cultural psychology to understand cultural dynamics. *American Psychologist, 76*(6), 1054.

Popper, K. R. (1963). *Conjectures and refutations: The growth of scientific knowledge.* New York: Routledge and Kegan Paul.

Ramesh, A., & Gelfand, M. J. (2010). Will they stay or will they go? The role of job embeddedness in predicting turnover in individualistic and collectivistic cultures. *Journal of Applied Psychology, 95*(5), 807.

Ronen, S., & Shenkar, O. (2013). Mapping world cultures: Cluster formation, sources and implications. *Journal of International Business Studies, 44*(9), 867–897.

Sampson, E. E. (1978). Scientific paradigms and social values: Wanted—a scientific revolution. *Journal of Personality and Social Psychology, 36*(11), 1332.

Taras, V., Kirkman, B. L., & Steel, P. (2010). Examining the impact of culture's consequences: A three-decade, multilevel, meta-analytic review of Hofstede's cultural value dimensions. *Journal of Applied Psychology, 95*(3), 405.

Varnum, M. E., & Grossmann, I. (2021). The psychology of cultural change: Introduction to the special issue. *American Psychologist, 76*(6), 833.

WCED. (1987). *Our common future*. Oxford: Oxford University Press.

Williamson, T. (2008). The good society and the good soul: Plato's *Republic* on leadership. *The Leadership Quarterly, 19*(4), 397–408.

Wright, T. A., & Goodstein, J. (2007). Character is not "dead" in management research: A review of individual character and organizational-level virtue. *Journal of Management, 33*(6), 928–958.

Yong, K., Mannucci, P. V., & Lander, M. W. (2020). Fostering creativity across countries: The moderating effect of cultural bundles on creativity. *Organizational Behavior and Human Decision Processes, 157*, 1–45.

Zellmer-Bruhn, M., & Gibson, C. B. (2014). How does culture matter? A process view of cultural interaction in groups. In M. Yuki & M. Brewer (Eds.), *Frontiers of culture and psychology series: Culture and group processes* (pp. 166–194). New York: Oxford University Press.

CHAPTER 2

Culture and Organizations: Theoretical and Methodological Perspectives

Ronald Fischer *and* Maria Cristina Ferreira

Abstract

We provide a review of recent theoretical and methodological advances in the field of culture and organizations. First, we review clusters of culture definitions and discuss major frameworks that have guided international business research. Complementary to these etic approaches, we highlight emic studies that provide culture-specific insights into effective work behaviors. We then describe recent advances in complex systems and evolutionary research that advance our understanding of both cultural similarities and differences, specifically focusing on explanations of why cultural differences may emerge in specific situations and points in time. We finish by discussing methodological and theoretical challenges for the next decade. Some of these challenges, such as the issue of cultural bias and equivalence, are well recognized but continue to pose significant challenges. Other areas, such as big data and massive improvements in statistical computing as well as increasing multiculturalism, offer new opportunities and challenges for organizational researchers.

Key Words: cross-cultural differences, norms, values, definition of culture, normology, emic-etic, cross-cultural bias, invariance, multi-level, cultural evolution

Introduction

In this chapter, we provide a brief history of the theoretical and methodological challenges in the study of culture and organizations, focusing not only on studies that examined national culture but also on recent culture-specific informal work behaviors and polycultural dynamics. Hofstede's (1980) seminal work continues to influence theorizing about culture and organizations, with both large numbers of studies following the overall paradigm and an increasing number of critical voices of the paradigm and proposing innovative attempts to move forward and charter new horizons. To provide some structure, we first briefly review foundational value research and focus on normology as a new approach to the study of cultural differences. We then present challenges associated with conceptualizing culture as shaped by national boundaries, outline some key insights from emic management research, and describe recent advances from an evolutionary perspective that can help integrate current research. We discuss theoretical and methodological issues together, as theory and methods rely on each other. In the final section, we reiterate a few core methodological advances and challenges for future research.

Using a Values Lens to Study Culture

Since the beginnings of the scientific study of culture in anthropology, defining culture has been challenging. In an early review of definitions of culture, Kroeber and Kluckhohn (1952) listed more than 150 definitions. Faulkner et al. (2006) updated this list and identified seven major clusters of definitions used in the social sciences. The first cluster focuses on structural or pattern definitions, typically referring to culture as a system or framework of elements (ideas, behaviors, or symbols, e.g., Rohner, 1984). The second cluster centers on functions, that is, origins of culture and cultural differences. This aspect of culture studies has attracted more research recently, with the emergence of the cultural evolution as a separate line of inquiry. These two clusters are often combined within anthropology as a functional-structural school, and they have been the dominant paradigm within cross-cultural management and international business research (Patel, 2015; Søderberg, 2020; Taras et al., 2010). The third cluster of definitions focuses on process: the social construction of culture and how culture influences social and psychological processes (e.g., Rohner, 1984). A fourth cluster defines culture in terms of products and the artefacts produced by cultural processes. This material approach has had some influence on the international marketing literature. A fifth cluster views culture in terms of refinement or "cultivation," which follows the French approach to culture as civilization (Kuper, 1999), but it is becoming more prevalent in evolutionary-inspired research that differentiates humans from other animals. The sixth cluster defines culture in terms of identity or group belonging, and the seventh explains it in terms of power and ideologies. This last approach has been most strongly aligned with critical and postmodern definitions of dominance and fragmentation, which has influenced some discussions of international management research (see Peterson et al., 2018). As this diversity of definitions shows, no consensus has been reached as to what culture might be; international business and management research is no exception in using diverse perspectives. In the present review, much of the work falls within the structural-functional perspective, but we will discuss alternative approaches where appropriate (see Fischer, 2012, for a more detailed discussion).

In the structure or pattern approach, the most common focus has been on examining culture and cultural differences via an emphasis on shared values (Taras et al. 2016). Through socialization, members of a given society internalize certain cultural values, which are therefore shared. The downstream effects of these shared values are then reflected in behaviors characteristic of that society (Leung & Morris, 2015) or even in the artefacts created by members of that cultural community.

Hofstede's (1980, 2001) seminal value study continues to define international business research. Approximately 50 years ago, Hofstede gathered data from workers in a large multinational organization (IBM) located across 53 countries and regions. He initially proposed four dimensions: (1) individualism versus collectivism, which refers to the degree to which people in a given country would rather act as individuals, giving priority to their own interests, or as members of the group to which they belong, thus prioritizing the interests of those groups (for updates on this dimension, see Minkov et al., 2017); (2) power distance, which concerns the relationship with authority, that is, the degree to which members of society accept the unequal distribution of power and large differences in status; (3) uncertainty avoidance, which is defined as the degree to which members of different cultural groups feel threatened by unknown or ambiguous situations and try to avoid them, thus opting for more structured situations; and finally (4) masculinity and femininity, which refer to the level to which societies value assertiveness, competitiveness, and achievement of goals versus interpersonal relationships and care for others, as well as the extent to which occupational roles are differentiated according to gender stereotypes. Hofstede and Bond (1988) added a fifth dimension, called long-term orientation, and captured the extent to which societies place greater emphasis on values oriented toward the past and/or the present compared to values oriented to the future, such as persistence and regulation of relationships by status. Hofstede et al. updated these dimensions in 2010 by adding a sixth dimension, which captures the distinction between indulgence (valuing free gratification of desires and following impulses to enjoy life and have fun) and restraint (valuing the suppression of needs and regulation behavior through social prohibitions). (For elaborations on this dimension, see Minkov et al., 2018; for a verification with new data, see Minkov, 2018; Minkov et al., 2019.)

Additional value frameworks inspired by Hofstede have also been proposed in the last few decades. Within psychology, the most prominent value approach was developed by Schwartz, who proposed different measurement instruments at the individual (Schwartz, 1992, Schwartz et al., 2012) and culture levels (Schwartz, 1994). At the country level, Schwartz differentiated between seven different types of values (conservatism, intellectual autonomy, affective autonomy, hierarchy, control, egalitarian commitment, and harmony), which differ along three bipolar dimensions projected into a two-dimensional representation. The first dimension, conservatism versus autonomy, differentiates societies in which individuals value being connected with others from societies in which individuals value being autonomous and express their thoughts and emotions (intellectual and affective autonomy). The second dimension, hierarchy versus egalitarian commitment, distinguishes between cultural groups in which individuals are socialized to fulfill the rules and obligations associated with their roles (hierarchy) and groups in which socialization is based on voluntary cooperation with others in a relatively more egalitarian context (egalitarian commitment). Finally, the third dimension is mastery versus harmony, which differentiates societies in which people actively seek to dominate and modify their natural and social environment (mastery) from those in which individuals accept the world as it is and seek to preserve it as it is (harmony).

In management research, the project GLOBE (Global Leadership and Organizational Behavior Effectiveness), led by House et al. (2004), stands out as the most ambitious project in Hofstede's shadow. House et al. (2004) collected data with managers from 62 nations, extending five of Hofstede's dimensions into nine distinct dimensions. Individualism–collectivism is split into two: institutional collectivism is characterized by the adoption of values and practices that emphasize collective action and distribution of resources, while in-group collectivism is limited to the expression of loyalty and cohesion among individuals of specific smaller groups, such as, for example, the family or the organization. Power distance, future orientation (Hofstede's long-term orientation), and uncertainty avoidance remain as distinct dimensions. Masculinity and femininity in Hofstede's framework are broken up into a series of dimensions, including gender egalitarianism (the extent to which professions and roles are gender-stereotyped) and assertiveness (the extent to which assertiveness and competition are being valued). Two new dimensions are performance orientation (the degree to which society encourages excellence in performance) and humane orientation (the extent to which society reinforces altruism and care for others). Although the studies by Hofstede (1980, 2001), Schwartz (1994), and House et al. (2004) have used different items and terms to identify possible cultural dimensions, the overall pattern suggests the relatively close resemblance of a number of core value dimensions that can be repeatedly identified in large-scale survey studies.

Inspired by Hofstede's framework at the culture level as well as the emerging evidence of a convergence of dimensions across different large-scale studies, researchers started developing a multitude of individual-level measures that could be used for measuring the cultural orientations of individuals. Taras et al. (2009) reviewed 121 instruments for measuring cultural values and identified 26 facets that could, for the most part, be grouped according to the original four cultural dimensions proposed by Hofstede (1980; 2001). One of the continuing debates in the literature is whether the individual and culture-level dimensions are capturing the same content and meaning (the problem of isomorphism) and whether or not the associations of constructs at each level are similar (the problem of homology) (see Fischer et al., 2010; Fischer & Poortinga, 2012). To date, this debate has not been resolved, although more recent studies have reported increasing evidence that dimensions at individual and culture levels tend to show greater convergence, pointing toward empirical similarity (see Fischer & Poortinga, 2012; House et al., 2004).

The identification of these major dimensions in independent studies has led to a large body of research focusing on the work-relevant correlates of these dimensions, which has been summarized in both meta-analyses and qualitative reviews. Taras et al. (2010), in their quantitative review of previous studies, demonstrated the importance of these cultural dimensions for understanding behavior at individual, group, and organizational levels. Their meta-analysis suggested that, although individualism–collectivism has attracted the most research attention, other dimensions such as power distance and uncertainty avoidance are of central importance for understanding and managing work-related attitudes and emotions across cultural contexts. However, cultural values had little predictive power in explaining behavioral indicators such as performance, absenteeism, and turnover, which led Taras et al. to conclude that cultural values were more strongly associated with attitudes than with behaviors. They also found that the effect of values on organizationally relevant variables was dependent on other factors, including education, age, and the extent to which norms within a society were tightly or loosely organized (Gelfand et al., 2011; see below). Taken together, these findings suggest that cultural values are important for work attitudes and beliefs; that research needs to move beyond individualism–collectivism but also that behaviors are less well predicted than attitudes by values and that the effect of values may be facilitated or constrained by other factors.

Value frameworks in line with Hofstede's tradition have also been used to explain, for example, the successes and failures in the mergers and acquisitions of companies (Rozen-Bakher, 2018), the human resources practices adopted in multinational companies (Aycan et al., 2000), the adaptation of expatriates to different cultures (Froese & Peltokorpi, 2011), the dynamics of multicultural teams (Stahl et al., 2010), organizational change (Kirsch et al., 2012), conflict (Vaara et al., 2012), negotiation (Tu, 2015), and leadership behaviors (Hanges et al., 2016).

These studies have explicitly or implicitly assumed a culture-fit approach to culture and organizations. Considered from a multilevel perspective, individual actors coordinate their actions, which give rise to larger scale units that are more than the sum of its parts (Gao et al., 2015). The current consensual wisdom is that global managers should adapt their management strategies to the local context (e.g., Gelfand et al., 2007). A considerable body of research highlights the contingency of the effectiveness of management strategies on an organization's environmental and cultural context (Adler & Gundersen, 2008; Gelfand et al., 2007; Tsui et al., 2007). Organizations should elicit higher performance if the organizational practices match the cultural preferences (e.g., values) of the local workforce (Adler & Gundersen, 2008; Hofstede, 1980, 2001) and the technological environment (Ellis et al., 2002). The theoretical foundations for fitting organizational practices to environmental contingencies can be found in diverse meta-theories such as the structural contingency approach (Burns & Stalker, 1961) and the culture-fit theory (Aycan et al., 2000). These broad contingency approaches have become a dominant management strategy that underlies much of strategic management and international business (Katsikeas et al., 2006).

Focusing on organizational research conducted with the individual level version of Schwartz's values (1992; Schwartz et al., 2012), Arieli and colleagues (2020) reviewed value research in organizational settings and proposed a framework that puts values at the core of organizational behavior. In line with definitions of values (Schwartz, 1992), they argued that values drive work orientation, vocational interest and career choices, which then causally influences a range of work-relevant behaviors of interest to managers. For example, Arieli et al. (2020) review studies showing that openness to change versus conservative values correlate with creativity and innovation behavior, proactive work behavior, initiatives for organizational change, and more positive reactions to organizational change initiatives. Self-transcendence (vs. self-enhancement) values correlate with altruistic behavior, cooperation, and more amiable conflict resolutions (for an overview, see Table 1 in Arieli et al.). However, one of the central limitations of this research is that

Table 2.1 Definitions of culture

Type	Culture as . . .	Organizational scholarship
Structure/ Patterns	Patterns or structure differentiating groups related to ways of life, cognition (including thoughts, beliefs, meanings, attitudes, values, interpretations, etc.), behaviors, relations, or institutions	Dominant, different emphasis on what is being shared: values (Hofstede, 1980, House et al., 2004; Schwartz, 1994); social axioms (Leung & Bond, 2004), norms (Fischer, 2006; Gelfand et al., 2011, 2017; Leung & Morris, 2015)
Functions	Focus on the functions and outcomes of culture, including providing guidance on what and how to learn about the world, providing a sense of belonging, an avenue for self-expression, to evaluate others, or a means to exert control	Dominant in cross-national research (e.g., Gelfand et al., 2011; Hofstede, 1980; Leung & Morris, 2015; Schwartz 1994)
Process	Focus on the practice of "culture," including the acts of differentiating one group from another, the acts of sense-making, and producing meaning in life; how to relate to others and deal with the social world, how to negotiate power and social hierarchies, etc.	Underlies diverse perspectives, guiding principle in value research (e.g., Hofstede, 1980; Schwartz, 1994)
Product	Product of meaningful activity, including objects of art, architecture, texts, and other artefacts produced as a result of culture	Particularly relevant in international marketing and advertising (e.g., Lamoreaux & Morling, 2012; Morling & Lamoreaux, 2008)
Refinement	A form of "cultivation" or refinement, including moral or cognitive distinctions, but also as distinguishing humans from other animals	Not common in organizational research, becoming more common via evolutionary approaches (e.g., Fischer, 2017; Gelfand et al., 2017; Kashima et al., 2019)
Group membership	Belonging to a specific nation or group, providing an identity	Diverse groups, including discussions of national culture boundaries (Minkov & Hofstede, 2012), but also interpretative approaches (e.g., Gertsen & Zølner, 2020)
Power/Ideology	Focus on processes of political and ideological dominance, including classifications in terms of dominance or hegemony; but also postmodern notions of fragmentation	Interpretative and critical approaches to management (Gertsen & Zølner, 2020; Patel, 2015; Primecz et al., 2016)

most of it has focused on correlational associations with attitudes and self-reported work behavior, which are often of small magnitude and open to alternative interpretation. This raises questions about the practical use of value research for organizational decision makers (Fischer, 2020), as already noted by the earlier meta-analysis by Taras et al. (2010).

In summary, research on values inspired by Hofstede's seminal project continues to shape organizational research. The large number of studies conducted since the 1980s has been synthesized and summarized in reviews and meta-analyses published in the last decade, demonstrating both the insights gained and the limits of cultural values to explain work behavior. In the coming years, we can expect further maturation and elaboration of some of the key insights gained.

Using a Normative Lens for Studying Culture

The realization that values may not explain cultural differences to the extent that was expected based on the theoretical definitions of culture has triggered a search for alternative ways of operationalizing culture. Norm-based approaches to culture assume that culture influences individuals' attitudes and behaviors through the norms that individuals develop about their social group (Leung & Morris, 2015). Norm research has a long tradition in sociology and social psychology, which was largely focused on behavior (Cialdini et al., 1990; Jasso & Opp, 1997). The reinvigoration of norm research in cross-cultural research has been shaped by a more cognitive turn, focusing on the intersubjectivity of the perceptions and experience of norms: members within a given sociocultural context form shared perceptions of their own actions and the actions of others around them, leading to an active construction of an intersubjective reality of generalized and shared beliefs about what is appropriate within a specific cultural context (cultural codes). This collectively created intersubjective reality guides the behavior of individuals and may not correspond to individual beliefs (Chiu et al., 2010). It also allows a more careful examination of the processes that lead to the emergence of such an intersubjectively shared norm perception. In addition, it permits separating individual preferences and values from normative influences on behavior (Fischer, 2006; Fischer et al., 2009; Shteynberg et al., 2009).

The intersubjective approach ties the effectiveness of norms to the perceived consensus of members of a given society on the most prominent ideas in that society (Chiu et al., 2010; but see Fischer, 2012, for a critical perspective on norm consensus). This approach allows flexible and dynamic patterns of behaviors, as cultural behavior is not driven by an automatic internalization of certain cultural traits, but rather by an actively constructed collective effort that may undergo modifications, depending on the environmental changes. The intersubjective norm approach through its collective constructions can also explain the persistence of behavioral norms in the face of large-scale migration and adaptation. The reason is that behavioral adaptations to the host country's perceived norms are dependent on motivational factors, including the degree to which the individual evaluates the culture of their destination country more or less favorably (Hong & Cheon, 2017).

One classic distinction of norms is the differentiation into descriptive versus injunctive norms (Cialdini et al., 1990). Descriptive norms are associated with cognitions about what is socially prevalent, that is, about what people actually do. Injunctive or prescriptive norms, on the other hand, concern cognitions about what is socially appropriate or approved, that is, about what people should and should not do. Morris, Hong et al. (2015) argued that descriptive norms are more likely to guide behavior when the right course of action is ambiguous and social evaluations are highly salient, whereas injunctive norms are likely to guide behavior in public contexts with clear expectations. They further predicted that normative influences depend on the culture's degree of tightness–looseness (see Gelfand et al., 2011). Injunctive norms are likely to be more salient when a society has tight norms—that is, when norms are clearly specified and rigorously enforced. In contrast, descriptive norms are likely to be more salient for behavior in loose cultures in which norms are less clearly demarcated and less strongly enforced (Li et al., 2017). However, contrary to these expectations, Smith (2017) in a recent country-level study found that helping behavior was more strongly related to descriptive norms in contexts classified as more tightly regulated. One possible explanation is that distinct information on descriptive versus injunctive norms may not always be available to individuals. Hence, information about one type of standard is absent, and people tend to apply the other type (Leung & Morris, 2015). In many practical situations, it may also be challenging to clearly differentiate descriptive and injunctive norms. If all members of a group adhere to a norm, it could indicate either a descriptive or an injunctive norm. Without further information on punishments of norm violations or moral judgments, it is impossible to distinguish between them.

With regard to the dynamics of norm adherence, mechanisms of social approval and incentives to avoid sanctions for violating social norms are thought to be critical (Harrington & Gelfand, 2014). Sanctions allow norms to stabilize within groups, explaining their persistence over time (Shteynberg et al., 2009). Compliance with norms is greater when the group's identity is more prominent, when the individual's reputation is taken into account, and when people have a greater need of cognitive closure (Gelfand & Jackson, 2016).

Integrating these insights with work on cognitive and motivational theories, Morris, Hong et al. (2015) proposed normology as the science of norms with an integrative and dynamic model of antecedents and consequences of norms at the micro (changes in individual cultural assumptions) and macro level (changes in cultural practices and institutions). Bringing together the various perspectives in the literature, Morris and colleagues proposed that at the micro level, norms are formed via situational pressures and maintained via the approval or disapproval of behaviors using conditioning processes based on reward and punishment. At the macro level, they contended that some patterns and practices are codified, formalized, and sanctioned by the social groups and become rules that are institutionalized (in which case informal practices become codified as explicit rules or norms). These processes of institutionalization can take the form of formalization or sacred group traditions. Formalization refers to repeated behaviors within a collective, which become normative and codified (a classic example is the emergence of left- vs. right-lane traffic). Sacralization, in contrast, is the emergence of group traditions in which repeated behaviors take on a sacred status and become non-negotiable (classic examples include religious traditions regarding food or labor restrictions that have implications for business organizations). The repetition of behavior therefore becomes encoded in the group's official discourse, embedded in their social structures, and formally sanctioned. In order to manage organizations more effectively across cultures and to accommodate the rapidly changing demographic and technological realities, Morris and colleagues argue that normative dynamics at both the micro and macro level need to be considered.

Attempts to operationalize norms across cultures have generally followed Hofstede's example by using value dimensions as the starting point for conceptualizing the content of cultural norm dimensions and evaluating them through self-reports. The GLOBE project (House et al., 2004) is the earliest systematic attempt to conceptualize norms. In addition to the nine dimensions of values mentioned above (asking managers "how things should be"), the researchers also asked participants to rate how "things are," reflecting the perception of prevalent behaviors and practices in their country. Focusing responses by managers on what other people in a society are doing, the research focus shifted toward descriptive norms (Fischer, 2006). One of the major challenges has been to interpret the relationship between these normative perceptions and cultural values, as the two sets do not necessarily positively correlate and in some cases, they even show a strongly negative correlation. Preliminary attempts have been made to integrate the convergence and divergence of normative and value processes (Fischer, 2006).

In summary, the last decades have seen the emergence of normology as an active field of organizational research. There are still limited measurement frameworks (Chiu et al., 2010), but it is possible to develop theory-guided measures of norms (Fischer et al., 2009; Gelfand et al., 2011; Yao et al., 2017), which allows a better understanding and mapping of cultural differences and relevant organizational dynamics (Morris, Hong, et al., 2015).

Moving Beyond Value and Norm Lenses

Moving beyond value and norm research, researchers have tried to differentiate cultures using additional approaches. Most salient among these efforts is the social axioms paradigm (Leung & Bond, 2004). Social axioms are generalized, shared beliefs about the life goals of individuals and their social world. They thus constitute the basic premises that individuals use to guide their behavior in different situations. Leung and Bond developed an instrument for measuring axioms and conducted an investigation in 41 countries in which they identified five individual belief dimensions: *social cynicism* (distrust of social institutions and the actions of others, resulting from negative assessments of human nature and social events); *social complexity* (belief that there are multiple solutions to social issues and, therefore, several ways to achieve desirable results); *reward for application* (belief that effort, knowledge, and careful planning lead to positive results and help to avoid negative results); *religiosity* (belief in spiritual forces and the positive effects of religion on people's lives); and *fate control* (belief that life events, though predetermined, influence their consequences). Social axioms showed low correlations with values (Leung et al., 2007) and explained differences between countries not explained by values (Bond et al., 2004). Regarding the implications for organizations, it was observed that social axioms showed greater predictive power than the values in relation to different methods of conflict resolution (Bond et al., 2004). This work has been influential for intersubjective norm research and has contributed to development of the dynamic situation approach, which we discuss in further detail below.

Building on both normative and value research, Leung and Cohen (2011) proposed a cultural typology that distinguishes between three types of norms that reflect different motivational systems. These systems vary according to the self-worth sources, leading to distinct dignity, face, and honor cultures. In the dignity culture, self-definition stems from self-assessments of one's own achievements, whereas in face culture, self-definition is based on external evaluations and the recognition of the other and in honor culture, self-definition is associated with both external and internal assessments. For Yao et al. (2017), the culture of dignity stems from social independence, the face culture from social interdependence, and the honor culture from both. Yao et al. developed and validated a measurement model for these three types of cultural norms and demonstrated that the differences between them explained the differences in the use of integrative and distributive negotiation strategies. Smith et al. (2020) examined the individual and culture-level dynamics of these cultural norms in a nomological net at both individual and national levels and found that individual level dynamics are particularly important for understanding self-reported behavior such as conflict resolution and norm adherence. Hence, these normative dynamics can be unpackaged across levels and linked back to the salient motivations and concerns of both the individuals and collectivism within which the individual is operating.

Cultural Distance and Beyond

A second line of research in reaction to the prevalence of research focusing on dimensions of cultural values focuses on patterns or overarching profiles of culture. One of the most widely used approaches is based on the concept of cultural distance in which value dimensions are combined and the relative differences between samples is the focus of attention. The gold standard for this approach has been Kogut and Singh's (1988) use of Hofstede's country classification (1980, 2001) to create a distance index between the country of origin and the country of destination. This construct has gained great acceptance in international business (Shenkar, 2012) and has been applied, for example, in the study of foreign entry (Barkema et al., 1996), firm internationalization (Beugelsdijk et al., 2018), adaptation of management innovations in foreign subsidiaries (Alofan et al., 2020), and cross-border acquisitions (Popli et al., 2016). However, more recently, the use of a cultural distance index for comparing cultures has been questioned (Beugelsdijk et al., 2018).

Moving beyond cultural distance and analyzing data from 10 large-scale studies on cross-country cultural differences, Ronen and Shenkar (2013) identified 11 relatively distinct cultural clusters: Latin America; Latin Europe; Eastern Europe; Nordic; Germanic; Anglo; Confucian; Far East; African; Near East; and Arab. Beugelsdijk et al. (2017) calculated a composite cultural-distance index using the dimensions of three cultural frameworks (Hofstede, GLOBE, and Schwartz) and found that the resulting cultural-distance scores match the cultural classification of countries in specific cultural zones by Ronen and Shenkar (2013).

A number of meta-analyses have also summarized the effect of cultural distance on various indices of multinational firm performance (e.g., Beugelsdijk et al., 2018; Morschett et al., 2010). These meta-analyses point toward the complexity of cultural distance as a construct, suggesting that although cultural distance has a measurable effect on firm performance and business decisions, these effects may be dependent, among other variables, on industry, type of cultural dimension considered, and the cultural framework used for calculating cultural distance. Concerning, for example, the moderation by type of industry, Morschett et al. (2010) observed that the relationship between income level of the host country and entry mode depends on the industry type. Service companies exhibited a negative relationship between income level and wholly owned subsidiaries, while manufacturing companies showed a positive relationship. Similarly, Popli et al. (2015) found that cultural distance has a stronger effect in the case of knowledge-intensive service firms because a higher uncertainty is associated with these firms than with capital-intensive service firms.

Considering the mixed findings in contemporary cultural distance research, Beugelsdijk et al. (2018) reviewed assumptions and problems of this kind of research and offered a series of recommendations for calculating, theorizing, and applying cultural distance measures. First, cultural distance measures can be constructed in a number of ways. The choice of calculation may not make that much of a difference, but what variance is being considered and how strongly the individual dimensions are intercorrelated are likely to have an impact on the overall index. Cultural distance metrics calculated on correlated dimensions are likely to bias difference metrics, and since most large-scale databases are constructed to capture particular theoretical domains, any cultural distance measure is likely to be biased.

An alternative has been to use an agnostic composite index such as Kogut and Singh's overall distance index, taking into account all available country-level indicators. Such an agnostic approach using composite scales about the importance or relevance of individual dimensions for calculating distance shows that we need more work on the theoretical mechanisms for establishing a cultural distance theory. Such a theory would allow a precise statement of the theoretical processes and mechanisms that clarify the nature of cultural distance for the problem at hand, be it entry mode choice, firm performance, or location choice.

The intercorrelation of cultural dimensions and variables together with the lack of a precise theory that drives the choice and method of calculating distance require greater transparency. In addition, distance metrics are silent on the relevant level and the direction of analysis: Should distance be considered at the firm level or the country level? Are distance effects symmetrical, or could distance effects have different implications when changing the direction? The work on tightness–looseness (Gelfand et al., 2006) may provide the clearest example of this—moving from a cultural loose to a culturally tight environment may have different implications than in reverse.

Moving beyond cultural distance metrics, cultural archetype models have tried to capture cultural variability across levels. Venaik and Midgley (2015) conceptualized cultural archetypes as a configuration of fundamental values, shared by groups of individuals not only within the same country, but also between countries. It represents the value configurations of ideal individuals that capture shared value orientations within specific subgroups. The composition and distribution of such archetypes is thought to provide new insights into cultural dynamics. Using complex multidimensional statistics on value data from Japan, the United States, China, and India, they identified four archetypes in Japan, the United States, and China, and six archetypes in India.

In a subsequent study, Midgley et al. (2018) used data from the World Values Survey across 52 countries and identified five global archetypes, which were universally applicable and captured cultural diversity both within and across countries. The main characteristics of each archetype are as follows: Archetype 1 (A1) is represented by people who give greater importance to all socially oriented values and to self-oriented values of self-direction and achievement. Archetype 2 (A2) is characterized not only by greater importance to all socially oriented values, as in A1, but also by moderate to high importance to the self-oriented value of hedonism. Archetype 3 (A3) is made up of people who give greater importance to all self-oriented values, with the exception of power and to a lesser extent achievement, as well as to the socially oriented value of benevolence. Archetype A4 (A4) is characterized by greater importance to self-oriented as well as socially oriented values. Archetype 5 (A5) includes individuals who give minor importance to all values, except to power, which they consider to be moderately important.

The distribution of these archetypes within countries can explain the observed cultural variability between countries. Hence, archetype theory provides a new methodology for addressing cultural differences beyond cultural distance measures, seeking to reconcile the tension between homogeneity and heterogeneity within and between countries. In the context of organizations, this theory implies that common management strategies can be adopted for groups and individuals who share the same cultural archetype, even if they differ in terms of nationality, ethnicity, religion, and so on (Venaik & Midgley, 2015).

Culture-Specific Work Behaviors

So far, we have discussed cultural dimensions as if they were universally applicable to all human populations and organizations. This perspective contrasts with a separate line of research that has focused on emic or indigenous approaches to culture, that is, theories and models to explain culture-specific ways of organizing and managing. These developments are not recent and can be traced back to post-World War II, postcolonial movements (Leung, 2009; Smith, 2008). In the past decade, there has been a marked increase in the number of investigations dedicated to analyzing emic constructs and their influence on organizations. These approaches typically fall within the structural-functional approach of culture definitions that we discussed above, as they often focus on locally relevant and efficient ways of resolving problems in culturally appropriate ways. Here we will focus on two major examples that have attracted much recent research, *jeitinho brasileiro* and *guanxi*, characteristic traits, respectively, of Brazilian and Chinese cultures. For broader discussions and listings of relevant culture-specific management strategies, see Ledeneva (2018).

The first trait analyzed here, *jeitinho brasileiro,* is best translated as the "little Brazilian way." It is associated with flexible and often norm-breaking problem-solving strategies used by individuals to deal with the excessive formality, bureaucracy, and hierarchy of Brazilian society as a means of achieving otherwise unattainable goals (Ferreira et al., 2012). This informal problem-solving approach has become a central part of Brazil's national identity, with both positive aspects, such as creativity and sympathy, and negative aspects associated with the infringement of norms and corruption (Ferreira et al., 2012; Fischer et al., 2014; Rodrigues et al., 2011). Using behavioral scenarios, Ferreira et al. (2012) found a three-dimensional structure, with creativity, norm infringement, and corruption components. Miura et al. (2019) found a simpler structure when treating *jeitinho* as an individual difference, personality-like variable. They distinguished a *jeitinho simpatico* (friendly way), associated with the tendency to seek positive interactions and find creative solutions, from a *jeitinho malandro* (tricky or deceptive way), associated with interpersonal deception and trickery in social interactions. Interestingly, even though these are culturally specific problem-solving behaviors, they can be predicted using universal value, personality, moral beliefs, and political attitude scales (Ferreira et al., 2012; Miura et al., 2019, Resende & Porto, 2020) that can help identify and mitigate both negative and positive effects.

Much of the business literature has focused on the negative aspects, such as corrupt behavior in buyer–supplier relationships and the breaking of rules and regulations or negotiation of business contracts (Duarte, 2006; Fischer et al., 2014). The informality of *jeitinho* may also impact international negotiations, with foreigners needing to adjust to these more personal and improvised negotiation strategies (Duarte, 2006). Experiments have shown that the intention to accept bribes or to behave in corrupt ways in working populations can be situationally activated, even with otherwise noncorruption-related images if they can trigger concepts associated with *jeitinho* (Fischer et al., 2014). This effect is enhanced in individuals who strongly identify with Brazil, highlighting the identity component of this behavior. However, Resende and Porto (2020) indicated that the negative impact of norm infringement and corruption aspects of *jeitinho* on ethical behavior was attenuated when individual had strong internalized moral identities. Nevertheless, political crises can reinforce preexisting predispositions (Fischer et al., 2022).

Within Chinese communities, *guanxi* is grounded in relationships between two people, defined by mutual commitment, loyalty, and obligation (Chen & Chen, 2004). Such personal relationships, generally maintained with family members, friends, and neighbors, are commonly used not only for people to achieve their own goals, but also to make decisions in the context of work (Chen et al., 2017). *Guanxi* thus implies long-term mutual obligations and the granting of favors by both parties, motivated by existing ties between members of the dyad (Luo, 2000) and by the desire to maintain harmony between them (Hwang, 1997).

Guanxi can have both positive consequences, such as bonds of affection and trust between the parties, and negative consequences, including fraud, nepotism, and favoritism (Gu et al., 2008). In organizational contexts, *guanxi* influences the relationship between leaders and subordinates (Chen & Tjosvold, 2007), including more privileged treatment of subordinates (Law et al., 2000), greater confidence in leaders (Chen et al., 2004), and nonabusive practices by leaders (Liu & Wang, 2013).

These informal social influences and problem-solving strategies may share important psychological components. In a series of studies, Smith et al. (2012) compared *jeitinho* and *guanxi* with other strategies such as *wasta* (Arabic cultures), *svyazi* (Russian), and pulling strings (British). Smith found common elements among these emic constructs, which typically involve using personal relationships or social status to solve problems encountered in hierarchical and bureaucratic contexts. Yet, these emic strategies also often have unique and culture-specific nuances. With regard to *guanxi* and *jeitinho*, Torres et al. (2015) found that despite their common aspects as problem-solving strategies, *jeitinho* is characterized as an attempt to treat other people as equals, as a way to overcome the barriers present in a hierarchical society. It does not require previous ties between those involved in the social relationship and using *jeitinho* can generate new social connections. In contrast, *guanxi* is based on preexisting and long-lasting relationships in a hierarchical social system in which higher-status individuals use their social position for their own benefits.

The deepening of studies on the emic aspects of culture can help develop approaches that integrate emic and ethical concepts and theories (Leung, 2009) as a way to better understand the similarities and differences between cultures. The search for emic constructs has grown in recent years, and a plethora of concepts have been identified (see Ledeneva, 2017). Of particular note for cross-cultural researchers and practitioners are the recent advances in identifying emic personality dimensions (e.g., Cheung et al., 2011; Fischer, 2017), especially since they may strongly influence legislation on employment recruitment and testing practices. For example, South African legislation requires that locally relevant and valid tests for all cultural and ethnic groups be used for recruitment and training purposes. This requirement has led to the development of emic personality instruments (Fetvadjiev et al., 2015). Studies that pay greater attention to these culture-specific ways of management with an explicit investigation of universal psychological processes underlying these behaviors (e.g., Miura et al., 2019) may contribute to the construction of a truly global and universal management science (Gelfand et al., 2017).

Evolutionary and Dynamic Approaches to Culture and Organizations

A Dynamic Situated Model of Culture

Using a situational approach and seeking to reconcile research focusing on values and norms, Leung and Morris (2015) proposed a dynamic and situated approach to culture incorporating values, norms and cultural schemas (cognitive structures associated with cultural scripts). They recognized that values, norms, and schemas are differentially affected by situational conditions and therefore are likely to result in nuanced relationships with work behavior. As a result of these interdependencies of psychological dynamics on the situational context, certain behavior patterns in a given culture may prove to be more stable and long-lasting. Others may vary widely across different situations, depending on the situationally activated schemas and norms. For example, on the one hand, values are predicted to be more strongly related to attitudes and behavior in situations of reduced tightness (higher looseness) and anonymity. On the other hand, norms are likely to be more prominent in situations of greater tightness and when behavior is dependent on social approval. In addition, tasks that involve ethical issues are more likely to activate values, whereas tasks that require decision making are likely to activate cognitive schemas. These predictions have largely been confirmed by relevant studies. For example, at the individual level, Fischer and Boer (2015) found that values are more strongly related to behavioral traits (e.g., personality traits) in contexts characterized by reduced normative tightness. At the country level, Smith (2017) found that in more tightly organized nations, cultural values were less strongly related to altruistic behavior (e.g., helping strangers) but more strongly related to behaviors regulating emotions.

Culture Evolution: Micro-Dynamics

Cultural dynamics has emerged as a major field of study over the last decade. Kashima et al. (2019) recently summarized major insights from this interdisciplinary work. Kashima (2016) outlined how the social transmission of individually held information shapes the emergence and maintenance of cultural systems. Cultural dynamics are mediated through language and communication sequences. Individuals need to communicate their subjective representations during social interactions in which the subjectively held information needs to be accepted by the receiver and becomes validated (i.e., "grounded"; see Kashima et al., 2007). In order to achieve a socially relevant objective, both the sender and the receiver must agree with each other about the shared information for the current purpose. This grounding enables interpersonal understanding. The jointly established grounding of information is in turn interpreted by both individuals and is stored in memory. Hence, the interpersonal grounding becomes intrapersonal once more and through repeated interactions and productions of subjective information, an intersubjectively shared reality is constructed. Artefacts—that is, enduring objects that can be observed by multiple actors—also help in grounding information and increase intersubjective representations of cultural information. Through these recurring cycles of language-based interactions, individuals start to converge in their intrapersonal subjective understanding of their world, which allows cultures to emerge. The insight gained through these micro-level analyses of language-based interactions vis-à-vis cognitive constraints through memory and perception systems enable clearer insights into how cultural information both stabilizes and changes cultural systems through repeated cycles of interactions between actors that have shared intentionality about common goals (Tomasello & Carpenter, 2007).

These micro-dynamic examinations as well as the dynamic model proposed by Leung and Morris (2015) also fit with emerging insights from cognitive psychology using a dynamic conception of culture as being composed of multiple knowledge structures. These structures can be activated or suppressed, depending on context demands (Molinski, 2007). Such dynamics help to explain the work behaviors of migrant and bicultural individuals. Hong et al. (2000) were the first to point out that bicultural individuals change their behavior through cultural frame shifting. Each cultural context is internalized through repeated interaction sequences with other members of the same cultural environments. A cultural script is being developed that is automatically and subconsciously being activated through situational clues and driven by cultural expectations. Bicultural individuals or individuals with a migration background will have developed multiple cultural frames that can be situationally activated.

The previously available cultural information facilitates information exchange, so that cultural shared information is typically more likely to be reproduced during interactions. In addition, culturally novel information is less likely to be passed on because it is more likely to interrupt the smooth information exchange, requiring more attention and memory resources (Clark & Kashima, 2007). As a consequence, culturally conforming information is more likely to be socially transmitted, leading to stabilization of cultural information within a community, increased cohesion with other group members, but decreased information sharing during social interactions. To the extent that the need for informativeness during interaction increases, the likelihood of sharing novel information increases, with accompanying costs for interpersonal cohesion. Understanding these patterns can help to provide a theoretical framework for observation that cultural diversity in teams increases task conflicts and decreases social cohesion, while at the same time increasing creativity and innovation via the introduction of novel information (Stahl et al., 2010. In summary, the evolutionary-based micro-level analyses of social interactions in the production and maintenance of cultural systems can help to provide a theoretical framework for examining organizational dynamics in a changing global environment.

Cultural Evolution: Macro-Dynamics

In addition to these micro-level dynamics, macro-level changes can also be examined. Starting from a different point of departure, Gelfand et al. (2006 and 2011) developed a multilevel theory of tightness–looseness, focusing on the degree to which norms are enforced or sanctioned in the event of norm violations in different societies. Gelfand et al. (2011) measured behavioral observations of norm tightness versus looseness in 33 societies and linked societal-level differences to ecological, economic, and social conditions. For example, societies with fewer natural resources are subject to greater risks of natural disasters and a higher prevalence of disease. They also suffer more threats to their territories and need to regulate collective responses more efficiently, which in turn leads to tighter rules to address and overcome these adversities. Societies not exposed to the same ecological challenges do not need to coordinate collective actions to the same degree, thereby permitting looser cultural norms and greater tolerance for norm violation (for a replication of these threat effects, see Jackson et al., 2020). From early childhood, individuals within both tight and loose cultures are socialized by institutions that reinforce the strength or weakness of these societal norms (Gelfand et al., 2017). These patterns were observed across nations in the original 2011 study and were replicated when examining variation within nations, such as across different states in the United States (Harrington & Gelfand, 2014).

Moving beyond observations and testing the theoretical assumptions using evolutionary game theory (Pan et al., 2021; Roos et al., 2015), we find that in a number of simulations high levels of threat created pressures to adopt stronger norms for organizing social interactions. Low levels of threat, on the contrary, were responsible for weaker norms. In sum, research has shown that threats are influential in the evolution of tightness in different societies (Gelfand et al., 2020).

These normative differences affect other societal-level dynamics that are of direct relevance and interest for managers. For example, when compared to looser societies, tighter societies tend to be ruled by more authoritarian governments, show less respect for political rights and civic freedoms, and tend to have higher rates of religiosity. At the individual level, people within tighter cultures display greater need for structure, are more prevention focused, and are less open (Gelfand et al., 2011). As a result, Gelfand et al. (2006) proposed that in tighter societies, organizational cultures favor the adoption of rules and predictability. This leads to more highly controlled and regulated recruitment, selection, and training practices as well as more developed performance monitoring systems. In contrast, organizations located in looser societies are likely to have organizational cultures that endorse flexibility and experimentation, as well as less controlled organizational practices. Adjustment of expatriates and organizational mergers may be more challenging when organizations and individuals vary in terms of tightness versus looseness.

Several investigations have shown the relevance of tightness versus looseness for organizational creativity (Chua et al., 2015), negotiations (Gunia et al., 2011), leadership perceptions (Aktas et al., 2016), entrepreneurship (Lettau, 2016), and adjustment of expatriates (Geeraert et al., 2019). As noted earlier, cultural tightness also appears to strengthen the effects of cultural values on work outcomes (Taras et al., 2011).

Other studies have pointed to the evolution of cultural dynamics (Ralston et al., 2006; Taras et al., 2012; Van Hoorn, 2019). Taras and colleagues' (2012) meta-analysis of studies using Hofstede's measures showed that the rank order of nations on these dimensions changed from the 1970s to the 2000s and that the validity of Hofstede's dimensions has steadily decreased over the decades. This finding highlights that relying on decades-old data may not be appropriate for data collected today. The most relevant study tracking societal-level changes in representative samples was launched by the World Values Survey, which has monitored the beliefs and values of citizens in over 81 societies since the 1980s (see Inglehart & Baker, 2000). The theories presented in this survey are driven by political science's modernization theories (Welzel, 2014) as well as behavioral ecology theories (Fischer, 2017, 2021; Inglehart, 2018; Sng et al., 2018). These analyses have now suggested consistent shifts in values and behaviors in large populations across the world that seem to follow similar trajectories, given systematic changes in economic and technological conditions (Welzel, 2014). The COVID-19 pandemic as an acute threat has already produced value shifts over a relatively short time period (Daniel et al., 2021). Recent investigations of political crises suggest that culture-specific problem-solving strategies such as *jeitinho* can be reinforced and shift cultural dynamics (Fischer et al., 2022). Using insights from evolutionary biology and psychology, we can pinpoint salient mechanisms within the social, economic, and ecological environment. These mechanisms can lead to macro-level changes via changed motivational dynamics at the individual level (Fischer, 2017) and can be modeled by game-theoretical principles (Pan et al., 2021). However, a large random element may not necessarily prioritize functional reactions to changes in social, economic, and historical conditions. Indeed, group selection theories may predict that solutions to real or imagined problems are not necessarily adaptive but instead provide the variability for cultural selection to work (Mesoudi, 2009).

Qualitative Approaches to Culture

Qualitative approaches and critical incidence techniques (Flanagan, 1954) in intercultural work encounters have been critical for identification of salient cultural dimensions in the European tradition (Thomas, 1988; Fink & Meierewert, 2001). This approach has more heavily influenced the management practices of European-based multinational companies than companies in the English-speaking world. This so-called cultural standard method can provide novel opportunities for paradigm interplays that provide synergies and a bridge between both positivist and interpretative paradigms (e.g., Romani et al., 2011). Birkinshaw et al. (2011) showed that qualitative methods are particularly useful for understanding and interpreting the cultural, institutional, and organizational contexts produced by globalization and their impact on firms' cross-cultural transactions. Moreover, they can allow for new conceptualizations and interpretations of culture, and they can also provide a better understanding of the micro-processes associated with cross-cultural interactions within specific institutional contexts (see Romani et al., 2011). Moore and Brannen (2018) outlined a comparative ethnographic method for international human resource management. They highlighted the often-explicit comparative nature of early anthropological research and reported how this research has shaped our understanding of culture. The shifts in research practice that took place in the second half of the twentieth century led to a reorientation of anthropological and ethnographic methods, with more emphasis shifted to reflexivity and reflection on the position of the researcher. Nevertheless, the comparative angle never completely vanished. Moore and Brannen emphasize that by contextualizing experience in terms of both cultural similarity and difference, ethnographic methodologies can play an important role. Hence, the focus on the lived experience of managers may provide unique novel insights and learning opportunities.

As an example, note that Hinds et al. (2014) focused on the role of language along group faultlines (Lau & Murnighan, 1998) in global teams. Their ethnographic and interview-based work revealed that faultlines are more likely to emerge around language competencies in global teams when a power struggle arises. When there is an established hierarchy between teams and among team members, faultlines are unlikely to erupt into more open tension and conflict and differences in language competencies are more likely to be tolerated. In contrast, when teams are in open competition for projects and status, language competencies in the dominant language can provide the proverbial lightning rod for group faultlines to emerge.

Drawing on extensive qualitative and mixed-method research, Cramton et al. (2021) used the script concept to examine breakdowns in complex work projects conducted by teams from different cultural backgrounds. These breakdowns can provoke delays and even project failure. Cramton et al. defined coordination scripts as cognitive and behavioral patterns related to individuals' comprehensions of their tasks and their roles (role structure scripts), their expectations about the temporal structures of coordination (temporal structure scripts) as well as the cues workers recognize in their interactions with others (cue scripts). These scripts are shaped by institutional differences at industry and organization levels. Scripts are also influenced by cultural coordination templates, which differ across national cultures and guide the preferences for coordination's scripts that are specific to certain institutional contexts. Cramton et al. outlined four cultural coordination templates. (1) The US coordination template, marked by pragmatic and friendly goal-directed flexibility that aims to overcome sticking points in task coordination; (2) the German coordination template, characterized by deliberate expert synchronization (each individual has a well-defined role for performing tasks in which they are expert) and by confrontational integration of expert inputs as a way to avoid task coordination problems; (3) the Indian coordination template, marked by adaptive responsiveness to rank ties using flexibility and improvisation in responding to problems signalized by superiors more than to a stated schedule; and (4) the Japanese coordination template, characterized by an emphasis on cultivation of consensus across domains as a way to harmonize relationships among people, although rank also matters. Cramton et al. (2021) state that in-depth studies can identify the multiple factors that influence task coordination in global work projects across diverse institutional contexts. Qualitative methods have significant potential to broaden and expand contemporary theories derived from quantitative methods (see Søderberg, 2020).

Methodological Innovations and Challenges

In our brief final section, we revisit some of the methodological innovations, but we also focus on some of the continuing challenges. We begin with one of the greatest opportunities, the digital transformation. The availability of big data approaches across virtually all areas of organizational functioning has opened unprecedented options for research. For example, it is now possible to conduct psychological diagnostics across temporal and geographical distances (e.g., Du et al., 2023; Fischer et al., 2020) and to identify patterns in hiring discrimination at the population level (Hangartner et al., 2021). These opportunities also raise significant ethical challenges (Sivarajah et al., 2017). It remains to be seen whether ethical guidelines in Western societies will provide greater protection of individuals (which is highly desirable) but ultimately drive research from academia toward industry or other legal contexts, which are less stringently regulated. The recent controversies surrounding Cambridge Analytica in which data harvested through Facebook apps was sold and used for political purposes without consent by the individuals are a case in point. This area promises significant growth and raises major ethical and moral questions that need to be addressed.

In line with these data analytical revolutions, the rapid advances in multivariate statistics have allowed more sophisticated analyses of the complex relationships between individuals, organizations, institutions, and national cultures, in particular multilevel models that can more adequately capture these relationships (Van Herk & Fischer, 2017). We also have more high-quality mixed-method studies that combine quantitative and qualitative insights to advance our understanding of working in global teams (e.g., Gibson et al., 2019). Experimental studies, though still rare in management, are important in producing a sounder understanding of the causal dynamics of relationships that are typically based on cross-sectional observational data (see Fischer & Karl, 2020, but see also Pearl & MacKenzie, 2018 for alternative views on causality). The studies on cultural norms and cognition in psychology that we reviewed earlier in this chapter show that important inroads can be made using experimental designs. Therefore, greater methodological power and precision have facilitated theoretical breakthroughs regarding culture and organizations.

At the same time, the last few years have also been marked by greater concerns about transparency and methodological rigor as well as about the replicability of empirical research. This replication crisis has undermined public confidence in the scientific process and the relevance of science for solving social, including organizational, problems. Preregistration is one important step in enhancing the transparency and validity of organizational scholarship. One concerning sign is that many of the studies reviewed here have a higher number of confirmed than disconfirmed hypotheses. This is worrisome because the ratio of confirmed to unconfirmed hypotheses should not be biased to this degree. Preregistration helps to a priori specify hypotheses and analytical plans to safeguard against the problems associated with the researcher's degree of freedom (Simmons et al., 2011). In addition, more complex statistical results such as multilevel models, including interactions, require more and clearer description. For example, moderation effects should be plotted clearly showing the interaction on appropriate scales, simple effects in the context of interactions need to be reported, and reporting effect sizes should be common practice. The issue concerning the relative size of cultural differences only became apparent when researchers started paying more attention to cross-cultural effect sizes. We urge researchers to be more careful in reporting and contextualizing their research findings.

An additional challenge for international research is the need to establish the validity of the instruments and testing whether procedures are appropriate and relevant for all populations and samples included. Without valid and reliable measurement instruments, interview schedules, coding schemes, or observation guidelines, researchers will inevitably reach inappropriate conclusions about the topic at hand. Translation guidelines and checklists have been refined and further developed in recent years. One important innovation, the TRAPD methodology (Translation, Review, Adjudication, Pretesting and Documentation; Harkness, 2003), overcomes many of the shortcomings of translation–backtranslation. Unfortunately, however, translation–backtranslation remains the dominant translation method in major international business journals (Chidlow et al., 2014). Excellent guidelines and checklists are available for both item generation and translation, and we strongly encourage researchers to use these resources (e.g., European Social Survey, no date; International Test Commission, 2018, Jowell et al., 2007).

Data collection and data analysis also need to be carefully conducted to control and rule out bias and establish invariance or equivalence. This work was developed within the context of psychometric testing but is more broadly applicable (e.g., see the application to experimental research in Fischer & Karl, 2020). These ideas would also be applicable with regard to training or organizational interventions in cross-national contexts more broadly because they define the criteria needed to identify the target problem to be addressed and to guide thinking concerning how a specific management problem may manifest itself within and across cultural contexts. Within the unified bias and equivalence framework (see Fischer & Karl, 2019; Van de Vijver & Leung, 2021), researchers' first step is to explore the conceptual or philosophical status of the variable of interest and how it may differ within and across cultural groups. What constitutes high performance, or what is intrinsic motivation? To aim is to identify the functional equivalence of concepts to be compared and measured across cultural contexts. Without the functional equivalence of concepts assuming some unity (see Patel, 2015), there is little scope to continue with explicit comparisons. This also links directly back to the discussion of possible culture-specific constructs and the emic-etic issue we discussed above.

The second step is to generate observable indicators that can measure both the general and specific cultural aspects of the construct of interest. Would intrinsic motivation manifest itself in the same way across different cultural contexts? Culturally specific and relevant items or indicators of the construct (e.g., of intrinsic motivation) need to be identified within and across cultures, which are then translated into survey items. Researchers need to consider that the intended instrument captures the whole domain or range of the construct of interest. Are all relevant domains and expressions of intrinsic motivation captured in the new instrument? If not, the instrument is thought to suffer from domain underrepresentation because it does not cover all context-specific expressions of the construct (e.g., intrinsic motivation). This second step is typically labeled structure equivalence. These two steps are often combined under the label of construct equivalence (although conceptually it makes sense to separate the philosophical from the operational step).

These steps are typically guided by qualitative and ethnographic work. Once an instrument is being applied and data is being collected, statistical procedures can be applied to examine the statistical comparability of the data. Both the strength of the relationship between each indicator and the overall construct (e.g., factor loading or item discrimination), as well as the purity of the item (does the indicator capture other construct content independent from the construct of interest, which leads to differences in item intercepts or item difficulty) can be tested statistically. To the extent that an instrument demonstrates similar relationships between each indicator and the intended theoretical construct across cultural groups, metric equivalence is achieved. To the extent that the indicators only capture variance due to the construct of interest (e.g., no intercept differences or differences in item difficulty), then the researcher has identified conditions of full score or scalar equivalence, and mean scores can be directly compared across groups. In recent years, significant progress has been made in identifying statistical procedures that can be applied to answer these questions (see Boer et al., 2018 for a general overview). Despite major progress in the number and diversity of available methods, many researchers still do not report relevant information to demonstrate how results can be interpreted and whether the reported results are cross-culturally valid (Boer et al., 2018; Fischer & Karl, 2019). Results cannot be interpreted due to possible biases if invariance is not demonstrated (Fischer et al., 2022). This is a major area for further improvement. Powerful conceptual and statistical tools have been developed, and we strongly encourage intercultural business researchers to make greater use of them.

Theoretical Challenges

Beyond Culture Fit

As we discussed earlier, culture-fit and broad contingency theories continue to dominate thinking within a functional-structural mode of culture research. Yet, such conventional wisdom may not adequately reflect the complex realities of contemporary organizations, which, as we have outlined in this chapter, operate in environments that are often subject to contradictory and conflict demands. The assumption of internally coherent cultural systems is not well aligned with conceptualizations of cultures as open systems and the emergent realization that cultures develop and change following classic evolutionary dynamics (Kashima et al., 2019). Examining cultural processes across multiple levels (individual to organization to country) simultaneously has started to provide new insights confirming that broad contingency and culture-fit approaches may be too simplistic to capture the dynamics facing modern organizations.

For example, a recent 17-country study involving 267 organizations focused on uncertainty dynamics (Fischer et al., 2019). Certainty is an epistemic human need, and dealing with uncertainty will take up crucial cognitive resources. Humans have evolved within specific evolutionary environments that have shaped our cognitive systems, prioritizing safety and security in our immediate environments and focusing our attention on immediate threats to survival and uncertainty. Given these cognitive limitations, in the context of perceived uncertainty, employees use available cognitive resources to cope with perceived uncertainty to regain a sense of control. Therefore, they are unlikely to engage in discretionary or high-performance behaviors that would require additional cognitive demands. As a consequence, desirable behavior such as organizational citizenship behavior (Kenrick et al., 2010) is likely to be reduced.

As discussed above, contingency and culture-fit theory predict that organizations in high-uncertainty contexts should adopt their practices and organizational culture to match this high level of uncertainty. From an evolutionary and systems perspective, a different hypothesis would be plausible. In highly uncertain environments, organizational formalization can compensate and buffer negative effects of uncertainty by providing structure and clarity. This will increase employees' sense of control and reduce their need to expend cognitive resources on coping with uncertainty. According to ideas from normology, clear normative perceptions of rules and procedures allow employees to rely on perceived norms of greater formalization as a form of "social autopilot" (in the form of "I know what is expected of me because I see what others are doing and how the organization runs"; Morris, Hong, et al., 2015). In contrast to culture-fit arguments, organizations can actively counter contextual effects by increasing formalization, which in turn facilitates higher levels of OCB in countries with high uncertainty through freeing up cognitive resources and reducing levels of anxiety due to contextual uncertainty.

These hypotheses were supported in a three-level analysis across samples from all inhabited continents. Discretionary behavior focusing on making suggestions and improving work conditions increased with organizational formalization, but this effect was only observed in high-uncertainty contexts (Fischer et al., 2019). Hence, culture-fit arguments might be too simplistic when accounting for the complex realities organizations are facing. Greater nuance and attention to cognitive capacities and constraints within specific contexts and how organizations may help employees achieve their full potential are needed. Researchers should develop theoretical models that can incorporate these distinct demands and provide more comprehensive models of organizational functioning across different levels of analysis.

Culture Equals Nation?

Much of the current research is conducted with the idea that citizenship and culture are exchangeable. Having arrived at this point in our review, we need to revisit some core assumptions that have guided much cross-cultural management and business research to date. Studies on national differences using either value or norm dimensions are guided by a number of core assumptions: (1) that modern geographical boundaries are appropriate to delimit different cultures; (2) that culture is shared by the members of a given country, hence leading to assumptions of consensual and homogeneous cultures which can be statistically described using the mean of a distribution of responses; and (3) that culture is relatively stable and consistent over long periods of time (Leung & Morris, 2015; Steel & Taras, 2010; Taras et al., 2009). These assumptions have been increasingly challenged by empirical and theoretical arguments.

First, the assumption that the culture is homogeneous has been challenged by the observation that there is greater variation within any given culture than between cultures (Fischer & Schwartz, 2011; Taras et al., 2011). Fischer and Schwartz (2011) summarized value data from both specific occupational populations (teachers) and nationally representative samples and found that, except for values related to religiosity, 80% or more of the variance was due to individual differences and not to cultural differences as captured by country boundaries. In a meta-analysis of 558 studies that had used Hofstede's framework, Taras et al. (2016) reported that 79 to 84% of the variance in value scores was within countries and a maximum of 21% of the variance was due to between-country differences. Occupational differences explained 50% of the variance in power distance scores, and education and generational differences between samples were more meaningful than country for understanding differences in uncertainty avoidance, power distance, and individualism values. These patterns suggest that factors such as socioeconomic level, ethnicity, religion, age cohorts, and profession, as well as political variables such as levels of equality and freedom, often better explain differences between samples than country (Ronen & Shenkar 2013; Taras et al., 2016).

In defense of using the nation-state, a number of studies have demonstrated that country is a better empirical boundary for classifying cultural orientations of individuals compared to ethnic or religious affiliation (see Minkov & Hofstede, 2012, 2014). Within Europe, van Herk and Poortinga (2012) found little evidence that regions within a country were important in explaining cultural differences. Similar to the work by Minkov and Hofstede, they found that economic and political conditions associated with national boundaries were more relevant for explaining value differences within modern Europe. Peterson and colleagues (Peterson & Sonderson, 2014; Peterson et al., 2018) provide a cautious outlook on the continuing relevance of national country borders as a useful proxy for delineating relevant cultural boundaries for management and international business research using their FICE (Functional, Institutional, and Critical Event) framework.

Peterson and colleagues differentiate three major groups of theories that have an immediate relevance for the salience and relevance of national boundaries. Functional explanations rely on the assumption (shared with most value and normative culture researchers, see the structural-functional definitions of culture above) that societies have to solve a number of problems of survival. Further, the characteristic or customary way of resolving these problems can be captured in the dominant values or norms expressed by individuals in the same societal boundary. Functional explanations can include rational (e.g., societies actively identifying, selecting, and executing ways to meet present and anticipated future challenges) or ecological theories (e.g., societies react to ecological challenges, and those societies that do not meet those challenges cease to exist, hence, this is a pure evolutionary explanation). Common theories in this domain fall into the group of modernization theories (Inglehart & Welzel, 2005).

The second group consisting of institutional theories focuses on the central role of institutions in creating meaning and legitimacy (see Kara & Peterson, 2012). This approach is akin to the dominance definitions of culture that we introduced at the beginning of this chapter and is shared by critical and interpretative scholars (see Gertsen & Zølner, 2020; Romani et al., 2020). According to neo-institutional theorists (e.g., Scott, 1995), governmental institutions foster an internal national culture that facilitates interactions within the country's boundaries; influence governmental policies and practices that shape behavior in response, and through shared language and communication systems (including road networks, electronic communication technologies, and mass media) promote and facilitate exchange of information within boundaries. All of this sets up center–periphery relationships that gravitate toward a shared common language within contemporary national boundaries. Institutional theories do not assume that the behavior and practices by institutional actors is functional or rational. Even though specific ways of solving problems may have been functional in the past, through institutionalization and enforcement or even coercion of actions within the system, the behavioral responses can become dysfunctional and irrational (Scott, 1995).

Finally, critical event explanations of cultural boundaries use complexity and chaos models that focus on major, cataclysmic events that are hard to predict and rarely occur (see Kara & Peterson, 2012, for an overview). These models are more common in history and sociology as ways to explain major disruptions that are either difficult to foresee or driven by complex constellations of actors and groups. Classic examples are wars and economic disasters that result from gradual degradation of social and institutional relations, which lead to either reinforcement or change of national boundaries. Singular events of a critical nature (e.g., natural disasters, economic collapse, and individual life histories of leaders that can shape the trajectory of a group) can often dramatically shape national histories and have a lasting impact on behavior. Some attempts have been made to model larger underlying dynamics using dynamic systems models (for an example focusing on U.S. history, see Turchin, 2017).

The FICE framework is relevant in that it simultaneously supports the continuing use of national boundaries as a legitimate focus of international business research (as national institutions have a significant effect on communication and management activities within national boundaries) and points to the processes that can break this alignment between "culture" and country boundaries. It highlights the complex functional, institutional, and critical events that are taking place at a subnational level and may lead to significant local cultural centers that do not well align with national boundaries. Bringing together political science theory and applying it to management research makes this a valuable framework for further exploration of the utility of national boundaries. Missing within the FICE model is a more explicit embrace of dynamics from evolutionary biology and behavioral ecology. Using well-established evolutionary dynamics can provide the micro- and macro-mechanisms through which these different theories described within the FICE model are operating (see Kashima et al., 2019). Hence, more theory-driven research may identify the origins and dynamics of both subnational and regional clusters that go beyond national country boundaries (see Inglehart & Baker, 2000).

Polyculturalism

Implicit in the previous section is another major challenge for contemporary culture theory. Modern societies are becoming increasingly complex and characterized by multiple cultural influences and dynamics. Morris, Chiu, et al. (2015) proposed the term *polyculturalism* to capture the complex interactions between cultural traditions and the resultant impact on individuals, making cultural influences on individuals partial and plural. In other words, individuals absorb the elements not only of their nominal culture of origin, but also of other cultures with which they interact (Morris, Chiu, et al., 2015). As a result, they develop beliefs about the interactions and mutual influences between cultural groups, which will affect their attitudes and behaviors in intercultural contexts (Rosenthal & Levy, 2010). The concept of polyculturalism is not equivalent to multiculturalism, which tends to emphasize the distinctiveness, integrity, and need to preserve different cultural traditions (Rosenthal & Levy, 2013). Polyculturalism accepts the fluidity and hybridism that exist between different cultural groups, while multiculturalists see this situation as a threat to preserving the authenticity of cultural groups (Hong et al., 2016).

Recently, several studies have pointed out that polyculturalism can emerge as a positive predictor of intergroup processes and increase intergroup contact of ethnically and culturally diverse groups (e.g., Bernardo et al., 2019; Rosenthal & Levy, 2016). Experimental studies also demonstrated that polyculturalism is associated with preferences for different cultural experiences (Cho et al, 2017) and increases cultural accommodation (Cho et al., 2018).

These positive effects may be more likely in contexts that are already characterized by high levels of cultural diversity. Therefore, these results may not be found in contexts with greater cultural homogeneity (Bernardo et al., 2019). The empirical evidence available to date demonstrates that a dynamic perspective in line with polyculturalism may provide novel insights into work conditions in global teams and intercultural contexts.

Final Remarks

We reviewed major developments in the study of culture and organizations since the start of the new millennium, marked by major transitions in the global management and international business landscape. We have seen a diversification of research traditions, and using general systems and evolutionary perspectives within a transdisciplinary research framework, we have started to provide novel insights into cultural dynamics.

Five Theoretical Principles

1. Cultural processes are dynamic and are grounded in ecological, economic, and social conditions. Cultures change through both micro- and macro-level dynamics that are shaped and validated through repeated social interaction cycles between individuals and institutions.
2. Cultural dynamics should be studied using multiple theoretical and empirical lenses, focusing on values, norms, and cognition.
3. Basic cultural dimensions have broad validity, but individual differences often explain more variance in specific behaviors than broad cultural dimensions.

4. Culture-specific informal problem-solving strategies are important for understanding management and work behavior in specific contexts, but these strategies can be seen as driven by universal behavioral processes displayed in specific social, economic, and historical contexts.
5. Culture is situationally grounded: Greater attention needs to be paid to the micro-dynamics of culture, including local traditions and norms that may help to explain work behavior in addition to national culture.

Five Key Practical Implications

1. National culture does not explain more variance than individual differences: Avoid essentializing culture; also avoid simplistic cultural stereotypes, and try to understand the motivations and cognitions of each employee.
2. Building strong group identity and establishing routines early on during global teams/projects is essential for better work performance, for it helps to set expectations, establishes norms, and creates a shared mindset.
3, Management practices can be used to buffer the possible negative impacts of the social, economic, and cultural environment.
4. Attention should be paid to what employees value and what they do. The mismatch can be informative about complexities and possible intervention points from a managerial perspective.
5. Attention should be given to contemporary cultural and social dynamics. Cultures are dynamic and are changing with shifting social, economic, and technological realities.

References

Adler, N. J., & Gundersen, A. (2008). *International dimensions of organizational behavior* (5th ed.). Cincinnati, Ohio: Thomson South-Western.

Aktas, M., Gelfand, M., & Hanges, P. (2016). Cultural tightness–looseness and perceptions of effective leadership. *Journal of Cross-Cultural Psychology, 47*, 294–309. doi:10.1177/0022022115606802

Alofan, F., Chen, S., & Tan, H. (2020). National cultural distance, organizational culture, and adaptation of management innovations in foreign subsidiaries: A fuzzy set analysis of TQM implementation in Saudi Arabia. *Journal of Business Research, 109*, 184–199. doi: 10.1016/j.jbusres.2019.11.037

Arieli, S., Sagiv, L., & Roccas, S. (2020). Values at work: The impact of personal values in organizations. *Applied Psychology: An International Review, 69*(2), 230–275. https://doi.org/10.1111/apps.12181

Aycan, Z., Kanungo, R., Mendonca, M., Yu, K., Deller, J., Stahl, G., & Kurshid, A. 2000. Impact of culture on human resource management practices: A 10 country comparison. *Applied Psychology, 49*, 192–221.

Barkema, H.G., Bell, J.H.J., & Pennings, J. (1996). Foreign entry, cultural barriers, and learning. *Strategic Management Journal*, 17, 151–166. doi: 10.1002/(SICI)1097-0266(199602)17:2<151::AID-SMJ799>3.0.CO;2-Z

Bernardo, A. B., Salanga, M. G., Tjipto, S., Hutapea, B., Khan, A. H., & Yeung, S. (2019). Polyculturalism and attitudes toward the continuing presence of former colonizers in four postcolonial Asian societies. *Frontiers in Psychology, 10*, 1335. doi: 10.3389/fpsyg.2019.01335

Beugelsdijk, S., Ambos, B., & Nell, P. C. (2018). Conceptualizing and measuring distance in international business research: Recurring questions and best practice guidelines. *Journal of International Business Studies, 49*, 1113–1137. https://doi.org/(...)57/s41267-018-0182-4

Beugelsdijk, S., Kostova, T., Kunst, V., Spadafora, E., & van Essen, M. (2018). Cultural distance and firm internationalization: A meta-analytical review and theoretical implications. *Journal of Management, 44*, 89–130. doi: 10.1177/0149206317729027

Beugelsdijk, S., Kostova, T., & Roth, K. (2017). An overview of Hofstede-inspired country level culture research in international business since 2006. *Journal of International Business Studies, 48*, 30–47. doi: 10.1057/s41267-016-0038-8

Birkinshaw, J., Brannen, M., & Tung, R. (2011). From a distance and generalizable to up close and grounded: Reclaiming a place for qualitative methods in international business research. *Journal of International Business Studies, 42*, 573–581. doi: 10.1057/jibs.2011.19

Boer, D., Hanke, K., & He, J. (2018). On detecting systematic measurement error in cross-cultural research: A review and critical reflection on equivalence and invariance tests. *Journal of Cross-Cultural Psychology, 49*, 713–734. doi:10.1177/0022022117749042

Bond, M. H., Leung, K., Au, A., Tong, K.-K., & Chemonges-Nielson, Z. (2004). Combining social axioms with values in predicting social behaviours. *European Journal of Personality, 18*(3), 177–191. https://doi.org/10.1002/per.509

Burns, T., & Stalker, G. M. 1961. *The management of innovation.* London: Tavistock.

Chen, C. C., Chen, Y. R., & Xin, K. (2004). Guanxi practices and trust in management: A procedural justice perspective. *Organization Science, 15*, 200–209. doi: 10.1287/orsc.1030.0047

Chen, C. C., Gaspar, J. P., Friedman, R., Newburry, W., Nippas, M. C. V., Xin, K., & Parent, R. (2017). Paradoxical relationships between cultural norms of particularism and attitudes toward relational favoritism: A cultural reflectivity perspective. *Journal of Business Ethics, 145*, 63–79. doi: 10.1007/s10551-015-2843-6

Chen, N. Y., & Tjosvold, D. (2007). Guanxi and leader member relationships between American managers and Chinese employees: Open-minded dialogue as mediator. *Asia Pacific Journal of Management, 24*, 171–189. doi: 10.1007/s10490-006-9029-9

Chen, X. P., & Chen, C. C. (2004). On the intricacies of the Chinese *guanxi*: A process model of *guanxi* development. *Asia Pacific Journal of Management, 21*, 305–324. doi: 10.1023/B:APJM.0000036465.19102.d5

Cheung, F. M., van de Vijver, F. J. R., & Leong, F. T. L. (2011). Toward a new approach to the study of personality in culture. *American Psychologist, 66*(7), 593–603. https://doi.org/10.1037/a0022389

Chidlow, A., Plakoyiannaki, M. E., & Welch, C. (2014). Translation in cross-language international business research: Beyond equivalence. *Journal of International Business Studies, 45*(5), 562–582.

Chiu, C. Y., Gelfand, M. J., Yamagishi, T., Shteynberg, G., & Wan, C. (2010). Intersubjective culture: The role of intersubjective perceptions in cross-cultural research. *Perspectives on Psychological Science, 5*, 482–493. doi:10.1177/1745691610375562

Cho, J., Morris, M. W., & Dow, B. (2018). How do the Romans feel when visitors "Do as the Romans Do"? Diversity ideologies and trust in evaluations of cultural accommodation. *Academy of Management Discoveries, 4*, 11–31. doi: 10.5465/amd.2016.0044

Cho, J., Morris, M. W., Slepian, M. L., & Tadmor, C. T. (2017). Choosing fusion: The effects of diversity ideologies on preference for culturally mixed experiences. *Journal of Experimental Social Psychology, 69*, 163–171. doi: 10.1016/j.jesp.2016.06.013

Chua, R. Y. J., Roth, Y., & Lemoine, J.-F. (2015). The impact of culture on creativity: How cultural tightness and cultural distance affect global innovation crowdsourcing work. *Administrative Sciences Quarterly, 60*, 189–227. doi: 10.1177/0001839214563595

Cialdini, R. B., Reno, R. R., & Kallgren, C. A. (1990). A focus theory of normative conduct: Recycling the concept of norms to reduce littering in public places. *Journal of Personality and Social Psychology, 58*, 1015–1026. doi:10.1037/0022-3514.58.6.1015

Clark, A. E., & Kashima, Y. (2007). Stereotypes help people connect with others in the community: A situated functional analysis of the stereotype consistency bias in communication. *Journal of Personality and Social Psychology*, 93(6), 1028–1039.

Cramton, C. D., Köhler, T., & Levitt, R. E. (2021). Using scripts to address cultural and institutional challenges of global project coordination. *Journal of International Business Studies, 52*, 56–77. doi: 10.1057/s41267-020-00337-7

Daniel, E., Bardi, A., Fischer, R., Benish-Weisman, M., & Lee, J. A. (2021). Changes in personal values in pandemic times. *Social Psychological and Personality Science, 13*(2), 572–582. https://doi.org/10.1177/1948550621102402

Du, A. H., Karl, J. A., Fetvadjiev, V., Luczak-Roesch, M., Pirngruber, R., & Fischer, R. (2023). Tracing the evolution of personality cognition in early human civilizations: A computational analysis of the Gilgamesh epic. *European Journal of Personality*. https://doi.org/10.1177/08902070231161869

Duarte, F. (2006). Exploring the interpersonal transaction of the Brazilian jeitinho in bureaucratic contexts. *Organization*, 13, 509–528. doi: 10.1177/1350508406065103

Ellis, S., Almor, T., & Shenkar, O. (2002). Structural contingency revisited: Toward a dynamic system model. *Emergence, 4*, 51–85.

European Social Survey. (no date). Translation. https://www.europeansocialsurvey.org/methodology/ess_methodology/translation/

Faulkner, S. L., Baldwin, J. R., Lindsley, S. L., & Hecht, M. L. (2006). Layers of meaning: An analysis of definitions of culture. In J. R. Baldwin, S. L. Faulkner, M. L. Hecht, & S. L. Lindsley (Eds.), *Redefining culture: Perspectives across the disciplines* (pp. 27–51). Mahwah, NJ: Lawrence Erlbaum.

Ferreira, M. C., Fischer, R., Porto, J. B., Pilati, R., & Milfont, T. (2012). Unraveling the mystery of Brazilian jeitinho: A cultural exploration of social norms. *Journal of Cross-Cultural Psychology, 38*, 331–344. doi: 10.1177/0146167211427148

Fetvadjiev, V. H., Meiring, D., Van de Vijver, F. J. R., Nel, J. A., & Hill, C. (2015). The South African Personality Inventory (SAPI): A culture-informed instrument for the country's main ethnocultural groups. *Psychological Assessment*, 27, 827–837. doi:10.1037/pas0000078

Fink, G., & Meierewert, S. (Eds.). (2001). *Interkulturelles Management: Osterreichische Perspektiven*. Vienna: Springer-Verlag.

Fischer, R. (2006). Congruence and functions of personal and cultural values: Do my values reflect my culture's values? *Personality and Social Psychology Bulletin, 32*, 1419–1431. doi: 10.1177/0146167206291425

Fischer, R. (2012). Intersubjective culture: Indeed intersubjective or yet another form of subjective assessment? *Swiss Journal of Psychology* (Special Issue: Personality and Culture), *71*, 13–20. doi: 0.1024/1421-0185/a000067

Fischer, R. (2017). *Personality, values, culture: An evolutionary perspective*. Cambridge: Cambridge University Press.

Fischer, R. (2020). What is the practical utility of value research for organizational practitioners in a global context? *Applied Psychology: An International Review, 69*, 276–283. doi: 10.1111/apps.12190

Fischer, R. (2021). Origins of values differences: A two-level analysis of economic, climatic and parasite stress explanations in the value domain. *Cross-Cultural Research, 55*(5), 438–473. https://doi.org/10.1177/00220 22109332738

Fischer, R., & Boer, D. (2015). Motivational basis of personality traits: A meta-analysis of value-personality correlations. *Journal of Personality, 83*, 491–510. doi: 10.1111/jopy.12125

Fischer, R., Ferreira, M. C., Assmar, E., Redford, P., Harb, C., Glazer, S., & Achoui, M. (2009). Individualism-collectivism as descriptive norms. *Journal of Cross-Cultural Psychology, 40*, 187–213. doi: 10.1177/0022022109332738.

Fischer, R., Ferreira, M. C., Milfont, T. L., & Pilati, R. (2014). Culture of corruption? The effects of priming corruption images in a high corruption context. *Journal of Cross-Cultural Psychology, 45*, 1594–1605. doi: 10.1177/0022022114548874.

Fischer, R., Ferreira, M. C., van Meurs, N., Gok, K., Jiang, D. Y., Fontaine, J., & Abubakar, A. (2019). Does organizational formalization facilitate voice and helping organizational citizenship behavior? It depends on (national) uncertainty norms. *Journal of International Business Studies, 50*, 125–134. https://doi.org/10.1057/s41267-017-0132-6

Fischer, R., & Karl, J. A. (2019). A primer to (cross-cultural) multi-group invariance testing possibilities in R. *Frontiers in Psychology*. 10.3389/fpsyg.2019.01507

Fischer, R., & Karl, J. A. (2020). Experimental methodologies. In B. Szkudlarek, J. Osland, D. Caprar, & L. Romani (Eds.), *The SAGE handbook of contemporary cross-cultural management* (pp. 111–126). London: SAGE.

Fischer, R., Karl, J. A., Fontaine, J. F., & Poortinga, Y. (2022). Evidence of validity does not rule out systematic bias: A commentary on nomological noise and cross-cultural invariance. *Sociological Methods and Research*. https://doi.org/10.1177/00491241221091756

Fischer, R., Karl, J. A., Luczak-Roesch, M., Fetvadjiev, V. H., & Grener, A. (2020) Tracing personality structure in narratives: A computational bottom-up approach to unpack writers, characters, and personality in historical context, *European Journal of Personality, 34*(5), 917–943. doi: https://doi.org/10.1002/per.2270

Fischer, R., Karl, J. A., & Pilati, R. (2022). Cultural syndromes in a changing world: A longitudinal investigation of Brazilian *Jeitinho* social problem-solving strategies. *Personality and Social Psychology Bulletin, 48*(10), 1423–1437. doi: 10.1177/01461672211043385. Epub 2021 Sep 16. PMID: 34528500.

Fischer, R., & Poortinga, Y. (2012). Are cultural values the same as the values of individuals? An examination of similarities in personal, social and cultural value structures. *International Journal of Cross-Cultural Management, 12*, 157–170. doi: 10.1177/1470595812439867

Fischer, R., & Schwartz, S. H. (2011). Whence differences in value priorities? Individual, cultural, or artifactual sources. *Journal of Cross-Cultural Psychology, 42*, 1127–1144. doi: 10.1177/0022022110381429

Fischer, R., Vauclair, C. M., Fontaine, J. R., & Schwartz, S. H. (2010). Are individual- and culture-level value structures different? Testing Hofstede's legacy with the Schwartz Value Survey. *Journal of Cross-Cultural Psychology, 41*, 135–151.

Flanagan, J. C. (1954). The critical incident technique. *Psychological Bulletin, 51*, 327–358.

Froese, F. J., & Peltokorpi, V. (2011) Cultural distance and expatriate job satisfaction. *International Journal of Intercultural Relations, 35*, 49–60. doi: 10.1016/j.ijintrel.2010.10.002

Gao, W., Qiu, L., Chiu, C. Y., & Yang, Y. Y. (2015). Diffusion of opinions in a complex culture system: Implications for emergence of descriptive norms. *Journal of Cross-Cultural Psychology*, 46, 1252–1259.

Geeraert, N., Li, R., Ward, C., Gelfand, M., & Demes, K. A. (2019). A tight spot: How personality moderates the impact of social norms on sojourner adaptation. *Psychological Science, 30*, 333–342. doi: 10.1177/0956797618815488

Gelfand, M. J., Aycan, Z., Erez, M., & Leung, K. (2017). Cross-cultural industrial organizational psychology and organizational behavior: A hundred-year journey. *Journal of Applied Psychology, 102*, 514–529. doi: 10.1037/apl0000186

Gelfand, M. J., Caluori, N., Jackson, J. C., & Taylor, M. K. (2020). The cultural evolutionary trade-off of ritualistic synchrony. *Philosophical Transactions of the Royal Society B, 375*, 20190432. doi: 10.1098/rstb.2019.0432

Gelfand, M. J., Erez, M., & Aycan, Z. (2007). Cross-cultural organizational behavior. *Annual Review of Psychology, 58*, 479–514.

Gelfand, M. J., Harrington, J. R., & Jackson, J. C. (2017). The strength of social norms across human groups. *Perspectives on Psychological Science, 12*, 800–809. doi: 10.1177/1745691617708631. PMID: 28972845.

Gelfand, M. J., & Jackson, J. C. (2016). From one mind to many: The emerging science of cultural norms. *Current Opinion in Psychology, 8*, 175–181. doi: 10.1016/j.copsyc.2015.11.002

Gelfand, M. J., Nishii, L. H., & Raver, J. L. (2006). On the nature and importance of cultural tightness-looseness. *Journal of Applied Psychology, 91*, 1225–1244. doi: 10.1037/0021-9010.91.6.1225

Gelfand, M. J., Raver, J. L., Nishii, L., Leslie, L. M., Lun, J., Lim, B. C., & Aycan, Z. (2011). Differences between tight and loose cultures: A 33-nation study. *Science, 332*, 1100–1104. doi: 10.1126/science.1197754

Gertsen, M. C., & Zølner, M. (2020). Interpretive approaches to culture: What is interpretative cross-cultural management research? In B. Szkudlarek, L. Romani, D. V. Caprar, & J. S. Osland (Eds.), *The SAGE handbook of contemporary cross-cultural management* (pp. 34–50). London: SAGE.

Gibson, C. B., Dunlop, P. D., & Cordery, J. L. (2019). Managing formalization to increase global team effectiveness and meaningfulness of work in multinational organizations. *Journal of International Business Studies, 50*, 1021–1052. https://doi.org/10.1057/s41267-019-00226-8

Gu, F. F., Hung, K., & Tse, D. K. (2008). When does guanxi matter? Issues of capitalization and its dark sides. *Journal of Marketing, 72*, 12–28. doi: 10.1509/jmkg.72.4.12

Gunia, B. C., Brett, J. M., Nandkeolyar, A. K., & Kamdar, D. (2011). Paying a price: Culture, trust, and negotiation consequences. *Journal of Applied Psychology, 96*, 774–789. doi: 10.1037/a0021986

Hangartner, D., Kopp, D., & Siegenthaler, M. (2021). Monitoring hiring discrimination through online recruitment platforms. *Nature, 589*, 572–576. https://doi.org/10.1038/s41586-020-03136-0

Hanges, P. J., Aiken, J. R., Park, J., & Su, J. (2016). Cross-cultural leadership: Leading around the world. *Current Opinion in Psychology, 8*, 64–69. doi: 10.1016/j.copsyc.2015.10.013

Harrington, J. R., & Gelfand, M. J. (2014). Tightness–looseness across the 50 United States. *Proceedings of the National Academy of Sciences, 111*, 7990–7995. doi: 10.1073/pnas.1317937111

Hinds, P., Neeley, T., & Cramton, C. (2014). Language as a lightning rod: Power contests, emotion regulation, and subgroup dynamics in global teams. *Journal of International Business Studies, 45*, 536–561. https://doi.org/10.1057/jibs.2013.62

Hofstede, G. (1980). *Culture's consequences: International differences in work related values.* Beverly Hills, CA: SAGE.

Hofstede, G. (2001). *Culture's consequences: Comparing values, behaviors, institutions and organizations across nations.* Thousand Oaks, CA: SAGE.

Hofstede, G., & Bond, M. H. (1988). The Confucius connection: From cultural roots to economic growth. *Organizational Dynamics*, 16, 4–21. doi: 10.1016/0090-2616(88)90009-5

Hofstede, G., Hofstede, G. J., & Minkov, M. (2010). *Cultures and organizations: Software of the mind* (3rd. ed.). New York: McGraw-Hill.

Hong Y. Y., & Cheon, B. K. (2017). How does culture matter in the face of globalization? *Perspectives on Psychological Science, 12*, 810–823. doi:10.1177/1745691617700496

Hong, Y. Y., Morris, M. W., Chiu, C. Y., & Benet-Martínez, V. (2000). Multicultural minds: A dynamic constructivist approach to culture and cognition. *American Psychologist, 55*, 709–720. doi: 10.1037// 0003-066X.55.7.709

Hong, Y. Y., Zhan, S., Morris, M. W., & Benet-Martínez, V. (2016). Multicultural identity processes. *Current Opinion in Psychology, 8*, 49–53. doi: 10.1016/j.copsyc.2015.09.020

House, R. J., Hanges, P. J., Javidan, M., Dorfman, P. W., & Gupta, V. (Eds) (2004). *Culture, leadership and organizations: The GLOBE study of 62 societies.* Thousand Oaks, CA: SAGE.

Hwang, K. K. (1997). Guanxi and mientze: Conflict resolution in Chinese society. *Intercultural Communication Studies, 7*, 17–40. doi: 10.1.1.596.4829

Inglehart, R. (2018). *Cultural evolution.* Cambridge: Cambridge University Press. doi: 10.1017/9781108613880

Inglehart, R., & Baker, W. E. (2000). Modernization, cultural change, and the persistence of traditional values. *American Sociological Review, 65*, 19–51. doi: 10.2307/2657288

Inglehart, R., & Welzel, C. (2005). *Modernization, cultural change, and democracy: The human development sequence.* Cambridge: Cambridge University Press. doi: 10.1017/CBO9780511790881

International Test Commission. (2018). Guidelines for translating and adapting tests (Second Edition). *International Journal of Testing, 18*(2), 101–134. doi: 10.1080/15305058.2017.1398166

Jackson, J. C., Gelfand, M., & Ember, C. R. (2020). A global analysis of cultural tightness in non-industrial societies. *Proceedings of the Royal Society B: Biological Sciences, 287*(1930), 20201036. doi: 10.1098/ rspb.2020.1036

Jasso, G., & Opp, K. D. (1997). Probing the character of norms: A factorial survey analysis of the norms of political action. *American Sociological Review, 62*, 947–964. doi: 10.2307/2657349

Jowell, R., Roberts, C., Fitzgerald, R., & Eva, G. (Eds.). (2007). *Measuring attitudes cross-nationally: Lessons from the European Social Survey.* Thousand Oaks, CA: SAGE. ISBN 978-1-4129-1981-4

Kara, A., & Peterson, M. F. (2012). The dynamic societal cultural milieu of organizations: Origins, maintenance and change. In L. Tihanyi, T. M. Devinney, & T. Pedersen (Eds.), Institutional theory in international business and management. *Advances in International Management*, 25 (pp. 341–371). Bingley, UK: Emerald Group Publishing Ltd. https://doi.org/10.1108/S1571-5027(2012)0000025020

Kashima Y. (2016b). Culture and psychology in the 21st century: Conceptions of culture and person revised. *Journal of Cross-Cultural Psychology, 47*(1), 4–20.

Kashima, Y., Bain, P. G., & Perfors, A. (2019). The psychology of cultural dynamics: what is it, what do we know, and what is yet to be known? *Annual Review of Psychology, 70*, 499–529. https://doi.org/10.1146/ annurev-psych-010418-103112

Kashima, Y., Klein, O., & Clark, A. E. (2007). Grounding: Sharing information in social interaction. In K. Fiedler (Ed.), *Frontiers of social psychology. Social communication* (pp. 27–77). Hove, UK: Psychology Press.

Katsikeas, C. S., Samiee, S., & Theodosiou, M. (2006). Strategy fit and performance consequences of international marketing standardization. *Strategic Management Journal, 27*, 867–890.

Kenrick, D. T., Griskevicius, V., Neuberg, S. L., & Schaller, M. (2010). Renovating the pyramid of needs contemporary extensions built upon ancient foundations. *Perspectives on Psychological Science, 5*, 292–314.

Kirsch, C., Chelliah, J., & Parry, W. (2012). The impact of cross-cultural dynamics on change management. *Cross Cultural Management, 19*, 166–195. doi: 10.1108/13527601211219865

Kogut, B., & Singh, H. (1988). The effect of national culture on the choice of entry mode. *Journal of International Business Studies, 19*, 411–432. doi: 10.1057/palgrave.jibs.8490394

Kroeber, A. L., & Kluckhohn, C. (1952). *Culture: A critical review of concepts and definitions.* Cambridge, MA: Peabody Museum of American Archaeology and Ethnology, Harvard University.

Kuper, A. (1999). *Culture: The anthropologists' account.* London: Harvard University Press.

Lamoreaux, M., & Morling, B. (2012). Outside the head and outside individualism-collectivism: Further meta-analyses of cultural products. *Journal of Cross-Cultural Psychology, 43*(2), 299–327. https://doi.org/10.1177/0022022110385234

Lau, D. C., & Murnighan, J. K. (1998). Demographic diversity and faultlines: The compositional dynamics of organizational groups. *Academy of Management Review, 23*, 325–340.

Law, K. S., Wong, C., Wang, D., & Wang, L. (2000). Effect of supervisor–subordinate guanxi on supervisory decisions in China: An empirical investigation. *International Journal of Human Resource Management, 11*, 751–765. doi: 10.1080/09585190050075105

Ledeneva, A. (2017). *The global encyclopaedia of informality* (Vol. 1). London: University College London Press. https://doi.org/10.14324/111.9781911307907

Ledeneva, N. (2018). *The global encyclopaedia of informality, Vol 1: Towards understanding of social and cultural complexity*. London: UCL Press. https://www.uclpress.co.uk/products/86227

Lettau, C. (2016). The effect of cultural tightness-looseness on effectuation or causation strategies of novice entrepreneurs in Germany. Bachelor's thesis. University of Twente, The Netherlands.

Leung, A. K. Y., & Cohen, D. (2011). Within- and between-culture variation: Individual differences and the cultural logics of honor, face and dignity cultures. *Journal of Personality and Social Psychology, 100*, 507–526. doi: 10.1037/a0022151

Leung, K. (2009). Never the twain shall meet? Integrating Chinese and Western management research. *Management and Organization Review, 5*(1), 121–129. https://doi.org/10.1111/j.1740-8784.2008.00135.x

Leung, K., Au, A., Huang, X., Kurman, J., Niit, T., & Niit, K. K. (2007). Social axioms and values: A cross-cultural examination. *European Journal of Personality, 21*, 91–111. doi: 10.1002/per.615

Leung, K., & Bond, M. H. (2004). Social axioms: A model for social beliefs in multicultural perspective. *Advances in Experimental Social Psychology, 36*, 119–197. doi: 10.1016/S0065-2601(04)36003-X

Leung, K., & Morris, M. W. (2015). Values, schemas, and norms in the culture-behavior nexus: A situated dynamics framework. *Journal of International Business Studies, 46*, 1028–1050. doi: 10.1057/jibs.2014.66

Li, R., Gordon, S., & Gelfand, M. J. (2017). Tightness–looseness: A new framework to understand consumer behavior. *Journal of Consumer Psychology, 27*, 377–391. doi: 10.1016/j.jcps.2017.04.001.

Liu, X. Y., & Wang, J. (2013). Abusive supervision and organizational citizenship behavior: Is supervisor–subordinate guanxi a mediator? *International Journal of Human Resource Management, 24*, 1471–1489. doi: 10.1080/09585192.2012.725082

Luo, Y. (2000). *Guanxi and business*. Singapore: World Scientific.

Mesoudi, A. (2009). How cultural evolutionary theory can inform social psychology and vice versa. *Psychological Review, 116*(4), 929–952. https://doi.org/10.1037/a0017062

Midgley, D. F., Venaik, S., & Christopoulos, D. (2018). Culture as a configuration of values: An archetypal perspective. In A. Gunnthorsdottir & D. A. Norton (Eds.), Experimental economics and culture (Vol. 20, pp. 63–88). Bingley, UK: Emerald Publishing Ltd. doi: 10.1108/S0193-230620180000020004

Minkov, M. (2018). A revision of Hofstede's model of national culture: Old evidence and new data from 56 countries. *Cross Cultural and Strategic Management, 25*, 231–256. doi: 10.1108/CCSM-03-2017-0033

Minkov, M., Bond, M. H., Dutt, P., Schachner, M., Morales, O., Sanchez, C., Jandosova, J., Khassenbekov, Y., & Mudd, B. (2018). A reconsideration of Hofstede's Fifth dimension: New flexibility versus monumentalism data from 54 countries. *Cross-Cultural Research, 52*(3), 309–333. https://doi.org/10.1177/1069397117727488

Minkov, M., Dutt, P., Schachner, M., Jandosova, J., Khassenbekov, Y., Morales, O., & Blagoev, V. (2019). What would people do with their money if they were rich? A search for Hofstede dimensions across 52 countries. *Cross Cultural and Strategic Management, 26*, 93–116. doi: 10.1108/CCSM-11-2018-0193

Minkov, M., Dutt, P., Varma, T., Schachner, M., Morales, O., Sanchez, C. J., & Mudd, B. (2017). A revision of Hofstede's individualism-collectivism dimension: A new national index from a 56-country study. *Cross-Cultural and Strategic Management, 24*, 386–404. doi: 10.1108/CCSM-11-2016-0197

Minkov, M., & Hofstede, G. (2012). Is national culture a meaningful concept: Cultural values delineate homogeneous national clusters of in-country regions. *Cross-Cultural Research, 46*, 133–159. doi: 10.1177/1069397111427262

Minkov, M., & Hofstede, G. (2014). Nations versus religions: Which has a stronger effect on cultural values at the group level? *Management International Review, 54*, 801–824. doi: 10.1007/s11575-014-0205-8

Miura, A. M., Pilati, R., Milfont, L. T., Ferreira, M. C., & Fischer, R. (2019). Between simpatia and malandragem: Brazilian jeitinho as an individual difference variable. *PLoS ONE, 14*, e0214929. doi: 10.1371/journal.pone.0214929

Molinsky, A. L. (2007). Cross-cultural code-switching: The psychological challenges of adapting behavior in foreign cultural interactions. *Academy of Management, 32*, 622–640. doi: 10.5465/amr.2007.24351878

Moore, F., & Brannen, M. Y. (2018). The anthropological comparative method as a means of analysing and solving pressing issues in comparative HRM. In C. Brewster, W. Mayrhofer, & E. Farndale (Eds.), *Handbook of research on comparative human resource management* (pp. 108–124). London: Elgar Online.

Morling, B., & Lamoreaux, M. (2008). Measuring culture outside the head: A meta-analysis of individualism–collectivism in cultural products. *Personality and Social Psychology Review, 12*, 199–221.

Morris, M. W., Chiu, C. Y., & Liu, Z. (2015). Polycultural psychology. *Annual Review of Psychology, 66*, 631–659. doi: 10.1146/annurev-psych-010814-015001

Morris, M. W., Hong, Y. Y., Chiu, C. Y., & Liu, Z. (2015). Normology: Integrating insights about social norms to understand cultural dynamics. *Organizational Behavior and Human Decision Processes, 129*, 1–13. doi: 10.1016/j.obhdp.2015.03.001

Morschett, D., Schramm-Klein, H., & Swoboda, B. (2010). Decades of research on market entry modes: What do we really know about external antecedents of entry mode choice? *Journal of International Management, 16*, 60–77.

Pan, X., Gelfand, M., & Nau, D. (2021). Integrating evolutionary game theory and cross-cultural psychology to understand cultural dynamics. *American Psychologist, 76*(6), 1054–1066. https://doi.org/10.1037/amp0000851

Patel, T. (2015). Crossing disciplinary, epistemological and conceptual boundaries in search of better cultural sense-making tools, *Journal of Organizational Change Management, 28*, 728–748.

Pearl, J., & MacKenzie, D. (2018). *The book of why: The new science of cause and effect*. New York: Basic Books.

Peterson, M. F., & Søndergaard, M. (2014). Countries, within-country regions, and multiple-country regions in international management: A functional, institutional, and critical event (FICE) perspective. *Management International Review, 54*, 781–800. doi: 10.1007/s11575-014-0228-1

Peterson, M. F., Søndergaard, M., & Kara, A. (2018). Traversing cultural boundaries in IB: The complex relationships between explicit country and implicit cultural group boundaries at multiple levels. *Journal of International Business Studies, 49*, 1081–1099. doi: 10.1057/s41267-017-0082-z

Popli, M., Akbar, M., Kumar, V., & Gaur, A. (2016). Reconceptualizing cultural distance: The role of cultural experience reserve in cross-border acquisitions. *Journal of World Business, 51*, 404–412. doi: 10.1016/j.jwb.2015.11.003.

Primecz, H., Mahadevan, J., & Romani, L. (2016). Why is cross-cultural management blind to power relations? Investigating ethnicity, language, gender and religion, *International Journal of Cross-Cultural Management, 16*(2), 127–136.

Ralston, D. A., Pounder, J., Lo, C. W. H., Wong, Y. Y., Egri, C. P., & Stauffer, J. (2006). Stability and change in managerial work values: A longitudinal study of China, Hong Kong, and the U.S. *Management and Organization Review, 2*, 67–94. https://doi.org/10.1111/j.1740-8784.2006.00031.x

Resende, M. M., & Porto, J. B. (2020). Brazilian jeitinho and moral identity: Impact on ethical behaviour at work. *Trends in Psychology, 28*, 148–164. doi: 10.9788/s43076-019-00006-1

Rodrigues, R. P., Milfont, T., Ferreira, M. C., Porto, J., & Fischer, R. (2011). Brazilian jeitinho: Understanding and explaining an indigenous psychological construct. *Interamerican Journal of Psychology, 45*, 27–36.

Rohner, R. P. (1984). Toward a conception of culture for cross-cultural psychology. *Journal of Cross-Cultural Psychology, 15*, 111–138. doi: 10.1177/0022002184015002002

Romani, L., Boussebaa, M., & Jackson, T. (2020). Critical perspectives on cross-cultural management. In B. Szkudlarek, L. Romani, D. Caprar, & J. Osland, *The SAGE handbook of contemporary cross-cultural management* (pp. 51–65). London: SAGE.

Romani, L., Primecz, H., & Topçu, K. (2011). Paradigm interplay for theory development: A methodological example with the Kulturstandard method, *Organizational Research Methods. 14*(3), 432–455.

Ronen, S., & Shenkar, O. (2013). Mapping world cultures: Cluster formation, sources and implications. *Journal of International Business Studies, 44*, 867–897. doi: 10.1057/jibs.2013.42

Roos, P., Gelfand, M., Nau, D., & Lun, J. (2015). Societal threat and cultural variation in the strength of social norms: An evolutionary basis. *Organizational Behavior and Human Decision Processes, 127*, 14–23. doi: 10.1016/j.obhdp.2015.01.003

Rosenthal, L., & Levy, S. R. (2010). The colorblind, multicultural, and polycultural ideological approaches to improving intergroup attitudes and relations. *Social Issues and Policy Review, 4*(1), 215–246. https://doi.org/10.1111/j.1751-2409.2010.01022.x

Rosenthal, L., & Levy, S. R. (2013). Thinking about mutual influences and connections across cultures relates to more positive intergroup attitudes: An examination of polyculturalism. *Social and Personality Psychology Compass, 7*, 547–558. doi: 10.1111/spc3.12043

Rosenthal, L., & Levy, S. R. (2016). Endorsement of polyculturalism predicts increased positive intergroup contact and friendship across the beginning of college. *Journal of Social Issues, 72*, 472–488. doi: 10.1111/josi.12177

Rozen-Bakher, Z. (2018). How do each dimension of Hofstede's national culture separately influence M&A success in cross-border M&As? *Transnational Corporations Review, 10*, 131–146. doi: 10.1080/19186444.2018.1475089

Schwartz, S. H. (1992). Universals in the content and structure of values: Theoretical advances and empirical tests in 20 countries. *Advances in Experimental Social Psychology, 25*, 1–65.

Schwartz, S. H. (1994). Beyond individualism/collectivism: New cultural dimensions of values. In U. Kim, H. C. Triandis, C. Kagitcibasi, S. Choi, & G. Yoon (Eds.), *Individualism and collectivism: Theory, method and application* (pp. 85–119). Thousand Oaks, CA: SAGE.

Schwartz, S. H., Cieciuch, J., Vecchione, M., Davidov, E., Fischer, R., Beierlein, C., Ramos, A., Verkasalo, M., Lonnqvist, J. E., Demirutku, K., Dirilen-Gumus, O., & Konty, M. (2012). Refining the theory of basic individual values. *Journal of Personality and Social Psychology, 103*, 663–688.

Scott, W. R. (1995). *Institutions and organizations*. Thousand Oaks, CA: SAGE.

Shenkar, O. (2012). Cultural distance revisited. *Journal of International Business Studies, 43*, 1–11. doi: 10.1057/palgrave.jibs.8490982

Shteynberg, G., Gelfand, M. J., & Kim, K. (2009). Peering into the "magnum mysterium" of culture: The explanatory power of descriptive norms. *Journal of Cross-Cultural Psychology, 40*, 46–69. doi: 10.1177/0022022108326196

Simmons, J. P., Nelson, L. D., & Simonsohn, U. (2011). False-positive psychology: Undisclosed flexibility in data collection and analysis allows presenting anything as significant. *Psychological Science, 22*, 1359–1366. doi:10.1177/0956797611417632

Sivarajah, U., Kamal, M. M., Irani, Z., & Weerakkody, V. (2017). Critical analysis of big data challenges and analytical methods. *Journal of Business Research, 70*, 263–286. https://doi.org/10.1016/j.jbusres.2016.08.001.

Smith, P. B. (2008). Indigenous aspects of management. In P. B. Smith, M. F. Peterson, & D. C. Thomas (Eds.), *The handbook of cross-cultural management research* (pp. 319–332). Thousand Oaks, CA: Sage.

Smith, P. B. (2017). Cultural values versus cultural norms as predictors of differences in helping behaviors and in emotion regulation: A preliminary nation-level test related to the Leung-Morris model. *Management and Organization Review, 13*, 739–766. doi: 10.1017/mor.2017.51

Smith, P. B., Easterbrook, M. J., Koc, Y., Lun, V. M., Papastylianou, D., Grigoryan, L., Torres, C., & and others. (2020). Is an emphasis on dignity, honor and face more an attribute of individuals or of cultural groups? *Cross-Cultural Research, 55*, 95–126.

Smith, P. B., Torres, C. V., Leong, C. H., Budhwar, P., Achoui, M., & Lebedeva, N. (2012). Are indigenous approaches to achieving influence in business organizations distinctive? A comparative study of guanxi, wasta, jeitinho, svyazi, and "pulling strings." *International Journal of Human Resource Management, 23*, 333–348. doi; 10.1080/09585192.2011.561232

Sng, O., Neuberg, S. L., Varnum, M. E. W., & Kenrick, D. T. (2018). The behavioral ecology of cultural psychological variation. *Psychological Review, 125*(5), 714–743. https://doi.org/10.1037/rev0000104

Søderberg, A. M. (2020). Reflexive chapter: Towards greater methodological awareness and researcher reflexivity. In B. Szkudlarek, L. Romani, D. V. Caprar, & J. Osland (Eds.), *The SAGE handbook of contemporary cross-cultural management* (pp. 171–178). London: SAGE.

Stahl, G. K., Maznevski, M. L., Voigt, A., & Jonsen, K. (2010). Unraveling the effects of cultural diversity in teams: A metaanalysis of research on multicultural work groups. *Journal of International Business Studies, 41*, 690–709. doi: 10.1057/jibs.2009.85

Steel, P., & Taras, V. (2010). Culture as a consequence: A multi-level multivariate meta-analysis of the effects of individual and country characteristics on work-related cultural values. *Journal of International Management, 16*, 211–233. doi: 10.1016/j.intman.2010.06.002

Taras, V., Kirkman, B., & Steel, P. (2010). Examining the impact of culture's consequences: A three decade, multi-level, meta-analytic review of Hofstede's cultural value dimensions. *Journal of Applied Psychology, 95*, 405–439. doi: 10.1037/a0018938

Taras, V., Rowney, J., & Steel, P. (2009). Half a century of measuring culture: Approaches, challenges, limitations, and suggestions based on the analysis of 112 instruments for quantifying culture. *Journal of International Management, 15*, 357–373.

Taras, V., Steel, P., & Kirkman, B. L. (2011). Three decades of research on national culture in the workplace: Do the differences still make a difference? *Organizational Dynamics, 40*, 189–198. doi: 10.1016/j.orgdyn.2011.04.006

Taras, V., Steel, P., & Kirkman, B. (2012). Improving national cultural indices using a longitudinal meta-analysis of Hofstede's dimensions. *Journal of World Business, 47*, 329–341. doi: 10.1016/j.jwb.2011.05.001

Taras, V., Steel, P., & Kirkman, B. L. (2016). Does country equate with culture? Beyond geography in the search for cultural boundaries. *Management International Review, 56*, 455–487. doi: 10.1007/s11575-016-0283-x

Thomas, A. (1988). Untersuchungen zur Entwicklung eines interkulturellen Handlungstrainings in der Managerausbildung. *Psychologische Beitrage, 30*, 147–165.

Tomasello, M., & Carpenter, M. (2007). Shared intentionality. *Developmental Science, 10*, 121–125. https://doi.org/10.1111/j.1467-7687.2007.00573.x

Torres, C. V., Alfinito, S., Galvão, C. A. S. P., & Tse, B. C. Y. (2015). Brazilian *jeitinho* versus Chinese *guanxi*: Investigating their informal influence on international business. *Revista de Administração Mackenzie, 16*, 77–99.

Tsui, A. S., Nifadkar, S. S., & Ou, A. Y. (2007). Cross-national, cross-cultural organizational behavior research: Advances, gaps, and recommendations. *Journal of Management, 33*, 426–478.

Tu, Y. T. (2015). A cross-cultural comparison of Brazil, Russia, India, and China (BRIC) on negotiation styles. *The Anthropologist, 19*, 457–467. doi: 0.1080/09720073.2015.11891680

Turchin, P. (2017). *Ages of discord: A structural-demographic analysis of American history*. Chaplin, CT: Beresta Books LLC.

Vaara, E., Sarala, R., Stahl, G. K., & Björkman, I. (2012). The impact of organizational and national cultural differences on social conflict and knowledge transfer in international acquisitions. *Journal of Management Studies, 49*, 1–27. doi: 10.1111/j.1467-6486.2010.00975.x

van de Vijver, F., & Leung, K. (2021). *Methods and data analysis for cross-cultural research* (2nd ed.; Culture and Psychology). V. Fetvadjiev, J. Fontaine, J. He, & Y. Poortinga (Eds.). Cambridge: Cambridge University Press.

van Herk, H., & Fischer, R. (2017). Multilevel cultural issues. In H. van Herk & C. J. Torelli (Eds.), *Cross cultural issues in consumer science and consumer psychology: Current perspectives and future directions* (pp. 191–211). Cham: Springer. doi: 10.1007/978-3-319-65091-3_11

van Herk, H., & Poortinga, Y. (2012). Current and historical antecedents of individual value differences across 195 regions in Europe. *Journal of Cross-Cultural Psychology, 43*, 1229–1248. https://doi.org/10.1177/0022022111429719

van Hoorn, A. (2019). Generational shifts in managerial values and the coming of a unified business culture: A cross-national analysis using European Social Survey data. *Journal of Business Ethics, 155*(2), 547–566. https://doi.org/10.1007/s10551-017-3488-4

Venaik, S., & Midgley, D. F. (2015). Mindscapes across landscapes: Archetypes of transnational and subnational culture. *Journal of International Business Studies, 46*, 1051–1079. doi: 10.1057/jibs.2015.11

Welzel, C. (2014). *Freedom rising: Human empowerment and the quest for emancipation*. New York: Cambridge University Press.

Yao, J., Ramirez-Marin, J., Brett, J., Aslani, S., & Semnani-Azad, Z. (2017). A measurement model for dignity, face, and honor cultural norms. *Management and Organization Review, 13*, 713–738. doi: 10.1017/mor.2017.49

PART II

Culture and Organizational Entry

CHAPTER

3 Recruiting and Selecting with Culture in Mind: Insights and Emerging Issues

Ann Marie Ryan *and* Eva Derous

Abstract

Organizations operate in a global marketplace for talent. Multinational organizations have moved to adopt centralized employee selection systems, to improve their selection of those for cross-cultural assignments, and to broaden the scope of their recruitment efforts across borders. In all of these efforts, it is important to consider culture in design and implementation efforts. While much has been written on topics such as establishing the measurement equivalence of selection tools across cultures, ensuring positive applicant reactions, and the like, there are emerging issues that require greater theoretical and practical focus. After providing a high-level review of the research to date on culture and recruitment and employee selection, we focus on several focal areas related to assessing cultural competencies in selection, cultural equivalence of selection tools, and use of technologically enhanced methods across cultures. We end with recommendations for future research and practice.

Key Words: recruitment, selection, applicant reactions, technology enhanced methods, cultural competency assessment

Globalization has been the trend in business for the last half century as the flow of goods, services, and people has shifted radically as a result of social and technological change. Recently, however, analysts have suggested that a "slowbalization" (PwC, 2020) is underway in which the trend is continuing but has slowed significantly. Currently, the COVID-19 pandemic is expected to contribute further to this slower pace (The Economist, 2020). Economic instability, conflict, and climate change continue to influence migration patterns in acute ways, but also, in addition, longer-term demographic and economic trends are fueling migration, resulting in almost 272 million international migrants annually (International Organization for Migration, 2019). While this level is higher than that in the past, most people (96.5%) continue to reside in the country in which they were born (International Organization for Migration, 2019). While barriers to doing business across borders are being eliminated through legislative and technological advances, growth in isolationist trends has accelerated (e.g., Brexit, Trump presidency policies; Tarrance, 2019). The global spread of COVID-19 also shows how connected businesses are globally, as supply chain disruptions became evident relatively quickly (Haren & Simchi-Levi, 2020), but the pandemic opened the world to greater cross-border collaborative remote work (Liu-Farrer et al., 2020). It is in this context that we discuss the role of culture in employee recruitment and selection.

Our aim in this chapter is to provide a brief overview of prior research on culture and employee recruitment and hiring, while focusing largely on emerging research topics and needs given the globalization and migration context just described. Besides noting where theory and empirical research are lacking, we also highlight what we know and do not know regarding some key practical questions for those developing and administering recruitment and selection across borders. While culture can and should be considered in recruiting and selecting within a particular country, we focus on selection of those whose roles require considerable cross-cultural interactions, such as workers on multinational teams; those on expatriate assignments; those in offshore service centers (e.g., call centers); and others whose roles regularly call for interaction with people from cultures different from their own culture of origin.

Brief History and Overview

Research on the intersections of culture and recruitment and selection has focused on three particular areas. First, there has long been an interest in understanding how to recruit and select those best suited for working outside one's home country (see Caligiuri & Paul, 2010, for a review). For example, Wilson (1961) discussed the particular challenges of selecting individuals for cross-cultural work, noting the importance of understanding motives such as one's relationship with one's own culture (e.g., sailors seeking to get away from home life rather than a desire to experience other cultures) as well as idealistic views of the ease of making such transitions.

Second, researchers have focused on how to adapt existing selection and recruitment systems to fit with different cultural contexts (see Ryan & Tippins, 2010). For example, Love et al. (1994) described adapting design and validation procedures in developing a selection system for hiring workers for a Japanese American joint venture manufacturing facility in order to fit with Japanese management philosophy (e.g., not using questionnaires to gather examples of ineffective performance; not having performance appraisal data as a criterion).

Third, there is also a long history of cross-cultural comparison studies on applications of selection tools, including frequency of use, validities, and decision making (see Ryan et al., 2017, for a review). For example, Triandis (1963) noted differences in the weighting of applicant characteristics by Greek and American personnel directors, with Americans giving more weight to race and Greeks to age in decisions. More recently, Billings and Dages (2018) demonstrated the validity of an integrity assessment across Mexican, South African, and U.S. contexts. Within these last two categories, there has been a longstanding focus on use of measures cross-culturally, including attention to measurement equivalence (e.g., Hambleton, 2005; Meade & Lautenschlager, 2004; van de Vijver, 2002) translation quality and cultural sensitivity (Brislin, 1986), prototypical recruiting and hiring practices by country (e.g., Clark, 1993; Huo et al., 2002; Krause & Thornton, 2009; Salgado & Anderson, 2002; Shackleton & Newell, 1994), and differences in applicant reactions by country (e.g., Anderson et al., 2010; Steiner & Gilliland, 1996, 2001).

A major challenge often noted in all these areas is that in much of the early research, while conclusions about the role of culture are drawn, typically culture was inferred (e.g., based on country) rather than assessed. Over time, researchers began to incorporate more direct consideration of culture in how recruitment and selection do and should occur. For example, Ryan et al. (1999) surveyed 959 organizations across 20 countries regarding selection practices to assess how cultural values might relate to use of testing and other selection methods; this effort was followed up in 2017 with a survey of 1153 HR professionals in 23 countries (Ryan et al., 2017). Both studies came to relatively similar conclusions regarding the small role of culture in selection practices relative to other potential influences (e.g., GDP) on differences in how selection is carried out across countries (see also Prince & Kabst, 2019; Ryan et al., 2015). For example, Ryan et al. (2017) noted that the considerable variability within countries in practices and differences was not explained by societal level standing on cultural values.

A number of comprehensive reviews of the research on culture and recruitment (e.g., Allen & Vardaman, 2017; Miller & Tucker, 2015; Ryan & Delaney, 2017); culture and applicant perceptions (e.g., Anderson et al., 2010; Anderson & Witvliet, 2008; König et al., 2015; Ryan et al., 2009); expatriate recruitment and selection (Caligiuri & Paul, 2010); and development and implementation of global selection systems (Ryan & Tippins, 2010) were published that had grounding in frameworks of cultural values. While these works do not focus solely on culture (e.g., considerations of language, law, and economic factors are addressed), they indicate that both researchers and those in selection practice recognize that culture may be an important consideration in understanding how and why we recruit and select in the ways we do, as well as recognize how culture can facilitate or hinder efforts toward global similarity in organizational practices in recruitment and selection.

Despite this attention, it is hard to draw a long list of conclusions from these reviews other than "culture might matter" and "pay attention to culture." One reason for this difficulty may be the quantity and quality of the empirical literature on this topic: too few large-scale studies that span multiple cultures, relatively few studies that actually assess culture rather than infer differences via proxies (e.g., country), and too few studies grounded in theory (both theory regarding culture and theory regarding selection and recruitment). Further, drawing inferences from findings with one selection tool (e.g., cognitive ability) or one recruitment method (e.g., job boards), often studied in a two-country comparison, and applying them more broadly to all selection or recruitment methods across many cultural contexts does not provide a strong base from which to make conclusions.

In general, though, these reviews find (1) much greater similarity in actual and desired recruiting and selection practices than differences, (2) clear evidence that tools for many of the constructs traditionally assessed in selection settings can be developed to be transportable across borders, given sufficient rigor in the process, and (3) the capacity for multinational corporations (MNCs) to use global strategies and approaches to recruiting and selection, with adaptation based on context actually more often due to economic, education, and legal reasons than to culture per se.

Because substantial review pieces already exist in these areas, in the rest of this chapter we focus on three specific areas of research that have received increased attention, with the hope of being more definitive in prescriptions regarding practice implications and research needs. First, we take a quick look at specific issues where researchers have indicated cultural influences may be of greatest concern in the current landscape of employee selection: regarding social desirability in applicant responses, in the increasing use of contextualized items in assessments, and in assessing interpersonal skills. Second, we discuss the assessment of cultural competencies for selection purposes, which is an important topic in expatriate selection as well as in MNC selection more broadly. Third, we note how the technological revolution in recruitment and selection affects when and how culture is (or should be) considered. We end with thoughts on how to better infuse theoretical frameworks on culture into this applied research area.

Culture's Influence in Recruiting and Selection

The approach to developing a recruitment or assessment tool to be used across cultures is relatively well established in terms of mechanics or steps to take; less well considered is how theory on culture might inform these processes. For example, in recruitment, the marketing literature provides considerable guidance as to how to make determinations of culture adaptations (Baack & Singh, 2007; Hermeking, 2005) in recruitment websites, materials, and activities. There is ample practitioner advice on candidate sourcing across cultures (see Griffeth et al., 2014, for a review). There is some cross-cultural comparative research on organizational image (Caligiuri & Paul, 2010; Gowan, 2004). However, surprisingly little research has been embedded in theories of culture that systematically consider culture's influence on attracting applicants, maintaining applicant interest, and influencing offer acceptance (Allen & Vardaman, 2017; Ma & Allen, 2009). Ma and Allen (2009) proposed the value-based recruitment (VBR) model, which is grounded in signaling theory (Spence, 1973) and person-organization fit theory (Kristof-Brown et al., 2005), as a way to inform how culture may play a role in applicant behavior and job choice. Specifically, they detail culture as having influence on what signals applicants attend to from an organization as well as how those signals are interpreted and factored into their job choice decisions. While this theoretical groundwork has existed for over a decade, we have yet to see it widely applied. Recently, Banks et al. (2019), drawing on signaling theory, illustrated how organizations generally standardize signals (e.g., inclusiveness, employee development) across domestic, international, and foreign language websites. However, they did not find that cultural distance between domestic and international operations influenced standardization; that is, culture did not appear to be the reason for any differences in what was signaled, although there were some differences in relative emphasis based on context (i.e., signals sent in foreign languages were more customized).

Similarly, the approach to developing a selection tool or system to be used across cultural contexts has been detailed in terms of considering cultural influences on what work is done, how to best assess individual attributes (e.g., educational system differences lead to differences in the meaning of what various degrees and certifications mean), how to assess measurement equivalence, and the like (see Ryan & Tippins, 2009, 2010, for reviews). While the need for cross-cultural equivalence is clearly acknowledged and approaches for examining cross-cultural equivalence of assessments are well discussed, the sharing of information on the results of these examinations is surprisingly limited. In part, this is due to proprietary or custom methods where a desire to produce generalizable knowledge does not exist. But we surmise that it is also due to more mechanical (i.e., take a tool, translate, give in a few countries, examine) and less theoretical approaches in this area. The latter would involve clear hypotheses as to *why* culture might affect responses; most efforts in the selection area are focused on eliminating any differences with less emphasis on forecasting when or why they occur.

In terms of specific findings, considerable research has focused on the cross-cultural equivalence of cognitive ability tests and personality measures. Indeed, the literature on things like cognitive ability assessment across languages and countries is substantial, although it is often focused on socioeconomic status (SES) and factors other than culture (e.g., Burhan et al., 2017; Rindermann & Ceci, 2018). Van de Vijver (2002), in a meta-analysis, showed that the mean score differences on cognitive ability tests across countries was near zero. However, research also shows that if cultural context is embedded into cognitive ability items (e.g., culturally specific familiarity in a reading passage), it can affect scores (Scherbaum et al., 2017). For example, van de Vijver's (1997) meta-analysis showed that Western cognitive ability tasks produced larger cross-national differences than when tasks developed in a local culture were used in comparisons. In general, in practice there is little concern regarding cross-cultural equivalence if proper consideration is given to removing nonequivalent items and appropriate norms (which may be local, regional, or global) are used to interpret scores.

Similarly, personality researchers have long been engaged in studying the cross-cultural universality of personality structure (see Cheung, 2004; Church, 2008; Nye et al., 2008; Schmitt et al., 2007; Thielmann & Hilbig, 2019), the assessment of intercultural personality traits (like the Multicultural Personality Questionnaire; van der Zee et al., 2003) as well as the appropriateness of culture-specific, regional, or global norms (Bartram, 2008; Ramesh et al., 2008). Nevertheless, little is known about how personality leads to intercultural success (see work on the Affect-Behavior-Cognition model [ABC model] as an exception; van der Zee & van Oudenhoven, 2013; Ward et al., 2001). Like cognitive ability tests, the use of personality instruments cross-culturally is not precluded if appropriately vetted and implemented. Discussions of other selection methods also note issues of equivalence and cultural differences (interviews, e.g., Lim et al., 2014; Manroop et al., 2013; biodata, Dalessio et al., 1996).[1] For example, Lim et al. (2014) noted that deferral to authority, display of negativity, and inclusion of personal content in interview responses are all culturally driven aspects of speaking style that can be misattributed by interviews to a lack of interviewee competence or fit. As another example, Dalessio et al. (1996) demonstrated that a biodata scoring key could be transported across U.S. and UK/Republic of Ireland contexts. However, several issues are not method specific but apply to considerations of culture in hiring processes more broadly: culture and socially desirable responding, culture and context fidelity, and culture and interpersonal interactions in assessments. In each of these instances, one can think of culture as not only directly impacting scores on a selection tool but also as moderating predictor-criterion relationships for measures that involve potential socially desirable responding, are high in context richness, or require interpersonal interaction. We discuss each of these in turn.

CULTURE AND SOCIALLY DESIRABLE RESPONDING

When using selection methods that involve self-report, there is a longstanding concern about socially desirable responding and faking (McFarland & Ryan, 2006; Melchers et al., 2020; Ziegler, 2011). Researchers have established practical ways of addressing this concern through the use of multidimensional forced-choice items (Cao & Drasgow, 2019), warnings (Converse et al., 2008), explicit measures (e.g., conditional reasoning; LeBreton et al., 2007), and overclaiming knowledge techniques (Dunlop et al., 2020). However, the role of culture in social desirability needs more central consideration. Research on this topic can be clustered into two streams: The first showing cultural differences in levels of self-presentation, faking, and socially desirable responding, and the second looking more specifically at cultural differences in what is considered socially desirable behavior. Both have implications for hiring.

As an example of the first stream, investigations have found culture to relate to levels of responding in a variety of contexts with a variety of measures. It is well established that a bias toward acquiescence varies in relation to culture (Johnson et al., 2005; Keillor et al., 2001; Middleton & Jones, 2000). It is also well established that mean differences across countries on social desirability scales in research settings are found (e.g., Hult et al., 1999; Tsushima, 1969) and those scales are not always cross-culturally equivalent (e.g., Baltes et al., 1969). Hiemstra et al. (2013) found that culture moderated qualification–evaluation relationships in that Dutch and immigrant job seekers presented their qualifications differently in resumes based on cultural norms on self-presentation.

---

[1] Vocational interests and culture are covered in Chapter 4.

Some studies have also indicated cultural differences in levels of socially desirable responding in selection contexts. Fell and König (2016) conducted a 43-nation study on cross-cultural differences in applicant faking on personality measures and found that culture was related to faking, though often in nonhypothesized directions. For example, they found positive country-level correlations between faking levels and uncertainty avoidance, future orientation, human orientation and assertiveness, and a negative relationship between faking levels and in-group collectivism. Also, Fell and König (2016) examined cross-cultural differences with regard to applicant faking in interviews in 31 countries and found considerable differences in attitudes toward faking in job interviews. They found positive correlations between attitudes toward faking and power distance, in-group collectivism, humane orientation, and negative correlations with uncertainty avoidance and gender egalitarianism. Sandal et al. (2014) found differences across 10 countries in the endorsement of using self-presentation tactics in interviews, with those in countries emphasizing embeddedness, mastery, and hierarchy indicating greater importance for self-presentation in the interview. Of note in this study were the inclusion of self-presenting tactics that would be more relevant in non-Western parts of the world and the finding that Americans score high on all tactics. In an examination of self-presentation in the application process across Switzerland, Iceland, and the United States, König et al. (2011) considered how cultural differences in endorsement of modesty values relate to the prevalence of self-presentation behaviors in the selection process (applying, testing, interviewing). In this study, the biggest differences were in serious self-presentation behaviors (e.g., fabrications on resume), although there were large differences overall. As the authors note, considering modesty and other value differences may be important in hiring, as global norms for any method where self-presentation is involved (which are most hiring methods!) can lead to poor selection decision making. In sum, research in the last decade has highlighted the need to recognize differences in socially desirable responding/self-presentation across cultures in many selection methods (application, resume, interview, personality tests) and the importance for researchers to better articulate *how* culture relates to those differences. More specifically, there is some evidence that differences in faking across countries may be driven by economic differences in addition to cultural values. In comparing the self-presentation of United Arab Emirates applicants to American, European, and Chinese applicants, Husain et al. (2018) noted that cultural values of modesty may be overtaken when economic conditions create greater challenges in securing employment. König et al. (2021) found that economic inequality within countries, rather than GDP and unemployment rate, related to faking across 20 countries.

As examples of the second stream of research on which behaviors are considered desirable, He et al. (2015) studied 20 countries and found that seeing positive traits as desirable is more universal, whereas denial of negative self-descriptions has more cross-cultural variability. Using data from 34 countries and based on the GLOBE cultural dimensions and the theory of purposeful behavior (Barrick et al., 2013), which outlines how personality relates to goals, Ryan et al. (2021) found few connections between culture and the desirability of personality aspects (i.e., a lower-level structure than a trait), with the exception that higher social desirability ratings were given for cooperativeness, sensitivity, and assertiveness in Confucian Asian, South Asian, and sub-Saharan contexts compared to Germanic European, Eastern European, Latin American, and Latin European contexts. They note, however, that some specific items did have high variability in social desirability. Further, while we focused on social desirable responding (SDR) and noncognitive measures here, it has long been noted that the definitions of cheating, plagiarism, and the like differ across cultures (McCabe, 2002). Research also shows cultural differences in impression management tactics in interviewing (Derous, 2017). It seems that one of the key ways culture may impact applicant behavior during the hiring process is through the influence on what is expected and normative behavior.

These findings suggest that selection system designers and users should not only focus on decreasing the ability to fake, socially desirable responding, or self-presentation falsely through methods such as multi-dimensional pairwise preference formats for items, warnings, and checking of information. They should also be accounting for cross-cultural comparisons of the effectiveness of these methods. Another suggestion (e.g., Derous, 2017; Fell et al., 2016) is cross-cultural training of recruiters and interviewers so as to increase awareness of cultural difference in self-presentation norms.

CULTURE AND CONTEXT FIDELITY

Selection assessments provide stimuli (test items, interview questions) to which individuals respond, and we know that culture influences how we interpret and respond to events (Markus & Kitayama, 1998). Research has shown differences between collectivistic cultures and individualist cultures in the extent to which individuals behave in consistent ways across situations (more in individualistic cultures) (Church, 2008). Those in individualistic societies tend to give more decontextualized explanations for behavior and events (Morris & Peng, 1994). That is, context matters more to behavioral choices and behavior evaluations in Asian versus European and North American cultures.

One area where selection research is just starting to consider culture is in how contextualization of assessments influences responses. In a highly regarded paper, Lievens and Sackett (2017) described a modular approach to considering selection procedures. One of the key factors involved differentiating predictor methods being contextualized or the extent to which detailed context information is provided to those taking an assessment. For example, providing a general context in a situational interview question or situational judgment item might be contrasted with richer contextualization in games and assessment center exercises. For some methods, technology can lead to increases in contextualization (e.g., a video situational judgment test [SJT] vs. a written item). Lievens and Sackett (2017) frame increased contextualization as worthy of further research because of its potential positive effects (e.g., applicant reactions) and negative effects (e.g., on cognitive load).

One might also question whether increased contextualization might have different effects across cultures. That is, beyond an effect of adding less culturally irrelevant or unfamiliar content (e.g., showing a video where individual engage in unfamiliar activities), those cultures that attend more to contextual cues (e.g., context-sensitive self in Asian cultures, Kashima et al., (2004); high-/low-context communication differences, see Kittler et al., 2011, for a review) may perform differently than those for whom context is seen as less relevant information. Further, research by Krumm et al. (2015) showed that one can distinguish SJT items as tapping into context-independent (generic customer service behaviors) and context-dependent knowledge (e.g., expectations in fine-dining service), and argue that more context-independent items may suffice for many purposes. As they note, one may want to consider how culture comes into play, and research is slowly emerging in this regard.

Because traditional SJTs are highly contextualized assessment tools, they may be particularly prone to cultural differences (Corstjens et al., 2017; Lievens, 2013). A wide range of research suggests that the effectiveness of a given behavior in response to a work situation might differ by culture (e.g., Adler et al., 1986; Smith et al., 1998). Researchers have begun to recognize that "the right way to respond" may vary by culture, but the patterns here can be quite complex (e.g., some situations are universal in terms of perceived correct responses; some are more culturally bound). Burke et al. (2013) described developing an SJT for use with customer service store representatives using an emic–etic approach, in which 75% of the content overlapped across versions used across three countries. Stemler et al. (2016) described the development and validity of sales and managerial SJTs in India as illustrating the cross-cultural usefulness of the approach. However, Lievens et al. (2015) examined the transportability of an SJT measuring integrity from the United States to Spain and illustrated the need to examine item scenario realism, item option endorsement, and scoring key and criterion-related validity. While overall there were positive conclusions regarding transportability, several item stems and options indicated differences across cultures. A similar note of caution regarding using SJTs across cultures was raised by Schmitt et al. (2019) who found culture to be related to differential item functioning between Chinese and American students. Of note, their study indicated that culture affects not only getting the right response but how various distractors are evaluated (i.e., the desirability of "wrong" behavioral choices). Because general domain knowledge SJTs are designed to measure general procedural knowledge, they might be better suited to be used cross-culturally than the more traditional SJTs that are highly contextualized in nature. However, these general procedural knowledge SJTs might also capture some cultural values (Corstjens et al., 2017).

While SJTs have been the focus of some cross-cultural work, highly contextualized formats are increasingly used with other selection methods as technology advances lead to greater use of simulations, games, virtual reality/augmented reality environments, and just generally greater realistic contexts in assessment items (Adler et al., 2018). Hawkes et al. (2018) noted that richness and fidelity in enhanced assessment content can increase construct-irrelevant variance in scores; culture may explain some of that variance.

CULTURE AND INTERPERSONAL INTERACTION

There is a substantial body of research on cross-cultural interpersonal interactions and the influence of culture on things like emotional intelligence (Shao et al., 2015), emotional labor (Allen et al., 2014), conflict handling styles (Gunkel et al., 2016), interpersonal distances (Sicorello et al., 2019), and the like. Although this research has relevance for the wide range of assessments that tap interpersonal skills (e.g., customer service skills, leadership), selection research has been surprisingly lagging in integrating this work.

One example of where this work can be applied is regarding interviewing. This research has focused on specific ways in which judgments of applicants might vary across cultures (Lim et al., 2014; Manroop et al., 2013), as well as differences in how applicants might approach the interview (Derous, 2017). For example, Tsai et al. (2019) found differences in hireability perceptions across countries that align with cultural differences in how emotional facial expressions are evaluated. Specifically, because European Americans value high arousal positive states more than Hong Kong Chinese, they evaluate individuals with more excited facial expressions as more affiliative than those with calm facial expressions. Overall, as research suggests, emotion perception may be more culturally universal, but emotion understanding and emotion regulation are more culturally specific (Shao et al., 2015); one can outline an agenda for research on how interviewee performance and interpretation of it may be affected by culture.

Other methods that focus on interpersonal interactions, such as assessment centers, simulations, and interpersonally oriented SJTs, might similarly be designed with greater consideration of cultural differences in these areas. For example, a common roleplay situation (and also a common SJT and interview question) involves conflict with a customer or with another employee. Research shows that cultural differences in preferring dominating and avoiding conflict styles (Gunkel et al., 2016) would suggest potential cultural differences in how these items are approached as well as how responses are evaluated. For example, actors and avatars convey ethnicity, gender, and other personal attributes that may relate to what is a culturally appropriate response in a conflict context (Golubovich & Ryan, 2021). According to van der Maesen de Sombreff and Abell (2001), in some cultures, differential importance is attached to content in interpersonal exchanges, depending on the nature of relationships; that is, culture affects both how things are said and what is said.

Summary. We have pointed to three areas where research suggests culture will have direct and moderating influences in a selection context. Researchers have noted, however, that there are limited published studies that specifically assess whether the criterion-related validity of selection assessments holds across countries (although proprietary work on specific instruments exists) (Lievens, 2006). As we noted at the start of this section, theory as to why culture might moderate relations should be foundational to such efforts.

Selecting for Cultural Competence

A common theme in writings regarding the selection of expatriates, as well as the selection of those working in MNCs more broadly, is the need for cultural competence, or related concepts (e.g., cultural intelligence, cultural agility) that focus on abilities, skills, motivations, and tendencies to function effectively in culturally diverse contexts. Because much of the expatriate selection research focuses on adjustment and turnover, ease of cultural adaptation has often been considered as an outcome to be predicted from individual factors such as prior experience and family circumstances (see Bhaskar-Shrinivas et al., 2005, and Mol et al., 2005 for meta-analytic reviews). Hundreds of works have been published on the meaning of these constructs, the psychometric qualities of associated measures, as well as their relation to important outcomes (for recent reviews, see Andresen & Bergdolt, 2017; Fang et al., 2018; Ott & Michailova, 2018).

When it comes to evaluating these cultural competencies and attributes in selection contexts, however, there are important practical considerations that may render swaths of this research uninformative. First, in employee selection, the focus is on assessing attributes that are relatively stable and that cannot be easily trained. Some research suggests that intercultural work experience leads to increases in cultural competence constructs (see elsewhere in this volume as well as in Koo Moon et al., 2012; Kurpis & Hunter, 2017). In addition, some studies specifically focus on training interventions to enhance cultural competence (e.g., Alexandra, 2018; Rosenblatt et al., 2013; Taras et al., 2013), all of which suggests the malleability of at least some aspects of cultural competencies.

Given the indicators of trainability of cultural competence and the large amount of training available that purports to be able to help individuals increase their cultural competence, it is important to consider whether it is better to "buy or build" when it comes to staffing on cultural competence. For managerial skills, work by DeOrtentiis et al. (2018) suggests that building managers (i.e., using internal hires and developing them) is cheaper and more effective, but the answer to this question for cultural competence may be complex. Mol et al. (2009), for instance, showed that the willingness of prospective MNC employees to become expatriates could be predicted based on personal dispositions such as core self-evaluations, personality traits (i.e., emotional stability, extraversion, openness, and conscientiousness), foreign language ability, biodata (e.g., countries visited on holiday), and expatriate specific predictors (i.e., high cultural flexibility, intercultural sensitivity, uncertainty tolerance, category width, and implicit cultural adaptability theories). This research suggests that the ability to predict expatriation willingness could be assessed at the time employees enter the organization to help MNCs ensure there will be an adequate number of qualified applicants to select from for future assignments, that is, to "buy" cultural competence upfront. Further, in terms of building, does a week-long training program provide a sufficient level of skill to positively affect the performance of an individual about to be sent on an overseas assignment for 3 months? For an individual who interacts on the phone regularly with individuals of varied cultural backgrounds? Or does a sufficient level of competence only emerge after relatively extensive immersive experiences?

Thus, while some research suggests "build" or do not select on this, other research suggests "buy" or make cultural competences and related attributes a core component of selection. The right answer may vary depending on the type and criticality of the role, length of assignment, cultural distance from the culture of origin, as well as individual dispositions (like one's entity vs. increment beliefs on cultural adaptation; Mol et al., 2009). For example, if an organization regularly selects individuals for overseas assignments of a year or more in length in cultures relatively distant from a home country (e.g., China and the United States), they may want to ensure that a pool of qualified candidates exists by "buying" cultural competence upfront as well as investing in quality preassessment training. For an organization with more short-term, unique assignments (e.g., someone for 2 months in Sydney and another for 4 months in Shanghai), perhaps only brief training coupled with selection focused on a few key attributes is sufficient.

Second, at the heart of justifying the use of any measure in a selection context is its job relatedness. While cultural agility may be seen as a desirable trait, using measures to screen individuals out requires clear evidence of a connection to the job, such as documented job analytic evidence that the job requires cross-cultural interactions or that the measure is predictive of job performance, turnover, or other outcomes. To establish job-relatedness some studies connect cultural competence constructs to performance, although many works use self-reported performance, which would not be viewed as a credible outcome measure in selection research. Evidence does exist using criteria other than self-ratings (e.g., van Der Zee et al., 2004, with student performance in diverse teams; Presbitero, 2016, with performance of call center workers; Jyoti & Kour, 2015 and Jyoti & Kour, 2017, predicting supervisor ratings). Rockstuhl and Van Dyne (2018) conducted a meta-analysis of cultural intelligence (CQ) predicting outcomes and reported R^2 of CQ measures with task performance of .19, .23 with citizenship performance, .25 with adaptive performance and .13 with leadership performance (all observer-rated outcome measures). However, they note a complexity in the findings when considering specific factors (e.g., metacognitive CQ) separately that warrant further research. There is also a significant stream of research on predictors of expatriate adjustment, which has in turn been linked to expatriate performance and turnover (see meta-analyses by Mol et al., 2005, and Bhaskar-Shrinivas et al., 2005, which establish adjustment-performance links). Finally, some studies examine the concept of multicultural personality (i.e., traits that relate to seeking out novel experiences and to cultural intelligence, Liao & Thomas, 2020) that show connections to performance outcomes (Fang et al., 2018; van Oudenhoven et al., 2003; Ward et al., 2009). Thus, ample evidence suggests value in examining cultural competence in employee selection when the role calls for it.

Third, selection practitioners would also want to know whether adding a cultural competence measure to an existing selection system is worthwhile—that is, whether the measure provides a sufficient increment in prediction above what is already in use to be worth additional time and cost. Some researchers have found that cultural competence measures may provide incremental validity beyond Big Five personality traits (Huff et al., 2014; Shu et al., 2017); others have found that intercultural competence is incrementally different from more general interpersonal competence (Fang et al., 2018). However, other researchers concluded that the incremental validity of cultural competence measures (like the Cultural Intelligence Scale; Ang et al., 2007) in predicting cultural adjustment is limited (Ward et al., 2009). The degree of incremental validity beyond personality may be less when personality measures are contextualized to working in a multicultural way (like the Multicultural Personality Questionnaire; van der Zee et al., 2003). Overall, greater support for incremental value over tools in use is likely needed. Note that is unlikely that cultural competence measures alone would be sufficient in selecting an individual for an international assignment; one would also need to consider technical competence for the specific role, international experience, language skills, and the like (see Bhaskar-Shrinivus et al., 2005 and Mol et al., 2005 for meta-analytic reviews). Further, much of the expatriate selection literature focuses on family adjustment and expatriate failure (e.g., Caligiuri et al., 2009; Mendenhall & Oddou, 1985), which involves factors such as family circumstances that are best addressed through self-selection by the candidate rather than selection by the organization.

Fourth, there are considerable differences in approaches to assessing these cultural constructs. In selection contexts, organizations face constraints on applicant time, assessment costs, and ease of assessment administration so that trade-offs can occur (the "validity per minute of testing time" trade-off; Hardy et al., 2017). Related to our first point, one can assess past experiences (interactions with those of other cultures, pursuit of culturally diverse activities), or one can assess aptitude (interest in other cultures, ability to sense how to act in intercultural contexts, foreign language ability). An organization can use self-report and relatively short measures, create structured interview questions, or invest in interactive simulations. The relative gains in accuracy from different methods of assessing the same construct are important to those deciding selection system design. Further, when hiring an individual to work in a particular cultural context (e.g., hiring an American to work in Japan), does one focus on culture-specific knowledge and skills or culture-general aptitudes and competencies, or both? (Fang et al., 2018). In the training literature, culture-general assimilators have been found to be more effective for increasing intercultural competence across cultures (Bhawuk, 1998), but an organization may seek to do targeted hiring for working in certain markets and may be better off with assessing culture-specific competence than broader skills and abilities.

Relatedly, a major challenge is that some of the more popular and well-researched measures, such as the Cultural Intelligence Scale (CQS; Ang et al., 2007; Van Dyne et al., 2008), use self-report Likert scale response items, which are associated with socially desirable responding and faking in selection contexts. Many organizations eschew the use of self-report measures for assessing personal characteristics, and have moved to techniques such as multi-dimensional forced-choice items (Cao & Drasgow, 2019) as a means of more accurate assessment. This concern over self-report measures extends beyond socially desirable responding to broader issues of self-report accuracy. For example, Kumas-Tan et al., (2007) noted that what is measured with self-report is individuals' confidence in oneself and feelings of comfort with others, rather than their actual capabilities. Some efforts have been made in this regard; for example, Ascalon et al. (2008) developed an SJT for selection purposes to assess cross-cultural empathy and ethnocentrism, and Rockstuhl et al. (2015) examined intercultural multimedia SJT predictive validity (see also Miller & Tucker, 2015, for an intercultural competence SJT assessing culture-general knowledge, empathic communication skills, and an open, nonjudgmental attitude, used for training evaluation). There is a need for methods of assessing cross-cultural competencies that work well in the constraints of a selection environment; most measures in the research literature are not well suited for contexts where individuals may be motivated to respond in socially desirable ways in order to obtain a position.

Summary: In a selection context, where there are always trade-offs in terms of efficiency (cost, time) and gathering more information on an individual, questions regarding what should be done to consider intercultural competence will vary according to the organization's strategy for recruitment and selection. Some organizations may decide that a focus on more general interpersonal competence, multicultural personality, and intercultural experience in hiring, supplemented with training in intercultural competence is the best strategy, whereas others may invest heavily in evaluating culture-specific knowledge as well as cultural competence at the start, such as when hiring for a key expatriate role, knowing that the cost of a poor hiring decision necessitates this upfront investment. Regardless of strategic considerations, we see a need for more research on measuring cross-cultural competence through means other than self-report and considering the incremental validity of cross-cultural competence beyond other common selection tools and foci (e.g., personality, interpersonal skills assessments).

Technologically Enhanced Recruitment and Assessment and Culture

Technology has radically changed the landscape of recruiting as applicants gain information about openings and organizations via technology (e.g., job boards, social media, organizational career websites) and apply for openings that way (Howardson & Behrend,

2014; Ryan & Delaney, 2017). As applicants from different cultures may react differently to recruitment activities (Ma & Allen, 2009), the question of how technology might "override" or exacerbate cultural influences deserves consideration.

As an example, recruitment research has long noted that the importance of personal connections culturally (e.g., *guanxi* in China, *Blat* in Russia, *wasta* in the Arabic world, *sifarish* in Pakistan) plays a role in the extensiveness of use of employee referrals as a source in recruiting and hiring across cultures. For example, Ko and Liu (2017) describe how the strategic use of *guanxi* in recruitment by firms in China can make hiring more convenient and enhance the person–organization fit but can also lead firms to fail to attend to the most appropriate candidate for the job. Im and Chen (2020), in an analysis in 97 cultures, indicated that uncertainty avoidance was a key correlate of favoritism, while familism and future orientation were correlates of nepotism/cronyism. Of interest, they note that favoritism may be driven more by a rational decision in cultures with higher distrust of others, whereas nepotism/cronyism is more about in-group preferences as culturally normative. Similarly, use of social media in recruitment poses interesting questions, as it may lead to greater reliance on weak social ties, not just strong ones, in obtaining jobs (Miller & Guo, 2014). Further, as Nadeem and Kayani (2019) discuss in their analysis of *sifarish* in hiring in Pakistan, a rigorous transparent selection process, which technology might aid, can allow for network-based referrals in culturally appropriate ways while still screening out unqualified individuals on merit bases.

As another example, technology has radically changed the emphasis on employer brand (Lievens & Slaughter, 2016; Theurer et al., 2018) in recruiting as more information is available to job seekers and as organizations seek to differentiate themselves through technology-mediated messaging. However, we know that culture relates to the emphasis placed on reputation and prestige (Caligiuri & Paul, 2010). With the internet allowing for "word of mouse" (Van Hoye & Lievens, 2007) to supplement or even supplant "word of mouth" from friends and family, technology may exacerbate or dampen culture's effects on preferred recruitment sources, preferred organizational attributes, and other elements of the recruitment process. For example, the internet affords more continual access to individuals and media on a global basis, exposing individuals to different norms and expectations regarding hiring processes. Job boards and company review sites provide wider access to information than what can be gained in one's immediate social circle.

In terms of efficiency, Bartram (2011) describes how technology has strongly impacted the globalization of testing. Rather than print copies of tests and scoring keys that must be warehoused and shipped, assessments can now be updated and delivered around the globe much more easily. Further, technology has allowed individuals not only to receive more information (i.e., reducing power distance), but also to distinguish themselves as individuals (i.e., reduce collectivism; Salehan et al., 2018). As technology changes cultures and potentially drives cultural convergence, cultures also influence technology adoption and innovation (e.g., government control of the internet). Both trends have implications for selection and recruitment.

Cultural considerations may come into play as technology enables us to expand the sources of information used in assessing an individual. As one example, the use of social media in recruitment and assessment has emerged (Vaughn et al., 2019), with some researchers cautioning about such use due to cross-cultural differences in social media site choices usage and content (Schmidt & O'Connor, 2016; Shields & Levashina, 2016). For example, Wang and Liu (2019) showed that cultural differences in privacy risk and control affect engagement in social media. El Ouirdi et al. (2016) demonstrated that Dutch recruiters evaluated nonprofessional content on social media more negatively than Italian recruiters. By using social media in recruitment and selection without considering cultural influences, candidate evaluations can be inaccurate and misleading.

Technology also has led to expanded use of algorithmic scoring of assessments, with the potential for cultural bias. One example would be in algorithmic scoring of video interviews (Langer et al., 2017; Mejia & Torres, 2018), where tone, gestures, facial expressions, and verbal content are scored. Our earlier discussion of culture and interview self-presentation indicates where problems might arise in this regard. Indeed, as a specific example, Bencharit et al. (2019) illustrated that culture influenced words used in applications as well as nature of smiles shown in video-recorded interview introductions in terms of conveying high (excited) and low (calm) positive arousal. Training a dataset without sufficient representations of all cultural groups can lead to biased algorithms (Barocas & Selbst, 2016; Merler et al., 2019). Further, culture may influence the acceptance of technology in hiring, as studies have indicated that non-Western cultures focus more on ease of use whereas Western cultures emphasize usefulness in evaluating technologies (Schepers & Wetzels, 2007).

In sum, technology is not only changing how we recruit and assess, but how and when culture might affect those perceptions. However, we also would echo an observation by Steiner voiced in 2012: "it seems likely that few cultural insights will be gained by continuing to focus on selection methods. If the focus of international studies were on the psychological constructs that are considered important to assess, we might find many more interesting cultural influences' (p. 754). Thus, our focus should not be on the methodological innovations of technology, but on reactions to changes to what constructs are being assessed, as that is where culture may play a larger moderating role.

Summary

In Table 3.1 we note key findings and key practical implications derived from our review, although we have only really scratched the surface of the ways culture can affect recruitment and selection processes. As we note early in the chapter, there is considerable research on cross-cultural differences in methods and practices, in how to ensure equivalence and set up global systems, and on some specific topics related to assessment. However, what we do not know is also substantial, and given the continued growth in recruitment and selection

Table 3.1 Key findings and practical implications
Findings
1. Globally, actual and desired recruiting and selection practices are much more similar than different.
2. Assessments of cultural competencies and multicultural personality can have value in predicting expatriate adjustment, performance, and turnover.
3. Culture relates to the extent and nature of socially desirable behavior by influencing what is considered expected and normative behavior, which affects how performance on selection tools should be considered.
4. The extent of contextualization within many selection methods (e.g., SJTS, interviews, simulations) will likely have differential effects on performance across cultures.
5. Culture influences many elements of interpersonal interactions (e.g., emotional expression, conflict handling, communication norms) and that influence will then affect assessment methods that involve interpersonal interaction (e.g., interviews, SJTs).
Practical Implications
1. Cognitive ability and personality assessments can be developed for use across borders, given sufficient rigorous attention to measurement equivalence, appropriate norms, and adaptations for economic, legal, and cultural constraints.
2. Employers might select for cultural competencies and related attributes (e.g., personality and dispositional characteristics associated with competence) so that they have a pool that may be more interested in and capable of gaining from cross-cultural competency training.
3. Consideration should be given to whether culture-specific knowledge and skills, culture-general aptitude and competencies, or both, should be the focus of selection.
4. Recruiters and interviewers should be trained to increase awareness of cultural differences in self-presentation that may affect performance in selection processes.
5. Technology can override or exacerbate cultural influences in selection and assessment context, and thus requires thoughtful implementation.

across cultures, following through on topics such as culture and social desirability, context, interpersonal interactions, and technology will be highly beneficial to organizations. While there are challenges to doing cross-cultural research in this area—particularly issues associated with the proprietary and customized nature of many selection processes, as well as the challenges of sufficient sample sizes for research at the organizational and country level—we hope readers are not dissuaded from adding to our knowledge base.

References

Adler, N. J., Doktor, R., & Redding, S. G. (1986). From the Atlantic to the Pacific century: Cross-cultural management reviewed. *Journal of Management, 12*(2), 295–318. https://doi.org/10.1177/014920638601200210

Adler, S., Boyce, A. S., & Caputo, P. M. (2018). Employment testing. In J. C. Scott, D. Bartram, & D. H. Reynolds (Eds.), *Next generation technology-enhanced assessment: Global perspectives on occupational and workplace testing* (pp. 3–35). Cambridge: Cambridge University Press.

Alexandra, V. (2018). Predicting CQ development in the context of experiential cross-cultural training: The role of social dominance orientation and the propensity to change stereotypes. *Academy of Management Learning & Education, 17*(1), 62–78. https://doi.org/10.5465/amle.2015.0096

Allen, D. G., & Vardaman, J. M. (2017). Recruitment and retention across cultures. *Annual Review of Organizational Psychology and Organizational Behavior, 4*(1), 153–181. https://doi.org/10.1146/annurev-orgpsych-032516-113100

Allen, J. A., Diefendorff, J. M., & Ma, Y. (2014). Differences in emotional labor across cultures: A comparison of Chinese and U.S. service workers. *Journal of Business and Psychology, 29*(1), 21–35. https://doi.org/10.1007/s10869-013-9288-7

Anderson, N., Salgado, J. F., & Hülsheger, U. R. (2010). Applicant reactions in selection: Comprehensive meta-analysis into reaction generalization versus situational specificity. *International Journal of Selection and Assessment, 18*(3), 291–304. https://doi.org/10.1111/j.1468-2389.2010.00512.x

Anderson, N., & Witvliet, C. (2008). Fairness reactions to personnel selection methods: An international comparison between the Netherlands, the United States, France, Spain, Portugal, and Singapore. *International Journal of Selection and Assessment, 16*(1), 1–13. https://doi.org/10.1111/j.1468-2389.2008.00404.x

Andresen, M., & Bergdolt, F. (2017). A systematic literature review on the definitions of global mindset and cultural intelligence—merging two different research streams. *The International Journal of Human Resource Management, 28*(1), 170–195. https://doi.org/10.1080/09585192.2016.1243568

Ang, Soon, Van Dyne, L., Koh, C., Ng, K. Y., Templer, K. J., Tay, C., & Chandrasekar, N. A. (2007). Cultural intelligence: Its measurement and effects on cultural judgment and decision making, cultural adaptation and task performance. *Management and Organization Review, 3*(3), 335–371. https://doi.org/10.1111/j.1740-8784.2007.00082.x

Ascalon, E., Schleicher, D. J., & Born, M. P. (2008). Cross-cultural social intelligence. *Cross Cultural Management: An International Journal, 15*(2), 109–130. https://doi.org/10.1108/13527600810870570

Baack, D. W., & Singh, N. (2007). Culture and web communications. *Journal of Business Research, 60*(3), 181–188. https://doi.org/10.1016/j.jbusres.2006.11.002

Baltes, P., K., E., & Schaie, K. W. (1969). Intra- and intercultural factor structures of social desirability ratings by American and German college students. *Multivariate Behavioral Research, 4*(1), 67–78. https://doi.org/10.1207/s15327906mbr0401_5

Banks, G. C., Woznyj, H. M., Wesslen, R. S., Frear, K. A., Berka, G., Heggestad, E. D., & Gordon, H. L. (2019). Strategic recruitment across borders: An investigation of multinational enterprises. *Journal of Management, 45*(2), 476–509. https://doi.org/10.1177/0149206318764295

Barocas, S., & Selbst, A. D. (2016). Big data's disparate impact. *California Law Review, 104*, 671–732.

Barrick, M. R., Mount, M. K., & Li, M. (2013). The theory of purposeful work behavior: The role of personality, higher-order goals, and job characteristics. *Academy of Management Review, 38*, 132–153. https://doi.org/10.5465/amr.2010.0479

Bartram, D. (2008). Global norms: Towards some guidelines for aggregating personality norms across countries. *International Journal of Testing, 8*(4), 315–333. https://doi.org/10.1080/15305050802435037

Bartram, D. (2011). International issues, standards, and guidelines. In N. T. Tippins & S. Adler (Eds.), *Technology-enhanced assessment of talent* (pp. 224–250). San Francisco: Jossey-Bass.

Bencharit, L. Z., Ho, Y. W., Fung, H. H., Yeung, D. Y., Stephens, N. M., Romero-Canyas, R., & Tsai, J. L. (2019). Should job applicants be excited or calm? The role of culture and ideal affect in employment settings. *Emotion, 19*(3), 377–401. https://doi.org/10.1037/emo0000444

Bhaskar-Shrinivas, P., Harrison, D. A., Shaffer, M. A., & Luk, D. M. (2005). Input-based and time-based models of international adjustment: Meta-analytic evidence and theoretical extensions. *Academy of Management Journal, 48*(2), 257–281. https://doi.org/10.5465/amj.2005.16928400

Bhawuk, D. P. S. (1998). The role of culture theory in cross-cultural training. *Journal of Cross-Cultural Psychology, 29*(5), 630–655. https://doi.org/10.1177/0022022198295003

Billings, S. W., & Dages, K. D. (2018). Cross-cultural validity of integrity assessments for lower-level and higher-level jobs. *International Journal of Selection and Assessment, 26*(1), 66–74. https://doi.org/10.1111/ijsa.12198

Brislin, R. W. (1986). The wording and translation of research instruments. In W. J. J. Lonner & W. Berry (Eds.), *Field methods in cross cultural research* (pp. 137–164). Thousand Oaks, CA: SAGE.

Burhan, N. A. S., Yunus, M. M., Tovar, M. E. L., & Burhan, N. M. G. (2017). Why are cognitive abilities of children so different across countries? The link between major socioeconomic factors and PISA test scores. *Personality and Individual Differences, 105*, 95–106. https://doi.org/10.1016/j.paid.2016.09.043

Burke, E., Vaughan, C., & Glennon, R. (2013). Employment testing and assessment in multinational organizations. In K. F. Geisinger, B. A. Bracken, J. F. Carlson, J.-I. C. Hansen, N. R. Kuncel, S. P. Reise, & M. C. Rodriguez (Eds.), *APA handbook of testing and assessment in psychology, Vol. 1. Test theory and testing and assessment in industrial and organizational psychology* (pp. 579–609). Washington, DC: American Psychological Association. https://doi.org/10.1037/14047-032

Caligiuri, P., & Paul, K. (2010). Selection in multinational organizations. In J. L. Farr & N. T. Tippins (Eds.), *Handbook of employee selection* (pp. 781–800). New York: Routledge.

Caligiuri, P., Tarique, I., & Jacobs, R. (2009). Selection for international assignments. *Human Resource Management Review, 19*(3), 251–262. https://doi.org/10.1016/j.hrmr.2009.02.001

Cao, M., & Drasgow, F. (2019). Does forcing reduce faking? A meta-analytic review of forced-choice personality measures in high-stakes situations. *Journal of Applied Psychology, 104*(11), 1347–1368. https://doi.org/10.1037/apl0000414

Cheung, F. M. (2004). Use of western and indigenously developed personality rests in Asia. *Applied Psychology, 53*(2), 173–191. https://doi.org/10.1111/j.1464-0597.2004.00167.x

Church, A. T. (2008). Current controversies in the study of personality across cultures. *Social and Personality Psychology Compass, 2*(5), 1930–1951. https://doi.org/10.1111/j.1751-9004.2008.00132.x

Clark, T. (1993). Selection methods used by executive search consultancies in four European countries: A survey and critique. *International Journal of Selection and Assessment, 1*(1), 41–49. https://doi.org/10.1111/j.1468-2389.1993.tb00082.x

Converse, P. D., Oswald, F. L., Imus, A., Hedricks, C., Roy, R., & Butera, H. (2008). Comparing personality test formats and warnings: Effects on criterion-related validity and test-taker reactions. *International Journal of Selection and Assessment, 16*(2), 155–169. https://doi.org/10.1111/j.1468-2389.2008.00420.x

Corstjens, J., Lievens, F., & Krumm, S. (2017). Situational judgement tests for selection. In Harold W. Goldstein, E. D. Pulakos, J. Passmore, & C. Semedo (Eds.), *The Wiley Blackwell handbook of the psychology of recruitment, Selection and employee retention* (pp. 226–246). Hoboken, NJ: John Wiley. https://doi.org/10.1002/9781118972472

Dalessio, A. T., Crosby, M. M., & McManus, M. A. (1996). Stability of biodata keys and dimensions across English-speaking countries: A test of the cross-situational hypothesis. *Journal of Business and Psychology, 10*(3), 289–296. https://doi.org/10.1007/BF02249604

DeOrtentiis, P. S., Van Iddekinge, C. H., Ployhart, R. E., & Heetderks, T. D. (2018). Build or buy? The individual and unit-level performance of internally versus externally selected managers over time. *Journal of Applied Psychology, 103*(8), 916–928. https://doi.org/10.1037/apl0000312

Derous, E. (2017). Ethnic minorities' impression management in the interview: Helping or hindering? *Frontiers in Psychology, 8*, 86. https://doi.org/10.3389/fpsyg.2017.00086

Dunlop, P. D., Bourdage, J. S., de Vries, R. E., McNeill, I. M., Jorritsma, K., Orchard, M., Austen, T., Baines, T., & Choe, W.-K. (2020). Liar! Liar! (when stakes are higher): Understanding how the overclaiming technique can be used to measure faking in personnel selection. *Journal of Applied Psychology, 105*(8), 784–799. https://doi.org/10.1037/apl0000463

El Ouirdi, M., Pais, I., Segers, J., & El Ouirdi, A. (2016). The relationship between recruiter characteristics and applicant assessment on social media. *Computers in Human Behavior, 62*, 415–422. https://doi.org/10.1016/j.chb.2016.04.012

Fang, F., Schei, V., & Selart, M. (2018). Hype or hope? A new look at the research on cultural intelligence. *International Journal of Intercultural Relations, 66*, 148–171. https://doi.org/10.1016/j.ijintrel.2018.04.002

Fell, C. B., & König, C. J. (2016). Cross-cultural differences in applicant faking on personality tests: A 43-nation study. *Applied Psychology, 65*(4), 671–717. https://doi.org/10.1111/apps.12078

Fell, C. B., König, C. J., & Kammerhoff, J. (2016). Cross-cultural differences in the attitude toward applicants' faking in job interviews. *Journal of Business and Psychology, 31*(1), 65–85. https://doi.org/10.1007/s10869-015-9407-8

Golubovich, J., & Ryan, A. M. (2021). Performance on video-based situational judgment test items: Simulated interracial interactions. *Journal of Business and Psychology, 36*, 693–711. https://doi.org/10.1007/s10869-020-09697-1

Gowan, M. A. (2004). Development of the recruitment value proposition for geocentric staffing. *Thunderbird International Business Review, 46*(6), 687–708. https://doi.org/10.1002/tie.20031

Griffeth, R. W., Tenbrink, A., & Robinson, S. (2014). Recruitment sources: A review of outcomes. In. Y. T. Yu & D. M. Cable (Eds.), *The Oxford handbook of recruitment* (pp. 215–250). New York: Oxford University Press.

Gunkel, M., Schlaegel, C., & Taras, V. (2016). Cultural values, emotional intelligence, and conflict handling styles: A global study. *Journal of World Business, 51*(4), 568–585. https://doi.org/10.1016/j.jwb.2016.02.001

Hambleton, R. K. (2005). Issues, designs and technical guidelines for adapting tests into multiple languages and cultures. In R. K. Hambleton, P. F. Merenda, & C. D. Speilberger (Eds.), *Adapting educational and psychological tests of cross-cultural assessment* (pp. 3–38). Mahwah, NJ: Lawrence Erlbaum.

Hardy, J. H., Gibson, C., Sloan, M., & Carr, A. (2017). Are applicants more likely to quit longer assessments? Examining the effect of assessment length on applicant attrition behavior. *Journal of Applied Psychology, 102*(7), 1148–1158. https://doi.org/10.1037/apl0000213

Haren, P., & Simchi-Levi, D. (2020). How coronavirus could impact the global supply chain by mid-March. *Harvard Business Review, 28(February)*. https://hbr.org/2020/02/how-coronavirus-could-impact-the-global-supply-chain-by-mid-march?ab=hero-subleft-1

Hawkes, B., Cek, I., & Handler, C. (2018). The gamification of employee selection tools: An exploration of viability, utility, and future directions. In J. C. Scott, D. Bartram, & D. H. Reynolds (Eds.), *Next generation technology-enhanced assessment: Global perspectives on occupational and workplace testing* (pp. 288–316). Cambridge: Cambridge University Press.

He, J., van de Vijver, F. J. R., Dominguez Espinosa, A., Abubakar, A., Dimitrova, R., Adams, B. G., Aydinli, A. Atitsogbe, K., Alonso-Arbiol, I. Bobowik, M., Fischer, R., Jordanov, V., Mastrotheodoros, S., Neto, F., Ponizovsky, Y. J., Reb, J., Sim, S., Sovet, L., Stefenel, D., & Villieux, A. (2015). Socially desirable responding. *Cross-Cultural Research, 49*(3), 227–249. https://doi.org/10.1177/1069397114552781

Hiemstra, A. M. F., Derous, E., Serlie, A. W., & Born, M. P. (2013). Ethnicity effects in graduates' résumé content. *Applied Psychology, 62*(3), 427–453. https://doi.org/10.1111/j.1464-0597.2012.00487.x

Hermeking, M. (2005). Culture and internet consumption: Contributions from cross-cultural marketing and advertising research. *Journal of Computer-Mediated Communication, 11*(1), 192–216. https://doi.org/10.1111/j.1083-6101.2006.tb00310.x

Howardson, G. N., & Behrend, T. S. (2014). Using the internet to recruit employees: Comparing the effects of usability expectations and objective technological characteristics on internet recruitment outcomes. *Computers in Human Behavior, 31*, 334–342. https://doi.org/10.1016/j.chb.2013.10.057

Huff, K. C., Song, P., & Gresch, E. B. (2014). Cultural intelligence, personality, and cross-cultural adjustment: A study of expatriates in Japan. *International Journal of Intercultural Relations, 38*, 151–157. https://doi.org/10.1016/j.ijintrel.2013.08.005

Hult, G. T. M., Keillor, B. D., & Lafferty, B. A. (1999). A cross-national assessment of social desirability bias and consumer ethnocentrism. *Journal of Global Marketing, 12*(4), 29–43. https://doi.org/10.1300/J042v12n04_03

Huo, Y. P., Huang, H. J., & Napier, N. K. (2002). Divergence or convergence: A cross-national comparison of personnel selection practices. *Human Resource Management, 41*(1), 31–44. https://doi.org/10.1002/hrm.10018

Husain, Z., Dayan, M., Pathak, R. D., Langer, M., & König, C. J. (2018). How much self-presentation behavior do applicants from the United Arab Emirates exhibit? *International Journal of Selection and Assessment, 26*(2–4), 191–195. https://doi.org/10.1111/ijsa.12225

Im, H., & Chen, C. (2020). Cultural dimensions as correlates of favoritism and the mediating role of trust. *Cross Cultural and Strategic Management, 27*(3), 417–445. https://doi.org/10.1108/CCSM-09-2019-0165

International Organization for Migration. (2019). *World migration report 2020*. International Organization for Migration. https://publications.iom.int/system/files/pdf/wmr_2020.pdf

Johnson, T., Kulesa, P., Cho, Y. I., & Shavitt, S. (2005). The relation between culture and response styles. *Journal of Cross-Cultural Psychology, 36*(2), 264–277. https://doi.org/10.1177/0022022104272905

Jyoti, J., & Kour, S. (2015). Assessing the cultural intelligence and task performance equation. *Cross Cultural Management: An International Journal, 22*(2), 236–258. https://doi.org/10.1108/CCM-04-2013-0072

Jyoti, J., & Kour, S. (2017). Cultural intelligence and job performance. *International Journal of Cross Cultural Management, 17*(3), 305–326. https://doi.org/10.1177/1470595817718001

Kashima, Y., Kashima, E., Farsides, T., Kim, U., Strack, F., Werth, L., & Yuki, M. (2004). Culture and context-sensitive self: The amount and meaning of context-sensitivity of phenomenal self differ across cultures. *Self and Identity, 3*(2), 125–141. https://doi.org/10.1080/13576500342000095a

Keillor, B. D., Owens, D., & Pettijohn, C. (2001). A cross-cultural/cross national study of influencing factors and socially desirable response biases. *International Journal of Market Research, 43*(1), 1–19. https://doi.org/10.1177/147078530104300101

Kittler, M. G., Rygl, D., & Mackinnon, A. (2011). Special review article: Beyond culture or beyond control? Reviewing the use of Hall's high-/low-context concept. *International Journal of Cross Cultural Management, 11*(1), 63–82. https://doi.org/10.1177/1470595811398797

Ko, W. W., & Liu, G. (2017). Overcoming the liability of smallness by recruiting through networks in China: a guanxi-based social capital perspective. *The International Journal of Human Resource Management, 28*(11), 1499–1526. https://doi.org/10.1080/09585192.2015.1128467

König, C. J., Langer, M., Fell, C. B., Pathak, R. D., Bajwa, N. ul H., Derous, E., . . . Ziem, M. (2021). Economic predictors of differences in interview faking between countries: Economic inequality matters, not the state of economy. *Applied psychology-an international review-psychologie appliquee-revue internationale, 70*(3), 1360–1379. https://doi.org/10.1111/apps.12278

König, C. J., Fell, C. B., Steffen, V., & Vanderveken, S. (2015). Applicant reactions are similar across countries. *Journal of Personnel Psychology, 14*(4), 213–217. https://doi.org/10.1027/1866-5888/a000142

König, C. J., Hafsteinsson, L. G., Jansen, A., & Stadelmann, E. H. (2011). Applicants' self-presentational behavior across cultures: Less self-presentation in Switzerland and Iceland than in the United States. *International Journal of Selection and Assessment, 19*(4), 331–339. https://doi.org/10.1111/j.1468-2389.2011.00562.x

Koo Moon, H., Kwon Choi, B., & Shik Jung, J. (2012). Previous international experience, cross-cultural training, and expatriates' cross-cultural adjustment: Effects of cultural intelligence and goal orientation. *Human Resource Development Quarterly, 23*(3), 285–330. https://doi.org/10.1002/hrdq.21131

Krause, D. E., & Thornton, G. C., III (2009). A cross-cultural look at assessment center practices: Survey results from Western Europe and North America. *Applied Psychology, 58*(4), 557–585. https://doi.org/10.1111/j.1464-0597.2008.00371.x

Kristof-Brown, A. L., Zimmerman, R. D., & Johnson, E. C. (2005). Consequences of individuals' fit at work: A meta-analysis of person-job, person-organization, person-group, and person-supervisor fit. *Personnel Psychology, 58*(2), 281–342. https://doi.org/10.1111/j.1744-6570.2005.00672.x

Krumm, S., Lievens, F., Hüffmeier, J., Lipnevich, A. A., Bendels, H., & Hertel, G. (2015). How "situational" is judgment in situational judgment tests? *Journal of Applied Psychology, 100*(2), 399–416. https://doi.org/10.1037/a0037674

Kumas-Tan, Z., Beagan, B., Loppie, C., MacLeod, A., & Frank, B. (2007). Measures of cultural competence: Examining hidden assumptions. *Academic Medicine, 82*(6), 548–557. https://doi.org/10.1097/ACM.0b013e3180555a2d

Kurpis, L. H., & Hunter, J. (2017). Developing students' cultural intelligence through an experiential learning activity. *Journal of Marketing Education, 39*(1), 30–46. https://doi.org/10.1177/0273475316653337

Langer, M., König, C. J., & Krause, K. (2017). Examining digital interviews for personnel selection: Applicant reactions and interviewer ratings. *International Journal of Selection and Assessment, 25*(4), 371–382. https://doi.org/10.1111/ijsa.12191

LeBreton, J. M., Barksdale, C. D., Robin, J., & James, L. R. (2007). Measurement issues associated with conditional reasoning tests: Indirect measurement and test faking. *Journal of Applied Psychology, 92*(1), 1–16. https://doi.org/10.1037/0021-9010.92.1.1

Liao, Y., & Thomas, D. C. (2020). *Cultural intelligence in the world of work.* New York: Springer International Publishing. https://doi.org/10.1007/978-3-030-18171-0

Lievens, F. (2006). The ITC guidelines on computer-based and internet-delivered testing: Where do we go from here? *International Journal of Testing, 6*, 189–194.

Lievens, F. (2013). International situational judgment tests. In J. A. Weekley & R. E. Ployhart (Eds.), *Situational judgment tests: Theory, Measurement, and application* (pp. 279–300). Mahwah, NJ: Lawrence Erlbaum. https://doi.org/10.4324/9780203774878

Lievens, F., Corstjens, J., Sorrel, M. Á., Abad, F. J., Olea, J., & Ponsoda, V. (2015). The cross-cultural transportability of situational judgment tests: How does a US-based integrity situational judgment test fare in Spain? *International Journal of Selection and Assessment, 23*(4), 361–372. https://doi.org/10.1111/ijsa.12120

Lievens, F., & Sackett, P. R. (2017). The effects of predictor method factors on selection outcomes: A modular approach to personnel selection procedures. *Journal of Applied Psychology, 102*(1), 43–66. https://doi.org/10.1037/apl0000160

Lievens, F., & Slaughter, J. E. (2016). Employer image and employer branding: What we know and what we need to know. *Annual Review of Organizational Psychology and Organizational Behavior, 3*(1), 407–440. https://doi.org/10.1146/annurev-orgpsych-041015-062501

Lim, C.-H., Chavan, M., & Chan, C. (2014). "Culture": The elephant in the room in structured behavioral selection interview. *International Journal of Intercultural Relations, 42*, 1–24. https://doi.org/10.1016/j.ijintrel.2014.07.004

Liu-Farrer, G., Yeoh, B., & Baas, M. (2020). Social construction of skill: An analytical approach toward the question of skill in cross-border labour mobilities. *Journal of Ethnic and Migration Studies, 47*, 1–15. doi: 10.1080/1369183X.2020.1731983

Love, K. G., Bishop, R. C., Heinisch, D., & Montei, M. S. (1994). Selection across two cultures: Adapting the selection of American assemblers to meet Japanese job performance demands. *Personnel Psychology, 47*(4), 837–846. https://doi.org/10.1111/j.1744-6570.1994.tb01580.x

Ma, R., & Allen, D. G. (2009). Recruiting across cultures: A value-based model of recruitment. *Human Resource Management Review, 19*(4), 334–346. https://doi.org/10.1016/j.hrmr.2009.03.001

Manroop, L., Boekhorst, J. A., & Harrison, J. A. (2013). The influence of cross-cultural differences on job interview selection decisions. *The International Journal of Human Resource Management, 24*(18), 3512–3533. https://doi.org/10.1080/09585192.2013.777675

Markus, H. R., & Kitayama, S. (1998). The cultural psychology of personality. *Journal of Cross-Cultural Psychology, 29*(1), 63–87. https://doi.org/10.1177/0022022198291004

McCabe, D. L. (2002). Cheating on tests: How to do it, detect it, and prevent it. [Review of the book Cheating on tests: How to do it, detect it, and prevent it, by Gregory J. Cizek.] *The Journal of Higher Education, 73*(2), 297–298. https://doi.org/10.1353/jhe.2002.0021

McFarland, L. A., & Ryan, A. M. (2006). Toward an integrated model of applicant faking behavior. *Journal of Applied Social Psychology, 36*(4), 979–1016. https://doi.org/10.1111/j.0021-9029.2006.00052.x

Meade, A. W., & Lautenschlager, G. J. (2004). A Monte-Carlo study of confirmatory factor analytic tests of measurement equivalence/invariance. *Structural Equation Modeling: A Multidisciplinary Journal, 11*(1), 60–72. https://doi.org/10.1207/S15328007SEM1101_5

Mejia, C., & Torres, E. N. (2018). Implementation and normalization process of asynchronous video interviewing practices in the hospitality industry. *International Journal of Contemporary Hospitality Management, 30*(2), 685–701. https://doi.org/10.1108/IJCHM-07-2016-0402

Melchers, K. G., Roulin, N., & Buehl, A. (2020). A review of applicant faking in selection interviews. *International Journal of Selection and Assessment, 28*(2), 123–142. https://doi.org/10.1111/ijsa.12280

Mendenhall, M., & Oddou, G. (1985). The dimensions of expatriate acculturation: A review. *Academy of Management Review, 10*(1), 39–47. https://doi.org/10.5465/amr.1985.4277340

Merler, M., Ratha, N., Feris, R. S., & Smith, J. R. (2019). *Diversity in faces.* arxiv:1901.10436

Middleton, K. L., & Jones, J. L. (2000). Socially desirable response sets: The impact of country culture. *Psychology and Marketing, 17*(2), 149–163. https://doi.org/10.1002/(SICI)1520-6793(200002)17:2<149::AID-MAR6>3.0.CO;2-L

Miller, J. K., & Guo, G. C. (2014). Recruitment: International cross-cultural perspective. In K. Y. T. Yu & D. M. Cable (Eds.), *The Oxford handbook of recruitment* (pp. 402–422). New York: Oxford University Press.

Miller, J. W., & Tucker, J. S. (2015). Addressing and assessing critical thinking in intercultural contexts: Investigating the distance learning outcomes of military leaders. *International Journal of Intercultural Relations, 48*, 120–136. https://doi.org/10.1016/j.ijintrel.2015.07.002

Mol, S. T., Born, M. Ph., Willemsen, M., van der Molen, H., & Derous, E. (2009). When selection ratios are high: Predicting the expatriation willingness of prospective domestic entry-level job applicants. *Human Performance, 22*(1), 1–22. https://doi.org/10.1080/08959280802540437

Mol, S. T., Born, M. P., Willemsen, M. E., & Van Der Molen, H. T. (2005). Predicting expatriate job performance for selection purposes. *Journal of Cross-Cultural Psychology, 36*(5), 590–620. https://doi.org/10.1177/0022022105278544

Morris, M. W., & Peng, K. (1994). Culture and cause: American and Chinese attributions for social and physical events. *Journal of Personality and Social Psychology, 67*(6), 949–971. https://doi.org/10.1037/0022-3514.67.6.949

Nadeem, S., & Kayani, N. (2019). Sifarish: Understanding the ethical versus unethical use of network-based hiring in Pakistan. *Journal of Business Ethics, 158*(4), 969–982. https://doi.org/10.1007/s10551-017-3709-x

Nye, C. D., Roberts, B. W., Saucier, G., & Zhou, X. (2008). Testing the measurement equivalence of personality adjective items across cultures. *Journal of Research in Personality, 42*(6), 1524–1536. https://doi.org/10.1016/j.jrp.2008.07.004

Ott, D. L., & Michailova, S. (2018). Cultural intelligence: A review and new research avenues. *International Journal of Management Reviews, 20*(1), 99–119. https://doi.org/10.1111/ijmr.12118

Presbitero, A. (2016). Cultural intelligence (CQ) in virtual, cross-cultural interactions: Generalizability of measure and links to personality dimensions and task performance. *International Journal of Intercultural Relations, 50*, 29–38. https://doi.org/10.1016/j.ijintrel.2015.11.001

Prince, N. R., & Kabst, R. (2019). Impact of national culture on organizations' use of selection practices. *Employee Relations: The International Journal, 41*(6), 1145–1161. https://doi.org/10.1108/ER-10-2018-0284
PWC. (2020, January). Global economy watch: Predictions for 2020: "Slowbalisation" is the new globalisation. *PWC*. https://www.pwc.com/gx/en/issues/economy/global-economy-watch/assets/pdfs/predictions-2020.
Ramesh, A., Hazucha, J. F., & Bank*, J. (2008). Using personality data to make decisions about global managers. *International Journal of Testing, 8*(4), 346–366. https://doi.org/10.1080/15305050802435110
Rindermann, H., & Ceci, S. J. (2018). Parents' education is More important than their wealth in shaping their children's intelligence: Results of 19 samples in seven countries at different developmental levels. *Journal for the Education of the Gifted, 41*(4), 298–326. https://doi.org/10.1177/0162353218799481
Rockstuhl, T., Ang, S., Ng, K.-Y., Lievens, F., & Van Dyne, L. (2015). Putting judging situations into situational judgment tests: Evidence from intercultural multimedia SJTs. *Journal of Applied Psychology, 100*(2), 464–480. https://doi.org/10.1037/a0038098
Rockstuhl, T., & Van Dyne, L. (2018). A bi-factor theory of the four-factor model of cultural intelligence: Meta-analysis and theoretical extensions. *Organizational Behavior and Human Decision Processes, 148*, 124–144. https://doi.org/10.1016/j.obhdp.2018.07.005
Rosenblatt, V., Worthley, R., & MacNab, B. (2013). From contact to development in experiential cultural intelligence education: The mediating influence of expectancy disconfirmation. *Academy of Management Learning and Education, 12*(3), 356–379. https://doi.org/10.5465/amle.2012.0199
Ryan, A. M., Boyce, A. S., Ghumman, S., Jundt, D., Schmidt, G., & Gibby, R. (2009). Going global: Cultural values and perceptions of selection procedures. *Applied Psychology, 58*(4), 520–556. https://doi.org/10.1111/j.1464-0597.2008.00363.x
Ryan, A. M., Bradburn, J., Bhatia, S., Beals, E., Boyce, A. S., Martin, N., & Conway, J. (2021). In the eye of the beholder: Considering culture in assessing the social desirability of personality. *Journal of Applied Psychology, 106*(3), 452–466. https://doi.org/10.1037/apl0000514
Ryan, A. M., & Delaney, T. (2017). Attracting job candidates to organizations. In J. L. Farr & N. T. Tippins (Eds.), *Handbook of employee selection* (2nd ed., pp. 165–181). New York: Routledge.
Ryan, A. M., Inceoglu, I., Bartram, D., Golubovich, J., Grand, J., Reeder, M., Derous, E., Nikolaou, I., & Yao, X. (2015). Trends in testing: Highlights of a global survey. In I. Nikolaou & J. K. Oostrom (Eds.), *Employee recruitment, selection, and assessment. Contemporary issues for theory and practice* (pp. 136–153). East Sussex, UK: Psychology Press.
Ryan, A. M., McFarland, L., & Baron, H. (1999). An international look at selection practices: Nation and cultures as explanations for variability in practice. *Personnel Psychology, 52*(2), 359–392. https://doi.org/10.1111/j.1744-6570.1999.tb00165.x
Ryan, A. M., & Tippins, N. T. (2009). *Designing and implementing global selection systems.*: Hoboken, NJ: Wiley Blackwell.
Ryan, A. M., & Tippins, N. T. (2010). Global applications of assessment. In J. C. Scott & D. H. Reynolds (Eds.), *Handbook of workplace assessment: Evidence-based practices for selection and developing organizational talent* (pp. 577–606). Hoboken, NJ: John Wiley.
Ryan, A. M., Reeder, M. C., Golubovich, J., Grand, J., Inceoglu, I., Bartram, D., Derous, E., Nikolaou, I., & Yao, X. (2017). Culture and testing practices: Is the world flat? *Applied Psychology, 66*(3), 434–467. https://doi.org/10.1111/apps.12095
Salehan, M., Kim, D. J., & Lee, J.-N. (2018). Are there any relationships between technology and cultural values? A country-level trend study of the association between information communication technology and cultural values. *Information and Management, 55*(6), 725–745. https://doi.org/10.1016/j.im.2018.03.003
Salgado, J., & Anderson, N. (2002). Cognitive and GMA testing in the European Community: Issues and evidence. *Human Performance, 15*(1–2), 75–96. https://doi.org/10.1080/08959285.2002.9668084
Sandal, G. M., van de Vijver, F., Bye, H. H., Sam, D. L., Amponsah, B., Cakar, N., Franke, G. H., Ismail, R., Kjellsen, K., Kosic, A., Leontieva, A., Mortazavi, S., & Tien-Lun Sun, C. (2014). Intended self-presentation tactics in job interviews. *Journal of Cross-Cultural Psychology, 45*(6), 939–958. https://doi.org/10.1177/0022022114532353
Schepers, J., & Wetzels, M. (2007). A meta-analysis of the technology acceptance model: Investigating subjective norm and moderation effects. *Information & Management, 44*(1), 90–103. https://doi.org/10.1016/j.im.2006.10.007
Scherbaum, C. A., DeNunzio, M. M., Oliveira, J., & Ignangni, M. (2017). Race and cultural differences in predictors commonly used in employee selection and assessment. In H. W. Goldstein, E. D. Pulakos, J.

Passmore, & C. C. Semedo (Eds.), *The Wiley Blackwell handbook of the psychology of recruitment, selection and employee retention* (pp. 400–421). Hoboken, NJ: John Wiley.

Schmidt, G. B., & O'Connor, K. W. (2016). Legal concerns when considering social media data in selection. In R. Landers & G. Schmidt (Eds.), *Social media in employee selection and recruitment* (pp. 265–287). Cham: Springer. https://doi.org/10.1007/978-3-319-29989-1_13

Schmitt, D. P., Allik, J., McCrae, R. R., & Benet-Martínez, V. (2007). The geographic distribution of Big Five personality traits. *Journal of Cross-Cultural Psychology, 38*(2), 173–212. https://doi.org/10.1177/0022022106297299

Schmitt, N., Prasad, J. J., Ryan, A. M., Bradburn, J. C., & Nye, C. D. (2019). Culture as a determinant of option choice in a situational judgement test: A new look. *Journal of Occupational and Organizational Psychology, 92*(2), 330–351. https://doi.org/10.1111/joop.12251

Shackleton, V., & Newell, S. (1994). European management selection methods: A comparison of five countries. *International Journal of Selection and Assessment, 2*(2), 91–102. https://doi.org/10.1111/j.1468-2389.1994.tb00155.x

Shao, B., Doucet, L., & Caruso, D. R. (2015). Universality versus cultural specificity of three emotion domains. *Journal of Cross-Cultural Psychology, 46*(2), 229–251. https://doi.org/10.1177/0022022114557479

Shields, B., & Levashina, J. (2016). Comparing the social media in the United States and BRIC nations, and the challenges faced in international selection. In R. Landers & G. Schmidt (Eds.), *Social media in employee selection and recruitment.* Cham: Springer. https://doi.org/10.1007/978-3-319-29989-1_8

Shu, F., McAbee, S. T., & Ayman, R. (2017). The HEXACO personality traits, cultural intelligence, and international student adjustment. *Personality and Individual Differences, 106*, 21–25. https://doi.org/10.1016/j.paid.2016.10.024

Sicorello, M., Stevanov, J., Ashida, H., & Hecht, H. (2019). Effect of gaze on personal space: A Japanese–German cross-cultural study. *Journal of Cross-Cultural Psychology, 50*(1), 8–21. https://doi.org/10.1177/0022022118798513

Smith, P. B., Dugan, S., Peterson, A. F., & Leung, W. (1998). Individualism: Collectivism and the handling of disagreement. A 23 country study. *International Journal of Intercultural Relations, 22*(3), 351–367. https://doi.org/10.1016/S0147-1767(98)00012-1

Spence, A. M. (1973). Job market signaling. *The Quarterly Journal of Economics, 87*(3), 355. https://doi.org/10.2307/1882010

Steiner, D. D. (2012). Personnel selection across the globe. In N. Schmitt (Ed.). *The Oxford handbook of personnel assessment and selection.* New York: Oxford University Press.

Steiner, D. D., & Gilliland, S. W. (1996). Fairness reactions to personnel selection techniques in France and the United States. *Journal of Applied Psychology, 81*(2), 134–141. https://doi.org/10.1037/0021-9010.81.2.134

Steiner, D. D., & Gilliland, S. W. (2001). Procedural justice in personnel selection: International and cross-cultural perspectives. *International Journal of Selection and Assessment, 9*(1&2), 124–137. https://doi.org/10.1111/1468-2389.00169

Stemler, S. E., Aggarwal, V., & Nithyanand, S. (2016). Knowing what NOT to do is a critical job skill: Evidence from 10 different scoring methods. *International Journal of Selection and Assessment, 24*(3), 229–245. https://doi.org/10.1111/ijsa.12143

Taras, V., Caprar, D. V., Rottig, D., Sarala, R. M., Zakaria, N., Zhao, F., Jiménez, A., Wankel, C., Lei, W. S., Minor, M. S., Bryła, P., Ordeñana, X., Bode, A., Schuster, A., Vaiginiene, E., Froese, F. J., Bathula, H., Yajnik, N., Baldegger, R., & Huang, V. Z. (2013). A global classroom? Evaluating the effectiveness of global virtual collaboration as a teaching tool in management education. *Academy of Management Learning and Education, 12*(3), 414–435. https://doi.org/10.5465/amle.2012.0195

Tarrance, V. L. (2019, April 10). Measuring the fault lines in current US foreign policy. *Gallup.* https://news.gallup.com/opinion/polling-matters/248354/measuring-fault-lines-current-foreign-policy.aspx

The Economist. (2020). *Globalisation unwound: Has Covid-19 killed globalisation?* https://www.economist.com/leaders/2020/05/14/has-covid-19-killed-globalisation

Theurer, C. P., Tumasjan, A., Welpe, I. M., & Lievens, F. (2018). Employer branding: A brand equity-based literature review and research agenda. *International Journal of Management Reviews, 20*(1), 155–179. https://doi.org/10.1111/ijmr.12121

Thielmann, I., & Hilbig, B. E. (2019). No gain without pain: The psychological costs of dishonesty. *Journal of Economic Psychology, 71*, 126–137. https://doi.org/10.1016/j.joep.2018.06.001

Triandis, H. C. (1963). Factors affecting employee selection in two cultures. *Journal of Applied Psychology, 47*(2), 89–96. https://doi.org/10.1037/h0049334

Tsai, J. L., Blevins, E., Bencharit, L. Z., Chim, L., Fung, H. H., & Yeung, D. Y. (2019). Cultural variation in social judgments of smiles: The role of ideal affect. *Journal of Personality and Social Psychology, 116*(6), 966–988. https://doi.org/10.1037/pspp0000192

Tsushima, W. T. (1969). Responses of Irish and Italians of two social classes on the Marlowe-Crowne social desirability scale. *The Journal of Social Psychology, 77*(2), 215–219. https://doi.org/10.1080/00224545.1969.9919867

Van de Vijver, F. J. R. (2002). Cross-cultural assessment: Value for money? *Applied Psychology, 51*(4), 545–566. https://doi.org/10.1111/1464-0597.00107

Van der Maesen de Sombreff, P. E. M., & Abell, P. (2001). Interview en arbeidsproeven bij allochtone sollicitanten [Job interview and sample tests with immigrant applicants]. In N. Bleichrodt & F. van de Vijver (Eds.), *Diagnostiek bij allochtonen. Mogelijkheden en beperkingen van psychologische tests* (pp. 157–175). Lisse, the Netherlands: Swets & Zeitlinger.

Van der Zee, K., Atsma, N., & Brodbeck, F. (2004). The influence of social identity and personality on outcomes of cultural diversity in teams. *Journal of Cross-Cultural Psychology, 35*(3), 283–303. https://doi.org/10.1177/0022022104264123

Van der Zee, K., & van Oudenhoven, J. P. (2013). Culture shock or challenge? The role of personality as a determinant of intercultural competence. *Journal of Cross-Cultural Psychology, 44*(6), 928–940. https://doi.org/10.1177/0022022113493138

Van der Zee, K., Zaal, J. N., & Piekstra, J. (2003). Validation of the Multicultural Personality Questionnaire in the context of personnel selection. *European Journal of Personality, 17*(February), S77–S100. https://doi.org/10.1002/per.483

Van Dyne, L., Ang, S., & Koh, C. (2008). Development and validation of the CQS. In S. Ang & L. Van Dyne (Eds.), *Handbook of cultural intelligence: Theory, measurement, and applications* (pp. 16–40). Armonk, NY: M. E. Sharpe.

Van Hoye, G., & Lievens, F. (2007). Investigating web-based recruitment sources: Employee testimonials vs word-of-mouse. *International Journal of Selection and Assessment, 15*(4), 372–382. https://doi.org/10.1111/j.1468-2389.2007.00396.x

van Oudenhoven, J. P., Mol, S., & Van der Zee, K. I. (2003). Study of the adjustment of Western expatriates in Taiwan ROC with the Multicultural Personality Questionnaire. *Asian Journal of Social Psychology, 6*(2), 159–170. https://doi.org/10.1111/1467-839X.t01-1-00018

Vaughn, D., Petersen, N., & Gibson, C. (2019). The use of social media in staffing. In R. N. Landers (Ed.), *The Cambridge handbook of technology and employee behavior* (pp. 232–268). New York: Cambridge University Press. https://doi.org/10.1017/9781108649636.011

Vijver, F. Van De. (1997). Meta-analysis of cross-cultural comparisons of cognitive test performance. *Journal of Cross-Cultural Psychology, 28*(6), 678–709. https://doi.org/10.1177/0022022197286003

Wang, X., & Liu, Z. (2019). Online engagement in social media: A cross-cultural comparison. *Computers in Human Behavior, 97*, 137–150. https://doi.org/10.1016/j.chb.2019.03.014

Ward, C., Bochner, S., & Furnham, A. (2001). *The psychology of cultural shock*. New York: Routledge.

Ward, C., Fischer, R., Zaid Lam, F. S., & Hall, L. (2009). The convergent, discriminant, and incremental validity of scores on a self-report measure of cultural intelligence. *Educational and Psychological Measurement, 69*(1), 85–105. https://doi.org/10.1177/0013164408322001

Wilson, A. T. M. (1961). Recruitment and selection for work in foreign cultures. *Human Relations, 14*(1), 3–21. https://doi.org/10.1177/001872676101400101

Ziegler, M. (2011). Applicant faking: A look into the black box. *Industrial and Organizational Psychology, 49*, 29–37. https://doi.org/http://www.siop.org/tip/july11/06ziegler.aspx

CHAPTER 4

Cross-Cultural Studies of Career Theories

Frederick T. L. Leong, Weiqiao Fan, Mengting Li, *and* Ting Wang

Abstract

To address the challenges of WEIRD science (Henreich et al., 2010) in vocational psychology. we adopted the framework of cultural validity and cultural specificity delineated by Leong and Brown (1995). Using this framework. this chapter provides a critical review of cross-cultural studies of career theories, including the career developmental theory, career trait and factor theory, social cognitive career theory, and career decision-making theory. Empirically, the cultural validity and cultural specificity of these career theories were supported across cultures. However, most evidence was based mainly on cross-sectional research design, and the corresponding longitudinal evidence is very much needed in future studies. The implications for career theory and practice across cultures are discussed, as are limitations of current research and promising directions for future research.

Key Words: career theories, cultural validity, cultural specificity, WEIRD samples

Introduction

In a classic paper in the domain of cross-cultural psychology, Henreich, Heine, and Norenzayan (2010) conducted a review of the comparative database from across the behavioral sciences and noted that "behavioral scientists routinely publish broad claims about human psychology and behavior in the world's top journals based on samples drawn entirely from Western, Educated, Industrialized, Rich, and Democratic (WEIRD) societies" (p. 61). They also noted that these researchers also assumed that either there is little variation across human populations or that these "standard subjects" are as representative of the species as any other populations. Henreich et al.'s (2010) findings suggest that members of WEIRD societies are among the least representative populations one could find for generalizing about humans. They went on to conclude that "Behavioral scientists now face a choice—they can either acknowledge that their findings in many domains cannot be generalized beyond this unusual subpopulation (and leave it at that), or they can begin to take the difficult steps to building a broader, richer, and better-grounded understanding of our species" (pp. 82–83).

Clearly, the problems of WEIRD samples also apply to career theories and models and call into question the cultural validity of these models for non-WEIRD samples as well as the neglect of culture-specific explanatory models in vocational psychology, which is concerned with psychological factors that influence vocational choices, development, and adjustment. In a chapter written for the *Handbook of Vocational Psychology* (Walsh & Osipow, 1995), Leong and Brown (1995) noted that the theoretical advances in cross-cultural career research have been represented by examinations of cultural validity and cultural specificity. They argued that these two dimensions could serve as components of a unifying theoretical framework for understanding cross-cultural career theories and research. According to Leong and Brown (1995), cultural validity is concerned with the validity of theories and models across other cultures in terms of the construct, concurrent, and predictive validities of these models for culturally different individuals (non-WEIRD samples). Specifically, do the relevant constructs have the same meaning across cultures? Are the predicted consequences of certain behaviors or cognitions the same for Chinese as for Americans or other populations? Cultural specificity, on the other hand, is concerned with concepts, constructs, and models that are specific to certain cultural groups in terms of their role in explaining and predicting behavior. These culture-specific variables are being identified through indigenous psychologies (Kim, Yang, & Kuo, 2006). For example, what effect does filial piety have on the career choices of Chinese youths? (This question refers to how children should fulfill parents' expectations, maintain absolute obedience to parents, and care for elders in the family, whereas parents are responsible for teaching and disciplining their children in a Chinese context; Jorgensen et al., 2017.)

According to Leong and Hardin (2002), culture-specific variables in vocational psychology can serve two functions. First, they can be useful in filling in the cultural gaps in Western-based models of vocational psychology generated from WEIRD samples. For this function, these culture-specific constructs are believed to provide incremental validity to the understanding and prediction of vocational behavior among culturally different populations. Second, culture-specific variables, independent of Western models, can be useful variables for understanding the vocational psychology of indigenous populations independent of their references to U.S. White European American samples. For this function, these culture-specific variables can serve as competing explanatory models to the Western-based models that are currently dominant in vocational psychology.

As Leong and Brown (1995) had pointed out, it is the integration of cultural validity and these cultural specificity approaches that will best advance our knowledge of the vocational psychology of clients in varying cultures. The basic premise of Leong and Brown's (1995) framework is that research that emphasizes cultural validity at the expense of cultural specificity addresses only half of the problem. Conversely, relying solely on cultural specificity studies would be to assume—without empirical research—that Western-oriented career theories and models would not work for a particular sample in a specific country.

In this chapter, we seek to address the challenge of overcoming WEIRD science (Henreich et al., 2010) in vocational psychology by using the framework of cultural validity and cultural specificity delineated by Leong and Brown (1995) to provide a critical review of cross-cultural studies of career theories and models: (1) the career developmental theory (Super), (2) the career trait and factor theory (Holland), (3) the social cognitive career theory (Bandura), and (4) the career decision-making theory (Gati and others).

Cross-cultural Studies in Developmental Theory (Super)

By specifying career development stages from early adolescence through to retirement age, Super and his colleagues devoted their initial efforts to theorizing about and studying individuals' career development from a lifespan perspective (Super, 1990). Career development is viewed as a lifelong process, and career maturity is defined as the extent to which an individual has mastered the developmental tasks appropriate to their career stage. These individuals are capable of making career decisions, preparing alternative careers, relating their present behavior to future goals, possessing high levels of self-reliance in making career decisions, and acknowledging the demands of reality.

Building on Super's formulation, Crites (1978) developed a model that includes both affective and cognitive dimensions. The cognitive dimensions of career maturity were represented by career-choice competences (i.e., career decision-making skills). As for the affective dimension, it is represented by attitudes toward career development. The Career Maturity Inventory (Crites, 1978) has been prominently employed in the research literature. One item sample is that "I don't know what courses I should take in school" (reversed). Meanwhile, in the late 1960s and early 1970s, work by Super and other colleagues had begun on constructing the Career Development Inventory (CDI), which arose directly from Super's formulation of career development tasks appropriate for the "Exploration" stage from midadolescence into early adulthood (e.g., Super et al., 1981).

As the pivotal construct in career development theory, career maturity has been cross-culturally examined and validated in the ethnic groups and outside the United States (e.g., Moracco, 1976; Watson et al., 1995) in the past half century. The cross-cultural investigation of career maturity was undertaken in response to concerns about the relative inattention to the cultural context of career development and recommendations for research into the interrelationships of the segments of lifespan, life-space theory of career development (Super, 1990). This section briefly summarized the cross-cultural findings with the framework of cultural validity and specificity (Leong & Brown, 1995) and examined if career maturity is a universal construct cross culturally.

Since the 1960s, many researchers have explored the cultural group differences of career maturity in the United States. Most studies concluded that White American samples reported a higher level of career maturity than did other ethnic/minority groups in the United States (e.g., Crites, 1978; Leong, 1991). For example, Dillard and Perrin (1980) examined the cultural group differences among Black, two Puerto Rican, and four Anglo counselors and found that Anglos had higher differences than Blacks. Leong (1991) found that White Americans displayed much greater career maturity than did Asian Americans. In addition, Lundberg et al. (1997) also reported that Anglo Americans displayed much greater career awareness and occupational knowledge that contributed to successful career planning in comparison to Mexican Americans.

Like the work for career maturity within the United States, studies also reported monotonic progression of career maturity in the samples from a number of countries (e.g., Fouad, 1988; Moracco, 1976; Patton et al., 2004). Participants from other cultures/countries largely showed a lower level of career maturity than did their counterparts from the United States, especially White samples. For example, Fouad (1988) found that Israeli students scored lower on almost all the subscales as well as the total Attitude Scale than U.S. students. This finding is similar to Moracco's (1976) report that American students living in Lebanon scored higher on career maturity than Arab students. In addition, Lee (2001) also reported that American students tend to be more mature than Korean students in career attitudes.

Since most studies have found that European Americans have higher levels of career maturity, many scholars have concluded that this is a cross-culturally universal concept of career development. Many researchers have also assumed the broad applicability of the career maturity construct across different national contexts without conducting cross-cultural validation studies. For example, Patton et al. (2004) indicated that students in higher school grades scored higher on the four subscales of Career Exploration, Career Planning, World of Work Knowledge, and Career Decision Making than students in lower grades in Australia and South Africa. Lee (2001), with a Korean student sample, also found that the construct of career maturity proposed by Crites (1978) CAMI was basically supported among Korean populations.

As shown in the above-mentioned literature, however, European Americans have often been reported to significantly score higher on career maturity than do non-White participants, including those from the United States and other countries. This may suggest that the construct of career maturity proposed by Super and Crites and their colleagues, may be an individualism-related career concept, not only because it is originally derived from White American cultures, but also because it mainly reflected the dimension of career maturity in the corresponding independent cultural context. In other words, career maturity should also be understood from the standpoint of cultural specificity.

Lawrence and Brown (1976) suggested that self-concept may have a different impact on career maturity for those individuals from different ethnic/minority backgrounds, and Super's self-concept theory has more validity when referring to white males than when referring to blacks in the U.S. context. Similarly, Hardin et al. (2001) also argued that high-acculturation Asian Americans and those with lower interdependent self-construal did not differ from European Americans in maturity of career choice attitudes. However, one's career development or maturity in a collective cultural background (e.g., China,

Japan, Korea) means not only gradually constructing their own career, but also learning how to integrate their careers with their families or significant others' career development.

Lee (2001) also argued that the difference between the U.S. and Korean samples in overall maturity is likely due to differences in cultures. Career-related activities or attitudinal development are not the main task assigned by their family or society to Korean high school students to achieve. Another possible reason for lower scores on career maturity for Korean male students concerns external influences on the career decision making of individuals. Korean societies stress duty to family or group on occupational choice (Leong, 1993; Markus & Kitayama, 1991). Since Korean culture puts more emphasis on group opinions than on personal interest, parental opinions play a very important role in career choice (Leong, 1993). If a population characteristic is such that important decisions are made by one's family, one may not develop a high level of career maturity. The influence of family on Chinese American, West German, African, and South Asian youth has also been highlighted in the literature (Freeman, 1993; Ma & Yeh, 2005).

In addition, a considerable body of work from South Africa has consistently shown that Black youth are less mature than their White counterparts (Watson et al., 1995). As a result, some researchers have identified the issue relevant to career maturity from a perspective of cultural specificity. For example, Stead and Watson (1998) suggest that, due to the unique features of South African society, the career maturity construct may be inappropriate. Instead, these researchers suggest a focus on role maturity as this broader emphasis would allow a particular culture or individual to define salient roles. Similarly, Bang (2016) and Ham and Lim (2017) highlighted the cultural specificity of career maturity through adapting the existing Western-based career maturity inventory (e.g., the Career Maturity Inventory; Savickas & Porfeli, 2011), or they developed culturally relevant inventory (e.g., the Korean version of the Career Maturity Inventory for Elementary Students; Chung et al., 2011) in Korean societies.

In summary, the above review on the association of family or related factors on career maturity actually highlights the importance of taking contextual factors into account as part of Super's construct, as was the idea of adjustment as a component of mature behavior. However, in the quest to substantiate his theories about stages and tasks, Super's early comments on the importance of contextual and contingency factors have typically been overlooked. Super (1990) himself proposed a change in terminology from: career maturity" to "career adaptability," a term which he believed better conveyed the range of career-related attitudes, knowledge, and skills at the various stages and transition points in career development.

Cross-cultural Studies in Trait and Factor Theory (Holland)

As the most popular typology of vocational interest with a trait and factor perspective, John L. Holland's (1985; 1997) theory of vocational personalities and work environments provided a circular structure of Realistic, Investigative, Artistic, Social, Enterprising, and

Conventional (RIASEC) interests. In Holland's theory, persons can be categorized as one of six personality types. In a similar way, the environments of college campuses, fields of study, work positions, and occupations can be classified using the same RIASEC system, The hexagonal model has been well examined and validated in the U.S. context (Gottfredson, 2009; Prediger, 1982; Ryan et al., 1996). However, results from non-U.S. samples are often variant across different cultures worldwide (Rounds & Tracey, 1996). Some significant cultural differences among different racial groups within the U.S. context or among different cultures worldwide were empirically supported.

Holland's hexagonal model is generally assessed using a number of different vocational interest surveys, including the two measures Holland developed—the Vocational Preference Inventory in 1953 and the Self-Directed Search (SDS) in 1970 (revised in 1977, 1985, and 1994)—and the Position Classification Inventory (PCI) developed by Holland and Gottfredson in 1991. Some measures developed by other authors have also been reflected in Holland's RIASEC typology, such as the Strong Interest Inventory (Hanson & Campbell, 1985), the Strong Campbell Interest Inventory (Campbell, 1977), and the revised Unisex Edition of the ACT Interest Inventory (UNIACT; Swaney et al., 1995). In addition, in terms of Holland's RIASEC typology, a number of translated or indigenously revised instruments have also been developed and examined cross-culturally worldwide.

In addition, also from a perspective of trait theory, Tracey (2002) has proposed an alternative typology involving eight types: Social Facilitating, Managing, Business Detail, Data Processing, Mechanical, Nature/Outdoors, Artistic, and Helping as the octant model. Being characterized by the People/Things and Data/Ideas dimensions (Prediger, 1982), these eight types were created into a spherical model, which was an expansion beyond Holland's six types and assessed with the Personal Globe Inventory (PGI; Tracey, 2002). The PGI has been employed to examine the vocational interests cross-culturally.

Accordingly, the question on the validity of the hexagonal and alternative models of vocational interests has also been proposed to be a question of cross-cultural relevance. Based on the assessment by those above-mentioned measures of vocational interests, this section briefly reviewed the cross-cultural relevance with the following two topics: (1) cross-cultural comparison within the U.S. cultural context; and (2) cross-cultural comparison worldwide and indigenous examination outside the U.S. context.

Cross-cultural Comparison within the U.S. Cultural Context

In view of the United States' special history, in addition to the White group (Caucasians), there are different ethnic minorities in the country, such as Asian Americans, Middle Eastern Americans, Hispanic and Latino Americans, and African Americans. Although they come from different cultural matrices and certain specific vocational interest differences are presented, the unique American cultures have also shaped some of their common career development characteristics (e.g., McCurtis Witherspoon & Speight, 2009).

Accordingly, the circular structure of RIASEC interests across the U.S. ethnic groups has been empirically supported, and Holland's (1994, 1997) model adequately represents the vocational interest structures of both sexes in all the diverse ethnic samples in general (e.g., Kantamneni, 2014). For example, Day et al. (1998) confirmed the circular structure of Holland's interest types across racial-ethnic groups (African Americans, Mexican Americans, Asian Americans, Native Americans, and Caucasians) using the UNIACT (Swaney et al., 1995). Similarly, Kantamneni (2014) empirically found that a circular RIASEC order is applicable to Asian American, Middle Eastern American, and Native American students and employed adults, regardless of gender, when measured by the 2005 Strong Interest Inventory. With the Vocational Preference Inventory (Holland, 1985), Ryan et al. (1996) confirmed the identical structure of vocational interest across African American and White high school students.

In addition, some structural or dimensional differences of the RIASEC were found within U.S. settings. For example, one exception reported by Hansen et al. (1999) is that Holland's structural model was not completely confirmed in a Chicano/Latino sample. Specifically, the plotted configurations of the male Chicano/Latino group demonstrated the RIASEC ordering hypothesized by Holland. However, for the female Chicana/Latina sample, the Social-Enterprising (SE) types were inverted. Data for both the female and male samples also deviated from Holland's hexagonal solution. In another study, Avilés and Spokane (1999) compared the general occupational interests with the 1985 revision of the Strong Interest Inventory (Hanson & Campbell, 1985) among African American, Hispanic, White, and Spanish Primary Language (SPL) students. They found significant differences among ethnic groups. Comparisons among racial groups indicated that SPL students expressed significantly higher interests in several of the General Occupational Themes when compared with Hispanic and White students. Specifically, SPL students expressed higher interests on the Investigative and Artistic occupational themes than did White and Hispanic students, and higher interests than did White students in the Social, Enterprising, and Conventional themes. In addition, Hispanic students evidenced significantly higher interest scores of the Conventional theme than did White students.

Cross-cultural Comparison Worldwide and Indigenous Examination Outside U.S. Cultures

Beyond the ethnic group differences within the U.S. context, some earlier research (e.g., Rounds & Tracey, 1996) did not find the cross-culture structural equivalent of Holland's circular order model. Some other studies found that that vocational interest types showed different influences on one's career development in different cultural settings. For example, Fan et al. (2012) reported that the Enterprise interest type significantly mediated the association between Social Potency (as one personality factor that assessing traits related to Extraversion together with several Openness-related scales that were constructed in Chinese contexts) and career exploration in the Hong Kong sample. However, the Artistic interest type was the mediator in the American sample. A recent international collaborative study by Glosenberg et al. (2019) found that the predictions of vocational interests on individuals' career development (i.e., person-vocation fit) have been moderated by cultural backgrounds (e.g., individualism) and that the circular model of vocational interests is less valid in settings of lower economic development. More concretely, this study provides evidence that the international use of a vocational interest inventory developed in one economic context (e.g., the United States) might not be appropriate for use in other economic contexts.

In addition, as for the PGI, even Glosenberg et al. (2019) found it was cross-culturally supported, and some inconsistent findings were also reported in the literature. For example, in a comparison between Switzerland and Burkina Faso samples, the French version of the PGI only reached metric invariance, suggesting that country-specific norms should be used for this inventory (Atitsogbe et al., 2018). Therefore, it seems that a universal vocational interest structure may not exist across cultures worldwide because cultures and other social-background variables (e.g., economic development) affected the validity of vocational interests (Glosenberg et al., 2019). Accordingly, a lot of indigenous examinations of vocational interests have been conducted through revisions or modifications for Holland's RIASEC interest model outside the U.S. context (e.g., China, Japan, Korea, India, Romania, Portugal, Spain, Israel, Serbia, South African, Canada, and Italy; see Fang et al., 1996; Farth et al., 1998; Ferreira & Hood, 1995; Long et al., 2006; Morgan et al., 2015; Poitras et al., 2012; Wille et al., 2010).

Theoretically, on the one hand, these works reflect the understanding of Holland's theory and other related models (e.g., Tracy's work) from a perspective of cultural validity; on the other hand, some other studies reflect the cultural specificity of vocational interests. In general, studies of careers from individualistic value perspectives are culture specific and should not be presented as cross-culturally valid, especially for those from collectivistic cultures. In light of the classical interest model such as the RIASEC model and spherical model derived from individualistic cultures such as the United States, which significantly moderated the validity of these models, we developed our reviews in terms of individualism and collectivism based on Hofstede's (2003) cross-cultural theory.

First, some research statistically supported the cultural validity across individualism and collectivism contexts. In the collectivist backgrounds, Long et al. (2006) reported a study at a Japanese college student sample. Using the translated Personal Globe Inventory (PGI; Tracey, 2002), Occupational Tide scales, the RIASEC, octant, and spherical structure of the PGI Occupational Title, scales were statistically supported. Similarly, although the cultural value of tradition plays an important role in Chinese vocational interests, Farth et al. (1998) still demonstrated the cross-cultural validity of Holland's models of six interests in a Hong Kong college student sample: (1) Holland's model as operationalized by UNIACT has considerable external validity; and (2) the internal structure of the UNIACT was generally consistent with Holland's formulations.

In another study of individualistic contexts, Poitras et al. (2012) confirmed the construct validity of the French Canadian version of the Self-Directed Search—Activities Section, and showed that the psychometric qualities of the French Canadian version are equivalent to those of the original English version. Furthermore, a significant external validity of the RIASEC interest model in predicting Germans' job change was reported by Wille et al. (2010) with a longitudinal design. In addition, with the Serbian version of the PGI (Tracey, 2002), Tracey's octagonal and spherical models were supported in a Serbian sample. At the same time, Holland's hexagonal model also fit the data very well, but the fit of Gati's and Rounds–Tracey's models of relations between RIASEC types was either nonsignificant or very low.

Second, some cultural-related findings and indigenous work reflect the importance of cultural specificity in understanding vocational interest in a specific cultural context. Based on Holland's original framework of vocational interests, some indigenous measures have been established and then validated; however, the RIASEC model has been kept. For example, Fang et al. (1996) developed the Chinese Vocational Interest Inventory of Holland type, which was more suited to Chinese conditions by removing four items in the original Holland's Inventory that did not fit the national conditions in China (for example, participating in religious service activities). Morgan et al. (2015) developed the South African Career Interest Inventory (SACII) and validated the structural validity of Holland's circular/hexagonal model in the South African context, including both college student and adult samples. Ferreira and Hood (1995) also demonstrated the construct validity of Holland's hexagonal model of vocational interest structure in Portugal by examining a self-developed inventory—the 174-item Inventario de Interesses Vocacionais. A similar work was conducted in the Argentinean context with a Spanish version of the Alternate Forms Public Domain (AFPD) RIASEC markers by Cupani et al. (2019). They found that the AFPD has an adequate internal structure and can be used to accurately assess the six basic types proposed by Holland.

In addition, the related works by other scholars (e.g., Zhang et al., 2013; Tang, 2001) basically confirmed the structure of the RIASEC model, but some concrete culturally related features were found as well. For instance, Zhang et al. (2013) found a strong fit for the eight types (assessed by the PGI-S; Tracey, 2010) and RIASEC models in a diverse Chinese student sample. Concurrent validity of the RIASEC scores from the PGI-S was examined as they covaried with the Self-Directed Search (SDS; Holland, 1994). However, the SDS demonstrated poor structural validity and thus was not an appropriate criterion. In another Chinese college student sample, although Tang (2001) largely demonstrated the circular model of RIASEC with some gender differences, the Basic Interest Scales of the Strong Interest Inventory 1994 version did not exactly resemble the original classification.

A group of empirical studies on individualism backgrounds investigated the RIASEC competing structural conceptions: Holland's (1997) circular interest model, Gati's (1979) hierarchical model, and Rounds and Tracey's (1996) alternative hierarchical model, were reported, with some mixed results. In a German context, Nagy et al. (2010) investigated the three competing structural conceptions by the randomization test of hypothesized order relations (RTOR) and confirmatory factor analysis (CFA). However, RTOR supported all three representations, whereas CFA supported only Holland's model.

To sum up, on the one hand, it seems that we could not find a robust typology of the vocational interest validity examination across individualism and collectivism contexts, and on the other hand, the structure of vocational interests has been largely demonstrated only across cultural settings. This may reflect the cultural validity of vocational interests in general. Simultaneously, some inconsistent results on the structure of vocational interests and some indigenous research work of vocational interests show that the cultural specificity should also be a pivotal construct for practically understanding vocational interests in a specific cultural background.

Cross-cultural Studies in Social Cognitive Theory (Bandura)

Because traits such as Holland's vocational interests are relatively universal, stable, and lasting attributes, it is difficult to reflect the variability of personal-environmental interactions, which will underestimate people's ability to change, develop, and adaptation. However, the social cognitive career theory (SCCT) highlights the interplay of personality and affective, environmental, and person-cognitive variables in understanding complex vocational behaviors and promoting positive psychosocial adjustment. On the basis of Bandura's (1986) general social cognitive theory, SCCT was introduced to the field of vocational psychology in 1994 (Lent et al., 1994). In the past 25 years, Lent and his collaborators have gradually established five sub-SCCT models. The first three interlocking SCCT models were developed to explicate interest development, career choice, and performance attainments and persistence in a given career domain (Lent et al., 1994). The fourth model was later presented to shed light on the process of pursuing educational and work satisfaction (or well-being) (Lent & Brown, 2006). Furthermore beyond the focus of the contents of career behaviors in the previous fourth models, Lent and Brown (2013) proposed the SSCT career self-management model for illuminating those process aspects of career behavior, such as decision making, job searching, and role transitioning across the lifespan.

Career self-efficacy, outcome expectations, and goals are three central constructs of the SCCT (Lent et al., 1994). The five models discussed earlier represent multivariate, unifying frameworks that emphasize the interplay of personality and affective, environmental, and person-cognitive variables in understanding complex vocational behaviors and promoting positive psychosocial adjustment. These models attracted attention from researchers and practitioners in the United States and other countries and have become a popular base for vocational research and intervention across the world. Existing research has largely offered empirical support for the five SCCT models in the United States and non-U.S. samples, and several key meta-analysis articles have also been published recently (Brown et al., 2008, 2011; Lent & Brown, 2019). This section aimed to briefly review those related studies based on the five SCCT models in the framework of cultural validity and specificity (Leong & Brown, 1995), relying on the findings of both individual studies and recently meta-analytic investigations.

Models of Educational and Occupational Interest and Choice. Because the interest model is a built-in component of the choice model, these two models have often been explored together in the literature. Although the original SCCT models incorporated such traditional "work personality" variables as interests and values, they mainly sought to clarify the nature and functions of contextual influences on career behavior, including interest development and choice-making. Since they were introduced (Lent et al., 1994), a large body of related empirical studies have been conducted, which have been well validated across cultural groups both within and outside the U.S. context (see Lent & Brown, 2019; Sheu & Bordon, 2017, for reviews). The issue of culture has been thoroughly dealt with, including the cultural validity and specificity in theory and career-related practice.

First, interests or choice goals were largely explained by outcome expectation and career self-efficacy worldwide (e.g., Lent et al., 1994, 2018). For example, a group of empirical studies from Asian samples (e.g., Chiu, 2012) supported SCCT hypotheses regarding the relations among self-efficacy, outcome expectations, interest, and choice goals across different career domains and student populations. In European populations, Lent and colleagues (e.g., Lent et al., 2010) tested the choice model across Holland's six occupational themes (R, I, A, S, E, and C) among high school students in Italy and Portugal. They found that the integrated interest-choice model fit the data well across Holland types and generally supported the hypotheses that self-efficacy and outcome expectations jointly predict interests and that interests mediate the relations of self-efficacy and outcome expectations to choice consideration (Lent et al., 2010).

In addition, according to Sheu et al.'s (2010) meta-analysis from 45 independent samples, self-efficacy and outcome expectations accounted for between 37% (Realistic theme) and 67% (Social theme) of the variance in interests, with both predictors explaining significant unique variation in each Holland interest theme. In a recent meta-analysis, Lent et al. (2018) concluded that self-efficacy and outcome expectations explained 46% of the variance in STEM interests and that both variables contributed similarly to the prediction of interests (path coefficients, respectively, of .42 and .37). Some other studies also found that interests partly mediate the relations of self-efficacy and outcome expectations to choice goals (Lent et al., 1994; also see Lent et al., 2018; Sheu et al., 2010, for reviews). Similarly, with a meta-analysis for outside the U.S. samples, Sheu and Bordon (2017) also concluded that empirical syntheses of the interest and choice models were largely supported among Asian, European, and other non-U.S. regions such as Canada, Australia, and countries in Africa and the Middle East.

Second, race/ethnicity differences of the SCCT interest and choice models within the U.S. context (e.g., McCurtis Witherspoon & Speight, 2009) were reported. In the review by Lent et al. (2018), some cultural-related differences were reported. For example, career barriers were more strongly negatively related to self-efficacy in racial/ethnic majority than minority samples. Career supports were more strongly and positively related to outcome expectations and goals in majority than in minority samples. Outcome expectations were more highly related to interests in majority samples, though outcome expectations were more strongly linked to goals in minority samples. For another example, McCurtis Witherspoon and Speight (2009) found that gender and self-efficacy are the best predictors of interest in traditional occupations, including education and the social sciences in American blacks.

Third, beyond the cultural validities of the SCCT interest and choice models, the issue of cultural specificity has also been highlighted in some individual empirical studies. For example, the roles of family support and acculturation have been emphasized among the vocational interest development depending on the Holland theme among Asian American populations (Hui & Lent, 2018). Lent et al. (2010) found that, contrary to SCCT, however, social supports and barriers related to choice consideration indirectly, through self-efficacy rather than directly among Portuguese high school students. A study in the East African community showed that Rwandan students rely mainly on career decision-making self-efficacy to take action on their preferred career paths; Kenyan students seem to behave according to their levels of performance (Takahashi, 2018).

Model of Performance Attainment and Persistence. SCCT's performance model shows that the ability and quality of past performance predict future academic or occupational performance and persistence through self-efficacy and performance goals. According to Bandura (1986), self-efficacy helps determine what people can achieve with their abilities, partly by encouraging performance goals that focus and motivate their efforts toward goal attainment. Based on a large body of empirical studies on this model from both academic and nonacademic works (e.g., Chiu, 2012; Lent et al., 1994), a number of meta-analyses have examined the relations of social cognitive variables to performance (e.g., Brown et al., 2008, 2011; Lent & Brown, 2019; Sheu & Bordon, 2017). Accordingly, some basic conclusions have been derived for statistically supporting this performance model across culturally. As Brown and his colleagues (2011) report, the social cognitive predictors together account for 20% in work performance (Brown et al., 2011), 19% in academic performance, and 28% in academic persistence (Brown et al., 2008) across behavioral domains. Lent and Brown (2019) also point out that the available meta-analytic findings suggest that, unlike fully mediating the relation of ability to interests, self-efficacy only partially mediated the relation of ability to perform. Consistent with social cognitive assumptions (Bandura, 1986), self-efficacy, which is informed by ability/past performance, may help determine how well students are able to deploy their skills. Success at complex academic tasks profits both from ability and from the confidence that one can harness it well to meet performance challenges. These findings largely supported the cultural validity of the SCCT performance model.

Unlike the examination of the performance model from a perspective of cultural validity, however, it has received limited attention with the perspective of cultural specificity. For example, in a Mexican American high school student sample, Garriott et al. (2016) examined the role of family-related variables in the performance model. They found that Familism predicted performance accomplishments and perceived family support, while perceived family support predicted self-efficacy and goals. This might be due to the tendency for academic or work performance to be viewed from a universalist or etic perspective. There is a need for more cross-cultural comparisons on the performance model from a culture-specific perspective, particularly for the samples from Europe and Southeast Asian or South Asian countries (Sheu & Bordon, 2017).

Model of Academic and Work Domain Satisfaction. The SCCT satisfaction and well-being model (Lent & Brown, 2006) shows that work and academic satisfaction (i.e., the degree to which one likes or is happy with one's educational or work experiences) are influenced, in part, by self-efficacy beliefs, outcome expectations, and goal mechanisms. Satisfaction at school or work is seen as a function of the degree to which people are making progress at their personally valued goals (e.g., performing well in a college major, developing leadership skills), along with their goal and task-related self-efficacy and outcome expectations.

This model has been largely supported across cultures. Both the predictions of the model for academic/college major satisfaction among college students (e.g., Sheu et al., 2014) and for work satisfaction of employed adults (e.g., Lee & Shin, 2017) in both the U.S. and non-U.S. samples have been empirically supported. For instance, the satisfaction model explained 49–67%, 47–66%, and 46–57% of the variance, respectively, in academic satisfaction, academic stress, and life satisfaction among Asian samples (Sheu et al., 2014).

In addition, Lent et al. (2014) offered preliminary evidence for the validity of the satisfaction model for college students and adults in Africa and the Middle East. Sheu et al. (2018) have been exploring invariance of the model across racial/ethnic groups (in the United States) and nationality, and they reported that the basic model, when collapsed over the academic and work domains, appears to fit well in each group comparison, accounting for large portions of the variation in domain and life satisfaction across grouping variables. These findings support the cultural validity of the academic and work satisfaction SCCT model.

However, some other results for the satisfaction model have been reported, which may suggest that the satisfaction model should be further investigated from a perspective of cultural specificity. Perhaps due to the characteristics of multiculturalism in Europe (e.g., the difference between Western Europe and Southern Europe), existing cross-sectional and longitudinal research conducted in Europe did not produce consistent findings regarding the mediating roles of self-efficacy and goal progress in the satisfaction model (Sheu & Bordon, 2017). Related to the collective cultural background, that interdependent self-construals significantly predict Asian students' academic satisfaction may indicate the benefit of adding one's cultural orientation to the satisfaction model (Sheu et al., 2014).

Model of Career Self-management. The career self-management model (Lent & Brown, 2013) was proposed later and differs from prior SCCT models in that it focuses on process rather than the content aspects of career development. The self-management model was developed to predict how people make school- and work-related choices and manage other important developmental tasks, challenges, and crises, regardless of the occupations they enter. The self-management model highlights the process by which individuals manage specific tasks entailed by various occupational contexts such as career exploration, decision making, job searching, identity management, transitions, and management of multiple roles (Lent & Brown, 2006). In this model, consistent with other SCCT models, person (e.g., race/ethnicity, personality traits) and contextual variables (e.g., supports, socioeconomic conditions) are posited to be linked to self-efficacy beliefs, outcome expectations, goals, and actions via several routes—directly, indirectly, and/or as moderators.

Because the self-management model has been developed recently, most model testing has been conducted among U.S. college samples (e.g., Lim et al., 2016; Tatum, 2018), and the model has begun to be examined mainly in U.S. backgrounds. As reviewed by Brown and Lent (2019), the career self-management model has been well tested and has shown utility in predicting self-management actions, disclosure status outcomes, decisional outcomes, and job search outcomes in U.S. settings. However, additional cross-cultural evidence has not been reported in the literature except for the study conducted by Kim et al. (2019).

Under the framework of the career self-management model and with an extended focus on job search self-efficacy (JSSE) and its relevant variables, Kim et al. (2019) found that JSSE was more strongly related to job search action in collectivist cultures than in individualist ones. Due to "face" concerns, individuals in collectivist cultures may experience stronger emotions in the job search process than people in individualist cultures because job security and connectedness to other members are more important considerations in collectivist than in individualist cultures (Probst & Lawler, 2006). It has also been found that those who are unemployed in the long term may feel more stressed and suffer more negative mental health effects than those unemployed short-term. This is because as the job search process is prolonged, job seekers tend to internalize pessimism about their employability (Thompson et al., 2017). The stronger relationship between JSSE and search action in more vulnerable groups, collectivist cultures, and the long-term unemployed group, supports previous suggestions that JSSE is a factor that helps one to continuously engage in job searching behaviors even in a prolonged search process or after subsequent setbacks.

In summary, those SCCT submodels have been largely demonstrated across cultural groups within the United States or non-U.S. settings in terms of cultural validities.

However, in consideration of the cultural relevance of career development, the issue of cultural specificity would need to be highlighted for the SCCT in future research.

Cross-cultural Studies in Career Decision-Making Theories (Gati and Others)

Modern changes in society have increased the difficulties individuals face during the complex decision-making process in career transitions (Gati et al., 1996). Career indecision is thus considered as one of the central career research topics and has been widely studied. Based on decision theory, Gati et al. (1996) developed a general theoretical taxonomy of career decision-making difficulties, which may lead to an individual's career indecision. The taxonomy divided these difficulties into three major categories: lack of readiness, lack of information, and inconsistent information. Gati et al. (1996) also developed the Career Decision-making Difficulties Questionnaire (CDDQ) to empirically test the proposed theoretical taxonomy. This questionnaire has been translated into several different languages and is used in various countries, including the United States, China, Turkey, and France (e.g., Willner et al., 2015).

To extend Gati et al.'s (1996) model of cognition-related facets of career decision-making difficulty, Saka et al. (2008) proposed a model of the emotional and personality-related aspects of career decision-making difficulties, which includes three major clusters: pessimistic views, anxiety, and self-concept and identity. To empirically test the proposed model, Saka et al. (2008) developed the Emotional and Personality-related Career decision-making Difficulties questionnaire (EPCD). This questionnaire was translated into different languages and has been used in various countries, such as China, Greece, Turkey, Korea, and the United States (Hou et al., 2016; Saka et al., 2008).

Cross-cultural studies in career indecision fall into three categories: construct structure, levels, and concurrent validity across cultures (e.g., Willner et al., 2015).

First, regarding the structure of career indecision, research showed that its structure may be culturally specific. Gati et al. (1996) reported that the external conflict scale was clustered under the inconsistent information dimension for the Israeli sample but under the lack of readiness dimension for the American sample. Mau (2001) reported a nonsignificant loading of the lack of motivation scale to the lack of readiness dimension for the Taiwanese sample, whereas there was a significant loading for the American sample. The structural validity of the EPCD has also been tested cross-culturally (Saka et al., 2008). However, the uncrystallized identity scale was clustered under the self-concept and identity dimension for the Israeli sample but under the anxiety dimension for the American sample (Saka et al., 2008).

Second, with regard to the cultural differences/similarities in the levels of career indecision/career decision-making difficulties, both cross-ethnic and cross-national studies were reported in the literature. For cross-ethnic research, Mau (2004) reported greater difficulties (measured by CDDQ) of Asian American students than did the White American students, African American students, and Hispanic American students, in both high school and college samples. However, a study by Lopez and Ann-Yi (2006) reported no significant difference in career indecision as measured by the Career Decision Scale among African, White, and Hispanic American female students.

Most cross-national studies were conducted to compare American and other cultures, and they found lower career indecision for the American than for other samples. For example, when comparing American and Asian samples, Mau (2001) indicated that American undergraduate students perceived less career decision-making difficulties (as measured by the CDDQ) and lower career indecision (as measured by the CDS) than did the Taiwanese undergraduate students. South Korean high school students were found to obtain higher career indecision scores (as measured by Career Indecision Profile) than did the U.S. undergraduates (Abrams et al., 2015). Saka et al. (2008) also reported higher emotional and personality-related difficulties (as measured by Emotional and Personality Career Difficulties Scale) among Israeli adults than among U.S. undergraduates.

When comparing American samples and European samples, Tagay (2014) reported more career decision-making difficulties (as measured by CDDQ) in American high school students than did the Turkish high school students. Italian high school students displayed higher career indecision, as measured by CIP, than did the U.S. undergraduates (Carr et al., 2014). Meanwhile, French-speaking undergraduates were found to obtain significantly higher neuroticism/negative affectivity scores than did the U.S. undergraduates (Carr et al., 2014).

In addition, the other two multicultural studies also reported lower career indecision scores for American samples than for other samples. When comparing U.S., Israeli, and Chinese samples, Willner et al. (2015) found that Chinese undergraduates perceived higher career decision-making difficulties (as measured by CDDQ) than did the U.S. undergraduates, U.S. adults, and Israeli adults. Among seven countries (Australia, Canada, China, India, South Africa, the United Kingdom, and the United States), Levin et al. (2020) reported that Australia and the United States exhibited the lowest total CDDQ scores, and China and India the highest.

Though limited, some cross-national studies explore cultural differences/similarities in career indecision levels across other cultures other than the United States. For example, Atitsogbe et al. (2018) found that Burkinabe undergraduates reported higher levels of career decision-making difficulties (as measured by CDDQ) than did the Swiss undergraduates and adult workers. South Korean high school students were found to receive higher neuroticism/negative affectivity scores (as measured by CIP) than did Chinese secondary students (Roche et al., 2017). No significant difference was found on career indecision, as measured by the Career Factors Inventory, between Israeli and Canadian undergraduates (Kofler, 2015). No significant differences in career decision-making difficulties (as measured by the CDDQ) were found among 12th-grade students in East Jerusalem, areas in the West Bank under the Palestinian National Authority, and Israel (Hijazi et al., 2004).

With regard to the concurrent validity of career indecision across cultures, cross-ethnic research reported that African Americans' career indecision (as measured by CDS) was predicted by career coping and educational barriers, whereas White Americans' career indecision was predicted by educational barriers, career coping, and career self-efficacy (Lopez & Ann-Yi, 2006). Educational barriers and career coping reflected respondents' perceived efficacy in coping with educational and career-related barriers such as negative comments about their racial/ethnic background, lack of educational preparation, and money problems. A cross-national study reported a similar pattern of associations between the career decision-making profiles and difficulties (as measured by CDDQ) in U.S. undergraduates, U.S. adults, Israeli adults, and Chinese undergraduates with only a few unique cultural differences (Willner et al., 2015). Specifically, a correlation between greater speed of making final decisions and fewer difficulties involving Lack of Information was only found in the U.S. sample; the desire to please others was found to predict Inconsistent Information only in the Israeli sample; and a correlation between greater Consulting with others and fewer difficulties was only found in the Chinese sample.

Some cross-national studies also explore the concurrent validity of career indecision within other cultures than the U.S. context. For example, correlations between vocational interest differentiation and consistency indices and career decision-making difficulties (as measured by the CDDQ) were only observed among Swiss students and adult workers but not among Burkinabe students (Atitsogbe et al., 2018). According to Patton et al. (2004), for both South African and Australian secondary school students, the more work and nonwork barriers they perceived, the greater indecision (as measured by CDS) they would experience. However, the association between work and nonwork barriers and career certainty (as measured by CDS) was only found among South African secondary school students (Patton et al., 2004).

In general, although previous cross-cultural studies showed structural validity levels and concurrent validity of career indecision across cultures, there are still some suggestions for future studies. First, the cultural diversity in previous research is limited; most researchers focused on a comparison between the U.S. and other contexts (e.g., Willner et al., 2015; Mau, 2001), thus leading to calling for exploring career indecision differences among other cultures in the future. Second, several studies recruited participants from both different cultural backgrounds and different age levels (e.g., Abrams et al., 2015; Carr et al., 2014), which may weaken the credibility of cultural explanations for the career indecision difference. Third, longitudinal studies are suggested to be conducted to test the cultural difference in the developmental pattern of career indecision. Fourth, studies exploring the predictive validity of career indecision across cultures are suggested to be conducted in the future.

Conclusion

In response to the problem identified by Henreich et al (2010) regarding how psychological science has been skewed toward a restricted sample of Western, Educated, Industrialized, Rich, and Democratic (WEIRD) societies, we have sought to expand the scope of career theories by reviewing cross-cultural studies. WEIRD samples have created the twin challenges regarding the cultural validity of these career theories as well as the lack of culture-specific variables such as those identified by indigenous psychologies (Kim, Yang, & Kuo, 2006). We hope that this review will move us forward to a more inclusive vocational psychology with greater generalizability.

Our review has identified several key limitations of existing research on culture and careers. Consistent with Henreich et al.'s (2010) findings regarding WEIRD samples, our literature search for this chapter revealed a dearth of studies regarding cultural and racial minorities in the field of vocational psychology. We also found that the majority of empirical studies in the field used primarily WEIRD samples and assumed that the findings were universal. It is important to note that without a comparative cross-cultural design, all studies in vocational psychology consisting of a sample from one culture is in fact an indigenous study. As Leong and Brown (1995) pointed out, the cultural validity of these indigenous studies need to be examined across other cultures if we are to avoid creating a science based on pseudo-etics and WEIRD samples.

In our review of the cultural validity studies of major Western career models such as Super's theory (1990), Holland's theory (1985, 1997), and social cognitive career theory (Lent et. al., 1994), these studies tended to examine the internal validity (e.g., the measurement model or measurement equivalence more than the external validity (e.g., the predictive validity) of the models. Clearly, more external validity studies are needed in terms of culture and careers. At the same time, these studies need to identify more culturally relevant and culturally sensitive criterion measures to test for the external validity of these Western models. In other words, we need to examine the measurement equivalence not only of the predictor variables (as formulated in these Western models) but also the outcome variables. Theoretically, job satisfaction, as an individual difference variable, would have a different nomological network (Cronbach & Meehl, 1955) in individualistic versus collectivistic cultures. Job satisfaction is likely to have different meaning for persons with interdependent self-construal in contrast to those with independent self-construal. As Hardin et al. (2001) found, Asians with lower acculturation and higher levels of interdependent self-construal tend to be assessed as having lower levels career maturity, as measured by Crites's (1978) Western model.

There are several new fruitful directions for the field of vocational psychology in moving beyond WEIRD samples. It is our hope that our current review of culture and career studies will stimulate further interest in expanding the theoretical foundations of vocational psychology beyond WEIRD samples. Earlier, Henreich et al. (2010) issued the challenge of countering WEIRD science by "building a broader, richer, and better-grounded understanding of our species." To build this broader and better grounded set of career theories, we propose that researchers need to adopt a dual strategy of testing (and not assuming) the cultural validity of these theories based on WEIRD samples for non-WEIRD populations. At the same time, these cultural validity studies need to be

Table 4.1 Theoretical and practical implications from this review

A. Theoretical Implications
1. Improve the generalizability of our career theories by studying non-WEIRD samples.
2. Study BOTH the external and internal validity of Western models when examining the cultural validity of these models.
3. Increase exploration of culture-specific/indigenous outcome variables relative to predictor variables.
4. Develop measures for operationalizing culture-specific/indigenous variables in expanding career theories beyond the current Western focus.
5. Test for the incremental validity of culture-specific constructs in predicting career choice, career adaptability, and career development in non-WEIRD samples.
6. Conduct more longitudinal studies to counter the present dominance of cross-sectional studies.
B. Practical Implications
1. Become aware of the impact of ethnocentrism in our practice, such as using career theories based on WEIRD samples with clients from non-WEIRD cultures.
2. Counter the culture-blind approach in practice by assuming that models and findings from WEIRD samples will automatically, without validation, apply to everyone.
3. Acquire knowledge about culture-specific constructs that may influence the careers of non-Western clients.
4. Use culture-specific constructs to improve culturally appropriate career counseling and interventions
5. Culturally adapt Western career theories to accommodate for cultural differences among non-WEIRD clients.

combined with culture-specific studies to explore the influence of the indigenous process and outcome variables. For example, does colorism (skin tone) moderate implicit bias in how African American clients are treated by career counselors or human resource professionals conducting selection interviews?

In terms of measurement, researchers also need to take a dual approach to evaluating the cross-cultural measurement equivalence of tests and instruments developed on WEIRD samples for non-WEIRD samples. At the same time, taking a culture-specific approach, they need to also develop more measures for operationalizing culture-specific/indigenous variables in expanding career theories beyond the current Western focus. With these established and properly validated measures of culture-specific constructs, the next step would be to test their incremental validity in predicting career choice, career adaptability, and career development in non-WEIRD samples, as suggested by Leong and Lee (2006) in their cultural accommodation model. This model consists of accommodating for culture-specificity when using Western-based models of counseling and psychotherapy.

Finally, we have identified five key theoretical implications and five key practical implications in our review (see Table 4.1).

References

Abrams, M. D., Lee, I. H., Brown, S. D., & Carr, A. (2015). The career indecision profile: Measurement equivalence in the United States and South Korea. *Journal of Career Assessment, 23*, 225–235.

Atitsogbe, K. A., Moumoula, I. A., Rochat, S., Antonietti, J. P., & Rossier, J. (2018). Vocational interests and career indecision in Switzerland and Burkina Faso: Cross-cultural similarities and differences. *Journal of Vocational Behavior, 107*, 126–140.

Avilés, R. M. D., & Spokane, A. R. (1999). The vocational interests of Hispanic, African American, and White middle school students. *Measurement and Evaluation in Counseling and Development, 32*, 138–148.

Bandura, A. (1986). *Social foundations of thought and action: A social cognitive theory*. Englewood Cliffs, NJ: Prentice-Hall.

Bang, N. M. (2016). Cross-cultural validation of the career maturity inventory: A Korean form. PhD (Doctor of Philosophy) thesis, University of Iowa. https://doi.org/10.17077/etd.z3y3u3r0

Brown, S. D., & Lent, R. W. (2019). Social cognitive career theory at 25: Progress in studying the domain satisfaction and career self-management models. *Journal of Career Assessment, 27*, 563–578.

Brown, S. D., Lent, R. W., Telander, K., & Tramayne, S. (2011). Social cognitive career theory, conscientiousness, and work performance: A meta-analytic path analysis. *Journal of Vocational Behavior, 79*, 81–90. doi:10.1016/j.jvb.2010.11.009

Brown, S. D., Tramayne, S., Hoxha, D., Telander, K., Fan, X., & Lent, R. W. (2008). Social cognitive predictors of college students' academic performance and persistence: A meta-analytic path analysis. *Journal of Vocational Behavior, 72*, 298–308. doi:10.1016/j.jvb.2007.09.003

Campbell, D. P. (1977). *Manual for the Strong-Campbell Interest Inventory* (2nd ed.). Palo Alto, CA: Stanford University Press.

Carr, A., Rossier, J., Rosselet, J. G., Massoudi, K., Bernaud, J. L., Ferrari, L., & Roche, M. (2014). The Career Indecision Profile: Measurement equivalence in two international samples. *Journal of Career Assessment, 22*, 123–137.

Chiu, M. S. (2012). Identification and assessment of Taiwanese children's conceptions of learning mathematics. *International Journal of Science and Mathematics Education, 10*, 163–191. doi:10.1007/s10763-011-9283-2

Chung, I. J., Im, J. Y., & Hwang, M. H. (2011). Development of career maturity scale for elementary schoolers. *The Journal of Elementary Education, 24*, 169–194.

Crites, J. O. (1978). *Career maturity inventory: Theory and research handbook*. Monterey, CA: CTBL McGraw-Hill.

Cronbach, L., & Meehl, P (1955). Construct validity in psychological tests. *Psychological Bulletin, 52*, 281–302.

Cupani, M., Morán, V. E., Azpilicueta, A. E., Piccolo, N. V., & Artuso, F. (2019). Alternate Forms Public Domain RIASEC markers for interests and self-Efficacy: Spanish version. *Electronic Journal of Research in Educational Psychology, 17*, 359–382.

Day, S. X., Rounds, J., & Swaney, K. (1998). The structure of vocational interests for diverse racial-ethnic groups. *Psychological Science, 9*, 40–44.

Dillard, J. M., & Perrin, D. W. (1980). Puerto Rican, Black, and Anglo adolescents' career aspirations, expectations, and maturity. *Vocational Guidance Quarterly, 28*(4), 313–321. https://doi.org/10.1002/j.2164-585X.1980.tb01004.x

Fan, W., Cheung, F. M., Leong, F. T., & Cheung, S. F. (2012). Personality traits, vocational interests, and career exploration: A cross-cultural comparison between American and Hong Kong students. *Journal of Career Assessment, 20*, 105–119.

Fang, L., Bai, L., & Lin, W. (1996). Construction of the Chinese vocational interest inventory of Holland type. *Acta Psychologica Sinica, 28*, 113–119.

Farth, J. L., Leong, F. T. L., & Law, K. S. (1998). Cross-cultural validity of Holland's model in hong kong. *Social Science Electronic Publishing, 52*, 425–440.

Ferreira, J. A. A., & Hood, A. B. (1995). The development and validation of a Holland-type Portuguese Vocational Interest Inventory. *Journal of Vocational Behavior, 46*, 119–130.

Fouad, N. A. (1988). The construct of career maturity in the United States and Israel. *Journal of Vocational Behavior, 32*, 49–59.

Freeman, S. C. (1993). Donald Super: A perspective on career development. *Journal of Career Development, 19*, 255–264.

Garriott, P. O., Reiter, S., & Brownfield, J. (2016). Testing the efficacy of brief multicultural education interventions in white college students. *Journal of Diversity in Higher Education, 9*, 158.

Gati, I. (1979). A hierarchical model for the structure of vocational interests. *Journal of Vocational Behavior, 15*, 90–106.

Gati, I., Krausz, M., & Osipow, S. H. (1996). A taxonomy of difficulties in career decision making. *Journal of Counseling Psychology, 43*, 510–526. https://doi.org/10.1037/0022-0167.43.4.510

Glosenberg, A., Tracey, T. J., Behrend, T. S., Blustein, D. L., & Foster, L. L. (2019). Person-vocation fit across the world of work: Evaluating the generalizability of the circular model of vocational interests and social cognitive career theory across 74 countries. *Journal of Vocational Behavior, 112*, 92–108.

Gottfredson, G. D. (2009). John L. Holland (1919–2008). *American Psychologist, 64*, 561.

Ham, K. A., & Lim, H. W. (2017). Career maturity and quality of life in Korean adolescents: A cross-lagged panel design. *The Career Development Quarterly, 65*, 250–263.

Hansen, J. I. C., Sarma, Z. M., & Collins, R. C. (1999). An evaluation of Holland's model of vocational interests for Chicana (o) and Latina (o) college students. *Measurement and Evaluation in Counseling and Development, 32*, 2–13.

Hanson, J. C., & Campbell, D. P. (1985). *Manual for the strong interest inventory*. Palo Alto, CA: Stanford University Press.

Hardin, E. E., Leong, F. T., & Osipow, S. H. (2001). Cultural relativity in the conceptualization of career maturity. *Journal of Vocational Behavior, 58*, 36–52.

Henrich, J., Heine, S. J., & Norenzayan, A. (2010). The weirdest people in the world? *Behavioral and Brain Sciences, 33*, 61–83.

Hijazi, Y., Tatar, M., & Gati, I. (2004). Career decision-making difficulties among Israeli and Palestinian Arab high-school seniors. *Professional School Counseling, 8*(1), 64–72.

Hofstede, G. (2003). *Culture's consequences: Comparing values, behaviors, institutions and organizations across nations*. Thousand Oaks, CA: SAGE.

Holland, J. L. (1985). *Making vocational choices: A theory of vocational personalities and work environments* (2nd ed.). Englewood Cliffs, NJ: Prentice-Hall.

Holland, J. L. (1994). *The self-directed search*. Odessa, FL: Psychological Assessment Resources.

Holland, J. L. (1997). *Making vocational choices: A theory of vocational personalities and work environments* (3rd ed.). Psychological Assessment Resources.

Hou, Z. J., Li, X., Liu, Y. L., & Gati, I. (2016). The emotional and personality-related career decision-making difficulties questionnaire—Validation of the Chinese version. *Journal of Career Assessment, 24*, 366–379.

Hui, K., & Lent, R. W. (2018). The roles of family, culture, and social cognitive variables in the career interests and goals of Asian American college students. *Journal of Counseling Psychology, 65*, 98.

Jorgensen, N. A., Nelson, L. J., & Duan, X. (2017). Perceived parenting practices and adjustment: Moderation by cultural values in Chinese emerging adults. *Emerging Adulthood, 5*, 371–376. https://doi.org/10.1177/2167696817694800

Kantamneni, N. (2014). Vocational interest structures for Asian Americans, Middle-Eastern Americans and Native Americans on the 2005 strong interest inventory. *Journal of Vocational Behavior, 84*, 133–141.

Kim, J. G., Kim, H. J., & Lee, K. H. (2019). Understanding behavioral job search self-efficacy through the social cognitive lens: A meta-analytic review. *Journal of Vocational Behavior, 112*, 17–34.

Kim, U., Yang, Y. K., & Kuo, H. K. (2006). *Indigenous and cultural psychology: Understanding people in context*. New York: Springer.

Kofler, D. (2015). Career indecision among Israeli and Canadian undergraduate students. Master dissertation, University of Toronto.

Lawrence, W., & Brown, D. (1976). An investigation of intelligence, self-concept, socioeconomic status, race, and sex as predictors of career maturity. *Journal of Vocational Behavior, 9*, 43–52.

Lee, E. S., & Shin, Y. J. (2017). Social cognitive predictors of Korean secondary school teachers' job and life satisfaction. *Journal of Vocational Behavior, 102*, 139–150.

Lee, K. H. (2001). A cross-cultural study of the career maturity of Korean and United States high school students. *Journal of Career Development, 28*, 43–57.

Lent, R. W., & Brown, S. D. (2006). On conceptualizing and assessing social cognitive constructs in career research: A measurement guide. *Journal of Career Assessment, 14*, 12–35.

Lent, R. W., & Brown, S. D. (2013). Social cognitive model of career self-management: Toward a unifying view of adaptive career behavior across the life span. *Journal of Counseling Psychology, 60*, 557–568. https://doi.org/10.1037/a0033446.

Lent, R. W., & Brown, S. D. (2019). Social cognitive career theory at 25: Empirical status of the interest, choice, and performance models. *Journal of Vocational Behavior, 115*, 103316.
Lent, R. W., Brown, S. D., & Hackett, G. (1994). Toward a unifying social cognitive theory of career and academic interest, choice, and performance. *Journal of vocational behavior, 45*, 79–122.
Lent, R. W., Paixao, M. P., Da Silva, J. T., & Leitão, L. M. (2010). Predicting occupational interests and choice aspirations in Portuguese high school students: A test of social cognitive career theory. *Journal of Vocational Behavior, 76*, 244–251.
Lent, R. W., Sheu, H., Miller, M. J., Cusick, M. E., Penn, L. T., & Truong, N. N. (2018). Predictors of science, technology, engineering, and mathematics choice options: A meta-analytic path analysis of the social-cognitive choice model by gender and race/ethnicity. *Journal of Counseling Psychology, 65*, 17–35.
Lent, R. W., Taveira, M., Pinto, J. C., Silva, A. D., Blanco, A′., Faria, S., & Gonçalves, A. M. (2014). Social cognitive predictors of well-being in African college students. *Journal of Vocational Behavior, 84*, 266–272.
Leong, F. T. L. (1991). Career development attributes and occupational values of Asian American and White American college students. *Career Development Quarterly, 39*, 221–230.
Leong, F. T. L. (1993). The career counseling process with racial-ethnic minorities: The case of Asian Americans. *The Career Development Quarterly, 42*, 26–40.
Leong, F. T. L. & Brown, M. (1995). Theoretical issues in cross-cultural career development: Cultural validity and cultural specificity. In W. B. Walsh & S. H. Osipow's (Eds.), *Handbook of vocational psychology* (pp. 143–180) (2nd ed.). Hillsdale, NJ: Lawrence Erlbaum.
Leong, F., & Hardin, E. E. (2002). Career psychology and Asian Americans: Cultural validity and cultural specificity. In G. C. Nagayama Hall & S. Okazaki (Eds.), *Asian American psychology: The science of lives in context* (pp. 131–152). Washington, DC: American Psychological Association.
Leong, F. T. L., & Lee, S. H. (2006). A cultural accommodation model of psychotherapy: Illustrated with the case of Asian-Americans. *Psychotherapy: Theory, Research, Practice, and Training*, 43, 410–423.
Levin, N., Braunstein-Bercovitz, H., Lipshits-Braziler, Y., Gati, I., & Rossier, J. (2020). Testing the structure of the Career Decision-Making Difficulties Questionnaire across country, gender, age, and decision status. *Journal of Vocational Behavior, 116*, 103365. https://doi.org/10.1016/j.jvb.2019.103365
Lim, R. H., Lent, R. W., & Penn, L. T. (2016). Prediction of job search intentions and behaviors: Testing the social cognitive model of career self-management. *Journal of Counseling Psychology, 63*, 594.
Long, L., Watanabe, N., & Tracey, T. J. (2006). Structure of interests in Japan: Application of the personal globe inventory occupational scales. *Measurement and Evaluation in Counseling and Development, 38*, 222–236.
Lopez, F. G., & Ann-Yi, S. (2006). Predictors of career indecision in three racial/ethnic groups of college women. *Journal of Career Development, 33*, 29–46.
Lundberg, D. J., Osborne, W. L., & Miner, C. U. (1997). Career maturity and personality preferences of Mexican-American and Anglo-American adolescents. *Journal of Career Development, 23*, 203–213.
Ma, P. W. W., & Yeh, C. J. (2005). Factors influencing the career decision status of Chinese American youths. *The Career Development Quarterly, 53*, 337–347.
Markus, H. R., & Kitayama, S. (1991). Culture and the self: Implications for cognition, emotion, and motivation. *Psychological Review, 98*, 224–253.
Mau, W. C. (2001). Assessing career decision-making difficulties: A cross-cultural study. *Journal of Career Assessment, 9*, 353–364. https://doi.org/10.1177/106907270100900403
Mau, W. C. (2004). Cultural dimensions of career decision-making difficulties. *The Career Development Quarterly, 53*, 67–77. https://doi.org/10.1002/j.2161-0045.2004.tb00656.x
McCurtis Witherspoon, K., & Speight, S. L. (2009). An exploration of African Americans' interests and self-efficacy beliefs in traditional and nontraditional careers. *Journal of Black Studies, 39*, 888–904.
Moracco, J. C. (1976). Vocational maturity of Arab and American high school students. *Journal of Vocational Behavior. 8*, 367–373.
Morgan, B., de Bruin, G. P., & de Bruin, K. (2015). Constructing Holland's hexagon in South Africa: Development and initial validation of the South African Career Interest Inventory. *Journal of Career Assessment, 23*, 493–511. doi:10.1177/1069072714547615
Nagy, G., Trautwein, U., & Lüdtke, O. (2010). The structure of vocational interests in Germany: Different methodologies, different conclusions. *Journal of Vocational Behavior, 76*, 153–169.
Patton, W., Creed, P. A., & Watson, M. (2004). Perceived work related and non-work related barriers in the career development of Australian and South African adolescents. *Australian Journal of Psychology, 55*, 74–82.

Poitras, S. C., Guay, F., & Ratelle, C. F. (2012). Using the self-directed search in research: Selecting a representative pool of items to measure vocational interests. *Journal of Career Development, 39*, 186–207.

Prediger, D. J. (1982). Dimensions underlying Holland's hexagon: Missing link between interests and occupations? *Journal of Vocational Behavior, 21*, 259–287.

Probst, T. M., & Lawler, J. (2006). Cultural values as moderators of employee reactions to job insecurity: The role of individualism and collectivism. *Applied Psychology, 55*, 234–254. https://doi.org/10.1111/j.1464-0597.2006.00239.x

Roche, M. K., Carr, A. L., Lee, I. H., Wen, J., & Brown, S. D. (2017). Career indecision in China: Measurement equivalence with the United States and South Korea. *Journal of Career assessment, 25*, 526–536.

Rounds, J., & Tracey, T. J. G. (1996). Cross-cultural structural equivalence of RIASEC models and measures. *Journal of Counseling Psychology, 43*, 310–329. doi:10.1037/0022-0167.43.3.310

Ryan, J. M., Tracey, T. J., & Rounds, J. (1996). Generalizability of Holland's structure of vocational interests across ethnicity, gender, and socioeconomic status. *Journal of Counseling Psychology, 43*, 330.

Saka, N., Gati, I., & Kelly, K. R. (2008). Emotional and personality-related aspects of career-decision-making difficulties. *Journal of Career Assessment, 16*, 403–424.

Savickas, M. L., & Porfeli, E. J. (2011). Revision of the career maturity inventory: The adaptability form. *Journal of Career Assessment, 19*, 355–374.

Sheu, H., & Bordon, J. J. (2017). SCCT research in the international context: Empirical evidence, future directions, and practical implications. *Journal of Career Assessment, 27*, 58–74.

Sheu, H. B., Chong, S. S., Chen, H. F., & Lin, W. C. (2014). Well-being in Taiwanese and Singaporean college students: Cross-cultural validity of a modified social cognitive model. *Journal of Counseling Psychology, 61*, 447–460.

Sheu, H., Lent, R. W., Brown, S. D., Miller, M. J., Hennessy, K. D., & Duffy, R. D. (2010). Testing the choice model of social cognitive career theory across Holland themes: A meta-analytic path analysis. *Journal of Vocational Behavior, 76*, 252–264. doi:10.1016/j.jvb.2009.10.015

Sheu, H., Lent, R. W., Phrasavath, L., Lui, A. M., Wang, X. T., Cho, H., & Morris, T. R. (2018, August). SCCT satisfaction model—A meta-analytic review. Paper presented at the meeting of the American Psychological Association, San Francisco, CA.

Stead, G. B., & Watson, M. B. (1998). The appropriateness of Super's career theory among black South Africans. *South African Journal of Psychology, 28*, 40–43.

Super, D. E. (1990). A life-span, approach to career development. In D. Brooks & L. Brown (Eds.), *Career choice and development: Applying contemporary theories to practice* (pp. 197–261). San Francisco: Jossey-Bass.

Super, D. E., Thompson, A. S., Lindeman, R. H., Jordaan, J.-P., & Myers, R. A. (1981). *Career Development Inventory*. Palo Alto, CA: Consulting Psychologists Press.

Swaney, K. B., Lamb, R., Prediger, D., & American College Testing Program. (1995). *Technical manual: Revised unisex edition of the ACT Interest Inventory (UNIACT)*. ACT.

Tagay, Ö. (2014). Career decision-making difficulties in Turkey and the USA. *International Journal of Recent Advances in Multidisciplinary Research, 2*, 232–239.

Takahashi, T. (2018). Career guidance in Rwanda and Kenya: Focusing on career decision-making process. *Psychology and Education: An Interdisciplinary Journal, 55*, 74–85.

Tang, M. (2001). Investigation of the structure of vocational interests of Chinese college students. *Journal of Career Assessment, 9*, 365–379.

Tatum, A. K. (2018). Workplace climate and satisfaction in sexual minority populations: An application of social cognitive career theory. *Journal of Counseling Psychology, 65*, 618–628.

Thompson, M. N., Dahling, J. J., Chin, M. Y., & Melloy, R. C. (2017). Integrating job loss, unemployment, and reemployment with social cognitive career theory. *Journal of Career Assessment, 25*, 40–57. https://doi.org/10.1177/1069072716657534.

Tracey, T. J. (2002). Personal Globe Inventory: Measurement of the spherical model of interests and competence beliefs. *Journal of Vocational Behavior, 60*, 113–172.

Tracey, T. J. (2010). Relation of interest and self-efficacy occupational congruence and career choice certainty. *Journal of Vocational Behavior, 76*, 441–447.

Watson, M. B., Stead, G. B., & De Jager, A. C. (1995). The career development of black and white South African university students. *International Journal for the Advancement of Counselling, 18*, 39–47.

Wille, B., De Fruyt, F., & Feys, M. (2010). Vocational interests and Big Five traits as predictors of job instability. *Journal of Vocational Behavior, 76*, 547–558.

Willner, T., Gati, I., & Guan, Y. (2015). Career decision-making profiles and career decision-making difficulties: A cross-cultural comparison among US, Israeli, and Chinese samples. *Journal of Vocational Behavior, 88*, 143–153.

Zhang, Y., Kube, E., Wang, Y., & Tracey, T. J. (2013). Vocational interests in China: An evaluation of the Personal Globe Inventory—Short. *Journal of Vocational Behavior, 83*, 99–105.

CHAPTER

5 Culture and Learning, Training, and Development

Julie V. Dinh *and* Eduardo Salas

Abstract

Given an increasingly diverse and global workforce, successful organizations must understand and address the role of culture in employee learning, training, and development. To this end, we begin by reviewing the instructional systems design (ISD) model as a guiding framework. We then discuss cultural influences on learning and the challenges that they may pose at each stage in the development of educational interventions. We review considerations and solutions that training science may offer. Finally, we synthesize interdisciplinary bodies of literature to highlight relevant theoretical principles and best practices for the workplace. The chapter concludes by identifying and describing future areas for research.

Key Words: culture, training, development, education, learning, instruction, evaluation

Introduction

Thanks to advances in technology and transportation, workplaces are becoming increasingly diverse and geographically dispersed (e.g., U.S. Bureau of Labor Statistics, 2018). These trends pose unique challenges for organizations and their human resources management programs. One particularly important area involves learning, training, and development. In this chapter, we review how organizations can optimally develop employee competencies within multicultural workforces.

This chapter explores the ways in which organizations' learning, training, and development functions can respond to globalization. Notably, trainings themselves can focus on culture as the primary content area (e.g., expatriate or diversity training). For those who are interested in training with culturally focused content, we recommend Bezrukova and colleagues' (2012, 2016) narrative review and meta-analysis on diversity trainings and Morris and Robie's (2001) meta-analysis on cross-cultural training for more comprehensive information in these areas. Here, however, we examine culture as a holistic influence on employee education. Please also note that we discuss both cultural and global contexts in this chapter; the former refers to culture at the local, organizational, and idiosyncratic levels, whereas the latter emphasizes multinational considerations. We begin with a primer on the learning, training, and development sciences before examining its intersection with culture.

A Primer on Learning, Training, and Development Sciences

It is first helpful to understand fundamental concepts from the learning, training, and development sciences. Given the scope of the literature, this section is not to meant to be a comprehensive summary; rather, it serves as an outline of elements that will help direct our review of culture's impact. Throughout this section, we define important concepts and highlight key questions from the learning, training, and development literature.

We use the Instructional Systems Development (ISD) model (Branson et al., 1975) to guide this chapter. Since its development, the ISD model has been commonly and widely used due to its comprehensive structure (Swezey & Llaneras, 1997). In keeping with Salas et al. (2006), we use this model to organize our conversation around culture and training rather than as an endorsement of this particular system above others. With the ISD as a framework, we will discuss how culture influences each of these stages and how we may use theory to guide learning, training, and development later in practice.

The ISD model is composed of five stages: analysis, design, development, implementation, and evaluation. *Analysis* refers to the critical step of understanding one's audience: collecting and analyzing data to understand the needs of the organization. Training *design* involves creating the structural elements of the training: the when, where, why, and how. During the third and fourth stages, *development* and *implementation*, the training is piloted, refined, and executed. *Evaluation* is an important phase that focuses on assessing the effectiveness of the program itself. Importantly, the training process need not end at evaluation. Training experts also examine long-term *transfer* of training outcomes into the real-world environment (e.g., Salas et al., 2006). Each of these stages will be discussed in further detail in the chapter.

Historically, the training sciences have posed questions at many of these levels. Much debate has centered around a question regarding training design—how can we create the most effective programs? It bears noting that many responses to this question, and indeed a large portion of the mainstream training literature, have originated from Western scholars and practitioners. As scholarship becomes more global and accessible, we expect that the training science literature will become more representative and inclusive. Regardless, our review of theory and best practices should be interpreted with these factors in mind.

Although training and learning can be very idiosyncratic, there do appear to be some universal truths. Several meta-analyses, across different content areas and industries, have identified best practices in training (e.g., Bezrukova et al., 2016; Hughes et al., 2016; Lacerenza et al., 2017; Reyes et al., 2019). A common theme is the importance of instructional system design as a holistic process. Administrators should complete each step thoroughly to get the most "return on investment." For example, the needs analysis is a critical and fundamental, but often overlooked, step that informs the remainder of the stages of training. As will be made clear in the rest of the chapter, one must understand the training audience fully in order to deliver programming with truly impactful results.

Learning, training, and development are not monolithic entities, nor do they have universal standards. In most cases, programs should be highly specialized depending on content and context. Training, learning, and development should not be a "one-size-fits-all" product. Programming can look very different depending on content requirements; for example, a diversity workshop will be designed and implemented very differently than a safety training. Different industries may also depend on specific types of learning. Client-facing companies will likely involve more interpersonal development than would a manufacturing firm. This points back to the importance of all the stages of the ISD model, particularly the training needs analysis, in developing robust interventions. It also suggests that some areas of learning, training, and development may be more sensitive to culture than others. As a result, administrators should keep in mind that, depending on the industry context and programming goals, culture may be more or less impactful.

For the purposes of this chapter, we take a bird's eye view of learning, training, and development. When and where appropriate, we draw attention to considerations for specific sectors or types of training. Otherwise, we discuss learning, training, and development in generalities. Our goal is to point to ways in which culture can influence learning, training, and development within organizations at large.

Clarifying Culture

Similarly, we use a broad definition of culture. We operationalize culture as the "integrated pattern of human behavior that includes thoughts, communications, actions, customs, beliefs, values and institutions" of a social or work group (Cross et al., 1989, p. 28; Triandis & Suh, 2002). Throughout this chapter, we examine dimensions of culture according to Hofstede's (2011) conceptualizations: individualism and collectivism; power distance; uncertainty avoidance; masculinity and femininity; long- and short-term orientation; and indulgence and restraint. We also look at more recent dimensions of culture, given their application within the learning, training, and development sciences. Notably, while culture is often considered on the national scale, including in Hofstede's (2011) model, culture is observed on many levels: within groups, teams, organizations, industries, and geographic regions. Training developers should also examine culture as it exists on levels beyond the national stage, including organizationally and regionally, and on finer-grained scales.

Culture influences behavior and learning through multiple avenues. We describe principles rooted in cultural social sciences and how they may impact individual learning and training preferences. In the following sections, we discuss how aspects of culture can be observed and evaluated at each stage of the ISD. This chapter is not an exhaustive summary of findings; rather, it is intended to provide insight into substantial considerations.

Given the large body of evidence supporting the interaction between culture and learning, the training sciences can contribute meaningful theory and best practices.

Training Analysis and Trainee Motivation

The first consideration in training and development, *training analysis*, ensures that programs respond to the needs of the organization, task, and individual. A proper needs analysis collects and analyzes data to inform the goals and design of the training (Brown, 2002). As the first stage of the ISD, training analysis takes place before any other activities.

One important consideration during this temporal stage is motivation, or an individual's predisposition and drive to learn. The assessment and understanding of trainee motivation is an important antecedent to training effectiveness (Baldwin et al., 1991; Baldwin & Magjuka, 1997). Although motivation is often discussed at the individual level, group dynamics, including culture, can often influence motivation. Demographic variables, such as age and gender, may alter training motivation, which then has downstream effects in training effectiveness (Mathieu & Martineau, 1997). These trends suggest that sociocultural identification also may have impact. Indeed, trainees' cultural backgrounds may inform their perceptions of organizational training.

Cultural Influences

Several dimensions of culture can influence trainee motivation. These include individualism versus collectivism and masculinity versus femininity.

Cultures can be characterized by their level of individualism or collectivism. Individualistic cultures emphasize single members' autonomy and independence (Triandis & Gelfand, 1998). At the opposite end of the spectrum, collectivism broadly refers to a communal orientation. Collectivistic cultures are comprised of members who prioritize their goals and shape their behavior based on their interdependence with their in-groups (Mills & Clark, 1982). Collectivistic values thus include the maintenance of relationships and social networks. Together, these two constructs touch upon the deep structures of cultures (Greenfield, 1999), influencing multilevel outcomes from childhood development to societal policies.

Unsurprisingly, then, individualistic and collectivistic tendencies can shape the dynamics of learning and training. Prior to training, such deep structures can influence motivation. For example, hygiene factors, like salary, job security, and working conditions, may create dissatisfaction in the work environment when absent or impaired. Certain motivators, like recognition and advancement, can actively promote better performance when present. Iguisi (2009) found that workers from collectivistic cultures weighted hygiene factors more heavily, whereas individualistic employees were more incentivized by motivators. Deep structures, by shaping value systems, can thus determine individual pursuits related to learning.

Differential motivating forces can lead to substantial effects downstream and at higher levels. For example, studies have found a positive relationship between individualistic cultures and economic markers, such as GDP, venture capital investments (Gantenbein et al., 2019), and household access to financial services (Lu et al., 2021). Although some studies have also suggested that individualism is associated with greater group member satisfaction, a recent study finds that this effect may be due instead to the construct of an "open society," which encourages tolerance, trust, civic engagement, and minimization of materialistic pressure (see Krys et al., 2019 for a review). Furthermore, some scholars have linked individualism with a number of negative developments, including high death tolls during the COVID-19 pandemic and the devaluing of higher education institutions (e.g., Marginson, 2020). With regard to collectivism, this orientation has been linked to both positive phenomena (e.g., higher team performance; Bell, 2007; Jackson et al., 2006) and negative events (e.g., decreased innovation; see Černe et al., 2013 for a review). Indeed, there appear to be costs and benefits associated with either end of the individualism–collectivism spectrum.

It is thus imperative for stakeholders to understand the culturally rooted drivers of their workforce in order to optimize training incentive structures and overall organizational success. The culture literature has often focused on individualism and collectivism, examining it at length in the context of learning, training, and development. However, other cultural dimensions have also attracted substantial scholarship.

A burgeoning area of scholarship looks at culture along a spectrum from masculinity to femininity. This dimension refers to the division of emotional roles between women and men. In masculine societies, genders are clearly emotionally and socially differentiated, such that men are assertive, ambitious, factual, decision making, and in leadership positions (with women in the reverse). Feminine societies, on the other hand, are more fluid and equivalent in distinguishing social roles, with more expressive, balanced, and shared decision making between genders (Hofstede, 2011).

Components of masculinity and femininity have been explored under various guises, including assertiveness. For example, one line of research examined the inclusion of cultural components in assertiveness training programs. It found that cultural context may be an important mediator of assertive (i.e., masculine) behavior (Comas-Diaz & Duncan, 1985). Given that assertiveness training may be at odds with feminine cultures, the researchers recommended that future studies examine the role of cultural factors in these types of training. Such advice can apply to several different types of programming.

Recommendations

Training analysis involves identifying the needs of the program at multiple levels, which can shape training strategic requirements, goals, and design (Brown, 2002; Salas et al., 2012). Many analyses involve data collection, focusing on the task, individual, and organization relevant to the training; however, research suggests that cultural contexts may merit close consideration as well. During this stage, trainers should consider the extensive body of research suggesting cross-cultural differences in motivation and learning. Given the evidence regarding individualism versus collectivism and masculinity versus feminism, program developers should make efforts to understand motivational patterns within their target audience. Furthermore, culturally based learning preferences should be included when collecting and analyzing data; we will discuss these preferences in more detail next in the "Training Design" section.

It can also be helpful to create an organizational environment conducive to trainee motivation. As discussed previously, incentivization may vary based on culture. For example, individuals from collectivistic societies may be motivated by the participation of colleagues, given the social focus on belonging; conversely, employees from individualistic cultures may respond more readily to the unique rewards and recognition tied to learning and performance. In this way, firms themselves can create organizational cultures that incorporate their broader values.

Training Design

Training design involves identifying the structural principles of the training: developing learning objectives, applying performance measures, and outlining the training timeline. During this phase, best practices in learning and training should guide the design of the program. Although there are many types of training design, we can group strategies into four major categories: *information-based* or didactic, which focuses on delivering information; *demonstration-based,* which targets the demonstration of specific skills and abilities; *practice-based* or experiential, wherein opportunities to exercise competencies are offered; and *feedback-based,* incorporating reactions, responses, and guidance from trainers and observers (Salas & Cannon-Bowers, 2000; Weaver et al., 2010). Researchers have recommended combining these four strategies as an effective approach to training design (Salas et al., 2012).

Within the domain of demonstration-based, experiential learning, scholars have further identified four cyclic stages: *abstract conceptualization*, or the application of logic and analysis of situations; *active experimentation*, which involves trying out various approaches; *concrete experience*, born from the opportunity to gather information and make judgments based on new experiences; and *reflective observation*, for example, watching and observing all sides of an issue in order to understand meaning and act (Joy & Kolb, 2009). These theories make up only a small part of the extensive learning and education literature but will be especially useful in understanding training design.

In determining specific strategies, research suggests that culture may influence optimal learning behaviors. Because culture is an experience-based social phenomenon, it inherently influences the ways in which individuals process and internalize information from the environment and stimuli. To illustrate, Franchi (2002) found that there may be cultural differences in particular learning strategies. Study participants from Colombia and Puerto Rico preferred experiential training techniques (e.g., round robin); in comparison, U.S. learners also indicated a desire for experiential strategies but via role-play experiences. Indeed, there are many culturally informed learning preferences, as well as methods of designing accommodating programs.

Cultural Influences

In this section, we refer to several learning modalities. Table 5.1 summarizes Kolb (2014)'s holistic model of experiential learning modes, which will be discussed in tandem with culture-based preferences. Notably, experiential learning involves all four modes, wherein a learner experiences, reflects, thinks, and acts. According to Joy and Kolb (2009) and as shown in Figure 5.1, "immediate or concrete experiences give rise to observations and reflections that are assimilated and distilled into abstract concepts from which new implications for action are drawn. When these implications are actively tested new experiences are created again" (p. 71).

In the context of training and learning, several facets of culture have been shown to impact learning preferences. In particular, prior research has connected individualistic learning with hands-on, experiential techniques, and vice versa. In a study on the learning styles of accounting students, Joy and Kolb (2009) found that culture significantly influenced a person's preferences for type and level of engagement during learning. Specifically, collectivistic trainees preferred reflective modes, while more individualistic students favored active learning. These results were supported by semistructured interviews with civil servants, which found that respondents from individualistic countries preferred experiential learning (Hassi, 2013). These results further emphasize the connection

Table 5.1 Types of learning strategies from experiential learning theory, based on Joy and Kolb (2009)

Mode	Learning strategy	Characterization
Grasping experience	Concrete experience	• Are open to new experiences. • Are dependent on people contact for gathering information. • Are intuitive and make judgments based on feelings.
	Abstract conceptualization	• Use a logical and analytical approach to a learning situation. • Seek theories and generalizations.
Transforming experience	Reflective observation	• Watch and observe all sides of an issue in order to understand its meaning. • Take time to act.
	Active experimentation	• Prefer to try things out. • Are more willing to take risks. • Are practical and application-oriented.

Sources: Auyeung & Sands, 1996; Barmeyer, 2004; Kolb & Kolb, 2005.

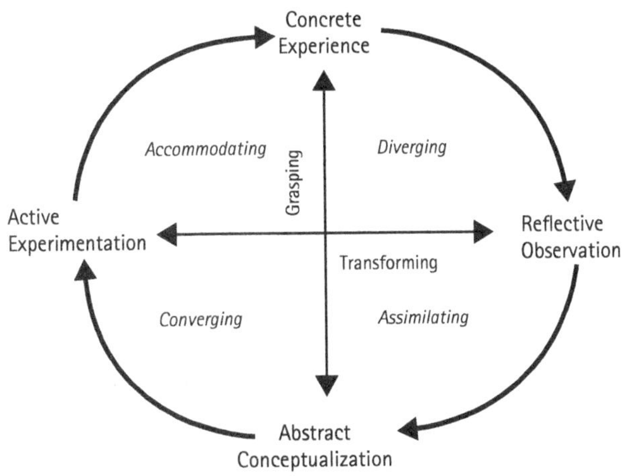

Figure 5.1. Experiential learning cycle, from Joy and Kolb (2009).

between culture and learning, both of which depend on social absorption of knowledge and information.

Additionally, masculinity and femininity dimensions may also impact individual learning preferences, particularly those that involve the often-gendered experiences of thinking and feeling. Feminine cultures were linked with a preference for abstract learning styles, which involves applying logic and analysis to seek theories and generalizations (Joy & Kolb, 2009). Masculinity was positively correlated with specific learning strategies, including reflection (Joy & Kolb, 2009); such strategies transform an experience by watching and observing all sides of an issue before acting. Masculine cultures have also been shown to prefer abstraction and experimenting (Kim, 2015). These preferences may be intuitive given cultural definitions of masculinity that focus on fact gathering, decision making, and action.

Researchers of culturally based learning preferences have also examined the influence of time orientation. Long- and short-term orientation refers to how people within cultures focus their efforts: on the future (long-term orientation), or the present and past (short-term orientation; Hofstede, 2011). Studies have shown that, in cultures with long-term orientations, learners indicate preferences for abstraction (Joy & Kolb, 2009; Kim, 2015). Indeed, learning through conceptualization may be more readily accessible within cultures that promote envisioning of the future.

Indulgence and restraint may also impact trainee preferences. This cultural dimension relates to the motivational and self-control aspects of culture. Indulgent cultures seek out gratification of basic human desires related to enjoying life, while restrained cultures focus more on the exercise of control thereof. Research has shown that indulgent cultures may seek out training methods that incorporate experiencing and thinking, as opposed to acting and reflecting (Kim, 2015). Although more research is necessary in this area, results so far suggest that individuals from cultures that emphasize gratification readily respond to learning strategies that make content more immediately accessible.

Power distance has also been shown to have some effects on training, learning, and development. Power distance refers to the extent to which groups resolve the basic problem of human inequality, such that cultures high in power distance encourage hierarchy and authority, and vice versa. It is important to note that power distance affects all members of the culture, including those in less authoritative positions; followers (as well as leaders) accept and expect the inequitable distribution of power (Hofstede, 2011). Given its influence on perceptions of authority (e.g., organizations, trainers, leaders, and administration), we intuit that power distance may influence individual investment in training and development programs. Research has supported these connections. For example, Kim (2015) found that learning preferences correlated with many national cultural dimensions. Of Hofstede's six cultural dimensions, power distance was most closely linked to distinct learning styles. For example, power distance was shown to correlate with active experimentation, reflective observation, and abstract conceptualization, depending on the national population (Kim, 2015). Other studies have taken a finer-grained approach when examining power distance and training strategies (see Yang et al., 2009, for a review). In particular, high-power distance cultures were associated with top-down nonparticipatory training methods, such as presentations and lectures. Conversely, individuals from low-power distance cultural backgrounds preferred participatory instructional methods (e.g., group building). Given that power distance dictates how individuals relate to one another, this dimension thus intuitively impacts how individuals learn in group contexts.

Another area of culture that may impact training design is uncertainty avoidance. Uncertainty avoidance relates to a culture's level of stress in the face of unknown futures (Hofstede, 2011). For example, Francis (1995) noted that, in cultures with low uncertainty avoidance, trainers are allowed to admit that they do not have all the answers; moreover, trainees are comfortable with ambiguity and are encouraged to creatively problem-solve and resolve conflict. However, the literature has demonstrated mixed findings. Intuitively, it may seem that learners from uncertainty-avoidant cultures may desire more tangible and concrete definitions when processing new information. Indeed, scholarly work has found evidence in support of this (Kim, 2015). On the other hand, some data suggest that uncertainty-avoidant individuals will rely more greatly on abstract conceptualization over concrete experience in order to more fully grasp an experience while learning (Joy & Kolb, 2009). More specifically, these individuals may prefer abstraction to be able to generalize, thereby avoiding the uncertainty that may accompany more concrete learning methods (Joy & Kolb, 2009). These conflicting findings suggest the importance of nuance, as well as the function of training needs analysis, in designing appropriate training programs.

Overall, it should be no surprise that cultural aspects factor into information-processing styles. However, culturally based preferences can extend beyond design principles, influencing perspectives toward content areas themselves. For example, in Holladay and Quinones's

(2005) and Hassi's (2013) studies, trainees from more individualistic countries (i.e., Australia, France, Germany, the United Kingdom, and the United States) reacted more positively to diversity training than their peers from collectivistic countries (i.e., India, Japan, and Singapore). Because diversity training often inherently draws attention to differences among employees, individualistic people may be more likely to embrace them as indicators of independence and uniqueness. Conversely, collectivistic counterparts would place greater value on the interdependencies and similarities within a group. Indeed, the way individuals perceive themselves within systems may also impact how they interpret and assess the acceptability of training program goals, particularly those that deal with interpersonal dynamics.

Recommendations

Training design refers to the planning of the training, including objectives, progression, and evaluation, as well as the identification of potential pain points. Researchers (e.g., Francis, 1995) have posited that individuals favor particular techniques based on cultural dimensions, recommending that trainers adjust design strategies accordingly. For example, workers from societies that are deferential to authority (high-power distance) and intolerant of the unknown (strong uncertainty avoidance) prefer didactic techniques, such as lecture-based learning. Conversely, individuals from lower power distance and weak uncertainty avoidance cultures may seek out more experiential programming.

As a result of the connection between culture and learning, education scholars believe that teachers must be aware of how students' cultures impact their learning styles, as "matching the contextual conditions for learning to the cultural experiences of the learner increases task engagement and hence increases task performance" (Allen & Butler, 1996, p. 317). Indeed, Gay (1994, p. 2) expanded:

> Teachers must understand cultural characteristics [. . .] so they can develop instructional practices that are more responsive to cultural pluralism. Cultural characteristics of particular significance in this undertaking are communication styles, thinking styles, value systems, socialization processes, relational patterns, and performance styles.

Clearly, the creation of sensitive education requires a holistic understanding of cultural preferences.

In light of these connections, programming can be tailored at fine-grained levels. These modifications can be observed at the task level. For instance, Francis (1995, p. 104) illustrates:

> [For those from cultures with a preference for avoiding risk,] techniques can be improvised to reduce the risk level. A fishbowl, for example, might become a whole-group activity that is videotaped and played back to the whole group to review and discuss, allowing all participants to feel equal risk.

Trainers can thus consider the idiosyncrasies of interpersonal dynamics within cultures and apply design principles accordingly.

Culture can even determine the optimal modalities through which training is delivered. Franchi (2002) also found several relationships between national cultural dimensions and training characteristics, including perceptual modalities. Perceptual modalities refer to an individual's preference for sensory intake and processing. That is, trainees can prefer auditory, visual and/or tactile and kinesthetic (e.g., hands-on) means of learning and education. For example, individuals from high-power distance cultures indicated learning styles that favored tactile and kinesthetic modalities. Uncertainty avoidance was linked to a preference for auditory and visual modalities and an aversion to tactile platforms. Finally, highly individualistic workers disfavored visual mediums. However, further investigation, including from interdisciplinary cognitive fields, is required to tease apart the mechanisms behind these potential differences.

Recent research has also shown that internalizing cognition and externalized behaviors may also influence learning preferences and outcomes. In a series of studies, Kim (2002) investigated Western and Eastern cultural beliefs regarding talking out loud while thinking. Talking impaired the performance of Asian Americans, but not European Americans, in solving reasoning problems; this effect may potentially relate to Asian Americans' less frequent use of internal speech compared to European Americans. In the context of training, learning, and development, then, managers may want to consider activities that enhance their trainees' modes of processing information.

In addition to tailoring training to the audience's culture, trainers can use delivery strategies that are inherently adaptable and specialized. Table 5.2 describes some of these design elements. Given their responsiveness to the individual, many of these strategies provide opportunities for interactivity and feedback that are especially valuable to diverse audiences.

Culture and Training Development and Implementation

Training comes to life during *training development*. In this stage, the training itself is built using the strategies identified during design. This phase can also involve pilot testing, which helps identify weaknesses prior to full deployment of the training (Salas et al., 2006). We will discuss development in conjunction with the next stage, which involves a similar focus on applying the training temporally.

Training implementation refers to the execution and delivery of the program itself. Here, contextual, mechanical, and logistical variables come to light. For example, location and trainees will materialize based on administrative resources and trainer decision making. Importantly, however, these phases should work in concert so that they support overall training effectiveness. A comprehensive needs analysis would have identified potential issues and guided the design and development of the training, such that implementation

Table 5.2 Examples of design strategies

Design strategy	Definition	Cultural considerations	Future directions
360 degree feedback	Multilevel evaluations by superiors, peers, and direct reports (Bird & Osland, 2005)	Individuals may often suffer gaps in performance and development due to cross-cultural difficulties. In response, this technique provides holistic and multidimensional feedback that can bolster effectiveness (Smither et al., 2005). However, organizations must be careful in designing and conducting these initiatives (e.g., framing 360 degree feedback as a developmental and constructive experience).	Studies suggest that cultural features may factor into the implementation and interpretation of 360 degree feedback (e.g., Brutus et al., 2006). Organizations may want to examine how certain cultural dimensions (such as power distance) influence trainee reactions and receptivity to 360 degree feedback.
Behavioral role modeling	Demonstration of target behaviors	This technique is used to train a variety of psychomotor and interpersonal skills, especially in cross-cultural contexts (Ross et al., 2010). It has been shown to shape desirable workplace behaviors (Taylor et al., 2005). One reason for its effectiveness may be the accessibility of behavioral role modeling to diverse audiences, given that trainees can observe and internalize demonstrated skills.	Compared to other training techniques, behavioral role modeling has been less commonly explored. This represents a gap in the literature that could be served by future work. For example, researchers and practitioners may want to examine how organizational culture and leadership style may impact the effectiveness of behavioral role modeling.
Coaching	Individual feedback and guidance	Supplementing training with coaching can provide personalized attention to trainees who desire specific experiences. For example, individuals who have had a difficult time acclimating to a particular national or organizational culture may benefit from training with a mentor who serves as role model.	Given the intimate and personalized nature of coaching, it may be worthwhile to investigate how individual cultural differences and preferences factor into the nature of these dyadic relationships.
Multimedia models of instruction	Multiple modes of instruction (e.g., scheduled webinars, in-person presentations, and online modules)	Using diverse delivery strategies can improve employee access to training. Although it is always best to design training based on the specific needs of the trainee, there may be culturally diverse audiences whose members each process information differently. In these circumstances, multiple methods may increase the likelihood that training is broadly responsive to the needs of multicultural audiences.	Following the COVID-19 pandemic, virtual forms of training have become increasingly common. Within this modality, there are various strategies (e.g., didactic vs. interactive and synchronous vs. asynchronous). Researchers may examine which configurations are optimally effective for specific learner cultures.

(*continued*)

Table 5.2 Continued			
Design strategy	**Definition**	**Cultural considerations**	**Future directions**
Simulation	A "working representation of reality" that models processes in abstracted, simplified, or accelerated ways (Galvão et al., 2000, p. 1962)	Simulations may provide multicultural trainees with valuable opportunities to practice key skills and receive tangible feedback. Simulations may provide individuals from different cultures with the opportunity to safely practice target skills and abilities.	In addition to being a training design strategy, simulations also provide an opportunity for meta-science. Trainers can use simulations to pilot and develop their programs, including on culturally diverse audiences. For example, many of the future directions discussed in this table can be explored using this strategy.
Social support	Administrative and peer support of participation	Social support can strengthen commitment to training and employees' maintenance of learned interventions. This is especially true for individuals who have not yet acculturated into their surrounding environments and social networks.	Social support may be especially instrumental for individuals from more communal backgrounds (i.e., collectivistic cultures). The role of cultural power dynamics may also determine which types and sources of social support are most effective.

goes smoothly. This highlights the overlap between some phases, given that they are not mutually exclusive (Salas et al., 2006). Indeed, these stages in particular draw synergistically from one another.

Cultural Influences

When considering training development and implementation, organizations may want to consider who exactly is conducting the training. Individuals have reacted differently to trainings, depending on the background of the trainees and instructors. Trainer–trainee concordance has been shown to enhance performance outcomes (e.g., Dobbs, 1983; Steiner et al., 1991; Towler & Dipboye, 2001), since mismatch may reduce the ability of the trainer to convey course material effectively (Osman-Gani & Zidan, 2001). For example, in diversity trainings, individualistic trainees showed no preference toward a particular trainer, whereas their collectivistic counterparts preferred trainers whose cultural background matched their own (Holladay & Quinones, 2005). Indeed, because collectivistic individuals perceive outgroup members unfavorably, they may see trainers from another group in a negative light; meanwhile, individualistic cultures would be indifferent (Holladay & Quinones, 2005). This research thus adds to the body of evidence that cultural variables, such as individualism and collectivism, can impact the overall preferences and self-perceptions of learners.

Recommendations

Development and implementation refer to the refinement, execution, and delivery of the training, wherein the mechanics of delivery are prepared. As evinced by the literature, individuals may have preferences in content and trainer characteristics based on their cultural background. The literature suggests that certain practices can help "even out" these tendencies. For example, in a cross-cultural classroom, trainers and learners may want to adopt active learning—focusing not only on technical aspects of course delivery, but also understanding diverse students' expectations and perceptions (Stefanic et al., 2020). Given how cultural perspectives color the trainee experiences, training programs should consider the needs of their audience when deciding on logistical and design issues.

In addition to ensuring that the trainer is appropriate for the audience and content, organizations should also use appropriate systems of deployment. An important consideration in development and implementation is platform, particularly given the increasing utilization of technology. One study explored cultural aspects as they influenced acceptance and usage of internet-based training platforms. Researchers recommend that trainers from individualistic and weak uncertainty avoidance cultures focus on specific user interface and design elements, including those with a focus on work tasks and gamified navigation. Conversely, collectivistic and high uncertainty avoidance educators should develop introductory courses and programs to gain experience and self-efficacy, in addition to creating technical support options (Sánchez-Franco et al., 2009). Given that work is moving to more virtual formats in today's world, administrators should also consider that online environments may also develop their own cultures (including norms and learning curves) in and of themselves. For example, those from younger generations can more quickly adapt to certain modalities, whereas those with less exposure to technology may require additional scaffolding. Evolving and generationally linked cultures of technological proficiency may thus influence the acceptability and accessibility of virtual platforms. Practitioners would thus be well served by understanding the goals and optimal modalities of their audience.

Culture and Training Evaluation

Training does not end once trainees walk out the door. Comprehensive *training evaluation* of outcomes ensures that organizations can properly assess impact and adapt their programming in the long term. Within organizations, educational programming can be assessed using a multilevel rubric. Kirkpatrick (1959, 1996) identified four types of training outcomes: *reactions*, or trainees' attitudinal responses to the program; *learning*, which are changes in knowledge or skills; *transfer*, which occurs when training is utilized and influences behaviors on the job; and organizational *results*, or the program's effect on organizational objectives. These criteria have been used across the organizational sciences to assess the holistic impact of training effectiveness.

Cultural Influences

Thus far, this chapter has largely focused on subjective learning preferences and experiences. Importantly, however, studies have shown that the effects of deep cultural structures extend beyond the trainee, affecting multilevel training outcomes. A laboratory experiment and a six-month field experiment showed support, at both the group and individual level of analysis, for hypotheses predicting that: for individualists, self-focused training would have a stronger impact on self-efficacy and performance than would group-focused training; and for collectivists, group-focused training would have a stronger impact on self-efficacy and performance than would individual-focused training (Earley, 1994). Indeed, the independent nature of individualists and the interdependent focus of collectivists may lend themselves to these training format tendencies and effects. This research suggests that culturally based training structures can affect the ways in which individuals perceive their abilities, as well as their objective performance.

Additionally, it is important to understand that cultural dynamics and outcomes can also interact with one another. According to learning theories (e.g., Dweck, 1986; Grant & Dweck, 2003), learners can be motivated based on a goal orientation toward: performance, or a desire to meet performance standards and avoid errors; and/or mastery or learning, driven by mastery of the target skill regardless of errors during learning. Several studies have further examined the relationship between culture and goal orientation. For example, in examining engineers undergoing technical training at a large multinational corporation, Rogers and Spitzmueller (2009) found that collectivists exhibited higher levels of training transfer intentions and motivation to learn. However, when collectivism was combined with a performance goal orientation, its effects on training outcomes were diminished. Other research has also found similar complex, related relationships. Cultural learning values moderated the relationship between goal orientation and performance and adaptation to change (Unger-Aviram & Erez, 2016). Within expatriates, mastery orientation positively influenced academic and social self-efficacy (Gong & Fan, 2006) and both types of orientation interacted with previous international experience and predeparture cross-cultural training on cultural intelligence (Moon et al., 2012). Altogether, this suggests that trainers should consider how to frame and evaluate learning with respect to cultural profiles.

The links between culture, motivation, and outcomes are also witnessed in group settings. Cultural diversity more positively relates to team performance when team members embrace learning and are not driven to perform at relatively high levels (Pieterse et al., 2013). Organizations can also develop environments that help foster training effectiveness. When employees hold positive perceptions of their organization's learning culture, they are also more willing to transfer training; the provision of performance coaching can also enhance this linkage (Banerjee et al., 2017). Other organizational aspects, including its structural flexibility (Chatterjee et al., 2018), psychological safety and openness to error reporting (Duryan et al., 2020), and emphasis on educating employees about stakeholders and clients (Cegarra-Navarro et al., 2019) can also encourage transfer of learned competencies. Overall, these lines of research suggest that educational programming should take into consideration the goal orientation profiles of their learners and adjust accordingly. Careful attention to these issues can ensure that training assessment is comprehensive and accurate.

Recommendations

It is necessary to take a multilevel approach to determine true training effectiveness. Organizations must examine the context that surrounds its goals—assessing long-term effects systematically, in order to establish patterns and behavioral motives (Unsworth et al., 2013). These influential contexts naturally include the cultures within and outside of the organization.

Kirkpatrick's (1959, 1996) model of training evaluation can also help systematically understand the multilevel impacts of trainings. When examining trainee reactions, organizations should keep in mind that individuals may react to trainings based on their own idiosyncratic or cultural antecedents. Reactions are often measured by self-report surveys, making them a particularly convenient metric of success. Indeed, diverse trainees may provide useful subjective information on the accessibility of a particular program.

When there are diverse learners in the audience, however, satisfaction and enjoyment may not be the best predictors of actual learning. There should also be evaluation of learning, including across competencies of knowledge, behavior, and attitudes. When possible, trainers should triangulate methods in order to ensure that these outcomes are being measured accurately and comprehensively. For example, knowledge tests may also be supplemented with a clinical observation to assess how well trainees have integrated training objectives.

The next section takes a deeper dive into the third Kirkpatrick criterion of training transfer. Importantly, the transfer of trained abilities into the workplace influences actual organizational results. Indeed, when organizations are evaluating interventions, they are most often interested in actual changes to the bottom line. This return on investment can predict the direction of development initiatives, and the organization as a whole, going forward.

Training Transfer

Salas and colleagues (2006) augmented the ISD model by incorporating one of Kirkpatrick (1959, 1996)'s criteria as a sixth phase: *training transfer*. Specifically, they argued that the transfer of training competencies into the actual task environment is an important component of the process. Research has suggested that transfer may be influenced by cultural factors and beliefs. For example, leaders invest in trainings based on a number of national and organizational factors, including culture-related values and beliefs (Subedi, 2006). In turn, perceptions of managerial investment may impact trainee motivation to perform and ultimately enhance outcomes, including transfer. Accordingly, we adopt Salas et al.'s (2006) approach in the inclusion of training transfer as part of the ISD model.

Cultural Influences

The literature on training transfer is often underrepresented relative to other Kirkpatrick training criteria. However, some scholars have investigated the impact of culture on training transfer. Research supports the notion that culture influences individual approaches to work and professional development. For example, cultural values can impact the extent to which workers translate job satisfaction into affective commitment. One relevant cultural dimension is traditionality: the commitment to, respect for, and acceptance of the customs and norms of a traditional society (Schwartz, 1992), including respect for authority, filial piety, male domination, and a general sense of powerlessness (Yang et al., 1989). People who are culturally more traditional tend to transfer their satisfaction with their job into stronger commitment, compared to those lower in cultural traditionality (Zhang & Zheng, 2009). It thus follows that traditionality increases organizational commitment and, ergo, learning. Given increasing attention around this construct, future research may want to examine traditionality as a more distal driver of learning effectiveness.

Cultures may also shape individual self-appraisal (see Aslani et al., 2016 for a review). In dignity cultures, self-worth is based on individual achievements (Schwartz, 1994); in face cultures, such value is evaluated per others' assessments of the individual's fulfillment of social role obligations (Heine, 2001; Ho, 1976; Kim & Cohen, 2010). Additionally, researchers have also suggested a third category. Honor cultures assign self-worth based on both reputation and the individual's own perceptions of others' thoughts (Mandelbaum, 1988). Evaluation of oneself can factor into motivation, preferences, and experiences; these can, in turn, influence how individuals engage in learning, training, and development. Research has shown that trainees from dignity cultures benefit from training with low structure and error encouragement, whereas those from face cultures perform more positively with high structure training and error avoidant instructions. That is, individuals who are more sensitive to peer evaluation may be more motivated to follow universal rubrics, including completing objective instructions and avoiding errors. Ultimately, this research found that trainee cultural background interacts with training structure and error instructions, ultimately predicting the transfer of training (Salmon, 2016). This line of investigation is especially promising, given that it examines cultural antecedents and tangible, behavioral training outcomes.

Finally, uncertainty avoidance may play a role in learning, training, and development transfer. In particular, it can impact how trainees approach content areas and achieve behavioral outcomes. One study found that uncertainty avoidance moderated the transfer of safety training, as measured through accident and injury reduction. Interestingly, a culture's tendency to avoid uncertainty may paradoxically lead to greater uncertainty and thus negatively influence transfer of safety training (Burke et al., 2008). This potentially counterintuitive finding speaks to the complexity of culture, education, and content, underscoring the need for additional work investigating these intersections.

Recommendations

The final step in the training process is the successful transfer of competencies into the work environment. The concept of informal learning suggests that training can and should continue to occur on the job. To this end, firms should provide opportunities for practice and feedback. For example, organizations can strengthen transfer through knowledge management practices, which involve the sharing of information. Collectivistic cultures may be more likely to engage in such sharing behaviors, wherein managers draw upon the interdependent predisposition of individuals and create cultures centered around cooperation and employee involvement (Ribiere & Zhang, 2010). Accordingly, knowing one's organizational culture, as well as the cultures of the individuals who comprise the workforce, can help managers optimally align these transfer environments.

Organizations can powerfully promote transfer by encouraging the acquisition and use of target skills (Bird & Osland, 2005). However, trainers must be cautious when assessing transfer long term. Notably, administrators and trainees both tend to overgeneralize skills transfer when self-reporting training effectiveness (Chiaburu et al., 2010). As a result, skills should be continually reinforced to avoid negative repercussions and ensure that transfer has reliably occurred.

Overall, trainers can develop culturally responsive training programs in myriad ways. The aforementioned culture and learning-related literatures can be synthesized to create robust training programs across cultures. Table 5.3 summarizes five key practical implications born from the science-based literature. Please note that many of these practices can be used at both the organizational cultural and multinational global contexts.

Table 5.3 Five practical implications

	Practical implications
1.	Training needs analyses must include consideration of culture, as it manifests on individual, work group, organizational, and regional and national levels.
2.	Effective training design strategies will respond to culturally informed learning preferences of individuals; see Table 5.2 for examples of strategies.
3.	Leadership should streamline and adapt training delivery mechanics to the needs of the audience, including through trainer characteristics and platform accessibility.
4.	Training and development should be evaluated with the consideration of cultural backgrounds, both subjectively (e.g., trainees' reactions toward instructors, programming design, and content areas) and objectively (as seen in learning and performance outcomes).
5.	Organizations should adapt their cultures, including through leadership and incentive structures, to create work environments that encourage successful transfer of competencies post-training.

Conclusions, Controversies, and Future Directions

In this chapter, we reviewed various cultural concepts that have been examined by interdisciplinary training research, including those that merit future investigation. Table 5.4 summarizes several key theoretical findings from the literature to date.

As the workplace becomes increasingly global, it will be critical to incorporate cross-cultural considerations into training, learning, and development. The earlier sections have outlined instructional design elements, detailed the influence of culture on learning, and listed ways in which administrators can develop culturally responsive programming. However, work remains to be done in these areas, including the resolution of several areas of controversy.

As previously mentioned, culture influences learning, and it can be useful to adapt instructional strategies in this regard. However, culturally based strategies can not only be helpful but harmful, depending on the manner of deployment. In this regard, we turn to the traditional elementary and secondary education literature and its discussion on assisting minority students: "Some teachers and scholars bristle at the notion that [racial and ethnic minority] students need different forms of instruction to succeed" (Teach for America, 2011). We may carry over these sentiments into organizational contexts. The inappropriate adaptation of training design and material may hurt learners by not adding value (e.g., overly general strategies), ignoring intragroup diversity, and propagating biases (Teach for America, 2011). To this end, scholars and practitioners should carefully discern the extent to which training design and delivery is adapted to cultural groups. Again, we emphasize the necessity of a training needs analysis, such that course design can be appropriately tailored to the specific audience and their cultural profile.

Table 5.4 Five key theoretical principles

	Theoretical principle
1.	The Instructional Systems Design (Branson et al., 1975) model categorizes the stage involved in the training process, each of which is influenced by contextual considerations: analysis, design, development, implementation, evaluation, and transfer.
2.	Cultural values and practices influence trainee motivation, including learning and transfer of knowledge and skills.
3.	Culture affects the ways in which individuals absorb and process information, including by influencing learning preferences and, consequently, optimal design strategies.
4.	Research suggests that learning, training, and development are influenced by cultural dimensions, such as: individualism and collectivism; power distance; uncertainty avoidance; masculinity and femininity; long- and short-term orientation; and indulgence and restraint (Hofstede, 2011).
5.	Training evaluation should incorporate contextual concerns and incorporate multiple levels of assessment, including: trainees' reactions; learning of knowledge, skills, and attitudes; transfer of learned competencies to the target environment; and results at higher levels, including within the workgroup, department, and organization (Kirkpatrick, 1959, 1996).

Moreover, this chapter discusses preexisting cultural lenses (e.g., derived from one's social communities). These powerful and all-encompassing cultural dynamics can often overpower the influence that organizations wield. Although firms can only do so much within their realm of control, they can still exercise some cultural influence through creating work climates. Organizational culture and strong leadership can play a role in individuals learning and transferring their training (Mathieu & Martineau, 1997). Indeed, "elements of the post-training environment can encourage (e.g., rewards, job aids), discourage (e.g., ridicule from peers), or actually prohibit the application of new skills and knowledge on the job (e.g., lack of necessary equipment)" (Tannenbaum & Yukl, 1992, p. 420). Still, the exact role and scope of a specific organization's culture in shaping and sustaining learning can be more difficult to characterize. It would be useful for experts in this area to examine real-world and multilevel cultural contexts (including temporally lagged study designs) when investigating instructional effectiveness.

Relatedly, we must consider the reality of the modern, multinational workplace. Within any organization's labor force, multiple intersecting cultural identities may be present, which may naturally conflict. Moreover, individuals may identify with several and diverse cultures, given the increasingly multicultural population across the globe. Indeed, there is a growing body of literature on people who "code-switch" between conflicting cultural identities (Brannen & Thomas, 2010; Huynh et al., 2011; Terhune, 2006). It is not yet fully understood how individuals may navigate these influences in learning, training, and development contexts.

Relatedly, it would be useful to understand what psychological processes occur when a learner must navigate between potentially disparate intersecting cultural influences. What mechanisms are at play when individuals adapt to different instructional environments? The literature on stereotype threat may hold interesting lessons and directions, given that scholars have found that particular identities can be prompted or activated prior to learning and thereby influence outcomes (Steele, 1997). To this end, Lisak et al. (2016) suggest that global leaders can foster shared identities within multicultural teams; doing so can motivate team members to adopt inclusive communication behaviors and enhance progress toward innovation goals. Indeed, today's organization represents an arena wherein many cultural identities may confront and/or cooperate with one another, both within and between employees. Optimistically, we believe that diverse identities can also be leveraged by effective management.

In summary, culture can impact learning, training, and development at multiple levels and through several avenues. However, significant work remains to be done in this area, which we expect will continue as the workplace becomes increasingly global and multicultural. Thus far, research suggests that culture may heavily color trainees' perceptions and experiences, ranging from motivation to learning preferences and performance. Scholars may continue to explore these effects, as operationalized by cultural dimensions such as individualism and collectivism, power distance, uncertainty avoidance, and others. Training functions will also benefit by considering cultural contexts in the analysis, design, development, implementation, evaluation, and transfer of training. Ultimately, researchers and practitioners can and should work in concert and interdisciplinarily to develop science-based and culturally responsive interventions.

Acknowledgments

The authors would like to thank Sanjana Krishnan and Ksenia Plotnikova for their assistance in developing this work. This material is based on work supported by the National Science Foundation Graduate Research Fellowship Program under Grant No. 1842494. Any opinions, findings, and conclusions or recommendations expressed in this material are those of the author(s) and do not necessarily reflect the views of the National Science Foundation. This research was also funded in part by the National Aeronautics and Space Administration, Grant No. #NNX16AP96G to Rice University (Principal Investigator: Eduardo Salas).

References

Allen, B. A., & Butler, L. (1996). The effects of music and movement opportunity on the analogical reasoning performance of African American and White school children: A preliminary study. *Journal of Black Psychology, 22*(3), 316–328.

Aslani, S., Ramirez-Marin, J., Brett, J., Yao, J., Semnani-Azad, Z., Zhang, Z.-X., Tinsley, C., Weingart, L., & Adair, W. (2016). Dignity, face, and honor cultures: A study of negotiation strategy and outcomes in three cultures. *Journal of Organizational Behavior, 37*(8), 1178–1201. https://doi.org/10.1002/job.2095

Auyeung, P., & Sands, J. (1996). A cross cultural study of the learning style of accounting students. *Accounting and Finance, 36*(2), 261–274.

Baldwin, T. T., & Magjuka, R. J. (1997). Training as an organizational episode: Pretraining influences on trainee motivation. *Improving Training Effectiveness in Work Organizations, 3*, 99–127.

Baldwin, T. T., Magjuka, R. J., & Loher, B. T. (1991). The perils of participation: Effects of choice of training on trainee motivation and learning. *Personnel Psychology, 44*(1), 51–65.

Banerjee, P., Gupta, R., & Bates, R. (2017). Influence of organizational learning culture on knowledge worker's motivation to transfer training: Testing moderating effects of learning transfer climate. *Current Psychology, 36*(3), 606–617. https://doi.org/10.1007/s12144-016-9449-8

Barmeyer, C. I. (2004). Learning styles and their impact on cross-cultural training: An international comparison in France, Germany and Quebec. *International Journal of Intercultural Relations, 28*(6), 577–594. https://doi.org/10.1016/j.ijintrel.2005.01.011

Bell, S. T. (2007). Deep-level composition variables as predictors of team performance: A meta-analysis. *Journal of Applied Psychology, 92*(3), 595–615. https://doi.org/10.1037/0021-9010.92.3.595

Bezrukova, K., Jehn, K. A., & Spell, C. S. (2012). Reviewing diversity training: Where we have been and where we should go. *Academy of Management Learning and Education, 11*(2), 207–227. https://doi.org/10.5465/amle.2008.0090

Bezrukova, K., Spell, C. S., Perry, J. L., & Jehn, K. A. (2016). A meta-analytical integration of over 40 years of research on diversity training evaluation. *Psychological Bulletin, 11*. http://psycnet.apa.org/journals/bul/142/11/1227/

Bird, A., & Osland, J. S. (2005). Making sense of intercultural collaboration. *International Studies of Management and Organization, 35*(4), 115–132.

Brannen, M. Y., & Thomas, D. C. (2010). Bicultural individuals in organizations: Implications and opportunity. *International Journal of Cross Cultural Management, 10*(1), 5–16. https://doi.org/10.1177/1470595809359580

Branson, R. K., Rayner, G. T., Cox, J. L., Furman, J. P., King, F. J., & Hannum, W. H. (1975). Interservice procedures for instructional systems development (5 vols.) (No. TRADOC Pam 350-30 NAVEDTRA 106A; NTIS No. ADA 019 486 through ADA 019 490). Ft. Monroe, VT: Army Training and Doctrine Command.

Brown, J. (2002). Training needs assessment: A must for developing an effective training program. *Public Personnel Management, 31*(4), 569–578.

Brutus, S., Derayeh, M., Fletcher, C., Bailey, C., Velazquez, P., Shi, K., Simon, C., & Labath, V. (2006). Internationalization of multi-source feedback systems: A six-country exploratory analysis of 360-degree feedback. *The International Journal of Human Resource Management, 17*(11), 1888–1906. https://doi.org/10.1080/09585190601000071

Burke, M. J., Chan-Serafin, S., Salvador, R., Smith, A., & Sarpy, S. A. (2008). The role of national culture and organizational climate in safety training effectiveness. *European Journal of Work and Organizational Psychology, 17*(1), 133–152. https://doi.org/10.1080/13594320701307503

Cegarra-Navarro, J., Jiménez-Jiménez, D., & García-Pérez, A. (2019). An integrative view of knowledge processes and a learning culture for ambidexterity: Toward improved organizational performance in the banking sector. *IEEE Transactions on Engineering Management, 68*(2), 408–417. https://doi.org/10.1109/TEM.2019.2917430

Černe, M., Jaklič, M., & Škerlavaj, M. (2013). Decoupling management and technological innovations: Resolving the individualism–collectivism controversy. *Journal of International Management, 19*(2), 103–117. https://doi.org/10.1016/j.intman.2013.03.004

Chatterjee, A., Pereira, A., & Bates, R. (2018). Impact of individual perception of organizational culture on the learning transfer environment. *International Journal of Training and Development, 22*(1), 15–33. https://doi.org/10.1111/ijtd.12116

Chiaburu, D. S., Sawyer, K. B., & Thoroughgood, C. N. (2010). Transferring more than learned in training: employees' and managers' (over) generalization of skills. *International Journal of Selection and Assessment, 18*(4), 380–393.

Comas-Diaz, L., & Duncan, J. W. (1985). The cultural context: A factor in assertiveness training with mainland Puerto Rican women. *Psychology of Women Quarterly, 9*(4), 463–476. https://doi.org/10.1111/j.1471-6402.1985.tb00896.x

Cross, T. L., Bazron, B. J., Dennis, K. W., & Isaacs, M. R. (1989). *Towards a culturally competent system of care: A monograph on effective services for minority children who are severely emotionally disturbed.* Washington DC: Child and Adolescent Services System Program Technical Assistance Center, Georgetown University Child Development Center. http://eric.ed.gov/?id=ED330171

Dobbs, J. H. (1983). Does behavior modeling work outside the US? *Training and Development Journal, 37*(10), 53–54.

Duryan, M., Smyth, H., Roberts, A., Rowlinson, S., & Sherratt, F. (2020). Knowledge transfer for occupational health and safety: Cultivating health and safety learning culture in construction firms. *Accident Analysis and Prevention, 139*, 105496. https://doi.org/10.1016/j.aap.2020.105496

Dweck, C. S. (1986). Motivational processes affecting learning. *American Psychologist, 41*(10), 1040.

Earley, P. C. (1994). Self or group? Cultural effects of training on self-efficacy and performance. *Administrative Science Quarterly, 39*(1), 89–117. https://doi.org/10.2307/2393495

Franchi, J. (2002). *Comparison of learning and performance styles of cross-cultural populations in a global corporate organization.* [Doctoral dissertation, Florida State University].

Francis, J. L. (1995). Training across cultures. *Human Resource Development Quarterly; Hoboken, 6*(1), 101.

Galvão, J. R., Martins, P. G., & Gomes, M. R. (2000). Modeling reality with simulation games for a cooperative learning. *2000 Winter Simulation Conference Proceedings (Cat. No. 00CH37165), 2*, 1692–1698.

Gantenbein, P., Kind, A., & Volonté, C. (2019). Individualism and venture capital: A cross-country study. *Management International Review, 59*(5), 741–777. https://doi.org/10.1007/s11575-019-00394-7

Gay, G. (1994). *At the essence of learning: Multicultural education.* Bloomington, IL: Kappa Delta Pi.

Gong, Y., & Fan, J. (2006). Longitudinal examination of the role of goal orientation in cross-cultural adjustment. *Journal of Applied Psychology, 91*(1), 176–184. https://doi.org/10.1037/0021-9010.91.1.176

Grant, H., & Dweck, C. S. (2003). Clarifying achievement goals and their impact. *Journal of Personality and Social Psychology, 85*(3), 541.

Greenfield, P. (1999). *Three approaches to the psychology of culture: Where do they come from? Where can they go?* Asian Association for Social Psychology, Taiwan.

Hassi, A. (2013). Case method in employee training: Comparative insights from Canada and Morocco. *International Journal of Teaching and Case Studies, 4*(1), 36–56. https://doi.org/10.1504/IJTCS.2013.053404

Heine, S. J. (2001). Self as cultural product: An examination of East Asian and North American selves. *Journal of Personality, 69*(6), 881–905.

Ho, D. Y. (1976). On the concept of face. *American Journal of Sociology, 81*(4), 867–884.

Hofstede, G. (2011). Dimensionalizing cultures: The Hofstede model in context. *Online Readings in Psychology and Culture, 2*(1), 2307–0919.

Holladay, C. L., & Quinones, M. A. (2005). Reactions to diversity training: An international comparison. *Human Resource Development Quarterly, 16*(4), 529–545.

Hughes, A. M., Gregory, M. E., Joseph, D. L., Sonesh, S. C., Marlow, S. L., Lacerenza, C. N., Benishek, L. E., King, H. B., & Salas, E. (2016). Saving lives: A meta-analysis of team training in healthcare. *Journal of Applied Psychology, 101*(9), 1266–1304. https://doi.org/10.1037/apl0000120

Huynh, Q.-L., Nguyen, A.-M. D., & Benet-Martínez, V. (2011). Bicultural identity integration. In S. J. Schwartz, K. Luyckx, & V. L. Vignoles (Eds.), *Handbook of identity theory and research* (pp. 827–842). New York: Springer.

Iguisi, O. (2009). Motivation-related values across cultures. *African Journal of Business Management, 3*(4), 141–150.

Jackson, C. L., Colquitt, J. A., Wesson, M. J., & Zapata-Phelan, C. P. (2006). Psychological collectivism: A measurement validation and linkage to group member performance. *Journal of Applied Psychology, 91*(4), 884.

Joy, S., & Kolb, D. A. (2009). Are there cultural differences in learning style? *International Journal of Intercultural Relations, 33*(1), 69–85.

Kim, H. S. (2002). We talk, therefore we think? A cultural analysis of the effect of talking on thinking. *Journal of Personality and Social Psychology, 83*(4), 828.

Kim, S. H. (2015). *A cross cultural study on white-collar workers' learning styles in a multinational corporation* [Master's thesis, The Graduate School of Seoul National University].

Kim, Y.-H., & Cohen, D. (2010). Information, perspective, and judgments about the self in face and dignity cultures. *Personality and Social Psychology Bulletin, 36*(4), 537–550.

Kirkpatrick, D. L. (1959). Techniques for evaluating training programs. *Journal of the American Society of Training Directors, 13*, 3–9.

Kirkpatrick, D. L. (1996). Great ideas revisited. *Training and Development, 50*(1), 54–59.

Kolb, A. Y., & Kolb, D. A. (2005). Learning styles and learning spaces: Enhancing experiential learning in higher education. *Academy of Management Learning and Education, 4*(2), 193–212.

Kolb, D. A. (2014). *Experiential learning: Experience as the source of learning and development.* Upper Saddle River, NJ: FT press.

Krys, K., Uchida, Y., Oishi, S., & Diener, E. (2019). Open society fosters satisfaction: Explanation to why individualism associates with country level measures of satisfaction. *The Journal of Positive Psychology, 14*(6), 768–778. https://doi.org/10.1080/17439760.2018.1557243

Lacerenza, C. N., Reyes, D. L., Marlow, S. L., Joseph, D. L., & Salas, E. (2017). Leadership training design, delivery, and implementation: A meta-analysis. *Journal of Applied Psychology, 102*(12), 1686.

Lisak, A., Erez, M., Sui, Y., & Lee, C. (2016). The positive role of global leaders in enhancing multicultural team innovation. *Journal of International Business Studies, 47*(6), 655–673.

Lu, W., Niu, G., & Zhou, Y. (2021). Individualism and financial inclusion. *Journal of Economic Behavior & Organization, 183*, 268–288. https://doi.org/10.1016/j.jebo.2021.01.008

Mandelbaum, D. G. (1988). *Women's seclusion and men's honor: Sex roles in North India, Bangladesh, and Pakistan.* Tucson: University of Arizona Press.

Marginson, S. (2020). The relentless price of high individualism in the pandemic. *Higher Education Research and Development, 39*(7), 1392–1395. https://doi.org/10.1080/07294360.2020.1822297

Mathieu, J. E., & Martineau, J. W. (1997). Individual and situational influences on training motivation. *Improving Training Effectiveness in Work Organizations, 193*, 221.

Mills, J., & Clark, M. (1982). Exchange and communal relationships. In L. Wheeler (Ed.), *Review of personality and social psychology* (Vol. 3, pp. 121–144). Thousand Oaks, CA: SAGE.

Moon, H. K., Choi, B. K., & Jung, J. S. (2012). Previous international experience, cross-cultural training, and expatriates' cross-cultural adjustment: Effects of cultural intelligence and goal orientation. *Human Resource Development Quarterly, 23*(3), 285–330. https://doi.org/10.1002/hrdq.21131

Morris, M. A., & Robie, C. (2001). A meta-analysis of the effects of cross-cultural training on expatriate performance and adjustment. *International Journal of Training and Development, 5*(2), 112–125.

Osman-Gani, A. M., & Zidan, S. S. (2001). Cross-cultural implications of planned on-the-job training. *Advances in Developing Human Resources, 3*(4), 452–460.

Pieterse, A. N., Van Knippenberg, D., & Van Dierendonck, D. (2013). Cultural diversity and team performance: The role of team member goal orientation. *The Academy of Management Journal, 56*(3), 782–804.

Reyes, D. L., Dinh, J.V., Lacerenza, C. N., Marlow, S. L., Joseph, D. L., & Salas, E. (2019). The state of higher education leadership development program evaluation: A meta-analysis, critical review, and recommendations. *The Leadership Quarterly, 30*(5), 101311.

Ribiere, V. M., & Zhang, Q. (2010). Expertise and mistakes, to share or not to share? A cross cultural study of in-group /out-group relationships on knowledge sharing. *Proceedings of the 2010 43rd Hawaii International Conference on System Sciences.* Institute of Electrical and Electronics Engineers. https://doi.org/10.1109/HICSS.2010.195

Rogers, A., & Spitzmueller, C. (2009). Individualism–collectivism and the role of goal orientation in organizational training. *International Journal of Training and Development, 13*(3), 185–201. https://doi.org/10.1111/j.1468-2419.2009.00326.x

Ross, K. G., MacNulty, C., Bencaz, N. A., & Thornson, C. A. (2010). *Framing cross-cultural competence (3C) learning outcomes in a competency model.* Patrick Air Force Base, FL: Defense Equal Opportunity Management Institute. [Doctoral dissertation, University of Maryland, College Park]. https://apps.dtic.mil/sti/citations/AD1056239

Salas, E., & Cannon-Bowers, J. A. (2000). The anatomy of team training. In S. Tobias & J. D. Fletcher (Eds.), *Training and retraining: A handbook for business, industry, government, and the military* (pp. 312–335). Macmillan.

Salas, E., Tannenbaum, S. I., Kraiger, K., & Smith-Jentsch, K. A. (2012). The science of training and development in organizations what matters in practice. *Psychological Science in the Public Interest, 13*(2), 74–101. https://doi.org/10.1177/1529100612436661

Salas, E., Wilson, K. A., Priest, H. A., & Guthrie, J. W. (2006). Design, delivery, and evaluation of training systems. *Handbook of Human Factors and Ergonomics, 3*, 472–512.

Salmon, E. D. (2016). *Culture training match: Testing the interaction between trainee cultural background and training design on stress reactions and transfer of training* (2016-99020-015). ProQuest Information & Learning.

Sánchez-Franco, M. J., Martínez-López, F. J., & Martín-Velicia, F. A. (2009). Exploring the impact of individualism and uncertainty avoidance in Web-based electronic learning: An empirical analysis in European higher education. *Computers and Education, 52*(3), 588–598. https://doi.org/10.1016/j.compedu.2008.11.006

Schwartz, S. H. (1992). Universals in the content and structure of values: Theoretical advances and empirical tests in 20 countries. In M. P. Zanna (Ed.), *Advances in experimental social psychology* (Vol. 25, pp. 1–65). Elsevier.

Schwartz, S. H. (1994). *Beyond individualism/collectivism: New cultural dimensions of values.* In U. Kim, H. C. Triandis, Ç. Kâğitçibaşi, S.-C. Choi, & G. Yoon (Eds.), *Individualism and collectivism: Theory, method, and applications* (pp. 85–119). Sage Publications, Inc.

Smither, J. W., London, M., & Reilly, R. R. (2005). Does performance improve following multisource feedback? A theoretical model, meta-analysis, and review of empirical findings. *Personnel Psychology, 58*(1), 33–66. https://doi.org/10.1111/j.1744-6570.2005.514_1.x

Steele, C. M. (1997). A threat in the air: How stereotypes shape intellectual identity and performance. *American Psychologist, 52*(6), 613.

Stefanic, I., Campbell, R. K., Russ, J. S., & Stefanic, E. (2020). Evaluation of a blended learning approach for cross-cultural entrepreneurial education. *Innovations in Education and Teaching International, 57*(2), 242–254.

Steiner, D. D., Dobbins, G. H., & Trahan, W. A. (1991). The trainer-trainee interaction: An attributional model of training. *Journal of Organizational Behavior, 12*(4), 271–286.

Subedi, B. S. (2006). Cultural factors and beliefs influencing transfer of training. *International Journal of Training and Development, 10*(2), 88–97. https://doi.org/10.1111/j.1468-2419.2006.00246.x

Swezey, R. W., & Llaneras, R. E. (1997). Models in training and instruction. In G. Salvendy (Ed.), *Handbook of human factors and ergonomics* (2nd ed., pp. 514–577). John Wiley & Sons.

Tannenbaum, S. I., & Yukl, G. (1992). Training and development in work organizations. *Annual Review of Psychology, 43*(1), 399–441.

Taylor, P. J., Russ-Eft, D. F., & Chan, D. W. (2005). A meta-analytic review of behavior modeling training. *Journal of Applied Psychology, 90*(4), 692.

Teach for America. (2011). "Cultural learning styles": Should students' culture inform instructional choices? In *Diversity, community, and achievement* (pp. 85–92). Teach for America.

Terhune, C. P. (2006). Biculturalism, code-switching, and shifting. *International Journal of Diversity in Organisations, Communities and Nations*, *5*(6), 9–16.

Towler, A. J., & Dipboye, R. L. (2001). Effects of trainer expressiveness, organization, and trainee goal orientation on training outcomes. *Journal of Applied Psychology*, *86*(4), 664.

Triandis, H. C., & Gelfand, M. J. (1998). Converging measurement of horizontal and vertical individualism and collectivism. *Journal of Personality and Social Psychology*, *74*(1), 118–128. https://doi.org/10.1037/0022-3514.74.1.118

Triandis, H. C., & Suh, E. (2002). Cultural influences on personality. *Annual Review of Psychology*, *53*, 133–160.

U.S. Bureau of Labor Statistics. (2018). *Labor force characteristics by race and ethnicity, 2017* (No. 1076; BLS Reports). https://www.bls.gov/opub/reports/race-and-ethnicity/2017/pdf/home.pdf

Unger-Aviram, E., & Erez, M. (2016). The effects of situational goal orientation and cultural learning values on team performance and adaptation to change. *European Journal of Work and Organizational Psychology*, *25*(2), 239–253. https://doi.org/10.1080/1359432X.2015.1044515

Unsworth, K. L., Dmitrieva, A., & Adriasola, E. (2013). Changing behaviour: Increasing the effectiveness of workplace interventions in creating pro-environmental behaviour change. *Journal of Organizational Behavior*, *34*(2), 211–229.

Weaver, S. J., Rosen, M. A., DiazGranados, D., Lazzara, E. H., Lyons, R., Salas, E., Knych, S. A., Mckeever, M., Adler, L., Barker, M., & others. (2010). Does teamwork improve performance in the operating room? A multilevel evaluation. *Joint Commission Journal on Quality and Patient Safety*, *36*(3), 133–142.

Yang, B., Wang, Y., & Drewry, A. W. (2009). Does it matter where to conduct training? Accounting for cultural factors. *Human Resource Management Review*, *19*(4), 324–333. https://doi.org/10.1016/j.hrmr.2009.03.002

Yang, K.-S., Yu, A.-B., & Yeh, M. H. (1989). Chinese individual modernity and traditionality: Construct definition and measurement. *Proceedings of the Interdisciplinary Conference on Chinese Psychology and Behavior*, 145–169.

Zhang, J., & Zheng, W. (2009). How does satisfaction translate into performance? An examination of commitment and cultural values. *Human Resource Development Quarterly*, *20*(3), 331–351.

CHAPTER

6 Culture and Performance Management at Individual and Team Levels

Zeynep Aycan *and* Elif Gizem Demirag Burak

Abstract

This chapter reviews the cross-cultural literature to identify the trends and gaps in three phases of the performance management (PM) process for individual employees and teams in organizations: (1) goal setting, (2) performance appraisal (methods, biases, and feedback), and (3) rewards and reinforcements. The review suggests the convergence of some of the PM practices in recent years (e.g., preference for merit- and individual-based reward schemes) and identifies emic themes such as *moqi, guanxi, wasta,* and *evil eye*. Several conclusions have been drawn from the review. First, the effect of culture is better conceptualized as a moderator between the PM and outcomes at the organizational and individual levels. Second, there are differences between espoused values and actual practices in PM. Third, there are two pathways through which culture influences PM practices: perceived fairness and justice, and self-related assumptions underlying PM practices. The chapter concludes with practical implications for domestic and multinational concerns.

Key Words: performance management, culture, goal setting, performance appraisal, rewards, reinforcements, organizational level, individual level

Introduction

Performance management (PM) is a series of activities that seek to enhance employee and team performance in organizations. The PM processes ensure that the tasks are achieved by accomplishing positive changes in employee behavior and retaining the efficiency and effectiveness of individuals and teams. The PM framework adopts behavioral modification principles and lays out a process that comprises three key steps: (1) goal setting (to identify the appropriate work behavior), (2) performance appraisal (to assess the maintenance of appropriate work behavior) and feedback as knowledge of the positive and negative outcomes of the behavior (to modify the inappropriate behavior), and (3) reward or punishment (to reinforce the appropriate behavior and extinguish the inappropriate ones). In this chapter, we will review the cross-cultural research literature on these topics. The review includes research comparing across countries as well as those focusing on single-country contexts. We also include studies on the PM practices of multinational corporations (MNCs), as a special case of managing cultural diversity in the same organizational setting. The chapter concludes with the theoretical and practical implications of research as well as future directions for cross-cultural studies on PM.

Determining Performance Criteria and Setting Goals

Performance Criteria

One of the most debated issues in Industrial and Organizational (IO) psychology is the criterion development. There is no consensus on how to define performance and its dimensions. As "good performance" is culture-bound, the criterion problem (cf. Campbell, 2012) is even harder to tackle in the cross-cultural context. According to some recent theoretical formulations (e.g., Campbell, 2012), the common dimensions of performance across work domains include job-specific knowledge and proficiency, communication competence, initiative, persistence and effort, mentorship/supervision, quality of output, productivity, interpersonal competence/teamwork facilitation, and administrative competence.

The validity of the Western performance models is yet to be tested across cultures. Indeed, scholars have already pointed out that our knowledge is limited in terms of how cultural and societal norms influence performance appraisal decisions (DeNisi & Murphy, 2017). Although research has demonstrated the existence of divergence in practices and policies across societies (e.g., Varma et al., 2008), whether cultural norms influence the effectiveness of these practices is not well known (DeNisi & Murphy, 2017). More cross-cultural research is needed for the performance management practices at individual and team levels.

Depending on the cultural context, different performance dimensions are included in the criterion domain. The process (e.g., effort, team processes) leading to results (e.g., quality and quantity of the output) may be considered equally important as the achieved results: "performance criteria in Chinese organizations tend to be generic, broad, and focus on effort and behavior instead of/as much as the outcome" (Cooke, 2008, p. 205). In collectivist and high-power distance cultures, outcomes may be important, but social and relational criteria (e.g., human nature, harmony in interpersonal relations, trustworthiness, respectful attitude, loyalty and deference toward superiors, effort and willingness to work, awareness of duties and obligations, gratitude, organizational citizenship, conformity, and contribution to team maintenance) are weighted heavily in evaluating employee performance (e.g., Rotundo & Xie, 2008; Varela & Premeaux, 2008). DeNisi and Sonesh (2011) argue that rating patterns signal the type of behaviors that are encouraged and discouraged in societies. For example, the authors found that Asian observers assign inflated ratings to provocativeness, egocentrism, and showing off, while they assign deflated ratings to submissiveness and obedience. The first set of behaviors is not endorsed in Asian cultures and rated as high, even though there are limited incidences of such behavior in employees, whereas the latter set of behaviors is encouraged and required to be shown even at a higher rate.

Specific elements of culture can deem it difficult to implement Western performance management systems in other countries (Nolan, 2011, 2015). For example, Gu and Nolan (2017) analyzed the perceived impact of *guanxi* (a system of social networking) on performance appraisal in banks with different ownership structures (e.g., state-owned bank, foreign-owned bank, and a city commercial bank). Interviews revealed that employee's *guanxi* relationships with managers, especially with older supervisors, were considered an important criterion in the performance evaluation. Some employees reported that they aimed to interact with managers even outside of the bank by visiting their homes and offering gifts to receive favorable evaluations.

Another culturally distinctive construct that can influence the difficulty of adapting Western models of performance appraisal across cultures is *wasta* (Harbi et al., 2017). *Wasta* is a Saudi Arabian concept that refers to personal relationship, connections, network, contact, and nepotism (Harbi et al., 2017, p. 2). Emphasizing the significant aspect of personal connections in Arab life, the term emphasizes "going in-between" and the importance of mediation (Smith et al., 2012, p. 3) in making decisions, transferring knowledge, and creating opportunity (Hutchings & Weir, 2006). Despite the Western performance appraisal system that was in place, actual performance evaluations were found to be significantly influenced by *wasta* in Saudi Arabia (Harbi et al., 2017).

Cross-cultural differences may also exist in the way the same criteria are interpreted, especially in the case of MNCs. For example, organizational commitment may imply "time spent in the organization" (i.e., years of work) in Japan, but "extra effort put in the job" in Oman; leadership may imply "cooperation and teamwork" in China, and "assertiveness and independence" in the United States (Caligiuri, 2006). The same challenge is evident in domestic organizations with a culturally diverse workforce; managers from diverse cultural backgrounds may use different interpretations of the same performance criteria in evaluating employees (De Cieri & Sheehan, 2008). Difficulty in defining the performance criteria is also due to the lack of specificity in job descriptions (see also Erez, 2010). Several reasons can explain why generic and nonspecific job descriptions and performance criteria are used in high power distance and collectivistic cultures. First, a broad job description gives superiors the liberty to ask for extra-role (and sometime off-the-job) responsibilities. Second, employees rely mainly on guidance from the supervisor to perform a task; therefore, no specific job description is needed. Third, setting specific performance criteria may limit the superior's discretion in evaluating employees. Fourth, in cultures where favoritism is high, a performance criterion is not set clearly so that superiors can use differential criteria depending on who is liked and who is not (cf. Vallance, 1999). Fifth, in fatalistic cultures, employees are not considered as having control over the work outcomes; therefore, job descriptions are kept generic and nonspecific (e.g., Aycan,

2005). Finally, specifying job requirements may be avoided to reduce employees' worries about failing in the job and facing punishment.

Setting Goals and Performance Expectations

The initial step of the PM is to set goals and establish the connection between these goals and organizational strategies. Goal-setting theory (Locke & Latham, 1984) suggests that the jointly set goals, which are specific, challenging, and acceptable, motivate employees more than simple, nonspecific goals set by the supervisors. The theory is based on the assumptions of individualistic cultures, such as independent self-construal (vs. interdependent), belief in self-determination and self-efficacy (vs. fatalism), and need for achievement and self-enhancement (vs. self-effacement). These underlying assumptions of the goal-setting theory limit its generalizability across cultures, as suggested by the following review under two headings: characteristics of goals to motivate employees and the method of goal setting.

Characteristics of Goals. Setting a goal instead of "doing your best" is confirmed to increase performance in many countries ranging from the Caribbean to Australia, Israel, and Sri Lanka (Punnett, 2004). Nevertheless, setting challenging and specific goals may be rejected in feminine and collectivistic cultures because these goals have the potential to increase competition and to highlight individual differences in organizations. These types of goals foster competitive work environments and lead to situations conducive to failure and the embarrassment of employees. Such goals are also unwelcome in fatalistic cultures. As Punnett (2004) argues: "where people feel that they have little control over their environment, the idea of setting a specific target may seem foolish at best and possibly thought of as going against God's will" (p. 150). Indeed, Geiger and colleagues' study in 10 countries (Australia, Canada, Hong Kong, India, Indonesia, Malaysia, Mexico, Oman, Singapore, and the United States) revealed that employees who believed achieving performance goals depended on their effort (i.e., expectancy belief) were more likely to be in cultures characterized by long-term orientation and individualism and less likely to be in cultures characterized by uncertainty avoidance and power distance (Geiger et al., 1998).

The type of goals people prioritizes in life and at work differ across cultures. Grouzet and colleagues (2005) suggested a goal categorization framework comparing two types of goals, which are intrinsic and extrinsic, along with self-transcendence and physical self-dimension. The authors found that although the structure of goal categorization was similar in 15 countries, the placement of goals in these categories was dissimilar. For example, individuals in economically underdeveloped countries placed financial goals close to safety-physical health goals and far from hedonism. In these types of countries, setting goals to achieve financial outcomes would be more motivating, compared to goals to enhance fun at work.

Few studies have investigated cross-cultural differences in goal orientation, namely, learning orientation versus performance orientation (Dweck, 1986). Evidence shows that in Confucian cultures these two opposite goal orientations are indeed positively associated (VandeWalle et al., 2001). The possibility that competing goals can jointly motivate employees should be taken into consideration in the PM practices of Asian cultures (e.g., Erez, 2013).

Method of Goal Setting. Is participative goal setting more effective than assigned goals in all cultures? Although participative goal setting enhances employee motivation in egalitarian cultures, this is not a common practice in high-power distance cultures. In power hierarchical and paternalistic cultures, employees assume that their superiors are more competent in deciding what is best for them and commit to assigned goals (Aycan, 2006). Sue-Chan and Mark Ong (2002) found that when goals are set jointly, employees from high-power distance cultures set significantly lower goals than those from low-power distance cultures. This is probably because employees in high-power distance cultures experience lower self-efficacy and perceive higher threat of losing face to their supervisors if ambitious goals cannot be achieved.

In an earlier seminal study, Erez and Earley (1987) found that Americans performed better than Israelis when the goals are assigned. The authors concluded that participative goal setting was beneficial to enhance performance in both cultures, but assigned goals increased goal acceptance and performance in the hierarchical culture (i.e., the United States, compared to Israel) (see also Latham et al., 1988). Using the psychoanalytic theory, Savani et al. (2012) studied cross-cultural differences in the internalization of goals that belong to significant others through goal priming. The findings revealed that Indian employees made choices aligned with the goals and expectations of primed authority figures, whereas American employees did not feel compelled to make the same choices expected by peers or authority figures. The cross-cultural difference found in this study could be explained by tightness–looseness (cf. Gelfand, 2018; Erez, 2013). In tight cultures, the tendency is to conform to the norm, whereas in loose cultures, the tendency is to follow one's own path or even the path that is against the recommendations of others. Indeed, the American participants evaluated the choice *less* favorably when it was perceived as recommended by the project manager than when there was no such prime (Savani et al., 2012). Asserting the self and challenging others, referred to as "influence goals," is more common in individualistic cultures, compared to suppressing the self and conforming to others, referred to as "adjustment goals" which is more common in collectivistic cultures (Tsai et al., 2007).

The diverse reactions to participative leadership can be rooted in the different understanding of what "participation" is. To illustrate, in high-power distance cultures, asking employees' opinions and making a decision that counters those opinions can be considered as participative leadership (Sagie & Aycan, 2003). However, this would be considered nonparticipative leadership in low-power distance cultures. As Kabasakal and Bodur (1998) stated, "employees expect management to make decisions, although they prefer that the manager asks their opinion before making decisions" (p. 14).

Performance-Appraisal: Methods, Biases, and Feedback

Performance-Appraisal Methods and Biases

The heated debate about the most reliable source of data for performance appraisal (PA) continues among scientists and practitioners. The most contested issues are whether to use multiple assessors in evaluating employee performance and what to do about the discrepancies in ratings obtained from the multisource feedback methods (MSF). The literature seems to conclude that discrepancies in ratings represent valuable information, rather than unwanted error in measurement (Levy et al., 2017). However, using multiple assessors in performance evaluation may not be aligned with cultural values and may evoke resistance to being evaluated by those other than the immediate supervisor. Indeed, the incongruence between societal culture and performance appraisal practices was found to be associated with higher turnover and absenteeism, especially when PA is used for personnel decisions rather than for feedback purposes (Peretz & Fried, 2012).

In low-power distant, individualistic, and assertive cultures, multisource feedback (e.g., 360-degree performance appraisal) is common (e.g., Chiang & Birtch, 2010; Shipper et al., 2007), while in high-power distance cultures, performance is evaluated by the superiors only (e.g., Peretz & Fried, 2012; Shipper et al., 2007). In these cultures, getting feedback from subordinates and peers on superiors' performance is considered a threat to the authority of supervisors (e.g., Ng et al., 2011). Even if such feedback is received, it is likely to be biased: "subordinates artificially inflate upward evaluation either as an expression of the assumption that " 'the boss's way is the best' or to avoid any hint of confrontation that a negative evaluation might engender eroding the credibility of ratings that subordinates provide in high power distant cultures" (Varela & Premeaux, 2008, p. 136).

Including peer evaluation and self-evaluation in the MSF system also presents challenges. In collectivist cultures, a 360-degree evaluation is feared to disturb group harmony because of the constant monitoring of the behaviors of peers (Shipper et al., 2007). While self-ratings produced the highest scores in MSFs in the U.S. samples, self-appraisal is neither desirable nor appropriate in collectivistic cultures (e.g., London, 2004). Emphasizing the "self" and personal achievements is not welcome in cultures where the norm is humility in the self-presentation (Wiersma & Van Der Berg, 1999). As an exception, in collectivistic cultures, self-ratings are found to be the highest among other sources of MSF in *people-oriented behaviors*, such as helping and supportiveness (Varela & Premeaux, 2008). Because such behaviors are strongly endorsed, self-ratings tend to be inflated to get the approval of superiors and colleagues. Another reason for deemphasizing personal achievements in collectivistic cultures may be the fear of envy from colleagues at work (see Duffy & Yu, 2018 for a review). In some cultures, this fear may reach a level of suspecting others to inflict harm to the high-achieving individuals, which is called the "evil eye" (cf., Gershman, 2015). It is a very common belief in the Middle East and North Africa (exceeding 80% of the participants in a survey in 2009—http://pewforum.org), but it is not unusual in the United States (16% in the same survey). To avoid the harm and to protect oneself from the evil eye, high achievers may tend to hide their successes or undermine their achievements. Future research should investigate the relationship between the belief in the evil eye and self-demotion in performance appraisal.

A new construct called worries about leadership (WAL) proposed by the first author may be relevant in any discussion of how leadership is viewed and evaluated (Aycan, 2015). WAL is an anticipated emotion about the possible negative consequence of accepting a leadership role. Psychophysiological studies showed that WAL is embodied (Aycan & Shelia, 2019). The embodied nature of WAL affects the way leadership performance is evaluated, and this relationship may be moderated by gender and culture. In a recent multilevel study, it was found that the leadership potential of high-WAL males was evaluated more favorably by their supervisors than that of high-WAL females (Karakulak et al., 2019). Similar moderation effects can be observed across cultures.

There is a dearth of research on performance evaluation biases in cross-cultural research (e.g., halo, leniency). Similar-to-me bias is found to be in effect to a greater extent in collectivistic than in individualistic cultures (e.g., Mishra & Roch, 2013). In a comprehensive study capturing leniency and halo biases in MSF ratings of naval officers in a leadership development program in Singapore, it was found that subordinate ratings were the most susceptible to biases, especially when subordinates endorsed power distance and collectivism values (Ng et al., 2011). Rater effects (raters' hierarchical level, power distance, and collectivism orientation) accounted for nearly 20% of the variance in halo and leniency biases when evaluating superiors' performance. Peers with collectivistic values (compared to individualistic ones) committed leniency bias but not halo bias.

Biases in performance appraisal may inflate the discrepancy among ratings of multiple assessors. In studies of leadership effectiveness, the self–other discrepancy was larger in cultures characterized by low assertiveness and power distance (Atwater et al., 2009). Some research shows that the discrepancy is particularly pronounced in certain behaviors, such as "decisiveness" in high- (compared to low-) power distant cultures (Eckert et al., 2010), and that it is associated with ineffectiveness and derailment to a greater extent in the United States than in Europe (e.g., Germany, Denmark, Italy, France) (Atwater et al., 2005; Gentry et al., 2007).

Biases in performance appraisal are not inconsequential. For example, Vietnamese employees in the Japanese subsidiary of an MNC reported lower job satisfaction than those in the U.S. subsidiary because in Japan there was a lack of transparency in performance appraisal, which decreased the perceived fairness in the organization (Vo & Stanton, 2011). Perceived bias in the performance appraisal process may also be influenced by cultural diversity in the workplace. In a study of Asian subsidiaries of a Japanese MNC (Yamazaki & Yoon, 2016), it was found that perceived bias in the performance appraisal process is higher in countries with more ethnic and religious diversity (e.g.,

Malaysia and Thailand) than in countries with less diversity (e.g., Japan and China). In a diverse context, there are doubts about the evaluators' willingness and ability to make objective judgments about the performance of employees irrespective of their stereotypes or prejudices about employees' ethnic and religious backgrounds. In the same study, in subsidiaries where performance appraisal is conducted in English (rather than in the native language), evaluators were direct and clear in their communication style, which increased the perception of fairness. These findings highlight the importance of language use and communication style in performance evaluations.

Performance-Related Feedback

Cross-cultural differences in the way feedback are given and received bring additional challenges to the delicate and important aspect of PM. Culture has a bearing on the openness and directness of seeking and giving feedback. In collectivistic and high-power distance cultures, there is a reluctance to seek feedback; superiors who are considered wise experts initiate the feedback process (e.g., Morrison et al., 2004). Research shows that in cultures where feedback from multiple sources may be ego-threatening, its utility is enhanced if only it is perceived to be constructive and coming from legitimate sources (Shipper et al., 2007).

In collectivistic cultures, feedback tends to be nonconfrontational, indirect, subtle, and nontransparent (Fletcher & Perry, 2001). Performance-related information is embedded in the context and indirectly communicated (i.e., high-context communication) (Gibson, 1997). Performance interviews are rarely conducted face to face, and direct and open communication is not common (Elenkov, 1998). This is mainly because employees tend to take direct and honest feedback personal, to resent the evaluator, and to withdraw from the relationship. In a recent study, an *emic* construct is introduced to explain the context where implicit feedback is preferred: *moqi* (Zheng et al., 2019). *Moqi* is a word composed of two Chinese characters, *mo* (silence) and *qi* (consensus), to mean "tacit understanding, implicit consent, and coordinated action in the absence of explicit verbal communication" in the subordinate–superior relationship (Zheng et al., 2019, p. 4). *Moqi* is enhanced when employees engaged in implicit feedback-seeking, especially when they are sensitive about sustaining a hierarchical relationship with their supervisors and maintaining face in this relationship. Stronger *moqi*, in turn, results in higher performance of subordinates and a higher likelihood of reward recommendation by superiors.

Let us examine how cross-cultural differences play out in positive and negative feedback. First, in collectivist cultures, positive feedback is expected to come from an external source (e.g., customers, auditors). When a manager praises their employees, it is perceived as self-serving (cf. Triandis, 1994). Second, some evidence suggests that positive feedback may not be as effective in Western cultures as it is in some Asian cultures because positive feedback is in line with the inflated view of self for Westerners and serves as a hygiene factor (i.e., expected and taken for granted) rather than a motivator (Lam et al., 2002).

Depending on the culture, failure is seen as either a threat to self-enhancement or an opportunity for self-improvement. American participants were found to switch to a new task upon receiving negative feedback signaling failure, whereas the Japanese persisted in the task even after they experienced failure (Heine & Raineri, 2009). The authors explain this difference by juxtaposing the self-enhancing motivation of Americans and the self-improvement motivation of Asians (see also Gaertner et al., 2012). Third, the utility of positive feedback was also found to be a function of the social status of the feedback giver and receiver in culturally diverse work organizations. Lawrence and colleagues (Lawrence et al., 2011) found that when positive feedback is provided to a member of a stigmatized cultural group by someone from a dominant group, it is perceived negatively and interpreted as if the evaluation had low expectation of the person being evaluated.

Giving and receiving negative feedback is challenging, regardless of the cultural context. However, certain circumstances may amplify the challenge. For example, in cultures where the distinction between work and life spaces is blurred (i.e. diffuse cultures; Trompenaars, 1993), negative feedback on one's work performance may be taken personally as an attack against one's personality. However, negative feedback may be motivating in cultures where emotional regulation is focused on prevention rather than promotion (e.g., Van Dijk & Kluger, 2011). In a recent study comparing participants from the United States and Hong Kong, the regulatory fit theory was supported to show that receiving a gain-framed feedback (i.e., "the company was able to gain $100,000 as profit this month; however, owing to your mistake, we earned $80,000 only") motivated promotion-focused participants while receiving a loss-framed feedback (i.e., "the company made $100,000 as profit this month; however, owing to your mistake, we have lost $20,000") motivated prevention-focused ones (Kung et al., 2016).

As discussed earlier, culture influences the biases in performance evaluations. In a rare example of cross-cultural research on evaluation biases in MSF, Ng and colleagues (2011) found that depersonalization of feedback (i.e., anonymous feedback) can be a remedy for evaluation biases in cultures sensitive to maintain harmonious relationships. A comparison between Chinese and Dutch participants showed that there is high satisfaction with feedback when the following conditions are matched: (1) *depersonalized* feedback is given to a *collectivistically* oriented *group* and (2) *personalized* feedback is given to *individualistically* oriented *individuals*. The mismatch among these conditions resulted in a perception of lower quality of the feedback and worsened the socioemotional relationship between the feedback giver and receiver.

Performance Improvement: The Role of Rewards

Cross-cultural Variations in the Type of Rewards

The type of rewards given to motivate employees for high performance differs across cultures. Let us first discuss financial incentives and rewards. One of the most popular performance-reward contingencies is the pay-for-performance scheme. According to the findings of the latest Cranet survey featuring HRM practices in 35 countries (the majority of the European Union countries plus Brazil, China, and Indonesia; Poór et al., 2017), pay-for-performance schemes were shown to be more popular than incentive plans based on financial participation (e.g., profit sharing, stock options). The number of organizations administering pay-for-performance schemes increased in the last cohort of the survey (2014–2016) compared to the previous one (2008–2010). These schemes are used more frequently to reward individual than group or team performance. However, it has been concluded that these schemes are far from being widespread.

Studying the PM practice of 171 subsidiaries of foreign-owned MNCs in Australia, Bartram and colleagues (Bartram et al., 2015) recently found that their PM practices follow global pressures for global institutional isomorphism, rather than home or host country norms. As such, some level of convergence among MNCs' PM practices are observed. In another study, profit-sharing and saving plans are associated with the intention to stay in the organization of Mexican employees in U.S.-owned plants in Mexico, while other pay forms (e.g., productivity bonus, overtime pay) increased turnover intention, probably because they signal performance pressure to employees who are low on performance orientation (Miller et al., 2001).

Are there valued outcomes to reward good performance other than pay or financial incentives? For instance, would praise from the supervisor be considered a valued outcome? In a comparative study of Japanese and American employees, regular expression of appreciation by managers as well as customer satisfaction were found to be associated with organizational performance in both countries, but the relationships were stronger in Japan than in the United States (Allen et al., 2004). Apart from incentives to individual performance outcomes, the key motivators in Japan and in high-tech industries included encouragement of initiative and risk-taking, autonomy on the job, pride in the work (Evans & Wolf, 2005), respect and recognition from the supervisor, good interpersonal relationships, and long-term employment (Fadil et al., 2005).

Silva and Caetano (2016) show that when applying the principles of justice in reward distribution, collectivist cultures tend to give priority to factors such as the employee's tenure, social skills, and *guanxi* relationships while individualistic cultures consider only the employee's efficiency and performance (Fischer & Smith, 2003). A recent study conducted by Gu et al. (2020) investigated employees' perceptions of *guanxi* connections on supervisor's performance rating and reward distribution in the banking sector in China. Employees working in the State Bank indicated that they found distribution of rewards unfair because the supervisor's performance evaluations were highly dependent on *guanxi*. They also indicated lower-level procedural and distributive justice perceptions toward the performance appraisals than the employees working the Foreign Bank and City Bank.

Promotion can be a valued reward for high performance. However, for employees in collectivist, high-power distance, or uncertainty avoidant cultures, promotion to a managerial position can be perceived negatively. Being promoted can separate a person from their work team; cause resentment and jealousy of other members of the team who did not get promoted; increase workload, responsibility, work hours, and risks to be taken (Corney & Richards, 2005). Indeed, Aycan and Shelia (2019) demonstrated that promotion to a leadership role can be worrisome for some individuals, even though they have high motivation to lead.

Method of Reward Distribution

Cross-cultural literature on reward distribution compares three main methods: equity, equality, and need. Earlier research indicated that in non-U.S. contexts, employees tended to prefer equality over equity in distributing rewards, suggesting the limited utility of the equity principle in motivating employees in collectivistic cultures (e.g., Gergen et al., 1980).

However, several meta-analyses shed doubt about this conclusion. In a meta-analysis, Sama and Papamarcos (2000) showed that employees in individualistic cultures preferred equity, while employees in collectivistic cultures preferred equality specifically for in-group members such as family, close friends, and relatives. Fischer and Smith's meta-analysis (2003) showed that individualism–collectivism was not related to preferences for reward allocation. These mixed results on the role of individualism–collectivism in reward distribution can be explained by the contextual moderators in the preferences for equity and equality. For example, earlier work by Leung (1997) suggested that when the reward allocator was also the reward recipient (e.g., the recipient is a member of the team), preference for equality can be observed in collectivistic cultures. However, if the reward allocator is not a recipient of rewards (e.g., an external agent), then equity would be preferred in both individualistic and collectivistic cultures.

Hysom and Fisek (2011) proposed the equity–equality equilibrium model (i.e., balance of equity and equality) to assess how situational factors interact with culture on the evaluation of justice perceptions. Through use of a vignette survey, fairness of the distribution of resources was evaluated in a comparison of students from the United States and Turkey. Each vignette included a description of a workgroup where the status differentiation was manipulated (e.g., age, education, experience) and participants were asked to indicate the fairest salary for each group member. Regardless of the culture, the study found that as the status differentiation increased, participants favored equality rather than equity to maintain social harmony and to avoid social tension. Therefore, the conflicting empirical evidence regarding the preference for equity or equality in different cultures exists, and more cross-cultural research on justice perceptions is needed.

The literature on the "need" criterion for reward distribution is meager. Employees were found to prefer need-based distribution in the conditions of high unemployment and collectivism (Fischer, 2004). Giacobbe-Miller et al. (1998) conducted a scenario-based experiment in which they compared American and Russian employees. The study reported that 59% of employees in the United States preferred the bonus to be distributed based on equity (i.e., performance levels), whereas 31% preferred equality among employees and 10% preferred the need. In contrast, only 8% of the Russian subjects preferred equity, 36% equality, and 55% need. All but three Russian participants stated that "need" should be the sole criterion for distributing the reward, whereas only three American participants held that opinion.

Diverging from earlier findings, research in recent years has tended to show that employees have increasingly been leaning toward the equity principle and pay-for-performance schemes. Several authors speak of shifting perspectives in competitive Asian economies, such as Korea: "45.2 percent of Korea firms with more than 100 employees have implemented an individual performance-based pay system, and . . . 22.6 percent are also planning to adopt the pay system in a year. This is indeed a notable growth considering only 3.6 percent of Korean companies used individual performance-based pay systems in 1997. The recent transformation suggests that Korean companies will have to confront emerging issues such as distributive justice as they approach a management paradigm characterized by performance orientation" (Chang & Hahn, 2006, p. 398).

Bozionelos and Wang (2007), found, contrary to expectations, that the younger generation of Chinese had a neutral (rather than negative) attitude toward equity-based rewards, that is, IBPRRS (individually based performance-related reward systems). Managers who participated in the interviews in this study expressed discomfort about the biases in their performance evaluations and viewed IBPRRS as a corrective step toward elevating fairness in the system. Similar findings were obtained by Du and Choi (2010) showing that pay-for-performance schemes are positively correlated with commitment and the organizational citizenship behavior (OCB) of Chinese employees when the performance evaluation system is perceived to be procedurally fair. He, Chen, and Zhang (2004) remind us that, from a historical perspective, Chinese people are no strangers to the equity principle. Their familiarity with it goes back to the beginnings of the CCP (Chinese Communist Party), which had advocated "to each according to work" idea in distributing limited resources. A meta-analysis (Jackson et al., 2013) of the relationship between leadership and commitment indeed shows a strong positive association between contingent-reward leadership and affective commitment. This relationship was especially strong in high- (compared to low-) power distant cultures (see also Allen et al., 2005; Wheeler, 2002).

Chiang and Birtch (2006) proposed a multidimensional framework for rewards and reward allocation to explore cross-cultural and national differences. Accordingly, "reward type" refers to the nature of reward (financial, nonfinancial, extrinsic, intrinsic); "reward system" refers to the method by which the organization determines the reward outcomes (seniority, performance, skill level, competencies); and "reward criterion" refers to the unit of reward allocation (individual vs. group; Chiang & Birtch, 2006, p. 576). Comparison of employees and managers in Hong Kong and Finland found that cross-cultural differences in preferences of reward type between the two countries were more pronounced than preferences in the reward system and reward criterion. In both countries, performance- and competency-based reward allocation (rather than seniority-based) to individuals (rather than groups) was preferred. A similar pattern emerged in their 2007 study, which compared Canadian, Hong Kong Chinese, British, and Finnish employees (Chiang & Birtch, 2007; see also Chiang & Birtch, 2012). The convergence among countries can be explained by the methodology of the study, which gauged participants' *preferences* rather than actual *practices* applied in their current organizations. This framework can also be used in future cross-cultural research to investigate the differences between values and practices in the intersections between types of rewards and their allocation methods.

Criteria for Reward Allocation

The input used in the equitable distribution of rewards is assumed to be job performance. However, inputs other than performance may be taken into account when rewarding employees. Early studies indicate that in high-power distance cultures, deserving a reward or a promotion depended on inputs such as seniority, social class, and age (e.g., Hundley & Kim, 1997). Seniority-based rewards increase predictability and certainty, especially in high-uncertainty avoidance cultures, while in countries with low uncertainty avoidance, performance, skill-based reward systems were preferred (Schuler & Rogovsky, 1998). However, in recent years, it has been shown that in economically developed and aging societies, seniority is also used to allocate rewards and promotions to create a noncompetitive organizational culture and promote long-term access to resources (Fischer, 2008).

Rewarding based on merit versus seniority has been debated especially in the Asian context (e.g., Budhwar & Khatri, 2001; Lowe et al., 2002). A shift from seniority-based rewards to merit-based ones seems to have occurred. For example, a seniority-based reward scheme negatively predicted organizational performance in Japan (Allen et al., 2004) and did not reduce turnover in Mexican maquiladoras (Miller et al., 2001). In the latest Cranet survey, China and Russia had higher scores in the use of performance-related pay than the UK and the United States. It was speculated that the postcommunist era emphasized the importance of employment relationships based on performance-oriented arrangements. In the Cranet survey of 2014–2015, levels of performance-related pay are generally higher than those found in the previous cohorts of the survey in most countries, suggesting that the trend toward performance-based pay persists (Poor et al., 2017).

An additional consideration in the decision of reward allocation is the reward unit as an individual versus team. In collectivistic cultures, reward schemes tend to reflect the norm of deemphasizing individual differences (e.g., Gluskinos, 1988). Financial incentives are highly contingent on the group's performance in China, Indonesia, and Taiwan, while this applies to a lower extent in Australia and the United States (Lowe et al., 2002). The success of the Japanese organizations is attributed to HR systems (including reward schemes) encouraging teamwork and discouraging competition (Allen et al., 2004).

However, the total quality management movement supporting team-based rewards that originated in Japan did not sit well with the individualistic U.S. culture and so failed to generate the same momentum for teamwork among U.S. workers (Allen et al., 2004). In a comparative study, organizational performance in the United States was associated with employee stock ownership and individual-based performance systems, while it was associated with team-based incentives in Japan (Allen et al., 2004). These findings have been corroborated by an experimental study (Leung et al., 2012) revealing that when the relative contribution of the group versus the individual to the group's outcome was made ambiguous, those from collectivistic cultures gave extra credit to the group, whereas those from individualistic cultures gave extra credit to the individual members. These authors argue that this difference is due to the way attribution is made about the source of a powerful agency that can influence the outcome and prevent failure—the group versus the individual. They also point out the role of epistemic motives: in collectivistic cultures, the group is seen as having the power to *prevent failure*, whereas in individualistic cultures, the individual is viewed as having the power to *attain success*—hence, the differences in the willingness to reward the group versus the individual for a positive outcome. Employees' behaviors in promoting maintenance of good interpersonal relationships and altruism are viable inputs for reward considerations (see also Bolino & Turnley, 2008). Other inputs, including loyalty, respect for authority, adherence to social norms, and helping behavior, were considered as inputs that were duly rewarded in collectivistic and hierarchical cultures (e.g., Du & Choi, 2010; Fadil et al., 2005).

What effect does the reward allocation method have on organizational outcomes? In a rare cross-cultural study addressing this question, Magnusson et al. (2014) collected data from top- to midlevel sales managers in 26 countries to investigate how cultural values moderated the relationship between reward alignment and sales collaboration. Their counterintuitive findings showed that the relationship between reward alignment and sales collaboration was stronger in individualistic and masculine cultures than it was in collectivistic and feminine cultures. More specifically, collaboration *and* firm performance were enhanced when the reward structure was aligned with the organization's overall objectives, especially in individualistic and masculine cultures. Managers in highly masculine and/or individualistic cultures achieved sales collaboration by designing a countercultural reward structure that promoted collaborative behavior, which otherwise would not have occurred naturally. The positive effect of such a reward structure was not as strong in organizations in feminine and collectivistic cultures because there was less of a need for such an intervention.

IMPLICATIONS AND FUTURE DIRECTIONS

Several theoretical and practical implications can be drawn from the research reviewed in this chapter. Let us start with theoretical implications. First, our review suggests that the effect of culture is better conceptualized as a moderator than the main effect between the PM practices and outcomes at the organizational and individual levels. For example, giving and receiving negative feedback on poor performance is generally avoided, but more so in collectivistic and power hierarchical cultures than in individualistic ones. In a few incidences, culture was considered the main effect influencing the PM process. For example, the cultural context has a direct impact on (1) what is considered desired work behaviors (e.g., interpersonal harmony), (2) what is deemed appropriate to be rewarded, and (3) what is as high as or even higher than work performance (e.g., units produced).

Second, the review also highlights the differences between espoused values and actual practices in PM. For example, when asked about preferences, managers in collectivistic and high-power distant cultures report a preference for equity-based rewards or performance-reward contingencies. However, the practice does not necessarily reflect such preferences. Instead, they are aligned with the cultural norms (e.g., downplaying individual differences in performance appraisal and rewarding). Future cross-cultural research should pay more attention to methodologically draw and theoretically explain the differences between preferences/values and practices concerning PM.

Third, according to the review, two pathways through which culture influences PM practices seem to emerge: (1) perceived fairness and justice in PM practices and (2) self-related assumptions underlying PM practices. Cultural context determines what is considered fair in goal-setting, evaluating, and rewarding employees, which, in turn, shape the design and implementation of PM practices. Culture also influences the way self is construed. Planning (i.e., goal setting), evaluation (i.e., performance appraisal), and reinforcement (i.e., rewarding) phases of PM are influenced by the way self is considered as independent or interdependent; motivation is enhanced through self-enhancement or self-effacement; and control of outcomes is possible through self-determination or subjugation to fate.

Another pathway through which culture influences PM practices has been proposed by Keles and Aycan (2011). Based on the premises of the Model of Culture Fit, Aycan et al. (2000) argued that PM practices are designed in accordance with the prevailing managerial assumptions about employee nature and behavior, which, in turn, are influenced by the cultural values. PM practices were classified in accordance to their (1) level of *structure* (i.e., whether PM is conducted in objective and systematic or unsystematic and subjective manner), (2) *focus* (i.e., whether the emphasis is placed on hard criteria, such as quality and quantity of outputs produced, or soft criteria, such as loyalty and good interpersonal relationships, and (3) level of *participation* (i.e., whether or not participation is encouraged to set performance goals and evaluate performance). Managers who implemented structured PM practices assumed that employees were goal-oriented. This assumption was, in turn, associated with the cultural value of performance orientation. Managers who emphasized hard criteria in evaluating performance assumed that employees were reactive by nature and had the responsibility to fulfill obligation toward others. These assumptions were associated with collectivism and paternalism values. Managers who implemented nonparticipative PM practices assumed that employees did not want to participate in decisions. This assumption reflected fatalism and power distance values in the cultural context. Future cross-cultural research should be guided by theoretical frameworks explaining how PM practices are influenced by culture directly (as the main effect) or indirectly (as a moderator).

The review has several practical implications as well. Domestic organizations in economically developing countries or those with a culturally diverse workforce find it difficult to adopt North American PM practices, which are grounded in individualistic, performance-oriented, and egalitarian cultural values and assumptions. The review suggests that in economically developing countries characterized by collectivism, high power distance, and uncertainty avoidance (Aycan, 2005), the challenges of implementing North American PM practices include resistance to or discomfort with (1) setting performance goals jointly with employees (the natural inclination is for the employee to implement the decision of the management team), (2) conducting upwards performance evaluations (the natural inclination is for only the supervisor to evaluate employees), (3) engaging in open and face-to-face feedback sessions to discuss the strengths and weaknesses of employee performance (the tendency is to avoid such sessions or do it indirectly with the mediation of HR), and (4) allocating performance-based rewards and recognition to deserving employees (the preference is to give rewards or recognition to teams and not to single out high-performing individuals). Western expatriates assigned to such country contexts experience these challenges in managing the performance of host country nationals (Adler & Aycan, 2018). Multinational corporations also face these challenges and develop interventions to offset their effects. The challenges are exacerbated in times of global crises like COVID-19, which heightened the stress levels of employees and managers who had to work virtually.

Despite these challenges, we remain optimistic about the future of PM. There are two reasons for our optimism. First, the review presented in this chapter implies that the preferences for workplace practices of so-called traditional societies (collectivistic, hierarchical, uncertainty avoiding) undergo a transformation. As found in the GLOBE project, a significant gap exists between how societies actually are and how they are aspired to be in these societies. The younger generations in countries deemed global players, such as China, India, Russia, and Brazil, seek and demand higher levels of transparency, fairness, and participation in workplace practices—especially those concerning performance management. Second, the North American PM literature suggests that the practices are also undergoing a transformation. Many critiques of existing PM systems have been presented (e.g., Murphy, 2020). For example, Deloitte's review suggested that organizations spend two million hours per year completing forms, holding meetings, and conducting performance reviews to produce outcomes that are less than satisfactory (Buckingham & Goodall, 2015). The trends in newly evolving team-based organizational structures include team-based PM, real-time and anonymous feedback from team members, weekly coaching sessions with managers, and peer coaching (Darino et al., 2020). Also recommended in difficult times, such as the time of the global pandemic, are showing compassion, focusing less on numerical ratings in evaluating employees, and treating poor performers with humility and kindness (Knight, 2020). These practices and changing trends in PM are indeed more compatible with the cultural values of collectivism, paternalism, and uncertainty avoidance.

The key recommendation for managing performance in MNCs is to find the right balance between global standardization (i.e., keeping the PM system the same in all subsidiaries) and local adaptation (i.e., tailoring the PM system to fit the cultural context of subsidiaries) (cf. Claus & Hand, 2009; Lazarova et al., 2017). Let us consider several examples of such a balancing act of MNCs (Aycan et al., 2014). First, it is important to keep the performance criteria the same across subsidiaries but to allow flexibility in the way they are measured in different cultures. "What" is being evaluated (e.g., behavioral competencies such as agility) may be the same in all subsidiaries. However, "how" they are evaluated (e.g., using superior as the sole evaluators vs. using a 360-degree evaluation system) should be sensitive to the cultural context. As discussed earlier, in high-power distance cultures, superiors do not prefer to be evaluated by their subordinates, and in collectivistic cultures, employees do not prefer to be evaluated by their colleagues. Therefore, in this cultural context, performance evaluation should be initially conducted as a top-down process (i.e., only supervisors evaluate employees). Later, the process may involve colleagues, but the feedback from colleagues may be used as information used for personal development rather than for performance evaluation. As employees get used to these initial applications of the multisource feedback system, MNCs can gradually implement the full 360-degree performance evaluation, if it is deemed strategically important to use multisource feedback. The key is to implement the so-called culturally inappropriate HR systems gradually in the organization and to avoid radical and quick changes. An alternative strategy is to *regionalize* HRM practices—that is, to design and/or implement different HRM systems for different country/cultural regions. This approach is midway between global standardization and localization. This strategy seems to have been adopted by the majority of MNCs. In this strategy, HRM practices are the same *within* the region but different *across* the regions.

Sumelius and colleagues (Sumelius et al., 2014) studied visibility, validity, and justice perception of managers of the performance appraisal system of Nordic MNCs in six subsidiaries. The findings revealed that "standardizing performance appraisal too much may result in employees paying less attention, and attaching less value to a system they perceive not to be relevant in their context, and thus highlight that MNCs cannot ignore the well-acknowledged dilemma of balancing standardization and localization of HRM practices (Rosenzweig & Nohria, 1994)" (p. 587). The key theoretical principles discovered in our review and the key practical implications are summarized in Table 6.1.

Table 6.1 Key theoretical principles and practical implications drawn from the review of cross-cultural literature on performance management
Theoretical principles
1. Culture is a *moderator* between PM practices and employee and organizational outcomes.
2. Cultural values and norms also directly impact how performance dimensions are defined and weighted in performance evaluation and reward allocation.
3. There are significant differences (especially in power hierarchical and collectivistic cultures) between espoused values and actual practices concerning PM.
4. Three pathways through which culture impacts PM practices are: (1) perceived justice, (2) the model of "self" underlying PM practices, and (3) managerial assumptions regarding employee nature and behavior.
5. The most important cultural dimensions influencing the PM process are individualism-collectivism, power distance, and uncertainty avoidance.
Practical implications
1. Adaptation of North American PM practices to collectivistic and power hierarchical cultures as needed, especially in the following areas: (1) involving employees in goal setting, (2) evaluating supervisors' and peers' performance, (3) giving and receiving performance feedback openly, and (4) allocating performance-based rewards.
2. Expatriate managers should receive training and coaching on cultural nuances and norms affecting performance evaluations and performance feedback. Expatriates should adopt a "coach-like leadership style" to manage the performance of local employees.
3. The congruence between cultural values and PM practices enhances employee satisfaction and fairness perception.
4. Multinational organizations should strike the right balance between global standardization and local adaptation of their PM practices. The best strategy would be the regiocentric approach.
5. Changing organizational structures shift the focus from individual employees to teams. Team-based tasks and goals, team members' evaluation of performance, and continuous peer coaching ease the transfer of PM practices to a wide range of cultures.

Future research should investigate the mediating mechanisms linking culture to PM practices. Several of these mediators have been suggested in the studies included in our review, but none of them have been explicitly tested. It can be proposed that cultural context influences the following mediating processes, which, in turn, determine the design and implementation of PM practices: (1) employees' perception of fairness in organizational practices (e.g., individualism is associated with perceived fairness of equity-based distribution of organizational resources, leading to a performance-reward contingency in PM); (2) managers' perception of trust to employees' honesty and integrity (e.g., power distance is associated with managers' low trust of employees' honesty and integrity, leading to top-down goal-setting practices in PM); and (3) managers' assumption about employee capacity to learn and develop (e.g., fatalism is associated with managers' assumption that employees' capacity to learn and develop is limited, leading to less likelihood of providing open and timely feedback on performance).

In many countries, the PM system is plagued by cynicism toward it. Managers and employees alike believe that activities such as goal setting and performance evaluation are useless and a waste of time (cf. Varma et al., 2008). The system is attacked for being unfair, especially in performance evaluation and reward distribution. Future research should investigate the effect of culture on coping with perceived unfairness and strategies to restore perceived injustice in the PM system.

Our review suggests that cultural dimensions used in cross-cultural PM research are limited to individualism–collectivism and power distance. Future research would benefit from utilizing the "performance orientation" dimension of the GLOBE project to capture the impact of culture on PM more directly than by using other cultural dimensions (House et al., 2004). One of the key challenges faced by managers operating in collectivistic and power hierarchical cultures is that employees experience a psychological barrier to giving and receiving feedback on performance. This may be related to the cultural dimension of assertiveness, which is low in these cultures compared to individualistic and performance-oriented ones (House et al., 2004). Future research should investigate how open and honest feedback can be provided in such cultures in a caring and nurturing way. The "radical candor" framework proposed by a practitioner, Kim Scott (2017), can be empirically tested across cultures. Scott advocates providing candid feedback while maintaining a caring relationship with employees. Paternalistic leadership seems to be the most conducive leadership style to providing radically candid feedback (Aycan et al., 2013). This proposition should be tested in future research.

In conclusion, our review demonstrates that although the cross-cultural literature on performance management and evaluation has made important strides, several important questions are yet to be addressed by future research. Acknowledging the strategic role that PM plays in globally interwoven work organizations, we hope that our review will guide scientists and practitioners to understand and navigate cultural nuances in the management of performance in teams operating across cultural and virtual borders.

References

Adler, N. J., & Aycan, Z. (2018). Cross-cultural interaction: What we know and what we need to know. *Annual Review of Organizational Psychology and Organizational Behavior, 5*(1), 307–333.

Allen, R. S., Takeda, M. B., White, C. S., & Helms, M. M. (2004). Rewards and organizational performance in Japan and the United States: A comparison. *Compensation and Benefits Review, 36*(1), 7–14.

Allen, R. S., Takeda, M., & White, C. S. (2005). Cross-cultural equity sensitivity: A test of differences between the United States and Japan. *Journal of Managerial Psychology, 20*(8), 641–662.

Atwater, L., Waldman, D., Ostroff, C., Robie, C., & Johnson, K. M. (2005). Self–other agreement: Comparing its relationship with performance in the US and Europe. *International Journal of Selection and Assessment, 13*(1), 25–40.

Atwater, L., Wang, M., Smither, J. W., & Fleenor, J. W. (2009). Are cultural characteristics associated with the relationship between self and others' ratings of leadership? *Journal of Applied Psychology, 94*(4), 876–886.

Aycan, Z. (2005). The interplay between cultural and institutional/structural contingencies in human resource management practices. *The International Journal of Human Resource Management, 16*(7), 1083–1119.

Aycan, Z. (2006). Paternalism: Towards conceptual refinement and operationalization. In K. S. Yang, K. K. Hwang, & U. Kim (Eds.), *Indigenous and cultural psychology: understanding people in context* (pp. 445–466). New York: Springer.

Aycan, Z. (2015). Leadership: Cultural perspectives and new directions. Keynote Address at the *European Association for Work and Organizational Psychology Congress*. Oslo, Norway.

Aycan, Z., Kanungo, R. N., & Mendonca, M. (2014). *Organizations and management in cross-cultural context*. Los Angeles: SAGE.

Aycan, Z., Kanungo, R., Mendonca, M., Yu, K., Deller, J., Stahl, G., & Kurshid, A. (2000). Impact of culture on human resource management practices: A 10-country comparison. *Applied Psychology: An International Review, 49*(1), 192–221.

Aycan, Z., Schyns, B., Sun, J. M., Felfe, J., & Saher, N. (2013). Convergence and divergence of paternalistic leadership: A cross-cultural investigation of prototypes. *Journal of International Business Studies, 44*(9), 962–969.

Aycan, Z., & Shelia, S. (2019). "Leadership? No, thanks!" A new construct: Worries about leadership. *European Management Review, 16*(1), 21–35.

Bartram, T., Boyle, B., Stanton, P., Sablok, G., & Burgess, J. (2015). Performance and reward practices of multinational corporations operating in Australia. *Journal of Industrial Relations, 57*(2), 210–231. https://doi.org/10.1177/0022185614564372

Bolino, M. C., & Turnley, W. H. (2008). Old faces, new places: Equity theory in cross-cultural contexts. *Journal of Organizational Behavior: The International Journal of Industrial, Occupational and Organizational Psychology and Behavior, 29*(1), 29–50.

Bozionelos, N., & Wang, L. (2007). An investigation on the attitudes of Chinese workers towards individually based performance-related reward systems. *The International Journal of Human Resource Management, 18*(2), 284–302.

Buckingham, M., & Goodall, A. (2015). Reinventing performance management. *Harvard Business Review, 93*(4), 40–50.

Budhwar, P. S., & Khatri, N. (2001). A comparative study of HR practices in Britain and India. *International Journal of Human Resource Management, 12*(5), 800–826.

Caligiuri, P. (2006). Developing global leaders. *Human Resource Management Review, 16*(2), 219–228.

Campbell, J. P. (2012). *Behavior, performance, and effectiveness in the twenty-first century*. In S. W. J. Kozlowski (Ed.), *Oxford library of psychology. The Oxford handbook of organizational psychology*, Vol. 1 (pp. 159–194). New York: Oxford University Press.

Chang, E., & Hahn, J. (2006). Does pay-for-performance enhance perceived distributive justice for collectivistic employees? *Personnel Review, 35*(4), 397–412.

Chiang, F. F., & Birtch, T. A. (2006). An empirical examination of reward preferences within and across national settings. *Management International Review, 46*(5), 573–596.

Chiang, F. F., & Birtch, T. (2007). The transferability of management practices: Examining cross-national differences in reward preferences. *Human Relations, 60*(9), 1293–1330.

Chiang, F. F., & Birtch, T. A. (2010). Appraising performance across borders: An empirical examination of the purposes and practices of performance appraisal in a multicountry context. *Journal of Management Studies, 47*(7), 1365–1393.

Chiang, F. F., & Birtch, T. A. (2012). The performance implications of financial and non-financial rewards: An Asian Nordic comparison. *Journal of Management Studies, 49*(3), 538–570.

Claus, L., & Hand, M. L. (2009). Customization decisions regarding performance management systems of multinational companies: An empirical view of Eastern European firms. *International Journal of Cross Cultural Management, 9*(2), 237–258.

Cooke, B. (2008). If critical management studies is your problem... *Organization, 15*(6), 912–914.

Corney, W. J., & Richards, C. H. (2005). A comparative analysis of the desirability of work characteristics: Chile versus the United States. *International Journal of Management, 22*(2), 159–165.

Darino, L., & Johnson, C. (2020). From me to we: The next shift in performance management. *McKinsey Organizational Blog*. https://www.mckinsey.com/business-functions/organization/our-insights/the-organization-blog/from-me-to-we-the-next-shift-in-performance-management

De Cieri, H. L., & Sheehan, C. R. (2008). Performance management in Australia. In A. Varma, P. S. Budhwar, & A. DeNisi (Eds.), *Performance management systems: A global perspective* (pp. 239–253). Abingdon, UK: Routledge.

DeNisi, A. S., & Murphy, K. R. (2017). Performance appraisal and performance management: 100 years of progress? *Journal of Applied Psychology, 102*(3), 421.

DeNisi, A. S., & Sonesh, S. (2011). The appraisal and management of performance at work. In S. Zedeck (Ed.), *APA handbooks in psychology. APA handbook of industrial and organizational psychology, Vol. 2. Selecting and developing members for the organization* (pp. 255–279). Washington, DC: American Psychological Association.

Du, J., & Choi, J. N. (2010). Pay for performance in emerging markets: Insights from China. *Journal of International Business Studies, 41*(4), 671–689.

Duffy, M. K., & Yu, L. (2018). Toxic emotions at work. In D. Ones, N. Anderson, C. Viswesvaran, & H. K. Sinangil (Eds.), *The SAGE handbook of industrial, work and organizational psychology* (pp. 487–498). Thousand Oaks, CA: SAGE.

Dweck, C. S. (1986). Motivational processes affecting learning. *American Psychologist, 41*(10), 1040–1048.

Eckert, R., Ekelund, B. Z., Gentry, W. A., & Dawson, J. F. (2010). "I don't see me like you see me, but is that a problem?" Cultural influences on rating discrepancy in 360-degree feedback instruments. *European Journal of Work and Organizational Psychology, 19*(3), 259–278.

Elenkov, D. S. (1998). Can American management concepts work in Russia? A cross-cultural comparative study. *California Management Review, 40*(4), 133–156.

Erez, M. (2010). Culture and job design. *Journal of Organizational Behavior, 31*(2/3), 389–400.

Erez, M. (2013). Cross-cultural issues in goal setting. In E. A. Locke & G. P. Latham (Eds.), *New developments in goal setting and task performance* (pp. 509–519). New York: Routledge.

Erez, M., & Earley, P. C. (1987). Comparative analysis of goal-setting strategies across cultures. *Journal of Applied Psychology, 72*(4), 658–665.

Evans, P., & Wolf, B. (2005). Collaboration rules. *Harvard Business Review, 83*(7), 96–104.

Fadil, P. A., Williams, R. J., Limpaphayom, W., & Smatt, C. (2005). Equity or equality? A conceptual examination of the influence of individualism/collectivism on the cross-cultural application of equity theory. *Cross Cultural Management: An International Journal, 12*(4), 17–35.

Fischer, R. (2004). Organizational justice and cultural values in Europe: Justice is in the eye of the beholder. In S. Schmidt & A. Thomas (Eds.), *Impact of values and norms on intercultural training and education* (pp. 83–92). Vienna: IDM.

Fischer, R. (2008). Rewarding seniority: Exploring cultural and organizational predictors of seniority allocations. *The Journal of Social Psychology, 148*(2), 167–186.

Fischer, R., & Smith, P. B. (2003). Reward allocation and culture: A meta-analysis. *Journal of Cross-Cultural Psychology, 34*(3), 251–268.

Fletcher, C., & Perry, E. (2001). Performance appraisal and feedback: A consideration of national culture and a review of contemporary and future trends. In N. Anderson, D. Ones, H. Sinangil, & C. Viswesvaran (Eds.), *International handbook of industrial, work and organisational psychology* (pp. 127–144). Beverly Hills, CA: Sage.

Gaertner, L., Sedikides, C., & Cai, H. (2012). Wanting to be great and better but not average: On the pancultural desire for self-enhancing and self-improving feedback. *Journal of Cross-Cultural Psychology, 43*(4), 521–526.

Geiger, M. A., Cooper, E. A., Hussain, I., O'Connell, B. T., Power, J., Raghunandan, K., & Sanchez, G. (1998). Using expectancy theory to assess student motivation: An international replication. *Issues in Accounting Education, 13*(1), 139–156.

Gelfand, M. J. (2018). *Rule makers, rule breakers: How culture wires our minds, shapes our nations and drive our differences.* New York: Simon & Schuster.

Gentry, W. A., Ekelund, B. R. Z., Hannum, K. M., & de Jong, A. (2007). A study of the discrepancy between self-and observer-ratings on managerial derailment characteristics of European managers. *European Journal of Work and Organizational Psychology, 16*(3), 295–325.

Gershman, B. (2015). The economic origins of the evil eye belief. *Journal of Economic Behavior and Organization, 110*, 119–144.

Gergen, K. J., Morse, S. J., & Gergen, M. M. (1980). Behavior exchange in cross-cultural perspective. *Handbook of Cross-Cultural Psychology, 5*, 121–153.

Giacobbe-Miller, J. K., Miller, D. J., & Victorov, V. I. (1998). A comparison of Russian and U.S. pay allocation decisions, distributive justice judgements, and productivity under different payment conditions. *Personnel Psychology, 51*(1), 137–163.

Gibson, C. B. (1997). Do you hear what I hear? A framework for reconciling intercultural communication difficulties arising from cognitive styles and cultural values. In P. C. Earley & M. Erez (Eds.), *New perspectives on international industrial and organizational psychology* (pp. 335–362). San Francisco: New Lexington Press.

Gluskinos, U. M. (1988). Cultural and political considerations in the introduction of Western technologies: The Mekorot project. *Journal of Management Development, 6*, 34–46.

Grouzet, F. M., Kasser, T., Ahuvia, A., Dols, J. M. F., Kim, Y., Lau, S., & Sheldon, K. M. (2005). The structure of goal contents across 15 cultures. *Journal of Personality and Social Psychology, 89*(5), 800–816.

Gu, F., & Nolan, J. (2017). Performance appraisal in Western and local banks in China: The influence of firm ownership on the perceived importance of guanxi. *The International Journal of Human Resource Management, 28*(10), 1433–1453.

Gu, F., Nolan, J., & Rowley, C. (2020). Organizational justice in Chinese banks: Understanding the variable influence of guanxi on perceptions of fairness in performance appraisal. *Asia Pacific Business Review, 26*(2), 169–189.

Harbi, S. A., Thursfield, D., & Bright, D. (2017). Culture, wasta and perceptions of performance appraisal in Saudi Arabia. *The International Journal of Human Resource Management, 28*(19), 1–19.

He, W., Chen, C. C., & Zhang, L. (2004). Rewards-allocation preferences of Chinese employees in the new millennium: The effects of ownership reform, collectivism, and goal priority. *Organization Science, 15*(2), 221–231.

Heine, S. J., & Raineri, A. (2009). Self-improving motivations and collectivism: The case of Chileans. *Journal of Cross-Cultural Psychology, 40*(1), 158–163.

House, R. J., Hanges, P. J., Javidan, M., Dorfman, P. W., & Gupta, V. (2004). *Culture, leadership, and organizations: The GLOBE study of 62 societies*. Thousand Oaks, CA: SAGE.

Hundley, G., & Kim, J. (1997). National culture and the factors affecting perceptions of pay fairness in Korea and the United States. *International Journal of Organizational Analysis, 5*(4), 325–341.

Hutchings, K., & Weir, D. (2006). Understanding networking in China and the Arab world: Lessons for international managers. *Journal of European Industrial Training, 30*, 272–290.

Hysom, S. J., & Fisek, M. H. (2011). Situational determinants of reward allocation: The equity–equality equilibrium model. *Social Science Research, 40*(4), 1263–1285.

Jackson, T. A., Meyer, J. P., & Wang, X. H. (2013). Leadership, commitment, and culture: A meta-analysis. *Journal of Leadership & Organizational Studies, 20*(1), 84–106.

Kabasakal, H., & Bodur, M. (1998). Leadership, values and Institutions: The case of Turkey, research paper. Istanbul, Turkey: Boğaziçi University.

Karakulak, A., Shelia, S., Baskurt, B., Koseoglu, G., & Aycan, Z. (2019). Worries about leadership: Is it a liability or advantage in leadership emergence for women and men? Paper presented at SIOP Symposium, Washington, DC.

Keles, S., & Aycan, Z. (2011). The relationship of managerial values and assumptions with performance management in Turkey: Understanding within culture variability. *The International Journal of Human Resource Management, 22*(15), 3080–3096.

Knight, R. (2020). How to do performance reviews remotely. *Harvard Business Review*, 1–9. https://hbr.org/2020/06/how-to-do-performance-reviews-remotely

Kung, F. Y., Kim, Y. H., Yang, D. Y. J., & Cheng, S. Y. (2016). The role of regulatory fit in framing effective negative feedback across cultures. *Journal of Cross-Cultural Psychology, 47*(5), 696–712.

Lam, S. S., Yik, M. S., & Schaubroeck, J. (2002). Responses to formal performance appraisal feedback: The role of negative affectivity. *Journal of Applied Psychology, 87*(1), 192–201.

Latham, G. P., Erez, M., & Locke, E. A. (1988). Resolving scientific disputes by the joint design of crucial experiments by the antagonists: Application to the Erez–Latham dispute regarding participation in goal setting. *Journal of Applied Psychology, 73*(4), 753–772.

Lawrence, J. S., Crocker, J., & Blanton, H. (2011). Stigmatized and dominant cultural groups differentially interpret positive feedback. *Journal of Cross-Cultural Psychology, 42*(1), 165–169.

Lazarova, M., Peretz, H., & Fried, Y. (2017). Locals know best? Subsidiary HR autonomy and subsidiary performance. *Journal of World Business, 52*(1), 83–96.

Leung, K. (1997). Negotiation and reward allocations across cultures. In P. C. Earley & M. Erez (Eds.), *New perspectives on international industrial/organizational psychology* (pp. 640–675). San Francisco: The New Lexington Press/Jossey-Bass Publishers.

Leung, A. K. Y., Kim, Y. H., Zhang, Z. X., Tam, K. P., & Chiu, C. Y. (2012). Cultural construction of success and epistemic motives moderate American-Chinese differences in reward allocation biases. *Journal of Cross-Cultural Psychology, 43*(1), 46–52.

Levy, P. E., Tseng, S. T., Rosen, C. C., & Lueke, S. B. (2017). Performance management: A marriage between practice and science—just say "I do". *Research in Personnel and Human Resources Management, 35*, 155–213.

Locke, E. A., & Latham, G. P. (1984). *Goal setting: A motivational technique that works!* Englewood Cliffs, NJ: Prentice-Hall.

London, M. (2004). *Job feedback: Giving, seeking, and using feedback for performance improvement* (2nd ed.). Mahwah, NJ: Lawrence Erlbaum.

Lowe, K. B., Milliman, J., De Cieri, H., & Dowling, P. J. (2002). International compensation practices: A ten-country comparative analysis. *Human Resource Management: Published in Cooperation with the School of Business Administration, The University of Michigan and in alliance with the Society of Human Resources Management, 41*(1), 45–66.

Magnusson, P., Peterson, R., & Westjohn, S. A. (2014). The influence of national cultural values on the use of rewards alignment to improve sales collaboration. *International Marketing Review, 31*(1), 30–50.

Miller, J. S., Hom, P. W., & Gomez-Mejia, L. R. (2001). The high cost of low wages: Does maquiladora compensation reduce turnover? *Journal of International Business Studies, 32*(3), 585–595.

Mishra, V., & Roch, S. G. (2013). Cultural values and performance appraisal: Assessing the effects of rater self-construal on performance ratings. *The Journal of Psychology, 147*(4), 325–344.

Morrison, E. W., Chen, Y. R., & Salgado, S. R. (2004). Cultural differences in newcomer feedback seeking: A comparison of the United States and Hong Kong. *Applied Psychology, 53*(1), 1–22.

Murphy, K. R. (2020). Performance evaluation will not die, but it should. *Human Resource Management Journal, 30*(1), 13–31.

Ng, K. Y., Koh, C., Ang, S., Kennedy, J. C., & Chan, K. Y. (2011). Rating leniency and halo in multisource feedback ratings: Testing cultural assumptions of power distance and individualism-collectivism. *Journal of Applied Psychology, 96*(5), 1033–1044.

Nolan, J. (2011). Good guanxi and bad guanxi: Western bankers and the role of network practices in institutional change in China. *The International Journal of Human Resource Management, 22*, 3357–3372.

Nolan, J. (2015). Guanxi. In T. Wright (Ed.), *Oxford bibliographies in Chinese studies*. New York: Oxford University Press. https://www.oxfordbibliographies.com/display/document/obo-9780199920082/obo-9780199920082-0115.xml?rskey=ZgMPVV&result=75

Peretz, H., & Fried, Y. (2012). National cultures, performance appraisal practices, and organizational absenteeism and turnover: A study across 21 countries. *Journal of Applied Psychology, 97*(2), 448–459.

Poor, J., Kovács, I. E., Mack, A., Poutsma, E., & Ligthart, P. (2017). Compensation benefits 2014–2015. *Cranet Survey on Comparative Human Resource Management. International Executive Report 2017*, 1–129. https://www.fdv.uni-lj.si/docs/default-source/cpocv-doc/cranet-international-report-2017.pdf?sfvrsn=4

Punnett, B. J. (2004). *International perspectives on organizational behavior and human resource management*. Armonk, NY: M. E. Sharpe.

Rosenzweig, P. M., & Nohria, N. (1994). Influences on human resource management practices in multinational corporations. *Journal of International Business Studies, 25*(2), 229–251.

Rotundo, M., & Xie, J. L. (2008). Understanding the domain of counterproductive work behaviour in China. *The International Journal of Human Resource Management, 19*(5), 856–877.

Sagie, A., & Aycan, Z. (2003). A cross-cultural analysis of participative decision-making in organizations. *Human Relations, 56*(4), 453–473.

Sama, L. M., & Papamarcos, S. D. (2000). Hofstede's IC dimension as predictive of allocative behaviors: A meta-analysis. *International Journal of Value-Based Management, 13*(2), 173–188.

Savani, K., Morris, M. W., & Naidu, N. V. R. (2012). Deference in Indians' decision making: Introjected goals or injunctive norms? *Journal of Personality and Social Psychology, 102*(4), 685–699.

Schuler, R. S., & Rogovsky, N. (1998). Understanding compensation practice variations across firms: The impact of national culture. *Journal of International Business Studies*, 29(1), 159–177.

Scott, K. (2017). *Radical candor: How to get what you want by saying what you mean*. New York: Macmillan.

Shipper, F., Hoffman, R. C., & Rotondo, D. M. (2007). Does the 360 feedback process create actionable knowledge equally across cultures? *Academy of Management Learning & Education, 6*(1), 33–50.

Silva, M. R., & Caetano, A. (2016). Organizational justice across cultures: A systematic review of four decades of research and some directions for the future. *Social Justice Research, 29*(3), 2.

Smith, P. B., Torres, C., Leong, C. H., Budhwar, P., Achoui, M., & Lebedeva, N. (2012). Are indigenous approaches to achieving influence in business organizations distinctive? A comparative study of Guanxi, Wasta, Jeitinho, Svyazi and Pulling Strings. *The International Journal of Human Resource Management, 23*, 333–348.

Sue-Chan, C., & Ong, M. (2002). Goal assignment and performance: Assessing the mediating roles of goal commitment and self-efficacy and the moderating role of power distance. *Organizational Behavior and Human Decision Processes, 89*(2), 1140–1161.

Sumelius, J., Björkman Ingmar, Ehrnrooth, M., Mäkelä Kristiina, & Smale, A. (2014). What determines employee perceptions of HRM process features? The case of performance appraisal in MNC subsidiaries. *Human Resource Management, 53*(4), 569–592.

Triandis, H. C. (1994). *Cross-cultural industrial and organizational psychology*. In H. C. Triandis, M. D. Dunnette, & L. M. Hough (Eds.), *Handbook of industrial and organizational psychology* (pp. 103–172). Washington, DC: Consulting Psychologists Press.

Trompenaars, F. (1993). *Riding the waves of culture*. London: The Economist Books.

Tsai, J. L., Miao, F. F., Seppala, E., Fung, H. H., & Yeung, D. Y. (2007). Influence and adjustment goals: Sources of cultural differences in ideal affect. *Journal of Personality and Social Psychology, 92*(6), 1102–1117.

Vallance, S. (1999). Performance appraisal in Singapore, Thailand and the Philippines: A cultural perspective. *Australian Journal of Public Administration, 58*(4), 78–95.

Van Dijk, D., & Kluger, A. N. (2011). Task type as a moderator of positive/negative feedback effects on motivation and performance: A regulatory focus perspective. *Journal of Organizational Behavior, 32*(8), 1084–1105.

VandeWalle, D., Cron, W. L., & Slocum, J. W., Jr. (2001). The role of goal orientation following performance feedback. *Journal of Applied Psychology, 86*(4), 629–640.

Varela, O. E., & Premeaux, S. F. (2008). Do cross-cultural values affect multisource feedback dynamics? The case of high power distance and collectivism in two Latin American countries. *International Journal of Selection and Assessment, 16*(2), 134–142.

Varma, A., Budhwar, P. S., & DeNisi, A. S. (Eds.). (2008). *Performance management systems: A global perspective*. Abingdon, UK: Routledge.

Vo, A., & Stanton, P. (2011). The transfer of HRM policies and practices to a transitional business system: The case of performance management practices in the US and Japanese MNEs operating in Vietnam. *International Journal of Human Resource Management, 22*(17), 3513–3527.

Wheeler, K. G. (2002). Cultural values in relation to equity sensitivity within and across cultures. *Journal of Managerial Psychology, 17*, 612–627.

Wiersma, U. J., ^& Van Der Berg, P. T. (1999). Influences and trends in human resource practices in the Netherlands. *Employee Relations, 21*(1–2), 63–80.

Yamazaki, Y., & Yoon, J. (2016). A cross-national study of fairness in Asia: How perceptions of a lack-of-group bias and transparency in the performance evaluation system relate to job satisfaction. *Human Resource Management, 55*(6), 1059–1077.

Zheng, X., Li, N., Brad Harris, T., & Liao, H. (2019). Unspoken yet understood: An introduction and initial framework of subordinates' moqi with supervisors. *Journal of Management, 45*(3), 955–983.

PART III

Culture and Individual Behavior in Organizations

CHAPTER 7

The Study of Work Motivation across Cultures: A Review and Directions for Future Research

Gilad Chen *and* Bradley L. Kirkman

Abstract

Despite decades of scholarly attention to theories of motivation, relatively little focus has been placed on cultural differences in motivation theories and constructs. To address this problem, we selectively review the motivation literature, focusing on theories and concepts involving goal-related processes and their antecedents. We then review research examining the main and moderating effects of national culture at individual and collective (i.e., team, organizational, national) levels of analysis. We offer five theoretical insights: (1) Motivation involves many complex, interrelated processes; (2) cultural differences affect various motivational processes and outcomes in distinct ways; (3) individualism–collectivism and power distance have dominated attention related to motivation compared to other cultural values; (4) cultural differences are not well integrated with comprehensive motivation models; and (5) there is a pressing need to better understand both cultural influences on self-regulation (i.e., goal-striving) processes and the role of collective-level cultural differences in motivational processes.

Key Words: motivation, culture, values, goal choice, goal striving, motivational states, levels of analysis

Scholars and practitioners have long been interested in the topic of work motivation, broadly defined as "a psychological process that influences how personal effort and resources are allocated to actions pertaining to work, including the direction, intensity, and persistence of these actions" (Kanfer et al., 2008, p. 5). There is now ample evidence that motivation constructs and processes explain individual as well as team differences in important work and career outcomes, ranging from attitudes and critical employee behaviors and performance to career success (for recent reviews, see Kanfer & Chen, 2016; Kanfer et al., 2008, 2017). However, as reviews of the literature attest, research on motivation in various social, work, and organizational settings has also led to a plethora of constructs and theories, with diverse focus on the meaning and function of motivational processes and constructs. In addition, less attention has been paid to how work motivation theories and research can be applied in different national cultural settings worldwide and how cultural differences impact motivation processes, necessitating a need for integrating motivation and culture research.

Based on this limitation and building on Kanfer and her colleagues' (Kanfer & Chen, 2016; Kanfer et al., 2008, 2017) organization of the literature, we briefly summarize the literature on work motivation and highlight core individual-level motivational constructs and theories. We specifically discuss theories and concepts involving goal-related processes (including goal choice and goal striving, which also capture behavioral and performance outcomes), and then we consider antecedents of goal processes. Following this brief review, we discuss various ways national cultural differences can impact work motivation processes and outcomes, as well how further integrating the motivation and cross-cultural management/psychology literatures can help advance both lines of research. As we will point out, the motivational framework and extant literature highlight multiple areas in which national cultural differences can impact important motivational processes and resulting behavioral and performance outcomes. Moreover, our review indicates areas where research gaps exist, and hence where additional research is needed to advance better understanding of national cultural influences on motivation in work settings.

Goal Choice

Goal choice involves the process by which individuals determine the direction, or courses of action, to which to direct their effort, including setting task-related goals and strategies for accomplishing those goals (Kanfer et al., 2008). The most widely studied theory of goal choice is goal-setting theory, developed by Locke and Latham (for reviews, see Locke & Latham, 1990, 2002). According to goal-setting theory, assignment of specific and difficult task goals enhances task performance by directing and sustaining effort and effort-related strategies toward task accomplishment. Although goal-setting research has shown that assigned goals have consistent positive effects on performance across a variety of tasks and settings, such positive effects have been shown to be more likely when individuals are (1) committed to a goal; (2) consider a goal important and relevant to their broader success; (3) believe they are capable of accomplishing a goal; and, (4) when tasks are less complex, better learned, and provide performance feedback to individuals (Kanfer & Ackerman, 1989; Latham et al., 1988; Locke & Latham, 2002).

Similar to goal-setting theory, theoretical and empirical work by Gollwitzer and his colleagues (e.g., 1990, 1999; Gollwitzer & Brandstatter, 1997; Gollwitzer et al., 1990) have theorized and shown that deliberate and conscious planning for action (i.e., involving goal and implementation intentions) can motivate and guide more successful goal pursuit and eventual performance. In addition, Kruglanski et al. (2015) have argued that goals, as desired future states, motivate behaviors toward that future state and lead to its attainment when the effort can overcome potential obstacles (e.g., competing goals, insufficient resources), and the desired state is something an individual wants, and not just likes (i.e., when the goal is something that is needed and desired). Thus, goal theories share the perspective that explicit, desirable goals divert and dedicate effort toward goal accomplishment.

Moving beyond Locke and Latham's goal-setting theory, Gollwitzer and Kruglanski's work cited earlier also emphasizes the importance of goal mindsets, or how individuals frame the goals they set. There is a voluminous literature on goal orientation, originating largely in Carol Dweck's research on mastery/learning versus performance goal orientation in educational and learning settings (Dweck, 1986). In this literature, individuals frame goals as opportunities to learn or master certain task domains and/or as opportunities to demonstrate competent performance on certain task domains. In later work, the literature proposed that these two goal orientations (i.e., learning and performance) can further capture approach and avoidance dimensions (i.e., "performance-prove" vs. "performance-avoid"), as well as trait-like (i.e., domain-generic and enduring) and state-like (i.e., domain-specific and malleable) attributes (for a review and integration, see DeShon & Gillespie, 2005). Goals, as most often conceptualized and operationalized in the goal-setting literature, focus mainly on task-specific, performance-approach goals. However, the literature on goal orientation also suggests that goals can differ more broadly in orienting individuals toward mastering or learning a task, as well as performing a task, approaching or avoiding certain tasks, and even as more enduring personal orientations that transcend specific task domains. Still, common to these literatures is the notion that goals help energize, direct, and guide individual task-related efforts and, ultimately, performance.

Goal Striving

Goal striving involves the process of engaging in the actual accomplishment of goals, which includes the regulation of cognitive, affective, and physical effort in goal pursuit, as well as processes involving changes and revisions made to goals and prioritization of effort across multiple goals (Kanfer et al., 2008; Lord et al., 2010; Neal et al., 2017). That is, while goal choice reflects the deliberate process of determining the direction of effort, goal-striving processes reflect more dynamic processes through which individuals allocate efforts toward goal accomplishment, revision, and/or prioritization.

Perhaps the most influential theory of goal striving is control theory (Carver & Scheier, 1982, 1998; Powers 1973). According to this theory, individuals are motivated to create an equilibrium between a desired state (e.g., a referent point, goal) and their input or effort directed toward that desired state. Individuals allocate efforts toward a target goal, and then once that goal is met, they reduce efforts toward that goal and/or divert their effort toward other goals. Likewise, over time, individuals re-divert effort toward goals when they perceive a discrepancy between where they stand relative to a goal. Control theory also proposes that the cycle of regulating effort toward goals can occur relative to referents residing at different levels of abstraction, generality, and time frames (e.g., it can operate over several years at the level of wanting to pursue certain career goals, as well as over milliseconds at the level of returning incoming balls in a tennis match; Lord et al., 2010). Control theory has led to informative research on how individuals regulate their effort across tasks when pursuing multiple goals simultaneously. This research has shown that individuals prioritize allocation of efforts toward goals under certain conditions, such as when (1) they are more likely and are closer to accomplish a goal, (2) goals are more important or otherwise satisfy stronger personal needs, and (3) deadlines for goal accomplishment are near (for reviews, see Lord et al., 2010; Neal et al., 2017).

Another important theory of goal striving is ego depletion theory (Baumeister et al., 1998), according to which individuals allocate personal resources not only toward goal accomplishment but also toward self-control (i.e., controlling disruptive emotions or thoughts that interfere with task engagement and accomplishment). For example, managers could find it more difficult to convey performance feedback successfully for an employee with whom they are angry, as controlling their anger toward their employee requires additional personal resources. Ego depletion theory argues that successful allocation of effort (and hence goal accomplishment) is more likely when one has access to more personal resources, such as when self-control requirements are lower. Supporting these theoretical ideas is research showing that individuals acted more ethically (Gino et al., 2011) and exerted more effort at work toward their goals (Lanaj et al., 2014) when self-control requirements were lower. However, meta-analyses have produced mixed support for this theory (see Hagger et al., 2010; Carter et al., 2015). In addition, Inzlicht et al. (2014) have argued that more research is needed to delineate possible moderators and boundary conditions for ego depletion effects.

A third stream of goal-striving research was stimulated by regulatory focus theory (Higgins, 1997, 2000). According to this theory, when pursuing goals, individuals adopt or focus on promotion or prevention strategies. When adopting a promotion strategy, individuals focus on maximizing gains and tend to work more quickly or complete a greater quantity of work. In adopting a prevention strategy, individuals focus on minimizing losses (or nongains) and act more vigilantly to enhance the quality and accuracy of their work. As Brockner and Higgins (2001) noted, promotion focus links goal-striving strategies to one's ideal self (i.e., focusing effort toward growth and development), whereas prevention focus links goal-striving strategies to one's ought self (i.e., focusing effort toward meeting duties and responsibilities). In line with these conceptual distinctions, Lanaj et al.'s (2012) meta-analysis found that promotion focus relates more positively to innovative performance than prevention focus, whereas prevention focus relates more positively to safety performance than promotion focus.

Integrative Models of Goal Processes

Collectively, theories of, and research on, goal choice and goal striving provide a basis for understanding the allocation of effort in pursuit of task goals and, hence, task performance. Moving beyond these theories, we find that other theories have sought to provide a more complete, integrative picture of why and how individuals direct and regulate task-related effort. These theories not only integrate principles of goal choice and goal striving, but also emphasize the importance of individuals' affective and cognitive reactions to their task environment in terms of assessing their capabilities and likelihood of handling tasks successfully, as well as reacting to task feedback as they pursue goals. In fact, theories of goal choice at least assume that goals impact performance through regulation of effort (Locke & Latham, 2002). Most theories of goal striving explicitly point out that individuals regulate their effort vis-a-vis personal goals. However, integrative models of goal processes go further in more fully articulating the interconnectedness not only between goal choice and goal striving processes, but also individual differences in abilities and conceptions of one's performance contexts.

In one influential integrative model—the resource allocation model—Kanfer and Ackerman (1989) sought to integrate goal processes (i.e., one's resource allocation processes), ability (i.e., one's resource capacity), and more proximal cognitive and emotional reactions as a function of goal pursuit. In testing their model, Kanfer and Ackerman found that (1) setting difficult performance goals promotes improved self-regulation processes and performance to a greater extent during later phases of skill acquisition (i.e., when the task is more, versus less, well-learned); (2) individual differences in ability moderate this pattern, such that individuals with greater cognitive abilities suffer less from performance goals at earlier stages of skill acquisition; and (3) attentional resources (i.e., higher task-related focus and lower negative and disruptive emotional reactions) help explain different effects of assigned goals on goal pursuit and performance. Overall, these findings indicate that self-regulation of effort in pursuit of goals requires attentional resources, which are more available when individuals perform well-learned tasks and/or have greater attentional resources (i.e., higher mental abilities).

In another integrative model—the multiple-goal pursuit model—Ballard et al. (2016) specified how individuals regulate effort in pursuit of simultaneous (i.e., multiple) goals. Their model examined how regulation of goal-directed effort depends first on the type of goal being pursued, and specifically, whether individuals pursue approach goals, such as meeting higher productivity targets, and/or shift their focus toward avoidance goals, such as minimizing safety incidents. Their model proposes that choosing between multiple different goals depends not only on the type of goal pursued (i.e., approach vs. avoidance), but also on how goal prioritization differs as a function of perceived risk and time sensitivity. Using multiple simulations, Ballard et al. (2016) found that, in general, individuals prioritize approach goals initially, but over time shift to prioritize avoidance goals. Individuals who simultaneously pursue two approach goals tended to focus on goals that require more effort (i.e., are further from being achieved), unless goals that are closer to being achieved have a looming deadline. This trend was more pronounced when they viewed both approach goals as less risky (i.e., when goal accomplishment is more certain). In contrast, those simultaneously pursuing two avoidance goals prioritized the goal that required less effort, regardless of perceived risk or accomplishment certainty. As a whole, Ballard et al.'s model indicates that goal framing interacts with deadlines and risk/certainty to influence how individuals prioritize their goal-directed effort across multiple goal pursuits.

Collectively, these and other integrative models of goal choice and goal striving indicate that goal-related processes are complex and interrelated, and they occur as part of a broader context. Specifically, individuals differ on various attributes that predispose them to value and prefer different goals, equip them with varying levels of ability required for certain goal accomplishment, and affect how they conceive of their own abilities and behavioral choices vis-a-vis the environment in which they operate. Likewise, the situations or contexts within which individuals pursue their goals impact goal choice and regulation of effort in goal pursuit, such as features that could constrain/limit or rather offer necessary encouragement and resources needed to achieve certain goals (e.g., Kanfer et al., 2017). As such, in the next section, we discuss various proximal (i.e., more direct) and distal (i.e., less direct) individual and contextual antecedents that have been shown to influence goal processes.

Antecedents of Goal Processes

Motivational States. As discussed in reviews of the motivation literature (e.g., Kanfer et al., 2017; Kanfer & Chen, 2016), the most proximal antecedents of goal choice and goal striving include motivational states, which broadly capture individuals' perceptions of their capability to be agentic and successfully pursue goals in a given task environment (Chen & Kanfer, 2006). Perhaps the most widely studied motivational state is self-efficacy, or individuals' belief in their capability to accomplish certain performance tasks (Bandura, 1997). According to Bandura's social cognitive theory, self-efficacy motivates individuals to pursue more challenging task goals and to persist in their effort to pursue such goals. Although there is ample evidence for the positive motivational influences of self-efficacy on task performance (e.g., Stajkovic & Luthans, 1998), some have argued that—over multiple performance engagements—self-efficacy can also negatively relate to subsequent effort and performance (Vancouver & Kendall, 2006). Specifically, building on control theory, Vancouver and colleagues attributed the negative effect of self-efficacy to the notion that more highly efficacious individuals believe that they have already performed at a desired level, relative to their aspiration level or goal, and hence allocate less effort during subsequent goal pursuit episodes (leading to lower performance). However, more recent evidence suggests that self-efficacy more positively relates to effort and performance when working on tasks that have clearer (i.e., less ambiguous) feedback regarding how one is doing on that task (Schmidt & DeShon, 2010). This suggests that those with higher efficacy still allocate greater effort in pursuit of goals when they are able to have a more accurate assessment of how well they do relative to their goals.

Building on social cognitive theory and integrating it with other theories, such as self-determination theory (Deci & Ryan, 1985), Thomas and Velthouse (1990) delineated the concept of psychological empowerment. Psychological empowerment captures four conceptually related motivational states, including *competence* (i.e., self-efficacy), *autonomy* (i.e., extent to which individuals can self-determine when and how they get their work done), *meaning* (i.e., extent to which individuals find their work intrinsically meaningful), and *impact* (i.e., extent to which individuals believe their work influences work unit or organizational outcomes). In line with theorizing regarding its component states, and regarding the overall psychological empowerment construct, Seibert et al.'s (2011) meta-analysis found that the four empowerment dimensions are highly related and similarly promote positive organizational behaviors (e.g., proactivity, citizenship). Collectively, this research indicates that individuals who have more favorable views of their capabilities to perform meaningful and impactful work are more likely to pursue and accomplish more challenging task goals.

Individual Differences. Early motivation research has focused on individual differences in needs, or the extent to which individuals are motivated to behave in ways that satisfy basic needs, such as safety and growth (e.g., Maslow, 1943; Alderfer, 1969). With developments in both motivation and personality theories, the focus in the motivation literature has shifted toward capturing individual differences in motivational tendencies or traits. According to Kanfer and Heggestad's (1997) extensive review of this literature, individual differences in motivational traits can be broadly classified as either achievement or anxiety traits. Achievement traits are approach-oriented, capturing tendencies to pursue more challenging goals that can either demonstrate existing competencies or master new ones and trigger efforts in pursuit of such goals. In contrast, anxiety traits are more avoidant-oriented and capture negative emotional reactions with regard to task pursuit (e.g., they divert attention away from task accomplishment, such as by worrying about failing on certain tasks).

Importantly, these two broad trait clusters—achievement and anxiety—also correspond to the type of goal orientations one adopts (i.e., learning, performance, and avoidant orientations), as well as the regulatory focus (i.e., promotion or prevention) one is predisposed to choose (Kanfer et al., 2017). Goal orientation and regulatory focus have been examined not only as states or midrange orientations, but also as stable, personality-like traits (Johnson et al., 2006; Payne et al., 2007). Further, the distinction between approach/achievement and avoidant/anxiety motivation helps explain differences in how individuals evaluate themselves, such as how they assess their capabilities and worth in general, across tasks and settings (Chang et al., 2012; Chen et al., 2004).

As Barrick et al. (2013) summarized, the literature has also identified individual differences in the type of motives or goals individuals strive to pursue at work, such as gaining affiliative or communion goals, acquiring power and status, attaining more independence or autonomy, and realizing personal growth and achievement. As we explain below, these types of goal striving could help identify how individual differences in cultural values impact various aspects of the goals individuals pursue. In particular, cultural differences are associated with differences in the types of goals and task pursuits individuals value and care about.

Contextual Antecedents. Finally, in addition to proximal influences of motivational states and more distal influences of individual difference traits, values, and motives, the actual environmental or contextual features within which individuals pursue their goals also impact goal processes. The literature has specifically identified differences in work design, team contexts, leader behaviors, and organizational climate and cultures as powerful antecedents of individual motivation, both through their impact on proximal motivational states and their direct impact of goal-directed behaviors.

From early theories of job design to more recent ones that focus on the nature of work requirements (for a review, see Parker et al., 2017), the work design literature has identified various ways in which work requirements impact goal choice and goal-striving processes, in part due to their impact on proximal motivational states. For example, building on principles from Hackman and Oldham's (1976) job characteristics model, Grant (2008) found support for the relational theory of job design by showing that enhancing fundraisers' task significance (by showing them the actual impact the money they raised had on scholarship recipients) led to greater effort and even more money raised. There is also evidence that jobs designed to provide employees with greater autonomy and more opportunity to make an impact in their organizations motivate employees to work harder, in part due to enhancing their level of psychological empowerment (Parker et al., 2017; Seibert et al., 2011).

There are also rich literatures on teams (Mathieu et al., 2017) and leadership (Lord et al., 2017) in organizations highlighting the profound impact of social influence on employee motivation. Given that interdependent teams capture the most immediate social context within which a significant amount of today's work takes place, it is not surprising that it is in teams where leaders and teammates exert motivational influences on individuals (Chen & Kanfer, 2006). For example, a study by Kark, Shamir, and Chen (2003) found that transformational leaders influence the extent to which members identify with team goals (which leads them to feel more psychologically empowered), but also with their leader's goals (which creates dependence on their leader). Kirkman and Rosen (1999) identified a set of leader empowering behaviors that motivate members of the leader's team to improve performance, as mediated by their collective sense of psychological empowerment. Chen and Kanfer (2006) delineated a systems-based theory of motivation in and of teams, according to which leaders and teams impact individual goal choice and goal striving processes both directly and through the development of team-level goal processes. For example, Chen et al. (2009) found that individual goal striving (i.e., task-directed effort and, ultimately, performance) in teams was positively influenced by individuals' self-efficacy beliefs and their team's engagement in coordinated goal striving processes.

Finally, at a broader level, contextual differences in culture and climate can also exert influences on employee motivation. Culture captures the shared beliefs, values, and assumptions in a unit (e.g., team, organization), whereas climate captures the enactment of policies and procedures (for reviews, see Ostroff et al., 2013; Schneider et al., 2017). Although organizational culture is distinct from national culture, the two share some attributes (e.g., capturing core beliefs and norms that guide behaviors) and content (e.g., capturing differences in how much relationships among people and power differentials are valued). According to Ostroff et al. (2013), organizational culture provides a foundational basis for other contextual features representing an organization, including its strategies, leadership structures, and climate. Climate, in turn, has been shown to exert more direct influences on motivational outcomes. For example, Wallace and Chen (2006) found that work units' safety climate (i.e., the extent to which unit leaders reinforced safety rules and procedures) positively related to employees' prevention focus and negatively related to employees' promotion focus. In turn, employees' promotion (prevention) focus positively (negatively) related to employee productivity and negatively (positively) related to employee safety behaviors.

Cultural Influences on Goal Processes

The review of the literature above indicates that motivation at work can be captured by two inter-related goal processes (i.e., goal choice and goal striving), which capture the direction, intensity, and persistence of effort across tasks and over time. However, these processes do not occur in a vacuum; rather, they operate and are affected by individual attributes (including motivational states and more distal individual differences) and the social and technical context within which individuals work. In line with this broad framework of motivation, individual differences in national cultural values and cultural variation at the collective level (i.e., team, organization, or nation) have been shown to impact motivational outcomes (for reviews, see Erez, 2018; Gelfand et al., 2007, 2017; Kirkman et al., 2006, 2017; Taras et al., 2010).

As we noted in our introduction, one key limitation of the motivation literature is that the majority of work motivation theories and research to date have been developed and tested in Western cultures. For example, as highlighted by Erez (2010), the job design literature has adopted a mostly individualistic perspective. In contrast, Erez noted that in more collectivistic societies, job designs such as quality circles in Japan or sociotechnical groups in Scandinavia have also been found to motivate effective work behaviors. Indeed, constructs developed in Western societies can neglect or leave out important features salient in other societal cultures (e.g., Farh et al., 1997). If constructs are universally supported across cultures, they are typically referred to as etic, whereas constructs that are culture-dependent or specific are referred to as emic (Morris et al., 1993). Accordingly,

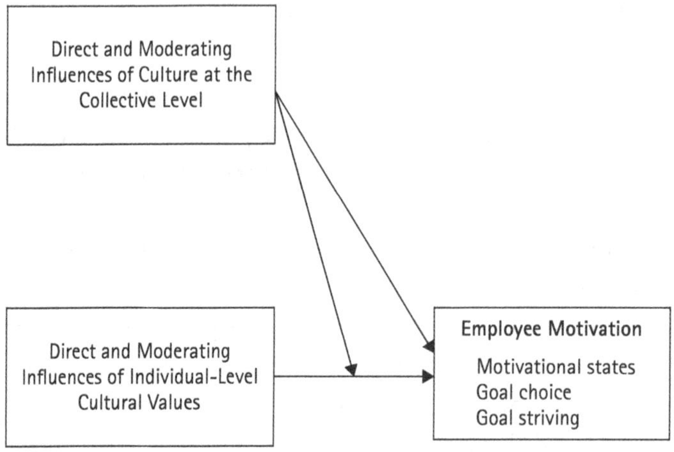

Figure 7.1. An integrative framework for studying cultural influences on work motivation.

in the next sections, we provide a selective review of specific evidence for cultural influences on motivational outcomes, including direct and moderating effects of individual-level cultural values and collective-level cultural differences. Figure 7.1 summarizes the broader framework delineated in the sections that follow, starting with direct and moderating influences of individual-level cultural values on individual-level motivation, and then moving to direct and moderating influences of culture at the collective (e.g., team or national) level on individual-level motivational processes.

Direct Effects of Individual Cultural Values

At the individual level, cultural values serve as an internal moral compass of how individuals should behave and interact in social and societal contexts (Hofstede, 1980; Kirkman et al., 2006, 2017). Individual cultural values include individualism–collectivism (i.e., the extent to which individual choice and accountability are emphasized in contrast to group needs, goals, and accountability; Stackhouse et al., 2018), power distance (i.e., the extent to which power is structured and ordered versus equally distributed and egalitarian, Stackhouse et al., 2018) and uncertainty avoidance (i.e., the extent to which a society feels threatened by uncertain and ambiguous situations and tries to avoid these situations by providing greater career stability and more formal rules and not tolerating deviant ideas and behaviors, Stackhouse et al., 2018), among others. As Gelfand et al. (2007, 2017) summarized, individuals' cultural values develop as a function of being socialized into one's society, as individuals learn from their parents, educators, and their broader society about behavioral norms and other societal expectations in social interactions. Similar to other individual differences (e.g., motivational traits), scholars have theorized and empirically found evidence that individual differences in cultural values can relate to goal-related processes, as well as to proximal motivational states. Of note,

Kirkman et al.'s (2006) review indicated that studies on cultural values have sometimes measured cultural values at the individual level directly (i.e., primary studies), and other times have compared relevant country differences (e.g., Americans vs. Japanese, who differ on such cultural values as power distance and individualism–collectivism) as proxies for individual differences in cultural values (i.e., secondary studies). For our purposes, we reviewed studies using both approaches. However, the validity of studies directly measuring individual-level cultural values is clearly higher, as country differences confound multiple cultural differences as well as noncultural variables (Kirkman et al., 2006; Taras et al., 2010).

Literature reviews indicate that individualism–collectivism has been the most widely studied cultural value, particularly with respect to motivational outcomes (Kirkman et al., 2006, 2017; Taras et al., 2010). For example, Jackson et al. (2006) suggested that collectivism is related to pursuing prosocial goals. Further, they showed that individuals higher on collectivism were more likely to help others (by engaging in more organizational citizenship behaviors) and less likely to harm others (by engaging in fewer counterproductive work behaviors). Taras et al.'s (2010) meta-analysis confirmed that those higher in collectivism were more likely to display organizational citizenship behaviors and help others and less likely to self-promote. Similarly, Chen et al. (2011) found that collectivism is positively related to individual motivation in teams, as reflected by positive relationships with team members' psychological empowerment, and in turn behaviors that contribute to team effectiveness. In addition, Lee et al. (2000) found that collectivism was positively related to prevention regulatory focus and negatively related to promotion regulatory focus.

Although less studied relative to collectivism, other cultural values can be expected to also impact motivational outcomes. For example, individuals higher on power distance are more likely to be motivated by goals assigned by superiors, as compared with self-set goals (cf. Erez, 2018). Indeed, Kirkman and Shapiro (2001a) found that those higher in power distance resisted working autonomously more so than those lower in power distance. Aycan et al. (2000) also found that managers were more reluctant to empower subordinates in high-power distance countries. These results indicate that, broadly, individuals higher on power distance are less motivated to satisfy autonomous needs and more motivated by top-down (as opposed to flatter) motivational interventions.

Uncertainty avoidance could also affect the manner in which individuals regulate their effort in pursuit of multiple goals, which in part is affected by the extent to which pursuing one goal over another involves risk (Ballard et al., 2016). Regarding motivational outcomes in teams, Taras et al. (2010) found that those higher in uncertainty avoidance also had higher levels of team commitment and preferences for teamwork—presumably because strong ties to a team and its members offer individuals more certainty and assurance regarding the future.

Moderating Effects of Individual Cultural Values

Researchers have also found evidence that cultural values moderate relationships involving individual-level motivational processes. Dorfman and Howell (1988) showed that directive leadership styles were more motivating for those followers who held more collectivistic values. Jung and Avolio (1999) found that collectivists generated more ideas in an experimental task when working under transformational, rather than transactional, leaders. In addition, individualists generated more ideas when working with transactional, rather than transformational, leaders. Jung and Avolio explained these findings by theorizing that transactional leaders emphasize meeting individual goals, whereas transformational leaders emphasize more collective goals. Nouri et al. (2015) also found that more collectivist Chinese employees generated more creative ideas when working alone, rather than in the presence of their supervisors. In addition, Earley (1994) found that, among more individualistic U.S. participants, more self-focused training enhanced self-efficacy, effort, and performance to a greater extent than did group-focused training, but that the opposite was found among more collectivistic participants from China and Hong Kong. Lam et al. (2002) found that participative decision making more positively related to individual performance among more collectivistic employees. These findings all indicate that individuals higher on collectivism react more positively to motivational interventions that emphasize the group and encourage group members' participation and involvement in important work processes. Finally, examining the moderating effect of multiple cultural values on the relationship between job characteristics and job satisfaction across 31 nations, Hauff et al. (2015) found that the relationship between job security and satisfaction was stronger in nations having higher power distance and masculinity but lower uncertainty avoidance. They also found that the relationship between having an interesting job and job satisfaction was stronger for nations higher in individualism.

Power distance has also been shown to moderate motivation-related processes and interventions. For example, Eylon and Au (1999) found that an empowerment intervention during an in-basket managerial simulation more positively enhanced performance among individuals who were lower, rather than higher, in power distance. Similarly, Robert et al. (2000) found that empowerment had more positive effects on employees in moderately low-power distance countries (i.e., Mexico, Poland, and the United States) and more negative effects in high-power distance ones (i.e., India). Across three studies, Hui et al. (2003) found weaker relationships between empowerment and job satisfaction when respondents were higher, rather than lower, in power distance. In another study, Kirkman et al. (2009) showed that employees lower in power distance were more likely to respond positively to their leaders (by viewing their leader as fairer and subsequently engaging in more citizenship behaviors) when their leaders engaged in more transformational leadership, whereas employees higher in power distance reacted positively to their leaders regardless of their transformational leadership behaviors. Erez and Earley (1987) found that power distance influenced individuals' receptivity to goal type (i.e., assigned, representative, or participative), such that relationships between both participative and representative goal setting and performance were stronger for those lower, rather than higher, in power distance. Together these findings indicate that power distance can moderate motivational interventions, such that individuals lower in power distance are more likely to expect their leaders and organizations to empower them and treat them more fairly. More broadly, the studies summarized above indicate that individual differences in cultural values "pre-wire" individuals to respond to motivational interventions differently.

Contextual Effects of Collective-Level Cultural Differences

Like individual-level effects, culture at higher levels of analysis (e.g., teams, organizations, nations) can impact the motivational processes and outcomes of individuals and collectives directly and/or as moderators. At higher levels of analysis, one way in which culture can be meaningful is as the aggregate/mean level of lower-level values. Teams, organizations, and countries can differ in individualism–collectivism, power distance, and other cultural values not only by averaging individuals within them, but also by formal and social structures that reinforce the values (e.g., social and/or technical systems that promote group well-being, or centralization of authority and power among fewer leaders in a more hierarchical structure).

Another meaningful way in which culture manifests at higher levels is through tightness–looseness, which Gelfand et al. (2006, p. 1226) define as "the strength of social norms and the degree of sanctioning within societies." In tighter societies (e.g., India, Malaysia, Pakistan), societal institutions promote narrower socialization to cultural values and norms with more constraint and systems of monitoring and sanctioning behavior. In contrast, looser societies (e.g., Israel, Netherlands, Ukraine) promote broader socialization to cultural values and norms, with less constraint and monitoring and sanctioning behavior. In culturally tighter societies, individuals will have less flexibility in exhibiting their cultural value attributes compared to culturally looser ones. In effect, tighter cultures provide fewer "situational affordances" to variability in individual motivational processes and outcomes (cf. Chen & Kanfer, 2006).

Direct Effects of Collective Cultural Values

Similar to individual-level studies of culture and motivation, research at higher levels of analysis has also linked culture to motivational outcomes and processes. With regard to the direct effects of culture on motivation, Eby and Dobbins (1997) found that teams higher on collectivism exhibited more cooperation, and cooperation mediated the relationship between team collectivism and team performance. Kirkman and Shapiro (2001b) found that team collectivism was negatively related to resistance to teams and that resistance to teams mediated the relationships between team collectivism and team cooperation, empowerment, and productivity. In a meta-analysis, Stahl et al. (2010) examined the impact of cultural value diversity on various team outcomes, finding that team cultural value diversity was positively related to team creativity, individual member satisfaction, and team conflict, and negatively related to team social integration. At the firm level, Kreiser et al. (2010) found that individualism, power distance, and uncertainty avoidance were all negatively related to proactive behavior in small- to medium-sized enterprises.

Gelfand et al. (2006) also provided a useful conceptual framework for the main effects of cultural tightness–looseness, suggesting that tightness–looseness will have direct effects on (1) organizational context (e.g., risk, life stage, size, public vs. private sector), (2) psychological adaptations through felt accountability (e.g., decision-making styles, psychological differentiation, shared cognition), and (3) work organization adaptations (e.g., organizational culture and practices). Gelfand et al. (2011) supported several of these propositions. All of this research suggests that when teams, units, or organizations share a collective sense of culture, these shared cultural beliefs will have direct effects on motivational processes—that is, collectives, like individuals, rely on cultural values to guide their behaviors and responses to the environment in which they operate.

Moderating Effects of Collective Cultural Values

Researchers have also found evidence that collective cultural values moderate relationships involving higher-level motivational processes. For example, Erez and Somech (1996) conducted an experiment with Israeli managers from kibbutzim (i.e., higher collectivism) and urban cities (i.e., higher individualism), finding that the kibbutzim versus urban distinction moderated the relationship between both type of goal (i.e., individual vs. group) and incentive (i.e., individual vs. group) and group performance, such that group performance loss was less likely in kibbutzim versus urban groups. The highest level of group performance occurred in the kibbutzim groups with a group goal and group incentives. Gibson (1999) found that group collectivism moderated the relationship between group efficacy and group performance, such that they were positively related when group collectivism was high but not when it was low. Lam et al. (2002) found that collectivism moderated the relationship between participative decision-making opportunity and group performance, such that they were positively related for groups high, but not low, in collectivism. At the organization level of analysis, Chatman and Barsade (1995) found that individualistic–collectivistic organizational cultures moderated the relationship between personal cooperation and cooperative behavior. More cooperative subjects in collectivistic cultures demonstrated more cooperative behavior than cooperative subjects in the individualistic organizational culture, and also less cooperative subjects in either the individualistic or collectivistic organizational culture.

In addition, Schaubroeck et al. (2007) found that team power distance and team collectivism moderated the effect of transformational leadership on team potency, such that higher-power distance and more collectivistic teams exhibited stronger positive effects of transformational leadership on team potency. Beyond cultural values research, Taras et al. (2010) also found that cultural tightness–looseness moderated the main effects of culture, such that effects are stronger for countries that are culturally tighter, compared to looser. These moderating effects of culture at the team, unit, and organization levels suggest that collectives should be expected to develop "shared" cultural beliefs that work to shape their reactions to motivational processes in ways that determine, in part, key outcomes such as collective performance.

Finally, there is also evidence that the contextual influences of cultural norms affect individuals differently, depending on various individual attributes. For example, Fu et al. (2007) found that individuals with higher need for closure are more motivated to conform to cultural norms (i.e., either Western or Eastern norms) regarding handling conflict. In particular, relative to those in Eastern cultures, individuals from Western cultures are more likely to adhere to norms such as choosing more direct and less relational strategies to resolve conflict. But such differences are greater among those with higher need for closure. Interestingly, the same effects held for bicultural individuals, such that they adhered to their respective cultural norms that were most situationally salient. For additional such evidence regarding the impact of cultural norms on bicultural individuals, see Hong et al. (2016).

Discussion

In this chapter, we have summarized the work motivation literature around a goal-related framework, which involves core goal processes and proximal and distal antecedents of goal processes. We then selectively reviewed the intersection between national cross-cultural management/psychology literatures and work motivation literature to identify specific areas in which cultural differences at the individual and collective levels have been shown to impact motivational processes and outcomes. We end the chapter with theoretical observations and insights, practical implications, and directions for future research, based on our review.

Theoretical Insights and Future Research

Table 7.1 summarizes the key theoretical insights gained from our review of the literature. Here, we elaborate on the key insights and discuss specific avenues that we believe are particularly important for future research. First, building on the work motivation literature, it is important to recognize that *motivation at work is not one thing—and not one concept.* Rather, motivation involves complex, interrelated processes that capture the (1) direction of where individuals chose to allocate their effort (i.e., goal choice), (2) manner in which individuals regulate their effort in pursuit of goals (i.e., goal striving), (3) complex interrelationships between goal choice and goal-striving processes, and (4) individual differences and situational factors that combine to impact goal-related processes. Considering motivation from this perspective is critically important, as understanding the complexity and intricacies of work motivation phenomena serves as a basis for understanding how and where to best integrate between motivation and cross-cultural literatures.

Table 7.1 Summary of key theoretical and practical insights
Theoretical Insights:
1. Motivation involves complex, interrelated processes that capture the (a) direction of effort (i.e., goal choice), (b) regulation of effort in pursuit of goals (i.e., goal striving), (c) complex interrelationships between goal choice and goal striving, and (d) personal and contextual drivers of goal-related processes.
2. Cultural differences at the individual and collective (team, organization, nation) levels shape motivational processes directly and as moderators.
3. Research on culture and motivation has focused primarily on individual-level collectivism and power distance. The motivational influences of other cultural values and culture at higher levels of analysis are less well known.
4. Research on cultural differences and motivation has not been well integrated to date. More research is needed to integrate these two literatures.
5. Two avenues are especially important for future research integrating cross-cultural differences with motivational processes: (a) cultural influences on self-regulation (i.e., goal-striving) processes; and (b) the roles cultural differences at the team, organizational, and national levels play in shaping motivational processes.
Practical Insights:
1. Employees and managers working in culturally diverse environments should modify their behaviors to fit cultural norms and expectations.
2. Organizational leaders should modify managerial practices to fit multiple cultures.
3. Employees and organizations need to appreciate that in more collectivistic cultures, team-based goals are relatively more valued than individual-based goals.
4. Organizations and leaders should allow sufficient time for newly formed global teams to learn about each other's preferences and styles, and for a common team identity to form.
5. Organizations should motivate employees to develop cultural competencies, such as by providing opportunities for global assignments and by recognizing employee success across cultural settings in promotion and reward systems.

Second, and related to the previous point, our review indicated that, indeed, *national cultural differences affect different motivational processes and outcomes in different ways.* In particular, our review indicated that individual differences in cultural values influence directly—as well as indirectly (i.e., as moderators)—goal-setting interventions (e.g., the efficacy of participation in goal setting, receptivity to supervisor assigned goals vs. self-set goals), receptivity to empowerment interventions, and motivational reactions to leadership behaviors. Broadly, we identified two consistent findings. First, collectivism enhances receptivity to more group-based motivational interventions and goal pursuits that help facilitate group outcomes and well-being. Second, power distance enhances the motivation to conform to authority, which can facilitate more motivational interventions emanating from higher authority levels. In this sense, the findings validate the functions of cultural differences in collectivism and power distance.

Third, in line with the broader cross-cultural literature (see Kirkman et al., 2006, 2017; Taras et al., 2010), *we know more about the roles of individual-level individualism–collectivism and power distance than other cultural dimensions* (both other values and cultural differences at the collective levels). Clearly, individuals and units are not made up of one or two cultural values in isolation. Rather, all entities consist of a constellation or mosaic of values that work in concert to influence important motivational processes and outcomes (Chao & Moon, 2005). Isolating only one or two values runs the risk of missing important variance in motivation. Furthermore, research should consider additional cultural concepts. For example, recent research on *guanxi* (e.g., Chen et al., 2013) and harmony (e.g., Leung et al., 2011), conducted primarily in Chinese contexts, can enrich our understanding of how goal processes differ as a function of how much emphasis individuals place in pursuing individual versus team (collective) goals.

A fourth and related insight from our review is that *national cultural differences are not well integrated with more comprehensive models of motivation—such* as the integrative models discussed. Instead, research has more selectively focused on a limited number of cultural differences (often focusing on one cultural value at a time—other than perhaps reviews of the literature) and one motivational outcome (e.g., responses to goal setting, motivational states). These two gaps, in combination, indicate perhaps the most exciting avenues for future research. That is, much more is needed to better understand the confluence of cultural influences on complex motivational phenomena. As an example, Ballard et al.'s (2016) integrative model of self-regulation across goals emphasizes the role of perceived risk in choosing among competing goals, suggesting that the uncertainty avoidance could likely impact such complex processes. Collectivism may also play a role in specific goal choices, leading individuals to prioritize goals in part based on whether they are instrumental to higher-order individual or collective goals.

Finally, building on our review, *two additional avenues are especially important for future research integrating national cross-cultural differences with motivational processes.* First, we need to better understand cultural influences on self-regulation (i.e., goal-striving) processes. Relative to goal choice and motivational states, we know far less about how cultural differences could affect the manner in which individuals regulate effort in pursuit of multiple goals, including goals involving career choices, work–family balance, and more (e.g., by influencing values individuals place on competing goals or outcomes). Second, we also need to better understand the role of collective-level cultural differences in motivational processes. This includes a strong need for cross-level studies that consider how cultural differences at the group, organization, and even national, level impact individual-level motivational processes (both directly and combined with individual-level cultural differences), and how collective cultural differences (such as collective-level values and tightness–looseness) shape collective-level motivational outcomes (e.g., the collective direction a team or an organization chooses to pursue).

Practical Implications

The intersection of motivation and national cross-cultural management/psychology research has important implications for managers charged with motivating employees, with two work situations of particular importance. First, expatriate managers, or those assigned to work and lead in countries other than their birth country, need to be cognizant of the various cultural values of those they are leading (Chen et al, 2010; Firth et al., 2014). As noted, differing cultural values are related to the manner in which employees choose goals and develop strategies to achieve them. For example, an expatriate from a highly individualistic country (e.g., Australia) working in a highly collectivistic country (e.g., Malaysia) could erroneously attempt to focus solely on individually targeted goals (common for countries high in individualism), which could actually demotivate those responding more positively to group-targeted goals (common for countries high in collectivism). In this situation, a manager could choose to use both individual- and group-targeted goals, making sure to put more emphasis on those goals having group attributes.

Second, many managers today are charged with leading global virtual teams, whose members are often spread out geographically in a number of different countries (Kirkman et al., 2012). In contrast to leading employees from a single different country, these managers are often faced with leading team members representing several different countries who could have a wide array of different cultural values (Gibson et al., 2014). Unlike expatriates, they cannot simply adjust their motivation efforts to "fit" the prevailing cultural values of a single country. In contrast, global virtual team leaders need to understand the cultural value differences between members of their teams and to develop motivational strategies that can "cut across" member preferences for how they prefer to be motivated. Research has also shown that promoting a high level of team identification can also motivate members to focus less on their differences and more so on their commonalities critical to goal accomplishment (Lisak et al., 2016; Van Der Vegt & Bunderson, 2005). For either expatriates or global virtual team leaders, the key is assessing and understanding the cultural values of those being led and then adapting motivational techniques to best match the specific situation.

References

Alderfer, C. P. (1969). An empirical test of a new theory of human needs. *Organizational Behavior and Human Performance, 4*, 143–175.

Aycan, Z., Kanungo, R. N., Mendonca, M., Yu, K., Deller, J., Stahl, G., & Kurshid, A. (2000). Impact of culture on human resource management practices: A 10-country comparison. *Applied Psychology: An International Review, 49*, 192–221.

Ballard, T., Yeo, G., Loft, S., Vancouver, J. B., & Neal, A. (2016). An integrative, formal model of motivation and decision making: The MGPM. *Journal of Applied Psychology, 101*, 1240–1265.

Bandura, A. (1997). *Self-efficacy: The exercise of control.* New York: Freeman.

Barrick, M. R., Mount, M. K., & Li, N. (2013). The theory of purposeful work behavior: The role of personality, higher-order goals, and job characteristics. *Academy of Management Review, 38*, 132–153.

Baumeister, R. F., Bratslavsky, E., Muraven, M., & Tice, D. M. (1998). Ego depletion: Is the active self a limited resource? *Journal of Personality and Social Psychology, 74*, 1252–1265.

Brockner, J., & Higgins, E. T. (2001). Regulatory focus theory: Implications for the study of emotions at work. *Organizational Behavior and Human Decision Processes, 86*, 35–66.
Carter, E. C., Kofler, L. M., Forster, D. E., & McCullough, M. E. (2015). A series of meta-analytic tests of the depletion effect: Self-control does not seem to rely on a limited resource. *Journal of Experimental Psychology: General, 144*, 796–815.
Carver, C. S., & Scheier, M. F. (1982). Control theory: A useful conceptual framework for personality–social, clinical, and health psychology. *Psychological Bulletin, 92*, 111–135.
Carver, C. S., & Scheier M. F. (1998). *On the self-regulation of Behavior*. New York: Cambridge University Press.
Chang, C.-H., Ferris, D. L., Johnson, R. E., Rosen, C. C., & Tan, J. A. (2012). Core self-evaluations: A review and evaluation of the literature. *Journal of Management, 38*, 81–128.
Chao, G. T., & Moon, H. (2005). The cultural mosaic: A metatheory for understanding the complexity of culture. *Journal of Applied Psychology, 90*, 1128–1140.
Chatman, J. A., & Barsade, S. G. (1995). Personality, organizational culture, and cooperation: Evidence from a business simulation. *Administrative Science Quarterly, 40*, 423–443.
Chen, C. C., Chen, X.-P., & Huang, S. (2013). Chinese guanxi: An integrative review and new directions for future research. *Management and Organization Review, 9*, 167–207.
Chen, G., Gully, S. M., & Eden, D. (2004). General self-efficacy and self-esteem: Toward theoretical and empirical distinction between correlated self-evaluations. *Journal of Organizational Behavior, 25*, 375–395.
Chen, G., & Kanfer, R. (2006). Toward a systems theory of motivated behavior in work teams. *Research in Organizational Behavior, 27*, 223–267.
Chen, G., Kanfer, R., DeShon, R. P., Mathieu, J. E., & Kozlowski, S. W. J. (2009). The motivating potential of teams: A test and extension of Chen & Kanfer's (2006) model. *Organizational Behavior and Human Decision Processes, 110*, 45–55.
Chen, G., Kirkman, B. L., Kim, K., Farh, C. I. C., & Tangirala, S. (2010). When does cross-cultural motivation enhance expatriate effectiveness? A multilevel investigation of the moderating roles of cultural distance and support. *Academy of Management Journal, 53*, 1110–1130.
Chen, G., Sharma, P. N., Edinger, S., Shapiro, D. L., & Farh, J. L. (2011). Motivating and de-motivating forces in teams: Cross-level influences of empowering leadership and relationship conflict. *Journal of Applied Psychology, 96*, 541–557.
Deci, E. L., & Ryan, R. M. (1985). *Intrinsic motivation and self-determination in human behavior*. New York: Plenum Press.
DeShon, R. P., & Gillespie, J. Z. (2005). A motivated action theory account of goal orientation. *Journal of Applied Psychology, 90*, 1096–1127.
Dorfman, P. W., & Howell, J. P. (1988). Dimensions of national culture and effective leadership patterns: Hofstede revisited. In R. N. Farmer & E. G. McGoun (Eds.), *Advances in international comparative management* (Vol. 3, pp. 127–149). Greenwich, CT: JAI Press.
Dweck, C. S. (1986). Motivational processes affecting learning. *American Psychologist, 41*, 1040–1048.
Earley, P. C. (1994). Self or group? cultural effects of training on self-efficacy and performance. *Administrative Science Quarterly, 39*, 89–117.
Eby, L. T., & Dobbins, G. H. (1997). Collectivistic orientation in teams: An individual and group-level analysis. *Journal of Organizational Behavior, 18*, 275–295.
Erez, M. (2010). Culture and job design. *Journal of Organizational Behavior, 31*, 389–400.
Erez, M. (2018). From local to cross-cultural to global work motivation and innovation. In M. Gelfand, C. Y. Chiu, and Y. Y. Hong, Y. Y. (Eds.), *Handbook of Advances in Culture and Psychology, Volume 7* (pp. 217–259). New York: Oxford University Press.
Erez, M., & Earley, P. C. (1987). Comparative analysis of goal-setting strategies across cultures. *Journal of Applied Psychology, 72*, 658–665.
Erez, M., & Somech, A. (1996). Is group productivity loss the rule or the exception? Effects of culture and group-based motivation. *Academy of Management Journal, 39*, 1513–1537.
Eylon, D., & Au, K. Y. (1999). Exploring empowerment cross-cultural differences along the power distance dimension. *International Journal of Intercultural Relations, 23*, 373–385.
Farh, J. L., Earley, P. C., & Lin, S. (1997). Impetus for action: A cultural analysis of justice and extra-role behavior in Chinese society. *Administrative Science Quarterly, 42*, 421–444.
Firth, B., Chen, G., Kirkman, B. L., & Kim, K. (2014). Newcomers abroad: Expatriate adaptation during early phases of international assignments. *Academy of Management Journal, 57*, 280–300.

Fu, J. H., Morris, M. W., Lee, S., Chao, M., Chiu, C., & Hong, Y. (2007). Epistemic motives and cultural conformity: Need for closure, culture, and context as determinants of conflict judgments. *Journal of Personality and Social Psychology, 92*, 191–207.

Gelfand, M. J., Aycan, Z., Erez, M., & Leung, K. (2017). Cross-cultural industrial organizational psychology and organizational behavior: A hundred year journey. *Journal of Applied Psychology, 102*, 514–529.

Gelfand, M. J., Erez, M., & Aycan, Z. (2007). Cross-cultural organizational behavior. *Annual review of psychology, 58*, 479–514.

Gelfand, M. J., Nishii, L. H., & Raver, J. L. (2006). On the nature and importance of cultural tightness-looseness. *Journal of Applied Psychology, 91*, 1225–1244.

Gelfand, M. J., Raver, J. L., Nishii, L., Leslie, L. M., Lun, J., Lim, B. C., Duan, L., Almaliach, A., Ang, S., Amadottir, J., Aycan, Z., Boehnke, K., Boski, P., Cabecinhas, R., Chan, D., Chhokar, J., D'Amato, A., Ferrer, M., Fischlmayr, I. C., . . . Yamaguchi, S. (2011). Differences between tight and loose cultures: A 33-nation study. *Science, 332*, 1100–1104.

Gibson, C. B. (1999). Do they do what they believe they can? Group efficacy and group effectiveness across tasks and cultures. *Academy of Management Journal, 42*, 138–152.

Gibson, C. B., Huang, L., Kirkman, B. L., & Shapiro, D. L. (2014). Where global and virtual meet: The value of examining the intersection of these elements in twenty-first century teams. *Annual Review of Organizational Psychology and Organizational Behavior, 1*, 217–244.

Gino, F., Schweitzer, M. E., Mead, N. L., & Ariely, D. (2011). Unable to resist temptation: How self-control depletion promotes unethical behavior. *Organizational Behavior and Human Decision Processes, 115*, 191–203.

Gollwitzer, P. M. (1990). Action phases and mind-sets. In E. T. Higgins & R. M. Sorrentino (Eds.), *Handbook of motivation and cognition: Foundations of social behavior* (Vol. 2, pp. 53–92). New York: Guilford Press.

Gollwitzer, P. M. (1999). Implementation intentions: Strong effects of simple plans. *American Psychologist, 54*, 493–503.

Gollwitzer, P. M., & Brandstaetter, V. (1997). Implementation intentions and effective goal pursuit. *Journal of Personality and Social Psychology, 73*, 186–199.

Gollwitzer, P. M., Heckhausen, H., & Steller, B. (1990). Deliberative and implemental mind-sets: Cognitive tuning toward congruous thoughts and information. *Journal of Personality and Social Psychology, 59*, 1119–1127.

Grant, A. M. (2008). The significance of task significance: Job performance effects, relational mechanisms, and boundary conditions. *Journal of Applied Psychology, 93*, 108–124.

Hackman, J. R., & Oldham, G. R. (1976). Motivation through the design of work: Test of a theory. *Organizational Behavior and Human Performance, 16*, 250–279.

Hagger, M. S., Wood, C., Stiff, C., & Chatzisarantis, N. L. D. (2010). Ego depletion and the strength model of self-control: A meta-analysis. *Psychological Bulletin, 136*, 495–525.

Hauff, S., Richter, N. F., & Tressin, T. (2015). Situational job characteristics and job satisfaction: The moderating role of national culture. *International Business Review, 24*, 710–713.

Higgins, E. T. (1997). Beyond pleasure and pain. *American Psychologist, 52*, 1280–1300.

Higgins, E. T. (2000). Making a good decision: Value from fit. *American Psychologist, 55*, 1217–1230.

Hofstede, G. (1980). *Culture's consequences: International differences in work-related values*. Beverly Hills, CA: SAGE.

Hong, Y., Siran, Z., Morris, M. W., & Benet-Martınez, V. (2016). Multicultural identity processes. *Current Opinion in Psychology, 8*, 49–53.

Hui, M. K., Au, K., & Fock, H. (2003). Empowerment effects across cultures. *Journal of International Business Studies, 35*, 46–60.

Inzlicht, M., Schmeichel, B. J., & Macrae, C. N. (2014). Why self-control seems (but may not be) limited. *Trends in Cognitive Sciences, 18*, 127–133.

Jackson, C. L., Colquitt, J. A., Wesson, M. J., & Zapata-Phelan, C. P. (2006). Psychological collectivism: A measurement validation and linkage to group member performance. *Journal of Applied Psychology, 91*, 884–899.

Johnson, R. E., Chang, C.-H., & Lord, R. G. (2006). Moving from cognition to behavior: What the research says. *Psychological Bulletin, 132*, 381–415.

Jung, D. I., & Avolio, B. J. (1999). Effects of leadership style and followers' cultural orientation on performance in group and individual task conditions. *Academy of Management Journal, 42*, 208–218.

Kanfer, R., & Ackerman, P. L. (1989). Motivation and cognitive abilities: An integrative/aptitude-treatment interaction approach to skill acquisition. *Journal of Applied Psychology, 74*, 657–690.

Kanfer, R., & Chen, G. (2016). Motivation in organizational behavior: History, advances and prospects. *Organizational Behavior and Human Decision Processes, 136*, 6–19.

Kanfer, R., Chen, G., & Pritchard, R. (2008). The three C's of work motivation: Content, context, and change. In R. Kanfer, G. Chen, & R. D. Pritchard (Eds.), *Work motivation: Past, present, and future* (pp. 1–16). New York: Routledge Academic.

Kanfer, R., Frese, M., & Johnson, R. E. (2017). Motivation related to work: A century of progress. *Journal of Applied Psychology, 102*, 338–355.

Kanfer, R., & Heggestad, E. D. (1997). Motivation traits and skills: A person-centered approach to work motivation. *Research in Organizational Behavior, 19*, 1–56.

Kark, R., Shamir, B., & Chen, G. (2003). The two faces of transformational leadership: Empowerment and dependency. *Journal of Applied Psychology, 88*, 246–255.

Kirkman, B. L., Chen, G., Farh, J. L., Chen, Z. X., & Lowe, K. B. (2009). Individual power distance orientation and follower reactions to transformational leaders: A cross-level, cross-cultural examination. *Academy of Management Journal, 52*, 744–764.

Kirkman, B. L., Gibson, C. B., & Kim, K. (2012). Across borders and technologies: Advancements in virtual teams research. In S. W. J. Kozlowski (Ed.), *Oxford Handbook of Industrial and Organizational Psychology* (Vol. 1, pp. 789–858). New York: Oxford University Press.

Kirkman, B. L., Lowe, K. B., & Gibson, C. B. (2006). A quarter century of *Culture's Consequences*: A review of empirical research incorporating Hofstede's cultural value framework. *Journal of International Business Studies, 37*, 285–320.

Kirkman, B. L., Lowe, K. B., & Gibson, C. B. (2017). A retrospective on *Culture's Consequences:* The 35-year journey. *Journal of International Business Studies, 48*, 12–29.

Kirkman, B. L., & Rosen, B. (1999). Beyond self-management: Antecedents and consequences of team empowerment. *Academy of Management Journal, 42*, 58–74.

Kirkman, B. L., & Shapiro, D. L. (2001a). The impact of cultural values on job satisfaction and organizational commitment in self-managing work teams: The mediating role of employee resistance. *Academy of Management Journal, 44*, 557–569.

Kirkman, B. L. & Shapiro, D. L. (2001b). The impact of team members' cultural values on productivity, cooperation, and empowerment in self-managing work teams. *Journal of Cross-Cultural Psychology, 32*, 597–617.

Kreiser, P. M., Marino, L. D., Dickson, P., & Weaver, K. M. (2010). Cultural influences on entrepreneurial orientation: The impact of national culture on risk taking and proactiveness in SMEs. *Entrepreneurship Theory and Practice, 34*, 959–984.

Kruglanski, A. W., Jasko, K., Chernikova, M., Milyavsky, M., Babush, M., Baldner, C., & Pierro, A. (2015). The rocky road from attitudes to behaviors: Charting the goal systemic course of actions. *Psychological Review, 122*, 598–620.

Lam, S. S. K., Chen, X. P., & Schaubroeck, J. (2002). Participative decision-making and employee performance in different cultures: The moderating effects of allocentrism-idiocentrism and efficacy. *Academy of Management Journal, 45*, 905–914.

Lanaj, K., Chang, C.-H., & Johnson, R. E. (2012). Regulatory focus and work-related outcomes: A review and meta-analysis. *Psychological Bulletin, 138*, 998–1034.

Lanaj, K., Johnson, R. E., & Barnes, C. M. (2014). Beginning the workday yet already depleted? Consequences of late-night smartphone use and sleep. *Organizational Behavior and Human Decision Processes, 124*, 11–23.

Latham, G. P., Erez, M. & Locke, E. A. (1988). Resolving scientific disputes by the joint design of crucial experiments by the antagonists: Application to the Erez–Latham dispute regarding participation in goal setting. *Journal of Applied Psychology, 73*, 753–772.

Leung, K., Brew, F. P., Zhang, Z.-X., & Zhang, Y. (2011). Harmony and conflict: A cross-cultural investigation in China and Australia. *Journal of Cross-Cultural Psychology, 42*, 795–816.

Lisak, A., Erez, M., Sui, Y., & Lee, C. (2016). The positive role of global leaders in enhancing multicultural team innovation. *Journal of International Business Studies, 47*, 655–673.

Locke, E. A., & Latham, G. P. (1990). *A theory of goal setting and task performance*. Englewood Cliffs, NJ: Prentice Hall.

Locke, E. A, & Latham, G. P. (2002). Building a practically useful theory of goal setting and task motivation: A 35-year odyssey. *American Psychologist, 57*, 705–717.

Lord, R. G., Day, D. V., Zaccaro, S. J., Avolio, B. J., & Eagly, A. H. (2017). Leadership in applied psychology: Three waves of theory and research. *Journal of Applied Psychology, 102*, 434–451.

Lord, R. G., Diefendorff, J. M., Schmidt, A. M., & Hall, R. J. (2010). Self-regulation at work. *Annual Review of Psychology, 61*, 543–568.

Maslow, A. H. (1943). A theory of human motivation. *Psychological Review, 50*, 370–396.

Mathieu, J. E., Hollenbeck, J. R., van Knippenberg, D., & Ilgen, D. R. (2017). A century of work teams in the *Journal of Applied Psychology*. *Journal of Applied Psychology, 102*, 452–467.

Morris, M. W., Leung, K., Ames, D., & Lickel, B. (1993). Views from inside and outside: Integrating emic and etic insights about culture and justice judgment. *Academy of Management Review, 24*, 781–796.

Neal, A., Ballard, T., & Vancouver, J. B. (2017). Dynamic self-regulation and multiple-goal pursuit. *Annual Review of Organizational Psychology and Organizational Behavior, 4*, 401–423.

Nouri, R., Erez, M., Lee, C., Liang, J., Bannister, B. D., & Chiu, W. (2015). Keeping the supervisor and peers out of sight: The effect of culture and the social work context on creativity. *Journal of Organizational Behavior, 36*, 899–918.

Ostroff, C., Kinicki, A. J., & Muhammad, R. S. (2013). Organizational culture and climate. In N. W. Schmitt, S. Highhouse, & I. B. Weiner (Eds.), *Handbook of psychology: Industrial and organizational psychology* (pp. 643–676). Hoboken, NJ: John Wiley.

Parker, S. K., Morgeson, F. P., & Johns, G. (2017). One hundred years of work design research: Looking back and looking forward. *Journal of Applied Psychology, 102*, 403–420.

Payne, S. C., Youngcourt, S. S., & Beaubien, J. M. (2007). A meta-analytic examination of the goal orientation nomological net. *Journal of Applied Psychology, 92*, 128–150.

Powers, W. T. (1973). *Behavior: The control of perception*. Chicago: Aldine.

Robert, C., Probst, T. M., Martocchio, J. J., Drasgow, F., & Lawler, J. J. (2000). Empowerment and continuous improvement in the United States, Mexico, Poland, and India: Predicting fit on the basis of dimensions of power distance and individualism. *Journal of Applied Psychology*, 85, 643–658.

Schaubroeck, J., Lam. S. K. K., & Cha, S. E. (2007). Embracing transformational leadership: Team values and the impact of leader behavior on team performance. *Journal of Applied Psychology, 92*, 1020–1030.

Schmidt, A. M., & DeShon, R. P. (2010). The moderating effects of performance ambiguity on the relationship between self-efficacy and performance. *Journal of Applied Psychology, 95*, 572–581.

Schneider, B., González-Romá, V., Ostroff, C., & West, M. A. (2017). Organizational climate and culture: Reflections on the history of the constructs in the *Journal of Applied Psychology*. *Journal of Applied Psychology, 102*, 468–482.

Seibert, S. E., Wang, G., & Courtright, S. H. (2011). Antecedents and consequences of psychological and team empowerment in organizations: A meta-analytic review. *Journal of Applied Psychology, 96*, 981–1003.

Stackhouse, M., Kirkman, B. L., Taras, V., & Steel, P. (2018). National culture and leadership research between 2003 and 2014: A review, synthesis, and directions for the next decade of cross-cultural leadership research. In N. Anderson, D. S. Ones, H. K. Sinangil, & C. Viswesvaran (Eds.), *Sage handbook of industrial, work, and organizational psychology* (Vol. 3, pp. 206–236). London: SAGE.

Stahl, G. K., Maznevski, M. L., Voigt, A., & Jonsen, K. (2010). Unraveling the effects of cultural diversity in teams: A meta-analysis of research on multicultural work groups. *Journal of International Business Studies, 41*, 690–709.

Stajkovic, A. D., & Luthans, F. (1998). Self-efficacy and work-related performance: A meta-analysis. *Psychological Bulletin, 124*, 240–261.

Taras, V., Kirkman, B. L., & Steel, P. (2010). Examining the impact of *Culture's Consequences*: A three-decade, multi-level, meta-analytic review of Hofstede's cultural value dimensions. *Journal of Applied Psychology, 95*, 405–439.

Thomas, K. W., & Velthouse, B. A. (1990). Cognitive elements of empowerment. *Academy of Management Review, 15*, 666–681.

Vancouver, J. B., & Kendall, L. (2006). When self-efficacy negatively relates to motivation and performance in a learning context. *Journal of Applied Psychology, 91*, 1146–1153.

Van Der Vegt, G. S., & Bunderson, J. S. (2005). Learning and performance in multidisciplinary teams: The importance of collective team identification. *Academy of Management Journal, 48*, 532–547.

Wallace, J. C., & Chen, G. (2006). A multilevel integration of personality, climate, self-regulation, and performance. *Personnel Psychology, 59*, 529–557.

CHAPTER

8 Culture and Job Attitudes

S. Arzu Wasti *and* Selin Eser Erdil

Abstract

We reviewed the cross-cultural job attitudes research spanning the last decade (2010–2020), most of which focused on the moderating role of national culture regarding the antecedents of job attitudes. The findings largely support the role of individualism versus collectivism as it relates to the impact of job demands, supervisor and organizational support, the effectiveness of different leadership styles, and the binding nature of extra-organizational ties (e.g., family embeddedness). Although the implications of fairness and work–life balance appear to have many generalizable aspects, findings speak to the moderating effect of gender egalitarianism and power distance on the predictive value of organizational practices that influence perceived fairness and inclusiveness. The scarce evidence on the outcomes of job attitudes suggests that the turnover intentions–turnover link is stronger in countries higher in individualism and power distance and lower in masculinity. Finally, several studies show the importance of incorporating economic, political, and regulatory differences, in addition to cultural values.

Key Words: national culture, cultural values, job attitudes, individiualism-collectivism, organizational commitment, job satisfaction, turnover intentions, perceived organizational support, job embeddedness

Job attitudes, which is an umbrella term encompassing favorable or unfavorable evaluations of one's job, have been and continue to be the bread and butter of organizational behavior (OB) research (Judge et al., 2017). As a result of the effort to comprehend Japan's increasing productivity in the late 1970s, job attitudes have also been one of the primary OB topics to garner cross-cultural interest (e.g., Marsh & Mannari, 1977). By 2009, Fischer and Mansell (2009) were able to gather 215 studies representing 48 countries to meta-analyze the role of culture in organizational commitment. This work was soon followed by Taras et al.'s (2010) meta-analysis, which showed that Hofstede's (2001) four dimensions correlated significantly with job attitudes and more strongly than they did with behaviors, suggesting that culture–behavior relationships may be mediated by attitudes. In this chapter, we review the cross-cultural job attitudes literature published after these two meta-analyses. In what follows, we present our methodology and findings, and we conclude with future directions.

Method

Focusing on the top 25 journals covering the fields of management, business, and applied psychology listed in the Web of Science, we conducted a bibliographic search for the 2010–2020 period. To increase the representation of non-U.S. journals, we included the *Journal of Cross Cultural Psychology, European Journal of Work and Organizational Psychology*, and *International Journal of Human Resource Management.* We adopted the definition of culture as the explicit and implicit patterns of historically derived and selected ideas, which are embodied in societal institutions and practices and inform interactions and individuals (Hamedani & Markus, 2019). Thus, we included comparative studies that explicitly prioritized cultural (e.g., values) as well as institutional differences (e.g., legal, economic structures). The final review included 54 comparative and 15 meta-analytic articles. We also included 29 non-U.S. single-country studies, which either measured culture at the individual level or were explicitly concerned with culture (e.g., inclusion of an emic variable). We evaluated the articles on several conceptual and methodological issues, which are summarized in Table 8.1. In view of space limitations, we applied judgment in the selection of articles included; however, the full list of articles is available from the authors.

Table 8.1 Conceptual and methodological practices identified from the review

	Yes		*No*		*Could Not Determine*	
	n	%	n	%		n
Development of the cross-cultural research question						
Emic/etic[a]						
Used emic approach?	5	6	78	94	0	83
Used imposed etic approach?	66	80	17	20	0	83
Used emic-etic (derived etic) approach?	12	14	71	86	0	83
Treatment of culture?						
Used country as a proxy for culture?	69	83	13	16	1	83
Used other delimiters besides country?	13	16	69	83	1	83
Culture justified by reference to Hofstede's framework?	34	41	48	58	1	83
If yes, was Hofstede country scores included in the empirical analysis?	3	9	31	91	0	34
Culture justified by reference to GLOBE's framework?	17	20	66	80	0	83
If yes, was GLOBE country scores included in the empirical analysis?	11	63	6	37	0	17
Culture justified by reference to European Values Survey (EVS)/ World Values Survey (WVS) framework?	2	2	81	98	0	83

Table 8.1 *Continued*

	Yes		No		Could Not Determine	n
	n	%	n	%		
If yes, were country scores of EVS/WVS included in the empirical analysis?	1	50	1	50	0	2
Culture treated as an individual-level construct?	12	14	71	86	0	83
Mentioned structural variables?	49	59	34	41	0	83
If yes, measured or controlled for structural variables?	13	27	36	73	0	49
Culture measured directly and aggregated to country level?[b]	4	7	50	93	0	54
Alignment of the research contexts? [b]						
Sample differences?						
Ignored demographic differences?	14	26	38	70	2	54
Ignored environmental/industry differences?	27	50	25	46	2	54
Ignored differences in experience levels?	20	37	32	59	2	54
Reported details about samples?	33	61	20	37	1	54
Matched samples?	18	33	35	65	1	54
Statistically controlled for differences?	36	67	16	30	2	54
Validation of research instrument?						
Used backtranslation?	47	60	29	37	2	78
Described procedures for ensuring semantic equivalence? [b]	12	22	37	69	5	54
Described procedures for ensuring measurement equivalence (ME)? [b]	28	52	19	35	7	54
Reported measurement equivalence of attitude constructs? [c]	24	86	4	14	0	28

Note. Schaffer and Riordan's (2003) Table 2 is adapted for this study. Meta-analyses are not coded. A total of 54 comparative and 29 single-country studies constitute the sample (n = 83) if not indicated otherwise.

[a] Imposed etic studies assume that shared frames of reference exist across cultures, whereas emic studies consider culture-specific frames of references when designing the study, determining constructs of interest and their measurement. Emic-etic or derived etic studies begin with an imposed etic approach but actively seek emic information in each country to better contextualize and adapt the study variables and their measures.

[b] Only comparative studies were evaluated (n = 54). Semantic equivalence was coded with reference to practices beyond backtranslation, such as pilot tests and consultation with bilingual experts and local collaborators to account for linguistic differences. Measurement equivalence was coded with reference to the reported statistical tests that established the equivalence of constructs and measures across the populations being compared.
[c]Measurement equivalence could not be tested for attitude constructs measured with one or two items.

Job Attitudes Research across Cultures: Overview of the Last Decade

Before reporting the substance of the review, a few observations from Table 8.1 are noteworthy. First, cross-cultural research on job attitudes enjoys greater methodological sophistication. For instance, the percentage of studies that test for measurement equivalence is twice that reported in Schaffer and Riordan's (2003) earlier review of comparative organizational studies. Second, researchers seem to consult a variety of frameworks beyond Hofstede (2001), such as the Global Leadership and Organizational Behavior Effectiveness (GLOBE) project (House et al., 2004) and the World Values Survey (WVS), suggesting a broader operationalization of culture. Yet, the vast majority of studies adopt an imposed-etic approach, which assumes culture-specific theories, constructs, and measures (usually developed in the United States or Canada) to be universal. Finally, most studies use country as a proxy for culture, thereby ignoring possible within-culture variance as well as neglecting other factors that may account for differences across national boundaries (Kirkman et al., 2017).

In terms of content, the last decade of research has largely focused on understanding the moderating role of culture, in particular individualism–collectivism (IC), on the antecedents of job attitudes. A few studies also tested culture's main effects on job attitudes. For instance, Meyer et al.'s (2012) meta-analysis covering 54 countries found that IC and power distance (PD) explained the greatest amount of variance in normative commitment (bond reflecting obligations), followed by affective commitment (bond characterized by affect) but not in continuance commitment (bond reflecting calculation of costs). Hausmann et al. (2013) showed that positive affectivity as a cultural variable served as an antecedent to affective commitment in 30 countries after controlling for job satisfaction and job role at the individual level, human development index, as well as Hofstede's four dimensions at the national level. Gamble and Tian (2015) found all three components of commitment to be lower in more developed regions in China. The relationships between affective commitment, normative commitment, and turnover intentions were not moderated by region, but the continuance commitment link to turnover intentions was stronger in more developed regions.

Regarding antecedents, we begin with the literature on job conditions (job demands and resources, including supervisor support), followed by leadership, organizational practices that influence perceived fairness and inclusiveness, and finally, the economic system.

Antecedents of Job Attitudes: Job Conditions

JOB DEMANDS

Researchers have explored how job demands predict job attitudes in different contexts, with the premise that employees in more individualistic contexts experience more strain. Yang et al. (2012) proposed that employees in individualistic countries may be especially frustrated by high workloads and lack of work-related resources because they stand in the way of their personal goals. In addition, they may be less inclined to seek support, owing to normative prescriptions to solve problems autonomously. Indeed, controlling for other Hofstede dimensions, GDP at the national level and number of weekly work hours at the individual level, the negative relationship with work demands, and undesirable job attitudes were stronger for individualistic than collectivistic countries.

Based on arguments that in collectivistic cultures people tend to be more concerned about how their emotions affect relationships with others, Nixon et al. (2020) showed that Turkish service employees' job attitudes suffered less in response to surface acting demands of emotional labor compared to their American counterparts. The interactions between individual-level collectivism and national culture suggested that only high collectivists in Turkey retained high organizational commitment across different levels of surface acting demands compared to low collectivists in Turkey as well as the American sample in total. Exploring beyond IC, König et al. (2011) predicted that job insecurity would have more detrimental effects on job attitudes in Switzerland, which is a high uncertainty avoidance (UA) country as opposed to the United States, a low UA country. Yet, they found the opposite, leading them to speculate on the differences regarding the social safety net in terms of unemployment insurance and health care systems. The researchers then undertook a 24-country study and showed that there were fewer negative reactions to job insecurity in terms of job satisfaction and affective commitment in low UA cultures and in countries with strong social safety nets, with the latter accounting for greater variance than UA (Debus et al., 2012).

Other research has also considered variables beyond national culture in predicting job attitudes from job demands. For instance, given the relatively lower national economic wealth in China, Liu et al. (2010) proposed that budget-related constraints would be more consequential for job satisfaction and turnover intentions in China than in the United States, but they found the relationships to be stronger in the United States. The authors speculated that in a resource-rich context like the United States such constraints might be more unsettling. Yet, in line with the lower wealth argument, Chinese and South Korean employees showed a stronger sensitivity to unfairness in the distribution of materialistic outcomes than Australian employees (Jiang et al., 2017). Finally, focusing on within-country variance in China, Nielsen et al. (2011) noted that the *hukou* status acted like a perfect proxy for occupational status, as it systematically segmented the urban job market into low-status, routine jobs (typically undertaken by migrant workers holding agricultural *hukou*) and higher-status jobs with clear career paths (which are mostly unavailable to migrant workers). Importantly, the authors observed that any benefit accruing from China's marketization was primarily advancing workers with higher-status jobs, thereby widening the satisfaction and subjective well-being gap within China.

JOB RESOURCES

Intrinsic job resources or human resource management systems that sustain job control, clear goals, and performance feedback appear to be more strongly linked to lower turnover intentions in individualistic cultures (Jang et al., 2018), and to job satisfaction in high-performance orientation (PO) cultures (Onyemah et al., 2010). Halliday et al. (2018) further explored job autonomy as a key resource for women in a 26-country study. Controlling for industry and GDP growth, they found significant negative indirect effects of job autonomy on turnover intentions in lower gender egalitarian (GE) countries and significant positive indirect effects in higher GE countries. This finding suggests that autonomy may act as a resource only when women are working under conditions of resource loss and high job demand.

Research on participative decision making has yielded mixed results, ranging from a positive effect across European Values Survey (EVS) participants (Pacheco & Webber, 2016) to a better fit in low UA and high-collectivism cultures (Jang et al., 2018) and to surprising results like greater reception in countries high on self-expression as well as traditionality, presumably because traditionality elevates the importance of work (Van der Westhuizen et al., 2012). Participative decision making was further found to buffer the negative impact of temporary contracts on job satisfaction across 23 European countries (Goñi-Legaz & Ollo-López, 2017). Relatedly, Fisher's (2014) 18-country study with data from a multinational corporation (MNC) tested whether the efficacy of empowerment and cooperative climate as moderators of the overload-organizational commitment relationship was dependent on the broader cultural context. Using Hofstede scores and the practice scores from the GLOBE project (House et al., 2004) for confirmation, Fisher (2014) showed that empowerment mitigated the negative relationship between overload and organizational commitment under conditions of low PD. Contrary to predictions, a cooperative climate did not mitigate this negative relationship under conditions of low individualism, which prompted Fisher to propose distinguishing between types of cooperation (instrumental vs. emotional support) in future research.

Indeed, the nature of support, or the role of interdependence in the workplace in predicting job attitudes, appears to be culture-dependent. Interpersonal interruptions or even face time have been argued to frustrate individualists as threats to their job autonomy (Liu et al., 2010; Masuda et al., 2012). In contrast, collectivists seem to have better job attitudes in interdependent contexts like team structures (e.g., So et al., 2011), though arguments regarding being susceptible to factors such as relationship conflict have been raised (Chen et al., 2011). It has also been proposed that employees in collectivist cultures might struggle with practices such as remote or flexible work as they may hurt intraorganizational informal networks by introducing temporal or spatial distance (e.g., Lai et al., 2022; Masuda et al., 2012).

More recently, the importance of support as a predictor of job attitudes has been investigated in the context of immigrant workers. Indeed, the precariousness of migrant lives and their work conditions are becoming central to OB as immigrants increasingly represent a greater proportion of workforces all around the world (Harrison et al., 2019). Focusing on China, Qin et al. (2019) argued that rural migrant workers experience cultural shock when adapting to urban society, while being separated from their family. Given weak laws, poor unionization, and a high PD culture, Qin et al. (2019) reasoned that their supervisor had an enormous influence on their retention and well-being. Yet, the authors proposed that having a personal relationship with the supervisor would attract considerable wrath or antipathy from the work group. Hence, the supervisory supportive climate and the collective resource available to all workers would be essential for employee retention. With multisource, multiphase data from a large Chinese construction group, they supported their arguments.

In another study, Ulusoy et al. (2016) compared Turkish immigrants in Germany to a sample of German natives in Germany and Turkish natives in Turkey. Immigration background per se did not affect job attitudes; instead, affective commitment was contingent on perceived psychological safety. The authors noted that having an immigrant background means being at risk of social exclusion and prejudice, and they argued that immigrants may be more sensitive to cues of inclusiveness. Indeed, the affective commitment of German and Turkish employees was less strongly related to psychological safety than was the case for Turkish immigrant employees. Ulusoy et al. (2016) speculated that the commitment of home country nationals may be based more on task self-efficacy or role clarity, as opposed to immigrant employees, who may interpret psychological safety as a sign of social belonging, particularly when they have a collectivist background but in an individualistic context.

On a related note, Frazier et al.'s (2017) meta-analysis found that the relationship between supportive work context and organizational commitment as mediated by psychological safety was stronger in high than in low UA cultures. Thus, beyond collectivism, a society's low tolerance for ambiguity may favor supportive work environments for desirable job attitudes.

Antecedents of Job Attitudes: Leadership

In an increasingly global business environment, the question regarding which leadership styles work across cultures and which are culture-bound has been pivotal. In a meta-analysis of the leader–member exchange (LMX), Rockstuhl et al. (2012) argued that the stronger deference to authority associated with vertical collectivism (VC) provided a basis to expect weaker effects of LMX on job attitudes, which they confirmed for job satisfaction and turnover intentions. However, the relationships between LMX and affective or normative commitment were not different in horizontal-individualistic (HI) and VC cultures. The authors speculated that the followers' commitment to the organization may have influenced the results. Testing the generalizability of another Western leadership construct, Stein et al. (2020) meta-analyzed the effects of servant leadership on job attitudes in China versus Anglo countries. They offered competing hypotheses, noting that servant leadership is not as authoritarian as the prototypical Chinese leadership, but it is congruent with Chinese norms for benevolence and ethics. Their results revealed no significant differences between Chinese and Anglo findings. Finally, another Western leadership construct, namely, empowering leadership, was tested in an international sample of hotel employees, and an overall positive impact of empowering leadership on affective commitment and voice was observed. Moreover, this effect was less positive among individuals high on PD values (Raub & Robert, 2013).

Regarding the generalizability of Eastern leadership constructs, Hiller et al.'s (2019) meta-analysis of paternalistic leadership revealed that Cheng et al.'s (2004) authoritarianism dimension measuring fear-inspiring authority and control was consistently negatively related to beneficial job attitudes. Yet, their benevolence (e.g., individualized care, forgivingness) and morality (e.g., not taking advantage) dimensions displayed the opposite pattern, as did the unitary benevolence measure of Aycan (2006). Impressively, 41% of this study's sample comprised non-English publications, thereby incorporating the results in contexts where paternalism has been argued to be preferred or popular. Another informative study as to the generalizability of Eastern leadership constructs was by Smith et al. (2014), who tested whether *guanxi*-type supervisor–subordinate relationships were culture-specific across Chinese and non-Chinese samples. Their analyses revealed that affective attachment (emotional connection with the supervisor) and deference (obedience toward the supervisor) subscales of *guanxi* demonstrated full metric invariance, whereas the personal life inclusion subscale, measuring the extent to which subordinates and supervisors are included in each other's private or family lives, had partial metric invariance. The affective attachment and deference to supervisor dimensions had cross-nationally invariant relationships with organizational commitment, but the personal life inclusion dimension was unrelated to desirable job attitudes, suggesting that this component may be experienced as a burden.

Supervisor–subordinate *guanxi* has also been the impetus for the only study to use the honor–dignity–face framework (Leung & Cohen, 2011). Cheng et al. (2015) argued that in dignity cultures such as the United States, where a person's worth is established by their internal integrity, subordinates would expect supervisor integrity and a fair exchange. In contrast, for face cultures like Taiwan, concern for social relationships may be more important than integrity. For both countries, the highest level of commitment to the supervisor was observed when both perceived supervisor integrity and support were high. For the American sample, perceived supervisor support increased supervisor commitment to a greater degree when a high degree of supervisor integrity was also perceived. For the Taiwanese employees, in contrast, high perceived support and low perceived integrity were almost as good as having both high support and high integrity, which the authors argued was due to the compensatory effect of *guanxi*.

Echoing research from Chinese contexts, Costigan et al. (2011) compared turnover intentions as an outcome of employee trust in supervisor versus top management with Polish, Russian, and American samples. Across the three samples, employee trust in upper management was more highly associated with turnover intentions than was supervisor trust, pointing to the greater role upper management might have for firm performance and job security. Finally, Loi et al. (2012) showed that a supervisor's affective commitment was an antecedent to subordinate affective commitment and that low PD at the individual level positively moderated this relationship. Thus, although high PD employees may be reverential toward their supervisors, they may not mimic their supervisor's affective mindset.

Antecedents of Job Attitudes: Fairness, and Inclusiveness of Organizational Practices

FAIRNESS

Justice is a primary concern in any work relationship. Shao et al. (2013) proposed that cultural differences would provide evidence of the differential validity of the various perspectives on justice. If the instrumental perspective, which holds that justice provides a mechanism for outcome maximization, is valid, individualism and masculinity would positively moderate the justice–outcomes relationship. In contrast, if the relational perspective, which posits individual value justice because it signals acceptance and ingroup status, is valid, then individualism and masculinity would weaken the justice–outcomes relationship. If the uncertainty management perspective on justice applies, naturally, UA would be a positive moderator. Finally, the moral perspective on justice would lead to the prediction that reactions to perceived injustices would be stronger in low-PD countries. With regard to job attitudes as outcomes, Shao et al.'s (2013) meta-analytic review only supported the instrumental perspective. Nonetheless, the moral perspective may also be relevant as other studies have found individuals from low-PD countries valued procedural justice to a greater extent than their counterparts in high-PD countries (e.g., Jiang et al., 2017; Summereder et al., 2014). Importantly, justice appears to have many generalizable aspects. For instance, consistency in decision procedures appears to be similarly related to turnover intentions across individuals from high versus low-PD countries (Summereder et al., 2014). Similarly, perceptions of transparency in performance evaluations was significantly related to job satisfaction in a Japanese MNC's five Asian subsidiaries (Yamazaki & Yoon, 2016), and procedural justice perceptions activated both social exchange and social identity motives across South Korean and U.S. samples (Cho & Treadway, 2011).

Recent studies have also explored an organization's fair treatment of external constituents. Dögl and Holtbrügge (2014) argued that in developed countries such as the United States and Germany, postmaterialistic values, such as environmental protection, gain importance compared to emerging economies such as China and India, where employees would be more committed to a company that satisfies their basic needs. Yet, environmental reputation had similar effects on organizational commitment across the board, leading Dögl and Holtbrügge to offer alternative explanations such as income differences not mattering that much, cultural values converging, or firm cultures being more similar than national cultures. Vlachos et al. (2014) compared salespeople in large companies in the Netherlands versus India regarding the impact of corporate social responsibility (CSR) initiatives in employee retention. Supporting their argument that CSR is a communitarian concern, CSR was more important in collectivist India. With data from a large MNC, Mueller et al. (2012) tested whether CSR influenced affective commitment across 17 countries. They proposed that in countries high on GLOBE's humane orientation (HO) values, which uphold altruism and high on institutional collectivism, which emphasize collective distribution of rewards and resources, the relationship between CSR and affective commitment would be stronger. In contrast, PD would weaken this relationship as low-PD countries would be aversive to power misuse. Controlling for gender, job satisfaction, differences in scale reliabilities and at the national level unemployment rate, the results supported all the predictions. Although not hypothesized, they also observed significant moderating effects of ingroup collectivism and future orientation (FO) suggesting that members of cultures that are not self-oriented and show a propensity to work toward long-term success are more likely to appreciate CSR.

FLEXIBLE AND FAMILY SUPPORTIVE WORK PRACTICES

With the established importance of family obligations in collectivist cultures and the rising female workforce participation in the developing world, where gender roles remain segregated, work-family conflict (WFC) has become attractive topic for comparative job attitudes research. Research attention has focused on whether this conflict is less evident in collectivist cultures primarily because work is seen as a contribution to the family unlike individualistic cultures, where they are seen as competing demands (Casper et al., 2011).

Differences aside, across many countries, WFC is related to job strain, and supervisor or organizational support in relation to work–family demands is predictive of desirable job attitudes (e.g., Agarwala et al., 2014; Allen et al., 2014; Billing et al., 2014; Haar et al., 2014; Lu et al., 2010; Stock et al., 2016). Even so, several studies speak to the moderating role of culture. Lu et al. (2010) confirmed that supervisor support played a greater role in the high PD Taiwanese context in curbing WFC compared to the UK. In a meta-analytic study, Zhang et al. (2018) found that work–family enrichment (WFE) and job satisfaction (but not turnover intentions or organizational commitment) were more strongly related in Eastern versus Western samples in support of their proposition that WFE would have more positive consequences in low masculinity, collectivist, and long-term oriented cultures, all of which are related to willingness to integrate work and family roles.

Studies on flexible work arrangements (FWA) or the work–life balance (WLB) and job attitudes have supported the idea that flexibility and the associated job autonomy pays off in individualistic cultures to a greater extent (e.g., Billing et al., 2014; Haar et al., 2014; Masuda et al., 2012). Lai et al. (2022) also found that access to and use of FWA were generally linked to higher levels of job satisfaction in the United States, in contrast to their Chinese sample, where the relationships were mostly insignificant, even though the data came from MNCs operating in both countries. Rather than values, Lai et al. (2022) argued that China's relatively low levels of prosperity may place economic survival above all other goals, and FWA could be viewed as a luxury. Indeed, legal or economic structures, especially welfare state regimes and statutory work–family policies have been found to be related to higher levels of supervisor and coworker work–family support (Beham et al., 2014). In a rare study that incorporated cultural, institutional, and organizational characteristics, Allen et al. (2014) found that paid sick leave had a small but significant negative relationship with WFC among working married couples in 12 industrialized nations after controlling for collectivist values. Family supportiveness of the work environment and the supervisor positively moderated the relationship between national policy and outcomes. This suggested that not being subject to repercussions for using one's legal rights was also consequential for one's well-being.

MISTREATMENT AND DISCRIMINATION

The cultures argued to be sensitive to interpersonal relationships have also been posited to be relatively passive in dealing with mistreatment. Although the empirical evidence was not always strong, researchers have maintained that collectivists might adopt nonadversarial conflict strategies to ostracism (Bedi, 2021) or that high PD (Loh et al., 2010) or low HO cultures (Giorgi et al., 2015) would respond less negatively to bullying. Regarding gender discrimination, Triana et al. (2017) found a negative and significant main effect between female gender of the supervisor and subordinate affective commitment in the Turkish but not in the U.S. sample. The authors noted that Turkey and the United States differ considerably in the prevalence of female managers (25% versus 51%), which may affect the acceptance of a female supervisor. Furthermore, because female employees expressed greater aversion to having a female supervisor, the authors posited that the relatively fewer opportunities for females in the upper echelons might be increasing the rivalry among women.

Arguing that employees would be less tolerant of gender discrimination in high GE countries as reflected in cultural values as well as institutions, in a later study Triana et al. (2019) conducted a meta-analysis. While, contrary to prediction, correlations between perceived gender discrimination and job attitudes were weaker in countries with more GE labor policies and practices, the cultural moderation hypothesis was supported. The authors speculated that in countries with more gender egalitarian labor policies and practices, employees may have alternative recourses to combat the discrimination, which in turn may attenuate the potential detriment to job attitudes.

Finally, Peltokorpi (2013) observed that although Japanese employees, especially those in large companies, were embedded through practices such as long-term employment, extensive socialization, strong mentorship by immediate supervisors, firm-specific training, and limited pension portability, female employees were less embedded in their organizations because of gender discrimination in Japanese companies.

Antecedents of Job Attitudes: The Economic Context

We conclude our review of the antecedents by reporting a handful of studies that incorporated the overall economic context to the prediction of job attitudes in various countries. Chen et al. (2012) showed that GDP per capita growth attenuated the positive relationship between job satisfaction and organizational commitment, and the negative relationship between organizational commitment and turnover intentions, indicating that employees may be more selective in evaluating their jobs when opportunities are abundant. Complementing this observation, Zeytinoglu et al.'s (2012) study on Turkish service sector employees failed to identify the negative effect of work demands on job attitudes, suggesting that the high unemployment rate in the country may have rendered employees impervious to conditions like unpaid overtime. In fact, Giorgi et al. (2015) went as far as to infer that employees put up with bullying in a turbulent economic environment. Yet, not all evidence points to poor economic conditions to have "buffering" effects. For instance, using the British Household Panel Survey, Çitçi and Bergen (2019) showed that people who enter the workforce when the unemployment rate is high have less job satisfaction even in later ages, compared to those who enter the workforce when the unemployment rate is lower.

Outcomes of Job Attitudes

The outcomes of job attitudes across cultures have been investigated to a much lesser extent. There appear to be three main clusters regarding outcomes: the first delineating the outcomes of turnover intentions, the second focusing on whether perceived organizational support (POS) translates into organizational citizenship behavior, and the third on the outcomes of job embeddedness.

OUTCOMES OF TURNOVER INTENTIONS

Our review identified two studies that tested the outcomes of turnover intentions. Mai et al. (2016) demonstrated that turnover intentions have behavioral implications beyond organizational exit such as deviant behaviors or OCBs. Using the psychological contracts framework, the authors found that in the United States, employees with turnover intentions experienced a weaker relational orientation and a stronger transactional orientation, which then resulted in fewer OCBs and more deviant behaviors. These findings were largely replicated with a Chinese sample except that there was no significant relationship between relational contract orientation and OCBs. The authors speculated that in China, OCBs were driven not by social exchange mechanisms but by the employees' perceived role within the organization. Indeed, Rockstuhl et al. (2020) also found that POS had stronger associations with felt obligation and organizational trust in HI cultures than VC cultures, but stronger associations with organizational identification in VC cultures compared to HI cultures.

In a multilevel meta-analysis, Wong and Cheng (2020) proposed that employees who are low (vs. high) in individualism as well as low in masculinity (vs. femininity) are less likely to translate their intention to leave or to stay into behavior because their original intention is more likely to be attenuated by group preferences. They further predicted that supervisors from lower (vs. higher) PD countries were more likely to help resolve their subordinates' problems because they would be more likely to learn of those problems and to talk openly to their own superiors to work them out. Because of its association with risk aversion, UA was posited to be inversely associated with turnover behavior. Wong and Cheng (2020) results showed that turnover intentions assessed at an initial time point positively predicted subsequent turnover behavior. Moreover, the positive turnover intentions–turnover link was stronger in countries higher in individualism, higher in PD, and lower in masculinity. The moderating effect of UA was only marginally significant. The authors repeated the analyses with GLOBE value and practice dimensions of ingroup collectivism, institutional collectivism, PD, UA, and GE but did not find significant results, which led them to raise concerns regarding GLOBE's construct validity (Taras et al., 2010).

OUTCOMES OF POS

One of the main debates regarding outcomes revolves around the role of collectivism in the POS–OCB relationship. Van Knippenberg et al. (2015) argued that collectivism would actually dampen the effect of POS on OCB because the reciprocity involved in social exchange relationships is based primarily on self-interest among two separate (i.e., not interdependent) entities. Indeed, their study with Dutch employees confirmed this argument. Other studies have found collectivism to have a positive impact on the POS–OCB relationship (De Clercq et al., 2019; Lam et al., 2016). These rival arguments served as a motivation for a very recent and rigorous meta-analysis covering 54 nations (Rockstuhl et al., 2020). Controlling for regulatory, political, and economic differences across countries, Rockstuhl et al. (2020) found that relationships between POS and attitudinal (affective commitment, normative commitment, job involvement, job security, turnover intentions) as well as behavioral (task performance, OCB) outcomes were stronger in VC than in HI cultures. In addition, culture explained 46% of the variance in POS effects on attitudinal (and 28% on behavioral) outcomes at the country level, over and above national institutional differences. Using U.S. and South Korean samples in separate studies, Kim et al. (2016) showed that the POS–OCB relationship was strengthened by perceptions of organizational competence, suggesting that competent organizations may provide more predictable environments, attributes that apparently are valued similarly across cultures.

OUTCOMES OF JOB EMBEDDEDNESS

Research on job attitudes typically examines the relations within the organization that bond the employees to their workplace. In contrast, job embeddedness, which is a more recent approach to understanding employee retention, takes into account both on-the-job and off-the-job forces (such as informal *links* to other people, overall *fit* with the community, and *sacrifices* associated with leaving). As such, this holistic construct has garnered considerable research interest, particularly about the role of IC. In fact, although no difference emerged regarding on-the-job embeddedness and turnover intentions, Jiang et al. (2012) found that the negative relation between off-the-job embeddedness and turnover intentions was significantly stronger in collectivistic than in individualistic countries.

In the first study of the job embeddedness model outside Western contexts with actual turnover data, Ramesh and Gelfand (2010) reported that the fit dimension of job embeddedness was a better predictor in the United States than in India, while the links dimension was a better predictor in India. They further showed that family embeddedness, a construct they introduced to capture the family's favorable appraisal of the focal employee's workplace by virtue of its prestige, connections, or benefits, predicted turnover in both cultures over and above job and community embeddedness. Since then, studies from other collectivist cultures have been identifying the contours of embeddedness. For instance, Hom and Xiao's (2011) insightful study revealed how *guanxi* ties reinforced on-the-job embeddedness, while the institutional constraints regarding household registration (*hukou*) and state employment systems that limit Chinese citizens' geographic mobility reinforced off-the-job embeddedness. In South Korea, Kwon (2017) showed that links to college alumni networks and region-based social circles predicted turnover intentions more than pay satisfaction or workload. Sender et al. (2018) argued that both on-the-job and off-the-job embeddedness would be more strongly related to turnover in collectivistic China than in individualistic Switzerland, but they found that on-the-job embeddedness reduced the likelihood of turnover more strongly in Switzerland. Additionally, on-the-job embeddedness did not buffer the relationship between unsolicited job offers and turnover in either country. These results highlighted the role of noncultural factors such as differences in tenure across samples as well as country or city size (e.g., regarding commute times; Kim & Park, 2017), as the latter factors influence whether job changes require or justify relocation.

In an informative interview study in Japan, Peltokorpi (2013) noted that off-work embeddedness involving hobbies or religion appeared to be minimal due to long hours at work and high-work centrality. Yet, caring for aging parents tied employees location-wise. In a follow-up study, Peltokorpi et al. (2015) tested the relationship between job embeddedness, turnover intentions, and turnover as moderated by demographics and value orientations in Japan. They concluded that the embeddedness construct has cross-cultural transportability, even to a relatively low-turnover national context. Collectivistic values did not moderate the relationships as originally predicted, but embeddedness had a stronger indirect impact on turnover for employees with lower risk aversion. Peltokorpi et al. (2015) proposed time orientation as another cultural variable to pursue.

Peltokorpi (2013) further suggested that several items of the American job embeddedness scale should be dropped or modified when applied in Japan. For instance, items assessing neighborhood safety or fitting into new communities do not appear to be as relevant in Japan. Similarly, the autonomy- or authority-related items in the original scale might not generalize to Japan. Similarly, Zhang et al. (2012a) argued that community embeddedness may have negligible effect in China, where there is a tradition of family rather than community orientation. Ramesh and Gelfand (2010) also questioned the generalizability of community embeddedness, especially to societies with low residential mobility such as India. Thus, Ramesh and Gelfand's family embeddedness construct, albeit with modifications regarding assumptions as to the presence of diffuse relationship (e.g., family knowing coworkers) appears to be more widely applicable (Wasti, 2002). Relatedly, occupational embeddedness, which refers to "the totality of forces that keep people in their present occupations" (Feldman & Ng, 2007, p. 353) promises to be a fruitful construct for cross-cultural research. For instance, Abdulla et al.'s (2011) study on the determinants of job satisfaction for the Dubai police revealed the greater importance of public prestige compared to intrinsic job factors or coworker relations. Because occupations have different degrees of prestige in diverse contexts and prestige itself is differentially valued across societies, occupational embeddedness may deserve further research attention.

Finally, although not treated in the framework of embeddedness by the researchers themselves, we cover the research on fit here, as fit has been proposed to be one of the forces increasing an employee's embeddedness. Lee and Antonakis (2014) argued that PD would moderate the relationship between person-job fit and job attitudes. In particular, they posited that individuals in high-PD contexts may incur psychological costs for not conforming to norms and feel intrinsically motivated when choices are made by trusted authority figures. Their results showed that individuals in the high-PD group (Taiwan, France, and Italy) were relatively satisfied even when their individual preferences were not fulfilled (low fit) compared to the low-PD group (Germany, UK, and Netherlands). Importantly, the authors underlined that fit may be defined differently across cultures. Indeed, Oh et al.'s (2014) meta-analysis further showed that relational fit (person-group and person-supervisor fit) was a better predictor of job attitudes in high-PD collectivist East Asia than in low-PD individualist North America, while the effect of rational fit (person-job and person-organization fit) was relatively stronger in North America (and to a lesser extent, Europe) than in East Asia. Jung and Takeuchi's (2014) study comparing Japan to South Korea further suggested that in cultures where the relationship with the supervisor is more interdependent or intense, the importance of person-organization fit in predicting job attitudes may be undermined.

Discussion

Despite suggestions as to cultures converging the process of globalization (Kirkman et al., 2017), our review does not suggest that the role of cultural differences in understanding work behavior is subsiding. As Rockstuhl et al. (2020) noted, globalization may be a more fragmented, incomplete, and discontinuous process, and perhaps will be more so post-COVID-19. Therefore, we conclude with several theoretical and practical implications that assume the continued importance of cultural differences (please see Table 8.2 for a summary).

Table 8.2 Summary of key theoretical and practical implications

Theoretical Implications 1. The influence of structural variables (e.g., unemployment rates, labor market conditions, or statutory benefits) deserve attention to complement the cultural perspective. 2. The cross-level direct or moderating effects of societal level variables on organizational or individual levels need to be further delineated and empirically captured to better predict job attitudes. 3. The conceptualization of *culture as values* can be fruitfully supplemented with a socioecological view, which defines *culture as social structures* that surround people and constrain their behavior. 4. More nuanced examination of collectivism can identify species as well as the intricacies of collectivism, which will advance our understanding of the complexity and diversity of organizational bonds. 5. The role of collective attitudes in focal employees' job attitudes can be incorporated by focusing on theories such as social information processing, family power dynamics, collective sense-making, theories of reasoned action, and social network analyses.
Practical Implications 1. Cultural change in younger generations toward greater individualism and joy is likely to be particularly challenging for organizational leaders in more collectivist, hierarchical, uncertainty avoidant, and tight cultures. 2. HR professionals and organizational leaders may need to adopt a more particularistic approach in the management of talent across international contexts while ensuring their legitimacy across the whole workforce. 3. HR professionals and organizational leaders should strive to create support mechanisms that would help immigrants effectively cope with workplace challenges like discrimination. 4. New work arrangements such as digitalization and remote work may be particularly challenging for the workforce of emerging and developing economies as well as collectivist, hierarchical, and high-context cultures. 5. Governmental protection programs and the regulation of the employment relationship can provide a social safety net supporting the positive job attitudes of vulnerable employees, particularly in developing economies.

Theoretical Directions

INTEGRATING THE CULTURALIST AND STRUCTURALIST PERSPECTIVES

As much as societal culture may be a strong moderator of the job attitudes nomological net, in many studies, differences in structural variables among the countries such as unemployment rates, labor market conditions, employee rights, and statutory benefits have been observed to be lurking as rival hypotheses. They are typically raised in the discussion, especially when the cultural predictions fail to pan out. Although research that links structural variables to psychological constructs is rare, there is enough evidence to take this concern seriously. For instance, employees have been found to be less critical of their organizations when macroeconomic conditions are faltering. Yet, they also appear to be less helping, more opportunistic, and more short-term-oriented during economic downturns (Sirola, 2020). Similarly, an employee's work experience under a welfare state is different from that in a market or a developing economy, also because employee attitudes toward favorable organizational practices vary depending on whether they are perceived to be at the discretion of management or legally enforced (Wasti et al., 2016). In incorporating structural differences, it will be important to clarify if and when the hypotheses will reflect deprivation-based preferences (e.g., extrinsic rewards being more important in less affluent countries) or habituation (e.g., individuals in less affluent countries being less reactive to lack of extrinsic rewards). Further, the so-called frog pond effects will need to be considered, as organizational experiences are likely to be evaluated by virtue of their relative standing in a particular context (Johns, 2006). For instance, working for an MNC is more likely to be embedding in a developing than an industrialized country. It is only through the integration of structural elements that the true effect of culture can be ascertained.

CAPTURING ORGANIZATIONAL- AND INDIVIDUAL-LEVEL MEDIATORS AND MODERATORS

Despite a considerable increase in the number of multilevel studies, comparative models of job attitudes will benefit from further delineating and in particular empirically capturing the mechanisms that reflect societal culture's cross-level influences on the organizational and individual levels. Currently, many models empirically leave out the mediating mechanisms. For instance, although employees in a high-PD country are found to be less confrontational regarding bullying, it is not clear whether it is because they blame themselves or it is not normative to complain or because they defer to powerholders (Loh et al., 2010). Similarly, if, contrary to expectations, more versus less affluent countries do not differ in their attitudes toward CSR, whether the more proximal organizational culture played a role cannot be determined (Dögl & Holtbrügge, 2014). It is essential that future models examine how societal-level variables have direct or moderating effects on lower-level (organization, team, individual) outcomes, as well as on relationships at lower levels (Gelfand et al., 2008).

BROADENING THE CULTURAL PERSPECTIVE

The most influential conceptualization of culture, and in particular IC, defines it as internalized values and preferences that drive individuals' behavior. However, this conceptualization is limited on several accounts; for instance, values appear to be less predictive of behavior in tight as opposed to loose cultures (Elster & Gelfand, 2021). Recently, the limitations of the culture-as-values view has generated calls for supplementing this argument with a socioecological view of culture, which defines culture as social structures that surround people and constrain their behavior (Liu et al., 2021). Consider the finding that Turkish employees exhibit behaviors such as helping peers (Zeytinoglu et al., 2012). According to the values account, this is because they cherish ingroup relationships, whereas the socioecological account would suggest that it is a fitting response in a resource-poor environment, with many family obligations but little institutional support. Similarly, while the values account posits those with authority are respected in high-PD cultures, Frazier et al. (2017) note that weak institutional environments (i.e., fragile or corrupt states, ineffective judicial systems) may make immediate leaders even more important. Broadening our understanding of culture as located "inside" as well as "in the world" (Hamedani & Markus, 2019) will greatly improve the predictive power of our models.

CAPTURING THE NUANCES OF COLLECTIVISM

It is natural that a subfield focused on organizational bonds has drawn so much on IC. Yet, it is also remarkable that a particular and uniform conceptualization of collectivism has been endorsed. This conceptualization highlights the importance of harmony and humility in relationships, which in effect is a characterization of Asian face collectivism and does not speak to other species such as honor collectivism (Leung & Cohen, 2011). While similar to face collectivists in that relatedness and garnering social respect are primary goals, honor cultures have historically emerged in contexts characterized by weak rule of law or portable economic wealth, which are associated with greater affordances regarding status contests, confrontation, and emotional expression. These differences call for more nuanced research, particularly with respect to peer relations as well as workplace aggression. Besides, the job attitudes literature has not focused on the intricacies of collectivism, thereby neglecting that interdependence binds and also blinds its parties (e.g., Liu et al., 2019) and results in chronic vigilance in managing the collective identity, dyadic relationships as well as self-interest (Qin et al., 2019). Going beyond the narrow conceptualization of collectivism can uncover the real complexity of the relationships as they unfold across cultures and in intercultural encounters.

RECOGNIZING COLLECTIVE DECISION MAKING

As with many mainstream OB theories, the literature on job attitudes has the individual as its central unit (Gelfand et al., 2008). Yet, this view is limited not only in terms of understanding other cultural contexts, but also in the United States, given that the workplace is one of the interdependent arenas of life. Consider, for instance, Liu et al.'s (2012) finding that coworkers' job satisfaction was predictive of the focal employee's turnover intentions in a U.S. sample. In that respect, the holistic and relational premises of job embeddedness are promising for future comparative job attitudes research. As Lee et al. (2017) noted, several theories can give a head start to better understand collective behavior, such as theories of social information processing, family power dynamics, collective sensemaking, theories of reasoned action, as well as social network analyses. Future studies should seek to answer the circumstances under which certain groups or group members (including family) wield greater influence on the focal employee's attitudes and decisions, how conflicting referent demands are resolved, as well as drawbacks and advantages of closed networks.

Practical Implications

CULTURAL CHANGE

The research emerging out of China is putting cultural change to the forefront of the researchers' as well as the managers' agenda. In particular, with Chinese organizations striving for globalization, competing with MNCs, with a new generation emerging from one-child families, exposed to Western values and working conditions in foreign firms, the question as to whether traditional Chinese management principles will continue to serve the workplace is paramount (e.g., Zhang et al., 2012b). However, the change imperative is not limited to China. Beugelsdijk and Welzel (2018) demonstrate a shift from collectivism toward individualism and from duty toward joy among younger generations across 110 countries. These changes are likely to be particularly challenging for more collectivist, hierarchical, uncertainty avoidant as well as tighter cultures (Gelfand et al., 2011). In loosening the particularistic, hierarchical, and tight practices, which the new generations appear to find constricting (Li et al., 2018), organizational leaders will also have to ensure that employees are not feeling abandoned (Humborstad et al., 2008) and will need to strike the right balance on the way to establishing more empowered systems.

TALENT MANAGEMENT

Global uncertainty, magnified with COVID-19, poses talent management as a critical challenge for HR professionals and organizational leaders. Cooke et al. (2014) propose a contingency framework and highlight the need to adopt a more particularistic approach in international contexts. Idiosyncratic deals (I-deals), which are negotiated work arrangements that benefit both the employer and employee, can serve this purpose (Liao et al., 2014). The I-deals literature suggests that employees in different cultures may interpret or value I-deals differently or I-deals may generate different reactions based on the prevalent fairness norms in the culture or the safety nets in the overall context (Wasti et al., 2022). Hence, when I-deals are used for retaining employees, it is important to ensure that their content is fitting the needs/goals of the employees in the particular context and that their implementation is well communicated across the workforce, ensuring their legitimacy.

IMMIGRANT EMPLOYEES

Our review highlighted the need to incorporate the challenging role transitions and adaptations that migrants experience to job attitudes and turnover models (e.g., Qin et al., 2019). Immigrants often face an identity struggle, accompanied by falling social status and rising insecurity, both within and outside of the work context (Harrison et al., 2019). Such a struggle might be more consequential regarding job attitudes, particularly if the new context holds a strikingly different culture than one's own. Moreover, national border closures and travel restrictions in the aftermath of COVID-19 may create unique challenges for the well-being and performance of immigrant employees. Research indicates that in the absence of a timely and proper intervention, fear and discrimination against outgroup members, such as immigrants, may be heightened during such a pandemic and the ensuing economic crisis (Van Bavel et al., 2020). Hence, nurturing organizational, supervisor, and coworker support mechanisms that help immigrant workers to effectively cope with challenging situations are critical.

NEW WORK ARRANGEMENTS

The health crisis created by COVID-19 had immediate implications in terms of work arrangements such as digitalization and remote work (International Labor Organization, 2020). Some of these changes are very likely here to stay. However, work arrangements such as remote work and flexible work hours, as well as integration of digital technology, may be experienced differently across contexts (Guan et al., 2020). Emerging and developing economies are typically characterized by limited WLB policies and precedents, segregated gender roles, and prevailing family obligations. Consequently, the role boundaries may be blurred more and have more negative consequences for workers with care responsibilities at home (Cho, 2020). Effective management of remote work resides within the companies. Not only should employees have the right to a good and safe working environment, they should also have the right to disconnect. However, for employees in collectivist and high-power distant cultures, this might become a daunting task as their concerns regarding role obligations may make it difficult to strike a balance. High-context cultures, which communicate in implicit, nonverbal ways or low-trust contexts, where the need to monitor is high, may find remote work particularly challenging. Creating channels for open dialogue between employer and employees to overcome these transitions is critical.

POLICY IMPLICATIONS

Although there is a debate regarding governmental involvement in the economy, the importance of strong social safety nets has become evident during the COVID-19 crisis. In particular, those living in developing countries may face more disruptive consequences in terms of massive unemployment and in turn, social cohesion (International Labor Organization, 2020). Protective measures such as wage subsidies, coupled with active labor market policies targeting retention of the employees, particularly those who are more vulnerable (e.g., employees with disabilities, migrant workers, and women), may be critical in these contexts. Our review has already revealed the positive influence of national policies regarding paid sick leave and access to health care (e.g., Allen et al., 2014; Debus et al., 2012), and it is easy to argue that their importance has been amplified in the COVID-19 crisis. It is only through a more holistic perspective on well-being that incorporates the whole society and the whole person that organizations can hope to achieve sustainable productivity.

References

Abdulla, J., Djebarni, R., & Mellahi, K. (2011). Determinants of job satisfaction in the UAE: A case study of the Dubai police. *Personnel Review, 40*(1), 126–146. https://doi.org/10.1108/00483481111095555

Agarwala, T., Arizkuren-Eleta, A., Castillo, E. D., Muniz-Ferrer, M., & Gartzia, L. (2014). Influence of managerial support on work–life conflict and organizational commitment: an international comparison for India, Peru and Spain. *The International Journal of Human Resource Management, 25*(10), 1460–1483. https://doi.org/10.1080/09585192.2013.870315

Allen, T. D., Lapierre, L. M., Spector, P. E., Poelmans, S. A. Y., O'Driscoll, M., Sanchez, J. I., Cooper, C. L., Walvoord, A. G., Antoniou, A., Brough, P., Geurts, S., Kinnunen, U., Pagon, M., Shima, S., & Woo, J. (2014). The link between National Paid Leave policy and work–family conflict among married working parents. *Applied Psychology: An International Review, 63*(1), 5–28. https://doi.org/10.1111/apps.12004

Aycan, Z. (2006). Paternalism. In U. Kim, K-S. Yang, & K-K. Hwang (Eds.), *Indigenous and cultural psychology* (pp. 445–466). New York: Springer.

Bedi, A. (2021). No herd for black sheep: A meta-analytic review of the predictors and outcomes of workplace ostracism. *Applied Psychology: An International Review, 70*(2), 861–904. https://doi.org/10.1111/apps.12238

Beham, B., Drobnicˇ, S., & Präg, P. (2014). The work–family interface of service sector workers: A comparison of work resources and professional status across five European countries. *Applied Psychology: An International Review, 63*(1), 29–61. https://doi.org/10.1111/apps.12012

Beugelsdijk, S., & Welzel, C. (2018). Dimensions and dynamics of national culture: Synthesizing Hofstede with Inglehart. *Journal of Cross-Cultural Psychology, 49*(10), 1469–1505. https://doi.org/10.1177/0022022118798505

Billing, T. K., Bhagat, R. S., Babakus, E., Krishnan, B., Ford, D. L., Jr., Srivastava, B. N., Rajadhyaksha, U., Shin, M., Kuo, B., Kwantes, C., Setiadi, B., & Nasurdin, A. M. (2014). Work–family conflict and organisationally valued outcomes: the moderating role of decision latitude in five national contexts. *Applied Psychology: An International Review, 63*(1), 62–95. https://doi.org/10.1111/j.1464-0597.2012.00526.x

Casper, W. J., Harris, C., Taylor-Bianco, A., & Wayne, J. H. (2011). Work–family conflict, perceived supervisor support and organizational commitment among Brazilian professionals. *Journal of Vocational Behavior, 79*(3), 640–652. https://doi.org/10.1016/j.jvb.2011.04.011

Chen, G., Sharma, P. N., Edinger, S. K., Shapiro, D. L., & Farh, J. (2011). Motivating and demotivating forces in teams: Cross-level influences of empowering leadership and relationship conflict. *Journal of Applied Psychology, 96*(3), 541–557. https://doi.org/10.1037/a0021886

Chen, H., Ford, D. L., Jr., Kalyanaram, G., & Bhagat, R. S. (2012). Boundary conditions for turnover intentions: Exploratory evidence from China, Jordan, Turkey, and the United States. *The International Journal of Human Resource Management, 23*(4), 846–866. https://doi.org/10.1080/09585192.2011.610968

Cheng, B. S., Chou, L. F., Wu, T. Y., Huang, M. P., & Farh, J. L. (2004). Paternalistic leadership and subordinate responses: Establishing a leadership model in Chinese organizations. *Asian Journal of Social Psychology, 7*(1), 89–117. https://doi.org/10.1111/j.1467-839X.2004.00137.x

Cheng, C., Jiang, D., Cheng, B., Riley, J. H., & Jen, C. (2015). When do subordinates commit to their supervisors? Different effects of perceived supervisor integrity and support on Chinese and American employees. *The Leadership Quarterly, 26*(1), 81–97. https://doi.org/10.1016/j.leaqua.2014.08.002

Cho, E. (2020). Examining boundaries to understand the impact of COVID-19 on vocational behaviors. *Journal of Vocational Behavior, 119*, 103437. https://doi.org/10.1016/j.jvb.2020.103437

Cho, J., & Treadway, D. C. (2011). Organizational identification and perceived organizational support as mediators of the procedural justice–citizenship behaviour relationship: A cross-cultural constructive replication. *European Journal of Work and Organizational Psychology, 20*(5), 631–653. https://doi.org/10.1080/1359432X.2010.487363

Çitçi, S. H., & Begen, N. (2019). Macroeconomic conditions at workforce entry and job satisfaction. *International Journal of Manpower, 40*(5), 879–893. https://doi.org/10.1108/IJM-02-2018-0048

Cooke, F. L., Saini, D. S., & Wang, J. (2014). Talent management in China and India: A comparison of management perceptions and human resource practices. *Journal of World Business, 49*(2), 225–235. https://doi.org/10.1016/j.jwb.2013.11.006

Costigan, R. D., Insinga, R. C., Berman, J. J., Kranas, G., & Kureshov, V. (2011). Revisiting the relationship of supervisor trust and CEO trust to turnover intentions: A three-country comparative study. *Journal of World Business, 46*(1), 74–83. https://doi.org/10.1016/j.jwb.2010.05.019

Debus, M. E., Probst, T. M., König, C. J., & Kleinmann, M. (2012). Catch me if I fall! Enacted uncertainty avoidance and the social safety net as country-level moderators in the job insecurity–job attitudes link. *Journal of Applied Psychology, 97*(3), 690–698. https://doi.org/10.1037/a0027832

De Clercq, D., Haq, I. U., & Azeem, M. U. (2019). Why happy employees help: How meaningfulness, collectivism, and support transform job satisfaction into helping behaviours. *Personnel Review, 48*(4), 1001–1021. https://doi.org/10.1108/PR-02-2018-0052

Dögl, C., & Holtbrügge, D. (2014). Corporate environmental responsibility, employer reputation and employee commitment: An empirical study in developed and emerging economies. *The International Journal of Human Resource Management, 25*(12), 1739–1762. https://doi.org/10.1080/09585192.2013.859164

Elster, A., & Gelfand, M. J. (2021). When guiding principles do not guide: The moderating effects of cultural tightness on value-behavior links. *Journal of Personality, 89(2)*, 325–337. https://doi.org/10.1111/jopy.12584

Feldman, D. C., & Ng, T. W. H. (2007). Careers: Mobility, embeddedness, and success. *Journal of Management, 33*(3), 350–377. https://doi.org/10.1177/0149206307300815

Fischer, R., & Mansell, A. (2009). Commitment across cultures: A meta-analytical approach. *Journal of International Business Studies, 40*, 1339–1358. https://doi.org/10.1057/jibs.2009.14

Fisher, D. M. (2014). A multilevel cross-cultural examination of role overload and organizational commitment: Investigating the interactive effects of context. *Journal of Applied Psychology, 99*(4), 723–736. https://doi.org/10.1037/a0035861

Frazier, M. L., Fainshmidt, S., Klinger, R. L., Pezeshkan, A., & Vracheva, V. (2017). Psychological safety: A meta-analytic review and extension. *Personnel Psychology, 70*(1), 113–165. https://doi.org/10.1111/peps.12183

Gamble, J., & Tian, A. W. (2015). Intra-national variation in organizational commitment: evidence from Chinese context. *The International Journal of Human Resource Management, 26*(7), 948–970. https://doi.org/10.1080/09585192.2012.722122

Gelfand, M. J., Leslie, L. M., & Fehr, R. (2008). To prosper, organizational psychology should . . . adopt a global perspective. *Journal of Organizational Behavior, 29*(4): 493–517. https://doi.org/10.1002/job.530

Gelfand, M. J., Raver, J. L., Nishii, L., Leslie, L. M., Lun, J., Lim, B. C., Duan, L., Almaliach, A., Ang, S., Arnadottir, J., Aycan, Z., Boehnke, K., Boski, P., Cabecinhas, R., Chan, D., Chhokar, J., D'Amato, A., Ferrer, M., Fischlmayr, I. C., . . . & Yamaguchi, S. (2011). Differences between tight and loose cultures: A 33-nation study. *Science, 332*(6033), 1100–1104. https://doi.org/10.1126/science.1197754

Giorgi, G., Leon-Perez, J. M., & Arenas, A. (2015). Are bullying behaviors tolerated in some cultures? Evidence for a curvilinear relationship between workplace bullying and job satisfaction among Italian workers. *Journal of Business Ethics, 131*, 227–237. https://doi.org/10.1007/s10551-014-2266-9

Goñi-Legaz, S., & Ollo-López, A. (2017). Temporary contracts, participation in decision making and job satisfaction in European workers. Is there a buffering effect? *International Journal of Manpower, 38*(6), 875–892. https://doi.org/10.1108/IJM-04-2016-0086

Guan, Y., Deng, H., & Zhou, X. (2020). Understanding the impact of the COVID-19 pandemic on career development: Insights from cultural psychology. *Journal of Vocational Behavior, 119*, 103438. https://doi.org/10.1016/j.jvb.2020.103438

Haar, J. M., Russo, M., Suñe, A., & Ollier-Malaterre, A. (2014). Outcomes of work–life balance on job satisfaction, life satisfaction and mental health: A study across seven cultures. *Journal of Vocational Behavior, 85*, 361–374. https://doi.org/10.1016/j.jvb.2014.08.010

Halliday, C. S., Paustian-Underdahl, S. C., Ordóñez, Z., Rogelberg, S. G., & Zhang, H. (2018). Autonomy as a key resource for women in low gender egalitarian countries: A cross-cultural examination. *Human Resource Management, 57*(2), 1–15. https://doi.org/10.1002/hrm.21874

Hamedani, M. G., & Markus, H. R. (2019). Understanding culture clashes and catalyzing change: A culture cycle approach. *Frontiers in Psychology, 10*, 1–7. https://doi.org/10.3389/fpsyg.2019.00700

Harrison, D. A., Harrison, T., & Schaffer, M. A. (2019). Strangers in strained lands: Learning from workplace experiences of immigrant employees. *Journal of Management, 45*(2), 600–619. https://doi.org/10.1177/0149206318790648

Hausmann, N., Mueller, K. Hattrup, K., & Spies, S. (2013). An investigation of the relationships between affective organisational commitment and national differences in positivity and life satisfaction. *Applied Psychology: An International Review, 62*(2), 260–285. https://doi.org/10.1111/j.1464-0597.2012.00500

Hiller, N. J., Sin, H., Ponnapalli, A. R., & Ozgen, S. (2019). Benevolence and authority as WEIRDly unfamiliar: A multi-language meta-analysis of paternalistic leadership behaviors from 152 studies. *Leadership Quarterly, 30*(1), 165–184. https://doi.org/10.1016/j.leaqua.2018.11.003

Hofstede, G. (2001). *Culture's consequences: Comparing values, behaviors, institutions and organizations across nations* (2nd ed.). Thousand Oaks, CA: SAGE.

Hom, P. W., & Xiao, Z. (2011). Embedding social networks: How guanxi ties reinforce Chinese employees' retention. *Organizational Behavior and Human Decision Processes, 116*(2), 188–202. https://doi.org/10.1016/j.obhdp.2011.06.001

House, R. J., Hanges, P. J., Javidan, M., Dorfman, P. W., & Gupta, V. (Eds.). (2004). *Culture, leadership, and organizations: The GLOBE study of 62 societies.* Thousand Oaks, CA: SAGE.

Humborstad, S. I. W., Humborstad, B., Whitfield, R., & Perry, C. (2008). Implementation of empowerment in Chinese high power-distance organizations. *The International Journal of Human Resource Management, 19*(7), 1349–1364. https://doi.org/10.1080/09585190802110224

International Labor Organization. (2020). *Policy brief: COVID-19 and the world of work.* Geneva: ILO. https://www.ilo.org/wcmsp5/groups/public/---dgreports/---dcomm/documents/briefingnote/wcms_743146.pdf

Jang, S., Shen, W., Allen, T. D., & Zhang, H. (2018). Societal individualism-collectivism and uncertainty avoidance as cultural moderators of the relationships between job resources and strain. *Journal of Organizational Behavior, 39*(4), 507–524. https://doi.org/10.1002/job.2253

Jiang, K., Gollan, P. J., & Brooks, G. (2017). Relationship between organizational justice, organizational trust, and organizational commitment: A cross-cultural study of China, South Korea and Australia. *The International Journal of Human Resource Management, 28*(7), 973–1004. https://doi.org/10.1080/09585192.2015.1128457

Jiang, K., Liu, D., McKay, P. F., Lee, T. W., & Mitchell, T. R. (2012). When and how is job embeddedness predictive of turnover? A meta-analytic investigation. *Journal of Applied Psychology, 97*(5), 1077–1096. https://doi.org/10.1080/09585192.2015.1128457

Johns, G. (2006). The essential impact of context on organizational behavior. *Academy of Management Review, 31*(2), 386–408. https://doi.org/10.5465/amr.2006.20208687

Judge, T. A., Weiss, H. M., Kammeyer-Mueller, J. D., & Hulin, C. L. (2017). Job attitudes, job satisfaction, and job affect: A century of continuity and of change. *Journal of Applied Psychology, 102*(3), 356–374. https://doi.org/10.1037/apl0000181

Jung, Y., & Takeuchi, N. (2014). Relationships among leader–member exchange, person–organization fit and work attitudes in Japanese and Korean organizations: testing a cross-cultural moderating effect. *The International Journal of Human Resource Management, 25*(1), 23–46. https://doi.org/10.1080/09585192.2013.778163

Kim, H., & Park, J. (2017). The effects of longer commutes, unsolicited job offers, and working in the Seoul metropolitan area on the turnover intentions of Korean employees. *International Journal of Manpower, 38*(4), 594–613. https://doi.org/10.1108/IJM-12-2015-0211

Kim, K. Y., Eisenberger, R., & Baik, A. K. (2016). Perceived organizational support and affective organizational commitment: Moderating influence of perceived organizational competence. *Journal of Organizational Behavior, 37*, 558–583. https://doi.org/10.1002/job.2081

Kirkman, B. L., Lowe, K. B., & Gibson, C. B. (2017). A retrospective on Culture's Consequences: The 35-year journey. *Journal of International Business Studies, 48*, 12–29. https://doi.org/10.1057/s41267-016-0037-9

König, C. J., Probst, T. M., Staffen, S., & Graso, M. (2011). A Swiss-US comparison of the correlates of job insecurity. *Applied Psychology: An International Review, 60*(1), 141–159. https://doi.org/10.1111/j.1464-0597.2010.00430.x

Kwon, H. W. (2017). A social embeddedness perspective on turnover intention: The role of informal networks and social identity evidence from South Korea. *Public Personnel Management, 46*(3), 263–287. https://doi.org/10.1177/0091026017717459

Lai, L., Besen, E., Sarkisian, N., & Xu, Q. (2022). A Sino-US comparison on workplace flexibility: evidence from multinational firms. *The International Journal of Human Resource Management, 33*(3), 561–593. https://doi.org/10.1080/09585192.2020.1737174

Lam, L. W., Liu, Y., & Loi, R. (2016). Looking intra-organizationally for identity cues: whether perceived organizational support shapes employees' organizational identification. *Human Relations, 69*(2), 345–367. https://doi.org/10.1177/0018726715584689

Lee, T. W., Hom, P. W., Eberly, M. B., Li, J. (J.), & Mitchell, T. R. (2017). On the next decade of research in voluntary employee turnover. *Academy of Management Perspectives, 31*(3), 201–221. https://doi.org/10.5465/amp.2016.0123

Lee, Y., & Antonakis, J. (2014). When preference is not satisfied but the individual is: how power distance moderates person–job fit. *Journal of Management, 40*(3), 641–675. https://doi.org/10.1177/0149206311436080

Leung, A. K.-Y., & Cohen, D. (2011). Within and between culture variation: Individual differences and the cultural logics of honor, face, and dignity cultures. *Journal of Personality and Social Psychology, 100*(3), 507–526. https://doi.org/10.1037/a0022151

Li, J., Wang, W., Sun, G., Jiang, Z., & Cheng, Z. (2018). Supervisor–subordinate guanxi and job satisfaction among migrant workers in China. *Social Indicators Research, 139*, 293–307. https://doi.org/10.1007/s11205-016-1471-6

Liao, C., Wayne, S. J., & Rousseau, D. M. (2014). Idiosyncratic deals in contemporary organizations: A qualitative and meta-analytical review. *Journal of Organizational Behavior, 37*, 9–29. https://doi.org/10.1002/job.1959

Liu, C., Nauta, M. M., Li, C., & Fan, J. (2010). Comparisons of organizational constraints and their relations to strains in China and the United States. *Journal of Occupational Health Psychology, 15*(4), 452–467. https://doi.org/10.1037/a0020721

Liu, D., Mitchell, T. R., Lee, T. W., Holtom, B. C., & Hinkin, T. R. (2012). When employees are out of step with coworkers: How job satisfaction trajectory and dispersion influence individual-and unit-level voluntary turnover. *Academy of Management Journal, 55*(6), 1360–1380. https://doi.org/10.5465/amj.2010.0920

Liu, S. S., Shteynberg, G., Morris, M. W., Talhelm, T., & Yang, Q. (2019). Ingroup vigilance in collectivistic cultures. *PNAS, 116*(29), 14538–14546. https://doi.org/10.1073/pnas.1817588116

Liu, S. S., Shteynberg, G., Morris, M. W., Yang, Q., & Galinsky, A. D. (2021). How does collectivism affect social interactions? A test of two competing accounts. *Personality and Social Psychology Bulletin, 47*(3), 362–376. https://doi.org/10.1177/0146167220923230

Loh, J., Restubog, S. L. D., & Zagenczyk, T. J. (2010). Consequences of workplace bullying on employee identification and satisfaction among Australians and Singaporeans. *Journal of Cross-Cultural Psychology, 41*(2), 236–252. https://doi.org/10.1177/0022022109354641

Loi, R., Lai, J. Y., & Lam, L. W. (2012). Working under a committed boss: A test of the relationship between supervisors' and subordinates' affective commitment. *The Leadership Quarterly, 23*(3), 466–475. https://doi.org/10.1016/j.leaqua.2011.12.001

Lu, L., Cooper, C. L., Kao, S., Chang, T., Allen, T. D., Lapierre, L. M., O'Driscoll, M. P., Poelmans, S. A. Y., Sanchez, J. I., & Spector, P. E. (2010). Cross-cultural differences on work-to-family conflict and role satisfaction: A Taiwanese-British comparison. *Human Resource Management, 49*(1), 67–85. https://doi.org/10.1002/hrm.20334

Mai, K. M., Ellis, A. P. J., Christian, J. S., & Porter, C. O. L. H. (2016). Examining the effects of turnover intentions on organizational citizenship behaviors and deviance behaviors: A psychological contract approach. *Journal of Applied Psychology, 101*(8), 1067–1081. https://doi.org/10.1037/apl0000115

Marsh, R., & Mannari, H. (1977). Organizational commitment and turnover: A prediction study. *Administrative Science Quarterly, 22*(1), 57–75. https://doi.org/10.2307/2391746

Masuda, A. D., Poelmans, S. A. Y., Allen, T. D., Spector, P. E., Lapierre, L. M., Cooper, C. L., Abarca, N., Brough, P., Ferreiro, P., & Fraile, G. (2012). Flexible work arrangements availability and their relationship with work-to-family conflict, job satisfaction, and turnover intentions: A comparison of three country clusters: *Applied Psychology: An International Review, 61*(1), 1–29. https://doi.org/ 10.1111/j.1464-0597.2011.00453.x

Meyer, J. P., Stanley, D. J., Jackson, T. A., McInnis, K. J., Maltin, E. R., & Sheppard, L. (2012). Affective, normative and continuance commitment levels across cultures: A meta-analysis. *Journal of Vocational Behavior, 80*, 225–245. https://doi.org/10.1016/j.jvb.2011.09.005

Mueller, K., Hattrup, K., Spiess, S., & Lin-Hi, N. (2012). The effects of corporate social responsibility on employees' affective commitment: A cross-cultural investigation. *Journal of Applied Psychology, 97*(6), 1186–1200. https://doi.org/10.1037/a0030204

Nielsen, I., Smyth, R., & Liu, Y. (2011). The moderating effects of demographic factors and hukou status on the job satisfaction–subjective well-being relationship in urban China. *The International Journal of Human Resource Management, 22*(6), 1333–1350. https://doi.org/10.1080/09585192.2011.559103

Nixon, A. E., Ceylan, S., Nelson, C. E., & Alabak, M. (2020). Emotional labor, collectivism and strain: a comparison of Turkish and US service employees. *Work and Stress, 34*(2), 168–188. https://doi.org/10.1080/02678373.2019.1598515

Oh, I., Guay, R. P., Kim, K., Harold, C. M., Lee, J., Heo, C., & Shin, K. (2014). Fit happens globally: A metaanalytic comparison of the relationships of person-environment fit dimensions with work attitudes and performance across East Asia, Europe and North America. *Personnel Psychology, 67*, 99–152. https://doi.org/10.1111/peps.12026

Onyemah, V., Rouziès, D., & Panagopoulos, N. G. (2010). How HRM control affects boundary-spanning employees' behavioural strategies and satisfaction: The moderating impact of cultural performance orientation. *The International Journal of Human Resource Management, 21*(11), 1951–1975. https://doi.org/10.1080/09585192.2010.505096

Pacheco, G., & Webber, D. (2016). Job satisfaction: How crucial is participative decision making? *Personnel Review, 45*(1), 183–200. https://doi.org/10.1108/PR-04-2014-0088

Peltokorpi, V. (2013). Job embeddedness in Japanese organizations. *The International Journal of Human Resource Management, 24*(8), 1551–1569. https://doi.org/10.1080/09585192.2012.723636

Peltokorpi, V., Allen, D. G., & Froese, F. (2015). Organizational embeddedness, turnover intentions, and voluntary turnover: The moderating effects of employee demographic characteristics and value orientations. *Journal of Organizational Behavior, 36*, 292–312. https://doi.org/10.1002/job.1981

Qin, X., Hom, P. W., & Xu, M. (2019). Am I a peasant or a worker? An identity strain perspective on turnover among developing-world migrants. *Human Relations, 72*(4), 801–833. https://doi.org/10.1177/0018726718778097

Ramesh, A., & Gelfand, M. J. (2010). Will they stay or will they go? The role of job embeddedness in predicting turnover in individualistic and collectivistic cultures. *Journal of Applied Psychology, 95*(5), 807–823. https://doi.org/10.1037/a0019464

Raub, S., & Robert, C. (2013). Empowerment, organizational commitment, and voice behavior in the hospitality industry: Evidence from a multinational sample. *Cornell Hospitality Quarterly, 54*(2), 136–148. https://doi.org/10.1177/1938965512457240

Rockstuhl, T., Dulebohn, J. H., Ang, S., & Shore, L. M. (2012). Leader–member exchange (LMX) and culture: A meta-analysis of correlates of LMX across 23 countries. *Journal of Applied Psychology, 97*(6), 1097–1130. https://doi.org/10.1037/a0029978

Rockstuhl, T., Eisenberger, R., Shore, L. M., Kurtessis, J. N., Ford, M. T., Buffardi, L. C., & Mesdaghinia, S. (2020). Perceived organizational support (POS) across 54 nations: A cross-cultural meta-analysis of POS effects. *Journal of International Business Studies, 51*, 933–962. https://doi.org/10.1057/s41267-020-00311-3

Schaffer, B. S., & Riordan, C. M. (2003). A review of cross-cultural methodologies for organizational research: A best-practices approach. *Organizational Research Methods, 6*, 169–215. https://doi.org/10.1177/1094428103251542

Sender, A., Rutishauser, L., & Staffelbach, B. (2018). Embeddedness across contexts: A two-country study on the additive and buffering effects of job embeddedness on employee turnover. *Human Resource Management Journal, 28*(2), 340–356. https://doi.org/10.1111/1748-8583.12183

Shao, R., Rupp, D. E., Skarlicki, D. P., & Jones, K. S. (2013). Employee justice across cultures: A meta-analytic review. *Journal of Management, 39*, 263–301. https://doi.org/10.1177/0149206311422447

Sirola, N. (2020). Individuals' responses to economic cycles: Organizational relevance and a multilevel theoretical integration. *Academy of Management Annals, 14*(2), 451–473. https://doi.org/10.5465/annals.2018.0124

Smith, P. B., Wasti, S. A., Grigoryan, L., Achoui, M., Bedford, O., Budhwar, P., Lebedeva, N., Leong, C. H., & Torres, C. (2014). Are guanxi type supervisor-subordinate relationships culture-general? An eight-nation test of measurement invariance. *Journal of Cross-Cultural Psychology, 45*(6), 921–938. https://doi.org/10.1177/0022022114530496

So, T. T. C., West, M. A., & Dawson, J. F. (2011). Team-based working and employee well-being: A cross-cultural comparison of United Kingdom and Hong Kong health services. *European Journal of Work and Organizational Psychology, 20*(3), 305–325. https://doi.org/10.1080/13594320903384821

Stein, A. M., Bell, C. M., & Min, Y. A. (2020). Does "the servant as leader" translate into Chinese? A cross-cultural meta-analysis of servant leadership. *European Journal of Work and Organizational Psychology, 29*(3), 315–329. https://doi.org/10.1080/1359432X.2019.1703681

Stock, R. M., Strecker, M. M., & Bieling, G. I. (2016). Organizational work-family support as universal remedy? A cross-cultural comparison of China, India and the USA. *The International Journal of Human Resource Management, 27*(11), 1192–1216. https://doi.org/10.1080/09585192.2015.1062039

Summereder, S., Streicher, B., & Batinic, B. (2014). Voice or consistency? What you perceive as procedurally fair depends on your level of power distance. *Journal of Cross-Cultural Psychology, 45*(2), 192–212. https://doi.org/10.1177/0022022113505356

Taras, V., Kirkman, B. L., & Steel, P. (2010). Examining the impact of Culture's Consequences: A three-decade, multilevel, meta-analytic review of Hofstede's cultural value dimensions. *Journal of Applied Psychology, 95*(3), 405–439. https://doi.org/10.1037/a0018938

Triana, M. D. C., Jayasinghe, M., Pieper, J. R., Delgado, D. M., & Li, M. (2019). Perceived workplace gender discrimination and employee consequences: A meta-analysis and complementary studies considering country context. *Journal of Management, 45*, 2419–2447. https://doi.org/10.1177/0149206318776772

Triana, M. D. C., Richard, O. C., & Yücel, İ. (2017). Status incongruence and supervisor gender as moderators of the transformational leadership to subordinate affective organizational commitment relationship. *Personnel Psychology, 70*, 429–467. https://doi.org/10.1111/peps.12154

Ulusoy, N., Mölders, C., Fischer, S., Bayur, H., Deveci, S., Demiral, Y., & Rössler, W. (2016). A matter of psychological safety: Commitment and mental health in Turkish immigrant employees in Germany. *Journal of Cross-Cultural Psychology, 47*(4), 626–645. https://doi.org/10.1177/0022022115626513

Van Bavel, J. J., Baicker, K., Boggio, P. S., Capraro, V., Cichocka, A., Cikara, M., Crockett, M. J., Crum, A. J., Douglas, K. M., Druckman, J. N., Drury, J., Dube, O., Ellemers, N., Finkel, E. J., Fowler, J. H., Gelfand, M., Han, S., Haslam, S. A., Jetten, J., . . . Willer, R. (2020). Using social and behavioral science to support COVID-19 pandemic response. *Nature Human Behavior, 4*, 460–471. https://doi.org/10.1038/s41562-020-0884-z

Van der Westhuizen, D., Pacheco, G., & Webber, D. (2012). Culture, participative decision making and job satisfaction. *International Journal of Human Resource Management, 23*(13), 2661–2679. https://doi.org/10.1080/09585192.2011.625967

Van Knippenberg, D., Van Prooijen, J., & Sleebos, E. (2015). Beyond social exchange: Collectivism's moderating role in the relationship between perceived organizational support and organizational citizenship behaviour. *European Journal of Work and Organizational Psychology, 24*(1), 152–160. https://doi.org/10.1080/1359432X.2013.858699

Vlachos, P. A., Panagopoulos, N. G., Theotokis, A., Singh, R., & Singh R. K. (2014). When do corporate social responsibility initiatives impact on customer-facing employees? Evidence from India and the Netherlands. *The International Journal of Human Resource Management, 25*(22), 3086–3112. https://doi.org/10.1080/09585192.2014.934884

Wasti, S. A. (2002). Affective and continuance commitment to the organization: Test of an integrated model in the Turkish context. *International Journal of Intercultural Relations, 26*, 525–550. https://doi.org/10.1016/S0147-1767(02)00032-9

Wasti, S. A., Ersoy, N. C., & Erdoğan, B. (2022). I-deals in context: a summary and critical review of I-deals literature around the Globe. In S. Anand & Y. Rofcanin (Eds.), *Idiosyncratic deals at work: Exploring individual, organisational and societal perspectives* (pp. 257–308). London: Palgrave Macmillan.

Wasti, S. A., Peterson, M. F., Breisohl, H., Cohen, A., Jørgensen, F., Rodrigues, A., Weng, Q., & Xu, X. (2016). Location, location, location: contextualizing workplace commitment. *Journal of Organizational Behavior, 37*, 613–632. https://doi.org/10.1002/job.2094

Wong, K. F. E., & Cheng, C. (2020). The turnover intention behavior link: A culture-moderated meta-analysis. *Journal of Management Studies, 57*(6), 1174–1216. https://doi.org/10.1111/joms.12520

Yamazaki, Y., & Yoon, J. (2016). A cross-national study of fairness in Asia: how perceptions of a lack-of-group bias and transparency in the performance evaluation system relate to job satisfaction. *Human Resource Management, 55*(6), 1059–1077. https://doi.org/10.1002/hrm.21707

Yang, L., Spector, P. E., Sanchez, J. I., Allen, T. D., Poelmans, S., Cooper, C. L., Lapierre, L. M., O'Driscoll, M. P., Abarca, N., Alexandrova, M., Antoniou, A., Beham, B., Brough, P., Çarikçi, I., Ferreiro, P., Fraile, G., Geurts, S., Kinnunen, U., Lu, C., . . . Woo, J. (2012). Individualism-collectivism as a moderator of the

work demands-strains relationship: A cross-level and cross-national examination. *Journal of International Business Studies, 43*, 424–443. https://doi.org/10.1057/jibs.2011.58
Zeytinoglu, I. U., Yılmaz, G., Keser, A., Inelmen, K., Uygur, D., & Özsoy, A. (2012). Job satisfaction, flexible employment and job security among Turkish service sector workers. *Economic and Industrial Democracy, 34*(1), 123–144. https://doi.org/10.1177/0143831X11434845
Zhang, M., Fried, D. D., & Griffeth, R. W. (2012a). A review of job embeddedness: Conceptual, measurement issues, and directions for future research. *Human Resource Management Review, 22*(3), 220–231. https://doi.org/10.1016/j.hrmr.2012.02.004
Zhang, Y., Farh, J., & Wang, H. (2012b). Organizational antecedents of employee perceived organizational support in China: A grounded investigation. *The International Journal of Human Resource Management, 23*(2), 422–446. https://doi.org/10.1080/09585192.2011.560886
Zhang, Y., Xu, S., Jin, J., & Ford, M. T. (2018). The within and cross domain effects of work-family enrichment: A meta-analysis. *Journal of Vocational Behavior, 104*, 210–227. https://doi.org/10.1016/j.jvb.2017.11.003

CHAPTER

9

Reconsidering Assumptions about Organizational Justice through the Lens of Culture and Moral Philosophy

Niti Pandey *and* Deborah E. Rupp

Abstract

This chapter reviews the scope and impact of organizational justice research through lenses that consider both culture and moral philosophy. Our review summarizes justice research by broad topical areas (employee-level issues, employment practices, and organizational characteristics), considering in particular the extant cross-cultural research to date within each category. Building on the work of Shao and colleagues (2013), we present a framework that further integrates multiple philosophical traditions (natural law, deontology, contractualism, utilitarianism, social recognition, Confucianism, Hinduism, and Buddhism) to more fully conceptualize justice motives as they are held across cultures. Our goal is to encourage new theorizing that examines justice as an organizing principle for social cooperation that is sensitive to cultural differences. We conclude by suggesting avenues for new research, specifically aimed at addressing emerging social issues affecting workers around the world.

Key Words: organizational justice, culture, cultural identity, moral philosophy, social justice

The year 2020 saw mass protests against systemic racism in the United States, triggered by incidents of police brutality against Black Americans, against the backdrop of a global pandemic. The resulting movement for social justice raised universal issues about systemic bias in our institutions and their practices not just in the United States but in many other countries. In the preceding years, #MeToo became a global social movement, highlighting systemic abuses of women across nations. The struggles for the rights of LGBTQ individuals saw new momentum highlighting long-endured injustices at an institutional level. These past few years have seen global changes and upheavals such as Brexit, the Hong Kong Democracy protests, women's rights expansions in Saudi Arabia and Iran, anti-immigration rhetoric and policy, and reimagined climate change movements like Fridays for Future. The pandemic revealed the fragility of employment, especially for low-income jobs, the lack of social safety nets, and the exploitation of gig workers. Many of these conversations took place in the context of organizations seen as unjust and as upholding practices that afford advantages to a select few and perpetuate systemic biases against many others based on unalterable characteristics such as race, sex, and identity. Organizations are central to our lives and are intertwined with all of these emerging social justice issues. Perhaps now is the opportune moment, more so than ever before, in these times of global upheaval, to revisit the scope and impact of organizational justice research, through lenses that consider both culture and moral philosophy.

John Rawls wrote: "Justice is the first virtue of social institutions, as truth is of systems of thought. . . . Many different kinds of things are said to be just and unjust; not only laws, institutions, and social systems, but also particular actions of many kinds, including decisions, judgments, and imputations" (1999b, p. 3) and that justice is "a complex of three ideas of liberty, equality, and reward for services contributing to the common good" (1999a, p. 48). Rawls's notion of justice as fairness was intended to illustrate the basic structure of society and the principles by which free and rational persons engage in social cooperation. *Organizational* justice has typically been viewed as employees' perception of fairness in how they are treated by their organization. Goldman and Cropanzano (2015) caution organizational researchers against using the terms *justice* and *fairness* interchangeably, claiming " 'justice' should refer to whether one adheres to certain rules or standards, while 'fairness' should refer to how one responds to perceptions of these rules (and rule compliance). . . . 'justice' denotes conduct that is morally required" (p. 313). Organizational justice research has largely examined perceptions of fairness to the exclusion of determining whether or not our social structures are just. In fact, there are increasing calls for justice researchers to reconcile the normative requirements of justice posed by philosophers with the concept of fairness as justice as studied by organizational scholars (Cuguero-Escofet & Fortin, 2014; Fortin, et al., 2016).

Justice as a virtue on which social institutions are based must naturally depend on *culture*. A recent review of culture and organizational justice raised the question of whether individuals from varying cultures value and react to the various dimensions of justice similarly (James, 2015). "Whose justice? Which rationality?" were questions raised by MacIntyre (1988), in his book by the same name, to illustrate how conceptual schemes and shared experiences result in distinct traditions of justice. Cross-cultural research often relies on Hofstede's (2011) conceptualization of culture along the dimensions of individualism–collectivism, power distance, uncertainty avoidance, masculinity–femininity, long- and short-term orientation, and indulgence–restraint. Most research examining the relationship between organizational justice and culture has tended to study one or more of these dimensions in the context of one or more countries. Trompenaars (1996) made a distinction between universalistic and particularistic cultures, stating that "Universalistic societies tend to feel that general rules and obligations are a strong source of moral reference . . . are inclined to follow the rules even when friends are involved and look for 'the one best way' of dealing equally and fairly with all cases. They assume that the standards they hold dear are the 'right' ones and they attempt to change the attitudes of others to match" (p. 52). He further described particularistic societies as "those where 'particular' circumstances are more important than rules . . . particular relationships (family, friends) are stronger than any abstract rule and the response may change according to circumstances and the people involved" (p. 53). If we are to extend the examination of organizational justice as a social virtue, such conceptualizations of culture are invaluable for understanding how justice motives might differ across societies, leading to varying expectations of fairness and justice in the organizational context.

Early cross-cultural justice research has examined how cultural values affect justice perceptions (Leung & Ling, 1986; Morris et al., 1999; Brockner et al., 2001; Leung, 2005), establishing the role of cultural differences in employees' perceptions of justice dimensions. More recently, in a meta-analytic review, Shao, Rupp, Skarlicki, and Jones (2013) developed a comprehensive framework for integrating justice and culture research. They identified gaps in extant research, examining the concept of justice across cultures and proposed relationships between various justice motives and cultural values. The framework we provide here builds upon this work by integrating the deeper philosophical roots of justice motives and how conceptualizations of justice might unfold on the basis of cultural values. We believe that by delving into various philosophies, both Eastern and Western, we can extend our understanding of organizational justice and develop a framework for guiding future research on organizational justice across cultures.

We start by summarizing justice research by broad topical areas, and then we focus our attention on cross-cultural studies within each. Then, building on the work of Shao and colleagues (2013), we present a framework to expand our understanding of the impact of culture on organizational justice by drawing on a variety of philosophical traditions to understand justice motives across cultures. While nearly any philosophical tradition can be aligned with some conception of justice, we discuss some dominant Western schools of thought, such as natural law, deontology, contractualism, utilitarianism, and social recognition theories of justice, as well as the tenets of justice in Eastern traditions such as Confucianism, Hinduism, and Buddhism. Our hope is to encourage thinking about justice research beyond perceptions of fairness and toward examining justice as an organizing principle for social cooperation that is sensitive to cultural differences. We suggest new directions for research specifically aimed at addressing emerging social issues affecting workers around the world. We do not seek to replicate past reviews. Rather, our goal is to review and expand upon cross-cultural justice research and understand the impact of culture on organizational justice.

State of Organizational Justice Research

Byrne and Cropanzano (2001) provided a comprehensive history of the concept of organizational justice, tracing its development over a relatively brief period of time and across three distinct waves (relative deprivation, distributive justice, and procedural justice). They examined the various theoretical frameworks that have led to development of the organizational justice construct as we know it (consisting of justice perceptions as they

Table 9.1 Common conceptualizations of justice—dimensions and motives	
Organizational Justice Dimensions (Colquitt, 2012)	
Distributive Justice	Fairness of decision outcomes
Procedural Justice	Fairness of decision-making processes
Interpersonal Justice	Communicating organizational procedures respectfully and properly
Informational Justice	Communicating organizational procedures truthfully and with adequate justifications
Organizational Justice Motives (Shao et al., 2013)	
Instrumental	Self-interest and outcome maximization drive individual concerns with justice issues
Relational	Self-worth, self-esteem, and social status drive individual concerns with fair treatment
Uncertainty Management	Needs for predictability and certainty through information drive individual perceptions of justice
Moral	Universal norms of ethics and morality drive individual concerns for justice

pertain to outcomes, procedures, and social interactions at work and measured according to normative rules associated with each; see Colquitt, 2001; Colquitt et al., 2001). More recently, Rupp et al. (2017) provided a timeline tracing the development of the concept of organizational justice and the emergence of dominant paradigms, stating that "despite the broad foundation built by classic justice theories, and despite common assumptions about the multidimensionality of justice, no systematic work has set out to map the full domain of employees' experiences of injustice" (p. 920). This assessment could not have come at a more apt time and echoes the call for making a distinction between justice and fairness. Table 9.1 presents the common ways in which organizational justice has been conceptualized, in terms of both dimensions and motives.

Although organizational justice has been regarded as a fairly new concept, with a relatively short development period, philosophers of all traditions have discussed the nature of justice ever since Plato's *Republic*. Their goal has been to provide an account of the essential nature of justice as a fundamental principle—such that adherence to or divergence from said principle determines whether something (whether it is a decision, an action, or a rule) is just or unjust. In the sections that follow, we review contemporary justice topics[1] and then progressively link them to both culture and these older, philosophical roots. Our review is organized into three broad topics: employee-level issues, employment practices, and organizational characteristics. In the area of employee-level issues, we briefly present the plethora of research examining employee justice perceptions. We then take

[1] For a comprehensive review of organizational justice research, see Cropanzano and Ambrose (2015).

a deeper look at employee emotions, identity, and sex as they pertain to organizational justice. Next, we review two areas of employment practices and justice—supervision and compensation. And finally, we examine organizational-level characteristics such as human resource management (HRM) practices in general, cultural social networks, and justice climate.

Employee-Level Issues

The individual-level antecedents and consequences of employee justice perceptions are the most commonly studied areas of organizational justice research. In this section, we briefly present some of the research examining a variety of employee-level issues in relation to justice dimensions, specifically examining a selection of cross-cultural studies. We then review, more extensively, employee emotions, identity, and sex, and discuss the implications of these findings for future cross-cultural research.

Justice Perceptions

A considerable number of studies have examined distributive, procedural, and interactional justice in the last decade, though the subset of those examining organizational justice as it pertains to a specific cultural setting, or across such settings, is considerably smaller. Biswas et al. (2013) studied managers and executives from Indian firms and found that both distributive and procedural justice were key antecedents of perceived organizational support, and subsequently employee engagement. Collecting data from 238 managers and executives from 12 organizations from the manufacturing and service sectors, they concluded that perceptions of justice are strong drivers for employee engagement as mediated by social exchange mechanisms such as perceived organizational support. Gupta and Singh (2013) discussed the cultural characteristics unique to India as they relate to the dimensions of organizational justice. Using data from 181 employees of multinational subsidiaries, they found that procedural justice was a concern for Indian employees. However, Indian employees deemed voice and impartial procedures as distinct dimensions of justice. They concluded by highlighting the importance of voice for the employees in their study, labeling it as "empowerment justice," in the context of a high-power distance society where there might be fewer opportunities to exercise employee voice. Thus, in high-power distance countries with particularistic values, organizations may have to pay attention to unique criteria applied by employees when assessing and experiencing justice.

In a cross-cultural study of university employees spanning China (n = 227), South Korea (n = 242), and Australia (n = 237), Jiang et al. (2017) studied the effects of organizational justice on trust and commitment, hoping to draw distinctions between Anglo and Confucian Asian cultures. Their results suggested that Chinese and South Korean workers' trust and affective commitment were more sensitive to distributive justice as compared to Australian workers and that all employees studied demonstrated higher trust and commitment when they perceived higher procedural justice. Lin and colleagues (2019), in a study of workers from Malaysia (*n* = 79), Cambodia (*n* = 244), the Philippines (*n* = 141), and China (*n* = 154), examined how employees form judgments about justice by measuring the extent to which they use different types of information. They found that while there were individual differences in how workers process information in making justice judgments, there were no significant differences in these patterns across cultures.

Lucas and colleagues (2016) studied university students from the United States (*n* = 210), Canada (*n* = 293), China (*n* = 240), and India (*n* = 178) to determine whether there were similarities across cultures in how justice beliefs are structured. Their results supported previous studies that have found universal similarity in personal justice beliefs or viewed justice in relation to fairness to one's self. They also found that procedural justice beliefs were stronger in Canada and China and that distributive justice beliefs were stronger in India and China. This research suggests the possibility that cultural values drive justice beliefs. Özbek et al. (2016) examined whether the relationship between justice and organizational citizenship behavior (OCB) was moderated by individualism in Kyrgyzstan, citing the general population's relative lack of knowledge about these concepts and the importance of the contextual effects of an economy emerging from the Soviet era. In analyzing data from 402 employees from two organizations, the author found that procedural justice was related to obedience, defined as the acceptance of organizational rules and regulations, and concluded that employees may not recognize why procedural justice is important since they are likely to display norms of organizational obedience learned in the Soviet era. The study found significant relationships between both distributive and interactional justice and OCB, which were further moderated by individualism.

Summereder and colleagues (2014) examined the effect of power distance on procedural justice, specifically voice and consistency, in a sample of students drawn from 10 different countries [Austria (*n* = 39), Germany (*n* = 35), Australia (*n* = 84), China (*n* = 32), Japan (*n* = 18), Indonesia (*n* = 16), Malaysia (*n* = 12), India (*n* = 10), Vietnam (*n* = 8), and the Philippines (*n* = 4)]. They found that power distance influences fairness evaluations relating to voice and consistency of decision process, such that individuals from low-power distance cultures are more likely to react positively (trust, low withdrawal cognition) to voice. They concluded that power distance was likely to have an impact on the voice aspect of procedural justice. Game and Crawshaw (2017) studied the attachment orientation and interpersonal justice perceptions of 205 "Anglo" and 136 "South Asian" MBA students who were employed full time. They found that employees perceive greater interpersonal injustice when they have greater levels of attachment anxiety. They further suggested that the relational motives of employees from collective cultures might foster a greater need for supportive relationships at work. Wong (2012) found job security, in addition to justice, to be a determinant of trust in Chinese joint ventures, while Loi et al. (2012) studied manufacturing workers in China and Macau, finding that perceptions of job insecurity decrease under conditions of high procedural justice and that low-power distance employees feel this effect more strongly under ethical leadership.

Ultimately, it would appear that the dimensions of justice (i.e., distributive, procedural, informational, interpersonal), at least to the extent that they are studied by researchers and recognized by employees as distinct and relevant, seem to be largely universally applicable across cultures. While some studies have attempted to unearth specific cultural differences in how organizational justice influences employee attitudes and behaviors, it appears that studies set in various national contexts have merely sought to replicate or expand on existing research in the field. Cross-cultural justice research would do well to consider factors that might be relevant to employees from different cultural contexts (such as job security, obedience mindset, voice, or attachment needs) and that may not have been considered within Western frameworks. The state of the research also suggests a need to shift our thinking beyond the traditional justice dimensions (i.e., distributive, procedural, interactional) to justice *motives* and to a deeper understanding of *how justice motives evolve within and across cultures*. This shift, by necessity, will allow us to question the motives by which just or unjust institutions and practices are designed and implemented across cultures, the values that are held in relative importance, and the outcomes that are seen as culturally desirable; and help the field move beyond the narrow view of justice as fairness.

Justice and Emotions

Researchers have examined how emotions are related to organizational justice. Barsky et al. (2011) reviewed research on how emotions influence the formation of fairness judgments. They proposed that organizational events could trigger emotional reactions in employees, which in turn influence how employees make fairness judgments. In their proposed framework, they argue for the central role of emotions in the judgment-forming process as related to justice events and the relevance of emotions to people's reactions to justice events over time.

Barclay and Kiefer (2014) studied the mediating role of emotions on the relationship between justice and employee outcomes in two studies, with the first study using a sample of 136 Canadian employees and the second study using an online sample of 451 participants. They found that both positive and negative emotions mediated the relationship between organizational justice perceptions and behavioral outcomes. Specifically, their research suggests that positive emotions (stemming from justice) tend to enhance performance and helping behaviors, while negative emotions (stemming from injustice) tend to enhance withdrawal behaviors.

Grandey et al. (2015) proposed that the requirement of emotional labor could constitute violations of justice through the requirement of specific emotional displays at work. Johnson and colleagues (2014) found that behaviors requiring adherence to procedural justice can be emotionally draining and that employees can use positive interpersonal interactions to deal with this deficit. Research on justice and emotions seems to be conducted primarily in the Western context, with many studies utilizing undergraduate student samples (e.g., Stouten et al., 2013; Long & Christian, 2015; Dahling, 2017). This leaves a gap in our understanding of how culture-specific norms around emotions in the workplace can impact employees' perceptions of and reactions to fairness. To the extent that cultures can have specific norms surrounding the display of emotions, these studies all point to the potential relevance of cultural differences in the display and acceptance of emotions in the workplace. Future justice research should examine whether there are significant differences in employees' experiences of fairness in cultures that more strongly sanction deviance from culturally acceptable emotional norms in the workplace as opposed to cultures that allow more autonomy in emotional expression.

Justice and Identity

Just or unjust treatment in the workplace also impacts identity, as just practices validate individuals' feelings of self-worth. Johnson et al. (2010) studied how justice affects individual identity (sense of uniqueness and self-worth) or interdependent identity (derived from the quality of relationships with one's partner and group), regulatory focus (promotion versus prevention), and affect. They found that employees reacted to fair treatment with positive affect and strong interdependent identities and to unfair treatment with emotions such as anxiety and identities focused on the self. Similarly, Johnson and Lord (2010), using a sample of college students, demonstrated experimentally that participants who were treated fairly were more likely to trust and engage in cooperative exchanges with the fair party. Using data from 1,258 Swiss citizens, Johnston and colleagues (2016) studied the role of personal and general just world beliefs as they related to justice and well-being. They found that individuals' fundamental beliefs about (in)justice in their own lives tended to shape their justice perceptions in general. The fact that organizational justice can have implicit effects on the identity and self-worth of workers is a powerful idea worth pursuing given the social issues relevant today. In a meta-analytic study, Fisher (2013) examined justice across 36 countries and found systematic cross-national differences. Results suggested that income inequality and national values explained the variations in justice across cultures and that people may care more about justice based on their affiliation, esteem, and self-protection needs. The study found that the effectiveness of fair practices was impacted by collective identification with the group or organization. Cultural values are drivers of self-worth and identity formation (Erez & Earley, 1993), and just or unjust treatment can further affect how such identity is validated in the workplace. We recommend that future justice research examine how race and sex discrimination across different cultural settings influences employees' sense of identity.

Justice and Sex

In recent years, research has examined gender stereotypes in relation to organizational justice. Caleo (2016) questioned whether the rules of organizational justice are inherently gendered and demonstrated that there is inherent bias in how men and women engaging in unjust behaviors are evaluated. Using four experimental studies, the author found that when women violate the rules of interactional justice, they are more likely than men to be rated negatively and to receive fewer rewards. Additionally, while procedural justice rules violations were not found to be related to sex, results suggested that gender stereotypes drove assessments of interactional justice violations. In another study, recognizing the relevance of organizational culture, Caleo (2018) found that men who distributed resources equally among subordinates (behavior typically ascribed to women and in violation of equity principles) were penalized for behaving contrary to gender stereotypes. It is not evident whether these findings about gender norms are generalizable across cultures. As more women enter the workforce globally, a potential area of research would be to examine the role of cultural gender norms in justice perceptions.

Gender and justice have also been studied in the context of recruitment and selection. Brands and Fernandez-Mateo (2017) studied the underrepresentation of women in top management in the context of procedural justice and found that women tend to avoid seeking employment with an employer where they were previously and unfairly denied a job. In an experimental study, which manipulated job gender type, Gillespie and Ryan (2012) found that gender-based preferential selection was seen as procedurally unfair. These research studies have an implication for future research on the cultural influences on women's perceptions of fairness, as cultures that value egalitarianism may be less likely to hold gender-biased norms about just behaviors.

Research suggests that not only are women expected to uphold justice norms according to gender stereotypes, but their own perceptions of organizational justice are uniquely influenced by their distinct gendered experiences and the resulting outcomes. No other issue has borne this out more starkly than the recent reckoning of sexual harassment in the workplace. A small amount of organizational justice research has examined the various aspects of women's experiences in the workplace in relation to sexual harassment, abuse, and sex/gender based microaggressions. Butler and Chung-Yan (2011) examined the effect of justice type (i.e., dimension) on the likelihood that women would report sexual harassment at work and found that reporting was more likely to depend on perceptions of distributive and procedural justice. Their research suggests that when women perceive their organizations to be more just, they are more likely to report or deal with instances of sexual harassment. More recently, Rubino and colleagues (2018) examined how organizational justice climate impacts sexual harassment using large military samples. These authors suggest that an organization's justice climate has an impact on all types of discrimination and that it may be more beneficial to address sexual harassment as a form of unequal treatment. Their data indicated that justice climate had a negative relation to sexual harassment and moderated the effects of other antecedents (sex similarity, sexual harassment climate) on sexual harassment. In other words, this study suggests that in organizations that place a greater value on fairness and justice, employees are both less likely to encounter sexual harassment and less likely to be impacted by other factors that might lead to sexual harassment.

Perhaps this is another indicator of how organizational justice research has stepped away from the normative ideas of justice proposed by philosophers. As more evidence comes to light that the experiences of women are distinct from those of men in organizations, that these experiences stem from deep-rooted biases and stereotypes, and that they continually shape the outcomes women experience at work, there is scope for organizational justice research to not only examine women's perceptions of fairness, but to also examine the extent to which organizations act justly on these issues through the creation of fair policies and procedures. The issue of fair treatment of women in the workplace has become a global one that likely resonates with working women across cultures. The paucity of cross-cultural research on this topic is a timely gap in the literature for future justice researchers to fill. Similarly, opportunities abound for examining the experiences of individuals from underrepresented race and ethnic groups in organizations, on which justice research seems to be (ironically) silent. Organizational justice research has the potential to have significant positive impact on the design of just rules and practices and the creation of ethical and moral workplaces.

Justice and Employment Practices

In this section, we examine cross-cultural justice research on two specific employment practices, supervision and compensation. We specifically examine the concept of abusive supervision across cultures since we believe it is an under-researched area (Tepper et al., 2017) and an issue that is of social significance in light of the social justice issues of the times. Similarly, compensation practices can have far-reaching impacts on workers' livelihoods and social issues such as income inequality, pay disparity, and worker exploitation through poor wages.

Justice and Supervision

Abusive supervision is defined as "subordinates' perceptions of the extent to which supervisors engage in the sustained display of hostile verbal and nonverbal behaviors, excluding physical contact" (Tepper, 2000, p. 178). Recent research has focused on abusive supervision in Asia, specifically in China. In a meta-analytic study, Zhang and Liao (2015) found that power distance moderated the relationship between abusive supervision and employee outcomes (including justice perceptions), such that employees in Asian countries were more likely to accept abusive supervision as an integral part of the supervisor–subordinate relationship. Similarly, Vogel and colleagues (2015) collected data from 363 respondents from Anglo cultures (Australia and the United States) and 588 respondents from Confucian cultures (Singapore and Taiwan) and found that culture influenced perceptions of supervisor fairness. Employees from "Anglo" cultures were more likely to perceive abusive supervision as having a negative impact on interpersonal justice. In a second study of 69 respondents from the United States and 209 from Taiwan, they further found that the relationship between abusive supervision and interpersonal justice was moderated by power distance, such that high-power distance cultures were more likely to tolerate abusive supervision. Wei and Si (2013) studied 198 employee–supervisor dyads in a multinational company in China and found abusive supervision to be linked to a host of counterproductive work behaviors. Low et al. (2019) studied the mediating effect of injustice perceptions on the relationship between abusive supervision and counterproductive work behaviors in 216 nurses in Malaysia. Additionally, they found moderating effects for power distance, such that the relationship between abusive supervision and perceived injustice was stronger for those low on power distance. Thus, power distance seems to have an effect on how employees perceive the justness of their supervisors' actions. Wang and Chan (2019) found support for the mediating effect of interactional justice on the relationship between abusive supervision and work outcomes for Chinese employees and reported that ethical leadership was more likely to accentuate justice perceptions. These studies lend support for cultural differences in expectations about the nature of workplace relationships, with relational, high-power distance cultures more likely to tolerate interpersonal injustice in order to maintain relational structures.

Wang and colleagues (2017) examined the mediating role of interactional justice and the moderating role of collectivist orientation on the relationship between ethical leadership and loyalty to supervisors in a sample of 550 Chinese subordinates and 110 of their immediate supervisors. Their results suggest that employees with strong collectivist orientation experience stronger loyalty to their supervisors when they perceive their supervisors to be more ethical. Justice perceptions have also been examined as having a moderating influence on the relationship between leadership and employee performance (He et al., 2017; Reb et al., 2019) and as an outcome of LMX differentiation (Liu et al., 2014). Studying teams of employees in China, Liu and colleagues (2014) found that when leaders treated team members differently, it led to a decrease in trust and consequently procedural justice perceptions. In an extensive study examining personality and supervisor justice rule compliance, Huang and colleagues (2017) found that the personality of a subordinate might have an impact on whether a supervisor treats them justly.

Findings such as these raise important questions for cultural differences in justice perceptions and other related concepts such as the overall justice climate, especially in collectivist cultures. Lavelle and colleagues (2018), in an examination of multi-foci justice (i.e., justice coming from various sources such as one's supervisor, the organization as a whole, or coworkers) and counterproductive behaviors suggested that supervisory unfairness was likely to result in counterproductive behaviors specifically targeted at supervisors. Clearly, cultural values such as power distance and collectivism have an impact on how employees perceive the fairness of their treatment by their supervisors and how they might react to mistreatment when it occurs. That is, while the concept of abusive supervision may be universal, it is possible that there might be cultural variations in how employees react to such supervisory behaviors (Mackey et al., 2017 Vogel et al., 2015). More research is needed that examines whether employees in high-power distance cultures make allowances for supervisory behaviors based on social norms of hierarchy. Other future research might consider how employees' specific responses to supervisory mistreatment varies by culture. Just as resulting justice perceptions to the same objective supervisor treatment could be the same or different among those with differing cultural values, so too could reactions take an attitudinal versus behavioral route (as well as the long-term consequences of differing reactions).

Justice and Compensation

Employees' perceptions of pay fairness is among the oldest forms of organizational justice research (see Rupp et al., 2017); and more recent work has considered such issues within various cultural settings. Hartmann and Slapnicar (2012) studied the perceptions of the pay fairness (both distributive and procedural) of 139 Slovenian bank managers (Slovenia scores high on collectivism and power distance) and found that when pay transparency was low, intrinsic motivation was more likely dependent on procedural justice, and when pay transparency was high, it was more likely dependent on distributional justice. Chien et al. (2010) found that procedural justice moderated the relationship between performance-based pay and job performance in a sample of 258 Taiwanese workers. Shaffer et al. (2013) studied 78 expatriates from nine countries living in Hong Kong and found perceptions of equity to be a significant determinant of pay satisfaction. In a longitudinal study spanning 10 years, Huang (2016) examined compliance and fairness in the pay systems of automotive companies in China under various ownership structures (such as state-owned, privately owned, foreign joint ventures). Results showed that "companies managed employees' perceptions of distributive fairness by introducing a 'fair' procedure of variable pay and adopting job evaluation techniques and job-based pay . . . to transform egalitarian pay structures into hierarchical structures and to widen pay differential among different jobs" (p. 2177). Huang acknowledged that host nation HRM practices tend to become more similar to Western HRM practices with increased foreign investment in an industry. Studies such as these raise the possibility that Western management practices, diffused through multinational corporations and joint ventures, may have a transformative effect on the cultural values of host nation employees. At the very least, such practices are likely to come across as unjust within specific cultural frames. It may also be important for justice researchers to explore the extent to which cultural values differentially impact justice perceptions in general (about social issues such as discrimination or climate change) and those specifically related to work (specific workplace practices and policies). In addition to what employees perceive are fair or unfair practices in the treatment of themselves and their coworkers, it might be fruitful to examine whether there are cultural similarities or differences in what employees think are the moral obligations of organizations in their society.

Shen and Xie (2018) studied Chinese expatriates of a Chinese subsidiary in the United Arab Emirates and found that compensation disparities had an effect on distributive justice when employees compared themselves to those working in mainland China or for other advanced multinationals but not in comparison to locals. Arya and colleagues (2019) found in a sample from South Africa that the relationship between core self-evaluations and pay satisfaction was mediated by justice perceptions and was stronger for women. Shoaib and Baruch (2019) sampled academics in Pakistan and found that justice perceptions mediated the relationship between desire for incentives and deviant behaviors. Villanueva-Flores and colleagues (2015) studied discrimination in compensation faced by employees with disabilities in Andalusia and found that perceptions of compensation inequality due to disability led to perceptions of discrimination. This particular study (the only one we found that sampled employees with disabilities) brings into sharp relief the reality that organizational justice research has done little to understand the unique justice-related experiences of individuals with disabilities.

Together, these studies suggest that unique contextual factors might help us understand how organizational justice unfolds in various cultures and countries in relation to compensation practices. There have long been calls for organizational researchers to examine social issues such as poverty reduction (Burt & Carr, 2011; Carr et al., 2014). Future justice research should carefully consider broader societal and cultural contexts when examining how organizational practices influence perceptions of justice and fairness, and as income inequality continues worldwide, including the effects of cultural values such as long-term orientation and indulgency restraint. Issues of pay parity, living wages, and the role of organizations in developing and administering just compensation policies should be researched from multiple perspectives beyond individual perceptions of fairness.

Justice and Organizational Characteristics

In this section, we review studies that have examined organizational-level characteristics and their impact on justice. We specifically look at studies that have broadly examined HRM practices in relation to discrimination and justice. We then review research on organizational social networks in two cultural contexts. Finally, we explore the emerging research in the area of justice climate. Our review of these topics suggests ideas for future research examining the importance of nondiscriminatory practices and respect for cultural identities as mechanisms for promoting just workplaces.

Justice and HRM Practices

Some studies have examined organizational justice in the context of organization-wide or organizational-level practices. Wood et al. (2013) studied the role of procedural and distributive justice in mediating the relationship between workplace discrimination and employee well-being. Using a sample of 2,258 employees working in mental health organizations in the United Kingdom, and asking about generalized discrimination from managers, coworkers, patients, and visitors ("Do you believe that you have experienced any form of discrimination at work from source x in the past 12 months?" p. 633), they found that while discrimination from managers had a stronger negative effect on well-being, perceptions of justice mediated this relationship for discrimination from managers and visitors. There is a need to advance multi-foci justice research in organizations as employees' sense of just treatment is not limited to their interactions with any one entity. Additionally, research should examine cultural variations in multi-foci justice to determine whether employees place greater importance on just treatment from employers, coworkers, or customers, and which cultural values drive any distinctions.

Dhanani et al. (2018) conducted a meta-analytic review of workplace discrimination and proposed that justice perceptions mediate the relationship between discrimination in the workplace and employee attitudes, behaviors, and health. Citing past research, they point to a lack of clarity about how discrimination against specific targets (i.e., based in race, sex, age, etc.) impacts outcomes. They found that both justice perceptions and stress mediate the relationship between discrimination and negative outcomes. More interestingly for future justice research, they found that when employees observe discrimination, rather than experience it, they are more strongly affected, suggesting that workplace discrimination of any type has a negative impact on all employees. Findings such as these point us toward the importance of understanding the scope of both third-party justice perceptions and justice climate and thinking about justice as an organizationally driven construct rather than an individualized experience.

In the cross-cultural domain, research has examined how discrimination and inequalities between the working conditions of expatriates and host country nationals of multinational firms can affect perceptions of justice. Oltra et al. (2013), drawing upon Rawlsian justice theory, propose a normative (i.e., nonperceptual) framework for assessing justice in the work arrangements of multinational organizations. They conclude that for multinational organizations, justice needs to be based in universal ethical values, rather than fairness standards that vary across countries and are impacted by cultural values. In a comparison of culturally similar countries, Harcourt and colleagues (2013) compared the employment-at-will practices of the United States with the just cause dismissal system of New Zealand. They concluded that New Zealand's just cause dismissal practices offered more just outcomes, with appropriate remedies when due process was followed in the event of an unfair outcome. Finally, in a study of 1,219 Canadian employees, Tremblay and colleagues (2010) found that HRM practices such as information sharing, performance feedback, skills development, and nonmonetary rewards can impact perceptions of procedural justice and consequently employee behaviors. Cross-cultural justice research could certainly benefit from examining how HRM practices, whether they are adopted from multinationals or are local in nature, can have an effect on fairness and justice in organizations, in varying cultural contexts.

*Justice and Social Networks (*Guanxi, Wasta*)*

Organizational justice focuses on the perceptions of justice and fairness by the members of an organization. Those perceptions are informed by the person's own sense of justice. Recent studies have examined whether broad cultural differences might exist to explain how people form these perceptions of fairness. For example, Chen and colleagues (2011) examined procedural justice perceptions within the Chinese *guanxi* system (the social networks that facilitate business dealings) at both the interpersonal and group level. They found that the existence of interpersonal *guanxi* practices (individual employees engaging with managers to curry favor) led to higher levels of procedural justice perceptions by employees. However, when the decisions of managers were systematically based on *guanxi*, perceptions of procedural justice became more negative. Based on these findings, the authors caution against making broad generalizations about culture and justice perceptions and note that even employees in collectivist cultures may be driven by individualistic motives.

Gadelrab and colleagues (2018) studied organizational justice across nine Arab countries. to measure the universality of the four justice dimensions and found that all four dimensions (distributive, procedural, interactional, and informational) were valid across Arab cultures. Using a measure developed specifically for Arab cultural perspectives of justice, the authors' results also supported earlier findings that it is more likely that the justice dimensions will be strongly correlated in hierarchical and collectivist cultures. Harbi and colleagues (2017) examined the effects of Arabic culture, specifically the practice of *wasta* (similar to *guanxi* and including contact and nepotism) in Saudi Arabia, within the context of collectivism and power distance, on perceptions of performance appraisal fairness in a company. Interestingly, the authors found that while organizational practices developed in the West may conflict with the *interpersonal* practices of the *wasta* tradition, there is also evidence that employees perceived such practices to be *procedurally* unfair. Harbi et al. concluded that employees may develop concerns about organizational justice by rejecting the unfairness inherent in some traditional practices. Khan et al. (2015) examined the moderating effect of the Islamic work ethic on the relationship between justice and job outcomes among Pakistani employees and found that perceptions of distributive justice reduced turnover intentions, while perceptions of procedural justice increased job satisfaction. This relationship was further moderated by the Islamic work ethic, such that individuals high on this cultural value were less likely to be influenced by the absence of distributive fairness.

Justice Climate

Recent justice research has considered the construct of justice climate. Justice climate has been defined as "a distinct group-level cognition about how a work group as a whole is treated" (Naumann & Bennett, 2000, p. 882). This concept is attractive for conceptualizing the treatment of various employee groups by organizations and is likely to lend itself as a useful framework for examining whether or not organizations adhere to rules and standards in the treatment of *all* groups. In a meta-analytic study, Whitman and colleagues (2012) found that distributive justice climate ("shared perceptions of reward and resource distribution fairness," p. 778) was strongly related to productivity, and customer satisfaction and interactional justice climate ("shared perceptions of fair interpersonal treatment by organizational authorities," p. 779) was strongly related to unit-level processes such as cohesion and OCB. The significance of collective understandings of workplace fairness might have implications for organizations in collectivist cultures. For example, Schimnke et al. (2015) found that shared moral values had a significant effect on justice climate. They examined employees' shared moral values at the department level in relation to both procedural and overall justice climate and found that shared moral values were strongly associated with the overall justice climate. Additionally, procedural justice climate tended to be higher in larger departments.

Cole, Carter, and Zhang (2013) examined whether the extent to which team effectiveness was driven by leader–team congruence on power distance values. They hypothesized a model in which procedural justice climate mediates the relationship between power distance congruence and team performance and OCB. Using a sample of employees from two service companies in China, they found that a mismatch in the power distance values of leaders and teams led to lower perceptions of justice.

Buengeler and Hartog (2015) examined the moderating role of interactional justice climate on the relationship between national diversity (culture or race) and team performance in the context of a multinational enterprise in Germany, with a sample of employees representing eight different nationalities. They proposed that both interactional justice climate level (the average of team members' justice perceptions) and strength (the level of consensus in justice perceptions) would moderate the national diversity–team performance relationship. The authors found evidence that when the manager was perceived by the team as demonstrating high interactional justice, national diversity had a positive impact on team performance. Lin (2015) studied the effect of procedural justice climate on individual outcomes on a sample of Chinese workers, proposing that procedural justice climate would be positively related to positive affect at both individual and group levels, moderated by emotional contagion, and consequently resulting in greater satisfaction, knowledge sharing, and decreased turnover intentions. Results showed that the procedural justice climate influenced group and individual affect. Research findings such as these suggest that cross-cultural differences might be ameliorated by the deliberate cultivation of a strong justice climate.

Rubenstein et al. (2019) decry the static nature of justice climate research and present a framework viewing justice more dynamically. Studying 4,348 employees over a 4-year period, they found that instances of fair or unfair treatment are often evaluated taking into consideration both past and expected future treatments. Similarly, Rupp and Paddock (2010) present a temporal process model whereby over time, group members, individually, vicariously, and collectively experience justice-related events, eventually creating shared notions of justice climate, which influence outcomes at multiple levels of analysis. The idea of organizational justice climate developing over time is appealing since it allows for the possibility of meaningfully creating just climates through interventions. Justice climates can be influenced by the actions of organizations toward specific employee groups, the actions of employees as they interact with one another, as well as the evolution of organizational practices over time.

The cultural values of group members would be important to consider as well. For example, justice climate (in contrast to individual-level justice perceptions) may be more relevant for driving employee attitudes and behaviors in more collectivist contexts, where the treatment of the group may be seen as paramount. In multicultural contexts (in contrast to culturally homogeneous groups), specific justice climates might be slower to emerge/converge if different forms of justice are more or less relevant for individuals with varying cultural values (as suggested by Fisher, 2016). Future research is needed to expand our understanding of how justice climate develops over time and the effects of cultural values in the creation, perpetuation, or modification of justice climate.

Reconceptualizing Justice Research through the Lens of Moral Philosophy

Shao et al. (2013) proposed a theoretical framework to integrate justice and culture research. They begin with the various motives for why individuals might be concerned with justice—instrumental (motive of self-interest and outcome maximization), relational (motive of belongingness), uncertainty management (need for certainty), and moral (universal norm of ethics and morality). They then present a framework that links the justice motives to various cultural values, proposing conditions under which justice motives will be stronger or weaker. For example, instrumental motives for justice are likely to be stronger in individualistic and masculine societies and relational motives in collectivistic and feminist societies. Similarly, they propose that uncertainty management motives for justice will be stronger in cultures with a strong need for certainty while moral motives for justice will be strongly related with power distance. They then conducted a meta-analysis on the justice-outcome relationships detected in past research, considering the cultural value scores of the countries where the primary data reported in each study were collected (which they expected to moderate specific justice–outcome relationships). While their study found support for many aspects of their framework, interactions also emerged that deviated from expectations. Overall, they found that justice–outcome relationships were strongest when participants worked within cultures associated with individualism, femininity, uncertainty avoidance, and low power distance.

Such a conceptualization of justice across cultures seems to be a better way of making sense of cultural variations in justice perceptions than merely examining the effects of cultural dimensions in the workplace in a single country or in a comparative way. This framework moves us closer to understanding justice as it has been proposed by philosophers of various traditions and understanding organizational justice, not just as fairness perceptions but also as true characteristics of institutions and relationships structured for the common good.

We next add to and extend the framework of Shao and colleagues (2013) by identifying numerous Western and Eastern philosophical traditions as the foundations of these justice motives. We specifically examine the Western philosophical traditions of Rawls, deontology (Kant), Utilitarianism, natural law, and more recent feminist traditions. We then explore the Eastern philosophical traditions of Hinduism, Confucianism, and Buddhism and discuss how they are grounded in fundamentally different values. Most organizational justice research has stemmed from a Rawlsian (Western) philosophical tradition. Justice research can be enriched by examining other traditions to better understand the fundamental values that drive employees in various cultures; and there is room for organizational researchers to view both justice and culture from the lens of Eastern philosophical traditions. Table 9.2 presents a framework for conceptualizing the role of the various philosophical traditions in developing the various justice motives as they relate to various cultural values.

Western Philosophical Traditions

Examining the major ideas of the philosophical theories of justice will enable linkages to be made between the conceptual divisions within (1) types of organizational justice perceptions (distributive, procedural, informational, interpersonal; Folger & Cropanzano, 1998); (2) types of justice motives held by individuals (instrumental, relational, and deontic; Fischer, 2016); and (3) the governing values of cultures (individualism–collectivism, power distance, masculine–feminine, uncertainty avoidance, long or short term, indulgence, or restraint; Hofstede, 2011).

Rawls famously states that "the fundamental idea in the concept of justice is fairness," but that these are not the same notions (1999a, p. 47). Rawls's approach is succinctly articulated by two principles that "express justice as a complex of three ideas: liberty, equality, and reward for services contributing to the common good" (p. 48). The first principle states the need for equal rights (as liberties) for all. The second principle concerns the distribution of, among other things, wealth and power in society, and demands that any inequality in the distribution of primary goods must be held to the standard that it improves the lot of the least well-off members of society over and above what a more equal distribution would do. While that may seem counterintuitive, the idea is that by

Table 9.2 Foundational philosophical traditions linking justice motives and cultural dimensions

Cultural Values	Justice Motives			
	Instrumental	Relational	Uncertainty Management	Moral
Individualism	Libertarianism (value individual rights because they maximize self-interest)	Natural Law (Nussbaum, Sen)	Natural Law (Hobbes, Locke)	Deontology
Collectivism	X	Hinduism	Confucianism	Confucianism Marxism
Masculinity	Egoism (aggressive pursuit of self-interest)	Objectivism (Randian–self-worth, a function of competition with others)	Neoliberalism (competition leads to fairness and reduced uncertainty)	Deontology
Femininity	X	Care Ethics	Sentimentalism (Hume, Baier)	Feminism (Jaggar)
Low-Power Distance	Hedonism (individual pursuit of pleasure)	Communitarianism	Utilitarianism	Deontology Rawls
High-Power Distance	X	Plato (self-worth from place in social hierarchy)	X	Hinduism Confucianism
Low Uncertainty Avoidance	Relativism (no shared universal norms, no rigid rules)	Buddhism	Rawls Utilitarianism	Buddhism
High Uncertainty Avoidance	X	X	Hinduism	Hinduism

Note: Instrumental motives are inherently nonmoral in that they justify the sacrificing of justice in the pursuit of self-interest. These motives are not discussed in depth here. Additionally, these justice motives and cultural values can also be tied to social and political structures such as fascism (high-power distance—instrumental), totalitarianism (high-uncertainty avoidance—instrumental), or democratic pluralism (low-uncertainty avoidance—uncertainty management). However, such a discussion is beyond the scope of this review.

allowing some individuals to gain more wealth or power in society, they might advance society as a whole such that there is more for everyone. While there may be inequality in the society, the persons with the least still are doing better than if we had not allowed any inequality in the distribution of resources.

Rawls (1999a) recognized the sense of justice to be the core component of an individual's moral psychology, but he believed this sense of justice arises from various forms of guilt that emerge from our connections to the institutions to which we belong, the persons with whom we are associated, and our relationship to the principles of justice themselves. This suggests that Rawls's social institutional approach to justice can make sense of the justice perceptions within institutions. The governing values of cultures can be seen to intersect with Rawls's theory in complex ways. It can be used to justify power inequalities, but it also demands that such inequalities be justified to the least powerful members. Inevitably, the demands of equality would minimize power distance. Likewise, the individualism–collectivism dimension is complicated for Rawls, whose classical liberal notions of individualism and equal rights means that increases in individual power, wealth, and status over a more egalitarian standard must be justified by their service to the common good.

Utilitarianism (the greatest amount of good for the greatest number) uses a notion of justice that is connected to the notion of equality, or the idea that the interests of each sentient being are morally equivalent to the like interests of other sentient beings. Utilitarianism's focus on the end goal of the greatest good or greatest happiness of the greatest number tends toward egalitarianism and the just distribution of resources. The utilitarian viewpoint helps us understand the instrumental motive for justice where fairness leads to output maximization. Utilitarianism holds individualism as an instrumental value that is in the service of the collective good. To the extent that reduction of power distance is consistent with the greater good for the greater number, then utilitarians would endorse such an egalitarian approach. If we consider the utilitarian calculations that are intended to guide an organization to the greatest happiness of the greatest number, then the elimination of uncertainty, focus on long-term ends, and restraint for the sake of the common good would seem to be the most prudent, and thus just, path (Hofstede, 2011). Hence, cultures that emphasize those values might be seen to function from the utilitarian perspective.

The major competing theory to the utilitarian is the deontological or Kantian approach. For Kant (1996), justice concerns the political domain of "right" (*Recht*), which is based on his moral theory of the innate dignity of individual persons and the values of freedom and rationality. Kant's moral theory is rooted in a single universal principle (which has several forms) called the categorical imperative, which holds that actions are right insofar as they can be thought of as a universal law acceptable to all persons or wrong insofar as they would result in the misuse of persons. Being acceptable or misusing a person is understood in terms of respecting the individual's freedom and rationality. Kant's conception of justice dictates a well-ordered system in which individual rights are clearly demarcated and based on the notions of equal liberty and equal respect. Justice researchers can draw upon these notions of equal liberty and equal respect to examine the role of institutions in relation to social justice issues such as systemic race and sex discrimination in the workplace.

Kantian deontology forms a natural and attractive philosophical basis for viewing organizational justice in terms of systems that respect the rights of workers and treat all workers with respect. The governing values of culture that align best with this tradition are individualism and restraint (Hofstede, 2011). The traditional moral and justice theories like Kant's and Rawls's may also be associated with the "masculine" cultural values over "feminine" values (Hofstede, 2011), based on their assertive conceptions of rights as demarcations of individual spaces of action, as opposed to a tradition that focuses on care and sentiment. Thus, interpersonal justice perceptions will be driven by a focus on cognitive relations such as respect or noninterference, as opposed to perceptions that are rooted in emotion, affect, or sentiment.

Both deontological and Rawlsian conceptions are part of the *contractarian* conception of moral and political theories. By contrast, several types of *communitarian* conceptions of justice have emerged recently and focus on the centrality of noncontractual relationships and the common social good. One diverse tradition of justice that pulls together many threads that the previous theories overlook is feminism. Alison Jaggar (1983) has argued for a socialist or Marxist conception of feminist justice in which she critiques patriarchy and capitalism and views justice as stemming from an ongoing social dialogue. Annette Baier (1994) has aligned feminism with the British sentimentalist tradition and thinkers such as David Hume who believed that justice is an expanding circle of trust-based relations.

"Care ethics," a situational ethics that focuses on maintaining emotional and social bonds between people, also contributes significantly to alternative conceptions of justice (Gilligan, 1993). These (and many other) third-wave feminist approaches to morality and politics can be thought of as promoting a conception of justice that sees the preservation of caring social relations and the establishment of relations of trust to be of central importance. Through criticism of the notion of gender itself, these views attack social structures of inequality and injustice and promote a notion of justice that is deeply rooted in the interpersonal and distributive perceptions of justice. Feminist conceptions of justice, with their stress on recovering the social, emotional, and embodied connections that bind us to others, also draw from twentieth-century European philosophy, such as phenomenology, existentialism, and postmodernism (Butler, 2011). Such views place primacy on relational justice motives. The feminist tradition of relational justice would appear to resonate with cultures that stress the collective, the reduction of power distance, and the affective and interpersonal values associated with the feminine. Furthermore, it can be thought of as embracing weak uncertainty avoidance, through the acceptance of our finite, embodied perspectives, our dependency on others, and skepticism about traditional norms of power and control. This would be in contrast to deontological, Rawlsian, and utilitarian justice traditions, which would align with cultures that practice strong uncertainty avoidance.

Modern neo-Aristotelian conceptions of justice, advocated most famously by philosopher Martha Nussbaum (2000) and economist Amartya Sen (2009), combine many of the previously discussed views. Natural law places a strong emphasis on individual rights, given by nature, which for many pre-nineteenth-century thinkers is synonymous with their being given by God. Thinkers such as Nussbaum (2000) and Sen (2009) focus on the material conditions and distribution of social goods because they recognize the importance of developing human virtues and virtuous communities. Nussbaum and Sen have called their approach the capabilities approach, and their conception of justice is simply to make sure that persons and their communities have access to "central" capabilities such as mental and physical health, reproductive rights, recreation and the environment, and the classical rights of free conscience, movement, and association.

Eastern Philosophical Traditions

While the preceding discussion has focused on Western philosophical traditions, justice is not merely a Western concept. Eastern philosophical traditions have their own approaches to conceptualizing justice. Starting with the Hindu tradition, the concept of dharma expresses "the principles which we have to observe in our daily life," which constitute our "social relations" (Radhakrishnan, 1947). The notion captures a holistic conception that the fulfillment of social duties is also care of the soul and the development of spiritual values. The notion of dharma "has been variously translated as 'duty,' 'religion,' 'justice,' 'law,' 'ethics,' 'religious merit,' 'principle' and 'right' " (Flood, 1996). Additionally, "the basic principle of dharma is the realization of the dignity of the human spirit" (Radhakrishnan, 1947, p. 107). While recognizing that the Hindu tradition has a long and diverse history, there are several unmistakable parallels between Hindu thinking on justice and the deontological tradition (Krishnan, 1992). The fulfillment of law, ritual, and duty and a notion of karma associated with successful or unsuccessful following of those laws suggests an embrace of procedural justice perceptions and deontic justice motives. In spite of those parallels with deontology, the Hindu tradition does not accept the individualistic value culture of that tradition. Its acceptance of a metaphysical picture of the human soul as connected to the divine challenges the individual-collective division. It also would not accept a clear division between indulgence and restraint, given that it recognizes pleasure (*kama*) as an important value but also advocates for spiritual enlightenment (*moksha*; Brannigan, 2000). Similarly, its spiritual tradition differs from Western liberal traditions by being willing to accept greater power distance in society because it regards true equality to be reserved for the domain of the spiritual (Mohanty, 2000). This might lead us to see the Hindu tradition as akin to one of the oldest Western justice traditions, Platonism (Chand, 1939). For Plato, justice in a social setting was defined as following a hierarchical system of law, which allowed social divisions to fulfill their functions. But that system of worldly inequality was compatible with a notion of justice as a virtue that comes from inner peace and perfection of the soul. Thus, it is evident that even our conceptualizations of cultural dimensions (individualism–collectivism, hedonism, power distance, etc.) clearly stem from a Western understanding of moral-cultural values.

In China, the tradition of Confucian thought also does not accept many Western distinctions. The Confucian tradition advocates for certain personal virtues and political values, each of which is easily associated with notions of justice pertaining to one's relations to others, obedience to laws and traditions, and concern for the greater good, as well as the development of one's own moral personality (Duvert, 2018). Confucian humanism has both a strong sense of duty as articulated in its notion of "filial piety" and "proper conduct" (*li*)[2] in society (Chan, 1963). Conscientiousness and consideration of others is also central to being human according to Confucianism, aligning it with more social, communitarian, and sentimentalist traditions (Yu-Lan, 1976). Furthermore, Confucius's emphasis on the benefits of good governance for a flourishing society would seem to align with the utilitarian tradition. This complexity means that aligning the Confucian notion of justice with a particular set of justice perceptions or motives is difficult. In terms of its relation to culture, it is clearly collectivist, accepting of great power distance, keenly aware of uncertainty, and pursuing long-term organizational goals.

In many ways, the same diversity of moral values and overturning of Western moral distinctions is found in the Buddhist tradition. While the Dalai Lama has argued for the centrality of happiness to Buddhist thought, it is clearly a reflective or inner state of peace quite distinct from the notion associated with utilitarianism (HH Dalai Lama & Cutler, 2009). The Buddhist Eight-Fold Path clearly identifies a set of actions that are morally right and duties that we have to others and to society, yet these actions are explained in very general terms that are not a clear-cut set of rules or foundational principles (Mitchell, 2002). The development of certain virtues and the fostering of relationships with others are clearly the heart of the theory, aligning it more with the values of the feminist tradition. The Buddhist notion of justice, thought of in terms of the various right actions prescribed by the Eight-Fold Path, clearly focuses on interactional justice perceptions and relational justice motives. The cultural values that would align with it are collectivism, minimized power distance, and feminism.

Conclusions and Takeaways

We began this chapter with the hope of examining some ways in which justice research could be moved beyond an examination of employees' perceptions of fairness and toward an examination of justice as a foundational concept on which social institutions are based. In Table 9.1, we presented the common ways in which organizational justice has been conceptualized to demonstrate the need to move from the traditional dimensions of justice to broader motives of justice in order to understand the impact of culture. In Table 9.2, we presented the philosophical roots of various justice motives as discussed by both Eastern and Western thinkers and began to develop a deeper appreciation of why cultural values may lead to differences in how organizational justice may be researched through a unique lens of culture and moral philosophy. Our conceptualization in this table can be used to guide future research on culture and organizational justice to understand how

[2] This is similar to the concept of social tightness–looseness or "the strength of social norms and degree of social sanctioning within societies." See Gelfand et al., 2006, for a discussion.

Table 9.3 Five key theoretical ideas found in culture and organizational justice research
Five Key Theoretical Principles
1. *Organizational Justice and* ***Identity***: Cultures value personal characteristics (such as sex, race, age, and disability) differently, and organizational practices can perpetuate advantages or disadvantages for specific groups of employees. Workplace discrimination will have an impact on employees' sense of self-worth and identity.
2. *Organizational Justice and* ***Behaviors***: Culturally sanctioned behaviors, such as the display of emotions, or culturally acceptable norms around relationships (e.g., acceptable supervisor-subordinate interactions), will have an effect on justice perceptions and acceptance of organizational practices.
3. *Organizational Justice and* ***Equality/Social Justice***: Cultural differences in shared values and justice motives around equality and social justice will impact how employees view the role of workplaces as social institutions responsible for creating just and equal societies.
4. *Organizational Justice and* ***Impact of Diffusion***: Diffusion of and adherence to Western management practices in host country nations that are inconsistent with shared cultural values can impact perceptions of fairness.
5. *Organizational Justice and* ***Cultural Identity***: Cultural moral traditions can form the basis of conceptualizations of justice, and these justice motives, as a fundamental part of cultural identity, will influence and be impacted by how organizations and institutions create practices and treat people.

organizational practices can be viewed as just or unjust based on values and outcomes that are held to be culturally desirable and important.

In our review of recent research on organizational justice across cultures, we were able to focus on issues that lend themselves to future inquiry. Table 9.3 summarizes some of the key takeaways regarding culture and organizational justice, which when examined through the lens of moral philosophy (especially feminist and Eastern traditions), can provide insights into what employees value and how they conceptualize just social structures. Justice is fundamentally about how we treat each other, and our review suggests that justice in organizations (whether structural or perceived) has an impact on both employee well-being and work behaviors. We find the role of culture especially important for the formation and maintenance of employees' self-worth and identity and related to their personal characteristics (like sex or disability). Cultural norms around behaviors that have an impact on well-being, such as display of emotions by employees or abusive behaviors by supervisors, could also drive perceptions of fairness. Recent social events have brought into focus the need for organizational justice research to study the impact of organizational rules and practices on racial and ethnic minorities. Future research should address the role of workplaces as institutions that perpetuate social injustices and the role of such institutions in creating just practices. Research should also focus on organizational practices that can be brought to bear on the real social issues of today such as living wages and pay equality. And finally, our review suggests that the diffusion and subsequent entrenchment of Western management practices may have transformative

Table 9.4 Five main practical implications for future research on justice and culture
Five Practical Implications
1. **Employee Well-being:** Just treatment can affect employee mental and physical health, and organizations should understand the implications of creating a positive justice climate, addressing issues of discrimination, emotional labor, and inequality. By doing so, organizations become just institutions in and of themselves.
2. **Supervision and Leadership:** Addressing abusive supervision and encouraging ethical leadership will require creating organizational practices that challenge cultural norms. This may require a cautious move away from culturally particularistic practices.
3. **Discrimination:** Just practices and the fair treatment of all is a core issue for organizations. Care should be taken to design practices that address issues of discrimination based in race, sex, disability, and identity. At the same time, cultural values should be considered when designing practices that promote equality in a way that is not contrary to the underlying philosophical approaches of a society.
4. **Design of HR Practices:** HR practices should be designed taking into consideration what is valued in each society, and care should be taken when transferring practices from one cultural context to another. This means paying attention to the underlying cultural motives that are not purely instrumental, but also relational and moral.
5. **Corporate Social Responsibility (CSR):** As organizations around the world engage in CSR practices, and as justice research increasingly delves into the field of CSR, organizations should pay attention to cultural values to ensure stakeholder buy-in.

effects on individuals' cultural values. Research should examine how management practices can impact employees' cultural identity through the push for assimilation into the firm's culture and impact their sense of worth and well-being. By focusing on multi-foci justice, such research can examine a broader scope of justice perceptions and not be limited to employees' interactions with single (or aggregate) entities. Table 9.4 presents some practical suggestions for considering organizational justice from multiple perspectives and moving beyond seeing justice as purely perceived fairness, judged through the lens of individual self-interest. The issues being addressed by organizations all around the world today and over the next few decades mean a much larger and varied scope for justice and culture research.

Ultimately, it would appear that justice researchers, when examining broader social issues such as racial injustice, inequality, or discrimination, need to step away from the traditionally evoked Utilitarian and deontic theories of justice and seek guidance from the feminist and Eastern traditions to understand how organizations can foster just relations and structures. When we look at studies of cultural values using Western frameworks, such as those developed by Hofstede, we come to realize that the role of culture in understanding the notion of organizational justice is not as simple as demarcating employees based on discrete national cultural values. Rather, it is to fully understand our core moral values that form our cultural identities, which we carry into our workplace.

References

Arya, B., Mirchandani, D. A., & Harris, M. M. (2019). Personality and pay satisfaction: exploring the influence of organizational justice and gender in South Africa. *The International Journal of Human Resource Management, 30*(2), 219–250.

Baier, A. (1994). *Moral prejudices: Essays on ethics.* Cambridge, MA: Harvard University Press.

Barclay, L. J., & Kiefer, T. (2014). Approach or avoid? Exploring overall justice and the differential effects of positive and negative emotions. *Journal of Management, 40*(7), 1857–1898.

Barsky, A., Kaplan, S. A., & Beal, D. J. (2011). Just feelings? The role of affect in the formation of organizational fairness judgments. *Journal of Management, 37*(1), 248–279.

Biswas, S., Varma, A., & Ramaswami, A. (2013). Linking distributive and procedural justice to employee engagement through social exchange: A field study in India. *The International Journal of Human Resource Management, 24*(8), 1570–1587.

Brands, R. A., & Fernandez-Mateo, I. (2017). Leaning out: How negative recruitment experiences shape women's decisions to compete for executive roles. *Administrative Science Quarterly, 62*(3), 405–442.

Brannigan, M. (2000). *The pulse of wisdom: The philosophies of India, China, and Japan.* Belmont, CA: Wadsworth.

Brockner, J., Ackerman, G., Greenberg, J., Gelfand, M. J., Francesco, A. M., Chen, Z. X., Leung, K., Bierbrauer, G., Gomez, C., Kirkman, B. L., & Shapiro, D. (2001). Cultural and procedural justice: The influence of power distance on reactions to voice. *Journal of Experimental Social Psychology, 37*, 300–315.

Buengeler, C., & Den Hartog, D. N. (2015). National diversity and team performance: The moderating role of interactional justice climate. *The International Journal of Human Resource Management, 26*(6), 831–855.

Burt, C. D., & Carr, S. C. (2011). Organizational psychology and poverty reduction: The multi-dimensionality of the aid worker experience. *Journal of Managerial Psychology, 26*(6), 444–452.

Butler, A. M., & Chung-Yan, G. A. (2011). The influence of sexual harassment frequency and perceptions of organizational justice on victim responses to sexual harassment. *European Journal of Work and Organizational Psychology, 20* (6), 729–754.

Butler, J. (2011). *Gender trouble: Feminism and the subversion of identity.* New York: Routledge.

Byrne, Z. S., & Cropanzano, R. (2001). The history of organizational justice: The founders speak. In R. S. Cropanzano (Ed.), *Justice in the workplace: From theory to practice*, Volume *2* (pp. 3–26). Mahwah, NJ: Lawrence Erlbaum.

Caleo, S. (2016). Are organizational justice rules gendered? Reactions to men's and women's justice violations. *Journal of Applied Psychology, 101*(10), 1422–1435.

Caleo, S. (2018). When distributive justice and gender stereotypes coincide: Reactions to equity and equality violations. *Journal of Applied Social Psychology, 48*(5), 257–268.

Carr, S. C., Thompson, M., Dalal, A. K., de Guzman, J. M., Gloss, A., Munns, L., & Steadman, A. (2014). Psychology and poverty reduction: A global special issue. *International Perspectives in Psychology, 3*(4), 215–237.

Chan, W. (1963). *A sourcebook in Chinese philosophy.* Princeton, NJ: Princeton University Press.

Chand, B. (1939). The Platonic concept of justice compared with the Hindu concept of Dharma. *Proceedings of the Indian History Congress, 3*, 204–213.

Chen, Y., Friedman, R., Yu, E., & Sun, F. (2011). Examining the positive and negative effects of guanxi practices: A multi-level analysis of guanxi practices and procedural justice perceptions. *Asia Pacific Journal of Management, 28*(4), 715–735.

Chien, M. S., Lawler, J. S., & Uen, J. F. (2010). Performance-based pay, procedural justice and job performance for R&D professionals: Evidence from the Taiwanese high-tech sector. *The International Journal of Human Resource Management, 21*(12), 2234–2248.

Cole, M. S., Carter, M. Z., & Zhang, Z. (2013). Leader-team congruence in power distance values and team effectiveness: The mediating role of procedural justice climate. *Journal of Applied Psychology, 98*(6), 962–973.

Colquitt, J. A. (2001). On the dimensionality of organizational justice: a construct validation of a measure. *Journal of Applied Psychology, 86*(3), 386–400.

Colquitt, J. A. (2012). Organizational justice. In S. W. Kozlowski (Ed.), *The Oxford handbook or organizational psychology.* (Vol. 1, pp. 526–547). New York: Oxford University Press.

Colquitt, J. A., Conlon, D. E., Wesson, M. J., Porter, C. O., & Ng, K. Y. (2001). Justice at the millennium: A meta-analytic review of 25 years of organizational justice research. *Journal of Applied Psychology, 86*(3), 425.
Cropanzano, R. S., & Ambrose, M. L. (2015). *The Oxford handbook of justice in the workplace.* New York: Oxford University Press.
Cugueró-Escofet, N., & Fortin, M. (2014). One justice or two? A model of reconciliation of normative justice theories and empirical research on organizational justice. *Journal of Business Ethics, 124*(3), 435–451.
Dahling, J. J. (2017). Exhausted, mistreated, or indifferent? Explaining deviance from emotional display rules at work. *European Journal of Work and Organizational Psychology, 26*(2), 171–182.
Dhanani, L. Y., Beus, J. M., & Joseph, D. L. (2018). Workplace discrimination: A meta-analytic extension, critique, and future research agenda. *Personnel Psychology, 71*(2), 147–179.
Duvert, C. (2018). How is justice understood in Confucianism? *Asian Philosophy, 28*(4), 295–315.
Erez, M., & Earley, P. C. (1993). *Culture, self-identity, and work.* New York: Oxford University Press.
Fischer, R. (2013). Belonging, status, or self-protection? Examining justice motives in a three-level cultural meta-analysis of organizational justice effects. *Cross-Cultural Research, 47*(1), 3–41.
Fischer, R. (2016). Justice and culture. In C. Sabbagh & M. Schmitt (Eds.), *Handbook of social justice theory and research* (pp. 459–475). New York: Springer.
Flood, G. (1996). *An introduction to Hinduism.* Cambridge: Cambridge University Press.
Folger, R. G., & Cropanzano, R. (1998). *Organizational justice and human resource management* (Vol. 7). Thousand Oaks, CA: SAGE.
Fortin, M., Nadisic, T., Bell, C. M., Crawshaw, J. R., & Cropanzano, R. (2016). Beyond the particular and universal: Dependence, independence, and interdependence of context, justice, and ethics. *Journal of Business Ethics, 137*(4), 639–647.
Gadelrab, H. F., Alkhadher, O., Aldhafri, S., Almoshawah, S., Khatatba, Y., El Abiddine, F. Z., & Slimene, S. (2018). Organizational justice in Arab countries: Investigation of the measurement and structural invariance. *Cross-Cultural Research, 54*(1), 3–27.
Game, A. M., & Crawshaw, J. R. (2017). A question of fit: Cultural and individual differences in interpersonal justice perceptions. *Journal of Business Ethics, 144*(2), 279–291.
Gelfand, M. J., Nishii, L. H., & Raver, J. L. (2006). On the nature and importance of cultural tightness-looseness. *Journal of Applied Psychology, 91*(6), 1225–1224.
Gillespie, J. Z., & Ryan, A. M. (2012). Gender-based preferential selection: Influences of perceptions of procedurally unfair advantage on performance and self-evaluations. *Journal of Applied Social Psychology, 42,* E150–E179.
Gilligan, C. (1993). *In a different voice: Psychological theory and women's development.* Cambridge, MA: Harvard University Press.
Goldman, B., & Cropanzano, R. (2015). "Justice" and "fairness" are not the same thing. *Journal of Organizational Behavior, 36*(2), 313–318.
Grandey, A. A., Rupp, D., & Brice, W. N. (2015). Emotional labor threatens decent work: A proposal to eradicate emotional display rules. *Journal of Organizational Behavior, 36*(6), 770–785.
Gupta, V., & Singh, S. (2013). An empirical study of the dimensionality of organizational justice and its relationship with organizational citizenship behaviour in the Indian context. *The International Journal of Human Resource Management, 24*(6), 1277–1299.
Harbi, S. A., Thursfield, D., & Bright, D. (2017). Culture, wasta and perceptions of performance appraisal in Saudi Arabia. *The International Journal of Human Resource Management, 28*(19), 2792–2810.
Harcourt, M., Hannay, M., & Lam, H. (2013). Distributive justice, employment-at-will and just-cause dismissal. *Journal of Business Ethics, 115*(2), 311–325.
Hartmann, F., & Slapničar, S. (2012). Pay fairness and intrinsic motivation: The role of pay transparency. *The International Journal of Human Resource Management, 23*(20), 4283–4300.
He, W., Fehr, R., Yam, K. C., Long, L. R., & Hao, P. (2017). Interactional justice, leader–member exchange, and employee performance: Examining the moderating role of justice differentiation. *Journal of Organizational Behavior, 38*(4), 537–557.
HH Dalai Lama & Cutler, H. (2009). *The art of happiness,* 10th Anniversary Edition. New York: Penguin.
Hofstede, G. (2011). Dimensionalizing cultures: The Hofstede model in context. Online Readings in Psychology and Culture, Unit 2. Retrieved fromhttp://scholarworks.gvsu.edu/orpc/vol2/iss1/8

Huang, J. L., Cropanzano, R., Li, A., Shao, P., Zhang, X. A., & Li, Y. (2017). Employee conscientiousness, agreeableness, and supervisor justice rule compliance: A three-study investigation. *Journal of Applied Psychology, 102*(11), 1564.
Huang, W. (2016). Responsible pay: managing compliance, organizational efficiency and fairness in the choice of pay systems in China's automotive companies. *The International Journal of Human Resource Management, 27*(18), 2161–2181.
Jaggar, A. M. (1983). *Feminist politics and human nature.* Lanham, MD: Rowan and Littlefield.
James, K. (2015). Culture and organizational justice: State of the literature and suggestions for future directions. In R. S. Cropanzano & M. L. Ambrose (Eds.), *The Oxford handbook of justice in the workplace* (pp. 273–290). New York: Oxford University Press.
Jiang, Z., Gollan, P. J., & Brooks, G. (2017). Relationships between organizational justice, organizational trust and organizational commitment: A cross-cultural study of China, South Korea and Australia. *The International Journal of Human Resource Management, 28*(7), 973–1004.
Johnson, R. E., Chang, C. H., & Rosen, C. C. (2010). "Who I am depends on how fairly I'm treated": Effects of justice on self-identity and regulatory focus. *Journal of Applied Social Psychology, 40*(12), 3020–3058.
Johnson, R. E., Lanaj, K., & Barnes, C. M. (2014). The good and bad of being fair: Effects of procedural and interpersonal justice behaviors on regulatory resources. *Journal of Applied Psychology, 99*(4), 635–650.
Johnson, R. E., & Lord, R. G. (2010). Implicit effects of justice on self-identity. *Journal of Applied Psychology, 95*(4), 681–695.
Johnston, C. S., Krings, F., Maggiori, C., Meier, L. L., & Fiori, M. (2016). Believing in a personal just world helps maintain well-being at work by coloring organizational justice perceptions. *European Journal of Work and Organizational Psychology, 25*(6), 945–959.
Kant, I. (1996). Toward perpetual peace. In M. Gregor (Ed.), *Practical philosophy* (pp. 317–351). Cambridge: Cambridge University Press.
Khan, K., Abbas, M., Gul, A., & Raja, U. (2015). Organizational justice and job outcomes: Moderating role of Islamic work ethic. *Journal of Business Ethics, 126*(2), 235–246.
Krishnan, L. (1992). Justice research: The Indian perspective. *Psychology and Developing Societies, 4*(1), 39–71.
Lavelle, J. J., Harris, C. M., Rupp, D. E., Herda, D. N., Young, R. F., Hargrove, M. B., & Mahan, G. C. (2018). Multifoci effects of injustice on counterproductive work behaviors and the moderating roles of symbolization and victim sensitivity. *Journal of Organizational Behavior, 39*(8), 1022–1039.
Leung, K. (2005). How generalizable are justice effects across cultures? In J. Greenberg & J. A. Colquitt (Eds.), *Handbook of organizational justice* (pp. 555–586). Mahwah, NJ: Lawrence Erlbaum.
Leung, K., & Lind, E. A. (1986). Procedural justice and culture: Effects of culture, gender, and investigator status on procedural preferences. *Journal of Personality and Social Psychology, 50*(6), 1134–1140.
Lin, H. C., Bruning, P. F., Cole, N. D., Flint, D. H., Ngin, C., & Supangco, V. (2019). Exploring justice judgment patterns in Asia: A four country multi-group latent class analysis. *The International Journal of Human Resource Management, 30*(2), 306–336.
Lin, X. (2015). How does procedural justice climate influence individual outcomes? An affective perspective. *Asia Pacific Journal of Management, 32*(3), 771–800.
Liu, D., Hernandez, M., & Wang, L. (2014). The role of leadership and trust in creating structural patterns of team procedural justice: A social network investigation. *Personnel Psychology, 67*(4), 801–845.
Loi, R., Lam, L. W., & Chan, K. W. (2012). Coping with job insecurity: The role of procedural justice, ethical leadership, and power distance orientation. *Journal of Business Ethics, 108*, 361–372.
Long, E. C., & Christian, M. S. (2015). Mindfulness buffers retaliatory responses to injustice: A regulatory approach. *Journal of Applied Psychology, 100*(5), 1409.
Low, Y. M., Sambasivan, M., & Ho, J. A. (2019). Impact of abusive supervision on counterproductive work behaviors of nurses. *Asia Pacific Journal of Human Resources, 59*(2), 250–278.
Lucas, T., Kamble, S. V., Wu, M. S., Zhdanova, L., & Wendorf, C. A. (2016). Distributive and procedural justice for self and others: Measurement invariance and links to life satisfaction in four cultures. *Journal of Cross-Cultural Psychology, 47*(2), 234–248.
MacIntyre, A. C. (1988). *Whose justice? Which rationality?* (Vol. 239). London: Duckworth.
Mackey, J. D., Frieder, R. E., Brees, J. R., & Martinko, M. J. (2017). Abusive supervision: A meta-analysis and empirical review. *Journal of Management, 43*(6), 1940–1965.
Mitchell, D. (2002). *Buddhism: Introducing the Buddhist experience.* New York: Oxford University Press.
Mohanty, J. N. (2000). *Classical Indian philosophy.* Lanham, MD: Rowman & Littlefield.

Morris, M. W., Leung, K., Ames, D., & Lickel, B. (1999). Views from inside and outside: Integrating emic and etic insights about culture and justice judgment. *Academy of Management Review, 24*(4), 781–796.

Naumann, S. E., & Bennett, N. (2000). A case for procedural justice climate: Development and test of a multilevel model. *Academy of Management Journal, 43*(5), 881–889.

Nussbaum, M. (2000). *Woman and human development: The capabilities approach.* Cambridge: Cambridge University Press.

Oltra, V., Bonache, J., & Brewster, C. (2013). A new framework for understanding inequalities between expatriates and host country nationals. *Journal of Business Ethics, 115*(2), 291–310.

Özbek, M. F., Yoldash, M. A., & Tang, T. L. P. (2016). Theory of justice, OCB, and individualism: Kyrgyz citizens. *Journal of Business Ethics, 137*(2), 365–382.

Radhakrishnan, S. (1947). *Religion and society.* London: George Allen and Unwin.

Rawls, J. (1999a). *Collected papers*, ed. Samuel Freeman. Cambridge: Cambridge University Press.

Rawls, J. (1999b). *A theory of justice*, revised edition. Cambridge, MA: Harvard University Press.

Reb, J., Chaturvedi, S., Narayanan, J., & Kudesia, R. S. (2019). Leader mindfulness and employee performance: A sequential mediation model of LMX quality, interpersonal justice, and employee stress. *Journal of Business Ethics, 160*(3), 745–763.

Rubenstein, A. L., Allen, D. G., & Bosco, F. A. (2019). What's past (and present) is prologue: Interactions between justice levels and trajectories predicting behavioral reciprocity. *Journal of Management, 45*(4), 1569–1594.

Rubino, C., Avery, D. R., McKay, P. F. Moore, B. L., Wilson, D. C., VanDriel, M. S., Witt, L. A., & McDonald, D. P. (2018). And justice for all: How organizational justice climate deters sexual harassment. *Personnel Psychology, 71*(4), 519–544.

Rupp, D. E., & Paddock, E. L. (2010). From justice events to justice climate: A multi-level temporal model of information aggregation and judgment. *Fairness and Groups, 13*, 245–273.

Rupp, D. E., Shapiro, D. L., Folger, R., Skarlicki, D. P., & Shao, R. (2017). A critical analysis of the conceptualization and measurement of organizational justice: Is it time for reassessment? *Academy of Management Annals, 11*(2), 919–959.

Schimnke, M., Arnaud, A., & Taylor, R. (2015). Ethics, values, and organizational justice: Individuals, organizations, and beyond. *Journal of Business Ethics, 130*(3), 727–736.

Sen, A. (2009). *The idea of justice.* Cambridge, MA: Harvard University Press.

Shaffer, M., Singh, B., & Chen, Y. P. (2013). Expatriate pay satisfaction: The role of organizational inequities, assignment stressors and perceived assignment value. *The International Journal of Human Resource Management, 24*(15), 2968–2984.

Shao, R., Rupp, D. E., Skarlicki, D. P., & Jones, K. S. (2013). Employee justice across cultures: A meta-analytic review. *Journal of Management, 39*(1), 263–301.

Shen, K. N., & Xie, X. (2018). Moving from the developing to the developed: Compensation disparities of Chinese expatriates. *Asia Pacific Journal of Human Resources, 56*(2), 260–285.

Shoaib, S., & Baruch, Y. (2019). Deviant behavior in a moderated-mediation framework of incentives, organizational justice perception, and reward expectancy. *Journal of Business Ethics, 157*(3), 617–633.

Stouten, J., Kuppens, P., & Decoster, S. (2013). Being angry for different reasons: The role of personality in distributive justice. *Journal of Applied Social Psychology, 43*(4), 795–805.

Summereder, S., Streicher, B., & Batinic, B. (2014). Voice or consistency? What you perceive as procedurally fair depends on your level of power distance. *Journal of Cross-Cultural Psychology, 45*(2), 192–212.

Tepper, B. J. (2000). Consequences of abusive supervision. *Academy of Management Journal, 43*(2), 178–190.

Tepper, B. J., Simon, L., & Park, H. M. (2017). Abusive supervision. *Annual Review of Organizational Psychology and Organizational Behavior, 4*, 123–152.

Tremblay, M., Cloutier, J., Simard, G., Chênevert, D., & Vandenberghe, C. (2010). The role of HRM practices, procedural justice, organizational support and trust in organizational commitment and in-role and extra-role performance. *The International Journal of Human Resource Management, 21*(3), 405–433.

Trompenaars, F. (1996). Resolving international conflict: Culture and business strategy. *Business Strategy Review, 7*(3), 51–68.

Villanueva-Flores, M., Valle-Cabrera, R., & Ramón-Jerónimo, M. A. (2015). Perceived compensation discrimination against physically disabled people in Andalusia. *The International Journal of Human Resource Management, 26*(17), 2248–2265.

Vogel, R. M., Mitchell, M. S., Tepper, B. J., Restubog, S. L., Hu, C., Hua, W., & Huang, J. C. (2015). A cross-cultural examination of subordinates' perceptions of and reactions to abusive supervision. *Journal of Organizational Behavior, 36*(5), 720–745.

Wang, H., Lu, G., & Liu, Y. (2017). Ethical leadership and loyalty to supervisor in China: The roles of interactional justice and collectivistic orientation. *Journal of Business Ethics, 146*(3), 529–543.

Wang, R., & Chan, D. K. S. (2019). Subordinate reactions to ethical leaders' abusive behavior: A multiple-wave study. *Asia Pacific Journal of Human Resources, 58*(3), 427–449.

Wei, F., & Si, S. (2013). Tit for tat? Abusive supervision and counterproductive work behaviors: The moderating effects of locus of control and perceived mobility. *Asia Pacific Journal of Management, 30*(1), 281–296.

Whitman, D. S., Caleo, S., Carpenter, N. C., Horner, M. T., & Bernerth, J. B. (2012). Fairness at the collective level: A meta-analytic examination of the consequences and boundary conditions of organizational justice climate. *Journal of Applied Psychology, 97*(4), 776.

Wong, Y. T. (2012). Job security and justice: Predicting employees' trust in Chinese international joint ventures. *The International Journal of Human Resource Management, 23*(19), 4129–4144.

Wood, S., Braeken, J., & Niven, K. (2013). Discrimination and well-being in organizations: Testing the differential power and organizational justice theories of workplace aggression. *Journal of Business Ethics, 115*(3), 617–634.

Yu-Lan, F. (1976). *A Short history of Chinese philosophy*, New York: Free Press.

Zhang, Y., & Liao, Z. (2015). Consequences of abusive supervision: A meta-analytic review. *Asia Pacific Journal of Management, 32*(4), 959–987.

CHAPTER

10 Culture and Creativity in Organizations: New Directions and Discoveries

Ella Miron-Spektor *and* Susannah B. F. Paletz

Abstract

Creativity is culture dependent. Culture influences how individuals and groups in organizations create new ideas and define and value creativity. In this chapter, we review recent research to highlight new developments in understanding individual and team creativity across cultures. Integrating different streams of research, we review research on cultural values, tightness–looseness, logic, and implicit theories. We discuss the effect of culture on the ability to generate novel and useful ideas and the impact of cultural systems on how people define, evaluate, and develop their creative ideas. Given the increasing reliance on multinational workforces and cross-country transitions of employees, we also consider the impact of multicultural experiences on creativity and the effectiveness and challenges of culturally diverse groups in innovative settings. Finally, we suggest several fruitful directions for future research, including expanding to different tasks, creative processes, and cultures.

Key Words: culture, creativity, tightness–looseness, values, implicit theories, diverse teams, multicultural

Rarely is there a more urgent need for people to be creative than at a time of crisis. In 2020, the COVID-19 pandemic generated a host of unique challenges for employees and employers worldwide. Pharmaceutical companies raced against time to develop new vaccines and treatments. Managers shifted to managing their workforce from afar, and parents had to find creative solutions to work from home while homeschooling their children (Kniffin et al., 2020; Pradies et al., 2021). Three years later, organizations in various industries cope with an energy crisis and a war in Europe, global political instability, and recession. With the pressing need for creativity in solving global challenges and everyday problems, it is vital to understand the role culture plays in nurturing creative behavior in organizations.

Creativity—the generation of novel ideas that are useful (Amabile et al., 1996)—is universal; yet, it also depends on context (Erez & Nouri, 2010; Leung & Wang, 2015; Loewenstein & Mueller, 2016). The context and situation influence the extent to which individuals engage in creativity and whether particular ideas are considered creative. Ideas are deemed novel if they are unique in a specific domain or context, and they are considered useful if they create potential value in a given organization or society (Csikszentmihalyi, 2014; Shalley et al., 2004). Given its context-dependence, creativity can range from incremental suggestions to radical breakthroughs (Madjar et al., 2011).

While most research has defined creativity in terms of its outcomes (i.e., novel and useful ideas), scholars have also considered the different stages in the creative process (Shalley et al., 2004). Creativity usually begins with the generation of ideas, allowing people to identify and define a problem and then gather relevant information through which they come up with new insights and alternative solutions. Through the elaboration of ideas, people evaluate their quality, consider potential pitfalls and advantages, and select a promising idea that is deemed more valuable than others. When successful, ideas are implemented into innovative products, services, or processes (Perry-Smith & Mannucci, 2017).

In the past 30 years, research on creativity and culture has flourished, and numerous studies have examined the influence of culture on creativity in various contexts and countries (Leung & Wang, 2015; Xie & Paik, 2019). Several special issues on culture and creativity were published (Kwan et al., 2018; Morris & Leung, 2010). Books were written on the interplay between culture and creativity (Gelfand, 2019; Spencer-Rodgers & Peng, 2018) and review papers on the topic (Maddux et al., 2020; Leung & Wang, 2015; Xie & Paik, 2019). While early studies examined cultural differences in generating new ideas (e.g., Jaquish & Ripple, 1984), more recent work showed that culture influences the type of ideas generated and how people define, perceive, and value creative solutions (Leung & Wang, 2015). Scholars have also examined the influence of multicultural experiences on creativity (Maddux et al., 2020), and the conditions under which culturally diverse teams can effectively innovate (e.g., Adler & Aycan, 2018; Mannix & Neale, 2005; Stahl et al., 2010).

This chapter reviews and integrates recent research on culture and creativity, focusing on the different streams of research and new findings. We start by documenting and explaining cross-cultural differences in creativity, and then we move to contemporary work to explore the influence of multicultural experiences and cultural diversity on creative thinking. Our review spans different levels of analyses and covers various theories and methods. We identify four main approaches used to understand the impact of culture on creativity: values, tightness–looseness, logics, and implicit theories. We discuss research on (1) the effect of cultural values, tightness, and logics on the ability to generate novel and useful ideas, and (2) the impact of cultural systems on the way people define creativity, emphasize novelty or usefulness, and develop their ideas. We provide a synthesis of what we currently know about culture and creativity, and we suggest several new directions for future research.

Research on Culture and Creativity

The increasing globalization of the workplace has motivated efforts to better understand how culture influences creativity. Culture is usually defined as a *shared system of learned meanings* (Rohner, 1984) and refers to values, norms, beliefs, and assumptions embraced by members of a given social unit (Schein, 1992). Culture can be dynamic and stable, a process, and an entity (Kashima, 2000a). It is often studied as if it is an unchanging force (stable, entity), but researchers readily admit that it grows and develops over time through human interaction (dynamic, process; Kashima, 2000b). Although most psychology research describes culture at the national level, culture exists at multiple levels, representing individuals nested within groups, organizations, and countries (Erez & Gati, 2004).

Research on culture and creativity has shifted focus over the years from a country-comparison approach to a more fine-grained understanding of how cultural systems shape the way people define and evaluate creativity and engage in the creative process. Scholars have examined how cultural diversity influences social dynamics to enable or impede creativity.

They have used a variety of methods. Early cross-cultural studies used creativity tests to compare individuals across cultures (Jacquish & Ripple, 1984–1985). Others used judges' evaluations of the novelty and usefulness of suggested ideas (Amabile, 1983) or decomposed creativity into distinct yet interrelated components: cognitive flexibility, fluency, originality, and elaboration (Nouri et al., 2014; Rietzschel et al., 2007). *Fluency* refers to the number of suggested ideas. Flexibility represents the number of distinct semantic categories people draw from when generating ideas, and originality refers to the rarity of the solution in a given sample or context. Fluency, flexibility, originality, and elaboration are divergent creative thinking types, whereas convergent creative thinking involves evaluating and choosing ideas (Rietzschel et al., 2007). More recent studies have employed new methodologies and tools, including qualitative and linguistic analysis (Jackson et al., 2019; Loewenstein & Mueller, 2016), scenario experiments and surveys of individuals (Paletz & Peng, 2008; Yue, 2003), experiments and surveys involving teams (Goncalo & Staw, 2006; Goncalo & Duguid, 2012), electroencephalography for testing brain activities (Mu et al., 2015), a meta-analysis (Watts et al., 2020), and big data using crowdsourcing platforms (Chua et al., 2015).

Early cross-cultural studies simply assessed whether one group performed better on American-made tests than others. Rather than presenting a theory of culture and creativity, these included attempts to replicate various creativity tests across cultures. While the tests were developed on a theoretical basis on what constituted creativity (e.g., fluency), cross-cultural replications were usually performed without any a priori hypotheses involving cross-cultural differences (van de Vijver & Leung, 2000). For example, a study that examined differences between Americans and people in East Asia on the Torrance Tests of Creative Thinking (TTCT) assessed ideational fluency, flexibility, and originality across five different age groups from 9 to 60 years of age (Jacquish & Ripple, 1984–1985).

Americans overall scored higher than the Chinese on fluency, flexibility, and originality. In contrast, Torrance and Sato (1979) found that Japanese outperformed Americans on every dimension of creativity except fluency (number of responses). These inconsistent findings revealed possible cultural biases in the assessment of creativity, as both the definitions and identification procedures are culture-specific (Ford & Harris, 1992); even tests with low verbal content may be biased (Torrance, 1968). Recent reviews that covered an even greater variety of the creativity testing literature concluded that although the majority of cultural differences studies show that Western participants score higher than Asian participants in various creative tests, these differences are not systematic and that creativity is affected by a wide range of contextual factors (Leung & Wang, 2015).

The next phase of research on cross-cultural creativity asked why and under what conditions there might be differences. Numerous studies have tried to address these questions by drawing on different theoretical perspectives, suggesting that individual and societal endorsement of specific cultural values influences creativity. Others indicated that social structure or the particular cultural logics that guide social interactions and tolerance of conflicts and contradictions impact creativity. Scholars also suggested that possible differences in creativity arise not from the motivation to suggest new ideas but rather from distinct implicit theories held by people from different cultures about creativity. The implicit theories shape the way they define and value creative ideas. Next, we review research representing each of these approaches.

Theoretical Approaches to Culture and Creativity

Cultural Values

Numerous studies on culture and creativity adopted a values-based approach (e.g., Erez & Nouri, 2010b; Morris & Leung, 2010; Schwartz, 1999), assuming that endorsed values and norms can account for observed differences in creativity within and across cultures. Most of them used Hofstede's framework (2001): They examined whether the extent to which a given society emphasizes the values of collectivism/individualism, power distance, uncertainty avoidance, and masculinity–femininity influences how its members engage in creative behavior and the ways they produce novel and useful ideas (e.g., Bechtoldt et al., 2010; Erez & Nouri, 2010; Nouri et al., 2014; Shane, 1992).

The values of individualism and collectivism define the way individuals view themselves in relation to others. Individualism includes focusing on individual freedom and oneself or on one's family/immediate social group rather than larger groups, whereas collectivism entails a focus on and efforts toward benefiting others, particularly ingroups (Triandis, 1989). Members of individualistic societies are motivated to engage in creative endeavors and favor radical ideas, which enable them to stand out and demonstrate their distinctiveness (Lan & Kaufman, 2012). For example, Shane (1992) analyzed the number of inventions per capita in 33 countries and noted that individualistic and nonhierarchical cultures were more creative than collectivistic hierarchical ones. Individualistic societies value autonomy and uniqueness and encourage people to express themselves and stand out by generating and sharing creative ideas (Westwood & Low, 2003). In contrast, field and experimental studies suggest that members are expected to conform to and preserve their group in collectivistic societies by suppressing their uniqueness (Goncalo & Staw, 2006; Markus & Kitayama, 1991; Mok & Morris, 2010; Westwood & Low, 2003). For this reason, researchers have argued that members of collectivistic societies generate incremental and less risky ideas (Leung & Wang, 2015).

A similar pattern is found in teams. Goncalo and Staw (2006) sought to understand the effect of individualistic and collectivistic orientations on group creativity. Challenging earlier assumptions, they examined whether—when they were expected to be creative—members of collectivist-oriented groups would feel conformity pressure to stand out from their group and suggest original ideas (Nemeth & Gonacalo, 2004). They primed team members with individualistic or collectivistic orientations and instructed them to generate creative or practical solutions to a business problem. Their creativity was then evaluated by judges who rated the novelty of the ideas, as well as their fluency, and flexibility on divergence. Interestingly, they found that individualistic groups were more creative than collectivistic groups, but only when they were instructed to generate creative rather than practical ideas. The creativity of both groups was similar when they were instructed to generate practical ideas. Their analysis also revealed differences in the creative process. While collectivistic groups tended to agree on a single idea, individualistic groups combined elements from several suggested ideas, which resulted in more novel solutions (Goncalo & Staw, 2006).

A follow-up study using a similar methodology found that the effect of individualistic or collectivistic group orientations on group creativity was dependent on the experienced pressure to conform and team members' personalities. When conformity pressure was high, individualistic norms promoted creativity, but only in groups composed of less creative characters. In groups with high average creative personalities, individualistic norms increased creativity regardless of conformity pressure (Goncalo & Duguid, 2012). Other studies tested how the collectivistic orientation of a group interacted with the individual orientation of its members. Choi and colleagues found that a combination of collectivistic value orientation and primed independent self-construal increased the fluency and originality of generated ideas relative to when the collectivistic value orientation was combined with an interdependent self-construal. However, in individualistic groups there were no differences in the level of these creativity indicators between those who were primed with independent or interdependent self-construal (Bechtoldt et al., 2012; Choi et al., 2018, 2019). In general, these and other studies suggest that the value of individualism is conducive to individual and group creativity and that collectivism can lead to creativity in some circumstances.

Power distance has also been widely studied in relation to creativity. The value of power distance refers to the extent to which differences in hierarchy are accepted and expected in a given society (Hofstede, 2001). In countries with high-power distance, individuals are less likely to speak their minds to someone higher up; hence, power distance may impede creativity and innovation. At the national level, Shane (1992) reported a negative correlation between power distance and the number of inventions per capita, even when controlling for economic factors. Others have suggested that the innovation in countries with high-power distance (such as Japan) is adaptive and mainly aims at improving quality and efficiency (e.g., "Quality Circles" and "Just-in-Time"; Jacobs & Herbig, 1998). At the group level, Yuan and Zhou (2015) offer a theoretical model to describe the effect of perceived status differentiation on group processes, individual psychological states, and creativity. They propose that members of groups with high-power distance will be less likely to share ideas and engage in constructive conflict: In general, high-status members contribute more ideas than low-status members, and the teams defer to the high-status members, which may lead them to consider fewer alternative ideas and select suboptimal solutions.

Uncertainty avoidance refers to "the extent to which the members of a culture feel threatened by uncertain or unknown situations" (Hofstede, 2001, p. 161). Nations scoring high on uncertainty avoidance tend to have well-defined rules and regulations that promote certainty and security (such as laws, technology, and religion). People in high uncertainty-avoidance cultures report experiencing higher levels of anxiety, stress, and neuroticism compared with low uncertainty-avoidance cultures. To them, "what is different, is dangerous." In contrast, in cultures with low uncertainty avoidance, people violate rules for pragmatic reasons, they feel comfortable with ambiguity, and they see conflict as a natural part of life (Kaasa & Vadi, 2010). Creative endeavors involve risk and uncertainty, and thus several studies suggest that countries with higher uncertainty avoidance are less innovative. For example, a study of European countries documented moderate negative correlations between the level of uncertainty avoidance and innovation activity as measured by patent applications (Kaasa & Vadi, 2010). A more fine-grained analysis of the creative process suggests that when generating ideas, individuals in cultures that are high on uncertainty avoidance prefer useful ideas to novel ones (Adair & Xiong, 2018). A meta-analysis of the leadership and innovation literature in 17 countries concluded that uncertainty avoidance strengthened the relationship between transformational leadership and innovation (Watts et al., 2020). In such cultures, because people avoid the uncertainty associated with innovation, a transformational leaders' role in promoting employee innovation is more significant.

Masculinity refers to the extent to which a culture values assertiveness and is driven by competition, achievement, and success (Hofstede, 1980). More masculine societies emphasize achievement, performance, and purposefulness, whereas more feminine cultures focus on people and the quality of life, preserving the environment, and helping others (Hofstede 1980). Studies that examined the relationship between masculinity and creativity at the national level have yielded inconsistent findings. While some found no relationship between masculinity and innovation (e.g., number of inventions patented, Shane, 1992), others found a negative correlation between masculinity and the number of patents issued (Kaaza & Vadi, 2010), or a positive relationship using the Global Innovation Index (GII; Khan & Cox, 2017). Nakata and Sivakumar (1996) tried to reconcile these findings by distinguishing between the idea generation and implementation phases, positing that masculinity distinctly affects the different stages of the innovation process. Given that a lower degree of masculinity enables greater psychological safety, trust, and cooperation, high femininity cultures should excel in idea generation. However, at the idea-implementation stage, the focus is on producing reliable and cost-efficient products, and thus a high degree of masculinity will enable the assembling of new products within given organizational constraints.

Together, these studies suggest that the relationship between cultural values and creativity depends on the particular value and is often moderated by other factors, such as the phase of creativity or individual self-construal. Although some findings have been replicated across studies and contexts, the heavy focus on values in cross-cultural research may lead to inaccurate conclusions, given that such research reduces the notion of culture to a single value. This approach may ignore additional influences such as specific cultural norms, social networks, and social structure (Gelfand et al., 2006; Goncalo et al., 2020).

In response, recent research has developed a more intricate perspective, integrating the value and structure approaches. For example, in a study that combined a meta-analysis with a qualitative comparative analysis, Yong et al. (2020) suggested that culture is a multidimensional construct and developed theory on cultural bundles, that is, "the cultural value dimensions that characterize a given country, and the strength of the norms enforcing these values" (p. 1). Thus, rather than examining cultural values in isolation, Yong and colleagues (2020) argue that culture should be examined as bundles of the cultural values of individualism, masculinity, uncertainty avoidance, and power distance, together with cultural tightness (norm strength). They suggest that these bundles moderate the relationship between creativity and the three components from the componential theory of creativity (Amabile & Pratt, 2016): domain-relevant skills, creativity, relative skills, and task motivation. Using artifact-corrected meta-analyses, they identified cultural bundles and then considered the strength of the norms enforcing the values in the bundles. Creativity was measured in a variety of subjective (self-and other-assessments) and objective (e.g., patents) ways. They found that with bundles characterized by high cultural tightness, the positive effect of the domain-relevant skills, creativity relative skills, and task motivation components on creativity was stronger as the number of cultural value dimensions in the bundle promoted the development of that component. Specifically, the cultural values of masculinity and uncertainty avoidance emphasize the importance of domain-relevant skills (i.e., the knowledge, expertise, and skills associated with a particular domain); the cultural values of individualism and masculinity emphasize creativity-relevant skills (i.e., cognitive styles and personality characteristics that are conducive to creative thinking); and the cultural values of individualism, power distance, and masculinity emphasize task motivation (i.e., the internal drive to solve a problem because it is interesting in itself). In bundles with a high degree of looseness, cultural values that discouraged the use of a component resulted in a stronger relationship between that component and creativity. Yong and colleagues (2020) attributed this to the fact that individuals in loose cultures are less likely to be sanctioned for deviating from cultural values, so they do not need values to promote specific components. Their innovative work suggests that the effect of culture cannot be fully understood by focusing on cultural dimensions in isolation.

Other researchers distinguished between within- and between-cultural variance and emphasized the situation's importance (Leung & Cohen, 2011). For instance, Nouri and her colleagues (2014) suggested that the effect of power distance on creativity depends on the context of whether individuals perform a creativity task in the presence of peers or a supervisor. In China, participants generated less original ideas in the presence of their supervisors than when working alone. In the United States, participants generated more ideas (higher fluency) when working with supervisors compared to working with peers. The authors suggested that in the presence of a supervisor or peers, social values are more salient than when working alone. Thus, the effect of culture varies depending on the situation. When the situation includes strong behavioral cues such as rewards on creative ideas, the impact of cultural differences on creativity may be weaker (Gelfand et al., 2007).

One potential criticism is the methodological challenges involved in measuring values cross-culturally (Peng et al., 1997). Cultural values are usually derived from individuals reporting on questionnaires, which are susceptible to various types of consistent errors. Respondents from different cultures may compare themselves to relevant others when making judgments, such that a Chinese who considers herself individualistic will score herself higher than similarly individualistic Americans simply because she is comparing herself to collectivistic Chinese norms (Peng et al., 1997). Researchers may wrongly assume that people across different cultures will similarly understand and use the endpoints of a Likert scale and have similar response styles (Peng et al., 1997). Arabs taking a test in Arabic were less likely to use middle categories than Arabs taking the test in English, Americans taking the test in English, and Japanese taking the test in either English or Japanese (Kuroda & Suzuki, 1989). Those speaking Japanese tended to use the middle categories the most. Some cross-cultural psychologists recommend using ipsatization to control for country-level means and/or standard deviations (Smith et al., 2006), but it is unclear how common this technique is in creativity research.

Cultural Tightness versus Looseness

The theory of cultural tightness–looseness has proven useful in understanding cultural differences in creativity. Tightness–looseness refers to the strength of social norms and the extent to which deviating from and violating norms carry social sanctions (Gelfand et al., 2006). According to Gelfand and her colleagues (2006), tight cultures such as Pakistan, Singapore, and Malaysia have clear and pervasive norms: These cultures are relatively ordered and cohesive, and promote convergent thinking and conformity that may hinder creativity. In contrast, in loose cultures such as Australia and Brazil, there is usually less order and cohesion, yet greater tolerance for change. In loose societies, the range of acceptable behaviors is wider, and they are considered more inclusive of and open to various perspectives.

Cultural tightness–looseness shapes the way members of that society are socialized and can explain cultural differences in creativity. For instance, Harrington and Gelfand (2014) found that cultural tightness was negatively correlated with the number of patents and artists in American states. Similarly, a longitudinal study using linguistic analysis of texts found that American norms loosened from 1800 to 2000 (Jackson et al., 2019). Over the years, Americans used more language related to rule deviation and challenging norms, and less language related to the setting of and conforming to rules. This trend was reflected in a gradual increase in creativity and innovation, as indicated by the rate of patents, feature film production, and baby-naming conformity (Jackson et al., 2019). However, others found the opposite effect. In their analysis of 31 provinces in China, Chua et al. (2019) found that provinces with tighter cultures enjoyed faster economic growth, greater tolerance toward the LGBT community, and higher rates of incremental but not radical creativity. The authors suggest that cultural tightness might be associated with different factors in different cultural contexts. People in culturally tighter provinces reported higher levels of self-monitoring, greater conscientiousness, and less openness to experience, while the opposite was found in looser provinces. Unlike America, in China, cultural tightness appears to have been associated with urbanization and economic growth, as tighter provinces (e.g., Guangdong, Shanghai, Beijing, and Zhejiang) are more strongly regulated by the government.

Given that creators may produce solutions for problems that emerge in other countries, Chua et al. (2015) sought to examine whether cultural alignment and distance in terms of tightness–looseness between the original and foreign countries influenced the willingness to engage in creativity and its potential success. They hypothesized that individuals from tight cultures would be less willing to engage in creative tasks in countries that were very different from their own. Using data from crowdsourcing platforms for competitions for consumer-product brands, they found that individuals from tight cultures were less likely to engage in and succeed at creativity relative to those from looser cultures. Furthermore, this effect was stronger when the cultural distance between the creator's country and the foreign target country was greater. Interestingly, they found that tight cultures were less receptive to ideas from foreign countries but more receptive to ideas from creators from similar cultures.

Another exciting study combined a new social norm violation paradigm with cross-cultural electroencephalography to examine the neural mechanism underlying the detection of norm violations in different cultures (Mu et al., 2015). Assuming that individuals in tight cultures tend to adhere to social norms and are more sensitive to others' violations than those from loose cultures, the study examined whether individuals from tight and loose cultures reacted differently to norm violation. Analysis of EEG recording from Chinese and American participants revealed a culture-general neural marker of detecting norm violations (i.e., activation in the central and parietal regions), but it also found some cultural differences between these groups. Specifically, they recorded activity in the frontal-temporal regions among Chinese, but not for the U.S. participants. This study also revealed that a frontal event-related potential of about 400 ms (N400) was associated with lower levels of creativity, yet higher self-control levels (Mu et al., 2015).

In sum, while cultural tightness is negatively associated with creativity and innovation in a global context or at the country level, the relationship between the two within specific countries may depend on how tightness is manifested and the type of creativity examined. Most studies suggest a negative association between cultural tightness and creativity, yet the relationship may be stronger with radical creativity than incremental creativity (Chua et al., 2019).

Cultural Logic

In addition to cultural values and structure, cultural logic has been used to explain individual and cultural differences in creativity (e.g., Leung & Cohen, 2011; Miron-Spektor et al., 2015). This new framework, which integrates theories of social identity and culture to understand how people in distinct cultures develop their self-worth independently or interdependently of others, distinguishes between three main cultural logics: face, dignity, and honor (Aslani et al., 2016; Kim & Nam, 1998; Leung & Cohen, 2011). In *face* cultures, individuals develop their self-worth based on how others see them (Kim & Nam, 1998). They feel obliged to cooperate and preserve each other's face, carefully observe formalities, and avoid direct conflict (Leung & Cohen, 2011). In contrast, the cultural logic of *dignity* assumes that each individual has inherent worth that cannot be granted or taken by others, and that all people are equals. In those cultures, others' perceptions can be viewed as a threat to autonomy in defining themselves (Kim et al., 2010). Finally, to feel respected, people in *honor* cultures are expected to show assertiveness, boldness, and confidence and to be able to handle conflicts. Cultures of honor tend to emerge in looser and more competitive societies that have a lot of rules but weak institutions (Nowak et al., 2015). In such environments, people behave according to reciprocity norms and are expected to pay back both positive and negative gestures (Leung & Cohen, 2011).

Research on cultural logic and creativity is in its infancy. New ideas may seem weird, uncertain, or risky and can be ridiculed and rejected. A few studies suggest that the fear of losing face may hold people back from suggesting new ideas. These studies offered face logic endorsement as a new explanation for differences in creativity within and across cultures. Using participants from Japan, Israel, and the United States, Miron-Spektor et al. (2015) showed that the concern for face or the extent to which saving face is considered important in the culture was negatively correlated with novelty and fluency but not the appropriateness of ideas. Specifically, in three studies, they measured the extent to which participants endorsed the logic of face or how they are concerned with losing face. Using a social-affirmation manipulation that asked participants to reflect on social events that enhanced or hindered their perceived social image, the authors showed that the negative relationship between face concern and creativity was attenuated when people felt valued and respected by others.

Another type of cultural logic refers to the way people cope with contradictions and accept different perspectives (Xie & Paik, 2019). Rooted in early Western and Eastern philosophies, the way people reason about contradictions is guided by tacit ontologies and epistemologies about the nature of the world. The literature on cross-cultural differences suggests that compared to Westerners, the Chinese see the world in constant flux, in which the part can only be understood in relation to the whole. When facing contradictions such as competing propositions and demands, they search for the middle way, assuming that some truth can be found in each of the opposing elements. This tacit ontology that contradictions need not be resolved, the world is continually changing, and holism has been called naïve dialectical thinking (Peng & Nisbett, 1999).

In contrast, the Western tradition since Aristotle presumes the constancy of the world and decontextualization of elements from their broader context (Peng & Nisbett, 1999). When facing contradictions, Westerners are more likely to try to choose or prioritize elements, assuming that they cannot coexist, or they will search for a synergetic solution (Lewis, 2000; Miron-Spektor et al., 2011). Building on these distinctions, research on dialectical thinking, paradox, and creativity has offered new insights into how culture shapes creative thinking (for a review, see Paletz et al., 2018a). For instance, when people face contradictions, such as the need to develop a radically novel idea that is also seen as useful to others (McCarthy et al., 2018; Miron-Spektor & Erez, 2017), different cognitive frames may be used (Miron-Spektor & Paletz, 2020). Paradoxical frames that recognize and accept contradictions prompt Western participants to search for synergetic, creative solutions (Miron-Spektor & Argote, 2008; Miron-Spektor et al., 2011). However, East Asians were less likely to benefit from paradoxical frames, as their tendency to avoid conflicts and extremes may prevent them from scrutinizing the paradox to find synergetic solutions that fully address both demands (Leung et al., 2018).

Just as with Yong and her colleagues' (2020) study on cultural bundles, it is possible that the strength of norms, or tightness–looseness, may serve as a moderator—or even a confound—for the effects of cultural logics. For instance, the lack of benefit of paradoxical frames may be due to perceived tight social norms regarding conflict or extremes rather than naïve dialectical thinking. By comparing a greater number of cultures with more variety in terms of both logics and tightness–looseness (e.g., tight dignity cultures, loose naïve dialectical cultures), researchers can determine the relative importance of these different culture constructs on creativity.

Implicit Theories

One early approach to understanding cultural differences in performance on creativity tests asked whether laypeople from different cultures conceive of creativity in the same way. Initial studies on implicit theories of creativity asked participants to list traits and activities associated with creativity (e.g., Kapur et al., 1997; Paletz et al., 2011; Runco & Johnson, 2002; Yue & Rudowicz, 2002). For example, Yue (2003) argued that Chinese have a "meritorious evaluation bias" (p. 151), such that individuals nominated to be high on creativity are also likely to have high social contribution scores (e.g., politicians, scientists) due to having collectivist goals of social contribution. Other researchers compared participants across cultures directly, finding that the rate of different traits or activities differed across different samples (e.g., Paletz et al., 2011; Runco & Johnson, 2002). For instance, Paletz et al. (2011) found that Caucasian American undergraduates, and to a lesser degree, Asian American undergraduates, had a greater association of creativity with more internal traits, activities, and professions (e.g., mental processes, philosophy) than did Japanese and Chinese undergraduates, who were more likely to mention and rate as creative traits, activities, and professions expressed more externally (e.g., scientist, team manager). Like Yue (2003), Paletz and colleagues argued that the internal/external focus differences were due to differences in individualism and collectivism across the West/East divide. In summarizing a special issue, Niu and Kaufman (2013) described potential differences between Chinese and American notions of creativity. They argued that Americans consider creativity to be rare, distinctive, and individual- and self-focused, whereas Chinese consider creativity to be attainable, indicate excellence, be contextualized, prioritize usefulness and acceptability, and the environment- and other-focused.

While the primary definition of creativity entails novelty and appropriateness (Amabile et al., 1996; Amabile & Pillemer, 2012), it was based on Western research on creativity in the 20th century. The effect of individualistic values on creativity has been attributed not only to the emphasis those cultures put on uniqueness, but also to different assumptions about what is considered creative. Research on implicit theories of creativity suggests that questioning these assumptions is essential. Many researchers, drawing on theory and historiometric analyses, have argued that novelty should be relatively valued and emphasized in the West, and appropriateness valued and emphasized as part of creativity in the East, due to the emphasis on individualistic versus collectivistic norms (Erez & Nouri, 2010; Hempel & Sue-Chan, 2010; Lan & Kaufman, 2012; Morris & Leung, 2010; Simonton & Ting, 2010). However, few studies have tested this hypothesis explicitly and empirically with large, modern samples. Paletz and Peng

(2008) obtained a sample of over 450 undergraduate students from two universities in the United States, two universities in Japan, and a university in China to test this theory. Using within-subject experimental scenario methods in two product domains (cooking meals and textbooks), they found that the novelty manipulation was equally important for ratings of creativity across all the participant samples. Counter to theory, the Chinese participants, compared to the Japanese and American participants (who included Asian Americans), were more influenced by the higher novelty manipulations in terms of their rated *desire* for the products. Appropriateness was relatively more important for the American and Japanese participants than the Chinese participants for both their rated desire and evaluations of the products' creativity. These counterintuitive findings were explained as potentially caused by the particular socioeconomic moment of data collection when both the United States and Japan were in recessions. Still, China was undergoing enormous economic growth (2002–2003). The lack of significant differences between the Japanese and American samples, in particular, suggested that differences and similarities in implicit theories of creativity may have other explanations than national or historical culture.

Loewenstein and Mueller (2016) expanded this research to examine a greater range of cues than novelty and appropriateness that could indicate creativity, such as moral goodness and social harmony, bringing the older research on traits and activities to bear when judging creative products. Across three studies and 2,140 participants from China and the United States, they found that Chinese participants used more cues and thus held a much broader view of creativity relative to Americans. While members of both cultures found cues such as "breakthrough" and "surprise" to indicate creativity, the Chinese also considered cues such as "feasible," "mass-market," and "harmony" as indicators of creativity. This study represents a paradigm shift to the idea that the breadth or narrowness of cues itself is the main difference in Chinese versus American modern implicit theories of creativity.

Recent research has investigated the relationship between cultural values and implicit theories. Adair and Xiong (2018) focused on values as a mediator between culture and implicit theories. They found that when asked to consider the importance of practicality and novelty in evaluating a creative idea (together out of 100%), Chinese students at a Canadian university assigned a larger weight to practicality than novelty, whereas Caucasian Canadian students did not assign a significantly different percentage. The relatively higher uncertainty avoidance in the Chinese sample mediated their novelty scores, while power distance and individualism–collectivism did not. Their second study replicated the first, but with bicultural Chinese Canadian undergraduates, and found that the importance of novelty was mediated by uncertainty avoidance. This and other studies (Grigoryan et al., 2018) suggest that—looking to the future—the effects of values on implicit theories and implicit theories on other factors could be studied in a more complex and holistic fashion to understand how culture affects creativity.

Multicultural Experiences and Creativity

Globalization and technological developments have triggered an interest in creative collaboration between people from different cultures and locations. Indeed, a growing body of research has explored the effect of multicultural experiences on creativity (for a review, see Maddux et al., 2020). Multicultural experiences refer to "exposure to or interactions with elements and/or members of a different culture(s)" (Maddux et al., 2020, p. 5), including living abroad, having a bicultural identity, working in culturally diverse teams, or having a culturally diverse professional network. Leung et al. (2008) first introduced the effect of multicultural experiences on creativity. It was followed by a comprehensive empirical investigation of the underlying psychological processes and boundary conditions that account for this relationship.

The exposure to different cultural systems increases the range of available cognitive scripts and behaviors that give rise to creativity. Multicultural experiences enable individuals to transfer knowledge from one context to another, create new combinations, and identify novel functions to familiar elements. Empirical findings support this theory, showing that time spent outside one's home country, the number of different countries visited, how distinct the cultures are from each other, the number of foreign languages spoken, and parents' birthplaces increase individual creativity, tested using different types of creativity tasks (Godart et al., 2015; Leikin & Tovli, 2014; Leung & Chiu, 2010; Maddux & Galinsky, 2009; Maddux et al., 2010; Puente-Diaz et al., 2019; Tadmor et al., 2012). Even brief exposure to knowledge from two different cultures (Chinese and American) can boost creative thinking (Cheng et al., 2011). For example, Mok and Morris (2010) exposed Chinese American biculturals to either Asian or Western cultural images to activate their Asian or Western mindset, respectively, just before completing a divergent thinking task. Integrated biculturals (those who identified with both Asian and American cultures and saw them as compatible) exposed to American cultural cues generated more novel ideas than those exposed to Asian cultural cues. The most substantial benefits of such exposure were found among individuals who incorporated two or more cultural identities. The two identities were inconsistent with one another and well integrated (Saad et al., 2013; Tadmor et al., 2012).

Scholars also considered moderating factors of the multicultural experience–creativity link, including personal and contextual characteristics. For example, several studies suggest that the positive effect of multicultural experiences on creativity is more vital for people who have higher cultural intelligence (Earley & Ang, 2003) and a lower need for closure (De keersmaecker et al., 2016). Studies also revealed contextual influences, including when the foreign culture is threatening or too different from one's own culture or when people from tight cultures need to innovate in loose contexts (Cheng et al., 2011; Chua et al., 2015; Gocłowska et al., 2018; Godart et al., 2015). Conversely, when people believe that ideas from different cultures are incompatible and cannot be integrated, such as in situations of "ambient cultural disharmony" (Chua, 2013), multicultural experiences can deter creative thinking. Finally, multicultural experiences are especially beneficial for creativity when working on culturally diverse teams. In these settings, individuals who have experience in different cultures serve as "cultural brokers" or "bridges" who facilitate information sharing and improve communication between members from different cultures that contribute to group creativity (Backmann et al., 2020; Jang, 2017).

Cross-Cultural Teams and Creativity

Cross-cultural teams are increasingly a topic of study (Adler & Aycan, 2018; Gelfand et al., 2007). All the effects described in this review may occur in the context of groups: differences in values, implicit theories of creativity, and multicultural experiences can all impact the creativity of individuals within a team. Multicultural teams can include members from different cultures that represent different nations or regions (e.g., Scandinavia), but also different regions within countries (e.g., southern versus northern Yemen) and different subcultures within a country, such as professions, minority groups, migrant groups, or age cohorts (Adler & Aycan, 2018; Paletz et al., 2018b). Harrison and Klein (2007) proposed three types of diversity: *separation*, when team members hold opposing positions; *variety*, when team members represent different groups with different kinds of information; and *disparity*, when team members may be better or worse on a particular dimension. Multicultural diversity is generally conceived as the first type, where different individuals have different backgrounds and identities (Harrison & Klein, 2007; van Knippenberg & Schippers, 2007). Thus, maximal diversity in variety would indicate a greater variety of backgrounds. However, diversity can also mean different levels or disparity, such as when individuals are higher or lower on individualism.

Cultural diversity, generally studied as heterogeneity (to some degree) versus homogeneity, has long been thought to lead to greater team creativity (Adler & Aycan, 2018; Jang, 2017). A meta-analysis of different kinds of diverse teams suggests that culturally diverse teams are more creative than more culturally homogeneous teams (Stahl et al., 2010). Culturally heterogeneous teams may have lower overall performance or have communication and other process difficulties, but effective leadership, formal rhythms, and coordinating processes; attending to cultural identities can improve performance and processes (see review, Gelfand et al., 2007). A study of multicultural dyads suggests that divergent tasks can benefit low-task specificity (task clarity), whereas high-task specificity can benefit convergent tasks (Nouri et al., 2013). Different cultural backgrounds can also offer different perspectives, ways of looking at problems, and a greater range of solutions (Adler & Aycan, 2018; Li et al., 2014). Drawing from information-processing theory, the argument for the creativity of diverse teams is that greater cultural diversity provides a greater variety of "deep-level" underlying psychological characteristics, such as different mental models and background information, both task- and team-relevant (e.g., Mannix & Neale, 2005; Paletz et al., 2018b; Stahl et al., 2010; van Knippenberg & Schippers, 2007). Although this diversity can also prompt task conflict (Stahl et al., 2010), researchers often argue that when properly harnessed such that relationship conflict is minimized, this can lead to greater creativity in culturally diverse teams (see Adler & Aycan, 2018; Li et al., 2014; Paletz et al., 2018b for reviews).

That said, not all types of diversity are the same, given different cultural values, historical power differences, minority/majority differences, and the greater cultural and national context (Adler & Aycan, 2018; Garvin et al., 2008; Jang, 2017; Roberson, 2019). In a study that analyzed the team meetings of engineering designers, Paletz et al. (2018c) pitted diversity theory against cross-cultural theory. They found that when their Southeast Asian colleagues joined a team of Scandinavians, they were more likely to use insight and promotion words, in line with prior research on cultural diversity and creativity; however, these more diverse teams also experienced fewer micro-conflicts. The authors argued that the relatively lower number of micro-conflicts was due to the diverse teams' cultural values composition being more collectivistic. Although small, this study suggests that team configuration, not just heterogeneity, matters to creativity (Miron-Spektor et al., 2011, 2012). The configuration of a team is not just "diverse versus not diverse"; it can include diverse teams that have a higher or lower mean or range of different cultural values, teams with different proportions of minority versus majority groups from within a population, and so on.

Additional theories beyond the information-processing theory have implications for culturally diverse team creativity (e.g., Jang, 2017; Janssens & Brett, 2006). Edmondson and Harvey (2018) proposed integrating knowledge diversity and creativity research with theory on cross-boundary teaming. Such models of diverse teams could also include psychological safety, specific organizational contexts, and internal boundaries. For instance, team interactions need to be examined within real contexts. Making differences salient in the service of diversity must be paired with a method of bridging such differences, as deep conversations regarding diversity are challenging and can cause interpersonal conflict (Edmondson & Harvey, 2018) that may not be of the sort that is conducive to creativity. Thus, research on knowledge boundaries and psychological safety may have useful insights for diverse teams.

Researchers have recently proposed different models for cross-cultural teams to succeed. Adler and Aycan (2018) offer a two-dimensional framework for different approaches to cross-cultural interaction: One dimension is about how much to include others' cultural approaches, and the second is the emphasis on one's own cultural approach. Their model suggests that high levels of embracing both one's own and the others' culture could be synergistic improvisation. Jang (2017), in a parallel effort, proposed the idea of cultural brokerage in creative teams, suggesting that while cultural insiders can act as bridges between cultures, integrating existing cultural perspectives, cultural outsiders can elicit cultural perspectives by asking explicitly about relevant cultural ideas. Jang (2017) found evidence of partial mediation for eliciting, but not integrating, behaviors between the type of multicultural team member and team performance in idea-generation tasks.

Janssen and Brett (2006) propose a more complex fusion model of collaboration for global teams, where unique contributions are valued and integrated. However, this collaboration must take into account power differences and who is most fluent in the dominant language. This model uses a metaphor of fusion cuisine, drawing on the principles of respect for the different ingredients, valuing combination and variety, a goal of creative dishes, and the preservation of the cultural identity of the ingredients. The task of the multicultural group is to elicit unique information from team members as well as a shared, convergent decision considering cultural differences in values, teamwork, and advocacy and conflict norms. Common values are not created through compromise or integration, nor are they simply accepted from the dominant subgroup. To us, this model involves a dialectical approach, holding paradox rather than resolving contradictions in values between team members.

This theory suggests that cultural intelligence could be used to leverage the broader backgrounds of culturally diverse teams. Using this model, Crotty and Brett (2012) found that in 37 multinational teams, team members who had high levels of the dimension of cultural intelligence called "cultural metacognition" (e.g., thinking about cultural differences in thinking) had higher levels of fusion teamwork and creativity, particularly when the overall team cultural metacognition was also high. Fusion teamwork was positively related to perceived team creativity. Similarly, separate research demonstrated that in cross-cultural dyads, the highest cultural metacognition in the dyads was positively associated with perceptions that the counterpart would be a good partner in creative collaboration, mediated by the felt trust (Chua et al., 2012).

Underlying all these studies of diversity within teams is the assumption that different cultural backgrounds lead to different types of background information. Future work in this area could more carefully study the levels of heterogeneity (e.g., maximal variety versus some diversity), the specific cultural compositions of homogeneity and heterogeneity, and the role of moderators such as cultural intelligence.

Discussion

Research on culture and creativity takes different approaches, examining cultural values, tightness, logics, and implicit theories. We have reviewed relevant work and focused on new theoretical developments. New frameworks consider both within- and between-cultural variance, examine cultural bundles, and recognize the role of the context and situation. Recent studies have also advanced our understanding of multicultural experiences (Maddux et al., 2020) and cultural diversity in global teams (Jang, 2017).

This chapter offers several theoretical and practical contributions (see Table 10.1). First, our review suggests that the impact of culture on creativity is far greater than initially assumed. Despite some universal elements, culture defines not just what ideas are considered creative, but also how much focus is given to each of the creativity dimensions in different situations. Traditionally, research on culture has examined whether endorsing

Table 10.1 Key findings of research on culture and creativity

Key findings
1. *Culture defines creativity*: Culture defines what is considered creative, but also how much focus is given to different dimensions of creativity (e.g., novelty vs. usefulness).
2. *Cultural dimensions and configurations*: Specific cultural values and logics as well as different configurations of cultural values and their tightness impact creativity.
3. *Situation impacts the effects of culture on creativity*: Situational cues such as rewards and authority figures can make cultural values salient.
4. *Levels of analysis*: The effects of culture on creativity manifest differently for individuals, teams, and organizations.
5. *Cultural diversity can promote creativity*: However, the extent depends on the cultural configuration of the team and the ability to integrate ideas from diverse perspectives.
Practical Implications for Organizations about Culture and Creativity
1. *Take culture into consideration when importing interventions*: Interventions developed for improving creativity in one country may not be as effective in another cultural context.
2. *Consider cultural distance when selling ideas*: Consciously think about whether ideas from one culture can be incorporated into another culture, based on the cultural distance.
3. *Form diverse teams*: Consider not only the cultural heterogeneity but the specific cultural configurations and how to leverage those configurations.
4. *Adopt culturally relevant practices to save face*: Establish anonymous channels for suggesting ideas and require respect for others.
5. *Encourage cultural intelligence*: Encourage and train for cultural intelligence to help teams leverage diversity, particularly cultural metacognition and having groups make explicit their assumptions about creativity.

a particular value explained differences in creativity, but recent work has revealed the complexity of culture and stresses the importance of understanding particular *configurations* of values and their relationship with creativity. Current research also considers the tightness or looseness of a given culture, generally suggesting that loose cultures enable creativity. Research on cultural logics have added a new perspective, suggesting that the amount of autonomy people have in defining themselves predicts their willingness to engage in creativity and their preference for novel or useful ideas (Miron-Spektor et al., 2015).

In addition, the effect of culture on creativity depends on the situation. Situational cues (e.g., rewards, authority figure) make cultural values more salient and thus may strengthen the effect of particular values on creativity. Furthermore, the effect of culture is manifested in different ways at different levels of analysis (Erez & Gati, 2004). Creativity benefits from diverse knowledge and information, and thus exposure to different cultures may contribute to the development of new ideas. In teams, collaborating with people from various countries could foster team creativity. Yet, the extent to which cultural diversity enables creativity depends on the specific cultural configuration (Paletz et al., 2018c) and the ability to integrate ideas from disparate cultural perspectives (Chua, 2013).

From a practical point of view, managers who wish to foster creativity should take culture into account. For instance, interventions for enhancing creativity developed in Western countries may not be as effective in East Asian cultures (Leung et al., 2018). They should also consider the distance between cultures when trying to sell new ideas in other cultures and the extent to which ideas from one culture can be integrated with their own ideas (Chua, 2013; Chua et al., 2015). When forming diverse teams, they should consider not only the heterogeneity of the group but also the specific cultural configuration of its members. Indeed, while a diverse team that included members from collectivistic cultures was more creative than when the members were from more individualistic cultures, the more diverse team had fewer conflicts, counter to prior research on diversity but in line with predictions from cross-cultural psychology (Paletz et al., 2018c). Further, organizations should be aware of their members' concerns to save face, which may prevent them from suggesting ideas. In such cases, they should use anonymous channels for suggesting ideas and encourage respect for others (Miron-Spektor et al., 2015). Another practical suggestion for culturally diverse teams is to encourage experiences that increase cultural intelligence, specifically cultural metacognition, so that teams can leverage their diversity (Crotty & Brett, 2012). Individuals and groups, before they embark on creative activities, could also make explicit their unspoken assumptions about creativity.

Future Directions

The recent growth in research on culture and creativity points to exciting new directions. At a basic level, new work could examine different kinds of cultures. Researchers have focused on investigating East–West differences, or even China-U.S. differences, but they could go beyond those countries. As the research on tightness–looseness suggests, many countries are less well studied concerning culture and creativity. Researchers across the rich diversity of nations within Africa, Latin America, the Middle East, and South and Southeast Asia are sure to have insights into creativity as it occurs locally and globally (e.g., Kahleefa et al., 1996, 1997). Even within countries and regions, there can be differences and similarities that would enable us to better understand both culture and creativity.

Researchers could use different tasks, including those generated by scholars from non-American cultures, and, in general, take cultural variation into account when developing new and using existing creativity tasks. A study could elicit tasks to examine, for instance, creative combination processes in such different cultures as Japan, Madagascar, South Africa, Thailand, and Brazil. Another study that would challenge the foundations of creativity psychology further would question whether different creative processes have been overlooked in the West but could be identified in other parts of the world. For instance, Leung and her colleagues (2018) suggested that ideas developed through the middle ground logic, which is prevalent in East Asia, are more incremental because they tend to "preserve attributes of its constitutes . . . rather than generating a higher-order synergy" (Leung et al., 2018, p. 5). More research is needed to understand the different kinds of creative cognitive processes such as problem finding, evaluation, and championing in different cultures. The observed differences in creative outcomes result from differences in the motivation to engage in creativity and from the way people perform creativity tasks. For instance, people from different cultures focus on different aspects of creativity (i.e., novelty vs. usefulness), and they value and feel emotionally connected to different types of ideas (Lazar et al., 2022).

Future research could also examine different ways of looking at culture. For example, Morris, Chiu, and Liu (2015) introduced polycultural psychology as "a network conception of culture in which cultural influence on individuals is partial, and plural and cultural traditions interact and change each other" (p. 632). This approach would suggest that we examine a greater variety of cultural influences at once and the dynamism between cultures. No individual or country is categorically one kind of culture (Morris et al., 2015): Above and beyond the research on biculturals, an American in America could also be in a subculture that is influenced by tropes in the Japanese media and video games. Future research could go deeper by using more than one approach for understanding culture and building on other theories. For instance, the way people from different cultures interpret and feel threatened by conflict may influence their creativity (Paletz et al., 2014). We should also consider the impact of intercultural tensions and disharmony that may hinder peoples' ability to connect ideas from disparate cultures (Chua, 2013), and potential coping mechanisms that can help people feel more comfortable with contradictions (Miron-Spektor et al., 2018). Another related topic worth exploring is whether and why cultural pluralism, or the extent to which "members of diverse ethnic, racial, religious, or social groups maintain and develop their traditional culture or special interest within the confines of a common civilization" is beneficial for creativity (Kwan, 2018, p. 324).

More research is needed to understand the psychological processes through which original, yet useful, ideas and insights are achieved in different cultures. Existing research mainly focuses on creative outcomes, such as the number and type of generated ideas (De Dreu, 2010). We do not yet understand the different processes through which such ideas emerge in different cultures. In general, we should test whether creativity theories developed in Western culture apply to other cultures. Finally, it is important to understand the interaction between culture, the situation, and the context, as new evidence suggests that some of the cultural differences only occur in situations in which the norms are salient (Nouri et al., 2014). For instance, Liou and Lan (2018) found that although Americans and Taiwanese were equally capable of generating original and useful ideas when working in groups, Americans selected more original ideas, whereas Taiwanese selected more useful ideas. More research is needed to determine whether cultural differences in creativity are greater in situations in which creative behavior is voluntary as opposed to required as part of one's task or role. It is possible that members of tight cultures are as creative as members of loose cultures when expected and appreciated for their creativity (Montag et al., 2012; Unsworth, Wall, & Carter, 2005).

Although research on culture and creativity employs various research methods, future research can benefit a meta-analysis of findings from different studies and cultures and use multiple indicators and predictors of creativity. Scholars can also use an abductive approach to explore the impact of culture on creativity to enable new findings that challenge existing research paradigms and conceptions. Researchers can also conduct qualitative analyses and ethnographic studies to gain a deeper understanding of creativity in different cultures. In particular, we know relatively little about how creativity unfolds over time and whether there are cultural differences in the perception of creativity as a malleable or fixed trait that determines the ability to develop and sustain creativity over time (Miron-Spektor et al., 2021).

Finally, it is essential to test whether current frameworks apply to extreme conditions such as creativity at times of crisis. For example, it has been suggested that cultural tightness is more beneficial to creativity during crises such as the most recent pandemic, in which following governmental restrictions in a coordinated manner is essential for public health (Pradies et al., 2021). Future research can advance our understanding of both the pathway through which individuals and groups are creative in different cultures and the specific situations in which their creativity emerges.

Conclusion

Culture and creativity is a growing area of research with direct implications for how we work, innovate, and solve global problems. Our review of the literature on potential cultural influences on creativity has examined values, conceptions of creativity, and multicultural experiences, as well as research on diverse teams. In a context of increasing globalization and migration, and the unrelenting changes of the twenty-first century, understanding the impact of culture on creativity is not only important but imperative.

References

Adair, W. L., & Xiong, T. X. (2018). How Chinese and Caucasian Canadians conceptualize creativity: The mediating role of uncertainty avoidance. *Journal of Cross-Cultural Psychology, 49*(2), 223–238. https://doi.org/10.1177/0022022117713153

Adler, N. J., & Aycan, Z. (2018). Cross-cultural interaction: What we know and what we need to know. *Annual Review of Organizational Psychology and Organizational Behavior, 5*, 307–333.

Amabile, T. M. (1983). The social psychology of creativity: A componential conceptualization. *Journal of Personality and Social Psychology, 45*(2), 357–376. https://doi.org/10.1037/0022-3514.45.2.357

Amabile, T. M., Conti, R., Coon, H., Lazenby, J., & Herron, M. (1996). Assessing the work environment for creativity Reproduced with permission of the copyright owner. Further reproduction prohibited without permission. *Academy of Management Journal, 39*(5), 1154–1184.

Amabile, T. M., & Pillemer, J. (2012). Perspectives on the social psychology of creativity. *Journal of Creative Behavior, 46*(1), 3–15. https://doi.org/10.1002/jocb.001

Amabile, T. M., & Pratt, M. G. (2016). The dynamic componential model of creativity and innovation in organizations: Making progress, making meaning. *Research in Organizational Behavior, 36*, 157–183. https://doi.org/10.1016/j.riob.2016.10.001

Aslani, S., Ramirez-Marin, J., Brett, J., Yao, J., Semnani-Azad, Z., Zhang, Z.-X., Tinsley, C., Weingart, L., & Adair, W. (2016). Dignity, face, and honor cultures: A study of negotiation strategy and outcomes in three cultures. *Journal of Organizational Behavior, 37*(8), 1178–1201. https://doi.org/10.1002/job.2095

Backmann, J., Kanitz, R., Tian, A. W., Hoffmann, P., & Hoegl, M. (2020). Cultural gap bridging in multinational teams. *Journal of International Business Studies, 51*, 1283–1311. https://doi.org/10.1057/s41267-020-00310-4

Bechtoldt, M. N., Choi, H. S., & Nijstad, B. A. (2012). Individuals in mind, mates by heart: Individualistic self-construal and collective value orientation as predictors of group creativity. *Journal of Experimental Social Psychology, 48*(4), 838–844. https://doi.org/10.1016/j.jesp.2012.02.014

Bechtoldt, M. N., De Dreu, C. K. W., Nijstad, B. A., & Choi, H. S. (2010). Motivated information processing, social tuning, and group creativity. *Journal of Personality and Social Psychology, 99*(4), 622–637. https://doi.org/10.1037/a0019386

Cheng, C.-Y., Leung, A. K.-Y., & Wu, T.-Y. (2011). Going beyond the multicultural experience-creativity link: The mediating role of emotions. *Journal of Social Issues, 67*(4), 806–824. https://doi.org/10.1111/j.1540-4560.2011.01729.x

Choi, H. S., Cho, S. J., Seo, J. G., & Bechtoldt, M. N. (2018). The joint impact of collectivistic value orientation and independent self-representation on group creativity. *Group Processes and Intergroup Relations, 21*(1), 37–56. https://doi.org/10.1177/1368430216638539

Choi, H.-S., Seo, J.-G., Hyun, J., & Bechtoldt, M. (2019). Collectivistic independence promotes group creativity by reducing idea fixation. *Small Group Research, 50*(3), 381–407. https://doi.org/10.1177/1046496419827990

Chua, R. Y. J. (2013). The costs of ambient cultural disharmony: Indirect intercultural conflicts in social environment undermine creativity. *Academy of Management Journal, 56*(6), 1545–1577. https://doi.org/10.5465/amj.2011.0971

Chua, R. Y. J., Huang, K. G., & Jin, M. (2019). Mapping cultural tightness and its links to innovation, urbanization, and happiness across 31 provinces in China. *Proceedings of the National Academy of Sciences of the United States of America, 116*(14), 6720–6725. https://doi.org/10.1073/pnas.1815723116

Chua, R. Y. J., Morris, M. W., & Mor, S. (2012). Collaborating across cultures: Cultural metacognition and affect-based trust in creative collaboration. *Organizational Behavior and Human Decision Processes, 118*(2), 116–131. https://doi.org/10.1016/j.obhdp.2012.03.009

Chua, R. Y. J., Roth, Y., & Lemoine, J. F. (2015). The impact of culture on creativity: How cultural tightness and cultural distance affect global innovation crowdsourcing work. *Administrative Science Quarterly, 60*(2), 189–227. https://doi.org/10.1177/0001839214563595

Crotty, S. K., & Brett, J. M. (2012). Fusing creativity: Cultural metacognition and teamwork in multicultural teams. *Negotiation and Conflict Management Research, 5*(2), 210–234. https://doi.org/10.1111/j.1750-4716.2012.00097.x

Csikszentmihalyi, M. (2014). *The systems model of creativity.* New York: Springer.

De Dreu, C. K. W. (2010). Human creativity: Reflections on the role of culture. *Management and Organization Review, 6*(3), 437–446. https://doi.org/10.1111/j.1740-8784.2010.00195.x

De keersmaecker, J., Van Assche, J., & Roets, A. (2016). Need for closure effects on affective and cognitive responses to culture fusion. *Journal of Cross-Cultural Psychology, 47*(10), 1294–1306. https://doi.org/10.1177/0022022116666375

Earley, P. C., & Ang, S. (2003). *Cultural intelligence: An analysis of individual interactions across cultures.* Palo Alto, CA: Stanford University Press.

Edmondson, A. C., & Harvey, J. F. (2018). Cross-boundary teaming for innovation: Integrating research on teams and knowledge in organizations. *Human Resource Management Review, 28*(4), 347–360. https://doi.org/10.1016/j.hrmr.2017.03.002

Erez, M., & Gati, E. (2004). A dynamic, multi-level model of culture: From the micro level of the individual to the macro level of a global culture. *Applied Psychology, 53*(4), 583–598. https://doi.org/10.1111/j.1464-0597.2004.00190.x

Erez, M., & Nouri, R. (2010). Creativity: The influence of cultural, social, and work contexts. *Management and Organization Review, 6*(3), 351–370. https://doi.org/10.1111/j.1740-8784.2010.00191.x

Ford, D. Y., & Harris, J. J., I. (1992). The elusive definition of creativity. *Journal of Creative Behavior, 26*(3), 186–198.

Garvin, D. A., Edmondson, A. C., & Gino, F. (2008). Is yours a learning organization? *Harvard Business Review, 86*(3), 109–116.

Gelfand, M. (2019). *Rule makers, rule breakers: Tight and loose cultures and the secret signals that direct our lives.* New York: Scribner.

Gelfand, M. J., Erez, M., & Aycan, Z. (2007). Cross-cultural organizational behavior. *Annual Review of Psychology, 58*(1), 479–514. https://doi.org/10.1146/annurev.psych.58.110405.085559

Gelfand, M. J., Nishii, L. H., & Raver, J. L. (2006). On the nature and importance of cultural tightness-looseness. *Journal of Applied Psychology, 91*(6), 1225–1244. https://doi.org/10.1037/0021-9010.91.6.1225

Godowska, M. A., Damian, R. I., & Mor, S. (2018). The diversifying experience model: taking a broader conceptual view of the multiculturalism–creativity link. *Journal of Cross-Cultural Psychology, 49*(2), 303–322. https://doi.org/10.1177/0022022116650258

Godart, F. C., Maddux, W. W., Shipilov, A. V., & Galinsky, A. D. (2015). Fashion with a foreign flair: Professional experiences abroad facilitate the creative innovations of organizations. *Academy of Management Journal, 58*(1), 195–220. https://doi.org/10.5465/amj.2012.0575

Goncalo, J. A., & Duguid, M. M. (2012). Follow the crowd in a new direction: When conformity pressure facilitates group creativity (and when it does not). *Organizational Behavior and Human Decision Processes, 118*(1), 14–23. https://doi.org/10.1016/j.obhdp.2011.12.004

Goncalo, J. A., & Staw, B. M. (2006). Individualism-collectivism and group creativity. *Organizational Behavior and Human Decision Processes, 100*(1), 96–109. https://doi.org/10.1016/j.obhdp.2005.11.003

Goncalo, J. A., Staw, B. M., Fairbank, J. F., Williams, S. D., Cheryan, S., Ziegler, S. A., Montoya, A. K., Jiang, L., Cuddy, A. J. C., Fiske, S. T., Glick, P., Kleinmintz, O. M., Goldstein, P., Mayseless, N., Abecasis, D., Shamay-Tsoory, S. G., Abraham, M., Kruger, J., Dunning, D., . . . Kouchaki, M. (2020). Individual differences in uses of humor and their relation to psychological well-being: Development of the humor styles questionnaire. *Journal of Applied Psychology, 25*(1), 347–366. https://doi.org/10.1177/0021886319888267

Grigoryan, L. K., Lebedeva, N., & Breugelmans, S. M. (2018). A cross-cultural study of the mediating role of implicit theories of innovativeness in the relationship between values and attitudes toward innovation. *Journal of Cross-Cultural Psychology, 49*(2), 336–352. https://doi.org/10.1177/0022022116656399

Harrington, J. R., & Gelfand, M. J. (2014). Tightness-looseness across the 50 united states. *Proceedings of the National Academy of Sciences of the United States of America, 111*, 7990–7995. http://dx.doi.org/10.1073/pnas.1317937111

Harrison, D. A., & Klein, K. J. (2007). What's the difference? Diversity constructs as separation, variety, or disparity in organizations. *Academy of Management Review, 32*(4), 1199–1228.

Hempel, P. S., & Sue-Chan, C. (2010). Culture and the assessment of creativity. *Management and Organization Review, 6*(3), 415–435. https://doi.org/10.1111/j.1740-8784.2010.00189.x

Hofstede, G. (1980). Culture and organizations. *International Studies of Management and Organization, 10*(4), 15–41. https://doi.org/10.1080/00208825.1980.11656300

Hofstede, G. H. (2001). *Culture's consequences: Comparing values, behaviors, institutions and organizations across nations* (2nd ed.). Thousand Oaks, CA: SAGE.

Jackson, J. C., Gelfand, M., De, S., & Fox, A. (2019). The loosening of American culture over 200 years is associated with a creativity–order trade-off. *Nature Human Behaviour, 3*(3), 244–250. https://doi.org/10.1038/s41562-018-0516-z

Jacobs, L., & Herbig, P. (1998). Japanese product development strategies. *Journal of Business and Industrial Marketing, 13*(2), 132–154. https://doi.org/10.1108/08858629810213351

Jang, S. (2017). Cultural brokerage and creative performance in multicultural teams. *Organization Science, 28*(6), 993–1009. https://doi.org/10.1287/orsc.2017.1162

Janssens, M., & Brett, J. M. (2006). Cultural intelligence in global teams: A fusion model of collaboration. *Group and Organization Management, 31*(1), 124–153. https://doi.org/10.1177/1059601105275268

Jaquish, G. A., & Ripple, R. E. (1984). A life-span developmental cross-cultural study of divergent thinking abilities. *International Journal of Aging & Human Development, 20*, 1–20.

Kaasa, A., & Vadi, M. (2010). How does culture contribute to innovation? Evidence from European countries. *Economics of Innovation and New Technology, 19*(7), 583–604. https://doi.org/10.1080/10438590902987222

Kapur, R., Subramanyam, S., & Shah, A. (1997). Creativity in Indian science. *Psychology and Developing Societies, 9*(2), 161–187. https://doi.org/10.1177/097133369700900202

Kashima, Y. (2000a). Conceptions of culture and person for psychology. *Journal of Cross-Cultural Psychology, 31*, 14–32. 10.1177/0022022100031001003

Kashima, Y. (2000b). Maintaining cultural stereotypes in the serial reproduction of narratives. *Personality and Social Psychology Bulletin, 26*(5), 594–604.

Khaleefa, O. H., Erdos, G., & Ashria, I. H. (1996). Creativity in an indigenous Afro-Arab Islamic culture: The case of Sudan. *Journal of Creative Behavior, 30*(4), 268–282.
Khaleefa, O. H., Erdos, G., & Ashria, I. H. (1997). Traditional education and creativity in an Afro-Arab Islamic culture: The case of Sudan. *Journal of Creative Behavior, 31*(3), 201–211.
Khan, R., & Cox, P. (2017). Country culture and national innovation. *Archives of Business Research, 5*(2), 85–101. https://doi.org/10.14738/abr.52.2768
Kim, J. Y., Cohen, D., & Au, W. T. (2010). The jury and abjury of my peers: The self in face and dignity cultures. *Interpersonal Relations and Group Processes, 98*(6), 904–916.
Kim, J. Y., & Nam, S. H. (1998). The concept and dynamics of face: Implications for organizational behavior in Asia. *Organization Science, 9*(4), 522–534. https://doi.org/10.1287/orsc.9.4.522
Kniffin, K., Narayanan, J., Anseel, F., Antonakis, J., Ashford, S., Bakker, A., Bamberger, P., Bapuji, H., Bhave, D., Choi, V., Creary, S., Demerouti, E., Flynn, F., Gelfand, Mi., Greer, L., Johns, G., Kesebir, S., Klein, P., Lee, S. Y., . . . van Vugt, M. (2020). COVID-19 and the workplace: Implications, issues, and insights for future research and action. *American Psychologist, 76*(1), 63–77. https://doi.org/10.31234/osf.io/gkwme
Kuroda, Y., & Suzuki, T. (1989). Language and attitude: A study in Arabic, English, and Japanese on the role of language in cross-cultural thinking. In D. M. Topping, D. C. Crowell, & V. N. Kobayashi (Eds.), *Thinking across Cultures: The Third International Conference on Thinking* (pp. 147–161). Mahwah, NJ: Lawrence Erlbaum.
Kwan, L. Y. Y. (2018). Institutional and value support for cultural pluralism is stronger in innovative societies with demanding climate. *Journal of Cross-Cultural Psychology, 49*(2), 323–335. https://doi.org/10.1177/0022022117746773
Kwan, L. Y. Y., Leung, A. K. Y., & Liou, S. (2018). Culture, creativity, and innovation. In *Journal of Cross-Cultural Psychology* (Vol. 49, Issue 2, pp. 165–170). Thousand Oaks, CA: SAGE. https://doi.org/10.1177/0022022117753306
Lan, L., & Kaufman, J. C. (2012). American and Chinese similarities and differences in defining and valuing creative products. *The Journal of Creative Behavior, 46*(4), 285–306. https://doi.org/10.1002/jocb.19
Lazar, M., Miron-Spektor, E., & Mueller, J. (2022). Love at first insight: An attachment perspective on early-phase idea selection. *Organizational Behavior and Human Decision Processes, 172*, 104168.
Leikin, M., & Tovli, E. (2014). Bilingualism and creativity in early childhood. *Creativity Research Journal, 26*(4), 411–417. https://doi.org/10.1080/10400419.2014.961779
Leung, A. K. Y., & Chiu, C. Y. (2010). Multicultural experience, idea receptiveness, and creativity. *Journal of Cross-Cultural Psychology, 41*(5), 723–741. https://doi.org/10.1177/0022022110361707
Leung, A. K.-Y., & Cohen, D. (2011). Within- and between-culture variation: Individual differences and the cultural logics of honor, face, and dignity cultures. *Journal of Personality and Social Psychology, 100*(3), 507–526.
Leung, A. K. Y., Liou, S., Miron-Spektor, E., Koh, B., Chan, D., Eisenberg, R., & Schneider, I. (2018). Middle ground approach to paradox: Within-and between-culture examination of the creative benefits of paradoxical frames. *Journal of Personality and Social Psychology, 114*(3), 443–464. https://doi.org/10.1037/pspp0000160
Leung, A. K. Y., Maddux, W. W., Galinsky, A. D., & Chiu, C. Y. (2008). Multicultural experience enhances creativity: The when and how. *American Psychologist, 63*(3), 169–181. https://doi.org/10.1037/0003-066X.63.3.169
Leung, K., & Wang, J. (2015). *A cross-cultural analysis of creativity*. In C. E. Shalley, M. A. Hitt, & J. Zhou (Eds.), *Oxford library of psychology. The Oxford handbook of creativity, innovation, and entrepreneurship* (pp. 261–278). New York: Oxford University Press.
Lewis, M. W. (2000). Exploring paradox: Toward a more comprehensive guide. *Academy of Management Review, 25*(4), 760–776. https://doi.org/10.5465/AMR.2000.3707712
Li, C., Kwan, L. Y.-Y., Liou, S., & Chiu, C.-Y. (2014). Culture, group processes, and creativity. In M. Yuki & M. Brewer (Eds.), *Culture and group processes* (pp. 143–165). New York: Oxford University Press.
Liou, S., & Lan, X. (2018). Situational salience of norms moderates cultural differences in the originality and usefulness of creative ideas generated or selected by teams. *Journal of Cross-Cultural Psychology, 49*(2), 290–302. https://doi.org/10.1177/0022022116640897
Loewenstein, J., & Mueller, J. (2016). Implicit theories of creative ideas: How culture guides creativity assessments. *Academy of Management Discoveries, 2*(4), 320–348. https://doi.org/10.5465/amd.2014.0147

Maddux, W. W., Adam, H., & Galinsky, A. D. (2010). When in Rome . . . learn why the Romans do what they do: How multicultural learning experiences facilitate creativity. *Personality and Social Psychology Bulletin, 36*(6), 731–741. https://doi.org/10.1177/0146167210367786

Maddux, W. W., & Galinsky, A. D. (2009). Cultural borders and mental barriers: The relationship between living abroad and creativity. *Journal of Personality and Social Psychology, 96*(5), 1047–1061. https://doi.org/10.1037/a0014861

Maddux, W. W., Lu, G. J., Affinito, S. J., & Galinsky, A. D. (2020). Multicultural experiences: A systematic review and new multicultural experiences multicultural experiences. *Academy of Management Annals, 15*(2), 345–376.

Madjar, N., Greenberg, E., & Chen, Z. (2011). Factors for radical creativity, incremental creativity, and routine, noncreative performance. *Journal of Applied Psychology, 96*(4), 730–743. https://doi.org/10.1037/a0022416

Mannix, E., & Neale, M. A. (2005). What differences make a difference? The promise and reality of diverse teams in organizations. *Psychological Science in the Public Interest, Supplement, 6*(2), 31–55. https://doi.org/10.1111/j.1529-1006.2005.00022.x

Markus, H. R., & Kitayama, S. (1991). Culture and the self: Implications for cognition, emotion, and motivation. American Psychological Association. *Psychological Review, 98*(2), 224.

McCarthy, M., Chen, C. C., & McNamee, R. C. (2018). Novelty and usefulness trade-off: Cultural cognitive differences and creative idea evaluation. *Journal of Cross-Cultural Psychology, 49*(2), 171–198. https://doi.org/10.1177/0022022116680479

Miron-Spektor, E., & Argote, L. (2008). The effect of paradoxical cognition on individual and team innovation. *Academy of Management Proceedings*. https://doi.org/10.5465/ambpp.2008.33718126

Miron-Spektor, E., & Erez, M. (2017). Looking at creativity through a paradox lens. In W. K. Smith, M. W. Lewis, P. Jarzabkowski, & A. Langley (Eds.), *Handbook of organizational paradox: Approaches to plurality, tensions and contradictions* (December Issue, p. 434). New York: Oxford University Press.

Miron-Spektor, E., Erez, M., & Naveh, E. (2011). The effect of conformist and attentive-to-detail members on team innovation: Reconciling the innovation paradox. *Academy of Management Journal, 54*(4), 740–760. https://doi.org/10.5465/AMJ.2011.64870100

Miron-Spektor, E., Erez, M., & Naveh, E. (2012). To drive creativity, add some conformity. *Harvard Business Review, 90*(3), 1–2. https://hbr.org/archive-toc/BR1203

Miron-Spektor, E., Gino, F., & Argote, L. (2011). Paradoxical frames and creative sparks: Enhancing individual creativity through conflict and integration. *Organizational Behavior and Human Decision Processes, 116*(2), 229–240. https://doi.org/10.1016/j.obhdp.2011.03.006

Miron-Spektor, E., Ingram, A., Keller, J., Smith, W. K., & Lewis, M. W. (2018). Microfoundations of organizational paradox: The problem is how we think about the problem. *Academy of Management Journal, 61*(1), 26–45. https://doi.org/10.5465/amj.2016.0594

Miron-Spektor, E., & Paletz, S. B. F. (2020). Collective paradoxical frames. In L. Argote & J. Levine (Eds.), *The Oxford handbook of group and organizational Learning* (p. 429). Oxford, UK: Oxford University Press. https://doi.org/10.1093/oxfordhb/9780190263362.013.32

Miron-Spektor, E., Paletz, S. B. F., & Lin, C. C. (2015). To create without losing face: The effects of face cultural logic and social-image affirmation on creativity. *Journal of Organizational Behavior, 36*(7), 919–943. https://doi.org/10.1002/job.2029

Miron-Spektor, E., Vashdi, D. R., & Gopher, H. (2022). Bright sparks and enquiring minds: Differential effects of goal orientation on the creativity trajectory. *Journal of Applied Psychology, 107*(2), 310–318. https://doi.org/10.1037/apl0000888

Mok, A., & Morris, M. W. (2010). An upside to bicultural identity conflict: Resisting groupthink in cultural ingroups. *Journal of Experimental Social Psychology, 46*(6), 1114–1117. https://doi.org/10.1016/j.jesp.2010.05.020

Montag, T., Maertz, C. P., & Baer, M. (2012). A critical analysis of the workplace creativity criterion space. *Journal of Management, 38*(4), 1362–1386. doi: 10.1177/0149206312441835

Morris, M. W., Chiu, C. Y., & Liu, Z. (2015). Polycultural psychology. *Annual Review of Psychology, 66*, 631–659. https://doi.org/10.1146/annurev-psych-010814-015001

Morris, M. W., & Leung, K. (2010). Creativity east and west: Perspectives and parallels. *Management and Organization Review, 6*(3), 313–327. https://doi.org/10.1111/j.1740-8784.2010.00193.x

Mu, Y., Kitayama, S., Han, S., & Gelfand, M. J. (2015). How culture gets embrained: Cultural differences in event-related potentials of social norm violations. *Proceedings of the National Academy of Sciences, 112*(50), 15348–15353

Nakata, C., & Sivakumar, K. (1996). National culture and new product development: An integrative review. *Journal of Marketing, 60*(1), 61–72. https://doi.org/10.1177/002224299606000106

Nemeth, C. J., & Gonacalo, J. A. (2005). Influence and persuasion in small groups. In T. C. Brock & M. C. Green (Eds.), *Persuasion: Psychological Insights and Perspectives* (pp. 171–194). London: SAGE. https://doi.org/10.1177/0020764011408651

Niu, W., & Kaufman, J. C. (2013). Creativity of Chinese and American cultures: A synthetic analysis. *The Journal of Creative Behavior, 47*(1), 77–87. https://doi.org/10.1002/jocb.25

Nouri, R., Erez, M., Lee, C., Liang, J., Bannister, B. D., & Chiu, W. (2014). Social context: Key to understanding culture's effects on creativity. *Journal of Organizational Behavior,* 36, 899–918.

Nouri, R., Erez, M., Rockstuhl, T., Ang, S., Leshem-Calif, L., & Rafaeli, A. (2013). Taking the bite out of culture: The impact of task structure and task type on overcoming impediments to cross-cultural team performance. *Journal of Organizational Behavior, 34*(6), 739–763. https://doi.org/10.1002/job.1871

Nowak, A., Gelfand, M. J., Borkowski, W., Cohen, D., & Hernandez, I. (2015). The evolutionary basis of honor cultures. *Psychological Science, 27*(1), 12–24.

Paletz, S. B. F., Bogue, K., Miron-Spektor, E., & Spencer-Rodgers, J. (2018a). Dialectical thinking and creativity from many perspectives: Contradiction and tension. In J. Spencer-Rodgers & K. Peng (Eds.), *The psychological and cultural foundations of East Asian cognition* (pp. 267–308). New York: Oxford University Press.

Paletz, S. B. F., Miron-Spektor, E., & Lin, C. C. (2014). A cultural lens on interpersonal conflict and creativity in multicultural environments. *Psychology of Aesthetics, Creativity, and the Arts, 8*(2), 237–252. https://doi.org/10.1037/a0035927

Paletz, S. B. F., Pavisic, I., Miron-Spektor, E., & Lin, C.-C. (2018b). Diversity in creative teams: Reaching across cultures and disciplines. In L. Y.-Y. Kwan, S. Liou, & A. K.-Y. Leung (Eds.), *Handbook of culture and creativity: Basic processes and applied* innovations (pp. 169–206). New York: Oxford University Press.

Paletz, S. B. F., & Peng, K. (2008). Implicit theories of creativity across cultures: Novelty and appropriateness in two product domains. *Journal of Cross-Cultural Psychology, 39*(3), 286–302. https://doi.org/10.1177/0022022108315112

Paletz, S. B. F., Peng, K., & Li, S. (2011). In the world or in the head: External and internal implicit theories of creativity. *Creativity Research Journal, 23*(2), 83–98. https://doi.org/10.1080/10400419.2011.571181

Paletz, S. B. F., Sumer, A., & Miron-Spektor, E. (2018c). Psychological factors surrounding disagreement in multicultural design team meetings. *CoDesign, 14*(2), 98–114. https://doi.org/10.1080/15710882.2017.1378685

Peng, K., & Nisbett, R. E. (1999). Culture, dialectics, and reasoning about contradiction. *American Psychologist, 54*(9), 741–754. https://doi.org/10.1037/0003-066X.54.9.741

Peng, K., Nisbett, R. E., & Wong, N. Y. C. (1997). Validity problems comparing values across cultures and possible solutions. *Psychological Methods, 2*(4), 329–344. https://doi.org/10.1037/1082-989X.2.4.329

Perry-Smith, J. E., & Mannucci, P. V. (2017). From creativity to innovation: The social network drivers of the four phases of the idea journey. *Academy of Management Review, 42*(1), 53–79. https://doi.org/10.5465/amr.2014.0462

Pradies, C., Carmine, S., Pina Cunha, M., Gaim, M., Keegan, A., Miron-Spektor, E., Nielsen, R. K., Pouthier, V., Sharma, G., Sparr, J., Vince, R., & Keller, J. (2021). The lived experience of paradox: How individuals navigate tensions during the pandemic crisis. *Journal of Management Inquiry, 30*(2), 154–167.

Puente-Diaz, R., Toptas, S. D., Cavazos-Arroyo, J., Wimschneider, C., & Brem, A. (2019). Creative potential and multicultural experiences: The mediating role of creative self-efficacy. *The Journal of Creative Behavior, 54*(4), 815–823. https://doi.org/10.1002/jocb.408

Rietzschel, E. F. , De Dreu, C. K. W., & Nijstad, B. A. (2007a). Personal need for structure and creative performance: The moderating influence of fear of invalidity. *Personality and Social Psychology Bulletin, 33*(6), 855–866.

Rietzschel, E. F., Nijstad, B. A., & Stroebe, W. (2007b). Relative accessibility of domain knowledge and creativity: The effects of knowledge activation on the quantity and originality of generated ideas. *Journal of Experimental Social Psychology, 43*, 933–946.

Roberson, Q. M. (2019). Diversity in the workplace: A review, synthesis, and future research agenda. *Annual Review of Organizational Psychology and Organizational Behavior, 6*(1), 69–88. https://doi.org/10.1146/annurev-orgpsych-012218-015243

Rohner, R. P. (1984). Toward a conception of culture for cross-cultural psychology. *Journal of Cross-Cultural Psychology*, 15(2), 111–138. https://doi.org/10.1177/0022002184015002002

Runco, M. A., & Johnson, D. J. (2002). Parents' and teachers' implicit theories of children's creativity: A cross-cultural perspective. *Creativity Research Journal, 14*(3-4), 427–438. https://doi.org/10.1207/S15326934CRJ1434_12

Saad, C. S., Damian, R. I., Benet-Martínez, V., Moons, W. G., & Robins, R. W. (2013). Multiculturalism and creativity. *Social Psychological and Personality Science, 4*(3), 369–375. https://doi.org/10.1177/1948550612456560

Schein, E. H. (1992). *Organizational culture and leadership*. San Francisco: Jossey-Bass.

Schwartz, S. H. (1999). A theory of cultural values and some implications for work. *Applied Psychology, 48*(1), 23–47. https://doi.org/10.1080/026999499377655

Shalley, C. E., Zhou, J., & Oldham, G. R. (2004). The effects of personal and contextual characteristics on creativity: Where should we go from here? *Journal of Management, 30*(6), 933–958. https://doi.org/10.1016/j.jm.2004.06.007

Shane, S. A. (1992). Why do some societies invent more than others? *Journal of Business Venturing, 7*(1), 29–46. https://doi.org/10.1016/0883-9026(92)90033-N

Simonton, D. K., & Ting, S. S. (2010). Creativity in Eastern and Western civilizations: The lessons of historiometry. *Management and Organization Review, 6*(3), 329–350. https://doi.org/10.1111/j.1740-8784.2010.00188.x

Smith, P. B., Bond, M. H., & Kağitçibaşi, Ç. (2006). *Understanding social psychology across cultures: Living and working in a changing world*. Thousand Oaks, CA: SAGE.

Spencer-Rodgers, J., & Peng, K. (2018). *The psychological and cultural foundations of East Asian cognition*. New York: Oxford University Press.

Stahl, G. K., Mäkelä, K., Zander, L., & Maznevski, M. L. (2010). A look at the bright side of multicultural team diversity. *Scandinavian Journal of Management, 26*(4), 439–447. https://doi.org/10.1016/j.scaman.2010.09.009

Tadmor, C. T., Galinsky, A. D., & Maddux, W. W. (2012). Getting the most out of living abroad: Biculturalism and integrative complexity as key drivers of creative and professional success. *Journal of Personality and Social Psychology, 103*(3), 520–542. https://doi.org/10.1037/a0029360

Tadmor, C. T., Satterstrom, P., Jang, S., & Polzer, J. T. (2012). Beyond individual creativity. *Journal of Cross-Cultural Psychology, 43*(3), 384–392. https://doi.org/10.1177/0022022111435259

Torrance, E. P. (1968). Testing the educational and psychological development of students from other cultures and subcultures. *Review of Educational Research, 38*(1), 71–76.

Torrance, E. P., & Sato, S. (1979). Figural creative thinking abilities of United States and Japanese majors in education. *Creative Child and Adult Quarterly, 4*(4), 216–221.

Triandis, H. C. (1989). The self and social behavior in differing cultural contexts. *Psychological Review, 96*(3), 506–520. https://doi.org/10.1037/0033-295X.96.3.506

Unsworth, K. L., Wall, T. D., & Carter, A. (2005). Creative requirement: A neglected construct in the study of employee creativity? *Group & Organization Management, 30*(5), 541–560.

van de Vijver, F. J. R., & Leung, K. (2000). Methodological issues in psychological research on culture. *Journal of Cross-Cultural Psychology, 31*, 33–51. 10.1177/0022022100031001004

van Knippenberg, D., & Schippers, M. C. (2007). Work group diversity. *Annual Review of Psychology, 58*(1), 515–541. https://doi.org/10.1146/annurev.psych.58.110405.085546

Watts, L. L., Steele, L. M., & Den Hartog, D. N. (2020). Uncertainty avoidance moderates the relationship between transformational leadership and innovation: A meta-analysis. *Journal of International Business Studies, 51*(1), 138–145. https://doi.org/10.1057/s41267-019-00242-8

Westwood, R., & Low, D. R. (2003). The multicultural muse: Culture, creativity and innovation. *International Journal of Cross-Cultural Management, 3*(2), 235–259.

Xie, G., & Paik, Y. (2019). Cultural differences in creativity and innovation: Are Asian employees truly less creative than western employees? *Asia Pacific Business Review, 25*(1), 123–147. https://doi.org/10.1080/13602381.2018.1535380

Yong, K., Mannucci, P. V., & Lander, M. W. (2020). Fostering creativity across countries: The moderating effect of cultural bundles on creativity. *Organizational Behavior and Human Decision Processes, 157*, 1–45. https://doi.org/10.1016/j.obhdp.2019.12.004
Yuan, F., & Zhou, J. (2015). Effects of cultural power distance on group creativity and individual group member creativity. *Journal of Organizational Behavior, 36*(7), 990–1007. https://doi.org/10.1002/job.2022
Yue, X. D. (2003). Meritorious evaluation bias: How Chinese undergraduates perceive and evaluate Chinese and foreign creators. *Journal of Creative Behavior, 37*, 151–178.
Yue, X. D., & Rudowicz, E. (2002). Perception of the most creative Chinese by undergraduates in Beijing, Guangzhou, Hong Kong, and Taipei. *Journal of Creative Behavior, 36*(2), 88–104. https://doi.org/10.1002/j.2162-6057.2002.tb01058.

CHAPTER 11

Culture and Workplace Deviance

Jana L. Raver

Abstract

Research and theory on culture and workplace deviance (including related constructs; e.g., bullying, aggression, counterproductive work behavior, harassment, incivility, abusive supervision) were rare until a decade ago, but this is now a flourishing area of scholarship. This chapter comprehensively reviews this body of research published since 2011. Key themes, findings, theoretical foundations, and methodologies are highlighted, along with the dilemmas and controversies surrounding the disparate treatment of workplace deviance in the literature. Key themes include evidence that several measures of workplace deviance are cross-culturally generalizable; increased methodological sophistication including tests of measurement equivalence and measuring theorized cultural mechanisms; and the emergence of larger multinational studies published by teams of global collaborators. Promising areas of inquiry for future research are also provided, grounded within theoretical principles that will advance scholarship. The chapter concludes with a synthesis of practical implications for organizational leaders and practitioners stemming from the current body of work.

Key Words: deviance, culture, cross-cultural, workplace, bullying, harassment, counterproductive work behavior, aggression, abusive supervision, incivility

Research on workplace deviance and related constructs (e.g., bullying, aggression, counterproductive work behavior, harassment, incivility, abusive supervision) has flourished over the past 25 years, moving from a peripheral topic to a mainstay of organizational behavior and organizational psychology scholarship (Mackey et al., 2021; Robinson et al., 2017). The umbrella term for this body of work used in this chapter, *workplace deviance*, was first defined by Robinson and Bennett in 1995 as the, "voluntary behavior of organizational members that violates significant organizational norms, and in so doing, threatens the well-being of the organization and/or its members" (p. 556). Evidence has accumulated quickly, and many organizational and individual antecedents to enacting deviance have been uncovered (see Mackey et al., 2021 for a recent meta-analysis), along with consistently strong evidence on the harm employees experience when they are mistreated with deviance enacted by others at work (see Bowling & Beehr, 2006; Einarsen et al., 2020; Robinson et al., 2017).

Despite the strong advances that have been made in understanding workplace deviance, remarkably little attention has been given to how societal culture affects the enactment and experience of this phenomenon until recently. The paucity of cross-cultural research and theorizing has been lamented in the broader psychological literature on human aggression as well (Bond, 2004). Fortunately, the tide has turned and within the past decade scholars have responded to calls for increased attention to cross-cultural research on workplace deviance (e.g., Raver & Barling, 2008; Schilpzand et al., 2016) by greatly increasing the number and quality of publications on this topic. The result is that there is now a sufficiently robust body of work on societal culture differences in workplace deviance to warrant a comprehensive literature review. To my knowledge, only one prior publication has summarized the literature on cultural differences in workplace aggression (Li & Lim, 2017), but the scope of this current review is broader and numerous additional studies have been discovered. The time is ripe for a review of this literature, with the goal of synthesizing what we know and stimulating future work in this area.

This chapter has four primary goals. The first aim is to provide readers with a comprehensive overview of the current literature on culture and workplace deviance, focusing predominantly on research published in the past decade. Second, in reviewing the literature, I aim to identify the key themes, findings, theoretical foundations, and methodologies, as well as the dilemmas and controversies surrounding the disparate treatment of workplace deviance in the literature. Third, after summarizing the existing literature, I identify promising areas of inquiry for future research, grounded within theoretical principles that will advance scholarship. The final aim is to synthesize practical implications for organizational leaders and practitioners stemming from the current body of work. The chapter begins with a brief overview of the nature of workplace deviance constructs and early research on culture and deviance.

Foundations of Culture and Workplace Deviance Research

Workplace Deviance Constructs

Workplace deviance research gained traction in the 1990s with the introduction of numerous related constructs in both North America and Europe nearly simultaneously, including workplace bullying (Einarsen et al., 1994), deviance (Robinson & Bennett, 1995), mobbing (Zapf et al., 1996), violence (Barling, 1996), misbehavior (Vardi & Wiener, 1996), sexual harassment (Fitzgerald et al., 1997), retaliation (Skarlicki & Folger, 1997), revenge (Bies et al., 1997), petty tyranny (Ashforth, 1997), antisocial behavior (Giacalone & Greenberg, 1997), emotional abuse (Keashly et al., 1997), aggression (Neuman & Baron, 1998), incivility (Andersson & Pearson, 1999), abusive supervision (Tepper, 2000), counterproductive work behavior (Fox et al., 2001), and social undermining (Duffy et al., 2002), among others. Deviant behaviors consist of both organizationally-targeted (e.g., theft, sabotage, time theft, reputation harm) and interpersonally-targeted (e.g., harassing others, rudeness, uncivil language, ethnic slurs) misconduct at work, and ranges in severity as well (Robinson & Bennett, 1995). The first decade of work in this domain focused on specifying construct domains and definitions, establishing prevalence of the phenomena, developing valid and reliable measures, and then exploring predictors of enacting deviance as well as outcomes of experiencing it (for reviews, see Bennett & Robinson, 2003; Fox & Spector, 2005; Kidwell & Martin, 2005; O'Leary-Kelly et al., 2000; Raver & Barling, 2008; Robinson & Greenberg, 1998). Although scholars have lamented the construct proliferation and have produced evidence on conceptual and empirical convergence across construct labels (Hershcovis, 2011; Hershcovis & Reich, 2013), research on distinct constructs has persisted, given the unique meanings and manifestations of each type of misconduct (cf. Ferris et al., 2017; Nielsen & Einarsen, 2018). However, given the similar nomological networks of the constructs within this body of work, it is wise to learn from theory and research on related constructs. Accordingly, the approach in this chapter is to synthesize the existing literature on culture and many similar constructs under the umbrella rubric of workplace deviance to learn from the full body of literature but to specify in the review each focal construct investigated.

In addition to workplace deviance taking on interpersonally-directed versus organizationally-directed forms, research in this area generally takes one of two stances, namely, enacted deviance versus experienced deviance (see Spector & Fox, 2005). Experiencing interpersonally-targeted deviance is described through construct labels such as workplace aggression, bullying, incivility, harassment, mobbing, abusive supervision, emotional abuse, ostracism, and victimization, among others. I will use specific construct labels when possible, but when referring to this set of constructs in combination, I will use the term *mistreatment*, as the term *deviance* is rarely used in the literature from the target's perspective. This is not intended as a new construct but as an umbrella term to encompass the full range of behaviors that targets experience, including acts that are minor versus severe, active versus passive, direct versus indirect, intentional versus unintentional, personally versus work-directed, acute versus chronic, and physical versus verbal (see Raver & Barling, 2008, for a review of dimensionality). Research on enacting deviance against individuals (i.e., mistreating others) is often conducted under these same construct labels, but for research that examines organizationally-directed misconduct, scholars typically use the broader terms of workplace deviance, counterproductive work behavior (CWB), antisocial behavior, and/or misbehavior. As Mackey et al. (2021) note in their recent review, the construct domain of CWB is larger than deviance because of the requirement that deviant acts violate significant organizational norms; minor interpersonal conflicts and small acts of defiance are not generally considered deviant. Accordingly, this chapter also focuses on acts that are widely construed as misconduct at work, but societal discrepancies in conceptual equivalence are discussed in more depth below.

Early Work on Culture and Deviance

Despite workplace deviance drawing interest among scholars and practitioners globally and the emergence of country-specific studies in several nations (e.g., Lee, 1998; Einarsen 2000; Mikkelsen & Einarsen, 2002; Nielsen et al., 2009; Resch & Schubinski, 1996; Sheehan et al., 1999; Yeung & Griffin, 2008), early research rarely paid explicit attention to societal culture and cultural differences. Rather, early studies focused on workplace bullying to document its nature and prevalence in a specific cultural context, often with an aim to influence public policy (see Einarsen et al., 2003). What soon became apparent is that the manifestations, etiology, and outcomes of mistreatment were similar across countries; yet variations in prevalence rates by country suggested that cultural influences may be at play (Eurofound, 2016; Nielsen et al., 2010).

An exception to this trend was research on culture and sexual harassment, in which scholars adopted more sophisticated cross-cultural research methodologies in the late 1990s and early 2000s. Gelfand et al. (1995) first conducted a comparative test of the structure of sexual harassment across cultures and settings, establishing measurement of the Sexual Experiences Questionnaire (SEQ; Fitzgerald et al., 1988) in the United States and Brazil. Wasti and colleagues (2000) explicitly theorized about cultural influences on the meaning of sexual harassment and its nomological network in the United States and Turkey. Using a rigorous set of analyses, they established measurement equivalence of the SEQ in both samples, as well as the relational equivalence of Fitzgerald et al.'s (1997) model of sexual harassment; the antecedents (e.g., organizational context, job gender context) and consequences (e.g., job satisfaction, health conditions) were parallel in both cultures. Although the results largely supported cross-cultural generalizability, Wasti et al. (2000) emphasized that behavioral manifestations of sexual harassment may differ across cultures, so the SEQ may not capture all emic (culture-specific) behaviors. Several additional studies (e.g., Cortina & Wasti, 2005; Merkin, 2008; Sigal et al., 2005; Wasti & Cortina, 2002) and theory papers in the 2000s (e.g., Luthar & Luthar, 2002, 2007) explicitly studied culture and sexual harassment. Unfortunately, these methodological sophistications and theoretical attention to the role of culture remained uniquely situated within the sexual harassment literature until they were adopted within the larger body of research on workplace deviance, as will be seen below.

Overall, early findings hinted that greater attention was needed to understanding cultural influences on workplace deviance. Yet as Bond (2004, p. 73) noted, "there have been remarkably few such cross-cultural studies" due to the logistical challenges of cross-cultural work as well as the lack of conceptual agreement on what constitutes aggressive (or deviant) behavior. In the late 2000s, scholars began to theorize more explicitly about national culture as a factor in workplace aggression (Irani & Oswald, 2009), with cross-cultural empirical studies appearing shortly thereafter. This shift in the larger workplace deviance literature toward explicitly focusing on culture represents the point of departure for the current review.

The Current Literature

Discovering research and theory on culture and workplace deviance published in the past decade entailed searching both the PsycInfo and Business Source Premier databases for papers on the intersection of these two phenomena. In addition to *culture*, searches included numerous terms that constitute workplace deviance: *deviance, counterproductive work behavior, misbehavior, antisocial behavior, aggression, revenge, retaliation, bullying, harassment, incivility, mistreatment, abuse, mobbing, insults, ostracism, undermining, rudeness, victimization*, and their derivatives. The search parameters also included *organization* and/or *work* to specifically focus on deviance in an organizational or workplace context. Potentially relevant articles resulting from these searches were then further refined based on these additional criteria: (1) the research or theory needed to be focused on societal (country-level) culture, not just within-country ethnocultural groups or organizational culture; (2) the paper needed to focus explicitly on culture, not just report research on non-United States samples; (3) the paper needed to be published in a journal or book; and (4) the paper needed to be published in and/or translated to English. These criteria resulted in 43 papers on culture and workplace deviance published since 2011. The focus will be on papers from the past decade, but earlier work will be selectively discussed to highlight foundational research and theory.

These papers can be further categorized as being cross-cultural/comparative (22 papers) versus culture-specific (14 studies) in their content, in addition to 7 theory and/or literature review articles. Within both the comparative and the culture-specific literature, there was a strong focus on understanding the meaning and equivalence of deviance across cultures. Thus, this review will begin by exploring research on both the universal (*etic*) and culture-specific (*emic*; Triandis, 1994) nature of workplace deviance. The comparative papers took one of three forms. First, two studies and two theory papers conceptualized culture as having a direct effect on national rates of workplace deviance. A second cluster of studies conceptualized culture as a qualifier of target reactions to experiencing workplace mistreatment. The final set of studies conceptualized culture as a qualifier of the antecedents to enacting deviance. The descriptions of specific study details in this narrative review are necessarily selective due to space constraints; the full set of papers included in this review are provided in References.

The Nature and Comparability of Deviance across Cultures

The first major question that arises when one is undertaking cross-cultural research on workplace deviance is whether this phenomenon is comparable across countries (Bond, 2004). Research in the past decade has made strides toward understanding which elements of workplace deviance are universal (etic) versus recognizing culture-specific (emic) manifestations (Triandis, 1994). This research includes several studies on conceptual and measurement equivalence, as well as emic studies aimed at unpacking specific cultures' manifestations of deviance and related constructs.

Measurement Equivalence Studies. Studies adopting an etic lens on the universality of workplace deviance have established measurement equivalence for several constructs. For example, Hu et al. (2011) established the measurement equivalence of Tepper's (2000) popular abusive supervision measure across samples from Taiwan and the United States. In addition, Coyne and colleagues (2013) established conceptual, linguistic, and structural equivalence across the United Kingdom, the Netherlands, Turkey, and Greece for a measure of voluntary work behavior that measured both interpersonal and organizational CWB (along with Organizational Citizenship Behavior; OCB). They concluded that their findings show more convergence than divergence across cultures with respect to the dimensionality and correlates of CWB and OCB, albeit the scale may have only captured etic elements of CWB and OCB. In a study of ethical leadership and bullying, Ahmad (2018) also established measurement equivalence between Australia and Pakistan for the Negative Acts Questionnaire Revised (NAQ-R; Einarsen et al., 2009), the most frequently employed workplace bullying measure. These studies echo earlier findings discussed above on the equivalence of sexual harassment across cultures (Wasti et al., 2000). These works might seemingly encourage the conclusion that the experience of deviance is universal, but numerous studies on culture-specific nuances of deviance contest this conclusion. As Gelfand et al. (2002) argued, even if factor-analytic techniques illustrate that measurement models are similar across cultures, construct invariance cannot be ruled out, as the focal construct may be deficient in other cultures.

Comparative Studies of Conceptual Equivalence. Comparative research on conceptual equivalence is most prevalent in the body of work on workplace bullying, perhaps because bullying research emerged simultaneously in several nations in the 1990s and 2000s (see Einarsen et al., 2003). Early discussions of country differences in bullying were based on inferences drawn from disparate samples across countries (e.g., Jennifer et al., 2003). In one of the first studies specifically designed to examine cross-cultural differences, Escartin and colleagues (2011) sampled participants from Costa Rica and Spain to inductively compare their understandings of bullying. Their results found that Costa Rican employees perceived bullying as having a stronger physical (versus psychological) component, but the sources of bullying (supervisors versus subordinates) and direct versus indirect strategies of bullying were similar across countries. Two- or three-country comparison studies on employees' experiences and understanding of bullying have also appeared for Australia, India, and Turkey (D'Cruz et al., 2016), as well as Estonia and Finland (Meriläinen et al., 2019). The qualitative study by D'Cruz and colleagues (2016) evidenced remarkable convergence in the etiology, manifestations, and coping with bullying across three countries. Differences emerged for the source of bullying—where it was more likely to come from superiors only in India and Turkey versus superiors and peers in Australia—as well as the absence of grievance procedures for targets in India and Turkey. They interpreted their findings as a manifestation of power distance discrepancies between countries. Meriläinen et al. (2019) found more evidence of cultural divergence, showing that bullying at universities in Estonia take direct forms consisting of threats of blame, violence, humiliation, or ridicule, whereas in Finland it takes more indirect forms, especially negative work-related remarks. They speculated that these differences may be due to the comparatively lower collectivism, higher power distance, and lower humane orientation in Estonia.

Salin and colleagues (2019) offered a more comprehensive exploration of the cross-national similarities and differences in perceptions and conceptualizations of workplace bullying among HR professionals in a 13-country qualitative study. They theoretically sampled countries such that representatives of all 10 cultural clusters identified in the GLOBE study (House et al., 2004) were included. They developed an in-depth interview based on a global team of collaborators using a combined etic–emic strategy (Berry, 1969; Triandis & Triandis, 1962), such that measures of bullying from several countries were combined to represent bullying. Coding of HR professionals' interviews explored the types of bullying behaviors, criteria for what constitutes bullying, and what makes the behavior more versus less acceptable.

Results from Salin et al. (2019) revealed that all types of workplace bullying (e.g., personal harassment, work-related harassment, social exclusion, physical violence) emerged but varied in their centrality across countries. Work-related (e.g., persistent criticism, unreasonable deadlines) and personal-related (e.g., insults, put-downs) forms of harassment emerged frequently in spontaneous descriptions of bullying in most countries, but work-related acts were more ambiguous. Whether work-related acts constituted bullying varied based on the country's performance orientation. High performance orientation countries (e.g., the United States, China, and Austria) tended to accept work-related acts, whereas these acts were perceived as bullying in low-performance orientation countries (e.g., Gulf countries, Argentina, and Finland). Cultures also differed in their perceptions of social exclusion, such that it only emerged as an element of bullying in Austria, Finland, and to some extent Poland. African and Gulf country participants did not see exclusion as central to bullying, which the authors speculate may be linked back to in-group collectivism levels, but this deserves future research attention. Moreover, in high power distance countries such as India, Nigeria, and Turkey, bullying was seen to emerge from superiors and was conceptualized as an abuse of power, but paradoxically it was also accepted as part of supervisory privileges (i.e., an "entitlement to abuse") and targets were expected to suffer in silence. Finally, the research found that spreading rumors diverged in conceptual equivalence, where Gulf country participants as well as those from Turkey and Finland perceived it as especially heinous, which is consistent with the logic of honor cultures in which self-worth is based on reputation (Leung & Cohen, 2011). Overall, Salin et al. (2019) represents a rich comparative investigation of the conceptual equivalence of bullying, with clear theoretical logic for both the country sampling and interpretation of findings.

In addition to these bullying studies, research has investigated Wasti et al.'s (2000) suggestion of culture-specific meanings of sexual harassment. Specifically, Toker (2016) studied United States and Turkish participants' perceptions of ambiguous forms of sexual harassment. They established that United States participants perceived sexist behaviors to be more harassing, whereas Turkish participants regarded sexual and insinuation-of-interest behaviors to be more harassing.

The preceding studies on conceptual equivalence were largely exploratory, but research on aggression has more formally assessed the comparable meaning of deviance using multidimensional scaling (MDS) techniques. Specifically, Severance and colleagues (2013) drew from the cultural logics of honor, dignity, and face (Leung & Cohen, 2011)—which specify sources of self-worth and social standing as being derived from self- (dignity) versus other-generated (honor, face) evaluations—to examine the conceptual equivalence of aggression in four countries (Pakistan, Israel, Japan, and the United States). Severance et al. (2013) theorized that certain dimensions of aggression are universal, whereas a society's degree to which it emphasizes honor, dignity, and/or face should elicit cultural specificity in the meaning of aggressive behaviors. Their MDS results revealed that damage to self-worth and direct versus indirect were universally present, and a physical versus verbal dimension emerged in three of the four countries (the United States excepted). Interestingly, the specific behaviors that constituted the damage to self-worth dimension diverged in theoretically coherent ways, such that it was construed as an honor violation in Pakistan and Israel (e.g., damage to social standing, social exclusion) but not elsewhere (see also Maitner et al., 2017, on the United Arab Emirates). Likewise, Japanese construals of damage to self-worth were more imbued with morality, respect, and threat, consistent with face concerns in this society. In addition, infringement to personal resources only emerged in dignity-focused Israeli and United States societies. A dimension reflecting degree of threat only emerged in Pakistan. Taken together, Severance et al. (2013) show that even when universal dimensions of aggression emerge, specific behaviors vary and are imbued with differential meanings across cultures, which are linked to honor, face, and dignity cultural logics.

Culture-Specific Manifestations of Deviance. The preceding comparative studies begin to illustrate the culture-specific manifestations of workplace deviance, but several emic papers have delved more deeply into the particulars of how deviance is enacted and/or experienced in specific cultures. One set of studies looks at the enactment and experience of deviance in Confucian East Asian cultures. Rotundo and Xie (2008) first conducted an emic study on CWB in China, arguing that Confucian virtues that teach controlling selfish behaviors will lead counterproductive actions to be seen as inappropriate in China, albeit the specific acts might differ. They inductively generated a list of CWB in China, and then using MDS, they found that the structure of CWB—consisting of an interpersonal-organizational dimension and a high- versus low-task relevance dimension—was similar to that seen in Western studies (see Gruys & Sackett, 2003;

Robinson & Bennett, 1995). Seo et al. (2012) also employed the logic of Confucian virtues to unpack South Korean manifestations of bullying, where local terminology implies group action against an individual (akin to "mobbing" in Europe; Leymann, 1996) and Confucian deference to social hierarchy encourages tolerance of mistreatment by superiors. Liu and Wang (2013) argued that traditional Chinese values and a high level of power distance have led abusive supervision to be a popular form of management in China, especially when supervisor–subordinate *guanxi* (i.e., personal relationships) is of low quality. Fang et al. (2016) also described Confucian virtues—particularly the importance of being patient with unreasonable situations—as promoting a culture of accepting bullying as normative among Taiwanese nurses. These and other emic studies (Hon & Lu, 2016; He et al., 2019; Zheng et al., 2017) highlight how Confucian values and power distance may encourage high levels of mistreatment and coercion from supervisors. Yet, paradoxically, employees in these cultures may tolerate such abuse from authorities as normative (see also Salin et al., 2019). Perceptions of bullying and misconduct in China and Korea may be more likely to emerge when it is done by a group against someone (Seo et al., 2012), and/or it is perceived as selfish behavior (Rotundo & Xie, 2008).

Few emic studies have been published on enacting and experiencing deviance in Latin cultures. One exception is Giorgi et al.'s (2015) study on the tolerance of bullying among Italian workers. They argued that Latin European countries are low on humane orientation (as defined by GLOBE; Javidan et al., 2006) and so do not expect compassionate or kind workplace behaviors. They found that job satisfaction in Italy decreases under exposure to bullying but only to a certain point, which they suggest means it is tolerated as more normative. As noted earlier, Escartin and colleagues (2011) compared bullying in Latin Europe and Latin America, finding that both cultures conceptualized bullying as being both top-down and bottom-up mistreatment.

In a study in South Africa, Motsei and Nkomo (2016) interviewed HR professionals, targets, and bystanders to understand their definitions of bullying and how organizational and structural factors facilitate it. They drew from Salin's (2003) framework of organizational antecedents, which specifies motivating structures (e.g., internal competition, reward systems), precipitating processes (e.g., organizational changes), and enabling structures (e.g., power imbalances) that may trigger bullying. Their results evidenced support for Salin's (2003) model with the exception of enabling processes. In South Africa, enabling processes emphasized leadership and organizational culture (e.g., "tough" leadership, getting results); structural power imbalances were inherent in the South African experience of bullying. Interviewees also highlighted societal, economic, and political features of the South African context as influences on bullying. Specifically, targets attributed the reasons they were bullied to social identities (i.e., race, gender, religion, education, tenure) and the associated ingroup versus outgroup dynamics. South African legislation, which cites bullying as a type of harassment, likely influences the emic conceptualization of bullying as overlapping with social identity-based harassment and discrimination in this context. Finally, economic conditions, which lead to tough internal competition and employees enduring unfair labor practices, also emerged as macro determinants of bullying. Motsei and Nkomo's (2016) study is notable as one of the few that highlights socio-structural determinants of workplace deviance (see also Amin & Darrag, 2011, and Knapp et al., 2019, for reviews of socio-structural influences on sexual harassment in Egypt and Russia, respectively).

Finally, Wasti and Erdas (2019) explored the construal of workplace incivility in Turkey, highlighting how the cultural logic of honor cultures (Leung & Cohen, 2011) plays out in this context. Being honorable means being trustworthy but also having a reputation for toughness, not being taken advantage of, and being able to protect one's self and family (Nisbett & Cohen, 1996). Like face cultural logics, honor focuses on external evaluations of one's self-worth, but face cultures tend to emerge in stable hierarchies that are largely cooperative; honor cultures emerge in more unstable and competitive contexts, necessitating stronger norms for positive and negative reciprocity (Leung & Cohen, 2011). Consistent with this theorizing, their inductive generation of incivility behaviors showed universals, but also emic manifestations such as perceiving taking credit for success, disruptive behavior in shared spaces, and both professional *and* social exclusion to be uncivil. Like Confucian East Asian cultures, Turkey has high power distance, but Turkish employees perceived mistreatment from supervisors and peers to be equally abhorrent. The authors interpret this finding to be consistent with the injunctive norm in honor cultures that those of higher status should bestow warmth and generosity toward subordinates.

Summary. Research on culture and workplace deviance in recent years has focused heavily on understanding the universal as well as culture-specific nature of deviance, and several conclusions from this body of work are apparent. First, all comparative studies on workplace deviance constructs (including CWB, abusive supervision, incivility, bullying, and aggression) have reached the conclusion that these constructs are at least partially universal in nature. Universal elements of workplace deviance appear to include the interpersonal versus organizational dimension of CWB (Coyne et al., 2013), the general categories of workplace bullying behaviors (Salin et al., 2019), the direct versus indirect nature of aggression (Meriläinen et al., 2019; Severance et al., 2013), as well as the etiology and coping strategies for bullying (D'Cruz et al., 2016). In addition, the general factor structures of measures of CWB (Coyne et al., 2013), abusive supervision (Hu et al., 2011), workplace bullying (Ahmad, 2018), and sexual harassment (Wasti et al., 2000) have also been found to be culturally invariant.

Second, divergent and culture-specific elements have emerged from the comparative and emic bodies of research as well. For example, physical versus verbal manifestations of bullying are not universal (Escartin et al., 2011; Severance et al., 2013), nor are infringements on personal resources (Severance et al., 2013), the centrality of social exclusion to bullying (Salin et al., 2019), the extent to which superiors and coworkers are both sources of mistreatment (Salin et al., 2019; Wasti & Erdas, 2019), or recourses to address bullying (D'Cruz et al., 2016).

Third, even when the nature or dimensionality of deviance constructs is generalizable across cultures, the specific behaviors that constitute the construct often differ (Severance et al., 2013). For example, mistreatment is often tied to one's social identity group, and yet the specific groups being targeted are culture specific, embedded within societal power structures and inequalities (see D'Cruz et al., 2016; Motsei & Nkomo, 2016). Likewise, simply because construct measures are invariant cross-culturally does not mean that they capture culture-specific misconduct behaviors (Wasti et al., 2000; Wasti & Erdas, 2019).

Finally, even when behavioral measures are invariant across cultures (e.g., abusive supervision; Hu et al., 2011), employees' perceptions of experiencing these behaviors as inappropriate misconduct may vary. For example, abusive supervision measures may not translate into parallel conclusions that one was actually abused because cultures differ in how much they tolerate superiors wielding power in domineering ways (Giorgi et al., 2015; Liu & Wang, 2013; Fang et al., 2016; Seo et al., 2012). Similarly, the prevalence of workplace bullying varies depending on whether behavioral measures or self-labeling was used, and the degree of correspondence between these metrics varies across countries. This suggests cultural differences in the understanding of whether specific behaviors should be labeled as bullying (Eurofound, 2016; Nielson & Einarsen, 2018). Thus, parallel behaviors do not carry the same meanings as norm-violating misconduct across cultures, and so targets may not react equivalently. These initial studies on the culturally contingent manifestations and meanings of workplace deviance set the stage for investigations of culture as moderators of targets' reactions to experiencing mistreatment as well as the triggers for enacting deviance, as will be seen below. Before turning to culture as a moderator, I first review studies and theory on how culture may directly influence countries' overall rates of workplace deviance.

Cultures' Prevalence of Workplace Deviance

Two large-scale comparative studies, as well as two theory papers, have built the case for societal culture being directly associated with countries' rates of workplace deviance. Compared to the predominantly exploratory nature of the literature reviewed thus far, scholarship on the cultural determinants of workplace deviance rates is more theoretically developed. Much of the theoretical logic in these papers is seen throughout studies on culture as a moderator as well; thus, they will be reviewed in more depth as a basis for the rest of the literature review.

Irani and Oswald (2009) were the first to theorize how national culture may influence countries' workplace aggression rates. Their paper is also one of the few that bridges psychological theories on what motivates aggressive behavior with cultural frameworks (House et al., 2004; Hofstede, 1980, 2001; Hofstede & Bond, 1988). Specifically, they delineate how aggression may first be understood from the lens of Bandura's (1973) social learning theory as behaviors learned in a social context. Both the theory of reasoned action (Fishbein & Ajzen, 1975) and the theory of planned behavior (Ajzen, 1991) also help us to understand cultural influences on the tendency to enact aggression, as peoples' own behavioral intentions are influenced by how referent others view a given behavior. Irani and Oswald (2009) use these psychological theories to explain how employees' personal tendencies toward aggression are influenced by cultural values in the sociocultural context because of internalized societal expectations and behavior modeling. For power distance, they theorize that the inequality of opportunity leads to frustration among less powerful members, but upward expression of aggression is forbidden so that employees will engage in peer-directed aggression; this will be coupled with high rates of supervisory aggression (cf. Seo et al., 2012). Irani and Oswald's (2009) arguments for individualism propose a straightforward relationship between high individualism and aggressive behavior, given individualists' tendencies to stand up for themselves and lower concerns for group harmony and goals. Cultural masculinity is also proposed to have a direct positive relation to workplace aggression due to the lower emphasis on positive interpersonal relations in these cultures. Finally, they argue that uncertainty avoidance will also be positively related, as Hofstede (1980) characterized these cultures as being aggressive. However, because of an intolerance toward risk, they will manifest as covert acts. Some of the theoretical tenets from Irani and Oswald (2009) have been supported, whereas others are less consistent with the evidence reviewed below.

In their theory paper on culture and workplace bullying, Jacobson and colleagues (2014) drew from the GLOBE framework (House et al., 2004) and focused specifically on three cultural dimensions that they argued would be most salient for understanding workplace bullying: (1) assertiveness, (2) power distance, and (3) ingroup collectivism. For assertiveness, which refers to a cultural tendency to be tough, dominant, and aggressive in social relationships (House et al., 1999), they argued for a direct positive relationship with societal prevalence rates of workplace bullying. Their theoretical arguments for individualism–collectivism were more nuanced than Irani and Oswald (2009) in that they clarified the focus on ingroup collectivism, which refers to the degree to which individuals express pride, loyalty, and cohesiveness within their organizations, families, and circles of friends. They assert that ingroup collectivism should be associated with lower levels of bullying and that bullying will take more covert (versus overt) forms and be more group-based in collectivistic societies (cf. Seo et al., 2012). Finally, arguments for power distance largely mirrored those of Irani and Oswald (2009), with the added specification that bullying will be more overt in high power distance cultures.

Both Van de Vliert et al. (2013) and Power et al. (2013) empirically assessed links between national culture and workplace harassment/bullying, and both are notable for the multinational scope of the research (44 and 14 countries, respectively), measuring cultural values rather than using country as a proxy of culture, and testing theoretical tenets. Power and colleagues (2013) examined the acceptability of both work-related bullying

(WRB) and physically intimidating bullying (PIB) in a comparative study inclusive of six GLOBE country clusters, focused on cultural practice measures (i.e., actual values held by cultures rather than aspirational values; House et al., 2004). They theorized that three cultural practice dimensions are most aligned with bullying behaviors: humane orientation, performance orientation, and future orientation. Their results showed that performance orientation (i.e., being highly results-driven) was positively associated with the acceptability of both WRB and PIB. Future orientation (i.e., focusing on the future, valuing long-term relationships) was negatively associated with both types of bullying. Humane orientation (i.e., valuing kindness, caring, fairness) was only negatively associated with the acceptability of WRB. They further compared six GLOBE cultural clusters and discovered that Confucian Asia is significantly higher than other country clusters (e.g., Latin America, sub-Saharan Africa) on the acceptability of both WRB and PIB, which they argued is due to the comparatively strong performance orientation in that country cluster. Interestingly, the Anglo cluster and the Confucian Asia cluster were non-significantly different on all three cultural values but there was significantly less acceptance of bullying in Anglo cultures, perhaps due to their strong fairness concerns.

To this point, theory and research have adopted a cultural values approach to studying cross-cultural differences, but Van de Vliert et al. (2013) offered and tested the climato-economic explanation of culture as a viable alternative. The climato-economic explanation of culture (Van de Vliert, 2009) posits that threatening climatic demands, coupled with poor national income resources, results in environments that focus on survival and threats. Consistent with the logic of displaced aggression (Neuman & Baron, 2011), people in such difficult environments are likely to lash out at others as a manifestation of their frustrations in coping with hardships. The results of their 44-nation comparative study support this hypothesis. Indeed, the interaction of climatic demands and national wealth accounted for 13% of the cross-national variation in severe forms of workplace harassment such as physical abuse or violence. Van de Vliert and colleagues (2013) examined power distance as well as alternative economic indicators as rival hypotheses and concluded that "cultural power distance . . . did not account for any variation in employee harassment, let alone reduce its climato-economic covariation" (p. 114). Thus, contrary to the theorizing above, this empirical test found no support for a relationship between power distance and country rates of workplace harassment. This evidence in support of a climato-economic basis for aggression, rather than cultural values, is compelling and suggests that researchers should dedicate far greater attention to countries' environmental, economic, and socio-structural characteristics as key determinants of workplace deviance (cf. Motsei & Nkomo, 2016), a point to which I return in the section on future directions.

Cultural Differences in Responses to Being Mistreated

Much of the empirical work on cross-cultural differences in workplace deviance has adopted the target's perspective, exploring how culture may qualify the extent to which targets experience negative outcomes after experiencing bullying, abusive supervision, and/or incivility. Research in this space has adopted a cultural values approach to exploring cross-cultural differences (House et al., 2004; Hofstede, 1980). More specifically, studies can be clustered into those focused on power distance and those focused on individualism-collectivism.

Power Distance as a Qualifier of Target Outcomes. Loh and colleagues (2010) were first to conduct a comparative study of the extent to which target outcomes of workplace bullying are culturally contingent. They reasoned that high power distance cultures accept status differences between bosses and subordinates as the norm, and so targets of bullying in such cultures are less likely to be distressed (Irani & Oswald 2009). Although they did not explicitly measure power distance, instead using country as a proxy, their results supported this logic such that Australian employees targeted with bullying reported stronger negative affect and feelings of alienation than Singaporean employees. In a similar vein, Casimir et al. (2012) found that bullied Australian schoolteachers evidenced higher negative affect and physical symptoms than a comparable sample of schoolteachers in Uganda. Casimir et al. also theorized about power distance but used country as a proxy. Unfortunately, then, this early empirical evidence on workplace bullying presents no direct support that power distance is a reason for culturally contingent outcomes.

Studies on abusive supervision have also theorized that employees in high power distance cultures will be more tolerant of supervisory abuse and thus will be less impaired when they receive it. Vogel and colleagues (2015) presented two comparative studies of Anglo versus Confucian East Asian cultures that support the moderating role of power distance in the relationship between abusive supervision and interpersonal justice, such that the negative effects were stronger for Anglo participants. They also measured power distance in the second study, evidencing that this cultural value was the explanatory mechanism beneath the cultural differences. Two meta-analyses also hypothesized power distance as a moderator of the effects of abusive supervision. This was supported but only tested indirectly by Zhang and Liao (2015) by comparing North American versus Asian countries in their sample. In their meta-analysis, Park et al. (2019) operationalized power distance through Hofstede et al.'s (2010) cultural values measures and found that the negative relationship between abusive supervision and supervisory-focused justice was stronger in low (compared to high) power distance cultures. Finally, although it is not a cross-cultural study, Lian et al. (2012) is frequently cited as presenting evidence on the moderating role of power distance. They found that not only is abusive supervision less likely to be seen as unfair by those who hold high power distance values, such targets are also more likely to mirror that behavior by enacting interpersonal deviance.

Contrary to these studies, one sexual harassment study theorized on how high power distance may lead to more negative reactions for targets of sexual harassment in Pakistan compared to the United States (Merkin & Shah, 2014). Merkin and Shah argue that Pakistan's high power distance, high collectivism, and paternalistic norms make it difficult for working women to report and address sexual harassment, leading to lower job satisfaction, turnover, and absenteeism. Their results (using country as a proxy for culture) were consistent with these arguments, highlighting how culture may not uniformly moderate all types of workplace deviance in the same way.

Collectivism as a Qualifier of Target Outcomes. A second set of studies has focused on the theoretical logic of collectivism qualifying the effects of workplace mistreatment on targets' outcomes. Two early studies outside the workplace domain are relevant in that they theorized on face and face loss in collectivistic cultures, which adds more nuance to the fairly straightforward effects theorized by Irani and Oswald (2009) and Jacobson et al. (2014). Specifically, both Kam and Bond (2008) and Hui and Bond (2009) argued that interpersonal harm may result in loss of face, which is the deterioration of one's social image and is associated with status loss (Brown & Levinson, 1987; Ho, 1976). This is particularly likely to happen in collectivistic East Asian cultures, where maintaining face is a central concern for preserving social harmony (Zane & Yeh, 2002). Both studies compared United States versus Hong Kong Chinese participants' relational responses to loss of face following interpersonal harm, including measures of retaliation and avoidance (Kam & Bond, 2008) and forgiveness (Hui & Bond, 2009). Kam and Bond (2008) showed that Hong Kong Chinese were more likely than Americans to report anger (but not shame) and relationship deterioration following face loss. Surprisingly, Chinese were less likely to retaliate despite their anger, likely because of the direct effect of shame on inhibiting retaliation. They did not directly measure collectivism, but this contribution was offered in Hui and Bond (2009). Their results also showed culturally contingent responses to face loss, but a measure of individuals' interdependent (collectivist) versus independent (individualistic) self-construals (Triandis & Gelfand, 1998) failed to explain this effect. Hui and Bond (2009) concluded that the cultural differences observed in this research cannot be explained by participants' interdependent and independent self-construals, so the collectivism logic was not supported. Instead, they encouraged future research on the moderating role of power distance.

In a comparative study on incivility in China and the United States, Chen et al. (2019) first established measurement equivalence for a new scale and then showed that United States employees' levels of negative affect and job satisfaction were more strongly linked with incivility than were employees in China. They did not measure cultural values but interpreted these findings as being consistent with collectivistic employees' job satisfaction being more influenced by the overall group and organization, rather than their own interpersonal experiences. Ahmad and Kaleem (2020) similarly used country (Australia and Pakistan) as a proxy to test their arguments that employees in collectivistic cultures receive more support from peers when bullied and that these social supports help with coping (Hobfoll et al., 1990). Their results show that both well-being and turnover were more strongly linked with bullying experiences in Australia than in Pakistan.

None of the preceding studies found direct empirical support for the moderating role of collectivism in targets' outcomes, but a study by Chi et al. (2019) does so and helps to clarify the nature of collectivism that is relevant. They argue that in many collectivistic cultures (e.g., China), relational outcomes are determined more by whether one has a concrete relationship with another (i.e., in-relation versus out-relation), rather than having shared membership in abstract groups such as organizations, communities, or countries. Like Liu et al. (2019), Chi et al. assert that collectivism does not guarantee harmony among group members. Instead, group collectivism encourages vigilance toward ingroup members' intentions, which are not always altruistic. As a result, Chi et al. (2019) argue that the more relevant and proximal determinant of people's reactions to offenses in Taiwan is what they label "relational collectivism." They proposed and found that offenses from in-relation others (e.g., friends) elicit significantly fewer negative emotions and subsequent revenge cognitions compared to offenses from out-relation others (e.g., strangers) in Taiwan, but no such differences emerged for United States participants. That is, Taiwan Chinese reacted more harshly to out-relation others after an offense, whereas United States participants showed no such particularism (see also Fulmer & Gelfand, 2015, on the severity of the violation by an in-group member as another key factor). Chi et al. (2019) and Liu et al. (2019) both highlight the importance of carefully considering the specific form of collectivism relevant in the cultural context and not presuming that collectivism equates with harmony.

Summary. We can reach two main conclusions from the preceding studies on culture as a moderator of the relationship between targets' experiences of mistreatment and their outcomes. First, several studies have established that cultural power distance moderates the relationship between abusive supervision and targets' outcomes, particularly supervisory-focused justice perceptions (see also Pandey & Rupp, chapter 9). Evidence on targets' outcomes of workplace bullying (e.g., negative affect, physical symptoms) is also consistent with theoretical arguments for power distance, but scholars have not yet included measures of power distance in research to directly test this. Measuring power distance and demonstrating its explanatory power are important avenues for future research on bullying and related constructs. In future work, it will be helpful to compare sources of mistreatment (e.g., supervisor versus coworker), as power distance arguments are most theoretically aligned with supervisory abuse.

Second, research positing a moderating role of collectivism in targets' outcomes has rarely found support for this argument. Researchers have interpreted cultural differences as being due to collectivism, but without measures of the underlying values, these findings are speculative. One study that measured collectivism found that it did not explain the cultural differences that emerged (Hui & Bond, 2009). Chi et al. (2019) offers the most promising line of inquiry on collectivism, more clearly specifying the nature of the relationship between the perpetrator and target. This more nuanced approach may help to explain when and why collectivists react more strongly to the experience of being mistreated.

Cultural Differences in Enacting Deviance

Cross-cultural research on actors' enactment of workplace deviance is rarer than studies from the target's perspective, but a handful of studies have begun to establish support for cultural contingencies. Liu et al. (2009) represents a rare example of incivility research that focuses on factors that encourage actors to behave in an uncivil manner. Similar to Power and colleagues' (2013) arguments about countries' high performance orientation eliciting greater workplace bullying, Liu et al. (2009) made the case that individual achievement orientation (i.e., the intent to achieve goals that are mainly self-focused) has a similar positive relationship with the tendency to enact incivility. They further argued that this individual tendency to enact incivility will be tempered by collectivism. Results of a comparative study in Taiwan and the United States, in which they measured collectivism, fully supported these arguments. Grijalva and Neuman's (2015) meta-analysis on narcissism and enacting CWB also provided support for collectivism attenuating individual tendencies toward misbehavior. Specifically, their second study on an international convenience sample showed that the relationship between narcissism and CWB was only positive in countries with low ingroup collectivism (as operationalized through country scores from the GLOBE study; Gelfand et al., 2004).

The remaining work on culture and the enactment of deviance is more fragmented but deserves mention. Menard et al. (2011) found that the relationship between organizational commitment and enacting psychological/physical violence was moderated by country (Canada vs. Belgium), where only Belgian employees' misconduct was attenuated when commitment was high. They interpret these findings to be consistent with both power distance and uncertainty avoidance; the latter is interesting as theory about uncertainty, and norm compliance is rare in the extant literature. Shkoler et al. (2019) tested a model of leader–member exchange (LMX) and team member exchange (TMX) as antecedents to CWB via one study in Israel and the other in the United States (i.e., noncomparable samples). They found that envy moderated relationships between LMX/TMX and CWB in the United States sample but not in the Israeli sample. They speculated that the combination of Israel's collectivism and lower power distance encourages direct, informal, and highly expressive communication, and because of this, the quality of relationships is not as important. Finally, a rich study by Zoogah and Zoogah (2020) delved into determinants of negative deviant behavior (NDB; e.g., coercion, theft, bribery, manipulation to extract property) in Ghana and Botswana. They proposed ethnos oblige theory, arguing that cultural values of benevolence toward one's ethnic group encourages (and indeed obligates) employees to enact NDB as a means to increase ingroup benefits and resources. Their results support the logic that in both countries, when individuals anticipate that others are depending on them, they are more likely to engage in NDBs as a way to enhance their careers and become better providers.

The first conclusion apparent from reviewing the literature on culture and enacting deviance is that comparative research on this topic is rare; future theory and research on cross-cultural differences in enacting workplace deviance are sorely needed. Nonetheless, one finding is consistent across two studies thus far. Specifically, ingroup collectivism appears to dampen individuals' personal tendencies toward enacting CWB and incivility, which is logically coherent as these deviant acts can be construed as selfish acts for personal gain. The additional studies in this area represent compelling initial lines of inquiry in need of future development.

Discussion and Future Research Directions

The first research and theory on culture and workplace deviance appeared less than 15 years ago but it is now a flourishing area of scholarship with dozens of papers published. This progress is notable given the logistical and ethical challenges of conducting research on workplace deviance in one culture, let alone across multiple cultures (cf., Bond, 2004). The pace of research has been facilitated in large part by evidence that several popular measures of mistreatment are cross-culturally generalizable, coupled with strong interest in this topic among scholars globally. The key findings in this body of work were summarized at the end of each section in this review, but it is also helpful to synthesize those findings into a set of five core theoretical implications (see Table 11.1).

The methodological sophistication of research on culture and deviance is also improving. Many authors are now including tests of measurement equivalence before testing

Table 11.1 Summary of key theoretical implications for culture and workplace deviance
1. The structure of organizational deviance constructs examined so far has universal elements, but the specific behavioral manifestations and underlying dimensionality are culturally nuanced. Differences in dimensionality are associated with cultural values, especially power distance, humane orientation, in-group collectivism, and future orientation.
2. Cultural logics of honor, dignity, and face influence the nature of deviance and reactions to being targeted. Honor cultures are especially concerned about upholding politeness and avoiding social damage, but face loss in face cultures also results in higher anger and retaliation cognitions than in dignity cultures. Retaliation against offenders in honor cultures is normatively accepted. Expectations of fair and dignified treatment apply to all relationships in honor cultures; supervisors are not given more leeway to behave in abusive ways.
3. Confucian virtues in East Asian cultures may encourage greater tolerance for and normative acceptance of workplace mistreatment from supervisors. Even when mistreatment comes from colleagues, the virtues teach acceptance and tempering one's own reactions to adverse experiences to avoid behaving in a shameful way. This is particularly true when mistreatment comes from relationally close others.
4. Cultural values are directly linked with cultures' acceptance of bullying (i.e., performance orientation, future orientation, humane orientation). They also attenuate targets' responses to abusive supervision (i.e., power distance) as well as dispositional tendencies toward enacting incivility and CWB (i.e., collectivism).
5. Countries' climate and wealth predict levels of workplace harassment above and beyond cultural values. Theory and research on the ecological, economic, and socio-structural determinants of workplace deviance across cultures is sorely needed.

hypotheses, albeit invariance does not rule out construct deficiency (Gelfand et al., 2002). A combined emic-etic approach may be preferable if the focal aim is to unpack the nature of the phenomenon globally (see Salin et al., 2019, for an example). Scholars are also beginning to move beyond using country as a proxy for culture by including measures of theorized cultural mechanisms as part of their study design (e.g., Chi et al., 2019) or using country values from established frameworks such as GLOBE (e.g., Park et al., 2019; Power et al., 2013). This trend should continue, as country differences can be due to any number of cultural, structural, economic, or ecological differences (cf. Van de Vliert et al., 2013). Another sign of methodological advancement is the appearance of larger multinational studies published by teams of global collaborators (e.g., Power et al., 2013; Salin et al., 2019). Such larger-scale studies enable more complete tests of hypotheses and rule out idiosyncratic differences between countries that threaten the validity of inferences drawn from two-country comparisons (Gelfand et al., 2002). Theoretical sampling of countries is rarely discussed in this literature, but Power et al. (2013) and Salin et al. (2019) had very diverse samples, enabling comparisons of GLOBE country clusters. Finally, research on culture and deviance has already emerged in world regions that have historically been underrepresented in organizational scholarship (e.g., Latin America: Escartin et al., 2011; sub-Saharan Africa: Zoogah & Zoogah, 2020). This suggests a truly global interest in this important topic, which bodes well for building multinational research teams.

With regard to future directions, one important area for future scholars to attend to more closely is building theoretical arguments that bridge cultural theories with theories of human aggression and/or deviance. Theorizing in this literature is "light," consisting largely of descriptions of cultural frameworks to justify cultural contingencies in already established relationships. What is needed is better theoretical coherence between theory on how/why people behave in deviant ways or react to mistreatment in particular ways (i.e., theory of the phenomenon) and cultural theory. For example, Bandura's social learning theory provides an explanatory framework for how aggression emerges (Irani & Oswald, 2009); this theory of the phenomenon can be coupled with theory on power distance, for example, to explain the conditions under which aggression will be modeled and against whom in certain cultures (cf., Lian et al., 2012). Another example is Samnani's (2013) theoretical framework that bridged Festinger's (1957) cognitive consistency theory with cultural theory to explain how bullying can become prolonged, depending on the targets' culturally-influenced resistance responses. Several scholars have called for better theorizing and have offered suggestions of related literatures that may help to better frame the phenomenon, its antecedents and consequences (e.g., Bond, 2004; Nielsen & Einarsen, 2018;). Promising, more theoretically rich literatures from which to draw include those on human aggression (e.g., Tedeschi & Felson, 1994), conflict in organizations (e.g., Raver & Barling, 2008), organizational justice (Pandey & Rupp, chapter 9), and intergroup relations (e.g., Argyle et al., 1986; Tajfel, 1974).

Another important direction for future research is to move beyond solely focusing on Hofstede (1980, 2001) and/or GLOBE (House et al., 2004) dimensions of cultural values as the basis for understanding cultural differences. Studying cultural differences has become nearly synonymous with studying cultural values. However, solely operationalizing culture as values risks a subjectivist bias, where culture is reduced to something inside people's heads (Gabrenya, 1999; Georgas & Berry; 1995). What is needed is work that adopts a structuralist view, understanding culture as a larger set of social structures, norms, and institutions that emerge as adaptations to a particular ecological milieu and history. Only a handful of papers in the current literature review explicitly reviewed or theorized on such structural societal factors (Amin & Darrag, 2011; Knapp et al., 2019; Motsei & Nkomo, 2016; Van de Vliert et al., 2013); more work on the structural characteristics of cultures is needed. Examining deviance as a function of cultural tightness–looseness (i.e., the strength of norms and sanctioning of deviant behavior), which was developed through a structuralist lens (Gelfand et al., 2006; 2011), is an especially promising future direction for workplace deviance research. The construct specifically focuses on the degree to which cultures constrain deviant behavior, so it should be directly relevant to rates of workplace deviance cross-culturally, as well as outcomes experienced by those who act in deviant ways.

The prior discussion hints at another important future direction, namely, the development of theory and larger-scale studies on the enactment of workplace deviance cross-culturally. There is a curious imbalance within the comparative literature, such that studies on targets' experiences of being mistreated with deviance are fourfold greater in number than studies on employees enacting deviance. Theories have not yet been published on cultural differences in the dispositions, motives, experiences, or perceptions that motivate employees to act deviantly, so this is an area ripe for discovery. With that said, much of the literature on motives for enacting deviance shares conceptual similarities with the literature on reactions to organizational (in)justice, as deviance is a common dependent variable used in that research. Thus, conceptual and empirical integration with justice research might be a viable path forward (Pandey & Rupp, chapter 9). Larger-scale research on dispositional antecedents to enacting deviance is also needed, especially in light of the promising findings on collectivism attenuating this relationship.

Finally, comparative research is needed on a broader array of workplace deviance constructs as the literature is currently dominated by studies on bullying, abusive supervision, and to a lesser extent, incivility and sexual harassment. For example, ostracism is a newer addition to scholarship on workplace deviance (Ferris et al., 2008) and has not yet been the focus of cross-cultural research. Given Salin and colleagues' (2019) finding that social exclusion is only part of the workplace bullying experience in some cultures, coupled with evidence on how social exclusion is part of the damage to self-worth in honor cultures (Severance et al., 2013), ostracism should evidence culturally contingent nomological networks. Comparative studies that examine both minor (e.g., incivility) and severe (e.g., bullying) forms of workplace deviance would also be beneficial. From the actor's perspective, it is surprising to see the absence of culture studies, looking at both interpersonally and organizationally directed CWB in conjunction. These are just a few examples of constructs and dilemmas that are popular in the larger domestic workplace deviance literature that could be explored from a cross-cultural perspective. My hope is that this synthesis helps to inspire a proliferation of new research on culture and deviance.

Practical Implications and Conclusion

Scholarly interest in workplace deviance (especially bullying) emerged from practitioners' increased recognition of the harm caused to targets of mistreatment (e.g., Leymann, 1996). Policy and law experts drew from scholarly evidence that documented the nature of the problem and advocated for organizational and legal policies to prevent workplace mistreatment (e.g., O'Rourke & Antioch, 2016). As a result, many countries (e.g., Australia, Belgium, Canada, Finland, France, Germany, the Netherlands, Norway, Sweden, Turkey, and the United Kingdom) have anti-bullying or anti-harassment legislation in place to forbid these behaviors and to better protect workers (Lippel, 2010). Nonetheless, the problem still persists. For example, a large-scale study of Europeans surveyed about their prior month at work indicated that, on average, 11% experienced verbal abuse, 6% endured humiliating behavior, and 4% were threatened (Eurofound, 2016). Organizational leaders and practitioners are also deeply concerned about organizationally-targeted misconduct such as sabotage, reputational harm, theft, and fraud, and they often aim to instill better behavior through ethics training and codes of conduct (e.g., Chen et al., 2018). Interest in this topic is truly global, and yet the phenomenon is not identical around the world, as we have seen in this chapter. For multinational firms and others working with multinational populations, many of the findings described in this chapter may help our understanding of intercultural challenges and inconsistencies. A summary of the practical implications is provided in Table 11.2 and is discussed further below.

From a practical perspective, it is first important to note that the actual behaviors that employees consider to be workplace mistreatment are not identical globally (e.g., Salin et al., 2019; Severance et al., 2013). This can lead to intercultural misunderstandings and difficulties with implementing employee codes of conduct or disciplinary tools across more than one cultural group. Rather than putting in place codes of conduct against specific behaviors, it may be better to describe workplace mistreatment as consisting of several dimensions of misconduct, coupled with country-specific (and organization-specific) behavioral examples. These are akin to "themes" that characterize the types of misconduct you may see and want to highlight as inappropriate. First, these behaviors can be characterized based on whether the organization or individual(s) were targeted. The organizational versus interpersonal dimension of workplace deviance has been strongly supported universally, so most corporate policies should address both types of misconduct. For anti-bullying or anti-harassment policies, further specification of the types of behavior can

Table 11.2 Summary of practical implications for culture and workplace deviance
1. Organizational deviance is frequently reported around the world, and employees can direct this misbehavior at either the organizations or interpersonally. When other employees experience this mistreatment, the behaviors they endure can universally be characterized as (1) personal versus work-directed, (2) verbal versus physical, and (3) direct versus indirect. Organizational policies and codes of conduct should provide country-relevant behavioral examples for each of these dimensions of mistreatment.
2. Several manifestations of mistreatment are not evaluated the same way across cultures. Social exclusion may be strongly perceived as damage to self-worth in honor cultures, more than elsewhere. Concerns about morality and respect are more likely to be considered damage to self-worth in face cultures. Infringements on personal resources are more likely to be considered aggressive in dignity cultures.
3. Countries are not equally likely to hear reports of supervisors versus coworkers as sources of mistreatment. Abusive supervision is more likely in high power distance countries, but ironically, it is more tolerated and less harmful to targets in such countries. It may be underreported in high power distance cultures, but it should not be presumed to not exist. Targets are still harmed and likely to turn over even if they do not report it.
4. The etiology and harm to bullying targets are very similar across cultures, but countries' legal environments affect the recourses available to targets of mistreatment and their expectations for treatment. Multinational firms are advised to implement codes of conduct that adopt the most stringent country's legal standards when using global virtual teams.
5. Cultures with a high performance orientation are more likely to have employees who are bullied. Likewise, individuals with a strong achievement orientation and narcissists are more likely to harm others and the organization. Pushing toward higher and higher achievement is linked with higher workplace deviance.

be characterized as (1) personal versus work-directed, (2) verbal versus physical, and (3) direct versus indirect. Behavioral examples of these dimensions should make clear that someone can be bullied through repeated harsh criticism of one's work, through only verbal remarks, and through covertly harming someone behind their back. Multinational firms should be clear in providing examples in their policies or codes of conduct that fit each of these more universal dimensions of mistreatment, in addition to incorporating culture-specific forms.

It is also important for scholars to recognize in their policy work and training that several manifestations of mistreatment are not evaluated in the same way across cultures. Intercultural conflicts and misunderstandings may be especially likely to occur when employees' underlying considerations of what constitutes a threat to self-worth are not the same (e.g., Severance et al., 2013). Specifically, social exclusion and reputational threats may be most strongly perceived as damage to self-worth in honor cultures, leading to retaliation and severe conflict escalation. Those from face culture are more likely than others to be deeply concerned about morality and respect, whereas those people from dignity cultures are more likely than others to be concerned about others infringing on their personal resources or spaces at work. For mediators and other conflict resolution practitioners, this knowledge may be particularly helpful in being able to intervene and de-escalate workplace conflicts where people from divergent cultures may have had no idea of the cultural meanings attached to their offensive behavior.

Another practical implication pertains to the reported prevalence of abusive supervision cross-culturally. If cross-national surveys show that employees in high power distance cultures report lower levels of workplace mistreatment from supervisors, that result should be interpreted with caution. The results of studies in this literature review have consistently shown that people in high power distance cultures are more likely to tolerate abuse from supervisors. They report less severe outcomes than those in low power distance cultures, but they still do experience harm. Targets in high power distance cultures often have to suffer silently, comforted slightly by the normative nature of abusive supervision. If multinational firms aim to put in place anti-bullying and anti-harassment policies globally, they may need to exert extra effort toward educating managers in high power distance cultures about better leadership styles, coupled with providing additional resources and anonymous reporting channels for victims.

Even though the sources of workplace mistreatment may vary cross-culturally, the etiology of how it is triggered by individual and situational forces and the harm it causes is very similar across countries (D'Cruz et al., 2016). Countries differ remarkably in their legal and policy environments, which means that targets of bullying in one country are often operating under a far more supportive legislative environment than targets in a different country. This issue can become very challenging in multinational firms, particularly with the rise of global virtual teams. If employees in one country are supported by anti-bullying legislation, whereas those in a different country are not but they work on a global team together, this can pose challenges for disciplinary and legal action. In multinational firms using global virtual teams, members of such teams may be operating with very different expectations for fair and respectful treatment, as influenced by their local legal frameworks against mistreatment. It would be advisable for such firms to implement anti-harassment or anti-bullying policies and codes of conduct that adopt the most stringent country's legal standards.

A final practical implication stemming from this review is the importance of performance orientation and/or achievement orientation in workplace mistreatment. Performance pressure is not universally accepted. Those from highly performance-oriented cultures exhibit behaviors that they may think are motivating or goal-directed, but they may be perceived by others as pushy, overly harsh, aggressive, or coercive. This tendency may be further amplified by personality, such that highly achievement-oriented individuals are more likely to enact deviance. This too can lead to conflicts on multicultural teams and can be the source of bullying complaints in which the "perpetrator" is deeply confused about why they were accused. Multinational firms should encourage leaders in performance-oriented cultures to be clear about work expectations while also tempering the urge to push people toward ever higher achievement or overwork.

With this comprehensive review, I have had the opportunity to integrate the extant scholarship on workplace deviance and related constructs with the aims of building knowledge synthesis, stimulating future research on this important phenomenon, and helping multicultural organizations better manage deviance. The amount of knowledge accumulated in recent years is substantial, and scholars can now draw from this synthesized knowledge base in their future work. I look forward to reading the next decade of improved theory and research on the cross-cultural and culture-specific meanings, antecedents, and outcomes of workplace deviance.

References

Ahmad, S. (2018). Can ethical leadership inhibit workplace bullying across East and West: Exploring cross-cultural interactional justice as a mediating mechanism, *European Management Journal, 36*(2), 223–234.

Ahmad, S., & Kaleem, A. (2020). Zooming in on the workplace bullying and turnover intentions pathway: The role of well-being and a cultural boundary condition. *Personnel Review, 49*(2), 425–444.

Ajzen, I. (1991). The theory of planned behavior. *Organizational Behavior and Human Decision Processes, 50*, 179–211.

Amin, A., & Darrag, M. S. (2011). Sexual harassment in the Egyptian workplace: A literature review and research agenda. *Review of Management, 1*, 25–38.

Andersson, L. M., & Pearson, C. M. (1999). Tit for tat? The spiraling effect of incivility in the workplace. *Academy of Management Review, 24*, 452–471.

Argyle, M., Henderson, M., Bond, M. H., Iizuka, Y., & Contarello, A. (1986). Cross-cultural variations in relationship rules. *International Journal of Psychology, 21*, 287–315.

Ashforth, B. E. (1997). Petty tyranny in organizations: A preliminary examination of antecedents and consequences. *Canadian Journal of Administrative Science, 14*, 126–140.

Bandura, A. (1973). *Aggression: A social learning analysis*. Englewood Cliffs, NJ: Prentice-Hall.

Barling, J. (1996). The prediction, psychological experience and consequences of workplace violence. In G. VandenBos & E. G. Bulatao (Eds.), *Violence on the job: Identifying risks and developing solutions* (pp. 29–49). Washington, DC: American Psychological Association.

Bennett, R. J., & Robinson, S. L. (2003). The past, present and future of workplace deviance research. In J. Greenberg (Ed.), *Organizational behavior: The state of the science* (pp. 247–281). Mahwah, NJ: Lawrence Erlbaum.

Berry, J. W. (1969). On cross-cultural comparability. *International Journal of Psychology, 4*, 119–128.

Bies, R. J., Tripp, T. M., & Kramer, R. M. (1997). At the breaking point: Cognitive and social dynamics of revenge in organizations. In R. Giacalone & J. Greenberg (Eds.), *Antisocial behavior in organizations* (pp. 18–36). Thousand Oaks, CA: SAGE.

Bond, M. H. (2004). Culture and aggression: From context to coercion. *Personality and Social Psychology Review, 8*, 62–78.

Bowling, N. A., & Beehr, T. A. (2006). Workplace harassment from the victim's perspective: A theoretical model and meta-analysis. *Journal of Applied Psychology, 91*, 998–1012.

Brown, P., & Levinson, S. C. (1987). *Politeness: Some universals in language usage*. Cambridge: Cambridge University Press.

Casimir, G., McCormack, D., Djurkovic, N., & Nsubuga-Kyobe, A. (2012). Psychosomatic model of workplace bullying: Australian and Ugandan schoolteachers. *Employee Relations, 34*(4), 411–428.

Chen, C., Gotti, G., Kang, T., & Wolfe, M. C. (2018). Corporate codes of ethics, national culture, and earnings discretion: International evidence. *Journal of Business Ethics, 151*, 141–163.

Chen, Y., Wang, Z., Peng, Y., Geimer, J., Sharp, O., & Jex, S. (2019). The multidimensionality of workplace incivility: Cross-cultural evidence. *International Journal of Stress Management, 26*(4), 356–366.

Chi, S.-C. S., Friedman, R. A., Chu, C.-C., & Shih, H.-L. (2019). Chinese acceptance of mistreatment by in-relation offenders can be neutralized by triggering a "group" collectivism perspective. *European Journal of Work and Organizational Psychology, 28*(3), 384–398.

Cortina, L. M., & Wasti, S. A. (2005). Profiles in coping: Responses to sexual harassment across persons, organizations and cultures. *Journal of Applied Psychology, 90*, 182–192.

Coyne, I., Gentile, D., Born, M. P., Ersoy, N. C., & Vakola, M. (2013). The relationship between productive and counterproductive work behaviour across four European countries. *European Journal of Work and Organizational Psychology, 22*(4), 377–389.

D'Cruz, P., Paull, M., Omari, M., & Guneri-Cangarli, B. (2016). Target experiences of workplace bullying: insights from Australia, India and Turkey. *Employee Relations, 38*(5), 805–823.

Duffy, M. K., Ganster, D. C., & Pagon, M. (2002). Social undermining in the workplace. *Academy of Management Journal, 45*, 331–351.

Einarsen, S. (2000). Harassment and bullying at work: A review of the Scandinavian approach. *Aggression and Violent Behaviour: A Review Journal, 4*, 371–401.

Einarsen, S., Hoel, H., & Notelaers, G. (2009). Measuring exposure to bullying and harassment at work: Validity, factor structure and psychometric properties of the Negative Acts Questionnaire-Revised. *Work & Stress, 23*(1), 24–44.

Einarsen, S., Hoel, H., Zapf, D., & Cooper, C. L. (2003), *Bullying and emotional abuse in the workplace: International perspectives in research and practice*. London: Taylor & Francis.

Einarsen, S. V., Hoel, H., Zapf, D., & Cooper, C. L. (2020). *Bullying and harassment in the workplace: Theory, research and practice*. New York: CRC Press.

Einarsen, S., Raykness, B. I., & Matthiesen, S. B. (1994). Bullying and harassment at work and their relationships to work environment quality: An exploratory study. *European Journal of Work and Organizational Psychology, 4*, 381–401.

Escartín, J., Zapf, D., Arrieta, C., & Rodríguez-Carballeira, Á. (2011). Workers' perception of workplace bullying: A cross-cultural study. *European Journal of Work and Organizational Psychology, 20*(2), 178–205.

Eurofound. (2016). *Sixth European Working Conditions Survey—Overview report*. Publications Office of the European Union, Luxembourg.

Fang, L., Huang, S., & Fang, S. (2016). Workplace bullying among nurses in south Taiwan. *Journal of Clinical Nursing, 25*(17-18), 2450–2456.

Ferris, D. L., Brown, D. J., Berry, J. W., & Lian, H. (2008). The development and validation of the workplace ostracism scale. *The Journal of Applied Psychology, 93*, 1348–1366.

Ferris, D. L., Chen, M., & Lim, S. (2017). Comparing and contrasting workplace ostracism and incivility. *Annual Review of Organizational Psychology and Organizational Behavior, 4*, 315–338.

Festinger, L. (1957). *A theory of cognitive dissonance*. Stanford, CA: Stanford University Press.

Fishbein, M., & Ajzen, I. (1975). *Belief, attitude, intention, and behavior: An introduction to theory and research*. Reading, MA: Addison-Wesley.

Fitzgerald, L. F., Drasgow, F., Hulin, C. L., Gelfand, M. J., & Magley, V. J. (1997). Antecedents and consequences of sexual harassment in organizations: A test of an integrated model. *Journal of Applied Psychology, 82*, 578–589.

Fitzgerald, L. F., Shullman, S. L., Bailey, N., Richards, M., Swecker, J., Gold, Y., Ormerod, M., & Weitzman, L. (1988). The incidence and dimensions of sexual harassment in academia and the workplace. *Journal of Vocational Behavior, 32*, 152–175.

Fox, S., & Spector, P. E. (2005). *Counterproductive work behavior: Investigations of actors and targets*. Washington, DC: American Psychological Association.

Fox, S., Spector, P. E., & Miles, D. (2001). Counterproductive work behavior (CWB) in response to job stressors and organizational justice: Some mediator and moderator tests for autonomy and emotions. *Journal of Vocational Behavior, 59*, 291–309.

Fulmer, C. A., & Gelfand, M. J. (2015). Trust after violations: Are collectivists more or less forgiving? *Journal of Trust Research, 5*, 109–131.

Gabreyna, W. (1999). Psychological anthropology and the "levels of analysis" problem: We married the wrong cousins. In J. C. Lasry, J. Adair, & K. Dion (Eds.), *Latest contributions to cross-cultural psychology* (pp. 333–351). Lisse: Swets & Zeitlinger.

Gelfand, M. J., Bhawuk, D. P., Nishii, L. H., & Bechtold, D. J. (2004). Individualism and collectivism. In R. J. House, P. J. Hanges, M. Javidan, P. W. Dorfman, & V. Gupta (Eds.), *Leadership, culture, and organizations: The GLOBE study of 62 societies* (pp. 437–512). Thousand Oaks, CA: SAGE.

Gelfand, M. J., Fitzgerald, L. F., & Drasgow, F. (1995). The structure of sexual harassment: A confirmatory factor analysis across cultures and settings. *Journal of Vocational Behavior, 47*, 164–177.

Gelfand, M. J., Nishii, L. H., & Raver, J. L. (2006). On the nature and importance of cultural tightness-looseness. *Journal of Applied Psychology, 91*(6), 1225–1244.

Gelfand, M. J., Raver, J. L., & Ehrhart, K. H. (2002). Methodological issues in cross-cultural organizational research. In S. G. Rogelberg (Ed.), *Handbook of research methods in industrial and organizational psychology* (pp. 216–246). Malden, MA: Blackwell.

Gelfand, M. J ., Raver, J. L., Nishii, L., Leslie, L. A., Lun, J., Lim, B. C., Duan, L., Almaliach, A., Ang, S., Arnadottir, J., Aycan, Z., Boehnke, K., Boski, P., Cabecinhas, R., Chan, D., Chhokar, J., D'Amato, A., Ferrer, M., Fischlmayr, I. C., . . . Yamaguchi, S. (2011). Differences between tight and loose cultures: A 33-nation study. *Science, 332*(6033), 1100–1104.

Georgas, J., & Berry, J. W. (1995). An ecocultural taxonomy for cross-cultural psychology. *Cross-Cultural Research, 29*, 121–157.

Giacalone, R. A., & Greenberg, J. (1997). *Antisocial behavior in organizations.* Thousand Oaks, CA: SAGE.

Giorgi, G., Leon-Perez, J., & Arenas, A. (2015). Are bullying behaviors tolerated in some cultures? Evidence for a curvilinear relationship between workplace bullying and job satisfaction among Italian workers. *Journal of Business Ethics, 131*(1), 227–237.

Grijalva, E., & Newman, D. A. (2015), Narcissism—CWB Relationship. *Applied Psychology: An International Review, 64*, 93–126.

Gruys, M. L., & Sackett, P. R. (2003). Investigating the dimensionality of counterproductive work behaviour. *International Journal of Selection and Assessment, 11*(1), 30–42.

He, P., Peng, Z., Zhao, H., & Estay, C. (2019). How and when compulsory citizenship behavior leads to employee silence: A moderated mediation model based on moral disengagement and supervisor–subordinate guanxi views. *Journal of Business Ethics*, 155(1), 259–274.

Hershcovis, M. S. (2011). Incivility, social undermining, bullying . . . Oh my! A call to reconcile constructs within workplace aggression research. *Journal of Organizational Behavior, 32*, 499–519.

Hershcovis, M. S., & Reich, T. C. (2013). Integrating workplace aggression research: Relational, contextual, and method considerations. *Journal of Organizational Behavior, 34*, S26–S42.

Ho, D. Y. F. (1976). On the concept of face. *American Journal of Sociology, 81*, 867–884.

Hobfoll, S. E., Freedy, J., Lane, C., & Geller, P. (1990). Conservation of social resources: social support resource theory. *Journal of Social and Personal Relationships, 7*(4), 465–478.

Hofstede, G. H. (1980). *Culture's consequences: International differences in work-related values* (1st ed.). Beverly Hills, CA: SAGE.

Hofstede, G. H. (2001). *Culture's consequences: International differences in work-related values* (2nd ed.). Beverly Hills, CA: SAGE.

Hofstede, G. H., & Bond, M. H. (1988). The Confucius connection: From cultural roots to economic growth. *Organizational Dynamics, 16*(4), 5–21.

Hofstede, G. H., Hofstede, G. J., & Minkov, M. (2010). *Culture and organizations— Software of the mind* (3rd ed.). New York: McGraw Hill Professional.

Hon, A. H. Y., & Lu, L. (2016). When will the trickle-down effect of abusive supervision be alleviated? The moderating roles of power distance and traditional cultures. *Cornell Hospitality Quarterly, 57*(4), 421–433.

House, R., Hanges, P. J., Javidan, M., Dorfman, P. W., & Gupta, V. (2004). *Culture, leadership and organizations: The GLOBE study of 62 societies.* Thousand Oaks, CA: SAGE.

House, R. J., Hanges, P. J., Ruiz-Quintanilla, S. A., Dorfman, P. W., Javidan, M., Dickson, M., Gupta, V. A., & Associates (1999). Cultural influences on leadership and organizations: project GLOBE. In W. H. Mobley, M. J. Gessner, & V. Arnold (Eds.), *Advances in global leadership* (pp. 171–233). Stamford, CT: JAI Press.

Hu, C., Wu, T.-Y., & Wang, Y.-H. (2011). Measurement equivalence/invariance of the abusive supervision measure across workers from Taiwan and the United States. *The Journal of Psychology: Interdisciplinary and Applied, 145*(2), 111–131.

Hui, V. K.-Y., & Bond, M. H. (2009). Target's face loss, motivations, and forgiveness following relational transgression: Comparing Chinese and US cultures. *Journal of Social and Personal Relationships, 26*(2–3), 123–140.

Irani, F. S., & Oswald, S. L. (2009). Workplace aggression: Is national culture a factor? *Business Renaissance Quarterly, 4*(1), 63–89.
Jacobson, K. J., Hood, J. N., & Van Buren, H. J. (2014). Workplace bullying across cultures: A research agenda. *International Journal of Cross-Cultural Management, 14*(1), 47–65.
Javidan, M., Dorfman, P. W., de Luque, M. S., & House, R. J. (2006). In the eye of the beholder: Cross cultural lessons in leadership from project GLOBE. *The Academy of Management Perspectives, 20*, 67–90.
Jennifer, D., Cowie, H., & Ananiadou, K. (2003). Perceptions and experience of workplace bullying in five different working populations. *Aggressive Behavior, 29*(6), 489–496.
Kam, C. C., & Bond, M. H. (2008), Role of emotions and behavioural responses in mediating the impact of face loss on relationship deterioration: Are Chinese more face-sensitive than Americans? *Asian Journal of Social Psychology, 11*, 175–184.
Keashly, L., Harvey, S., & Hunter, S. (1997). Emotional abuse and role state stressors: Relative impact on resident assistants' stress. *Work and Stress, 11*, 35–45.
Kidwell, R. E., Jr., & Martin, C. L. (2005). *Managing organizational deviance.* Thousand Oaks, CA: SAGE.
Knapp, D. E., DuBois, C. L. Z., Hogue, M., Astakhova, M. N., & Faley, R. H. (2019). Russian workers' experiences and perceptions of sexual harassment severity. *The International Journal of Human Resource Management, 30*, 2049–2076.
Lee, D. (1998). An analysis of workplace bullying in the UK. *Personnel Review, 29*(5), 593–610.
Leung, A. K. Y., & Cohen, D. (2011). Within and between-culture variation: Individual differences and the cultural logics of honor, face, and dignity cultures. *Journal of Personality and Social Psychology, 3*, 507–526.
Leymann, H. (1996). The content and development of mobbing at work. *European Journal of Work and Organizational Psychology, 5*, 165–184.
Li, X., & Lim, S. (2017). Cross-cultural differences in workplace aggression. In N. A. Bowling & M. S. Hershcovis (Eds.), *Current perspectives in social and behavioral sciences. Research and theory on workplace aggression* (pp. 245–268). New York: Cambridge University Press.
Lian, H., Ferris, D. L., & Brown, D. J. (2012). Does power distance exacerbate or mitigate the effects of abusive supervision? It depends on the outcome. *Journal of Applied Psychology, 97*(1), 107–123.
Lippel, K. (2010). The law of workplace bullying: An international overview. *Comparative Labor Law & Policy Journal, 32*, 1–13.
Liu, S. S., Morris, M. W., Talhelm, T., & Yang, Q. (2019). Ingroup vigilance in collectivistic cultures. *Proceedings of the National Academy of Sciences,* 116(29), 14538–14546.
Liu, W., Chi, S.-C. S., Friedman, R., & Tsai, M.-H. (2009). Explaining incivility in the workplace: The effects of personality and culture. *Negotiation and Conflict Management Research, 2*(2), 164–184.
Liu, X.-Y., & Wang, J. (2013). Abusive supervision and organizational citizenship behaviour: Is supervisor–subordinate guanxi a mediator? *The International Journal of Human Resource Management, 24*(7), 1471–1489.
Loh, J., Restubog, S. L. D., & Zagenczyk, T. J. (2010). Consequences of workplace bullying on employee identification and satisfaction among Australians and Singaporeans. *Journal of Cross-Cultural Psychology, 41*, 236–252.
Luthar, H. K., & Luthar, V. K. (2007). A theoretical framework explaining cross-cultural sexual harassment: Integrating Hofstede and Schwartz. *Journal of Labor Research, 28*, 169–188.
Luthar, V. K., & Luthar, H. K. (2002). Using Hofstede's cultural dimensions to explain sexually harassing behaviours in an international context. *International Journal of Human Resource Management, 13*, 268–284.
Mackey, J. D., McAllister, C. P., Ellen, B. P., III, & Carson, J. E. (2021). A meta-analysis of interpersonal and organizational workplace deviance research. *Journal of Management, 47*(3), 597–622.
Maitner, A. T., Mackie, D. M., Pauketat, J. V. T., & Smith, E. R. (2017). The impact of culture and identity on emotional reactions to insults. *Journal of Cross-Cultural Psychology, 48*(6), 892–913.
Ménard, J., Brunet, L., Savoie, A., van Daele, A., & Flament, A. (2011). Crossnational deviance in the workplace: Diverging impact of organizational commitment in Canada and Belgium. *European Journal of Work and Organizational Psychology, 20*(2), 266–284.
Meriläinen, M., Käyhkö, K., Kõiv, K., & Sinkkonen, H. M. (2019) Academic bullying among faculty personnel in Estonia and Finland, *Journal of Higher Education Policy and Management, 41*(3), 241–261.
Merkin, R. S. (2008). The impact of sexual harassment on turnover intentions, absenteeism, and job satisfaction: Findings from Argentina, Brazil and Chile. *Journal of International Women's Studies, 10*, 73–91.

Merkin, R. S., & Shah, M. K. (2014). The impact of sexual harassment on job satisfaction, turnover intentions, and absenteeism: Findings from Pakistan compared to the United States. *Springer Plus, 3*, 1–13.

Mikkelsen, E. G., & Einarsen, S. (2002). Relationships between exposure to bullying at work and psychological and psychosomatic health complaints: The role of state negative affectivity and generalized self-efficacy. *Scandinavian Journal of Psychology, 43*, 397–405.

Motsei, N., & Nkomo, S. M. (2016). Antecedents of bullying in the South African workplace: Societal context matters. *Africa Journal of Management, 2*(1), 50–72.

Neuman, J. H., & Baron, R. A. (1998). Workplace violence and workplace aggression: Evidence concerning specific forms, potential causes, and preferred targets. *Journal of Management, 24*, 391–419.

Neuman, J. H., & Baron, R. A. (2011). Social antecedents of bullying: A social interactionist perspective. In S. Einarsen, H. Hoel, D. Zapf, & C. L. Cooper (Eds.), *Bullying and harassment in the workplace: Developments in theory, research and practice* (2nd ed., pp. 201–225). Boca Raton, FL: CRC Press.

Nielsen, M. B., & Einarsen, S. V. (2018). What we know, what we do not know, and what we should and could have known about workplace bullying: An overview of the literature and agenda for future research. *Aggression and Violent Behavior, 42*, 71–83.

Nielsen, M. B., Matthiesen, S. B., & Einarsen, S. (2010). The impact of methodological moderators on prevalence rates of workplace bullying. A meta-analysis. *Journal of Occupational and Organizational Psychology, 83*(4), 955–979.

Nielsen, M. B., Skogstad, A., Matthiesen, S. B., Glaso, L., Aasland, M. S., Notelaers, G., & Einarsen, S. (2009). Prevalence of workplace bullying in Norway: Comparisons across time and estimation methods. *European Journal of Work and Organizational Psychology, 18*, 81–101.

Nisbett, R. E., & Cohen, D. (1996). *Culture of honor: The psychology of violence in the South.* Boulder, CO: Westview Press.

O'Leary-Kelly, A. M., Duffy, M. K., & Griffin, R. W. (2000). Construct confusion in the study of antisocial work behavior. *Research in Personnel and Human Resources Management, 18*, 275–303.

O'Rourke, A., & Antioch, S. K. (2016). Workplace bullying laws in Australia: Placebo or panacea? *Common Law World Review, 45*(1), 3–26.

Park, H., Hoobler, J. M., Wu, J., Liden, R. C., Hu, J., & Wilson, M. S. (2019). Abusive supervision and employee deviance: A multifoci justice perspective. *Journal of Business Ethics, 158*(4), 1113–1131.

Power, J. L., Brotheridge, C. M., Blenkinsopp, J., Bowes-Sperry, L., Bozionelos, N., Buzády, Z., . . . & Ugochukwu Obiajulu Nnedumm, A. (2013). Acceptability of workplace bullying: A comparative study on six continents. *Journal of Business Research, 66*(3), 374–380.

Raver, J. L., & Barling, J. (2008). Workplace aggression and conflict: Constructs, commonalities, and challenges for future inquiry. In C. K. W. De Dreu & M. J. Gelfand (Eds.), *The psychology of conflict and conflict management in organizations* (pp. 211–244). Mahwah, NJ: Lawrence Erlbaum.

Resch, M., & Schubinski, M. (1996). Mobbing: Prevention and management in organizations. *European Journal of Work and Organizational Psychology, 5*, 295–307.

Robinson, S. L., & Bennett, R. J. (1995). A typology of deviant workplace behaviors: A multidimensional scaling study. *Academy of Management Journal, 38*, 555–572.

Robinson, S. L., & Greenberg, J. (1998). Employees behaving badly: Dimensions, determinants and dilemmas in the study of workplace deviance. In D. M. Rousseau & C. Cooper (Eds.), *Trends in organizational behavior* (Vol. 5, pp. 1–23). New York: John Wiley.

Robinson, S. L., Wang, W., & Kiewitz, C. (2017). Coworkers behaving badly: The impact of coworker deviant behavior upon individual employees. *Annual Review of Organizational Psychology and Organizational Behavior, 1*, 123–143.

Rotundo, M., & Xie, J. L. (2008). Understanding the domain of counterproductive work behaviour in China. *The International Journal of Human Resource Management, 19*(5), 856–877.

Salin, D. (2003). Ways of explaining workplace bullying: A review of enabling, motivating and precipitating structures and processes in the work environment. *Human Relations, 56*, 1213–1232.

Salin, D., Cowan, R., Adewumi, O., Apospori, E., Bochantin, J., D'Cruz, P., Djurkovic, N., Durniat, K., Escartín, J., Guo, J., Išik, I., Koeszegi, S. T., McCormack, D., Monserrat, S. I., & Zedlacher, E. (2019). Workplace bullying across the globe: a cross-cultural comparison. *Personnel Review, 48*(1), 204–219.

Samnani, A. K. (2013) The early stages of workplace bullying and how it becomes prolonged: The role of culture in predicting target responses. *Journal of Business Ethics, 113*, 119.

Schilpzand, P., De Pater, I. E., & Erez, A. (2016). Workplace incivility: A review of the literature and agenda for future research. *Journal of Organizational Behavior, 37*, S57–S88.

Seo, Y. N., Leather, P., & Coyne, I. (2012), South Korean culture and history: The implications for workplace bullying, *Aggression and Violent Behavior, 17*(5), 419–422.

Severance, L., Bui-Wrzosinska, L., Gelfand, M. J., Lyons, S., Nowak, A., Borkowski, W., Soomro, N., Soomro, N., Rafaeli, A., Treister, D. E., Lin, C.-C., & Yamaguchi, S. (2013). The psychological structure of aggression across cultures. *Journal of Organizational Behavior, 34*(6), 835–865.

Sheehan, M., Barker, M., & Rayner, C. (1999). Applying strategies for dealing with workplace bullying. *International Journal of Manpower, 20*, 50–56.

Shkoler, O., Rabenu, E., Tabak, F., & Lebron, M. J. (2019). Leader- and team-member exchanges and their relationships with organizational and interpersonal counterproductive work behaviors: Moderation by envy and group size in Israel and USA. *Journal of Work and Organizational Psychology, 35*(3), 145–156.

Sigal, J., Gibbs, M. S., Goodrich, C., Rashid, T., Anjum, A., Hsu, D., Perrino, C. S., Boratav, H. B., Carson-Arenas, A., van Baarsen, B., van der Pligt, J., & Pan, W. K. (2005). Cross-cultural reactions to academic sexual harassment: Effects of individualist vs. collectivist culture and gender of participants. *Sex Roles, 52*, 201–215.

Skarlicki, D. P., & Folger, R. (1997). Retaliation in the workplace: The roles of distributive, procedural, and interactional justice. *Journal of Applied Psychology, 82*, 434–443.

Spector, P. E., & Fox, S. (2005). *Counterproductive workplace behavior: Investigations of actors and targets*. Washington, DC: American Psychological Association.

Tajfel, H. (1974). Social identity and intergroup behaviour. *Social Science Information/sur les sciences sociales, 13*(2), 65–93.

Tedeschi, J. T., & Felson, R. B. (1994). *Violence, aggression, and coercive actions*. Washington, DC: American Psychological Association.

Tepper, B. J. (2000). Consequences of abusive supervision. *Academy of Management Journal, 43*, 178–190.

Toker, Y. (2016). Perception differences in ambiguous forms of workplace sexual harassment: A comparison between the United States and Turkey. *The Journal of Psychology, 150*, 625–643.

Triandis, H. C. (1994). *Culture and social behavior*. New York: McGraw-Hill.

Triandis, H. C., & Gelfand, M. J. (1998). Converging measurement of horizontal and vertical individualism and collectivism. *Journal of Personality and Social Psychology, 74*, 118–128.

Triandis, H. C., & Triandis, L. M. (1962). A cross-cultural study of social distance. *Psychological Monographs: General and Applied, 76*, 21.

Van de Vliert, E. (2009). *Climate, affluence, and culture*. New York: Cambridge University Press.

Van de Vliert, E., Einarsen, S., & Nielsen, S. B. (2013). Are national levels of employee harassment cultural covariations of climato-economic conditions? *Work and Stress, 27*(1), 106–122.

Vardi, Y., & Wiener, Y. (1996). Misbehavior in organizations: A motivational framework. *Organization Science, 7*, 151–165.

Vogel, R. M., Mitchell, M. S., Tepper, B. J., Restubog, S. L. D., Hu, H., Hua, W., & Huang, J-C. (2015). A cross-cultural examination of subordinates' perceptions of and reactions to abusive supervision. *Journal of Organizational Behavior, 36*, 720–745.

Wasti, S. A., Bergman, M. E., Glomb, T. M., & Drasgow, F. (2000). Test of the cross-cultural generalizability of a model of sexual harassment. *Journal of Applied Psychology, 85*, 766–778.

Wasti, S. A., & Cortina, L. M. (2002). Coping in context: Sociocultural determinants of responses to sexual harassment. *Journal of Personality and Social Psychology, 83*, 394–405.

Wasti, S. A., & Erdaş, K. D. (2019). The construal of workplace incivility in honor cultures: Evidence from Turkey. *Journal of Cross-Cultural Psychology, 50*(1), 130–148.

Yeung, A., & Griffin, B. (2008). Workplace incivility: Does it matter in Asia? *People and Strategy, 31*, 14–19.

Zane, N., & Yeh, M. (2002). The use of culturally-based variables in assessment: Studies on loss of face. In K. S. Kurasaki, S. Okazaki, & S. Sue (Eds.), *Asian American mental health: assessment theories and methods* (pp. 123–138). New York: Kluwer Academic/Plenum Publishers.

Zapf, D., Knorz, C., & Kulla, M. (1996). On the relationship between mobbing factors, and job content, social work environment, and health outcomes. *European Journal of Work and Organizational Psychology, 5*, 215–237.

Zhang, Y., & Liao, Z. (2015). Consequences of abusive supervision: A meta-analytic review. *Asian Pacific Journal of Management, 32*, 959–987.

Zheng, W., Wu, Y.-C. J., Chen, X., & Lin, S.-J. (2017). Why do employees have counterproductive work behavior? The role of founder's Machiavellianism and the corporate culture in China. *Management Decision, 55*(3), 563–578.

Zoogah, D. B., & Zoogah, R. B. (2020. Benevolence and negative deviant behavior in Africa: The moderating role of centralization. *Journal of Business Ethics, 161*, 783–813.

CHAPTER

12 Occupational Stress in the Global World

Paul E. Spector

Abstract

The study of occupational stress had its beginning primarily in Scandinavia and Northern Europe and has only recently spread to the rest of the world. This chapter summarizes research that addresses cross-cultural and cross-national (CC/CN) occupational stress research. It begins with a discussion of typical design approaches, specifically collecting data in one country; collecting data in two or more countries, which allows comparisons of means and correlations; collecting data in multiple countries and analyzing at the country level (i.e., country means); and multilevel studies that analyze data at both the person and country level. Some studies use country as a proxy for culture (cross-national), whereas others include a cultural variable (cross-cultural). A review of the CC/CN literature found 32 studies. This literature is fragmented, making it difficult to draw firm conclusions. The review showed that even with rigorous backtranslation procedures, instruments do not always maintain psychometric properties. People in individualistic societies report higher levels of well-being, and stronger stressor-strain relationships. The same occupational stressor can manifest itself differently across countries.

Key Words: cross-cultural, cross-national, emotional labor, measurement invariance, occupational stress, scale development

The study of occupational stress began in earnest in the 1980s primarily in Scandinavian Europe. The cultural values of the region emphasized people's health and well-being, and perhaps no domain of life has more impact on people than the workplace. In the ensuing decades, the study of occupational health spread throughout the Western world and North America, and then to Eastern societies such as China, as concerns about employee health and wellness took hold. Most of that research was conducted in single countries, with little attention paid to culture or nationality, but a growing number of researchers have been exploring stress from a broader perspective. My purpose in this chapter is to take a global perspective on the issue of occupational stress, summarizing what the academic research literature has revealed so far with a particular focus on the past decade.

The Nature of Occupational Stress

Occupational stress is the study of environmental and social conditions at work (stressors) that lead to adverse behavioral, physical, and psychological effects (strains). Many working conditions can serve as stressors, but a relatively small number have received much research attention. Some stressors are related to tasks, such as role ambiguity, role conflict, and work overload (Katz & Kahn, 1978). Other stressors are related to the social environment, such as abuse and harassment (Brown et al., 2011). Job stressors have been associated with strain responses that can be immediate, such as emotional reactions, or cumulative, such as stress-related illnesses.

A common framework used to consider the connection between stressful conditions at work and strains is the transactional stress model (Lazarus, 1991). According to this model, environmental conditions and events are perceived and appraised by employees. The immediate primary appraisal determines if the condition or event is threatening. If so, secondary appraisal is an analysis of the best means of coping with the stressor. The individual might decide to use a problem-solving approach to constructively handle the stressor, for example, asking a coworker to help if there is too much work to do. Alternately, the person might decide to use an emotion-focused approach to deal with the strain. This could be through escaping the situation by leaving work early or by engaging in a relaxing activity, such as having a drink with a colleague after work.

Two additional elements have been suggested as potential buffers of stressor effects on strains: control and social support. Control is the degree to which an employee can determine how, when, and where a job is performed. When an employee has control over a situation, problem-focused approaches will appear more feasible. The control-demand model suggests that control will buffer the stressor-strain relationship so that under high control, there will be less of a detrimental effect of stressors (Karasek, 1979). However, although there is evidence that control relates directly to strains (Spector, 1986), tests of the moderating effect have been inconsistent (de Lange, Taris, Kompier, Houtman, & Bongers, 2003).

Social support is the extent to which an employee can rely on others for help. It can be instrumental support that helps with work demands and problems, or it can be emotional support that helps the person cope with being upset (Beehr & Glazer, 2001). In a sense, instrumental support focuses on reducing stressors, whereas emotional support focuses on reducing strains. As with control, there is evidence that having social support can reduce strains, but results are equivocal about moderating effects (Viswesvaran, Sanchez, & Fisher, 1999). One reason is that social support is not always effective, and under some conditions it can make matters worse (Gray et al., 2020).

Cross-Cultural and Cross-National Studies

Although they are often used interchangeably, there is an important distinction between cross-cultural and cross-national (CC/CN) studies. Cross-cultural studies deal with an aspect of culture that might vary among individuals either within a larger social unit such as a company or country or across social units. Such studies will isolate one or more cultural variables to study at the individual or social unit level. This could involve looking at the culture variable as it relates to stressors or strains at the person level. Alternately, this could look at culture from a higher unit level to see if stressors are higher in units, most often countries, that are higher or lower on a cultural variable. It is also possible to view culture from a moderator perspective to see if a cultural variable moderates, say, the stressor-strain relationship.

Cross-national studies merely involve the comparison of people from different countries, for example, to see if there are country differences in stressors and strains or in stressor-strain relationships. One should not, however, equate country and culture, as people within countries can be variable on culture, and cultures can be shared across national boundaries. Studies that merely compare countries should be considered cross-national, whereas studies that make comparisons based on cultural variables can be considered cross-cultural. In some cases, researchers will compare countries known to be high versus low on a cultural variable and draw inferences to culture. Although such speculative inferences are a good basis for hypothesis generation, they are not based on adequate cross-cultural evidence.

In the organizational literature, cross-cultural studies have focused on a narrow range of cultural variables, usually values. The most well-known cultural value scheme is Hofstede's (2001) that isolated five dimensions: individualism–collectivism, long-term orientation, masculinity–femininity, power distance, and uncertainty avoidance. Of the five, individualism–collectivism has received most of the research attention.

Types of CC/CN Studies

Several research approaches and designs can address CC/CN issues in stress. Qualitative approaches can be quite useful in the study of culture, as they allow for an in-depth exploration of cultural context. This type is valuable when trying to understand how cultural differences might be relevant in workplace stress, or when investigating culture-specific (emic) aspects as opposed to general principles (etic). Interviews and focus groups, an important tool for the study of culture, have been underutilized in studies of occupational stress dominated by quantitative survey methods.

Quantitative CC/CN studies have used a variety of research approaches and designs. Spector, Liu, and Sanchez (2015) discussed six research designs that can be found in this domain. **Single-country** studies investigate workplace stress in a single place. These are most typically used to see if results in one country or region, typically North America or Western Europe, can be replicated in a culturally dissimilar country. Xie (1996), for example, conducted a test of the demand–control model (Karasek, 1979) in China for the purpose of determining if it would be supported outside of the West. Most studies performed around the world, however, do not have a specific CC/CN purpose, as location is just one element of convenience sampling. Researchers are likely to have connections for data collection within the country of their residence. Accumulating studies of the same variables across studies done in different places can allow for comparisons, although it can be difficult to find equivalent studies that use the same measures and sample the same industries and occupations.

A **two-country** study expands on the single-country study by collecting data in two places to allow a direct comparison. An advantage is that the nature of the samples can be controlled (e.g., engineers or nurses) so that occupation and other sample differences are not confounded with country. They also can assure that measures and procedures are similar. With both the single-country and two-country designs, conclusions are limited to cross-national differences, for they provide little basis to draw conclusions about culture. Choosing countries that are culturally dissimilar (most often China versus the United States) can allow for cultural speculations but not conclusions. For example, Nixon, Ceylan, Nelson, and Alabak (2019) conducted a comparative study of emotional labor and strain to contrast Turkey and the United States.

Multicountry studies expand into multiple countries and can include a measure of culture, such as cultural values. The cultural variable can be assessed internal to the study itself, or it can be assessed externally from archival sources, such as Hofstede (2001). With this type of study, countries can be classified into groups along a cultural dimension, such as individualism–collectivism (IC), to see if groups vary according to culture. This can be done by including an internal measure of culture in the study itself. Sometimes country samples are aggregated to regions to enhance statistical power by boosting sample sizes. An example of this approach is Glazer and Amren (2018), who investigated social support and stress in 25 countries that were collapsed into nine regions.

A **country-level** design is one in which data on culture and the variables of interest are collected from multiple countries and then are aggregated to the country level. This design could address questions about whether stressors and/or strains are higher or lower in countries that vary on a culture variable, such as power distance. An external source can be used to assess the country's culture, such as using Hofstede's (2001) country data to classify countries, or measures of cultural variables can be included in the study and aggregated to the country level. For example, Spector et al. (2001) assessed IC, locus of control, and strains in 24 country samples, and then they analyzed results at the country (mean for each country) level.

A **multilevel** design is one in which data from a sample of people is collected from a group of countries; thus people are nested in a country. Such studies can include a measure of culture, either internally or externally. Such a design allows for the use of multilevel statistics that test for relationship differences (e.g., stressors vs. strains) across countries and determine whether cultural variables can explain differences in relationships. These designs provide flexibility to combine data at the person level with data at the country level. An example of this design with an external measure of culture is Yang et al. (2012)

who investigated the mean level of country individualism as a moderator of the stressor-strain relationships at the employee level.

An additional type of CC/CN study focuses on scale development across multiple countries or in establishing measurement equivalence/invariance or ME/I (Vandenberg & Lance, 2000) of scales across countries. This latter type of study is quite prevalent in demonstrating that the psychometric properties of a scale developed in one place and language, usually North America in English, will be maintained after translation and exportation to another country. Sometimes ME/I evidence is contained within research reports that have a substantive purpose, such as Liu et al.(2010) who provided ME/I tests for their measures in a study of stressor-strains in China and the United States.

Review of the CC/CN Literature

This chapter takes a contemporary view of the CC/CN occupational stress literature to summarize the current state of the art. This was accomplished by conducting a PsychInfo search focusing on the most recent decade (since 2009) and supplementing with some notable prior work. Although much of the occupational stress research is conducted globally, relatively little of it is truly cross-national (explicit comparison of countries) or cross-cultural (identification of cultural factors in stress). The search using keywords (cross-cultural OR cross-national) AND (job, occupational OR work stress) uncovered 32 sources that I was able to locate.

Almost all the research in this review used a survey method, and in all but a few cases, the survey was quantitative with the use of rating scales. The regions of the world where such work occurs is quite limited, with few studies conducted in Latin America, Africa, or Eastern Europe. By far the most popular country in CC/CN studies outside of North America was China, followed by South Korea. In terms of topics, the most frequently studied stress variable was burnout, followed by some aspect of autonomy or control. The only aspects of culture uncovered in the review concerned cultural values, in almost all cases IC. Samples came from a narrow set of industries and occupations, most notably, counselors, managers, nurses, teachers, and university employees. Most studies that compared countries were limited to two or three, with a handful looking at eight or more.

Scale Development Studies

One of the most important questions in CC/CN research is the extent to which instruments can be exported from the source country in which it was developed to other places. The establishment of measurement equivalence/invariance (ME/I) shows that the factor structure of an instrument is maintained after translation and use in a target country (Spector et al., 2015). Equivalence of factor structure between samples using the source language from which the scale was developed and the target language into which the scale is translated is considered a basic requirement for treating different language versions as equivalent. However, there are different levels of ME/I (Vandenberg & Lance,

2000). The most restrictive and hardest to achieve is homogeneity of the item covariance matrices between the two samples. Equivalence indicates that both language versions have equivalent item variances and equivalent levels of inter-item correlation. If covariance matrices are equivalent, so too will be the factor structure. Less restrictive forms of ME/I are more often used, as they are easier to achieve (Schmitt & Kuljanin, 2008). Metric invariance requires that the factor loading matrices from the two samples have similar values. Configural invariance only requires that both samples have the same number of factors and that the same items load on the factors.

Although most instruments come from English-speaking countries, some have been developed elsewhere. It is important to establish ME/I before interpreting results, and in some cases, instrument modification is required.

Many research reports about occupational stress and other topics include an analysis of ME/I to justify comparisons across countries. For example, Liu et al. (2007) exported into Chinese several established English-language scales, such as the job autonomy subscale of the Job Diagnostic Survey (Hackman & Oldham, 1975), the Interpersonal Conflict at Work Scale and the Organizational Constraints Scale (Spector & Jex, 1998), the job satisfaction subscale from the Michigan Organizational Assessment Questionnaire (Cammann et al., 1979), and the organizational frustration scale by Peters et al. (1988). Using a structural equation modeling approach, they established a reasonable level of ME/I based on the adequate fit of models designed for this purpose.

My review uncovered several papers that were focused specifically on developing translations of scales or establishing ME/I for multiple-language versions of specific scales. Some studies merely attempted to demonstrate that a scale developed in English would have ME/I when translated into another language. For example, Chen et al. (2018) translated a multidimensional workplace incivility scale into Chinese and showed that the factor structure was maintained in a Chinese sample. Their findings that correlations of subscales with criteria were not the same could be interpreted with some confidence that the scales were reflecting similar constructs. Other studies compared factor structures across two countries. For example, Bova et al. (2015) compared Dutch and Italian samples on the Demand-Induced Strain Compensation Questionnaire (de Jonge et al., 2007), finding evidence for ME/I and similar patterns of correlations with burnout and musculoskeletal disorders.

The majority of papers I located examined the transportability of burnout measures. Most notable is a series of papers by San Min Lee and colleagues to develop translations of the English-language Counselor Burnout Inventory (Lee et al., 2007). They established that the psychometric properties (factor structure and internal consistency) of the five-dimension scale was maintained when exported to Hong Kong (Puig et al., 2014; Shin et al., 2013), Japan (Puig et al., 2014; Yagi et al., 2011), Korea (Carrola et al., 2012; Puig et al., 2014), and the Philippines (Puig et al., 2014). Lee and colleagues were able to demonstrate configural invariance (the least restrictive form of ME/I) across five countries

(Carrola et al., 2012; Puig et al., 2014), but only in a Korean sample they did not find the more restrictive scaler invariance that requires factor loadings to be the same (Carrola et al., 2012). They concluded that some items needed to be modified for use in Korea.

Likewise, transportability to Chinese was found for the Copenhagen Burnout Inventory (Fong et al., 2014). For the Maslach Burnout Inventory (Maslach, 1998), however, although the original three factors were found for samples in China, Ghana, and Pakistan, reasonable ME/I could only be established after dropping some items (Aboagye et al., 2018).

The most systematic attempt to examine ME/I for a scale came from the Collaborative International Study of Managerial Stress (CISMS) project, which was a two-phase study of more than 14,000 managers from 39 countries. Jang et al. (2017) used data from the second phase to investigate ME/I for the Satisfaction with Life Scale (Diener et al., 1985) across 26 culturally dissimilar countries spanning Asia, Europe, Latin America, and North America. They found that configural but not scalar invariance held across all countries, suggesting that the items all fit the same factors but that factor loading values were not the same.

The literature on scale development and transportability is haphazard and inconsistent. Papers vary in the statistical methods reported, with some comparing independent factor analyses, and others conducting formal ME/I tests. In most cases, the translations are ad hoc; that is, they are performed for the particular study. Systematic studies of transportability are uncommon, and usually a small number of countries are compared. Explorations of cultural or linguistic issues that might affect transportability are difficult to find (for an example with a job satisfaction measure see Liu et al., 2004). Since most tests of ME/I are embedded in studies of substantive and not measurement issues, locating specific language versions of popular scales can be difficult and requires contacting authors. One resource that contains translations of scales used in stress research is the assessment section of my website: https://paulspector.com/assessments/pauls-no-cost-assessments/. However, most of the translations were provided by people who used it in their research (e.g., a doctoral dissertation) conducted in a single country. They might have used rigorous backtranslation approaches (Hinkin, 1998) that would have provided accurate translations of scale content, but without having a sample taking the original scale in the source language, rigorous ME/I tests would not have been possible.

National Differences

Most CC/CN studies merely make country comparisons, with no explicit attempt to tie differences in means or relationships to assessed cultural variables. This approach can be a good first step in establishing what is similar and what differs among countries. However, it fails to provide much insight into why differences might occur, although often authors will speculate about what might be a reasonable explanation. In most cases, the speculations are limited to values, most notably IC. As with the assessment domain, the sampling of studies is generally not systematic, and studies are likely chosen on the basis of availability rather than for theoretical reasons. This makes it difficult to develop ideas about what might drive differences because there are not enough comparisons of the same countries to see patterns. An exception is a comparison of China with North America and other Anglo countries where many studies can be found.

Several studies have compared a small number of countries to see if relationships among variables are consistent. Combined, they suggest that many relationships are not universal. For example, Glei et al. (2013) compared men and women in three countries on perceived stress and biomarkers of cardiovascular disease. They found a positive relationship in Russia for both genders, a positive relationship for women but not men in the United States, and a negative (reversed) relationship for men but not women in Taiwan. Pal and Saksvik (2008) studied nurses and physicians in Norway and India. Demands and perceived stress correlated significantly in Norway but not India; social support correlated with perceived stress in India but not Norway. Levine et al. (2011) found that correlations between negative emotions and counterproductive work behavior (behavior that harms organizations or people in organizations; see Spector & Fox, 2005) varied across China, Romania, and the United States. The correlation between negative mood and CWB directed against people was significantly larger in China than in the other two countries. Although not significantly different from one another, the correlation was significant for the United States and nonsignificant for Romania. These three studies document that the correlations among stress-related constructs are not consistent, but the range of countries is limited.

On the other hand, some studies showed consistency in relationships among constructs across countries. For example, Salavecz et al. (2010) tested the effort–reward imbalance model (Siegrist, 1996) in six countries (Czech Republic, Germany, Hungary, Poland, Russia, and the United Kingdom). They classified employees into one of four categories from low to high effort–reward imbalance, and utilizing logistic regression they tested models that degree of imbalance would predict health. For all six countries, imbalance was statistically significantly related to health, but the magnitude of the effect varied considerably, with Hungary having an odds ratio more than three times that of Russia.

Although most comparative studies involve a small number of countries, two stand out for having investigated more than two dozen (Glazer & Amren, 2018; Spector et al., 2002). Although they might not have shed light on culture, these studies demonstrated that results are not necessarily universal. Spector et al. (2002) used data from phase 1 of the CISMS study that investigated the role of work locus of control (Spector, 1988) in the relationship of workplace stress with job satisfaction, physical strain, and psychological strain. Results across 26 countries showed that whether results were similar depended on the specific strain. Relationships of work locus of control were most consistent across countries with job satisfaction and least consistent with physical health symptoms.

Glazer and Amren (2018) was a study of stressors, positive job attitudes, and social support among 1,796 employees of a multinational company spanning 25 countries placed into nine regions. They showed that the regions differed in mean levels of stressors and strains, as well as correlations among them. The most striking finding had to do with the potential buffering (moderator) effect of social support on the stressor-strain relationship. Although these effects were expected, they were only significant in three of the regions. In the United States/Canada region, there was a buffering effect where the negative relationship between stressors and strains was reduced under conditions of high support. In Germanic and Latin Europe, however, there was a reverse buffering effect; that is, there was a larger stressor-strain slope for those with high rather than low social support. As they speculated about feasible regional differences that might explain the differences in results, they noted that the CC/CN literature needs to broaden the range of cultural variables that are considered to provide a deeper understanding of culture effects.

National Differences in the Nature of Stressors

One notable series of studies by Cong Liu and colleagues investigated Chinese-U.S. differences in stressors and strains that looked at how the nature of the stressors might differ across the two countries. Their use of a mixed-method approach combining open-ended questions with rating scales allowed for a more nuanced understanding of stressors than is typically found with quantitative methods alone. This series of studies found that the mean level of autonomy was higher in the United States than in China (Liu et al., 2007; Nauta et al., 2010), whereas mean levels of overall interpersonal conflict (Liu et al., 2007), conflict with supervisors (Liu et al., 2011), and overall organizational constraints (Liu et al., 2007) did not differ between the two countries. The qualitative results, however, suggested that while overall stressors of interpersonal conflict and organizational constraints did not differ, the nature of these stressors did (Liu et al., 2007). Specifically, when asked to relate a stressful experience at work, Americans and Chinese reported different types of conflict and constraints. Chinese were more likely to describe indirect conflicts, such as social undermining and talking behind the person's back rather than arguing and directly confronting, which was typical of Americans. Chinese were more likely to report constraints due to the context of work (e.g., inadequate training), whereas Americans were more likely to describe constraints due to poor teamwork. Furthermore, even though Americans reported higher quantitative levels of autonomy than Chinese, Americans were also more likely than Chinese to relate stressful incidents due to lack of autonomy.

Relationships between stressors and strains showed some mixed results in that some specific stressor-strain relationships were similar, whereas others were significantly different. In part, this might be due to complex interactions among stressors and other variables. For example, for Americans autonomy buffered the relationship between supervisor conflict and negative emotions, whereas for Chinese there was a reverse-buffering effect in that the negative impact of conflict only occurred for individuals who perceived high levels of autonomy (Liu et al., 2011). For Americans having low autonomy was associated with higher psychological strain for those low, but not those high in self-efficacy. For Chinese, the results were opposite. Having low autonomy was associated with high strain for those with high and not low self-efficacy. In other words, autonomy is important for Americans with low self-efficacy, but for Chinese it is harmful for those with low self-efficacy.

We can go beyond stressor-strain relationships to investigate how people who differ culturally might cope with stress. Zhang and Long (2006) argued that the IC of a society can influence the approaches that people take to deal with stress. In individualist societies, people engage in active coping that can involve directly confronting others. In collectivist societies, people tend to take indirect approaches that can include avoiding the situation and controlling one's internal reaction. In the workplace, we might ask if one form of coping is more effective than the other regardless of culture, or does culture determine which approach works best in mitigating the detrimental effects of stressors on strains?

This line of research shows that merely comparing stressors across countries is insufficient to understand the role of culture and nationality. Transporting scales developed in one place to another is taking an etic approach to the study of stress, investigating the universality of general principles. However, this approach ignores the emic perspective of identifying country- or culture-specific differences that can be important. Samples from two places might have similar levels of overall stressors, but the nature of those stressors can be different. Clearly, the field needs more qualitative approaches in a variety of countries to provide a more complete understanding of the nature of stressors across countries and cultures.

Emotional Labor in a CC/CN Context

Emotion display rules and how people regulate their emotions are very much linked to culture (Mesquita & Delvaux, 2013). Not surprisingly, there is a cultural component to how emotions are displayed and regulated at work as people interact with one another. Emotional labor is concerned with both explicit and implicit organizational demands that employees express positive emotions and avoid expressing negative emotions, most notably in customer service interactions (Grandey & Melloy, 2017). Further, when confronted with offensive or unpleasant behavior by customers, employees are expected to suppress responding with anger or irritation. Two forms of emotional labor are distinguished by whether the employee changes the emotion (deep acting) or fakes the emotion (surface acting).

It has been well established in primarily Western studies that only surface acting is detrimental to employee well-being (Grandey & Melloy, 2017). Given that people's emotion regulation strategies can be molded by cultural experience (Matsumoto et al., 2008), it seems reasonable to expect differences in how emotional labor might affect people in different countries, particularly contrasting countries generally considered to be individualist versus collectivist. (Mesquita & Delvaux, 2013, refer to countries in which people tend to be independent versus interdependent.)

Mesquita and Delvaux (2013) argue that people from individualist societies like the United States will differ in their emotional labor from people from collectivist societies, such as East Asia. They described a study in which Americans and Japanese were asked about their likely responses to someone being offensive. Americans, on the one hand, noted that they would likely respond aggressively, which would be a way to protect their individual identities. Japanese, on the other hand, noted that they would attempt to see the other person's point of view, and they would make an effort to maintain a good relationship. Whereas the Americans focused on their own feelings and responded to the person in kind, the Japanese adjusted to the needs of the other person and worked to maintain harmony. If we take this study into a work setting where display rules require maintaining a positive demeanor, the Japanese response to a rude customer would require little additional labor because such a response would be automatic and shaped by cultural norms since childhood. Americans, however, would have to engage in labor to avoid responding in a more natural, aggressive manner. They noted that Latin Americans are also concerned with harmony and will avoid conflict and negative emotions directed toward others.

Although most studies of emotional labor focus on deep and surface acting, Quiñones-García et al. (2013) pointed out that it is not clear how much actual emotional effort is needed to engage in such behavior. They developed the Emotional Effort Scale (EEF) to assess exactly that. In a sample of Spanish customer service workers, they found that the EFF related more strongly to surface than deep acting, suggesting it required more effort. Consistent with their point that labor should focus on effort, they showed that the EEF related more strongly to burnout than did either form of acting and that acting did not explain incremental variance in burnout beyond that explained by effort. In other words, what mattered was not the type of acting per se, but rather the effort it took for an employee to engage in emotional labor.

If it is the case that compared to people from individualist societies, people from collectivist societies find expression of positive emotions and suppression of negative emotions more natural, we would expect that emotional labor would require less effort and be less stressful in collectivist countries (Mesquita & Delvaux, 2013). Studies compared individualist U.S. with collectivist China (Allen et al., 2014) and Turkey (Nixon et al., 2019) in the relationships of deep and surface acting with burnout. In both studies, for Americans correlations of burnout were stronger for surface than deep acting. For both Chinese and Turkish samples, correlations were larger in magnitude for deep acting than for surface acting. Furthermore, the correlation between surface acting and burnout was larger in the American samples ($r = .27$ for the United States vs. $r = -.03$ for Turkey; $r = .52$ for the United States vs. $r = .15$ for China), suggesting that engaging in surface acting was more stressful for Americans, as we might expect.

Most of the emotional labor literature focuses on the detrimental and stressful effects of having to express certain emotions at work, particularly if those emotions are not actually felt. Indeed a meta-analysis shows that surface acting was associated positively with emotion strains such as burnout and negatively related to job satisfaction (Hülsheger & Schewe, 2011). Deep acting had little relationship to emotional strain or job satisfaction. However, this is not the entire story. As the limited cross-cultural literature suggests, the effects of emotional labor are very much linked to culture, and the detrimental effects of surface acting are apparently stronger in individualist society, where almost all of the studies contained in the meta-analysis were conducted. Furthermore, it is not entirely clear that emotional labor is necessarily detrimental to employees. Brockmann's (2013) qualitative study of English and German customer service employees found that emotion work can be seen by the employee as part of the job, leading to feelings of competence and enjoyment. Consistent with this finding, the Hülsheger and Schewe (2011) meta-analysis found that personal accomplishment was positively correlated with deep acting, suggesting that people get a sense of satisfaction from successfully using emotion regulation strategies with customers. Further, deep acting was shown to be related to job satisfaction in Chinese (Nixon et al., 2011) and Turkish (Nixon et al., 2019) samples.

Stress Studies Including a Measure of Culture

The stress studies that compared countries have in some cases identified differences that led to speculation about the reasons. Many of these explanations make intuitive sense and provide a good starting point from which to investigate cultural hypotheses. A limited number of studies explicitly incorporated a measure of a cultural variable that could put to the test some of the speculations. Most such studies assessed culture values, most notably IC. In some cases, values were assessed in the samples collected; in other cases, external indexes of values at the country level were incorporated into the analysis.

Country-level Values. Perhaps the first large-scale attempt to link country-level values to occupational stress was the 1995 study by Peterson et al. This 21-country study linked four of Hofstede's (2001) values (IC, masculinity, power distance, and uncertainty avoidance) to role stressors of ambiguity, conflict, and overload. Although the sample size was quite small (21 countries), they were able to find significant relationships of role ambiguity and role overload with IC and power distance, but only with all four values entered into a regression analysis. Compared to collectivist countries, employees in individualist countries had higher means on role ambiguity and lower means on role overload. Conversely, employees in high-power distance countries had lower mean role ambiguity and higher mean role overload than their low-power distance country counterparts.

Attempts to replicate the Peterson et al. findings have not been successful. In an 18-country study, Fisher (2014) failed to find a significant relationship between any of the

Hofstede values and role overload while using multilevel modeling statistics. Likewise, Yang et al. (2012) utilized multilevel modeling analyses in a 24-country study (phase 2 of CISMS) of IC, workload, and strain. They found a significant connection between IC and workload, but in the opposite direction as Peterson et al. (1995). It is difficult to determine why these studies varied in their results, but one major issue is the relatively small number of country units being compared, and the inclusion of different subsets of countries.

Results linking IC to well-being have been more consistent. In a meta-analysis, Fischer and Boer (2011) found that the national level of well-being (anxiety, burnout, and mental health) was positively associated with country-level individualism. Yang et al. (2012) found that IC was significantly related to emotional strain in the same direction as Fischer and Boer, but not with job satisfaction, turnover intentions, or physical health. Similarly, Fisher (2014) failed to find a significant relationship of IC or the three other Hofstede values with organizational commitment.

The final issue is whether stressor-strain relationships differ by country culture. Yang et al. (2012) investigated relationships of organizational constraints and workload with job satisfaction, turnover intentions, emotional strain, and physical health. They found that for both job satisfaction and turnover intentions, but not emotional strain or physical health, relationships were stronger for individualist countries. Thus, the differential impact of stressors was limited mainly to attitudes.

Person-level Values. The limited number of studies that included a measure of culture values provided comparisons of the United States with China (Li, Wu, & Johnson, 2018), Colombia (Cendales & Gómez Ortiz, 2019), and South Korea (Klassen et al., 2010). All three studies showed that person-level IC results varied across samples. For example, Li et al. found that job stress was associated with individualism, but only for the American sample. Klassen et al. reported that collectivism was associated with job satisfaction, but only for the Korean sample and not the American or Canadian. Cendales et al. found that control buffered the effects of demands on strain, but only for people high on individualism in the Colombian sample. A second sample that combined Americans and Colombians failed to replicate the buffering effect.

Why results of person-level values varied across countries is not clear, but there are some limitations to these studies that need to be considered. First, the measures used to assess IC were not the same across studies, so it is difficult to know if they were assessing the same thing. Further, in two of the studies, the North American samples (Canada and the United States), which are widely considered individualist, had higher collectivism scores than the two Asian samples (China and South Korea) that are widely considered collectivist. This finding suggests potential problems with the assessment; most notably that means these scales might not be comparable across countries due to cultural differences in how people respond to scales (Spector et al., 2015). At the current time we can conclude that results might vary across countries, but the reasons are not clear.

What Can We Conclude?

Although the study of stress from a CC/CN perspective is more than 25 years old, a limited number of conclusions can be reached. Unfortunately, there are too few studies, and the field is rather disjointed and haphazard. We know that country and culture are important and can influence the stress process, but it is not always clear how. We know that results are sometimes the same and sometimes different when data are collected internationally, and we have seen some systematic differences based on country-level and person-level culture. Although tentative, this review has revealed a few conclusions about occupational stress from a CC/CN perspective.

Table 12.1 lists 10 key takeaways from this review, five of which are key principles and five are practical implications. The bottom line from these 10 points is that culture and nationality matter in many ways; we cannot assume that findings from one place will hold in another. Although some findings might generalize, others do not. This is true for exporting instruments from one place to another, as well as in investigating the occupational stress process. It seems that IC is an important aspect of culture and that individualists apparently have higher levels of overall well-being than collectivists, while at the same time they can be more reactive to stressors. This seeming paradox might be explained by

Table 12.1 Key principles and practical implications

Key principles
1. Even with the most careful translation procedures, there is no guarantee that measures will behave equivalently in two countries. Items might load on the same factors, but factor loadings are often different.
2. Burnout measures show good transportability, although some items might have to be deleted or modified.
3. People in individualistic societies demonstrate higher levels of well-being than people in collectivistic societies.
4. Stressor-strain relationships are stronger in individualistic than collectivistic societies.
5. The same stressor might manifest itself differently in different countries.
Key practical implications
1. We cannot assume that a measure when translated will maintain measurement equivalence/invariance. This should always be checked when exporting scales. This is especially important when those scales are used to make policy decisions.
2. We should be flexible in our leadership approaches because what might be stressful in one country might not be in another. This is particularly true about emotion display rules.
3. People in collectivist societies might be better able to cope with certain types of job conditions, such as dealing with difficult customers.
5. The importance of autonomy and control can be culturally determined, so the amount of control versus direction should be chosen with culture in mind.
6. The CC/CN research literature is fragmented and incomplete, so one should not blindly apply results from North America and Western Europe to other regions of the world.

both economic and social mechanisms. Collectivists are more likely than individualists to focus on the well-being of others and might sacrifice their own well-being for the good of the group, so their overall well-being is lower. On the other hand, collectivists might have better social support which can buffer the negative effects of stressors. Of course, it is also possible that some of the differences are due to measurement artifacts, such as cultural differences in how rating scales are used (Spector et al., 2015).

From a practical perspective, the CC/CN literature provides guidance about how to approach the management of global organizations. It is clear that the same approaches would not be advised across culturally dissimilar countries. Although the literature might be short on specifics, it does suggest that one should not make assumptions that what works well in one place will work well in another. It suggests that managers should be flexible in their approaches and be proactive in asking questions to better understand the local situation. Optimal leadership approaches concerning autonomy and empowerment are very likely to vary across countries. North American approaches—offering autonomy and holding people accountable for success—might prove to be overly stressful for people in collectivist societies where more directive approaches are expected.

The Way Forward

Perhaps the most striking aspect of the CC/CN occupational stress literature is how disjointed it is. Of course, international comparative research is difficult to accomplish for a variety of reasons, so it is not surprising that efforts are not more systematic. For example, country choices in individual studies can be more the product of the availability of samples than of preplanning. This makes it difficult to draw contrasts between countries because there are too few studies of the same country, and the studies that exist are too different in terms of variables, instruments, and the nature of samples. What we need are systematic studies that sample countries that vary along meaningful cultural dimensions. We also need more large-scale studies that contain enough countries that vary in meaningful ways to isolate the potential impact of cultural variables at the country level. In my review, I found only three papers that described such studies, ranging from 18 to 24 countries. Clearly, we need more of this type of study.

Some basic questions need to be addressed in the CC/CN stress literature. First, how do countries differ in levels of stressors and strains, and what is the contribution of culture to such differences? Care must be taken in making mean comparisons so that we can distinguish experiences from reporting styles (Spector et al., 2015). The existing studies suggest that people in individualist countries are higher in well-being. This might be correct, but there is reason to be cautious in interpreting this finding. Iwata and colleagues (e.g., Iwata et al., 1995) conducted a series of studies to understand why Japanese score higher on depression than Americans. Is it because the incidence of depression is higher in Japan, or is it something else? Iwata et al. found that Americans and Japanese respond differently to positively but not negatively worded items on depression scales and that the differences in overall depression are entirely due to the positively worded items. Since the negatively worded items reflect depressive symptoms, their results showed that depression levels were the same in the two countries. The extent to which this finding might apply to other Asian countries, to other countries considered collectivistic, or to scales of other constructs is not clear.

Second, are there differences in stressor-strain relationships across countries and cultures? Again, my review failed to find consistent patterns, but there are too few comparative studies of the same stressor-strain variables from which to draw firm conclusions. A further complication is that even if there were a sufficient number of comparative studies, they tend to use different measures and sample different populations. An alternative approach to studying country differences would be to conduct a meta-analysis of stressor-strain relationships and code for country. This would increase the number of comparisons but at the cost of consistency of methods.

Third, are moderators of stressor-strain relationships the same across county and culture? For example, does control serve as a buffer of stressor-strain relationships universally? This is a tough question to address since studies within North America and Western Europe have been inconsistent (de Lange et al., 2003), so it would take a large number of studies to reach a firm conclusion. One important issue with moderator studies is the insufficiency of statistical power due to inadequate sample sizes in most studies. Failure to find a moderator effect is inconclusive with the typical sample sizes in stress research. In their meta-analysis of occupational health psychology papers, Spector and Pindek (2016) found that the mean sample size was under 300, which is insufficient to achieve adequate power for moderator tests. What is needed are studies with sufficiently large sample sizes that tests of moderators will be conclusive.

Fourth, most cultural variables studied are values, which can be assessed at the person or country level. We need to investigate whether we get the same results at each level. My review located a few studies at each level, but what are needed are studies that assess the same values at both levels to provide a clearer picture of whether results of, say, person-level IC are the same across countries, or if they differ depending on country-level values. In other words, does the general level of IC in a society moderate the relationship of person-level IC with other variables?

Fifth, IC is generally studied as a unidirectional construct that ignores differences among societies that share the same level of IC. Little attention has been given to more complex conceptions of IC. For example, Triandis and Gelfand (1998) distinguish horizontal from vertical individualism and collectivism. Horizontal IC characterizes societies in which individuals are considered similar to one another. Vertical IC characterizes societies in which people are viewed as being dissimilar based on their position in the social hierarchy. A more complex five-dimension conception of IC was developed by Khoury (2009). He identified dimensions of Responsibility (who is responsible and affected by someone's actions), Affiliation (the personal importance of the group versus the individual), Social

Welfare (whether the group or individual is responsible for people's welfare), Religion (whether religious activities are group or individual focused), and Achievement (whether people pursue group versus individual goals).

Sixth, the study of culture has focused on a narrow set of values that provide no more than a superficial glimpse into cultural differences that might affect stress and well-being. One potential cultural variable that seems relevant is the culture of honor (Cohen et al., 1999). A culture of honor is one in which men are expected to be tough and quick to defend themselves over physical and psychological affronts with physical violence. According to Cohen et al., it arises when people live in a hostile environment with little formal law enforcement. An obvious question for a stress researcher is whether people who live in such cultures would find the need for aggressive response to provocation stressful, and would this background level of stress exacerbate the effects of other stressors? Slavin et al. (1991) went beyond values in providing a detailed analysis of how cultural variables might impact different aspects of the stress process from the nature of stressors through the strain response. Their factors included poverty, political power, minority group status, marital practices, and religious beliefs.

Seventh, we need to be careful not to take observed differences among countries at face value but instead will consider alternative explanations. It is generally assumed that countries differ in values—for example, Western countries are individualistic whereas Eastern countries are collectivistic. Results have been inconsistent, however, in that some studies find the reverse in their samples. There are several potential reasons. First, people within countries likely vary in their values, which might be associated with age, education level, and occupation. If, for example, samples across countries contain people from different occupations, there will be a confound that makes it difficult to determine if observed differences in values are due to country or occupation. Thus, the nature of samples might determine the level of values, and if samples differ in their characteristics country is confounded with other variables, which might produce unexpected results. Furthermore, different studies use different instruments to assess what are intended to be the same values, and this can result in differences. There are construct validity issues with some scales that might not reflect the same construct when exported to another country (van de Vijver & Leung, 1997). As we saw with burnout scales, sometimes translation will maintain psychometric properties and sometimes not.

Conclusions

The study of CC/CN occupational stress is still in its infancy. Although individual studies are found throughout the world, relatively few are designed specifically to investigate the role of culture and nationality. We know from what has been done that sometimes there are sample differences and sometimes there are not. Most of the explanations that have been suggested are limited to cultural values, and mainly IC. This is a good start, but we need to go beyond values to more completely understand why results might differ among countries and regions (Glazer & Amren, 2018). A more complete understanding will require the use of a variety of research approaches. A good place to start would be with qualitative studies better suited to the study of context than merely comparing results from quantitative rating scales. Such methods can expand our studies from the etic to emic in focusing on how constructs such as stressors or social support might differ from place to place. For example, Kim, Sherman, and Taylor (2008) discussed how Americans seek more social support than Asians in response to stressors. Furthermore, the effectiveness of social support in buffering the stressor-strain relationships can vary among cultural groups (Park et al., 2013; Shavitt et al., 2016).

As the world has become increasingly global, it is important that we better understand how the stress process might differ from place to place. Such knowledge will help us build theories that can explain the impact of culture and nationality, and it will inform how we can best manage organizations in the global environment.

References

Aboagye, M. O., Qin, J., Qayyum, A., Antwi, C. O., Jababu, Y., & Affum-Osei, E. (2018). Teacher burnout in pre-schools: A cross-cultural factorial validity, measurement invariance and latent mean comparison of the Maslach Burnout Inventory, Educators Survey (MBI-ES). *Children and Youth Services Review, 94*, 186–197.

Allen, J. A., Diefendorff, J. M., & Ma, Y. (2014). Differences in emotional labor across cultures: A comparison of Chinese and US Service workers. *Journal of Business and Psychology, 29*(1), 21–35.

Beehr, T. A., & Glazer, S. (2001). A cultural perspective of social support in relation to occupational stress. In P. L. Perrewé & D. C. Ganster (Eds.), *Research in occupational stress and well being* (Vol. 1, pp. 97–142). New York: JAI.

Bova, N., De Jonge, J., & Guglielmi, D. (2015). The demand-induced strain compensation questionnaire: A cross-national validation study. *Stress and Health: Journal of the International Society for the Investigation of Stress, 31*(3), 236–244.

Brockmann, M. (2013). Learning cultures in retail: Apprenticeship, identity and emotional work in England and Germany. *Journal of Education and Work, 26*(4), 357–375.

Brown, L. P., Rospenda, K. M., Sokas, R. K., Conroy, L., Freels, S., & Swanson, N. G. (2011). Evaluating the Association of Workplace Psychosocial Stressors with occupational injury, illness, and assault. *Journal of Occupational and Environmental Hygiene, 8*(1), 31–37.

Cammann, C., Fichman, M., Jenkins, D., & Klesh, J. (1979). The Michigan Organizational Assessment Questionnaire. Unpublished manuscript, University of Michigan, Ann Arbor.

Carrola, P. A., Yu, K., Sass, D. A., & Lee, S. M. (2012). Measurement invariance of the Counselor Burnout Inventory across cultures: A comparison of US and Korean counselors. *Measurement and Evaluation in Counseling and Development, 45*(4), 227–244.

Cendales, B. E., & Gómez Ortiz, V. (2019). Cultural values and the job demands–control model of stress: A moderation analysis. *International Journal of Stress Management, 26*(3), 223–237.

Chen, Y., Wang, Z., Peng, Y., Geimer, J., Sharp, O., & Jex, S. (2018). The multidimensionality of workplace incivility: Cross-cultural evidence. *International Journal of Stress Management, 26*(4), 356–366.

Cohen, D., Vandello, J., Puente, S., & Rantilla, A. (1999). "When you call me that, smile!" How norms for politeness, interaction styles, and aggression work together in Southern culture. *Social Psychology Quarterly, 62*(3), 257–275.

de Jonge, J., Dormann, C., Van Vegchel, N., Von Nordheim, T., Dollard, M., Cotton, S., & Van den Tooren, M. (2007). *DISQ 2.0: The DISC Questionnaire English version 2.0.* Eindhoven: Eindhoven University of Technology.

de Lange, A. H., Taris, T. W., Kompier, M. A., Houtman, I. L., & Bongers, P. M. (2003). "The very best of the millennium": Longitudinal research and the demand-control-(support) model. *Journal of Occupational Health Psychology, 8*(4), 282–305.

Diener, E., Emmons, R. A., Larsen, R. J., & Griffin, S. (1985). The Satisfaction with Life Scale. *Journal of Personality Assessment, 49*(1), 71.
Fischer, R., & Boer, D. (2011). What is more important for national well-being: Money or autonomy? A meta-analysis of well-being, burnout, and anxiety across 63 societies. *Journal of Personality and Social Psychology, 101*(1), 164–184.
Fisher, D. M. (2014). A multilevel cross-cultural examination of role overload and organizational commitment: Investigating the interactive effects of context. *Journal of Applied Psychology, 99*(4), 723–736.
Fong, T. C. T., Ho, R. T. H., & Ng, S. M. (2014). Psychometric properties of the Copenhagen Burnout Inventory—Chinese version. *The Journal of Psychology: Interdisciplinary and Applied, 148*(3), 255–266.
Glazer, S., & Amren, M. (2018). Culture's implications on support as a moderator of the job stressor–outcome relationship. *International Journal of Stress Management, 25*(S1), 7–25.
Glei, D. A., Goldman, N., Shkolnikov, V. M., Jdanov, D., Shkolnikova, M., Vaupel, J. W., & Weinstein, M. (2013). Perceived stress and biological risk: Is the link stronger in Russians than in Taiwanese and Americans? *Stress: The International Journal on the Biology of Stress, 16*(4), 411–420.
Grandey, A. A., & Melloy, R. C. (2017). The state of the heart: Emotional labor as emotion regulation reviewed and revised. *Journal of Occupational Health Psychology, 22*(3), 407–422.
Gray, C. E., Spector, P. E., Lacey, K. N., Young, B. G., Jacobsen, S. T., & Taylor, M. R. (2020). Helping may be harming: Unintended negative consequences of providing social support. *Work and Stress, 34*(4), 359–385.
Hackman, J., & Oldham, G. R. (1975). Development of the Job Diagnostic Survey. *Journal of Applied Psychology, 60*(2), 159–170.
Hinkin, T. R. (1998). A brief tutorial on the development of measures for use in survey questionnaires. *Organizational Research Methods, 1*, 104–121.
Hofstede, G. (2001). *Culture's consequences* (2nd ed.). Thousand Oaks, CA: SAGE.
Hülsheger, U. R., & Schewe, A. F. (2011). On the costs and benefits of emotional labor: A meta-analysis of three decades of research. *Journal of Occupational Health Psychology, 16*(3): 361–389.
Iwata, N., Roberts, C. R., & Kawakami, N. (1995). Japan-U.S. comparison of responses to depression scale items among adult workers. *Psychiatry Research, 58*(3), 237–245.
Jang, S., Kim, E. S., Cao, C., Allen, T. D., Cooper, C. L., Lapierre, L. M., O'Driscoll, M. P., Sanchez, J. I., Spector, P. E., Poelmans, S. A. Y., Abarca, N., Alexandrova, M., Antoniou, A.-S., Beham, B., Brough, P., Carikci, I., Ferreiro, P., Fraile, G., Geurts, S., . . . Woo, J.-M. (2017). Measurement invariance of the Satisfaction with Life Scale across 26 countries. *Journal of Cross-Cultural Psychology, 48*(4), 560–576.
Karasek, R. A., Jr. (1979(. Job demands, job decision latitude, and mental strain: Implications for job redesign. *Administrative Science Quarterly, 24*(2), 285–308.
Katz, D., & Kahn, R. L. (1978). *The social psychology of organizations* (2nd ed.). New York: John Wiley.
Khoury, H. A. (2009). *The moderating influence of cultural dimensions on the relationship between role stressors, job satisfaction, and organizational commitment.* ProQuest Information & Learning.
Kim, H. S., Sherman, D. K., & Taylor, S. E. (2008). Culture and social support. *American Psychologist, 63*(6), 518–526.
Klassen, R. M., Usher, E. L., & Bong, M. (2010). Teachers' collective efficacy, job satisfaction, and job stress in cross-cultural context. *Journal of Experimental Education, 78*(4), 464–486.
Lazarus, R. S. (1991). Psychological stress in the workplace. *Journal of Social Behavior and Personality, 6*(7), 1–13.
Lee, S. M., Baker, C. R., Cho, S. H., Heckathorn, D. E., Holland, M. W., Newgent, R. A., Ogle, N. T., Powell, M. L., Quinn, J. J., Wallace, S. L., & Yu, K. (2007). Development and initial psychometrics of the Counselor Burnout Inventory. *Measurement and Evaluation in Counseling and Development, 40*(3), 142–154.
Levine, E. L., Xu, X., Yang, L.-Q., Ispas, D., Pitariu, H. D., Bian, R., Ding, D., Capotescu, R., Che, H., & Musat, S. (2011). Cross-national explorations of the impact of affect at work using the state-trait emotion measure: A coordinated series of studies in the United States, China, and Romania. *Human Performance, 24*(5), 405–442.
Li, C., Wu, K., & Johnson, D. E. (2018). The impact of balance-focused attitudes on job stress: Gender differences evidenced in American and Chinese samples. *International Journal of Psychology, 53*(1), 31–39.
Liu, C., Borg, I., & Spector, P. E. (2004). Measurement equivalence of the German Job Satisfaction Survey used in a multinational organization: Implications of Schwartz's culture model. *Journal of Applied Psychology, 89*(6), 1070–1082.

Liu, C., Nauta, M. M., Li, C., & Fan, J. (2010). Comparisons of organizational constraints and their relations to strains in China and the United States. *Journal of Occupational Health Psychology, 15*(4), 452–467.

Liu, C., Spector, P. E., Liu, Y., & Shi, L. (2011). The interaction of job autonomy and conflict with supervisor in China and the United States: A qualitative and quantitative comparison. *International Journal of Stress Management, 18*(3), 222–245.

Liu, C., Spector, P. E., & Shi, L. (2007). Cross-national job stress: A quantitative and qualitative study. *Journal of Organizational Behavior, 28*(2), 209–239.

Maslach, C. (1998). A multidimensional theory of burnout. In C. L. Cooper (Ed.), *Theories of organizational stress* (pp. 68–85). Oxford: Oxford University Press.

Matsumoto, D., Yoo, S. H., & Nakagawa, S. (2008). Culture, emotion regulation, and adjustment. *Journal of Personality and Social Psychology, 94*(6), 925–937.

Mesquita, B., & Delvaux, E. (2013). A cultural perspective on emotion labor. In A. A. Grandey, J. M. Diefendorff, & D. E. Rupp (Eds.), *Emotional labor in the 21st century: Diverse perspectives on emotion regulation at work* (pp. 251–272). New York: Routledge/Taylor & Francis Group.

Nauta, M. M., Liu, C., & Li, C. (2010). A cross-national examination of self-efficacy as a moderator of autonomy/job strain relationships. *Applied Psychology: An International Review, 59*(1). 159–179.

Nixon, A. E., Ceylan, S., Nelson, C. E., & Alabak, M. (2019). Emotional labour, collectivism and strain: a comparison of Turkish and U.S. service employees. *Work and Stress, 34*(2), 168–188.

Nixon, A. E., Yang, L.-Q., Spector, P. E., & Zhang, X. (2011). Emotional labor in China: Do perceived organizational support and gender moderate the process? *Stress and Health: Journal of the International Society for the Investigation of Stress, 27*(4), 289–305.

Pal, S., & Saksvik, P. O. (2008). Work-family conflict and psychosocial work environment stressors as predictors of job stress in a cross-cultural study. *International Journal of Stress Management, 15*(1), 22–42.

Park, J., Kitayama, S., Karasawa, M., Curhan, K., Markus, H. R., Kawakami, N., Miyamoto, Y., Love, G. D., Coe, C. L., & Ryff, C. D. (2013). Clarifying the links between social support and health: Culture, stress, and neuroticism matter. *Journal of Health Psychology, 18*(2), 226–235.

Peters, L. H., O'Connor, E. J., Eulberg, J. R., & Watson, T. W. (1988). An examination of situational constraints in Air Force work settings. *Human Performance, 1*(2), 133–144.

Peterson, M. F., Smith, P. B., Akande, A., Ayestaran, S., Bochner, S., Callan, V., Jesuino, J. C., D'Amorim, M., Francois, P.-H., Hofmann, K., Koopman, P. L., Mortazavi, S., Munene, J., Radford, M., Ropo, A., Savage, G., & Setiadi, B. (1995). Role conflict, ambiguity, and overload: A 21-nation study. *Academy of Management Journal, 38*(2). 429–452.

Puig, A., Yoon, E., Callueng, C., An, S., & Lee, S. M. (2014). Burnout syndrome in psychotherapists: A comparative analysis of five nations. *Psychological Services, 11*(1), 87–96.

Quiñones-García, C., Rodríguez-Carvajal, R., Clarke, N., & Moreno-Jiménez, B. (2013). Development and cross-national validation of the Emotional Effort Scale (EEF). *Psicothema, 25*(3), 363–369.

Salavecz, G., Chandola, T., Pikhart, H., Dragano, N., Siegrist, J., Jöckel, K. H., Erbel, R., Pajak, A., Malyutina, S., Kubinova, R., Marmot, M., Bobak, M., & Kopp, M. (2010). Work stress and health in Western European and post-communist countries: An East-West comparison study. *Journal of Epidemiology and Community Health, 64*(1), 57–62.

Schmitt, N., & Kuljanin, G. (2008). Measurement invariance: Review of practice and implications. *Human Resource Management Review, 18*(4), 210–222.

Shavitt, S., Cho, Y. I., Johnson, T. P., Jiang, D., Holbrook, A., & Stavrakantonaki, M. (2016). Culture moderates the relation between perceived stress, social support, and mental and physical health. *Journal of Cross-Cultural Psychology, 47*(7), 956–980.

Shin, H., Yuen, M., Lee, J., & Lee, S. M. (2013). Cross-cultural validation of the Counselor Burnout Inventory in Hong Kong. *Journal of Employment Counseling, 50*(1), 14–25.

Siegrist, J. (1996). Adverse health effects of high-effort/low-reward conditions. *Journal of Occupational Health Psychology, 1*(1), 27–41.

Slavin, L. A., Rainer, K. L., McCreary, M. L., & Gowda, K. K. (1991). Toward a multicultural model of the stress process. *Journal of Counseling and Development, 70*(1), 156–170.

Spector, P. E. (1986). Perceived control by employees: A meta-analysis of studies concerning autonomy and participation at work. *Human Relations, 39*(11), 1005–1016.

Spector, P. E. (1988). Development of the work locus of control scale. *Journal of Occupational Psychology, 61*(4), 335–340.

Spector, P. E., Cooper, C. L., Sanchez, J. I., O'Driscoll, M., Sparks, K., Bernin, P., Bussing, A., Dewe, P., Hart, P. M., Lu, L., Miller, K., De Moraes, L. F. R., Ostrognay, G. M., Pagon, M., Pitariu, H., Poelmans, S., Radhakrishnan, P., Russinova, V., Salamatov, V., . . . Yu, S. (2001). Do national levels of individualism and internal locus of control relate to well-being: An ecological level international study. *Journal of Organizational Behavior, 22*(8), 815–832.

Spector, P. E., Cooper, C. L., Sanchez, J. I., O'Driscoll, M., Sparks, K., Bernin, P., Bussing, A., Dewe, P., Hart, P. M., Lu, L., Miller, K., De Morales, L. R., Ostrognay, G. M., Pagon, M., Pitariu, H. D., Poelmans, S. A., Radhakrishnan, P., Russinova, V., Salamatov, V. . . . Yu, S. (2002). Locus of control and well-being at work: How generalizable are Western findings? *Academy of Management Journal, 45*(2), 453–466.

Spector, P. E., & Fox, S. (2005). The stressor-emotion model of counterproductive work behavior. In S. Fox & P. E. Spector (Eds.), *Counterproductive work behavior: Investigations of actors and targets* (pp. 151–174). Washington, DC: American Psychological Association.

Spector, P. E., & Jex, S. M. (1998). Development of four self-report measures of job stressors and strain: Interpersonal Conflict at Work Scale, Organizational Constraints Scale, Quantitative Workload Inventory, and Physical Symptoms Inventory. *Journal of Occupational Health Psychology, 3*(4), 356–367.

Spector, P. E., Liu, C., & Sanchez, J. I. (2015). Methodological and substantive issues in conducting multinational and cross-cultural research. *Annual Review of Organizational Psychology and Organizational Behavior, 2*(1), 101–131.

Spector, P. E., & Pindek, S. (2016). The future of research methods in work and occupational health psychology. *Applied Psychology: An International Review, 65*(2), 412–431.

Triandis, H. C., & Gelfand, M. J. 1998. Converging measurement of horizontal and vertical individualism and collectivism. *Journal of Personality and Social Psychology, 74*(1), 118–128.

van de Vijver, F. J. R., & Leung, K. (1997). *Methods and data analysis for cross-cultural research*. Thousand Oaks, CA: SAGE.

Vandenberg, R. J., & Lance, C. E. (2000). A review and synthesis of the measurement invariance literature: suggestions, practices, and recommendations for organizational research. *Organizational Research Methods, 3*(1), 4–70.

Viswesvaran, C., Sanchez, J. I., & Fisher, J. (1999). The role of social support in the process of work stress: A meta-analysis. *Journal of Vocational Behavior, 54*(2), 314–334.

Xie, J. L. (1996). Karasek's model in the People's Republic of China: Effects of job demands, control, and individual differences. *Academy of Management Journal, 39*(6), 1594–1618.

Yagi, D. T., Lee, J., Puig, A., & Lee, S. M. (2011). Cross-cultural validation of factor structure in the Japanese Counselor Burnout Inventory. *Japanese Psychological Research, 53*(3), 281–291.

Yang, L.-Q., Spector, P. E., Sanchez, J. I., Allen, T. D., Poelmans, S., Cooper, C. L., Lapierre, L. M., O'Driscoll, M. P., Abarca, N., Alexandrova, M., Antoniou, A.-S., Beham, B., Brough, P., Çarikçi, I., Ferreiro, P., Fraile, G., Geurts, S., Kinnunen, U., Lu, C.-Q., . . . Woo, J.-M. (2012). Individualism-collectivism as a moderator of the work demands-strains relationship: A cross-level and cross-national examination. *Journal of International Business Studies, 43*(4), 424–443.

Zhang, D., & Long, B. C. (2006). A multi-cultural perspective on work-related stress: Development of a collective coping scale. In P. T. P. Wong & L. C. J. Wong (Eds.), *Handbook of multicultural perspectives on stress and coping* (pp. 555–576). New York: Springer.

PART IV

Culture and Social Dynamics in Organizations

CHAPTER

13 Culture and Trust in Organizational Contexts

C. Ashley Fulmer, Nicole Gillespie, Donald L. Ferrin, *and* Emmy Denison

Abstract

Understanding the interface of trust and culture is critical as employees and organizations continue to communicate and interact across groups and borders. In this chapter, we review the literature on culture and trust in organizational settings, focusing primarily on research published since 2010. We examine the influences of culture on trust, within-culture differences in trust, as well as trust in intercultural relationships. Further, recognizing that trust can influence culture such that the culture–trust relationship is recursive, we also discuss research on trust as culture and cultural context. Following the review, we identify theoretical implications, such as exploring trust as a determinant of culture development and the effects of cultural change on trust, as well as practical implications in the areas of artificial intelligence, HR analytics, political and societal divisions, and trust pedagogies and interventions. Research on culture and trust is thriving in organization science, with many exciting opportunities still awaiting investigation.

Key Words: trust, culture, cross-cultural differences, intercultural interactions, organizations

The relationship between trust and culture has been studied across a range of scientific fields, including management (Chua et al., 2012; Ferrin & Gillespie, 2010; Huff & Kelley, 2003), information systems (Cyr, 2008), psychology (Yuki et al., 2005), and economics (Bohnet et al., 2010; Bornhorst et al., 2010; Croson & Buchan, 1999). A previous review of research on the effects of culture on trust found that culture can influence the amount or level of trust, the meaning of trust, its and consequences, and its mediating and moderating roles (Ferrin & Gillespie, 2010). The need for understanding trust vis-à-vis culture is critical as employees and organizations continue to communicate and interact in person or virtually across groups and borders.

In this chapter, we focus on research at the intersection of trust and culture in organizational settings. Consistent with the aim of the volume, we review research conducted primarily during the past decade since 2010 on the complex influences of culture on trust toward a wide range of organization-relevant referents, particularly trust in coworkers, leaders and subordinates, team members, and management, organizations, and companies.

Our review builds on previous reviews examining the influence of culture on trust (Diez et al., 2010; Ferrin & Gillespie, 2010). However, as both culture and trust are dynamic and malleable (Fulmer & Gelfand, 2012; McGrath et al., 1992), we also recognize that trust can influence culture: that is, the relationship is recursive. Consequently, we will also consider that the behaviors and interactions that stem from trust in organizational settings can send signals about values and norms that may eventually shape cultures and individuals' cultural values. Finally, recognizing that both trust and culture can be defined in a variety of ways, are multidimensional, and manifest at and across multiple levels, our review includes a broad set of studies revealing how scholars have defined and pursued relatively specific research questions within these much broader research domains.

We begin by briefly defining trust and providing an overview of early research on trust and culture. Next, we review research published primarily over the past decade in four relevant areas: (1) cultural influences on trust, (2) within-culture differences in trust, (3) trust in intercultural relationships, and (4) trust as culture and cultural context. We searched databases, including Business Source Complete, PsychINFO, and ABI/Inform, for peer-reviewed articles published over the last decade and, after reviewing their abstracts, included those that focused on culture and trust. We conclude our chapter by identifying five theoretical principles and five practical implications uncovered by our review.

Definition of Trust

Much of the research on trust in organizational settings has coalesced around the trust definitions proposed by Mayer et al. (1995) and Rousseau et al. (1998), which refer to trust as the trustors' willingness to accept vulnerability toward the trustee based on positive expectations of the trustee. Mayer et al. (1995) specified that this willingness to accept vulnerability arises from positive expectations of trustworthiness in three dimensions: *ability*, referring to competencies and skills in a given domain; *benevolence*, or goodwill toward the trustor; and *integrity*, a set of principles deemed acceptable by the trustor (Mayer et al., 1995). Further, the positive expectations upon which trust is based can include both cognition- and affect-based expectations where cognition-based expectations are based on knowledge and reasons and affect-based expectations are based on relational connections (McAllister, 1995). In addition, individuals and groups may differ in their levels of trust propensity or generalized trust, which refers to an individual's general tendency to trust others (Rotter, 1971; Yamagishi & Yamagishi, 1994). Across the trust literature, scholars frequently define and operationalize trust and trustworthiness using one or more of the above concepts. Accordingly, consistent with the approaches in prior reviews (Ferrin & Gillespie, 2010; Fulmer & Gelfand, 2012), rather than including in our review only those studies that used a common, narrow definition of trust, we have included in our review studies that have used any of the above definitions, as well as other definitions in the literature that are conceptually or operationally similar to the definition by Mayer et al. (1995) and Rousseau et al. (1998).

Definition of Culture

Diverse definitions of culture have been offered, including "the collective programming of the mind" (Hofstede, 1991, p. 5), and "unstated assumptions, standard operating procedures, and ways of doing things" (Triandis, 1994, p. 6). More recently, culture has been defined as a group property that reflects collective meaning systems such as language, norms, and customs, as well as how groups arrange and perpetuate themselves and distinguish themselves from other groups (Baldwin et al., 2006). Culture can exist at multiple levels of analysis, including the societal level within a region or nation, at the institutional, organizational, and group levels, and as assumptions, values, and beliefs at the individual level (e.g., Wasti & Önder, 2021). We expect that the recursive relationships between culture and trust can be observed in both within-culture and cross-cultural relationships.

Dynamic Relationships between Culture and Trust

The relationships between culture and trust are likely to be both dynamic and recursive. Elements of national-societal culture are likely to influence the trust-related attitudes, beliefs, and behaviors of individual members, as well as those of groups and organizations in the society. In addition to these direct relationships, national-societal cultures are also likely to influence the systems and structures in the society that, in turn, affect the trust of the cultural members, groups, and organizations. That said, individuals can also form and maintain personal values and beliefs that are distinct from a given culture within which they are embedded. This has become increasingly common as individuals are exposed to multiple cultures and subcultures, for example, cultures related to age, politics and profession, exposure to additional cultures via work or travel, and individuals identifying as bicultural or multicultural (Chao & Moon, 2005; Hong et al., 2007). In addition, research on cultural tightness–looseness (Gelfand et al., 2011) informs us that cultures that are relatively loose permit or even encourage members to depart from cultural norms. Depending on the context, members may also subscribe to different cultural values at different times, for example, as they move from one culture to another culture as well as from one group to another group. In these various ways, individuals' trust is influenced by the broader cultures within which they are embedded, as well as the contexts that make particular cultural effects salient. However, these dynamics also result in heterogeneity in the trust experienced and manifested by individuals, groups, and organizations.

Meanwhile, trust can also influence culture. Individuals' trust, influenced by cultures at different levels as described above, also affects their perceptions, behaviors, and interactions. The feedback they receive from interacting with others and the reactions they have to this feedback in turn influence their trust and trust-related behaviors, as well as their personal cultural values and beliefs. Collectively then, it is likely that the trust among members of a cultural group and the consequent behaviors can result in shared beliefs, norms, and patterns of behaviors that also influence culture at the group, organizational, and even societal levels. While such a culture change is generally slow, the process may accelerate as people actively shape their environment, sharing and advocating their ideas and forming and supporting groups and organizations that affirm their values and approaches to trust. The way people trust can thus become normalized and institutionalized, and these trust changes become a part of the culture.

While both of the above processes are logically understandable and intuitively compelling, we note that scholars have focused primarily on the first, and mostly neglected the second. Therefore, with this review, we also hope to highlight the opportunity to focus research on how trust may be not only influenced by culture, but also influence cultural development.

Cultural Influences on Trust

Recent research on cross-cultural influences on trust has considered the extent to which the meaning, dimensions, and importance of trust may differ across cultures, the influence of culture on trust, and whether culture may moderate the effects of trust on hypothesized outcomes. Such studies typically operationalize culture at the national or societal level. One line of studies examines the understanding and importance of trust dimensions across cultures. For example, in both China and Turkey, the role of benevolence has been found to be a particularly important element of trust due to the collectivist norms of both cultures and, in both cultures, the tendency of trust relationships at work to go beyond the professional domain to include personal time and space (Wasti et al., 2011). In considering descriptions of trustworthy subordinates and leaders in South Africa and Canada, Kwantes et al. (2018) found that integrity was most important across the two cultures and roles. In contrast, ability was more strongly emphasized in descriptions of trustworthy subordinates in South Africa, whereas it was more strongly emphasized in descriptions of trustworthy leaders in Canada.

Comparing managers in Germany and China, Muethel and Hoegl (2012) found that German managers' conceptualizations of trust emphasize openness and reliability, while Chinese managers' conceptualizations of trust emphasize shared understanding and morality. Focusing on the organizational level, Chathoth et al. (2011) reported that although integrity, commitment, and dependability are critical dimensions of employees' trust in their organization in both India and the United States, Indian employees perceived integrity to be more important for trust in the organization than commitment and dependability as compared to U.S. participants.

Differences due to national-level culture are not always observed, however. In both Sweden and Slovenia, managers' actions, such as adequately solving problems and supporting, appreciating, and trusting their employees, were the strongest predictors of subordinate trust, compared to other factors such as working conditions and perceptions of team goals (Andersen & Kovač, 2012). Yamaguchi (2013) found that employees' generalized trust toward teams and work groups in their organizational setting mediated the relationship between team autonomy and employee outcomes such as job satisfaction and organizational commitment, and this pattern did not differ between the United States and Japan. And Xu et al. (2016) found that the factors that predicted perceived organizational trustworthiness were similar across U.S. and Chinese managers and business faculty members.

The effects of culture on trust have also been examined in multicountry studies. Examining data from 25 countries, Deephouse et al. (2016) found that corporate reputation, which included the general public's trust in the company, was positively related to the national cultural dimension of power distance but negatively related to the national cultural dimension of masculinity. In countries high on power distance, the general public is likely to be more comfortable with the hierarchical nature of corporations and more trusting toward them than people in countries low on power distance. The finding that trust toward corporations was negatively associated with the country's level of masculinity was contrary to the researchers' predictions; the researchers speculated that corporations in more feminine societies may have values and implement practices that are more focused on benefits to employees and society, which could cause the public to trust them more. In another survey that examined cultural values across 97 countries, Im and Chen (2020) found that countries high in collectivism, power distance, and uncertainty avoidance tended to have lower levels of generalized trust, which, in turn, was related to greater favoritism in institutional practices in the society. The authors suggested that for countries with cultural values associated with lower generalized trust, favoring trusted ingroups might be seen as a rational business decision. Other research has found that, across 18 countries, when country-level collectivism is low rather than high, followers' OCBs influence leaders' trustworthy behaviors through leaders' affective trust in the followers (Reiche et al., 2014).

Some research efforts have attempted to understand how culture and related factors influence trust in a given cultural context. In China, for example, leaders' level of conflict avoidance was found to be positively related to followers' trust in the leader, which appears to be consistent with the culture's emphasis on face and respect (Yang & Li, 2017). Further, consistent with Confucian values of hierarchy and relationalism, employee affective trust was found to mediate between benevolent and moral paternalistic leadership and employee in-role and extra-role performance among leader–follower dyads in Taiwan (Chen et al., 2014). Other research has examined the relationship between organizational control and employee trust. In Singapore, whose culture is characterized as high in control and compliance, Verburg et al. (2018) found that employee trust in the organization mediated the positive effects of three forms of control (process, outcome, and normative) on employee job performance and citizenship behavior. Other research found that Nigeria's culture of hierarchy and short-term orientation, combined with the country's economic instability, are associated with low interpersonal trust within the organization, which in turn is reflected in authoritarian management practices and perceptions that employees may leave the organization at any moment to pursue other opportunities (Bamgboje-Ayodele & Ellis, 2015).

Culture can serve not only as a pervasive contextual difference that influences levels of trust; it can also moderate the effects of trust on other outcomes. Costigan et al. (2011) showed that the relationship between employees' affect-based trust in their coworkers and proactive behaviors such as speaking out and making independent judgments was stronger in higher-power distance cultures than in lower-power distance cultures. They argued that trust in one's coworkers plays a stronger role in higher-power distance cultures such as Turkey and Russia in determining whether or not an employee feels comfortable being creative and taking initiative in their job, as compared to lower-power distance cultures such as the United States and Poland where enterprising behavior is more closely related to individual initiative than concerns about violating the organizational hierarchy.

In a meta-analysis, Li et al. (2014) found that the effect of trust between interorganizational partners on knowledge transfers was stronger in cultures with high collectivism and power distance than in cultures with low collectivism and power distance. And focusing on reactions toward takeovers, Stahl et al. (2012) examined German and Singaporean employees and found that the relative importance of the different factors for employee trust in the acquiring firm, such as collaboration history and mode of takeover, varies across the two countries. For example, due to the higher culture-level collectivism in Singapore, positive collaboration history between firms was a stronger predictor for trust in the acquiring firm for Singaporean employees than for German employees. In contrast, because of the emphasis on joint decision making in Germany, the friendliness of the takeover was a stronger predictor for trust in the acquiring firm for German employees than for Singaporean employees.

There also appear to be contexts in which cross-cultural differences and their impact on trust become more salient or pronounced. This is consistent with a culture-by-context perspective that looks beyond the cultural main effects on trust to understand how contexts modify the effects of cultures (Gelfand & Cai, 2004; Gelfand et al., 2013; Hong et al., 2000). For example, cultural differences in trust become more salient when considering the role of long-term relationships and approaches to risks in trust. Özer et al. (2014) found that, in the absence of future interactions, Chinese partners exhibited less trust and trustworthiness than the U.S. partners in supply chain relationships. With regard to risk, research has shown that risk mitigation aimed at lowering the cost of betrayal increased trust in the United States, but not in Jordan where risk prevention is preferred to decrease the likelihood of betrayal given that repeated interactions and reputation concerns are the norms in a tribal society (Al-Ississ & Bohnet, 2016). A high-risk context may even reverse typically observed cultural patterns. For example, because of a lack of effective governance in China's relatively new diamond industry, diamond merchants in China tend to adopt a more transactional and even antagonistic approach in business transactions, as compared to diamond merchants in Western markets who generally adopt a strong relational approach (Berger et al., 2018). Reflecting this transactional environment, the authors found a negative relationship between interpersonal trust (*xinren*) and firm performance in the diamond industry in China.

Another notable example is the context of leader–follower relationships. As an example, employees in Anglophone cultures rated abusive supervision as less fair than employees in Confucian Asian cultures, and as a result had lower trust in the leader than employees in Confucian Asian cultures (Vogel et al., 2015). This suggests that leader–follower relationships may entail different roles and expectations across cultures. Similarly, Rockstuhl et al. (2012) found that the relationship between leader–member exchange (LMX) and trust was stronger in horizontal-individualistic cultures than in vertical-collectivistic cultures.

The contexts of conflicts, trust violations, and trust repair represent yet another context in which cultural differences emerge. There is also evidence that people across cultures may react to trust violations differently. For example, Friedman et al. (2018) found that Americans were more likely to lower perceptions of behavioral integrity following a broken promise than Indians, Koreans, and Taiwanese, and the difference between the United States and India was stronger when the person who broke the promise was a superior rather than a subordinate. Eckerd et al. (2016) similarly found that compared to Chinese, Americans trusted less and were less willing to work with the partner after a psychological contract breach. They theorized that this was due to the United States' individualism and short-term orientation, both of which make Americans intolerant toward equity imbalances, while China's collectivism and long-term orientation make Chinese more flexible and tolerant of temporary imbalances. The effects of violations on collectivists and their trust also depend on the magnitude of the violation and the relational context between the trustor and trustee, such that trust dissolution and repair are more difficult for collectivists after a large ingroup violation (Fulmer & Gelfand, 2015). In terms of trust repair, Maddux et al. (2011) found that apologies addressing integrity were more effective for trust repair in Japan than in the United States, but apologies addressing competence were more effective for trust repair in the United States than in Japan. The authors proposed that the difference is due to different approaches to apologies in the two cultures. In Japan, apologies are more likely to be offered when one isn't involved in the original violation, whereas in the United States apologies are more likely to be associated with personal blame.

Within-Culture Differences in Trust

While most research on culture and trust has focused on differences across national and societal cultural contexts, some research has also examined cultural differences within a society, region, country, or group. To understand these differences within a country or region, most of these studies focus on cultural differences measured at the regional or individual level rather than using country-level cultural variables. For example, within the United States, generalized trust at the state level was found to mediate the relationship between state-level cultural values of hierarchy and unfair labor practices adopted by the businesses within a state, such that states high on hierarchical values had lower generalized trust, resulting in more business practices undermining employee rights in those states (Hogler et al., 2013). Within China, where the country has experienced cultural transitions resulting in heterogeneity in traditional versus modern values, Zhao et al. (2017) found that traditionality was associated with identity-based trust, while modernity was associated with calculus-based trust in generalized interpersonal relationships.

Culture at the individual level also acts as a moderator that leads to differences related to trust within a country or society. Li et al. (2017) found that, among Chinese employees high on traditionality, the negative effect of differentiated empowering leadership, where leaders provide the followers with different levels of autonomy and authority, on trust in leaders was weaker than among employees low on traditionality. Within-cultural differences may also interact with individuals' trust in influencing outcomes. In another study with Chinese employees, Zhang and Zhou (2014) found that the relationship between empowering leadership and employee creativity is stronger when employees are high on individual-level uncertainty avoidance and trust the leader at the same time.

Trust in Intercultural Relationships

A number of studies have focused specifically on trust in intercultural settings. This includes, for instance, when people from diverse cultural backgrounds work on a project together or when expatriate employees or managers work in locations with different cultures from which they are accustomed.

Intercultural trust relationships in organizations face unique challenges. For instance, one study surveying Chinese senior executives found that their affect-based trust was higher when they worked with foreign partners of the same cultural ethnicity or of cultures that were more similar to their own (Jiang et al., 2011). However, the pattern for cultural similarity and difference is not always consistent. In particular, when people interact with others from different cultures, they can be subject to cultural stereotypes, such that perceptions of cooperation about people from a country influence trust in a partner from that country positively as well as negatively (Danik, 2014). For example, Özer et al. (2014) found that in supply chain relationships, because Chinese partners perceived the U.S. partner to be more trusting and trustworthy, the Chinese partners were more likely to trust them.

In international strategic alliances, financial support from the local government was found to be related to lower trust toward the local partner, but the negative relationship was weaker with increased interactions between partners (Christoffersen & Robson, 2017). In some cases, people may engage in specific tactics to manage cross-cultural trust. Ado et al. (2017) documented that, when interacting with Chinese joint venture partners, African partners elected to use informal channels and even secret connections to manage trust that the Chinese partners may not be aware of. And in the area of mediation, Salmon et al. (2013) found that manipulative mediation, a strategy that is effective in difficult negotiations, which pushes disputants to reach an agreement through the use of threats and rewards, produced more efficient agreement when an intercultural dyad had lower trust, but not when an intercultural dyad had higher trust.

Other studies focus specifically on expatriates working in host organizations with a different culture. Zaheer and Kamal (2011) proposed that differences in home and host cultures could manifest at the dyadic level, influencing trust building and trust repair in case of violations. They further found that trust violations would be more severe and trust repair more difficult for cross-cultural exchange relationships when the host culture has lower rather than higher levels of trust. On the other hand, cultural similarity has been found to promote trust between cross-cultural negotiators from emerging and developed countries (Debabi, 2010).

Despite these challenges, expatriates can find ways to build trust amidst cultural differences. Research indicates that expatriate managers and their local counterparts build trust initially based on competence, which progresses to be more affect-based over time through the expatriate managers' cultural intelligence (CQ) (Ang & Tan, 2016). In the case of American managers working in Chinese firms, Chen et al. (2018) found that American managers who endorsed collectivistic values more strongly were better able to build trust with Chinese employees. If the managers also endorsed lower-power distance, they were better able to understand the perspectives of their employees, and the combination led to increased cooperative conflict management.

Intercultural trust has also been studied in the context of multicultural teams, including virtual teams, where cultural differences are still present as interactions occur remotely via technology (Mockaitis et al., 2012) but may manifest differently from in-person intercultural exchanges. Findings, however, can be complex. For example, Mach and Baruch (2015) and Mockaitis et al. (2012) found that in samples from cross-cultural project teams where, across teams, members were from 30 countries of origin, collectivistic orientation at the team level leads to team trust. At the individual level, Lowry et al. (2010) found that individualism has a positive effect on individuals' trust toward team members consisting of Chinese and U.S. members. Based on their interviews of team members in an American-Polish startup joint venture, Gerbasi and Latusek (2015) found that despite having frequent in-person interactions and a common professional identity that should have facilitated trust among team members, the joint venture still struggled to bridge the gap in trust between the American members' preference for diffused generalized trust and the Polish members' preference for in-depth relational trust. It is important to note that cultural differences are not only obstacles to overcome; they can also contribute to higher performance. In a sample of hotel employees, Nazarian et al. (2017) observed that different national cultures among employees in a hotel promoted a balanced organizational culture that was characterized by a high level of mutual trust that offered more flexibility and improved the organization's performance.

Increased knowledge about other cultures has been identified as a factor that can help build trust in intercultural contexts. Research conducted in Canada and China showed that diversity in one's social interactions in the community is positively associated with one's social trust in the workplace (Cui et al., 2015). People exposed to different cultural contexts can even adjust their perceptions of the person breaking a promise based on the cultural context where the violation occurred (Friedman et al., 2018). For expatriate managers, to the extent that they engage in behaviors focused on building trust and bridging divides by adopting a nonpartisan attitude, they can be more successful in promoting organizational identification among local employees (Oh et al., 2018). A group's openness to diversity in values, languages, and information also leads to higher group trust in multicultural settings (Lauring & Selmer, 2012). Further, both CQ and cultural adaptation facilitate trust in culturally diverse teams (Chang et al., 2014; Henderson et al., 2018). When individuals have higher CQ, they have higher affective trust in their intercultural ties and share more new ideas in intercultural relationships (Chua et al., 2012). And cultural adaptation, particularly by the lower-power party, can serve to increase trust in cross-cultural collaborations (Labarca, 2014).

Trust as Culture and Cultural Context

Research has also considered trust as an element of culture and consequently also as a cultural context. Trust as culture refers to the overall level of generalized trust—the extent to which one trusts others in general—among individuals who make up the culture. This level of trust is expected to influence behavior in at least two ways. First, one's individual behaviors are influenced in part by one's own propensity to trust, and consequent aggregate behaviors are likely to be influenced by an aggregate propensity to trust. Second, individuals are likely to decide on their trust-related behaviors in part based on the context, particularly on the level of generalized trust among others in the culture, as that may be reflected in norms about when and where to trust, norms about reciprocation of trust, and so on. Generalized trust in a society and its societal culture are therefore related as generalized trust is shaped by the shared assumptions, values, and beliefs of the society (Goodell, 2017). For example, You (2012) found that societal-level fairness and equality (democracy, freedom from corruption, and relatively equal and unskewed income distribution) have a stronger association with generalized trust than ethnic homogeneity.

As a context, trust as culture exerts influences on organizational behaviors, as contexts represent "situational opportunities and constraints that affect the occurrence and meaning of organizational behavior as well as functional relationships between variables" (Johns, 2006, p. 386). For instance, in Europe, Meier et al. (2019) showed that countries with higher levels of generalized trust had a greater division of labor within organizations than countries with lower levels of generalized trust. In high-trust cultures, workers are able to specialize and trust that their coworkers will fulfill their specified duties, leading to an efficient division of labor; whereas in low-trust cultures, workers may repeat each other's work due to lower trust in their coworkers.

Looking at the top-down effect of culture-level trust, research has suggested that the cultural context of trust in which an organization is embedded has a direct effect on how members of the organization perceive the trustworthiness of its international joint venture partners (Ertug et al., 2013). Negotiation research has shown that lower generalized trust among Indian negotiators leads to poorer outcomes as compared to American negotiators with higher generalized trust (Gunia et al., 2011). Considering the levels of generalized trust and cultural tightness–looseness, Brett et al. (2017) theorized that the interaction between the two cultural factors explains differences in negotiation strategies. Higher generalized trust at the societal level is positively related to individuals' likelihood of making angel investments (Ding et al., 2015) and is negatively related to CEO compensation levels, proportion of equity-based compensation, and income disparity between executive and employee compensation (Kanagaretnam et al., 2016). Meta-analyses indicate that the relationship between firm internalization and firm performance is stronger in countries with higher generalized trust in others from foreign countries than in countries with lower generalized trust in others from foreign countries (Marano et al., 2016). Another meta-analysis showed that the extent of family firms' internationalization depends on the firm's level of home country trust in people from other nations (Arregle et al., 2016).

Evidence also indicates that trust as culture also acts as a moderator. A study examining the relationship between stock ownership and financial performance in Europe found that the relationship was stronger in countries high on societal generalized trust (e.g., Denmark) where employees were less concerned about other employees' freeriding and were more committed to contributing to the organization, as compared to those lower on social generalized trust (e.g., Portugal; Kang & Kim, 2018). Trust as culture also moderates the relationship between firm corruption and tax compliance, such that as generalized trust increases, the negative relationship between corruption (in the form of unofficial payments) and tax compliance weakens (Alon & Hageman, 2013). In addition, research on family and nonfamily firms found that while family firms and nonfamily firms are equally profitable in high-trust societies, family firms performed better in profitability and sales growth in low-trust societies (Carr & Bateman, 2010). The authors suggest that the increased organizational control inherent in family firms is particularly beneficial in low-trust contexts.

Review Summary

In our review of the literature on culture and trust over the past 10 years, we found that much of the research on culture and trust addresses cultural differences and their possible connections to trust levels, meaning, and dimensions. A substantial body of research has also focused on the influences of cultural values and dimensions on trust, as well as their moderating effects on trust and employee and organizational outcomes. What emerges is that there are complex relationships between culture and trust that are observable when comparing different countries. But there remains a lack of a systematic theoretical stance to explain the myriad patterns of findings. Several contexts, including those that involve long-term relationships, high levels of risk, leader–follower relationships, and trust violations and repairs, appear to amplify cross-cultural differences in trust. The contextual focus may provide one avenue where future research can continue to provide a more systematic understanding of trust across cultures.

By comparison, research on the within-cultural relationships between culture and trust is relatively sparse. Studies in this area tend to focus on individual-level cultural dimensions and the relationship to individual-level trust or the effects of trust on outcomes. This area is ripe for further research, with room to expand the literature base by studying group, organizational, and regional level variations in cultures and trust.

It is encouraging to see the growing and diverse research studies of trust in intercultural relationships. Studies have explored various intercultural contexts and forms of exchanges such as strategic alliances, expatriate assignments, and multicultural virtual teams. Our review also found that a good number of studies have provided recommendations for trust development in intercultural exchanges across the individual, team, and organizational levels. Finally, our review identified a stream of research that conceptualizes trust as a cultural context. Research in this stream typically focuses on generalized trust, with the assumption that it is shared among members of a culture or society. As our review shows, culture as context influences a variety of employee behaviors and organizational practices, both directly and as a moderator. While culture influences interpersonal trust and generalized trust, trust in turn influences cultural member behaviors and organizational practices. In this way, trust provides a feedback loop to influence culture over time and potentially exert a recursive effect on culture. This is a fascinating and promising direction for future research. There remain several other substantive opportunities and important considerations for new research in the culture and trust intersection, as we discuss next.

Discussion

Our review indicates that research on trust and culture has continued to expand, focusing on the interplay of trust and culture not only within a given level but across levels. Thus, the domain of trust and culture research is remarkably broad, and within that broad domain, scholars continue to identify and pursue interesting and important specific research questions.

We conclude with five theoretical implications and five practical implications that arise from our review. Table 13.1 lists the implications.

Table 13.1 Theoretical and practical implications from the review

Theoretical Implications	– Trust perceptions and behaviors as a determinant of cultural change and development
	– Effects of cultural change on trust of culture group members
	– Need for further systematic research and focus on intercultural exchanges
	– Cross-cultural and intercultural trust research on distrust, felt trust, trust motivation, and trust and affect
	– Emerging methods as opportunities for research on trust and culture
Practical Implications	– Trust-related reactions toward the use of artificial intelligence
	– Management of trust in HR Analytics
	– Trust across political and social-cultural divisions
	– Cross-fertilization for trust pedagogies and interventions
	– Potential of trust to override cultural differences

Theoretical Implications

1. **Trust as a determinant of culture.** Our review indicates that culture impacts a range of trust-related outcomes at the individual, group, and organizational levels. However, we know relatively little about how trust perceptions and behaviors among individuals and groups may impact broader culture change and development over time. Research on the relationship between trust and institution building offers preliminary support that a bidirectional relationship exists between trust and institution building (Nikolakis & Nelson, 2018). Lumineau and Schilke (2018) likewise proposed that organizational structures and trust in members of the organization influence each other (see also McEvily et al., 2021. Given the likelihood that trust impacts the formal structures (e.g., regulations and monitoring) and informal structures (e.g., interaction patterns and networks) of a cultural group, changes in trust levels among individuals and groups are likely to result in changes in interaction patterns, norms and expectations, values and beliefs, and ultimately systems and processes, that are likely to ultimately constitute a change in culture, whether within organizations or even within societies. Unfortunately, the complexity and long timescale of these processes and effects are likely to pose significant challenges for empirical examination.
2. **Effects of cultural change on trust.** Finally, the fact that cultures continually evolve has important implications for trust. In fact, evidence suggests that trust is malleable in responding to changes of cultures. For example, Slater and Robson (2012) found that while Japanese cultural values support trust in interfirm relationships in Japan, as traditional cultural values

changed and eroded over time, the interfirm trust relationships weakened. Research on first-generation immigrants highlights that those who migrated from low-trust to high-trust countries showed higher trust than nonmigrants from their country of origin, which indicates that individuals' generalized trust is also influenced by experience, even in adulthood (Dinesen, 2012). Further, culture-level shared goals for socializing children (e.g., focusing on civility or practicality) have been found to moderate the influence of individuals' trust in ingroup and outgroup members on their generalized trust (Jing & Bond, 2015). In this way, different foci of children's socialization also play a role in influencing societal trust. Cultural changes thus present critical opportunities to influence the trust of cultural group members. Further research is therefore warranted to better understand these effects and processes.

3. **Need for further systematic research.** An earlier comprehensive review (Ferrin & Gillespie, 2010) of the empirical research on trust and culture examined whether mean levels of trust, the determinants, consequences and functions (mediation and moderation) of trust, and the meaning of trust vary across cultures. They found evidence of cross-cultural differences, particularly in relation to generalized trust toward others, and also saw evidence of trust universals across cultures. The evidence led the authors to conclude that trust operates as both a variform universal (i.e., while the general principle of trust holds across cultures, some specific manifestations differ across cultures; Dickson et al., 2001; Lonner 1980) and a variform functional universal (i.e., relationships among trust and associated variables are confirmed across cultures, but their magnitude or directions may vary across cultures; see Bass, 1997). The research summarized in this review has broadened and deepened the existing evidence base. Our assessment is that the research on trust and culture produced in the last decade reinforces the pattern of results and conclusions found in the prior review: trust functions as a variform universal and variform functional universal. Going forward, we reiterate Ferrin and Gillespie's call for further systematic research, particularly in the area of trust in intercultural exchanges.
4. **Emerging and neglected streams of research.** We highlight several emerging, or neglected but nevertheless important, streams of trust research that are likely to have important cultural manifestations. Cross-cultural and intercultural research could fruitfully focus on the role of vulnerability in trust (Fulmer et al., 2023), distrust, which entails confident negative expectations of another (Lewicki et al., 1998); felt trust or the feeling of being trusted (Lau et al., 2014; Baer et al., 2015); trust calibration and the accuracy of trust and felt trust (e.g., Campagna et al., 2019; Schilke & Huang,

2018); trust motivation (van der Werff et al., 2019); and trust and emotions (e.g., Williams, 2001; 2007). Future studies should also examine the interaction between individual-level trust and cultural-level trust. For example, research has shown that a match between cultural- and individual-level characteristics increases subject well-being (Fulmer et al., 2010). In each of these areas, cross-cultural and intercultural analyses are likely to reveal fascinating trust differences and dynamics.

5. **Emerging methods as opportunities.** Each of the foundational literatures of this review, culture and trust, has its own unique methodological challenges. Culture research, for instance, has to grapple with issues of cross-cultural construct and measurement equivalency, the fact that culture is multidimensional and multilevel and takes different but interdependent forms across levels. Trust research has to grapple with the fact that trust phenomena are by nature multiparty (trustor and trustee at a minimum), multidimensional and multilevel, and trust development processes are inherently difficult to understand, model, and assess. Scholars working at the intersection of trust and culture potentially face both sets of challenges simultaneously. Our review indicates that researchers have tended to navigate these challenges by defining relatively narrow questions that can be addressed with relatively simple, traditional methods. Consequently, some of the cutting-edge methods that have arisen in the two separate literatures such as agent-based models (Nooteboom, 2015) and evolutionary game-theoretic models (Pan et al., 2020) in the culture literature, and the actor–partner interdependence models (Ferrin et al. 2008), discontinuous growth models (Korsgaard et al., 2018), multiwave latent growth models (van der Werff & Buckley, 2017), and network methods (Taselli & Kilduff, 2018; Jones & Shah, 2021; McEvily et al., 2021) in the trust literature, have yet to see much adoption in research on trust and culture (see Fulmer & Gelfand, 2015, for an exception). Adoption of such methods represents an opportunity to explore some yet more interesting and challenging questions in the trust and culture domain.

Practical Implications

1. **Artificial intelligence.** Much of the research conducted in the last decade on trust and culture has focused on contexts and phenomena that have already been extensively studied in the two respective literatures. Focusing on such "mainstream" topics and contexts is, of course, extremely valuable. However, we would like to highlight the potential value of also focusing on emerging trust and culture issues. On the trust side, organizational leaders'

increasing use of artificial intelligence for personnel decisions, in the face of the technology's well-recognized tendency to make and perpetuate decisions that are culturally, racially, or ethnically biased (Chouldechova, 2017; Ledford, 2019), is likely to raise additional questions about the extent to which organizational leaders can or should be trusted. Yet, this practice also presents an opportunity for leaders to "solve" this dilemma by developing ways to use technologies that are unbiased and can demonstrate ability, benevolence, and integrity. We expect cultural differences in the trust-related reactions of employees to the use of AI in the workplace.

2. **HR Analytics.** Similarly, the extensive adoption of analytics in society, including the use of HR analytics in organizations (e.g., Edwards & Edwards, 2019), represents a level of monitoring that in its comprehensiveness and intrusiveness could scarcely have been imagined when scholars earlier began to systematically consider how trust and monitoring might be interrelated (Ferrin et al., 2007). Again, research could fruitfully explore how leaders could use HR analytics in a way that demonstrates, rather than undermines, perceptions of their ability, benevolence, and integrity. This is particularly important for trust among employees with diverse experiences, backgrounds, and group memberships and in multicultural and intercultural settings, as HR and people analytics can also introduce and perpetuate biases in the workplace (Whiteman, 2020).
3. **Cultural dynamics and trust.** Within many countries, political and societal issues such as populism, patriotism, and social justice have become strong sources of cultural identity and have caused cultural divisions that are sometimes greater than 'traditional' cultural differences of national background, language, and cultural values. These emerging politically and societally based divisions have the potential to damage existing trust relationships and impede the building of new trust relationships within organizations and society. Research could fruitfully focus on how trust could be maintained or built in the presence of such deep, often adversarial, cultural differences.
4. **Cross-fertilization for trust pedagogies and interventions.** Culture and trust areas of scholarship differ dramatically in their development of interventional and pedagogical methods: over the decades, culture researchers and practitioners have developed and implemented numerous tools, including culture simulations (e.g., BaFa' BaFa', Shirts, 1974), cross-cultural training including training in cultural attribution and cultural awareness (e.g., Littrell & Salas, 2005), and cultural intelligence (e.g., Gelfand et al., 2008). In contrast, trust scholars have made much less headway in terms of developing pedagogic or interventional approaches (e.g., Ferrin, 2013). Considering that one important outcome of cultural training and

interventions is to build strong relationships among parties in cross-cultural settings, trust scholars may be able to gain insights from culture scholars on how trust pedagogies and interventions can be developed and/or trust and culture scholars could work together to embed trust-building into existing culture pedagogical and interventional tools.

5. **The potential of trust to override cultural differences.** One key distinction between trust and culture is their degree of stability over time: Culture, by definition, tends to be stable over long periods of time, whether as an individual value or a set of shared beliefs, norms, or values. In contrast, trust, while often enduring in nature, can also be built or lost very quickly. Consequently, trust may provide a useful practical "answer" to the question of how to secure cooperation and positive relationships in the face of cultural differences. Given the commonly observed effects of trust, such as higher risk-taking and increased cooperation (Colquitt et al., 2007; Ferrin et al., 2007), trust has the potential to bridge cultural differences between individuals and groups. For example, research on international joint ventures has found that while different cultures led to different conflict resolution strategies, trust between the joint venture partners played a more important role in the choice of conflict resolution strategies, thus overriding the effects of cultures (Nguyen et al., 2016). This may be due to the fact that trust can foster cooperation even in the face of differences. For instance, researchers have found that top management teams high on team trust have lower relational conflict spillover from task conflict that could arise from different perspectives (Simons & Peterson, 2000). Thus, when cultural differences are potentially divisive, a focus on trust-building may provide a route to cooperation and more positive relationships.

References

Ado, A., Su, Z., & Wanjiru, R. (2017). Learning and knowledge transfer in Africa-China JVs: Interplay between informalities, culture, and social capital. *Journal of International Management, 23*(2), 166–179. doi:10.1016/j.intman.2016.11.003

Al-Ississ, M., & Bohnet, I. (2016). Risk mitigation and trust: Experimental evidence from Jordan and the United States. *Journal of Economic Psychology, 53*, 83–98. doi:10.1016/j.joep.2015.12.010

Alon, A., & Hageman, A. M. (2013). The impact of corruption on firm tax compliance in transition economies: Whom do you trust? *Journal of Business Ethics, 116*(3), 479–494. doi:10.1007/s10551-012-1457-5

Andersen, J. A., & Kovač, J. (2012). Why European subordinates trust their managers. *Organizacija, 45*(6), 300–308. doi:10.2478/v10051-012-0029-x

Ang, F., & Tan, H. H. (2016). Trust building with Chinese host country nationals. *Journal of Global Mobility, 4*(1), 44–62. doi:10.5465/ambpp.2015.11563abstract

Arregle, J., Duran, P., Hitt, M. A., & Essen, M. V. (2016). Why is family firms' internationalization unique? A meta-analysis. *Entrepreneurship Theory and Practice, 41*(5), 801–831. doi:10.1111/etap.12246

Baer, M. D., Dhensa-Kahlon, R. K., Colquitt, J. A., Rodell, J. B., Outlaw, R., & Long, D. M. (2015). Uneasy lies the head that bears the trust: The effects of feeling trusted on emotional exhaustion. *Academy of Management Journal, 58*(6), 1637–1657. doi:10.5465/amj.2014.0246

Baldwin, J. R., Faulkner, S. L., & Hecht, M. L. (2006). A moving target: The illusive definition of culture. Redefining culture: Perspectives across the disciplines. In J. R. Baldwin, S. L. Faulkner, M. L. Hecht, & S. L. Lindsley (Eds.), *Redefining culture: Perspectives across the disciplines* (pp. 3–26). Mahwah, NJ: Lawrence Erlbaum.

Bamgboje-Ayodele, A., & Ellis, L. (2015). Knowledge management and the Nigerian culture – A round peg in a square hole? *The African Journal of Information Systems, 7*(1), 1–16.

Bass, B. M. (1997). Does the transactional-transformational leadership paradigm transcend organizational and national boundaries? *American Psychologist, 52*(2), 130–139. doi:10.1037/0003-066X.52.2.130

Berger, R., Herstein, R., Silbiger, A., & Barnes, B. R. (2018). Is guanxi universal in China? Some evidence of a paradoxical shift. *Journal of Business Research, 86*, 344–355. doi:10.1016/j.jbusres.2017.07.016.

Bohnet, I., Herrmann, B., & Zeckhauser, R. (2010). Trust and the reference points for trustworthiness in gulf and Western countries. *Quarterly Journal of Economics, 125*(2), 811–828. doi:10.1162/qjec.2010.125.2.811

Bornhorst, F., Ichino, A., Kirchkamp, O., Schlag, K. H., & Winter, E. (2010). Similarities and differences when building trust: The role of cultures. *Experimental Economics, 13*(3), 260–283. doi:10.1007/s10683-010-9240-x

Brett, J. M., Gunia, B. C., & Teucher, B. M. (2017). Culture and negotiation strategy: A framework for future research. *Academy of Management Perspectives, 31*(4), 288–308. doi:10.5465/amp.2015.0195

Campagna, R. L., Dirks, K. T., Knight, A. P., Crossley, C., & Robinson, S. L. (2019). On the relation between felt trust and actual trust: Examining pathways to and implications of leader trust meta-accuracy. *Journal of Applied Psychology, 105*(9), 994–1012. doi:10.1037/apl0000474

Carr, C., & Bateman, S. (2010). Does culture count? Comparative performances of top family and non-family firms. *International Journal of Cross Cultural Management, 10*(2), 241–262. doi:10.1177/1470595810370907

Chang, H. H., Hung, C., & Hsieh, H. (2014). Virtual teams: Cultural adaptation, communication quality, and interpersonal trust. *Total Quality Management and Business Excellence, 25*(11–12), 1318–1335. doi:10.1080/14783363.2012.704274

Chao, G. T., & Moon, H. (2005). The cultural mosaic: A metatheory for understanding the complexity of culture. *Journal of Applied Psychology, 90*(6), 1128–1140. doi:10.1037/0021-9010.90.6.1128

Chathoth, P. K., Mak, B., Sim, J., Jauhari, V., & Manaktola, K. (2011). Assessing dimensions of organizational trust across cultures: A comparative analysis of U.S. and Indian full service hotels. *International Journal of Hospitality Management, 30*(2), 233–242. doi:10.1016/j.ijhm.2010.09.004

Chen, N., Chao, M. C., Xie, H., & Tjosvold, D. (2018). Transforming cross-cultural conflict into collaboration. *Cross Cultural and Strategic Management, 25*(1), 70–95. doi:10.1108/ccsm-10-2016-0187

Chen, X.-P., Eberly, M. B., Chiang, T.-J., Farh, J.-L., & Cheng, B.-S. (2014). Affective trust in Chinese leaders: Linking paternalistic leadership to employee performance. *Journal of Management, 40*(3), 796–819. doi:10.1177/0149206311410604

Chouldechova, A. (2017). Fair prediction with disparate impact: A study of bias in recidivism prediction instruments. *Big Data, 5*, 153–163.

Christoffersen, J., & Robson, M. J. (2017). Money can't buy me trust: Evidence of exogenous influences crowding out process-based trust in alliances. *British Journal of Management, 28*(1), 135–153. doi:10.1111/1467-8551.12189

Chua, R. Y., Morris, M. W., & Mor, S. (2012). Collaborating across cultures: Cultural metacognition and affect-based trust in creative collaboration. *Organizational Behavior and Human Decision Processes, 118*(2), 116–131. doi:10.1016/j.obhdp.2012.03.009

Colquitt, J. A., Scott, B. A., & Lepine, J. A. (2007). Trust, trustworthiness, and trust propensity: A meta-analytic test of their unique relationships with risk taking and job performance. *Journal of Applied Psychology, 92*(4), 909–927. doi:10.1037/0021-9010.92.4.909

Costigan, R. D., Instinga, R. C., Berman, J. J., Kranas, G., & Kureshov, V. A. (2011). A cross-cultural study of coworker trust. *International Journal of Commerce and Management, 21*(2), 103–121. doi:10.1108/10569211111144328

Croson, R., & Buchan, N. (1999). Gender and culture: International experimental evidence from trust games. *American Economic Review, 89*(2), 386–391. doi:10.1257/aer.89.2.386

Cui, V., Vertinsky, I., Robinson, S., & Branzei, O. (2015). Trust in the workplace: The role of social interaction diversity in the community and in the workplace. *Business and Society, 57*(2), 378–412. doi:10.1177/0007650315611724

Cyr, D. (2008). Modeling web site design across cultures: Relationships to trust, satisfaction, and e-loyalty. *Journal of Management Information Systems, 24*(4), 47–72. doi:10.2753/MIS0742-1222240402

Danik, L. (2014). Perception of cooperation and trust in international cooperation. A study on Polish exporters and importers cooperation with partners from China and Germany. *Oeconomia, 13*(4), 55–65. https://ssrn.com/abstract=2878821

Debabi, M. (2010). Contribution of cultural similarity to foreign products negotiation. *Cross Cultural Management: An International Journal, 17*(4), 427–437. doi:10.1108/13527601011086612

Deephouse, D. L., Newburry, W., & Soleimani, A. (2016). The effects of institutional development and national culture on cross-national differences in corporate reputation. *Journal of World Business, 51*(3), 463–473. doi:10.1016/j.jwb.2015.12.005

Dickson, M. W., Hanges, P. J., & Lord, R. G. (2001). Trends, developments and gaps in cross-cultural research on leadership. *Advances in Global Leadership, 2*, 75–100.

Dietz, G., Gillespie, N., & Chao, G. T. (2010). Unravelling the complexities of trust and culture. In M. N. K. Saunders, D. Skinner, G. Dietz, N. Gillespie, & R. J. Lewicki (Eds.), *Organizational trust: A cultural perspective* (pp. 3–41). New York: Cambridge University Press.

Dinesen, P. T. (2012). Does generalized (dis) trust travel? Examining the impact of cultural heritage and destination-country environment on trust of immigrants. *Political Psychology, 33*(4), 495–511. doi:10.1111/j.1467-9221.2012.00886.x

Ding, Z., Au, K., & Chiang, F. (2015). Social trust and angel investors' decisions: A multilevel analysis across nations. *Journal of Business Venturing, 30*(2), 307–321. doi:10.1016/j.jbusvent.2014.08.003

Eckerd, S., Boyer, K. K., Qi, Y., Eckerd, A., & Hill, J. A. (2016). Supply chain psychological contract breach: An experimental study across national cultures. *Journal of Supply Chain Management, 52*(3), 68–82. doi:10.1111/jscm.12101

Edwards, M. R., & Edwards, K. A. (2019). *Predictive HR analytics: Mastering the HR metric* (2nd ed.). London: Kogan Page Limited.

Ertug, G., Cuypers, I. R., Noorderhaven, N. G., & Bensaou, B. M. (2013). Trust between international joint venture partners: Effects of home countries. *Journal of International Business Studies, 44*(3), 263–282. doi:10.1057/jibs.2013.6

Ferrin, D. L. (2013). On the institutionalisation of trust research and practice: Heaven awaits!. *Journal of Trust Research, 3*(2), 146–154. doi:10.1080/21515581.2013.822669

Ferrin, D. L., Bligh, M. C., & Kohles, J. C. (2007). Can I trust you to trust me? A theory of trust, monitoring, and cooperation in interpersonal and intergroup relationships. *Group & Organization Management, 32*(4), 465–499. doi:10.1177/1059601106293960

Ferrin, D. L., Bligh, M. C., & Kohles, J. C. (2008). It takes two to tango: An interdependence analysis of the spiraling of perceived trustworthiness and cooperation in interpersonal and intergroup relationships. *Organizational Behavior and Human Decision Processes, 107*(2), 161–178. doi:10.1016/j.obhdp.2008.02.012

Ferrin, D. L., & Gillespie, N. (2010). Trust differences across national-societal cultures: Much to do, or much ado about nothing. In M. Saunders, D. Skinner, G. Dietz, N. Gillespie, & R. Lewicki (Eds.), *Organizational trust: A cultural perspective* (pp. 42–86). Cambridge: Cambridge University Press. doi:10.1017/CBO9780511763106.003

Friedman, R., Hong, Y., Simons, T., Chi, S. C., Oh, S. H., & Lachowicz, M. (2018). The impact of culture on reactions to promise breaches: Differences between East and West in behavioral integrity perceptions. *Group and Organization Management, 43*(2), 273–315. doi:10.1177/1059601116678101

Fulmer, C. A., & Gelfand, M. J. (2012). At what level (and in whom) we trust. *Journal of Management, 38*(4), 1167–1230. doi:10.1177/0149206312439327

Fulmer, C. A., & Gelfand, M. J. (2015). Trust after violations: Are collectivists more or less forgiving? *Journal of Trust Research, 5*(2), 109–131. doi:10.1080/21515581.2015.1051050

Fulmer, C. A., Gelfand, M. J., Kruglanski, A. W., Kim-Prieto, C., Diener, E., Pierro, A., & Higgins, E. T. (2010). On "Feeling Right" in cultural context: How person-culture match affects self-esteem and subjective well-being. *Psychological Science, 21*, 1563–1569. doi:10.1177/0956797610384742

Fulmer, C. A., Gillespie, N., Liu, L. A., Schafheitle, S., Gawk, J., & Hong, S. H. (2023). *Navigating vulnerability: A multidisciplinary review and roadmap forward.* Manuscript submitted for publication.

Gelfand, M. J., & Cai, D. A. (2004). Cultural structuring of the social context of negotiation. In M. J. Gelfand & J. M. Brett (Eds.), *The handbook of negotiation and culture* (pp. 238–254). Stanford, CA: Stanford University Press.

Gelfand, M. J., Imai, L., & Fehr, R. (2008). Thinking intelligently about cultural intelligence. In S. Ang & L. Van Dyne (Eds.), *Handbook on cultural intelligence: Theory, measurement, and applications* (pp. 375–388). Armonk, NY: M. E. Sharpe.

Gelfand, M. J., LaFree, G., Fahey, S., & Feinberg, E. (2013), Culture and extremism. *Journal of Social Issues, 69*(3), 495–517. doi:10.1111/josi.12026

Gelfand, M. J., Raver, J. L., Nishii, L., Leslie, L. A., Lun, J., Lim, B. C., Duan, L., Almaliach, A., Ang, S., Arnadottir, J., Aycan, Z., Boehnke, K., Boski, P., Cabecinhas, R., Chan, D., Chhokar, J., D'Amato, A., Ferrer, M., Fischlmayr, I. C., . . . Yamaguchi, S. (2011). Differences between tight and loose cultures: A 33-nation study. *Science, 332*(6033), 1100–1104. doi:10.1126/science.1197754

Gerbasi, A., & Latusek, D. (2015). Trust-building in international business ventures. *Baltic Journal of Management, 10*(1), 30–51. doi:10.1108/bjm-04-2013-0056

Goodell, J. W. (2017). Trust and governance: The conditioning role of national culture. *Finance Research Letters, 23*, 80–86. doi:10.1016/j.frl.2017.02.008

Gunia, B. C., Brett, J. M., Nandkeolyar, A. K., & Kamdar, D. (2011). Paying a price: Culture, trust, and negotiation consequences. *Journal of Applied Psychology, 96*(4), 774–789. doi:10.1037/a0021986

Henderson, L. S., Stackman, R. W., & Lindekilde, R. (2018). Why cultural intelligence matters on global project teams. *International Journal of Project Management, 36*(7), 954–967. doi:10.1016/j.ijproman.2018.06.001

Hofstede, G. (1991). *Cultures and organizations: Software of the mind.* New York: McGraw-Hill.

Hogler, R., Henle, C., & Gross, M. (2013). Ethical behavior and regional environments: The effects of culture, values, and trust. *Employee Responsibilities and Rights Journal, 25*(2), 109–121. doi:10.1007/s10672-013-9215-0

Hong, Y., Morris, M. W., Chiu, C., & Benet-Martínez, V. (2000). Multicultural minds: A dynamic constructivist approach to culture and cognition. *American Psychologist, 55*(7), 709–720. doi:10.1037/0003-066x.55.7.709

Hong, Y.-Y., Wan, C., No, S., & Chiu, C.-Y. (2007). Multicultural identities. In S. Kitayama & D. Cohen (Eds.), *Handbook of cultural psychology* (pp. 323–345). New York: Guilford Press.

Huff, L., & Kelley, L. (2003). Levels of organizational trust in individualist versus collectivist societies: A seven-nation study. *Organization Science, 14*(1), 81–90. doi:10.1287/orsc.14.1.81.12807

Im, H., & Chen, C. (2020). Cultural dimensions as correlates of favoritism and the mediating role of trust. *Cross Cultural and Strategic Management, 27*(3), 417–445. doi:10.1108/CCSM-09-2019-0165

Jiang, C. X., Chua, R. Y., Kotabe, M., & Murray, J. Y. (2011). Effects of cultural ethnicity, firm size, and firm age on senior executives' trust in their overseas business partners: Evidence from China. *Journal of International Business Studies, 42*(9), 1150–1173. doi:10.1057/jibs.2011.35

Jing, Y., & Bond, M. H. (2015). Sources for trusting most people: How national goals for socializing children promote the contributions made by trust of the in-group and the out-group to non-specific trust. *Journal of Cross-Cultural Psychology, 46*(2), 191–210. doi:10.1177/0022022114557488

Johns, G. (2006). The essential impact of context on organizational behavior. *Academy of Management Review, 31*(2), 386–408. doi:10.5465/amr.2006.20208687

Jones, S., & Shah, P. (2021). The tangled ties of trust: A social network perspective on interpersonal trust. In N. Gillespie, C. A. Fulmer, & R. J. Lewicki (Eds.), *Understanding trust in organizations: A multilevel perspective* (pp. 205–232). New York: Routledge.

Kanagaretnam, K., Khokhar, A., & Mawani, A. (2016). Linking societal trust and CEO compensation. *Journal of Business Ethics, 151*(2), 295–317. doi:10.1007/s10551-016-3211-x

Kang, S., & Kim, A. (2018). Employee stock ownership and financial performance in European countries: The moderating effects of uncertainty avoidance and social trust. *Human Resource Management, 58*(6), 641–655. doi:10.1002/hrm.21942

Korsgaard, M. A., Kautz, J., Bliese, P., Samson, K., & Kostyszyn, P. (2018). Conceptualising time as a level of analysis: New directions in the analysis of trust dynamics. *Journal of Trust Research, 8*(2), 142–165. doi:10.1080/21515581.2018.1516557

Kwantes, C. T., Idemudia, E. S., & Olasupo, M. O. (2018). Power distance and trustworthiness in organizations: A comparative study of students' perceptions in two countries. *North American Journal of Psychology, 20*(2), 397–414.

Labarca, C. (2014). International business and trust: The Sino-Chilean experience. *International Journal of Cross Cultural Management, 14*(3), 323–342. doi:10.1177/1470595814542258

Lau, D. C., Lam, L. W., & Wen, S. S. (2014). Examining the effects of feeling trusted by supervisors in the workplace: A self-evaluative perspective. *Journal of Organizational Behavior, 35*(1), 112–127. doi:10.1002/job.1861

Lauring, J., & Selmer, J. (2012). Openness to diversity, trust and conflict in multicultural organizations. *Journal of Management and Organization, 18*(6), 1870–1894. doi:10.5172/jmo.2012.1870

Ledford, H. (2019). Millions of black people affected by racial bias in health-care algorithms. *Nature, 574*(7780), 608–609. doi: 10.1038/d41586-019-03228-6

Lewicki, R. J., McAllister, D. J., & Bies, R. J. (1998). Trust and distrust: New relationships and realities. *The Academy of Management Review, 23*(3), 438–458. doi:10.2307/259288

Li, J. H., Chang, X. R., Lin, L., & Ma, L. Y. (2014). Meta-analytic comparison on the influencing factors of knowledge transfer in different cultural contexts. *Journal of Knowledge Management, 18*(2), 278–306. doi:10.1108/jkm-08-2013-0316

Li, S., Huo, Y., & Long, L. (2017). Chinese traditionality matters: Effects of differentiated empowering leadership on followers' trust in leaders and work outcomes. *Journal of Business Ethics, 145*(1), 81–93. doi:10.1007/s10551-015-2900-1

Littrell, L. N., & Salas, E. (2005). A review of cross-cultural training: Best practices, guidelines, and research needs. *Human Resource Development Review, 4*(3), 305–334. doi:10.1177/1534484305278348

Lonner, W. J. (1980). A decade of cross-cultural psychology: JCCP, 1970–1979. *Journal of Cross-Cultural Psychology, 11*(1), 7–34. doi:10.1177/0022022180111002

Lowry, P. B., Zhang, D., Zhou, L., & Fu, X. (2010). Effects of culture, social presence, and group composition on trust in technology-supported decision-making groups. *Information Systems Journal, 20*(3), 297–315. doi:10.1111/j.1365-2575.2009.00334.x

Lumineau, F., & Schilke, O. (2018). Trust development across levels of analysis: An embedded-agency perspective. *Journal of Trust Research, 8*(2), 238–248. doi:10.1080/21515581.2018.1531766

Mach, M., & Baruch, Y. (2015). Team performance in cross cultural project teams: The moderated mediation role of consensus, heterogeneity, faultlines and trust. *Cross Cultural Management: An International Journal, 22*(3), 464–486. doi:10.1108/ccm-10-2014-0114

Maddux, W. W., Kim, P. H., Okumura, T., & Brett, J. M. (2011). Cultural differences in the function and meaning of apologies. *International Negotiation, 16*(3), 405–425. doi:10.1163/157180611x592932

Marano, V., Arregle, J., Hitt, M. A., Spadafora, E., & Essen, M. V. (2016). Home country institutions and the internationalization-performance relationship. *Journal of Management, 42*(5), 1075–1110. doi:10.1177/0149206315624963

Mayer, R. C., Davis, J. H., & Schoorman, F. D. (1995). An integrative model of organizational trust. *Academy of Management Review, 20*(3), 709–734. doi:10.5465/amr.1995.9508080335

McAllister, D. J. (1995). Affect- and cognition-based trust as foundations for interpersonal cooperation in organizations. *Academy of Management Journal, 38*(1), 24–59. doi:10.5465/256727

McEvily, B., Zaheer, A., & Soda, G. (2021). Network Trust. In N. Gillespie, C. A. Fulmer, & R. J. Lewicki (Eds.), *Understanding trust in organizations: A multilevel perspective* (pp. 179–204). New York: Routledge.

McGrath, R. G., Macmillan, I. C., Yang, E. A., & Tsai, W. (1992). Does culture endure, or is it malleable? Issues for entrepreneurial economic development. *Journal of Business Venturing, 7*(6), 441–458. doi:10.1016/0883-9026(92)90019-n

Meier, S., Stephenson, M., & Perkowski, P. (2019). Culture of trust and division of labor in nonhierarchical teams. *Strategic Management Journal, 40*(8), 1171–1193. doi:10.1002/smj.3024

Mockaitis, A. I., Rose, E. L., & Zettinig, P. (2012). The power of individual cultural values in global virtual teams. *International Journal of Cross Cultural Management, 12*(2), 193–210. doi:10.1177/1470595812439868

Muethel, M., & Hoegl, M. (2012). The influence of social institutions on managers' concept of trust: Implications for trust-building in Sino-German relationships. *Journal of World Business, 47*(3), 420–434. doi:10.1016/j.jwb.2011.06.001

Nazarian, A., Atkinson, P., & Foroudi, P. (2017). Influence of national culture and balanced organizational culture on the hotel industry's performance. *International Journal of Hospitality Management, 63*, 22–32. doi:10.1016/j.ijhm.2017.01.003

Nguyen, H. L., Larimo, J., & Ali, T. (2016). How do ownership control position and national culture influence conflict resolution strategies in international joint ventures? *International Business Review, 25*(2), 559–568. doi:10.1016/j.ibusrev.2015.09.006

Nikolakis, W., & Nelson, H. (2018). Trust, institutions, and indigenous self-governance: An exploratory study. *Governance, 32*(2), 331–347. doi:10.1111/gove.12374

Nooteboom, B. (2015). Agent-based simulation of trust. In F. Lyon, G. Möllering, & M. N. K. Saunders (Eds.), *Handbook of research methods on trust* (pp. 40–49). Northampton, MA: Edward Elgar Publishing.

Oh, H., Lee, S., & Oh, S. H. (2018). Expatriate managers' cross-cultural motivation and host country national employees' attitudes. *Social Behavior and Personality: An international journal, 46*(5), 841–860. doi:10.2224/sbp.6515

Özer, Ö, Zheng, Y., & Ren, Y. (2014). Trust, trustworthiness, and information sharing in supply chains bridging China and the United States. *Management Science, 60*(10), 2435–2460. doi:10.1287/mnsc.2014.1905

Pan, X., Nau, D., & Gelfand, M. (2020, November). Cooperative norms and the growth of threat: Differences across tight and loose cultures. In *2020 7th International Conference on Behavioural and Social Computing (BESC)* (pp. 1–6). IEEE.

Reiche, B. S., Cardona, P., Lee, Y., & Canela, M. Á. (2014). Why do managers engage in trustworthy behavior? A multilevel cross-cultural study in 18 countries. *Personnel Psychology, 67*(1), 61–98. doi:10.1111/peps.12038

Rockstuhl, T., Dulebohn, J. H., Ang, S., & Shore, L. M. (2012). Leader–member exchange (LMX) and culture: A meta-analysis of correlates of LMX across 23 countries. *Journal of Applied Psychology, 97*(6), 1097–1130. doi:10.1037/a0029978

Rotter, J. B. (1971). Generalized expectancies for interpersonal trust. *American Psychologist, 26*(5), 443–452. doi:10.1037/h0031464

Rousseau, D. M., Sitkin, S. B., Burt, R. S., & Camerer, C. (1998). Not so different after all: A cross-discipline view of trust. *Academy of Management Review, 23*(3), 393–404. doi:10.5465/amr.1998.926617

Salmon, E. D., Gelfand, M. J., Çelik, A. B., Kraus, S., Wilkenfeld, J., & Inman, M. (2013). Cultural contingencies of mediation: Effectiveness of mediator styles in intercultural disputes. *Journal of Organizational Behavior, 34*(6), 887–909. doi:10.1002/job.1870

Schilke, O., & Huang, L. (2018). Worthy of swift trust? How brief interpersonal contact affects trust accuracy. *Journal of Applied Psychology, 103*(11), 1181–1197. doi:10.1037/apl0000321

Shirts, G. (1974). BaFa' BaFa' [educational game]. Del Mar, CA: Simulation Training Systems.

Simons, T. L., & Peterson, R. S. (2000). Task conflict and relationship conflict in top management teams: The pivotal role of intragroup trust. *Journal of Applied Psychology, 85*(1), 102–111. doi:10.1037/0021-9010.85.1.102

Slater, S., & Robson, M. J. (2012). Cultural interpretations of destructive acts and trust in Japanese supply channel relationships. *International Business Review, 21*(3), 357–368. doi:10.1016/j.ibusrev.2011.04.003

Stahl, G. K., Chua, C. H., & Pablo, A. L. (2012). Does national context affect target firm employees' trust in acquisitions? *Management International Review, 52*(3), 395–423. doi:10.1007/s11575-011-0099-7

Tasselli, S., & Kilduff, M. (2018). When brokerage between friendship cliques endangers trust: A personality-network fit perspective. *Academy of Management Journal, 61*(3), 802–825. doi:10.5465/amj.2015.0856

Triandis, H. C. (1994). *Culture and social behavior.* New York: McGraw-Hill.

van der Werff, L., & Buckley, F. (2017). Getting to know you: A longitudinal examination of trust cues and trust development during socialization. *Journal of Management, 43*(3), 742–770. doi:10.1177/0149206314543475

van der Werff, L., Legood, A., Buckley, F., Weibel, A., & de Cremer, D. (2019). Trust motivation: The self-regulatory processes underlying trust decisions. *Organizational Psychology Review, 23*(2–3), 99–123. doi:10.1177/2041386619873616

Verburg, R. M., Nienaber, A.-M., Searle, R. H., Weibel, A., Den Hartog, D. N., & Rupp, D. E. (2018). The role of organizational control systems in employees' organizational trust and performance outcomes. *Group and Organization Management, 43*(2), 179–206. doi:10.1177/1059601117725191

Vogel, R. M., Mitchell, M. S., Tepper, B. J., Restubog, S. L., Hu, C., Hua, W., & Huang, J. (2015). A cross-cultural examination of subordinates' perceptions of and reactions to abusive supervision. *Journal of Organizational Behavior, 36*(5), 720–745. doi:10.1002/job.1984

Wasti, S. A., Tan, H. H., & Erdil, S. E. (2011). Antecedents of trust across foci: A comparative study of Turkey and China. *Management and Organization Review, 7*(2), 279–302. doi:10.1111/j.1740-8784.2010.00186.x

Wasti, S. A., & Önder, Ç. (2021). Employee trust in organizations across cultures: A multilevel model. In N. Gillespie, C. A. Fulmer, & R. J. Lewicki (Eds.), *Understanding trust in organizations: A multilevel perspective* (pp. 334–357). New York: Routledge.

Whiteman, H. (2020). 7 Ways HR can build a fairer, data-informed culture. *Harvard Business Review*. https://hbr.org/2020/11/7-ways-hr-can-build-a-fairer-data-informed-culture

Williams, M. (2001). In whom we trust: Group membership as an affective context for trust development. *Academy of Management Review, 26*(3), 377–396. doi:10.5465/amr.2001.4845794

Williams, M. (2007). Building genuine trust through interpersonal emotion management: A threat regulation model of trust and collaboration across boundaries. *Academy of Management Review, 32*(2), 595–621. doi:10.5465/amr.2007.24351867

Xu, B., Xu, F., Caldwell, C., Sheard, G., & Floyd, L. (2016). Organizational trustworthiness – empirical insights from a Chinese perspective. *Journal of Management Development, 35*(8), 956–969. doi:10.1108/jmd-03-2015-0035

Yamagishi, T., & Yamagishi, M. Trust and commitment in the United States and Japan. *Motivation and Emotion, 18*(2), 129–166 (1994). doi:10.1007/BF02249397

Yamaguchi, I. (2013). A Japan–US cross-cultural study of relationships among team autonomy, organizational social capital, job satisfaction, and organizational commitment. *International Journal of Intercultural Relations, 37*(1), 58–71. doi:10.1016/j.ijintrel.2012.04.016

Yang, I., & Li, M. (2017). Can absent leadership be positive in team conflicts? *International Journal of Conflict Management, 28*(2), 146–165. doi:10.1108/ijcma-12-2015-0083

You, J. (2012). Social trust: Fairness matters more than homogeneity. *Political Psychology, 33*(5), 701–721. doi:10.1111/j.1467-9221.2012.00893.x

Yuki, M., Maddux, W. W., Brewer, M. B., & Takemura, K. (2005). Cross-cultural differences in relationship-and group-based trust. *Personality and Social Psychology Bulletin, 31*(1), 48–62. doi:10.1177/0146167204271305

Zaheer, A., & Kamal, D. F. (2011). Creating trust in piranha-infested waters: The confluence of buyer, supplier and host country contexts. *Journal of International Business Studies, 42*(1), 48–55. doi:10.1057/jibs.2010.49

Zhang, X., & Zhou, J. (2014). Empowering leadership, uncertainty avoidance, trust, and employee creativity: Interaction effects and a mediating mechanism. *Organizational Behavior and Human Decision Processes, 124*(2), 150–164. doi:10.1016/j.obhdp.2014.02.002

Zhao, N., Shi, Y., Xin, Z., & Zhang, J. (2017). The impact of traditionality/modernity on identification- and calculus-based trust. *International Journal of Psychology, 54*(2), 237–246. doi:10.1002/ijop.12445

CHAPTER

14 Leaders, Followers, and Culture: The Entangled Triangle

Paul J. Hanges, Emily E. Forgo, *and* Alexander I. Butler

Abstract

In this chapter, we highlight the role that DeRue's (2011) leader–follower double-interact model plays as a critical, but previously unexplored, mediator for the societal culture-leader/follower interaction relationships. In the proposed model described in this chapter, societal culture influences the frequency and dispersion with which group members can temporarily enact and practice their leadership styles (i.e., DeRue's double-interact patterns). As a result of these cultural modifications, the double-interact patterns will affect (1) leader and follower schema content, structure, and accessibility; (2) leader and follower identity development and centrality; and (3) regulatory fit or nonfit among group members. All of these factors have been shown to be very important factors affecting leader–follower interactions. Throughout this chapter, several hypotheses for future research are discussed.

Key Words: context, double interacts, followers, leader identity, leadership, regulatory focus, relational perspectives, societal culture

> A leader is best when people barely know he exists. When his work is done, his aim fulfilled, they will say: we did it ourselves." —Lao Tzu

> A genuine leader is not a searcher for consensus but a molder of consensus. —Martin Luther King Jr.

> A good leader inspires people to have confidence in the leader. A great leader inspires people to have confidence in themselves. Eleanor Roosevelt

> The art of leadership is a serious matter. One must not lag behind a movement, because to do so is to become isolated from the masses. But one must not rush ahead, for to rush ahead is to lose contact with the masses. He who wished to lead a movement must conduct a fight on two fronts—against those who lag behind and those who rush ahead. —Joseph Stalin

The question of what good leadership is has been debated for centuries. As these quotations illustrate, the answers to this question vary substantially, and a portion of these differences can be traced to the societal culture from which it was derived. For example, the quote from Lao Tzu is consistent with the historically more collectivistic Chinese culture. Whereas the quotes from Eleanor Roosevelt and Martin Luther King Jr. emphasized the impact of one individual on the self-concept and opinions of others and are consistent with more individualistic societies. The quote from Stalin is interesting in that it appears to be a mixture of both collectivism (e.g., the masses have already begun a movement) and individualism (i.e., the leader focuses on the people who lag behind and those who have gone too far ahead).

In the present chapter, we discuss the interconnection between culture and leadership. Early social science leadership research ignored the role of contextual variables, such as culture, on leadership. Instead, these researchers sought to identify universal leadership attributes (Zaccaro et al., 2018). However, starting in the mid-1960s, research increasingly recognized the role of context in leadership (Ayman & Lauritsen, 2018; Liden & Antonakis, 2009). Of the various contextual factors discussed in the contingency leadership literature (e.g., task structure, resource availability, follower characteristics), we focus on societal culture in this chapter. Culture can influence the kind of leadership behavior and style that is desired and enacted in different societies (Dorfman et al., 2012; House et al., 2004), and it can moderate the effectiveness of different leadership styles (Hanges et al., 2016).

We depart from the prior leadership literature in a number of ways. First, the original work on contingency leadership incorporated followers and their characteristics as components of the context that leaders evaluate and react to. Instead, we follow more recent trends in the literature by pulling followers out of the contextual background and therefore highlight their essential role in the leadership process. Thus, our perspective on leadership in this chapter is consistent with John C. Maxwell's quote that said, "If you think you are leading, but there is no one following, then you're only taking a walk." Leaders and followers are both necessary but insufficient components in the leadership process.

Second, we borrow DeRue's (2011) general model of adaptive leadership. This model highlights a concept called the "double interact," which DeRue views as the most basic unit of the leader–follower relationship. We discuss this model and use it to identify the most likely points in the leader–follower relationship in which culture intervenes.

In summary, we will focus on the relationships between leaders, followers, and culture. These three components have been previously described as part of the leadership triangle. For example, in their discussion of the toxic triangle, Padilla et al. (2007) argued that destructive leadership occurs when certain kinds of leaders interact with certain kinds of followers in certain contexts. In our view of this triangle, the three sides are difficult to separate. As was indicated earlier and will be discussed in more detail in the next section, leaders and followers are essential elements of this concept called leadership. Leadership does not exist unless there are both leaders and followers. Further, we will discuss how culture not only influences the subsequent leader–follower interactions that occur, but leader–follower interactions also influence subsequent group or organizational culture.

Thus, we believe that the three sides of this triangle are truly entangled. We now turn to the definition of leadership that that is central to this chapter.

Co-Creation of the Leader-Follower Process: A Relational-Based Perspective.

As we discussed, the early contingency leadership models conceptualized followers as part of the context that leaders considered when making decisions (Blanchard et al., 1993, 2013; Fiedler, 1967; House & Mitchell, 1975). These early models can be described as having taken a leader-centric perspective (Brown, 2018). In other words, these theories focused on the agency of the leader, whereas followers were viewed as passive objects in the contextual background.

The deficiencies of a leader-centric perspective have been increasingly evident over the past two decades. It is now commonly recognized that leadership is not a stable property of one individual but, rather, is best thought of as an emergent phenomenon of dyads or group interactions (e.g., Vroom & Jago, 2007). In all relationships of two (i.e., dyads) or more people, influence has the potential to flow bidirectionally (i.e., all interacting individuals can influence all other interacting individuals). Leaders are those people in a dyad or group that are more influential, on average, than others. In other words, leadership exists and becomes more salient as a dyad's or group's influence process becomes more asymmetric (i.e., one person is more influential on others than the reverse). Leaders influence the attitudes, motives, behaviors, and value saliency of followers (Hanges et al., 2000, 2005, 2016). However, as suggested by our emphasis on the notion that influence flows bidirectionally, followers are not passive recipients of the leader's influence. Followers actively engage with the leader, and they influence the leader's behavior, values, attitudes, and beliefs over time (Brown, 2018). This reverse influence direction is emphasized in the followership literature, and the recognition of the agency of followers has grown over the years (Chaleff, 1995; Kellerman, 2008; Kelley, 2008; Lapierre & Carsten, 2014; Riggio et al., 2008).

We further conceptualize this leader–follower bidirectional influence process as dynamic as opposed to static. That is, we believe that a group's influence pattern or network emerges and changes over time. Thus, in this chapter, we use the relational-based perspective when thinking about leaders and followers. This perspective focuses on the interpersonal behaviors of leaders and followers and pays less attention to their specific roles (DeRue & Ashford, 2010; Uhl-Bien et al., 2014). It is a dynamic perspective because it emphasizes that leaders and followers jointly co-create the leadership process over time (Uhl-Bien et al., 2014). The relational-based perspective is consistent with the literature on the dynamic systems approaches of individual and group processes as well as adaptive leadership and complexity leadership approaches (Aiken et al., 2019; Cronin & Vancouver, 2019; Grand et al., 2016; Hanges et al., 2000, 2005; Marion, 1999; Uhl-Bien & Marion, 2007; Vallacher & Nowak, 1994; Vallacher et al., 2002). Followers are fully integrated into the adaptive/complexity leadership perspectives (Fairhurst & Grant, 2010), and leadership is viewed as an emergent phenomenon that operates at the dyadic or group level of analysis. In summary, for purposes of this chapter, we define the leader–follower process as a dyadic or group level phenomenon that emerges as a result from the dynamic, asymmetric influence process actively co-created by both leaders and followers over time.

With this definition, we turn to a discussion of DeRue's (2011) double-interact model. We will discuss how this model is consistent with our definition of the leader–follower process. We will outline this model and then use it to identify the various points by which culture influences this process.

Double-Interact Episodes as the Basic Unit of Leadership and Followership Interactions

DeRue specified his dynamic model of adaptive leadership in 2011. Consistent with the relational-based perspective, DeRue (2011) focuses on leader–follower relationships in his model and deemphasizes the role of legitimate power or hierarchical positions. Consistent with our definition of leader–follower relationships, DeRue rejected the leader-centric perspective and emphasizes leadership as an emergent phenomenon that results from bidirectional influence processes.

According to DeRue (2011), the basic unit of interaction in leadership is the interdependent and interlocking acts of leading and following. A person can only enact leading or following as a function of whether other group members grant that person those roles (DeRue & Ashford, 2010). Figure 14.1 illustrates the roles that a group of three members take over four different time periods. As shown in this figure, Person A is enacting the leader role at Time 1, while the other two group members are enacting the follower role. At Times 2 and 3, the leader role is enacted by Person C and Person B, respectively. Persons A and B are enacting the follower role at Time 2, and Persons A and C are enacting the follower role at Time 3. Finally, Person A is enacting the leader role at Time 4. This figure illustrates that the exact role that a particular group member claims at any given time period depends on the rest of the group members granting that role to the given group member. Given that taking on these roles are contingent and dependent on the other group members, DeRue (2011) calls this basic leadership interaction a "double interact." The likelihood that a particular group member claims and is granted either the leader or follower role is a function of whether all the group members share the same leader/follower schema, the extent to which the claiming group member's behavior and attributes fits this common leader/follower schema, and the history of claiming and the granting of these roles in the group (DeRue & Ashford, 2010).

DeRue differentiates double interacts in terms of two dimensions: (1) magnitude of leading/following and (2) dispersion of leadership. The first dimension, magnitude, refers to the frequency of leading/following double-interact episodes that occur among

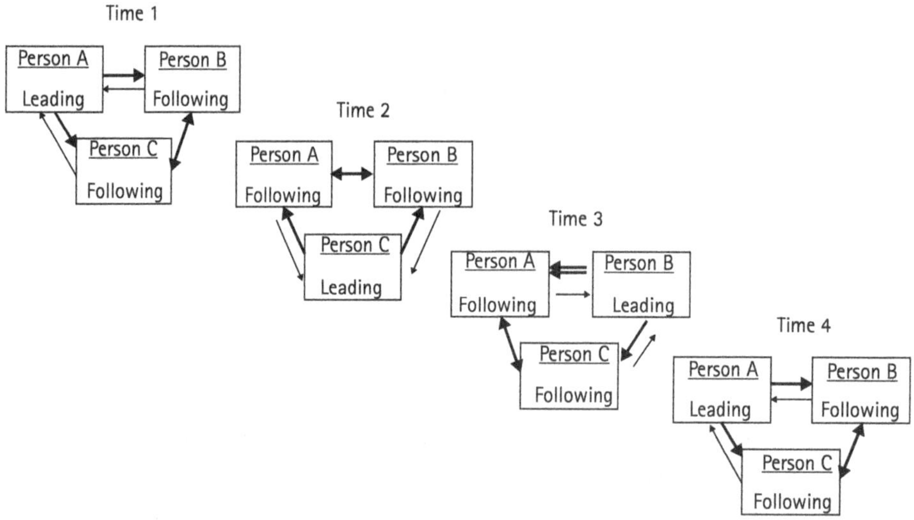

Figure 14.1. Illustration of DeRue's (2011) double-interact episodes over time. *Note*: At any period of time, all group members have influence over all other group members. The differential level of influence between leaders and followers is shown by the size and weight of the arrows coming from and pointing toward one of the group members. The greater influence of leaders over followers is represented by the darker and heavier arrows. The lighter arrows indicate that, while followers influence the leader, their influence is to a substantially smaller degree.

members of a group. A high magnitude of double-interact episodes indicates that leadership is very important for the group and that leader/follower role exchanges occur frequently (DeRue, 2011). A low magnitude of double-interact episodes in a group could be due to disagreements among group members about a particular group member's right or potential to enact the leadership role. It could also be due to leadership not being relevant for the group (e.g., the task does not require group members to coordinate their efforts) or a lack of leadership (e.g., management by exception, laissez-faire leadership). For example, the group in Figure 14.1 has a high magnitude of double-interact episodes because, during every period sampled, someone was enacting the role of the leader while others took on the role of the follower.

The second dimension DeRue used to differentiate a group's double interacts is dispersion. This dimension reflects the percentage of time that the leadership role is primarily enacted by one group member (i.e., low dispersion) versus shared across multiple group members over time (i.e., high dispersion). For example, the group in Figure 14.1 has a high level of dispersion because, over the four time periods, every group member was granted the leader role at least once.

Before discussing how culture affects the double interacts, we want to quickly discuss one implication of DeRue's (2011) model. DeRue indicated that different group or organizational culture as well as other aspects of the context will emerge as a function of magnitude and dispersion of double interacts over time. For example, imagine the context and culture that would emerge in a group in which one member maintains the leadership role over time by using intimidation and ridicule. Compare the context and culture that would emerge in a group in which multiple members share the leader role over time. The nature of a group's double interact influences the kinds of contexts and culture seen in the group. As we will discuss next, context and culture also influence the type of double-interact patterns seen in a group. In general, we expect that societal-level culture will exert greater influence on most leader–follower double interacts[1] whereas leader–follower double interacts would exert somewhat more influence on group or organizational culture. The main implication of DeRue's model is that the causal connections between leaders, followers, and context/culture are truly entangled and constantly influencing each other over time. Questions about causal direction between leaders,' followers', and culture's influence are problematic given the entanglement among these variables.

Double Interacts and Culture

DeRue's (2011) double-interact model can be used as a framework for understanding how societal culture impacts leader–follower relationships. In particular, we believe that a key mechanism by which culture influences the leader–follower process, but one that hasn't received attention in the research literature, is culture's influence on the dispersion and magnitude of the double–interaction patterns.[2] For example, groups from societies with a power distance culture (i.e., societies in which the unequal distribution of power and privileges are accepted)[3] probably have fewer individuals enacting the leader role (i.e., low double–interact dispersion) compared to groups in more egalitarian societies (i.e., a society lacking social stratification and one that values equal access to resources and prestige). Further, group members in power distance cultures probably experience more frequent leader–follower events (i.e., higher double-interact magnitude) compared to group members in more egalitarian societies. Similarly, groups in societies that have an assertive culture (i.e., societies in which assertive, confrontational, and aggressive interactions are viewed as positive and socially acceptable) also probably have less dispersion of double interacts than groups in less assertive cultures. The groups in assertive cultures probably use more aggressive and abusive tactics (e.g., bullying, ridiculing) to maintain the leader role for themselves and to discourage other group members from attempting to claim that

---

[1] For example, Kemal Atatürk, the founding father of the Republic of Turkey, changed the culture of Turkish society during the early part of the 20th century. His large-scale political, economic, and cultural reforms led to the replacement of the prior Turkish culture with a more secular one. The long-term viability of this secular culture, however, started to be questioned in 2007 with the election of the Justice and Development Party. In 2015, the Turkish Parliament speaker indicated that "secularism would not have a place in a new constitution." Thus, the inertia of values, norms, and beliefs of the citizens can work against a leader's efforts to change societal culture over the long run.

[2] There are other mechanisms through which culture influences leader–follower interactions (e.g., culture increases the salience of values and norms). However, we believe that culture's influence on the double interacts is especially important at the formation of leader and follower relationships in a group.

[3] Javidan et al. (2004).

role. In other words, societal culture affects the dispersion and magnitude of double interacts as well as the style used in groups to maintain double-interact dispersion and magnitude over time. Many hypotheses regarding specific cultural variables and their influence on these two properties of double interacts can be generated. It should be noted, however, that the effect of culture on the magnitude and dispersion of double interacts has not yet been empirically tested.

Proposed Mechanism for Culture's Influence on Leader and Follower Schemas

The exact mechanism by which societal culture influences the leader–follower double interacts as well as leader and follower schemas has not been studied. However, we can draw upon institutional theory and research as well as some of the findings from the information processing approach to leadership to identify a potential mechanism. First, regarding linking societal culture to the magnitude and pattern of double interacts, we can draw from institutional theory and in particular, the work of Hambrick and his colleagues (Crossland & Hambrick, 2007; 2011; Hambrick & Finkelstein, 1987). Their work has demonstrated that organizational factors (e.g., organizational slack, passive board, entrenched culture), environmental characteristics (e.g., lack of regulations and speed of growth in industry), and societal culture influence leader behavior primarily by restricting managerial discretion. Managerial discretion refers to the tolerance granted to executives, leaders, and managers to devise and implement creative solutions to organizational problems (Hambrick & Finkelstein, 1995). Executives, leaders, and managers working in organizations that have a strong and established culture, or in highly regulated industries, or in culturally tight societies have less latitude than executives, leaders, and managers working in organizations with weak or unentrenched cultures, in nonregulated industries, or in culturally loose societies. We predict that the variability of observed double interact claiming and granting patterns would be reduced (lower dispersion) in such organizations, industries, and cultures due to the leader role only being granted to the appointed leader. After all, it is probably unacceptable for executives, leaders, and managers to be provided the latitude to grant the leader role to other group members when managerial discretion is restricted. In other words, we expect that participative leadership (i.e., high dispersion) will not occur when managerial discretion is minimalized.[4] In addition to cultural tightness, Crossland and Hambrick (2011) found that societies high on uncertainty avoidance, power distance, and collectivistic cultures also restrict managerial discretion when compared to societies lower on these dimensions. Thus, institutional theory and research has provided the first link of our proposed mechanism: societal culture influences double-interact patterns via loosening/restricting managerial discretion.

---

[4] It is possible that participant leadership would occur when managerial discretion is limited if the content of the organizational culture, industry regulations, or societal culture explicitly endorses this leadership style.

To complete the path from culture to leader-follower interactions, we can draw upon the work of the GLOBE project (House et al., 2004, 2014). House et al. (2004) showed that societal culture influences the content (i.e., expected behaviors and attributes) of leadership schemas. The content of a schema is determined by personal experiences as well as individual-level and societal-level values. A person's experience is a function of the magnitude and dispersion of the double interacts that they have encountered. Thus, exposure to double-interact patterns results in schema content. House et al. (2014) adds to this argument because they showed that societal culture affects actual leader behavior through the mediating mechanism of content in leadership schemas shared by individuals in a society. It is the culturally specified shared content in the leadership schemas that influences actual leader behavior (House et al., 2014). While prior research has connected culture to managerial discretion and leader schema to leader behavior, the connecting path through leader–follower double interacts has not been tested and needs to be verified. Thus, one mechanism by which culture influences leader–follower interaction is by changing the shared leader and follower schema content via the enhancement or restriction of double–interact patterns experienced by group members in a society.

In addition to shaping the shared leader and follower schema content, culture might also influence leader-follower interactions by influencing one's identity. Indeed, culture has repeatedly been shown to shape one's identity (Abrams & Hogg, 1990; Erez & Gati, 2004: Roccas & Brewer, 2002). The centrality and strength of one's leader and follower identities are a major factor in determining whether someone emerges as a leader or as a follower in group interactions (Epitropaki et al., 2017). For example, Erez and her colleagues (Erez & Early, 1993; Erez & Gati, 2004; Lisak & Erez, 2015; Lisak et al., 2016) have found that people with a strong global leadership identity (i.e., being a member of the global community is central to self-concept) emerge as leaders of multicultural groups. In the present chapter, we add to this literature by connecting societal culture's influence on identity via the leader–follower double–interact mechanism. The complexity and centrality of leader and follower identities increase as group members have more opportunities to enact and develop their leader and follower identities over time. We argue that these changes in leader and follower identities are a result of the mechanism shown in Figure 14.2.

Finally, research has found that regulatory focus is an important predictor for understanding goal-oriented behavior. Higgins's (1998) regulatory focus theory states that people are either promotion focused or prevention focused. Promotion-focused individuals focus on growth, aspirations, and their ideal self, whereas prevention-focused individuals focus on avoiding punishment by accomplishing their duties and responsibilities. These individuals focus on what "ought" to be done in a situation. Regulatory focus has been found to be an important mechanism in leader–follower interactions. We will discuss how culture can increase the salience of a promotion or prevention focus and how double–interact patterns can increase the match between leader and follower's regulatory focus.

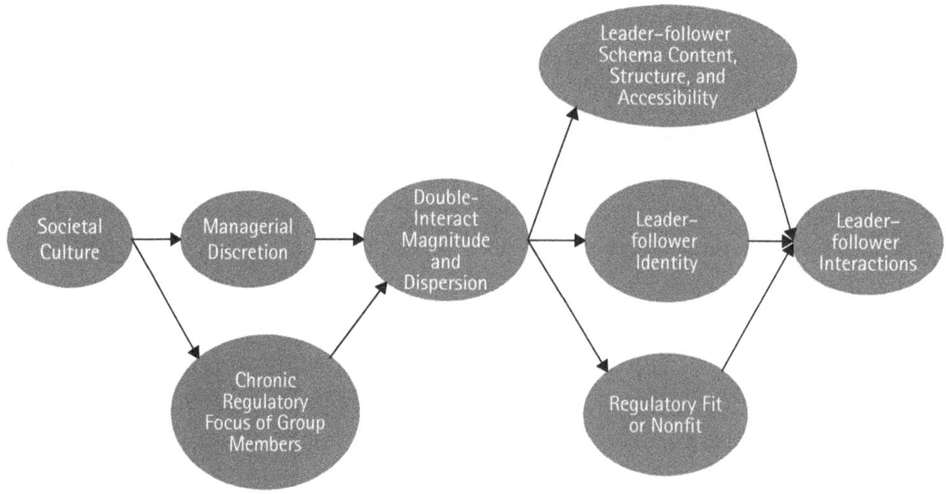

Figure 14.2. Proposed mechanism by which societal culture influences leader–follower interactions.

In summary, we maintain that DeRue's (2011) double-interact model provides a useful framework for understanding how culture affects leader–follower processes. We will focus on the three mechanisms to support our argument. The full hypothesized culture to leader–follower interaction mechanism is shown in Figure 14.2. For ease of discussion, we limit our focus to societal-level culture in this chapter. As mentioned earlier, group and organizational culture have a more complex and bidirectional relationship with leader–follower double interacts. Discussion of culture below the societal level will have to be covered in a different chapter.

Culture and Culturally Endorsed Leadership Schemas

Robert Lord and his colleagues (e.g., Lord et al., 1982, 1984; Lord & Brown, 2004) first proposed the information-processing explanation for leadership perception and effectiveness approximately 40 years ago. Specifically, Lord and colleagues argued that the beliefs about and attributes of leaders are clustered together in cognitive structures called schemas (Lord et al., 1984). The information-processing explanation says that attribution of leadership regarding others is a function of an automatic matching process between the attributes and behavior of the other person against the content of the observer's (i.e., follower's) leadership schema. The better the match, the more likely it is that the observed person will be labeled a leader by the observer–follower (Lord & Maher, 1991). Once the label of "leader" is ascribed to the observed person, that person gains social power (Cronshaw & Lord, 1987), and the label triggers causal attributions and assumptions of the person's ability to motivate and direct others (Konst et al., 1999). The process by which we label some group members as leaders is the same process by which we label other group members as followers (Carsten et al., 2010; Shondrick & Lord, 2010).

The content of both leader and follower schemas will differ across individuals as a function of each person's experiences, values, and personality (Lord & Brown, 2004). However, despite individual variation in schema content, people from preexisting intact groups often share aspects of their schemas due to common group experiences, values, and personality (Schneider, 1987). Nisbett et al. (2001), for example, found cultural differences in the use of cognitive processes where Westerners were more likely to use analytic processes, while East Asian individuals were more likely to use holistic processes. Research has also found the role of culture in the development of various schemas, including descriptions used to describe one's team (Gibson & Zellmer-Bruhn, 2001) and displays of creativity when in the presence of a supervisor or peer (Nouri et al., 2014). In the leadership literature, Erez and Earley (1993), Dorfman (1996), Hanges et al. (2000), House et al. (1997), Shaw (1990), Triandis (1993), and others have also argued that culture is a major determinant of the commonality in leadership schemas; empirical work has supported this argument (e.g., Den Hartog et al., 1999; Dickson et al., 2001; Dorfman, 1996; Erez & Earley, 1993; Hanges et al., 2000, 2005; House et al., 2004; Shaw, 1990; Triandis, 1993). Given the work showing that culture affects a variety of different schemas, we expect that follower schemas will be similarly affected by societal culture.

Shaw (1990) outlined three mechanisms by which societal culture influences leader schemas.[5] First, societal culture could affect the attributes and behaviors believed to be typical of leaders (i.e., schema content). Second, societal culture could affect the cognitive complexity and differentiation among the schema content (i.e., schema structure). Finally, Shaw (1990) proposed that culture could affect the level of automaticity involved in processing leadership encounters. As we review next, researchers have tested Shaw's (1990) proposed mechanisms, although they have primarily focused on the first mechanism. We believe that all of Shaw's mechanisms are affected by culture as shown in Figure 14.2. The cognitive research literature has repeatedly found that the content, structure, and accessibility of schemas change as a function of the frequency of experiences accessing and using a schema. We therefore expect that different double-interact patterns (e.g., magnitude and dispersion) across societies will influence the content, structure, and accessibility of leader (and follower) schemas.

Empirical Findings

As mentioned, most of the prior empirical work on cross-cultural leader schemas has focused primarily on the first of Shaw's (1990) mechanisms (Hanges et al., 2000, 2005, 2016; House et al., 2004, 2014) although some preliminary work has explored the second (Hanges et al., 2000, 2005). The Global Leadership and Organizational Behavior Effectiveness (GLOBE) project (Chhokar et al., 2007; House et al., 2004) found that the

[5] Shaw's (1990) three mechanisms is a general conceptualization of culture's effect on schemas, and it probably generalizes to the effect of culture on follower schemas as well.

content of desired leadership characteristics differed as a function of societal culture as well as the industry and culture of the organization from which respondents were sampled.

Specifically, using their international collaborators, the GLOBE team identified over 100 positive and negative leadership attributes. Survey respondents in this study came from 62 different societies (Dorfman et al., 2012; House et al., 2004). The separate attributes, after being averaged to the societal level of analysis, were found to collapse into 21 first-order leadership scales referred to as culturally endorsed leadership theory (CLTs) scales.[6] These first-order dimensions could be subsequently collapsed into the following six second-order dimensions (a.k.a. Global CLTs): (1) autonomous (i.e., independent and individualistic), (2) charismatic (e.g., inspirational, motivational, and high-performance expectations for followers, (3) humane-oriented (supportive, compassionate, and generous), (4) participative (followers are involved in decision making), (5) self-protective (status and face-saving behaviors), and (6) team-oriented (team building and implementation of a common goal).

Many dimensions of societal culture were found to relate to the Global CLTs.[7] For example, the charismatic CLT was positively related to cultural dimensions such as performance orientation (i.e., societal cultures vary in encouraging and rewarding innovation and stressing excellence and performance improvement), humane orientation (i.e., societal differences in encouraging and rewarding fairness, altruism, and caring), in-group collectivism (i.e., societal differences in stressing pride, loyalty, and cohesiveness for groups and families), gender egalitarianism (i.e., societal differences in minimizing gender inequality), and future orientation (i.e., societal differences in encouraging and rewarding planning and delaying gratification). The participative CLT was positively related to cultural dimensions such as performance orientation, humane orientation, and gender egalitarianism but negatively related to the uncertainty avoidance (i.e., societal differences on the stressing of social norms, rules, and procedures to reduce the unpredictability of the future) cultural dimension. Finally, the team-oriented CLT was positively related to such cultural dimensions as performance orientation, humane orientation, in-group collectivism, and future orientation.

Subsequent work added Gelfand's construct of cultural tightness (Gelfand et al., 2006, 2011; Harrington & Gelfand, 2014) to the GLOBE database. Specifically, Atkas et al. (2016) tested whether cultural tightness (i.e., societal differences in having strong norms and lack of tolerance for deviating from these norms) adds unique variance in the prediction of the Global CLTs over and beyond the GLOBE organizational and societal cultural

[6] All of the GLOBE leadership scales were developed at the country level of analysis. Using various statistics, such as the intraclass correlation coefficient, findings demonstrated that these scales could be aggregated to the country level of analysis and could be used to reliably differentiate societies (Hanges & Dickson, 2004, 2006).

[7] We use the GLOBE cultural dimensions (House et al., 2004; Javidan et al., 2004) as well as the Schwartz (2006) cultural value dimensions in this chapter.

dimensions. They found that cultural tightness added more variance in the prediction of the autonomous CLT (positive relationship), charismatic CLT (negative relationship), and team-oriented CLT (negative relationship). In other words, autonomous CLTs were viewed as more effective in tight versus loose societies. Charismatic and team-oriented CLTs, on the other hand, were viewed as less effective in tight versus loose societies.

One kind of leadership style not examined in the original 2004 GLOBE study was paternalistic leadership. This leadership style is a combination of leader benevolence and leader authoritarianism (Aycan, 2006). This type of leader shows individualized consideration and care for their followers, while also exerting substantial control over subordinates' behavior and retaining decision-making power for themselves (Mansur et al., 2017). Paternalistic leaders try to create a family atmosphere at work by establishing close, personal relationships with their followers and becoming involved in the nonwork aspects of followers' lives. Like parents in traditional families, paternalistic leaders expect loyalty and deference from their followers (Aycan, 2015).

Paternalistic leadership style is not universally endorsed (Mansur et al., 2017). It is more strongly endorsed in countries with higher cultural values of power distance and collectivism such as Asian, Middle Eastern (Aycan et al., 2013; Mansur et al., 2017), African (Matando, 2012; Wanasika et al., 2011), and Latin American (Castaño et al., 2015; Davila & Elvira, 2012) countries, as well as Turkey and Taiwan (Gumusluoglu et al., 2019) than in Western societies (Gelfand et al., 2007). Further, Aycan et al. (2013) found that the content of paternalistic leadership, authoritarian leadership, and nurturant-task leadership[8] schemas overlapped for respondents from higher-power distance and collectivistic societal cultures compared to the content overlap of these three schemas for respondents from lower-power distance and collectivistic societal cultures. Consistent with our argument in this chapter, Aycan et al. (2013) used DeRue's double interact model to explain why respondents from some countries might have greater content overlap among these three schemas than respondents from other countries.

While research has found that paternalistic leadership is more strongly endorsed in non-***W***estern, ***E***ducated, ***I***ndustrialized, ***R***ich, and ***D***emocratic societies (WEIRD) countries, it should be noted that the components of paternalistic leadership are differentially emphasized throughout the world. For example, China tends to emphasize the benevolent more than the authoritarian component, whereas the opposite trend is found in Mexico (Mansur et al., 2017). Further, even though paternalistic leadership is reported to be not typically endorsed in Western societies, empirical work has found that aspects of this style are endorsed in these societies (Hiller et al., 2018; Wang et al., 2018). Clearly, the relationship between culture and paternalistic leadership is subtle.

---

[8] In contrast to paternalistic leadership, nurturant-task leaders want high follower task performance in exchange for caring and supportive leadership.

A few papers explored the impact of societal culture on Shaw's (1990) second mechanism, schema structure. Hanges et al. (2001) explicitly sought to test the structure hypothesis. They predicted that the importance or centrality of leader attributes will shift as a function of societal culture. MBA students from three countries (Germany, the United States, and Mexico) were provided with the same set of leader attributes and asked to independently rate the perceived similarity of these attributes. Hanges et al. (2001) found that, consistent with Shaw (1990), the central attributes in the leadership schemas significantly varied in a fashion consistent with societal culture. Specifically, the leadership attributes of "excellence-oriented," "visionary," "motivational," and "inspirational" were more central for schemas obtained from societies that had more performance orientation and future orientation cultures. The attributes of "win–win problem solver," "collaborative," "team-builder," and "group-oriented" were more central in societies that held more collectivist values. Overall, these results were consistent with the hypothesized link between societal culture and leader schema structure.

In another study, Nishii et al. (2004) hypothesized that cognitive consistency is more important in societies with more individualistic cultures that stress *analytical* systems of thought, whereas societies that are more collectivist stress *holistic* systems of thought. Individuals in collectivistic societies switch between multiple schemas as a function of the context in which they are situated. Nishii et al. (2004) reasoned that the constant switching between multiple, potentially contradictory schemas would result in leadership schemas in collectivistic societies being less hierarchically structured and having more central attributes than leadership schemas in individualistic societies. Data was collected from MBS students located in Germany, Singapore, Thailand, and the United States. Their results were consistent with these hypotheses. Societal culture was found to change leader schema structure and content accessibility.[9]

Finally, a study by Chen et al. (2016) found that societal culture moderated the centrality and importance of social competence (i.e., interpersonally skillful, and sensitive to social skills) and task competence (e.g., accomplishing tasks and intelligence) leadership attributes. These authors predicted that social competence would be more important in the collectivistic East Asian cultures than in the more individualistic North American cultures. Consistent with their predictions, social competence was strongly associated with leader trust in China, whereas task competence was more strongly associated with leader trust in the United States.

There is evidence that the positive consequences of people's behavior match societal-level shared leadership schemas. House et al. (2014) sampled over 1,000 CEOs and over 5,000 top management team (TMT) members in 24 countries to test whether CEO behavior that matches CLTs results in positive outcomes. These researchers had two

---

[9] Central attributes/behaviors in schemas are more easily accessible. Accessible attributes/behaviors are processed faster and more automatically than less accessible (less central) attributes/behaviors.

measures of organizational effectiveness: (1) TMT dedication that reflected TMT levels of morale and motivation; and (2) firm competitive performance ratings by each organization's chief financial officer. Consistent with predictions, the fit between CEO behavior and the CLTs was positively related to both TMT dedication and firm competitive performance.

House et al. (2014) collected data across 26 societies from over 1,000 CEOs and 5,000 members of their TMTs. The TMT members rated their CEO's leader behavior as well as the morale of the TMT and organizational effectiveness. They found that CEO behavior was directly predicted by societal-level shared leadership schema content and that societal culture indirectly influenced CEO behavior through its influence on the shared content of schemas. When CEO behavior matched the content of the societal-level shared leadership schemas, the TMTs reported higher levels of morale and dedication than CEOs whose behavior was discrepant from the societal-level leadership schemas.

While the House et al. (2014) study did not include measures of magnitude or dispersion, its results suggest that societal culture should influence double-interact patterns. For example, House et al. (2014) found that participative CEO leadership behavior was related to both TMT dedication and organizational effectiveness. We believe that it is reasonable to hypothesize that CEOs who have leader–follower double-interact patterns with higher magnitudes and dispersions would be perceived as more participative than leaders with lower magnitudes and dispersion levels.

In another study, Kennedy (2018) suggested that sometimes a misfit between actual leader behavior and shared leadership schemas might be allowed. For example, people typically forgive and tolerate the cultural transgressions of expatriate leadership behavior as a function of the expatriate leader's reputation, the followers' degree of empathy, and the severity of the transgression. Cultural transgressions are more likely to be tolerated if the expatriate's transgression is consistent with the local stereotype about what leadership behavior from the expatriate's home country would be.

Finally, research has shown that national culture moderates some of the outcomes predicted by leader–member exchange (LMX) theory. This theory predicts that positive outcomes (e.g., follower performance, citizenship behaviors, attitudes) are enhanced and negative outcomes (e.g., turnover) are diminished as the quality of leader–follower interactions improves (Erdogan & Bauer, 2015; Northouse, 2019). Comparing data collected from the United States and South Korea, Lee et al. (2014) found that the relationship between LMX quality and follower attitudes toward organizational change (i.e., affective commitment and consultation) differed cross culturally. Litano et al. (2016) found that societal culture moderated the relationship between LMX quality and perceptions of work interfering with family life. In particular, they found that the negative relationship between LMX quality and work interference with family was stronger in societies with lower-power distance cultures compared to higher-power distance cultures. Finally, Rockstuhl et al.'s meta-analysis (2012) of 23 countries revealed that societal culture moderated the relationships between LMX quality and a host of follower attitudes (e.g., justice perceptions, employee satisfaction, and turnover intentions). Specifically, the LMX quality–attitude relationships were stronger in countries with horizontal-individualistic (i.e., countries that are low on both power distance and collectivism) societal cultures than in countries with vertical-collectivistic (i.e., countries that are high on both power distance and collectivism) societal cultures. Interestingly, this meta-analysis revealed that societal culture did not moderate all the LMX quality relationships. Culture was not found to moderate either the LMX quality-task performance relationship or the LMX quality-organizational commitment relationship.

In summary, there is support for three mechanisms as specified by Shaw (1990). Most of the empirical culture-leadership schema evidence focused on culture's impact on schema content. Clearly, the kinds of attributes and characteristics in the leader schema are influenced by societal culture. There is also some evidence for the second Shaw (1990) mechanism, societal culture affecting the structure of leader schemas. Finally, while we did not explicitly discuss any leader–follower literature supporting the idea that societal culture affects leader/follower schema accessibility, there is strong indirect evidence for this mechanism. For example, Nishii et al.'s (2004) finding that societal culture influences attribute centrality is supportive of this mechanism. Attribute centrality should be related to the chronic level of salience and ease of access of attributes in the mind of leaders and followers. Further, Leung and Morris's (2015) demonstration that culture primes and increases the saliency and subsequent accessibility of nonleadership schemas as well as other broader psychological traits is also suggestive that societal culture should influence schema accessibility (e.g., Gibson & Zellmer-Bruhn, 2001; Nisbett et al., 2001; Nouri et al., 2014). We expect that groups from high-power distance and uncertainty avoidant cultures will probably have more frequent leader–follower double-interact episodes because the leader has either the right to exert power (high-power distance societies) and/or exercise leadership by one individual reduces uncertainty (high-uncertainty avoidant societies). Thus, we expect that the leader schema will be more accessible in such societies compared to societies with lower levels of these cultural dimensions. We expect that the follower schema will be accessible for the majority of group members in these societies because of frequent enactment of the follower role. We expect that the same pattern of results will occur in culturally tight compared to culturally loose societies. Therefore, societal culture's influence on the accessibility of leader/follower schema is likely to be found but needs to be established.

In the next section, we discuss how the claiming and granting process also creates and develops group members' identity as leader or as follower. The literature on leader–follower interactions has increasingly discussed the importance of leader and follower identities for understanding leader/follower behavior in a particular context (Epitropaki et al., 2017; Van Knippenberg et al., 2004.

Leader and Follower Identities

Leader and follower identities are subcomponents of a person's overall self-concept, also known as self-views or self-construal (Day & Dragoni, 2015). The self-concept refers to all the personal beliefs that an individual has about themselves (Van Knippenberg et al., 2004). For example, self-beliefs include knowledge about what we personally value, what we believe, judge, and feel about different topics, people, or contexts, the areas we excel in, and the areas where we struggle (self-efficacy), as well as our aspirations for and fears of possible future versions of oneself (Petriglieri & Stein, 2012; Van Knippenberg et al., 2004). The self-concept can best be thought of as a system or collection of self-schemas that are hierarchically organized, with some self-schemas being central and others more peripheral to the individual (Lord et al., 1999; Markus & Wurf, 1987; Sedikides, 1995). The more central or core self-schemas are well developed, connected to central values, and accessible across multiple contexts, and they have specific memories of experiences and events connected with them (Lord & Brown, 2004). The more peripheral self-schemas are accessed in a limited number of situations and are usually less formed and vaguer than the central self-concepts (Lord & Brown, 2004).

The centrality and strength of a group member's leader and follower identities are a major factor in determining whether someone will emerge as a leader or as a follower in group interactions in particular contexts (Epitropaki et al., 2017). Leadership style and the manner by which group members influence each other is also influenced by the content of group members' leader and follower identities (Epitropaki et al., 2017). Leader identity is the part of one's self-concept that relates to being a leader or how one thinks of oneself as a leader (Day & Dragoni, 2015; Day & Harrison, 2007). It includes leader schemas, personal experiences as a leader, and thoughts about oneself as a leader in the future (Epitropaki et al., 2017). Similarly, follower identity can be defined as the part of one's self-concept that relates to being a follower and how one thinks of oneself as a follower. It includes followership schemas, personal experiences as a follower, and thoughts about oneself as a follower in the future (Epitropaki et al., 2017). These identities evolve over time as a function of varied experiences that allow people to gain insight regarding the type of leader or follower they are or want to become in the future (Day & Dragoni, 2015; Epitropaki et al, 2017).

These identities strengthen and develop over time because of our interactions in social contexts and how we react to each other (DeRue & Ashford, 2010; Lord & Brown, 2004; Lord et al., 1999; Markus & Sentis, 1982; Van Knippenberg et al., 2004). The process of creating these identities is called performing identity work (Ibarra & Petriglieri, 2010; Sveningsson & Alvesson, 2003). It involves people thoughtfully experimenting with possible alternative versions (aka provisional selves) of leadership and followership each time they have an opportunity to enact one of these roles (Day & Harrison, 2007; Day & Dragoni, 2015; DeRue & Ashford, 2010; Ibarra, 1999; 2004; Snow & Anderson, 1987). People retain the parts of these experiments that are reinforced by others and reject those parts that are not. As the leader and follower identities develop and start to generalize over contexts and time, they become linked to the person's core values, and thus, the identity becomes more central to the person's self-concept (Day & Dragoni, 2015).

Brewer and Gardner (1996) conceptualized self-identities as being structured across three levels of analysis: (1) individual; (2) relational (dyadic); and (3) collective (i.e., group/organization/community) levels. Not surprisingly, researchers have also talked about leader and follower identities as being similarly structured (Epitropaki et al., 2017; Lord & Brown, 2004). The individual level focuses on the individual's beliefs regarding their personal attributions and the person's perceived efficacy of successfully performing as a leader or follower compared to others (Epitropaki et al., 2017). Identity is internalized and becomes a stable and salient aspect of one's self-concept at this level (DeRue & Ashford, 2010). The early leadership literature that sought to identify universal leader attributes (e.g., intelligent, talkative, decisive) is reflective of this level of identification. The relational level, on the other hand, focuses on dyadic relationships between the individual and others (DeRue & Ashford, 2010; Lord & Brown, 2004). Consistent with the double interact model, leader and follower identities strengthen as a function of group members endorsing and granting the person's claim of a particular identity (DeRue & Ashford, 2010). The leader–member exchange (LMX) theory is reflective of this level of identification (Day & Dragoni, 2015). Finally, the collective level focuses on the groups the individual feels meaningful connection to. This level emphasizes the similarity of the self, and other members of the collective- and group-level characteristics are ascribed to the self (Van Knippenberg et al., 2004). Leader and follower identity at this level is strengthened when there is a collective endorsement of the identity for the individual. When the collective component of an identity is salient, the individual is more likely to take the collective's interest to heart (van Knippenberg et al., 2004).

The connection between the double-interact patterns and the development of identities has been noted above, as well as discussed by DeRue and Ashford (2010). Specifically, with each episode of claiming and granting roles, people can experiment with a particular provisional self. Parts of the provisional self will be kept or discarded depending on whether they accomplish (fail to accomplish) their task, receive positive (negative) feedback from the group, and devote time and thought to learning from their experience. The testing of these provisional selves continues over time, and the identities that are enacted frequently and positively received grow stronger. The relational level identity develops or fails to develop as a function of the other members of the group either granting or rejecting the claims by a member. Finally, the collective level identity develops as people in the community grant the role that is being claimed. This identity is strengthened as others in the community recognize the member as leader or follower.

Culture and Identity

Societal culture clearly affects the identities held by individuals (Abrams & Hogg, 1990; Erez & Gati, 2004: Roccas & Brewer, 2002). For example, Markus and Kitayama (1991) have argued that people in Asian cultures tend to have identities at the relational or collective level, whereas people from the United States tend to have identities at the individual level. Thinking about the implications of Markus and Kitayama's work on double-interact patterns, we expect higher levels of dispersion (more shared or distributed leadership) in collectivist cultures than in individualistic cultures. Since frequency of enacting roles develops identities and makes them more central, we hypothesize that leader and follower identities might be equally developed and central in individuals from collectivistic rather than individualistic societies.

There are other cultural dimensions beyond individualism/collectivism, however, that could affect leader and follower identities. Unfortunately, the effect of these additional cultural dimensions on either leader or follower identities have not been empirically verified. However, we could hypothesize that groups from cultures with high levels of power distance would show higher magnitude and lower dispersion compared to groups from low-power distance cultures. We expect that groups from cultures with higher levels of power distance would have a higher frequency of double-interact episodes than groups from cultures that are lower in power distance because followers from groups that are high in power distance probably expect their leader to frequently provide direction. We also hypothesize that the frequency of dispersion in high-power distance cultures will be lower than in low power distance cultures because in high power distance cultures it is antitheoretical for the leader in such cultures to give away their power and privilege. Given these two hypotheses, we would also expect sizable differences in the centrality and strength of the follower identity for the average citizen compared to the centrality and strength of the leader identity for average citizens in highpower distance cultures.

The same set of hypotheses probably applies to high uncertainty avoidance cultures. The certainty resulting from the same group leader (high dispersion) and frequent leader–follower episodes (low magnitude) would be highly desired in uncertainty avoidance cultures. Due to the low dispersion of the leader role, we also expect that the average citizen in such cultures would have high levels of centrality and strength for the follower identity but not for the leader identity. The same pattern of result is expected for tighter as opposed to looser cultures.

For humane orientation cultures, however, we expect the opposite double-interact pattern. Humane orientation culture emphasizes fairness and generosity. Thus, we expect that there will be higher dispersion and lower magnitude of double-interact patterns in these cultures compared to societies lower in humane orientation. In humane orientation cultures, the average citizen probably has relatively equal levels of centrality and strength for their leader and follower identities compared to lower humane orientation cultures.

In summary, we reviewed the literature on leader and follower identities. These identities have been shown to predict several group outcomes. Consistent with Figure 14.2, we discussed how culture might influence leader and follower identities through DeRue's (2011) double-interact model. Several hypotheses regarding identity centrality and strength were suggested. In the next section of this chapter, we discuss the connection between the double-interact model and the motivational processes individuals use to achieve their desired goals.

Regulatory Focus, Leadership, and Culture

Self-regulation and regulatory focus have been increasingly discussed as potential mediators of the leader–follower influence process (Kark & Van Dijk, 2019). Self-regulation refers to the process by which people align their behavior to facilitate attaining their goals and/or standards (Brockner & Higgins, 2001). Regulatory focus theory, first proposed by Higgins in 1998, postulates that people align their goal-oriented behavior in different ways, depending on whether they are more focused on maximizing gains as opposed to minimizing losses (Higgins, 2014; Higgins & Pinelli, 2020). In other words, people either have a promotion-focused orientation or a prevention-focused orientation. Promotion-focused individuals regulate their behavior to maximize their chances of attaining some desired goal or endpoint. They are focused on their growth, aspirations, and their ideal self (Johnson et al., 2017; Kark & Van Dijk, 2007). Prevention-focused individuals, on the other hand, regulate their behavior to minimize their chances of losing already obtained status or performance. These individuals focus on avoiding punishment by accomplishing their duties and responsibilities and focusing on oughts (Kark & Van Dijk, 2007, 2019).

Each of these two orientations not only affects individuals' behavior and performance, but they also differentially affect peoples' perceptions, motivations, decision making, and emotions (Kark & Van Dijk, 2007, 2019). Promotion-focused individuals are more likely to pay attention to the presence or absence of rewards. They incorporate this information to design a strategy and a set of tactics (Scholer et al., 2019; Scholer & Higgins, 2008, 2013) that tend to be innovative, creative, and risky (Johnson et al., 2017). These individuals value change, and they tend to be more creative and willing to take risks. Emotionally, they can range from elation to dejection, depending upon goal attainment (Johnson et al., 2017). Prevention-focused individuals, on the other hand, are more likely to pay attention to the presence or absence of punishments and are focused on their obligations and responsibilities—what they ought to do (Johnson et al., 2017; Kark & Van Dijk, 2007, 2019). They are particularly sensitive to errors and/or potential injuries, and so they are more risk averse and security seeking (Johnson et al., 2017; Kark & Van Dijk, 2019). Their emotions can range from anxiety to calmness (Kark & Van Dijk, 2019).

To understand how regulatory focus affects behavior, researchers have conceptualized regulatory focus as three separate, but hierarchically arranged, motivational levels: (1) the system level, (2) the strategic level, and (3) the tactical level (Johnson et al., 2015; Higgins, 1997). The system level is at the top of this hierarchy and refers to the overall orientation that people use when approaching their goal (i.e., promotion versus prevention focus). The strategic level is in the middle of this hierarchy, and it refers to whether people tend to rely on eagerness strategies (promotion-focused) or vigilant strategies (prevention-focused).

For example, assume that Person A works at the National Science Foundation and Person A's task is to select proposals to fund for the next year. If Person A had a promotion focus, they would choose more eagerness strategies such as funding a proposal that is less likely to succeed, provided that the potential benefit of the project working is high. On the other hand, if Person A had a prevention focus, they would choose more vigilant strategies such as funding proposals whose potential benefit is lower but have a higher chance of succeeding. The tactical level is the lowest level in this hierarchy, and it refers to explicitly incorporating contextual constraints in their preferred strategy so that they can either maximize gains or minimize losses. For example, as indicated earlier, promotion-focused individuals working at NSF might select the riskiest proposals to fund because they were using eagerness strategies to achieve their goals. However, when contextual factors indicate that caution is warranted, then these individuals probably would make the tactical choice to reject the riskiest proposals despite their promised benefit.

Finally, both promotion and prevention focus orientations can be split into a portion that is stable and chronic (trait) versus a portion that is more susceptible to situational (state) fluctuations. The chronic portion of these orientations generalizes over time and across contexts. Changes in situational factors do not affect this portion of regulatory focus orientations. Rather, contextual factors influence the more situational dependent portion of these orientations. Factors such as the leadership style in a group, the structure of an organization's reward system, the organizational climate, organizational culture, or the type of task being performed have been shown to push a person's regulatory focus orientation one way or the other (Scholer et al., 2019). It is important to note, however, that eager and vigilant tactics that coincide with promotion and prevention orientations, respectively, are still used regardless of whether a person's behavior is primarily being driven by the situational or chronic portion of their regulatory focus (Higgins & Spiegel, 2004).

Given this background on regulatory focus, we can now turn to groups and discuss how regulatory focus operates in leader–follower relationships. The leaders' regulatory focus influences their behavior, their leadership style, and their outcomes (Brockner & Higgins, 2001; Kark & Van Dijk, 2007). When the leader has a chronic promotion orientation, the leader engages in exploration behavior such as risk taking, conducting searches of their environment for opportunities, and experimentation with and testing of alternative courses of action (Ahmadi et al., 2017; Tuncdogan et al., 2015). Not surprisingly, the CEO's promotion focus was positively related to firm engagement in exploration and exploitation (Kamerlander et al., 2015). The leaders' chronic regulatory focus affects their motivation to lead as well as their enacted leadership style (Kark & Van Dijk, 2007). For example, Johnson et al. (2017) found that a leader's chronic promotion focus was positively related to transformational leadership style, whereas prevention focus was positively related to management by exception style.

We incorporated the role of culture in the group member's chronic regulatory orientation in our proposed mechanism. As can be seen in Figure 14.2, the chronic regulatory orientation that individuals bring to a group before it is formed should affect the early claiming and granting double-interact patterns observed in that group. Indeed, we predict that groups predominantly composed of promotion-oriented members will show higher levels of dispersion than groups composed of predominantly prevention-oriented members. Also, we predict that groups with predominantly promotion-oriented members will have more frequent double-interact episodes than groups predominantly composed of prevention-oriented members.

However, once the double-interact pattern operates for some time, the state level of a group member's regulatory focus converges as group members attempt to fit in to groups and the environment. For example, research has found that people adjust their regulatory focus as a function of the encountered leadership style (Righetti et al., 2011), as well as contextual factors such as the organization's reward system and task requirements (Righetti et al., 2011). We also expect that adjustment of state-level regulatory focus is also a function of double-interact patterns of claiming and granting. This adjustment and convergence in regulatory styles over time is called regulatory fit. In all likelihood, regulatory fit occurs at the strategic and tactical levels of regulatory focus. Thus, a transformational leader who repeatedly emphasizes gains resulting from achieving difficult goals causes their more prevention-focused followers to adopt riskier strategies and tactics over time (Johnson et al., 2015). This adjustment and convergence happens quite rapidly, with one study reporting leader–follower orientation convergence after only 3 months (Sassenberg & Hamstra, 2017). When regulatory fit exists, positive outcomes, such as higher task engagement, higher motivation, and greater feelings that everything is going well, will occur (Johnson et al., 2015).

Of course, regulatory fit doesn't always occur. The follower's chronic portion of regulatory focus limits the range of change that can occur in their state regulatory focus. When regulatory nonfit occurs, followers become disengaged and demotivated, and they feel that things are not going well (Avnet et al., 2013; Higgins, 2008; Camacho et al., 2003, Cesario et al., 2004). Benjamin and Flynn (2006) found that the effectiveness of transformational leadership was greater for followers with a promotion focus (regulatory fit) than for followers with a prevention focus (regulatory nonfit). Figure 14.2 shows that we expect regulatory fit or nonfit to be influenced by double-interact patterns over time.

In all likelihood, groups composed of regulatory nonfit members will split into subgroups. Individuals with the same regulatory fit will collapse into similar subgroups, and the nonfitting members will probably join more compatible subgroups. We expect that there will be more claiming and granting among people who share their regulatory orientation (regulatory fit) than among people who do not (regulatory nonfit). If that prediction is supported by future research, we would also expect that the average level of centrality and strength of leader and follower identities should be relatively equivalent for the average group members in regulatory fit subgroups. In contrast, for regulatory nonfit subgroups, the level of centrality and strength of the follower identity should be greater for the average group member than the centrality and strength of the leader identity. Using LMX terminology, we find that the regulatory fit subgroup would be the ingroup, whereas the regulatory nonfit subgroup would be considered the outgroup (Dansereau et al., 1975; Northouse, 2019).

Culture and Regulatory Focus

As indicated previously, contextual factors can affect the situational or state portion of regulatory focus. Regulatory focus changes as a function of the nature of the tasks one is working on, and it has been found that the average level of regulatory focus is different in different occupations. Crises tend to also change the regulatory orientation of both leaders and followers (Stam et al., 2018; Van Dijk et al.,2013). Similar to these contextual factors, societal culture has also been shown to influence regulatory orientation. However, unlike other contextual factors, Higgins (2008) indicated that the long-term effects of societal culture change the chronic portion of regulatory focus. Research has found that people from individualistic cultures are more promotion-oriented and less prevention-oriented compared to individuals from collectivist cultures (Elliot et al., 2001; Kark & Van Dijk, 2019; Lee et al., 2000). Individualistic and collectivistic cultures have also been found to moderate the relationship between regulatory focus and a variety of dependent variables, such as attitudes and perceptions of one's enemies (Li & Masuda, 2016), the most effective way to deliver negative feedback (Kung et al., 2016), the most effective method to communicate health information (Uskul et al., 2008), socially desirable responding (Lalwani & Chiu 2009), and preferences for enriched information or impoverished information when making decisions (Zhang & Mittal, 2007). Our proposed mechanism shown in Figure 14.2 incorporates Higgins' (2008) proposal and this empirical work that cultures influence individuals' chronic regulatory style.

Almost all the literature on regulatory orientation and societal culture has focused on the individualism/collectivism dimension. However, much like implicit leader–follower schemas literature and the leader–follower identity literature, other societal culture dimensions (e.g., tightness–looseness, uncertainty avoidance) probably also affect regulatory focus. For example, given the focus on the ideal self in promotion orientation and the focus on the ought self in the prevention focus, we posit that people from achievement-oriented cultures would show stronger levels of promotion orientation than prevention orientation compared to people from less achievement-oriented cultures. Also, it is reasonable to expect that prevention orientation would be stronger in tighter rather than looser cultures because tight cultures stress conforming to behavioral norms and what ought to be done. Probably the same relationships would be expected in uncertainty avoidance and power distance cultures. Indeed, Bozer and Delegach (2019) proposed that prevention focus is stronger in societies higher in uncertainty avoidance. Unfortunately, this hypothesis regarding uncertainty avoidance has yet to be empirically tested. Finally, we expect that promotion orientation, rather than prevention orientation, would be stronger in future-oriented cultures.

Discussion

In this chapter, we used a relational-based perspective to discuss the entangled nature of leadership, followership, and culture. Unlike the previously used leader-centric perspective, followers are full partners in the relational-based perspective. Indeed, it is the continued and dual influence of leaders and followers on each that causes the emergence of the dyadic-level or group-level phenomenon referred to as leadership in the literature (Uhl-Bien et al., 2014). More precisely, we defined leadership in this chapter as the dyadic-level or group-level phenomenon that emerges as a result of the dynamic, asymmetric influence process actively co-created by both leaders and followers over time. This definition stresses that the interrelationship between leaders and followers is dynamic. Their relationship and expectations about each other evolve and change over time due to the continued interaction and mutual influence on each other (Eidelson, 1997; Hanges et al., 2000).

We created and proposed a mechanism by which societal culture flows through mediating pathways to influence leader–follower interactions. This mechanism was captured in Figure 14.2. As can be seen in this figure, DeRue's (2011) double-interact mechanism is at the center of the dynamic process. Of course, multiple pathways are documented in other papers and chapters describing societal culture's influence on leader–follower interactions. We focused on the double-interact mechanism in this chapter because (1) its contribution has not been discussed in the prior cross-cultural leadership literature and (2) the claiming and granting process central to this mechanism conceptually leads to many of the factors that researchers have focused on as precursors to leader and follower emergence and behavioral style. We argued that the magnitude and dispersion of double-interact patterns in groups determines (1) the content, structure, and accessibility of leader–follower schemas, (2) the development and centrality of leader–follower identities, and (3) any modification and convergence of the individual group member's strategic and tactical levels of state-level regulatory focus, resulting in either regulatory fit or nonfit. Rather than performing an in-depth review of the massive literature for each of these outcomes, we choose to briefly review each outcome so that we can focus on the mediating role that double-interact patterns play in the culture—the leader–follower relationship. Several hypotheses for future research were provided, and of course, only future empirical research will determine the viability of our model and these hypotheses.

We included Figure 14.2 because we thought it would aid in communicating the components and mechanism outlined by our conceptual model. However, we recognize that this figure may produce an unintended negative impression regarding whether we truly believe in the dynamic nature of our model. This false impression is possible because the Figure 14.2 model shows a unidirectional flow of influence starting from societal culture going through managerial discretion to double-interact patterns. The double-interact patterns are shown to affect (1) leader content, structure, and accessibility, (2) leader and follower identity; and (3) regulatory fit/nonfit and then finally to affect leader–follower interactions. A more accurate depiction of the dynamic nature of our model probably would have required the addition of feedback loops and double-headed arrows. However, we chose not to so because we were concerned that making Figure 14.2 more realistic would have added confusion, and the gain in realism would not have been worth the sacrifice in effective communication. We justified Figure 142's unidirectional flow of influence because the figure includes societal culture and not group/organizational culture. Given the multigenerational transmission of culture, societal culture probably has a greater effect on the observed double-interact patterns seen in a culture than the reverse. While a single group's double-interact patterns may influence societal culture, it probably doesn't have much of an effect (but see footnote 1 above).

The dynamic and entangled nature of culture, leadership, and followership is clearly seen when group- or organizational-level, rather than societal-level, culture is involved. Patterns of claiming and granting in a group change and evolve over time. These claiming and granting patterns result in the development of group norms and common interpretations of the actions taken by group members and the group leader over time. The more common interpretations and the implied values underlying these behaviors are discussed and shared among existing and new group members. Eventually, these shared interpretations of norms, values, and behaviors become entrenched. Group and organizational culture is defined as the shared perceptions among members of some collective regarding the collective's norms, values, and beliefs. The existing culture is communicated to new members through explanatory stories, factual or not, or by longer-term employees sharing past interpretations to help new members interpret the group's practices and rituals. In this way, culture is perpetuated as well as informative for new members regarding the "correct way to perceive, think, and feel" about organizational events and practices (Schein, 2010, p. 18).

In true dynamic fashion, the group and organizational culture, once formed, subsequently restricts the patterns of claiming and sharing that are acceptable or seen as appropriate in the future. Either formal pressure or informal social pressure discourages members from trying new double-interact patterns. Attempts to introduce a more participative leadership style that involves allowing more group members to share the leader role (i.e., increased dispersion) or attempts to introduce a more autocratic leadership style that involves restricting who can enact the leader role (i.e., less dispersion) will be rejected if they are inconsistent with the previously formed group-level or organizational-level culture. Thus, the entangled nature of culture, leadership, and followership is revealed when thinking about group-level or organizational-level culture.

Of course, the dynamic interplay of culture, leadership, and followership needs to be empirically verified. Indeed, while we identified several avenues of future research throughout this chapter, we can also generate hypotheses surrounding the dynamics of our proposed mechanism. For example, De et al. (2017) studied the dynamics of cultural change and proposed that the cultural tightness of a society can slow down the rate at which cultural norms evolve and change over time. They hypothesized that the need for greater coordination seen in culturally tight societies will cause "cultural inertia" (i.e., increased resistance to changing shared norms despite contextual pressure to change the norms) and slow down the "exploration rate" (i.e., attempts to try new strategies to resolve contextual pressure to change norms). These authors supported their arguments using a technique known as agent-based modeling, which are computer simulations that examine where a system ends up as a result of dynamic processes and slight changes in the system's starting point. Agent-based modeling is beneficial for exploring the implications of dynamical processes such as the culture, leadership, and followership process we described in this chapter. Borrowing from De et al.'s (2017) arguments, we can also hypothesize that the rate of change and flexibility of leader and follower behavior, as well as group and organizational culture, will be reduced in culturally tight as opposed to culturally loose societies.

Our field has started to recognize the importance of applying and incorporating dynamical systems theory perspective into a variety of topics in psychology and organizational behavior (e.g., Cronin & Vancouver, 2019; Hanges et al., 2000, 2006; Kozlowski & Chao, 2018; Kozlowski et al., 2013; Shaw, 1997; Trop & Trop, 2018; Uhl-Bien & Marion, 2007; Uhl-Bien et al., 2007; Vallacher et al., 2002; Vancouver et al., 2020). However, conceptual arguments for our proposed model can only go so far. Empirical support for the dynamical perspective of Figure 14.2 is needed and will require changes in the preferred research designs, as well as the development of new analytic methods. Currently, researchers have used both qualitative and quantitative methods to study system dynamics (Aiken et al., 2018). The empirical exploration of dynamic processes requires a preference for longitudinal over cross-sectional research designs.

Of course, as illustrated in the aforementioned De et al. (2017) paper as well as other research studies (e.g., Will, 2016), agent-based modeling, along with other computational modeling techniques, will prove to be useful for uncovering and communicating new insights and future empirical hypotheses when studying dynamic processes. Computational modeling and other forms of simulations are also typically the most impactful when these models are paired with empirical studies of actual behavior (e.g., Cronin & Vancouver, 2019; Vancouver & Purl, 2017; Zhou et al., 2019).

In conclusion, we have argued that leadership, followership, and culture are truly interconnected. Culture influences the type of leader–follower interactions that occur, but leader–follower interactions also influence subsequent group or organizational culture. Leadership is not a property of individuals, but rather it emerges from group interaction patterns over time. We used DeRue's (2011) concept of double interacts to capture the dynamic process that entangles the influence of leaders, followers, and culture. Several hypotheses concerning societal culture and the magnitude and dispersion of double interact patterns were presented as well as hypotheses regarding leader–follower double interacts and leader–follower schemas, identity, and regulatory focus.

Key Findings

- DeRue's (2011) leader–follower double interacts is an important, but previously unexplored, mediator of societal culture's influence on leader–follower interactions.
- Societal culture influences the frequency (i.e., magnitude) and extent to which group members share the leader role (i.e., dispersion) of the leader–follower double-interact pattern.
- The magnitude and dispersion of leader–follower double-interact patterns affect the content, structure, and accessibility of group members' leadership and followership schemas.
- The magnitude and dispersion of leader–follower double–interact patterns influence the development of leader and follower identities as well as the centrality of these identities to the self-concept of group members.
- Chronic regulatory focus orientation affects the leader–follower double-interact patterns, which subsequently produce either regulatory fit or non-fit.

Practical Implications

- All group members, regardless of their official title, are active agents in the process known as leadership. Leadership style is behaviorally manifested by the magnitude and dispersion of leader–follower double-interact patterns.
- The development of future organizational leaders is enhanced when followers are granted sufficient opportunities to enact the "leader" role in their groups and create their identity as leaders.
- Changing the magnitude and dispersion of leader–follower double-interact patterns occurring in an organization can be a powerful tool for modifying group and organizational culture.
- Modification of the observed leader–follower double-interact patterns can improve (diminish) organizational outcomes by increasing regulatory fit (non-fit).
- The scope of change that can be made to leader–follower double-interact patterns is limited by societal culture but also by current group and organizational culture. However, group and organizational culture are modifiable when the organizational leadership supports changes in the magnitude and dispersion of leader–follower double-interact pattern

Author's Note: Please send all correspondence to the first author (phanges@umd.edu). We would like to thank Carolina Cardozo, Virginia Cheng, Jordan E. Epistola, Nivedhitha Kishore, and Kira Cohen for their assistance in conducting the literature review.

References

Abrams, D. E., & Hogg, M. A. (1990). *Social identity theory: Constructive and critical advances*. New York: Springer-Verlag.

Ahmadi, S., Khanagha, S., Berchicci, L., &, Jansen, J. J. (2017). Are managers motivated to explore in the face of a new technological change? The role of regulatory focus, fit, and complexity of decision-making. *Journal of Management Studies, 54*(2), 209–237.

Aiken, J. R., Hanges, P. J., & Chen, T. (2019). The means are the end: Complexity science in organizational research. In S. E. Humphreys & J. M. LeBreton (Eds.), *The handbook of multilevel theory, measurement, and analysis* (pp. 115–140). Washington, DC: American Psychological Association.

Aktas, M., Gelfand, M. J., & Hanges, P. J. (2016). Cultural tightness–looseness and perceptions of effective leadership. *Journal of Cross-Cultural Psychology, 47*(2), 294–309.

Avnet, T., Laufer, D., & Higgins, E. T. (2013). Are all experiences of fit created equal? Two paths to persuasion. *Journal of Consumer Psychology, 23*(3), 301–316.

Aycan, Z. (2006). Paternalism: Towards conceptual refinement and operationalization. In U. Kim, K.-S. Yang, & K.-K. Hwang (Eds.), *Indigenous and cultural psychology: Understanding people in context* (pp. 445–466). New York: Springer Science + Business Media. https://doi.org/10.1007/0-387-28662-4_20

Aycan, Z. (2015). Paternalistic leadership. *Wiley Encyclopedia of Management*, 1–2.

Aycan, Z., Schyns, B., Sun, J., Felfe, J., & Saher, N. (2013). Convergence and divergence of paternalistic leadership: A cross-cultural investigation of prototypes. *Journal of International Business Studies, 44*, 962–969.

Ayman, R., & Lauritsen, M. (2018). Contingencies, context, situation, and leadership. In J. Antonakis & D. Day (Eds.), *The nature of leadership* (3rd ed.) (pp. 138–166). Thousand Oaks, CA: SAGE.

Benjamin, L., & Flynn, F. J. (2006). Leadership style and regulatory mode: Value from fit? *Organizational Behavior and Human Decision Processes, 100*, 216–230.

Blanchard, K. H., Zigarmi, D., & Nelson, R. B. (1993). Situational Leadership® after 25 years: A retrospective. *Journal of Leadership Studies, 1*(1), 21–36.

Blanchard, K. H., Zigarmi, P., & Zigarmi, D. (2013). Leadership and the one minute manager Updated. New York: HarperCollins.

Bozer, G., & Delegach, M. (2019). Bringing context to workplace coaching: A theoretical framework based on uncertainty avoidance and regulatory focus. *Human Resource Development Review, 18*(3), 376–402. https://doi.org/10.1177/1534484319853098

Brewer, M. B., & Chen, Y. R. (2007). Where (who) are collectives in collectivism? Toward conceptual clarification of individualism and collectivism. *Psychological Review, 114*(1), 133–151.

Brewer, M. B., & Gardner, W. (1996). Who is this" We"? Levels of collective identity and self representations. *Journal of Personality and Social Psychology, 71*(1), 83–93.

Brockner, J., & Higgins, E. T. (2001). Regulatory focus theory: Implications for the study of emotions at work. *Organizational Behavior and Human Decision Processes, 86*(1), 35–66.

Brown, D. J. (2018). Chapter 4: In the minds of followers: Follower-centric approaches to leadership. In J. Antonakis & D. Day (Eds.), *The nature of leadership* (3rd ed.) (pp. 82–108). Thousand Oaks, CA: SAGE.

Camacho C. J., Higgins, & E.T., Luger, L. (2003). Moral value transfer from regulatory fit: "What feels right is right" and "what feels wrong is wrong." *Journal of Personality and Social Psychology, 84*, 498–510.

Carsten, M. K., Uhl-Bien, M., West, B. J., Patera, J. L., & McGregor, R. (2010). Exploring social constructions of followership: A qualitative study. *The Leadership Quarterly, 21*(3), 543–562.

Castaño, N., Sully de Luque, M. F., Wernsing, T., Ogliastri, E., Shemueli, R. G., Fuchs, R. M., & Robles-Flores, J. A. (2015). El Jefe: Differences in expected leadership behaviors across Latin American countries. *Journal of World Business, 50*(3), 584–597.

Cesario, J., Grant, H., & Higgins, E. T. (2004). Regulatory fit and persuasion: transfer from "feeling right." *Journal of Personality and Social Psychology, 86*(3), 388–404.

Chaleff, I. (1995). *The courageous follower: Standing up to and for our leaders*. Oakland, CA: Berrett-Koehler.

Chen, F. F., Jing, Y., Lee, J. M., & Bai, L. (2016). Culture matters: The looks of a leader are not all the same. *Social Psychological and Personality Science, 7*(6), 570–578.

Chhokar, J. S., Brodbeck, F. C., & House, R. J. (2007). *Culture and leadership across the world: The GLOBE book of in-depth studies of 25 societies*. New York: Routledge.

Cronin, M. A., & Vancouver, J. B. (2019). The only constant is change: expanding theory by incorporating dynamic properties into one's models. In S. E. Humphreys & J. M. LeBreton (Eds.). *The handbook of multilevel theory, measurement, and analysis* (pp. 89–114). Washington, DC: American Psychological Association.

Cronshaw, S. F., & Lord, R. G. (1987). Effects of categorization, attribution, and encoding processes on leadership perceptions. *Journal of Applied Psychology, 72*(1), 97–106. doi: 10.1037/0021-9010.72.1.97
Crossland, C., & Hambrick, D. C. (2007). How national systems differ in their constraints on corporate executives; A study of CEO effects in three countries. *Strategic Management Journal, 28*(8), 767–789.
Crossland, C., & Hambrick, D. C. (2011). Differences in managerial discretion across countries: How nation-level institutions affect the degree to which CEOs matter. *Strategic Management Journal, 32*, 797–819.
Dansereau, F., Graen, G., & Haga, W. J. (1975). A vertical dyad linkage approach to leadership in formal organizations: A longitudinal investigation of the role making process. *Organizational Behavior and Human Decision Processes, 13*, 46–78.
Davila, A., & Elvira, M. M. (2012). Humanistic leadership: Lessons from Latin America. *Journal of World Business, 47*, 548–554.
Day, D. V., & Dragoni, L. (2015). Leadership development: An outcome-oriented review based on time and levels of analyses. *Annual Review of Organizational Psychology and Organizational Behavior, 2*, 133–156.
Day, D. V., & Harrison, M. M. (2007). A multilevel, identity-based approach to leadership development. *Human Resource Management Review, 17*(4), 360–373.
De, S., Nau, D. S., & Gelfand, M. J. (2017, May). Understanding norm change: An evolutionary game-theoretic approach. In *Proceedings of the 16th Conference on Autonomous Agents and Multiagent Systems* (pp. 1433–1441).
Den Hartog, D. N., House, R. J., Hanges, P. J., Ruiz-Quintanilla, S. A., Dorfman, P. W., Abdalla, I. A., Adetoun, B. S., Aditya, R. N., Agourram, H., Akande, A., Akande, B. E., Akerblom, S., Altschul, C., Alvarez-Backus, E., Andrews, J., Arias, M. E., Arif, M. S., Ashkanasy, N. M., Asllani, A., . . . , Zhou, J. (1999). Culture specific and cross-culturally generalizable implicit leadership theories: Are attributes of charismatic/transformational leadership universally endorsed? *The Leadership Quarterly, 10*(2), 219–256.
Derue, D. S. (2011). Adaptive leadership theory: Leading and following as a complex adaptive process. *Research in Organizational Behavior, 31*, 125–150. doi: 10.1016/j.riob.2011.09.007
DeRue, D. S., & Ashford, S. J. (2010). Who will lead and who will follow? A social process of leadership identity construction in organizations. *Academy of Management Review, 35*(4), 627–647.
Dickson, M. W., Hanges, P. J., & Lord, R. G. (2001). Trends, developments, and gaps in cross-cultural research on leadership. *Advances in Global Leadership, 2*(2), 75–100.
Dorfman, P. W. (1996). International and cross-cultural leadership research. In J. Punnitt & O. Shanker (Eds.), *Handbook for international management research* (pp. 267–349). Malden, MA: Blackwell.
Dorfman, P. W., Javidan, M., Hanges, P. J., Dastmalchian, A., & House, R. J. (2012). GLOBE: A twenty year journey into the intriguing world of culture and leadership. *Journal of World Business, 47*(4), 504–518. doi: 10.1016/j.jwb.2012.01.004
Eidelson, R. J. (1997). Complex adaptive systems in the behavioral and social sciences. *Review of General Psychology, 1*(1), 42–71.
Elliot, A. J., Chirkov, V. I., Kim, Y., & Sheldon, K. M. (2001). A cross-cultural analysis of avoidance (relative to approach) personal goals. *Psychological Science, 12*(6), 505–510.
Epitropaki, O., Kark, R., Mainemelis, C., & Lord, R. G. (2017). Leadership and followership identity processes: A multilevel review. *The Leadership Quarterly, 28*(1), 104–129.
Erdogan, B., & Bauer, T. N. (2015). Leader–member exchange theory. *International Encyclopedia of the Social and Behavioral Sciences* (pp. 641–647). https://doi.org/10.1016/b978-0-08-097086-8.22010-2
Erez, M., & Earley, P. C. (1993). *Culture, self-identity, and work*. New York: Oxford University Press.
Erez, M., & Gati, E. (2004). A dynamic, multi-level model of culture: From the micro level of the individual to the macro level of a global culture. *Applied Psychology: An International Review, 53*(4), 583–598.
Fairhurst, G. T., & Grant, D. (2010). The social construction of leadership: A sailing guide. *Management Communication Quarterly, 24*(2), 171–210. doi: 10.1177/0893318909359697
Fiedler, F. E. (1967). *A theory of leadership effectiveness*. New York: McGraw-Hill.
Gelfand, M. J., Erez, M., & Aycan, Z. 2007. Cross-cultural organizational behavior. *Annual Review of Psychology, 58*, 479–515.
Gelfand, M. J., Nishii, L. H., & Raver, J. L. (2006). On the nature and importance of cultural tightness-looseness. *Journal of Applied Psychology, 91*(6), 1225.
Gelfand, M. J., Raver, J. L., Nishii, L., Leslie, L. M., Lun, J., Lim, B. C., Duan, L., Almaliach, A., Ang, S., Arnadottir, J., Aycan, Z., Boehnke, K., Boski, P., Cabecinhas, R., Chan, D., Chhokar, J., D'Amato, A., Ferrer, M., Fischlmayr, I. C., . . . Yamaguchi, S. (2011). Differences between tight and loose cultures: A 33-nation study. *Science, 332*(6033), 1100–1104.

Gibson, C. B., & Zellner-Bruhn, M. E. (2001). Metaphors and meaning: An intercultural analysis of the concept of teamwork. *Administrative Science Quarterly, 46*(2), 274–303

Grand, J. A., Braun, M. T., Kuljanin, G., Kozlowski, S. W. J., & Chao, G. T. (2016). The dynamics of team cognition: A process-oriented theory of knowledge emergence in teams. *Journal of Applied Psychology, 101*(10), 1353–1385.

Gumusluoglu, L., Karakitapoğlu-Aygün, Z., & Changya, C. (2019). Angels and devils?: How do benevolent and authoritarian leaders differ in shaping ethical climate via justice perceptions across cultures? *Business Ethics, 29*(2), 388–402.

Hambrick, D. C. & Finkelstein, S. (1987). Managerial discretion: A bridge between polar views of organizational outcomes. *Research in Organizational Behavior, 9*, 369–406.

Hanges, P. J., Aiken, J. R., Park, J., & Su, J. (2016). Cross-cultural leadership: Leading around the world. *Current Opinion in Psychology, 8*, 64–69.

Hanges, P. J., & Dickson, M. W. (2004). The development and validation of the GLOBE culture and leadership scales. In R. House, P. J. Hanges, P.W. Dorfman, M. Javidan, & V. Gupta (Eds.), *Culture, leadership, and organizations: The GLOBE study of 62 societies* (pp. 122–151). Thousand Oaks, CA: SAGE.

Hanges, P. J., & Dickson, M. W. (2006). Agitation over aggregation: Clarifying the development of and the nature of the GLOBE scales. *The Leadership Quarterly, 17*(5), 522–536.

Hanges, P. J., Dorfman, P. W., Shteynberg, G., & Bates, A. L. (2005). Culture and leadership: A connectionist information processing model. *Advances in Global Leadership, 4*, 71–37.

Hanges, P. J., Higgins, M., Dyer, N. G., Smith-Major, V., Dorfman, P. W., Brodbeck, F. C., . . . Prieto, L. (2001). Influence of cultural values on leadership schema structure. In P. J. Hanges & M. J. Gelfand (Co-Chairs), *Applications of pathfinder to understanding cognition in organizational psychology*. Symposium presented at the 16th annual Society of Industrial and Organizational Psychology conference. San Diego, CA.

Hanges, P. J., Lord, R. G., & Dickson, M. W. (2000). An information-processing perspective on leadership and culture: A case for connectionist architecture. *Applied Psychology: An International Review, 49*(1), 133–161.

Harrington, J. R., & Gelfand, M. J. (2014). Tightness–looseness across the 50 united states. *Proceedings of the National Academy of Sciences, 111*(22), 7990–7995.

Higgins, E.T. (1997). Beyond pleasure and pain. *American Psychologist, 52*(12), 1280–1300

Higgins, E. T. (1998). Promotion and prevention: Regulatory focus as a motivational principle. *Advances in Experimental Social Psychology, 30*, 1–46.

Higgins, E. T. (2008). Culture and personality: Variability across universal motives as the missing link. *Social and Personality Psychology*, 608–634. doi: 10.1111/j.1751-9004.2007.00075.x.

Higgins, E. T. (2014). Promotion and prevention: How "0" can create dual motivational forces. *Dual-Process Theories of the Social Mind, 1*, 423–436.

Higgins, E. T., & Pinelli, F. (2020). Regulatory focus and fit effects in organizations. *Annual Review of Organizational Psychology and Organizational Behavior, 7*, 25–48.

Higgins, E. T., & Spiegel, S. (2004). Promotion and prevention strategies for self-regulation. In R. F. Baumeister & K. D. Vohs (Eds.), *Handbook of self-regulation: Research, theory, and applications* (pp. 171–187). The Guilford Press.

Hiller, N. J., Sin, H., Ponnapalli, A., & Ozgen, S. (2018). Benevolence and authority as WEIRDly unfamiliar: A multi-language meta-analysis of paternalistic leadership from 152 studies. *The Leadership Quarterly, 30*(1). doi: 10.1016/j.leaqua.2018.11.003

House, R. J., Dorfman, P. W., Javidan, M., Hanges, P. J., & de Luque, M. F. S. (2014). *Strategic leadership across cultures: GLOBE study of CEO leadership behavior and effectiveness in 24 countries*. Thousand Oaks, CA: SAGE.

House, R. J., Hanges, P. J., Javidan, M., Dorfman, P. W., & Gupta, V. (2004). *Culture, leadership, and organizations: The GLOBE study of 62 societies*. Thousand Oaks, CA: SAGE.

House, R. J., & Mitchell, T. R. (1975). Path-goal theory of leadership. *Contemporary Business, 3* (Fall), 81–98.

House, R. J., Wright, N. S., & Aditya, R. N. (1997). Cross-cultural research on organizational leadership: A critical analysis and a proposed theory. In P.C. Earley & M. Erez (Eds.), *New perspectives on international industrial and organizational psychology* (pp. 535–625). New Lexington Press.

Ibarra, H. (1999). Provisional selves: Experimenting with image and identity in professional adaptation. *Administrative Science Quarterly*, 44, 764–791.

Ibarra, H. (2004). *Working identity: Unconventional strategies for reinventing your career*. Harvard Business School Press.

Ibarra, H., & Petriglieri, J. L. (2010). Identity work and play. *Journal of Organizational Change Management, 23*(1), 10–25.

Javidan, M., Dorfman, P., & Gupta, V. (2004). Culture, leadership, and organizations: The GLOBE study of 62 societies. In R. J. House, P. J. Hanges, M. Javidan, P. W. Dorfman, & V. Gupta (Eds.), *Culture, leadership, and organizations: The GLOBE study of 62 societies* (pp. 29–48). Thousand Oaks, CA: SAGE.

Johnson, P. D., Smith, M. B., Wallace, J. C., Hill, A. D., & Baron, R. A. (2015). A review of multilevel regulatory focus in organizations. *Journal of Management, 41*(5), 1501–1529.

Johnson, R. E., King, D. D., Lin, S.-H. J., Scott, B. A., Walker, E. M. J., & Wang, M. (2017). Regulatory focus trickle-down: How leader regulatory focus and behavior shape follower regulatory focus. *Organizational Behavior and Human Decision Processes, 140*, 29–45.

Kammerlander, N., Burger, D., Fust, A., & Fueglistaller, U. (2015). Exploration and exploitation in established small and medium-sized enterprises: The effect of CEOs' regulatory focus. *Journal of Business Venturing, 30*(4), 582–602.

Kark, R., & Van Dijk, D. (2007). Motivation to lead, motivation to follow: The role of the self-regulatory focus in leadership processes. *Academy of Management Review, 32*(2), 500–528.

Kark, R., & Van Dijk, D. (2019). Keep your head in the clouds and your feet on the ground: a multifocal review of leadership–followership self-regulatory focus. *Academy of Management Annals, 13*(2), 509–546.

Kellerman, B. (2008). Followership: how followers are creating change and changing leaders. Cambridge, MA: Harvard Business School Press.

Kelley, R. E. (2008). Rethinking followership. In R. E. Riggio, I. Chaleff, & J. Lipman-Blumen (Eds.), *The Warren Bennis signature series. The art of followership: How great followers create great leaders and organizations* (pp. 5–15). San Francisco: Jossey-Bass/Wiley.

Kennedy, J. C. (2018). Forbearance of culturally inappropriate leadership behaviors: a conceptual model. *Journal of Global Mobility: The Home of Expatriate Management Research.*

Konst, D., Vonk, R., & Van der Vlist, R. (1999). Inferences about causes and consequences of behavior of leaders and subordinates. *Journal of Organizational Behavior: The International Journal of Industrial, Occupational and Organizational Psychology and Behavior, 20*(2), 261–271.

Kozlowski, S. W., & Chao, G. T. (2018). Unpacking team process dynamics and emergent phenomena: Challenges, conceptual advances, and innovative methods. *American Psychologist, 73*(4), 576–592.

Kozlowski, S. W. J., Chao, G. T., Grand, J. A., Braun, M. T., & Kuljanin, G. (2013). Advancing multilevel research design: Capturing the dynamics of emergence. *Organizational Research Methods, 16*, 581–615.

Kung, F. Y. H., Kim, Y., Yang, D. Y. J., & Cheng, S. Y. Y. (2016). The role of regulatory fit in framing effective negative feedback across cultures. *Journal of Cross-Cultural Psychology, 47*(5).

Lalwani, A. K., & Chiu, C. (2009). Motivated response styles: The role of cultural values, regulatory focus, and self-consciousness in socially desirable responding. *Journal of Personality and Social Psychology, 96*(4), 870–882.

Lapierre, L. M., & Carsten, M. K. (2014). Followership: what is it and why do people follow? Somerville, MA: Emerald Group Publishers.

Lee, A. Y., Aaker, J. L., & Gardner, W. L. (2000). The pleasures and pains of distinct self-construals: The role of interdependence in regulatory focus. *Journal of Personality and Social Psychology, 78*(6), 1122.

Lee, K., Scandura, T. A., & Sharif, M. M. (2014). Cultures have consequences: A configural approach to leadership across two cultures. *The Leadership Quarterly, 25*(4), 692–710. https://doi.org/10.1016/j.leaqua.2014.03.003

Leung, K., & Morris, M. W. (2015). Values, schemas, and norms in the culture-behavior nexus: A situated dynamics framework. *Journal of International Business Studies, 46*, 1028–1050.

Li, L. M. W., & Masuda, T. (2016). The role of regulatory focus in how much we care about enemies: Cross-cultural comparison between European Canadians and Hong Kong Chinese. *Journal of Cross-Cultural Psychology, 47*(1).

Liden, R. C., & Antonakis, J. (2009). Considering context in psychological leadership research. *Human Relations, 62*(11), 1587–1605.

Lisak, A., & Erez, M. (2015). Leadership emergence in multicultural teams: The power of global characteristics. *Journal of World Business, 50*(1), 3–14.

Lisak, A., Erez, M., Sui, Y., & Lee, C. (2016). The positive role of global leaders in enhancing multicultural team innovation. *Journal of International Business Studies, 47*(6), 655–673.

Litano, M. L., Major, D. A., Landers, R. L., Streets, V. N., & Bass, B. L. (2016). A meta-analytic investigation of the relationship between leader-member exchange and work-family experiences. *The Leadership Quarterly, 27*(5), 802–817.

Lord, R. G., & Brown, D. J. (2004). *Leadership processes and follower self-identity*. Mahwah, NJ: Lawrence Erlbaum.

Lord, R. G., Brown, D. J., & Freiberg, S. J. (1999). Understanding the dynamics of leadership: The role of follower self-concepts in the leader/follower relationship. *Organizational Behavior and Human Decision Processes, 78*(3), 167–203.

Lord, R. G., Foti, R. J., & De Vader, C. L. (1984). A test of leadership categorization theory: Internal structure, information processing, and leadership perceptions. *Organizational behavior and human performance, 34*(3), 343–378.

Lord, R. G., Foti, R. J., & Phillips, J. S. (1982). A theory of leadership categorization. In J. G. Hunt, U. Sekaram, & C. A. Schriesheim (Eds.), *Leadership: Beyond establishment views* (pp. 104–121). Carbondale: Southern Illinois University Press.

Lord, R. G., & Maher, K. J. (1991). *Leadership and information processing: Linking perceptions and performance.* New York: Routledge.

Mansur, J., Sobral, F., & Goldszmidt, R. (2017). Shades of paternalistic leadership across cultures. *Journal of World Business, 52*(5), 702–713.

Marion, R. (1999). *The edge of organization: chaos and complexity theories of formal social systems.* Thousand Oaks, CA: SAGE.

Markus, H. R., & Kitayama, S. (1991). Culture and the self: Implications for cognition, emotion, and motivation. *Psychological Review, 98*, 224–253.

Markus, H. R., & Sentis, K. (1982). The self in social information processing. In J. Suls (Ed.), *Psychological perspectives on the self* (Vol. 1, pp. 41–70). Hillsdale, NJ: Lawrence Erlbaum.

Markus, H., & Wurf, E. (1987). The dynamic self-concept: A social psychological perspective. *Annual Review of Psychology, 38*(1), 299–337.

Matondo, J. P. M. (2012). Cross-cultural values comparison between Chinese and Sub-Saharan Africans. *International Journal of Business and Social Science, 3*(11), 38–45.

Nisbett, R. E., Peng, K., Choi, I., & Norenzayan, A. (2001). Culture and systems of thought: Holistic versus analytic cognition. *Psychological Review, 108*(2), 291–310.

Nishii, L. H., Gelfand, M. J., Ang, S., Lange, S., & Taveesin, J. (2004). Culture, systems of thought, and leadership: Holistic and analytical thinking and the structure of leadership schemas in the U.S., Germany, Singapore, and Thailand. Unpublished manuscript.

Northouse, P. G. (2019). *Leadership: theory and practice* (8th ed.). Thousand Oaks, CA: SAGE.

Nouri, R., Erez, M., Lee, C., Liang, J., Bannister, B. D., & Chiu, W. (2014). Social context: Key to understanding culture's effects on creativity. *Journal of Organizational Behavior*, 36(7), 899–918.

Padilla, A., Hogan, R., & Kaiser, R. B. (2007). The toxic triangle: Destructive leaders, susceptible followers, and conducive environments. *The Leadership Quarterly, 18*(3), 176–194. doi: 10.1016/j.leaqua.2007.03.001

Petriglieri, G., & Stein, M. (2012). The unwanted self: Projective identification in leaders' identity work. *Organization Studies, 33*(9), 1217–1235.

Riggio, R. E., Chaleff, I., & Lipman-Blumen, J. (2008). *The art of followership: How great followers create great leaders and organizations.* San Francisco: Jossey-Bass.

Righetti, F., Finkenauer, C., & Rusbult, C. (2011). The benefits of interpersonal regulatory fit for individual goal pursuit. *Journal of Personality and Social Psychology, 101*, 720–736.

Roccas, S., & Brewer, M. B. (2002). Social identity complexity. *Personality and Social Psychology Review, 6*(2), 88–106.

Rockstuhl, T., Dulebohn, J. H., Ang, S., & Shore, L. M. (2012). Leader–member exchange (LMX) and culture: A meta-analysis of correlates of LMX across 23 countries. *Journal of Applied Psychology, 97*(6), 1097–1130. https://doi.org/10.1037/a0029978

Sassenberg, K., & Hamstra, M. R. W. (2017). The intrapersonal and interpersonal dynamics of self-regulation in the leadership process. *Advances in Experimental Social Psychology, 55*, 193–257.

Schein, E. H. (2010). *Organizational culture and leadership* (Vol. 2). Chichester, UK: John Wiley & Sons.

Schneider, B. (1987). The people make the place. *Personnel Psychology, 40*(3), 437–453.

Scholer, A. A., Cornwell, J. F., & Higgins, E. T. (2019). Regulatory focus theory and research. In R. M. Ryan (Ed.), *The Oxford handbook of human motivation* (47–66). London: Oxford University Publications.

Scholer, A. A., & Higgins, E. T. (2008). Distinguishing levels of approach and avoidance: An analysis using regulatory focus theory.

Scholer, A. A., & Higgins, E. T. (2013). Dodging monsters and dancing with dreams: Success and failure at different levels of approach and avoidance. *Emotion Review, 5*(3), 254–258.

Schwartz, S. H. (2006). A theory of cultural value orientations: Explication and applications. *International Studies in Sociology and Social Anthropology, 5*(2–3), 137–182.

Sedikides, C. (1995). Central and peripheral self-conceptions are differentially influenced by mood: Tests of the differential sensitivity hypothesis. *Journal of Personality and Social Psychology, 69*, 759–777.

Shaw, J. B. (1990). A cognitive categorization model for the study of intercultural management. *Academy of Management Review, 15*(4), 626–645.
Shaw, P. (1997). Intervening in the shadow systems of organizations: Consulting from a complexity perspective. *Journal of Organizational Change Management, 10*, 235–250.
Shondrick, S. J., & Lord, R. G. (2010). Implicit leadership and followership theories: Dynamic structures for leadership perceptions, memory, and leader-follower processes. In G. P. Hodgkinson & J.K. Ford (Eds.). *International Review of Industrial and Organizational Psychology, 25*, 1–33.
Snow, D. A., & Anderson, L. (1987). Identity work among the homeless: The verbal construction and avowal of personal identities. *American Journal of Sociology, 92*, 1336–1371.
Stam, D., van Knippenberg, D., Wisse, B., & Nederveen Pieterse, A. (2018). Motivation in words: Promotion- and prevention-oriented leader communication in times of crisis. *Journal of Management, 44*(7), 2859–2887.
Sveningsson, S., & Alvesson, M. (2003). Managing managerial identities: Organizational fragmentation, discourse, and identity struggle. *Human Relations, 56*(10), 1163–1193.
Triandis, H. C. (1993). The contingency model in cross-cultural perspective. In M. M. Chemers, & R. Ayman (Eds.), *Leadership theory and research: Perspectives and directions*. (167–188). New York: Academic Press.
Trop, J. L., & Trop, G. (2018). Self psychology and the concept of the nuclear self: A dynamic systems perspective. *Psychoanalysis, Self, and Context, 13*, 160–170.
Tuncdogan, A., Van Den Bosch, F., & Volberda, H. (2015). Regulatory focus as a psychological microfoundation of leaders' exploration and exploitation activities. *The Leadership Quarterly, 26*(5), 838–850.
Uhl-Bien, M., & Marion, R. (2007). *Complexity leadership: Part 1: Conceptual foundations*. IAP.
Uhl-Bien, M., Marion, R., & McKelvey, B. (2007). Complexity leadership theory: Shifting leadership from the industrial age to the knowledge era. *The Leadership Quarterly, 18*, 298–318.
Uhl-Bien, M., Riggio, R. E., Lowe, K. B., & Carsten, M. K. (2014). Followership theory: A review and research agenda. *The Leadership Quarterly, 25*(1), 83–104.
Uskul, A. K., Sherman, D. K., & Fitzgibbon, J. (2008). The cultural congruency effect: culture, regulatory focus, and the effectiveness of gain- vs. loss-framed health messages. *Journal of Experimental Social Psychology*. doi: 10.1016/j.jesp.2008.12.005
Vallacher, R., & Nowak, A. (1994). *Dynamical systems in social psychology*. New York: Academic Press.
Vallacher, R., Read, S. J., & Nowak, A. (2002). The dynamical perspective in personality and social psychology. *Personality and Social Psychology Review, 6*(4), 264–273.
Van Dijk, D., Seger-Guttmann, T., & Heller, D. (2013). Life-threatening event reduces subjective well-being through activating avoidance motivation: A longitudinal study. *Emotion, 13*(2), 216.
Vancouver, J. B., & Purl, J. D. (2017). A computational model of self-efficacy's various effects on performance: Moving the debate forward. *Journal of Applied Psychology, 102*(4), 599–616.
Vancouver, J. B., Wang, M., & Li, X. (2020). Translating informal theories into formal theories: The case of the dynamic computational model of the integrated model of work motivation. *Organizational Research Methods, 23*(2), 238–274.
Van Knippenberg, D., Van Knippenberg, B., De Cremer, D., & Hogg, M. A. (2004). Leadership, self, and identity: A review and research agenda. *The Leadership Quarterly, 15*(6), 825–856.
Vroom, V. H., & Jago, A. G. (2007). The role of the situation in leadership. *American Psychologist, 62*(1), 17–24. doi: 10.1037/0003-066x.62.1.17
Wanasika, I., Howell, J. P., Littrell, R. F., & Dorfman, P. W. (2011). Managerial leadership and culture in Sub-Saharan Africa. *Journal of World Business, 46*(2), 234–241.
Wang, A. C., Tsai, C. Y., Dionne, S. D., Yammarino, F. J., Spain, S. M., Ling, H. C., Huang, M. P., Chou, L. F., & Cheng, B. S. (2018). Benevolence-dominant, authoritarianism-dominant, and classical paternalistic leadership: Testing their relationships with subordinate performance. *The Leadership Quarterly, 29*(6), 686–697. doi: 10.1016/j.leaqua.2018.06.002
Will, T. E. (2016). Flock leadership: Understanding and influencing emergent collective behavior. *Leadership Quarterly*, 27, 261–279.
Zaccaro, S. J., Dubrow, S., & Kolze, M. (2018). Leader traits and attributes. In J. Antonakis & D. Day (Eds.), *The nature of leadership* (pp. 29–55). Thousand Oaks, CA: SAGE.
Zhang, Y., & Mittal, V. (2007). The attractiveness of enriched and impoverished options: Culture, self-construal, and regulatory focus. *Personality and Social Psychology Bulletin, 33*(4).
Zhou, L., Wang, M., & Vancouver, J. B. (2019). A formal model of leadership goal striving: Development of core process mechanisms and extensions to action team context. *Journal of Applied Psychology, 104*(3), 388–410.

CHAPTER

15 The Technology-Enabled, Task-Specific, and Time-Variant Role of Culture in Teams

Cristina B. Gibson, Terence Chia, *and* Rukman Singh

Abstract

This chapter examines the role of culture in organizational teams, moving beyond the direct effects of culture that was the focus of prior reviews to evidence the more complex interaction of culture with other team features, including technology, task, and time. We explore questions such as: Can technology level the playing field such that culture takes a back seat? Or does technology play a catalytic role and accentuate cultural differences? Does team task type modify the influence of culture in guiding team processes? Does the effect of culture change over the lifespan of a team? We address these questions by reviewing and integrating the literature in the past decade. Theoretical and practical implications, as well as new research directions, are discussed.

Key Words: culture, team, technology, team task, time

Introduction

For many decades, both scholars and managers have recognized the salient and multifaceted role that culture plays in work teams. Indeed, culture is often defined as the interactive patterns of groups of people providing frames of reference, commonly held values, and expectations regarding interpersonal behaviors (Lytle et al., 1995). As a form of deep-level diversity, culture is often derived from place of birth and early socialization, but it can have numerous sources (Kirkman et al., 2017). Individuals may be born and raised in one country but have a strong cultural influence at home (and thus throughout formative childhood years) by a parent from another country, and yet be educated and work in a third cultural setting. Exposure to all these sources are likely to shape their expectations for working in teams (Gibson & Zellmer-Bruhn, 2001).

When culture is shared in teams, it can embed commonly held norms for interpersonal interactions and work processes (Earley & Gibson, 2002; Huang et al., 2017; Stanko & Gibson, 2009). Differences in culture among members of work teams can bring about creative controversy that sparks innovation or conflict that derails the team, making it impossible for work to be moved forward (Gibson et al., 2014, 2021). In essence, work teams constitute an intercultural interaction space that provides both the opportunity for recognition of cultural cues and the occasion for culturally adaptive responses (Zellmer-Bruhn & Gibson, 2014).

The literature that addresses culture in teams over the last decade is varied and rich and has been summarized in several comprehensive reviews (e.g., Gibson et al., 2009, 2014; Gibson & McDaniel, 2010; Hinds et al., 2011, Kirkman et al., 2017; Stahl et al., 2010; Stanko & Gibson, 2009; Zellmer-Bruhn & Gibson, 2014; Zhou & Shi, 2011). We acknowledge the contributions of these reviews but argue that the time has come to shift the focus to a more complex role that culture can play in teams—how *culture interacts with other team features*. We examine three such features that recent research indicates interact with culture in teams: technology, task type, and time. This approach corresponds with recent conceptual work that indicates the importance of examining when and how culture matters for organizational phenomena (Gibson et al., 2009; Zellmer-Bruhn & Gibson, 2014).

Historical Focus of Prior Reviews

Prior reviews have focused on the role of culture broadly in organizations, including in teams, leadership, and conflict (e.g., Feitosa et al., 2018; Gibson & McDaniel, 2010; Kirkman et al., 2017), culture as an element of diversity in teams (e.g., Jackson et al., 2003; Stahl et al., 2010; Zhou & Shi, 2011); and teams that are global because they operate across national boundaries (Gibson et al., 2014; Hinds et al., 2011; Stanko & Gibson, 2009; see Table 15.1 for a summary).

For example, Gibson and McDaniel (2010) reviewed studies that had documented cultural differences in a variety of organizational behaviors, including teaming. They noted that studies in that early part of the decade had primarily documented contrasts in team behaviors in different countries. For example, during conflict management, teams in the United States preferred to engage in mutual interests, while teams in Germany had a preference for using established rules and regulations to address conflict. These studies often invoked a cultural explanation for country differences but rarely measured culture. When culture was a specific focus, it was most often the orientation toward individualism–collectivism, with studies documenting that teams in highly collectivistic countries tended to be more cooperative than those in individualistic countries. Among other future research directions, the authors of these prior reviews called for more research on the relative influence of alternative predictors. Among these predictors are other societal or organizational level factors, such as how jobs are designed or the physical work environment, as these factors are likely to influence behavior in addition to culture and to move beyond individualism–collectivism in examining cultural differences (Kirkman et al., 2017). Similarly, Feitosa et al. (2018) argued for future research that is more specific when characterizing different aspects of teams' cultural environment by considering theories of situation strength and trait activation. Situation strength represents the degree

Table 15.1 Summary of prior reviews

Citation	Overview of Findings from Past Research	Example Suggestions for Future Research
Gibson, C. B., & McDaniel. D. M. (2010). Moving beyond conventional wisdom: Advancements in cross-cultural theories leadership, conflict, and teams. *Association for Psychological Science, 5*(4), 450–462.	1. Teams • Cultural differences in team members—collectivistic (more cooperative; strong interpersonal orientation) versus individualistic (egalitarian). 2. Leadership • Charismatic leadership: negatively associated with power distance; not equally endorsed across cultures 3. Empowerment: negatively associated with satisfaction for high-power distance; managers in fatalistic and high-power distance environments do not engage in it; 4. Conflict • Low-context communicate threats versus high-context reciprocate to threats • Members high on collectivism and hierarchy and low on explicit contracting tend to use power strategies (force conciliation based on social status).	• Findings warn against unilateral application of management across cultures • Rather than seeing personal life and non-work roles as disjointed from organizational behavior, view these particulars as integrated. • Consider the relative influence of alternative predictors, including other societal or organizational level factors that are likely to influence behavior.
Stahl, G. K., Maznevski, M., Voigt, A., & Jonsen, K. (2010). Unraveling the effects of cultural diversity in teams: A meta-analysis of research on multicultural work groups. *Journal of International Business Studies, 41*(4), 690–709.	1. Culture diversity raises barriers to convergence, and increases the forces of divergence in teams. 2. More diverse teams experience process gain of increased creativity, but also process loss of increases conflict 3. Heterogeneous teams experience higher communication satisfaction than homogeneous teams. However, cultural diversity was associated with decreased communication effectiveness in teams with longer tenure.	• Research should continue to examine areas in which we can fine-tune our understanding of processes. This can be achieved by systematically studying how moderators can affect these processes. • Research has not yet been able to isolate process-oriented moderator variables from structural moderators. Therefore, future studies should focus on such variables. • Conduct a closer examination of whether certain diversity attributes are more salient in some cultural contexts than in others.

Hinds, P., Liu, L., & Lyon, J. (2011). Putting the global in global work: An intercultural lens on the practice of cross-national collaboration. *The Academy of Management Annals*, *5*(1), 135–188.	1. Many variables such as adaptation and individual differences play a part in the dynamic nature of culture. 2. National culture has been largely ignored when studying virtual teams and global work. A few studies that have included this component suggest that • Teams struggled to develop a shared way of understanding • Teams with low or high levels of national diversity performed better than those with a moderate level of national diversity • National diversity decreased innovation, especially in the absence of a psychologically safe climate. 3. Practices must converge to ensure collaboration, but an alternative is a hybrid culture	• Although evidence suggests that culture may matter for adaptation, the characteristics that determine when and with whom adaptation will occur are still under studied. • Two unexamined assumptions: (a) the design of collaboration technologies is free from cultural bias; and (b) globally diverse members of a team will interpret and use a shared technology in the same way. • Culture must be considered dynamically. • Behavioral and contextual view of culture points our attention not only to value systems but also to study work practices as cultural production themselves
Zhou, W., & Shi, X. (2011). Culture in groups and teams: A review of three decades of research. *International Journal of Cross Cultural Management, 11*(1), 5–34.	1. Team members from individualistic cultures: • Were associated with resistance to teams • Reported higher self-efficacy beliefs • Were more positive toward job complexity and autonomy • Generated more ideas with a transactional leader • Worked better alone 2. Team members from collectivistic cultures: • Evaluated an ingroup team member more generously • Supported charismatic leadership • Generated more ideas with a transformational leader • Showed no signs of social loafing and work better in groups than alone 3. Conflict—Diversity shapes conflict, and that conflict, in turn, shapes performance, with racial diversity being positively associated with emotional conflict.	• Investigate values beyond individualism–collectivism • Researchers must demonstrate that all of the constructs in cross-cultural studies have validity in each cultural group included. • Incorporate a dynamic view of culture.

(*Continued*)

Table 15.1 *Continued*

Citation	Overview of Findings from Past Research	Example Suggestions for Future Research
Ravlin, E. C., Ward, A. K., & Thomas, D. C. (2014). Exchanging social information across cultural boundaries. *Journal of Management*, *40*(5), 1437–1465.	1. Due to ambiguous power dynamics, social information exchange and conflicts within the team did not benefit from traditional approaches to how work was structured and carried out. 2. During negotiations in a team and dyad setting, origins of culture and timing of events influenced specific behaviors where cultural stereotypes can affect how negotiators are being perceived.	• Research should address power differences in the context of cross-cultural social information exchange.
Han, S. J., & Beyerlein, M. (2016). Framing the effects of multinational cultural diversity on virtual team processes. *Small Group Research*, *47*(4), 351–383.	1. Task-related challenges due to cultural diversity: • Task-related communication • Coordination difficulties • Clarification of expectations due to differences in norms • Sharing of knowledge to prevent information bottlenecks 2. Socioemotional-related challenges due to cultural diversity: • Overcoming biases from stereotype and in/outgroup dynamics. • Building relationships • Developing trust • Intercultural learning	• Research should focus on interpersonal processes and how they relate to long-term team outcomes (e.g., group emotion, group efficiency) in multinational virtual teams. • Research should differentiate team processes from emergent states to surface differences in actual activities undertaken by the team and the socioemotional states experienced by the team.

Kirkman, B. L., Lowe, K. B., & Gibson, C. B. (2017). A retrospective on culture's consequences: The 35-year journey. *Journal of International Business Studies, 48*, 12–29.	1. Cross-cultural research is inherently multilevel. 2. Cultural effects will be moderated by individual differences, group-level features, and situational characteristics. 3. Interaction of individualism–collectivism and power distance likely influences preferences for reward allocations, among other phenomena.	• Explore other "containers" of culture besides country—do not assume that culture equals country • Move beyond self-report, survey-based assessments of culture and isolating only one or two values. • Investigate cultural change—do not assume that culture is static. • Broaden the conceptualization and operationalization of culture to go beyond using values.
Feitosa, J., Grossman, R., & Salazar, M. (2018). Debunking key assumptions about teams: The role of culture. *American Psychologist, 73*(4), 376–389.	Culture plays a role in assumptions guided by teaming framework—forming, functioning, and finishing. 1. Forming • The role of trust in team effectiveness can be better understood only if researchers consider contextual cross-cultural differences. • Regardless of differences, members can contribute to the team under trait-activating conditions. 2. Functioning • While virtuality can be a source of challenges to teams, it can be turned into a strength by making differences within the team less salient. • Due to cross-cultural differences, conflict management strategies need to consider the cultural contexts. • Teams that are high in individualism and have low-power distance best utilize empowering leadership. 3. Finishing: • Teams that are culturally diverse can overcome their challenges by developing cultural intelligence.	• Integrate cultural differences in team members' attitudes, beliefs, and values with the team's context so as to understand how cultural factors are influenced by the team performance context. • Aim to be more specific when characterizing different aspects of a team environment by considering theories of situation strength and trait activation.

to which the situation has constraints (Meyer et al., 2010); if a situation is governed by strict rules, behaviors will also be heavily constrained by these rules, such that the role of culture is weaker.

Reviews that focus on research investigating culture as an element of diversity in teams document that when cultural differences exist within a team, they often coincide with different preferences for specific teamwork practices, and this can bring about internal team conflict (e.g., see Zhou & Shi, 2011). For example, Zhou and Shi review research showing that diverse teams may have some members (i.e., those with individualistic orientations) that prefer to work alone and separate responsibilities into independent and discrete tasks; while other members (i.e., those with collectivistic orientations) will desire extensive collaboration. When the team fails to reach an agreement about how to proceed, it may lead to turnover, conflict, or other inefficiencies. Two important areas for future research identified in these reviews were to incorporate intervening processes and temporal dynamics in studies of culture and teams (Stahl et al., 2010).

Finally, a third set of prior reviews examines global teams that operate across national boundaries (e.g., Han & Beyerlein, 2016; Hinds et al., 2011; Ravlin et al., 2014). While studies reviewed by these authors do sometimes incorporate the role of culture, it often takes a back seat to geographic dispersion and the accompanying time zone, political, or status differences represented on the team (Stanko & Gibson, 2009). One persistent finding pertaining to diversity in global teams is that teams with a low level of national diversity (e.g., only one nation represented) or high levels of national diversity (e.g., four or five nations represented) performed better than those with a moderate level of national diversity (e.g., two or three nations represented; e.g., see Gibson & Vermeulen, 2003). When teams have low diversity, similarity of thinking smooths team functioning. With high diversity, there is unlikely to be strong subgroups emerging to create factions. But teams with moderate diversity benefit from neither. Another common focus in these reviews is on the importance of learning and information sharing (Hans & Beverlein, 2016; Ravlin et al., 2014). Among other future research directions, the authors of these reviews recommend that studies of culture in teams should investigate cultural adaptations that occur in global teams. They also recommend that cultural differences in technology use or preferences is a promising direction for future investigation (Hinds et al., 2011; Hans & Beverlein, 2016).

Review of the Last Decade

The prior reviews point to the need for a more nuanced understanding of the role of culture in teams, which incorporates how culture interacts with other features of the team, such as technology, task, or time. To summarize and integrate the literature that has addressed these nuances over the last decade, we conducted a comprehensive search for articles containing the search terms *culture* and *team* published in 85 journals in organization science, psychology, and management between 2009 and 2019. Initially, this search

Table 15.2 Initial screening and subsequent inclusion of articles by journal

Journal	# of Articles Identified	# Included after Screening
Academy of Management Annals	3	1
Academy of Management Learning and Education	2	1
Academy of Management Discoveries	2	1
Academy of Management Journal	4	1
American Psychologist	1	0
Annual Review of Organizational Psychology and Organizational Behavior	3	0
Communication in Monographs	1	0
Group & Organization Management	2	2
Human Performance	1	0
Human Relations	5	3
Human Resource Management	1	1
Human Resource Management Review	2	2
International Journal of Human Resource Management	4	4
International Journal of Intercultural Relations	5	2
Journal of Applied Psychology	1	1
Journal of Business and Psychology	1	0
Journal of Cross-Cultural Psychology	2	1
Journal of International Business Studies	8	7
Journal of International Management	6	4
Journal of Management	1	1
Journal of Organizational Behavior	6	3
Journal of World Business	4	2
Organization Science	3	2
Organizational Behavior and Human Decision Processes	2	0
Organizational Dynamics	1	0
Small Group Research	1	0
Strategic Management Journal	2	0
Total	**74**	**39**

identified a total of 74 articles across 27 of these journals that addressed the interaction of culture with technology, task, and time in teams (see Table 15.2). However, careful screening of these articles indicated that many were investigating diversity more broadly, without specific reference to culture; others made only passing reference to teams, but this was not a central focus; and still others were book reviews. This screening revealed that 39 articles addressed the manner in which culture interacted with technology, task, and time in teams. This included 9 conceptual papers and 30 empirical papers. In the next section, we review the key findings of these studies.

Culture and Technology in Teams

The articles we review in this set speak to the question, how does culture and communication technology (devices, applications, and systems that support the transmittal of messages, information, and virtual presence, including e-mail, teleconferencing, instant messaging, and document repositories, Majchrzak et al., 2005) interact in teams? Some of these articles suggest that technology "levels the playing field" such that culture should play less of a role in teams (e.g., Gibbs et al. 2013; Hajro et al., 2017), while others suggest that having to rely on technology in a team exacerbates cultural differences (e.g., Hinds et al., 2011). We first review four articles that address conceptual issues relating to technology, culture, and teams, followed by eight empirical articles in this area that were revealed in our search.

Conceptual Work. Important conceptual work in this area argues that teams will adopt and use technology differently based on culture (Kramer et al., 2016). Drawing upon Hofstede's cultural values orientations and Triandis's cultural typology, these scholars offer a number of propositions that predict the extent to which teams in certain cultures will rely on virtual tools that are synchronous versus asynchronous and have high task-related information value. For example, Kramer et al. (2016) argued that teams characterized by individualism (as opposed to collectivism) and masculinity are more likely to rely on virtual tools that are asynchronous; teams are characterized by high uncertainty avoidance, and long-term orientation will prefer utilizing a virtual tool with high informational value. In terms of Triandis's typology, Kramer et al. (2016) propose, for example, that overall reliance on virtual tools is lower for those teams characterized by vertical and horizontal collectivism, affectivity, diffuseness, and high context than for those teams characterized by vertical and horizontal individuality, neutrality, specificity, and low context.

Other conceptual work has proposed that in globally dispersed virtual teams, cultural characteristics at a national level influence team leadership behaviors (Muethel & Hoegl, 2010). For example, scholars have developed the idea that a society's performance orientation, learning orientation, uncertainty avoidance, assertiveness, institutional collectivism, and humane orientation are positively related to shared leadership behaviors in virtual teams. In contrast, they argue that a society's level of power distance is negatively related to such behaviors. This highlights that contextual cultural characteristics can be a source of influence for different individuals from different parts of the world; virtual teams have to be aware of these underlying influences that might exacerbate cultural differences within the team.

Developing trust in virtual teams is a challenging task to undertake because of the lack of face-to-face contact and uncertainties when engaging in communication with team members from another culture by use of technology. Brandl and Neyer (2009) proposed that cross-cultural training can aid cognitive adjustment for members in virtual teams. Specifically, the authors argued that training virtual teams to cope with culturally related uncertainties using technology would be more effective in providing team members with template concepts of cultures, which might fuel stereotype behaviors.

A final conceptual piece that investigated the interaction of technology and culture in teams explored the presence of multicultural brokers in global virtual teams (Eisenberg & Mattarelli, 2017). These scholars note that members' cultural identities may be threatened in global virtual teams, which is likely to decrease knowledge sharing. However, having multicultural brokers in virtual teams is likely to attenuate this relationship, but only up to a certain point, after which such brokers may have a negative impact. Further, the authors argue that it is not just the mere presence of a multicultural broker that improves the relationship between identity threats and team knowledge sharing. Rather, it is when the broker brings cultural intelligence, familiarity with coworkers from different subgroups, and naturally emerge (rather than are formally appointed), that processes are improved.

Empirical Work. Our literature search revealed eight empirical articles published from 2009 to 2019 which explored how culture and technology interacted within virtual teams. For example, Taras et al. (2019) conducted a study of 804 global virtual teams and found that given the reliance on technology in these teams, different forms of diversity had different impacts on team effectiveness, in terms of task outcomes and psychological outcomes, such as the psychological well-being of team members and the level of satisfaction toward team members during and after the team project (Hackman, 1987). They found that contextual diversity (focused on the characteristics of a situation) had a positive relationship with task outcomes, while personal diversity (focused on the characteristics of a person, including culture) had a negative relationship with psychological outcomes. They reasoned that personal diversity, such as cultural differences in the teams, were particularly difficult to navigate using technology.

Communication technology such as text messages and email can be efficient, but omission of contextual information might lead message recipients to form negative perceptions of the sender. With a total of 435 university students from the United States, Vignovic and Thompson (2010) conducted an experiment to test how errors in messages can surface these attributions. Results indicated that negative perceptions were formed against the sender, but the negativity dissipated when recipients were told that the senders were from another culture. This suggests that situational information is important to set the context and assist with relationship building when communicating virtually.

Tenzer and Pudelko (2016) conducted 54 interviews with monolingual and multilingual virtual teams to determine if language differences affect how an individual collaborates and processes different viewpoints during a team meeting. Findings indicated that multilingual virtual teams experienced a cognitive load, which reduced team performance. As a result, the authors suggested that media synchronicity theory needs to incorporate the multilingual nature of many virtual teams. In particular, the findings highlight the importance of balanced redundant communication and suggest that companies need to provide both adequate media infrastructure and education regarding adding the infrastructure into routine usage.

A study by Collins et al. (2017) used a mixed-method approach to research virtual teams in Indonesia, Taiwan, and Vietnam. The researchers found that cultural intelligence, cultural openness, self-efficacy, interpersonal trust, leadership, and language ability can significantly affect individual knowledge-sharing willingness and knowledge-sharing behavior. The analyses of case study interviews revealed that communication style has a huge influence on virtual team cooperation. Negative virtual team interactions (e.g., late responses and absences) affected willingness to share personal knowledge, and most team members were willing to share personal information only if they received some in exchange. Similar findings were obtained by Glikson and Erez (2019) in their study of the emergence of communication climates in virtual teams.

Klitmøller and Lauring (2012) analyzed interaction between 14 Danish and Indian project teams made up of 61 members working in a multinational corporation. Many members working in these teams had English as a second language and there was variance in verbal accents. When a team had a high degree of cultural and language differences, face-to-face interaction was preferable for sharing equivocal knowledge (information that has no definite answer and has scope for ambiguity) because it allowed the members to use nonverbal signs and physically move or touch objects. On the other hand, virtual communication was as desirable as face-to-face interaction for canonical information (numbers or different types of straightforward data). When face-to-face communication was not possible, rich media communication (such as video conferences) were more effective than lean media (such as emails) for equivocal knowledge sharing. However, with extreme language differences, lean media were more effective than rich media. This was a surprising find as it contradicted media richness theory, which advocates that rich media is better for equivocal knowledge. However, the authors found that lean media minimized the occurrence of cultural cues that can potentially lead to misinterpretations and conflict. According to this study, managers in multinational corporations (MNCs) should use the right media in the proper context. Furthermore, while considering the appropriate media, managers and employees must consider the content of the information along with important variables such as differences in cultural difference and spoken language commonality.

Using an ethnographic approach, Gibbs (2009) explored the tensions that took place in a global virtual software team. After analyzing semistructured and in-depth interviews with participants from different nationalities, she proposed a tension-centered model of global team interaction. Gibbs (2009) found that the way team members managed these tensions can lead the team to a productive or destructive outcome. When teams choose to approach these tensions by adopting a selection strategy (where team members choose one side of the argument and completely ignore the other side) or a withdrawal strategy (where team members keep to themselves and do not voice concerns), the outcomes of these strategies were unproductive. In contrast, when virtual teams adopted transcendence strategies (where team members were open to ambiguities and were inclusive when exploring opposing ideals), the outcomes were productive. Based on these findings, Gibbs (2009) proposed that it is not necessary to replicate conditions of collocated teams in terms of maximizing cohesion and shared understanding. Rather, this tension-centered team interaction model suggests the important need to be open to ambiguity and to approach opposing views in an inclusive and positive manner.

Finally, Gibson, Dunlop, and Raghav (2020) examined the extent to which global virtual team members experienced compatibility or conflict among their cultural, professional, organization, and team identities in a sample of 122 workers of a multinational mineral refining firm, who worked across five locations globally. Findings revealed that the higher the tolerance for ambiguity and resilience, and the stronger the team identification, the less the intrapersonal identity conflict experienced, and the more the workers thrived at work, experiencing simultaneously greater learning and physical vitality. Identity conflict explained variance in thriving beyond the variance explained by the strength of identification with specific identities, such as national cultural identity or team identity.

Culture and Team Task

The articles we reviewed in this set address the question, does culture play a different role in teams based on the task being conducted or the type of team? Universalists predict that culture often plays an antecedent role, determining team task processes (e.g., see Stahl et al., 2010 for a review), while others see culture as a moderator, with team task being the primary determinant of team processes and culture amplifying or attenuating this effect (e.g., Gibson et al., 2014; Huang et al., 2017). In this section, we review four conceptual articles that address how culture and team task interact, followed by 14 empirical articles that address these issues. Most of the studies that investigated culture and team tasks focused on tasks that involve generating knowledge and negotiating. These are but two of the four quadrants of task types as defined in McGrath's task circumplex (1984). The other two quadrants—intellective and judgment tasks (choose quadrant) and psychomotor tasks (execute quadrant)—were relatively neglected in the literature. Other studies examined contexts where teams engaged in a variety of tasks, such as automotive production teams.

Conceptual Work. The conceptual piece by Butler et al. (2018) stressed the importance of human resource management practices in shaping the task context for global teams. They argued that HR managers should meticulously manage the situational strength of their HRM system so as to preserve within-group behavioral variability and protect differences, while at the same time offsetting conflicting demands for members in global teams who belong to different cultures. The tasks of global teams often involve generating diverse ideas; hence, the authors argue for the importance of social interaction skills and intercultural skills. The search for new competencies has implications for the "breadth and depth" of the human capital pool from which HR managers recruit global teams and for how they organize, lead, and develop global teams.

Mockaitis et al. (2018) proposed a model for the manner in which human resource managers can assist global teams, given that their primary task often involves responding to local context needs, while also integrating across the organization. As a result, global teams are also knowledge coordinators and network builders for the organization. They argue that collaboration both internally and externally is the key to creating a positive climate of diversity in such teams.

Gibbs et al. (2017) provided a conceptual integration of research investigating the impact of team task and type on global virtual team processes. The review distinguished between student and organizational teams and field and laboratory research. Among other themes, their review revealed that variance in team members' nationality had a positive, negative, or curvilinear relationship with team performance, depending on various team processes. Most importantly, the overlapping alignment of diversity characteristics within a team had a stronger impact than team diversity itself because this overlap resulted in faultlines, which impacted power dynamics. Further, when compared to student samples, organizational samples documented more positive benefits from team diversity. They reason that this is because teams in organizational samples are more motivated to build a shared team identity to overcome challenges stemming from cultural diversity for the purpose of meeting the firm's objectives, while student samples may not see the benefits.

The interaction of culture with generating and creative team tasks has also received substantial attention in the literature. Leung and Wang (2015) provide a theoretical analysis of how cultural diversity may serve as both a benefit and liability as teams work on creative tasks. Cultural diversity broadens the potential perspectives on the team but can also create cultural identity threats (when team members view the presence of other cultural groups as a threat to an individual's cultural identity) and identity fragmentation (the lack of a shared cultural identity). In turn, Leung and Wang (2015) argue that this can hinder knowledge sharing and integration among team members, which can negatively impact team creativity. Leung and Wang (2015) also proposed interaction effects for other task characteristics, including communication technology realism (the extent to which the communication technology replicates the communication in collocated teams), task interdependence (the extent to which team members rely on each other for information exchange), task complexity, and task intellectiveness (the extent to which the task has demonstrably correct decisions and solutions such as engineering and accounting problems). They argue that these characteristics reduce the negative effects of cultural diversity on creativity in teams.

Empirical Work. Our review revealed 13 empirical articles that examined the interaction of culture with team task. Continuing along the theme of understanding creative tasks, Wang and colleagues (2019) conducted a meta-analysis that included 47 studies. They found that surface- and deep-level diversity had differential effects in teams. Deep-level diversity (involving unobservable attributes, including culture values, personalities, and attitudes) were positively related to team creativity. Surface-level diversity (involving readily detectable demographic attributes that explicitly differentiate social category membership, such as nationality) had a nonsignificant relationship with team creativity. Additionally, team virtuality, task complexity, and task interdependence displayed varied moderating effects, depending on whether surface or deep-level diversity was captured (Wang et al., 2019). For example, the relationship between deep-level diversity and creativity was positive and significant for co-located (but not virtual) teams; there was no moderating effect of virtuality for the relationship between surface-level diversity and creativity. The same was true for highly interdependent tasks (i.e., the relationship between deep-level diversity and creativity was positive and significant only for highly interdependent tasks; there was no moderating effect of task interdependence for the relationship between surface-level diversity and creativity).

Following the topic of creativity, Shin and colleagues (2016) conducted a cross-sectional study of 104 teams across 14 companies located in South Korea. The researchers found that an open-system culture (a culture that is outwardly focused and flexible), is positively associated with creative team performance. They also found that team culture is vital to team performance after controlling for leadership and task characteristics. Jang (2017) addressed how multicultural teams leverage their knowledge to be creative through cultural brokerage, which is the facilitation of interactions between individuals across cultural boundaries. Jang (2017) found that team members with multicultural backgrounds (i.e., cultural insiders and outsiders) boost the creative performance of culturally diverse teams by improving team processes. Specifically, among those who are multicultural, cultural insiders (those who have a background that overlaps with others in the team) engaged in integrating knowledge from different cultures, while cultural outsiders (those whose background does not overlap) engaged in eliciting knowledge from different cultures. Both types of brokerage activities enhanced team creativity performance.

A study conducted by Tadmor et al. (2012) found that multicultural experience can positively impact creativity in a dyadic teamwork task. A two-step methodology was used whereby researchers conducted individual and dyadic brainstorming sessions with 114 university students. Half of the subject pool was Caucasian, and the other half was Asian. In the dyadic brainstorming task, participants were paired up with someone else who was ethnically different. The researchers controlled for individual creativity, along with a variety of individual differences, and the results indicated that dyadic creativity was strongest when both partners had high levels of multicultural experience. This study revealed that the creative utility of multicultural experience extends beyond the individual level by enhancing collective creativity through a super-additive effect.

Nouri et al. (2013) examined the influence of two types of task structure—high- versus low-task specificity—on the relationship between cultural diversity and operational and creative task performance. The results of two experimental studies found that on operational tasks, high-task specificity reduced the negative effect of cultural diversity on team processes and team task performance. In contrast for creative tasks, low-task specificity promoted team creativity with original ideas because a less rigid environment allowed for exploration and creative thinking. This study highlights the importance of aligning task specificity to task type in culturally diverse teams.

In a study of team innovation, Huang et al. (2017) examined the cultural orientation toward traditionalism in teams—that is, placing importance on preserving old ways of doing things over breaking precedent and forging new approaches. Across two different samples, one consisting of aerospace teams and the other in a laboratory experiment, the authors found that idea generating benefited the most from high diversity on team traditionalism, whereas idea implementing benefited the most from high average levels of team traditionalism. Previous studies examining the culture–innovation link theorized about the overall construct of innovation, which may have obscured the more fine-grained predictions generated by separating out these two innovation dimensions.

Also focusing on teams engaged in innovation tasks, Hinds et al. (2014) explored how differences in language fluency created an ingroup/outgroup dynamic in six global teams from a software development company. Results from their ethnographic study revealed that even though language fluency, geographical location, and nationality may have caused faultlines to form, it was power struggles within the teams that caused destructive faultlines to surface.

Hajro et al. (2017) also examined how culture enters into knowledge management tasks in multicultural teams, highlighting the role of the diversity climate in the organization in which teams are embedded. They conducted 143 interviews across 43 nationalities, supplemented by participant observation and public documentation. They found that the type of diversity climate that prevails in an organization encourages/constraints knowledge exchange, which in turn was related to team effectiveness. When diversity climate encouraged oscillation across both assertive (perspectives and information were clear and unambiguous) and cooperative (implicit, suggestive, or explanatory, expressing willingness to remain open to others' ideas) knowledge exchange, teams were most effective. Their study primarily implies that the way in which culture will play out in teams is at least partially driven by the diversity climate that is developed at the organizational level. This is particularly true for knowledge management tasks, which require diverse knowledge to be combined and shared.

Other learning-related tasks have also received attention in the literature on culture in teams. Cooper (2013) unpacked the relationship between demographic dissimilarities among team members due to ethnicities, races, or nationalities, and their learning within the team. To test the hypotheses, 177 team members from various organizations, ranging from small businesses to large Fortune 500 companies, responded to an online survey. Results showed that when perceived cultural value dissimilarity was high (i.e., the extent to which an individual perceives themselves to hold different values from their team), demographic dissimilarity was more negatively related to learning. The degree to which team members reported relational identification with other members also moderated this relationship.

Among those studies that examined teams engaging in a variety of McGrath's (1984) task types, Tenzer et al. (2014) investigated the influence of language barriers on the formation of trust in a large German automotive corporation, using a qualitative study based on 90 interviews with 15 multinational teams. The authors found that individuals with high language proficiency perceive team members who face language barriers as less competent, which is related to the formation of trust in the team.

In two utility companies located, respectively, in Canada and India, Mahajan and Toh (2017) investigated operational teams and examined how power distance and uncertainty avoidance moderated the relationship between political behaviors and interpersonal citizenship behaviors in teams. A total of 410 participants took part in this study. The authors found that team culture has a strong influence on an individual's interpersonal citizenship behaviors.

Cooperative, highly interdependent tasks have also received attention in the literature on culture in teams. Tian et al. (2015) examined performance on these tasks when team leaders have very different skill levels compared to team members (leader–member skill distance). A mixed-method research design consisting of 30 qualitative interviews and quantitative data derived from basketball teams from two different countries were utilized. Teams from the United States' National Basketball Association were sampled to represent teams from an individualistic culture, and teams from the China Basketball Association were sampled to represent teams from a collectivistic culture. The researchers found that, in China, the greater the leader–member skill distance, the better the team performance, and team cooperation negatively affected this relationship. Within the United States, the relationship between leader–member skill distance and performance followed an inverted U shape, and team cooperation amplified the effect.

Lee et al. (2018) examined collaborative team tasks in culturally diverse teams to understand how identity configurations (e.g., home identity, host identity, and global identity) relate to cultural intelligence and the leadership perception of members. Using data from 196 professionals who came from 35 different nationalities, they found that when global identity was weak, and the other two culture-specific identities (i.e., home identity and host identity) were equally strong or equally weak, individuals demonstrated higher cultural intelligence and were more likely to be perceived as leaders in global work. In addition, when global identity was strong, the influence of home identity and host identity on cultural intelligence and leadership perception was weaker.

Finally, the meta-analysis by Roh and colleagues (2019) examined how top management teams with diverse backgrounds make strategic decisions, specifically, how they engage in information exchange and conflict. The authors found that cultural characteristics based on nationality and the industry sector environment were significant moderators of top management team diversity dynamics. For example, collectivism in national culture weakened the effects of diversity on social categorization; likewise, industry munificence and industry dynamism also weakened the association between diversity and social categorization within top management teams.

Culture and Time in Teams

Articles reviewed in our final set address the question, does the effect of culture change over time in teams? Some scholars have found that culture primarily influences teams early in the team's life or for workers who have newly entered international teams (e.g., Gibson et al., 2019), while other scholars suggest that the effect is more pervasive (e.g., Hajro & Pudelko, 2010; Tenzer et al., 2014). In this section we review one conceptual article and eight empirical articles that address how culture interacts with time in work teams.

Conceptual Work. Addressing a broad array of features of diversity beyond simply national cultural diversity, Srikanth et al. (2016) shed light on the "double-edge sword" of diversity in teams by emphasizing the importance of dynamic effects over time; they suggested that static views showing the positive or negative effects of diversity are incomplete. They propose that any analysis of diversity must also take into consideration the timing and flow of diversity's effects and that diversity has different short- and long-term effects. For example, initial negative experiences with diversity can develop into dangerous patterns or diffuse into having little effect, or even a positive effect on performance.

Empirical Work. The empirical studies in this set also emphasize that early experiences with culture in teams can change over time and that members and teams often adapt. Those members with the ability to do so are an important asset. For example, Simkhovych (2009) examined the relationship between intercultural effectiveness, which is the ability to relate to people from different cultural backgrounds for the purpose of reaching mutually beneficial outcomes, and the performance of international development project teams. In particular, cultural empathy (an interest in other people and sensitivity toward others' feelings and beliefs) played a significant role. An individual's age, education, and length of international experience also affected the level of intercultural effectiveness.

Based on a 2-year longitudinal mixed-methods study of Jamaican-Indian software development teams, Barrett and Oborn (2010) noticed early on in the teams that an open work climate and interdependence among Jamaicans and Indians existed. These team interactions allowed for flexible use of timelines and requirement specifications. In a subsequent phase, team members utilized formal coordination and control mechanisms, as an Indian project leader asserted his managerial authority and charted strict deadlines for the project. This had an adverse effect in terms of interaction across team members, as tacit knowledge sharing across team members shifted to a more explicit knowledge-sharing environment at an individual level. In the final stage, "us and them" boundaries emerged and resulted in task and relational conflict. The authors concluded that when cultural boundaries built on negative stereotyping were established, team dynamics suffered owing to exacerbated cross-cultural differences online.

Haas and Cummings (2015) investigated whether international or noninternational differences among team members mattered more in teams over time. A 2-year longitudinal mixed-methods approach examined 289 teams in a large multinational corporation. Results indicated that the differences that matter more to the team actually depended on whether the differences are position-based (e.g., proximity or hierarchical structure) or person-based (nationality or demographic). Position-based differences created a bigger barrier to knowledge seeking among team members. With regard to the role of time, the authors found that past relations from a prior team helped reduce these barriers.

In a qualitative study, Zakaria (2016) analyzed an archive of over 1,600 emails generated by the United Nations World Summit on Information Society (WSIS) Civil Society. From this analysis, Zakaria (2016) found that many members of global teams modified their behaviors over time in accordance to the purpose, roles, situation, and person with whom they were communicating during a distributed decision-making process. Focusing on 50 active global virtual team members, Zakaria (2016) revealed that 70% engaged in a consistent pattern of behaviors as predicted by their national identity (high context vs. low context); 12% exhibited inconsistent behaviors (contradictory to their national identity); and 18% switched their behaviors during the email collaboration. In other words, members were capable of, and actively engaged in, adaptation of their culturally prescribed behavior in the global virtual teams.

Based on a qualitative analysis of 132 ethnographic interviews and a series of onsite team observations, Cramton and Hinds (2014) identified the adaptation over time that took place in global teams when members confronted challenges associated with cultural differences. The researchers proposed an embedded model of cultural adaptation in global teams where a key focus is on the dynamic processes that bridge global team members to local institutions, norms, and practices that can also help mold and guide the integration processes between the team and the local environment. They discovered that people who adapted their behavior often found their efforts to be out of alignment with people and institutions in their local context. Global team members who interacted with local team members were found to cause contradictions and set off ripple effects. For example, Cramton and Hinds (2014) noted that when global team managers from a Western background applied their participative management style and annual review processes to an Indian context, local Indian team members rejected this approach, which alarmed the managers. Members who had worked across cultures helped to create a bridge between the two teams.

Erez et al. (2013) shed light on cultural intelligence, global identity, and trust in a longitudinal study involving 312 virtual multicultural teams made up of 1,221 postgraduate students from 12 countries. The researchers found that cultural intelligence and global identity significantly increased over time, whereas local identity did not. These effects remained 6 months after completion of a 4-week project. The level of trust within the teams also enhanced the association between team members' cultural intelligence and global identity. Finally, also highlighting the importance of development over time, a study by Lisak and Erez (2015) compared emergent leaders to nonleaders in multicultural teams. From a sample of 317 MBA students from 32 different nationalities grouped to 81 multicultural teams, the authors found that emergent leaders scored higher in three global characteristics—cultural intelligence, global identity, and openness to cultural diversity.

Two final noteworthy articles in this set examined the importance of multicultural teams remaining fluid, with a structure not as fixed as in traditional teams, but not as loosely structured as communities of practice or networks. Santistevan and Josserand (2018) conducted interviews and observations with 40 global sales teams in the complex matrix structure of a large technology multinational. They found that when the work of the teams is dynamic, using a "meta-team structure" that adapts to activities of operational practices and a common mindset that provides guidelines for member behavior and expectations is more effective than strict traditional static team structures.

Gibson et al. (2019) examined global multicultural teams from a large mining and resources organization operating across 44 countries, using interviews, observations, and a quantitative two-wave survey. They found that structure was helpful for the teams, but only to the extent that such formalization promoted knowledge sharing across members from different cultures. Importantly, the timing of when such structure was provided mattered. Implementing rules and procedures in the setup of the teams and projects, rather than during subsequent interactions, and utilizing protocols to help establish the global team as a source of identity, increased knowledge sharing and in turn effectiveness. Finally, they found that members' personal need for structure moderated the effect of team formalization on how meaningful individuals found their work within the team.

Summary

Five Key Theoretical Principles

1. As a means of extending media richness theory, theories regarding the choice of communication technology in teams must incorporate factors beyond the complexity of the message to include language difference represented on the team (Klitmøller & Lauring, 2012).
2. Cultural brokers play an important role in enabling teams to address potential challenges, but their success depends on the use of technology, which enables interpersonal trust to build, and their contributions are likely to be different, depending on how their background overlaps with members of the team (Eisenberg & Mattarelli, 2017; Jang, 2017).
3. Multilevel influences predict team knowledge exchange in multicultural teams, including the diversity climate in the organization, as well as team features and processes. Hence, interventions or policies must be targeted across levels. Extending optimal distinctiveness theory, diversity climates that encourage teams to oscillate between convergence and divergence allow for both uniqueness and belonging to emerge (Hajro et al., 2017).

4. The team innovation literature has long recognized that innovation is composed of subphases involving idea generating and implementing (West, 2002). However, recent research shows that culture (specifically, the orientation toward traditionalism) differentially affects these two phases, such that low traditionalism is associated with greater idea generation and high traditionalism is associated with more effective implementation (Huang et al., 2017).
5. Identification processes feature prominently in multicultural teams, including global identities and local identities, as well as the potential conflict among members' multiple identities, which may result in diminished thriving in such teams. Members with multiple identities can serve to unite the team across identity groups (Erez et al., 2013; Liask & Erez, 2015; Gibson et al., 2021).

Five Practical Implications

1. While considering the appropriate media, managers and employees must consider the content of the information along with important variables such as cultural differences in spoken language. Highly diverse teams likely benefit from lean media for complex ideas, but rich media may enhance cohesion (Kramer et al., 2016; Muethal & Hogel, 2010).
2. Virtual teams do not necessarily need to replicate conditions of collocated teams in terms of maximizing cohesion and shared understanding. Rather, they can be productive when they adopt transcendence strategies, where team members are open to ambiguities and are inclusive when exploring opposing ideals (Gibbs, 2009).
3. Cultural diversity can enhance creativity, but managers must consider the degree to which constraints are placed on the team's task. If task instructions are too specific, then creativity will suffer (Nouri et al., 2013).
4. Because average level of cultural orientations such as traditionalism and diversity on these orientations have opposite effects for idea generating versus. implementing, leaders might consider allocating idea-generation tasks versus implementation tasks to teams with different team compositions (Huang et al., 2017).
5. Incorporating a dynamic view to support cultural differences may mean providing more structure for global teams at the start of their work together and then loosening the extent to which processes are formalized as the team's interaction unfolds (Gibson et al., 2019).

New Research Directions

We next highlight important avenues for future research suggested by our review. These avenues lie at the intersection of the three themes: technology, task, and time. That is, by exploring how these features of teams interact both together and with culture, we can extend theory and practice in novel and important ways. First, we discuss opportunities for extending theory, followed by promising methodological techniques that will propel the field forward.

Theoretical Avenues

First, we encourage research that extends current approaches to understanding how team-level cultures are enacted and in particular the role of national culture and team leader imprinting on these processes over time. Kim and Toh (2019) found that team leaders enact team-level cultures based on their previous intercultural cultural experiences and by transferring cultures from their former groups to their current groups. These team cultures may be self-reinforcing, especially in tight cultures where members are strict in enforcing norms within the group (Gelfand et al., 2006).

Given the findings reviewed above regarding the importance of specific competencies and skills such as cultural intelligence and cultural brokerage, we see this as promising research that develops theory regarding how leaders with (and without) these skills imprint team cultures. We imagine that cultural imprinting might occur more often when leaders do not have these skills. If this is the case and the leader transfers negative past culture to current culture, or applies antiquated solutions to current problems, leaders and employees may miss out on tailoring a strategy or plan to the current environment that would be more effective. Research into the antecedents of team culture, as well as the adaptability of team cultures, needs to be deepened as we unravel these questions.

Second, we encourage research that examines the use of technology over time in teams across cultures. Kramer et al.'s work (2016) on cultural proclivities toward certain technologies implies that teams may become entrenched in a certain way of communicating and completing tasks. Participating in technology-reliant teams may pose an undue burden on team members from certain cultures that are never face to face, which could perpetuate a form of ethnocentrism. We know that team members who are located miles away from the headquarters may be disadvantaged because of the lack of physical presence (Trope & Liberman, 2003). Being physically present at the workplace has been recognized to be beneficial to employees because it creates a positive impression of competence among their colleagues (Munck, 2001). It is also associated with higher performance appraisals (Elsbach et al., 2010) and higher remuneration (Howell et al., 2016).

Further, Cristea and Leonardi (2019) found that headquarters' managers admitted to the reluctance of choosing an employee who is not physically co-located because the managers believed that an onsite team member would be more reliable. As a result of this perceived lack of recognition, team members who are not located onsite compensate by working long hours and being continually available to demonstrate both their commitment and their wish to stay connected in another time zone. Despite the advent of instantaneous technology promising greater connectivity and increasing efficiency and productivity, an unintended consequence is the abetment of longer working hours. This may affect the workforce unevenly, such that members from certain cultures are consistently adversely affected. Over time, this can lead to unhealthy work arrangements for these employees and result in poor work outcomes, which can eventually negatively impact the organization. We encourage future research that documents these processes to raise awareness of the potential ill effects of patterned technology use across cultures in teams.

Methods

Numerous mixed-methods studies have been conducted over the past decade. Such designs allow for triangulation across archival, qualitative, and quantitative data, or the opportunity to enrich and extend one method with another (Gibson, 2017). When conducting team-level research and investigating the effects of culture on teams, researchers can contribute to the literature by bridging emerging findings to observations from the field and strengthen this with laboratory studies to build on field observations and establish causality (see Kim & Toh, 2019). In terms of longitudinal methodologies, management science scholars can consider utilizing analytical approaches that are common in other disciplines—for example, the use of survival analysis that is commonly used in epidemiology, when accounting for fluidity in membership. This approach can account for team members who have dropped off to another team and account for team members who are included midway or only for a certain phase of the project, given that their specialization is relevant for just a specific duration, or can model the mixture of part-time and full-time members (Hoverstad et al., 1990). Employing a different methodological approach can open doors to different questions within the same research domain. For example, Somers and Birnbaum (1999) provided robust commentary on the differences in employee turnover research when comparing between-survival analysis and traditional research methodological approaches. The traditional approach reproduced findings that were already present in the research domain, while utilization of survival analysis methodology revealed new associations.

An unintended consequence of the massive shift to an online work routine due to the pandemic is the creation of archival data. Organizations have deployed video conferences as a stand-in for physical meetings, and sometimes these sessions are recorded and stored. As a result, recorded sessions that involve deliberation and decision making are now being captured in unprecedented volumes. While reviewing recording meetings is not a new practice, the sudden uptake of video conferencing means that such data is broader and more readily available. Video conference sessions can be a source of rich data compared to written meetings or recorded teleconferences. Scholars can tap into this resource, adding methods research design for future research to their mix.

Conclusion

Undeniably, culture is important in the workplace, and the field is now ripe to extend our focus and build our understanding of how culture interacts with team features such as technology, task type, and time. In doing so, we can develop both theory and recommendations for practice that incorporate these nuances with greater precision, ultimately increasing the effectiveness of teams that span cultures.

References

Barrett, M., & Oborn, E. (2010). Boundary object use in cross-cultural software development teams. *Human Relations, 63*(8), 1199–1221.

Brandl, J., & Neyer, A.-K. (2009). Applying cognitive adjustment theory to cross-cultural training for global virtual teams. *Human Resource Management, 48*(3), 341–353.

Butler, C. L., Minbaeva, D., Mäkelä, K., Maloney, M. M., Nardon, L., Paunova, M., & Zimmermann, A. (2018). Towards a strategic understanding of global teams and their HR implications: an expert dialogue. *The International Journal of Human Resource Management, 29*(14), 2209–2229.

Collins, N., Chou, Y.-M., Warner, M., & Rowley, C. (2017). Human factors in East Asian virtual teamwork: A comparative study of Indonesia, Taiwan and Vietnam. *The International Journal of Human Resource Management, 28*(10), 1475–1498.

Cooper, D. (2013). Dissimilarity and learning in teams: The role of relational identification and value dissimilarity. *International Journal of Intercultural Relations, 37*, 628–642.

Crampton, C. D., & Hinds, P. J. (2014). An embedded model of cultural adaptation in global teams. *Organization Science, 25*(4), 1056–1081.

Cristea, I. C., & Leonardi, P. M. (2019). Get noticed and die trying: Signals, sacrifice, and the production of face time in distributed work. *Organization Science, 30*(3), 552–572.

Earley, P. C., & Gibson, C. B. (2002). *Multinational work teams: A new perspective.* New York: Routledge.

Eisenberg, J., & Mattarelli, E. (2017). Building bridges in global virtual teams: The role of multicultural brokers in overcoming the negative effects of identity threats on knowledge sharing across subgroups. *Journal of International Management, 23*, 399–411.

Elsbach, K. D., Cable, D. M., & Sherman, J. W. (2010). How passive "face time" affects perceptions of employees: Evidence of spontaneous trait inference. *Human Relations, 63*(6), 735–760.

Erez, M., Lisak, A., Harush, R., Glikson, E., Nouri, R., & Shokef, E. (2013). Going global: Developing management students' cultural intelligence and global identity in culturally diverse virtual teams. *Academy of Management Learning and Education, 12*(3), 330–355.

Feitosa, J., Grossman, R., & Salazar, M. (2018). Debunking key assumptions about teams: The role of culture. *American Psychologist, 73*(4), 376–389.

Gelfand, M. J., Nishii, L. H., & Raver, J. L. (2006). On the nature and importance of cultural tightness-looseness. *Journal of Applied Psychology, 91*(6), 1225–1244.

Gibbs, J. (2009). Dialectics in a global software team: Negotiating tensions across time, space, and culture. *Human Relations, 62*(6), 905–935.

Gibbs, J. L., Grushina, Y., Gibson, C. B., Dunlop, P., & Cordery, J. (2013). *Language, culture, status, and identity: Understanding factors that encourage or limit global team participation.* [Paper presentation] Australian and New Zealand Communication Association Conference: Global networks global divides (pp. 1–21). ANZCA.

Gibbs, J. L., Sivunen, A., & Boyraz, M. (2017). Investigating the impacts of team type and design on virtual processes. *Human Resource Management Review, 27*(4), 590–603.

Gibson, C. B. (2017). Elaboration, generalization, triangulation, and interpretation. *Organizational Research Methods, 20*(2), 193–223.

Gibson, C. B., Dunlop, P. D., & Cordery, J. L. (2019). Managing formalization to increase global team effectiveness and meaningfulness of work in multinational organizations. *Journal of International Business Studies*, 50(6), 1021–1052.

Gibson, C. B., Dunlop, P. D., & Raghav, S. (2021). Navigating identities in global work: Antecedents and consequences of intrapersonal identity conflict. *Human Relations, 74*(4), 556–586.

Gibson, C. B., Huang, L., Kirkman, B. L., & Shapiro, D. L. (2014). Where global and virtual meet: The value of examining the intersection of these elements in twenty-first century teams. *Annual Review of Organizational Psychology and Organizational Behavior, 1*, 217–244.

Gibson, C. B., Maznevski, M. L., & Kirkman, B. L. (2009). When does culture matter? In R. S. Bhagat & R. M. Steers (Eds.), *Cambridge handbook of culture, organizations, and work* (pp. 46–68). Cambridge: Cambridge University Press.

Gibson, C. B., & McDaniel, D. M. (2010). Moving beyond conventional wisdom: Advancements in cross-cultural theories of leadership, conflict, and teams. *Perspectives on Psychological science, 5*(4), 450–462.

Gibson, C., & Vermeulen, F. (2003). A healthy divide: Subgroups as a stimulus for team learning behavior. *Administrative Science Quarterly, 48*(2), 202.

Gibson, C. B., & Zellmer-Bruhn, M. E. (2001). Metaphors and meaning: An intercultural analysis of the concept of teamwork. *Administrative Science Quarterly, 46*(2), 274.

Glikson, E., & Erez, M. (2019). The emergence of a communication climate in global virtual teams. *Journal of World Business, 55*(6), 101–112.

Haas, M. R., & Cummings, J. N. (2015). Barriers to knowledge seeking within MNC teams: Which differences matter most? *Journal of International Business Studies, 46*(1), 36–62.

Hackman, J. R. (1987). The design of work teams. In J. W. Lorsch (Ed.), *Handbook of organizational behavior* (pp. 315–342). Englewood Cliffs, NJ: Prentice-Hall.

Hajro, A., Gibson, C. B., & Pudelko, M. (2017). Knowledge exchange processes in multicultural teams: Linking organizational diversity climates to teams' effectiveness. *Academy of Management Journal, 60*(1), 345–372.

Hajro, A., & Pudelko, M. (2010). An analysis of core-competences of successful multinational team leaders. *International Journal of Cross Cultural Management, 10*(2), 175–194.

Han, S. J., & Beyerlein, M. (2016). Framing the effects of multinational cultural diversity on virtual team processes. *Small Group Research, 47*(4), 351–383.

Hinds, P., Liu, L., & Lyon, J. (2011). Putting the global in global work: An intercultural lens on the practice of cross-national collaboration. *The Academy of Management Annals, 5*(1), 135–188.

Hinds, P. J., Neeley, T. B., & Cramton, C. D. (2014). Language as a lightning rod: Power contests, emotion regulation, and subgroup dynamics in global teams. *Journal of International Business Studies, 45*(5), 536–561.

Hoverstad, R., Moncrief III, W. C., & Lucas, G. H., Jr. (1990). The use of survival analysis to examine sales force turnover of part-time and full-time sales employees. *International Journal of Research in Marketing, 7*(2-3), 109–119.

Howell, L. P., Elsbach, K. D., & Villablanca, A. C. (2016). The role of compensation criteria to minimize face-time bias and support faculty career flexibility: An approach to enhance career satisfaction in academic pathology. *Academic Pathology, 3*, 1–9.

Huang, L., Gibson, C. B., Kirkman, B. L., & Shapiro, D. L. (2017). When is traditionalism an asset and when is it a liability for team innovation? A two-study empirical examination. *Journal of International Business Studies, 48*(6), 693–715.

Jackson, S. E., Joshi, A., & Erhardt, N. L. (2003). Recent research on team and organizational diversity: SWOT analysis and implications. *Journal of Management, 29*(6), 801–830.

Jang, S. (2017). Cultural brokerage and creative performance in multicultural teams. *Organization Science, 28*(6), 993–1009.

Kim, Y. J., & Toh, S. M. (2019). Stuck in the past? The influence of a leader's past cultural experience on group culture and positive and negative group deviance. *Academy of Management Journal, 62*(3), 944–969.

Kirkman, B. L., Lowe, K. B., & Gibson, C. B. (2017). A retrospective on culture's consequences: The 35-year journey. *Journal of International Business Studies, 48*(1), 12–29.

Klitmøller, A., & Lauring, J. (2012). When global virtual teams share knowledge: Media richness, cultural difference and language commonality. *Journal of World Business, 48*, 398–406.

Kramer, W. S., Shuffler, M. L., & Feitosa, J. (2016). The world is not flat: Examining the interactive multidimensionality of culture and virtuality in teams. *Human Resource Management Review, 27*(4), 604–620.

Lee, Y., Masuda, A. D., Fu, X., & Reiche, S. (2018). Navigating between home, host, and global: Consequences of multicultural team members' identity configuration. *Academy of Management Discoveries, 4*(2), 180–201.

Leung, K., & Wang, J. (2015). Social processes and team creativity in multicultural teams: A socio-technical framework. *Journal of Organizational Behavior, 36*, 1008–1025.

Lisak, A., & Erez, M. (2015). Leadership emergence in multicultural teams: The power of global characteristics. *Journal of World Business, 50*, 3–14.
Lytle, A. L., Brett, J. M., Barsness, Z. J., Tinsley, C. H., & Janssens, M. (1995). A paradigm for confirmatory cross-cultural research in organizational behavior. *Research in Organizational Behavior, 17*, 167–214.
Mahajan, A., & Toh, S. M. (2017). Group cultural values and political skills: A situationist perspective on interpersonal citizenship behaviors. *Journal of International Business Studies, 48*(1), 113–121.
Majchrzak, A., Malhotra, A., & John, R. (2005). Perceived individual collaboration know-how development through information technology–enabled contextualization: Evidence from distributed teams. *Information Systems Research. 16*, 9–27.
McGrath, J. E. (1984). *Groups: Interaction and performance*. Englewood Cliffs, NJ: Prentice-Hall.
Meyer, R. D., Dalal, R. S., & Hermida, R. (2010). A review and synthesis of situational strength in the organizational sciences. *Journal of Management, 36*, 121–140.
Mockaitis, A. I., Zander, L., & Cieri, H. D. (2018). The benefits of global teams for international organizations: HR implication. *The International Journal of Human Resource Management, 29*(14), 2137–2158.
Muethel, M., & Hoegl, M. (2010). Cultural and societal influences on shared leadership in globally dispersed teams. *Journal of International Management, 16*, 234–246.
Munck, B. (2001). Changing a culture of face time. *Harvard Business Review, 79*(10), 125–130.
Nouri, R., Erez, M., Rockstuhl, T., Ang, S., Leshem-Calif, L., & Rafaeli, A. (2013). Taking the bite out of culture: The impact of task structure and task type on overcoming impediments to cross-cultural team performance. *Journal of Organizational Behavior, 34*(6), 739–763.
Ravlin, E. C., Ward, A.-K., & Thomas, D. C. (2014). Exchanging social information across cultural boundaries. *Journal of Management, 40*(5), 1437–1465.
Roh, H., Chun, K., Ryou, Y., & Son, J. (2019). Opening the black box: A meta-analytic examination of the effects of top management team diversity on emergent team processes and multilevel contextual influence. *Group and Organization Management, 44*(1), 112–164.
Santistevan, D., & Josserand, E. (2018). Meta-teams: Getting global work done in MNEs. *Journal of Management, 45*(2), 510–539.
Shin, Y., Kim, M., Choi, J. N., & Lee, S. H. (2016). Does team culture matter? Roles of team culture and collective regulatory focus in team task and creative performance. *Group and Organization Management, 41*(2), 232–265.
Simkhovych, D. (2009). The relationship between intercultural effectiveness and perceived project team performance in the context of international development. *International Journal of Human Resource Management, 33*, 383–390.
Somers, M. J., & Birnbaum, D. (1999). Survival versus traditional methodologies for studying employee turnover: differences, divergences and directions for future research. *Journal of Organizational Behavior, 20*(2), 273–284.
Srikanth, K., Harvey, S., & Peterson, R. (2016). A dynamic perspective on diverse teams: Moving from the dual-process model to a dynamic coordination-based model of diverse team performance. *Academy of Management Annals, 10*(1), 453–493.
Stahl, G. K., Maznevski, M. L., Voigt, A., & Jonsen, K. (2010). Unraveling the effects of cultural diversity in teams: A meta-analysis of research on multicultural work groups. *Journal of International Business Studies, 41*(4), 690–709.
Stanko, T. L., & Gibson, C. (2009). *The role of cultural elements in virtual teams*. In R. B. Bhagat and R. M. Steers (Eds.), *Cambridge handbook of culture, organizations, and work* (pp. 272–304). Cambridge: Cambridge University Press.
Tadmor, C. T., Satterstrom, P., Jang, S., & Polzer, J. T. (2012). Beyond individual creativity: The superadditive benefits of multicultural experience for collective creativity in culturally diverse teams. *Journal of Cross-Cultural Psychology, 43*(3), 384–392.
Taras, V., Baack, D., Caprar, D., Dow, D., Froese, F., Jimenez, A., & Magnusson, P. (2019). Diverse effects of diversity: Disaggregating effects of diversity in global virtual teams. *Journal of International Management, 25*(4), 100689.
Tenzer, H., & Pudelko, M. (2016). Media choice in multilingual virtual teams. *Journal of International Business Studies, 47*(4), 427–452.
Tenzer, H., Pudelko, M., & Harzing, A. W. (2014). The impact of language barriers on trust formation in multinational teams. *Journal of International Business Studies, 45*(5), 508–535.

Tian, L., Li, Y., Li, P. P., & Bodla, A. A. (2015). Leader-member skill distance, team cooperation, and team performance: A cross-culture study in a context of sport teams. *International Journal of Intercultural Relations, 49*, 183–197.

Trope, Y., & Liberman, N. (2003). Temporal construal. *Psychological Review, 110*(3), 403–421. https://doi.org/10.1037/0033-295x.110.3.403

Vignovic, J. A., & Thompson, L. F. (2010). Computer-mediated cross-cultural collaboration: Attributing communication errors to the person versus the situation. *Journal of Applied Psychology, 95*(2), 265.

Wang, J., Cheng, GH-L., Chen, T., & Leung, K. (2019). Team creativity/innovation in culturally diverse teams: A meta-analysis. *Journal of Organizational Behavior, 40*, 693–708.

West, M. A. (2002). Sparkling fountains or stagnant ponds: An integrative model of creativity and innovation implementation in work groups. *Applied Psychology, 51*(3), 355–387.

Zakaria, N. (2016). Emergent patterns of switching behaviors and intercultural communication styles of global virtual teams during distributed decision making. *Journal of International Management, 23*, 350–366.

Zellmer-Bruhn, M. E., & Gibson, C. B. (2014). How does culture matter? A contextual view of intercultural interaction in groups. In M. Yuki & M. Brewer (Eds.), *Culture and group processes* (pp. 342–402). New York: Oxford University Press.

Zhou, W., & Shi, X. (2011). Culture in groups and teams: A review of three decades of research. *International Journal of Cross Cultural Management, 11*(1), 5–34.

CHAPTER 16

Culture and Communication

Suraj Sharma *and* Leigh Anne Liu

Abstract

Human cultural values and norms are developed and maintained through communication between and within individuals and between and within groups. The relationship between culture and communication is complex and challenging to study. On one hand, communication is the carrier of human interaction and culture, as values and norms are shared among its members through communication. On the other hand, culture may dictate how we communicate, since values and norms may prescribe our thinking and communication styles. In this chapter, we review the extant literature on culture and communication and explore how they influence and coevolve over time. We then propose new directions of research with theoretical and practical implications.

Key Words: culture, communication, cognition, emotion, holistic thinking, analytical thinking

> *It is extraordinary the way people, music and cultures develop. The paths and experiences that guide them are unpredictable. Shaped by our families, neighborhoods, cultures and countries, each of us ultimately goes through this process of incorporating what we learn with who we are and who we seek to become. As we struggle to find our individual voices, I believe we must look beyond the voice we've been assigned and find our place among the tones and timbre of human expression.*
>
> —*Yo-Yo Ma*

This quote by Yo-Yo Ma illustrates the ever-complex dynamics between culture and communication within individuals, interpersonally, and across social groups. The relationship between culture and communication is a compelling part of social life that infiltrates every aspect of our being. Although it is challenging to disentangle the interactions between culture and communication, we explore these mechanisms in the literature in order to

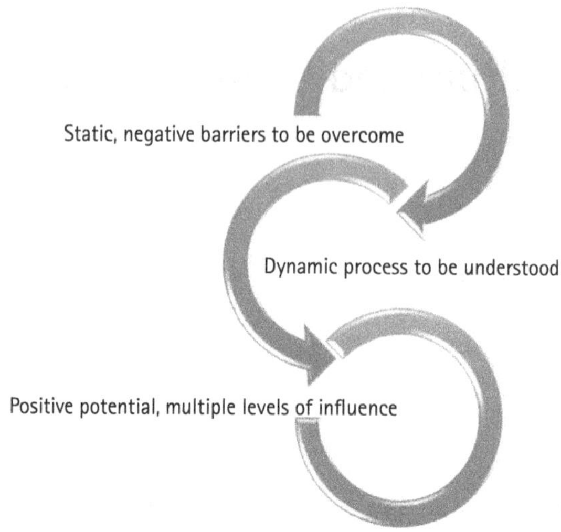

Figure 16.1. The evolution of culture phenomenology in communication research.

offer insights to advance the field forward. In this chapter, we first analyze the literature on culture and communication from two perspectives: how culture affects communication and how communication affects culture. We then offer ideas on future research, before summarizing the takeaways of this chapter.

How Culture Affects Communication

Research on how culture influences communication has evolved from simple comparisons of two cultural styles in communication (e.g., Hall, 1959, 1976) to a more sophisticated treatment of dynamic interactions among intra- versus intercultural interactions in various settings (e.g., Adair et al., 2015; Liu et al., 2010). Figure 16.1 depicts the progression of the role culture plays in communication research, evolving from static, negative barriers to be overcome in communication to dynamic processes to be understood and to potentially positive and multiple levels of influence on communication. Although the purpose of communication is to understand and be understood, earlier studies on culture and communication necessarily focused on deciphering the differences across cultures.

Cultural Differences as Barriers of Communication

The first stage of culture and communication research started with Edward Hall's (1959, 1976) anthropology work on culture, perception of time and space, and high- or low-context communication styles. Hall explains that members of different cultures vary in their orientations toward time. Some focus on the past, whereas others anchor communications on the present or future. Regarding perception of space, *proxemics* suggests that comfortable personal space differs across cultures. Hall also described that members of high-context cultures communicate with implicit and indirect messages that heavily emphasize the situation for interpretation while those in low-context cultures communicate with direct and explicit messages that are less sensitive to the specific situation.

Another early theoretical foundation of cultural differences was holistic versus analytical thinking styles. *Holistic* thinking style, on the one hand, refers to a systematic consideration of both internal attributes and external situations, as well as overall patterns, contexts, and relationships. *Analytical* thinking style, on the other hand, is characterized by focusing on ascribed factors and disentangling internal and external elements in phenomena (Nisbett, 2003; Nisbett et al., 2001). A case in point can be found in the different approaches of Eastern and Western medicine. For example, when a person has stomach issues, Eastern medicine addresses the cause holistically and may view it as an imbalance of the person's energy and will use experience-based treatments, such as acupuncture, which aim to rebalance these energies. The Western approach to the same problem would be a much more focused analysis of the stomach and use of treatments consistent with an empirically backed, scientific lens with stomach-specific medications or surgery. Applied to communication situations, Kim (2002) examined the relationships between talking and thinking among European Americans and East Asians and found that "thinking out loud" or talking helps European Americans resolve reasoning problems but doesn't necessarily make East Asians better problem solvers. These examples highlight the effects of culture on cognitive reasoning, which then subsequently affect individuals from these culture's communicative processes. These kinds of fundamental differences between cultures have become sources of miscommunication and misunderstanding, which are reflected in the studies of how culture influences communication at this stage.

Scholars focused on the subjective perceptions of cultural differences, which were then assumed to be negative barriers to effective communication. For example, Adler and Graham (1989) found that American, Canadian, and Japanese individuals differ when they are facing challenges of language, nonverbal behaviors, values, and patterns of thought while communicating with each other. They noted that American negotiators behave similarly regardless of whether the opponents were Japanese or American, while Japanese negotiators seem to be more tuned in to changing contexts, and thus adjust their behaviors accordingly. Similarly, Brett and Okumura (1998) found that intercultural negotiators achieve fewer desirable outcomes than intracultural negotiators, possibly because intercultural dyads encounter more difficulties to cooperation (Matsumoto & Hwang, 2011; Tse et al., 1994). Based on an ethnographic study in global teams, Hinds et al. (2014) found that, as an important proxy of culture, language, especially language asymmetry in global teams, amplified power differences and geographic distribution among team members and triggered negative tensions. Therefore, cultural differences were viewed as a barrier due to challenges associated with decoding language, nonverbal cues, and/or intentions of cooperation.

Research on cultural values also offered implications for communication. For example, collectivism might influence how collaborative a communicator is and how likely one is to share information with others (Cai et al., 2000). Cultural norms of implicit rules and guidelines may also predict tactics and strategies for interactions. For example, Adair et al. (2001) found that Japanese negotiators use *positional strategies,* such as pointing out limitations of alternatives to engage and influence their counterparts, while U.S. negotiators use more *direct strategies* to share information. *Face negotiation theory* (Oetzel & Ting-Toomey, 2003; Ting-Toomey & Dorjee, 2018; Zhang et al., 2019) links individual identity, relationship with others, and conflict management styles to propose different patterns of communication, depending on the need to defend, protect, or accommodate one's own and the other party's face, or socially embedded identity. Consequently, individuals need to adjust their communicating behaviors in order to be more effective in intercultural interactions (e.g., Adair et al., 2001; Kim, 1988; Weiss, 1994). In sum, studies in this stage focused on cultural comparisons in communication and have generally found relatively *stable and static* cultural influences on communication (Oyserman et al., 2002; Morling & Lamoreaux, 2008).

Culture as a Dynamic Process in Communication

In the second stage of culture and communication research, researchers started to look beyond values or simplified norms to study how internalized norms (Liu, Friedman, & Chi, 2005; Brett et al., 2007), experience and cognitive mental networks (Liu et al., 2010, 2012), and motivations (De Drue & Carnevale, 2003; Liu et al., 2012) influenced patterns of communication and interpersonal dynamics. These communication patterns and dynamics include temporal sequences (Adair & Brett, 2005), consensus building (Liu et al., 2012), multiparty communication (Adair & Liu, 2011), social distance bridging (Kern et al., 2012), information exchange strategies (Gunia et al., 2011), and nonverbal communication (Semnani-Azad & Adair, 2011). These studies began to treat the phenomenology of culture *as a dynamic and contextualized process,* considering multiple interaction effects among culture, motivations, and behaviors. A few studies used culture priming, or situational variation and flexibility (Trafimow, Triandis, & Goto, 1991, Brewer & Gardner, 1996; Hong et al., 2000; Oyserman et al., 2009; Oyserman & Lee, 2008), to explore the dynamic and contextualized nature of culture and cultural cognitive frames. One of the most notable examples is Hong et al.'s (2000) dynamic constructivist view of cultural influence in which individual interpretation of the meaning of a message flexibly depends on the variation of the context or situation. The same person may interpret a message in culturally different ways if they are primed by a typical American or Chinese cultural image.

Following the dynamic constructivist view of cultural influence on behavior, this group of studies found that depending on individual attributes (e.g., cognitive or social motivations) or situational factors (e.g., inter- or intracultural partners), how individuals communicate to reach agreements takes different patterns (Liu et al., 2012). In intracultural situations, reaching consensus is a necessary pathway for joint gains in two-party negotiations, while in intercultural negotiations, individual cognitive adaptation has a stronger effect on joint gains (Liu et al., 2012). Similarly, Adair and Liu (2011) suggested that in multiparty communication, the consensus-building process evolves through phases of information accumulation, examination, and accommodation, depending on cultural heterogeneity, group size, and individuals' integrative and distributive mindsets.

To summarize, while the first stage of studies on culture and communication merely acknowledged the significance of negative contextual influence, this cluster of studies fully considered cultural influence on communication as situational, flexible, and varied, as evident in the multiple interaction patterns found in these papers. The next stage of research on culture's influence of communication not only builds on the complexity of these relationships but also explores culture's positive effects on individual communicators.

Culture's Positive and Multiplicity Influence on Communication

In the most recent stage of culture and communication research, scholars continue to explore the multiplicity of culture and have so far discovered even more sophisticated mechanisms of culture's influence on communication. For example, Imai and Gelfand (2010) examined cultural intelligence, the capability of knowing and behaving in culturally complex situations, in intra- and intercultural negotiations. The role of culture or cultural phenomenology in communication research has evolved from culture being treated as a barrier to be overcome by communicators to culture now offering opportunities for personal competency development and pluralistic influences (e.g., Liu & Adair, 2017; Liu et al., 2018). For example, Erez et al. (2013) found that communication in global virtual teams increased cultural intelligence and global identity over a 4-week time period and that these effects were retained 6 months later. Liu et al. (2013) suggested that multicultural experience and a communicator's global identity versus local identity may also make a difference in the process and outcomes of interpersonal communication, especially while interacting with culturally different others. Specifically, they found that broad (but not deep) multicultural experience is associated with a higher degree of local identity, which can lead such individuals to achieve better outcomes in intracultural negotiations. On the other hand, deep, and both deep and broad multicultural experience is linked to higher global identity, which is beneficial for intercultural negotiations.

Adair et al. (2015) expanded the notions of high- and low-context communication by examining the patterns of communication tendencies with a more sophisticated study design and measures. They showed that understanding nonverbal cues in message, relationship, time, and space is especially beneficial for intercultural communications. In global virtual teams, Glikson and Erez (2020) investigated communication messages of participants and found that self-disclosure of relational messages, rather than task messages, helped create a psychologically safe communication climate for the team, which is positively related to team performance. By coding the content of early asynchronous text messages among members of 60 global virtual teams, Glikson and Erez (2020) linked communication to relationship building in intercultural settings. Their findings suggest that in virtual intercultural communications, where relationship building might be extra challenging, sharing relational messages at the beginning of interactions may be especially conducive for a positive communication climate and, ultimately, more productive team outcomes.

Researchers also examined the impact of communication media, such as email, on communication strategies and processes (Rosett et al., 2011). Rosett and colleagues (2011) examined the emails of intra- and intercultural negotiations by Hong Kong Chinese and Americans. They found that in distributive situations, reduced social awareness by media may lead Hong Kong Chinese email negotiators to be more competitive than Americans and more effective than face-to-face situations. They concluded that culture's nuanced influence on media use is of utter importance in the digital age.

Other studies explored the dynamics between specific communication properties, such as quality of communication experience in intra- versus intercultural contexts (Liu et al., 2010). These authors found that *quality of communication experience*, measured by the degree of clarity, responsiveness, and comfort encountered by individuals, interacts with communication context in predicting outcomes. For example, in intercultural negotiations between Americans and Chinese, there was an asymmetrical experience between the two parties where Americans reported more comfort and Chinese reported more clarity. Although higher degrees of clarity, responsiveness, and comfort predicted better outcomes in all situations, the effects were much stronger in intercultural settings.

This group of studies has advanced from previous stages and has begun appreciating culture as a source of individual development, such as the potential for building cultural intelligence or multicultural experience. Cultural intelligence and multicultural experience are, in turn, constructive for communication outcomes, including producing a higher degree of satisfaction and creating both economic and subjective values. To summarize, although the research on culture's influence on communication has evolved from simply mapping out cultural differences in behavioral patterns to a more sophisticated treatment of cultural influence with significant consideration of contextual factors, they remain fragmented, the studies are largely comparative, and as a result there is considerable potential for future research.

How Communication Affects Culture

While culture has clear impacts on the communication process and outcomes of participants involved, it is also reproduced, contested, and changed through the communicative events of the participants within a culture as well. In this sense, culture affects communication but is also affected and changed by communication, leading culture to be constantly evolving at various levels. For example, at the individual level, Lau, Chiu, and Lee (2001) proposed a reciprocal relationship between communication and shared reality in social knowledge and representation. Social knowledge and interpretation by communication partners evolve from a joint propagation of the communicative process and context. In other words, when individuals communicate, they simultaneously construct a common ground in their messages and responses through a psychologically parallel process.

Kashima (2000) reviewed and "recovered" legendary psychologist Fredric C. Bartlett's metatheory of culture as a "universal configurationist," treating culture as a configuration of universal components with culturally specific patterns and dynamic interactions within contexts. In other words, social interactions significantly affect culture. In this view, culture is and can be shaped and transmitted through communication within and between groups. Analyzing an example of a football player's story in multiple communication chains, Lyons and Kashima (2001) described the process of how individual communication activities enforced stereotype-consistent storylines, which collectively produced meaning. This dynamic process of meaning production, reproduction, and convergence formed the foundation of culture as a meaning system. Kashima, Lyons, and Clark (2013) further demonstrated that interpersonal conversations are important venues that maintain cultural stereotypes. In two experiments, Kashima and colleagues found that although stereotype-inconsistent information may attract attention, stereotype-consistent information is more likely to be emphasized, narrated, and discussed. Together, Kashima and colleagues have expanded Bartlett's metatheory of culture and offered specific empirical evidence on how communication affects cultural processes.

At a social collective level, Kashima and colleagues (2021) report that communication driven by political ideology entrenches and exacerbates polarization in societies through collective cognition. By examining political discourses through ideological commitment to an opinion, ideologically filtered interpretation, and communication in social networks, they found that polarizing opinions and interpretations are accelerated and amplified by communication and social networks, especially when disagreeable ties were cut off (Kashima et al., 2021).

In international joint ventures, Brannen and Salk (2000) found that organizational work culture evolves through a negotiated process between individuals' sense-making and the structure of organizational events based on ranges of cultural assumptions and normative orientations. A negotiated work culture emerges over time as the result of compromises in human resource management, meeting in the middle in operations, innovating new ideas for both partner groups, and dividing labor (Brannen & Salk, 2000).

Digging deeper into the social cognitive mechanisms of how communication interacts with culture, there seem to be three key mediums through which communication interacts and shapes culture: (1) language, (2) nonverbal communication and emotions/emotional expression, and (3) music. Here we elaborate on how these mediums of communication both influence and are influenced by culture and how these effects apply to organizational contexts.

Language

Holtgraves and Kashima (2008) define language as a "semiotic tool for meaning making and exchange" (p. 73). Language provides a systematic means of communicating highly abstract ideas and represents one of the principal ways that humans communicate with each other. Humans use language to enable interactions for social coordination and survival (Ko, 2016). As a culturally transmitted system, language evolves together with cultural change (Tallerman, 2005), and at the same time, culture evolves as a result of language use (Chomsky, 1965, 2010). Language and culture are thus dynamically coupled, perpetually shaping each other. While language is a powerful medium for the creation, maintenance and transmission of culture, research shows that language systems of a particular culture may also affect the cognitions of the participants within that culture (Ji et al., 2004; Hamers & Blanc, 2000; Markman & Hutchinson, 1984; Whorf, 1956; Logan, 1986). The language(s) one learns within their culture appears to have a profound impact on shaping how they perceive, order, and categorize the many diverse stimuli within any given environment or context (Vygotsky, 1962, Hamers & Blanc, 2000; Ji et al., 2004).

This provocative idea is not without debate within the literature. At the center of this debate is the *Sapir–Whorf linguistic relativity hypothesis*, whose main theme is that culture, through language, has the ability to influence how an individual thinks (Ji et al., 2004). The two views originating from this hypothesis are linguistic determinism and linguistic relativity, with each contending a different degree of power that language exerts on the cognitive processes of its speakers (Huang & Tse, 2017; Hardin & Banaji, 1993; Hunt & Agnoli, 1991; Kay & Kempton, 1984). *Linguistic determinism* refers to "the view that the structure of language strongly influences or fully determines the way its native speakers perceive the world" (Huang & Tse, 2017, p. 4). While this powerfully deterministic view has been largely disconfirmed (e.g., Berlin & Kay, 1969; Heider, 1972; Heider & Olivier, 1972), the linguistic relativity view, which differs in the magnitude of influence language exerts on cognition, remains a fruitful topic for language researchers. *Linguistic relativity* "postulates that the structural differences between languages are generally paralleled by nonlinguistic cognitive differences in the native speakers of the two languages" (Huang & Tse, 2017, p. 4). Overall, the question boils down to whether or not people think in language, and if they do, how it shapes thought.

Early debates on this hypothesis looked at physically perceptive domains such as "color, number, space, time and musical pitch" (Huang & Tse, 2017, p. 4). A popular example of debate in this field looks at the differing perceptions of colors in languages that differ in the number of words they use to differentiate different colors. While some languages, such as Dugum Dani, may only have two basic color terms to differentiate between black and white (Heider, 1972), other languages, such as Russian and Turkish, have up to 12 basic color terms (Ozgen & Davies, 1998; Huang & Tse, 2017). *Universalists* are researchers that hold that color-perceptive capabilities are universal and innate (e.g., Berlin & Kay, 1969; Franklin & Davies, 2004), while *linguistic relativity hypothesis* supporters contend that language plays a role in an individual's ability to cognitively differentiate and categorize colors (Roberson et al., 2000; Winawer et al., 2007). For example, Winawer et al. (2007) found that Russians, whose language differentiates between lighter blue and darker blue, were faster at differentiating these colors than individuals from English-speaking countries who have just one broad word for these two colors.

Another example of the impact of language on cognition would be Kashima and Kashima's study (1998) on the differences between individuals who use languages that allow for *pronoun dropping* compared to languages that do not. Languages differ in the use of person-indexing pronouns, which are called *deixis*. Examples of deixis within the English language are "I" and "you." In some languages, such as Chinese and Japanese, linguistic rules allow for the dropping of pronouns, "despite the absence of verb inflections and the grammatical rule of subject–verb agreement" (Kashima & Kashima, 1998, p. 464; Hinds, 1982; Huang, 1984; Li & Thompson, 1976). Reasons for why this pronoun dropping occurs is not without extensive debate (e.g., Berman, 1990, 1992; Bloom, 1990; Valian, 1990).

The *cognitive grammar view* (Langacker, 1987) contends that "a deictic expression indexes elements in the particular situation where the speech takes place . . . [and] describes a relationship between the speaker and the speech context, that is, the manner in which the speaker relates to the social context of the speech" (Kashima & Kashima, 1998, p. 465; Langacker, 1987, pp. 128–132). This *construal relationship* then causes a perceptive shift in the focal point of what is being expressed. For example, expressions with explicit first-person singular pronouns (1PS) such as I, and second-person singular (2PS) pronouns, explicitly cause individuals to become the salient focus of the expression. Languages that then allow for the dropping of these pronouns allow the speakers to emphasize or deemphasize the self or other and the contextual environment in communicative events (Kashima & Kashima, 1998). Kashima and Kashima (1998) found evidence of coinciding cultural differences with these linguistic differences, such as finding lower levels of individualism in cultures whose languages allow for pronoun dropping.

In organizational settings, Liu et al. (2015) found that relational metaphors used by international joint venture partners to describe their relationships, whether it is equal or hierarchical, will interact with equity structures of the joint venture in shaping the quality of the relationship and their achievement of strategic goals over time. In other words, the use of an equal relational metaphor, such as a "modern marriage," rather than a hierarchical one, such as a "patriarchal family," would contribute to higher-quality relationships and a more productive work culture in joint ventures. Additionally, in an extensive case study of a Japanese multinational enterprise, Neeley (2017) showed that an intentional mandate of a common language not only changed individual employees' values and identities, but also transformed the organizational culture into a more global one. Therefore, although rooted in cultures, common languages and strategic use of language can facilitate the construction of or reshaping of new organizational cultures.

Nonverbal Communication and Emotions

While linguistic communication represents an extraordinary human capability for abstract communication, verbal communication is not the only way that humans are able to communicate. In fact, it is estimated that nonverbal behavior accounts for around 60 to 90% of human communication (Mehrabian, 2017). Nonverbal mechanisms of communication involve body language, gesture, and emotional expression, all of which are anchored on the capacity for empathy. The literature on these nonverbal communicative capabilities can provide additional insight into cultural differences and similarities of communication. Emotion, emotional expression, and empathy provide a foundational ability for tuning into reading both nonverbal behaviors and verbal behaviors to maximize the accurate deciphering of what it is another individual is trying to communicate (and even may not be consciously trying to communicate).

Emotions serve as a powerful device for effective nonverbal communication. They are complex *feelings* that are deeply social in nature. Social systems benefit from the capacity of individuals to experience and express emotions (Keltner & Haidt, 1999), so collective emotional expressions may become normative in a culture. In this sense, display *rules* for how emotions are conveyed and interpreted in a certain culture are likely passed on to future generations and solidify the cultural norm of emotional expression. There must exist a physiological mechanism, or a form of body language, for expressing emotions in order for them to be read by others. Answers to the questions "What are emotions" and "where do they come from" remain a hot topic of debate within the literature, with deep implications for the culture and communication field. To understand the interaction between culture and communication, specifically related to emotions and emotional expression, it is necessary to understand the current debate within the literature regarding the nature versus nurture origin of emotions.

Different researchers from different emotional theory camps differ in the universality versus cultural specificity of felt emotion and emotional expression. For example, *basic emotion theorists* believe, for the most part, that felt and expressed emotion is largely universal, whereas *social construction theorists* believe the other extreme, that felt and expressed emotion is largely culturally specific. The *basic emotions perspective* views emotions as an innate and universal process that serves as "motivational amplifiers" (Tomkins, 1962). In this view, emotions serve to cause a certain reaction "to tasks that require change in some way" (Warrenburg, 2020, p. 4). Basic emotion theorists believe that emotions are innate and present at or shortly after birth and are thus universal. Sadness, for example, is a functional state with a specific and shared coinciding feeling, activated physiologies and expressions that serve to communicate that feeling, or the awareness of that feeling to another individual (Ekman, 1992; Tomkins, 1962). Similarly, the emotion of disgust, together with its associated nonverbal body cues, also seems to be produced universally in reaction to something offensive or revolting, perhaps to communicate to another individual that something is potentially dangerous (Trompenaars & Turner, 1997). It would make sense for feelings and expressions of sadness and disgust to be universally felt and recognized given their evolutionary importance to survival.

Social construction theorists view emotions as entirely a social artifact that is the product of the cultural context in which they exist and that aid in the performance of culturally specific tasks (Mesquita et al., 2016). How one emotionally reacts to any given stimulus, to social construction theorists, is largely dependent on the social consequences of this emotional experience and the normativity of what emotion other individuals from that culture typically feel (Warrenburg, 2020; Mesquita et al., 2016). For these theorists, each culture has specific emotions that aid in the success of that individual. For example, the independent versus collective cultural differences between Western and Eastern cultures, respectively, have an impact on what emotions will be felt in any given situation (Mesquita et al., 2016). Individuals learn through constant exposure within their environment and are thus "a 'social reality' [that] depend[s] on the collective intentionality of a group of people" (Warrenburg, 2020, p. 32; Barrett, 2017; Mesquita et al., 2016) and are ultimately heavily informed and impacted by the norms and values of the cultural context. Therefore, when individuals from one culture enter into another culture, *emotional acculturation* occurs, where the individual begins to learn and experience new emotional states consistent with this new cultural context (Barrett, 2017).

Research into determining cultural differences regarding the ability to read emotional expressions from cultures that are the same and different from one's own culture has posed two conflicting models: the *cultural equivalence model* and the *cultural advantage model of emotion recognition*. On the one hand, the *cultural equivalence model of emotion recognition* aligns more closely with basic emotion theorists, who contend that because emotional communication is largely rooted physiologically in making individuals more evolutionarily equipped for survival, individuals will be able to equally evaluate the emotional expressions of both ingroup and outgroup members regardless of what culture they belong to (Darwin, 1872; Preston & de Waal, 2002). On the other hand, the *cultural advantage model of emotion recognition* believes that individuals are more evolutionarily equipped for survival through the ability of individuals from the same ingroup to be better at reading the emotional expressions of other individuals from the ingroup compared to the outgroup (Anderson & Keltner, 2002; Thibault et al., 2006). In organizational life, although emotions are reactions to happenings within a context, collective emotions are also building blocks for organizational actions that eventually form norms and construct culture over time.

An early review of culture and emotions by Mesquita and Frijda (1992) situated cultural variations in emotions within a framework of the *cognitive-process model of emotions*. In this view, "whether cultural differences or similarities are found depends to an important degree on the level of description of the emotional phenomena" (p. 179). This model breaks the emotional response of an individual into a process of *elicitation* and *manifestation* containing various stages that allow for a deeper dive into each and show whether differences or similarities between cultures exist within them. These stages are, first, the *antecedent events*, which may differ across cultures, thus affecting what individuals within each culture expect and are sensitive to. The second stage, *event coding*, explains that individuals from within a culture will code and categorize events in a schematic way facilitated by their culture, thus affecting how the event will be emotionally appraised. In the third stage, or the *appraisal stage*, events are "appraised with respect to their implications for the subject's well-being and his or her possibilities for coping with the event" (Mesquita & Frijda, 1992, p. 180). The fourth stage would be the *physiological reaction patterns* that explain how an emotional response is both due to and affected by physiological responses to a stimulus. The fifth stage is described as *action readiness*, where "emotional states involve changes in action readiness" (Mesquita & Frijda, 1992, p. 180). For example, the emotional state of fear may elicit a survival instinct composed of cognitions that aid self-protection. The sixth stage is *emotional behavior*. Once an emotional state is generated, behaviors are generated by the individual, depending on the "availability and expected effectiveness of the various behavior patterns" (Mesquita & Frijda, 1992, p. 180). Lastly, the seventh stage is *regulation*, which "refers to both inhibitory control and voluntary enhancement" (Mesquita & Frijda, 1992, p. 180). Thus, by adding more nuance to the particular stages involved in an individual's emotional state, research into culture and emotions is better able to dissect and understand cultural similarities and differences. While culture provides a framework vital to how an individual learns to organize their reality and what expectations of behavior are deemed acceptable for that given context, there still appears to be a shared, biologically based innate emotional expression system across all humans.

Matsumoto and Hwang (2019) have elaborated on this model and proposed the *biocultural model of emotion*. This model reconciles the differences and similarities across cultures through the idea that a "biologically-based, core emotion system is calibrated, regulated, and elaborated by culture and culture learning" (p. 501). These researchers conducted a study comparing the spontaneous emotional expression of blind and sighted Judo athletes and found evidence for universal facial expressions of emotions based on a core biological system. Because blind individuals who were unable to learn what facial expressions are associated with what emotions in the context of their cultures exhibited the same facial expressions as those sighted, there is evidence for this basic emotional system. This substantiates the idea that, at least some emotional expressions, served an evolutionary, phylogenetic advantage to communicate with and be understood by others. At the same time, this does not deny cultural specificities; "the interaction between biology and culture in human emotions allows for complex social networks and relationships, and enhances the meaning of normal, daily activities" (p. 512). With emotions and emotional expressions being explicated as a key human tool for nonverbal communication, it is thus vital to explore the importance of an important communication tool that seems able to convey deep, nonverbal messages and to evoke powerful emotional responses in nearly every culture around the world, *music* (Wallmark et al., 2018; Vuoskoski & Eerola, 2017).

Music

Music is a powerful, almost magical tool important in conveying highly abstract ideas and emotions, but it is ultimately social in nature. As Wallmark et al. (2018) state, "by disclosing the affective and cognitive states of actual or imagined human actors, musical engagement can function as a mediated form of social encounter, even when listening by ourselves" (p. 1). Although music is an intense manifestation of cultural variations, we believe that musical practice is a particularly insightful domain to investigate the mechanisms of how this communication medium ultimately shapes and advances the cultural setting it exists in.

While the capacity to create, utilize, and enjoy music as a communicative medium for meaning and emotion appears to be universal, the musical practice, both in how and what meaning is communicated, is deeply entrenched within its cultural context. A national anthem both reflects and projects the salient features of the country's characters. Iconic musicians such as the Beatles and the Grateful Dead both lead and symbolize the spirit of the time, with widespread resonance of the messages carried through their melodies, harmonies, rhythms, and lyrics. Organizations often choose music in advertising, company websites, or lobbies to aid the expression of their products' properties and shape organizational climate for consumers, employees, and business associates. In this sense, as an integral part of cultural expression, music coevolves with culture. Additionally, there is ample evidence of how music and musical practice have affected and shaped the culture in which it exists, such as the musical event Woodstock (Lovesey, 2020). Woodstock was a music and arts festival that epitomized, affected, and was affected by the cultural context in which it existed. As Lovesey (2020) states, Woodstock "registered a paradigm shift in cultural, intellectual, and musicological history" (p. 121).

Evidence for further communicative implications of music come from Wallmark et al. (2018) in their study of the neurophysiological effects of trait empathy and music. Recent studies have suggested that empathy "is related to emotional identification and feelings of intimacy or social connectedness" (Leman, 2007, p. 122; Berthoz & Jorland, 2004). Leman (2007) states that "listening to music can be seen as a socializing activity in the sense that it may train the listener's self in social attuning at empathic relationships" (p. 126). While empathy is a vital mechanism central to all communicative mediums, within this study, empathy was hypothesized to be a key mechanism in how music is perceived and processed. Wallmark et al. (2018) conducted a study that examined the fMRIs of individuals differing on cognitive and affective trait empathy levels and found physiological evidence for a link between empathy and music, explicating music as a potentially fruitful avenue for further investigating and understanding cultural similarities and differences in communication.

Evolutionarily, it would make sense for acculturation and socialization processes to include musical practices for groups and organizations to have a mechanism for enhancing cohesion and coordination. As Sun Tzu (2012) states in *The Art of War*, "Gongs and drums and banners and flags make the army hear with the same ear and see with the same eye" (p. 45). Embodied listening of a group of people may cause the harmonization of movement among the individuals, in turn causing an "increased liking between interaction partners" (Leman, 2007, p. 126), in what Lakin et al. (2003) refer to as the *chameleon effect of nonconscious mimicry*. A group with strong cohesion and effective communication capabilities could, at least historically, engage in more complex and collective coordinated action, positioning groups that leverage these capabilities as more adept for survival. In this sense, music serves as a form of nonverbal communication that promotes a "sense of groupishness" that enables conflict management, bonding, and collective survival of the group (Brown, 2000; Cross & Morley, 2010; Cross, 2007).

To summarize, music has been an unsung communication tool in shaping, maintaining, and creating cultural norms and taste, ranging from national anthems to cultural icons. Visionary organizations have already started strategic manipulation of sound in workspace for senses of community and creativity (e.g., Krukowski, 2019). Together, language, nonverbal communication, emotion, and music not only dynamically influence and interact with culture, but also offer new and fertile avenues of studying culture and communication.

Future Research for Culture and Communication

Although communication is an essential activity in human and organization life across cultures, research on culture and communication has largely taken a static, fragmented, and de-contextualized view. Szkudlarek et al. (2020) offer a comprehensive critique on communication in international business and point out that the existing literature does not address the dynamic and contextualized nature of communication. For example, they note that the extant works in the field tend to overly rely on etic dimensions that do not capture within-culture dynamics, or the situational complexity of communication, and may cause superficial and even misleading findings. One of the reasons, we speculate, is that the field of communication has been dominated by the Western analytical thinking style that focuses on decontextualized and discrete inquiries (Nisbett et al., 2001). Moving forward, processual, relational, and contextual perspectives of research on culture and communication promise to provide a more holistic inquiry of the field (Szkudlarek et al., 2020; Liu et al., 2021; Corner et al., 2021). Specifically, Liu et al. (2021) suggest that communicators in multicultural relationships might switch, expand, and fuse their culturally typical communal or exchange schemata of relationships. As an important aspect of intercultural competency, Corner et al. (2021) maintain that when communicating with foreign counterparts, especially those based in emerging markets, individuals need to consider the perspectives and uncertainties embedded within the context, as well as initiating and cultivating relationships. Future empirical research is needed to fill these gaps and test the propositions of studying culture and communication in processual, embedded relationships, and contextualized situations that can provide dynamic, holistic findings on the interactions between culture and communication.

Research in culture and communication has gradually shifted from a static, compartmentalized understanding into one that is more dynamic, context dependent, and process oriented whereby individuals iteratively negotiate meaning. For future research, we propose that research on culture and communication could be oriented more holistically, specifically, (1) temporally, (2) spatially, (3) inter- and intrapersonally, and (4) inter- and intraculturally.

By *temporally*, we refer to an increased emphasis being placed on the chronical conditions that gave rise to the circumstances and environments in which communicative events exist. Culture and communicative capabilities, mediums, and meanings are the result of thousands of years of constant evolution and still continue to evolve dynamically. A shift from a view that treats communication and culture as a static cross section to one that is processual would yield fruitful avenues for future research (Szkudlarek et al., 2020; Cramton et al., 2021). Past research in culture and communication that views communicative events as static and isolated snapshots miss out on the richness of the "interactive, evolving, and complex" nature of communication processes in reality (Szkudlarek et al., 2020, p. 6). Both the capabilities for communication and the implied meaning of communicative tools are the result of constant iterative sense-making processes negotiated by the many different participants across many different mediums. Future research should investigate how "past experiences, individual predispositions and situational contingencies affect the communication process" (Szkudlarek et al., 2020 p. 6). Methodologies that utilize longitudinal data may yield prolific insights for the study of culture and communication.

By *spatially*, we refer to an increased emphasis on the specific contextual and environmental circumstances where communication occurs. Past research has been largely decontextualized, overlooking the specific contexts in which communication events occur and the effects these contexts may have on communication. Varner (2000) argues that "the multiplicity of contexts is crucial for making sense of communicative processes" (Szkudlarek et al., 2020, p. 3). An example of such a context is the tight versus loose norms in societies, which in a way dictated the communication of responses and actions by countries in coping with the COVID-19 pandemic (e.g., Gelfand et al., 2021).

Additionally, many scholars have shown that media types and mediums play a role in communicative interactions and outcomes (e.g., Klitmøller & Lauring, 2013; Daft & Lengel, 1986) and called for research to include a more diverse range of media platforms (Ishii, Lyons, & Carr, 2019). Future research should investigate how different mediums yield different communicative outcomes, such as across digital platforms, musical formats, or in-person communicative events and what the variables within these mediums contribute, culturally, emotionally, and cognitively to these outcomes. Further, Keller and Tian (2021) advocate for studying the interconnected paradoxes between linguistic tensions embedded in organizational paradoxes. An example is that linguistic tensions such as explicit versus implicit messages can complicate organizational management paradoxes, such as control versus autonomy. Therefore, the multiplicity of contextual influence holds the promise of sophisticated inquiries in future research on culture and communication.

By calling for research to be more *interpersonal* and *intrapersonal*, we refer to an increased emphasis being placed on communicative events that occur between individuals and even *within* individuals. Interpersonal communication involves negotiations of meaning. Much of the past literature on communication has focused on the organizational or group level, such as investigating "knowledge characteristics, organizational culture, and the perceived importance of sender and receiver attitudes, motivation or communication skills" (Szkudlarek et al., 2020, p. 4; Minbaeva, 2007; Morgulis-Yakushev et al., 2018). Focusing on the integration of organizational level and individual level and viewing communicative events and processes from a multilevel perspective presents an avenue that may probe at the deep nuance involved in communicative events.

Within the individual level, a focus on intrapersonal communication may also help generate novel and exciting insights into the study of communication and culture. Interfacing an individual's many identities and changing the salience and availability of self-construal schemas and its impact on culture and communication provide a fruitful avenue for research. Intrapersonal negotiation may occur through introspective avenues such as meditation but may also be facilitated through altered states of consciousness such as through music, mind altering substances and one's environmental context. Researchers have begun investigating and elaborating on the "multiple selves" theory. Angyal (1965) proposed that "the mind is made up of subsystems which interact, resulting in setting and shifting sets" (Lester, 2012, p. 1). Thus, individuals may simultaneously have many "selves" that hold different priorities, which contribute to an inner dialogue in the process of decision making. Different selves have different goals, different priorities, and ultimately different cognitions that are most saliently accessible, especially for individuals with multiple cultural identities and experiences. These selves may be primed by cultural artifacts within the environment, emotional states, or the salient identities of their peers. Thus, it is important to understand different selves and states of consciousness for a more holistic understanding of communication. This view emphasizes the need to understand communicative events within the environments and contexts in which they exist, as well as the cognitive and emotional states of the individual, whether primed by existing stimuli within their environment, and the effects on communicative processes and outcomes.

Lastly, we propose that research in culture and communication be expanded more to investigate *intercultural and intracultural communication*. Both communication and communication competence are the result of a relational exchange between two individuals. As discussed earlier, no communicative event between individuals happens in a vacuum, and each of these individuals will bring to the table a set of existing predispositions and preexisting assigned meanings, which may heavily impact communication. For example, although intercultural communication has been studied (e.g., Imai & Gelfand, 2010; Liu et al., 2010, 2012), a more dialectical approach is needed to recognize the dynamic and interactive nature in complex situations (Corner et al., 2021; Martin, 2015; Szkudlarek et al., 2020). Thus, further research should infuse more culturally diverse views in understanding, holistically, what individuals bring from their own culture and how that, in turn, affects the communicative events.

Existing literature, however, on cross-cultural perspectives has seemingly missed out on the dynamic nature and complexity of intercultural communication, especially in complex temporal and special situations. While previous studies have been insightful in their own way, with a few exceptions of qualitative studies (e.g., Brannen & Salk, 2000), almost all intercultural communication studies (e.g., Brett & Okumura, 1998; Imai & Gelfand, 2010; Liu et al., 2010, 2012) used lab studies with single or repeated negotiation simulations. Longitudinal, contextualized, and both qualitative and quantitative field experiments might better capture the evolving forces in inter- and intracultural interactions (Brannen et al., 2017; Lee et al., 2020; Casrnir, 1999; Nardon, 2017). In order to better understand the dynamic and fluid nature of intercultural and intracultural communicative events, moving from comparative methodologies such as surveys, to diverse and rich methodologies such as "narrative analysis (e.g., Gertsen & Søderberg's, 2011), ethnographic field studies (e.g., Moore & Mahadevan, 2020), in-depth cases (e.g., Piekkari et al., 2020), critical analysis (e.g., Romani et al., 2020) or even experimental designs (Fischer & Karl, 2020)" may be better suited (Szkudlarek et al., 2020, p. 2).

Table 16.1 Five key takeaways

Takeaways
Theoretical implication
Dynamic constructivist View
1. Research should continue to emphasize the importance of context and interactions with contexts
2. Research should investigate how various cultures within an individual resonate or conflict with each other based on context
Holistic thinking
1. Research should view communication and communicative events more holistically where various factors interact and affect each other
2. Context and other mediums should be jointly analyzed to better understand cultural differences and similarities
Social cognitive theory
1. Schemata and mental models can be used to explore the impact and effectiveness of communication

(continued)

Table 16.1 *Continued*
2. Felt emotion should be emphasized in determining how individuals make sense during communication
Cultural evolution perspective
1. Both cultures and individuals' identities are dynamically evolving, and the coevolution process is worth studying
2. Future research should investigate the interplay between and within individuals of different cultures and subcultures
Communication mediums
1. Communication consists of various interwoven and overlapping mediums
2. Language, body language, emotional expression, music, art, theater, and other artistic mediums have unique mechanisms of communicating ideas which future research can better dissect
3. Different cognitions and emotions may be associated with different communication mechanisms
Practical implication
Dynamic constructivist View
1. Managers should be sensitive to the impact of context on employees
2. Cognitive frames associated with work from home may greatly differ from working in office
Holistic thinking
1. Strategic communication with foreign business partners and customers should consider not only the content of the product but also relationships, historical perspectives, and other factors in the ecosystem
Social cognitive theory
1. Greater emphasis should be placed on emotional regulation
2. Greater empathy and mindfulness can be utilized during communication for more effective outcomes
Cultural evolution perspective
1. Individuals and populations are becoming more complex as they are exposed and become adjusted to various cultures and subcultures
2. Managers should remain sensitive to these complexities
Communication mediums
3. Strategic communicators may manipulate conscious and subconscious receptors of communication through a combination of mediums.
4. There might be convergence and divergence of communication medium use across cultures, which could be consequential for outcomes of intercultural communication

We summarize main takeaways on Table 16.1 and below.

Five Key Takeaways

1- **Dynamic Constructivist View—Individuals** are composed of various overlapping and interwoven cultures with different associated norms and values that may become more or less cognitively salient depending on the context. Contexts are composed of various cues, which are then associated with existing cultural frames within an individual (Hong et al., 2000). Accordingly, different contexts will prime different cultural identities by causing a cultural frame and its associated cognitions to become more salient and enacted, affecting subsequent communicative events. Future research should remain highly sensitive to cues within a context and its effects on an individual's cognitive frame.

2- **Holistic Thinking—Previous** research on culture and communication, dominated by Western theories and research norms, focus more on the analytical traditions and perspectives. Krukowski (2019) showed that an integration of space and sound communicates to both the conscious and the unconscious mind and created a new kind of work culture at WeWork and the Yard in New York. Future research should consider a more holistic perspective that better integrates elements of communication such as language, emotion, music, and contexts into organization studies.

3- **Social Cognitive Theory—Culture** and communication research should further deploy the use of a social cognitive theory (Fiske & Taylor, 1991) that examines mental models before and after communicative events and the valence and arousal of emotions associated with certain cognitions for a more nuanced understanding of communicative processes and outcomes. Felt emotions will determine how individuals engage in sensemaking (Maitlis et al., 2013), that is, how cues are extracted into existing frames, largely effecting how information will be communicated and understood by both parties in a communicative event.

4- **Cultural Evolution Perspective—Cultural** identities, within both individuals and societies are not a static monolith but are instead composed of a constellation of subparts that are constantly changing and evolving (e.g., Wilson, 2002). Cultures are composed of many subcultures that are constantly interacting, causing them to gradually evolve. Individuals within these cultures are constantly negotiating and co-constructing realities with each other, within and between their cultures and communities. Individuals are then also composed of various interconnected identities that are dynamically interacting as an individual constructs their identity. Future research should examine how cultures change and evolve due to the interactions of the subcultures that compose them, as well as how individuals constantly change and evolve as they gradually negotiate a sense of self through the many cultures and subcultures they belong to. Doing so would require examining cross and intracultural communication at both the group and individual level for a more detailed understanding of culture and communication.

5- **Communication Mediums—Different** mediums of communication may offer different insights into cultural differences and similarities. By grounding each medium into its given context and exploring each, a more thorough analysis of culture and communication can be conducted. Language, nonverbal body language, emotions and emotional expression, music, and other cultural artifacts provide fruitful and incredibly interesting avenues for future investigation. These different mediums consist of different psychological and physiological mechanisms that are interwoven and that should be holistically taken into consideration to further understand communicative similarities and differences of the capabilities of individuals from both different and the same cultures.

References

Adair, W. L., & Brett, J. M. (2005). The negotiation dance: Time, culture, and behavioral sequences in negotiations. *Organization Science, 16*(1), 33–51.

Adair, W. L., & Liu, L. A. (2011). Building shared mental models in multicultural multiparty negotiations: The dynamic process. *Research on Managing Groups and Teams, 14*, 57–78.

Adair, W. L., Buchan, N., Chen, X.-P., & Liu, D. (2015). A model of communication context and measure of context dependence. *Academy of Management Discovery, 2*(2), 198–217.

Adair, W. L., Okumura, T., & Brett, J. M. (2001). Negotiation behaviors when cultures collide: The US and Japan. *Journal of Applied Psychology, 86*(3), 371–385.

Adler, N. J., & Graham, J. L. (1989). Cross-cultural interaction: The international comparison fallacy? *Journal of International Business Studies, 20*(3), 515–537.

Anderson, C., & Keltner, D. (2002). Open peer commentary: The role of empathy in the formation and maintenance of social bonds. *Behavioral and Brain Sciences, 25*(1), 21–22.

Angyal, A. (1965). *Neurosis and treatment.* New York: John Wiley.

Barrett, L. F. (2017). *How emotions are made: The secret life of the brain.* New York: Houghton Mifflin Harcourt.

Berlin, B., & Kay, P. (1969). *Basic color terms: Their universality and evolution.* Berkeley: University of California Press.

Berman, L. A. (1992). First person identities in Indonesian conversational narratives. *Journal of Asian Pacific Communication, 3*, 3–14.

Berman, R. A. (1990). On acquiring an (S)VO language: Subjectless sentences in children's Hebrew. *Linguistics, 28*, 1135–1166.

Berthoz, A., & Jorland, G. (Eds.). (2004). *L'Empathie.* Paris: Jacob.

Bloom, P. (1990). Subjectless sentences in child language. *Linguistic Inquiry, 21*(4), 491–504.

Brannen, M. Y., Gómez, C., Peterson, M. F., Romani, L., Sagiv, L., & Wu, P. C. (2017). People in global organizations: Culture, personality, and social dynamics. In H. W. Lane, M. L. Maznevski, M. E. Mendenhall, & J. McNett (Eds.), *The Blackwell handbook of global management* (pp. 26–54). Malden, MA: Blackwell.

Brannen, M. Y., & Salk, J. (2000). Partnering across borders: Negotiating organizational culture in a German-Japanese joint venture. *Human Relations, 53*(4), 451–487.

Brett, J. M., & Okumura, T. (1998). Inter-and intracultural negotiation: US and Japanese negotiators. *Academy of Management Journal, 41*, 495–510.

Brett, J. M., Tinsley, C. H., Shapiro, D. L., & Okumura, T. (2007). Intervening in employee disputes: How and when will managers from China, Japan, and the US act differently? *Management and Organizational Review, 3*(2), 183–204.

Brewer, M. B., & Gardner, W. (1996). Who is this "We"? Levels of collective identity and self representations. *Journal of Personality and Social Psychology, 71*(1), 83–93.

Brown, S. (2000). The "musilanguage" model of music evolution. In N. Wallin, B. Merker, and S. Brown (Eds.), *The origins of music* (pp. 271–300). Cambridge, MA: MIT Press.

Cai, D. A., Wilson, S. R., & Drake, L. (2000). Culture in context: Individualism/collectivism, negotiator role, framing, and paths to integrative agreements. *Human Communication Research, 26*, 591–617.
Casrnir, F. L. (1999). Foundations for the study of intercultural communication based on a third-culture building model. *International Journal of Intercultural Relations, 23*, 91–116.
Chomsky N. (1965). *Aspects of the theory of syntax*. Cambridge, MA: MIT Press.
Chomsky, N. (2010). Poverty of stimulus: Unfinished business. Transcript of a presentation given at Johannes-Gutenberg University, Mainz.
Corner, A. J., Liu, L. A., & Bird, A. (2021). Intercultural competencies for emerging markets: A contextualized approach. *International Business Review, 30*(3), 101792.
Cramton, C. D., Köhler, T., & Levitt, R. E. (2021). Using scripts to address cultural and institutional challenges of global project coordination. *Journal of International Business Studies*, 52(1), 56–77.
Cross, I. (2007). Music and cognitive evolution. In L. Barrett & R. Dunbar (Eds.), *Oxford Handbook of Evolutionary Psychology*. Oxford Library of Psychology 2012. https://doi.org/10.1093/oxfordhb/9780198568308.013.0045, accessed 20 March 2023.
Cross, I., & Morley, I. R. M. (2010). The evolution of music: Theories, definitions and the nature of the evidence. In S. Malloch and C. Trevarthen (Eds.), *Communicative Musicality: Exploring the Basis of Human Companionship* (No. 5, pp. 61–81). New York, NY: Oxford University Press.
Daft, R. L., & Lengel, R. H. (1986). Organizational information requirements, media richness and structural design. *Management Science, 32*(5), 554–571.
Darwin, C. (1872). *The descent of man, and selection in relation to sex* (Vol. 2). D. Appleton.
De Dreu, C. K. W., & Carnevale, P. J. (2003). Motivational bases of information processing and strategy in conflict and negotiation. In M. P. Zanna (Ed.), *Advances in experimental social psychology* (Vol. 35, pp. 235–291). Amsterdam: Elsevier Academic Press. https://doi.org/10.1016/S0065-2601(03)01004-9
Ekman, P. (1992). An argument for basic emotions. *Cognition and Emotion*, 6(3–4), 169–200.
Erez, M., Lisak, A., Harush, R., Glikson, E., Nouri, R., & Shokef, E. (2013). Going global: developing management students' cultural intelligence and global identity in virtual culturally diverse teams. *The Academy of Management Learning and Education Journal*, 12 (3), 330–355.
Fischer, R., & Karl, J. A. (2020). Experimental methods in cross-cultural management. In B. Szkudlarek, L. Romani, D. Caprar, and J. S. Osland (Eds.), *The SAGE handbook of cross-cultural management* (pp. 111–126). London: SAGE.
Fiske, S. T., & Taylor, S. E. (1991). *Social cognition*. New York, NY: Mcgraw-Hill Book Company.
Franklin, A., & Davies, I. R. L. (2004). New evidence for infant colour categories. *British Journal of Developmental Psychology, 22*, 349–377.
Gelfand, M. J., Jackson, J. C., Pan, X., Nau, D., Pieper, D., Denison, E., Dagher, M., Van Lange, P. A. M., Chiu, C.-Y., & Wang, M. (2021). The relationship between cultural tightness–looseness and COVID-19 cases and deaths: A global analysis. *The Lancet Planetary Health, 5*(3), e135–e144.
Gertsen, M. C., & Søderberg, A. M. (2011). Intercultural collaboration stories: On narrative inquiry and analysis as tools for research in international business. *Journal of International Business Studies, 42*(6), 787–804.
Glikson, E., & Erez, M. (2020). The emergence of a communication climate in global virtual teams. *Journal of World Business, 55*(6), 1–10.
Gunia, B. C., Brett, J. M., Nandkeolyar, A., & Kamdar, D. (2011). Paying a price: Culture, trust, and negotiation consequences. *Journal of Applied Psychology, 96*(4), 774–789.
Hall, E. T. (1959). *The silent language*. New York: Random House.
Hall, E. T. (1976). *Beyond culture*. New York: Doubleday.
Hamers, J. F., & Blanc, M. H. A. (2000). *Bilinguality and bilingualism* (2nd ed.). Cambridge: Cambridge University Press.
Hardin, C., & Banaji, M. R. (1993). The influence of language on thought. *Social Cognition, 11*, 277–308.
Heider, E. R. (1972). Universals in color naming and memory. *Journal of Experimental Psychology, 93*, 10–20.
Heider, E. R., & Olivier, D. C. (1972). The structure of the color space in naming and memory for two languages. *Cognitive Psychology, 3*, 337–354.
Hinds, J. (1982). *Ellipsis in Japanese*. Edmonton, Canada: Linguistic Research.
Hinds, P. J., Neeley, T., & Cramton, C. D. (2014). Language as a lightning rod: Power contests, emotion regulation, and subgroup dynamics in global teams. *Journal of International Business Studies, 45*(5), 536–561.
Holtgraves, T. M., & Kashima, Y. (2008). Language, meaning, and social cognition. *Personality and Social Psychology Review, 12*(1), 73–94.

Hong, Y. Y., Morris, M. W., Chiu, C. Y., & Benet-Martinez, V. (2000). Multicultural minds: A dynamic constructivist approach to culture and cognition. *American Psychologist, 55*(7), 709–720.

Huang, J. (1984). On the typology of zero anaphora. *Ohak Yongu* [Language Research], 20, 85–105.

Huang, Y., & Tse, C. S. (2017). Linguistic relativity in conceptual metaphors. *Psychology of bilingualism: The cognitive and emotional world of bilinguals.* In A. Ardila, A. Cieślicka, R. Heredia, and M. Rosselli (Eds.), *Psychology of bilingualism. The bilingual mind and brain book series* (pp. 3–26). Cham: Springer.

Hunt, E., & Agnoli, F. (1991). The Whorfian hypothesis: A cognitive psychology perspective. *Psychological Review, 98*, 377–389.

Imai, L., & Gelfand, M. J. (2010). The culturally intelligent negotiator: The impact of cultural intelligence (CQ) on negotiation sequences and outcomes. *Organizational Behavior and Human Decision Processes, 112*, 83–98.

Ishii, K., Lyons, M. M., & Carr, S. A. (2019). Revisiting media richness theory for today and future. *Human Behavior and Emerging Technologies, 1*(2), 124–131.

Ji, L. J., Zhang, Z., & Nisbett, R. E. (2004). Is it culture or is it language? Examination of language effects in cross-cultural research on categorization. *Journal of Personality and Social Psychology, 87*(1), 57.

Kashima, Y. (2000). Recovering Bartlett's social psychology of cultural dynamics. *European Journal of Social Psychology, 30*(3), 383–403.

Kashima, Y., Lyons, A., & Clark, A. (2013). The maintenance of cultural stereotypes in the conversational retelling of narratives. *Asian Journal of Social Psychology, 16*(1), 60–70.

Kashima, E. S., & Kashima, Y. (1998). Culture and language: The case of cultural dimensions and personal pronoun use. *Journal of Cross-Cultural Psychology, 29*(3), 461–486.

Kashima, Y., Perfors, A., Ferdinand, V., & Pattenden, E. (2021). Ideology, communication and polarization. *Philosophical Transactions of the Royal Society B, 376*(1822), 20200133.

Kay, P., & Kempton, W. (1984). What is the Sapir-Whorf hypothesis? *American Anthropologist, 86*, 65–79.

Keller, J., & Tian, P. (2021). The organizational paradox of language. In R. Bednarek, M. P. Cunha, J. Schad, and W. R. Smith. (Eds.), *Interdisciplinary dialogues on organizational paradox: Investigating social structures and human expression, Part B* (*Research in the Sociology of Organizations, Vol. 73b*) (pp. 101–122). Bingley, UK: Emerald Publishing Limited.

Keltner, D., & Haidt, J. (1999). Social functions of emotions at four levels of analysis. *Cognition and Emotion, 13*(5), 505–521.

Kern, M. C., Lee, S., Aytug, Z., & Brett, J. M. (2012). Bridging social distance in intercultural negotiations: "You" and the bicultural negotiator. *International Journal of Conflict Management, 23*(2), 173–191.

Kim, H. S. (2002). We talk, therefore we think? A cultural analysis of the effect of talking on thinking. *Journal of Personality and Social Psychology, 83*(4), 828–842.

Kim, Y. Y. (1988). *Communication and cross-cultural adaptation.* Clevedon, UK: Multilingual Matters.

Klitmøller, A., & Lauring, J. (2013). When global virtual teams share knowledge: Media richness, cultural difference and language commonality. *Journal of World Business, 48*, 398–406.

Ko, K. H. (2016). Origins of human intelligence: The chain of tool-making and brain evolution. *Anthropological Notebooks, 22* (1), 5–22.

Krukowski, D. (2019). The ideal conditions for sound art and office productivity aren't so far apart. *The New Yorker*, March 4. https://www.newyorker.com/culture/cultural-comment/the-ideal-conditions-for-sound-art-and-office-productivity-arent-so-far-apart/amp

Lakin, J. L., Jefferis, V. E., Cheng, C. M., & Chartrand, T. L. (2003). The chameleon effect as social glue: Evidence for the evolutionary significance of nonconscious mimicry. *Journal of Nonverbal Behavior, 27*(3), 145–162.

Langacker, R. W. (1987). *Foundations of cognitive grammar* (Vol. 1). Stanford, CA: Stanford University Press.

Lau, I. Y-M., Chiu, C-Y., & Lee, S-L. (2001). Communication and shared reality: Implications for the psychological foundations of culture. *Social Cognition, 19*, 350–371.

Lee, E. S., Nguyen, D. C., & Szkudlarek, B. (2020). Global migration and cross-cultural management: Understanding the past, moving towards the future. In B. Szkudlarek, L. Romani, D. V. Caprar, and J. S. Osland (Eds.), *The SAGE handbook of contemporary cross-cultural management* (pp. 409–423). London: SAGE.

Leman, M. (2007). *Embodied music cognition and mediation technology.* Cambridge, MA: MIT press.

Lester, D. (2012). A multiple self theory of the mind. *Comprehensive Psychology, 1*, 2–9.

Li, Ci. N., & Thompson, S. A. (1976). Subject and topic: A new typology of language. In C. N. Li (Ed.), *Subject and topic* (pp. 457–489). New York: Academic Press.

Liu, L. A., & Adair, W. L. (2017). Intercultural communication in international negotiation. In Y. Y. Kim and K. McKay-Semmler (Eds.), *The International Encyclopedia of Intercultural Communication* (pp. 1–14). Hoboken, NJ: Wiley-Blackwell.

Liu, L. A., Adair, W. L., & Bello, D. C. (2015). Fit, misfit, and beyond fit: Relational metaphors and semantic fit in international joint ventures. *Journal of International Business Studies, 46*(7): 830–849.

Liu, L. A., Adair, W. L., Tjosvold, D., & Poliakova, E. (2018). Understanding intercultural dynamics: Integrating insights from competition and cooperation in complex contexts. *Cross Cultural and Strategic Management, 25*(1), 2–31.

Liu, L. A., Chiu, C. Y., & Zhang, Z.-X. (2021). Dynamic transformation of communal and exchange schemata in multicultural relationships. *Cross Cultural & Strategic Management, 28*(2), 368–383.

Liu, L. A., Chua, C. H., & Stahl, G. (2010). Quality of communication experience: Definition, measurement, and implications for intercultural negotiations. *Journal of Applied Psychology, 95*(3), 469–487.

Liu, L. A., Friedman, R. A., Barry, B., Gelfand, M. J., & Zhang, Z-X. (2012). The dynamics of consensus building in intracultural and intercultural negotiations. *Administrative Science Quarterly, 57*(2), 269–304.

Liu, L. A., Friedman, R. A., & Chi, S-c. (2005). "*Ren Qing*" versus the "Big 5": The need for culturally sensitive measures of individual difference in negotiation. *Management and Organization Review, 1*(2), 225–247.

Liu, L. A., Ma, L., Chua, C.-H., Zhang, Z.-X., & Barzantny, C. (2013). The confluence of cultural richness and global identity in intracultural and intercultural negotiations. *Academy of Management Proceedings, 1*, 841–846.

Logan, R. F. (1986). *The alphabet effect*. New York: Morrow.

Lovesey, O. (2020). Introduction to "Woodstock University": The idea of Woodstock. *Popular Music and Society, 43*(2), 121–125. doi:10.1080/03007766.2019.1687679

Lyons, A., & Kashima, Y. (2001). The reproduction of culture: Communication processes tend to maintain cultural stereotypes. *Social Cognition, 19*(3: Special issue), 372–394.

Maitlis, S., Vogus, T. J., & Lawrence, T. B. (2013). Sensemaking and emotion in organizations. *Organizational Psychology Review, 3*(3), 222–247.

Markman, E., & Hutchinson, J. (1984). Children's sensitivity to constraints on word meaning: Taxonomic versus thematic relations. *Cognitive Psychology, 16*, 1–27.

Martin, J. N. (2015). Revisiting intercultural communication competence: Where to go from here. *International Journal of Intercultural Relations, 48*, 6–8.

Matsumoto, D., & Hwang, H. S. (2011). Cooperation and competition in intercultural interactions. *International Journal of Intercultural Relations, 35*(5), 677–685.

Matsumoto, D., & Hwang, H. S. (2019). Culture, emotion, and expression. In K. D. Kieth (Ed.), *Cross-cultural psychology: Contemporary themes and perspectives* (pp. 501–515). Hoboken, NJ: John Wiley.

Mehrabian, A. (2017). *Nonverbal communication*. New York: Routledge.

Mesquita, B., Boiger, M., & De Leersnyder, J. (2016). The cultural construction of emotions. *Current Opinion in Psychology, 8*, 31–36.

Mesquita, B., & Frijda, N. H. (1992). Cultural variations in emotions: A review. *Psychological Bulletin, 112*(2), 179.

Minbaeva, D. (2007). Knowledge transfer in multinational corporations. *Management International Review, 47*, 567–593.

Moore, F., & Mahadevan, J. (2020). Ethnography and cross-cultural management. In B. Szkudlarek, L. Romani, D. V. Caprar, and J. S. Osland (Eds.), *The Sage handbook of contemporary cross-cultural management* (pp. 128–140). London: SAGE.

Morgulis-Yakushev, S., Yildiz, H. E., & Fey, C. F. (2018). When same is (not) the aim: A treatise on organizational cultural fit and knowledge transfer. *Journal of World Business, 53*, 151–163.

Morling, B., & Lamoreaux M. (2008). Measuring culture outside the head: A meta-analysis of individualism–collectivism in cultural products. *Personality and Social Psychology Review, 12*(3), 199–221.

Nardon, L. (2017). *Working in a multicultural world: A guide to developing intercultural competence*. Toronto, Canada: University of Toronto Press.

Neeley, T. (2017). *The language of global success: How a common tongue transforms multinational organizations*. Princeton, NJ: Princeton University Press.

Nisbett, R. E. (2003). *The geography of thought: How Asians and Westerners think differently . . . and why*. New York: The Free Press.

Nisbett, R. E., Peng, K., Choi, I., & Norenzayan, A. (2001). Culture and systems of thought: holistic versus analytic cognition. *Psychological Review, 108*(2), 291.

Oetzel, J., & Ting-Toomey, S. (2003). Face concerns in interpersonal conflict: A cross-cultural empirical test of the face-negotiation theory. *Communication Research, 36*, 599–624.

Oyserman, D., Coon, H. M., & Kemmelmeier, M. (2002). Rethinking individualism and collectivism: Evaluation of theoretical assumptions and meta-analyses. *Psychological Bulletin, 128*(1), 3–72.

Oyserman, D., & Lee, S. W. S. (2008). Does culture influence what and how we think? Effects of priming individualism and collectivism. *Psychological Bulletin, 134*(2), 311–342.

Oyserman, D., Sorensen, N., Reber, R., & Chen, S. X. (2009). Connecting and separating mind-sets: Culture as situated cognition. *Journal of Personality and Social Psychology, 97*(2), 217–235.

Ozgen, E., & Davies, I. R. L. (1998). Turkish color terms: Tests of Berlin and Kay's theory of color universals and linguistic relativity. *Linguistics, 36*, 919–956.

Piekkari, R., Welch, C., & Zølner, M. (2020). The uneasy relationship between the case study and cross-cultural management. In B. Szkudlarek, L. Romani, D. Caprar, & J. S. Osland (Eds.). *The SAGE handbook of cross-cultural management* (pp. 156–170). London: SAGE.

Preston, S. D., & de Waal, F. B. M. (2002). Empathy: Its ultimate and proximate bases. *Behavioral and Brain Sciences, 25*, 1–72.

Roberson, D., Davies, I., & Davidoff, J. (2000). Color categories are not universal: Replications and new evidence from a stone-age culture. *Journal of Experimental Psychology: General, 129*, 369–398.

Romani, L., Mahadevan, J., & Primecz, H. (2020). Methods of critical cross-cultural management. In B. Szkudlarek, L. Romani, D. Caprar, & J. S. Osland (Eds.), *The SAGE handbook of cross-cultural management* (pp. 141–155). London: SAGE.

Rosette, A. S., Brett, J. M., Barsness, Z., & Lytle, A. L. (2011). When cultures clash electronically: The impact of email and social norms on negotiation behavior and outcomes. *Journal of Cross-Cultural Psychology, 43*(4), 628–643.

Semnani-Azad, Z., & Adair, W. L. (2011). The display of "dominant" nonverbal cues in negotiation: The role of culture and gender. *International Negotiation, 16*(3), 451–479.

Szkudlarek, B., Osland, J. S., Nardon, L., & Zander, L. (2020). Communication and culture in international business–Moving the field forward. *Journal of World Business, 55*(6), 101–126.

Tallerman, M. (Ed.) (2005). *Language origins: Perspectives on evolution*. Oxford: Oxford University Press.

Thibault, P., Bourgeois, P., & Hess, U. (2006). The effect of group-identification on emotion recognition: The case of cats and basketball players. *Journal of Experimental Social Psychology, 42*, 676–683.

Ting-Toomey, S., & Dorjee, T. (2018). *Communicating across cultures*. New York: Guilford Publications.

Tomkins, S. (1962). *Affect imagery consciousness: Volume I: The positive affects*. New York: Springer.

Trafimow, D., Triandis, H. C., & Goto, S. G. (1991). Some tests of the distinction between the private self and the collective self. *Journal of Personality and Social Psychology, 60*(5), 649–655.

Trompenaars F., & Turner, C. (1997). *Riding the waves of culture: Understanding diversity in global business*. New York, NY: McGraw-Hill.

Tse, D. K., Francis, J., & Walls, J. (1994). Cultural differences in conducting intra- and inter-cultural negotiations. *Journal of International Business Studies, 25*(3), 537–555.

Tzu, S. (2012). *The art of war*. Vij Books India Pvt Ltd.

Valian, V. (1990). Null subjects: A problem for parameter-setting models of language acquisition. *Cognition, 35*, 105–122.

Varner, I. I. (2000). The theoretical foundation for intercultural business communication: A conceptual model. *The Journal of Business Communication, 37*, 39–57.

Vuoskoski, J. K., & Eerola, T. (2017). The pleasure evoked by sad music is mediated by feelings of being moved. *Frontiers in Psychology, 8*, 439.

Vygotsky, L. S. (1962). *Thought and language*. Cambridge, MA: MIT Press.

Wallmark, Z., Deblieck, C., & Iacoboni, M. (2018) Neurophysiological effects of trait empathy in music listening. *Frontiers in Behavioral Neuroscience, 12*, 66.

Warrenburg, L. A. (2020). Comparing musical and psychological emotion theories. *Psychomusicology: Music, Mind, and Brain. 30*(1), 1–19.

Weiss, S. E. (1994). Negotiating with Romans: Part 1. *Sloan Management Review, 35*(2), 51–61.

Whorf, B. L. (1956). *Language, thought, and reality*. Cambridge, MA: Technology Press of MIT.
Wilson, M. (2002). Six views of embodied cognition. *Psychonomic Bulletin & Review, 9*, 625–636.
Winawer, J., Witthoft, N., Frank, M. C., Wu, L., Wade, A. R., & Boroditsky, L. (2007). Russian blues reveal effects of language on color discrimination. *Proceedings of the National Academy of Sciences of the United States of America, 104*, 7780–7785.
Zhang, Q., Oetzel, J., Ting-Toomey, S., & Zhang, J. (2019). Making up or getting even? The effects of face concerns, self-construal, and apology on forgiveness, reconciliation and revenge in the United States and China. *Communication Research, 46*(4), 503–524.

CHAPTER

17 Culture and Conflict and Negotiation Strategy

Jeanne M. Brett

Abstract

This chapter summarizes research and theory documenting cultural differences in the use of strategy in deal making and conflict management negotiations. Negotiation is the process by which parties with conflicting goals try to reach agreement. Negotiation strategy is the goal-directed behavior that people use when negotiating (Weingart et al., 1990). The strategy of sharing information is not effective in generating joint gains in non-Western cultures because of low trust. Negotiators can use multi-issue offers to generate insight into the counterpart's priorities and joint gains, but doing so may require second-order processing of information from the offers. Cultural differences in how people express emotion and communicate may generate misunderstanding and conflict escalation. A major opportunity for future research is to use the emerging science of artificial intelligence (AI) and negotiation to understand strategic adjustment in intercultural negotiations.

Key Words: culture, negotiation strategy, information sharing, multi-issue offers, joint gains, emotional expression, conflict escalation, artificial intelligence

This chapter summarizes research and theory documenting cultural differences in the use of negotiation strategy. Negotiation is the process by which two or more parties with conflicting goals, interests, or priorities try to reach an agreement. Negotiation strategy comprises the goal-directed behaviors that negotiators engage in when trying to reach agreement (Weingart et al., 1990). Most of the empirical research on culture and negotiation strategy is *comparative intracultural;* it contrasts the behavior and outcomes of negotiators from one culture to those of negotiators from another culture. There is less *intercultural* research comparing the behavior and outcomes of negotiators from one culture trying to reach agreement with negotiators from another culture. Given the paucity of the intercultural research, it is addressed only in the section on opportunities for future research. Overviews of current intercultural research are presented in both Gunia and colleagues' 2016 *Current Opinion in Psychology* paper and Brett's (2022) forthcoming chapter 5 in *Handbook of Advances in Cultural Psychology.*

Deal making and dispute resolution negotiations vary in several ways (Brett, 2014). All disputes are conflicts, not all conflicts rise to the level of a dispute—a claim made by one party, rejected by another (Felsteiner et al., 1980–1981). In this text, I review the culture and deal making and the culture and conflict management negotiation strategy research, including third parties. I do not review research on cultural differences in conflict management styles (e.g., Blake & Mouton, 1964; Pruitt & Rubin, 1986; Kilmann & Thomas, 1977; Rahim, 1983).

Culture and Deal-Making Negotiations

Cultural Differences in the Use of Negotiation Strategy

John Graham (1983, 1985, 1993, 1995; Graham et al., 1994; Graham & Mintu-Wimsat, 1997) pioneered comparative culture and negotiation strategy research. He used nationality as an indicator of culture and studied how negotiators from different cultures used strategy and the relationship between their use of strategy and their outcomes. Graham collected data using a three-issue simulation with two trade-offs and one distributive issue. His dependent variable was individual gains. Using negotiators' postnegotiation self-reports of problem-solving behavior and in some studies, their verbal and nonverbal behaviors, Graham documented cultural differences in problem solving and in individual gains.

Decades after Graham's pioneering work, Brett et al. (2017) reviewed the comparative culture research on negotiation strategy and outcomes. Foundational negotiation theory (Walton & McKersie, 1965) identifies two types of strategy, distributive and integrative, and two important outcomes, individual gains and joint gains—the total value created and subsequently divided between negotiators by their agreement. Because agreements involving high joint gains tend to create advantageous economic outcomes for all negotiators, generate satisfaction, and facilitate relationships and agreement implementation, joint gains are an important metric of the effectiveness of negotiations (Raiffa, 1982).

Negotiation researchers have assigned various labels to the two primary types of negotiation strategy. In this chapter, I use the terms *value creation* and *value claiming* (Lax & Sebenius, 1986). Negotiators using value claiming, also called distributive strategy, focus narrowly on maximizing their own outcomes, how much value they claim for themselves. They engage in behaviors (tactics), such as argument, persuasion, and threats, while trying to influence the counterpart to make concessions favorable to themselves (Weingart et al., 1990). Value-claiming strategy predicts negotiators' individual gains (Hüffmaier et al., 2014). Negotiators using value-creating or integrative strategy, also called problem solving, (De Dreu et al., 2001) focus on both their own outcomes and those of their counterparts. They engage in behaviors (tactics) such as sharing and comparing information about their own and the counterpart's interests (motives) and priorities (what is more and less important to negotiators) in order to propose trade-offs. Value-creating strategy predicts negotiators' joint gains (Kong et al., 2014), but only in Western culture samples (Brett et al., 2020).

The comparative cultural research on negotiation strategy and joint gains largely follows Graham's lead using national boundaries to define cultural boundaries. Brett and colleagues (2017) used the statistical results of 22 comparative culture studies to classify a culture as value creating or value claiming prototypical or dominant. For example, three studies reported data comparing Chinese and U.S. negotiators' use of strategy (Aslani et al., 2016; Dong, 2006; Liu, 2009). In all three studies, the Chinese negotiators used value claiming statistically more frequently than the U.S. negotiators, and the U.S. negotiators used value creating statistically more frequently than the Chinese negotiators. A fourth study (Lügger et al., 2015) compared German and Chinese negotiators. The Chinese again used value claiming statistically more frequently than the Germans, and the Germans used value creating statistically more frequently than the Chinese. Patterns of results were remarkably consistent across studies, samples, and simulations. In classifying a national culture as value creating or value claiming prototypical, these authors emphasized that they did *not* mean that all negotiators in that culture only used value-creating (claiming) strategy and never used another strategy. However, they concluded that the available research implied that negotiators from some cultures devote relatively more of their strategic negotiation focus to value creating than value claiming and vice versa. They classified negotiators from Western culture nations (e.g., Germany, Israel, Norway, Sweden, and the United States) as *value creating prototypical*, while those from East Asian cultures (e.g., China, Hong Kong, Japan, and Thailand) and South Asian and Middle Eastern cultures (e.g., India, Qatar) as *value claiming prototypical*. The limited studies reporting on the use of negotiation strategy within Latin cultures showed value creating prototypical in Brazil and value claiming prototypical in Mexico and Spain.

Culture and negotiation studies have used many different constructs to explain national cultural differences with limited success. This may be due to the lack of a theoretically grounded framework linking cultural constructs (e.g., individualism–collectivism) to the context of negotiation strategy (Kirkman et al., 2006). For example, why would a culture of individualism facilitate negotiators using value-creating strategy relatively more frequently than negotiators in more collectivist cultures?

Brett and colleagues (2017) suggest that understanding cultural differences in the prototypical use of negotiation strategy requires understanding the relationship between the context of negotiation and two cultural constructs, trust and tightness–looseness. Negotiation has both competitive and cooperative elements (Pruitt, 1981; Lax & Sebenius, 1986). Negotiators have to cooperate to reach agreement because they are by definition interdependent; yet, they must compete to promote and protect their interests. The competitive element of the negotiation is not always consistent with cultural norms associated either with cultural levels of trust or cultural tightness–looseness. However, Brett and colleagues (2017) propose that the intersection between these two cultural constructs does

Table 17.1 High- and low-trust and tight and loose culture differences in negotiation strategy

	Trust	
	High	Low
Tight	East Asia Strategy: Value claiming; Multi-issue offers	Middle East South Asia Strategy: Value claiming
Loose	West Strategy: Value creating	Latin America Strategy: Value claiming; Value creating

explain culturally prototypical patterns of use of negotiation strategy. See Table 17.1. This table organizes the national cultural prototypical use of negotiation strategy by World Values Survey (WVS) data on national cultural levels of trust (Haerpfer et al., 2020) and Gelfand and colleagues' (Gelfand et al., 2021) data on national cultural levels of tightness–looseness.

Trust is an important predictor of the use of negotiation strategy (Kong et al., 2014). Negotiators who trust their counterparts not to exploit shared information about interests and priorities tend to use value-creating strategy. Trust enables negotiators to accept the vulnerability inherent in exchanging such information. Conversely, negotiators who do not trust tend to engage in value-claiming strategy, as they are unwilling to accept the vulnerabilities inherent in exchanging information and may even disbelieve information shared by the counterpart (Gunia et al., 2011).

Levels of trust vary across cultures (Branzei et al., 2007; Delhey & Newton, 2005; Yamagishi et al., 1998), but this variation does not seem to be attributable to differences in the core conceptualization of trust. Terms such as reliability, benevolence, responsibility, integrity, and dependability turn up repeatedly in studies comparing the conceptualization of trust across cultures (Ferrin & Gillespie, 2010). However, national culture levels of trust, as measured by the WVS, do not fully explain the patterns of use of negotiation strategy (Brett et al., 2017). For example, the WVS reports trust to be high in China and other East Asian cultures, but the negotiation strategy data show that value claiming is prototypical in East Asian cultures. Likewise, the WVS reports trust to be extremely low in Latin American cultures, such as Brazil, but research shows that value-creating strategy is prototypical among Brazilian negotiators.

The intersection of cultural levels of trust and of tightness–looseness does, however, explain the pattern of prototypical use of negotiation strategy. The trust by tightness–looseness explanation separates high-trust national cultures in East Asia from those in the West and low-trust South Asian and Middle Eastern national cultures from national cultures in Latin America. Tightness–looseness refers to the strength of a culture's social norms and the degree to which compliance is socially monitored and deviance is sanctioned (Gelfand et al., 2006, 2011, 2018, 2021). East Asian, Middle Eastern and South Asian cultures tend to be very tight, Latin American cultures, looser, and Western cultures, the loosest, with some exceptions (Gelfand et al., 2011). Cultural tightness–looseness influences everyday social interaction. People living in tight cultures look to the prevailing social norm governing the context. They adjust their own behavior to the context's norms and sanctions. People living in looser cultures still have social norms to guide their behaviors, but as monitoring and sanctioning are less intense than in tight cultures, people in looser cultures have relatively more behavioral choice than people in tighter cultures. This difference between tight and loose cultures not only has implications for people's own behavior, but it also affects their ability to predict the behavior of others. Because there is less behavioral flexibility in tight cultures and more behavioral flexibility in loose cultures, it is easier to predict people's behaviors in tight than in loose cultures. Consider a normal curve around a culture's prototypical use of negotiation strategy. In tight cultures, the variance around the prototype should be narrower, and in loose cultures that variation should be wider. The upshot is that relative to people in tighter cultures, people in looser cultures engage in more behavioral improvisation (Gelfand et al., 2011). Improvisation signals a behavioral intention and stimulates a response from which the improviser can interpret the intention of the other.

Cultural differences in tightness–looseness explain the prototypical use of negotiation strategy in the diagonals shown in Table 17.1: why in high-trust, tight cultures, such as China, negotiators rely heavily on value-claiming strategy and in low-trust, looser cultures such as Brazil, negotiators rely heavily on value-creating strategy. Considering the high-trust, tight quadrant, note that negotiation is a particular context for social interaction; negotiators are interdependent, and cooperative negotiators risk exploitation by their more competitive counterparts. Although the dominant norm for social interaction in high-trust, tight cultures, such as China is harmony (Aslani et al., 2016), the dominant norm in negotiation is competition. Trust that governs everyday social interaction does not carry into the negotiation context that operates in a different normative context, resulting in the prototypical negotiation strategy of value claiming (Brett et al., 2017). To be sure, negotiators in a low-trust culture such as Brazil risk exploitation just as do Chinese negotiators. However, even though low trust is pervasive in Brazilian culture, Brazil is a looser culture than China. Brazilians have to determine whether others are trustworthy in all types of social interaction, not just negotiation. They cannot rely on strong social norms to predict the behavior of others in everyday social interaction. They have to learn to evaluate others' trustworthiness. The skill set they develop to do so provides a basis for using value-creating strategy for evaluating the trustworthiness of another negotiator. (See Brett & Mitchell, 2019, for further discussion.)

The intersection of cultural trust and tightness–looseness provides a more straightforward theoretical interpretation of the prototypical use of negotiation strategy in the off-diagonal cells in Table 17.1 than trust alone. In everyday social interaction in loose Western cultures, trust is relatively high. That trust is grounded not only in an underlying cultural assumption that others are trustworthy, but also in extensive social experience (loose culture) testing whether that assumption is valid. This assumption and, importantly that loose culture experience, manifest in reliance on value-creating strategy in negotiation. Brett and Mitchell (2019) captured the perspectives of their Western culture interviewees on trusting a potential new business partner with a quote from one: *Trust but verify; people are not on the watch for distrust, but don't ignore signs either.* They reported that Western culture managers assumed their potential partners were trustworthy, but that they engaged in a lot of testing at the negotiation table to verify that assumption. In contrast, in tight, low-trust Middle Eastern and South Asian cultures, reliance on value-claiming strategy in negotiation is a rational defense of the risks of being taken advantage of in a context where competition is the norm in both everyday social interaction and negotiations. Brett and Mitchell (2019) captured the perspective of their Middle Eastern and South Asian culture interviewees on trusting a potential new business partner with a quote from one: *It's not, I trust, I verify; it's I verify first, then I trust.*

Brett and colleagues (2017) developed this cultural trust by a tightness–looseness theoretical framework for explaining prototypical use of negotiation strategy. They surveyed theory and evidence from a variety of studies ranging from trust game experiments that turned monitoring and sanctioning for defection on or off in samples of Japanese and U.S. decision makers (Yamagishi & Yamagishi, 1994), to a comparative cultural study of trust and use of negotiation strategy by Indian and U.S. negotiators (Gunia et al., 2011) and a comparative cultural study of Chinese, Qatari, and U.S. negotiators applying Leung and Cohen's (2011) face, honor, dignity cultural framework (Aslani et al., 2016). Brett and Mitchell's (2019) interview study of 81 managers from 33 national cultures investigating the process of deciding to trust a potential new business partner provided evidence consistent with the theoretical explanation of the effect of negotiating at the intersection of cultural levels of trust by tightness–looseness.

Culture Negotiation Strategy and Joint Gains

Value creating strategy facilitates and value claiming strategy impedes negotiators' joint gains (Kong et al., 2014), but only in in Western culture samples (Brett et al., 2021). Brett and colleagues (2021) based their conclusion on a meta-analysis of value creation and value-claiming negotiation strategy and joint gains. They used standard meta-analysis search techniques, supplemented by personal requests to authors (particularly when data appropriate for the meta-analysis appeared to have been collected but not published) to identify 46 papers. They assigned national cultures to regions based on the World Bank's classification of regions of economic activity (World Bank Annual Report, 2016). With appropriate controls for papers that reported multiple independent samples or studies and papers that reported coefficients for both value claiming and value creating and joint gains, the researchers estimated coefficients for value creating (value claiming) and joint gains from 45 (40) Western, 11 (10) East Asian, and 9 (8) Middle Eastern and South Asian samples. (There was not enough data to estimate a separate coefficient for Latin American cultures.) In Western culture samples, the value-creating coefficient was positive (.31) and significant; the value claiming coefficient was negative (–.15) and significant. In East Asian samples, the coefficients were not significant: value creating (.06); value claiming (.04). In Middle Eastern and South Asian samples, the coefficients were not significant: value creating (.10); value claiming (–.03). The differences between coefficients of Western and non-Western samples for both value creation and value claiming and joint gains were significant, but there were no significant differences between East Asian and Middle Eastern and South Asian coefficients. These meta-analytic results reveal two very important points about the theory of negotiation strategy and joint gains (Brett et al., 2021). First, given available data, value-creating strategy does not facilitate joint gains in non-Western cultural samples. Second, again given available data, value-claiming strategy does not have as strong a negative effect on joint gains in non-Western cultures as it does in Western cultures.

Multi-issue Offers: An Alternative Strategy for Joint Gains

These meta-analytic results raise two further questions about negotiation strategy and joint gains: Are non-Western culture negotiators just agreeing to settle for significantly lower joint gains than their Western culture counterparts do? If so, why? If not, what are they doing to generate joint gains, since they do not appear to be using value-creating strategy to that end? Current research suggests that at least East Asian negotiators are using multi-issue offers (MIOs) to reach joint gains.

Interest in multi-issue offers has ebbed and flowed historically. Kelley (1966) proposed using multi-issue offers in a systematic concession-making model. The model advises negotiators to make reciprocal concessions using multi-issue offers in which they concede on low-priority issues and hold firm on high-priority issues until no further trade-offs are possible. Using this model should generate joint gains by taking advantage of trade-offs, but will not necessarily generate insight into those trade-offs. Pruitt (1981) labeled this process heuristic trial and error processing (HT&E). Pruitt (1981) thought that negotiators could engage in second-level information processing to infer each other's interests and priorities when using HT&E or even when simply engaging in value-claiming negotiations. His reasoning was that negotiators do not make offers that are not in their own interests and that they do not try to influence the counterpart to make concessions on issues that are of no importance to them. Nevertheless, Pruitt (1981) admitted that he had never observed negotiators in his lab drawing inferences about priorities either from use of value-claiming strategy or HT&E. He did find that negotiators using HT&E reached high joint gains, but he concluded that they had stumbled into joint gains, because of the HT&E (Kelly, 1966) concession strategy. Then, in a very important empirical paper,

Weingart and colleagues (1990) reported a large, significant, negative correlation between use of multi-issue offers and joint gains. It is no wonder then that interest in MIOs waned. It is only with Yao and colleagues' (2020) current experimental research and meta-analysis that multi-issues offers may take their place as a third dominant negotiation strategy—and notably one that both high- and low-trust negotiators can use effectively and that will facilitate both individual and joint gains. MIOs facilitate individual gains because negotiators do not make offers that are not in their interests, which was Pruitt's (1981) point. However, MIOs also can facilitate joint gains, if across a series of offers, negotiators follow Kelley (1966) and Pruitt's (1981) logic of conceding on low-priority issues holding firm on high-priority issues.

Although many studies report the hegemony of Western versus non-Western culture joint gains, East Asian negotiators' joint gains are not always significantly lower than those of Western negotiators. In addition, lower joint gains among East Asians may be due to factors other than failing to generate insight into trade-offs via the value-creating strategy of information sharing (Yao et al., 2020). For example, East Asian negotiators tend to leave a compatible issue on the table for future negotiation, seeing it as a fine reason to have a subsequent negotiation built on the first one (Brett, 2007).

Evidence has mounted over the past two decades that East Asian negotiators may be using offers to generate joint gains. Brett and Okumura (1998) report that Japanese negotiators' joint gains were not significantly different from those of the U.S. negotiators. Adair and colleagues' (2001, 2007) further analysis of these data reveals that Japanese negotiators who achieved high joint gains used strategy very differently than Western culture negotiators. While the U.S. negotiators were exchanging information directly by asking and answering questions about priorities and interests, the Japanese negotiators were sharing information indirectly using single- and multi-issue offers (Adair et al., 2001). Further analysis of this same Japanese and U.S. data revealed that early offers facilitated joint gains for Japanese negotiators, but reduced joint gains for U.S. negotiators. In addition, the more information exchanged prior to the first offer facilitated joint gains in U.S. negotiations but impeded them in Japanese negotiations (Adair et al., 2007). These authors concluded that early offers represented information gathering among Japanese negotiators but that later offers represented information consolidation among U.S. negotiators.

Aslani and colleagues (2016) studied U.S., Qatari, and Chinese negotiators' use of information-sharing (value-creating) and influence (value-claiming), and they also measured insight (postnegotiation understanding of the counterpart's priorities) via self-report. The Chinese negotiators in this study were using strategy similarly to that of the Qatari negotiators—heavy use of influence, avoidance of information sharing—but they had more insight than the Qatari negotiators, and their joint gains were not significantly different from those of the U.S. negotiators who were relying on value-creating strategy. It is not clear what the Chinese negotiators were doing to generate joint gains, as this study did not measure MIOs.

Yao and colleagues (2020) answer this question with their own Chinese data. Like the Japanese managers in Adair and colleagues' studies (2001, 2007), Yao and colleagues' Chinese managers were using offers, especially MIOs to generate insight and joint gains. The theorizing underlying Yao and colleagues' studies integrates Pruitt's (1981) and Brett's (2014) theorizing that negotiators' processing information holistically can use indirect information to generate insight and joint gains. People with holistic mindsets focus on context and use associative reasoning to understand the relationship between a focal object and its context (Nisbett et al., 2001). In contrast, people with an analytic mindset focus on content and use linear reasoning to understand each element of an object (Nisbett et al., 2001). Nisbett and colleagues also generated substantial evidence that mindset varies systematically between Eastern and Western cultures, with East Asians more often categorized as holistic and Westerners as analytic (e.g., Chua et al., 2005; Masuda et al., 2008; Norenzayan et al., 2002).

Yao and colleagues' (2020) Study 2 tested a model that predicted a path of relationships from prenegotiation trust to use of strategy (e.g., value creating—information sharing about priorities; value claiming—use of influence attempts; single-issue offers (SIOs); and MIOs) to insight to joint gains. They also predicted that mindset would moderate the relationship between use of MIOs and insight. Their results with a Chinese managerial sample supported the model. Trust and mindset, measured prior to the negotiation, predicted both the use and effectiveness of negotiation strategy, leading to insight and joint gains. Low-trust negotiators were significantly more likely to use MIOs than high-trust negotiators. The more holistic mindset negotiators using MIOs were significantly more likely to generate insight from use of MIOs. Insight predicted joint gains. Yao et al.'s (2020) third study, an experiment manipulating trust by using undergrad negotiators and a different, less complex simulation, supported this result. In these Chinese samples, value-creating strategy predicted neither insight nor joint gains.

The Yao et al. (2020) studies suggest that Chinese negotiators can use multi-issue offers to generate insight when they process information holistically. The question is whether this effect is limited to the context of negotiating in China. Yao and colleagues' (2020) meta-analysis suggests that the MIO-joint gains effect generalizes across cultures. Data from 42 independent samples (35 intracultural, 6 intercultural, and 1 multicultural) (N = 1,728 dyads) embedded in 25 papers showed that MIOs predicted joint gains positively, SIOs predicted joint gains negatively, and in studies where the measure of offers aggregated across MIOs and SIOs, aggregate offers had no relationship with joint gains. The MIO strategy predicted joint gains after controlling for value-creating strategy (explicit information sharing). The positive effect of MIO strategy on joint gains was not significantly different in Western versus non-Western cultures, although the number of samples used to generate the non-Western culture coefficient was small (5).

Overall, Yao and colleagues' (2020) studies generate three conclusions. First, use of MIOs to generate insight is one strategic alternative to value creation for generating joint gains. Second, use of MIOs may be a particularly safe strategy for low-trust negotiators seeking joint gains. Third, using MIOs without using the direct information sharing of value creation may require second-order, holistic processing to generate insight and joint gains.

Honor: An Intermediate Step for Trust and Strategy and Joint Gains

Though limited, the data from Middle Eastern and South Asian culture negotiations compared to Western culture negotiations show both a heavier reliance on value-claiming strategy and lower joint gains (Aslani et al., 2016; Gelfand et al., 2015; Gunia et al., 2011). The trust by tightness–looseness theoretical framework provides one explanation for these results. Gelfand and colleagues' (2015) focus on relationship building in honor cultures provides another.

Not only are Middle Eastern and South Asian cultures low-trust, but their cultural tightness has a unique character, which Gelfand has elaborated (Gelfand et al., 2017; Gelfand, 2018). East Asian cultures are both ethnically homogeneous and tight cultures. Norms are shared, and monitoring and sanctioning are enforced across a broad swath of the population. This is not the case for South Asia and the Middle East, which Gelfand characterizes as heterogeneous and tight cultures. Imagine a homogeneous, tight culture as a single narrow, normal curve, but a heterogeneous, tight culture as multiple, separate, narrow, normal curves, packed together in three dimensions. In heterogeneous, tight cultures, people from different subcultures may live intermingled or in communities that rub against one another, but each subculture has its own institutional set of norms and systems of monitoring and sanctioning. People in different subcultures share norms, as data on cultural levels of trust and tightness–looseness have shown. However, the institutions that monitor and enforce normative behavior and sanction deviance do not cross subculture boundaries in heterogeneous, tight cultures. This theorizing suggests that in tight cultures, heterogeneity exacerbates low trust.

Aslani and colleagues (2013) characterize Middle Eastern and South Asian cultures as honor cultures, Western cultures as dignity cultures, and East Asian cultures as face cultures following the cultural logics of self-worth articulated by Leung and Cohen (2011). Descriptive norm data largely confirm this mapping of regions of the world to the psychological representation of self-worth represented by the honor/face/dignity cultural framework (Yao et al., 2017).

Self-worth refers to peoples' sense of their value in the society in which they live (Leung & Cohen, 2011). Very briefly, in dignity cultures self-worth is the individual's own assessment of their value; dignity manifests in a sense of achievement. In face cultures, self-worth depends on how others in the society view the individual's value; face manifests in a sense of social responsibility. In honor cultures, self-worth is the individual's assessment of how others view their value; honor manifests in the respect of others, which in turn is based on a reputation for measuring up to well-defined social norms and obligations but at the same time not appearing vulnerable to exploitation (Gelfand et al., 2015).

People generally strive for a consistent and stable view of self. The differences between self-worth based on dignity, face, or honor are subtle but important. Because dignity is the individual's own assessment, it is relatively unaffected by others' opinions and therefore is relatively stable. Because face is the assessment of others, the way to maintain a stable self-worth in a face culture is to fulfill the expectations of others. Because honor combines self and others' assessments of self-worth, it is much less stable than self-worth based on face or dignity.

Gelfand and colleagues (2015) are not suggesting use of an alternative strategic approach for negotiators in honor culture to reach joint gains. They simply propose an intermediate step to generate the counterpart's trust to facilitate information sharing, insight and joint gains. That intermediate step is to gain the counterpart's respect. Signaling respect involves acting to promote and protect honor. Gelfand and colleagues (2015) proposed that Middle Eastern negotiators need to promote honor by signaling integrity and willingness to abide by codes of loyalty, honesty, and trustworthiness, and they need to protect honor by signaling strength and willingness to deter aggression. Their empirical study contrasting Egyptian and U.S. negotiators reports that the U.S. negotiators outperformed the Egyptians with respect to joint gains, but the more the Egyptian negotiators used language reflecting honor promotion and honor protection, the higher their joint gains.

Gelfand and colleagues' (2015) theorizing and results are consistent with Brett and Mitchell's (2019) interview data, in which Middle Eastern and South Asian managers explained that new business relationships very much depended on respect for differences. (Recall that these are heterogeneous, tight cultures.) Interviewees described engaging in social interaction with prospective new business partners with the underlying agenda of actively assessing character, and of evaluating whether the potential partner was someone with whom they could work. Brett and Mitchell (2020) explain that extending hospitality to a potential business partner provides an opportunity to signal honor, but also determines if the potential partner reciprocates respect by graciously accepting hospitality.

Conflict Management

Fixed prices bring efficiencies to everyday buying and selling in most parts of the world, which means that many people engage much more frequently in conflict management negotiations with family, neighbors, and coworkers than in deal-making negotiations. Yet, the empirical research on negotiations is overwhelmingly set in the context of deal making rather than conflict management. The most likely reason is that deal making is easy to simulate; conflict is not. In the opening paragraphs of this chapter, I pointed out that the nature of negotiators' interdependence is different in deal making and conflict management negotiations. Conflict management negotiators are interdependent in terms of the agreement *and* the no agreement alternative; deal-making negotiators are interdependent only in terms of the agreement (Brett, 2014).

Interdependence is not the only reason why conflict management and deal-making negotiations are different. These two contexts for negotiation also differ in terms of why negotiators are at the table, what they are trying to accomplish with an agreement, and as a result, the emotions that negotiators bring to the table (Brett, 2014). In deal making, negotiators are each other's best possible partner. They want to reach an agreement that maximizes gains, and their counterpart is the best party to do that with—assuming the negotiators have analyzed their alternatives correctly. At least at the beginning, deal-making negotiators' emotions should be positive—we both have something to gain. In contrast, in conflict management negotiations, one or both parties perceives that the other is thwarting their goals or interests. The counterpart at the table is not the best possible partner but the worst one. The problem is that negotiators, trying to manage conflict, cannot just walk away from the negotiation the way disgruntled dealmakers can. When dealmakers disagree, each turns to its best alternative. When conflict management fails, each negotiator's no agreement option is in the hands of the other. The reason is interdependence of the no agreement alternatives (Brett, 2014). Furthermore, because conflict management negotiations occur after there has been a stalemate, the negotiation is about minimizing costs, not maximizing gains (as it is in deal making). This means that emotions are negative from the outset.

For all these reasons—interdependence, why negotiators are at the table, what they are trying to accomplish via negotiating, positive versus negative emotions—deal making and conflict management negotiations are different. However, it is extremely difficult to simulate the emotional differences that make conflict management so challenging. To be sure, the conflict management researcher can program a computer agent to express anger to a human participant (Van Kleef et al., 2004a), motivate anger in a second study after poor treatment in a preliminary study (Liu, 2009), or tell a study participant to express anger when playing a role (Schroth, 2008). However, study participants' simulated emotions are far from the intensity and negativity of emotions that overwhelm people who truly are in conflict (Friedman et al., 2004).

Adding culture to the research mix adds yet another level of complexity that has not been conquered empirically. There are systematic cultural differences in the emotions that people in different cultures feel and express (Mesquita et al., 2016). Events that stimulate anger in some cultures stimulate shame in other cultures (Boiger et al., 2013, 2014). The empirical research linking negotiation and emotions, especially anger, reveals many contingencies that affect whether anger generates concessions from the counterpart (see Brett & Thompson, 2016, for a review). The underlying theory is that anger expressions provide information about the firmness of positions (EASI model, Van Kleef, 2004b, 2009). However, the anger-concession effect does not seem to generalize to East Asian cultures

(Adam et al., 2010), to negotiations to manage conflict, or to construct a long-term deal-making relationship (Adam & Brett, 2015).

In contrast to the dearth of systematic comparative quantitative research on culture and conflict management, there has been quite a bit of qualitative descriptive research and theorizing. A place to start is Trompenaars's (1996) observation that culture generates functional solutions to problems of social interaction. Although the problem of social interaction–conflict—may be the same, the culturally grounded functional approach may be quite different. Brett (2018) organizes cultural differences in functional approaches to conflict management by the emotional expression, direct versus indirect confrontation, and the role of third parties observed in honor, face, and dignity cultures.

Recall that this honor, face, dignity framework distinguishes between cultural types in terms of the basis of self-worth—a person's sense of their own value in society. In honor cultures, self-worth rests on reputation—what persons think others think of them. In face cultures, self-worth rests on fulfillment of social roles—what others think of the person. In dignity cultures, self-worth rests on achievement—what the persons think of themselves. This cultural logic is particularly relevant to cultural differences in conflict management negotiations because conflict engages self-worth. Although not all conflict rises to the level of a dispute, conflict generally threatens people's sense of self-worth. Party A feels that party B is thwarting party A's interests, but Party B feels they are being fair and Party A has no right to make demands.

People from dignity cultures tend to focus on the substantive issues in conflict rather than the emotional ones (Sanchez-Burks, 2005), not because they do not feel negative emotions when thwarted, but because of a cultural norm that directs people in conflict in dignity cultures to separate the people from the problem (Fisher et al., 1993). In dignity cultures, resolving the emotional aspects of a conflict is not viewed as a means of resolving the substantive conflict, but resolving the substantive conflict should take care of the negative emotions (Brett et al., 2014).

In face cultures, the negative emotion associated with conflict is likely to be shame, not anger, and shame is likely to be suppressed, not expressed (Mesquita et al., 2016). Brett (2018) observes that in face cultures, shaming serves to cue norms of social responsibility and motivate the target to resolve the conflict typically by engaging in self-improvement. She suggests that the "thwarted" party who engages in shaming is not acting out of self-interest, as is a party who breaks norms and exhibits anger in dignity cultures. The party engaged in shaming is fulfilling their own social responsibility by encouraging others, who are not meeting the social standards, to adjust their behavior. Shaming behavior is very consistent with tight culture; face cultures are tight cultures.

Anger is a culturally normative response in cultures that emphasize that to be honorable a "person must meet the challenge and not shrink from it" (Kim et al., 2010, p. 905). Expressed anger seems to be a more common response to conflict in honor than in dignity cultures and certainly than in face cultures as well (Boiger et al., 2014; Nisbett

& Cohen, 1996; Cohen et al., 1996). In an interesting study contrasting the behavior of Dutch (dignity culture) and Spanish (honor culture) participants, parties from both cultures expressed anger in response to provocation. The Spanish were more likely than the Dutch to regard their honor as affronted, criticize the offender, and break off any relationship with the offender—an interpersonal response reflecting the protection of honor. In contrast, the Dutch were more likely than the Spanish to report shouting or breaking things—an impersonal response (Rodriguez Mosquera et al., 2000) reflecting an assertion of dignity.

How people confront conflict also seems to vary systematically with the honor, face, and dignity logics of self-worth. Theorizing distinguishes a continuum from direct to indirect confrontation. At the extreme of directness, the process of social interaction is direct as is the way parties communicate. For example, one will try to get the other's attention, tell the other what the problem is and that the other is responsible, and finally what the other should do to fix the problem. (It is notable that the subtitle of the classic article distinguishing conflicts and disputes [Felsteiner et al., 1980–1981] is Naming, Blaming, and Claiming, not Shaming.) If the two Western culture parties are unable to work out the problem for themselves, they may involve a third party, for example, a friend, parent, neighbor, boss, or even a professional mediator or an arbitrator, but the first aim in direct confrontation is to resolve the conflict without involvement of those not immediately engaged in the conflict (Tinsley & Weldon, 2003). When parties confront conflict directly, their communication is explicit, which means that the literal and semantic meaning of the language they use to express the conflict is similar (Grice, 1968). At the extreme of indirectness, both the process and the means of communication may be indirect. For example, one party may signal there is a problem through verbal or nonverbal communication, for example, a story or metaphor, where the intended meaning of the communication must be inferred from the context rather than from its literal semantic meaning (Brown & Levinson, 1987). Indirect confrontation, whether spoken or nonverbal, relies on cues (e.g., a subtle expression of anger or contempt) that leave the other party to notice the problem and to decide what to do about it. Indirect confrontation may also involve a third party early in the conflict. In general, when one party is explicit about the claim and the expected response, confrontation is direct; when the claim and expected response are more implicit—left for the other to notice and infer from symbolic nonverbal cues—confrontation is indirect (Brett, 2007, p. 141).

People in dignity cultures tend to confront conflict directly (Gelfand et al., 2004; Sanchez-Burks & Mor Barak, 2004). The dignity culture direct approach defines the conflict, identifies responsibility, and states how the conflict can be resolved to the satisfaction of the claimant (naming, blaming, and claiming). The possibility of being rejected does not threaten dignity because dignity is a self-assessment and is not dependent on what others think.

In contrast, people in face cultures tend to confront conflict indirectly (Gelfand et al., 2004). Recall that face depends on fulfilling social roles to the satisfaction of others. Signaling there is a problem indirectly allows both parties involved in the conflict to save face. By confronting indirectly, the claimant minimizes their own risk of losing face if the claim is denied. By signaling there is a conflict, but not explicitly placing responsibility or blame, or by saying exactly how the conflict should be resolved, the target's risk of losing face is also minimized. This indirect approach recognizes that a target may not always understand there is a conflict. It also assumes that when the conflict comes to the target's attention (perhaps by shaming), the target will act according to norms of social responsibility by resolving the conflict and restoring social harmony—an important norm in face culture (Oetzel & Ting-Toomey, 2003).

People in honor cultures exhibit direct and aggressive behavior when they perceive conflict that threatens their self-worth (Cohen & Nisbett, 1997; Rodriguez Mosquera et al., 2008). By exhibiting warmth and hospitality in everyday social interaction with others who pose no threat to self-worth, people in honor cultures build reputations for generosity (Nisbett & Cohen, 1996; Pitt-Rivers, 1968). However, by being defensive and aggressive toward those who pose a threat, people in honor cultures demonstrate that their generosity has limits and that they will not be taken advantage of (Aslani et al., 2013). Direct confrontation of conflict in an honor culture is not subtle. It assigns responsibility for the conflict, as is characteristic of direct confrontation in dignity cultures, and it assigns blame. The implication is that to resolve the conflict requires that the claimant's reputation be restored, most likely at the price of the target's loss of reputation (Brett, 2018).

Important differences associated with the confrontation of conflict in dignity, face, and honor cultures are how the target of confrontation is treated and the implications that treatment has for action. In dignity cultures, the target typically is assigned responsibility for the situation—which carries with it a certain expectation of action. In honor cultures, the person is blamed for the situation—which is a threat to reputation and a call for retaliation. In face cultures, the person is shamed for the conflict because of failure to fulfill social roles, which is also a call for action.

Third-Party Intervention

The literature on culture and third-party intervention into conflict is largely qualitative and descriptive. It suggests several insightful conclusions about how early third parties engage in the conflict, how much authority they have, and whom they involve in conflict management. This section relies heavily on research by James Wall and his students, who over a period of years talked to community members all over the world about third-party intervention into conflict. In summarizing his research, Wall concluded that all cultures use third parties to intervene in and resolve community conflict except when a society is so poor that people are "eating mud"; a society is dominated by norms of war and conquest; or a society does not have a sense of compromise—they lump conflict: "If I'm wrong, tell me I'm wrong, if I'm right, tell me I'm right." (J. Wall, personal correspondence, October 30, 2016). Wall went on to explain that unless societies have sufficient resources to feed their people, they do not have the excess resources to construct the institutional structures characteristic of civil societies. Nevertheless, third-party intervention in conflict is not limited to developed nations, and the social structures that manage conflict are not limited to government institutions.

Organizing Wall's research by the honor, face dignity framework of Leung and Cohen (2011) reveals rather systematic cultural differences in how early third parties become engaged in conflict, how much authority third parties have to resolve conflict, and whom they involve in the conflict management process.

In face cultures, third parties intervene early in conflict. Conflict implies that one or both parties think the other is not fulfilling social roles, posing a threat to social harmony. Because direct confrontation may escalate the conflict, presenting an even greater threat to social harmony, one or both parties, or a third-party member of the community, family, or workplace may seek the involvement of a third party—an indirect approach to confrontation. In this instance, the third party provides a buffer against conflicting parties' face loss. There is no dearth of potential third parties in face cultures: managers in the workplace, elders in the community or the family, even local authorities. Because third parties in face cultures have the task of not only managing the immediate conflict, but also of maintaining social harmony, face cultures give third parties substantial moral authority to resolve conflict and to involve parties beyond the protagonists who might be affected by the conflict or the resolution. Given what we know from the culture and emotion literature, it is no surprise that Wall found that in face cultures third parties may shame parties in conflict for failing to fulfill their social responsibilities. They may try to educate them about their responsibilities, press for concessions, and ask them to apologize and forgive (Wall, 1993; Wall et al., 1995, 2000; Wall & Callister, 1999). In honor cultures, third parties are likely to intervene early in conflict to try to minimize retaliation and escalation. Because honor extends beyond the individual to the family, family members may be the first to ask third parties to intervene (Wall et al., 2008, 2010). As in face cultures, there is no dearth of potential third parties in honor cultures; however, Wall and Callister (1999) report that religious leaders are frequent choices. Although religious leaders may have moral authority to resolve conflict, once family honor is threatened, it may require engagement between two potentially warring families to manage the conflict. Kozan and Ilter (1994) describe a different third-party approach to conflict management in the workplace based on interviews with over 300 managers in Turkey. In order to avoid direct confrontation in the workplace, because in honor culture, confronted conflict can escalate rapidly and take on "extreme forms" (p. 454), they found that managers preferred to try to help the parties in conflict find an acceptable resolution and if not would separate them by reassigning one or the other. These managers preferred not to intervene by telling the protagonists what to do to resolve the dispute. Perhaps they wanted to avoid risking the compromise of their own reputations, if the protagonists did not follow their direction.

In dignity cultures, third parties are likely to get involved after the parties have tried to resolve their conflict by speaking to each other directly. If they fail to reach agreement, there are informal options for third-party intervention, but much of third-party intervention in dignity cultures is institutionalized. Intervention comes after an impasse in direct confrontation, when one or the other party files or threatens to file a lawsuit—the consequence of the interdependence of the parties if they cannot reach agreement themselves. Dignity cultures tend to adhere to the principles of rule of law: that people and institutions are subject to and accountable to law and that law is fairly applied and enforced. Three types of third-party intervention are common and very highly developed in dignity cultures: courts, arbitration, and mediation. Courts are public institutions whose third-party judges make final and binding decisions to resolve the conflict based on the application of law. Arbitration is a private judicial system in which parties select a neutral arbitrator who makes a final and binding decision to resolve the conflict based on the application of contract terms to the conflict. Mediation can be public, an extension of a court, or private. Mediators are neutral third parties selected by the parties to facilitate the resolution of the conflict. Mediators do not have authority to impose an outcome on protagonists. The nature of the mediator's intervention can range from trying to help protagonists find a resolution of their conflict that addresses their underlying interests to advising the protagonists on how the mediator would rule on the dispute if the mediator were a judge.

A vast Western culture literature focuses on how to mediate and the effectiveness of mediation. A 2019 review of studies in Australia, Canada, England, Wales, Ireland, and the United States concluded that mediation settles cases and that people feel the process is fair. The review also concluded that the data are less clear about whether settlement at mediation is more frequent than settlement on the courthouse steps prior to going to trial. There are also conflicting data as to whether mediation increases compliance, reduces time to disposition, or actually reduces trial rates; cost savings and perceptions of savings (Mediation in Civil Justice, 2019). The conclusion about the effectiveness of mediation in settling conflict in a fair manner reflects the psychology of the process. Effective mediators are empathic, they listen, and they respect protagonists' emotions. Mediators understand that to facilitate a settlement they need to learn about the protagonists' interests and that to get protagonists to share interests, the protagonists need to trust the mediator. Mediators know to propose trade-offs and how to engage in reality testing concerning what happens if there is no settlement (Goldberg et al., 2017).

In sum, third-party intervention to resolve conflict is common across cultures. What varies are how early in the conflict third parties engage, how much authority they have, and whom they involve in the conflict management process. This variation is consistent with the underlying logics of self-worth in honor, face, and dignity cultures and the functional solutions different types of culture have developed to protect self-worth when threatened by conflict.

Theoretical Principles

Culture matters in how people negotiate deals and manage conflict! Trompaaners (1996) pointed out that different cultures devise different functional approaches to the same problem of social interaction. Buying and selling when prices are not fixed and managing conflict are problems of social interaction. That culture matters is no great surprise.

Although there is no single definitive cultural explanation for cultural differences in general, much less cultural differences in deal-making negotiation and conflict management, two psychological logics are promising. The intersection of cultural levels of trust by tightness–looseness maps onto cultural differences in the way negotiators use strategy in deal making. The honor, face, and dignity logic of self-worth maps onto cultural differences in the way parties in conflict interact.

Why these cultural explanations and not others? Negotiations regarding whether to buy or sell or to resolve conflict occur in a context that is quite different from the context of everyday social interactions. Negotiators are interdependent. One cannot just make a decision and impose it on the other. Both parties have to agree. Although deal making and conflict management negotiations share this characteristic of interdependence, the context of conflict management also has characteristics, such as interdependence of the no agreement alternative, negative emotion, and goal to minimize costs that distinguish it further from deal making. These characteristics of conflict management negotiations seem likely to be the reason why the honor, face, and dignity logic with its focus on the psychology of self-worth provides a parsimonious cultural explanation for differences in conflict management.

Opportunities for Future Research

This chapter focuses on negotiators' use of strategy to make deals and manage conflict. It does not cover many of the theoretical and practical questions that arise when considering the implication of culture for negotiation. Intercultural negotiation is the most obvious omission. From a negotiation strategy perspective, the most interesting question about intercultural negotiation for future research is how, why, and when negotiators deviate from their culturally prototypical use of strategy whether in the context of deal making or dispute resolution. To be sure, intercultural research has been extremely difficult to carry out with adequate sample sizes to allow contrasts between intra- and intercultural negotiations (e.g., Brett & Okumura, 1998). There may be an opportunity to address these research questions in the near future using online and AI technology. For example, one could program IAGO to negotiate as prototypically Japanese, following Adair et al., 2001; prototypically, Chinese following Yao et al., 2020; or prototypically, U.S. or Indian following Gunia et al., 2011 and have IAGO negotiate with an intra- or intercultural person. Eventually, after capturing enough data to model strategic change, IAGO could even negotiate with its AI programmed alternative cultural self. To be sure, negotiating online probably amplifies use of culturally prototypical strategy (Rosette et al., 2012), but that may not be bad thing, as in the future more and more intra- and intercultural negotiations are likely to be carried out electronically. IAGO (myiago.com) is a research project associated with the University of Southern California's Institute for Creative Technologies. IAGO's AI currently can handle a three-issue negotiation via Q&A and MIOs. Of course, this is just one idea for using advances in AI and negotiation to address fascinating questions about culture and use of negotiation and conflict management strategy.

Five Key Empirical Findings

1. Value-creating negotiation strategy, which is sharing information about negotiators' interests and priorities, is not effect-generating insight and joint gains in non-Western cultures. Value-claiming negotiation strategy, which is, trying to influence the counterpart to make concessions does not have as strongly negative an effect on joint gains in non-Western than Western cultures.
2. Multi-issue offers (MIOs) is an alternative strategy for negotiating joint gains. Negotiators who process information holistically can generate insight from MIOs.
3. The framework of cultural levels of trust by tightness–looseness explains patterns of cultural differences in the use of negotiation strategy.
4. Negotiators' displays of anger do not always generate concessions in negotiations, but they can backfire particularly in conflict management negotiations and in negotiation to set up long-term deal-making relationships.
5. The honor, face, dignity cultural logic explains cultural differences in the timing and authority of third-party intervention into conflict as well as the extent to which the third party involves others in the process.

Five Practical Implications

1. Learn to use multi-issue offers to generate insight and joint gains. Activate your holistic mindset!
2. Learn to build trust in different cultural contexts. Recognize that negotiators in non-Western cultures will not assume that the counterpart is trustworthy.
3. Learn to differentiate deal making and conflict management! Understand that negotiating deals and negotiating conflict start in different places and end in different places. Deals begin with positive emotions and the focus on maximizing gains. Deal making ends, if unsuccessful with each party's best alternative, which is free of control of the other party. Conflict begins with

negative emotions, anger and shame, and the focus on minimizing costs. Conflict management, if unsuccessful, ends with each party's worst alternative, which is under the control of the other party.

4. Learn to use third parties effectively. Manage the timing and authority of third-party intervention as well as the involvement of others' process.
5. Learn to take a cultural approach to negotiating. Everything researchers know about the process of deal making and conflict management varies systematically with culture. You don't need to know a lot more about culture than trust, tightness–looseness, and the logics of honor, face, and dignity to be able to recognize a counterpart's use of negotiation strategy as cultural and adjust to it.

References

Adair, W. L., Okumura, T., & Brett, J. M. (2001). Negotiation behavior when cultures collide: The United States and Japan. *Journal of Applied Psychology, 86*(3), 371–385.

Adair, W. L., Weingart, L. R., & Brett, J. M. (2007). The timing and function of offers in US and Japanese negotiations. *Journal of Applied Psychology, 92*(4), 1056–1068.

Adam, H., & Brett, J. M. (2015). Context matters: The social effects of anger in cooperative, balanced, and competitive negotiation situations. *Journal of Experimental Social Psychology, 61*, 44–58.

Adam, H., Shirako, A., & Maddux, W. W. (2010). Cultural variance in the interpersonal effects of anger in negotiations. *Psychological Science, 21*, 882–889.

Aslani, S., Ramirez, J., Semnani-Azad, Z., Brett, J. M., & Tinsley, C. (2013). Honor, face, and dignity cultures: Implications for conflict management. In M. Olekalns & W. Adair (Eds.), *Handbook of negotiation research* (pp. 249–282). Northampton, MA: Edward Elgar.

Aslani, S., Ramirez-Marin, J., Brett, J., Yao, J., Semnani-Azad, Z., Zhang, Z. X., Tinsley, C., Weingart, L., & Adair, W. (2016). Dignity, face, and honor cultures: A study of negotiation strategy and outcomes in three cultures. *Journal of Organizational Behavior, 37*(8), 1178–1201.

Blake, R., & Mouton, J. (1964). *The managerial grid: The key to leadership excellence.* Houston, TX: Gulf Publishing Co.

Boiger, M., Güngör, D., Karasawa, M., & Mesquita, B. (2014). Defending honour, keeping face: Interpersonal affordances of anger and shame in Turkey and Japan. *Cognition and Emotion, 28*(7), 1255–1269.

Boiger, M., Mesquita, B., Uchida, Y., & Feldman Barrett, L. (2013). Condoned or condemned: The situational affordance of anger and shame in the United States and Japan. *Personality and Social Psychology Bulletin, 39*(4), 540–553.

Branzei, O., Vertinsky, I., & Camp, R. D., II. (2007). Culture-contingent signs of trust in emergent relationships. *Organizational Behavior and Human Decision Processes, 104*(1), 61–82.

Brett, J. M. (2007). *Negotiating globally: How to negotiate deals, resolve disputes, and make decisions across cultural boundaries* (2nd ed.). San Francisco: Jossey-Bass.

Brett, J. M. (2014). *Negotiating globally: How to negotiate deals, resolve disputes, and make decisions across cultural boundaries* (3rd ed.). San Francisco: Jossey-Bass.

Brett, J. (2018). Intercultural challenges in managing workplace conflict—a call for research. *Cross Cultural and Strategic Management, 25*(1), 32–52.

Brett, J. M. (2020). Negotiation strategy. In M. Gelfand, C-Y Chiu, &Y-Y Hong (Eds.), *Advances in Culture and Psychology, 9* (pp. 245–289). New York: Oxford University Press.

Brett, J. M., Behfar, K., & Sanchez-Burks, J. (2014). Managing cross-culture conflicts: A close look at the implication of direct versus indirect confrontation. In N. M. Ashkanasy, O. B. Ayoko, & K. A. Jehn (Eds.), *Handbook of research in conflict management* (pp. 136–154). Northampton, MA: Edward Edgar Publishing.

Brett, J. M., Gunia, B. C., & Teucher, B. M. (2017). Culture and negotiation strategy: A framework for future research. *Academy of Management Perspectives, 31*(4), 288–308.

Brett, J. M., & Mitchell, T. (2019). Searching for trustworthiness: Culture, trust and negotiating new business relationships. *International Journal of Conflict Management, 31*(1), 17–39.

Brett, J. M., & Okumura, T. (1998). Inter and intra-cultural negotiation: U.S. and Japanese negotiators. *Academy of Management Journal, 41*(5), 495–510.

Brett, J. M., Ramirez-Marin, J., & Galoni, C. (2021). Negotiation strategy: A cross-cultural meta-analytic evaluation of theory and measurement. *Negotiation and Conflict Management Research, 14*(4).

Brett, J. M., & Thompson, L. (2016). Negotiation. *Organizational Behavior and Human Decision Processes, 136*, 68–79.

Brown, P., & Levinson, S. (1987). *Politeness: Some universals in language usage*. Cambridge: Cambridge University Press.

Chua, H. F., Boland, J. E., & Nisbett, R. E. (2005). Cultural variation in eye movements during scene perception. *Proceedings of the National Academy of Sciences, 102*, 12629–12633.

Cohen, D., & Nisbett, R. E. (1997). Field experiments examining the culture of honor: The role of institutions in perpetuating norms about violence. *Personality and Social Psychology Bulletin, 23*(11): 1188–1199.

Cohen, D., Nisbett, R. E., Bowdle, B. F., & Schwartz, N. (1996). Insult, aggression and the southern culture of honor: A "experimental ethnography." *Journal of Personality and Social Psychology, 70*(5), 945–960.

De Dreu, C. K., Evers, A., Beersma, B., Kluwer, E. S., & Nauta, A. (2001). A theory-based measure of conflict management strategies in the workplace. *Journal of Organizational Behavior, 22*(6), 645–668.

Delhey, J., & Newton, K. (2005). Predicting cross-national levels of social trust: Global pattern or Nordic exceptionalism? *European Sociological Review, 21*(4), 311–327.

Dong, R. (2006). How does culture influence the joint gains of a negotiation? A close study on the U.S. and Chinese intracultural negotiations. Northwestern University. Undergraduate Thesis.

Felsteiner, W. L. F, Abel, R. L., & Sarat, A. (1980–1981). The emergence and transformation of disputes: Naming, blaming, and claiming. *Law and Society Review, 15*, 631–654.

Ferrin, D. L., & Gillespie, N. (2010). Trust differences across national-societal cultures: Much to do, or much ado about nothing? In M. Saunders, D. Skinner, G. Dietz, N. Gillespie, & R. Lewicki (Eds.), *Trust across cultures: Theory and practice* (pp. 42–86). Cambridge: Cambridge University Press.

Fisher, R., Ury, W., & Patton, B. (1993). *Getting to yes*. New York: Penguin.

Friedman, R., Anderson, C. Brett, J., Olekalns, M. Goates, N., & Lisco, C. C. (2004). The positive and negative effects of anger on dispute resolution: Evidence from electronically-mediated disputes. *Journal of Applied Psychology, 89*, 369–376.

Gelfand, M. J. (2018). *Rule makers rule breakers: How tight and loose cultures wire our world*. New York: Scribner.

Gelfand, M. J., Harrington, J. R., & Fernandez, J. R. (2017). Cultural tightness-looseness: Ecological affordances and implications for personality. In T. Church (Ed.), *The Praeger handbook of personality across cultures* (Vol. 3, Ch. 8, pp. 207–235). Santa Barbara, CA: Praeger.

Gelfand, M. J., Jackson, J. C., Pan, X., Nau, D., Pieper, D., Denison, E., Dagher, M., Van Lange, P. A. M., Chiu, C-Y., & Wang, M. (2021). The relationship between cultural tightness–looseness and COVID-19 cases and deaths: A global analysis. *The Lancet Planetary Health, 5*(3), e135–e144.

Gelfand, M. J., Lim, B.-C. & Raver, J. (2004). Culture and accountability in organizations: variations in forms of social control across cultures. *Human Resource Management Review, 14*(1), 135–160.

Gelfand, M. J., Nishii, L. H., & Raver, J. L. (2006). On the nature and importance of cultural tightness-looseness. *Journal of Applied Psychology, 91*(6), 1225–1244.

Gelfand, M. J., Raver, J. L., Nishii, L., Leslie, L. M., Lun, J., Lim, B. C., et al. (2011). Differences between tight and loose cultures: A 33-nation study. *Science, 332*, 1100–1104.

Gelfand, M. J., Severance, L., Lee, T., Bruss, C. B., Lun, J., Abdel-Latif, A. H., Al-Moghazy, A. A., & Moustafa Ahmed, S. (2015). Culture and getting to yes: The linguistic signature of creative agreements in the United States and Egypt. *Journal of Organizational Behavior, 36*(7), 967–989.

Goldberg, S. B., Brett, J. M., & Brenneur, B. (2017). *How mediation works*. Bingley, UK: Emerald.

Graham, J. L. (1983). Business negotiations in Japan, Brazil, and the United States. *Journal of International Business Studies* (Spring/Summer), 47–62.

Graham, J. L. (1985). The influence of culture on the process of business negotiations: An exploratory study. *Journal of International Business Studies* (Spring), 79–94.

Graham, J. L. (1993). The Japanese negotiation style: Characteristics of a distinct approach. *Negotiation Journal* (April), 123–141.

Graham, J. L. (1995). Negotiation behaviors in Norway compared to eleven other cultures. *Essays in Marketing and Management: A Festchrift in Honour of Kjell Gronhaug*. Norway: Fagbokforlaget.

Graham, J. L., &. Mintu-Winsatt, A. (1997). Culture's influence on business negotiations in four countries. *Group Decision and Negotiation, 6*(5), 483–502.

Graham, J. L., Mintu, A. T., & Rodgers, W. (1994). Explorations of negotiation behaviors in ten foreign cultures using a model developed in the United States. *Management Science, 40*(1), 72–95.

Grice, H. P. (1968). Utterer's meaning, sentence-meaning and word meaning. *Foundations of Language, 4*, 225–242.

Gunia, B. Brett, J. M., & Gelfand, M. (2016). The science of culture and negotiation. *Current Opinion in Psychology, 8*, 78–83.

Gunia, B. C., Brett J. M., Nandkeolyar, A., & Kamdar, D. (2011). Paying a price: Culture, trust, and negotiation consequences. *Journal of Applied Psychology, 96*(4), 774–789.

Haerpfer, C., Inglehart, R., Moreno, A., Welzel, C., Kizilova, K., Diez-Medrano, J., Lagos, M., Norris, P., Ponarin, E., & Puranen, B. (2020). World values survey: Round seven-country–pooled datafile. Available at: http://www.worldvaluessurvey.org/WVSDocumentationWV7.jsp

Hüffmeier, J., Freund, P. A., Zerres, A., Backhaus, K., & Hertel, G. (2014). Being tough or being nice? A meta-analysis on the impact of hard-and soft-line strategies in distributive negotiations. *Journal of Management, 40*(3), 866–892.

Kelley, H. H. (1966). A classroom study of dilemmas in interpersonal negotiation. In K. Archibald (Ed.), *Strategic interaction and conflict* (pp. 49–73). Institute of International Studies, University of California, Berkeley.

Kilmann, R. H., & Thomas, K. W. (1977). Developing a forced-choice measure of conflict-handling behavior: The "Mode" instrument. *Educational and Psychological Measurement, 37*(2), 309–325.

Kim, M.-S., Lee, H.-R., Kim, I. D., & Hunter, J. E. (2004). A test of a cultural model of conflict styles. *Journal of Asian Pacific Communication, 14*(2), 197–222.

Kim, Y., Cohen, D., and Au, W.-T. (2010). The jury and abjury of my peers: The self in face and dignity cultures. *Journal of Personality and Social Psychology, 98*(6), 904–916.

Kirkman, B. L., Lowe, K. B., & Gibson, C. B. (2006). A quarter century of culture's consequences: A review of empirical research incorporating Hofstede's cultural values framework. *Journal of International Business Studies, 37*(3), 285–320.

Kong, D. T., Dirks, K. T., & Ferrin, D. L. (2014). Interpersonal trust within negotiations: Meta-analytic evidence, critical contingencies, and directions for future research. *Academy of Management Journal, 57*(5), 1235–1255.

Kozan, M. K., & Ilter, S. S. (1994). Third party roles played by Turkish managers in subordinates' conflicts. *Journal of Organizational Behavior, 15*(5), 453–466.

Lax, D. A., & Sebenius, J. K. (1986). *The manager as negotiator*. New York: The Free Press.

Leung, A. K. Y., & Cohen, D. (2011). Within and between culture variation: individual differences and the cultural logics of honor, face, and dignity cultures. *Journal of Personality and Social Psychology, 100* (3), 507–526.

Liu, M. (2009). The intrapersonal and interpersonal effects of anger on negotiation strategies: A cross-cultural investigation. *Human Communication Research, 35*(1), 148–169.

Lügger, K., Geiger, I., Neun, H., & Backhaus, K. (2015). When East meets West at the bargaining table: Adaptation, behavior and outcomes in intra-and intercultural German–Chinese business negotiations. *Journal of Business Economics, 85*(1), 15–43.

Masuda, T., Gonzalez, R., Kwan, L, & Nisbett, R. E. (2008). Culture and aesthetic preference: Comparing the attention to context of East Asian and Americans. *Personality and Social Psychology Bulletin, 34*(9). 1260–1275.

Mediation in civil justice: International evidence review. (2019). https://www.gov.scot/publications/international-evidence-review-mediation-civil-justice/pages/9/

Mesquita, B., Boiger, M., & De Leersnyder, J. (2016). The cultural construction of emotions. *Current Opinion in Psychology, 8*, 31–36.

Nisbett, R. E., & Cohen, D. (1996), *Culture of honor: The psychology of violence in the South*. Boulder, CO: Westview Press.

Nisbett, R. E., Peng, K., Choi, I., & Norenzayan, A. (2001). Culture and systems of thought: holistic vs. analytic cognition. *Psychological Review, 108*, 291–310.

Norenzayan, A., Smith, E. E., Kim, B. J., & Nisbett, R. E. (2002). Cultural preferences for formal versus intuitive reasoning. *Cognitive Science, 26*, 653–684.

Oetzel, J. G., & Ting-Toomey, S. (2003). Face concerns in interpersonal conflict. *Communication Research, 30*(6), 599–624.

Pitt-Rivers, J. (1968), *International encyclopedia of the social sciences.* New York: Macmillan, pp. 509–510.

Pruitt, D. G. (1981). *Negotiation behavior.* New York: Academic Press.

Pruitt, D. G., & Rubin, J. Z. (1986). *Social conflict: Escalation, impasse, and resolution.* Boston: Addison-Wesley.

Rahim, M. A. (1983). A measure of styles of handling interpersonal conflict. *Academy of Management Journal, 26*(2), 368–376.

Raiffa, H. (1982). *The art and science of negotiation.* Cambridge, MA: Harvard University Press.

Rodriguez Mosquera, P. M., Fischer, A. H., Manstead, A. S. R., & Zaalberg, R. (2008). Attack, disapproval, or withdrawal? The role of honour in anger and shame responses to being insulted. *Cognition and Emotion, 22*(8), 1471–1498.

Rodriguez Mosquera, P. M. R., Manstead, A. S. R., & Fischer, A. H. (2000). The role of honor related values in the elicitation, experience, and communication of pride, shame, and anger: Spain and the Netherlands compared. *Personality and Social Psychology Bulletin, 26* (7), 833–844.

Rosette, A. S., Brett, J. M., Barsness, Z., & Lytle, A. (2012). When cultures clash electronically: The impact of e-mail and social norms on negotiation behavior and outcomes. *Journal of Cross-cultural Psychology, 5*(2), 210–234.

Sanchez-Burks, J. (2005). *Protestant relational ideology: The cognitive underpinnings and organizational implications of an American anomaly.* In R. Kramer & B. Staw (Eds.), *Research in Organizational Behavior* (Vol. 26, pp. 265–305). Elsevier.

Sanchez-Burks, J., & Mor Barak, M. (2004). Interpersonal relationships in a global work context. In M. Mor Barak (Ed.), *Managing diversity in the age of globalization: Toward a worldwide inclusive workplace* (pp. 114–168). Thousand Oaks: SAGE.

Schroth, H. A. (2008). Some like it hot: Teaching strategies for managing tactical versus genuine anger in negotiations. *Negotiation and Conflict Management Research, 1*(4), 315–332.

Tinsley, C. H., & Weldon, E. (2003). Responses to a normative conflict among American and Chinese managers. *International Journal of Cross Cultural Management, 3*(2), 183–194.

Trompenaars, F. (1996). Resolving international conflict: Culture and business strategy. *Business Strategy Review, 7* (3), 51–68.

Van Kleef, G. A. (2009). How emotions regulate social life the emotions as social information (EASI) model. *Current Directions in Psychological Science, 18*, 184–188.

Van Kleef, G. A., De Dreu, C. K., & Manstead, A. S. (2004a). The interpersonal effects of anger and happiness in negotiations. *Journal of Personality and Social Psychology, 86*(1), 57–76.

Van Kleef, G. A., De Dreu, C. K., & Manstead, A. S. (2004b). The interpersonal effects of emotions in negotiations: a motivated information processing approach. *Journal of Personality and Social Psychology, 87*(4), 510–528.

Wall, J. (1993). Community mediation in China and Korea: Some similarities and differences. *Negotiation Journal, 9*(2), 141–153.

Wall, J., Arunachalem, V., & Callister, R. R. (2008). Third-party dispute resolution in India and the United States. *Journal of Applied Social Psychology, 38*(12), 3075–3100.

Wall, J., Beriker, N., & Wu, S. Y. (2010). Turkish community mediation. *Journal of Applied Social Psychology, 40* (8), 2019–2042.

Wall, J., Jr., Blum, M. E., & Jin, D. (2000). A response to Diamant's conflict and conflict resolution in China. *Journal of Conflict Resolution, 44*(4), 547–551.

Wall, J., & Callister, R. R. (1999). Malaysian community mediation. *Journal of Conflict Resolution, 43* (3), 343–365.

Wall, J., Sohn, D.-W., Cleeton, N., & Jin, D. J. (1995). Community and family mediation in the People's Republic of China. *International Journal of Conflict Management, 6* (1), 30–47.

Walton, R. E., & McKersie, R. B. (1965). *A behavioral theory of labor negotiations.* Ithaca, NY: Cornell University Press.

Weingart, L. R., Thompson, L. L., Bazerman, M. H., & Carroll, J. S. (1990). Tactical behavior and negotiation outcomes. *International Journal of Conflict Management, 1*(1), 7–31.

World Bank Annual Report. (2016). Retrieved from http://documents.worldbank.org/curated/en/782691475489708512/World-Bank-annual-report-2016-organizational-information-and-lending-dataappendixes.

Yamagishi, T., Cook, K. S., & Watabe, M. (1998). Uncertainty, trust, and commitment formation in the United States and Japan. *American Journal of Sociology, 104*(1), 165–194.

Yamagishi, T., & Yamagishi, M. (1994). Trust and commitment in the United States and Japan. *Motivation and Emotion, 18*(2), 129–166.

Yao, J., Brett, J. M., Zhang, Z. X., & Ramirez-Marin, J. (2021). Multi-issue offers strategy and joint gains in negotiations: How low-trust negotiators get things done. *Organizational Behavior and Human Decision Processes, 162*, 9–23.

Yao, J. J., Ramirez-Marin, J., Brett, J. M., Aslani, S., & Semnani-Azad, Z. (2017). A measurement model for dignity, face, and honor cultural norms. *Management and Organization Review, 13*(4), 713–738.

PART V

Culture at the Organizational Level

CHAPTER

18

Culture and Social Networks

Mo Wang *and* Yanran Fang

Abstract

In this chapter, we will first introduce the importance of investigating the relationship between culture and social networks. In answering the question of why the social network approach should be adopted to understand the central role of culture in impacting employee work behaviors, we highlight two core characteristics of culture and social networks that connect them: the multilevel structures and the dynamic processes. We then derive an overarching theoretical framework to explain how culture and social networks at multiple levels are mutually constitutive and coevolving. On the basis of this theoretical framework, we review the literature on the effects of culture on social networks, the roles of social networks in relation to culture and the acculturation process, and discuss new theoretical and empirical directions for future research. We also summarize five key theoretical principles and five practical implications that we discovered in our review. Future research questions and directions are proposed at the end of the chapter.

Key Words: culture, social network, multi-level nature, dynamic nature, mutual influence

A social network is defined as a set of nodes (or network members) that are tied by one or more types of relations (Wasserman & Faust, 1994). It depicts the processes in which individuals' acts, thoughts, and behaviors are impacted by relations and the lasting patterns formed by these relations (Marin & Wellman, 2011). The growing scholarly interest in applying social network approaches to studying employees' work behaviors in recent years highlights the importance of applying relational and structural perspectives to understanding social influence processes (Wasserman & Faust, 1994). In particular, social network approaches offer a series of theoretical principles for understanding the development of relationships, as well as a set of analytic tools to identify, describe, and explain relationships (e.g., Borgatti et al., 2009; Contractor et al., 2006).

Given that interpersonal communication and social influence processes serve as critical conduits for the creation and influence of culture in any defined population (González-Romá et al., 2002; Lehman et al., 2004; Pachucki & Breiger, 2010; Patterson, 2014), the social network approach offers advantages in depicting the critical role of culture in influencing human behaviors in social systems. In this chapter, we offer a multilevel and dynamic theoretical framework to delineate the interplay between culture and social networks. We begin our chapter by reviewing the two core characteristics of culture and social networks, which are the foundations of the close connections between them: the multilevel structures and the dynamic processes.

The Multilevel Nature of Culture and Social Networks

One of the metatheoretical dimensions of sociological theory is that social phenomena can be generally categorized as macro-phenomena and micro-phenomena (Mortensen, 1999). The key difference between the two forms of phenomena is that the number of actors is usually too large to allow simultaneous contact among actors in a macro-level system, whereas such contact, whether permanent or sporadic, is usually achievable in a micro-level environment (Mortensen, 1999). Additionally, macro-phenomena can be subdivided into a series of meso-level phenomena that manifest in organizations or other collective systems (Luhmann, 1977; Mortensen, 1999). By nature, both culture and social networks are inherently functioning and evolving in multilevel systems (i.e., spanning from the micro individual level to the meso team or organization level, and then to the macro societal and country level).

Specifically, representing a shared meaning system, culture may exist and impact peoples' attitudes and behaviors at multiple levels (Burke et al., 2008; Erez & Gati, 2004; Yammarino & Dansereau, 2011b). For instance, culture can be formed as national characters or ultimate values, local practices and norms (Erez & Gati, 2004), organizational culture or small-group climates (Yammarino & Dansereau, 2011a), and individual internal culture identification (Pachucki & Breiger, 2010) or cultural self-representation (Erez & Gati, 2004). Although culture was usually conceptualized and investigated as a collective property (especially with individual difference an irrelevant idea in the field of anthropology; Schneider et al., 2013), the literature on social and cultural psychology has extended the research of culture to a relatively micro level and investigated the development of an individual's internal perception or culture identification, as well as its role in impacting individual attitudes and behaviors (e.g., Repke & Benet-Martínez, 2017, 2018).

The multilevel nature of culture exacerbates the complexity of understanding human behaviors impacted by both external cultural environment and their own culture identification. Nevertheless, theoretical principles and analytic tools offered by the social network approach are well equipped to address this complexity. In general, social network studies have been applied to understanding multilevel systems from two interrelated perspectives. The sociocentric network (also known as the whole network; see Kilduff & Brass, 2010) approach is often applied to depicting the macro-level structure and functioning, whereas the egocentric network approach is often applied to depicting the micro-level structure and functioning. Specifically, the sociocentric network focuses on the complete or whole network connecting all actors in the actors' sets, thereby allowing scholars to take a macro perspective to capture network-level structural constructs (Carpenter et al., 2012). In contrast, the egocentric network is defined as "the social network surrounding ego, including the ties among ego's direct ties" (Kilduff & Brass, 2010, p. 356), which depicts the focal individual's personal network and usually reflects their perceived interpersonal environment (Borgatti & Foster, 2003; Repke & Benet-Martínez, 2019). Therefore, the social network approach is flexible in its applicability to different kinds of actors and to different kinds of interconnected social relationships (Brass et al., 2004; Scott & Carrington, 2011; Wasserman & Faust, 1994), offering a distinctive opportunity to understand the effects that could coexist and coevolve at different levels, such as the emergence and impacts of culture at different levels.

Taken together, both culture and social networks function as multilevel systems that incorporate complex social phenomena involving actors and connections of actors across different levels (e.g., the individual, group, organizational, and regional levels). Scholars in social sciences can therefore explore the emergence and effectiveness of culture by adopting a social network approach and vice versa.

The Dynamic Nature of Culture and Social Networks

Emerging from interpersonal communication and social influence, culture or collective norms are shown to stay relatively stable, but still, such collective beliefs or shared norms can evolve over a longer time span (Lehman et al., 2004). For instance, in the field of anthropology, Shennan (2000) suggested that culture change is one of the major influences of the fluctuation in regional populations, corroborating the argument that culture and people that compose the culture are reciprocally impacting each other (Hannerz, 1992). Further, analyzing the time-series data collected from 38 societies from 1981 to 1998 in World Value Surveys, Inglehart and Baker (2000) tracked the changes over time in the two dimensions of cross-cultural variation: (1) traditional versus secular-relational orientations toward authority, and (2) survival versus self-expression values. Specifically, they found a close relationship between economic development and a given society's increasing emphasis on secular-relational values and self-expression values in its culture, whereas economic collapse tended to push the emphasis toward traditional values and survival values. Such findings offer evidence showing the change of massive culture over time.

At the meso team or organizational level, culture was defined as "the dynamic product of a process of collective 'sense-making' where individuals communicate and agree common explanations for work-related events in an effort to understand, predict and control their environment" (Silvester et al., 1999, p. 4). In particular, considerable scholarly attention has been devoted to investigating the research question of "can organizational culture be managed and changed?" (Alvesson & Sveningsson, 2015, p. 46). Scholars hold different views on this research question. Specifically, scholars holding a relatively proactive perspective believe that organizational culture can be impacted under certain conditions; scholars holding a neutral perspective suggest that such change is difficult; whereas scholars holding a relatively passive perspective tend to believe that cultural change is usually beyond control (Alvesson & Sveningsson, 2015). Nevertheless, beyond such debates in the literature, the underlying assumption of this stream of research is that the meso-level culture is incrementally adaptive and is continuously in flux (Meyerson & Martin, 1987).

At a micro individual level, the dynamic nature of an individual's internal culture identification or cultural self-reflection indicates the process of acculturation. Such cultural change at the individual level reflects one of the broad domains of cross-cultural psychology: the psychology adaptations individuals make when they move between cultures (Berry, 1995, 2005). Specifically, acculturation is defined as a process of learning and internalizing cultural values and identities (Berry, 1980; Ryder et al., 2000; Volpone et al., 2018). A general consensus in immigration literature and expatriate literature is that cultural identity change is often associated with cross-cultural adaptation when relocating to a different cultural context. Such an acculturation process would profoundly impact the focal employees' work- and life-related consequences (e.g., Berry, 1997, 2005; Kraimer et al., 2012; Mao & Shen, 2015; Shaffer et al., 2012; Takeuchi et al., 2005, 2009; Wang & Takeuchi, 2007).

Similarly, social networks, including the state of actors and the connections between them can evolve following sociodynamic and psychological processes (e.g., selection preferences, opportunity structures, and social influence) over time (van der Hulst, 2011). In particular, focusing on the development of the connections among actors, selection preference was derived from the principle of homophily in which people tend to initiate contacts with other people who share similar characteristics (e.g., share similarities in terms of location, membership, and attribute; see Borgatti & Foster, 2003). For instance, collecting data from 205 psychology freshmen in their first semester at a large university, Selfhout et al. (2010) observed an increasing trend in participants' average number of friendship network ties over the first 3 months. They also found that such changes in their social networks depended on the extent to which the actors shared similar levels of agreeableness, extraversion, and openness. Similarly, literature on sociology also suggests that a similar cultural background, or the sense of belongingness to a similar culture, may initiate opportunities and offer incentives for individuals to establish social connections with each other (Van der Meer & Tolsma, 2014). Notably, such a selection preference based on cultural homophily is analogous to Harrison et al.'s discussion (2002) of interpersonal similarity based on values, attitudes, and beliefs. Specifically, according to Harrison et al. (2002), surface-level (dis)similarity (i.e., similarities in terms of race, sex, age, and marital status) functions through a social categorization mechanism, whereas deep-level (dis)similarity (i.e., similarities in terms of personalities, values, attitudes, beliefs) functions through the similarity attraction mechanism. Further, the impacts of deep-level (dis)similarity tend to be more salient over time via interpersonal interaction processes (Harrison et al., 2002). This notion further underscores the dynamic nature of interpersonal interaction and highlights the importance of incorporating time space in understanding the dynamic interplay between culture and the social network.

Opportunity structure emphasizes the structural opportunity for actors in different groups to build social ties, highlighting the importance of proximity among actors' geographic or social space in impacting their social network properties (Lehman et al., 2004; Zeng & Xie, 2008). Therefore, such propinquity usually manifests as population composition and organizational structure (An, 2011), depicting structural opportunity-based antecedents of the formation and development of different clusters or groups of social networks, beliefs, and behaviors (Borgatti et al., 2009; Lehman et al., 2004; Zeng & Xie, 2008). That is, people with greater opportunity to interact and communicate with each other are more likely to develop social ties with each other, such that their personal social networks tend to become similar, gradually overlap, and coalesce into clusters or groups of networks over time. Supporting such theorizing, in analyzing interactions (operationalized as e-mail communication) among 43,553 individuals at a large university, Kossinets and Watts (2006) found that interpersonal network evolution was largely impacted by organizational structure in which the networks were embedded (e.g., participants that shared the same classes). Specifically, this study highlights the importance of taking a social interaction-based perspective to understand new tie formation, as it found that the probability for two previous unconnected and distance-apart network members to develop a new tie diminished rapidly with the increase of interpersonal distance in the network (Kossinets & Watts, 2006). This finding corroborates the notion of structural opportunity that "individuals who are far apart in the network have no opportunity to interact and hence are very unlikely to form ties" (Kossinets & Watts, 2006, p. 88).

Social influence refers to an actor's ability to directly influence another actor's decision based on their communication (Ma et al., 2015) or social network properties such as relations and positions (Repke & Benet-Martínez, 2017, 2019). The social influence model therefore reveals the social contagion process in which the network-connected actors mutually impact one another's beliefs and actions (Robins et al., 2001). As such, the characteristics of network-connected actors are changeable over time, which could further result in the change in overall network pattern such as homogeneity (Borgatti et al., 2009). In particular, as almost every definition of culture suggests that the emergence and evolution of certain culture elements (e.g., identities, tastes, moral values) rely on the "shared" consensus regarding behavioral norms and cognitive values within a definable population (e.g., Lehman et al., 2004; Patterson, 2014), the coalesced attitudes and actions among tied actors unfolding in a social network reflect the essence of the development and evolution of culture.

Taken together, both culture and social networks tend to dynamically evolve and develop overtime. The above-mentioned sociodynamic and psychological processes incorporated in social network dynamics imply that both the formation of social ties among actors and the outcomes of various social network features are particularly relevant to the formation and emergent features of culture, reflecting the culture's dynamics at multiple levels. In particular, such dynamic interplay between culture and social networks was supported by Höllinger and Haler's work (1990). Specifically, they observed the increasingly critical role of nonkinship in social networks in modern societies such as those of Americans and Australians and argued that this change was driven by economic development and sociocultural characteristics, including cultural tradition, geographic mobility, and individualistic lifestyle (Höllinger & Haler, 1990). Therefore, social networks and culture can couple and explain each other at different levels in a coevolving manner.

An Overarching Theoretical Framework for Coupling Culture and Social Networks

Given the multilevel and dynamic nature of social networks and culture, integrating a social network perspective is of great importance in understanding the emergence of culture and the impact of culture on employees' work behaviors in organizations. Social network approaches, including both sociocentric and egocentric approaches, are critical in investigating the creation and effect of culture in organizational contexts. We summarize the relation between culture and social networks in the theoretical framework presented in Figure 18.1. In the next section, we describe and review prior research findings based on this theoretical framework. Specifically, we divide the previous literature into two sections: (1) the first section summarizes the effects of culture at different levels on social networks, and (2) the second section summarizes the different ways social networks can shape culture and acculturation process.

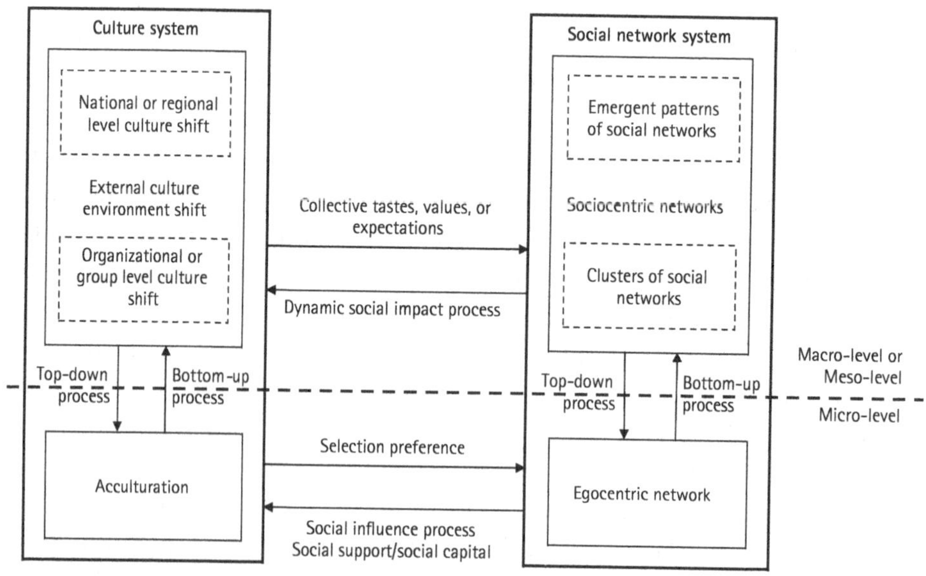

Figure 18.1. Theoretical framework of the relationship between culture and social network

Effects of Culture on Social Networks

IMPACTS OF MACRO-LEVEL CULTURE ON SOCIAL NETWORKS

The theoretical basis of the impacts of macro-level culture on social networks involves the essence of culture itself. Specifically, culture may be defined as the coalescence of distinctive shared beliefs and norms within a population (Lehman et al., 2004). Hence, the impacts or functions of any given culture are established on the basis of homogeneous attitudinal or behavioral patterns in a given population. A culturalist perspective suggests that the socially shared practices, norms, values, and other mental events are loosely organized around the core of cultural schemas of paradigms (Shore, 1998). It is these cultural schemas or paradigms that guide the construction of meaning across social life (Lehman et al., 2004), such as different properties of social networks.

Cultural factors such as shared tastes and moral frameworks create relational affinities that shape network structure (Mische, 2011). For example, taking a constructionist approach, Lizardo (2006) investigated the effects of cultural tastes on the formation and the sustentation of network relations. In particular, the strength of ties was incorporated in his study as an important property of personal network. The strength of ties was originally defined as "a (probably linear) combination of the amount of time, the emotional intensity, the intimacy (mutual confiding), and the reciprocal services which characterize the tie" (Granovetter, 1973, p. 1361). As such, strong ties are often characterized as "frequent, long-lasting, and affect-laden" (Krackhardt, 1992, pp. 218–219), whereas weak ties are usually "infrequent and distant" (Hansen, 1999, p. 84). In Lizardo's study (2006), he found that compared to "popular culture taste" which enjoys a relatively broader distribution of weak ties in social space, "highbrow culture taste" is more likely to be converted into social capital exclusively for strong-tie networks due to its inherently restricted and asset-specific nature.

Further, as collective cultural tastes or preferences usually differ from each other according to different geographic locations of population, scholarly attention has also been devoted to investigating the relationship between national culture preferences and general network structure (e.g., network density; Brass et al., 2004; Fischer & Shavit, 1995; Monge & Eisenberg, 1987; network homogeneity and network closure, Igarashi et al., 2008). For instance, in reviewing Monge and Eisenberg's work (1987), Brass and his colleagues (2004) noted that social network density and interconnectedness were usually greater in Japanese companies (i.e., they have greater network density and multiplexity) than in those organizations embedded in the national culture of individualism. As social network density is calculated as "the number of ties in a network divided by the maximum number of ties that are possible," and multiplexity refers to "the extent to which two actors are connected by more than one type of relationship" (Kilduff & Brass, 2010, p. 356), Monge and Eisenberg's research (1987) suggested that people impacted by different national cultures (represented as the emphasis on group orientation in Japan and on individualism in the United States, respectively) tend to form different patterns of personal networks.

Further, Xiao and Tsui (2007) theorized and empirically showed that people in collectivistic cultures preferred dense networks that reflected clear group membership rather than networks full of structural holes. Specifically, they suggested that people in collectivistic cultures (such as Chinese culture) value group members' commitments to the group in an exclusive way. Hence, impacted by such cultural preference, people tend to attach higher levels of trust to group members who have "simple and clear networks that represent clear group membership" (Xiao & Tsui, 2007, p. 5). On the contrary, people who span structural holes are those who stay at the boundary of different groups, rendering questions about their membership and "in-group" status. Indeed, in their research conducted in four high-tech companies in China, they found that individuals spanning structural holes were less likely to achieve favorable career advancement (Xiao & Tsui, 2007). Similarly, Ma et al. (2011) also highlighted the critical role of culture in impacting the effects of social network properties (i.e., structural holes and strength of ties in their study). Specifically, their research indicated that tie strength was negatively related to opportunity identification and that structural holes were positively related to opportunity identification in individualistic cultures, whereas the effect of tie strength was positive and the effect of structural holes was negative on opportunity identification in collectivist cultures (Ma et al., 2011).

In addition to the general socio-network structure, cross-cultural differences were shown to impact the contents of social ties such as the complexity or the amount of information that was taken into consideration within social interaction (e.g., Brannen & Salk, 2000; Choi et al., 2003; Chua et al., 2009; Gold et al., 2002; Morris et al., 2008; Salk & Brannen, 2000). For instance, Brannen and Salk have conducted a series of research studies in a German-Japanese joint venture, and they found significant differences regarding the emphasis allocated to interpersonal interactions between German managers and Japanese managers (Brannen & Salk, 2000; Salk & Brannen, 2000). Specifically, they concluded that German managers were more likely to follow the rule-based logics of "consensus and orderliness" (p. 193) by placing greater emphasis on expertise and responsibility in interacting with colleagues, whereas Japanese managers tend to place greater reliance on maintaining interpersonal contacts and harmony on an emotional level (Salk & Brannen, 2000). Similarly, in comparison with European North Americans, relational information such as interpersonal networks or community memberships were shown to be more impactful in shaping interpersonal interactions for East Asians. East Asians are therefore more likely to take a more holistic, more complex view when making social inferences (Choi et al., 2003). Additionally, Chua and his colleagues (2009) also found that the affect- and cognition-based trust were more intertwined for Chinese than for American managers, which, again, demonstrates the salient impact of the familial collectivistic culture at a macro level on the individual's social network features.

Conceptualized as a characteristic of a given culture, residential mobility has been recognized as a critical factor that shapes one's social network formation and the social network's key characteristics (e.g., Oishi, 2010; Oishi et al., 2013). Specifically, residential mobility refers to the number of moves an individual makes during a certain period of time at a micro level and to the proportion of residents who moved (or expect to move) during a certain period of time at a macro level (Oishi, 2010). Oishi and his colleagues (Oishi, 2010; Oishi et al., 2013) suggested that higher residential mobility should constrain the available context for people to maintain interpersonal relationships. They found that a higher level of residential mobility motivated people to expand their own social networks (Oishi et al., 2013) and drove one's social network to be more open and transient (i.e., easier to make friends but not necessarily long-lasting, Oishi, 2010).

IMPACTS OF MESO-LEVEL CULTURE ON SOCIAL NETWORKS

Meso-level culture can also shape the patterns or structures of social networks among individuals. This is because meso team culture or organizational culture usually represents shared expectations for the members in a given work unit,[1] which ought to impact most aspects of organizational life, including how employees interact with one another (Eckenhofer & Ershova, 2011; Ostroff et al., 2013). For example, in a case study of two Austrian organizations, Eckenhofer and Ershova (2011) explored the relationship between culture types on intra-organizational network structures. Drawing on the Competing Value Framework (CVF, Cameron & Quinn, 2011), their research suggested that among the four dimensions of organizational culture (i.e., clan culture, adhocracy culture, market culture, and hierarchy culture), clan culture was the most salient predictor of a solid network (i.e., a dense network characterized by trusting relationship). They also found that a solid network was less likely to form when the hierarchy dimension was a dominant component of the organizational culture.

Additionally, analyzing data collected by requiring 47 employees in the same organization to rate each other, Krackhardt and Kilduff (1990) found that a pair of employees who were friends had similar perceptions across the seven dimensions of organizational culture (i.e., flexible, tolerant; eats, sleeps, and breathes; prepared to cut corners; efficient, organized; aggressive, competitive; straightforward, blunt; and task-oriented), and they also argued that the development and emergence of employees' network patterns in the organization can be considered as the product of meso team or organizational culture. Taken together, these findings supported their theorizing that "people use the social network to find support for their own interpretations of experience" (Krackhardt & Kilduff, 1990, p. 146).

---

[1] Aligned with Ostroff, Kinicki, and Muhammad's work (2013, p. 644), work unit refers to "a collection of individuals that include, but are not limited to, strategic business units, divisions, departments, and teams within organizations."

IMPACTS OF MICRO-LEVEL CULTURE ON SOCIAL NETWORKS

At the micro level, scholarly attention has been devoted to investigating the roles of cultural identification (i.e., the sense of belong to a cultural group, Repke & Benet-Martínez, 2017) in impacting personal social networks. Specifically, the effects of culture on social networks at a micro level (i.e., individual level) mainly manifest in the emergence and formation of personal networks in a given context. These effects are largely based on the selection preference process reviewed earlier. Specifically, as people usually prefer to interact with others similar to themselves (Van der Meer & Tolsma, 2014), homogeneous cultural identification has been shown to play an essential role in shaping the development of personal social networks (Lehman et al., 2004). Similarly, in their systematic review of homophily in social networks, McPherson and his colleagues (2001) summarized that homophily (including sharing similar cultural tastes) serves as one of the major principles that structure network ties in many societies.

Additionally, sociologists have long been investigating the phenomenon associated with subculture in city life (Fischer, 1995). Specifically, subcultural theory suggests that subculture is one of the key characteristics of city life, as clusters of residents in a same city can differ from each other to a large extent (Fischer, 1995). Hence, population concentration generates a set of interconnected social networks, constituting clusters of people who share similar traits, adhere to the same values, and share a set of cultural tools (Fischer, 1995; Swidler, 1986). Therefore, initiated by similar cultural identity, individuals tend to build social connections with each other, thereby constituting a set of personal networks based on their preference selection processes. Over time, such beliefs and behaviors within the same cluster of social networks tend to be increasingly correlated, whereas beliefs and behaviors of different clusters of social networks tend to be distinct from each other (Lehman et al., 2004), rendering people in one cluster of social networks to behave differently in comparing to people in other clusters of social networks.

Role of Social Networks in Relation to Culture and Acculturation Process

IMPACTS OF SOCIOCENTRIC NETWORKS ON CULTURE AT A MACRO OR MESO LEVEL

Dynamic social impact theory (Latané, 1996) serves as the theoretical basis for understanding the impacts of social networks on the emergence, maintenance, and evolution of culture. Specifically, the dynamic social impact perspective suggests that the coalescence of shared beliefs and collective norms is simply the consequence of interpersonal communication, and such a dynamic emergent process is bounded by opportunities for individuals to interact with each other and the extent to which individuals are capable of impacting others (Latané, 1996, 1981; Lehman et al., 2004).

Prior research in sociology and social psychology has well documented that initially diverse beliefs and behavioral tendencies tend to coalesce over time through social influence processes. Thus, people in a given cluster are more likely to share similar beliefs or behavioral practices than people in other clusters (Brass et al., 2004; Cullum & Harton,

2007; Lehman et al., 2004). Indeed, in investigating the process of culture evolution, Cullum and Harton's work (2007) supported the prediction of dynamic social impact theory that the gradually formed homogeneity in attitudes and beliefs are the results of interpersonal influence processes. Therefore, social networks serve as conduits and incubators for the spread of ideas (McIntyre et al., 2004), attitude similarity (Brass et al., 2004), and homogeneity of beliefs (Borgatti & Foster, 2003). Building on these ideas, Hollenbeck and Jamieson (2015) underscored the importance of understanding the sociocentric network of employees across different departments in shaping cooperate culture. Specifically, they pointed out that organizations can benefit from identifying the channels of the spread of messages and social influences, such that they can effectively take appropriate actions when a "socially inappropriate culture starts taking shape in the organization," or when they "wish to promote a positive culture" among employees (Hollenbeck & Jamieson, 2015, p. 380).

In addition to conceptualizing individuals as actors in social networks, institutional theories have also allocated considerable attention to investigating how organizations as actors in interorganizational networks play a critical role in shaping cultures at the macro level. For instance, Abrahamson and Fombrun (1992) have argued that interorganizational network structure and dynamics serve as critical conduits that would impact the entire industry's culture over time. Further, Provan, Fish, and Sydow (2007) reviewed empirical research investigating interorganizational networks from a sociocentric perspective and summarized that interorganizational network ties offer opportunities for organizations to learn and imitate from each other, such that these connected organizations and network as a whole are learning and evolving together over time, thereby contributing to both organization and network effectiveness.

IMPACTS OF SOCIOCENTRIC NETWORKS ON CULTURE AT A MICRO LEVEL

There is actually a lack of research that directly investigates the impacts of social networks on an individual's acculturation process from a sociocentric perspective. Nevertheless, evidence exists that links the properties of a particular network system to how individuals learn and internalize collective values and identities. For example, scholars have suggested that societies differ from each other in terms of people's general preferences to establish connections with each other (Bhugra, 2004; Bhugra & Becker, 2005). Specifically, in collective societies (also known as sociocentric societies), individuals tend to establish strong ties with each other, which can further enhance the endorsement of collectivistic values and the salience of collective identity (Bhugra, 2004; Bhugra & Becker, 2005). In contrast, in individualistic societies (also known as egocentric societies), individuals prefer to establish weak and loose ties with each other, which can reinforce individualistic values and personal identity (Bhugra, 2004; Bhugra & Becker, 2005). Therefore, one potential impact of a sociocentric network on culture could manifest through the acculturation process. That is, general features of the whole network system in a given community (e.g., density and the multiplexity of social networks, as well as the general strength of social ties among members) could play an important role in shaping how a newcomer of the community communicates and interacts with other members in the community. As communication and interaction are essential in impacting the assimilation, integration, rejection, or deculturation process for the newcomer (Bhugra & Ayonrinder, 2004), general features of a given network system should be able to shape how an individual assimilates into an unfamiliar culture.

Further, people embedded in different forms of sociocentric networks are usually more familiar with and used to their own particular ways of interacting with each other. Thus, when relocating to another egocentric network to live or to work, people may encounter difficulties regarding acculturation, as they were not able to interact with other actors that share similar cultural and social characteristics with them. For instance, prior literature suggested that individuals may feel even more isolated and alienated when relocating from a collective society to an individualistic society (Bhugra, 2004), which may further lead to a lower level of identity and a lower sense of belonging toward the embedded environment (Bhugra & Becker, 2005; Ralph & Staeheli, 2011).

IMPACTS OF EGOCENTRIC NETWORKS ON CULTURE AT A MACRO OR MESO LEVEL

People differ in their ability to influence each other in social networks (Lehman et al., 2004), and such interpersonal difference can be partly explained by the positions that different actors hold in their social networks. As such, an individual who occupies a critical position in the social network would have greater opportunity to impact the development of the overarching beliefs and value in the network system. For example, literature on organizational culture showed that founders and top executive leaders (i.e., those who usually hold critical positions in the hierarchical structure) greatly impact the creation and development of organizational cultures (Rowlinson & Procter, 1999; Schein, 2010; Tsui et al., 2006). In addition to hierarchical status in the social network, individuals' network proximity and centrality were also shown to greatly impact their power of eliciting social influence on other connected actors in the network (Ibarra & Andrews, 1993; Venkataramani et al., 2016). In particular, network proximity reflects the structural opportunities or constraints that impact the extent to which individuals can interact with each other (i.e., being close to one another in the network; Brass et al., 2004; Ibarra & Andrews, 1993), whereas network centrality reflects the importance or power of the individual to interact in the network (i.e., being well connected or important in the network; see Borgatti, 2005; Ibarra & Andrews, 1993). In Ibarra and Andrews's research (1993), they found that friendship network proximity was significantly related to employees' perception of interdepartmental conflict, whereas advice network centrality was shown to be a stronger predictor of employees' perceptions of organizational conditions from different perspectives (including encouragement of risk taking, information access, individual acceptance, job autonomy, and interdepartmental conflicts). Similarly, examining the role of one's structural position within their social network in relation to the social influence processes, Venkataramani and her colleagues (2016) investigated the impact of employee workflow centrality on employee voice. This study showed that employees with a central position in the formal task network of project team were more likely to voice ideas and suggestions (Venkataramani et al., 2016). Further, they also found that the positive relationship between workflow centrality and voice was strengthened if the team leader held a central position in the team's friendship network and was weakened if the team leader or the focal employee held a central position in the team's avoidance network (Venkataramani et al., 2016).

Further, an individual's position in the social network can also impact the extent to which they are able to access diverse information, which would in turn, impact the network system as a whole (Mische, 2011). Such arguments were mainly derived from structural hole theory in social network analysis, which suggests that those brokerage positions between clusters offer diverse information for the network as a whole to evolve (Gargiulo & Benassi, 2000). For instance, conceptualized as "the act of facilitating interactions between actors across cultural boundaries" (Jang, 2017, p. 994), cultural brokerage in multicultural teams was found to enhance team creativity by both integrating and eliciting knowledge from different cultures. Therefore, actors who occupy brokerage positions would have greater opportunities to access to "fresh ideas" from different clusters, thereby bringing new information and resources to shape network-level properties such as creativity performance (e.g., Burt, 2004; Burt et al., 2013; Lingo & O'Mahony, 2010). It is notable that in addition to the focal actor's position in the network, the composition of their network (e.g., having network members with diverse cultural backgrounds) also shapes the extent to which the actor can access to diverse ideas. For example, analyzing the social network data collected from 210 college students and 72 media professionals in two separate samples, respectively, Chua's recent research (2018) reveals that the cultural diversity of one's social network was positive related to the likelihood of receiving culture-related novel ideas, which, in turn, had a positive impact on creativity on tasks.

Moreover, taking an egocentric perspective to look at interorganizational networks, prior literature also suggests that an organization's position in the interorganizational network would impact its systemic power by shaping the extent to which the focal organization has the privilege to access valuable information in the network (Schmidt & Keil, 2013; Zaheer & Bell, 2005). Therefore, an organization's position in its network can also influence its power to govern or to manage other network connected organizations (Provan et al., 2007), which could subsequently impact the shared understanding of values in the whole network system (Bazzoli et al., 1998).

IMPACTS OF EGOCENTRIC NETWORKS ON ACCULTURATION PROCESS AT A MICRO LEVEL

At a micro level, the social network was shown to play a critical role in shaping expatriates' and immigrants' acculturation process, especially in terms of reducing their short-term stress associated with resettlement. For example, when relocated to another country to work or live, social networks can offer informal, yet critical, resources in immigrants' job search process in the labor market and thus facilitate their integration into the host society (Drever & Hoffmeister, 2008; Sanders et al., 2002). Therefore, an actor's egocentric network often depicts the availability and richness of their social capital in a given environment, offering critical resources and supports for acculturation process.

Further, an immigrant's egocentric social network may not only help with the psychological adjustment and sociocultural adjustment process in an unfamiliar environment, but also impact their internal perceptions associated with cultural identity. For example, literature on immigration has long been investigating the development and effects of bicultural identity among immigrants across different cultural contexts (e.g., Benet-Martínez & Haritatos, 2005; Repke & Benet-Martínez, 2017, 2018, 2019). In particular, bicultural identity integration was conceptualized as "biculturals' subjective perception of how much their dual cultural identities intersect to overlap" (Benet-Martínez & Haritatos, 2005, p. 1019). Such bicultural identity integration was found to be particularly critical in the process of cultural frame switching (Benet-Martínez & Haritatos, 2005; Cheng et al., 2006). Over time, with the increasing social ties connected with local residents, an immigrant's secondary, host-culture identity would be gradually integrated into their primary ethnic identity (Mok et al., 2007), resulting in ultimate change in the focal immigrant's behavioral repertoire and their psychological and sociocultural adaptations to the new cultural environment (Berry, 2005).

Theoretical Principles and Practical Implications for Future Research

Theoretical Principles

Theoretical principles for future research on culture and social network are summarized in Table 18.1. The first theoretical principle that can be derived from our review and

Table 18.1 Theoretical principles for future research on culture and social network

Theoretical Principles
1. When studying relationship between culture and social networks, the levels of analysis need to be clearly specified.
2. When studying relationship between culture and social networks, the corresponding dynamic features need to be clearly specified.
3. Culture's impact on social networks can be decomposed into culture at the macro/meso level and at the micro level in impacting various network properties.
4. Social networks' impact on culture can be understood from both a sociocentric and egocentric perspective.
5. Higher levels of culture and social networks should be considered important contexts for the relationship between culture and social networks at lower levels.

proposed theoretical framework is that when studying relationships between culture and social networks, the levels of analysis need to be clearly specified. Specifically, both culture and social networks are functioning as multilevel systems that incorporate various constructs and complex social phenomena existing at different levels. As such, clearly specifying functional relationships among constructs at different levels allows scholars to precisely conceptualize target constructs and hypothesized relations, thereby delineating "a systematic framework for mapping the transformation across levels" (Chan, 1998, p. 234) and broadening our understanding of both topics.

Second, when studying the relationship between culture and social networks, the corresponding dynamic features need to be clearly specified. In particular, both culture and social networks are continuously developing and evolving over time. As such, it is of great importance to understand the time course of the interplay between culture and social networks. Longitudinal study design and computation modeling would show greater advantages in understanding the dynamics of elements in both culture and social network systems and their evolving processes.

Third, culture's impact on social networks can be decomposed into culture at the macro/meso level and at the micro level in impacting various network properties. Specifically, culture at a macro or meso level would shape social network structures and the content of social ties by establishing collective tastes, values, or expectations to guide actors' beliefs and actions in their interactions. Culture at a micro level tends to drive people's connection-building with each other through selection preference based on homogeneity. Thus, motivated by different research questions, scholars can adopt different theoretical lenses to look at the multifaceted effects of culture on social networks.

Fourth, the impact of social networks on culture can be understood from both a sociocentric and ego-centric perspective. In particular, sociocentric and egocentric perspectives in social network analysis, while interrelated, focus on different research questions. Taking a sociocentric approach to investigate the role of networks as a whole in impacting culture highlights the dynamic social impact process and social networks as conduits and incubators for the development of culture. Taking an egocentric perspective emphasizes the focal actor's social influence on other actors in the network and the potential cultural resources that the focal actor can access in their embedded environment. Therefore, the theoretical mechanisms and analytic tools that match both perspectives need to be integrated to address complex and multifaceted research questions associated with cultural system.

Fifth, higher levels of culture and social networks should be considered as important contexts for the relationship between culture and social networks at lower levels. For instance, the interplay between cultural identification and ego network can be impacted by the overarching cultural contexts or sociocentric network characteristics. The literature on culture and social networks can be further extended by examining these cross-level contextual effects.

Table 18.2 Practical implications for organizations and individuals that are facing cross-cultural challenges

Practical Implications
1. In considering the impacts of macro-level culture on interpersonal interaction preferences, organizations may need to pay more attention to the design of organizational structure when relocated or expanded to a different cultural context.
2. When assigning employees to other countries or different cultural contexts to work (assigning expatriates) or recruiting employees from other places to work for the organizations (recruiting migrant workers), organizations should leverage understanding about the social network features of such employees and implement feasible practices to accommodate their needs during the acculturation process.
3. Organizations may need to pay attention to both formal and informal networks among employees in order to facilitate a favorable meso-level culture or climate.
4. Individuals need to respect and comply with local culture preferences or moral values when going through the acculturation process and establishing personal social networks in the host society.
5. Leveraging the resources embedded in social networks in the host society should be particularly helpful for migrant workers, expatriates, and immigrants in their integration and adjustment process when relocated to another cultural context to live or to work.

Practical Implications

Our review also offers several practical implications for organizations and individuals that are facing cross-cultural challenges, and we summarize them in Table 18.2. First, considering the impacts of macro-level culture on interpersonal interaction preferences, organizations may need to pay more attention to the design of organizational structure when relocated or expanded to a different cultural context. Conceptualized as "the relatively stable and formal network of vertical and horizontal interconnections among jobs that constitute the organization" (Noe et al., 2016, p. 147), organization structure would largely impact the patterns regarding how employees interact with each other. As people in different cultural contexts tend to have different preferences when interacting with each other, a careful design of organizational structure should be able to motivate employees with different cultural backgrounds to collaborate with each other, thereby facilitating more favorable cross-cultural management outcomes.

Second, the critical roles of social networks in facilitating acculturation and social integration process offer implications for organizations in the field of expatriate and migrant worker management. That is, when assigning employees to other countries or different cultural contexts to work (assigning expatriates) or when recruiting employees from other places to work for the organizations (recruiting migrant workers), organizations should leverage understanding about the social network features of such employees and implement feasible practices (e.g., offering family-visiting holidays for expatriates or migrant workers, holding offsite events or team-building exercises, launching appropriate cross-cultural training programs, providing support in both work and nonwork domains) to accommodate their needs during the acculturation process (Cross et al., 2002; Li et al., 2019; Littrell & Salas, 2005; Qin et al., 2014; Takeuchi et al., 2005, 2009).

Third, given that social networks, whether formal or informal, are essential in the development of shared beliefs, organizations may need to focus on both formal and informal networks among employees in order to facilitate favorable meso-level culture or climate. For example, as "the actions and behaviors of organizational actors are created at the interstices of the formal and informal networks" (Soda & Zaheer, 2012, p. 767), organizations or managers hoping to create favorable shared values among employees should try to carve out assignments and work-flow processes that facilitate communication and cooperation via both formal and informal conduits in organizations (Cross et al., 2002).

Fourth, as individual attitudes and behaviors are expected to fit into cultural expectations, it is of great importance for individuals to respect and comply with local cultural preferences or moral values when going through the acculturation process and establish personal social networks in the host society. Therefore, before relocating to another cultural context to work, attending expatriate training and development programs (e.g., global mindset training) could help prepare expatriates or migrant workers for the challenges they may experience (Mendenhall & Stahl, 2000).

Fifth, given that the personal social network plays a critical role in the integration and adjustment process when one relocates to another cultural context to live or to work, leveraging the resources embedded in social networks in the host society should be particularly helpful for migrant workers, expatriates, and immigrants. As such, when relocating to a new environment to work or to live, it could be helpful for individuals to build up and expand their personal social networks in the new society, thereby assisting the focal individual to deal with the various challenges they may experience during the acculturation and adjustment process.

Future Research Questions and Directions

The theoretical framework presented in this chapter offers a springboard for future research to further advance both the culture and social network literature. Specifically, based on our overarching theoretical framework and review of previous literature, the impacts of sociocentric networks on an individual's acculturation process could pose a blind spot. Addressing this omission is critical, as social network properties at a relatively macro level may profoundly impact people's cultural identification over time, and such change in one's cultural identification lies at the core of the acculturation process. Therefore, broadening our understanding of the impacts of the whole network properties on the acculturation process would not only extend both the culture and social network literature, but also offer valuable and concrete practical implications for an organization's human resource management policies targeting expatriates and migrant workers.

As culture and social network shape each other at multiple levels and coevolve over time, we encourage future researchers to build on our theoretical framework and further empirically investigate the interplay between culture and social networks. For example, starting with the role of culture at a relatively macro level, it would be valuable to examine how specific values and norms may impact the specific features of egocentric and sociocentric networks (e.g., density, multiplexity, structural holes, centrality) and how they, in turn, reinforce these cultural values and norms. A more comprehensive investigation depicting the multilevel and dynamic-evolving nature of both culture and social network can further advance our understanding of the interplay between these two phenomena.

In addition to the mutual impacts of culture and social network on each other, future research can build on our theoretical model and examine the joint effects of different features of culture (e.g., cultural tightness–looseness, Gelfand et al., 2011; vertical and horizontal individualism–collectivism, Triandis & Gelfand, 1998) and social network properties on people's daily life. For example, in their recent research conducted in the United States with 13,789 Facebook users, Liu et al. (2018) found that individuals with denser networks were more likely to express positive emotions in culturally tight states, as compared to individuals in culturally loose states. Additionally, the research reported by Ma et al. (2011) can also serve as an example of investigating how the macro-cultural context and social network jointly impact peoples' work and life in a given cultural environment.

We also encourage future researchers to investigate the role of various organizational practices in impacting employees' social network formation and development, as well as its impacts on culture at different levels and vice versa. In this way, they can offer more concerted practical implications for human resource development and management practices in organizations. For example, as also suggested in the career management and vocational psychology literature (e.g., Bonsdorff et al., 2018; Jung & Takeuchi, 2018; Wang et al., 2011; Wang & Wanberg, 2017), a more "balanced" (Baruch & Vardi, 2016) and "interdependent" (Tams & Arthur, 2010) view to integrate organizational-based resources and individual-specific needs/preferences in expatriate management would greatly advance our knowledge in the field. For example, it would be both theoretically and practically meaningful to further examine how organizations can refine and improve their cross-cultural training programs to accommodate the fact that expatriates may have different network preferences and needs during their acculturation and adjustment process (Osman-Gani & Rockstuhl, 2008; Takeuchi, Li, & Wang, 2019).

References

Abrahamson, E., & Fombrun, C. J. (1992). Forging the iron cage: Interorganizational networks and the production of macro-culture. *Journal of Management Studies, 29*(2), 175–194.

Alvesson, M., & Sveningsson, S. (2015). *Changing organizational culture: Cultural change work in progress.* New York: Routledge.

An, W. (2011). Models and methods to identify peer effects. In J. Scott & P. J. Carrington (Eds.), *The SAGE handbook of social network analysis* (pp. 515–532). Thousand Oaks, CA SAGE.

Baruch, Y., & Vardi, Y. (2016). A fresh look at the dark side of contemporary careers: Toward a realistic discourse. *British Journal of Management, 27*(2), 355–372.

Bazzoli, G. J., Harmata, R., & Chan, C. (1998). Community-based trauma systems in the United States: an examination of structural development. *Social Science and Medicine, 46*(9), 1137–1149.

Benet-Martínez, V., & Haritatos, J. (2005). Bicultural identity integration (BII): Components and psychosocial antecedents. *Journal of Personality, 73*(4), 1015–1050.

Berry, J. W. (1980). Acculturation as varieties of adaptation. In A. Padilla (Ed.), *Acculturation: Theory, models and some new findings* (pp. 9–26). Boulder, CO: Westview Press.

Berry, J. (1995). Psychology of acculturation. In N. R. Goldberger & J. B. Veroff (Eds.), *The culture and psychology reader* (pp. 457–488). New York: New York University Press.

Berry, J. W. (1997). Immigration, acculturation, and adaptation. *Applied Psychology, 46*(1), 5–34.

Berry, J. W. (2005). Acculturation: Living successfully in two cultures. *International Journal of Intercultural Relations, 29*(6), 697–712.

Bhugra, D. (2004). Migration, distress and cultural identity. *British Medical Bulletin, 69*(1), 129–141.

Bhugra, D., & Ayonrinde, O. (2004). Depression in migrants and ethnic minorities. *Advances in Psychiatric Treatment, 10*(1), 13–17.

Bhugra, D., & Becker, M. A. (2005). Migration, cultural bereavement and cultural identity. *World Psychiatry, 4*(1), 18–24.

Borgatti, S. P., & Foster, P. C. (2003). The network paradigm in organizational research: A review and typology. *Journal of Management, 29*(6), 991–1013.

Borgatti, S. P. (2005). Centrality and network flow. *Social Networks, 27*(1), 55–71.

Borgatti, S. P., Mehra, A., Brass, D. J., & Labianca, G. (2009). Network analysis in the social sciences. *Science, 323*(5916), 892–895.

Brannen, M. Y., & Salk, J. E. (2000). Partnering across borders: Negotiating organizational culture in a German-Japanese joint venture. *Human Relations, 53*(4), 451–487.

Brass, D. J., Galaskiewicz, J., Greve, H. R., & Tsai, W. (2004). Taking stock of networks and organizations: A multilevel perspective. *Academy of Management Journal, 47*(6), 795–817.

Burke, C. S., Priest, H. A., Wooten, S. R., II, DiazGranados, D., & Salas, E. (2008). Understanding the cognitive processes in adaptive multicultural teams: A framework. In E. Salas, G. F. Goodwin, and C. S. Burke (Eds.), *Team effectiveness in complex organizations* (pp. 243–274). New York: Routledge.

Burt, R. S. (2004). Structural holes and good ideas. *American Journal of Sociology, 110*(2), 349–399.

Burt, R. S., Kilduff, M., & Tasselli, S. (2013). Social network analysis: Foundations and frontiers on advantage. *Annual Review of Psychology, 64*, 527–547.

Cameron, K. S., & Quinn, R. E. (2011). *Diagnosing and changing organizational culture: Based on the competing values framework.* Reading, MA: Addison-Wesley.

Carpenter, M. A., Li, M., & Jiang, H. (2012). Social network research in organizational contexts: A systematic review of methodological issues and choices. *Journal of Management, 38*(4), 1328–1361.

Chan, D. (1998). Functional relations among constructs in the same content domain at different levels of analysis: A typology of composition models. *Journal of Applied Psychology, 83*(2), 234–246.

Cheng, C.-Y., Lee, F., & Benet-Martínez, V. (2006). Assimilation and contrast effects in cultural frame switching: Bicultural identity integration and valence of cultural cues. *Journal of Cross-Cultural Psychology, 37*(6), 742–760.

Chua, R. Y. (2018). Innovating at cultural crossroads: How multicultural social networks promote idea flow and creativity. *Journal of Management, 44*(3), 1119–1146.

Chua, R. Y., Morris, M. W., & Ingram, P. (2009). Guanxi vs networking: Distinctive configurations of affect- and cognition-based trust in the networks of Chinese vs American managers. *Journal of International Business Studies, 40*(3), 490–508.

Choi, I., Dalal, R., Kim-Prieto, C., & Park, H. (2003). Culture and judgement of causal relevance. *Journal of Personality and Social Psychology, 84*(1), 46–59.

Contractor, N. S., Wasserman, S., & Faust, K. (2006). Testing multitheoretical, multilevel hypotheses about organizational networks: An analytic framework and empirical example. *Academy of Management Review, 31*(3), 681–703.

Cross, R., Nohria, N., & Parker, A. (2002). Six myths about informal networks-and how to overcome them. *MIT Sloan Management Review, 43*(3), 67–75.

Cullum, J., & Harton, H. C. (2007). Cultural evolution: Interpersonal influence, issue importance, and the development of shared attitudes in college residence halls. *Personality and Social Psychology Bulletin, 33*(10), 1327–1339.

Drever, A. I., & Hoffmeister, O. (2008). Immigrants and social networks in a job-scarce environment: The case of Germany. *International Migration Review, 42*(2), 425–448.

Eckenhofer, E. M., & Ershova, M. (2011). Organizational culture as the driver of dense intra-organizational networks. *Journal of Competitiveness, 3*(2), 28–42.

Erez, M., & Gati, E. (2004). A dynamic, multi-level model of culture: from the micro level of the individual to the macro level of a global culture. *Applied Psychology, 53*(4), 583–598.

Fischer, C. S. (1995). The subcultural theory of urbanism: A twentieth-year assessment. *American Journal of Sociology, 101*(3), 543–577.

Fischer, C. S., & Shavit, Y. (1995). National differences in network density: Israel and the United States. *Social Networks, 17*(2), 129–145.

Gargiulo, M., & Benassi, M. (2000). Trapped in your own net? Network cohesion, structural holes, and the adaptation of social capital. *Organization Science, 11*(2), 183–196.

Gelfand, M. J., Raver, J. L., Nishii, L., Leslie, L. M., Lun, J., Lim, B. C., Duan, L., Almaliach, A., Ang, S., Arnadottir, J., Aycan, Z., Boehnke, K., Boski, P., Cabecinhas, R., Chan, D., Chhokar, J., D'Amato, A., Ferrer, M., Fischlmayr, I. C., . . . & Yamaguchi, S. (2011). Differences between tight and loose cultures: A 33-nation study. *Science, 332*(6033), 1100–1104.

Gold, T., Gold, T. B., Guthrie, D., & Wank, D. (2002). *Social connections in China: Institutions, culture, and the changing nature of guanxi.* Cambridge: Cambridge University Press.

González-Romá, V., Peiró, J. M., & Tordera, N. (2002). An examination of the antecedents and moderator influences of climate strength. *Journal of Applied Psychology, 87*(3), 465–473.

Granovetter, M. S. (1973). The strength of weak ties. *American Journal of Sociology, 78*(6), 1360–1380.

Hannerz, U. (1992). *Cultural complexity: Studies in the social organization of meaning.* New York: Columbia University Press.

Hansen, M. T. (1999). The search-transfer problem: The role of weak ties in sharing knowledge across organization subunits. *Administrative Science Quarterly, 44*(1), 82–111.

Harrison, D. A., Price, K. H., Gavin, J. H., & Florey, A. T. (2002). Time, teams, and task performance: Changing effects of surface-and deep-level diversity on group functioning. *Academy of Management Journal, 45*(5), 1029–1045.

Hollenbeck, J. R., & Jamieson, B. B. (2015). Human capital, social capital, and social network analysis: Implications for strategic human resource management. *Academy of Management Perspectives, 29*(3), 370–385.

Höllinger, F., & Haller, M. (1990). Kinship and social networks in modern societies: A cross-cultural comparison among seven nations. *European Sociological Review, 6*(2), 103–124.

Ibarra, H., & Andrews, S. B. (1993). Power, social influence, and sense making: Effects of network centrality and proximity on employee perceptions. *Administrative Science Quarterly, 38*(2), 277–303.

Igarashi, T., Kashima, Y., Kashima, E. S., Farsides, T., Kim, U., Strack, F., . . . & Yuki, M. (2008). Culture, trust, and social networks. *Asian Journal of Social Psychology, 11*(1), 88–101.

Inglehart, R., & Baker, W. E. (2000). Modernization, cultural change, and the persistence of traditional values. *American Sociological Review, 65*(1), 19–51.

Jang, S. (2017). Cultural brokerage and creative performance in multicultural teams. *Organization Science, 28*(6), 993–1009.

Jung, Y., & Takeuchi, N. (2018). A lifespan perspective for understanding career self-management and satisfaction: The role of developmental human resource practices and organizational support. *Human Relations, 71*(1), 73–102.

Kilduff, M., & Brass, D. J. (2010). Organizational social network research: Core ideas and key debates. *Academy of Management Annals, 4*(1), 317–357.

Kossinets, G., & Watts, D. J. (2006). Empirical analysis of an evolving social network. *Science, 311*(5757), 88–90.

Krackhardt, D. 1992. The strength of strong ties: The importance of philos in organizations. In N. Nohria & R. G. Eccles (Eds.), *Networks and organizations: Structure* (pp. 216–239). Cambridge, MA: Harvard Business School Press.

Krackhardt, D., & Kilduff, M. (1990). Friendship patterns and culture: The control of organizational diversity. *American Anthropologist, 92*(1), 142–154.

Kraimer, M. L., Shaffer, M. A., Harrison, D. A., & Ren, H. (2012). No place like home? An identity strain perspective on repatriate turnover. *Academy of Management Journal, 55*(2), 399–420.

Latané, B. (1981). The psychology of social impact. *American Psychologist, 36*(4), 343–356.

Latané, B. (1996). Dynamic social impact: The creation of culture by communication. *Journal of Communication, 46*(4), 13–25.
Lehman, D. R., Chiu, C.-y., & Schaller, M. (2004). Psychology and culture. *Annual Review of Psychology, 55*, 689–714.
Li, G., Fang, Y., Song, Y., Chen, J., & Wang, M. (2019). Effects of family encouragement on migrant workers' return-to-hometown intention and turnover. *Career Development International, 25*(2), 165–185.
Lingo, E. L., & O'Mahony, S. (2010). Nexus work: Brokerage on creative projects. *Administrative Science Quarterly, 55*(1), 47–81.
Littrell, L. N., & Salas, E. (2005). A review of cross-cultural training: Best practices, guidelines, and research needs. *Human Resource Development Review, 4*(3), 305–334.
Liu, P., Chan, D., Qiu, L., Tov, W., & Tong, V. J. C. (2018). Effects of cultural tightness–looseness and social network density on expression of positive and negative emotions: A large-scale study of impression management by Facebook users. *Personality and Social Psychology Bulletin, 44*(11), 1567–1581.
Lizardo, O. (2006). How cultural tastes shape personal networks. *American Sociological Review, 71*(5), 778–807.
Luhmann, N. (1977). Differentiation of society. *Canadian Journal of Sociology, 2*(1), 29–53.
Ma, L., Krishnan, R., & Montgomery, A. L. (2015). Latent homophily or social influence? An empirical analysis of purchase within a social network. *Management Science, 61*(2), 454–473.
Ma, R., Huang, Y. C., & Shenkar, O. (2011). Social networks and opportunity recognition: A cultural comparison between Taiwan and the United States. *Strategic Management Journal, 32*(11), 1183–1205.
Mao, J., & Shen, Y. (2015). Cultural identity change in expatriates: A social network perspective. *Human Relations, 68*(10), 1533–1556.
Marin, A., & Wellman, B. (2011). Social network analysis: An introduction. In J. Scott & P. J. Carrington (Eds.), *The SAGE handbook of social network analysis* (pp. 11–25). Thousand Oaks, CA: SAGE.
McIntyre, A., Lyons, A., Clark, A., & Kashima, Y. (2004). The microgenesis of culture: Serial reproduction as an experimental simulation of cultural dynamics. In M. Schaller & C. S. Crandall (Eds.), *The Psychological Foundations of Culture* (pp. 227–258). Hillsdale, NJ: Lawrence Erlbaum.
McPherson, M., Smith-Lovin, L., & Cook, J. M. (2001). Birds of a feather: Homophily in social networks. *Annual Review of Sociology, 27*(1), 415–444.
Mendenhall, M. E., & Stahl, G. K. (2000). Expatriate training and development: Where do we go from here? *Human Resource Management, 39*(2-3), 251–265.
Meyerson, D., & Martin, J. (1987). Cultural change: An integration of three different views. *Journal of Management Studies, 24*(6), 623–647.
Mische, A. (2011). Relational sociology, culture, and agency. In J. Scott & P. J. Carrington (Eds.), *The SAGE handbook of social network analysis* (pp. 80–97). Thousand Oaks, CA: SAGE.
Mok, A., Morris, M. W., Benet-Martinez, V., & Karakitapoğlu-Aygün, Z. (2007). Embracing American culture: Structures of social identity and social networks among first-generation biculturals. *Journal of Cross-Cultural Psychology, 38*(5), 629–635.
Monge, P. R., & Eisenberg, E. M. 1987. Emergent communication networks. In F. M. Jablin, L. L. Putnam, K. H. Roberts, & L. W. Porter (Eds.), *Handbook of organizational communication: An interdisciplinary perspective* (pp. 304–342). Thousand Oaks, CA: SAGE.
Morris, M. W., Podolny, J., & Sullivan, B. N. (2008). Culture and coworker relations: Interpersonal patterns in American, Chinese, German, and Spanish divisions of a global retail bank. *Organization Science, 19*(4), 517–532.
Mortensen, N. (1999). Mapping system integration and social integration. In I. Gough & G. Olofsson (Eds.), *Capitalism and social cohesion* (pp. 13–37). London: Palgrave Macmillan.
Noe, R. A., Hollenbeck, J. R., Gerhart, B., & Wright, P. M. (2016). *Human resource management: Gaining a competitive advantage* (10th ed.). New York: McGraw-Hill Education.
Ostroff, C., Kinicki, A. J., & Muhammad, R. S. (2013). Organizational culture and climate. In N. W. Schmitt & S. Highhouse (Eds.), *Handbook of psychology* (2nd ed., Vol. 12*): Industrial and organizational psychology* (pp. 643–676). Hoboken, NJ: John Wiley.
Pachucki, M. A., & Breiger, R. L. (2010). Cultural holes: Beyond relationality in social networks and culture. *Annual Review of Sociology, 36*, 205–224.
Patterson, O. (2014). Making sense of culture. *Annual Review of Sociology, 40*, 1–30.
Provan, K. G., Fish, A., & Sydow, J. (2007). Interorganizational networks at the network level: A review of the empirical literature on whole networks. *Journal of Management, 33*(3), 479–516.

Oishi, S. (2010). The psychology of residential mobility: Implications for the self, social relationships, and well-being. *Perspectives on Psychological Science, 5*(1), 5–21.

Oishi, S., Kesebir, S., Miao, F. F., Talhelm, T., Endo, Y., Uchida, Y., Shibanai, Y., & Norasakkunkit, V. (2013). Residential mobility increases motivation to expand social network: But why?. *Journal of Experimental Social Psychology, 49*(2), 217–223.

Osman-Gani, A. M., & Rockstuhl, T. (2008). Antecedents and consequences of social network characteristics for expatriate adjustment and performance in overseas assignments: Implications for HRD. *Human Resource Development Review, 7*(1), 32–57.

Qin, X., Hom, P., Xu, M., & Ju, D. (2014). Applying the job demands–resources model to migrant workers: Exploring how and when geographical distance increases quit propensity. *Journal of Occupational and Organizational Psychology, 87*(2), 303–328.

Ralph, D., & Staeheli, L. A. (2011). Home and migration: Mobilities, belongings and identities. *Geography Compass, 5*(7), 517–530.

Repke, L., & Benet-Martínez, V. (2017). Conceptualizing the dynamics between bicultural identification and personal social networks. *Frontiers in Psychology, 8*(469), 1–19.

Repke, L., & Benet-Martínez, V. (2018). The (diverse) company you keep: Content and structure of immigrants' social networks as a window into intercultural relations in Catalonia. *Journal of Cross-Cultural Psychology, 49*(6), 924–944.

Repke, L., & Benet-Martínez, V. (2019). The interplay between the one and the others: Multiple cultural identifications and social networks. *Journal of Social Issues, 75*(2), 436–459.

Robins, G., Pattison, P., & Elliott, P. (2001). Network models for social influence processes. *Psychometrika, 66*(2), 161–189.

Rowlinson, M., & Procter, S. (1999). Organizational culture and business history. *Organization Studies, 20*(3), 369–396.

Ryder, A. G., Alden, L. E., & Paulhus, D. L. (2000). Is acculturation unidimensional or bidimensional? A head-to-head comparison in the prediction of personality, self-identity, and adjustment. *Journal of Personality and Social Psychology, 79*(1), 49–65.

Salk, J. E., & Brannen, M. Y. (2000). National culture, networks, and individual influence in a multinational management team. *Academy of Management Journal, 43*(2), 191–202.

Sanders, J., Nee, V., & Sernau, S. (2002). Asian immigrants' reliance on social ties in a multiethnic labor market. *Social Forces, 81*(1), 281–314.

Schein, E. H. (2010). *Organizational culture and leadership* (Vol. 2). Hoboken, NJ: John Wiley.

Schmidt, J., & Keil, T. (2013). What makes a resource valuable? Identifying the drivers of firm-idiosyncratic resource value. *Academy of Management Review, 38*(2), 206–228.

Schneider, B., Ehrhart, M. G., & Macey, W. H. (2013). Organizational climate and culture. *Annual Review of Psychology, 64*, 361–388.

Scott, J., & Carrington, P. J. (2011). *The SAGE handbook of social network analysis*. Thousand Oaks, CA: SAGE.

Selfhout, M., Burk, W., Branje, S., Denissen, J., Van Aken, M., & Meeus, W. (2010). Emerging late adolescent friendship networks and Big Five personality traits: A social network approach. *Journal of Personality, 78*(2), 509–538.

Shaffer, M. A., Kraimer, M. L., Chen, Y.-P., & Bolino, M. C. (2012). Choices, challenges, and career consequences of global work experiences: A review and future agenda. *Journal of Management, 38*(4), 1282–1327.

Shennan, S. (2000). Population, culture history, and the dynamics of culture change. *Current Anthropology, 41*(5), 811–835.

Shore, B. (1998). *Culture in mind: Cognition, culture, and the problem of meaning*. New York: Oxford University Press.

Silvester, J., Anderson, N. R., & Patterson, F. (1999). Organizational culture change: An inter-group attributional analysis. *Journal of Occupational and Organizational Psychology, 72*(1), 1–23.

Soda, G., & Zaheer, A. (2012). A network perspective on organizational architecture: Performance effects of the interplay of formal and informal organization. *Strategic Management Journal, 33*(6), 751–771.

Swidler, A. (1986). Culture in action: Symbols and strategies. *American Sociological Review, 51*(2), 273–286.

Takeuchi, R., Li, Y., & Wang, M. (2019). Expatriates' performance profiles: Examining the effects of work experiences on the longitudinal change patterns. *Journal of Management, 45*(2), 451–475.

Takeuchi, R., Wang, M., & Marinova, S. V. (2005). Antecedents and consequences of psychological workplace strain during expatriation: A cross-sectional and longitudinal investigation. *Personnel Psychology, 58*(4), 925–948.

Takeuchi, R., Wang, M., Marinova, S. V., & Yao, X. (2009). Role of domain-specific facets of perceived organizational support during expatriation and implications for performance. *Organization Science, 20*(3), 621–634.

Tams, S., & Arthur, M. B. (2010). New directions for boundaryless careers: Agency and interdependence in a changing world. *Journal of Organizational Behavior, 31*(5), 629–646.

Triandis, H. C., & Gelfand, M. J. (1998). Converging measurement of horizontal and vertical individualism and collectivism. *Journal of Personality and Social Psychology, 74*(1), 118–128.

Tsui, A. S., Zhang, Z.-X., Wang, H., Xin, K. R., & Wu, J. B. (2006). Unpacking the relationship between CEO leadership behavior and organizational culture. *The Leadership Quarterly, 17*(2), 113–137.

Van der Hulst, R. C. (2011). Terrorist networks: The threat of connectivity. In J. Scott & P. J. Carrington (Eds.), *The SAGE handbook of social network analysis* (pp. 256–270). Thousand Oaks, CA: SAGE.

Van der Meer, T., & Tolsma, J. (2014). Ethnic diversity and its effects on social cohesion. *Annual Review of Sociology, 40*(1), 459–478.

Venkataramani, V., Zhou, L., Wang, M., Liao, H., & Shi, J. (2016). Social networks and employee voice: The influence of team members' and team leaders' social network positions on employee voice. *Organizational Behavior and Human Decision Processes, 132*, 37–48.

Volpone, S. D., Marquardt, D. J., Casper, W. J., & Avery, D. R. (2018). Minimizing cross-cultural maladaptation: How minority status facilitates change in international acculturation. *Journal of Applied Psychology, 103*(3), 249–269.

von Bonsdorff, M. E., Zhou, L., Wang, M., Vanhala, S., von Bonsdorff, M. B., & Rantanen, T. (2018). Employee age and company performance: An integrated model of aging and human resource management practices. *Journal of Management, 44*(8), 3124–3150.

Wang, M., & Takeuchi, R. (2007). The role of goal orientation during expatriation: A cross-sectional and longitudinal investigation. *Journal of Applied Psychology, 92*(5), 1437–1445.

Wang, M., & Wanberg, C. R. (2017). 100 years of applied psychology research on individual careers: From career management to retirement. *Journal of Applied Psychology, 102*(3), 546–563.

Wang, M. O., Zhan, Y., McCune, E., & Truxillo, D. (2011). Understanding newcomers' adaptability and work-related outcomes: Testing the mediating roles of perceived p–e fit variables. *Personnel Psychology, 64*(1), 163–189.

Wasserman, S., & Faust, K. (1994). *Social network analysis: Methods and applications* (Vol. 8). Cambridge: Cambridge University Press.

Xiao, Z., & Tsui, A. S. (2007). When brokers may not work: The cultural contingency of social capital in Chinese high-tech firms. *Administrative Science Quarterly, 52*(1), 1–31.

Yammarino, F. J., & Dansereau, F. (2011a). Multi-level issues in evolutionary theory, organization science, and leadership. *The Leadership Quarterly, 22*(6), 1042–1057.

Yammarino, F. J., & Dansereau, F. (2011b). Multilevel issues in organizational culture and climate research. In N. M. Ashkanasy, C. P. M. Wilderom, & M. G. Peterson (Eds.), *The handbook of organizational culture and climate* (pp. 50–76). Thousand Oaks, CA: SAGE.

Zaheer, A., & Bell, G. G. (2005). Benefiting from network position: Firm capabilities, structural holes, and performance. *Strategic Management Journal, 26*(9), 809–825.

Zeng, Z., & Xie, Y. (2008). A preference-opportunity-choice framework with applications to intergroup friendship. *American Journal of Sociology, 114*(3), 615–648.

CHAPTER

19 National Culture and Strategic Management

William Q. Judge, Aiden Norouzi, *and* Matthew Farrell

Abstract

In this chapter, we review over a quarter century of scholarly organizational science literature that explores the influence of national social culture on strategic management processes and choices. While the literature discusses a wide array of cultural frameworks, we find that Hofstede's framework is by far the most popular one among strategy scholars. Notably, Kogut and Singh's (1988) cultural distance concept is the single most common construct used to examine the influence of culture on strategy. In our review of the strategic management literature, we examine the impact of national culture on strategic management processes and content. We find that the early literature treated culture primarily as an antecedent of strategy, but more recent literature more commonly positions it as a moderator of the relationship between an antecedent and strategy. We conclude our review by advancing five separate recommendations for strategy scholars and five recommendations for practitioners to consider.

Key Words: : national culture, strategic management, cultural frameworks, cultural distance, international strategy

Introduction

National social culture (hereafter referred to as simply "culture") is a societal factor that encompasses a set of beliefs, expected behaviors, and outcomes, which in turn influence organizational outcomes (Hofstede, 1980). The field of strategic management focuses predominantly on how organizations interact with their environment in order to enhance overall organizational effectiveness (Nag et al., 2007). Consequently, strategic management scholars have increasingly examined the role of national culture in the formation of strategic processes and choices in order to optimize organizational effectiveness. For example, Judge (2001), in his comparison of CEOs in the United States and Taiwan, found that CEO character is markedly influenced by the larger social culture in which they operate, despite the growth and homogenization of the global economy.

Like most social science disciplines, systematic examination of the role of culture in organizational processes and outcomes is a fairly recent development due to the expansion of the global economy (Gelfand et al., 2017). In the field's early days in the 1960s and

1970s, almost all systematic strategic management scholarship was focused on domestic organizations operating within a single culture. However, some pioneering scholars challenged the field to examine cross-national influences on strategy in the 1980s (e.g., Ronen & Shenkar, 1985).

With the rise of emerging economies and the decline of trade barriers, multinational firms and their strategies have become a major focus of strategic management research over the last 30 years (Kogut & Zander, 1993). Indeed, there is now a dedicated journal within the field devoted to cross-national strategic issues (*Global Strategy Journal*), and other well-established international business journals (e.g., *Journal of International Business Studies*, *Journal of World Business*) increasingly examine and publish strategic management scholarship. Of course, recent trends toward deglobalization may temporarily blunt the expansion of the global economy (e.g., Witt, 2019), but we frankly doubt that the need for cross-cultural understanding will ever abate in our globally connected world.

Despite the widely accepted notion that culture influences strategy-formation processes and content, we were able to find just one study that systematically reviewed the influence of national culture within the field of strategic management. That study, conducted by White et al., (2016), identified 10 subfields of study within international strategy. One of them—national culture—represented less than 6% of all international strategy studies. Unfortunately, that review was conducted over a relatively short period of time (2000–2013), and it did not attempt to unpack the specific relationship between culture and strategy. While there have been several prominent reviews of Hofstede's cultural framework (e.g., Beugelsdijk et al., 2017; Kirkman et al., 2006; Taras et al., 2010), no systematic review of the specific relationship between culture and strategy has been documented in this stream as well. Hence, this chapter seeks to fill that void in the literature.

Concepts and Terminology

Since this handbook focuses on the influence of culture on organizations and the early chapters of this book focus on that, we do not need to define national social culture or to describe and explain the wide variety of societal frameworks used to examine strategy formation and outcomes. In our review of the culture literature, we note that a wide variety of cultural frameworks were used, including (1) Hofstede (1980, 1991), (2) Schwartz (1992), and Project GLOBE (House et al., 2004).

The field of strategy is large and produces an impressive amount of literature each year. While the field has its origins in the need to enhance our cross-functional understanding of the organizational-environmental interface, this same cross-functional and multidisciplinary foundation has led to disagreement as to what exactly the boundaries of the field entail. The two foundational disciplines undergirding strategic management are economics and sociology, but these disciplines offer very different understandings and hence theories of the firm. Consequently, this relatively new field of study has an unusual disparity of conceptualizations of what constitutes the field.

In a rigorous and comprehensive study of the field, Nag et al. (2007, p. 944) concluded that "[t]he field of strategic management deals with the major intended and emergent initiatives taken by general managers on behalf of owners, involving utilization of resources, to enhance the performance of firms in their external environments."

Within the field, the literature is generally broken down into two subfields: (1) content studies dealing with the question—which strategy works best? and (2) process studies dealing with the question how do strategies form? Both subfields seek to better understand how general managers can enhance firm performance. Of course, some studies examine both process and content attributes in the same study, but most strategic management literature examines these two questions separately.

Consequently, the literature review that follows breaks down the cultural studies into two areas—culture's influence on *strategy content*, and on *strategy process*. Content studies look at particular strategies, such as a "low-cost/differentiation" approach (Porter, 1980), or a "diversified/undiversified" approach (Rumelt, 1984). Traditionally, these studies focus on the organization–environment interface, and they draw their insights from economics. In this study, we seek to understand how the external environment, in the form of culture, influences the selection or development of a particular firm strategy.

In contrast, process studies seek to understand how strategies are formed and the influence of this formation process on firm performance. Traditionally, these studies focus on the firm's boundaries, and their insights are drawn from the sociopsychological disciplines. In this study, we also seek to understand how the external environment, in the form of culture, influences the strategy-formation process and/or its subsequent influence on organizational outcomes.

Methodology

Population and Sample

We analyzed 2,560 studies that were either in press or already published from 1995 to 2020 in 31 distinct peer-reviewed strategic management, general management, or international business journals. In general, these journals have a relatively high-impact factor (Podsakoff et al., 2005) as well as a history of publishing national culture research (e.g., Kirkman et al., 2006; Rapp et al., 2010).

To assess the impact of national culture research on firm strategy, we searched the electronic databases ProQuest and ABI/Inform in order to conduct the review "systematically," following the recommendations outlined in Tranfield et al. (2003) and using these keywords: *national culture and social culture* combined with *firm strateg**. As such, we utilized a rather broad, comprehensive search strategy. In total, our search yielded 1,301 potential articles. After screening each article through careful review of the study abstracts in order to ensure relevance to both national culture and firm strategy, our final sample was 115 articles covering 131 empirical studies examining the relationship between culture and strategy. These articles and empirical relationships formed the basis of our review. Each article was then downloaded, and content was analyzed by multiple coders.

Research Results for Overall Sample

Because of the relatively large size of the overall sample and space limitations, we cannot include a detailed listing of each study in this chapter.[1] Instead, we chose to list a frequency analysis of the attributes of our overall sample. These analyses are presented in Tables 19.1 and 19.2.

Theory Building versus Testing

Our first interest was to determine if the studies took an inductive, theory-building approach or a deductive, theory-testing approach. Table 19.1 reveals that the vast majority (98.5%) of the published studies utilized a deductive, theory-testing approach in their research utilizing quantitative measures. As such, the literature is overwhelmingly deductive and quantitative in its theoretical approach.

Cultural Frameworks

In general, Table 19.1 also reveals that cross-cultural strategy research has relied primarily on Hofstede's multidimensional framework. Specifically, 77% of the studies utilized Hofstede's (1980) cultural dimensions. Of the remaining frameworks, 10% of the duties utilized GLOBE cultural dimensions (House et al., 2004), another 4% relied on Schwartz's (1992) cultural values framework, and 2% used Ronen and Shenkar's (1985) cultural clusters. Notably, 7% of the studies utilized some other cultural framework that was mostly unique to that particular study, often utilizing new survey items.

Theoretical Positioning

Our next task was to determine how culture was theoretically positioned within the study. In other words, we sought to understand if culture was positioned as an antecedent of strategy or a moderator of some antecedent and its relationship with strategy. Our review of the data in Table 19.1 showed that the vast majority of studies treated culture as a direct antecedent of strategy rather than an indirect moderator. Specifically, 84% of the studies in our review framed culture as an antecedent of strategy, while only 16% of the studies framed culture as a moderator. Notably, the examination of culture's moderating effects is a relatively recent trend in the literature.

Strategic Impact

We next sought to understand if these cultural studies primarily examined culture's influence on strategy content or strategy process. To make this determination, our research

---

[1] For readers interested in the full listing of the attributes of the articles, please contact the second author.

Table 19.1 Frequency analysis of attributes for all culture-strategy studies, 1995–2020 ($N = 131$)

Theory Testing versus Theory Building		
Framework	Frequency	Percentage
Theory testing, quantitative	129	98.5%
Theory building, qualitative	2	1.5%
Total	131	100%
Cultural Frameworks		
Framework	Frequency	Percentage
Hofstede	103	77%
GLOBE	13	10%
Schwartz	6	4%
Ronen & Shenkar	3	2%
Others	6	7%
Total	131	100%
Theoretical Positioning of Culture Construct		
Positioning	Frequency	Percentage
Antecedent	111	84%
Moderator	20	16%
Total	131	100%
Strategic Impact of Culture		
Strategy	Frequency	Percentage
Content	79	60%
Process	52	40%
Total	131	100%
Host Country Context		
Host Country	Frequency	Percentage
International	68	51%
USA	20	15%
China	18	14%
Others	25	20%
Total	131	100%
Cultural Measures		
Culture Type	Frequency	Percentage
Cultural Dimensions	56	43%
Cultural Distance	57	44%
Cultural Clusters	18	13%
Total	131	100%

Table 19.2 Frequency analysis of theories used for All culture-strategy studies, 1995–2020 (N = 131)

Theoretical Framework			
Theory	Frequency	Percentage	Seminal Citation
Agency theory	7	5%	Jensen & Meckling, 1976
Capital structure theory	2	1%	Modigliani & Miller, 1958
Dynamic capabilities perspective	3	2%	Teece, Pisano, & Shuen, 1997
Economic institutionalism theory	25	16%	North, 1990
Knowledge-based view	7	5%	Kogut & Zander, 1993
National character theory	2	1%	Clark, 1990
Ownership, location, internalization	3	2%	Dunning, 2009
Psychic distance theory	23	15%	Kogut & Singh, 1988
Resource-based view	5	3%	Wernerfelt, 1984
Real options theory	2	1%	Myers, 1977
Sociological institutionalism theory	24	15.5%	Scott, 1995
Structural contingency theory	2	1%	Schoonoven, 1981
Theory-building study	2	1%	Miles & Huberman, 1994
Transaction cost economics	22	14%	Coase, 1937
Uppsala model	6	4%	Johanson & Vahlne, 1977
No theoretical basis (blank)	10	6%	
Other theories only used once	9	6%	
Total	154	100%	

team read the article and categorized the operationalization as a strategy-content or strategy-process construct. With this approach, we found that 81 of the studies (~60%) examined culture's influence on strategy content, while only 50 of them (~40%) examined culture's influence on strategy processes. Notably, cross-cultural studies of strategy process are a relatively recent trend in the literature.

Host Country Context

In addition, we sought to better understand the host country context utilized by the authors of these cross-cultural studies. In some studies, multiple host countries are utilized. In these cases, we coded the article as "International." In other cross-cultural studies, a single host country is examined in terms of its relationship with other foreign cultures. When that was the case, researchers coded the context using the name of the host country.

Our data listed in Table 19.1 suggest that roughly half of the cross-cultural strategy studies (51%) were international. The second most common host country context was the United States, which constituted 15% of our studies. In a close third position, China was the host country context for 14% of the studies in our sample. Finally, 20% of the remaining studies were in other individual countries.

Cultural Measures

Further, we were curious to learn what type of cultural measures were utilized in the overall sample. As revealed in Table 19.1, cultural distance measures were the most common (44%), closely followed by individual cultural dimensions (43%). Cultural clusters were utilized in just 13% of the studies. Clearly, the literature has largely concentrated on cultural distance.

Theories Used

For the 131 studies that relied on a theoretical perspective to frame their study, we also categorized the literature in terms of the theory used. This listing is depicted in Table 19.2. As this table shows, a wide variety of theories were used, and no one study dominated this listing. Not surprisingly, institutional theory was the most popular theory used over the past 25 years. Specifically, 25 of our studies (16%) utilized the Economic Institutional Perspective, first described by North (1990), and 24 of our studies (15.5%) utilized the Sociological Institutional Perspective, first described by Scott (1995), to frame the study. The third most common theoretical framework utilized was Psychic Distance Theory (Kogut & Singh, 1988), which was used by 24 of the studies (15%). Finally, Transaction Cost Economics was the fourth most utilized framework, comprising 14% of the studies examined. As such, these four theoretical perspectives constituted over 60% of the studies.

The other studies drew from a wide range of other theories, drawing from the strategic management discipline (e.g., Real Options Theory, Resource Based View, Knowledge-Based View, and Dynamic Capabilities Perspective), as well as from the international business discipline (e.g., Ownership, Location, Internalization Theory, National Character Theory, and the Uppsala Model). Notably, 10 studies were published using no theoretical basis, and 9 studies were published using a single theory that has never been used a second time. Overall, the theoretical basis of the literature appears to be quite diverse.

To give the reader both a broad and a deep understanding for the literature, we included a selected listing of the articles examining the culture–strategy relationship over the past 26 years. We performed this selection by analyzing the citations for each article and then dividing the number of citations by the number of years that it could be cited so as not to bias our sample toward earlier articles that possessed a longer citation window. Remarkably, all of these studies have been cited more than 30 times per year since their publication, which is quite significant given the fact that many organizational science publications never get cited at all. In addition, we included most recent articles in these tables to show the current flow of studies in this field. The results are shown in Tables 19.3 and 19.4. Table 19.3 contains studies that focus on culture–strategy content, and Table 19.4 covers studies that focus on the culture–strategy process.

Table 19.3 Attributes of culture-strategy content studies, 1995–2020 (N = 37)

Article	Theoretical Basis	Framing		Culture					Host Context
		Framework	Positioning	PDI	IDV	MAS	UAI	Other	
Corporate Governance Strategy									
Griffin et al., 2017	Economic Institutional	Hofstede*	Antecedent	(–)	(+)	(–)	(–)		International
Corporate Social Responsibility Strategy									
Waldman et al., 2006	Sociological Institutionalism	GLOBE*	Antecedent	(–)				ICI (+)	International
Campbell et al., 2012	Sociological Institutionalism	Hofstede**	Antecedent					CD (-)	USA
Thanetsunthorn, 2014		Hofstede*	Antecedent	(O)	(–)	(–)	(+)		International
Young & Makhija, 2014	Sociological Institutional	GLOBE*	Antecedent					Benevolence (+); Egalitarianism (+)	USA
Kang et al., 2016	Sociological Institutional	Hofstede*	Antecedent		(–)	(–)	(+)		USA
Matthiesen & Salzmann, 2017	Sociological Institutional	GLOBE*	Moderator					Assertiveness (–); Humane Orient. (+); Institutional Collectivism (+)	International
Thanetsunthorn & Wuthisatian, 2018		Hofstede*	Antecedent	(–)	(–)	(–)	(+)	LTO (+);	International
Earning Discretion Choice Strategy									
Han et al., 2010	Sociological Institutional	Hofstede*	Antecedent		(+)		(–)		International
Entrepreneurial Strategy									
Thomas & Mueller, 2000	Psychic Distance	Hofstede**	Antecedent					CD (-)	International
Schlaegel et al., 2013		Hofstede*	Antecedent	(+)	(–)		(+)		International

(*continued*)

Table 19.3 Continued

Article	Theoretical Basis	Framing		Culture					Host Context
		Framework	Positioning	PDI	IDV	MAS	UAI	Other	
Entry Location Choice Strategy									
Quer et al. (2012)	Psychic Distance	Hofstede**	Antecedent					CD(+)	China
Entry Mode Strategy									
Barkema & Vermeulen, 1997	Economic Institutionalism	Hofstede*	Antecedent	(+)	(+)	(+)	(–)	LTO (-)	Netherlands
Hennart & Larimo, 1998	Transactions Cost	Hofstede**	Antecedent	(–)			(–)		USA, Japan, Finland
Brouthers & Brouthers, 2001	Transactions Cost	Hofstede*	Antecedent	(+)	(+)	(+)	(+)		International
Yiu & Makino, 2002	Psychic Distance	Hofstede**	Antecedent					CD (+)	Japan
Tihanyi et al., 2005	Psychic Distance	Hofstede**	Antecedent					CD(O)	International
Larimo & Arslan, 2013	Psychic Distance	Hofstede**	Antecedent					CD(O)	International
Dadzie & Owusu, 2015	Psychic Distance	Hofstede**	Antecedent					CD(+)	Ghana
Gollnhofer & Turkina, 2015	Psychic Distance	GLOBE**	Antecedent					CD(–)	France
Lo et al., 2016	Psychic Distance	Survey Data	Antecedent					CD(O)	Taiwan
Environmental Strategy									
Song et al., 2018	Stakeholder Theory	Hofstede*	Antecedent		(–)	(—)	(+)		USA
Financial Strategy									
La Rocca et al., 2019		Hofstede*	Moderator			(+)			International
Arantes et al, 2020		Hofstede*	Antecedent	(+)	(–)		(+)	LTO(-)	International
Kashefi-Pour et al., 2020		Hofstede* (GLOBE)	Moderator	(+)	(+)	(+)	(+)		International

Foreign Direct Investment Strategy									
Blomkvist & Drogendijk, 2013	Uppsala, Psychic Distance	Hofstede**	Antecedent					CD(-)	International
Siegel et al., 2013	Psychic Distance	Schwartz*	Antecedent					CD- Egalitarianism (–)	USA
Innovation Strategy									
Pesch & Bouncken, 2017	Psychic Distance	Survey Items	Antecedent					Perceived CD (+)	International
International Diversification Strategy									
Ketkar & Acs, 2013	Econ/Socio Institutional	Hofstede*	Antecedent		(O)	(–)	(–)		International
Yu et al., 2013	Sociological Institutional	Hofstede*	Antecedent					LTO(–)	International
Merger and Acquisition (M & A) Strategy									
Tihanyi et al., 2005	Psychic Distance	Hofstede**	Antecedent					CD (0)	International
Chakrabarti et al, 2009	Psychic Distance	Hofstede**	Antecedent					CD (+)	International
Rues & Lamont, 2009	Psychic Distance	Hofstede**	Antecedent					CD (+)	International
Operation Strategy									
Park & Paiva, 2018		Hofstede*	Antecedent	(O)	(+)		(O)	LTO(+)	International
Risk Management Strategy									
Ketkar & Acs, 2013	Econ/Socio Institutional	Hofstede*	Antecedent		(O)	(+)	(–)		International
Diez et al., 2018		Hofstede*	Antecedent	(+)	(+)	(+)	(–)	LTO (+)	International
An et al., 2020		Hofstede*	Antecedent		(+)				International

Notes:

* 'Culture' examined; ** 'Cultural Distance' (CD) examined; *** 'Cultural Cluster' (CC) examined

PDI – Hofstede's Power Distance Index UAI – Hofstede's Uncertainty Avoidance Index

IDV – Hofstede's Individualism Index LTO – Hofstede's Long-Term Orientation Index

MAS – Hofstede's Masculinity Index ICI – GLOBE's Institutional Collectivism Index

Table 19.4 Attributes of culture-strategy process studies, 1995–2020 (*N* = 22)

Article	Theoretical Basis	Framing		Culture					Host Context
		Framework	Positioning	PDI	IDV	MAS	UAI	Other	
Alliance Formation Process									
Choi & Contractor, 2016	Economic Institutionalism	Hofstede*	Antecedent	(-)				LTO (–)	USA
Corporate Control Process									
Puck et al., 2016	Psychic Distance	Hofstede**	Moderator					CD (+)	China
Corporate Governance Process									
Handley & Angst, 2015	Transactions Cost	Hofstede*	Moderator		(+)		(–)		USA
Feng et al., 2017	Econ/Socio Institutional	Hofstede*	Antecedent	(O)	(+)	(–)	(–)		International
Cao et al., 2018	Economic Institutional	Hofstede*	Moderator	(–)	(+)		(O)		International
Entry Mode Process									
Yao & Li, 2016	Psychic Distance	Hofstede**	Antecedent					CD (–)	China
Innovation Process									
Azar & Drogendijk, 2014	Psychic Distance	Hofstede**	Antecedent					CD (+)	International
Isomorphism Process									
Salomon & Wu, 2012	Psychic Distance	Hofstede**	Antecedent					CD (+)	USA
Knowledge Transfer Process									
Simonin, 1999	Knowledge Based View	Unique Survey Items	Antecedent					(+)	International
Jensen & Szulanski, 2004	Psychic Distance	Hofstede**	Antecedent					CD (–)	International
Sarala & Vaara, 2010	Psychic Distance	Globe**	Antecedent					CD (+)	Finland
M&A Strategy Decision-Making Process									
Nguyen & Belaounia, 2020	Psychic Distance	Hofstede**	Antecedent					CD (+)	France

Organizational Change Process									
Judge et al., 2015	Configuration Theory	Hofstede*	Antecedent				(–)		International
Le & Kroll, 2017	Psychic Distance	Hofstede**	Moderator					CD Intl Experience (+)	USA
Organizational Learning Process									
Skerlavaj et al., 2013	Organizational Learning	Hofstede*	Moderator	(+)	(–)	(–)	(–)		International
Organizational Trust Process									
Huff & Kelly, 2003	Sociological Institutional	Hofstede*	Antecedent		(+)				International
Pesche & Bouncken, 2017		Survey items	Antecedent						International
Thanetsunthorn & Wuthisatian, 2020		Hofstede*, Schwartz	Antecedent	(–)	(+)		(–)	LTO (+)	International
Social Ties and Identification Process									
Ellis, 2011	Psychic Distance	Hofstede**	Antecedent					CD (0)	China
Strategic Acquisition Process									
Dikova et al., 2010	Economic Institutionalism	GLOBE*	Antecedent	(–)					International
Strategic Leadership Behavior Process									
Elenkov et al., 2005	Sociological Institutional	Ronen & Shenkar***	Moderator					AGE (+)	International
Strategic Renewal Process									
Au et al., 2018	Dominant Logic	Hofstede*	Moderator	(+)			(–)		International

Notes:

* "Culture" examined; ** "Cultural Distance" (CD) examined; *** "Cultural Cluster" (CC) examined

PDI – Hofstede's Power Distance Index UAI – Hofstede's Uncertainty Avoidance Index

IDV – Hofstede's Individualism Index LTO – Hofstede's Long-Term Orientation Index

MAS – Hofstede's Masculinity Index ICI – GLOBE's Institutional Collectivism Index

AGE – Anglo, Germanic, and Eastern Slavic Index

Review of Culture–Strategy Studies

As discussed previously, the field of strategic management is often divided into content and process studies. Hence, our review follows this traditional division by examining first the strategy–content studies and then the strategy–process studies within our study period.

Culture–Strategy Content Studies

Culture–Entry Mode Strategy Studies. As can be seen from Table 19.3, the most common content issue examined in this subsample is the relationship between national culture and entry mode strategy used by firms to expand their international presence. Barkema and Vermeulen (1997) advanced this inquiry by examining how culture influences an entry mode strategy for firms outside of the Netherlands utilizing the economic institutionalism perspective. They found that the power distance, individualism, and masculinity scores for the home country were all positively related to the riskiness of the entry mode strategy chosen by the international firm. Furthermore, they found that the uncertainty avoidance and long-term orientation were both negatively related to the riskiness of the entry mode strategy.

Hennart and Larimo (1998) published the next study in this line of inquiry. Similar to Barkema and Vermeulen (1997), they sought to understand how culture influences entry mode strategy, but they utilized cultural distance measures based on just power distance and uncertainty avoidance, and they relied on different theoretical arguments drawn from the transaction cost and national character perspectives. They found that the greater the cultural distance, the less risky the entry mode strategy chosen by the multinational firm.

Next, Brouthers and Brouthers (2001) sought to explain the Cultural Distance Paradox. This paradox exists due to previous inconsistent findings whereby distance sometimes finds support for wholly-owned subsidiaries over all other entry strategies, while other studies find that distance suggests a preference for international joint ventures. When considering just cultural distance, joint ventures were found to be the preferred mode of entry. However, when they also considered the investment risk, wholly-owned ventures were the preferred mode of entry. Hence, they offered a resolution to the existing paradox by considering the level of investment risk within the context of foreign entry.

Yiu and Makino (2002) observed that previous research on the antecedents of entry mode choice had largely ignored the role of national institutions, instead emphasizing transaction cost explanations. Hence, their study attempted to blend both perspectives to explain choice of entry mode. They found support for the idea that, in addition to attempting to minimize transaction costs with their entry mode choices, firms will adapt to local norms by conforming to regulatory barriers and mimicking other entrants. Relevant to our study, the authors found that cultural distance interacts with regulative and normative institutions to influence entry mode strategy in the form of joint venture versus wholly-owned subsidiary choice. Specifically, greater cultural distance will tend to lead to the choice of a joint venture entry mode, particularly in the face of restrictive regulatory and normative institutions.

Tihanyi, Griffith, and Russell (2005) performed a meta-analysis on the effects of cultural distance on entry mode strategy. Based on a database of 67 scholarly studies, they found *no* systematic relationship between cultural distance and entry mode strategy. However, when they applied moderators, the effect of cultural distance became clearer. Specifically, they found a negative relationship between cultural distance and entry mode strategy when that relationship emanated from the United States but not from other countries. In addition, they found that a strong negative relationship between cultural distance and entry mode strategy when considered within a high-technology industry. Overall, this study greatly expanded our understanding of the role and influence of cultural distance on entry mode strategies, and it suggests that national culture is but one of several contextual factors.

More recently, Larimo and Arslan (2013) found that cultural distance had no systematic relationship to the wholly-owned subsidiary entry mode choice by Nordic firms investing in central and eastern European countries. Next, Dadzie and Owusu (2015) sought to understand how culture distance influences the greenfield investment entry mode decision by multinational firms in Ghana. They found that the greater the cultural distance, the more likely a greenfield investment was made. Gollnhofer and Turkina (2015) hypothesized and found that cultural distance would be negatively related to low-resource commitment entry strategies, such as international joint ventures by French retailers in other countries. And most recently, Lo et al. (2016) hypothesized that cultural distance would positively influence Taiwanese firms' entry mode decisions toward international joint ventures over wholly-owned subsidiaries. Similar to Larimo and Arslan (2013), they found no significant relationship. In sum, the cultural distance–entry mode inquiry continues to yield equivocal findings.

Culture-Mergers and Acquisitions (M&A) Strategy Studies. Within the international business literature, there is a line of inquiry seeking to understand what context is most favorable for international mergers and acquisitions. Tihanyi et al. (2005), in their meta-analysis, examined all previous empirical studies on this relationship. Similar to their entry mode findings, they discovered that there was no systematic linear relationship between national culture and international M&A decisions. However, they found a robust negative relationship between cultural distance and international diversification when the diversification effort took place after 1990 but not before that date.

Chakrabarti et al. (2009) next explored the relationship between cultural distance and international acquisition strategy performance. Specifically, they sought to find out whether cultural distance helps or hurts the long-term performance associated with international mergers and acquisitions. They found that while there is an announcement effect that is negative immediately after the merger announcement is made; the long-term performance of M&A is stronger for culturally distant firms.

Rounding out this M&A stream, Rues and Lamont (2009) explored cultural distance and its effects on international acquisition strategy. They argued that cultural distance had a "double-edged sword" influence on strategy—in some instances negative and in other instances positive. They found that cultural distance did indeed have a negative influence on short-term international acquisition performance but that its influence was positive with respect to mutual understanding and communication in the postacquisition integration process. Interestingly, they utilized GLOBE data for this study rather than the more traditional Hofstede data.

Culture-Corporate Social Responsibility Strategy Studies. A third area of interest within the culture-content literature was study of how national culture might influence CSR strategies by multinational firms. Specifically, Waldman et al. (2006) sought to understand how national culture might influence strategic leaders' views on corporate social responsibility (CSR) strategies. Specifically, they looked at three dimensions of culture: (1) institutional collectivism, (2) ingroup collectivism, and (3) power distance. As hypothesized, they found that institutional collectivism was positively associated with CSR strategies, while power distance was negatively associated with CSR strategies. Ingroup collectivism was found to be unrelated. Notably, this was the first top-cited organizational-level cultural study that broke from using Hofstedian dimensions and instead used GLOBE data.

Next, Campbell et al. (2012) sought to understand how the distance between home and host countries affects a foreign affiliate's CSR activities in a host country. They considered various attributes of distance, including Cultural, Administrative, Geographic, and Economic (i.e., CAGE) differences between home and host countries. Using Hofstede's (2001) cultural values and Kogut and Singh's (1988) cultural distance measure, they found that cultural distance was negatively associated with CSR activity by a foreign affiliate. In other words, the greater the cultural distance between home and host countries, the less likely the CSR strategy pursued by the foreign affiliate was similar to the home country strategy.

Thanetsunthorn (2014) sought to understand how national culture influences a firm's CSR activities. Using Hofstede data, she found that individualism and masculinity were negatively related to CSR activities, and uncertainty avoidance was positively associated with the extent of CSR. During that same year, Young and Makhija (2014) argued that the national institutional context in which national culture operates influences a firm's CSR activities. Using GLOBE data, they found that benevolence norms and egalitarian norms were positively related to the firm's CSR activities.

Kang et al. (2016) added to this stream by examining how culture influenced CSR activities within the global hospitality industry. Similar to Thanetsunthorn (2014), which also used Hofstede data, they found that individualism and masculinity norms were negatively associated with CSR activities, but uncertainty avoidance norms were positively associated with it. Matthiesen and Salzmann (2017) broke new ground by seeking to better understand the relationship between CSR activities and the cost of equity. They hypothesized that national culture moderates this relationship, and found that the GLOBE measures of assertiveness, human orientation, and institutional collectivism all influence the culture–cost of equity relationship. Finally, Thanetsunthorn and Wuthisatian (2018) basically replicated Thanetsunthorn's (2014) earlier work by examining just employee-related CSR, but they found that long-term orientation was also positively related. In sum, there is fairly strong empirical support for the relationship between culture and CSR, both as an antecedent and as a moderator.

Culture-Financial Strategy Studies. La Rocca et al. (2019) hypothesized and found that the masculinity norms within a society will influence the use of short-term debt by female managers. They found that female managers were more likely to utilize short-term debt to preserve financial flexibility in high-masculinity cultures. Next, Arantes et al. (2020) found that power distance and uncertainty avoidance were positively related to earnings management practices, and individualism and long-term orientation were negatively related. Finally, Kashefi-Pour et al. (2020) examined the well-established positive relationship between cash flow and its level of capital expenditures in a cross-national context. They found that power distance, individualism, masculinity, and uncertainty avoidance all positively moderate this already positive relationship. In sum, culture appears to clearly influence financial strategies within firms.

Culture-Risk Management Strategy Studies. Diez-Esteban et al. (2013) sought to understand how cultural norms influence corporate risk taking. They found that power distance, individualism, masculinity, and long-term orientation norms were all positively related to corporate risk taking; while uncertainty avoidance norms were negatively related. Reinforcing these findings, An et al. (2020) found that individualism norms were positively related to corporate risk measures. In sum, culture has been shown to influence corporate risk-taking.

Culture-Foreign Diversification Strategy Studies. Ketkar and Acs (2013) hypothesized that culture would influence the degree to which small firms internationalize their operations. They found that masculinity norms were positively related and uncertainty avoidance norms were negatively related to internationalization. Notably, they utilized hierarchical linear modeling to explore these nested relationships. In that same year, Yu et al. (2013) explored the moderating influence of cultural distance on the competitive intensity–alliance formation activity within the global automobile industry. They did not find any systematic relationship. In sum, cultural norms were found to have a direct influence on foreign diversification but no moderating influence.

Culture-Foreign Direct Investment Strategy Studies. Blomkvist and Drogendijk (2013) argued that cultural distance should negatively influence outward foreign direct investments by Chinese firms. They found empirical support for this hypothesis. Siegel et al. (2013) reported that cultural distance in egalitarianism would negatively influence foreign direct investment. In sum, cultural distance appears to have a rather robust influence on foreign direct investment.

Culture-Corporate Governance Strategy Study. Griffin et al. (2017) argued that two cultural norms, individualism and uncertainty avoidance, have a major influence on corporate governance practices throughout the world. They found that individualism had a positive influence and uncertainty avoidance had a negative influence on Anglo-American corporate governance practices.

Culture-Entrepreneurial Orientation Strategy Studies. Thomas and Mueller (2000) sought to understand the relationship between cultural distance and the amount of entrepreneurial activity at a national level. Specifically, they surveyed students in nine nations to determine whether there was a systematically negative relationship between cultural distance and aggregate entrepreneurial orientation within an economy. Based on their research, cultural distance was negatively related to national risk propensity, innovativeness, and energy level, thereby indicating yet another negative influence of cultural distance, this time with respect to strategic entrepreneurism. Schlaegel et al. (2013) explored entrepreneurial intentions by students in many countries. They found that power distance and uncertainty avoidance norms were positively related to entrepreneurial intent, and individualism was negatively related.

Culture-Operations Strategy Study. Park and Paiva (2018) explored how cultural differences may influence operations strategies in manufacturing firms from multiple countries. Specifically, they sought to explore cultural influences on (1) leadership for cross-functional integration, (2) manufacturing strategy linkage with overall corporate strategy, and (3) sophistication of manufacturing strategy formulation. Using rather simplistic statistical analyses, they found that the first two issues are positively influenced by power distance and individualism norms. However, the third aspect was positively influenced by individualism and long-term orientation.

Culture-Environmental Strategy Study. Song et al. (2018) sought to understand how national culture influences firm-level environmental strategies. They found that individualism and masculinity norms were negatively associated with environmental proactivity and uncertainty avoidance was positively associated. In sum, culture appears to also influence firms' approaches to the natural environment.

Culture-Innovation Management Strategy Study. Pesch and Bouncken (2017) sought to explore the double-edged sword of cultural distance on product innovativeness and speed to market within international strategic alliances. They found that perceived cultural distance could be mitigated internally through organizational trust and higher levels of internal communication to yield favorable innovation outcomes.

Culture-Earnings Discretion Choice Strategy Study. Han et al. (2010) explored the influence of national culture on earnings management discretion. They posited that national culture influences the proclivity of strategic leaders to "manage" their earnings liberally or conservatively. Building on Gray's (1988) model of the inextricable influence of Hofstede's cultural values on accounting practices, they found that the extent of individualism within a national culture is positively associated with earnings management discretion and that uncertainty avoidance is negatively related to this phenomenon. Notably, when the formal institution of investor protections is considered, these relationships get stronger.

Culture-Entry Location Choice Strategy Study. Finally, Quer et al. (2012) sought to understand how political risk and cultural distance influenced the location choices of Chinese MNCs. They found that political risk was unrelated, but cultural distance (operationalized as percentage of ethnic Chinese in a foreign country) was negatively related with location choice for outward foreign direct investment decisions.

Culture-Strategy Process Studies

Culture-Corporate Governance Process Studies. Handley and Angst (2015) examined the impact of national culture on the relationship between governance and outsourcing relationships. In general, outsourcing relationships can be controlled through contracts or trusting relationships. This study revealed that contractual governance is more effective in individualistic cultures and relational governance is more effective in societies with relatively high uncertainty avoidance. Next, Feng et al. (2017) found that corporate governance mechanisms generally work in individualistic societies, but they do not work in masculine or high-uncertainty avoidance cultures. Finally, Cao et al. (2018) conducted a meta-analysis of culture's influence on the exchange hazards–interfirm governance relationship. Overall, it was found that individualism positively moderated this relationship whereas power distance negatively moderated it. In sum, it appears that cultural context has a major influence on the corporate governance process.

Culture-Organizational Change Process Studies. Judge et al. (2015) sought to understand how external and internal organizational conditions influence its capacity for change. They found that uncertainty avoidance was one of several critical conditions that influence an organization's capacity for change in a global sample of initial public offering firms. Next, Le and Kroll (2017) explored the relationship between strategic change and firm performance. They found that the breadth of the CEO's cultural experience positively moderated this relationship.

Culture-Organizational Trust Process Studies. Huff and Kelley (2003) redirected attention to a single dimension of culture—that of individualism within a society. They reasoned that the cultural norms surrounding individualism would greatly influence internal trust norms operating within an organization as well as external trust (i.e., trust in suppliers, customers, and other persons external to the focal organization). After collecting data from six highly collectivist Asian nations and comparing data from one highly individualist nation (i.e., the United States), they found that individualistic societies possessed a higher overall propensity to trust and higher overall external trust, but that collectivistic cultures possessed higher ingroup trust within organizations.

Pesch and Bouncken (2017) sought to understand how perceived cultural distance influenced interorganizational trust processes. They found that the greater the cultural distance between the joint venture and its home country, the greater effort is expended to build interorganizational trust, primarily through greater levels of communication. More recently, Thanetshunthorn and Wuthisatian (2020) argued that national culture norms influence national trust norms, which in turn, influence organizational trust. They found that power distance and uncertainty avoidance were negatively associated and individualism and long-term orientation were positively associated with national trust norms.

Culture-Corporate Control Process Study. Puck et al. (2016) hypothesized that the relationship between the ownership mode and corporate control for a firm's foreign subsidiaries is moderated by cultural distance. They found that cultural distance weakens this relationship for wholly-owned subsidiaries and strengthens it for international joint ventures. Hence, the corporate control process appears to depend on the cultural distance of the subsidiary in the host country from its home country.

Culture-Innovation Process Study. Azar and Drogendijk (2014) explored the relationship between cultural distance and innovation processes within firms. They found that the greater the cultural distance between home and host country, the more likely that innovation processes will flourish in the foreign subsidiary. In sum, cultural distance is shown to provide an opportunity for learning and innovation.

Culture-Entry Mode Process Study. Multinational firms often operate within multiple foreign markets, and these markets can all be a source of learning. Yao and Li (2016) hypothesized that the cultural distance between home and host firms will moderate the firms' multimarket contact with foreign entry decisions. As hypothesized, they found that cultural distance weakened this relationship.

Culture-Alliance Formation Process Study. Choi and Contractor (2016) broke new ground by examining the relationship between culture and alliance formation structures and processes. They found that power distance and long-term orientation were negatively associated with the degree to which the alliance was integrated with the home country firm.

Culture-Organizational Learning Process Study. Skerlavaj et al. (2013) hypothesized that national cultural norms will have a direct and moderating influence on organizational learning processes. They did not find a direct influence, but power distance had a positive moderating influence and individualism, masculinity, and uncertainty avoidance had negative moderating influences on the information acquisition–organizational learning process.

Culture-Strategic Renewal Process Study. Au, Han, and Chung (2018) sought to understand how culture influences the strategic renewal process in a cross-national study. They found that power distance had a positive moderating influence and uncertainty avoidance had a negative moderating influence on the family CEO-strategic renewal process relationship.

Culture-Strategic Decision Process Study. Nguyen and Beloiunia (2020) sought to understand how cultural distance influences the strategic decision process when making cross-border merger and acquisition decisions. They found that the greater the cultural distance between the home and host country, the higher the level of cash used in payment for the target firm.

Culture-Knowledge Transfer Process Studies. As shown by Table 19.4, one of the most common culture-process studies examined the knowledge transfer process within multinational firms. Simonin (1999), utilizing unique survey items, sought to understand how culture influenced the knowledge transfer process within multinational firms. Using the knowledge-based view, he found that cultural distance positively influences the ambiguity surrounding the process. In other words, interfirm knowledge transfer becomes more difficult as cultural distance increases. However, this effect tends to be attenuated if the firm has prior collaborative experience, if the firm is larger, and if the duration of the alliance is longer. As such, this study broke new ground by identifying cultural distance as a hurdle in multinational alliances.

Jensen and Szulanski (2004) significantly advanced this stream by considering the more nuanced features of the knowledge transfer process. Specifically, they considered the recipient's motivation (i.e., openness to new knowledge) and the "stickiness" of the knowledge being transferred (i.e., the difficulty of transferring the knowledge in question). Consistent with their hypothesis, cultural distance was negatively associated with the recipient's motivation. However, contrary to expectations, cultural distance decreased knowledge stickiness. The authors offered as a possible explanation that recipients of knowledge would be less likely to adapt that knowledge to local conditions if it were more difficult to understand.

Sarala and Vaara (2010) next sought to understand how national and organizational cultural differences influenced the knowledge transfer process after an international merger or acquisition. Using GLOBE cultural practice measures, they found that national cultural differences had a direct and indirect influence on the knowledge transfer process. Specifically, they found that the greater the differences, the greater the amount of knowledge transfer that occurred. This suggests that cultural differences provide a greater learning opportunity for transacting parties from different nations. Notably, national cultural differences had a stronger influence than organizational cultural differences did.

Culture-Leadership Behavior Process Study. Elenkov et al. (2005) broke new ground by seeking to understand how strategic leadership behaviors influenced the innovation process within firms. Specifically, they considered how three cultural clusters (i.e., Anglo, Germanic, and Slavic) moderated the leader behavior–innovation process. They found that by considering the cultural context in which leaders operated, there was a deeper understanding of the effects of strategic leadership behaviors and their innovation influence. They also found that the national social culture moderated the relationship between the tenure heterogeneity of the top management team and the influence these executives had on administrative innovations.

Culture-Strategic Acquisition Process Study. Dikova et al. (2010) sought to understand why firms abandon cross-border acquisitions. In general, they found that differences in the formal and informal institutions associated with the two economies inhibited deal completion but that prior organizational learning mitigated that negative influence. With respect to this review, they found that differences in uncertainty avoidance and power distance hindered deal completion. Notably, they utilized GLOBE data for this study, arguing that it was superior to Hofstede data.

Culture-Opportunity Recognition Process Study. Ellis (2011) conducted a very ambitious study of how the social ties of entrepreneurs influenced the opportunity recognition process in cross-border expansions. In addition, he considered how geographic, cultural, and linguistic differences might influence that process. In sum, he found that geographic and linguistic differences had a much greater effect on the process than cultural differences did.

Culture-Isomorphism Process Study. Finally, Salomon and Wu (2012) sought to understand why some foreign firms imitate local firms and why others deviate from local norms. They hypothesized that the more "distant" the foreign firms were, the more they would imitate local firms in order to overcome the heightened liability of foreignness. They found that culturally distant foreign banks did in fact imitate local firms more than foreign banks which were more culturally proximate.

Discussion and Implications

We have provided a review of the past 26 years of literature examining the influence of national culture on firm strategies. We conclude with a discussion of the theoretical and practical implications of this review for future research.

Theoretical Implications

Clearly, these studies employ a wide variety of measures of culture, but Hofstede remains the most popular measure. In recent years, GLOBE measures have started replacing Hofstede, particularly with respect to cultural distance studies. In our view, GLOBE measures are superior in terms of methodological and theoretical rigor; therefore, when future research is conducted, the researcher should strongly consider using GLOBE measures. Similarly, previous strategy research has preferred utilizing dimensional cultural measures (i.e., Hofstede, GLOBE, and Schwartz) rather than more holistic measures (i.e., Ronen & Shenkar). This is ironic since the field of strategic management is supposed to take a more holistic approach to its research. In sum, our first theoretical implication is that future research should utilize GLOBE practice measures when taking a dimensional approach and consider using more holistic measures, such as cultural tighten–looseness (e.g., Gelfand & associates, 2011), when appropriate to the research question.

A second theoretical implication is that since culture is a contextual variable, it is more theoretically appropriate to frame it as a moderator rather than as an antecedent of strategic behavior and outcomes. As demonstrated by this review, the bulk of the strategic management literature has framed culture as an antecedent. More recent literature has taken the moderation approach. We think that this moderation approach is more theoretically appropriate since it allows us to reexamine the findings of single-culture studies in a multicultural context.

A third theoretical implication is that the cultural distance between home and host country clearly plays a major role in strategically managing multinational firms. This statement is true for both strategy content and process studies. Indeed, more is known about cultural distance than any other cross-cultural aspect of strategic management.

Over 94% of the studies examined in this review utilized an overarching theoretical framework, and the primary theoretical framework used in cross-cultural strategic management studies is institutional theory. Specifically, economic institutionalism was used 17% of the time, and sociological institutionalism was utilized 15.5% of the time. Clearly, a wide variety of theories were employed. However, we think that there is a great opportunity for qualitative theory-building work to examine the relationship between culture and strategy due to the glaring void in the literature and the promise of inductive work.

Finally, cutting-edge research suggests that both transnational and subnational cultures exist between and within a nation's boundaries (Venaik & Midgley, 2015). Consequently, there is an opportunity for future researchers to determine when and how national boundaries matter to the field or whether other metrics might be more appropriate.

Practical Implications

First and foremost, strategic leaders should generally take concrete steps to reduce the strategic risk associated when the "psychic distance" is relatively large between home and host countries. For example, when all else is equal, the firm should venture into a culture that is more similar to the home country when possible (Johanson & Vahle, 1977). Once in a foreign market, hiring local managers and investing in cross-cultural training can help remove obstacles to smooth operation. Forming alliances with local firms can also be a great source of learning and knowledge transfer.

Of course, entering culturally different markets can and does yield strategic benefits, especially if it confers first-mover advantages. Consequently, strategic leaders can leverage skill in dealing with cultural distance as a strategic advantage. For example, Smale (2016: 21) argues that firms do not have to be "prisoners to culture" and suggests that firms can be more innovative when they pay more attention to culture than their competition. While a recent meta-analysis of national culture and innovation shows that culture has a rather strong influence on exploratory innovation (Mueller, Rosenbusch, & Bausch,

2013), strategic leaders can and do beat the odds by taking on acceptable risks to generate value. Hence, firms venturing into culturally different economies can create a competitive advantage; it just is a riskier proposition.

Given the fast pace of business in the twenty-first century, managers will often underestimate the time it takes to learn to operate within a new culture. In general, the greater the cultural distances involved, the greater the amount of time this will take. That is, firms should allow cross-cultural investments more time to yield net benefits given greater cultural distance. In selecting and evaluating general managers of multinational subsidiaries, firms should take into account the constraints on discretion that the local culture imposes (Crossland & Hambrick, 2011).

The leadership pipeline within a firm should give greater attention to cross-cultural training and experience. Expatriate assignments should be encouraged and rewarded, with special attention to mainstreaming the expat back into the home country after a foreign assignment. Efforts should be made to assign local managers to foreign subsidiaries as soon as possible. Moving to a "transnational solution" whereby managers operate with a "matrix of the mind" is to be encouraged and rewarded (Bartlett & Ghoshal, 1990). And generally speaking, no multinational firm in the twenty-first century should be led by any CEO who has not first operated successfully in a cross-national context first.

In this age of pressure for more gender and ethnic diversity, cultural diversity should also be sought within the top management team and the board of directors within the home country. This can only be achieved if cultural biases can be confronted within the organization, and creativity through diversity is celebrated. While most large firms are only diversified within countries that are relatively close to their home location, cultural diversity can assist in helping firms to become truly global as well as successfully address the challenges associated with the enormous complexity of a global enterprise. While this endeavor will not be easy, those firms that achieve this first will create a sustainable competitive advantage.

Since "wicked" problems (Rittel & Webber, 1973) are increasingly global in nature (i.e., climate change, mass migration, global pandemics, the prospect of nuclear war), cross-cultural understanding within multinational firms can be part of the solution to global challenges. This can come in the form of strategic philanthropy that targets the source of these problems, collaboration with the public sector to address comprehensive win/win solutions, sabbaticals for managers that promote cross-cultural understanding, and opposition to corrupt governments that are causing these problems. Both the theoretical and practical implications of this review are summarized in Table 19.5.

Conclusions

Like many other fields of study, the field of strategic management is awakening to the powerful role of context as scholars seek to understand how its primary constructs behave. Because the multinational firms are a relatively new phenomenon, at least relative to domestic firms, the influence of national social culture has proven to be a key construct in the international strategic management

Table 19.5 Summary implications of the culture-strategy review
Theoretical Implications
1. Future research should use GLOBE cultural dimensions which are more rigorous than Hofstede dimensions.
2. Culture should be used as a moderator of strategic behavior and outcomes.
3. Cultural distance between home and host countries plays a major role in managing multinational firms.
4. There is a growing need to publish more qualitative theory-building work to examine the relationship between culture and strategy.
5. New research needs to be done to determine when and how national boundaries matter to the field of strategy.
Practical Implications
1. Managers need to seek to reduce strategic risk when psychic distance between home and host countries is large.
2. Managers can also benefit from cultural distance as a strategic advantage.
3. Managers need to consider that the greater the cultural distance, the greater the amount of time it takes to operate properly in a new cultural environment.
4. Cross-cultural training and experience is a key to success for multinational firms.
5. Cultural diversity within the top management team and the board of directors empowers firms' globalization capabilities.

literature. Strategy consultants like to argue that "culture eats strategy for lunch," implying that the best formulated strategies do not amount to much if implementation issues are not given priority by strategic leaders and general managers. Of course, this cultural reference refers to organizational culture. Imagine just how complicated life is when managing across multiple national social cultures. We hope that this review contributes to a deeper understanding of the theories and insights associated with business in the twenty-first century.

Acknowledgments: Professor Robert Pidduck provided valuable feedback on an earlier draft, which improved our contribution.

References

* *Indicates article was part of the 26-year empirical review*

** *Indicates article was one of the top 20 most cited articles in the 26-year review*

*Abdi, M., & Aulakh, P. S. (2012). Do country-level institutional frameworks and interfirm governance arrangements substitute or complement in international business relationships? *Journal of International Business Studies*, *43*(5), 477–497.

*Alexander, E. A. D. (2012). The effects of legal, normative, and cultural-cognitive institutions on innovation in technology alliances. *Management International Review*, *52*(6), 791–815.

*Allred, B. B., & Swan, K. S. (2004). Global versus multidomestic: Culture's consequences on innovation. *Management International Review*, *44*(1), 81–105.

An, Z., Cao, Z., Chen, Z., & Li, D. (2020). Does individualistic culture impact operational risk.? *European Financial Management*, *26*, 808–838.

Arantes, P. P. M., Peixoto, F. M., & Carvalho, L. (2020). Cultural determinants of corporate governance: a multi-country study. *Revista Eletrônica de Negócios Internacionais* (Internext), *15*(2), 56–71.

Arrantes, P. P., M., Peixoto, F. M., Carvalho, F., & Malaquias, F. F. O. (2020). Culture determinants of corporate governance: A multi-country study. *Review of International Business, 15*(2), 56–71.

*Au, K., Stone, H., & Hsi-Mei, C. (2018). The impact of sociocultural context on strategic renewal. *Cross Cultural and Strategic Management, 25*(4), 604–627.

*Azar, G., & Drogendijk, R. (2014). Psychic distance, innovation, and firm performance. *Management International Review, 54*(5), 581–613.

*Baik, B., Cho, K., Choi, W., & Kang, J.-K. (2015). The role of institutional environments in cross-border mergers: a perspective from bidders' earnings management behavior. *Management International Review, 55*(5), 615–646.

**Barkema, H. G., & Vermeulen, F. (1997). What differences in the cultural backgrounds of partners are detrimental for international joint ventures? *Journal of International Business Studies, 28*(4), 845–864.

*Barr, P. S., & Glynn, M. A. (2004). Cultural variations in strategic issue interpretation: Relating uncertainty avoidance to controllability in discriminating threat and opportunity. *Strategic Management Journal, 25*(1), 59.

Bartlett, C. A., & Ghoshal, S. (1990). *Managing across borders: The transnational solution*. Cambridge, MA: Harvard Business Press.

*Berard, C., & Delerue, H. (2010). A cross–cultural analysis of intellectual asset protection in SMEs. *Journal of Small Business and Enterprise Development, 17*(2), 167–183.

Beugelsdijk, S., Kostova, T., & Roth, K. (2017). An overview of Hofstede-inspired country-level culture research in international business since 2006. *Journal of International Business Studies, 48*(1), 30–47.

*Bhardwaj, A., Dietz, J., & Beamish, P. W. (2007). Host country cultural influences on foreign direct investment. *Management International Review, 47*(1), 29–50.

*Blomkvist, K., & Drogendijk, R. (2013). The impact of psychic distance on Chinese outward foreign direct investments. *Management International Review, 53*(5), 659–686.

*Boubakri, N., Mansi, S. A., & Saffar, W. (2013). Political institutions, connectedness, and corporate risk-taking. *Journal of International Business Studies, 44*(3), 195–215.

*Brock, D. M., Shenkar, O., Shoham, A., & Siscovick, I. C. (2008). National culture and expatriate deployment. *Journal of International Business Studies, 39*(8), 1293–1309.

**Brouthers, K. D., & Brouthers, L. E. (2001). Explaining the national cultural distance paradox. *Journal of International Business Studies, 32*(1), 177–189.

*Calza F., Cannavale, C., & Tutore, I. (2016). The important effects of national culture on the environmental proactivity of firms. *Journal of Management Development*, 35(8), 1011–30.

**Campbell, J. T., Eden, L., & Miller, S. R. (2012). Multinationals and corporate social responsibility in host countries: Does distance matter? *Journal of International Business Studies, 43*(1), 84–106.

*Cao, Z., Li, Y., Jayaram, J., Liu, Y., & Lumineau, F. (2018). A meta-analysis of the exchange hazards–interfirm governance relationship: An informal institutions perspective. *Journal of International Business Studies, 49*(3), 303–323.

**Chakrabarti, R., Gupta-Mukherjee, S., & Jayaraman, N. (2009). Mars–Venus marriages: Culture and cross-border M&A. *Journal of International Business Studies, 40*(2), 216–236.

*Chari, M. D., & Chang, K. (2009). Determinants of the share of equity sought in cross-border acquisitions. *Journal of International Business Studies, 40*(8), 1277–1297.

*Choi, J., & Contractor, F. J. (2016). Choosing an appropriate alliance governance mode: The role of institutional, cultural and geographical distance in international research & development collaborations. *Journal of International Business Studies, 47*(2), 210–232.

*Chui, A. C. W., Lloyd, A. E., & Kwok, C. C. Y. (2002). The determination of capital structure: Is national culture a missing piece to the puzzle? *Journal of International Business Studies, 33*(1), 99–127.

Clark, T. (1990). International marketing and national character: A review and proposal for an integrative theory. *Journal of Marketing, 54*(4), 66–79.

Coase, R. H. (1937). The Nature of the Firm. *Económica, n.s.4*, 386–405.

*Couto, J. P. A., & Vieira, J. C. (2004). National culture and research and development activities. *Multinational Business Review, 12*(1), 19–35.

Crossland, C., Hambrick, D. C., 2011 Differences in managerial discretion across countries: How nation-level institutions affect the degree to which CEOs Matter. *Strategic Management Journal, 32*(8), 797–819.

*Cuypers, I. R., & Martin, X. (2010). What makes and what does not make a real option? A study of equity shares in international joint ventures. *Journal of International Business Studies, 41*(1), 47–69.

*Dadzie, S. A., & Owusu, R. A. (2015). Understanding establishment mode choice of foreign manufacturing firms in Ghana. *International Journal of Emerging Markets, 10*(4), 896–920.

*Daniel, S. J. P., Cieslewicz, J. K. A. P., & Pourjalali, H. P. (2012). The impact of national economic culture and country-level institutional environment on corporate governance practices. *Management International Review, 52*(3), 365–394.

*Delios, A., & Henisz, W. J. (2003). Policy uncertainty and the sequence of entry by Japanese firms, 1980–1998. *Journal of International Business Studies, 34*(3), 227.

*Delios, A., Xu, D., & Beamish, P. W. (2008). Within-country product diversification and foreign subsidiary performance. *Journal of International Business Studies, 39*(4), 706–724.

*Demirbag, M., Tatoglu, E., & Glaister, K. W. (2008). Factors affecting perceptions of the choice between acquisition and greenfield entry: The case of Western FDI in an Emerging Market. *Management International Review, 48*(1), 5–38.

*Diez – Esteban, J. M., Farinha, J. B., Garcia-Gomez, C. D. (2018). How does national culture affect corporate risk-taking? *Eurasia Business Review, 9*(1), 49–68.

**Dikova, D., Sahib, P. R., & Van Witteloostuijn, A. (2010). Cross-border acquisition abandonment and completion: The effect of institutional differences and organizational learning in the international business service industry, 1981–2001. *Journal of International Business Studies, 41*(2), 223–245.

*Dionisis, S., Katsikeas, C. S., & Schlegelmilch, B. B. (2002). Drivers of commitment and its impact on performance in cross-cultural buyers-seller relationships: The importer's perspective. *Journal of International Business Studies, 33*(4), 757–783.

Dunning, J. H. (2009). Location and the multinational enterprise: John Dunning's thoughts on receiving the *Journal of International Business Studies* 2008 Decade Award. *Journal of International Business Studies, 40*(1), 20–34.

**Elenkov, D. S., Judge, W., & Wright, P. (2005). Strategic leadership and executive innovation influence: an international multi-cluster comparative study. *Strategic Management Journal, 26*(7), 665–665+.

*Ellis, P. D. (2008). Does psychic distance moderate the market size-entry sequence relationship? *Journal of International Business Studies, 39*(3), 351–369.

**Ellis, P. D. (2011). Social ties and international entrepreneurship: Opportunities and constraints affecting firm internationalization. *Journal of International Business Studies, 42*(1), 99–127.

*Erramilli, M. K. (1996). Nationality and subsidiary ownership patterns in multinational corporations. *Journal of International Business Studies, 27*(2), 225.

*Erramilli, M. K., Agarwal, S., & Seong-Soo, K. (1997). Are firm-specific advantages location-specific too? *Journal of International Business Studies, 28*(4), 735–757.

*Fan, T., & Phan, P. (2007). International new ventures: Revisiting the influences behind the 'born-global' firm. *Journal of International Business Studies, 38*(7), 1113.

*Feng, M., Kang, T., & Nabar, S. (2017). National societal values and corporate governance. *International Journal of Emerging Markets, 12*(2), 183–198.

*Flores, R. G., & Aguilera, R. V. (2007). Globalization and location choice: an analysis of US multinational firms in 1980 and 2000. *Journal of International Business Studies, 38*(7), 1187.

*Gaur, A., S., Ma, H., & Ge, B. (2019). MNC strategy, knowledge transfer context, and knowledge flow in MNEs. *Journal of Knowledge Management, 23*(9), 1885–1900.

Gelfand, M. J., Aycan, Z., Erez, M., & Leung, K. (2017). Cross-cultural industrial organizational psychology and organizational behavior: A hundred-year journey. *Journal of Applied Psychology, 102*(3), 514–534.

Gelfand, M. J., Raver, J., Nishi, L., et al. (2011). Differences between tight and loose cultures: A 33-nation study. *Science, 332*, 1100–1104.

*Gollnhofer, J. F., & Turkina, E. (2015). Cultural distance and entry modes: implications for global expansion strategy. *Cross Cultural Management, 22*(1), 21–41.

Gray, S. J. (1988). Towards a theory of cultural influence on the development of accounting systems internationally. *ABACUS*, 24, 1–15.

*Griffin, D., Guedhami, O., Kwok, C. C. Y., Li, K., & Shao, L. (2017). National culture: The missing country-level determinant of corporate governance. *Journal of International Business Studies, 48*(6), 740–762.

*Griffith, D. A., & Harvey, M. G. (2001). A resource perspective of global dynamic capabilities. *Journal of International Business Studies, 32*(3), 597–606.

*Griffith, D. A., Hu, M. Y., & Ryans, J. K., Jr. (2000). Process standardization across intra- and inter-cultural relationships. *Journal of International Business Studies, 31*(2), 303–323.

*Hackert, A. M., Krumwiede, D., Tokle, J., & Vokurka, R. J. (2012). Global corporate social practices and cultural dimensions. *Advanced Management Journal, 77*(4), 33–41.

*Hakanson, L., & Nobel, R. (2001). Organizational characteristics and reverse technology transfer. *Management International Review, 41*(4), 395–420.

*Hamilton, R. D., III, & Kashlak, R. J. (1999). National influences on multinational corporation control system selection. *Management International Review, 39*(2), 167–189.

**Han, S., Kang, T., Salter, S., & Yoo, Y. K. (2010). A cross-country study on the effects of national culture on earnings management. *Journal of International Business Studies, 41*(1), 123–141.

*Handley, S. M., & Angst, C. M. (2015). The impact of culture on the relationship between governance and opportunism in outsourcing relationships. *Strategic Management Journal, 36*(9), 1412.

*Hansen, M. T., & Løvås, B. (2004). How do multinational companies leverage technological competencies? Moving from single to interdependent explanations. *Strategic Management Journal, 25*(8/9), 801.

*Hashai, N. (2011). Sequencing the expansion of geographic scope and foreign operations by "born global" firms. *Journal of International Business Studies, 42*(8), 995–1015.

*Haxhi, I., & Van Ees, H. (2010). Explaining diversity in the worldwide diffusion of codes of good governance. *Journal of International Business Studies, 41*(4), 710–726.

**Hennart, J.-F., & Larimo, J. (1998). The impact of culture on the strategy of multinational enterprises: Does national origin affect ownership decisions? *Journal of International Business Studies, 29*(3), 515–538.

Hofstede, G. (1980). *Culture's consequences: National differences in thinking and organizing.* Beverly Hills, CA: SAGE.

Hofstede, G. (1991). Empirical models of cultural differences. In N. Bleichrodt & P. J. D. Drenth (Eds.), *Contemporary issues in cross-cultural psychology* (pp. 4–20). Lisse, the Netherlands: Swets & Zeitlinger.

Hofstede. G. (2001). *Cultures' consequences: Comparing values, behaviors, institutions across nations, 2nd edition.* Beverly Hills, CA: SAGE.

*Hofstede, G., Van Deusen, C. A., Mueller, C. B., & Charles, T. A. (2002). What goals do business leaders pursue? A study in fifteen countries. *Journal of International Business Studies, 33*(4), 785–803.

*Holtbrügge, D., & Berg, N. (2004). Knowledge transfer in multinational corporations: evidence from German firms. *Management International Review, 44*(3), 129–145.

House, R. J., Hanges, P. J., Javidan, M., Dorfman, P. W., & Gupta, V. (Eds.). (2004). *Culture, leadership, and organizations: The GLOBE study of 62 societies.* Thousand Oaks, CA: SAGE.

**Huff, L., & Kelley, L. (2003). Levels of organizational trust in individualist versus collectivist societies: A seven-nation study. *Organization Science, 14*(1), 81–90.

Jensen, M. C., & Meckling, W. H. (1976). Theory of the firm: Managerial behavior, agency costs and ownership structure. *Journal of Financial Economics, 3*(4), 305–360.

**Jensen, R., & Szulanski, G. (2004). Stickiness and the adaptation of organizational practices in cross-border knowledge transfers. *Journal of International Business Studies, 35*(6), 508–523.

Johanson, J., & Vahlne, E. J. (1977). The internationalization process of the firm: A model of knowledge development and increasing foreign market commitments. *Journal of International Business Studies,* 8: 23–32.

Jones, G. K., & Davis, H. J. (2000). National culture and innovation: Implications for locating global R&D operations. *Management International Review, 40*(1), 11–39.

Judge, W. Q. (2001). Is a leader's character culture-bound or culture-free? An empirical comparison of the character traits of American and Taiwanese CEOs. *Journal of Leadership Studies, 8*(2), 63–78.

*Judge, W. Q., Hu, H., Gabrielssen, J., Talaulicar, T., Witt, M., Zattoni, A., Lopéz-Iturriaga, F., Chen, J. J., Shukla, D., Quttainah, M., Adegbite, E., Rivas J. L., & Kibler, B. (2015). Configurations of capacity for change in entrepreneurial threshold firms: Imprinting and strategic choice perspectives, *Journal of Management Studies, 52*(4): 506–530.

*Kang, K. H., Lee, S., & Yoo, C. (2016). The effect of national culture on corporate social responsibility in the hospitality industry. *International Journal of Contemporary Hospitality Management, 28*(8), 1728–1758.

Kashefi-Pour, E., Amini, Sh., Uddin, M., & Duxbury, D. (2020). Does cultural difference affect investment-cash flow sensitivity? Evidence from OECD countries. *British Journal of Management,* 31, 636–658.

*Kashlak, R. J., Chandran, R., & Di Benedetto, C. A. (1998). Reciprocity in international business: A study of telecommunications alliances and contracts. *Journal of International Business Studies, 29*(2), 281–304.

*Ketkar, S., & Acs, Z. J. (2013). Where angels fear to tread: internationalization of emerging country SMEs. *Journal of International Entrepreneurship, 11*(3), 201–219.

*Kim, Y., & Gray, S. J. (2009). An assessment of alternative empirical measures of cultural distance: Evidence from the Republic of Korea: APJM APJM. *Asia Pacific Journal of Management, 26*(1), 55–74.

Kirkman, B. L., Lowe, K. B., & Gibson, C. B. (2006). A quarter century of culture's consequences: A review of empirical research incorporating Hofstede's cultural values framework. *Journal of International Business Studies, 37*(3), 285–320.

Kogut, B., & Singh, H. (1988). The effect of national culture on the choice of entry mode. *Journal of International Business Studies, 19*(3), 411–432.

Kogut, B., & Zander, U. (1993). Knowledge of the firm and the evolutionary theory of the multinational corporation. *Journal of International Business Studies, 24*(4), 625–645.

*Larimo, J., & Arslan, A. (2013). Determinants of foreign direct investment ownership mode choice: Evidence from Nordic investments in Central and Eastern Europe. *Journal of East European Management Studies, 18*(2), 232–263.

La Rocca, M., Neha, N., & La Rocca, T. (2019). Female management, overconfidence and debt maturity: European evidence. *Journal of Management and Governance*, 24, 713–747.

*Le, S., & Kroll, M. (2017). CEO international experience: Effects on strategic change and firm performance. *Journal of International Business Studies, 48*(5), 573–595.

*Li, D., & Glaister, K. W. (2007). National and corporate culture differences in international strategic alliances: Perceptions of Chinese partners. *Asia Pacific Journal of Management, 24*(2), 191.

*Li, J., Lam, K., & Qian, G. (2001). Does culture affect behavior and performance of firms? The case of joint ventures in China. *Journal of International Business Studies, 32*(1), 115–131.

*Li, K., Griffin, D., Yue, H., & Zhao, L. (2011). National culture and capital structure decisions: Evidence from foreign joint ventures in China. *Journal of International Business Studies, 42*(4), 477–503.

*Lo, F.-Y., Chiao, Y.-C., & Yu, C.-M. J. (2016). Network and institutional effects on SMEs' entry strategies. *Management International Review, 56*(4), 531–563.

*Luo, Y. (2007). An integrated anti-opportunism system in international exchange. *Journal of International Business Studies, 38*(6), 855–877.

*Luo, Y. (2007). Private control and collective control in international joint ventures. *Management International Review, 47*(4), 531–566.

*Luo, Y., Shenkar, O., & Mee-Kau, N. (2001). A dual parent perspective on control and performance in international joint ventures: Lessons from a developing economy. *Journal of International Business Studies, 32*(1), 41–58.

*Makino, S., & Neupert, K. E. (2000). National culture, transaction costs, and the choice between joint venture and wholly owned subsidiary. *Journal of International Business Studies, 31*(4), 705–713.

*Matthiesen, M.-L., & Salzmann, A. J. (2017). Corporate social responsibility and firms' cost of equity: How does culture matter? *Cross Cultural and Strategic Management, 24*(1), 105–124.

Miles, M. B., & Huberman, A. M. (1994). Qualitative data analysis: An expanded sourcebook. Beverly Hills, CA: SAGE.

Modigliani, F., & Miller, M. H. (1958). The cost of capital, corporation finance and the theory of investment. *American Economic Review, 48*(3), 261–297.

Mueller, V., Rosenbusch, N., & Bausch, A. (2013). Success patterns of exploratory and exploitative innovation: A meta-analysis of the influence of institutional factors. *Journal of Management, 39*(6), 1606–1636.

*Murphy, M. (2012). An integration of cultural frames of reference with the market entry decision. *Journal of International Business Research, 11*(1), 43–57.

Myers, S. C. (1977). Determinants of corporate borrowing. *Journal of Financial Economics, 5*(2), 147–175.

*Nachum, L. (2003). Liability of foreignness in global competition? Financial service affiliates in the city of London. *Strategic Management Journal, 24*(12), 1187.

Nag, R., Hambrick, D. C., & Chen, M. J. (2007). What is strategic management, really? Inductive derivation of a consensus definition of the field. *Strategic Management Journal, 28*(9), 935–955.

Nguyen, P., & Belaounia, S. (2020). Cultural distance and payment method in French cross-border acquisitions. *Management International, 24*(1), 109–126.

North, D. (1990). *Institutions, institutional change and economic performance*. New York: Cambridge University Press.

*Pan, Y. (1996). Influences on foreign equity ownership level in joint ventures in China. *Journal of International Business Studies, 27*(1), 1.

*Pan, Y. (2002). Equity ownership in international joint ventures: The impact of source country factors. *Journal of International Business Studies, 33*(2), 375–384.
*Pan, Y., & Tse, D. K. (1996). Cooperative strategies between foreign firms in an overseas country. *Journal of International Business Studies, 27*(5), 929–946.
*Park, C. L., & Paiva, E. L. (2018). How do national cultures impact the operations strategy process? *International Journal of Operations and Production Management, 38*(10), 1937–1963.
*Peng, G. Z., & Beamish, P. W. (2014). The effect of host country long term orientation on subsidiary ownership and survival: APJM APJM. *Asia Pacific Journal of Management, 31*(2), 423–453.
*Pesch, R., & Bouncken, R. B. (2017). The double-edged sword of cultural distance in international alliances. *Cross Cultural and Strategic Management, 24*(1), 33–54.
Podsakoff, P., MacKenzie, S., Bachrach, D., & Podsakoff, N. (2005). The influence of management journals in the 1980s and 1990s. *Strategic Management Journal, 26*(5), 473–88.
Porter, M. E. (1980). Generic competitive strategies. *Competitive strategy: Techniques for analyzing industries and competitors*, 35–46.
*Puck, J., Hödl, M. K., Filatotchev, I., Wolff, H.-G., & Bader, B. (2016). Ownership mode, cultural distance, and the extent of parent firms' strategic control over subsidiaries in the PRC. *Asia Pacific Journal of Management, 33*(4), 1075–1105.
*Puck, J. F., Holtbrügge, D., & Mohr, A. T. (2009). Beyond entry mode choice: Explaining the conversion of joint ventures into wholly owned subsidiaries in the People's Republic of China. *Journal of International Business Studies, 40*(3), 388–404.
**Quer, D., Claver, E., & Rienda, L. (2012). Political risk, cultural distance, and outward foreign direct investment: Empirical evidence from large Chinese firms. *Asia Pacific Journal of Management, 29*(4), 1089–1104.
Rapp, J. K., Bernardi, R. A., & Bosco, S. M. (2010). Examining the use of Hofstede's uncertainty avoidance construct in international research: A 25-year review. *International Business Research, 4*(1), 3–15.
*Reuer, J. J. (2002). Incremental corporate reconfiguration through international joint venture buyouts and selloffs. *Management International Review, 42*(3), 237–260.
Rittel, H. W. J., & Webber, M. W. (1973). Dilemmas in a general theory of planning. *Policy Sciences*, 4: 155–179.
*Rocca, M., Neha, N., & Rocca, T. (2019). Female management, overconfidence and debt maturity: European evidence. *Journal of Management and Governance, 24*, 1–35.
Ronen, S., & Shenkar, O. (1985). Clustering countries on attitudinal dimensions: A review and synthesis. *Academy of Management Review, 10*(3), 435–454.
**Reus, T. H., & Lamont, B. T. (2009). The double-edged sword of cultural distance in international acquisitions. *Journal of International Business Studies, 40*(8), 1298–1316.
Rumelt, R. P. (1984). Towards a strategic theory of the firm. *Competitive Strategic Management, 26*(3), 556–570.
**Salomon, R., & Wu, Z. (2012). Institutional distance and local isomorphism strategy. *Journal of International Business Studies, 43*(4), 343–367. doi:http://dx.doi.org/10.1057/jibs.2012.3
**Sarala, R. M., & Vaara, E. (2010). Cultural differences, convergence, and crossvergence as explanations of knowledge transfer in international acquisitions. *Journal of International Business Studies, 41*(8), 1365–1390.
*Scalera, V. G., Mukherjee, D., & Piscitello, L. (2018). Ownership strategies in knowledge-intensive cross-border acquisitions: Comparing Chinese and Indian MNEs, *Asia Pacific Journal of Management, 37*, 1–31.
*Schlaegel, C., He, X., & Engle, R. L. (2013). The direct and indirect influence of national culture on entrepreneurial intentions: A fourteen nation study. *International Journal of Management, 30*(2), 597–609.
*Schmitt, A., & Van Biesebroeck, J. (2013). Proximity strategies in outsourcing relations: The role of geographical, cultural and relational proximity in the European automotive industry. *Journal of International Business Studies, 44*(5), 475–503.
Schoonhoven, C. (1981). Problems with contingency theory: Testing assumptions hidden within the language of contingency "theory." *Administrative Science Quarterly, 26*(3), 349–377.
Schwartz, S. H. (1992). Universals in the content and structure of values: Theoretical advances and empirical tests in 20 countries. *Advances in Experimental Social Psychology, 25*(1), 1–65.
Scott, W. R. (1995). *Institutions and organizations*. Thousand Oaks, CA: SAGE.
*Shane, S., & Venkataraman, S. (1996). Renegade and rational championing strategies. *Organization Studies, 17*(5), 751–771.
*Shao, L., Kwok, C. C., & Guedhami, O. (2010). National culture and dividend policy. *Journal of International Business Studies, 41*(8), 1391–1414.

*Shao, L., Kwok, C. C., & Zhang, R. (2013). National culture and corporate investment. *Journal of International Business Studies, 44*(7), 745–763.

*Siegel, J. I., Licht, A. N., & Schwartz, S. H. (2013). Egalitarianism, cultural distance, and foreign direct investment: A new approach. *Organization Science, 24*(4), 1174–1194.

**Simonin, B. L. (1999). Transfer of marketing know-how in international strategic alliances: An empirical investigation of the role and antecedents of knowledge ambiguity. *Journal of International Business Studies, 30*(3), 463–490.

Skerlavaj, M., Su, C., & Huang, M. (2013). The moderating effects of national culture on the development of organisational learning culture: A multilevel study across seven countries. *Journal of East European Management Studies, 18*(1), 97–134.

*Slangen, A. H. L., & Beugelsdijk, S. (2010). The impact of institutional hazards on foreign multinational activity: A contingency perspective. *Journal of International Business Studies, 41*(6), 980–995.

*Slangen, A. H. L., & Hennart, J.-F. (2008). Do multinationals really prefer to enter culturally distant countries through greenfields rather than through acquisitions? The role of parent experience and subsidiary autonomy. *Journal of International Business Studies, 39*(3), 472–490.

Smale, T. (2016). Why national culture should be at the heart of innovation management. *Technology Innovation Management Review, 6*(4), 18–25.

*Song, R., Moon, S., Chen, H., & Houston, M. B. (2018). When marketing strategy meets culture: The role of culture in product evaluations. *Journal of the Academic Marketing Science, 46*(3), 384–402.

*Tang, L. (2012). The direction of cultural distance on FDI: Attractiveness or incongruity? *Cross Cultural Management Journal, 19*(2), 213–256.

Taras, V., Kirkman, B. L., & Steel, P. (2010). Examining the impact of culture's consequences: A three-decade, multilevel, meta-analytic review of Hofstede's cultural value dimensions. *Journal of Applied Psychology, 95*(3), 405.

Teece, D. J., Pisano, G., & Shuen, A. (1997). Dynamic capabilities and strategic management. *Strategic Management Journal, 18*(7), 509–533.

*Thanetsunthorn, N. (2014). Ethical organization: The effect of national culture on CSR. *Organization Development Journal, 32*(3), 89–109.

*Thanetsunthorn, N., & Wuthisatian, R. (2018). Cultural configuration models: corporate social responsibility and national culture: MRN MRN. *Management Research Review, 41*(10), 1137–1175.

Thanetsunthorn, N., & Wuthisatian, R. (2020). Trust and culture: Applications for organization development. *Organization Development Journal, 38*(1), 33–43.

**Thomas, A. S., & Mueller, S. L. (2000). A case for comparative entrepreneurship: Assessing the relevance of culture. *Journal of international business studies, 31*(2), 287–301.

**Tihanyi, L., Griffith, D. A., & Russell, C. J. (2005). The effect of cultural distance on entry mode choice, international diversification, and MNE performance: A meta-analysis. *Journal of International Business Studies, 36*(3), 270–283.

*Tong, T. W., & Reuer, J. J. (2007). Real options in multinational corporations: Organizational challenges and risk implications. *Journal of International Business Studies, 38*(2), 215–230.

*Tosi, H. L., & Greckhamer, T. (2004). Culture and CEO compensation. *Organization Science, 15*(6), 657–670.

Tranfield, D., Denyer, D., & Smart, P. (2003). Towards a methodology for developing evidence-informed management knowledge by means of systematic review. *British Journal of Management, 14*(3), 207–222.

*Tse, D. K., Pan, Y., & Au, K. Y. (1997). How MNCs choose entry modes and form alliances: The China experience. *Journal of International Business Studies, 28*(4), 779–805.

*Uhlenbruck, K. (2004). Developing acquired foreign subsidiaries: The experience of MNES in transition economies. *Journal of International Business Studies, 35*(2), 109–123.

*Venaik, S., Midgley, D. F. (2015). Mindscapes across landscapes: Archetypes of transnational and subnational culture. *Journal of International Business Studies*, 46, 1051–1079.

**Waldman, D. A., Sully de Luque, M., Washburn, N., House, R. J., Adetoun, B., Barrasa, A., & Grachev, M. (2006). Cultural and leadership predictors of corporate social responsibility values of top management: A GLOBE study of 15 countries. *Journal of International Business Studies, 37*(6), 823–837.

*Wan, W. P., & Hillman, A. J. (2006). One of these things is not like the others: What contributes to dissimilarity among MNE subsidiaries' political strategy? *Management International Review, 46*(1), 85–107.

*Wang, Ch. L., Lin, X., Chan, A. K. K., & Shi, Y. (2005). Conflict handling styles in international joint ventures: A cross-cultural and cross-national comparison. *Management International Review, 45*(1), 3–21.
*Wang, H., & Schaan, J.-L. (2008). How much distance do we need? Revisiting the "national cultural distance paradox." *Management International Review, 48*(3): 263–277.
Wernerfelt, B. (1984). A resource-based view of the firm. *Strategic Management Journal, 5*(2), 171–180.
White, G., Guldiken, O., Hemphill, T., He, W., & Sharifi Khoobdeh, M. S. (2016). Trends in international strategic management research from 2000 to 2013: Text mining and bibliometric analyses. *Management International Review*, 56: 35–65.
Witt, M. A. (2019). De-globalization: Theories, predictions, and opportunities for international business research. *Journal of International Business Studies, 50*(7), 1053–1077.
*Xu, D., Pan, Y., & Beamish, P. W. (2004). The effect of regulative and normative distances on MNE ownership and expatriate strategies. *Management International Review, 44*(3), 285–307.
*Yao, F. K., & Li, J. (2016). Multi-market contact and foreign entry location decisions in China. *Management International Review, 56*(1), 95–122.
**Yiu, D., & Makino, S. (2002). The choice between joint venture and wholly owned subsidiary: An institutional perspective. *Organization Science, 13*(6), 667–683.
*Young, S. L., & Makhija, M. V. (2014). Firms' corporate social responsibility behavior: An integration of institutional and profit maximization approaches. *Journal of International Business Studies, 45*(6), 670–698.
*Yu, T., Subramaniam, M., & Cannella, A. A., Jr. (2013). Competing globally, allying locally: Alliances between global rivals and host-country factors. *Journal of International Business Studies, 44*(2), 117–137.
*Zhang, C., Cavusgil, S. T., & Roath, A. S. (2003). Manufacturer governance of foreign distributor relationships: Do relational norms enhance competitiveness in the export market? *Journal of International Business Studies, 34*(6), 550.

CHAPTER

20 National Culture and Organizational Change

Noga Sverdlik *and* Shaul Oreg

Abstract

In this chapter, we examine the role of national culture for understanding organizational change. We review extant cross-cultural studies of organizational change and offer an integrative framework of micro and macro approaches. We then highlight the dimensions of national culture that are conceptually related to the notion of change and elaborate on a recently developed taxonomy of cultural change orientations, including the dimensions of cultural rigidity, cultural affective reactance, and cultural routine seeking. Drawing on this taxonomy we develop conceptual propositions linking national culture to key events and components in the evolution of organizational change, including the initiation of change, the change process, and recipients' responses to organizational change. We conclude by discussing the implications of our framework for theory and practice.

Key Words: organizational change, cultural change orientations, resistance to change, cultural values, national culture

Using broad brush strokes, we can classify the literature on organizational change into research with a focus on the strategic process of managing organizational change, which tends to have a macro orientation (e.g., Battilana & Casciaro, 2012; Burke & Litwin, 1992), and micro research, focusing on understanding change recipients' responses to change (e.g., Bartunek et al., 2006; Oreg et al., 2013), with some of the pioneering research in the field addressing aspects of both perspectives (e.g., Lewin, 1947). Macro approaches often take on the perspective of management and describe what change looks like, what are its triggers, how it evolves over time, and, consequently, how it should be managed. Much of the early writings from this perspective has been from a very applied orientation, resulting in sets of recipes and generic recommendations for how to manage change. Ample macro research has nevertheless been conducted, which consists largely of qualitative research of the contextualized aspects of organizational change and quantitative strategy research aimed at predicting changes in firm performance (e.g., Boeker, 1997).

In contrast, micro approaches to the study of organizational change have undertaken change recipients' perspective (Oreg et al., 2013) and have focused on describing and explaining the nature of recipients' affective, cognitive, and behavioral responses to change (for reviews see Choi, 2011; Oreg et al., 2011; Rafferty et al., 2013). Within both the macro and micro fields, some research has been conducted from a cross-cultural perspective. In the macro field, this research has aimed at linking aspects of national culture to the manner in which change evolves in organizations. In the micro field, the focus has been on using dimensions of national culture to explain differences in recipients' responses to change. We review this research next.

Cross-Cultural Studies of Organizational Change

Within both macro and micro approaches to the study of organizational change, the role of national culture has been studied only sporadically and generally indirectly. Even beyond the context of *organizational* change, the notion of change in research on national culture is addressed only to a limited degree, with much of this research aimed at explaining how and why national cultures change over time (e.g., Chiu et al., 2010; Greenfield, 2009; Grossmann & Varnum, 2015; Oishi & Graham, 2010). This research draws links between ecological changes, such as globalization and climate change, and gradual changes in national culture. None of these studies, however, addresses organizational change. We thus focus here on those studies that explicitly link national culture with changes in organizations.

Culture and the Management of Change

Within the scope of macro approaches to change, change is generally conceptualized and operationalized as organizational development (OD) interventions, thus offering a restricted view of organizational change. OD is a prominent American management tool, focusing on deliberate and planned implementation of change, aimed at enhancing organizational effectiveness (Jaeger, 1986). The research on OD and national culture highlights the importance of considering both the *content* of the changes implemented and the *process* of their implementation in a culturally sensitive manner (see link 1 in Figure 20.1). In *content* we refer to the kind of change implemented and the specific factors that are being changed. In *process* we refer to the manner in which the change unfolds. A number of studies have linked the content of the intervention with the cultural values that characterize countries (e.g., Fagenson-Eland et al., 2004; Jaeger, 1986). In a conceptual analysis, the success of change interventions was linked with the degree of congruence between the values that underlie the intervention and countries' position on Hofstede's (1980, 2001) cultural values (Jaeger, 1986). For example, Jaeger (1986) argues that the values in Scandinavian countries, which are relatively low on power distance, uncertainty avoidance, and masculinity, and relatively high on individualism, correspond most closely with OD values, and therefore OD interventions should be particularly well accepted there. Hofstede's cultural dimensions were similarly linked with the prevalence of the OD intervention types implemented in seven countries, as reported by OD practitioners (Fagenson-Eland et al., 2004). For example, practitioners from countries high

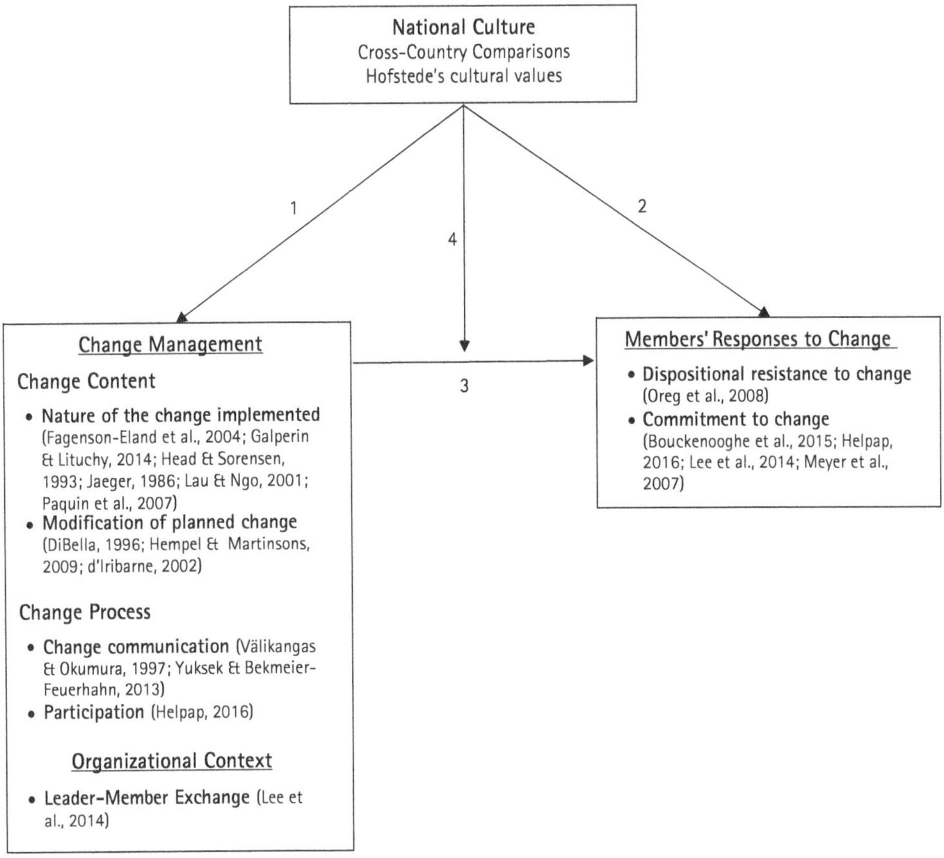

Figure 20.1. Summary of findings about national culture and organizational change.

on masculinity were more likely to report using OD training and development initiatives than those from low-masculinity countries. Overall, however, the patterns of relationships in this study were complex and only partially consistent with the theoretically expected relationships.

In another study, managers and OD practitioners, also from seven countries, were asked about the prevalence and effectiveness of change interventions in their countries. Respondents from countries that were higher on Hofstede's masculinity and uncertainty avoidance dimensions tended to report a higher prevalence and effectiveness of task-oriented (e.g., career planning, quality circles) versus process-oriented (e.g., T-groups, team-building) interventions (Head & Sorensen, 1993). The authors explain this by arguing that task-oriented interventions are of greater, and process-oriented interventions lesser, fit to masculine and uncertainty avoidant cultures, although they do not provide a rationale for this assertion. In yet another study, based in Hong Kong, using reports from HR representatives in 292 Chinese and international firms, European and U.S. firms were said to apply OD interventions more than were Chinese and Japanese ones (Lau & Ngo,

2001). No consistent differences across cultures were found, however, in the associations between these interventions and firms' performance.

In a study of OD interventions that emphasized employee involvement, implemented in 90 organizational units from seven countries, intervention success was associated with a combination of low power distance and high collectivism, which corresponds with the bottom-up and group-oriented process emphasized in the intervention (Paquin et al., 2007). In line with such findings, a conceptual analysis of human resource development interventions suggests that changes should be planned with target organizations' national (and organizational) culture in mind (Galperin & Lituchy, 2014).

A few qualitative studies provide evidence for this claim. For example, in a qualitative analysis of eight case studies of business process reengineering in Chinese organizations, the success of organizational reengineering initiatives was achieved only once adjustments were made to the original reengineering plans to increase the fit of their underlying values with those of Chinese culture, such as maintaining harmony within the organization and building strong relationships during the change (Hempel & Martinsons, 2009). In another study, of an international organization in which a planned change was implemented, organization members from different cultural groups adopted different interpretations of the change content and process, including interpretations of the goals of the change and its nature (DiBella, 1996). For example, whereas staff members from the Swiss office were concerned about their ability to control communications during the change, members from the South American regional office interpreted the change as an opportunity for improved participation in the change process. The authors therefore proposed that change agents should account for such differences when implementing changes. Similarly, the implementation of a change in two companies (one in Morocco and another in Mexico) succeeded, at least in part, due to adaptations of the change to the local national culture (d'Iribarne, 2002). In the Moroccan company, parallels were drawn between the values underlying the change and those of the local culture, highlighting dimensions of honesty, cooperation, and respect for people's contributions. In Mexico, the change was promoted through an emphasis on family-oriented values, through actions such as providing help to the community, which strongly resonated with Mexican values and norms.

Overall, the role of culture in these studies is considered by comparing either the implementation of organizational changes across several countries (e.g., Galperin & Lituchy, 2014; Paquin et al., 2007; Yüksek & Bekmeier-Feuerhahn, 2013) or the cultural values of the countries within which the organizational change is implemented with the values that underlie the change intervention (e.g., Hempel & Martinsons, 2009; Jaeger, 1986). In this latter way of considering culture, studies highlighted the contrast between the Western orientation of many change interventions and the non-Western cultures in which many of these changes have been introduced. Although a large-scale systematic investigation of the relationship between culture and the success of organizational change has yet to be conducted, the studies above draw attention to the importance of considering the role of national culture and its fit with the content or the change implemented.

Beyond the content of organizational changes, several studies considered cultural differences in the process through which changes are implemented (e.g., Välikangas & Okumura, 1997; Yuksek & Bekmeier-Feuerhahn, 2013). In a qualitative case study, comparing the implementation of a change in a Japanese and a U.S. company, company leaders differed in their approach to motivating followers to implement the change (Välikangas & Okumura, 1997). In the U.S. company, the CEO focused on goals that have to do with obtaining rewards or expressing one's personal values. In contrast, in the Japanese company the CEO focused on group cohesion and identification with company goals, and on creating consensus around the change. The U.S. leader's emphasis on individual outcomes and the emphasis of the Japanese leader on collective outcomes are consistent with key cultural values in each country. The study thus demonstrates links between organizations' cultural context and the process through which leaders' implement change. In line with such findings, in a recent conceptual model of culture and change communication, change agents are called to consider the cultural values of their organization's country when planning their change communication strategies (Yüksek & Bekmeier-Feuerhahn, 2013). The authors argue, for example, that in individualistic and low-power distance cultures, organization members will be more in tune with their personal goals and interests, will expect to participate in the change, and may therefore be skeptical about management's change impositions (Yüksek & Bekmeier-Feuerhahn, 2013).

Culture and Responses to Change

In reviews of the micro approaches to organizational change, culture is considered part of the "change context," which constitutes the conditions and atmosphere within which change is implemented and has been studied as a predictor of recipients' responses to change (Oreg et al., 2011). Although most of the research linking culture to responses to change has focused on *organizational* culture (e.g., Cartwright & Cooper, 1993; Jones et al., 2005), a small number of studies have considered the role of national culture in explaining differences in responses to change (link 2 in Figure 20.1; e.g., Bouckenooghe et al., **Lee, et al., 2014; Meyer et al., 2007**). In a few of the studies, this has been done by comparing change recipients' orientations toward change and responses to it across national cultures (Bouckenooghe et al., 2015; Meyer et al., 2007; Oreg et al., 2008). In a few other studies, national culture was viewed as a moderator of the effects of the organization's leadership on followers' responses to the change (e.g., Lee et al., 2014).

Within the first set of studies, one work focused on the construct of dispositional resistance to change—a trait pertaining to individuals' personality-based inclination to resist change—which was compared among participants from 17 countries (Oreg et al., 2008). Overall, the construct had the same structure and took on comparable meanings across countries. In two other studies, the structure of commitment to change

(Herscovitch & Meyer, 2002), and parts of its nomological net were tested first in Canada and India (Meyer et al., 2007) and then in eight countries, divided into North American (the United States and Canada) and non-North American (Pakistan, Belgium, Taiwan, China, Korea, and India) categories (Bouckenooghe et al., 2015). Although findings in Canada and India were similar to each other, some differences were found in the relationship between affective commitment to change—wanting to support a change based on its perceived benefits—and normative commitment to change—a sense of obligation to support the change (Meyer et al., 2007). Specifically, the data from India did not support the distinction between affective and normative commitment, which has been established among U.S. participants and supported by the Canadian data. The authors tentatively proposed that these differences may result from differences in these countries' degree of individualism–collectivism and power distance.

Similarly, a meta-analysis of 17 studies from eight countries provided overall support for the structure of the commitment to change scale and for the relationships between commitment to change and behavioral support for the change (Bouckenooghe et al., 2015). Yet in this study as well, differences were found between the North American and non-North American samples (Pakistan, Belgium, Taiwan, China, South Korea, and India) in the study, such that the accepted distinctions between scale dimensions were not as clearly supported in the non-North American samples (Bouckenooghe et al., 2015). As in Mayer et al.'s (2007) study, the distinction between affective commitment and normative commitment was not as clear in the non-North American samples. Similar to Meyer et al.'s (2007) suggestion, Bouckenooghe et al. (2015) propose that the particularly strong correlation between affective and normative commitment to change in non-North American countries may result from the higher levels of power distance in these countries and the generally higher levels of collectivism (except for in Belgium) compared with those in North America. As the authors explain, organizational changes in collectivist societies are more likely to be viewed as initiated in the interest of the collective. Being committed to and supporting the change, as reflected in affective commitment, will therefore be tightly linked with organization members' sense of their moral obligation to support the organization and the change, as reflected in their normative commitment to the change.

Affective commitment to change in non-North American samples presented particularly high correlations not only with normative commitment to change, but also with continuance commitment to the change—reflecting the acknowledgment of the costs associated with not supporting the change (Bouckenooghe et al., 2015). The authors propose that the greater acceptance of inequality that characterizes high-power distance cultures brings about a greater willingness to make personal sacrifices during the change (i.e., affective commitment), partly out of a sense that there are no alternatives to supporting the change (i.e., continuance commitment).

A couple of studies focused on the moderating effect of national culture on relationships between management approaches and followers' responses to change across cultures (link 4 in Figure 20.1; Helpap, 2016; Lee et al., 2014). The focus of one study was on employees' perceptions of their relationship with their manager (LMX, Graen & Uhl-Bien, 1995), which constitute an aspect of the organizational context within which change is implemented. Specifically, the relationship between LMX and followers' commitment to an organizational change was tested among U.S. and Korean employees (Lee et al., 2014). National affiliation moderated the effects of LMX on commitment to change, such that the relationships were significantly stronger in the United States. In addition, values of power distance similarly moderated the effects of LMX on employees' commitment to change, such that the relationship was stronger among followers with low-power distance values. In another study, power distance values similarly moderated the relationship between employees' perceptions of their opportunity to participate in the change process (conceptualized as their managers' participatory versus programmatic change communication strategy) and their commitment to change, such that here too, the effects were stronger among low-power distance followers (Helpap, 2016). In both of the above studies, however, these values were operationalized at the individual rather than national level. As such, they are similar to studies at the individual level in which personal values are used to explain differences in the relationships between change processes and responses to change (e.g., Sverdlik & Oreg, 2009, 2015). They do, nevertheless, point to a promising research direction at the culture level.

The studies above are important for drawing attention to the effects that national culture has on organizational change and organization members' responses to it. Yet the scarcity of research in this field leaves us with very limited insights. At the broadest level, we know that national culture has an effect on how change recipients respond to organizational change (see link 2 in Figure 20.1) and that part of this effect may come from the ties between national culture and the practices used in organizations for managing change (link 1), followed by the effects of these practices on change recipients' responses (link 3). A few of the studies also suggest that the effects of change management practices on organization members' responses may differ across national cultures (link 4). Very little has been conducted, however, to flesh out these general links. Doing so would require a more systematic focus on both the factors to consider within national culture and the processes through which these cultural factors shape how change unfolds and how organization members respond to it. We begin with the former point and explicitly examine those aspects of national culture that specifically pertain to the notion of change. We then follow by describing how some of these cultural aspects may influence organizational change processes and recipients' responses.

Cultural Change Orientation

To date, several taxonomies of national culture have been established, each comprising dimensions of culture through which societies can be characterized and compared to one another.[1] Most prominent among these taxonomies are the framework developed by Hofstede (1980, 2001), the GLOBE research group (House et al., 2004), Schwartz (2006), Inglehart (1997; Inglehart & Baker, 2000), and Gelfand et al. (2011) and the frameworks pertaining to the personality profiles of national cultures (Allik et al., 2017; Gebauer et al., 2015; McCrae & Terracciano, 2005). Each of these frameworks includes dimensions that are, in one way or another, related to the notion of change. Beyond links that can be drawn from any given cultural dimension and specific types of change (e.g., as described above, Hofstede's masculinity was linked with the success of task-oriented OD interventions; see Head & Sorensen, 1993), several of the dimensions from extant frameworks appear to be inherently related to the notion of change. Hofstede's (1980, 2001) uncertainty avoidance dimension, for example, pertains to change given that changes generally increase the degree of uncertainty that people experience. As another example, Schwartz's (1994) embeddedness dimension, which highlights societies' emphasis on maintaining ingroup solidarity and the *status quo,* is relevant to change given that, by definition, change challenges the status quo. Neither of the early taxonomies, however, was developed with the intent of specifically capturing cultures' orientation toward change. Accordingly, key aspects of a culture's orientation toward change may be missing or only indirectly represented in extant taxonomies.

Complementing extant taxonomies, we recently developed a cultural taxonomy, focusing explicitly on societies' orientation toward change (Oreg & Sverdlik, 2018). Corresponding to how several cultural taxonomies were developed, through the aggregation of society members' personal attributes (e.g., values, traits), the taxonomy of cultural change orientations was developed through the aggregation of society members' dispositional resistance to change (Oreg, 2003; Oreg et al., 2008). In this section, we describe the main conceptual and empirical analyses through which we established this taxonomy in our earlier research.

As noted above, dispositional resistance to change is a personality trait, representing individuals' personality-based orientation toward change. At the individual level, it comprises four dimensions (routine seeking, emotional reaction, short-term focus, and cognitive rigidity), each highlighting a different aspect of individuals' orientation toward change. The trait and its dimensions have been linked with individuals' attitudes and behaviors in numerous types of change situations, including in organizational and occupational contexts (e.g., Fugate & Soenen, 2018; Oreg, 2018; Oreg & Goldenberg, 2015; Soenen et al., 2017). To learn about cultures' orientation toward change, individuals' responses to the 17-item dispositional resistance to change scale (Oreg, 2003) were aggregated to the country level. Specifically, the responses of 6,487 individuals from 27 countries were aggregated. A multidimensional scaling analysis of the aggregated responses revealed three distinct cultural dimensions: cultural rigidity, affective reactance, and routine seeking (Oreg & Sverdlik, 2018).

Cultural rigidity reflects a society's disinclination to change established norms, beliefs, and ideas and is associated with an overall societal inaction. *Cultural affective reactance* represents

[1] This section is based on sections from Oreg and Sverdlik (2018).

the anxiety and vigilance that society members experience and exhibit, in particular toward the notion of change. *Cultural routine seeking* represents a society's emphasis and reliance on the structure that routines provide. More than an active search for new routines, this dimension represents the reliance on existing ones as a stepping stone to the society's development. Whereas, at the individual level, the construct's dimensions are generally tightly and positively linked with each other, at the culture level the three dimensions are distinct, with only a moderate *negative* correlation between cultural rigidity and routine seeking. Moreover, in contrast to the individual level, at the culture level, routine seeking takes on a somewhat paradoxical positive orientation toward change. Societies high on cultural routine seeking tend to exhibit progress and affluence, and individuals in these societies appreciate their routines and the convenience they provide. At the same time, they value progress and change, which can further enhance such convenience (Shove, 2003). This corresponds with the notion that at least some degree of structure is a prerequisite for innovation (Brown & Eisenhardt, 1998). Each of the three cultural change dimensions thus reflects a separate aspect of a society's orientation toward stability versus change. The countries' standing on the three change orientation dimensions is presented in Figure 20.2.

Figure 20.2. Biplot of countries mapped on to the three change orientation dimensions. *Note*: The dashed part of the axes represents their lower end. Figure adapted from Oreg and Sverdlik, 2018.

As part of the process for determining the meanings of the three dimensions, we tested their relationships with the dimensions of extant cultural taxonomies. These existing dimensions were used as conceptual anchors through which we could better interpret the meanings of the three change orientation dimensions and establish their nomological net. After briefly reviewing each of the taxonomies, we describe their conceptual links to the notion of change.

The Hofstede and GLOBE Taxonomies

Hofstede's (1980, 2001) research highlights five cultural dimensions—power distance, individualism–collectivism, femininity–masculinity, uncertainty avoidance, and long- versus short-term orientation. Partially based on Hofstede's taxonomy, the GLOBE project (House et al., 2004), aimed predominantly at identifying universal and culture-specific dimensions of leadership, proposed an extended cultural taxonomy including nine dimensions. Some of Hofstede's dimensions remained as originally conceptualized, whereas others were relabeled or split into specific subdimensions, and a few new dimensions were proposed. Power distance and uncertainty avoidance retained their labels; long-term orientation was relabeled as future orientation, collectivism was split into institutional collectivism and ingroup collectivism, masculinity–femininity was split into assertiveness and gender egalitarianism; and the dimensions *performance orientation* and *humane orientation* were added.

Of the nine dimensions, uncertainty avoidance and future orientation seem to be particularly relevant to the notion of stability versus change. In line with both Hofstede and the GLOBE project, the emphasis in uncertainty avoidance is on the degree to which societies rely on rules, norms, and practices.[2] Because change typically involves a degree of uncertainty, uncertainty avoidance is relevant for understanding change situations and the response to them.

The second change-related dimension within the Hofstede and GLOBE taxonomies is long-term/future orientation. In both taxonomies, this dimension reflects a societal emphasis on the future (versus the past and present) and adaptability, along with future-oriented activities and inclinations such as planning and a willingness to sacrifice short-term costs for future benefits (Hofstede, 2001; House et al., 2002). The long-term/future orientation dimension would therefore also seem to capture societies' openness to change.

---

[2] It is noteworthy, however, that there is a negative correlation between uncertainty avoidance as measured by Hofstede and in the GLOBE project, suggesting that each index captures a distinct aspect of the concept (Venaik & Brewer, 2010). Whereas Hofstede's index may capture the degree of stress that society members experience under uncertainty, the GLOBE index captures the degree to which society employs rule-oriented practices for dealing with uncertainty.

Schwartz's Cultural Dimensions

Schwartz's (2006) framework captures six cultural dimensions, positioned on three bipolar axes—embeddedness versus autonomy, mastery versus harmony, and hierarchy versus egalitarianism. Among these, the first two axes are relevant to the notion of change. Autonomy and embeddedness pertain to the degree to which societies highlight society members' autonomy versus their commitments to the collective. As noted above, embeddedness includes an emphasis on maintaining ingroup solidarity and the *status quo*. On the second axis, mastery reflects an emphasis on exploiting the environment for the betterment of society and its members through mastering, directing, and *changing* the environment. At the opposite end of the axis, harmony involves an emphasis on accepting and appreciating the world *as it is* (Schwartz, 2006). Thus, societies with an emphasis on autonomy and mastery may also tend to have a positive cultural orientation toward change, and those with an emphasis on embeddedness and harmony will tend to have a negative one.

Inglehart's Framework of Traditional and Secular Values

Inglehart (1997; Inglehart & Baker, 2000) proposed two bipolar cultural dimensions: one pertaining to traditional versus secular values and the other to survival versus self-expression values. The continuum of traditional versus secular values represents the importance given to religion in society and the degree to which it has become industrialized, involving bureaucratization and rationalization. Defined as such, these values could be linked to the notion of change in two contrasting ways. On one end of the continuum, the emphasis on tradition involves a society's preference for the status quo and should thus correspond with a preference for stability. Yet, on the other end of the continuum, the emphasis on bureaucracy and the formalization that characterize it suggests that secular societies may also prefer stability to change. Although both of these rationales make sense, a test of the competing hypotheses supported the latter rationale, whereby secularism was associated with the routine-seeking dimension of the cultural change orientation (Oreg & Sverdlik, 2018).

Cultural Tightness–Looseness

Using data from individuals in 33 countries, Gelfand and colleagues (2011) developed the notion of cultural tightness (versus looseness), which distinguished societies on the basis of the strength of their norms and tolerance for deviant behavior. Tighter cultures are characterized by stronger norms and less tolerance for deviation from them. Like Inglehart's dimension of traditionalism versus secularism, cultural tightness can also be said to be both positively and negatively associated with a preference for stability. On the one hand, the lack of tolerance for deviations from the status quo could be associated with a preference for stability and a disinclination toward change (Erez & Gati, 2004; Toh & Leonardelli, 2012). On the other hand, when changes are initiated by society leaders, the adherence to norms, often installed by leaders, may actually make members of tight cultures more supportive of the changes (Varnum & Grossmann, 2017). In one study, cultural tightness is conceptually linked with the likelihood of changes in societal norms (De et al., 2017). A series of computer simulations supported the idea that cultural tightness is negatively associated with a society's likelihood and rate of change in norms and with the willingness of its members to try out new strategies. In another set of simulations, changes in norms were less likely to occur in tight cultures, but once they occurred, their rate of change was faster in these cultures (De, Nau, Pan, & Gelfand, 2018). Although this link has yet to be tested with field data, it seems that the relationships between tightness–looseness and societal change is complex and can both impede and, under certain conditions, facilitate change. This may also explain why in our own data, tightness was not significantly related to societies' orientation toward stability versus change.

Country Big-Five Dimensions

Although not developed for distinguishing among cultures, the five-factor model of personality has been used at the aggregate level for characterizing cultures (Allik et al., 2017; Gebauer et al., 2015; McCrae & Terracciano, 2005). Among the five factors, the aggregation of openness to experience to the culture level is most relevant to the notion of change, such that cultures open to experiences could be expected to be similarly open to change.

Our earlier analyses supported several of the expectations described above. Specifically, with the exception of cultural tightness–looseness (Gelfand et al., 2011), dimensions from each of the taxonomies were correlated with at least one of the cultural change orientation dimensions (see Table 20.1). Cultural rigidity was negatively correlated with the GLOBE institutional collectivism dimension and was associated with Schwartz's axis of harmony versus mastery. Affective reactance was associated with Schwartz's axis of hierarchy versus egalitarianism, was negatively correlated with harmony and the extraversion cultural profile, and positively correlated with the neuroticism cultural profile. Routine seeking yielded the largest number of significant correlations with extant dimensions, including the negative correlation with GLOBE's power distance dimension, the positive correlation with GLOBE's uncertainty avoidance dimension, the positive correlation with Inglehart's secularism dimension, and associations with Schwartz's axis of autonomy (positive) versus embeddedness (negative).

These relationships helped to further interpret what each of the three change orientation dimensions reflects as well as the distinctions among them. Each change orientation dimension reflects a separate aspect of a society's position toward stability and change. Cultural rigidity captures a form of inaction and a reluctance to change beliefs and norms; in affective reactance, the emphasis is on the threats that change entails; and in routine seeking. the emphasis is on the benefits that stability provides. As we further describe in the next section, this latter dimension exemplifies that stability does not necessarily

Table 20.1 Descriptive statistics and Spearman correlations between change orientation dimensions and other cultural dimensions (adopted from Oreg & Sverdlik, 2018).

Variable	N	Mean	SD	Cultural Rigidity	Cultural Affective Reactance	Cultural Routine Seeking
Hofstede's Value Orientations						
Individualism (vs. Collectivism)	26	50.90	22.16	–.21	–.12	.40*
Uncertainty Avoidance	26	69.90	22.97	.17	.12	–.58**
Power Distance	26	57.31	20.47	.24	.14	–.42*
Masculinity–Femininity	26	49.73	22.39	–.06	.34	.06
Long-term Orientation	17	55.82	25.33	–.39	.05	.04
GLOBE Societal Practices						
Institutional Collectivism	19	4.19	.42	–.67**	.33	.52*
Ingroup Collectivism	19	4.79	.73	.32	–.10	–.49*
Uncertainty Avoidance	19	4.06	.57	–.24	–.15	.67**
Power Distance	19	5.15	.36	.43	–.21	–.72**
Gender Egalitarianism	19	3.42	.35	–.26	–.06	.16
Assertiveness	19	4.20	.34	.24	–.16	.08
Future	19	3.82	.42	–.27	–.10	.49*
Humane	19	3.87	.34	–.42	.32	.08
Performance	19	4.07	.41	–.15	.20	.42
Schwartz Values Orientations						
Affective Autonomy	27	3.60	.39	–.35	–.23	.39*
Intellectual Autonomy	27	4.47	.28	.02	–.32	.29
Egalitarianism	27	4.72	.29	.23	–.46*	.04
Harmony	27	4.09	.35	.40*	–.50**	–.24
Embeddedness	27	3.62	.27	.25	.24	–.41*
Hierarchy	27	2.29	.48	–.10	.56**	–.07
Mastery	27	4.00	.16	–.52**	.38	.17
Ingelhart's Value Dimensions						
Secularism (vs. Traditionalism)	24	.19	.53	–.13	.13	.53**
Self-expression (vs. Survival)	24	.23	.55	–.28	–.32	.33
Gelfand et al.'s Tightness (vs. Looseness)	18	5.66	2.65	.18	–.26	.00

(*continued*)

Table 20.1 *Continued*						
Variable	***N***	**Mean**	**SD**	**Cultural Rigidity**	**Cultural Affective Reactance**	**Cultural Routine Seeking**
Allik et al.'s / McCrae et al.'s Big-Five						
Cultural Profiles						
Neuroticism	20/ 21	51.14/ 49.80	4.42/ 1.77	.12/–.10	.54*/.17	–.31/–.18
Extraversion	20/ 21	47.75/ 50.08	4.72/ 2.41	.19/.08	–.70**/–.42	–.06/.10
Openness	20/ 21	50.64/ 50.03	3.43/ 1.82	–.06/–.07	–.24/–.09	.39/–.06
Agreeableness	20/ 21	49.77/ 49.87	3.20/ 1.66	–.22/.28	.08/–.15	.69**/–.19
Conscientiousness	20/ 21	49.55/ 49.97	3.34/ 1.62	.08/.40	–.11/–.46*	.01/–.28

*$p < .05$; **$p < .01$

exclude, and may sometimes even facilitate, development and change. Beyond the relationships with extant cultural dimensions, further evidence for the meaningfulness of the change orientation dimensions was obtained by demonstrating links between them and country-level indexes of change. We review these next.

Cultural Change Orientation and Societal Outcomes

The country-level outcomes we aimed to predict using the cultural change orientation dimensions were annual indexes of economic and technological change, and of social and environmental development (see Table 20.2), obtained from the World Bank World Development pool (http://data.worldbank.org/data-catalog/world-development-indicators) and the 2010 Rainbow Europe Map and Country Index (http://www.ilga-europe.org/rainboweurope/2010). Moreover, we also tested their relationships with the rate at which such indexes change. Of particular interest in our findings was the fact that whereas cultural rigidity and affective reactance tended to be associated with slower development and change, routine seeking was associated with greater change and progress. The focus on structure and routines, as captured in the routine-seeking dimension, seems to provide societies with an infrastructure and a secure base for exploring and further developing. In contrast, both cultural rigidity and affective reactance reflect a defensive stance, oriented toward inaction.

Specifically, in line with its focus on societies' disinclination to change established norms and ideas, cultural rigidity was negatively associated with the number of patent

Table 20.2 Spearman correlations between change orientation dimensions and country-level outcomes (adopted from Oreg & Sverdlik, 2018)

Variable	Cultural Rigidity	Affective Reactance	Routine seeking
1. GDP	$-.38^{\dagger}$	–.12	.21
2. Mobile cellular subscriptions	–.05	.07	$.41^{*}$
3. Number of patent applications	$-.45^{*}$	.02	.19
4. Research and development expenditure	$-.47^{*}$	–.07	$.62^{**}$
5. High-technology exports	$-.42^{*}$	–.08	$.45^{*}$
6. Entrepreneurial activity[1]	–.14	–.24	$.67^{**}$
7. Proportions of women in parliament[1]	–.09	$-.39^{*}$	$.54^{**}$
8. Alternative and nuclear energy	.06	$-.48^{*}$	–.03
9. LGB rights[2]	.04	$-.54^{*}$	$.66^{**}$
10. Subjective well being	–.36	$-.39^{*}$	$.56^{**}$

$^{\dagger}p = .052$; $^{*}p < .05$; $^{**}p \leq .01$

[1] Scores for this variable were only available for 26 countries; [2] Scores for LGB rights were only available for the 16 European countries in the Oreg and Sverdlik (2018) sample

applications in a country, a country's expenditure on research and development, exports of high-tech products, and a country's GDP. Cultural rigidity was similarly negatively associated with the rate at which these indexes of economic and technological development changed over a period of approximately 20 years. In line with its emphasis on a society's overall anxiety and vigilance about change, affective reactance was negatively associated with country-level well-being and with indexes of social and environmental change, such as in the proportion of women in parliament, LGB rights, and countries' use of alternative nuclear energy.

In contrast to the former two dimensions, cultural routine seeking was positively associated with country-level well-being and several indexes of economic and technological outcomes, including countries' high-tech exports, number of mobile cellular subscriptions, R&D expenditure, and entrepreneurial activity. It was also positively associated with the rate of growth in the latter three indexes. Most of the above relationships held while controlling for the dimensions of the other cultural taxonomies reviewed above and while controlling for GDP.

The evidence from our earlier research thus suggests that cultural change orientation can be used for predicting meaningful change-related outcomes at the country level. Moreover, each dimension is associated with a distinct set of cultural values and country-level outcomes. Cultural rigidity is aimed at maintaining stability, as reflected in a society's inaction and reluctance to change beliefs, norms, and procedures. Accordingly, it is negatively associated with indexes of economic and technological development. Affective reactance is also oriented toward stability, yet through societies' vigilance and anxiety about change, and it is negatively related to country-level well-being and to indexes of social and environmental change. Lastly, cultural routine seeking emphasizes the voluntary adoption of structure and routines while using these as the basis for a society's development. Accordingly, it is positively associated with country-level well-being and indexes of economic and technological development.

Given their specific focus on change and established insights about the role of national culture as an influential context within which changes in organizations unfold, the three change orientation dimensions may be useful for linking national culture and characteristics of organizational change and the responses to it. We conceptually develop such links in the following section.

Cultural Change Orientation and Organizational Change

To systematically link national culture to organizational change, we consider key events and components in the evolution of organizational change. We include in this evolution the initiation of change, the nature of the change, the process through which it is introduced and managed, and the nature of change recipients' responses to the change (see Table 20.3).

Table 20.3 Conceptual links between change orientation dimensions and key factors in organizational change

	Cultural rigidity	Affective reactance	Routine seeking
Change Initiation	Less likely	Less likely	More likely
Change Content / Type of Change			
Incremental versus Radical	Incremental	–	More incremental and radical
Social versus Technological	Fewer technological	Fewer social	More technological and social
Imposed versus Voluntary	–	More imposed	More voluntary
Change Process			
Communication	–	Less likely	More likely
Participation	–	Less likely	More likely
Organizational support	–	Less likely	More likely
Procedural justice	–	Less likely	More likely
Response to Change			
Valence	Negative	Ambivalent	Positive
Activation	Low	High	High
Type of response	Cognitive	Affective	Behavioral

Cultural Change Orientation and the Initiation of Organizational Changes

National cultural can be linked with the frequency at which organizational changes occur. The likelihood that a change will be initiated is influenced by several factors, including a cognitive openness to considering alternatives to the status quo, one's inherent feelings about change, and a solid base from which one can safely explore new territory. Each of these factors is shaped, in part, by the cultural emphases within a given society. Openness to alternatives, for example, may be influenced by the degree to which a given society relies on existing ideas and inertia versus highlighting progression and novelty. Such differences are captured in the dimension of cultural rigidity. Accordingly, we can expect the initiation of change to be less likely in organizations within culturally rigid societies.

The initiation of change is also less likely in cultures that predispose individuals to experience negative emotions toward the notion of change. As captured in cultural affective reactance, whereas some cultures may elicit positive emotions toward change, others tend to elicit anxiety and fear from it. Accordingly, changes should be less likely to be initiated in organizations within cultures high on affective reactance. In addition, in many contexts, a prerequisite to exploring new directions is a sense of stability and safety within one's current stance (Brown & Eisenhardt, 1997). Such stability is represented in the dimension of cultural routine seeking. Accordingly, the initiation of organizational change would be more likely in countries that are high on cultural routine seeking.

The findings we presented in Table 20.2, linking the three change orientation dimensions with indexes of country-level change, provide initial evidence for our propositions. Although the changes we listed are operationalized at the country, rather than organization, level, several of them reflect changes that took place or were initiated in organizations. Entrepreneurial activity, for example, reflects novel initiatives that originate in companies. Progressive social legislation and the use of alternative nuclear energy similarly reflect changes that take place in public and private organizations. This suggests that organizational changes are more likely to take place in countries low on affective reactance and cultural rigidity and high on routine seeking.

Once a change is initiated, several aspects of the change can be further influenced by national culture. As described in our review of the literature on national culture and change (see Figure 20.1), the key change-related factors that have been predicted by national culture thus far include the *change content*, *change process*, and recipients' *responses to the change* (see Table 20.3). These are also key factors in the psychological literature about organizational change (e.g., Oreg et al., 2011, 2013; Rafferty et al., 2013). We elaborate on each of these factors next.

Cultural Change Orientation and Change Content

Change content refers to the nature of the change and its elements. We focus here on three dimensions on which the content of the change can be differentiated: incremental versus radical, technological versus social, and voluntary versus imposed.

An established distinction is between changes that are incremental versus radical (the latter are also known as discontinuous, revolutionary or breakthrough change; e.g., Dewar & Dutton, 1986; Tushman & Anderson, 1986). The key difference between the two types of change is the degree to which the change enhances or destroys previous competencies and practices (Tushman & Anderson, 1986). Whereas incremental change builds on and extends or enhances existing practices, radical change renders extant practices useless because the change entails an entirely new approach. This distinction would thus be particularly important in culturally rigid societies, in which there is little openness to new ideas. Thus, the lower prevalence of changes in culturally rigid societies is likely to be particularly pronounced with respect to radical changes. In contrast, given the increased frequency at which changes are initiated in routine-seeking cultures, the prevalence of both incremental and radical organizational change can be expected to positively correlate with a society's cultural routine seeking.

As can be seen in the various national change indexes in Table 20.2, another distinction among types of change is between changes that are economic and technological in nature, which are least prevalent in culturally rigid societies, versus those that are social-environmental, which are least prevalent in affective reactant societies. Whereas the former changes appear to require a proactive stance and an overall openness to new ideas, the latter, comprising changes in the social order, involve individuals' affective orientation toward the notion of change. One can similarly distinguish between these kinds of changes in organizations. Given the findings described above, we would expect less development and implementation of new technologies in organizations within culturally rigid societies and fewer changes that involve a change to the organizational structure and distribution of power in organizations within affective reactant cultures. Moreover, in accordance with the overall increased likelihood of changes in high routine-seeking cultures, the prevalence of both technological and social changes is likely to be higher in organizations within national cultures high on routine seeking.

A third distinction that is particularly relevant to organizations is that between voluntary and imposed changes (Oreg & Sverdlik, 2011; Sverdlik & Oreg, 2009, 2015). Whereas both types of changes challenge the status quo, imposed changes also threaten change recipients' autonomy, whereas voluntary change provides the opportunity to express one's autonomy (Sverdlik & Oreg, 2015). The emphasis on autonomy that characterizes routine-seeking societies would thus suggest that the changes most likely to be implemented in these societies are voluntary. In contrast, the apprehension that is experienced toward change in affective reactant cultures, along with the hierarchical nature of these cultures, suggests that the changes most likely to be implemented in these societies are imposed. We summarize these predictions in Table 20.3.

Cultural Change Orientation and Change Process

As described above, the change process refers to the manner in which changes are introduced and implemented in the organization (Armenakis & Bedeian, 1999; Oreg et al., 2011). Key among attributes of the change process are the degree and quality of *communication* about the change, the degree to which change recipients are provided with opportunities to *participate* in planning and implementing the change, the amount of *support* the organization provides to help recipients cope with the change and its implications, and recipients' overall perception that the change was managed *fairly*. All four of these provide change recipients with a sense of control and autonomy in preparation for and during the change (see Table 20.3).

The emphasis on autonomy that characterizes cultural routine seeking and the apprehension and lack of autonomy that characterize affective reactance make these two cultural dimensions particularly relevant for predicting the process through which organizational changes are managed in a given cultural setting. Accordingly, one could expect the management of organizational changes in high-routine-seeking cultures to provide recipients with greater control (i.e., more communication, participation, support, and procedural justice) relative to organizations in low-routine-seeking cultures. In contrast, changes within high affective reactant cultures will be managed through a more restrictive and programmatic process than in low affective reactant cultures. This corresponds with our proposition above concerning the increased ratio of voluntary changes in routine-seeking cultures and of imposed changes in affective reactant ones.

Cultural Change Orientation and Responses to Change

The literature on responses to change draws attention to several dimensions of change recipient reactions to organizational change (e.g., Choi, 2011; Rafferty et al., 2013). Most straightforward, including the longest line of research (for a review, see Oreg et al., 2011), is the degree to which the response to change is positive versus negative (i.e., response valence). Over time, a greater degree of complexity in the response to change has been acknowledged, including distinctions between affective, cognitive, and behavioral responses (e.g., Oreg, 2006; Piderit, 2000), the existence of ambivalent responses (e.g., Oreg & Sverdlik, 2011; Sverdlik & Oreg, 2009), and more recently, an emphasis on the degree of activation of the response (Oreg et al., 2018). Accordingly, we draw links between the three cultural change orientation dimensions and each of these response dimensions.

With respect to response valence, one would expect the valence toward change to be positive in cultures high on routine seeking and negative in affective reactant and cultural rigid cultures. As we described above, the connotation of change in routine-oriented cultures tends to be positive, whereas the connotation of change in rigid and affective reactant cultures will tend to be negative. In affective reactant cultures, however, the inherent apprehension that society members experience may drive change recipients to behaviorally comply with change despite their negative affective response to it, which may manifest in an overall ambivalent response (see Table 20.3).

The distinction among types of change responses (i.e., affective, behavioral, cognitive) receives ample research attention and corresponds with the individual-level origins of the three cultural change orientation dimensions. As we described above, the cultural change orientation construct was derived from the country-level aggregation of individuals' responses to the dispositional resistance to change scale, which comprises behavioral, affective, and cognitive dimensions. As our analyses indicated (Oreg & Sverdlik, 2018), this distinction was maintained at the culture level, such that cultural rigidity emphasizes cognitive elements, (e.g., openness to new ideas); affective reactance captures an overall affective apprehension; and routine seeking represents the maintenance of behavioral practices. Accordingly, the type of response most relevant for representing recipients' responses to change in culturally rigid, affective reactant, and routine-seeking cultures should be cognitive, affective, and behavioral, respectively.

Finally, the various responses to change, whether positive or negative, can also be distinguished on the basis of their degree of activation (Oreg et al., 2018). Positive responses to change can range from enthusiastic support to passive compliance. Negative responses range from belligerent resistance to passive-aggressive foot-dragging. The inaction that characterizes cultural rigidity suggests that responses to change in culturally rigid societies would tend to be of low activation. In contrast, the elevated vigilance that characterizes affective reactant cultures suggests that activation of the response to changes in these cultures would tend to be high. With respect to routine seeking, we rely on both the literature linking perceived control to high response activation (e.g., Lazarus, 1991) and the emphasis on autonomy highlighted in these cultures to propose that the activation of responses to organizational change in routine-seeking cultures will be high.

Discussion

Despite ample evidence for the relevance of national culture on organizational processes (for reviews see Gelfand et al., 2017; Tsui et al., 2007), and the centrality of organizational change as a key organizational process, relatively little research has directly addressed the link between national culture and organizational change. We present in Figure 20.1 a summary of extant findings. Studies undertaking a macro approach to the study of change highlight the relationships between national culture and the types of change initiated, as well as the process through which they are managed. Only a few studies, however, have demonstrated these relationships empirically. Those that have do so by comparing changes conducted across a number of countries. As we described above, most of the scholarship on the topic used Hofstede's framework of cultural values as the means for either conceptually or empirically comparing changes across countries. Studies undertaking a micro approach demonstrate similarities and differences in individuals' orientation or attitude toward change across countries, but here too only very few studies have been conducted.

Two of the studies we found argue for a moderating effect of national culture, such that the relationship between the change process or change leadership and responses to change will vary across national cultures.

To better understand the role of national culture in shaping organizational change, much more research is required, with an effort to uncover characteristics of culture that pertain to change and the impact of these characteristics on the processes and outcomes of organizational change. With respect to the former effort, we reviewed extant taxonomies, focusing on those dimensions most relevant to the notion of change. We highlighted a recently developed taxonomy of cultural change orientations, discussed its three dimensions, and reviewed findings about their relationships with country-level change-related outcomes. We then proposed links between the three dimensions and key events or aspects of organizational change, namely, change initiation, change content, change process, and responses to change (see Table 20.3).

Future research could empirically test these proposed links. Specifically, relationships could be tested between country scores on the three change orientation dimensions and (1) the rates at which different types of changes are initiated in these countries, (2) patterns reflecting the manner in which changes are implemented, and (3) overarching trends in recipients' responses to these changes. Moreover, beyond the main effects that each of the change orientation dimensions may have, the dimensions may also have interactive effects. Cultural routine seeking, for example, which is positively associated with progress and development, may moderate the generally negative effects of the other two dimensions, such that their effects may be attenuated. In addition, although emotional reactance is not correlated with indexes of economic and technological change, it may nevertheless enhance the negative effects of cultural rigidity on these indexes.

More broadly, more research should be conducted for linking attributes of national culture with attributes of organizational change. Conducting such research poses a number of challenges such as composing indexes that represent country-level rates of change and obtaining data about change processes and responses to change in the context of comparable changes across a sufficiently large number of countries. Current investigations are predominantly based on a very small number of countries, which provide only anecdotal insights. Moreover, cross-cultural research of change should consider organizational changes beyond those that take place as part of OD endeavors. COVID-19 may have provided an opportunity for such research, given that similar organizational changes have been implemented around the world in response to pandemic-related restrictions (e.g., universities' transition to online teaching).

Beyond the main effects of national culture on attributes of organizational change, findings on the importance of fit between national culture and the nature of the changes introduced (e.g., Head & Sorensen, 1993) suggest that culture may also moderate relationships among attributes of organizational change, such as between the change process and recipients' responses to the change. Moreover, some dimensions of national culture may moderate the effects of other cultural dimensions on change-related outcomes. For example, tightness–looseness has been shown to moderate the effects of Hofstede's dimensions on a variety of organizational outcomes, such that effects tended to be stronger in tighter cultures (Taras et al., 2010). Tightness may accordingly amplify the effects of change-related cultural dimensions (e.g., cultural change orientation) on the process or outcomes of organizational change.

From a practical perspective, our conceptual analyses also provide insights for the implementation of organizational change (see Table 20.4), although we present these tentatively given the scant research on the subject. Perhaps the broadest of insights is about the importance of fit between national culture and both the types of changes implemented and the manner in which they are managed. Changes are more likely to succeed and

Table 20.4 Key theoretical principles and practical implications

Theoretical Principles
1. Fit between types of organizational changes and attributes of the national culture within which these changes are implemented contributes to the acceptance and success of the change.
2. Influences of culture on factors in the management and change and on responses to organizational change have been studied separately. Integrating insights from both literatures allows for consideration of mediated processes, whereby the change process mediates the effects of culture on the response to change.
3. The predominant taxonomies of cultural dimensions include several dimensions that in one way or another pertain to the notion of change.
4. Cultural differences can be conceptualized through societies' orientation toward change. Extant findings suggest three dimensions of such an orientation: cultural rigidity, affective reactance, and routine seeking.
5. Incorporating the cultural change orientation taxonomy into the literature on organizational change allows for the development of conceptual propositions about relationships between national culture and change content, change process, and the components of recipients' responses to change.
Practical Implications
1. The implementation of organizational change should be sensitive to the broader cultural context within which change is introduced.
2. Knowledge of the mechanisms through which societies maintain the balance between stability and change (e.g., rely on accepted modes of thinking, rely on established social structures, maintain routines) suggests the processes through which change can be most effectively managed.
3. Instilling in change recipients a sense of control through change communication and participation may be particularly useful in cultures that value autonomy, such as those high on cultural routine seeking.
4. Providing change recipients with support in preparation for and during organizational change may be particularly meaningful and effective in societies characterized by elevated levels of vigilance and apprehension, such as those high on affective reactance.
5. Structuring change around accepted ideas and modes of operations may be useful for promoting change in culturally rigid societies.

benefit change recipients when their initiation and design have been formulated while considering the national culture's attributes.

Other insights for implementing change can be drawn from considering the three cultural change orientation dimensions and from findings about the moderating effect of culture on the link between change process and responses to change. Specifically, participatory change processes may be especially important in societies that highlight the combination of routines and autonomy, such as in routine-seeking cultures. Similarly, supportiveness during change may be particularly meaningful in societies with higher levels of anxiety toward change, as represented in cultural change reactance. Finally, framing change in incremental terms, focusing on those aspects of the change that correspond with extant ideas, may be particularly useful in culturally rigid societies. More generally, we call for a more systematic consideration, by both practitioners and scholars, of the role of national culture in understanding organizational change.

References

Allik, J., Church, A. T., Ortiz, F. A., Rossier, J., Hřebíčková, M., De Fruyt, F., Realo, A., & McCrae, R. R. (2017). Mean profiles of the NEO personality inventory. *Journal of Cross-Cultural Psychology, 48*(3), 402–420.

Armenakis, A. A., & Bedeian, A. G. (1999). Organizational change: A review of theory and research in the 1990s. *Journal of Management, 25*(3), 293–315.

Bartunek, J. M., Rousseau, D. M., Rudolph, J. W., & DePalma, J. A. (2006). On the receiving end: Sensemaking, emotion, and assessments of an organizational change initiated by others. *Journal of Applied Behavioral Science, 42*(2), 182–206.

Battilana, J., & Casciaro, T. (2012). Change agents, networks, and institutions: A contingency theory of organizational change. *Academy of Management Journal, 55*(2), 381–398.

Boeker, W. (1997). Strategic change: The influence of managerial characteristics and organizational growth. *Academy of Management Journal, 40*(1), 152–170.

Bouckenooghe, D., M. Schwarz, G., & Minbashian, A. (2015). Herscovitch and Meyer's three-component model of commitment to change: Meta-analytic findings. *European Journal of Work and Organizational Psychology, 24*(4), 578–595.

Brown, S. L., & Eisenhardt, K. M. (1997). The art of continuous change: Linking complexity theory and time-paced evolution in relentlessly shifting organizations. *Administrative Science Quarterly, 42*(1), 1–34.

Brown, S. L., & Eisenhardt, K. M. (1998). *Competing on the edge: Strategy as structured chaos.* Cambridge, MA: Harvard Business Press.

Burke, W. W., & Litwin, G. H. (1992). A causal model of organizational performance and change. *Journal of Management, 18*(3), 523–545.

Cartwright, S., & Cooper, C. L. (1993). The psychological impact of merger and acquisition on the individual: A study of building society managers. *Human Relations, 46*(3), 327.

Chiu, C.-Y., Gelfand, M. J., Yamagishi, T., Shteynberg, G., & Wan, C. (2010). Intersubjective culture: The role of intersubjective perceptions in cross-cultural research. *Perspectives on Psychological Science, 5*(4), 482–493.

Choi, M. (2011). Employees' attitudes toward organizational change: A literature review. *Human Resource Management, 50*(4), 479–500.

d'Iribarne, P. (2002). Motivating workers in emerging countries: Universal tools and local adaptations. *Journal of Organizational Behavior, 23*(3), 243–256.

De, S., Nau, D. S., & Gelfand, M. J. (2017). *Understanding norm change: An evolutionary game-theoretic approach.* Paper presented at the Proceedings of the 16th Conference on Autonomous Agents and MultiAgent Systems, São Paulo Brazil.

De, S., Nau, D. S., Pan, X., & Gelfand, M. J. (2018). *Tipping points for norm change in human cultures.* Paper presented at the International Conference on Social Computing, Behavioral-Cultural Modeling and Prediction and Behavior Representation in Modeling and Simulation, Washington, DC.

Dewar, R. D., & Dutton, J. E. (1986). The adoption of radical and incremental innovations: An empirical analysis. *Management Science, 32*(11), 1422–1433.

DiBella, A. J. (1996). Culture and planned change in an international organization: a multi-level predicament. *International Journal of Organizational Analysis, 4*(4), 352–372.

Erez, M., & Gati, E. (2004). A dynamic, multi-level model of culture: from the micro level of the individual to the macro level of a global culture. *Applied Psychology, 53*(4), 583–598.

Fagenson-Eland, E., Ensher, E. A., & Burke, W. W. (2004). Organization development and change interventions: A seven-nation comparison. *The Journal of Applied Behavioral Science, 40*(4), 432–464.

Fugate, M., & Soenen, G. (2018). Predictors and processes related to employees' change-related compliance and championing. *Personnel Psychology, 71*(1), 109–132.

Galperin, B. L., & Lituchy, T. R. (2014). Human resource development in service firms across cultures. *Human Resource Development Review, 13*(3), 336–368.

Gebauer, J. E., Sedikides, C., Wagner, J., Bleidorn, W., Rentfrow, P. J., Potter, J., & Gosling, S. D. (2015). Cultural norm fulfillment, interpersonal belonging, or getting ahead? A large-scale cross-cultural test of three perspectives on the function of self-esteem. *Journal of Personality and Social Psychology, 109*(3), 526.

Gelfand, M. J., Aycan, Z., Erez, M., & Leung, K. (2017). Cross-cultural industrial organizational psychology and organizational behavior: A hundred-year journey. *Journal of Applied Psychology, 102*(3), 514.

Gelfand, M. J., Raver, J. L., Nishii, L., Leslie, L. M., Lun, J., Lim, B. C., Duan, L., Almaliach, A., Ang, S., Arnadottir, J., Aycan, Z. Boehnke, K., Boski, P., Cabechinhas, R., Chan, D., Chhokar, J., D'Amato, A., Ferrer, M., Fischlmayr, I. C., . . . Yamaguchi, S. (2011). Differences between tight and loose cultures: A 33-nation study. *Science, 332*(6033), 1100–1104.

Graen, G. B., & Uhl-Bien, M. (1995). Relationship-based approach to leadership: Development of leader-member exchange (LMX) theory of leadership over 25 years: Applying a multi-level multi-domain perspective. *The Leadership Quarterly, 6*(2), 219–247.

Greenfield, P. M. (2009). Linking social change and developmental change: Shifting pathways of human development. *Developmental Psychology, 45*(2), 401.

Grossmann, I., & Varnum, M. E. (2015). Social structure, infectious diseases, disasters, secularism, and cultural change in America. *Psychological Science, 26*(3), 311–324.

Head, T. C., & Sorensen, P. F. (1993). Cultural values and organizational development: A seven-country study. *Leadership & Organization Development Journal, 14*(2), 3–7. https://doi.org/10.1108/01437739310032656

Helpap, S. (2016). The impact of power distance orientation on recipients' reactions to participatory versus programmatic change communication. *The Journal of Applied Behavioral Science, 52*(1), 5–34.

Hempel, P. S., & Martinsons, M. G. (2009). Developing international organizational change theory using cases from China. *Human Relations, 62*(4), 459–499.

Herscovitch, L., & Meyer, J. P. (2002). Commitment to organizational change: Extension of a three-component model. *Journal of Applied Psychology, 87*(3), 474–487.

Hofstede, G. (1980). *Culture's consequences, international differences in work-related values.* Beverly Hills, CA: SAGE.

Hofstede, G. (2001). *Culture's consequences: comparing values, behaviors, institutions, and organizations across nations* (2nd ed.). Thousand Oaks, CA: SAGE.

House, R. J., Hanges, P. J., Javidan, M., Dorfman, P., & Gupta, V. (2004). *Culture, leadership, and organizations: The GLOBE study of 62 societies.* Thousand Oaks, CA: SAGE.

House, R. J., Javidan, M., Hanges, P. J., & Dorfman, P. (2002). Understanding cultures and implicit leadership theories across the globe: an introduction to project GLOBE. *Journal of World Business, 37*(1), 3–10.

Inglehart, R. (1997). *Modernization and postmodernization: Cultural, economic, and political change in 43 societies.* Princeton, NJ: Princeton University Press.

Inglehart, R., & Baker, W. E. (2000). Modernization, cultural change, and the persistence of traditional values. *American Sociological Review, 65*(1), 19–51.

Jaeger, A. M. (1986). Organization development and national culture: Where's the fit? *Academy of Management Review, 11*(1), 178–190.

Jones, R. A., Jimmieson, N. L., & Griffiths, A. (2005). The impact of organizational culture and reshaping capabilities on change implementation success: The mediating role of readiness for change. *Journal of Management Studies, 42*, 361–386.

Lau, C. M., & Ngo, H. Y. (2001). Organization development and firm performance: A comparison of multinational and local firms. *Journal of International Business Studies, 32*, 95–114.
Lazarus, R. S. (1991). Cognition and motivation in emotion. *American Psychologist, 46*(4), 352–367.
Lee, K., Scandura, T. A., & Sharif, M. M. (2014). Cultures have consequences: A configural approach to leadership across two cultures. *The Leadership Quarterly, 25*(4), 692–710.
Lewin, K. (1947). Frontiers in group dynamics: concept, method and reality in social science; social equilibria and social change. *Human Relations, 1*, 5–41.
McCrae, R. R., & Terracciano, A. (2005). Personality profiles of cultures: Aggregate personality traits. *Journal of Personality and Social Psychology, 89*(3), 407.
Meyer, J. P., Srinivas, E., Lal, J. B., & Topolnytsky, L. (2007). Employee commitment and support for an organizational change: Test of the three-component model in two cultures. *Journal of Occupational and Organizational Psychology, 80*(2), 185–211.
Oishi, S., & Graham, J. (2010). Social ecology: Lost and found in psychological science. *Perspectives on Psychological Science, 5*(4), 356–377.
Oreg, S. (2003). Resistance to change: Developing an individual differences measure. *Journal of Applied Psychology, 88*, 680–693.
Oreg, S. (2006). Personality, context, and resistance to organizational change. *European Journal of Work and Organizational Psychology, 15*, 73–101.
Oreg, S. (2018). Resistance to change and performance: Toward a more even-handed view of dispositional resistance. *The Journal of Applied Behavioral Science, 54*(1), 88–107.
Oreg, S., Bartunek, J. M., Lee, G., & Do, B. (2018). An affect-based model of recipients' responses to organizational change events. *Academy of Management Review, 43*(1), 65–86.
Oreg, S., Bayazit, M., Vakola, M., Arciniega, L., Armenakis, A. A., Barkauskiene, R., . . ., & van Dam, K. (2008). Dispositional resistance to change: Measurement equivalence and the link to personal values across 17 nations. *Journal of Applied Psychology, 93*(4), 935–944.
Oreg, S., & Goldenberg, J. (2015). *Resistance to innovation: Its sources and manifestations*. Chicago: University of Chicago Press.
Oreg, S., Michel, A., & By, R. T. (Eds.). (2013). *The psychology of organizational change: Viewing change from the employee's perspective*. Cambridge: Cambridge University Press.
Oreg, S., & Sverdlik, N. (2011). Ambivalence toward imposed change: The conflict between dispositional resistance to change and the orientation toward the change agent. *Journal of Applied Psychology, 96*(2), 337–349.
Oreg, S., & Sverdlik, N. (2018). Translating dispositional resistance to change to the culture level: Developing a cultural framework of change orientations. *European Journal of Personality, 32*(4), 327–352.
Oreg, S., Vakola, M., & Armenakis, A. A. (2011). Change recipients' reactions to organizational change: A sixty-year review of quantitative studies. *The Journal of Applied Behavioral Science, 47*(4), 461–524.
Paquin, A. R., Roch, S. G., & Sanchez-Ku, M. L. (2007). An investigation of cross-cultural differences on the impact of productivity interventions: The example of ProMES. *The Journal of Applied Behavioral Science, 43*(4), 427–448.
Piderit, S. K. (2000). Rethinking resistance and recognizing ambivalence: A multidimensional view of attitudes toward an organizational change. *Academy of Management Review, 25*(4), 783–794.
Rafferty, A. E., Jimmieson, N. L., & Armenakis, A. A. (2013). Change readiness: A multilevel review. *Journal of Management, 39*(1), 110–135.
Schwartz, S. (1994). Beyond individualism/collectivism: New cultural dimensions of values. In U. Kim, H. C. Triandis, C. Kagitcibasi, S.-C. Choi, & G. Yoon (Eds.), *Individualism and collectivism: Theory, method, and applications* (pp. 85–119). Newbury Park, CA: SAGE.
Schwartz, S. (2006). A theory of cultural value orientations: Explication and applications. *Comparative Sociology, 5*(2), 137–182.
Shove, E. (2003). Converging conventions of comfort, cleanliness and convenience. *Journal of Consumer Policy, 26*(4), 395–418.
Soenen, G., Melkonian, T., & Ambrose, M. L. (2017). To shift or not to shift? Determinants and consequences of phase shifting on justice judgments. *Academy of Management Journal, 60*(2), 798–817.
Sverdlik, N., & Oreg, S. (2009). Personal values and conflicting motivational forces in the context of imposed change. *Journal of Personality, 77*(5), 1437–1466.

Sverdlik, N., & Oreg, S. (2015). Identification during imposed change: The roles of personal values, type of change, and anxiety. *Journal of Personality, 83*(3), 307–319.
Taras, V., Kirkman, B. L., & Steel, P. (2010). Examining the impact of culture's consequences: A three-decade, multilevel, meta-analytic review of Hofstede's cultural value dimensions. *Journal of Applied Psychology, 95*(3), 405–439.
Toh, S. M., & Leonardelli, G. J. (2012). Cultural constraints on the emergence of women as leaders. *Journal of World Business, 47*(4), 604–611.
Tsui, A. S., Nifadkar, S. S., & Ou, A. Y. (2007). Cross-national, cross-cultural organizational behavior research: Advances, gaps, and recommendations. *Journal of Management, 33*(3), 426–478.
Tushman, M. L., & Anderson, P. (1986). Technological discontinuities and organizational environments. *Administrative Science Quarterly, 31*(3), 439–465.
Välikangas, L., & Okumura, A. (1997). Why do people follow leaders? A study of a US and a Japanese change program. *The Leadership Quarterly, 8*(3), 313–337.
Varnum, M. E., & Grossmann, I. (2017). Cultural change: The how and the why. *Perspectives on Psychological Science, 12*(6), 956–972.
Venaik, S., & Brewer, P. (2010). Avoiding uncertainty in Hofstede and GLOBE. *Journal of International Business Studies, 41*, 1294–1315.
Yüksek, S., & Bekmeier-Feuerhahn, S. (2013). Culture-Specific Objectives of Change Communication: An Intercultural Perspective. *Journal of Management and Change, 30/31*, 180–193.

PART VI

Cross-Cultural Organization Interfaces

CHAPTER 21

Culture and Work–Family Dynamics

Winny Shen *and* Kristen M. Shockley

Abstract

Awareness of the influence of culture has permeated work–family research since its inception. In this chapter, we first briefly review the history and evolution of cross-cultural work–family research, followed by a focus on the current state of work–family research in the last decade. Although cross-cultural work–family research has experienced stunning growth over the last three decades, it still tends to be heavily centered on a limited set of constructs (i.e., work–family conflict), use a narrow range of methods (i.e., quantitative cross-sectional survey research), concentrate on certain world regions (i.e., Anglo-Asian comparisons), and predictions are based predominantly on specific cultural values (i.e., individualism–collectivism). We identify key controversies in the literature and set an agenda for future research that expands our understanding of cross-cultural work–family concerns in multiple ways, including a call for a focus on process to refine theory-building and theory-testing and diversification of research designs and methods (e.g., experiments). Implications for theory and practice are also discussed.

Key Words: work-family, cross-cultural, national policies, cultural values

The Beginnings of Research on Culture and Work–Family Dynamics

The scientific study of the intersection of people's work and family lives gained initial traction in the 1980s and has become an increasingly prevalent area of research over the past four decades. Although the earliest work was U.S.-centric, researchers have long recognized the importance of cultural considerations in the work–family interface. Specifically, certain cultural values and national policies (e.g., collectivism, parental leave policies) dictate norms for how people behave at home and at work, in addition to how they view the dual management of work and family roles. This acknowledgment led to work–family studies conducted outside of the United States context beginning in the early 1990s (e.g., Aryee, 1992, in Singapore; Izraeli, 1993, in Israel).

Multi-sample comparative studies, where work–family variables are explicitly compared across cultures, started appearing in the literature beginning around the early 2000s (e.g., Aryee et al., 1999; Yang et al., 2000). This date also corresponds to when cross-cultural work–family research really took off in earnest and when studies in this domain started to accumulate at a rapid rate, which continues today. The literature has grown so substantially over the subsequent 20 years that there have been enough studies to conduct meta-analyses on both mean differences across cultures on central work–family constructs (i.e., work–family conflict; Allen et al., 2015) and on the moderating role of culture in the relationship between predictors and antecedents of work–family conflict (Allen et al., 2020; French et al., 2018).

Before moving on, it is imperative to first define key work–family constructs. The most commonly studied variable—in general and within cross-cultural work–family research in particular—is work–family conflict, defined as a "form of interrole conflict in which the role pressures from the work and family domains are mutually incompatible in some respect" (Greenhaus & Beutell, 1985, p. 77). Scholars often make distinctions between the directionality of conflict; work-interference-with-family (WIF) occurs when the work domain intrudes upon the family domain, and family-interference-with work (FIW) occurs when the family domain intrudes upon the work domain. Work–family balance is the second most commonly researched variable in cross-cultural work–family research (Shockley et al., 2017a). The study of work–family balance generally has been fraught with inconsistent operationalizations across studies (Casper et al., 2018), but it typically refers to the notion that work and family life are somehow integrated, harmonious, or free from substantial conflict (Frone, 2003). Finally, a few cross-cultural studies have measured variables such as work–family fit (i.e., how well one is able to integrate work and family) or work–family enrichment (i.e., the extent to which experiences and resources in one role enhance performance in the other role; see Greenhaus & Powell, 2006).

Interestingly, across these work–family constructs, family is rarely explicitly defined. Although work–family researchers often employ inclusion criteria in their studies that may reflect their own beliefs regarding who constitutes a family (e.g., married or cohabiting with a partner, having child care or elder care responsibilities), these criteria are highly variable across studies. Further, even when such criteria are used to delineate a sample, work–family measures that contain the term *family* rarely offer participants a definition of what is meant by the term, allowing for much individual interpretation. Thus, participants may potentially hold very different views from other participants and the researchers conducting these studies regarding who exactly is family. We return to this point in our section on future research directions.

Before delving into a more extensive review of this literature over the past decade, we first briefly review some of the seminal projects in cross-cultural work–family research. Several prominent studies emerged from the Collaborative International Study of Managerial Stress (CISMS), which consisted of two phases, over 40 researchers, and approximately 7,000 managers drawn from more than 20 countries in each phase (though not all countries and participants were included in all studies). The products of this project include a paper by Spector et al. (2004), who found that the relationship between work hours and WIF was stronger in the Anglo country cluster than in the more collectivistic

Latin or Asian country clusters. In a subsequent study, Spector et al. (2007) found that the relationship between work demands and strain-based WIF, as well as the relationship between strain-based WIF and job attitudes (i.e., job satisfaction and turnover intentions) tend to be stronger in the Anglo country cluster than the other three more collectivistic country clusters (e.g., Asian, Latin, and Eastern European). Finally, Masuda et al. (2012) found that flexible work arrangements were more likely to be available in the Anglo country cluster, and the relationship between the availability of different flexible work arrangements (e.g., flextime, part-time work) and outcomes (e.g., work–family conflict, turnover intentions) often differed across country clusters.

Another major effort was Project 3535, which consisted of three phases and nearly 3,000 organizationally employed parents in 10 countries. Project 3535 is unique in that it utilized a mixed-methods approach (i.e., focus groups and quantitative surveys), the project team aimed to take a balanced approach in exploring both etic and emic concepts, and constructs beyond work–family conflict were assessed. The results of this project is reported in a comprehensive book by Korabik et al. (2017). Some notable findings include evidence that, although work overload was more strongly associated with WIF and turnover intentions in more individualistic and gender egalitarian countries (e.g., the United States, Australia) than in collectivistic and traditional countries (e.g., China, Turkey), the opposite pattern was found for family overload, such that it was more strongly related to FIW and turnover intentions in more collectivistic and traditional countries. Additionally, the authors also found that family control was more strongly related to family-to-work positive spillover in monochronic cultures (e.g., Taiwan, China), where the preference is to complete tasks one at a time, than in polychronic cultures (e.g., India, Indonesia), where the preference is often to multitask. Finally, the authors found that effective coping strategies to managing work–family conflict differed across cultures. Specifically, setting priorities at home was generally associated with the lowest work–family conflict in individualistic and gender egalitarian countries, but differential gender-congruent approaches (i.e., a "superman" at work for men and a "superwoman" at home for women) were associated with the lowest work–family conflict in collectivistic and gender traditional countries.

The Current State of the Field: The Last Decade in Review

We now take a deep dive into the state of the cross-cultural work–family literature over the past 10 years. Specifically, we first review recent meta-analytic syntheses that highlight both how typical experiences of work–family conflict vary across national or cultural contexts and how these contexts shape associations between work–family variables and both antecedents and outcomes. Next, we discuss some prominent narrative reviews that focus on both conceptual and methodological issues in this literature. To complement these syntheses, we also discuss primary studies focusing on cross-cultural issues from the last couple of years and how this domain appears to be evolving, including new ways to conceptualize culture (other than nation).

Meta-Analytic Investigations of Cross-Cultural Work–Family Research

Reflecting the significant growth and maturation of the literature on cultural perspectives to understanding work–family issues, a number of prominent syntheses have emerged within the past decade. In the first synthesis, Allen et al. (2015) conducted a meta-analysis to examine whether experiences of work–family conflict differ across national contexts. Whereas average levels of FIW did vary across contexts, average levels of WIF did not appear to systematically differ based on cultural dimensions, institutional factors, or economic conditions, which the authors speculate could be because WIF may be more strongly affected by organizational-level variables than national-level variables. However, FIW was higher in more collectivistic cultures relative to more individualistic cultures, and this appeared to be driven by the Asian (vs. Latin American) collectivistic subgroup in particular, suggesting that stronger family ties that are viewed as obligations may tend to create conflict between roles. Additionally, the United States exhibited higher FIW than the other countries combined, perhaps reflecting its unique position as the only industrialized nation without national-level policies or supports for family care (e.g., paid family leave). Finally, individuals in countries with less gender equity (i.e., differential access to resources dependent on gender) also experienced higher levels of FIW.

Not only does culture impact average levels of work–family conflict, but it also shapes the magnitude of relationships between work–family conflict and its antecedents and outcomes. Using a meta-analytic approach, Allen et al. (2020) examined whether associations between work (family) hours or demands and WIF (FIW) differed across national contexts. Although specific cultural dimensions (i.e., individualism–collectivism, power distance, and uncertainty avoidance) did not moderate relations between work hours or demands and WIF, there was some evidence that these demands were more strongly related to WIF in the Confucian Asia regional cluster, and to a lesser extent, the Anglo regional cluster relative to the other regional clusters defined by the GLOBE project (Gupta & Hanges, 2004). Allen et al. argued that these two regional clusters share a strong performance orientation; therefore, this emphasis on performance excellence perhaps enhances relations between different types of work demands and WIF.

In contrast, individualism–collectivism and uncertainty avoidance moderated the relationship between family hours and FIW, such that this relationship was stronger in more individualistic or higher uncertainty avoidance countries (Allen et al., 2020). These findings support the authors' contentions that beliefs that work is undertaken to benefit the family and the more permeable boundaries and flexible roles that tend to characterize lower uncertainty avoidance cultures may help to mitigate the negative consequences of family responsibilities on FIW. Interestingly, although not moderated by specific cultural dimensions, comparisons across clusters reveal that the relationship between family demands and FIW was *stronger* in all other regional clusters compared to the Anglo cluster (with the exception of the South Asia cluster). Thus, relations between quantitative versus qualitative family demands and FIW may differ across national environments in unexpected ways that are worth greater future exploration.

In addition to demands, resources are also argued to be important antecedents to work–family conflict, helping to alleviate its occurrence. In their meta-analysis of relations between social support and work–family conflict, French et al. (2018) also examined the role of national culture. The most robust finding was for national unemployment, such that the negative relationship between work support and WIF was stronger in country contexts where levels of unemployment were higher. Moderating effects by cultural dimensions and additional economic factors were also uncovered, but only when outliers were removed. Specifically, in-group collectivism, assertiveness, and GDP each moderated the relationship between work support and WIF, such that the negative relationship was weaker in country contexts that were higher on in-group collectivism, lower on assertiveness, and lower on GDP, respectively. The first two moderating effects are in line with a utility-based perspective, suggesting that support is more beneficial in contexts where it is more needed (i.e., where support tends to be less socially obligated, and where achievement is strongly valued and likely requires the removal of barriers to success). However, this is not the case for GDP, which the authors explain by theorizing that in low-GDP countries, individuals are more concerned with meeting basic needs and necessities (e.g., food and shelter) than higher-order goals surrounding work or family. Finally, compared to the moderation effects observed for work support and WIF, it appears that associations between indicators of family support and FIW are relatively robust across national contexts.

Beyond theorized antecedents, Allen et al. (2020) also examined whether relations between work–family conflict and domain-specific (i.e., job and family) and life satisfaction differed across national environments. They showed that collectivism moderated negative relationships between WIF and job and life satisfaction, respectively, such that these associations were weaker in more collectivistic countries. Power distance also moderated the negative relationship between WIF and job satisfaction, such that associations were weaker in higher-power distance countries. Thus, it seems that the harmful effects of WIF may be lessened in vertical-collectivistic cultures relative to horizontal-individualistic cultures. In line with this argument, when examining regional clusters, Allen et al. found that the association between WIF and job satisfaction was stronger in the Anglo and Germanic Europe clusters relative to the other regional clusters. Although specific cultural dimensions did not moderate the negative relationship between FIW and family satisfaction, there did appear to be important variations in this relationship across regional clusters. Specifically, the relationship between FIW and family and life satisfaction, respectively, was stronger in the Nordic Europe cluster relative to the other regional clusters. Allen and colleagues theorized that given that Nordic countries have some of the most generous family supportive policies in the world, occurrences of FIW may be unexpected and tend to lead to more negative affective outcomes among workers, such as family and life dissatisfaction.

To summarize, cultural differences do seem to play a role in work–family experiences, particularly in altering the strength of relationships between work–family conflict and its correlates. The nature of how and when cultural values matter varies significantly based on the specific predictors and consequences examined. The trend that emerges most consistently is that the antecedents and consequences are more strongly related to WIF and FIW in more individualistic cultures compared to more collectivistic nations.

Prominent Narrative Reviews and the Evolution of the Field in Recent Years

In addition to the meta-analytic reviews described above that focused on specific relationships, comprehensive narrative reviews of this literature have also been undertaken in the past decade. Shockley et al. (2017a) reviewed the literature with a particular eye toward the theoretical logic and methodology used. Ollier-Malaterre and Foucreault (2017) also reviewed this literature, highlighting the fact that whereas psychologists tend to focus on various cultural dimensions, structural features of nations (i.e., laws, economic conditions, and social factors), which tend to be the focus of scholars in other fields (e.g., sociology, industrial relations, political science), also shape work–family experiences in key ways. They also highlight the need to integrate these two approaches in future work. Finally, Ollier-Malaterre and Foucreault noted that culture could impact not only the work–family experiences of individual workers, but also the work–family-focused strategies of companies and organizational outcomes.

One important finding from Shockley et al.'s (2017a) review is that the coverage of nations remains highly uneven, with limited cross-cultural work–family research incorporating countries from South Asia (e.g., Indonesia), the Middle East (e.g., Egypt), or sub-Saharan Africa (e.g., Kenya; for a more detailed review, see Shockley et al., 2018). In recent years, some additional studies have included African nations, but these three regions remain highly understudied. For instance, based on arguments centered on individualism–collectivism, Annor and Burchell (2018) examined whether associations between antecedents and consequences of WIF differed for workers in the United Kingdom (UK) and Ghana. They found that the relationship between job pressure and WIF was stronger for UK than Ghanaian workers, but the relationship between supervisor support and WIF was stronger for Ghanaian than UK workers. Further, in an experiment comparing participants from Spain and Ghana, Fernández-Cornejo et al. (2019) examined whether participants from both cultures would more severely penalize fathers than mothers for using family-friendly policies. The authors found that this penalty only held for the Ghanaian but not the Spanish participants, which they speculate could be due to cultural differences in gender egalitarianism between the two nations.

Cultural Dimensions . The reviews by both Shockley et al. (2017a) and Ollier-Malaterre and Foucreault (2017) reveal that studies in the cross-cultural work–family literature tend to predominantly derive predictions regarding differences in work–family conflict across national contexts based on individualism–collectivism. However, as described in greater detail later in our chapter, theorizing regarding the impact of this dimension on work–family conflict is often inconsistent across studies and scholars. In the past several years, theorizing based on country differences in individualism–collectivism is still prevalent in the literature. For example, supporting their arguments that collectivists may be more attuned to social norms as a means to maintain group harmony, Vaziri et al. (2019) found that the relationship between coworkers' work hours and one's WIF was stronger in cultural contexts that were higher on in-group collectivism.

Gender egalitarianism is the second most commonly invoked cultural dimension in cross-cultural work–family research (Ollier-Malaterre & Foucreault, 2017; Shockley et al., 2017a). In their meta-analysis, Shockley et al. (2017b) found that cultural gender egalitarianism did not moderate gender differences in either WIF or FIW. In contrast, in their eight country investigation, Beham et al. (2020) found that gender differences in work-to-family enrichment in favor of women were larger in more gender egalitarian countries. In the last couple of years, there continues to be a strong focus on country-level differences in gender equality when examining work–family issues. Much of this work uses various indices of gender equity (e.g., United Nations Gender Inequality Index) rather than cultural dimension scores of gender egalitarianism that reflects beliefs, which is more in line with a structural rather than a cultural approach.

More recent work on country-level gender equality often focuses on moderating effects. Kaufman and Taniguchi (2019) found that the positive relationship between possessing a more traditional gender ideology and having young children, respectively, and FIW is actually weaker in more gender-unequal countries. Davis (2020) found that the positive relationship between WIF and stress was stronger in countries higher in gender equality, and the positive relationship between FIW and stress was also stronger for women in these environments. In contrast to the prior two studies, which suggests that risk factors and negative consequences of conflict were generally attenuated in more gender-unequal countries, Riva et al. (2019) found that the positive relationship between work–life fit (i.e., congruence between work hours and commitments outside of work) and well-being was stronger in countries higher in gender equality. Finally, Halliday et al. (2018) found job autonomy to be an especially important resource for women to achieve work–life balance, particularly in countries higher in gender inequality.

Although theorizing or empirical assessment focused on individualism–collectivism and gender egalitarianism still tends to dominate the literature, there is evidence that there is a slow expansion beyond these foci in the literature. For example, Ferreira et al. (2020), who focused on Latin versus non-Latin country comparisons in WIF, found that non-Latin countries scored lower on WIF (contrary to their arguments). Zeng and

Chen (2020), who compared China and Finland on correlates of family-supportive organizational perceptions, found that managerial support for work–family balance was more strongly related to organizational dissent (which is similar to the construct of voice) in Finland than in China. Both studies drew heavily on performance orientation in their arguments regarding why they expected cultural differences. Similarly, Ollo-López and Goñi-Legaz (2017) and Ollier-Malaterre et al. (2020) highlighted the potential impact of cultural differences in humane orientation, the extent to which values such as altruism and compassion were emphasized. Specifically, partially supporting their hypothesis, Ollo-López and Goñi-Legaz (2017) found that humane orientation was negatively associated with work–family conflict, but only for men. In support of their hypothesis, Ollier-Malaterre et al. (2020) found that greater family-supportive organizational perceptions were associated with lower burnout in cultures higher in humane orientation. More generally, authors almost exclusively draw upon the cultural dimensions articulated by the GLOBE project in generating predictions, though a recent paper by Masuda et al. (2019) demonstrated that national differences in Schwartz's cultural value orientations incremented above GLOBE dimensions in predicting work–family conflict.

Additionally, in line with prior reviews (Shockley et al., 2017a), the vast majority of research continues to concentrate on work–family conflict. As a result, limited work has investigated cross-cultural differences in work–family enrichment or work–family balance. Further, research almost exclusively examines work–family variables rather than constructs that assess the broader work–life interface. Thus, we know virtually nothing about how work and other important life domains (e.g., friendships, leisure, education; Keeney et al., 2013) intersect across cultures.

Finally, in a development that we hope will continue to gain traction in the literature, some recent studies have expanded beyond perceptions of work–family conflict, enrichment, or balance to explore cross-cultural differences in variables such as flexible work arrangements and family-supportive supervisor behaviors. Peretz et al. (2018) found support for their arguments that use of flexible work arrangements would be more common in cultural contexts with congruent "modern" values (i.e., higher on individualism, future orientation, gender egalitarianism, humane orientation, performance orientation, and assertiveness, and lower on power distance and uncertainty avoidance) and that the use of flexible work arrangements would also be more effective in reducing absenteeism and turnover in these contexts. In a four-country examination, Bosch et al. (2018) found that the relationship between family-supportive supervisor behaviors and prosocial motivation at work was stronger in more gender egalitarian cultural contexts.

New Approaches to Examining Culture. In line with the broader literature on cross-cultural industrial/organizational psychology and organizational behavior (Gelfand et al., 2017), cross-cultural work–family research generally equates culture with country.

However, there appears to be growing recognition that this need not be the only level-of-analysis that work–family researchers interested in culture examine. For instance, Ammons et al. (2017) recently explored racial differences in work–family conflict in the United States. Their findings show that race seemed more influential for WIF, whereas gender was more influential for FIW. Specifically, on average, Latino/a workers reported lower levels of WIF than White and Black workers, and women (in all three racial groups) reported higher levels of FIW than men.

Some scholars have also argued that immigrants may be another population that can help us to understand the role of culture in work–family dynamics (Grzywacz et al., 2018). As an example, in a recent comparative qualitative study, Yilmaz et al. (2019) explored how work–family conflict may differ for native Belgian versus Turkish women professionals in Belgium. Demonstrating the complexity of culture, it seemed that Turkish women generally experienced higher family-related expectations from their extended family (e.g., parents), but also received more instrumental support from their extended family, particularly around child care than native Belgian women. Finally, it should be acknowledged that the acculturation stress experienced by many immigrants could also directly impact their work–family experiences (Lin & Lin, 2021).

Key Controversies in the Cross-Cultural Work–Family Literature

Given the rapid expansion of the cross-cultural work–family literature over the past two decades, a number of issues or key controversies have become increasingly apparent in the literature, which we review in this section. First, we discuss the issue of inconsistent theorizing regarding the role of various cultural dimensions. Second, we discuss difficulties in methods and measurement. Third, and relatedly, we describe associated statistical challenges involved in assessing cultural variables. Finally, we discuss the lack of attention paid to potential boundary conditions regarding culture-related findings in the work–family literature.

Inconsistent Theorizing Regarding the Role of Cultural Dimensions

One of the major controversies to be resolved in this literature is exactly how culture exerts its effect on the work–family interface. Myriad possibilities have been raised in the literature. Unfortunately, this has sometimes resulted in contradictory predictions regarding the impact of cultural dimensions on a given relationship (Shockley et al., 2017a). For example, Yang (2005) postulated that the negative relationship between WIF and well-being is weaker in cultures that are higher on collectivism because individuals in these environments should be more likely to see work as a means to benefit the family, and therefore, be more tolerant of spillover from work to family. In contrast, Aycan (2008) predicted that this same relationship should be stronger in more collectivistic cultures because family is the more valued domain in these settings. As a result, greater experiences of WIF may be seen as a failure to adequately protect one's valued family role. We further discuss the importance of testing theorized mechanisms empirically in the section on future research directions for cross-cultural work–family research.

Generally, cross-cultural work–family scholars have posited a wide variety of mechanisms—virtually all of which have not been empirically examined. First, it is most common for authors to focus on potential associations between cultural dimensions and the presence of work or family demands (e.g., work hours) or resources (e.g., family support) to support their predictions regarding both mean differences or the moderating effects of culture on work–family variables (Shockley et al., 2017a). These types of arguments are prevalent across cultural dimensions (e.g., cultural collectivism is related to greater work–family conflict due to more family demands—Oishi et al., 2015; cultural humane orientation is related to less work–family conflict due to greater social support—Powell et al., 2009). However, many scholars' theorizing often centers only on demands *or* resources, which ignores the fact that these are independent constructs, such that both may occur simultaneously at high levels in certain cultural settings.

Second, some authors have argued that cultural differences in work–family dynamics could be due to the differential permeability or rigidity of boundaries between work and family across cultures. Arguments regarding the key role of boundaries appear to be made, to date, primarily when discussing cultural differences in individualism–collectivism and uncertainty avoidance. For example, Allen et al. (2020) argued that negative relations between work–family conflict and satisfaction (i.e., job, family, or life) are weaker in more collectivistic cultures because work and family are more apt to be viewed as interdependent roles, and the positive relationship between work demands and WIF is stronger in higher uncertainty avoidance cultures because role boundaries are more strictly enforced by border keepers, leading to less flexibility in how workers can meet work–family needs. These boundary-based arguments can be a bit ambiguous in terms of whether these differences will likely lead to objective differences in the number of work–family intrusions, perceptual differences in work–family conflict, or both.

Third, authors have argued that values vary across cultures, and these value differences are often used to undergird predictions regarding the moderating effects of culture. One key way that values manifest is in the perceived importance of work and family domains. The cultural dimensions most commonly tied to these arguments are individualism–collectivism and performance orientation, such that cultures higher in individualism or performance orientation are argued to place greater value on the work domain. It could be the case that the negative consequences of perceived interference from work (family) to family (work) may be greater in cultures where the intruded-upon domain is more strongly valued.

Beyond how much work and family is valued within a cultural context, cultural values may also manifest in how work or family demands and resources are appraised. Typically, value-based predictions tend to take the form that a match between demands or resources with cultural values amplifies relationships with work–family constructs (e.g., French et al., 2018). However, French and colleagues actually found more support for the importance of *mismatch*. Specifically, rarer resources (i.e., social support) within a culture (i.e., more individualistic, assertive) were found to be more strongly related to reductions in work–family conflict, which from a utility-based perspective, may be because these resources were more useful or needed in that setting. Yet, there may be other potential explanations for this pattern of results. For example, rather than cultural differences in need, perhaps this effect is due to cultural differences in acclimation, such that individuals in cultural contexts where social support is common tend to take it for granted that this resource is available and are more habituated to its benefits to reducing work–family conflict. Future research should also ascertain whether this moderation effect is centered on the low versus high end of the social support continuum (i.e., differences across cultures in reactions to *lack* of social support versus *high* levels of social support).

Reconciling Difficulties in Method and Measurement

A critical component of any cross-cultural investigation is to ensure that measures are construct valid in each cultural context. This can be achieved by quantitatively testing for measurement equivalence using confirmatory factor analysis or item response theory (Hulin, 1987). In their review, Shockley et al. (2017a) assessed the proportion of cross-cultural work–family studies that tested for measurement equivalence and found that it was only 29%. Thus, in the majority of studies in this literature it is unclear whether observed cultural differences are due to true differences or to issues of measurement. Indeed, Project 3535 reported challenges in finding measures that were equivalent across all 10 cultures they focused on (Korabik et al., 2017). They ultimately limited the analyses presented in their book to only those constructs that did show equivalence, but this begs the question—what does it mean when constructs are not equivalent?

We contend that the lack of measurement equivalence may be signaling meaningful differences in constructs across cultures—and that these differences may be worthy of additional scrutiny rather than viewed only as an impediment to conducting cross-cultural comparisons. The use of cognitive task analysis (Robie et al., 2007) with participants from different cultures on work–family items that fail to demonstrate measurement equivalence may be especially illuminating. For example, Korabik et al. (2017) found that Grzywacz and Marks's (2000) measure of work–family positive spillover did not exhibit measurement invariance across their 10 cultures unless certain items were dropped. Thus, by asking participants in different cultures to "think aloud" their thought process when responding to these problematic items, we may better understand how and why individuals across cultures view and respond to these items differently.

Grzywacz et al.'s (2007) mixed-method study of Mexican and Guatemalan immigrants working in a poultry processing plant in the United States also nicely illustrates this concept. Specifically, in the quantitative part of their study, they translated a commonly used measure of WIF and found low levels of WIF among men and women (i.e., below 2 on a 5-point scale). However, the qualitative portion of their study revealed experiences that seem (at least to the authors based in the United States) to represent very high levels of WIF (e.g., having only a few hours per week to spend with children and being too tired then to interact with them). The qualitative reports also made it clear that because employment was of utmost importance, participants did not feel there was a choice—family had to accommodate. This lack of perceived choice could explain the low quantitative levels of WIF; people did not perceive these experiences as WIF because WIF was the expected status quo.

Thus, rather than always attempting to use translated measures in other cultural contexts, scholars may sometimes be better served by engaging in thorough qualitative, emic research (e.g., Rowan & Wulff, 2007) to create scales that uniquely capture the construct within that culture. However, we acknowledge that this still creates an issue when trying to directly compare cultures empirically. Future research needs to reconcile this tension between looking for consistency in views of work–family concepts to facilitate meaningful cross-cultural comparisons, while simultaneously recognizing that failure to view work–family issues in the same manner also constitutes an important way to understand and study the influence of culture.

Statistical Challenges Associated with Assessing Culture

Taxonomies, such as Hofstede (1984) and GLOBE (House et al., 2004), illustrate that the way to most comprehensively capture culture is to consider multiple dimensions at once. However, most work–family cross-cultural research only considers one cultural dimension in isolation (Shockley et al., 2017a). This obfuscates differences between countries that may be similarly high on one dimension but quite distinct on another. One example is (in-group) individualism–collectivism and humane orientation, both of which have been posited to be important cultural values for the work–family interface (Powell et al., 2009). Both Singapore and Thailand score high on collectivism, but Thailand is also high on humane orientation, whereas Singapore is quite low on this dimension. In this case, collectivism may act differently to impact work–family relations due to the moderating effect of humane orientation or vice versa.

Yet, from a statistical standpoint, including multiple cultural dimensions in studies can be problematic. Many cultural dimensions are highly correlated (e.g., in-group collectivism correlates $r = .61$ with power distance; Gupta et al., 2004), which creates multicollinearity concerns if they are included in the same linear regression model. One potential solution to dealing with this problem is to conduct ridge, LASSO (least absolute shrinkage and selection operator), or elastic net regression where the impact of collinearity on model parameters is reduced (Friedman et al., 2010). LASSO and elastic net can also be used for variable selection (e.g., when one has a number of potential cultural variables to consider) in that they shrink coefficients of variables that are not improving prediction to zero.

Another promising way to incorporate multiple dimensions in a more interpretable way is to use configural approaches that assess how patterns of cultural components combine to impact outcomes. Although some authors have started to examine configural approaches, this usually takes the form of comparing regional clusters (e.g., Allen et al., 2020). However, a potential drawback of using regional clusters is that this implicitly indicates that this configuration is *the* most important one across outcomes, which may not necessarily be the case. Thus, one way forward may be to use profile techniques that are explicitly criterion-focused (e.g., Davison & Davenport, 2002), which identifies the key cultural configuration associated with a particular outcome (e.g., the pattern most predictive of work–family conflict versus work–family enrichment may differ).

Lastly, another way to circumvent these statistical limitations is to be mindful of cultural values when selecting countries to include in a study. Project 3535 provides an illustration of best practices in this regard. They selected countries based on two dimensions they deemed relevant to work–family issues: gender egalitarianism and societal support systems. They then made sure that, collectively, the countries included in their investigation spanned a 2 x 2 matrix (high- versus low-gender egalitarianism and institutional versus non-institutional support types) of these factors, and that multiple countries were nested within each quadrant. This allowed for natural consideration of interactions between factors when making direct country comparisons (Korabik et al., 2017).

Lack of Consideration of Potential Boundary Conditions

In reviewing the cross-cultural work–family literature holistically, it is important to identify boundary conditions that may impact the conclusions we can draw about cultural differences. One example stems from research participants. Paralleling the broader work–family literature (e.g., Shen et al., 2018), most cross-cultural work–family studies include professional/managerial employees in urban or suburban settings to the neglect of blue-collar workers or workers in rural settings. This is problematic in two respects. First, there are profound differences in these settings that may call into question the broad generalizability of findings to others within that nation. For example, job characteristics such as autonomy, flexibility, and income are likely to be significantly higher in professional/managerial samples, which would afford different resources to help manage competing demands. Likewise, different resources may typically be available in urban versus rural settings, such as the number of jobs and child care centers or the nature of community relationships, which could also impact work–family or work–life outcomes. Second, cross-cultural comparisons should equate these features to the extent possible, so that any differences can more easily be attributed to the cultural context versus aspects of the job or socioeconomic status, which would play out in any cultural setting.

A related issue regarding the characteristics of samples is the consideration of life stage and/or career stage. Surprisingly, given the varied impact children of different ages have on family demands, life stage is often not taken into account in work–family research (Allen & Shockley, 2012) and cross-cultural studies are no exception. This is an important omission, as life stage may interact with culture to influence work–family outcomes. For example, the family responsibilities of single individuals in more collectivistic cultures may be quite different from their counterparts in more individualistic cultures. Similarly, work demands and resources also differ across career stages (e.g., early-, mid-, versus late-career) and are likely to impact work–family variables (e.g., conflict, facilitation; Demerouti et al., 2012). Culture or national context may further shape these relationships as well, given that countries can vary on when the majority of individuals leave school, enter the workforce, and exit the workforce (e.g., retire), as well as the types of career pathways available and the speed at which they are typically attained.

Another concern is the existence of distinct subgroups within nations. Some cross-cultural work–family researchers have explicitly taken this into account (e.g., study of Arab and Jewish teachers' work–family conflict in Israel, Cinamon, 2009), but in other contexts, differences may be less obvious. As one example, Eby et al. (2018) highlighted how states within the United States vary on a number of important values and attitudes that may have implications for the work–family interface, including with regard to gender, self-protection, religiosity, and political ideology. For example, people in the Deep South tend to have less egalitarian views about gender roles and less generous state-supported benefits (e.g., parental leave) compared to those in other regions. Thus, quite distinct conclusions might be drawn regarding cultural differences between the United States and other nations, depending on whether the sample is drawn from the Deep South versus other regions. This is generally an understudied area, and we recommend that authors conduct more research to understand these subgroup differences within nations, such as Africans, Coloureds, Indians, and Whites in South Africa, French versus English-speaking Canada, Sunni Muslims, Shia Muslims, and Kurds in Syria, and European versus. Maori New Zealanders. A related idea is to examine immigrants' work–family experiences to see whether they are more or less similar to the experiences of those in their country of origin versus current residence.

Lastly, the workplaces that employees are embedded within are often overlooked when interpreting cross-cultural work–family research. Some researchers conduct cross-cultural comparisons using a sample from a single multinational organization (e.g., IBM, Hill et al., 2003). Such studies may make it easier to equate job characteristics across samples, but also create challenges in that it may be difficult to isolate the effects of company culture from national culture. In other words, a lack of significant differences across people from different nations within a large, single organization might simply be due to the strong culture of the company overriding the effects of national culture. Additionally, little consideration is generally given regarding how organizational work–family policies may be used by workers to fill voids in national-level work–family policies. For example, although there is no national parental leave policy in the United States, some organizations do offer generous policies in this regard (e.g., Bank of America, Ernst & Young). Thus, cultural differences based on national-level policies may be obscured if researchers do not consider the use of organizational policies too.

New Directions for Cross-Cultural Work–Family Research

After reviewing the literature in detail and identifying key controversies that need to be resolved, in this section we turn to identifying exciting new directions for future cross-cultural work–family research. In particular, we discuss the need to expand our theoretical understanding, new methodological frontiers to be tackled, and additional questions to be addressed in future work. Finally, we end this section by describing the implications of cross-cultural work–family research for practice and the need for scholars to be more attuned to practitioners' concerns.

Expanding Our Theoretical Understanding

In line with observations made by Ollier-Malaterre and Foucreault (2017), we think one important way that future cross-cultural work–family research should seek to develop is via a greater conceptual integration of how cultural values and structural practices (e.g., legal, economic, and family structures) jointly influence variations in work–family management across cultures. This includes a deeper understanding of when these factors tend to be aligned as well as when they are more apt to be misaligned, and corresponding downstream consequences for work–family outcomes. This integration is also important because it will help to break down longstanding disciplinary siloes and allow for a more comprehensive understanding of how living within a given nation influences the work–family experiences of those within its borders.

We also encourage future work to explore other theoretical frameworks beyond those that are dominant in the literature—that is, those articulated by Hofstede (1984) and the GLOBE project (House et al., 2004). This could include integrating cultural dimensions not included in those taxonomies; for example, cultural tightness–looseness (i.e., strength of social norms and punishment for norm violations) has been shown to moderate the impact of cultural values on outcomes (Taras et al., 2010). Thus, given that culture often impacts mean levels of work–family variables or their associations with correlates, it seems plausible that these relationships could be further strengthened in tighter cultures. Alternatively, researchers could also explore other frameworks that may prove relevant to understanding cross-cultural differences in work–family experiences. As an example, Masuda et al. (2019) recently found that Schwartz's cultural value orientations incremented above GLOBE dimensions in explaining cross-cultural variation in work–family conflict. Finally, researchers could potentially look at other societal norms or cultural practices that are more unobtrusive but nevertheless might be highly telling.

For example, perhaps statistics related to cellphone use might give researchers important insight into the preferred or typical boundary management strategies of those within a given culture.

In our review of the literature, we find that much of the theorizing underlying cross-cultural work–family research tends to be quite vague, and authors often suggest multiple underlying mechanisms that are typically untested. We strongly call for future research to begin to test these mechanisms and by extension the theories that authors are utilizing to support their arguments. Further, existing arguments regarding mechanisms tend to center on differences across cultures in (1) demands or resources, (2) permeability of boundaries, and/or (3) values. However, other scholars have argued that culture can also exert its effects via other pathways that remain largely unexplored and discussed in the work–family literature. For example, Peterson and Barretto (2014) postulated that the main way that culture impacts members of that culture is via members' expertise and understanding (i.e., cognitive structures and schemas), with its impact on internalization of values being much more modest.

We also caution authors that mechanisms are not only key when explicating cross-cultural differences, but are important when considering cross-cultural *similarities*. In other words, if cross-cultural differences are expected but not found, it is equally important for scholars to understand why this is the case (e.g., could there be countervailing forces that were overlooked and what might those be) and not simply think there is nothing to be learned here. In fact, principles of equifinality suggest that even if members of two different cultures tend to experience similar work–family outcomes, they did not necessarily achieve it via the same underlying processes, which may be of significant theoretical interest.

Tackling New Methodological Frontiers

As articulated above, explicit testing of mechanisms is essential from a theoretical perspective, but doing so likely poses significant methodological challenges. Given the significant efforts needed to conduct cross-cultural work–family studies, one way to overcome some of the difficulties of testing mechanisms at the culture level could be to first focus on within-culture variation to see if the mechanisms that are argued to explain between-culture variation hold initially at this lower level of analysis (e.g., look at variation across states within the United States prior to examining variation across countries). However, it could be the case that mechanisms are ultimately not homologous across levels of analysis.

Alternatively, in addition to measuring posited mechanisms and testing for mediation via the calculation of indirect effects, we also encourage other creative ways to uncover mediating mechanisms. For example, it has long been recognized that manipulations or moderation can sometimes be a powerful way to understand underlying processes (e.g., Spencer et al., 2005). In particular, cross-cultural work–family scholars should seek to take advantage of natural experiments, such as changes in government policies or major events that may disrupt or strengthen theorized mechanisms. As an example, given the differential progression of the COVID-19 pandemic across countries, can this be used to scholars' advantage to sharpen our understanding of processes that underlie cross-cultural variations in work–family experiences? As an example, perhaps differences in the reopening of day care and schools across states in the United States or other countries could be used to understand the influence of child care on work–family variables. A recent study by Shockley et al. (2021) examined the child care strategies of dual-earner couples with young children in the United States during the pandemic, when child care suddenly became unavailable as schools and day cares closed. They found that the common strategy where the wife "did it all" resulted in the worst performance and well-being. However, given that this study was conducted in the United States, it would be interesting to examine whether the types, distributions, or effectiveness of the various work–family strategies varied across cultures.

Finally, we also call for future research that will expand the methodological toolkit used by cross-cultural work–family scholars, who currently rely heavily on cross-sectional surveys. We view the increasing use of meta-analytic methods as a positive development in this domain. However, other methods are also needed. For example, cross-cultural work–family research rarely employs experimental designs. However, to the extent that existing cross-cultural differences in work–family experiences are driven by cognitive- or value-based processes, experiments seem well positioned to elucidate such effects. As an example, perhaps experiments that prime different cultural identities among bicultural individuals could be very illuminating with regard to understanding cross-cultural differences in work–family management. In some cases, experiments may be more interpretable than field studies because this approach can often more easily ensure equivalence across participants (e.g., in a vignette, specifying equal family demands and work responsibilities across participants). Finally, to complement the self-report measures that tend to dominate the current literature, future cross-cultural work–family research can also incorporate physiological measures (e.g., blood pressure, cortisol) to examine how relations between work–family conflict and employee health may differ across cultures.

Additional Questions to Be Pursued

Issues of gender are deeply embedded both within a cultural context and work–family dynamics. Thus, we encourage future research that examines potential interactive relationships between gender and culture in shaping work–family variables and relationships. Although work and family has traditionally been conceptualized as "separate spheres," this is not the case for employees who work in a family business. Some scholars have sought to integrate the literatures on work–family and family business (e.g., Rothausen, 2009), but to our knowledge, a cross-cultural lens has not been further layered on this relationship, despite the fact that cultural variables (e.g., in-group collectivism) are theorized to shape the importance of family across cultures. Similarly, research indicates that many countries differ in their prevalence of various employment choices, such as self-employment and entrepreneurship (OECD, 2018). Thus, we generally call for additional research that examines how culture may shape relations between employment in different types of organizations or sectors and work–family dynamics.

Another important theoretical and methodological issue that future research centers need to unpack is the definition of family. As mentioned at the beginning of our chapter, family has historically been left undefined in work–family research. However, conceptualizations of family may differ across cultures, with individuals in more individualistic societies more apt to focus on the nuclear family, whereas family is likely to also encompass the extended family in more collectivistic societies. This may make future cross-cultural studies of elder care particularly telling, as ties to one's parents in adulthood may vary significantly across cultures, in contrast to child care responsibilities, which may be viewed more similarly across cultures. Further, macro-level changes in family structures, such as the declining marriage rate and geographic dispersion from one's natal home, may also increase the likelihood that individuals who share no genetic or legal ties may nevertheless consider themselves family. These differences could have important and interesting implications for both research and practice. As an example, will an organization that offers their employees assistance for elder care see an employee's desire to use these services for an elderly family member who is not their parent as legitimate? The answer probably depends on how the organization defines family, which is likely to be shaped by culture.

Considering Implications for Practice

We also believe that future cross-cultural work–family research needs to more deeply consider issues that are likely to be of greater concern to practitioners. This could include research that uncovers best practices in implementing work–family policies within multinational corporations. As an example, currently little empirical evidence is available on how to effectively deal with issues of fairness that might arise when the work–family supports offered by the organization vary across cultural contexts and the organization is operating in many different environments in terms of both cultural norms and legislative mandates. In the same vein, family adjustment is a key component of expatriate success (e.g., Lazarova et al., 2010) and is likely to be a very salient issue for multinational organizations. However, to date, relatively little has been done to integrate knowledge from the cross-cultural work–family literature with the expatriate literature to help multinational companies navigate the difficulties that may arise when their workers live abroad with their families for extended periods of time. For a recent review of this literature, see Dimitrova (2018), who calls for more research that expands beyond the expatriate's spouse to also include other family members (e.g., children).

Similarly, research has established that family-supportive supervisor behaviors are an important component of organizational support for work–family issues, and such behaviors can be successfully trained (e.g., Hammer et al., 2011). Additionally, there is a burgeoning body of work on the topic outside of the United States, where the construct and training program originated (for a review, see Kossek et al., 2018). However, to our knowledge, none of these studies takes a deep dive as to whether the *meaning* of family-supportive supervision differs across cultures, and correspondingly, how training programs may need to be adapted across cultures. Thus, difficulties in practice may arise when trying to implement such training programs across cultures in an effort to improve the work–family management of workers globally.

Table 21.1 Key theoretical principles and practical implications of cross-cultural work–family research
Key Theoretical Principles
1. National cultural differences in individualism–collectivism appears to impact both average levels of work–family conflict (i.e., FIW) and many relations between work–family conflict and correlates (i.e., family demands, work support, and satisfaction).
2. The effects of gender egalitarianism versus gender equity indices that reflect structural differences in access to resources by gender within a culture often differ in how they impact the same work–family constructs or relationships—highlighting that cultural versus structural approaches to studying work–family issues may not always converge.
3. Culture need not always be equated with nation; there can be significant subcultures within nations whose experiences at the work–family interface may vary significantly (e.g., states or provinces within a country, racial/ethnic groups, religious groups, language groups, immigrant groups).
4. Culture has been theorized to exert its effects on the work–family interface via multiple mechanisms, including but not limited to average levels of work and family demands and resources, differential permeability of work and family boundaries, and how much work and family are valued by individuals within that culture.
5. Conceptually, it is just as informative to understand processes that give rise to cross-cultural similarities in work–family relations relative to cross-cultural differences.
Key Practical Implications
1. It is difficult to come up with one-size-fits-all organizational work–family policies because how work and family are conceptualized and how people think they should intersect often vary significantly by culture.
2. In some situations, organizational culture may have a stronger impact on work–family relations than national culture; national culture may not be salient in all contexts.
3. It is important to establish measurement equivalence or invariance in order to ensure comparisons across cultures on work–family variables are meaningful.
4. To be able to assess the impact of culture, particularly the interaction or profile of multiple cultural variables, it is important to sample or include countries carefully to ensure sufficient representation of the full range or all combinations of interest.
5. It is important to recognize the heterogeneity that is often present within cultures and to consider how representative samples are of the culture as a whole when drawing inferences regarding cross-cultural differences or similarities.

Conclusion

In summary, a growing body of research on cross-cultural issues at the work–family interface indicates that typical experiences of work–family conflict, enrichment, and balance can differ across cultural contexts as can relations with facilitators and the consequences of these important variables. We summarize key insights from our chapter in Table 21.1, where we articulate five key theoretical principles and five important practical implications derived from our review of the extant literature on cross-cultural work–family research. Overall, although much has been learned over the past two decades, when research in this domain started to burgeon at a rapid rate, significant controversies—both theoretical and methodological—remain to be resolved in order to continue to move this field forward. Specifically, we contend that clear specification and explicit, and perhaps creative, testing of mediating mechanisms is needed to enhance theoretical development. Also needed is the exploration of additional theoretical approaches or cultural dimensions beyond the models that currently dominate the literature. Cross-cultural work–family research will be more likely to continue to prosper if future researchers expand their methodological toolkits beyond cross-sectional surveys and also seek to address the concerns of practitioners who seek to help workers and organizations around the world to successfully navigate work–family issues.

References

Allen, T. D., French, K. A., Dumani, S., & Shockley, K. M. (2015). Meta-analysis of work–family conflict mean differences: Does national context matter? *Journal of Vocational Behavior, 90*, 90–100. https://doi.org/10.1016/j.jvb.2015.07.006

Allen, T. D., French, K. A., Dumani, S., & Shockley, K. M. (2020). A cross-national meta-analytic examination of predictors and outcomes associated with work–family conflict. *Journal of Applied Psychology, 105*, 539–576. http://dx.doi.org/10.1037/apl0000442

Allen, T. D., & Shockley, K. M. (2012). Older workers and work–family issues. In J. W. Hedge & W. C. Borman (Eds.), *Oxford handbook of work and aging* (pp. 520–537). New York: Oxford University Press.

Ammons, S. K., Dahlin, E. C., Edgell, P., & Santo, J. B. (2017). Work–family conflict among Black, White, and Hispanic men and women. *Community, Work, and Family, 20*, 379–404. https://doi.org/10.1080/13668803.2016.1146231

Annor, F., & Burchell, B. (2018). A cross-national comparative study of work demands/support, work-to-family conflict and job outcomes: Ghana versus the United Kingdom. *International Journal of Cross-Cultural Management, 18*, 53–72. https://doi.org/10.1177/1470595817746195

Aryee, S. (1992). Antecedents and outcomes of work–family conflict among married professional women: Evidence from Singapore. *Human Relations, 45*, 813–837. https://doi.org/10.1177/001872679204500804

Aryee, S., Fields, D., & Luk, V. (1999). A cross-cultural test of a model of the work–family interface. *Journal of Management, 25*, 491–511. https://doi.org/10.1177/014920639902500402

Aycan, Z. (2008). Cross-cultural perspectives to work–family conflict. In K. Korabik, & D. Lero (Eds.), *Handbook of work–family conflict* (pp. 359–371). Cambridge: Cambridge University Press.

Beham, B., Drobnič, S., Präg, P., Baierl, A., & Lewis, S. (2020). Work-to-family enrichment and gender inequalities in eight European countries. *The International Journal of Human Resource Management, 31*, 589–610. https://doi.org/10.1080/09585192.2017.1355837

Bosch, M. J., Las Heras, M., Russo, M., Rofcanin, Y., Grau, I., & Grau, M. (2018). How context matters: The relationship between family supportive supervisor behaviours and motivation to work moderated by gender inequality. *Journal of Business Research, 82*, 46–55. https:// doi.org/10.1016/ j.jbusres.2017.08.026

Casper, W. J., Vaziri, H., Wayne, J. H., DeHauw, S., & Greenhaus, J. (2018). The jingle-jangle of work-nonwork balance: A comprehensive and meta-analytic review of its meaning and measurement. *Journal of Applied Psychology, 103*, 182–214. https://doi.org/10.1037/apl0000259

Cinamon, R. G. (2009). Role salience, social support, and work–family conflict among Jewish and Arab female teachers in Israel. *Journal of Career Development, 36*, 139–158. https://doi.org/10.1177/0894845309345849.

Davis, S. N. (2020). The work–family interface in a gendered cultural context: Cross-national analysis of work stress. *International Journal of Cross Cultural Management, 20*, 53–69. https://doi.org/10.1177/147059582 0904111

Davison, M. L., & Davenport, E. C., Jr. (2002). Identifying criterion-related patterns of predictor scores using multiple regression. *Psychological Methods, 7*, 468–484. https://doi.org/10.1037/1082-989X.7.4.468

Demerouti, E., Peeters, M. C. W., & van der Heijden, B. I. J. M. (2012). Work–family interface from a life and career stage perspective: The role of demands and resources. *International Journal of Psychology, 47*, 241–258. https://doi.org/10.1080/00207594.2012.699055

Dimitrova, M. (2018). Expatriation and the work–family interface. In Shockley, K. S., Shen, W., & Johnson, R. C. (Eds.), (2018). *The Cambridge handbook of the global work–family interface* (pp. 479–493). Cambridge: Cambridge University Press.

Eby, L. T., Vande Griek, O., Maupin, C. K., Allen, T. D., Gilreath, E., & Martinez, V. (2018). A cultures within culture perspective on work and family among United States employees. In K. M. Shockley, W. Shen, & Ryan C. Johnson (Eds.), *The Cambridge handbook of the global work–family interface* (pp. 405–423). Cambridge: Cambridge University Press.

Fernández-Cornejo, J. A., Britwum, A. O., Escot, L., Odoi, A., Palomo-Vadillo, M. T., Del Pozo-García, E., & Ayitey, D. A. (2019). Penalizing fathers who use family friendly measures: A comparative study with university students from Ghana and Spain. *Social Science Research, 82*, 204–220. https://doi.org/10.1016/ j.ssresearch.2019.04.006

French, K. A., Dumani, S., Allen, T. D., & Shockley, K. M. (2018). A meta-analysis of work–family conflict and social support. *Psychological Bulletin, 144*, 284–314. http://dx.doi.org/10.1037/bul0000120

Friedman, J., Hastie, T., & Tibshirani, R. (2010). Regularization paths for generalized linear models via coordinate descent. *Journal of Statistical Software, 33*, 1–22.

Frone, M. R. (2003). Work–family balance. In J. C. Quick & L. E. Tetrick (Eds.), *Handbook of occupational health psychology* (pp. 143–162). Washington, DC: American Psychological Association. https://doi.org/ 10.1037/10474-007

Gelfand, M. J., Aycan, Z., Erez, M., & Leung, K. (2017). Cross-cultural industrial organizational psychology and organizational behavior: A hundred-year journey. *Journal of Applied Psychology, 102*, 514–529. https:// doi.org/10.1037/apl0000186

Greenhaus, J. H., & Beutell, N. J. (1985). Sources of conflict between work and family roles. *Academy of Management Review, 10*, 76–88. https://doi.org/10.5465/amr.1985.4277352

Greenhaus, J. H., & Powell, G. N. (2006). When work and family are allies: A theory of work–family enrichment. *Academy of Management Review, 31*, 72–92. https://doi.org/10.5465/amr.2006.19379625

Grzywacz, J. G., Arcury, T. A., Marín, A., Carrillo, L., Burke, B., Coates, M. L., & Quandt, S. A. (2007). Work–family conflict: Experiences and health implications among immigrant Latinos. *Journal of Applied Psychology, 92*, 1119–1130. doi:10.1037/0021-9010.92.4.1119

Grzywacz, J. G., Gopalan, N., & Carlos Chavez, F. L. (2018). Work and family among immigrants. In K. M. Shockley, W. Shen, & Ryan C. Johnson (Eds.), *The Cambridge handbook of the global work–family interface* (pp. 454–478). Cambridge: Cambridge University Press.

Grzywacz, J. G., & Marks, N. F. (2000). Reconceptualizing the work–family interface: An ecological perspective on the correlates of positive and negative spillover between work and family. *Journal of Occupational Health Psychology, 5*, 111 126. https://doi.org/10.1037/1076-8998.5.1.111

Gupta, V., & Hanges, P. J. (2004). Regional and climate clustering of societal cultures. In R. J. House, P. J. Hanges, M. Javidan, P. W. Dorfman, & V. Gupta (Eds.), *Culture, leadership, and organizations: The GLOBE study of 62 societies* (pp. 95–101). Beverly Hills, CA: SAGE.

Gupta, V., Sully de Luque, M., & House, R. (2004). GLOBE unobtrusive measures for societal culture dimensions. In R. J. House, P. J. Hanges, M. Javidan, P. W. Dorfman, & V. (Eds.), *Culture, leadership, and organizations: The GLOBE study of 62 societies* (pp. 178–218). Beverly Hills, CA: SAGE.

Halliday, C. S., Paustian-Underdahl, S. C., Ordóñez, Z., Rogelberg, S. G., & Zhang, H. (2018). Autonomy as a key resource for women in low gender egalitarian countries: A cross-cultural examination. *Human Resource Management, 57*, 601–615. https://doi.org/10.1002/hrm.21874

Hammer, L. B., Kossek, E. E., Anger, W. K., Bodner, T., & Zimmerman, K. L. (2011). Clarifying work–family intervention processes: The roles of work–family conflict and family-supportive supervisor behaviors. *Journal of Applied Psychology, 96*, 134–150. doi: 10.1037/a0020927

Hill, E. J., Hawkins, A. J., Martinson, V., & Ferris, M. (2003). Studying "working fathers": Comparing fathers' and mothers' work–family conflict, fit, and adaptive strategies in a global high tech company. *Fathering, 1*, 239–261. doi:10.3149/fth.0103.239

Hofstede, G. (1984). *Culture's consequences* (2nd ed.). Beverly Hills, CA: SAGE.

House, R. J., Hanges, P. J., Javidan, M., Dorfman, P. W., & Gupta, V. (Eds.) (2004). *Culture, leadership, and organizations: The GLOBE study of 62 societies*. Beverly Hills, CA: SAGE.

Hulin, C. L. (1987). A psychometric theory of evaluations of item and scale translations: Fidelity across languages. *Journal of Cross-Cultural Psychology, 18*, 115–142. https://doi.org/10.1177/002200218701 8002001

Izraeli, D. N. (1993). Work/family conflict among women and men managers in dual-career couples in Israel. *Journal of Social Behavior and Personality, 8*, 371–388.

Kaufman, G., & Taniguchi, H. (2019). Gender equality and work–family conflict from a cross-national perspective. *International Journal of Comparative Sociology, 60*, 385–408. https://doi.org/10.1177/002071521 9893750

Keeney, J., Boyd, E. M., Sinha, R., Westring, A. F., & Ryan, A. M. (2013). From "work–family" to "work-life": Broadening our conceptualization and measurement. *Journal of Vocational Behavior, 82*, 221–237. https:// doi.org/10.1016/j.jvb.2013.01.005

Korabik, K., Aycan, Z., & Ayman, R. (2017). *The work–family interface in global context*. Routledge.

Kossek, E. E., Odle-Dusseau, H. N., & Hammer, L. B. (2018). Family supportive supervision around the globe. In K. M. Shockley, W. Shen, & R. C. Johnson (Eds.), *The Cambridge Handbook of the Global Work–Family Interface* (pp. 570–594). Cambridge: Cambridge University Press.

Lazarova, M., Westman, M., & Shaffer, M. A. (2010). Elucidating the positive side of the work–family interface on international assignments: A model of expatriate work and family performance. *Academy of Management Review, 35*, 93–117. https://doi.org/10.5465/amr.35.1.zok93

Lin, I.-H., & Lin, P.-S. (2021). Immigrants' experiences of work–family conflict in the U.S.: A systematic review. *Community, Work, and Family, 24*, 155–172. https://doi.org/10.1080/13668803.2020.1722063

Masuda, A. D., Poelmans, S. A. Y., Allen, T. D., Spector, P. E., Lapierre, L. M., Cooper, C. L., Abarca, N., Brough, P., Ferreiro, P., Fraile, G., Luo, L., Lu, C-Q., Siu, O. L., O'Driscoll, M. P., Simoni, A. S., Shima, S., & Moreno-Velazquez, I. (2012). Flexible work arrangements availability and their relationship with work-to-family conflict, job satisfaction, and turnover intentions: A comparison of three country clusters. *Applied Psychology: An International Review, 61*, 1–29.

Masuda, A. D., Sortheix, F. M., Beham, B., & Naidoo, L. J. (2019). Cultural value orientations and work–family conflict: The mediating role of work and family demands. *Journal of Vocational Behavior, 112*, 294–310. https://doi.org/10.1016/j.jvb.2019.04.001

OECD. (2018). *OECD labour force statistics 2017*. Paris: OECD Publishing. https://doi.org/10. 1787/oecd_lfs-2017-en

Oishi, A. S., Chan, R. K. H., Wang, L. L.-R., & Kim, J.-H. (2015). Do part-time jobs mitigate workers' work–family conflict and enhance wellbeing? New evidence from four East-Asian societies. *Social Indicators Research, 121*, 5–25. https://doi.org/10.1007/s11205-014-0624-8.

Ollier-Malaterre, A., & Foucreault, A. (2017). Cross-national work-life research: Cultural and structural impacts for individuals and organizations. *Journal of Management, 43*, 111–136. https://doi.org/10.1177/ 0149206316655873

Ollier-Malaterre, A., Haar, J. M., Sunyer, A., & Russo, M. (2020). Supportive organizations, work–family enrichment, and job burnout in low and high humane orientation cultures. *Applied Psychology: An International Review, 69*, 1215–1247. https://doi.org/10.1111/apps.12217

Ollo-López, A., & Goñi-Legaz, S. (2017). Differences in work–family conflict: Which individual and national factors explain them? *The International Journal of Human Resource Management, 28*, 499–525. https://doi.org/10.1080/09585192.2015.1118141
Peretz, H., Fried, Y., & Levi, A. (2018). Flexible work arrangements, national culture, organizational characteristics, and organizational outcomes: A study across 21 countries. *Human Resource Management Journal, 28*, 182–200. https://doi.org/10.1111/1748-8583.12172
Peterson, M. F., & Barreto, T. S. (2014). The like it or not proposition: Implications of societal characteristics for the cultural expertise and personal values of organizational members. *Journal of Organizational Behavior, 35*, 1134–1152. https://doi.org/10.1002/job.1977
Powell, G. N., Francesco, A. M., & Ling, Y. (2009). Toward culture-sensitive theories of the work–family interface. *Journal of Organizational Behavior, 30*, 597–616. https://doi.org/10.1002/job.568
Riva, E., Lucchini, M., & Russo, M. (2019). Societal gender inequality as moderator of the relationship between work-life fit and subjective well-being: A multilevel analysis across European countries. *Social Indicators Research, 143*, 657–691. https://doi.org/10.1007/s11205-018-1986-0
Robie, C., Brown, D. J., & Beaty, J. C. (2007). Do people fake on personality inventories? A verbal protocol analysis. *Journal of Business and Psychology, 21*, 489–509. https://doi.org/10.1007/s10869-007-9038-9
Rothausen, T. J. (2009). Management work–family research and work–family fit: Implications for building family capital in business. *Family Business Review, 22*, 220–234. https://doi.org/10.1177/0894486509337409
Rowan, N., & Wulff, D. (2007). Using qualitative methods to inform scale development. *The Qualitative Report, 12*, 450–466.
Shen, W., Shockley, K. M., & Johnson, R. C. (2018). Charting a path forward. In K. M. Shockley, W. Shen, & R. C. Johnson (Eds.), *The Cambridge handbook of the global work–family interface* (pp. 749–756). Cambridge: Cambridge University Press.
Shockley, K. M., Clark, M. A., Dodd, H., & King, E. B. (2021). Work–family strategies during COVID-19: Examining gender dynamics among dual-earner couples with young children. *Journal of Applied Psychology, 106*, 15–28. http://dx.doi.org/10.1037/apl0000857
Shockley, K. M., Douek, J., Smith, C. R., Yu, P. P., Dumani, S., & French, K. A. (2017a). Cross-cultural work and family research: A review of the literature. *Journal of Vocational Behavior, 101*, 1–20. https://doi.org/10.1016/j.jvb.2017.04.001
Shockley, K. M., French, K. A., & Yu, P. P. (2018). A comprehensive review and synthesis of the cross-cultural work–family literature. In K. M. Shockley, W. Shen, & Ryan C. Johnson (Eds.), *The Cambridge handbook of the global work–family interface* (pp. 9–68). Cambridge: Cambridge University Press.
Shockley, K. M., Shen, W., DeNunzio, M. M., Arvan, M. L., & Knudsen, E. A. (2017b). Disentangling the relationship between gender and work–family conflict: An integration of theoretical perspectives using meta-analytic methods. *Journal of Applied Psychology, 102*, 1601–1635. https://doi.org/10.1037/apl0000246
Spector, P. E., Allen, T. D., Poelmans, S. A., Lapierre, L. M., Cooper, C. L., O'Driscoll, M., Sanchez, J. I., Abarca, N., Alexandrova, M., Beham, B., Brough, P., Ferreiro, P., Fraile, G., Lu, C-Q., Lu, L., Moreno-Velazquez, I., & Pagon, M. (2007). Cross-national differences in relationships of work demands, job satisfaction, and turnover intentions with work–family conflict. *Personnel Psychology, 60*, 805–835. https://doi.org/10.1111/j.1744-6570.2007.00092.x
Spector, P. E., Cooper, C. L., Poelmans, S., Allen, T. D., O'Driscoll, M., Sanchez, J. I., Siu, O., Dewe, P., Hart, P., Lu, L., De Moraes, L. F. R., Ostrognay, G. M., Sparks, K., Wong, P., & Yu, S. (2004). A cross-national comparative study of work–family stressors, working hours, and well-being: China and Latin America versus the Anglo world. *Personnel Psychology, 57*, 119–142. https://doi.org/10.1111/j.1744-6570.2004.tb02486.x
Spencer, S. J., Zanna, M. P., & Fong, G. T. (2005). Establishing a causal chain: Why experiments are often more effective than mediational analyses in examining psychological processes. *Journal of Personality and Social Psychology, 89*, 845–851. https://doi.org/10.1037/0022-3514.89.6.845
Taras, V., Kirkman, B. L., & Steel, P. (2010). Examining the impact of Culture's consequences: A three-decade, multilevel, meta-analytic review of Hofstede's cultural value dimensions. *Journal of Applied Psychology, 95*, 405–439. https://doi.org/10.1037/a0018938

Vaziri, H., Benson, G. S., & Salazar Campo, M. (2019). Hardworking coworkers: A multilevel cross-national look at group work hours and work–family conflict. *Journal of Organizational Behavior*, 40, 676–692. https://doi.org/10.1002/job.2361

Yang, N. (2005). Individualism-collectivism and work–family interfaces: A Sino-U.S. comparison. In S. A. Y. Poelmans (Ed.), *Work and family: An international research perspective* (pp. 287–318). Hillsdale, NJ: Lawrence Erlbaum.

Yang, N., Chen, C. C., Choi, J., & Zou, Y. (2000). Sources of work–family conflict: A Sino-U.S. comparison of the effects of work and family demands. *Academy of Management Journal, 43*, 113–123. https://doi.org/10.5465/1556390

Yilmaz, S., Van de Putte, B., & Stevens, P. A. J. (2019). Work–family conflict: Comparing the experiences of Turkish and native Belgian women. *Community, Work, & Family, 22*, 284–301. https://doi.org/10.1080/13668803.2017.1360247

Zeng, C., & Chen, H. (2020). An exploration of the relationships between organizational dissent, employee burnout, and work–family balance: A cross-cultural comparison between China and Finland. *Communication Studies, 71*, 441–457. https://doi.org/10.1080/10510974.2020.1749864

CHAPTER

22 Culture and Consumer Behavior: A Review and Agenda for Future Research

Carlos J. Torelli, Jie (Doreen) Shen, *and* Maria A. Rodas

Abstract

Culture is a fundamental driver of consumer behavior. This chapter reviews the three most common approaches for incorporating culture into frameworks of consumer behavior and describes key findings about: (1) the effect of culture on consumers' attention and information processing, (2) the persuasiveness of culturally matched advertising messages, (3) the contexts in which culture is more likely to impact consumer behavior, and (4) the behavior of bicultural consumers. The chapter concludes with a discussion of a future research agenda that focuses on the study of the tightness–looseness (T-L) distinction for refining cultural predictions, the further integration of the different approaches to cultural research for understanding a variety of consumer phenomena in a globalized world, the adoption of a polycultural approach for explaining the behavior of multicultural consumers with knowledge about two or more cultures, and the potential insights from new methodologies borrowed from neuroscience, machine learning, and big data analyses.

Key Words: consumer behavior, culture, multicultural consumers, cross-cultural consumers, cultural adaptations, bicultural consumers

Culture, as a fundamental determinant of people's wants, drives consumer behavior (Kotler & Keller, 2009). As the world becomes increasingly globalized, both the demand side (i.e., consumer markets) and the supply side (i.e., brand offerings) of the global marketplace are also growing in cultural diversity. Cultural diversity in consumer markets is fueled by the emergence of China, India, and Brazil as engines of growth for the global economy (Nayyar, 2010), as well as by the immigration patterns changing the cultural landscape of developed markets (e.g., growth of Hispanics in the United States or of Muslim populations in Europe). The supply side has also grown in cultural diversity thanks to the emergence of global brands from every corner of the developed and developing world.

Supported by these global trends, a wide range of brands bring a variety of cultures to an increasingly diverse consumer population. In this context, how can we incorporate cultural variables into models of consumer behavior? How can companies develop strategies to successfully connect with consumers from different cultures? What future challenges will marketers face in such a complex environment? This chapter provides answers to these important questions.

Because culture is an elusive concept that has been defined in numerous ways in research across different intellectual traditions (Kroeber & Kluckhohn, 1952), we start by reviewing key approaches for incorporating culture into models of consumer behavior and by identifying the factors that explain the cultural patterning of consumers' preferences for products and brands. In the consumer behavior literature, three intellectual traditions have dominated the approach to cultural research: the dimensional approach, the dynamic constructivist approach, and the consumer theory of marketplace cultures. Each of these traditions focuses on specific defining aspects of culture and their consequences for consumer behavior. Upon reviewing these approaches, this chapter discusses the effects of culture on attention and information processing, the persuasiveness of culturally matched appeals, the processes by which brands acquire cultural meanings, and the responses of consumers to the cultural meanings in brands. Special attention is devoted to the novel phenomenon of culture mixing or the juxtaposition of multiple cultures in a single-product offering. Finally, the chapter concludes with a discussion of a future research agenda, as well as with a summary of the key findings and practical implications for organizations regarding culture and consumer behavior.

The Dimensional Approach to Culture

According to the dimensional approach to understanding the role of culture in consumer behavior, culture is conceptualized as shared elements "that provide the standards for perceiving, believing, evaluating, communicating, and acting among those who share a language, a historic period, and a geographic location" (p. 408; Triandis, 1996). This approach identifies and measures *patterns* of variations in these shared elements that are organized around a psychological theme, dimension, or syndrome (Hofstede, 1980; Triandis, 1995, 1996). The underlying assumption under the dimensional approach is that, although there may be hundreds of cultures spread throughout the world, they vary according to a handful number of dimensions. Uncovering these dimensions helps categorize them into groups that share the same pattern of beliefs, values, and cognitions, which in turn can be used for predicting attitudes and behaviors of individual group members. In the past decades, the majority of research has focused on the *individualism–collectivism* classification, followed by the *vertical* and *horizontal* subtypes of individualism and collectivism and the related dimension of power distance (see Shavitt et al., 2006).

Individualism–Collectivism Classification

This classification relates to the extent to which individuals view themselves as distinct from or connected to others. People who are from individualistic cultures, or who have an independent self-construal, tend to emphasize individual autonomy and separation from others, while people from collectivistic cultures, or who have an interdependent self-construal, tend to prioritize connectedness, social context, and relationships with ingroup members (Triandis, 1995). The individualism–collectivism classification can be used to predict how consumers attend to and process product information, as well as to identify advertisements that will be most persuasive.

Attention and Information Processing. Because individualism promotes an independent view of the self, people in individualistic cultures (e.g., Americans) tend to have a decontextualized view of the world that focuses on focal objects and their attributes. Thus, individualism fosters a tendency to focus on the attributes of an object, separate from its context, in order to assign it to a category and to use rules about the category to explain and predict the object's behavior (i.e., *analytic* thinking style, Nisbett et al, 2001). Individualists tend to judge new products introduced by existing brands on the basis of how close the new product is to existing products, or the extent to which the attributes of the parent brand transfer to the new product (Monga & John, 2007). In contrast, because collectivism fosters a view of the self as embedded within a larger social context, people in collectivistic cultures (e.g., East Asians) attend to the relationships between the self, others, and the environment, fostering a tendency to attend to social and environmental contexts as a whole, especially to relationships between focal objects and the environment, and predict events on the basis of such relationships. This way of thinking is often referred to as *holistic* thinking style (Nisbett et al., 2001). This approach affords an advantage in detecting broader connections between objects, even if subtle. Because they pay more attention to the environment, collectivists more easily identify relationships between an existing brand and a newly introduced product based on complementarity of use or overall reputation (i.e., more subtle connections). For example, Indian (i.e., collectivistic) consumers perceive a higher fit between a distant brand extension, such as a filing cabinet introduced by the Kodak brand, than American (i.e., individualistic) consumers do because collectivists are more able to identify the more subtle usage-based connection between Kodak and filing cabinets (i.e., filing cabinets can be used to store pictures) than individualists are (Monga & John, 2007).

Given individualists' tendency to process messages analytically, attending to focal images and attributes, relying in categorical knowledge, and making choices based on rules, advertisements in individualistic cultures would benefit from the use of white space as a way of making focal product images/attributes salient. In contrast, given collectivists' tendency to process ads holistically, attending to relationships between focal images/attributes and the context, advertisements in collectivistic cultures would benefit less from the use of white space; it would be more appropriate for ads to embed focal product images/messages in a background that contains reinforcing contextual information.

Persuasiveness of Culturally Matched Advertising Messages.

One of the most important findings under the dimensional approach, and more specifically the individualism–collectivism classification, is that advertising messages that match cultural value priorities are more persuasive than those that do not. This effect, however, is more evident for shared products (i.e., products for which the purchase decision and usage are likely to include family members and friends, such as laundry detergent and home appliances) than for personal products (i.e., products for which the purchase decision and usage are usually done by the individual, such as chewing gum and running shoes) (Han & Shavitt, 1994). A slogan for a detergent brand like "Solo cleans with a softness that you will love" is more persuasive in the individualistic U.S. culture, while "Solo cleans with a softness that your family will love" appeals to the values of a collectivistic culture like South Korea.

Similarly, individualists are better persuaded by information that addresses their promotion of regulatory concerns (i.e., messages about personal achievement, individuality, uniqueness, and self-improvement), whereas collectivists are better persuaded by information that addresses their prevention regulatory concerns (i.e., messages about harmony, group goals, conformity, and security; see Aaker & Lee, 2001). Furthermore, recent research shows that the practice by some firms of adopting asymmetric pricing (i.e., charging different consumers with different prices) is perceived to be less fair by collectivistic (vs. individualistic) consumers because such practice does not match the communal norms of firm benevolence endorsed by collectivists (Chen et al., 2018).

Vertical-Horizontal Distinction

The vertical-horizontal distinction emerges from the observation that American individualism differs from Australian individualism in much the same way that Japanese collectivism differs from the collectivism of the Israeli Kibbutz. Whereas individuals in vertical societies view the self as differing from others along a hierarchy and accept inequality, those in horizontal societies value equality and view the self as having the same status as others in society (Triandis, 1995). Thus, combining the horizontal-vertical distinction with the individualism–collectivism classification produces four cultural orientations: horizontal individualist, vertical individualist, horizontal collectivist, and vertical collectivist.

In vertical individualist societies like the United States, people tend to be concerned with the self-enhancement values of power and achievement, while in horizontal individualist cultures like Australia, people view themselves as equal and avoid status differentiation. In vertical collectivist societies like Japan, conservation values of tradition, conformity, and security are emphasized, while in horizontal collectivist cultural contexts like the Israeli Kibbutz, individuals endorse self-transcendence values that promote the welfare of others (Shavitt et al., 2006; Shavitt et al., 2010; Triandis & Gelfand, 1998).

Attention and Information Processing. Focusing on the vertical and horizontal distinctions, nested within the broader individualism–collectivism classification, affords a more nuanced understanding of culture. Specifically, the tendency by individualists to assign objects to categories and to make predictions about these objects based on category attributes is particularly pronounced among vertical individualists (who are chronically concerned about status and power) when responding to power cues. When presented with information about a focal object, vertical individualists who feel powerful tend to focus on information that is consistent with the stereotype of the category to which the object belongs, while ignoring inconsistent information—often referred to as *stereotyping processing* (Torelli & Shavitt, 2011). This occurs because attending to stereotypical information helps to confirm prior expectations and to reassert control, thereby protecting a powerful status (Fiske, 1993). For instance, when vertical individualists are presented with an advertisement for a status-enhancing financial advisory service, they recognize better, in a subsequent recognition task, information *congruent* with the stereotypical image of the status product (e.g., "financial experts graduated from the top-tier universities in the country") relative to their recognition of *incongruent* information (e.g., "When you visit Interbank offices, you will feel the warmth of your own home"; Torelli & Shavitt, 2011).

In contrast, as stated earlier, collectivists base their perceptions on a holistic view of the target object and its relationship to the social context. This tendency is particularly strong among horizontal collectivists (who are chronically concerned about interdependence and sociability) driven by power motives. Specifically, when presented with information about a focal object, horizontal collectivists motivated to use their power for the benefit of others (i.e., socialized power) tend to engage in *individuating processing*—or the tendency to individuate and understand others (Torelli & Shavitt, 2011). This involves attending to information that is incongruent with prior expectations, presumably because such information helps to form an accurate impression instrumental for helping others (Overbeck & Park, 2001). For instance, upon priming socialized power, horizontal collectivists presented with an advertisement for a nurturing dog food recognize better, in a subsequent recognition task, information *incongruent* with the stereotypical image of the nurturing product (e.g., "It has been reported that the company recently influenced distributors to stop carrying competitors' products") (Torelli & Shavitt, 2011).

Given vertical individualists' tendency to stereotype when influenced by power, advertisements that contain power themes would trigger stereotyping processing among vertical individualistic consumers, which in turn would prompt them to attend to information consistent with the categorical knowledge triggered by the focal product (e.g., the horsepower of a pick-up truck), while ignoring inconsistent information (e.g., the softness of the car seat cushion). In contrast, in view of the individuating processing exhibited by horizontal collectivists when motivated to help others, ads that cue responsibility themes would trigger individuating processing among horizontal collectivistic consumers, in turn prompting them to pay special attention to information that is inconsistent with the categorical knowledge triggered by the focal product.

Persuasiveness of Culturally Matched Advertising Messages. Although appeals to self-enhancement values and openness values seem equally appropriate in individualistic cultures, as both primarily refer to individual interests, a focus on the vertical-horizontal distinction helps us recognize that openness values are more appealing for consumers with a horizontal individualistic orientation, while they are less so for those with a vertical individualistic orientation. In contrast, appeals to self-enhancement values are more appealing for consumers with a vertical individualistic orientation, but less so for those with a horizontal individualistic orientation (Torelli et al., 2012). Similarly, appeals to self-transcendence values are more appealing for consumers with a horizontal collectivistic orientation but are less so for those with a vertical collectivistic orientation. In contrast, appeals to conservation values are more appealing for consumers with a vertical collectivistic orientation but are less so for those with a horizontal collectivistic orientation (Torelli et al., 2012).

Power Distance

Power distance is a cultural dimension that reflects the degree to which differences in power are expected and accepted (Hofstede, 2001). This dimension partially overlaps with the horizontal—vertical distinction, but there are also important conceptual and structural differences between them (Shavitt et al., 2006). From a conceptual standpoint, the horizontal/vertical distinction refers to a hierarchical arrangement of individuals, whereas power distance relates to differences in the acceptance of hierarchies as being valid or important in one's society. From a structural standpoint, although power distance is conceptualized as a single dimension (from high to low Power Distance Index; Hofstede, 1980, 2001), it is highly correlated with individualism–collectivism. Thus, countries high in power distance tend to also be collectivistic. More specifically, countries topping the list of power distance scores (e.g., China, India, Malaysia, and Mexico) are countries also characterized as vertical collectivists, whereas those lowest in power distance (e.g., Denmark, Sweden, and Norway) are countries also characterized as horizontal individualistic (Triandis, 1995; Triandis & Gelfand, 1998). Thus, the high-/low-power distance distinction partially overlaps with the distinction between vertical collectivism and horizontal individualism.

Attention and Information Processing. People who believe in power distance (i.e., high on power distance beliefs, or PDB) are comfortable with, and even desire, structure. Therefore, people who are high in PDB tend to categorize products, which affect their judgments. For example, recent research by Lalwani and Forcum (2016) found that people high in PDB are more likely to categorize products by price, resulting in ascribing higher quality to high-priced products. Other research has found that the interaction between PDB and psychological power states, or power cues, can affect people's attention focus and subsequent behavior. For example, Han et al. (2017) found that in low-PDB contexts, people high in psychological power tended to be self-focused, which led to less charitable giving; whereas in high-PDB contexts, people high (vs. low) in psychological power tended to be more other-focused, which led to more charitable giving.

Persuasiveness of Culturally Matched Advertising Messages. People high in PDB, given their tendency to expect and accept authority, are likely to be better persuaded by expertise and trustworthiness. Indeed, recent research demonstrates that people high in PDB tend to be better persuaded by celebrity endorsements (Winterich et al., 2018) and by company-designed products over user-designed products (Paharia & Swaminathan, 2019). Consumers high in PDB have a strong desire for status and thus show a stronger preference for status brands (Kim & Zhang, 2014), national (vs. private-label) brands (Wang et al., 2020), and upward (vs. downward) brand extension (Liu et al., 2015). Furthermore, people low in PDB express greater preference for transparency in brand information (Jain & Jain, 2018).

The Dynamic Constructivist Approach to Culture

Although the dimensional approach to culture helps to make predictions about perceptual, attentional, and evaluative tendencies of consumers, it is less useful for identifying specific contexts in which people will exhibit these tendencies. In this tradition, it is often implicitly assumed that culture is constantly operating in the background to trigger these tendencies across contexts. However, empirical evidence does not seem to support this notion, and suggests instead that consumers are strategic in their reliance on cultural cognitions for their judgments and behaviors (Briley & Aaker, 2006; Briley et al., 2000; Chiu & Hong, 2006). The dynamic constructivist approach to culture addresses this issue by considering that culture is not internalized as a highly general structure, such as a value orientation, but instead as a loose network of domain-specific knowledge structures, such as categories (e.g., individualist values and beliefs), implicit theories (e.g., an individual's behavior originates in internal dispositions), and cultural icons (e.g., the Statue of Liberty) linked to a central theme (e.g., American culture), which drive judgments and behaviors when made readily accessible by environmental stimuli (Hong et al., 2000). Thus, although people possess cultural knowledge, this knowledge drives behavior only when it is *activated*, or primed, by cues in the environment that make salient the application of the cultural knowledge network for the task at hand (Hong et al., 2001; Hong et al., 2000). The dynamic constructivist approach has been particularly useful for identifying contexts in which culture is an operative construct, as well as to model the behavior of bicultural consumers.

When Does Culture Matter?

Instead of considering culture as a dispositional trait that drives behavior across contexts, research on the dynamic constructivist approach has uncovered situations that render culture salient to guide consumer decisions. The cultural matching effects on advertising persuasiveness described earlier are more likely to emerge when information is processed in a cursory, spontaneous manner, when people are prone to form impressions based on commonly used cultural constructs. For instance, American (vs. Chinese) consumers are better persuaded by promotion than by prevention advertising messages when they relied on automatic processing (e.g., under time constraints or under cognitive load), but less so when they were encouraged to deliberate on the message (Briley & Aaker,

2006). Culture-based product decisions are also more likely to emerge when consumers are prompted to justify their choices through reasoned statements, which renders explanations based on cultural norms particularly salient in memory. For example, Hong Kong Chinese consumers are more likely to choose a compromise option, that aligns with the normative tendency to find "the middle way" fostered in Chinese culture, when prompted to justify their choices (Briley et al., 2000). Similarly, consumers with a salient collective self are more likely to favorably evaluate products that align with the preferences of others when prompted to justify their decisions to these others (Torelli, 2006).

The Behavior of Bicultural Consumers

As stated earlier, globalization has exponentially amplified people's interactions with lifestyles, customs, and traditions from different cultures. Consequently, the number of individuals who internalize knowledge from two (i.e., bicultural) or more (i.e., multicultural) cultures, as opposed to a single culture, is rapidly on the rise (Benet-Martínez et al., 2002). Based on the notion that culture drives behavior when it is activated, the dynamic constructivist approach helps to explain how bicultural individuals switch cultural frames according to the context. Cultural frame switching refers to the process by which biculturals respond to situationally salient cultural cues or contexts by activating cultural meaning systems. For example, for Hong Kong Chinese students, exposure to Chinese cultural symbols (e.g., a Chinese dragon) increases the degree to which they endorse Chinese values as compared to the exposure to American cultural symbols (e.g., the American flag) (Hong et al., 2000). Although some part of cultural frame switching is automatic, bicultural individuals also consciously choose between cultural frames to meet the cultural demands of the situation (Birman, 1994). For example, an Asian American consumer could alternate their cultural identities and be Asian at home and American at work (Forehand et al., 2002). Prior work has demonstrated such compartmentalization of cultural identities and frame switching across a wide range of cultures and populations (Lau-Gesk, 2003). Recent research has expanded to cultural switching among monocultural individuals exposed to the tenets of a foreign culture (e.g., European Americans living in Chinatown; Alter & Kwan, 2009). Cultural frame switching has market consequences, as consumers tend to favor products consistent with the accessible cultural frame. For instance, Mexican American consumers residing in the United States prefer songs from a Hispanic rock band as a way to connect with their Hispanic identity (Torelli et al., 2017).

Consumer Theory of Marketplace Cultures

Consumer culture theory (CCT) refers to a family of phenomenological and ethnographic approaches focused on the dynamic relations between consumers' actions, the marketplace, and cultural meanings. Rather than considering shared patterns of meanings in a given society, CCT investigates the heterogeneous distribution of cultural meanings, and how consumers use commercial products and images to make collective sense of their environments and guide their actions (Arnould & Thompson, 2005). This more granular approach to studying the interplay between culture and consumption has provided further insights into the ways in which consumers develop a sense of collective identity built around a brand. As we discuss in more detail in the next section, the study of marketplace cultures has helped illuminate the process by which abstract cultural categories are instantiated in products and brands to endow such entities with cultural meanings (Fournier & Alvarez, 2019; McCracken, 1986). Brand associations can be embedded within cultural myths or cultural models in a narrative form. For instance, the Mexican beer Corona strongly associated itself with the partying myth of the Mexican spring break, which helped Corona embody such cultural meaning (Holt, 2004). The consumer theory of marketplace cultures also affords a more nuanced understanding of how experiential consumption promotes collective identification grounded in shared cultural meanings. For example, consuming experiences built around the imaginary mountain men who trapped beavers in the Rocky Mountains of the American West not only provides a strong sense of community among consumers, but also strengthens the symbolic meaning of American values of freedom and individualism (Belk & Costa, 1998).

Consumers' Responses to Cultural Meanings in Products and Brands

Coke and *Pepsi* are brands with an almost identical core product offering, whose products are similarly priced, are sold through the same distribution channels, and adopt similar promotional strategies. Nonetheless, Coke consistently dominates Pepsi in brand rankings of best global brands. Recent research in consumer behavior argues that Coke's success can be attributed to its distinctive ability to achieve the status of an icon—both globally and nationally (Cross, 2002; Holt, 2004; Torelli, 2013).

As stated earlier, culture not only consists of values and beliefs, but also manifests itself in objects such as brands and products. Brands often acquire cultural meanings and come to embody the values and ideals nurtured by a cultural group. Thus, a brand's cultural meaning is defined in terms of shared agreement that the brand symbolizes an abstract cultural image (Torelli & Ahluwalia, 2012; Torelli et al., 2010; Torelli et al., 2020). For example, Ford has cultural meaning for Americans because of its strong association with the rugged individualism that characterizes American culture. Brands that are consensually perceived to symbolize an abstract cultural identity are regarded as *cultural icons*. Thus, iconic brands symbolize the beliefs, ideas, and values of a cultural group. Recent research in consumer behavior has focused on how brands acquire cultural meanings, as well as on the more favorable responses of consumers to the cultural meanings in brands.

How Do Brands Acquire Cultural Meanings?

The brand meaning-making process is a collective effort involving the marketer, consumers, and social influencers (e.g., mass media, celebrities, and social media influencers; Fournier & Alvarez, 2019). Brand meanings originate in the culturally constituted world and move into brands through several instruments such as advertising, the fashion system, and reference groups (McCracken, 1986). Consumers appropriate these brand meanings for constructing their individual identities (Escalas & Bettman, 2005), and in a dynamic process of social verification, subjective brand meanings take a concreteness that can be widely recognized by society at large (Holt, 2004; McCracken, 1986). In this interactive process, brands that are deemed better cultural carriers are publicly acknowledged as cultural icons. To illustrate this process, let us consider the cultural meaning of Elvis Presley, undoubtedly one of the most widely recognized American icons of the twentieth century.

Elvis, also known as "the King," was certainly not the first musician to embrace the newly popular sound of rock and roll. Black musicians of his time, such as Arthur Crudup or Big Bill Broonzy, had been performing the new rhythm well before it was Presley's style (Farley, 2004). However, for multiple reasons, none of these musicians developed the cultural meaning that Elvis did. Because these Black musicians did not embody the image, traits, and values of mainstream, segregated, White American culture in the 1950s, they could not become consensual expressions of cultural ideals of the time. Indeed, Sam Phillips, the head of Sun Records where Elvis recorded his first songs, has often said in interviews that the music industry was looking for a White boy who sang Black, who had the rhyming and soul to do R&B, and that Elvis was this boy (Guralnick, 1994). In addition to embodying traits that characterized American culture at the time, Elvis also embodied in a unique way the key dramas of sex, race, and class that had been suppressed in the conservative and conformist 1950s (Kellner, 2013). By embodying an emerging cultural myth, Elvis became a target of public discourse that facilitated consensus around his cultural meaning (Fournier & Alvarez, 2019; Holt, 2004).

Elvis's story illustrates how a brand, in this case a person brand, acquires cultural meaning by becoming a widely regarded symbol of a particular kind of story found to be valuable by people in a culture (Holt, 2004). Importantly, consumers of his time more easily agreed publicly on Elvis's cultural meaning due to his embodiment of valued cultural characteristics, allowing him to become a target of cultural discourse. In any culture, there is wide consensus about the importance of valued cultural characteristics, which contributes to the *shared reality*, or the totality of knowledge that is assumed to be known and shared by others (Wan et al., 2007). As a result, people have an inclination to transmit information that is consistent with the shared reality (Wan et al., 2010). Given the defining role of key cultural characteristics, members of the culture attend to the cultural significance of narratives that support them and evaluate these stories favorably as cultural narratives. Thus, narratives about actors (e.g., product or person brands) that personify cultural aspects are evaluated in cultural terms and hence are more favorably evaluated and more frequently transmitted (Kashima, 2000; Wan et al., 2010).

Iconic Brands Resonate with Consumers

The consumer is the central character in the process of creating brand meanings (Batra, 2019). Consumers internalize the cultural meaning of a brand through inferencing and semantic interpretation, as well as through identity processes. Social groups and brand communities "cultivate" a disposition among their members toward certain types of brand meanings (e.g., refinement for high-class individuals; Fournier & Alvarez, 2019). Furthermore, consumers appropriate and transmit desirable brand meanings for building their cultural identities. Because culture provides the individual with a strong sense of collective identity (Chiu & Hong, 2006), people are more likely to recruit cultural knowledge for their judgments and behaviors when enacting their cultural identity. Building upon the dynamic constructivist approach to culture, the identity-based motivation theory (Oyserman, 2009) proposes that identities not only include knowledge about group membership and a positive sense of ingroup connections, but also the readiness to act and make sense of the world in identity-congruent ways. In the context of cultural identities, the theory predicts that people will behave in culturally appropriate ways when acting on behalf of their cultural identity. For instance, when making an ethnic identity salient (vs. not), consumers evaluate advertisements targeted to the ethnic group more favorably (e.g., as depicted in copy and ad images; Forehand et al., 2002).

Because brands with cultural significance symbolize the values, beliefs, myths, and ideals of a cultural group, consumers with a heightened need to symbolize a cultural identity will judge iconic brands as highly instrumental for fulfilling such needs. By consuming a culturally symbolic brand, one emphasizes the possession of the cultural identity and the alignment with and adherence to the culture (Torelli et al., 2017). Thus, when a cultural identity is temporarily or chronically salient, consumers evaluate more favorably and are even willing to pay more for culturally meaningful brands. For example, recent research found that people born and raised in Minnesota valued *Target*, a Minnesota icon, more highly (as evidenced by their higher willingness to pay for a set of poker chips with the *Target* logo stamped on each chip) when their Minnesotan identity was made salient (Amaral & Torelli, 2018). Importantly, because a salient identity brings to mind identity-consistent decisions that do not require further reflection, the higher valuation of iconic brands occurs rather automatically and without conscious deliberation (Torelli, 2013). Indeed, the pleasing processing experience of consuming culturally symbolic brands has been found to underlie the enhanced brand valuation effects. This is illustrated in a study about brand extensions in which both the new product and the brand activate the same cultural identity. Participants in the study evaluated more favorably a new Tequila introduced by Corona (both the brand and the new product activate the Mexican cultural schema) compared to a Tequila introduced by a "beer manufacturer" (neutral condition in which culture is less salient). Furthermore, the more favorable attitudes toward Corona Tequila were mediated by the ease with which participants processed the new brand extension (Torelli & Ahluwalia, 2012). Over time, continued reliance on iconic brands for fulfilling salient cultural identity needs can contribute to developing strong self-brand relationships (Amaral & Torelli, 2018; Escalas & Bettman, 2005). In turn, forming a strong bond with a culturally symbolic brand can shield the brand against negative publicity when cultural identity needs are salient (Swaminathan et al., 2007).

The above discussion seems to suggest that identities are stable systems with clear boundaries and structures. However, current conceptualizations rooted in social cognition research assume a not-well-integrated structure and a highly contextualized definition of a social identity depending on what referent group is relevant in a given context (Oyserman, 2009). Indeed, identities not only can be "anchored" in different referent groups, but can also bridge various classifications (e.g., an ethnic and a national identity; Reed et al., 2012). Specifically, the boundaries that define a cultural group can be flexible and expanded to fulfill cultural identity goals. This is illustrated in research on cultural distinctiveness (Torelli et al., 2017) or the feeling of separation from the surrounding cultural environment that people often experience when visiting a foreign, unfamiliar culture. This feeling of separation is often accompanied by a desire to connect with familiar things from "home," which then expands consumers' ingroup boundaries to include a related cultural group within a broadened definition of home—subsequently triggering a strong pro-ingroup bias. This broadened definition allows them to fulfill the need to connect with home by favoring brands/products associated with the related cultural group. For example, Mexican immigrants living in the United States, who are more likely to be chronically high in cultural distinctiveness, preferred to listen to an Argentine over a Turkish song, compared to Mexicans living in their home country, who are less likely to experience cultural distinctiveness. This is due to the desire of Mexican immigrants to connect with "home," which prompts the expansion of the cultural boundaries that define their cultural group from Mexican to Latin American, and hence leads to favor an Argentinian product associated with this more broadly defined cultural identity (Torelli et al., 2017).

Multiculturalism in Products and Brands

In globalized markets, symbols of different cultures often occupy the same space at the same time. Unlike the priming of a single cultural frame discussed earlier in the chapter, exposure to symbols of multiple cultures, or *culture mixing*, activates not only one, but two or more cultural representations at the same time. Recent research has documented the basic cognitive and evaluative processes triggered by culture-mixed stimuli, as well as some of the factors that moderate consumers' responses to culture mixing in products and brands.

Cognitive and Evaluative Responses to Culture Mixing

When symbols of two cultures are present in the environment, the cognitive representations of both cultures will be activated (Chiu et al., 2009). In turn, the perceiver will attend to the defining characteristics that distinguish the two cultures, which in turn enlarges the perceived differences and incompatibility of the two cultures and renders culture salient as an organizing theme for judgments and decisions. These processes are less likely to occur when only one cultural representation is activated (i.e., monocultural priming), even when that representation is one of a foreign culture (Torelli et al., 2011). Thus, culture mixing draws attention to the conflict between the juxtaposed cultures, resulting in the expectation that cultures are discrete entities with relatively impermeable boundaries, and prompts individuals to judge the world according to the cultural view.

The effect of exposure to culture-mixed stimuli on the cognitive tendency to view the world in cultural terms is illustrated in a study about American consumers' responses to products associated with either a single culture (monocultural products) or two cultures (culture-mixed products; Torelli et al., 2011). In this study, American consumers exposed to culture-mixed products (e.g., iconic Mexican products that carry British brand names) perceived greater cultural differences than those exposed to monocultural products (e.g., culture-neutral products that carry prototypic British brand names). This effect emerges because exposure to the culture-mixed products simultaneously activates representations of Mexican and British cultures, which prompts using culture as an organizing theme for processing information, and hence increases perceived differences between cultures. This effect emerges not only for the target cultures (e.g., Mexican and British), but also for other cultures (e.g., Puerto Rican and Canadian). This tendency toward culture-based judgments is also evident in a study with Beijing Chinese consumers (Chiu et al., 2009). Participants evaluated a McDonald's hamburger advertisement that was either placed next to another McDonald's hamburger advertisement (monocultural priming) or next to a traditional Chinese moon cake advertisement (culture mixing). Following the manipulation, the participants were presented with two commercial messages for *Timex*, one appealing to individualist values and one to collectivist values. The participants then rated how likely it was that a Chinese consumer would choose the individualist and collectivist messages for designing a Chinese website for Timex. Accordingly, compared to those in the monocultural priming condition, those in the culture-mixed condition believed that the Chinese consumer would be more likely to behave according to their cultural prescriptions and choose the collectivist message.

Because experiencing conflict between incongruent concepts is an aversive state (Meyers-Levy & Tybout, 1989), consumers often evaluate culture-mixed products less favorably than monocultural ones. For instance, past research (Torelli & Ahluwalia, 2012) shows that Americans evaluate less favorably a culture-mixed product (*Sony cappuccino machines*–the Sony brand is iconic in Japan, whereas Cappuccino machines are iconic in Italy) than a monocultural one (*Sony toaster oven*—only the Japanese Sony is culturally symbolic), even when both products have similar levels of moderate fit with the Sony brand. Furthermore, the less favorable evaluations of the culture-mixed product are driven by the subjective experience of disfluency (i.e., feeling that the product is not "right"), triggered by the simultaneous activation of two different cultural schemas.

Personal and Situational Factors Affecting Responses to Culture Mixing

One way to mitigate the spontaneous negative reaction to culture-mixed products is to combine the two contrastive cultural images to reduce the perceived conflict, which might require mustering cognitive resources. Indeed, research suggests that thoughtful elaboration about cultural complexities (either spontaneously or temporarily induced) can attenuate consumers' negative reactions to culture-mixed products (Torelli et al., 2011). More generally, psychological and situational factors that induce openness to the novel experiences from intercultural encounters promote integrating the contrastive cultures and reducing conflict. For instance, Chen et al. (2016) demonstrate that openness to experience favorably impacts the creative benefits of experiencing culture mixing in the environment. Similarly, Keh et al. (2016) showed that endorsing autonomy values of stimulation and self-direction positively predicts favorable attitudes of Chinese consumers toward culture-mixed phonosemantic brand translations (i.e., from a Western language to Chinese that maintains the foreign-sounding name, while conveying the brand meaning in the Chinese language).

In contrast, factors that promote closemindedness or the protection of one of the cultural identities hinder the reconciliation needed to favorably evaluate culture mixing. Consistent with this notion, De keersmaecker et al. (2016) demonstrate that people who are high in need for cognitive closure, or those who need a firm answer in a psychologically ambiguous situation, are less favorable toward culturally mixed stimuli (e.g., fusion cuisine). Past research also suggests that a motivation to defend a stable cultural worldview free from ambiguity can promote negative responses to culture mixing (Torelli & Cheng, 2011). Indeed, Torelli and colleagues (2011) show that, when under the influence of a culture defense mindset triggered by thoughts of one's own death (i.e., mortality salience), people are particularly intolerant of contamination of brands symbolizing their culture when cued with culture mixing. In one of their studies, focused on inducing mortality salience, American participants evaluated a marketing plan of Nike (an American icon), which involved some questionable actions to increase its competitiveness in a foreign market (e.g., eliminating the "Swoosh" symbol and replacing the Nike brand name with the Arabic word for "Sportsmanship" to penetrate the Middle East market). Results showed that, only upon making mortality salient, participants evaluated the marketing plan less favorably after evaluating culture-mixed products (e.g., a Chinese brand of breakfast cereal) than after evaluating monocultural products (e.g., an American brand of breakfast cereal).

Accordingly, personal or situational factors that heighten the motivation to defend a valued cultural identity should incite unfavorable responses to culture mixing. Consistent with this notion, Cheon et al. (2016) showed that disgust toward ingroup–outgroup cultural mixing is particularly pronounced among those who endorse higher levels of patriotism. Similarly, Shi et al. (2016) demonstrated that individuals who highly identify with their heritage culture tend to exhibit implicit prejudice toward the foreign culture represented in a culturally mixed stimulus.

Conclusions and Future Directions

As marketing efforts become increasingly globalized, it is key for organizations to understand how the multiculturalism prompted by globalization impacts consumer behavior. Our review sheds light on the cultural factors that shape consumers' responses in a global marketplace, and it proposes alternatives for organizations to adapt their marketing strategies to address the consumer's cultural needs. However, many questions remain unanswered. What other cultural dimensions beyond the ones discussed in this chapter have the greatest potential to further refine our predictions of consumer behavior? How can we further integrate the different approaches to cultural research to develop a more comprehensive model of cross-cultural consumer behavior? What happens when more than two cultures influence consumer behavior? What new methodological insights can cultural researchers adopt?

Additional Cultural Dimensions

In trying to uncover the cultural dimensions that would provide a more nuanced understanding of consumer behavior, several dimensions have been proposed, such as uncertainty avoidance (Hofstede, 2001), religious beliefs, and tightness–looseness (Triandis, 1995). Recent research on the tightness–looseness distinction seems to offer the greatest potential (Li, Gordon, & Gelfand, 2017). *Tightness* (T) refers to cultures in which norms are clearly defined and there is little tolerance of deviant behavior, whereas *looseness (L)* relates to cultures in which norms are vague, and there is high tolerance of deviant behavior (Gelfand et al., 2011; Pelto, 1968; Triandis, 1995). According to Li, Gordon, and Gelfand (2017), it can be expected that ads in tighter cultures (e.g., Singapore) would emphasize adherence to societal standards, whereas ads in looser cultures (e.g., the United States) would focus more on taking risks. Lin, Dahl, and Argo (2017) identified four consumer-relevant research questions under the T-L framework, such as the examination of a potentially bidirectional relationship between tight/loose culture and consumer behavior.

Focusing on tightness–looseness can provide a more nuanced understanding of consumer behavior, especially by integrating it within existing cultural frameworks. For instance, it has been proposed that the T-L distinction seems particularly likely to shed light on the differences between societies that are high in vertical collectivism (Torelli & Rodas, 2017). This cultural syndrome might help to explain the differences between Asian versions of vertical collectivism in which it is normative to suppress the expression of emotions (e.g., Japan, a tight culture) and Latin American versions of the same cultural syndrome in which people freely express their emotions (e.g., Venezuela, a loose culture; Gelfand et al., 2011). More research can be conducted by incorporating multiple cultural dimensions and examining their impact on marketing-relevant factors.

Focusing on tightness–looseness could also provide novel insights on some of the phenomena discussed in this chapter, for example, cultural mixing. Recent research has found that people tighten cultural norms in response to ecological threats (Jackson et al., 2019). In one of their studies, the authors found that when people recall a threat such as a foreign attack or a major recession, they are more likely to vote for nationalists politicians, and this is mediated by stronger support for cultural tightness. Future research could explore whether these findings extend to cultural mixing, more specifically, whether ecological threats would result in more negative reactions to cultural mixing. Given the increased number of threats in the consumer's environment (e.g., COVID-19, global recessions, or political instability), understanding whether consumers are going to be more averse to culture mixing would be of value to managers of global brands.

Integrating Cultural Approaches to Refine Models of Consumer Behavior

Although the three different approaches to cultural research described in this chapter have contributed separately to a more nuanced understanding of how culture impacts consumer behavior, future research integrating these approaches can greatly help to develop a more comprehensive model of consumer behavior in a globalized world. For instance, although the consumer theory of marketplace cultures provides a framework for understanding how consumers develop a collective identity built around a brand, we still lack a thorough understanding of the process by which brands become cultural icons. We argue that this process can be illuminated by integrating this ethnographic approach with an experimental approach aimed at understanding how identity concepts are linked to cultural icons in a cultural knowledge network. Specifically, this integrated approach might help to clearly delineate what is cultural about an iconic brand. If what grants a brand an iconic status is the strength of association with values, beliefs, rituals, lay theories, and other cultural objects, marketers can manage the process of cultural meaning creation by associating the brand with this constellation of cultural elements (MacInnis et al., 2019). This integrated approach might also help to determine whether iconic brands can sustain changes and remake themselves while still retaining their iconic status. Increasingly relevant in this growing age of nationalism concerns, where consumers may stereotype other consumers based on their use of culturally symbolic products and brands, it is not clear how cultural stereotypes enhance, detract from, or alter brand meanings. For example, nationalism could either strengthen the shared cultural meanings of brands, or it could polarize views about those brands and the members of the cultures who use them, depending on their nationality. In this way, nationalism could hurt the equity of brands that had previously received support outside its country of origin.

Exposure to culture-mixed products triggers a variety of cognitive, emotional, and evaluative responses. Multiple situational and dispositional factors have been uncovered as moderators of the extent to which exclusionary or integrative responses are more likely to emerge. However, there is still the need for future research integrating these factors into a comprehensive framework. One fruitful approach might be the categorization of factors into those relating to the culture-mixed stimuli, the individual's dispositions, environmental factors, and sociocultural and psychological consequences (Hao et al., 2016). For instance, research focusing on features of the stimuli might try to explain how the "fusion" of cultures in a more or less harmonious way, or the strength of the symbolism of the features being mixed, can moderate responses to culture mixing. There is also need for research on how the organization in memory of multicultural knowledge guides people's responses to culture-mixed stimuli, as well as on the contexts in which exclusionary or integrative responses are more likely to emerge.

From Biculturalism to Polyculturalism

This chapter discussed how cultural influence is not stable and deterministic, but dynamic and dependent on the context. Because it is increasingly common for people to internalize more than one cultural knowledge network (e.g., bicultural individuals), situational cues can determine how people switch between cultural frames for making judgments and decisions. Although recent research suggests that the way in which two cultural frames are organized in memory can impact how people respond to cultural primes (e.g., the frames are integrated vs. kept separately; Mok & Morris, 2013), we still know very little about how knowledge of more than two cultures influences consumer behavior.

With globalization, it is increasingly common for people to acquire knowledge about multiple cultures. Polyculturalism has emerged as a novel approach to understand how a multicultural mind works (Morris et al., 2015). This approach proposes that most cultural learning happens implicitly through interaction with different cultures (e.g., via web browsing or when sharing with colleagues from different cultures). Hence, people take influences from multiple cultures and become conduits through which cultures can affect each other. Thus, cultural knowledge is conceived more like a set of "apps" that the individual unwittingly downloads and that can be "launched" to accommodate one's behavior to a given situation. People flexibly assimilate or contrast their responses to the accessible cultural knowledge in the service of their goals (e.g., adopting a foreign practice as a better solution to a problem) or driven by emotional connections to the accessible culture (e.g., admiration for the culture; Morris et al., 2015). The polycultural approach opens avenues for future research about how multicultural consumers navigate a global marketplace.

New Methodological Insights

Like many other areas in psychology, the field of cultural psychology is also being reinvigorated by methodological innovations. In particular, cultural neuroscience is a promising research discipline that has emerged to investigate cultural differences in psychological, neural, and genomic processes (Chiao et al., 2010). Cultural neuroscience specializes in developing culturally appropriate experimental tasks that can be applied in consumer behavior research in order to identify differences in the functional brain activity patterns associated with culture. This can help to further explain the nature of the processes underlying cross-cultural differences in consumer behavior via activation of specific areas of the brain. Another novel methodological approach to cultural research relates to the utilization of machine learning techniques (e.g., natural language processing) and the analyses of big data. An increasing number of empirical research studies have uncovered cross-cultural differences in various aspects of consumer preferences and behaviors, such as emoji usage (Guntuku et al., 2019), recognition of beauty in music (Claire, 2013), and color–emotion association (Jonauskaite et al., 2019). These findings eventually will help the tech industry develop AI systems that can incorporate cultural factors into their algorithms (Forbus, 2019). Future research can benefit from the adoption of these methodologies to further refine our understanding of cross-cultural consumer behavior.

Key Findings

1. *Cultural patterning of attention and perception:* Culture is associated with specific patterns that drive consumers' processing of advertising messages.
2. *Cultural matching effects:* Advertisements that match cultural value priorities or regulatory orientations are more persuasive.
3. *Situational effects of culture and frame switching:* Cultural influence is dynamic and context dependent.
4. *Cultural-identity driven consumption:* People consume products and brands to symbolize their cultural identities and fulfill salient cultural identity goals.
5. *Responses to culture mixing:* Exposure to culture-mixed products triggers a variety of cognitive, emotional, and evaluative responses. Culture mixing prompts perceptions that differences between cultures are greater than they would otherwise be.

Practical Implications for Organizations about Culture and Consumer Behavior

1. As marketing efforts become increasingly globalized, it is key for organizations to understand how the multiculturalism prompted by globalization impacts consumer behavior.
2. Adding themes that match the values of the culture makes ads more persuasive (e.g., ads with cues of power or status in the United States, and tradition and security in Japan and India).
3. Brands with values that are aligned with specific cultures (e.g., tradition in China) would benefit by imbuing ads with cultural cues (e.g., a Chinese dragon) to activate the brand-compatible cultural knowledge and make their ads more persuasive.
4. Corporations can build brands with cultural significance (i.e., iconic brands), which are instrumental in fulfilling consumers' cultural identity goals.

5. Culture-mixed products can elicit disgust, and they are often evaluated negatively (exclusionary responses). However, people can also respond favorably to culture-mixed products when they can integrate the contrastive cultural frames brought to mind (integrative responses).

References

Aaker, J. L., & Lee, A. Y. (2001). "I" seek pleasures and "we" avoid pains: The role of self-regulatory goals in information processing and persuasion. *Journal of Consumer Research, 28*(1), 33–49.

Alter, A. L., & Kwan, V. S. Y. (2009). Cultural sharing in a global village: Evidence for extracultural cognition in European Americans. *Journal of Personality and Social Psychology, 96*(4), 742–760. doi: 10.1037/a0014036

Amaral, N. B., & Torelli, C. J. (2018). Salient cultural identities and consumers' valuation of identity congruent brands: Consequences for building and leveraging brand equity. *Journal of Management and Training for Industries, 5*(3), 13–30. doi: 10.12792/JMTI.5.3.13

Arnould, E. J., & Thompson, C. J. (2005). Consumer culture theory (CCT): Twenty years of research. *Journal of Consumer Research, 31*(4), 868–882. doi: 10.1086/426626

Batra, R. (2019). Creating brand meaning: A review and research agenda. *Journal of Consumer Psychology, 29*(3), 535–546. doi: 10.1002/jcpy.1122

Belk, R. W., & Costa, J. A. (1998). The Mountain Man myth: A contemporary consuming fantasy. *Journal of Consumer Research, 25*(3), 218–240. doi: 10.1086/209536

Benet-Martínez, V., Leu, J., Lee, F., & Morris, M. W. (2002). Negotiating biculturalism: Cultural frame switching in biculturals with oppositional versus compatible cultural identities. *Journal of Cross-Cultural Psychology, 33*(5), 492–516.

Birman, D. (1994). Acculturation and human diversity in a multicultural society. In E. Trickett, R. J. Watts, & D. Birman (Eds.), *Human diversity: Perspectives on people in context* (pp. 261–284). San Francisco: Jossey-Bass.

Briley, D. A., & Aaker, J. L. (2006). When does culture matter? Effects of personal knowledge on the correction of culture-based judgments. *Journal of Marketing Research, 43*(3), 395–408.

Briley, D. A., Morris, M. W., & Simonson, I. (2000). Reasons as carriers of culture: Dynamic versus dispositional models of cultural influence on decision making. *Journal of Consumer Research, 27*(2), 157–178.

Chen, H., Bolton, L. E., Ng, S., Lee, D., & Wang, D. (2018). Culture, relationship norms, and dual entitlement. *Journal of Consumer Research, 45*(1), 1–20.

Chen, X., Leung, A. K.-Y., Yang, D. Y.-J., Chiu, C.-Y., Li, Z.-Q., & Cheng, S. Y.-Y. (2016). Cultural threats in culturally mixed encounters hamper creative performance for individuals with lower openness to experience. *Journal of Cross-Cultural Psychology, 47*(10), 1321–1334.

Cheon, B. K., Christopoulos, G. I., & Hong, Y.-Y. (2016). Disgust associated with culture mixing: Why and who? *Journal of Cross-Cultural Psychology, 47*(10), 1268–1285.

Chiao, J. Y., Hariri, A. R., Harada, T., Mano, Y., Sadato, N., Parrish, T. B., & Iidaka, T. (2010). Theory and methods in cultural neuroscience. *Social cognitive and affective neuroscience, 5*(2–3), 356–361.

Chiu, C.-Y., & Hong, Y.-Y. (2006). *Social psychology of culture*. New York: Psychology Press.

Chiu, C.-Y., Mallorie, L., Keh, H. T., & Law, W. (2009). Perceptions of culture in multicultural space: Joint presentation of images from two cultures increases in-group attribution of culture-typical characteristics. *Journal of Cross-Cultural Psychology, 40*(2), 282–300.

Claire, Q. (2013). Machine learning analysis of the cultural and cross-cultural aspects of beauty in music. Doctoral dissertation.

Cross, M. (2002). *A century of American icons*. Westport, CT: Greenwood Press.

De Keersmaecker, J., Van Assche, J., & Roets, A. (2016). Need for closure effects on affective and cognitive responses to culture fusion. *Journal of Cross-Cultural Psychology, 47*(10), 1294–1306.

Escalas, J. E., & Bettman, J. R. (2005). Self-construal, reference groups, and brand meaning. *Journal of Consumer Research, 32*(3), 378–389.

Farley, C. J. (2004). Elvis rocks. But he's not the first. *www.time.com,* Downloaded from http://www.time.com/time/arts/article/0,8599,661084,00.html on March 26, 2013.

Fiske, S. T. (1993). Controlling other people: The impact of power on stereotyping. *American Psychologist, 48*(6), 621–628.

Forbus, K. D. (2019). Creating AI systems that take culture into account. *The ethical machine*. Downloaded from https://ai.shorensteincenter.org/ideas/2019/1/14/creating-ai-systems-that-take-culture-into-account-aps9l.

Forehand, M. R., Deshpandé, R., & Reed, A. (2002). Identity salience and the influence of differential activation of the social self-schema on advertising response. *Journal of Applied Psychology, 87*(6), 1086–1099. doi: 10.1037/0021-9010.87.6.1086

Fournier, S., & Alvarez, C. (2019). How brands acquire cultural meaning. *Journal of Consumer Psychology, 29*(3), 519–534.

Gelfand, M. J., Raver, J. L., Nishii, L., Leslie, L. M., Lun, J., Lim, B. C., Duan, L., Almaliach, A., Ang, S., Arnadottir, J., Aycan, Z., Boehnke, K., Boski, P., Cabecinhas, R., Chan, D., Chhokar, J., D'Amato, A., Ferrer, M., Fischlmayr, I. C., . . . Yamaguchi, S. (2011). Differences between tight and loose cultures: A 33-nation study. *Science, 332*(6033), 1100–1104. doi: 10.1126/science.1197754

Guntuku, S. C., Li, M., Tay, L., & Ungar, L. H. (2019). Studying cultural differences in emoji usage across the east and the west. *Proceedings of the International AAAI Conference on Web and Social Media, 13*, 226–235.

Guralnick, P. (1994). *Last train to Memphis: The rise of Elvis Presley*. Boston: Little, Brown.

Han, D., Lalwani, A. K., & Duhachek, A. (2017). Power distance belief, power, and charitable giving. *Journal of Consumer Research, 44*(1), 182–195.

Han, S.-P., & Shavitt, S. (1994). Persuasion and culture: Advertising appeals in individualistic and collectivistic societies. *Journal of Experimental Social Psychology, 30*(4), 326–350.

Hao, J., Li, D., Peng, L., Peng, S., & Torelli, C. J. (2016). Advancing our understanding of culture mixing. *Journal of Cross-Cultural Psychology, 47*(10), 1257–1267.

Hofstede, G. H. (1980). *Culture's consequences: International differences in work-related values*. Newbury Park, CA: SAGE.

Hofstede, G. H. (2001). *Culture's consequences: Comparing values, behaviors, institutions and organizations across nations*. Thousand Oaks, CA: SAGE.

Holt, D. B. (2004). *How brands become icons: The principles of cultural branding*. Cambridge, MA: Harvard Business School Press.

Hong, Y.-Y., Ip, G., Chiu, C.-Y., Morris, M. W., & Menon, T. (2001). Cultural identity and dynamic construction of the self: collective duties and individual rights in Chinese and American cultures. *Social Cognition, 19*(3), 251–268.

Hong, Y.-Y., Morris, M. W., Chiu, C.-Y., & Benet-Martinez, V. (2000). Multicultural minds: A dynamic constructivist approach to culture and cognition. *American Psychologist, 55*(7), 709–720.

Jackson, J. C., van Egmond, M., Choi, V. K., Ember, C. R., Halberstadt, J., Balanovic, J., Basker, I. N., Boehnke, K., Buki, R., Fulop, M., Fulmer, A., Homan, A. C., Van Kleef, G. A., Kreemers, L., Schei, V., Szabo, E., Ward, C., & Gelfand, M. J. (2019). Ecological and cultural factors underlying the global distribution of prejudice. *PloS one, 14*(9), e0221953. doi: 10.1371/journal.pone.0221953

Jain, S. S., & Jain, S. P. (2018). Power distance belief and preference for transparency. *Journal of Business Research, 89*, 135–142.

Jonauskaite, D., Wicker, J., Mohr, C., Dael, N., Havelka, J., Papadatou-Pastou, M., Zhang, M., & Oberfeld, D. (2019). A machine learning approach to quantify the specificity of colour–emotion associations and their cultural differences. *Royal Society Open Science, 6*(9), 190741.

Kashima, Y. (2000). Maintaining cultural stereotypes in the serial reproduction of narratives. *Personality and Social Psychology Bulletin, 26*(5), 594–604.

Keh, H. T., Torelli, C. J., Chiu, C.-Y., & Hao, J. (2016). Integrative responses to culture mixing in brand name translations: The roles of product self-expressiveness and self-relevance of values among bicultural Chinese consumers. *Journal of Cross-Cultural Psychology, 47*(10), 1345–1360.

Kellner, D. (2013). The Elvis spectacle and the cultural industries. *Essays by Douglas Kellner, Graduate School of Education & Information Studies, UCLA, Downloaded from* http://pages.gseis.ucla.edu/faculty/kellner/2009_essays.html on March 26, 2013.

Kim, Y., & Zhang, Y. (2014). The impact of power-distance belief on consumers' preference for status brands. *Journal of Global Marketing, 27*(1), 13–29.

Kotler, P., & Keller, K. L. (2009). *A framework for marketing management* (4th ed.). Englewood Hills, NJ: Prentice-Hall.

Kroeber, A. L., & Kluckhohn, C. (1952). *Culture: A critical review of concepts and definitions.* Cambridge, MA: Harvard University Press.

Lalwani, A. K., & Forcum, L. (2016). Does a dollar get you a dollar's worth of merchandise? The impact of power distance belief on price-quality judgments. *Journal of Consumer Research, 43*(2), 317–333.

Lau-Gesk, L. G. (2003). Activating culture through persuasion appeals: An examination of the bicultural consumer. *Journal of Consumer Psychology, 13*(3), 301–315.

Li, R., Gordon, S., & Gelfand, M. J. (2017). Tightness–looseness: A new framework to understand consumer behavior. *Journal of Consumer Psychology, 27*(3), 377–391. doi: https://doi.org/10.1016/j.jcps.2017.04.001

Lin, L., Dahl, D. W., & Argo, J. J. (2017). Refining the tightness and looseness framework with a consumer lens. *Journal of Consumer Psychology, 27*(3), 392–397.

Liu, J., Ng, S., & Lim, E. (2015). *Moving up or down: power distance belief and the asymmetric effect of vertical brand extension.* Paper presented at the AP - Asia-Pacific Advances in Consumer Research, Duluth, MN.

MacInnis, D. J., Torelli, C. J., & Park, C. W. (2019). Creating cultural meaning in products and brands: A psychological perspective. *Journal of Consumer Psychology, 29*(3), 555–562.

McCracken, G. (1986). Culture and consumption: A theoretical account of the structure and movement of the cultural meaning of consumer goods. *Journal of Consumer Research, 13*(1), 71–84.

Meyers-Levy, J., & Tybout, A. M. (1989). Schema congruity as a basis for product evaluation. *Journal of Consumer Research, 16*(1), 39–54.

Mok, A., & Morris, M. W. (2013). Bicultural self-defense in consumer contexts: Self-protection motives are the basis for contrast versus assimilation to cultural cues. *Journal of Consumer Psychology, 23*(2), 175–188. doi: http://dx.doi.org/10.1016/j.jcps.2012.06.002

Monga, A. B., & John, D. R. (2007). Cultural differences in brand extension evaluation: The influence of analytic versus holistic thinking. *Journal of Consumer Research, 33*(4), 529–536.

Morris, M. W., Chiu, C.-Y., & Liu, Z. (2015). Polycultural psychology. *Annual Review of Psychology, 66*(1), 631–659. doi: 10.1146/annurev-psych-010814-015001

Nayyar, D. (2010). China, India, Brazil and South Africa in the world economy: Engines of growth. In A. U. Santos-Paulino & G. Wan (Eds.), *Southern engines of global growth* (pp. 9–27). New York: Oxford University Press.

Nisbett, R. E., Peng, K., Choi, I., & Norenzayan, A. (2001). Culture and systems of thought: Holistic versus analytic cognition. *Psychological Review, 108*(2), 291–310.

Overbeck, J. R., & Park, B. (2001). When power does not corrupt: Superior individuation processes among powerful perceivers. *Journal of Personality and Social Psychology, 81*(4), 549–565.

Oyserman, D. (2009). Identity-based motivation: Implications for action-readiness, procedural-readiness, and consumer behavior. *Journal of Consumer Psychology, 19*(3), 250–260.

Paharia, N., & Swaminathan, V. (2019). Who is wary of user design? The role of power-distance beliefs in preference for user-designed products. *Journal of Marketing, 83*(3), 91–107.

Pelto, P. J. (1968). The differences between "tight" and "loose" societies. *Trans-action, 5*(5), 37–40.

Reed, A., Forehand, M. R., Puntoni, S., & Warlop, L. (2012). Identity-based consumer behavior. *International Journal of Research in Marketing, 29*(4), 310–321. doi: 10.1016/j.ijresmar.2012.08.002

Shavitt, S., Lalwani, A. K., Zhang, J., & Torelli, C. J. (2006). The horizontal/vertical distinction in cross-cultural consumer research. *Journal of Consumer Psychology, 16*(4), 325–356.

Shavitt, S., Torelli, C. J., & Riemer, H. (2010). Horizontal and vertical individualism and collectivism: implications for understanding psychological processes. In M. J. Gelfand, C.-Y. Chiu, & Y.-y. Hong (Eds.), *Advances in culture and psychology* (Vol. 1, pp. 309–350). New York: Oxford University Press.

Shi, Y., Shi, J., Luo, Y. L., & Cai, H. (2016). Understanding exclusionary reactions toward a foreign culture: The influence of intrusive cultural mixing on implicit intergroup bias. *Journal of Cross-Cultural Psychology, 47*(10), 1335–1344.

Swaminathan, V., Page, K. L., & Gürhan-Canli, Z. (2007). "My" brand or "our" brand: The effects of brand relationship dimensions and self-construal on brand evaluations. *Journal of Consumer Research, 34*(2), 248–259.

Torelli, C. J. (2006). Individuality or conformity? the effect of independent and interdependent self-concepts on public judgments. *Journal of Consumer Psychology, 16*(3), 240–248.

Torelli, C. J. (2013). *Globalization, culture, and branding: How to leverage cultural equity for building iconic brands in the era of globalization.* London: Palgrave Macmillan.

Torelli, C. J., & Ahluwalia, R. (2012). Extending culturally symbolic brands: A blessing or a curse? *Journal of Consumer Research, 38*(5), 933–947.

Torelli, C. J., Ahluwalia, R., Cheng, S. Y.-y., Olson, N. J., & Stoner, J. L. (2017). Redefining home: How cultural distinctiveness affects the malleability of in-group boundaries and brand preferences. *Journal of Consumer Research, 44*(1), 44–61.

Torelli, C. J., & Cheng, S. Y.-y. (2011). Cultural meanings of brands and consumption: A window into the cultural psychology of globalization. *Social and Personality Psychology Compass, 5*, 251–262.

Torelli, C. J., Chiu, C.-Y., Tam, K.-p., Au, A. K. C., & Keh, H. T. (2011). Exclusionary reactions to foreign cultures: Effects of simultaneous exposure to cultures in globalized space. *Journal of Social Issues, 67*(4), 716–742.

Torelli, C. J., Keh, H. T., & Chiu, C.-Y. (2010). Cultural symbolism of brands. In B. Loken, R. Ahluwalia, & M. J. Houston (Eds.), *Brands and brand management: Contemporary research perspectives* (pp. 113–132). New York: Routledge.

Torelli, C. J., Oh, H., & Stoner, J. L. (2020). Cultural equity: Knowledge and outcomes aspects. *International Marketing Review, 38*(1), 99–123. doi: 10.1108/imr-12-2018-0366

Torelli, C. J., Ozsomer, A., Carvalho, S., Keh, H. T., & Maehle, N. (2012). Brand concepts as representations of human values: Do cultural congruity and compatibility between values matter? *Journal of Marketing, 76*(July), 92–108.

Torelli, C. J., & Rodas, M. A. (2017). Tightness–looseness: Implications for consumer and branding research. *Journal of Consumer Psychology, 27*(3), 398–404. doi: https://doi.org/10.1016/j.jcps.2017.04.003

Torelli, C. J., Rodas, M. A., & Stoner, J. L. (2017). The cultural meaning of brands. *Foundations and Trends® in Marketing, 10*(3), 153–214.

Torelli, C. J., & Shavitt, S. (2011). The impact of power on information processing depends on cultural orientation. *Journal of Experimental Social Psychology, 47*(5), 959–967. doi: 10.1016/j.jesp.2011.04.003

Triandis, H. C. (1995). *Individualism and collectivism*. Boulder, CO: Westview Press.

Triandis, H. C. (1996). The psychological measurement of cultural syndromes. *American Psychologist, 51*(4), 407–415.

Triandis, H. C., & Gelfand, M. J. (1998). Converging measurement of horizontal and vertical individualism and collectivism. *Journal of Personality and Social Psychology, 74*(1), 118–128.

Wan, C., Chiu, C.-Y., Tam, K.-P., Lee, S.-L., Lau, I. Y.-M., & Peng, S. (2007). Perceived cultural importance and actual self-importance of values in cultural identification. *Journal of Personality and Social Psychology, 92*, 337–354.

Wan, C., Torelli, C. J., & Chiu, C.-Y. (2010). Intersubjective consensus and the maintenance of normative shared reality. *Social Cognition, 28*(3), 422–446.

Wang, J. J., Torelli, C. J., & Lalwani, A. K. (2020). The interactive effect of power distance belief and consumers' status on preference for national (vs. private-label) brands. *Journal of Business Research, 107*, 1–12.

Winterich, K. P., Gangwar, M., & Grewal, R. (2018). When celebrities count: Power distance beliefs and celebrity endorsements. *Journal of Marketing, 82*(3), 70–86.

CHAPTER

23

Shifts in Research on Global Mobility

Mila B. Lazarova, B. Sebastian Reiche, *and* Callen C. Clegg

Abstract

This chapter provides a brief historical review and discusses seven major shifts that reflect contemporary expatriation research. The first shift concerns changing conceptualizations of the expatriation construct itself. Second, the portfolio of mobility options has been widening, with a matching shift in terminology from "managing expatriation" to "managing global mobility." Third, there is a notable shift from research that centers on expatriates themselves to research that accounts for other stakeholders, notably expatriate family members and members of the local community. Fourth, the definition of "expatriate success" has evolved to encompass a much more diverse set of variables going beyond traditional indicators, such as expatriate turnover. Fifth, what repatriation is and how repatriation is managed are also changing. The last two changes reflect shifts in, respectively, theory and methodological approaches, suggesting a widening pool of theoretical lenses and increasing methodological sophistication. Our chapter concludes with a discussion of key theoretical principles and practical implications derived from our review.

Key Words: expatriation, repatriation, global mobility, global work, international HRM, international staffing, international relocation

Introduction

Expatriation as a form of global mobility is one of the earliest themes of research on managing people on a global scale, and it has a history dating back decades. A Google Scholar search renders over tens of thousands of results pertaining to the word "expatriation," and an approximate third of these results have been published in the last decade alone. In this chapter, we discuss seven major shifts in contemporary expatriation research. First among these is broadening the notion of who is an *expatriate*. In contrast to the focus of "classic" studies on assigned corporate expatriates, recent research has adopted a broader view of expatriation that includes self-initiated expatriates (individuals who take up expatriation on their own accord rather than being sent abroad by their organization). Related to this shift is the second one, which concerns changes in reasons why organizations use expatriates and a related proliferation of *forms of global work*. Third, studies have shifted from primarily centering on expatriates to accounting for other important *stakeholders*, notably expatriate family members, local colleagues, the communities where expatriates work, and the wider organization.

Next, the definition of *expatriate success* has evolved. Previously captured through variables of interest to the organization (e.g., turnover), today's literature views success in terms of what is important to the individual (e.g., personal development, fulfillment of values). Fifth, what *repatriation* is and how repatriation is managed are also changing. Traditionally, repatriation was a well-demarcated stage signifying the completion of one's assignment, returning to headquarters, and resuming one's job responsibilities. However, today the end of one assignment may merely mark the beginning of another, with many careers increasingly characterized by an evolving sequence of international moves. The last two changes reflect shifts in, respectively, *theoretical and methodological approaches*. The shift in theories reflects a change in the lens through which expatriation and global mobility are being viewed and studied, and methodologically, we have seen a shift toward increased sophistication (e.g., multi-study, longitudinal, or mixed-methods designs).

We begin with the briefest of historical overviews of the field of expatriation, and then we describe each of these seven shifts. Given the scope of our chapter, we do not strive for comprehensiveness when describing emergent research themes, but rather we use select studies as illustrative examples of the respective shifts within the literature. We conclude with a discussion of key theoretical and practical implications and identify promising future research directions.

Brief Historical Overview

Global mobility, and more specifically expatriation, has been a major topic in management research for some time, and interest in the subject from sociological and historical perspectives can be found as early as the 1800s (Hay, 1814). Of course, the movement of people dates further back and is as old as humanity itself. It has been said that all of us can be linked back to one to two locations on the planet. During prehistoric times, human ancestors moved in order to look for greener pastures and survive ever-threatening weather conditions (Clark, 1992). Since then, the reasons why humans moved about the world have ranged from the pursuit of wealth (e.g., Egyptian merchants trading with distant ports in India during the earlier years of the first millennium; Andrade, 2017), proselytizing religions (Morris, 2018), crossing borders for political reasons (e.g., those in military service), or escaping catastrophic conditions (e.g., those seeking refuge following recent events in Syria). Because these individuals moved and lived outside of one's country of origin (i.e., in *ex-patria*), they were called *expatriates* (McNulty & Brewster, 2017). For many, a return home often involved lengthy perilous journeys back, and for some, it meant permanent settlement (Andrade, 2017). However, with the advance in technology and transportation in the post-World War II era, coupled with geopolitical changes, international movements became far more common (Baruch et al., 2016).

Concurrently, the globalization of business accelerated, with companies (mostly from Europe and North America) venturing beyond their neighboring countries. Once they did, they needed to dispatch employees to fulfill organizational tasks, leading to the birth of the modern-day "expatriate" (a term, which until recently, the business literature used as a shortcut for corporate expatriate). Organizations started to gain interest in a variety of different conditions under which said expatriates were most likely to attain success. Expatriation research got traction in the early 1950s and continued to gain steady ground in the following decades, viewing expatriation as a corporate-focused phenomenon and examining issues such as the use of expatriates (Edstrom & Galbraith, 1977; Harzing, 2001), expatriate selection (Caligiuri, 2000), adjustment (Black & Stephens, 1989), training (Mendenhall & Oddou, 1986), career development (Feldman & Thomas, 1992), and repatriation (Forster, 1994). Moving in lockstep with deepening globalization, economic integration, and technological innovation, since the turn of the twenty-first century, research has experienced even more rampant growth, with increased speed of publication and growing diversity of the issues studied (Brewster et al., 2014; McNulty & Selmer, 2017). It is this most recent research to which we turn next, deliberately focusing on work published over the course of the last decade.

Shift 1: Evolving Conceptualizations of the *Term Expatriate*

The early research focus on corporate expatriates reflected not only the sociopolitical and economic realities of the day but also a view of expatriation as occurring within an exclusive circle of predominantly male (Tharenou, 2010) technical experts and managerial employees. These employees were sent to foreign postings to advance company business, to transfer and develop knowledge and competencies, and to boost their careers (Baruch et al., 2016; Kraimer et al., 2016). Assignments were associated with a heightened status, and expatriation (typically of the assignee and his family) was supported by extensive relocation packages (Caligiuri & Bonache, 2016).

It was only in 1997 when Inkson et al. (1997) published a seminal paper on individuals undertaking 'overseas experiences' on their own, followed by Suutari and Brewster's (2000) paper on engineers "making their own way" that attention turned to those who are now commonly known as *self-initiated expatriates* (SIEs) (Doherty et al., 2013; Jokinen et al., 2008). Within a few years, articles on SIEs grew exponentially, rivaling, and by now likely outnumbering, all preceding research on corporate expatriation.

One of the first orders of business of this evolving subfield of research was defining what SIEs are and contrasting them with traditional, that is, corporate expatriates (and, on some occasions, with migrants). A host of primarily theoretical articles have rendered an array of different demarcation criteria (e.g., Andresen et al., 2014; McNulty & Brewster, 2017). Although driven by the call of conceptual clarity, each new article signals a fair dose of respectful collegial disagreement on the practicalities and accuracy of utilizing demarcation criteria suggested by its predecessors, ironically resulting in enhanced complexity rather than clarity. Scholars have also moved beyond merely distinguishing SIEs from corporate expatriates and have described specific SIEs, such as academic expatriates (Selmer et al., 2017), sports expatriates (Dolles & Egilsson, 2017), or "expat-preneurs" (Vance et al., 2016), among others.

Given this "definitionally dense" landscape, distinguishing between various forms of expatriation (and describing the diversity within each) is well beyond the scope of our chapter. While we do not want to oversimplify matters and encourage interested readers to explore the relevant literature, we use *corporate expatriates* (CEs, sometimes also referred to as classic, traditional, or assigned expatriates) to refer to those sent by, and with the support of, an organization to a country where the organization has a particular interest, for a predetermined amount of time, with the anticipation that they will be repatriated (i.e., will return) to their home country after assignment completion. In contrast, we refer to those who initiate and, for the most part, self-finance, relocating abroad to pursue personal development experiences on their own accord, often with no definite time frame in mind as *SIEs* (Shaffer et al., 2012, p. 1286).

Along the lines of searching for definitional clarity, researchers have also invested in numerous studies, which compare motivations to go abroad, adjustment levels, and respective antecedents of success between CEs and SIEs. For example, Alshahrani and Morley (2015) found that SIEs were more likely to have higher levels of previous nonwork mobility, international exposure at an early age, and more intercompany moves, and they were more likely to come from cultures with smaller differences to the host nation. In another example, looking at enrichment between work and private life, Ballesteros Leiva et al. (2018) suggest that CEs and SIEs show "distinct particularities"—for example, organizational support was positively related to CEs' work-to-personal-life enrichment, while SIEs' coworker support was negatively related to both work-to-personal-life and personal-life-to-work conflict.

Shift 2: Evolving Management of Global Mobility in Multinational Companies

The emerging interest in SIEs stems at least partly from changes in the broad economic, social, geopolitical, and technological landscape marked by events such as the fall of the Berlin Wall, the emergence of the European Union, the economic rise of the BRIC countries (Brazil, Russia, India, and China), market liberalization, the growth of multilateral institutions such as the World Trade Organization (WTO), the technological revolution, notably the advent of the internet and ways to connect to previously inaccessible parts of the world. While SIEs (under different names) have existed through the ages, becoming one became significantly easier over time, especially for those with transferable skills. As the number of globetrotting SIEs increased (or became more visible), so did scholarly attention directed at them.

But these same broad contextual changes also impacted how multinational companies (MNCs) conduct their business: access to foreign markets became easier, technological advances increased the speed of doing business, outsourcing and offshoring increased, supply chains diversified, and even small startup operations could build an international presence. Further, all organizations are pressured to decrease costs, especially in times of economic downturns. All these changes have had a profound impact on corporate expatriation. Importantly, while the need for globally mobile personnel has not decreased, the way mobility is managed is changing (Salt & Wood, 2012), with fewer expatriates stationed in far-flung locations for long periods of time and the emergence of more flexible approaches to global work. On the one end of the spectrum are international transfers, whereby employees are permanently transferred to another country rather than expatriated for a specified term. Next are various "flexpatriation" arrangements, domestically based jobs that also require employees to travel to and work in alternating locations on a regular basis (i.e., frequent travelers, commuters, and short-term assignments). Finally, there are employees referred to as global domestics—those whose jobs have international responsibilities that are fulfilled primarily though virtual and electronic communication and involve little, if any, physical mobility (e.g., work in global virtual teams; Mayerhofer et al., 2004; Shaffer et al., 2012).

Research on new types of "global assignees" has begun, but the majority of work to date remains descriptive, focusing mostly on identifying challenges and opportunities associated with each type of work. Such work arrangements have been shown to pose considerable pressures, including intense pace of work, reporting to more than one supervisor, difficulties adjusting given the limited amount of time spent in respective locations, as well as stress related to frequent travel and associated health concerns (Suutari et al., 2013). The unpredictability of work schedules and limited ability to exercise control over them have also been mentioned, as has the limited support they receive from the organization (Baker & Ciuk, 2015).

The reasons why MNCs send workers abroad have also shifted. Traditionally, expatriates were sent for control and coordination, filling positions that cannot be filled by locals, and management development (Edstrom & Galbraith, 1977; Harzing, 2001). While all three motives are still relevant, assignees are now also increasingly seen as critical for transferring knowledge across MNC locations (Chang et al., 2012). Defined broadly, knowledge transfer concerns the process through which an individual or a collective is affected by the experience of another. Specifically, it involves acquiring knowledge (especially tacit knowledge) in one situation and applying it to another. Expatriation is increasingly viewed from a knowledge transfer perspective as it is the movement of people across organizational units that provides an important channel for sharing and adapting complex knowledge across different contexts (Argote & Ingram, 2000). Changes in expatriation described in the preceding paragraphs notwithstanding, global assignees are no longer simply sent for operational reasons, but they can act as agents for knowledge management and organizational learning, as they can gather, generate, transfer, and integrate knowledge across MNC units. Interest in knowledge transfer, at both the individual and organizational level, has increased, and so has the recognition that expatriates can make significant contributions to knowledge transfer (Burmeister et al., 2018; Duvivier et al., 2019).

The global "war for talent" implicates another key shift in the way globally mobile individuals are being managed. Fueled by the previously identified heightened globalization and technological advancements, organizations worldwide are competing to attract employees from the same talent pools (Baruch et al., 2016). They are investing in global talent management (GTM), that is, assessing how to make the best use of their talent on a global scale and changing the ways in which they approach attracting, developing, and retaining employees to leverage their respective talent pools for organizational benefit (Collings et al., 2019). In this vein, the importance of treating international assignments as a developmental opportunity has been highlighted and so has the full integration of global mobility into the GTM cycle of the MNC (Caligiuri & Bonache, 2016). Related to this development has been a surge in research documenting the developmental role of international experiences (Dragoni et al., 2014). The literature has also emphasized that in order to secure return on investment, organizations must acknowledge the importance of retaining those who engage in global mobility to avoid the loss of knowledge and expertise gained during international experiences (McNulty & De Cieri, 2016).

Shift 3: Emerging Stakeholder Perspective

It has long been recognized that there are others besides expatriates themselves that have an impact on the expatriate experience. Early research discussed the importance of expatriate families reasoning that unhappy family members may become a source of stress for the expatriate, which may increase the likelihood of assignment failure (Bormann, 1968). More recently, research has drawn attention to the role of expatriate colleagues, and specifically, host country nationals (HCNs) with whom expatriates interact and work (Toh & DeNisi, 2005). Successful expatriate–HCN interactions can be an important source of social support and mentorship. HCNs can help enhance expatriates' cultural awareness; they can act as cultural interpreters and ease expatriates' culture shock; they can be a sounding board regarding important expatriate decisions relevant to the subsidiary; they can help expatriates break communication barriers with local constituents and connect expatriates to key local networks; they can be a rich source of information for both things trivial (e.g., best food market in town) and significant (e.g., how to prepare for a meeting with a local governmental official); if HCNs and expatriates develop personal relationships off the job, HCNs can help expatriates escape the "expatriate bubble" and can engage them in local activities (e.g., attending a sports game to support the local team; van Bakel et al., 2016). Thus, HCNs and their interactions with expatriates can contribute to expatriate adjustment and performance (Kang & Shen, 2018; Maertz et al., 2016), but they can also benefit organizations as they can facilitate the exchange of resources and tacit knowledge (van Bakel, 2019).

Although such interactions are dynamic and reciprocal, the literature to date has been mostly one-sided, focusing on how other actors affect the expatriate but only rarely considering how the expatriate affects them. In a seminal paper, Takeuchi (2010) drew attention to this shortcoming and called for moving away from "expatriate-centric" to multiple stakeholder models in adjustment research. His stance is consistent with earlier observations from research on HCNs, which suggested that the literature was showing a stark collective neglect of the HNCs' interests (Vance & Ring, 1994), a sentiment that is still being echoed today (van Bakel, 2019).

Our review suggests that although still largely expatriate-centric, over the last decade, research has indeed broadened its focus. Family members are studied most frequently, with spouses' experiences being examined as key variables of interest rather than merely as antecedent to expatriate adjustment/performance. For example, research has highlighted how spouses feel about international moves (Cho et al., 2013), the specific challenges they face during expatriation (e.g., marital stress, alcoholism; Cole & Nesbeth, 2014), the impact of disrupted spouse employment on spouse adjustment (Cole, 2011), the experiences of spouses who do not become expatriates but stay behind to take care of the family (Mutter & Thorn, 2019), and how spouses reconstruct their identity (McNulty, 2012).

Recent research has also examined the experiences of expatriates' children. De Sivatte and colleagues (2019), for example, found that children adapt well, being mostly interested in fitting in with other children, and that making friends is key to their adjustment. The authors highlight the role of children's social skills, academic self-efficacy, the level of the school in the host country, and the family support they receive as important for adjustment. Theoretical research has further suggested that the family unit be examined as a whole and that outcomes such as family satisfaction or well-being be studied (Takeuchi, 2010).

The literature has also made great strides toward describing the complexity of HCNs' experiences, recognizing that working with expatriates (who often understand little of the local context, especially early in their assignments) can be a burden for HCNs. For example, in a recent study, Fee (2020) discusses previously hidden costs associated with HCNs' work with expatriates, including a range of extra-role demands and more complex, as well as stressful, interpersonal interactions, which may lead to HCN withdrawal.

Recent research has suggested that HCNs differentiate themselves from expatriates (Belhoste & Monin, 2013), that their attitudes toward expatriates are not necessarily positive (e.g., Arman & Aycan, 2013), and that support is not automatically extended to expatriates (e.g., Peltokorpi, 2020). Further, research has also examined HCNs' perceived compensation disparity (e.g., Leung et al., 2014; Toh & DeNisi, 2005), issues pertaining to social categorization and identity (e.g., Varma et al., 2011), as well as interpersonal affect (Varma et al., 2009). Job attitudes of HCNs such as feelings of relative deprivation

(Toh & DeNisi, 2003), job satisfaction, organizational commitment (Hon & Lu, 2010), satisfaction with compensation, and turnover intentions (Chen et al., 2002) have also been studied. Conceptual papers have provided further ideas for future research on HCNs such as antecedents and consequences of HCNs' negative stereotyping of expatriates (Bonache et al., 2016), antecedents to HCN learning (Brewster et al., 2014), or the potential career implications for HCNs that are being mentored by an expatriate (van Bakel, 2019).

To a much lesser extent, research has also considered the subsidiary and/or the wider MNC as a stakeholder. In this vein, Plourde et al. (2014) showed that expatriates could help their host subsidiary capture the attention of the MNC headquarters. In another study, Chang et al. (2012) provided evidence that expatriate knowledge transfer competencies led to increased knowledge received by the subsidiary, which in turn was related to enhanced subsidiary performance. A body of literature has also developed around the idea of capturing return on investment of international assignments (McNulty & De Cieri, 2011) as an important way to assess their impact on organizations.

Finally, some scholars have suggested that the literature must take an even more macro perspective and view nation-states as stakeholders in global mobility, for example, by examining the impact of mobility on national competitiveness through considering how mobility contributes to brain gain (whereby some nations gain human capital through inbound migration), brain drain (whereby nations lose human capital through outbound migration), or brain circulation (reverse migration whereby individuals with—often enhanced—human capital move back to their country of origin, or more generally move between home, host and another country for work-related purposes; Baruch et al., 2016; Saxenian, 2005; Tung, 2016). However, to date, macro-level outcomes of global mobility remain primarily within the domain of economists and migration scholars rather than expatriation researchers.

Shift 4: Evolving Definitions of Success

Early expatriation research was typically conducted at the individual level but assessed "success" with variables of primary interest to the organization, notably turnover (intentions), with a clear theme of equating failure with premature turnover (i.e., an early return from a posting). Research also considered expatriate attitudes such as organizational commitment, satisfaction, and performance (Baruch et al., 2016). Adjustment, though not of direct interest to organizations, was studied most widely, based on the reasoning that it is the central antecedent of performance and job attitudes (Firth et al., 2014). Adjustment is most frequently conceptualized as a degree of comfort with (or the absence of stress related to) being an expatriate, with the majority of researchers drawing on work by Black and colleagues (Black et al., 1991; Black & Gregersen, 1991a, 1991b; Black & Stephens, 1989), who proposed three adjustment facets: adjustment (1) to work, (2) to interaction with HCNs, and (3) to the general cultural environment. Black et al.'s work is generally consistent with research on cross-cultural adaptation (e.g., Ward & Chang, 1997; Ward &

Kennedy, 1999) that speaks of psychological (i.e., psychological and emotional well-being and satisfaction) and sociocultural adjustment (reflecting a behavioral component, the ability to "fit in," acquire culturally appropriate skills, and negotiate interactive aspects of the host culture). Although Black et al.'s conceptualization and the related measurement have been critiqued and other conceptualizations and measurement approaches have been advanced (Haslberger et al., 2013; Lazarova et al., 2010; Shaffer et al., 2016), they still loom large. Research has explored various individual (e.g., self-efficacy), job (e.g., job discretion), organizational (e.g., logistical support), nonwork (e.g., spouse adjustment), and broader contextual factors (e.g., culture novelty) as antecedents of adjustment (Bhaskar-Shrinivas et al., 2005).

Of particular interest to readers of this volume, the literature has looked at the impact of being posted to a culturally different setting. Research has shown that cultural distance may stimulate creativity and innovation (e.g., Leung et al., 2008) but may also trigger stress, withdrawal cognitions, and reduced performance (Bhaskar-Shrinivas et al., 2005) and may weaken the relationship between cross-cultural motivation and adjustment (Chen et al., 2010). Research on the impact of cultural distance on adjustment remains inconclusive (Hemmasi & Downes, 2013). Some studies suggest that it may be just as difficult to adjust to culturally similar as to dissimilar countries (Furusawa & Brewster, 2016; Selmer & Lauring, 2009), and other studies show that some differences, even large ones, may be perceived positively by expatriates (Hippler et al., 2014). Research has also shown that the direction of transfer matters, with one study reporting that German expatriates in the United States were better adjusted than American expatriates in Germany (Selmer et al., 2007). More recently, scholars have examined the role of tightness (strong and rigidly imposed norms) of the host and home country cultures for adaptation and suggested that those living in a looser host culture and those originating from a tight home culture reported higher adaptation. Further, the negative impact on culture tightness of adjustment was buffered for sojourners who had higher agreeableness and honesty–humility (Geeraert et al., 2019).

Over the most recent decade, interest in these "traditional" success variables has remained strong. There has been new work on adjustment (Firth et al., 2014), adaptation (Geeraert et al., 2019), satisfaction (Froese & Peltokorpi, 2013), effectiveness (Chen et al., 2010) and retention (Ren et al., 2015), with some scholars noting that assessing whether an expatriate is effective requires examining multiple success indicators (Chen et al., 2010). Meanwhile, more recent research has taken a broader perspective, examining ever-expanding myriad outcomes, with a marked shift to variables reflecting individual (rather than organizational) success.

Assignments are now frequently viewed from a career lens. Studies have examined variables such as career advancement (Reiche et al., 2011), employability (Andresen, 2021), and the development of career capital/competencies (Dickmann et al., 2018). Assignments have been viewed as enriching experiences that help individuals acquire career capital and are thus associated with enhanced *subjective* or intrinsic career success (Dickmann et al., 2018; Suutari et al., 2018). Assessing *objective* or extrinsic career success (e.g., salary increased, promotions) outcomes has been trickier. Many corporate assignees experience career frustrations immediately upon repatriation (e.g., Kraimer et al., 2009), and studies have reported slower career progress of those who have undertaken global mobility (Hamori & Koyuncu, 2011). However, more recent research also highlights positive objective career outcomes (Breitenmoser et al., 2018; Conyon et al., 2018). Collectively, such research suggests that there are both career benefits and career downsides of global experiences (Mäkelä et al., 2016) and that mobility may have short-term career costs, with a career "payoff" occurring after a time lag (Biemann & Braakmann, 2013).

In addition to career outcomes, there has also been an increased interest in *work–life balance and well-being*. Studies have examined issues such as the reciprocal relationships among work–family conflict, emotional exhaustion, and psychological health complaints (Jensen & Knudsen, 2017), and work–life boundary pressures experienced by expatriates (Bader et al., 2018). Although present in research on traditional expatriates (Mäkelä et al., 2011), work–life balance tends to be examined more frequently in the case of flexpatriates and international business travelers, whose personal lives are more likely to get disrupted by the demands of shorter-term global mobility. Thus, research has suggested that compared to their domestic counterparts, international business travelers experience high work–family conflict (Jensen, 2014). The positive well-being consequences of mobility have also been identified, with Demel and Mayrhofer (2010) observing that while many flexpatriates reported limitations to private life, strain, and fatigue, they also spoke of fun and enjoyment. Some scholars explicitly adopt "positive work–family interface" frameworks (e.g., Lazarova et al., 2010), and suggest that the field will benefit from the study of expatriate thriving (Ren et al., 2015).

Global mobility has also been examined as a setting of identity transformation. Assignments can lead to profound changes in individuals and may affect how they view themselves and others, including their organization (Scurry et al., 2013; Shaffer et al., 2012). While expatriates strive to maintain some identification with their home culture, they must also undergo some revision of their identities as they attend to the distinct values, attitudes, and norms they experience (Maertz et al., 2016), if they are to be able to function effectively in and adjust to the host context. The literature has generally distinguished between four orientations toward such identity change (Berry, 1980, 1997): integration (identifying with both home and host cultures), assimilation (identifying with host but not home culture), separation (identifying with home but not host culture), and marginalization (identifying with neither home nor host culture).

Expatriates also need to make sense of the meaning and personal significance of differences and unexpected similarities encountered abroad concerning their own identities (e.g., Berger & Calabrese, 1975; Molinsky, 2013). This may involve the need to reduce the cognitive dissonance arising from exposure to foreign values, attitudes and norms that are inconsistent with their own. In this regard, research has pointed to different methods expatriates use to deal with such dissonance, including changing their own values, attitudes, and norms to fit the host context and conscious affirmation of positive aspects of the context that may overcome the dissonance or rejection of the host culture completely (Maertz et al., 2009). Other work has examined the specific type of identities expatriates develop or the predictors of expatriates' orientations toward identity transformation. For example, Adams and van der Vijver (2015) discussed whether expatriates develop a cosmopolitan perspective (developed after many cultural experiences) or a pragmatic perspective (maintaining one's identity and making only superficial adjustments in a new context). The role of one's social networks as they change during the period of expatriation on cultural identity transformation has also been explored, with different orientations toward identity transformation having a different impact on adjustment (Mao & Shen, 2015). Finally, research has pointed to the role of global identity—that is, the sense of belongingness to an overarching global community (Erez & Gati, 2004)—as a superordinate identity that may buffer the different orientations toward identity transformation (Harush et al., 2016; Lee et al., 2018).

The shift to broader understanding of success is likely due to the evolving understanding of careers (from hierarchical to boundaryless), changes in the labor market (e.g., rising employment insecurity), and the rise of alternative forms of mobility (as detailed previously). Gains in career capital, employability, and agency in managing one's career are desired currencies in most labor markets. Whereas the *raisons d'être* of corporate expatriation are control, coordination, transfer of skills/technology and management development, self-initiated expatriation is a way to improve one's own career prospects or lifestyle, or to follow one's passion. With the increase of SIEs, interest has shifted from commitment and retention to well-being, personal fulfillment, and identity transformation. Given that "traditional" expatriation involves long-term relocation, adjustment was a natural focus of research. In contrast, short-term mobility involves project work, family separation, increased stress levels due to tight travel schedules, jetlag, and working across locations—conditions where work–life balance becomes paramount.

Shift 5: Evolving Understanding of Repatriation

A fifth shift concerns repatriation. Traditionally, repatriation has been a well-demarcated final assignment stage: the completion of an international posting and return to one's home unit to resume "domestic" job responsibilities, with repatriation success captured by postassignment retention, repatriate satisfaction, and repatriation adjustment and performance (Kraimer et al., 2016). However, recent research has recognized that rather than an assignment endpoint and a return to "normality," repatriation often requires coping with substantive change in individuals themselves, their specific roles, and the broader organizational, nonwork and societal context (Akkan et al., 2020; Baruch et al., 2016). For example, in line with the earlier mentioned identity-related changes individuals experience as a result of expatriation, repatriates who develop an international employee identity while abroad experience identity strain when they perceive that their organization does not provide them with appreciable benefits relative to their colleagues who did not complete an international assignment, which can drive turnover (Kraimer et al., 2012).

Importantly, completing one assignment may often indicate the beginning of another international work arrangement, whether it crosses physical or psychological boundaries. This leads researchers to speak of "sequences of global work experiences" (McKouen et al., 2020; Shaffer et al., 2012). In this vein, research has examined individuals' motivations to take on another assignment upon return. Ho et al. (2015), for instance, found that repatriation dissatisfaction with career and life in their home country, the experience of reverse culture shock, and the expected career, family and quality-of-life outcomes from re-expatriation all explained returnees' intentions to self-initiate new expatriation. Cappellen and Janssens (2010) have also shown that individuals develop and enact their own career strategies, outside of their organization's career scripts, to secure global work experience.

Moving beyond single international postings to consider sequences of global work experiences has further led scholars to integrate global mobility with global careers research. Global careers can be viewed as a series of work arrangements that include some global work experiences (McKouen et al., 2020). Existing evidence that multiple assignments may in fact be detrimental for career advancement to senior executive positions (Hamori & Koyuncu, 2011), however, seems to suggest that multiple global work experiences by themselves do not necessarily make a global career more effective. Instead, the specific timing, duration, and transition between experiences are important, for both the individual and the organization. We also know that various individual-level factors such as international career orientation (Mäkelä et al., 2015) and having a proactive personality (Leiba-O'Sullivan, 2002) may influence whether employees aspire to global carers, and how they cope with the challenges inherent in global careers.

Finally, the very nature of the repatriation concept is challenged by new forms of global work. For some workers, such as global virtual team members or global domestics, repatriation is not a relevant consideration, while for others, such as international business travelers or short-term assignees, the return is a qualitatively different experience compared to that of long-term expatriates (see, e.g., Demel & Mayrhofer, 2010). Repatriation can also elicit new career activities, including entrepreneurial ventures. For example, Lin et al. (2016) found a positive association between returnees' acquisition of advanced knowledge from their host countries and their subsequent decisions to become entrepreneurs. This positive relationship was stronger when returnees perceived supportive policies for returnee entrepreneurship in the home country but weaker when returnees perceived difficulties in readjusting to the local norms and culture in their home countries. Conceptualizing the return as a trigger of other work experiences thus promises to integrate the global mobility literature into wider career research (Baruch et al., 2016).

Shift 6: Changing Theoretical Frameworks

Past reviews lamented that the global mobility field has remained theoretically underdeveloped (e.g., Thomas, 1998). While such concerns are still relevant to repatriation research (Akkan et al., 2020), much has changed in the wider domain of global mobility. As a result, many diverse theories have been deployed (Baruch et al., 2016, identified close to 30 different theoretical approaches) to the point that we may now be facing growing theoretical fragmentation.

Early research primarily adopted theories on stress (Black et al., 1991), psychological contract (Guzzo et al., 1994), perceived organizational support (Kraimer et al., 2001), or unmet expectations (Caligiuri et al., 2001), reflecting a focus on the perceived organizational experience of global mobility. By contrast, more recent studies have drawn on theoretical lenses as varied as boundaryless career theory (Lazarova & Cerdin, 2007), identity theory (Kraimer et al., 2012), social resources theory (Reiche, 2012), trait activation theory (Chen et al., 2010), embeddedness theory (Reiche et al., 2011), role theory (Shaffer et al., 2016), job demands and resources theory (Ren et al., 2013), and human capital theory (Ramaswami et al., 2016), among others. As a result, we now have a more detailed understanding of global mobility at the interface of the focal individuals, their intrapersonal experiences, relationships with key stakeholders, as well as the resulting individual and organizational outcomes.

The increase and shifting focus in theoretical bases underpinning mobility research has prompted the need for theoretical integration (e.g., Maertz et al., 2016). Research has started to test the boundary conditions of particular theoretical mechanisms by drawing on complementary or alternative theoretical lenses. For example, in his study examining the predictors of knowledge benefits upon repatriation, Reiche (2012) integrated social resources theory and social exchange theory arguments to explain repatriates' ability and motivation to access and transfer host unit knowledge, pointing to alternative mechanisms through which these knowledge benefits occur. Another means to achieve theoretical integration is to develop competing predictions based on different theoretical arguments. Georgakakis et al. (2016), for instance, integrated competing arguments from human capital and social network theories to investigate the U-shaped relationship between international experience and speed of career advancement.

Finally, research on global work is turning to process theories (Molinsky, 2013; Reiche et al., 2019). Scholars have pointed to the different phases of the assignment cycle (Bonache et al., 2001), and empirical research has examined processes integral to the experience of global mobility (Baruch et al., 2016), including acculturation and adjustment (Firth et al., 2014; Mendenhall & Oddou, 1985) and coping with stress (Westman & Etzion, 2002). However, it is surprising that process theories have not featured more prominently in the literature, given that global mobility is at its heart a temporal phenomenon. This shortcoming can be partly explained by the heightened methodological requirements, as discussed in the next section.

Recent examples of studies adopting a process perspective include Maertz and colleagues (2016), who integrate adjustment-related constructs into an episodic framework of outgroup interaction processing in order to conceptualize adjustment as a change process and theorize how adjustment processes unfold. Further, Duvivier et al. (2019) examine the combination and sequencing of different types of international assignments over time to meet the specific knowledge transfer needs in headquarters–subsidiary dyads. A process perspective would also allow scholars to examine how different global experiences evolve over time, for example, as a function of how the individual assignee adjusts to, is embedded in, or performs in the host context. Doing so may also help refine our understanding of the optimal time frames of different forms of global mobility.

Shift 7: Increasing Methodological Sophistication

A final shift concerns the research designs and empirical toolkits that contemporary expatriate scholars have adopted. Expatriate data have always been challenging to obtain, which may be one reason why about half of the empirical studies do not explicitly report their response rates (Tharenou, 2015). Further, given problems of survey fatigue generally, data access is becoming increasingly difficult. At the same time, we have witnessed a greater sophistication in the design and analytical approaches. Early expatriation research primarily conducted small, exploratory qualitative studies or cross-sectional field surveys with archival data or single informants. This approach limited the conclusions that can be drawn from the findings (Baruch et al., 2016). In addition, scholars have often mixed and jointly analyzed different types of international assignees in their samples (Tharenou, 2015). This may cancel out meaningful differences in findings across assignee types (e.g., Shaffer et al., 2016) and may have led to overly general models that cannot account for the particularities of specific samples.

Recent empirical studies have adopted a variety of approaches to address these limitations. First, not only do these studies provide more details about their samples, but scholars have also sought to overcome single-source bias by drawing on multiple data sources. For example, analyzing how expatriate competencies and subsidiary absorptive capacity influence the knowledge transfer process in MNCs, Chang et al. (2012) combined the use of archival data, surveys of expatriates, and surveys of local HR and line managers. Similarly, Dragoni and colleagues (2014) complemented self-report data with data by trained raters from assessment center activities to study under which conditions leaders' global work experiences relate to competency in strategic thinking. To the extent that data sources stem from different levels of analyses, researchers need to adopt multilevel approaches to data analysis, as in Chen et al.'s paper (2010) showing that expatriates' work adjustment mediates the positive relationship between cross-cultural motivation and job performance when expatriates are assigned to foreign subsidiaries with lower levels of subsidiary support and cultural distance.

More scholars have also adopted multiple study designs, which are a hallmark of psychology research more broadly. For example, Leonardelli and Toh (2011) draw on social categorization, social identity, and justice theories to demonstrate that local employees were more likely to provide knowledge to assist expatriate coworkers' adjustment when local-expatriate categorization and procedural justice from organizational authorities were high than when these variables were low. To do so, they conducted two separate studies, using alternative measures of procedural justice. They focused on procedural justice perceptions regarding specific organizational practices (Study 1) and more general perceptions of fair treatment in the organization (Study 2). Multiple study designs have also been used to develop new measurement scales and show evidence of their convergent, discriminant, nomological, and predictive validity (Shaffer et al., 2016).

As briefly illustrated in the previous section, an increasing number of studies have used time-lagged and longitudinal research designs to help support theoretical arguments about causality and change. Reiche (2012) collected data from inpatriates, defined as foreign subsidiary staff who are temporarily relocated to a multinational's headquarters, at two time points, 2 years apart, to examine the relationship between inpatriates' social capital at headquarters and knowledge benefits upon repatriation. Similarly, Ramaswami and colleagues (2016) used data obtained in two time points to show that repatriates only obtained positive compensation returns when they experienced more than one assignment; perceived acquired knowledge and skills to be utilized during post-repatriation periods; and were working at higher organizational levels.

Other scholars have adopted yet more intensive longitudinal designs that allow the study of changes over time. For example, data from 70 newly transferred expatriates across four separate time points showed that expatriates' motivational states and stress cognitions influenced their work adjustment patterns over time, in turn driving relevant assignment attitudes (Firth et al., 2014). These analyses continue to focus on variable-centered approaches to data analysis, which consider relationships among variables. Recent efforts, however, have also used intensive longitudinal designs, with the aim of identifying subgroups of assignees based on similarities on a specific variable and tracing the subgroups' evolution over time. Such a person-centered approach not only requires a more sophisticated research design in terms of multiple measurement occasions, but also calls for other data analytical approaches. For example, Takeuchi et al. (2019) draw on a four-wave, archival dataset of expatriates in China and latent class growth analysis techniques to identify four distinct change patterns of job performance, which could be attributed to three types of prior work experience (international, job, organizational): (1) U-curve, (2) learning-curve, (3) stable high-performing pattern, and (4) stable low- performing pattern.

Finally, the use of more sophisticated qualitative or mixed-method approaches is also on the rise. For example, although not strictly an expatriate sample, Molinsky (2013) adopted a grounded theory approach and a longitudinal sample of 50 foreign students over an 8-week period to study the psychological dynamics of how individuals expand their cultural repertoire during cultural adaptation. His study showed that integrative techniques to address the internal conflict experienced during adaptation, including self-licensing (i.e., adopting and embracing new cultural perspectives to interpret foreign behavior) and personalizing (i.e., slight behavioral adjustments to make new behaviors more familiar and comfortable to execute) were superior to instrumental techniques such as emphasizing the necessity of a behavior to fight through internal stress or attempts to ignore and suppress stress. Another example is Cole's (2011) mixed-method study of career-related predictors of spousal adjustment and the role of organizational assistance programs, where a field study first examined relevant predictors of spouse adjustment, and additional interviews unearthed spouses' specific needs of assistance programs. Taken together, the increased methodological sophistication has enabled scholars not only to study global mobility with greater granularity, but also to ask novel and different research questions.

Implications and Conclusion

The developments we have described in this chapter have contributed to the maturity and quality of the research domain. We conclude by specifying five key principles of theoretical guidance (see Table 23.1) and five areas of practical application (see Table 23.2) based on the shifts we identify.

Table 23.1 Theoretical implications summary

Implication
1. *Do not aim for new theory above all else*
2. *Consider theories that examine expatriation holistically*
3. *Account for multiple stakeholders*
4. *Acknowledge that there are many sides to success*
5. *Leverage novel methodological approaches*
Description
1. Refrain from introducing new theories for "theory's sake." Instead, aim for *sound* theory. Begin by seeking theoretical clarity through examining, applying, and extending available theories, including relevant theoretical work outside expatriation research.
2. Seek to apply or construct more complex theories, which reflect the holistic nature of expatriation and global mobility.
3. Consider the interests of a variety of diverse stakeholders involved in global mobility.
4. Consider the multifaceted nature of success by including various measures of success, acknowledging that the interests of all stakeholders may not always align; think of what may be considered success in the long run.
5. Consider utilizing a range of novel methodological approaches in order to enhance and extend the quality of global mobility research.

Table 23.2 Practical applications summary

Implication	Description
Strategic realignment and development of new competencies	MNCs must reevaluate and strategically realign vis-à-vis the necessary composition and function of globally mobile employees, which may require the development of analytical capabilities in order to leverage various metrics to aid strategic decision making.
Global mobility as means of developing talent	The developmental potential of the various forms of global mobility should be considered, combined and strategically exercised in order to develop talent within the organization, rather than viewing global mobility simply as a tool for executing projects.
Integration of global mobility and global talent management	Different forms of global mobility must be fully integrated with GTM and respective organizational processes and practices to leverage all potential benefits of having a globally mobile workforce.
Consideration of employee health and well-being	Organizations should be understanding and observant with regard to the potential strain that working internationally has on employees' health and well-being.
Adaptability in the face of uncertainty	Organizations must be ready to adapt their use of various forms of global mobility in the face of uncertainty and external shocks, and balance these against a steep rise in technological investments that may render certain forms of global mobility unnecessary in the future.

Theoretical Principles

A first principle that emerges from our review concerns the need to integrate rather than multiply the use of theoretical frameworks. Past literature called for higher theoretical sophistication, exploding into a storm of new theories, thereby swinging the pendulum to the other extreme: high—and perhaps too high—proliferation of novel theoretical frameworks. This is not a trivial matter, given that the overcomplication of theory constrains the ability to test the veracity of a theoretical model empirically, as well as to apply it in practice. While a sound theoretical basis and theoretical development are desired features of any paper, introducing a new theory for the sake of introducing a new theory, especially when examining a phenomenon or relationship that has been studied previously, is not optimal. We would argue that instead of increasing theoretical proliferation, we should first seek theoretical clarity. Good initial steps are thoughtfully applying, extending (or disproving) established theories (including relevant theories in related fields), and testing boundary conditions to enhance nuance and richness. Our first plea is therefore not to stop using sound theoretical fundaments, but rather to avoid increased complexity for complexity's sake. If, having engaged in these steps, we still find ourselves in a theoretical vacuum, then the doors to thoughtful theory building can open.

Second, while streamlining in order to rein in theoretical fragmentation and complexity is a good starting point, the shift away from the organizational benefit perspective of expatriates to a more inclusive body of literature also calls for the application of broader, more malleable theoretical frameworks. Global mobility does not occur in a vacuum and impacts many stakeholders. Baruch et al. (2016) recently applied ecosystem theory to guide research on globally mobile careers in a more holistic manner, within which they highlighted the interconnectedness and interdependency at multiple levels (i.e., micro, meso, and macro levels), while also emphasizing the fragmented nature of previously applied theories. Other researchers have used equally broad overarching theoretical frameworks such as the job demands–resources model or conservation of resources theory (e.g., Lazarova et al., 2010) to examine how a range of resources and demands that have been discussed in previous research influence expatriates' experiences. Such examples illustrate the importance of engaging in due diligence when selecting *sound* theory, rather than simply piling up many theories.

Third, it is important for scholars to continue to consider the interest of a variety of stakeholders involved in global mobility. As suggested by ecosystem theory, for example, we are all part of an overriding, interconnected system. This interconnectedness has a reciprocal effect on various actors, neither of whom can be looked at in isolation. While scholars are now examining a greater variety of stakeholders at the individual level (e.g., HCNs, family members), and are paying attention to the MNC as a relevant actor, we know little about how stakeholders at the societal level, including government agencies, regulators, and other institutions, may shape global mobility and its most salient outcomes.

Fourth, our review also echoes the call to explicitly acknowledge success as a multidimensional phenomenon (Brewster et al., 2014). For example, taking a multiple stakeholder perspective, one must consider that what is good for one stakeholder may not be good for every other stakeholder, for example, consider the case of a repatriate with increased competencies who quits her company for a better job. This will assuredly be considered a success for the individual, but it will be detrimental to the organization that has lost valuable skills and expertise; see Lazarova & Cerdin, 2007). Related to this point, multiple outcome variables ought to be considered simultaneously to advance a more holistic understanding of success. For example, should an expatriate who stays on the assignment but is not performing well be described as successful (Harzing, 1995)? Research must also consider what Brewster and colleagues (2014) label "the temporal consistency challenge" or the idea that what may appear to be a positive outcome at one point of time may not be perceived positively at a later point, or vice versa (e.g., think of an assignment that was beset by personal challenges early on, but the expatriate not only overcomes them but also builds resilience and useful skills over time).

Fifth, we would also call for leveraging novel methodological approaches to enable asking novel—and more interesting—questions. For example, collecting data through intensive longitudinal design (see e.g., Takeuchi et al., 2019) would allow researchers to identify subgroups of assignees based on similarities on a specific variable and trace the subgroups' evolution over time. This would allow us to rethink the type of research questions we ask and to pose novel questions, such as: what are emergent subgroups of SIEs as defined by their work role adjustment, international experience, or host country embeddedness, or how do assignees' identity configurations evolve over time?

Practical Applications

Given the changing landscape of global mobility that we have traced in our review and the more fundamental changes to mobility that may arise as a result of major global shocks such as the COVID-19 pandemic, which gripped the world in early 2020, there is a need for strategic realignment for MNCs and global mobility professionals alike. What should be the ideal composition of an organization's global staff, and how can it change in the future? Addressing these questions requires that the global mobility function develops greater strategic proficiency. Identifying relevant metrics can provide necessary raw material for doing so. However, the growing importance—and availability—of data also points to the need for global mobility professionals to develop their analytical literacy, which will require a change in the competency mix in global mobility teams and a shifting mindset toward critical causal reasoning and the willingness to continuously validate the key business drivers of global mobility.

Second, organizations are well advised to view global mobility as investing in the development of talent rather than as a cost to be contained. The importance of international experience for the ability to function in a new environment is well documented (e.g., Takeuchi et al., 2019). Thus, organizations should make good use of global mobility alternatives to develop their employees at various phases of their career. For instance, individuals could be assigned to work in a global virtual team with members from select locations as part of a cross-cultural training program. This would allow them to familiarize themselves with a certain culture before engaging in long-term assignments, thereby easing their subsequent adjustment process. There are of course other ways to develop people, including through repeated short-term business travel or through assignment of international task responsibilities without the need to relocate, as in the form of global domestics (Shaffer et al., 2012).

Third, global mobility practices need to be better aligned. "Novel" forms of mobility are not that new anymore. MNCs should have policies and support practices for these more flexible assignment types. Each form of global mobility involves different challenges, which must be overcome or supported appropriately. As noted, the use of global mobility should also be integrated with organizational processes pertaining to talent development, which can enhance an employee's sociocultural career capital. Thus, the integration of new types of global mobility must be appropriately integrated within broader organizational practices, such as global talent management, including succession planning and career development.

Fourth, our review has demonstrated that scholars—as reflected in both the questions they ask and the outcome variables they study—now think more holistically and pay more attention to employee well-being and health. One consistent theme in the mobility literature, across types of global work, has always been the recognition that global mobility can lead to mental and physical strain. We can only advise practitioners to *not* assume that their employees, despite opting into jobs involving high levels of mobility, are superhuman. While some may enjoy this lifestyle and flourish, keeping a close eye on their well-being is essential (De Cieri & Lazarova, 2021). This will ensure that individuals will be able to perform in a more sustainable manner, and can aid with their retention, thereby helping to keep the previously outlined invaluable knowledge and experience within the organization.

Finally, given the many uncertainties in the aftermath of COVID-19, the global mobility function also needs to be more adaptable. There are many plausible scenarios. For example, if barriers to international travel persist, the more traditional long-term expatriation might experience a renaissance relative to other more recent forms of global mobility. At the same time, we would also expect that many people have experienced substitutes to various forms of global work amidst the COVID-19 crisis, such as regular remote and (global) virtual teamwork. And while global companies like Hong Kong-based fintech firm Xapo, which are operating fully virtually without physical offices, have thus far been an exception, many more companies are—and will be—discussing how to reduce physical presence. As such, due to the crisis, we may see a catalytic influence on the speed at which more sophisticated technologies are implemented. This will make it easier for organizations to find appropriate, efficient working practices that will substitute or deem other forms of global mobility in certain professions as unnecessary costs.

Conclusion

People have been traveling and living abroad for their work for thousands of years. Despite the recent crisis in which we find ourselves, the likelihood of global mobility continuing in some way, shape, or form remains high. Research on global mobility has come a long way since the identification of expatriation as an important topic in the business management literature in the mid-20th century. We have suggested the major shifts that have occurred in research over the last decade, as well as some key theoretical and practical implications of these shifts. These ongoing transformations are a clear sign of maturation of the field of global mobility as a whole.

References

Adams, B. G., & van de Vijver, F. J. R. (2015). The many faces of expatriate identity. *International Journal of Intercultural Relations, 49*, 322–331.

Akkan, E., Reiche, B. S., & Lazarova, M. B. (2020). A "change" perspective of repatriation: Review and research recommendations. In B. Szkudlarek, J. Osland, D. Caprar, & L. Romani (Eds.), *SAGE handbook of contemporary cross cultural management* (pp. 439–451). London: SAGE.

Alshahrani, S. T., & Morley, M. J. (2015). Accounting for variations in the patterns of mobility among conventional and self-initiated expatriates. *The International Journal of Human Resource Management, 26*(15), 1936–1954.

Andrade, N. J. (2017). Drops of Greek in a multilingual sea: The Egyptian network and its residential presences in the Indian Ocean. *Journal of Hellenic Studies, 137*, 42–66.

Andresen, M. (2021). When at home, do as they do at home? Valuation of self-initiated repatriates' competences in French and German management career structures. *The International Journal of Human Resource Management, 32*(4), 789–821.

Andresen, M., Bergdolt, F., Margenfeld, J., & Dickmann, M. (2014). Addressing international mobility confusion—developing definitions and differentiations for self-initiated and assigned expatriates as well as migrants. *The International Journal of Human Resource Management, 25*(16), 2295–2318.

Argote, L., & Ingram, P. (2000). Knowledge transfer: A basis for competitive advantage in firms. *Organizational Behavior and Human Decision Processes, 82*(1), 150–169.

Arman, G., & Aycan, Z. (2013). Host country nationals' attitudes toward expatriates: Development of a measure. *International Journal of Human Resource Management, 24*(15), 2927–2947.

Bader, A. K., Froese, F. J., & Kraeh, A. (2018). Clash of cultures? German expatriates' work-life boundary adjustment in South Korea. *European Management Review, 15*(3), 357–374.

Baker, C., & Ciuk, S. (2015). "Keeping the family side ticking along": An exploratory study of the work-family interface in the experiences of rotational assignees and frequent business travellers. *Journal of Global Mobility, 3*(2), 137–154.

Ballesteros Leiva, F., Poilpot-Rocaboy, G., & St-Onge, S. (2018). Social support and life-domain interactions among assigned and self-initiated expatriates. *European Management Review, 15*(3), 293–313.

Baruch, Y., Altman, Y., & Tung, R. L. (2016). Career mobility in a global era: Advances in managing expatriation and repatriation. *Academy of Management Annals, 10*(1), 841–889.

Belhoste, N., & Monin, P. (2013). Constructing differences in a cross-cultural context: National distance, social differentiation or functional distinction. *Human Relations, 66*(12), 1529–1561.

Berger, C. R., & Calabrese, R. J. (1975). Some explorations in initial interaction and beyond: Toward a developmental theory of interpersonal communication. *Human Communication Research, 1*(2), 99–112.

Berry, J. (1997). Immigration, acculturation and adaptation. *Applied Psychology: An international Review, 46*(1), 5–68.

Berry, J. W. (1980). Acculturation as varieties of adaptation. In A. M. Padilla (Ed.), *Acculturation: Theory, models and some new findings* (pp. 9–25). Boulder, CO: Westview.

Bhaskar-Shrinivas, P., Harrison, D. A., Shaffer, M. A., & Luk, D. M. (2005). Input-based and time-based models of international adjustment: Meta-analytic evidence and theoretical extensions. *Academy of Management Journal, 48*(2), 257–281.

Biemann, T., & Braakmann, N. (2013). The impact of international experience on objective and subjective career success in early careers. *The International Journal of Human Resource Management, 24*(18), 3438–3456.

Black, J. S., & Gregersen, H. B. (1991a). The other half of the picture: Antecedents of spouse cross-cultural adjustment. *Journal of International Business Studies, 22*(3), 461–477.

Black, J. S., & Gregersen, H. B. (1991b). When Yankee comes home: Factors related to expatriate and spouse repatriation adjustment. *Journal of International Business Studies, 22*(4), 671–694.

Black, J. S., Mendenhall, M., & Oddou, G. (1991). Toward a comprehensive model of international adjustment: An integration of multiple theoretical perspectives. *Academy of Management Review, 16*(2), 291–317.

Black, J. S., & Stephens, G. K. (1989). The influence of the spouse on American expatriate adjustment and intent to stay in Pacific Rim overseas assignments. *Journal of Management, 15*(4), 529–544.

Bonache, J., Brewster, C., & Suutari, V. (2001). Expatriation: A developing research agenda. *Thunderbird International Business Review, 43*(1), 3–20.

Bonache, J., Langinier, H., & Zárraga-Oberty, C. (2016). Antecedents and effects of host country nationals negative stereotyping of corporate expatriates. A social identity analysis. *Human Resource Management Review, 26*(1), 59–68.

Bormann, W. A. (1968). The problem with expatriate personnel and their selection in international enterprises. *Management International Review, 8*(4/5), 37–48.

Breitenmoser, A., Bader, B., & Berg, N. (2018). Why does repatriate career success vary? An empirical investigation from both traditional and protean career perspectives. *Human Resource Management, 57*(5), 1049–1063.

Brewster, C., Bonache, J., Cerdin, J.-L., & Suutari, V. (2014,). Exploring expatriate outcomes. *The International Journal of Human Resource Management, 25*(14), 1921–1937.

Burmeister, A., Lazarova, M. B., & Deller, J. (2018). Repatriate knowledge transfer: Antecedents and boundary conditions of a dyadic process. *Journal of World Business*, *53*(6), 806–816.

Caligiuri, P., & Bonache, J. (2016). Evolving and enduring challenges in global mobility. *Journal of World Business*, *51*(1), 127–141.

Caligiuri, P. M. (2000). Selecting expatriates for personality characteristics: A moderating effect of personality on the relationship between host national contact and cross-cultural adjustment. *Management International Review*, *40*(1), 61–80.

Caligiuri, P. M., Phillips, J., Lazarova, M., Tarique, I., & Burgi, P. (2001). The theory of met expectations applied to expatriate adjustment: The role of cross-cultural training. *The International Journal of Human Resource Management*, *12*(3), 1–16.

Cappellen, T., & Janssens, M. (2010). Enacting global careers: Organizational career scripts and the global economy as co-existing career referents. *Journal of Organizational Behavior*, *31*(5), 687–706.

Chang, Y.-Y., Gong, Y., & Peng, M. W. (2012). Expatriate knowledge transfer, subsidiary absorptive capacity, and subsidiary performance. *Academy of Management Journal*, *55*(4), 927–948.

Chen, C. C., Choi, J., & Chi, S. C. (2002). Making justice sense of local-expatriate compensation disparity: Mitigation by local referents, ideological explanations, and interpersonal sensitivity in China-foreign joint ventures. *Academy of Management Journal*, *45*(4), 807–826.

Chen, G., Kirkman, B. L., Kim, K., Farh, C. I., & Tangirala, S. (2010). When does cross-cultural motivation enhance expatriate effectiveness? A multilevel investigation of the moderating roles of subsidiary support and cultural distance. *Academy of Management Journal*, *53*(5), 1110–1130.

Cho, T., Hutchings, K., & Marchant, T. (2013). Key factors influencing Korean expatriates' and spouses' perceptions of expatriation and repatriation. *The International Journal of Human Resource Management*, *24*(5), 1051–1075.

Clark, J. D. (1992). African and Asian perspectives on the origins of modern humans. *Philosophical Transactions: Biological Sciences*, *337*, 201–215.

Cole, N. (2011). Managing global talent: Solving the spousal adjustment problem. *International Journal of Human Resource Management*, *22*(7), 1504–1530.

Cole, N., & Nesbeth, K. (2014). Why do international assignments fail? *International Studies of Management & Organization*, *44*(3), 66–79.

Collings, D. G., Mellahi, K., & Cascio, W. F. (2019). Global talent management and performance in multinational enterprises: A multilevel perspective. *Journal of Management*, *45*, 540–566.

Conyon, M. J., Haß, L. H., Vergauwe, S., & Zhang, Z. (2018). Foreign experience and CEO compensation. *Journal of Corporate Finance*, *57*, 102–121.

De Cieri, H., & Lazarova, M. (2021). "Your health and safety is of utmost importance to us": A review of research on the occupational health and safety of international employees. *Human Resource Management Review*, *31*(4), 100790.

de Sivatte, I., Bullinger, B., Cañamero, M., & del Pino Martel Gomez, M. (2019). Children of expatriates: key factors affecting their adjustment. *Journal of Global Mobility*, *7*(2), 213–236.

Demel, B., & Mayrhofer, W. (2010). Frequent business travelers across Europe: Career aspirations and implications. *Thunderbird International Business Review*, *52*(4), 301–311.

Dickmann, M., Suutari, V., Brewster, C., Mäkelä, L., Tanskanen, J., & Tornikoski, C. (2018). The career competencies of self-initiated and assigned expatriates: assessing the development of career capital over time. *The International Journal of Human Resource Management*, *29*(6), 2353–2377.

Doherty, N., Richardson, J., & Thorn, K. (2013). Self-initiated expatriation: Career experiences, processes and outcomes. *Career Development International*, *18*(1), 6–11.

Dolles, H., & Egilsson, B. (2017). Sports Expatriates. In J. Selmer & Y. McNulty (Eds.), *Research Handbook of Expatriates* (pp. 350–367). Northampton, MA: Edward Elgar Publishing.

Dragoni, L., Oh, I.-S., Tesluk, P. E., Moore, O. A., VanKatwyk, P., & Hazucha, J. (2014). Developing leaders' strategic thinking through global work experience: The moderating role of cultural distance. *Journal of Applied Psychology*, *99*(5), 867–882.

Duvivier, F., Peeters, C., & Harzing, A. (2019). Not all international assignments are created equal: HQ-subsidiary knowledge transfer patterns across types of assignments and types of knowledge. *Journal of World Business*, *54*(3), 181–190.

Edstrom, A., & Galbraith, J. R. (1977). Transfer of managers as a coordination and control strategy in multinational organizations. *Administrative Science Quarterly*, *22*(2), 248–263.

Erez, M., & Gati, E. (2004). A dynamic, multi-level model of culture: from the micro level of the individual to the macro level of a global culture. *Applied Psychology: An international Review, 53*(4), 583–598.

Fee, A. (2020). How host-country nationals manage the demands of hosting expatriates: An exploratory field study. *Journal of Global Mobility, 8*(1), 25–54.

Feldman, D. C., & Thomas, D. C. (1992). Career management issues facing expatriates. *Journal of International Business Studies, 23*(2), 271–293.

Firth, B. M., Chen, G., Kirkman, B. L., & Kim, K. (2014). Newcomers abroad: Expatriate adaptation during early phases of international assignments. *Academy of Management Journal, 57*(1), 280–300.

Forster, N. (1994). The forgotten employees? The experiences of expatriate staff returning to the UK. *International Journal of Human Resource Management, 5*(2), 405–425.

Froese, F. J., & Peltokorpi, V. (2013). Organizational expatriates and self-initiated expatriates: Differences in cross-cultural adjustment and job satisfaction. *International Journal of Human Resource Management, 24*(10), 1953–1967.

Furusawa, M., & Brewster, C. (2016). IHRM and expatriation in Japanese MNCs: HRM practices and their impact on adjustment and job performance. *Asia Pacific Journal of Human Resources, 54*(4), 396–420.

Geeraert, N., Li, R., Ward, C., Gelfand, M., & Demes, K. A. (2019). A tight spot: How personality moderates the impact of social norms on sojourner adaptation. *Psychological Science, 30*(3), 333–342.

Georgakakis, D., Dauth, T., & Ruigrok, W. (2016). Too much of a good thing: Does international experience variety accelerate or delay executives' career advancement? *Journal of World Business, 51*(3), 425–437.

Guzzo, R. A., Noonan, K. A., & Elron, E. (1994). Expatriate managers and the psychological contract. *Journal of Applied Psychology, 79*, 617–626.

Hamori, M., & Koyuncu, B. (2011). Career advancement in large organizations in Europe and the United States: do international assignments add value? *International Journal of Human Resource Management, 22*(4), 843–862.

Harush, R., Lisak, A., & Erez, M. (2016). Extending the global acculturation model to untangle the culture mixing puzzle. *Journal of Cross-Cultural Psychology, 47*(10), 1395–1408.

Harzing, A.-W. (2001). Of bears, bumble-bees, and spiders: The role of expatriates in controlling foreign subsidiaries. *Journal of World Business, 36*(4), 366–379.

Harzing, A.-W. K. (1995). The persistent myth of high expatriate failure rates. *International Journal of Human Resource Management, 6*(2), 457–475.

Haslberger, A., Brewster, C., & Hippler, T. (2013). The dimensions of expatriate adjustment. *Human Resource Management, 52*(3), 333–351.

Hay, G. (1814). *A treatise on expatriation*. Washington, DC: A & G Way, Printers.

Hemmasi, M., & Downes, M. (2013). Cultural distance and expatriate adjustment revisited. *Journal of Global Mobility, 1*(1), 72–91.

Hippler, T., Caligiuri, P. M., Johnson, J. E., & Baytalskaya, N. (2014). The development and validation of a theory-based expatriate adjustment scale. *The International Journal of Human Resource Management, 25*(14), 1938–1959.

Ho, N. T. T., Seet, P.-S., & Jones, J. (2015). Understanding re-expatriation intentions among overseas returnees: An emerging economy perspective. *International Journal of Human Resource Management, 27*, 1938–1966.

Hon, A. H. Y., & Lu, L. (2010). The mediating role of trust between expatriate procedural justice and employee outcomes in Chinese hotel industry. *International Journal of Hospitality Management, 29*(4), 669–676.

Inkson, K., Pringle, J., Arthur, M. B., & Barry, S. (1997). Expatriate assignment versus overseas experience: Contrasting models of international human resource development. *Journal of World Business, 32*(4), 351–368.

Jensen, M. T. (2014). Exploring business travel with work–family conflict and the emotional exhaustion component of burnout as outcome variables: The job demands–resources perspective. *European Journal of Work and Organizational Psychology, 23*(4), 497–510.

Jensen, M. T., & Knudsen, K. (2017). A two-wave cross-lagged study of business travel, work–family conflict, emotional exhaustion, and psychological health complaints. *European Journal of Work and Organizational Psychology, 26*(1), 30–41.

Jokinen, T., Brewster, C., & Suutari, V. (2008). Career capital during international work experiences: contrasting self-initiated expatriate experiences and assigned expatriation. *International Journal of Human Resource Management, 19*(6), 979–998.

Kang, H., & Shen, J. (2018). Antecedents and consequences of host-country nationals' attitudes and behaviors toward expatriates: What we do and do not know. *Human Resource Management Review, 28*(2), 164–175.

Kraimer, M., Bolino, M., & Mead, B. (2016). Themes in expatriate and repatriate research over four decades: What do we know and what do we still need to learn? *Annual Review of Organizational Psychology and Organizational Behavior, 3*, 83–109.

Kraimer, M. L., Shaffer, M. A., & Bolino, M. C. (2009). The influence of expatriate and repatriate experiences on career advancement and repatriate retention. *Human Resource Management 48*(1), 27–47.

Kraimer, M. L., Shaffer, M. A., Harrison, D. A., & Ren, H. (2012). No place like home? An identity strain perspective on repatriate turnover. *Academy of Management Journal, 55*(2), 399–420.

Kraimer, M. L., Wayne, S. J., & Jaworski, R. A. (2001). Sources of support and expatriate performance: The mediating role of expatriate adjustment. *Personnel Psychology, 54*, 71–99.

Lazarova, M., Westman, M., & Shaffer, M. A. (2010). Elucidating the positive side of the work-family interface on international assignments: A model of expatriate work and family performance. *Academy of Management Review, 35*(1), 93–117.

Lazarova, M. B., & Cerdin, J. L. (2007). Revisiting repatriation concerns: Organizational support versus career and contextual influences. *Journal of International Business Studies, 38*(4), 404–429.

Lee, Y.-T., Masuda, A., Fu, X., & Reiche, B. S. (2018). Navigating between home, host, and global: Consequences of multicultural team members' identity configurations. *Academy of Management Discoveries, 4*, 180–201.

Leiba-O'Sullivan, S. (2002). The protean approach to managing repatriation transitions. *International Journal of Manpower, 23*(7), 597–616.

Leonardelli, G. J., & Toh, S. M. (2011). Perceiving expatriate coworkers as foreigners encourages aid: Social categorization and procedural justice together improve intergroup cooperation and dual identity. *Psychological Science, 22*(1), 110–117.

Leung, A. K.-Y., Maddux, W. W., Galinsky, A. D., & Chiu, C. Y. (2008). Multicultural experience enhances creativity: The when and how. *American Psychologist, 63*, 169–183.

Leung, K., Lin, X., & Lu, L. (2014). Compensation disparity between locals and expatriates in China: A multilevel analysis of the influence of norms. *Management International Review, 54*(1), 107–128.

Lin, D., Lu, J., Liu, X., & Zhang, X. (2016). International knowledge brokerage and returnees' entrepreneurial decisions. *Journal of International Business Studies, 47*(3), 255–318.

Maertz, C. P., Jr., Hassan, A., & Magnusson, P. (2009). When learning is not enough: A process model of expatriate adjustment as cultural cognitive dissonance reduction. *Organizational behavior and human decision processes, 108*, 66–78.

Maertz, C. P. J., Takeuchi, R., & Chen, J. (2016). An episodic framework of outgroup interaction processing: Integration and redirection for the expatriate adjustment research *Psychological Bulletin, 142*(6), 623–654.

Mäkelä, L., Kinnunen, U., & Suutari, V. (2015). Work-to-life conflict and enrichment among international business travelers: The role of international career orientation. *Human Resource Management, 54*(3), 517–531.

Mäkelä, L., Suutari, V., Brewster, C., Dickmann, M., & Tornikoski, C. (2016). The impact of career capital on expatriates' perceived marketability. *Thunderbird International Business Review, 58*(1), 29–39.

Mäkelä, L., Suutari, V., & Mayerhofer, H. (2011). Lives of female expatriates: Work-life balance concerns. *Gender in Management: An International Journal, 26*(4), 256–274.

Mao, J., & Shen, Y. (2015). Cultural identity change in expatriates: A social network perspective. *Human Relations, 68*(10), 1533–1556.

Mayerhofer, H., Hartmann, L. C., Michelitsch-Rield, G., & Kollinger, I. (2004). Flexpatriate assignment: A neglected issue in global staffing. *International Journal of Human Resource Management, 15*(8), 1371–1389.

McKouen, K. L., Shaffer, M. A., & Reiche, B. S. (2020). From global experiences to global careers: A review and future research agenda. In H. Gunz, M. B. Lazarova, & W. Mayrhofer (Eds.), *Routledge companion to career studies* (pp. 310–327). New York: Routledge.

McNulty, Y. (2012). 'Being dumped in to sink or swim': An empirical study of organizational support for the trailing spouse. *Human Resource Development International, 15*(4), 417–434.

McNulty, Y., & Brewster, C. (2017). Theorising the meaning(s) of "expatriate": Establishing boundary conditions for business expatriates. *The International Journal of Human Resource Management, 28*(1), 27–61.

McNulty, Y., & De Cieri, H. (2011). Global mobility in the 21st century: Conceptualising expatriate return on investment in global firms. *Management International Review, 51*, 897–919.

McNulty, Y., & De Cieri, H. (2016). Linking global mobility and global talent management: The role of ROI. *Employee Relations, 38*(1), 8–30.

McNulty, Y., & Selmer, J. (2017). Introduction: overview of early expatriate studies, 1952 to 1979. In Y. McNulty & J. Selmer (Eds.), *Research handbook of expatriates* (pp. 3–20). Northampton, MA: Edward Elgar Publishing.

Mendenhall, M. E., & Oddou, G. (1985). The dimensions of expatriate acculturation: A review. *Academy of Management Review, 10*(1), 39–47.

Mendenhall, M., & Oddou, G. (1986). Acculturation profiles of expatriate managers: Implications for cross-cultural training programs. *Columbia Journal of World Business, 21*(4), 73–79.

Molinsky, A. L. (2013). The psychological processes of cultural retooling. *Academy of Management Journal, 56*(3), 683–710.

Morris, J. (2018). China, Japan and Christian emissaries to Muslim lands. *Islam and Christian-Muslim Relations, 29*(2), 167–191.

Mutter, J., & Thorn, K. (2019). Global mobility and the career of the stay-at-home partner. *Journal of Global Mobility, 7*(1), 88–102.

Peltokorpi, V. (2020). Host country national employees' prosocial behavior toward expatriates in foreign subsidiaries: A common ingroup identity model perspective. *International Business Review, 29*(2), 101642.

Plourde, Y., Parker, S. C., & Schaan, J.-L. (2014). Expatriation and its effect on headquarters' attention in the multinational enterprise. *Strategic Management Journal, 35*(6), 938–947.

Ramaswami, A., Carter, N. M., & Dreher, G. F. (2016). Expatriation and career success: A human capital perspective. *Human Relations 69*(10), 1959–1987.

Reiche, B. S. (2012). Knowledge benefits of social capital upon repatriation: A longitudinal study of international assignees. *Journal of Management Studies, 49*(6), 1052–1077.

Reiche, B. S., Kraimer, M., & Harzing, A.-W. (2011). Why do international assignees stay? *Journal of International Business Studies, 42*(4), 521–544.

Reiche, B. S., Lee, Y.-T., & Allen, D. (2019). Actors, structure, and processes: A review and conceptualization of global work integrating IB and HRM research. *Journal of Management, 45*(2), 359–383.

Ren, H., Bolino, M. C., Shaffer, M. A., & Kraimer, M. L. (2013). The influence of job demands and resources on repatriate career satisfaction: A relative deprivation perspective. *Journal of World Business, 48*(1), 149–159.

Ren, H., Yunlu, D. G., Shaffer, M. A., & Fodchuck, K. M. (2015). Expatriate success and thriving: The influence of job deprivation and emotional stability. *Journal of World Business, 50*(1), 69–78.

Salt, J., & Wood, P. (2012). Recession and international corporate mobility. *Global Networks, 12*(4), 425–445.

Saxenian, A. L. (2005). From brain drain to brain circulation: Transnational communities and regional upgrading in India and China. *Studies in Comparative International Development, 40*(2), 35–61.

Scurry, T., Rodriguez Jenny, K., & Bailouni, S. (2013). Narratives of identity of self-initiated expatriates in Qatar. *Career Development International, 18*(1), 12–33.

Selmer, J., Chiu, R. K., & Shenkar, O. (2007). Cultural distance asymmetry in expatriate adjustment. *Cross Cultural Management: An International Journal, 14*(2), 150–160.

Selmer, J., & Lauring, J. (2009). Cultural similarity and adjustment of expatriate academics. *International Journal of Intercultural Relations, 33*(5), 429–436.

Selmer, J., Trembath, J.-L., & Lauring, J. (2017). Expatriate academics: An era of higher education internationalization In J. Selmer & Y. McNulty (Eds.), *Research handbook of expatriates* (pp. 335–349). Northampton, MA: Edward Elgar Publishing.

Shaffer, M. A., Kraimer, M. L., Chen, Y.-P., & Bolino, M. C. (2012). Choices, challenges, and career consequences of global work experiences: A review and future agenda. *Journal of Management, 38*(4), 1282–1327.

Shaffer, M. A., Reiche, B. S., Dimitrova, M., Lazarova, M., Chen, S., Westman, M., & Wurtz, O. (2016). Work- and family-role adjustment of different types of global professionals: Scale development and validation. *Journal of International Business Studies, 47*(2), 113–139.

Suutari, V., & Brewster, C. (2000). Making their own way: International experience through self-initiated foreign assignments. *Journal of World Business, 35*(4), 417–436.

Suutari, V., Brewster, C., Mäkelä, L., Dickmann, M., & Tornikoski, C. (2018). The effect of international work experience on the career success of expatriates: A comparison of assigned and self-initiated expatriates *Human Resource Management, 57*(1), 37–54.

Suutari, V., Brewster, C., Riusala, K., & Syrjäkari, S. (2013). Managing non-standard international experience: evidence from a Finnish company. *Journal of Global Mobility*, *1*(2), 118–138.

Takeuchi, R. (2010). A critical review of expatriate adjustment research through a multiple stakeholder view: Progress, emerging trends, and prospects. *Journal of Management*, *36*(4), 1040–1064.

Takeuchi, R., Li, Y., & Wang, M. (2019). Expatriates' performance profiles: Examining the effects of work experiences on the longitudinal change patterns. *Journal of Management*, *45*(2), 451–475.

Tharenou, P. (2010). Women's self-initiated expatriation as a career option and its ethical issues. *Journal of Business Ethics*, *95*(1), 73–88.

Tharenou, P. (2015). Researching expatriate types: The quest for rigorous methodological approaches. *Human Resource Management Journal*, *25*(5), 149–165.

Thomas, D. C. (1998). The expatriate experience: A critical review and synthesis. *Advances in International Comparative Management*, *12*, 237–273.

Toh, S. M., & DeNisi, A. S. (2003). Host country national reactions to expatriate pay policies: A model and implications. *Academy of Management Review*, *28*(4), 606–621.

Toh, S. M., & DeNisi, A. S. (2005). A local perspective to expatriate success. *Academy of Management Executive*, *19*(1), 132–146.

Tung, R. L. (2016). New perspectives on human resource management in a global context. *Journal of World Business*, *51*(1), 142–152.

van Bakel, M. (2019). It takes two to tango: A review of the empirical research on expatriate-local interactions. *The International Journal of Human Resource Management*, *30*(21), 2993–3025.

van Bakel, M., Gerritsen, M., & van Oudenhoven, J. P. (2016). The importance of relationship quality: Maximizing the impact of expatriate contact with a local host. *Thunderbird International Business Review*, *58*(1), 41–54.

Vance, C. M., McNulty, Y., Paik, Y., & D'Mello, J. (2016). The expat-preneur: Conceptualizing a growing international career phenomenon. *Journal of Global Mobility*, *4*(2), 202–224.

Vance, C. M., & Ring, P. S. (1994). Preparing the host country workforce for expatriate managers: The neglected other side of the coin. *Human Resource Development Quarterly*, *5*(4), 337–352.

Varma, A., Budhwar, P., & Pichler, S. (2011). Chinese host country nationals' willingness to help expatriates: The role of social categorization. *Thunderbird International Business Review*, *53*(3), 353–364.

Varma, A., Pichler, S., Budhwar, P., & Biswas, S. (2009). Chinese host country nationals' willingness to support expatriates: The role of collectivism, interpersonal affect and guanxi. *International Journal of Cross Cultural Management*, *9*(2), 199–216.

Ward, C., & Chang, W. C. (1997). "Cultural fit": A new perspective on personality and sojourner adjustment. *International Journal of Intercultural Relations*, *21*(4), 525–533.

Ward, C., & Kennedy, A. (1999). The measurement of sociocultural adaptation. *International Journal of Intercultural Relations*, *23*(4), 659–677.

Westman, M., & Etzion, D. (2002). The impact of short overseas business trips on job stress and burnout. *Applied Psychology: An international Review*, *54*(1), 582–592.

CHAPTER 24

National Culture and Alliances

Youtha Cuypers, Dorota Piaskowska, *and* Ilya R. P. Cuypers

Abstract

A large and diverse literature on the effects of national culture on cross-border alliances has developed in recent decades. This chapter provides a review and critical assessment of this literature and lays out a path for future research. First, we provide an overview of the evolution of scholarship on this topic, and we identify some trends in recent work. Second, we provide a roadmap for navigating this literature by conducting a structured and sequential review of how cultural traits and cultural distance affect each of the key stages in the life cycle of an alliance. Finally, we propose an agenda for future research by highlighting several overarching avenues worth pursuing in future research. We believe that our review of the impact of national culture on cross-border alliances offers valuable insights to both scholars and practitioners.

Key Words: joint ventures, alliances, cross-country collaborations, cultural distance, cultural traits, alliance governance

Introduction

In recent decades, we have witnessed an increasing number of firms entering into cross-border alliances, such as contractual alliances and joint ventures (JVs), to strengthen or sustain their competitive advantage (e.g., Ariño & Reuer, 2006). In line with this trend, numerous scholars from a variety of disciplines have sought to improve our understanding of various aspects of this important phenomenon. In this literature, *national culture* (hereafter *culture*) has emerged as one of the key factors that influence the formation, management, and success of cross-border alliances (Hennart & Zeng, 2002; Kogut & Singh, 1988; Pothukuchi et al., 2002). Specifically, numerous studies have shown that both culture in absolute terms, that is, the cultural attributes or traits of an alliance partner's home country (e.g., Kogut & Singh, 1988; Park & Ungson, 1997; Teegen & Doh, 2002), as well as the relative cultural distance between the partners (e.g., Barkema & Vermeulen, 1997; Choi & Contractor, 2016; Kogut & Singh, 1988) matter.

This chapter provides a review of the key themes in research on the effect of culture and cultural distance on cross-border alliances and highlights opportunities for future research. First, we provide an overview of the evolution of scholarship that has looked at culture and cross-border alliances. This analysis allows us to put our review in a historical context and identify trends in recent work. It also helps us set the scope of our review and clarify the core concepts. Second, we conduct a review of how culture and cultural distance affect specific aspects of cross-border alliances. Alliances involve a series of investment decisions, processes, and events, and this temporal sequence is commonly referred to as the "life cycle" of alliances (e.g., Reuer, 2000). By considering each of the key stages in this life cycle, we discuss the impact of culture on cross-border alliances in a structured, comprehensive, and sequential manner. We review prior research that has looked at each of the key alliance life-cycle stages, and for each of these stages, we differentiate between the impact of *cultural distance* and *culture traits* and propose avenues for future research. Finally, we conclude this chapter by highlighting a number of overarching avenues for future research.

Alliances: Definitions and Historical Perspective

We define (cross-border) alliances as voluntary arrangements between two or more independent firms (from different home countries) made with the intention to share, exchange, and/or jointly develop resources, products, or services (e.g., Dussauge et al., 2000; Gulati, 1998). This broad definition encompasses a wide variety of different types of alliances. More precisely, it encompasses alliances that are of a vertical nature, that is, between firms that are at different stages of the value chain; or alliances of a horizontal nature, that is, involving firms that operate in the same industry and are often considered to be competitors (e.g., Belderbos et al., 2012). Our broad definition of alliances includes both contractual alliances, in which the collaboration is governed by a contract, and equity joint ventures (EJVs), in which case two or more firms set up a new legal entity and contribute resources, including equity (e.g., Killing, 1983; Martin & Salomon, 2003). These different types of alliances have two commonalities that are particularly relevant for our review. First, they typically evolve along a number of common life-cycle stages, including (1) partner identification and selection, (2) alliance negotiations, (3) alliance design and governance choices, (4) postformation alliance management, and (5) alliance outcomes (e.g., stability, termination, and performance). Second, culture is likely to play an important role in most types of alliances and across the different stages (albeit possibly to a different degree as we will elaborate later), as they entail ongoing interactions between participants from different cultures. Hence, in the following sections of this chapter, we discuss the impact of culture on alliances in each of the alliance life-cycle stages.

Scholars and practitioners' interest in cross-border alliances took off after the Second World War when U.S. multinationals started to expand globally and to collaborate increasingly with foreign firms (Nippa & Reuer, 2019). Early work was dominated by economists and law scholars and focused on explaining general patterns of alliance formation, motivations, and the competitive and antitrust consequences of cross-border alliances (e.g., Dixon, 1962; Friedmann & Kalmanoff, 1961; Pfeffer & Nowak, 1976). This early research only scarcely touched upon issues related to culture and cultural differences between partners. Those scholars who nevertheless focused on cultural issues made notable contributions by highlighting the idea that studying culture in cross-border alliances was a relevant and interesting avenue of research. For example, Peterson and Shimada (1978) emphasized that cultural differences are a major source of managerial problems in Japanese-U.S. cross-border alliances.

It was not until after the publication of the seminal works by Hofstede (1980) and Kogut and Singh (1988) that scholars started to more systematically investigate the effects of culture and cultural distance on alliances. The conceptual advancements, as well as the data and measures provided by these works, triggered an explosion of studies, leading to numerous new insights into the effects of culture and cultural distance (Cuypers et al., 2018). Initially, most work in this stream of research focused on alliance governance choices (e.g., Gatignon & Anderson, 1988; Pan, 1996) and alliance survival (e.g., Brown et al., 1989; Park & Ungson, 1997; Parkhe, 1991). Since then, this literature has considerably broadened to the point that now each stage of the life cycle of alliances has been studied from a cultural perspective, albeit to varying extents. In addition, other cultural frameworks (e.g., House et al., 2004; Inglehart & Welzel, 2005; Schwartz, 1994) and ways to operationalize cultural distance have also emerged (e.g., Berry et al., 2010). However, in line with the broader international business literature on culture and cultural distance, the literature on cross-border alliances still largely relies on Hofstede's framework and Kogut and Singh's (1988) cultural distance index (Beugelsdijk et al., 2018; Cuypers et al., 2018). Therefore, we consider these as the default in our review, but we highlight explicitly that a study relies on an alternative cultural framework or measure of cultural distance when relevant.

In the following sections, we critically review work on the role of culture in each of the key alliance life-cycle stages and propose avenues for future research. In doing so, we differentiate between work that has looked at the impact of *cultural distance* and work that has looked at *cultural traits.*

Partner Selection

Selecting the right partner for an alliance is imperative to achieving the alliance's goals and avoiding the risk of opportunistic behavior, frequent renegotiations, and undesirable outcomes (Geringer, 1991). Yet, this stage has been underresearched in general, and most work takes a partner as a given and focuses on other aspects of the alliance (Nippa & Reuer, 2019).

A relatively small body of work has nevertheless investigated how culture affects partner selection, focusing mostly on *cultural distance.* In this line of research, several studies proposed that the likelihood of selecting a partner is negatively associated with cultural distance (e.g., Dasí-Rodríguez & Pardo-del-Val, 2015). They argued that firms prefer to avoid more culturally distant partners because of the increased coordination costs, higher chances of misunderstandings and conflict, and the additional difficulty in assessing such a partner. In contrast, some studies have proposed a positive association between cultural distance and the likelihood of selecting a partner. For example, Krammer (2018) found that firms are more likely to opt for more culturally distant partners when they enter in exploratory technological alliances as more culturally distant partners bring more unique knowledge and diversity to the table compared to less culturally distant partners. However, Krammer (2018) proposed that the opposite holds for exploitation alliances, which suggests that the effect of cultural distance on partner selection is complex and likely to be contingent on the type of alliance. There is also some work that simultaneously considered the benefits and cost of collaborating with a more culturally distant partner, and found an inverted U-shaped relationship between cultural distance and the likelihood of selecting a partner. Hence, only at moderate levels of cultural distance do the benefits of having a partner that provides access to more novel knowledge outweigh the challenges and costs associated with cultural distance (e.g., Joshi & Lahiri, 2015). Hence, while the exact relationship remains unclear, cultural distance plays an important role in partner selection.

The way *cultural traits* affect partner selection has also enjoyed some attention in the literature. Typically, these studies proposed that cultural traits affect which criteria firms use to select their partners. For example, early work by Peterson and Shimada (1978) argued that Japanese partners scrutinized the managers of their prospective American partners particularly closely, focusing predominantly on trust, character, and the nature of the relationships between them. In contrast, they argued that American partners focused predominantly on the formal agreement. These differences were explained by the specific cultural traits of the Japanese and Americans when it comes to fulfillment of obligations, with the Japanese expecting goodwill and benevolence to drive obligation fulfillment, while the Americans are more likely to demand that their counterpart meets contractual obligations. Later on, Geringer (1991) hinted at the possibility that the relative importance given to task- versus partner-related criteria may also vary across cultures. Hence, the limited body of research in this area suggests that the cultural traits of alliance partners might play a role in the partner selection process. However, it is important to note that these studies tended to focus on country-of-origin effects and attributed alliance partner selection preferences to differences in countries' cultures without divulging the effects of specific cultural traits.

While our review highlights the importance of culture for alliance partner selection, we nevertheless see several areas for future research on this topic (summarized in Table 24.1). First, we encourage future research to be more precise in terms of the mechanisms that link cultural distance and cultural traits to alliance partner selection. Much of the existing work relies on a mix of arguments and mechanisms to establish this relationship. However, if we want to improve our understanding of how and when culture matters in alliance partner selection, it is important to precisely theorize the specific mechanisms at play and to carefully isolate them empirically.

Table 24.1 Overview of specific areas for future research

PARTNER SELECTION
• Theorize and isolate empirically the mechanisms that link cultural distance and cultural traits to firms' partner selection. • Explore how sociological and psychological mechanisms (e.g., homophily) affect partner selection. • Disentangle the effects of cultural traits on partner selection from other country effects. • Separate the effects of culture on firms' location choice from the effects on partnering choices.
ALLIANCE NEGOTIATIONS
• Extend relevant insights from the broader cross-cultural negotiation literature to the alliance context. • Explore how cultural distance and cultural traits impact the negotiations in multiparty alliances. • Investigate other aspects of negotiations, such as the duration of negotiations. • Examine how a broader set of cultural traits affect negotiations.
ALLIANCE DESIGN AND GOVERNANCE CHOICES
• Investigate the effect of culture on the composition and functioning of JV boards and the steering committees in contractual alliances. • Examine how decision makers' cultural backgrounds and cultural perceptions affect alliance design.
POSTFORMATION ALLIANCE MANAGEMENT
• Explore how cultural traits affect different functional activities in alliances. • Further examine how cultural traits affect firms' propensity to trust their partners and manage alliances through trust. • Further examine how cultural differences can effectively be managed in alliances. • Investigate the effect of culture on the management of multiparty alliances.
ALLIANCE OUTCOMES
• Examine how cultural traits affect alliance performance. • Study mediation effects to tease out the mechanisms that link cultural distance and performance. • Resolve some of the mixed findings in the extant literature by theorizing with the level of analysis and type of performance in mind. • Incorporate the conditions and decisions in each alliance life-cycle stage when examining the performance implications of culture.

Second, future research may consider more sociological and psychological mechanisms that have been shown to be relevant in related contexts. For example, several forms of homophily—the tendency to associate with similar others (e.g., Ertug et al., 2018; Lawrence & Shah, 2020)—have been shown to influence partnering choices (e.g., Ahuja et al., 2009). Empirical research in other settings has established that culturally similar actors are more likely to associate with each other than with culturally dissimilar actors (e.g., Byrne, 1971). Therefore, it might be worth investigating whether cultural homophily is also driving alliance partner selection.

Third, most studies that have looked at the potential effects of cultural traits on partner selection have focused on explaining cross-country differences. Future research in this area could benefit from a more direct and systematic approach rather than simply comparing the choices of firms coming from different countries. A more systematic investigation of specific cultural traits is likely to yield valuable insights into which cultural traits actually matter and to what extent. Empirically, it would also allow us to disentangle the effects of cultural traits from other country effects (e.g., Beugelsdijk et al., 2017).

Finally, we cannot ignore the fact that in reality firms often decide to enter a particular market and then look for a suitable partner. This implies that the level of cultural distance we observe between partners may be the outcome of the location choice process and that partners may be selected based on criteria other than culture. It is important for future research to disentangle the effects of culture on the location choice from those on the partnering choice. This might be possible by looking at which foreign partners firms collaborate with in their domestic market, or by employing econometric techniques to separate the effect of culture on firms' location choice from the effect on partnering choices.

Alliance Negotiation

Alliance negotiations constitute a complex process, starting with the initial expression of interest, followed by negotiations regarding the best governance mode, the time horizon, and the division of responsibilities and outcomes. This process also includes renegotiations during the course of the collaboration, as unforeseen events unfold (e.g., Ariño et al., 2014; Ring & Van de Ven, 1994).

The relevance of *cultural distance* for negotiations in cross-border alliances is well established. The complexities inherent to alliance negotiations due to high levels of uncertainty and ambiguity are exacerbated by cultural distance in the cross-border context and may lead to impasses, prevent the alliance from being formed, or set the tone for a contentious ongoing collaboration (Kumar & Patriotta, 2011). Cross-cultural negotiations are particularly complicated due to a lack of behavioral transparency, differences in communication styles, varying expectations and interpretations of actions, as well as inherently different negotiation perspectives and tactics (Luo, 1999; Rao & Schmidt, 1998; Ribbink & Grimm, 2014). Using a survey-based measure developed by Boyacigiller (1990),[1] Rao and Schmidt (1998) found that as cultural distance increases, alliance negotiators appear to start acting like novice negotiators who attempt to gain compliance without really knowing what is the most suitable type of tactic to use, thereby increasing their use of both soft and hard tactics. Not only is it difficult to determine what the right tactics are in cross-cultural negotiations, it is also hard to interpret the behavior and intentions of others based on how they communicate. More precisely, differences in the directness of information sharing between negotiators from high-context cultures (less direct, more implicit) and those from low-context cultures (more direct, more explicit) are often interpreted

[1] Boyacigiller (1990) used a single survey item on a 5-point Likert scale to ask respondents to evaluate how long it would take the "average American" to adapt to the business milieu of a particular country.

as one party misrepresenting information, thereby causing conflict (Lee et al., 2006). In addition, Luo and Shenkar (2002) suggested that cultural distance also affects the scope of negotiations, as it is associated with higher term specificity and higher topic inclusiveness in contract negotiations.

In addition, the *cultural traits* of the negotiators or partner firms are also likely to be relevant. While there is a vast literature on the impact of cultural traits on cross-cultural negotiations in general (e.g., Gelfand & Realo, 1999; Gelfand et al., 2013b), research that has specifically focused on the impact of cultural traits on cross-cultural negotiations in the context of alliances remains scarce. Among notable exceptions is the study by Luo (1999), who argued that the cultural background of the negotiators influences JV negotiations. Luo cited the example of Chinese negotiators, who, influenced by cultural values rooted in Confucianism, tend to build flexibility into contracts during negotiations to avoid lawsuits and save face in the future. Moreover, in the context of Sino-U.S. joint ventures, Lin and Miller (2003) observed differences in the negotiation tactics used by the American and Chinese partners, which they attributed to differences in cultural traits related to individualism and collectivism, tolerance for ambiguity, and high- versus low-context cultures.

We again see several areas for future research (summarized in Table 24.1). As we have previously highlighted, empirical research on the role of cultural traits in the alliance negotiation stage remains relatively scarce. Hence, extending insights from the vast general cross-cultural negotiation literature to the context of alliances has the potential to advance the literature considerably. For example, research on cross-cultural negotiations in general has shown that North American negotiators suffer more from the so-called fixed-pie bias than, for example, the Japanese (Morris & Gelfand, 2004). This implies that North American negotiators see less room than Japanese negotiators for integrative negotiations in which parties try to create a win–win situation rather than to appropriate value at each other's expense. This is because the North American negotiators tend to (falsely) assume that their own interests are diametric to those of their counterpart. Such tendencies in judgment may be particularly relevant in the context of alliances where partners often engage in cooperative competition or "coopetition" (Brandenburger & Nalebuff, 2011). Specifically, the cultural traits of negotiators may determine how much weight they put on the cooperative or competitive aspects of the alliance context, which is likely to affect alliance negotiations.

There may be additional and broader opportunities to integrate the culture and negotiation literatures from psychology and organizational behavior with the international alliance literature. The idea that the context of the negotiations interacts with the cultural traits of the negotiator has been tested and supported in the general cross-cultural negotiation literature. More precisely, Gelfand et al. (2013a) found that the same situational context (in their case, team vs. solo negotiations) can have differential effects on negotiation outcomes across cultures by amplifying the cultural norms of negotiators. Situational factors can reinforce culturally normative negotiation behavior, but they can also trigger counternormative behavior by relieving negotiators from the need or expectation to follow cultural norms (Gelfand et al., 2013b). For example, Gelfand and Realo (1999) showed that explicit pressures on negotiators, such as those triggered by high levels of accountability, led to competitive behavior in individualistic cultures but more cooperative behavior in collectivist cultures. In other words, high accountability reinforces cultural-normative behavior. However, in situations in which accountability was not an issue, negotiators exhibited counter-normative behavior, with collectivists becoming more competitive than individualists. It would be interesting to explore the role of these, and other, contextual factors in cross-border alliance negotiations. Among the contextual factors specific to cross-border alliances, the industry in which the alliance is active or the activities the alliance engages in (e.g., R&D, marketing, manufacturing), may also affect how cultural traits and cultural distance impact alliance negotiations. For example, previous research has shown that the effect of culture on partner selection is contingent on the purpose of the alliance or the activities it will engage in (e.g., Krammer, 2018). Consequently, these contextual variables will likely also influence alliance negotiations. In sum, there seems to be ample opportunity for cross-fertilization between the literature on (cross-cultural) negotiations in psychology and organizational behavior and the international alliances literature to improve our understanding of how contextual factors reinforce or weaken the effects of culture in cross-border alliance negotiations.

Third, the vast majority of cross-cultural negotiation studies have focused on two-party negotiations. However, relatively little is known, in both the negotiation literature at large and the alliance negotiation literature in particular, on how culture matters in multi-party alliances. This is surprising since multiparty alliances are commonplace, especially in high-tech industries (e.g., Xia et al., 2012). The role of culture is likely to be more than simply additive in these more complex multiparty alliances. Future research could investigate how cultural distance and cultural traits impact the formation of coalitions in such negotiations.

Fourth, most of the literature on cross-cultural negotiation in general, and in the context of alliances, has focused on determining differences in negotiation tactics and on the gains created in general negotiation tasks. We also see potential for future research to look at other aspects of negotiations. For example, the alliance literature has paid little attention to the duration of negotiations and the likelihood that negotiations are actually completed, while work in the acquisition literature (e.g., Dikova et al., 2010) suggests that these are two important aspects of negotiations that are worth investigating. In the context of JVs, Luo and Shenkar (2002) hinted that culture impacts the length of negotiations, as they found that JV negotiations are lengthier between Chinese and Western firms than between Chinese and other Asian firms. Future research could investigate how cultural distance and cultural traits, such as long-term orientation and uncertainty avoidance, might impact the duration of negotiations and the likelihood that negotiations are completed successfully.

Finally, two of Hofstede's cultural dimensions, that is, individualism–collectivism and power distance, and the distinction between low- and high-context cultures seem to be particularly prevalent in the cross-cultural negotiations literature, both in the context of alliances and more generally. Hence, there is ample room for research that takes different dimensions into account, as well as research that studies the potential interplay between different dimensions, or between culture and other factors that determine negotiation behavior and outcomes. For example, the role of power asymmetry in negotiations and its effect on negotiation behavior and outcomes has been studied extensively (Dwyer & Walker, 1981; Rao & Schmidt, 1998). In addition, Wolfe and McGinn (2005) emphasized the importance of *perceived* relative power—determined by social contextual variables—in negotiations, as it impacts the behavior and subsequently, the integrative outcome of negotiations. Given that perceptions of power are shaped by context, it is likely that differences in power distance between the negotiation parties create asymmetries in the partners' perceptions of relative power, and thereby shape negotiation behavior and outcomes in cross-border alliance negotiations.

Alliance Design and Governance Choices

During the formation and structuring stage of an alliance's life cycle, the partner firms typically enter into a legal agreement that governs their joint activities and relationship (Contractor & Reuer, 2014). Such an agreement usually encapsulates how the alliance will be structured and governed. This, for example, plays an important role in safeguarding the partners against transaction and collaboration hazards (Kale & Singh, 2009). Thus, alliance structure and governance have long been regarded as key aspects of alliances and have been extensively studied.

In this area of research, the bulk of studies has focused on how *cultural distance* affects the formal governance of alliances. Most of this work fits in a broader stream of research that has looked at how cultural distance influences the choice between different entry modes.[2] Studies that specifically focus on the formal governance of alliances are typically one of two types. First, several studies (e.g., Globerman & Nielsen, 2007; Majocchi et al., 2013; Yamin & Golesorkhi, 2010) have researched the choice between equity-based alliances (i.e., collaborative agreements where two or more firms set up a new legal entity and contribute equity and other resources for the joint pursuit of economic goals) and contractual alliances (i.e., contractual agreements in which the partners contribute resources to the relationship for the joint pursuit of economic goals, excluding equity and without forming a separate legal entity). Second, a number of studies have also looked at firms'

---

[2] For meta-analytic reviews of this broader literature, see Beugelsdijk et al. (2018), Morschett et al. (2010), Tihanyi et al. (2005), and Zhao et al. (2004).

preferences for different levels of ownership in equity JVs, either considering the choice of minority, 50–50, and majority stakes, or the actual level of equity ownership partners take (e.g., Cuypers & Martin, 2010; Pan, 1996, 2002; Richards & Yang, 2007; Tsang, 2005).

Primarily building on insights from transaction cost theory, real options theory, and the resource-based view,[3] these studies have argued rather consistently that cultural differences increase the ambiguity, uncertainty, and complexity of international alliances. This in turn may increase the possibility of opportunistic behavior by one of the partners, coordination challenges, conflicts, and misunderstandings. However, it is less clear what impact such cultural distance-related challenges have on the choice between different types of alliances and ownership levels. On the one hand, several scholars have proposed that higher levels of cultural distance lead to a preference for more flexible and low-commitment modes such as contractual alliances (as opposed to EJVs) and minority EJVs (as opposed to majority EJVs) (e.g., Buckley et al., 2002; Gatignon & Anderson, 1988). This is because such alliances enable firms to access location-specific knowledge and networks of the partner, and provide opportunities to learn about the host market and about collaborating in a cross-cultural context with limited risk and downside exposure.

On the other hand, higher levels of cultural differences between partners and between the home and host markets increase the complexity of an alliance and may lead to firms choosing more protective, higher control modes such as EJVs (as opposed to contractual alliances) or majority EJVs (as opposed to minority EJVs). For example, Li et al. (2017) found partner complexity—stemming from the additional costs and risks that have to be managed when dealing with partners from different cultures—to increase the likelihood that an equity-based alliance is chosen over a contractual alliance.

These divergent arguments have been accompanied by mixed empirical findings, which may be attributable to several issues. First, it is plausible that different governance modes act as substitutes to deal with the challenges of cultural distance or that the optimal choice is contingent on other factors. Second, empirical issues, such as the choice of cultural framework to calculate cultural distance (e.g., Beugelsdijk et al., 2018), and the confounding of country effects with the effects of cultural distance (e.g., Harzing & Pudelko, 2016) may also have led to these mixed findings. Regardless of the cause, these mixed findings provide an opportunity for future research.

Several studies have taken a broader approach by studying how cultural distance affects other aspects of alliance design and governance choices, such as contractual design and the board of directors in EJVs. For example, Delerue and Sicotte (2019) found that alliance contracts are less detailed and have fewer monitoring clauses when the partners

[3] This body of work primarily draws from these three theories, as they have been, in general, among the most influential theories in strategic management and international business research, particularly in research on governance choices (e.g., Leiblein, 2003). We refer interested readers to a number of reviews, which provide a detailed overview of these theories (e.g., Kraaijenbrink et al., 2010; Trigeorgis & Reuer, 2017; Cuypers et al., 2021).

are more culturally distant (using an adapted version of Kogut and Singh's composite index based on nine dimensions from the GLOBE project). This illustrates the relevance of cultural distance for our understanding of EJV boards and alliance contracts.

There are also several studies that have looked at how *cultural traits* impact alliance design and governance. This research has relied mostly on Hofstede's cultural dimensions and found that uncertainty avoidance in particular has an influence on alliance structuring. Decision makers originating from uncertainty-avoidant cultures tend to prefer well-structured and predictable situations and therefore show a preference for high-equity ownership levels in cross-border EJVs (Erramilli, 1996; Pan, 2002). This effect is particularly strong in host countries with high levels of country risk (Richards & Yang, 2007). Similarly, because high power distance cultures tend to prefer hierarchical structures and centralized decision making, they also show a preference for high ownership levels (Erramilli, 1996; Morschett et al., 2010). Furthermore, individualistic and masculine cultures tend to be less inclined to use collaborative strategies than collectivistic and feminine cultures (Beugelsdijk et al., 2018; Steensma, Marino, & Weaver, 2000; Steensma, Marino, Weaver, & Dickson, 2000). This body of work suggests that the cultural traits of a partner also affect alliance design and governance choices.

Although alliance structuring and design is one of the most studied areas in the alliance literature, we still see several opportunities for future research. First, the literature on alliances is increasingly acknowledging the importance of studying the content and design of alliance contracts as well as the design and functioning of the board of directors of EJVs (e.g., Cuypers et al., 2017; Nippa & Reuer, 2019). A few studies (e.g., Delerue & Sicotte, 2019; Reuer et al., 2014) have started to explore how cultural distance affects these aspects of alliance design. However, several areas remain relatively unexplored. For example, future work could investigate how cultural distance and cultural traits, in particular, affect the composition and functioning of EJV boards. Furthermore, the impact of culture on the use and design of steering committees in contractual alliances remains open for investigation. This is particularly relevant as recent work has shown that these steering committees are an important structural aspect of contractual alliances (Reuer & Devarakonda, 2016).

Second, several studies have explored how cultural traits impact alliance structure and governance. These studies have investigated the impact of a limited set of cultural traits and have largely relied on Hofstede's cultural framework. Future research could investigate how other cultural traits, potentially drawing from different frameworks, might matter. In addition, it would be interesting to explore whether and how decision makers' cultural backgrounds and cultural perceptions affect alliance design. These factors have been shown to affect ownership structures of foreign subsidiaries (e.g., Piaskowska & Trojanowski, 2014; Taylor et al., 1998; Trąpczyński et al., 2020), but less is known about their effects on alliance governance and design.

Postformation Alliance Management

Once an alliance is formed, it needs to be managed efficiently for the partners to achieve their goals. Postformation alliance management refers to the practices, procedures, and other ways the alliance is managed after it is formed. It includes aspects such as how the partners coordinate activities, communicate with each other, develop their mutual relationship, trust, and collaborative routines, share knowledge, and make decisions. Culture has been shown to influence a range of these aspects of postformation alliance management (Beamish & Lupton, 2009), some of which we discuss next, starting with the body of work that has looked at *cultural distance*.

While scholars have long divulged the benefits of managing or governing through trust, this is particularly challenging in contexts characterized by cultural differences. Zaheer and Zaheer (2006) argued that the culturally determined asymmetries in the nature and levels of trust can negatively affect alliance performance. They therefore called for further research on the role of culture in determining the appropriate levels of investment in trust building versus monitoring mechanisms. In line with these arguments and based on a qualitative study involving Chinese and German managers, Muethel and Hoegl (2012) indeed found that the understanding of trust varied across cultures. While concepts such as credibility, honesty, and dependability were found to be essential for trust in both cultures, openness and reliability were only indicated as important components of trust by German managers, while shared understanding and morality were only associated with trust by their Chinese counterparts.

In addition, cultural distance negatively affects other aspects of alliances. More precisely, cultural differences have also been shown to negatively impact communication in alliances and the partners' ability to develop their relationship and interaction capabilities (Jean et al., 2010). Similarly, the establishment of processes and policies that encourage collaborative learning between alliance partners is hindered by cultural differences (Hennart & Zeng, 2002). Cultural distance also affects how partners resolve conflict. For example, Lin and Germain (1998) used a perceptual measure of cultural distance and found that the more JV managers indicated that they viewed their partners as being culturally similar, the more likely they were to use conflict resolution strategies that rely on entering into direct discussions, while getting concerns and issues out in the open and exchanging ideas and developing various courses of action. Cultural distance also appears to affect how much partners and their representatives, such as top managers and the board of directors of EJVs, are involved in the direct management of the EJV, and how various roles within the alliance are distributed and perceived in the alliance. For example, Reuer et al. (2014) found that the board of directors in international EJVs limit their involvement when the cultural distance between partners is high, and results are consistent both when cultural distance is measured based on the GLOBE project dimensions and on Hofstede's dimensions. Finally, Shenkar and Zeira (1992) found a positive association between cultural distance and the degree of role ambiguity and role conflict alliance CEOs face when managing the alliance.

While the above discussed body of work has focused on how cultural differences affect the management of alliances, there is also some research that has looked at how alliance management can mitigate the negative effects of cultural distance. For example, Varma et al. (2015) indicated that cross-border alliance management capabilities (cf. Kale et al., 2002) can help to mitigate the negative effects of cultural distance by stimulating mutual understanding between alliance partners, increasing partners′ abilities to coordinate tasks, share knowledge, and resolve conflicts. In line with this, Meschi (1997) proposed that the negative effects of cultural distance may weaken over time, when cultural integration is actively promoted and managed within the alliance.

There is also a limited body of work that has looked at how *cultural traits* affect the management of alliances. Wang et al. (2005), for example, examined how alliance partners' cultural traits determined the management of conflict during the collaboration. They found that, on the one hand, Asian alliance managers showed a greater preference for compromising conflict resolution strategies than their Western counterparts. Western managers, on the other hand, used more problem-solving tactics, which entail openly acknowledging and discussing conflicts, as well as strategies that use power to force others to comply, than Asian managers. These differences can at least partially be explained by the role of harmony and face saving in Asian cultures, as well as differences in terms of individualism–collectivism between Asian and Western cultures. Nevertheless, the role of culture in shaping alliance conflict resolution strategies is complex. For example, Nguyen and Larimo (2011) proposed that all of Hofstede's dimensions may affect alliance partners' preferences for different conflict resolution strategies. They postulated that compromise or problem-solving strategies, which entail making concessions or closely working together to get conflict resolutions, tend to be preferred by partners from feminine and low power distance cultures. Alliance partners from cultures characterized by high power distance, high uncertainty avoidance, individualistic, and/or low long-term orientation, are expected to exhibit a preference for forcing or legalistic strategies, where they, respectively, exert dominance or rely on the terms in the contract to resolve conflict.

Cultural traits also affect other aspects of the alliance management process. Johnson et al. (2001) showed that parent firm involvement in the EJV, through direct or indirect control, varies across cultures, as do the motivations to exert different types of control and their consequences in terms of conflict. More precisely, they found that parent companies from high power distance cultures (operationalized as firms from the Far Eastern cultural cluster in Ronen and Shenkar's [1985] cultural cluster typology) tend to engage in more direct control than parents from low power distance cultures (operationalized as firms from the Anglo cluster). Moreover, partners from low power distance cultures exhibited more resistance to direct control from their own parent than the JV partners from high power distance cultures. Partners' preferences in terms of human resource policies and practices (e.g., staffing decisions, appraisal and compensation policies, training practices) may also vary considerably according to the cultural traits of the partners (Baird et al., 1990; Schuler & Tarique, 2012). Also, some works have taken a temporal approach to understanding the effects of cultural traits on alliance management. For example, Rodriguez (2005) noted that over time the impact of partners' cultural traits may diminish as management and leadership styles start to converge and a "third culture" emerges (Rodriguez, 2005). "Third cultures" arise when groups from different cultures interact and cooperate, and start to construct a distinct third culture between them, which offers common ground and includes elements of both cultures (Casmir, 1993; Rodriguez, 2005). These third cultures may be imperative for the development of mutual understanding, accommodation, respect, and cooperation, and for assurance that the potential benefits of cultural differences can materialize (Pothukuchi et al., 2002).

Our review of the literature on culture and postformation management of alliances raised a number of important questions and directions for future research. To begin with, it is well established in the international HR literature that culture has a considerable impact on HR management practices (e.g., Aycan et al., 2000). Some of the insights from this literature have been extended to help us understand how human resources are managed in cross-border alliances (e.g., Schuler & Tarique, 2012). These extensions highlight the importance of studying how the management of specific functional activities in alliances is affected by culture. Future research could focus on other functional activities, such as marketing, operations, and R&D, and it could improve our understanding of how management of these activities in alliances is affected by culture. Collectively, future research in this area could also offer valuable insights into whether and how the impact of culture may vary across the different functional activities, which could help practitioners to decide on the scope of their cross-border alliances.

As we have highlighted above, trust plays an important role in the management of alliances. Future work could explore how cultural traits affect the formation of trust in alliances. Prior research has shown that the country of origin of a focal partner influences its propensity to trust its partners (e.g., Ertug et al., 2013). At the individual level, scholars have shown that the differences in the propensity to trust (i.e., people's predisposition toward trusting other people in general) across countries can be at least partially attributed to cultural traits (e.g., Ferrin & Gillespie, 2010; Huff & Kelley, 2003). Hence, the differences Ertug and colleagues (2013) found across countries in firms' propensity to trust their alliance partners might be due to differences across cultures. Therefore, it would be interesting to investigate whether cultural traits indeed determine firms' propensity to trust their partners in cross-border alliances and if so, which cultural traits have the greatest impact.

The bulk of the work we have discussed above looked at how culture affects the management of alliances. While there is a vast literature on managing cultural differences in the workplace (e.g., Taras et al., 2011), relatively few studies have looked specifically at how cultural differences in alliances can be managed (e.g., Meschi, 1997; Rodriguez, 2005). Given that the effective management of cultural differences is particularly important for practitioners, we suggest that future research more extensively investigates how cultural differences can best be managed and how behavior resulting from specific cultural traits that is not in the best interest of the alliance can be mitigated.

We would also encourage research to look beyond the dyadic alliances that are typically the focus of most studies. Multiparty alliances are common, especially in technology-driven industries, and they come with a higher level of complexity and often generate "unique dynamics" (Lavie et al., 2007, p. 578). Increased cultural diversity, the potential of culturally similar parties forming coalitions, and the dynamics that subsequently unfold are bound to create additional challenges for postformation alliance management and warrant further research.

Alliance Outcomes

The performance implications of cross-border alliances have been an important research topic in international business research (e.g., Ariño, 2003) and culture has been identified as an important factor that influences the performance of these alliances (e.g., Christoffersen et al., 2013; Robson et al., 2002). This research has typically considered the financial performance of the alliance or the parent firm, alliance longevity, stability in terms of governance structure, and perceptual measures of outcomes (for a review, see Christoffersen, 2013). As we will now highlight, findings in the literature on alliance outcomes seem to vary depending on how performance is measured.

By far, most of the work that has taken an interest in culture in this context has looked at the effects of *cultural distance* on performance, using measures such as alliance longevity and survival (e.g., Barkema & Vermeulen, 1997; Hennart & Zeng, 2002; Makino et al., 2007; Park & Ungson, 1997;), perceived satisfaction with the alliance (e.g., Pothukuchi et al., 2002), and investors' reaction to the announcement of an alliance (e.g., Merchant & Schendel, 2000). However, this body of work has yielded mixed findings (Christoffersen et al., 2013; Robson et al., 2002), with some studies finding a negative effect of cultural distance on performance (e.g., Barkema & Vermeulen, 1997; Hennart & Zeng, 2002; Makino et al., 2007); others finding the reverse (e.g., Park & Ungson, 1997; Pothukuchi et al., 2002); and still others finding no effect at all (e.g., Merchant & Schendel, 2000).

Much of the work that has found negative effects of cultural distance has argued that many international collaborations failed due to differences in objectives, communication issues, and operating methods, resulting from cultural differences (Geringer & Hebert, 1991; Killing, 1983). For example, comparing U.S.-Japanese JVs with Japanese-Japanese JVs, Hennart and Zeng (2002) found a negative relationship between cultural distance and IJV longevity, which they attributed to culturally distant partners having divergent managerial styles and goals and greater communication problems as compared to culturally proximate partners.

In contrast, several studies found a positive relationship between cultural distance and alliance performance. For example, Park and Ungson (1997) found that cultural distance has a positive effect on the longevity of JVs. Similarly, Pothukuchi et al. (2002) found that cultural distance has a positive effect on operational and strategic aspects of JV performance, while having no effect on the satisfaction of employees with the JV. In addition, some studies argued that only differences on specific cultural dimensions impact alliance performance. For example, Barkema and Vermeulen (1997) found that differences in uncertainty avoidance, masculinity, and long-term orientation between the partners' home countries have a negative effect on international JV survival, but differences in power distance and individualism do not. Zeira et al. (1997), on the other hand, found a positive effect of distance in terms of masculinity–femininity on the effectiveness of JVs (i.e., the extent to which it achieved goals and expectations in terms of market share, growth, and profitability). Similar to most other studies that found a positive effect of cultural differences on alliance outcomes, this was unanticipated. However, ex-post they linked this to Hofstede's (1985) arguments that an asymmetry between masculine and feminine cultures contributes to organization effectiveness, which could be beneficial for collaboration.

Reus and Rottig (2009) examined whether these mixed empirical findings can be partially attributed to the operationalization of the cultural distance construct. Their meta-analysis showed that in studies relying on subjective, self-reported measures of cultural distance the relationship was negative, while in studies using the Kogut and Singh's (1988) composite index, the effect of cultural distance on JV performance was positive. Similarly, they also found the effect to vary depending on how performance was measured. More precisely, studies relying on objective performance measures (e.g., longevity or cumulative abnormal returns) and on Kogut and Singh's composite measure of cultural distance, found a negative effect of cultural distance on performance. On the other hand, studies using subjective measures of performance (e.g., self-reported measures of satisfaction with the JV) reported a positive relationship between cultural distance and JV performance.

Prior research has devoted far less attention to how the *cultural traits* of the partners affect alliance outcomes. Among the few examples, Park and Ungson (1997) argued that certain cultural features, such as group identification, collective responsibility, loyalty, harmony, and a sense of reciprocal obligation, which are characteristics of collectivistic cultures, positively influence JV longevity. They also pointed out that as a cultural trait, time orientation, associated with the focus on short-term profitability, influences JV longevity. Their empirical analyses of U.S.-Japanese and domestic U.S. JVs showed that the former tended to last longer than the latter, as was expected given the Japanese partners' cultural traits. Others suggested that cultural traits such as uncertainty avoidance, masculinity versus femininity, and long- versus short-term orientation have a moderating effect on the relationship between a firm's positional advantage in its alliance network and alliance performance (Kang et al., 2018). A few studies have reported that cultural traits may also determine other performance-related aspects of alliances. For example, Teegen and Doh (2002) found that culture affects which alliance outcomes partners actually value, while Delerue and Simon (2009) pointed out that culture affects the perception of relational risk, which is also likely to influence alliance success. Gill and Butler (2003), in turn, found that trust, conflict, and dependence are key determinants of EJV stability, but their relative importance varies from culture to culture.

Despite this substantial body of work on culture and alliance performance, plenty of uncharted territory remains for future research. First, the effects of cultural traits on alliance performance remains a relatively unexplored area. However, cultural traits have been shown to impact the performance of other types of collaborations. For example, Kirkman and Shapiro (2001) found that several cultural traits affect individuals' job satisfaction in self-managing work teams. Magnusson et al. (2014) found that individualism and masculinity affect firms' sales performance by determining the extent to which salespeople collaborate across departments. Moreover, Steensma, Marino, and Weaver (2000) called for comparative research to determine how cultural traits influence alliance performance, after finding significant differences along national cultural dimensions in terms of entrepreneurs' willingness to use alliances. Hence, future research could explore in greater depth how cultural traits affect alliance performance.

Second, several studies introduce an intermediate construct such as trust or conflict to provide a specific theoretical mechanism through which cultural distance affects alliance performance. However, empirically very few studies actually look at mediation effects or are able to precisely tease out any specific mechanism that links cultural distance and performance. Therefore, future research could benefit substantially from studies that use mediation analysis to improve our understanding of how cultural distance and performance are actually linked. Similarly, exploring theoretically meaningful contingency factors might also help researchers to establish whether or not, or to what extent, a particular mechanism is actually at play. For example, a study proposing a trust-based baseline mechanism to link cultural distance with alliance performance might usefully contrast horizontal alliances (i.e., alliances with a competitor), where appropriation concerns are typically high, with alliances that do not involve a competitor. Such a study might reveal interesting insights about when trust may mediate the effect of cultural distance on alliance performance. Similarly, a study that focuses on a communication-related mechanism to link cultural distance with alliance performance might contrast the effect of cultural distance in certain types of alliances, such as R&D alliances that typically require more intense and frequent communication, with alliances that engage in less complex activities and have lower communication demands. In sum, mediation analysis and exploration of theoretically meaningful moderators might offer novel insights into which mechanisms actually drive the relationship between cultural distance and alliance performance. Furthermore, such an effort might also help resolve some of the empirical inconsistencies in the current literature.

Third, alliance performance has been conceptualized and measured in various ways (Ariño, 2003). Namely, in some studies it refers to the performance of the alliance itself, while in other studies it refers to the performance of the partners. Studies also have relied on a wide range of different measures: perceptual measures, measures that capture the survival and stability of the alliance, financial performance measures, or innovation performance, among others. Reus and Rottig's (2009) meta-analysis showed that some mixed findings are due to the different ways in which performance is operationalized. Therefore, we believe that theorizing more precisely, with the level of analysis (e.g., alliance performance vs. firm/partner performance) and type of performance in mind, would help resolve some of the mixed findings in the extant literature and would help us understand more clearly when the effects of cultural traits and distance are positive or negative.

Finally, we observed that studies that examine the performance implications of culture often do not sufficiently incorporate the conditions and decisions in each of the preceding alliance life-cycle stages. This is problematic as culture affects, as we have shown in our review so far, each of the stages in the alliance life cycle. For example, it has been extensively shown that culture affects how an alliance is structured and governed, and the broader alliance literature also has established that governance choices influence performance (e.g., Hoetker & Mellewigt, 2009). Hence, not incorporating alliance structure and governance choices in the analysis of how culture affects alliance performance might lead to omitted variable bias and inaccurate or even incorrect conclusions. Therefore, it is important that future research considers how culture impacts each of the preceding alliance stages when studying how culture affects alliance performance.

Key Insights and Broad Avenues for Future Research

We provided an overview of the literature on the role of cultural traits and distance in each alliance stage. Throughout this review, we made specific suggestions for future research. In addition, our review also helped us to identify several broader avenues for future research that would allow this body of work to advance beyond its current state. We elaborate on this below and provide an overview of these directions for future research in Table 24.2.

More Focus on the Role of Cultural Traits

Our review of the literature indicates that relatively few studies have focused on the alliance partners' (absolute) cultural traits compared to the number of studies that have looked at the effects of cultural distance. We see this lack of work as a clear opportunity for future research. However, we would like to emphasize two specific issues, which we believe are important to consider for future research.

First, researchers can draw from several cultural frameworks, each with their own dimensions (e.g., Hofstede, 1980; House et al., 2004; Schwartz, 1994), to study the effects of cultural traits. We observed that many studies focus on a subset of cultural dimensions, which is not surprising considering the large number of dimensions available

Table 24.2 Key insights for scholars and practitioners
Key Insights and Broad Avenues for Future Research
1. Investigate the effect of cultural traits on the various aspects of alliances.
2. Focus on the specific mechanisms that underlie the impact that cultural distance and cultural traits have on alliances.
3. Take a positive view and explore systematically the positive effects of cultural distance in cross-border alliances.
4. Improve theoretical and empirical integration across the different alliance stages.
5. Investigate how other culture-related concepts such as cultural intelligence, cultural sensitivity, and cultural tightness–looseness affect alliances.
Key Insights and Implications for Practice
1. Need to take a holistic approach to alliances, taking culture into account in all stages.
2. Introspectively examine own cultural traits and their impact on alliance-related decisions.
3. Invest in building competences such as cultural gap bridging and cultural intelligence.
4. Assess partner's perception of cultural distance and recognize potential asymmetries in how cultural differences are perceived.
5. Recognize potential benefits as well as complexities of managing multipartner alliances or portfolios of alliances in terms of culture.

across the different frameworks. However, in many studies the choice of cultural dimensions to focus on seems to be largely arbitrary and to lack a clear motivation. Hence, it often remains unclear why studies focus on certain dimensions as opposed to others. Therefore, we recommend that future studies provide a clear motivation for their focus. We believe this can best be done by starting from an overarching theoretical framework, which then informs which cultural dimensions are relevant to address the study's specific research question.

There might also be alternative, more inductive approaches that could help avoid looking at arbitrary cultural dimensions. For example, advances in machine learning methods such as LASSO (Least Absolute Shrinkage and Selection Operator) procedures and Random Forests algorithms would allow for theory development and an inductive selection of cultural dimensions that are relevant, followed by classical hypotheses testing (e.g., Puranam et al., 2018). Specifically, researchers could start with all available cultural dimensions and use machine learning on a first sample to identify which dimensions are relevant to build prediction models. Subsequently, the identified dimensions and associations could be used to develop theory, which could then be tested using conventional econometric techniques on a different holdout sample. Scholars have started to use such approaches in management research (e.g., Choudhury et al., 2021; Tidhar & Eisenhardt, 2020), and we see potential in applying these approaches to study the effects of cultural traits on alliances.

Second, we observed that many of the studies looking at the effect of cultural traits do so by looking at cross-border alliances (e.g., Lin & Miller, 2003). This might make it particularly challenging to empirically distinguish between the effects of cultural traits and cultural distance (e.g., Harzing & Pudelko, 2016). Hence, for scholars interested in studying the effects of cultural traits on alliances, comparative studies where domestic alliances in one country are compared with those in other countries might be beneficial. A comparative research design combined with matching approaches such as Coarsened Exact Matching (CEM) to reduce the potentially confounding influence of other characteristics of the alliance would allow the effects of cross-country differences in cultural traits to be isolated better than in many of the approaches we observed in past research.

More Focus on the Underlying Mechanisms

The body of work we have reviewed indicates that cultural factors influence most aspects of cross-border alliances. However, we often lack a clear understanding as to *why* this is the case. A wide range of theories such as transaction cost theory, the resource-based view, and organizational learning theory have been invoked to establish that cultural factors matter. This implies that there might be a plurality of mechanisms at play. Unfortunately, too many studies fall short in detailing the precise mechanisms through which cultural factors have an effect, and as a result, the actual mechanisms that are at play remain a black box (e.g., Maseland et al., 2018). For this body of literature to keep advancing, it is critical to better ground predictions in solid theoretical arguments and to be more precise in terms of the mechanisms that link specific cultural factors to an outcome variable. This would allow the literature to move beyond establishing that cultural factors matter and would instead improve our understanding of *why* and *how* these factors matter. This would also allow for more specific and sophisticated research designs that facilitate the distinction between the different mechanisms that might be at play.

This effort might also facilitate more research on how firms can mitigate some of the challenges they face when collaborating with firms from different cultures, or on how they can better exploit some of the benefits arising from such collaborations. For such research to prosper, it is important that the underlying mechanisms that create challenges or benefits are well understood in the first place. Once these mechanisms are more precisely identified and better understood, future research should be able to offer valuable insights into how these mechanisms in practice can be manipulated by firms. We believe this is particularly important for cultural research on alliances to be of practical relevance.

A More Positive View

The bulk of the literature on alliances considers cultural distance as negative, and it is commonly referred to as a source of friction, costs, challenges, or hurdles. This issue is not unique to work on alliances and exists in the broader international business literature (Stahl & Tung, 2015). However, it seems particularly prevalent in the literature on alliances. Therefore, we would like to encourage research that looks at the upside of cultural differences. For example, there is a considerable body of work that has focused on cross-border alliances from a learning perspective (e.g., Hamel, 1991). Typically, this body of work has seen cultural distance as a factor that increases the need to learn or that prevents partners from learning from each other. However, a small body of work has indicated that cultural differences expose partners to new practices and ways of thinking from which they might learn (e.g., Krammer, 2018). Cultural differences may also create opportunities to combine different practices and ways of thinking, which in turn may lead to innovation and the creation of completely novel ways of doing things (e.g., Pesch & Bouncken, 2017).

Collaborating with more culturally dissimilar partners may have yet other benefits. For example, it may allow people to behave in ways in which they normally would not be able to behave within the traditional boundaries of their organization, which may allow them to break away from the social constraints they usually face, and could lead to innovation or other benefits. This could be particularly valuable for firms from culturally "tight" societies, where deviations are typically sanctioned or not tolerated (Gelfand, Nishii, & Raver, 2006).

We hope these brief illustrations highlight that there is considerable upside to exploring the positive effects of cultural distance in cross-border alliances. We would encourage future research to explore when and how cultural differences can be an asset rather than a liability (e.g., Piaskowska, 2017). The M&A literature has already shown that this is indeed a fruitful avenue for research, and it provides insights into how firms can leverage the positive side of cultural distance (e.g., Dikova & Sahib, 2013; Reus & Lamont, 2009).

Better Integration across the Different Alliance Stages

Our review shows that culture and cultural distance matter for each key stage in the life cycle of alliances. At the same time, as is well established in the broader alliance literature (e.g., Beamish & Lupton, 2009), most of the alliance life-cycle stages also impact one or more of the subsequent stages in this life cycle (e.g., partner selection might affect subsequent alliance negotiations and postformation management). While it is beyond the scope of this review to establish all the possible relationships between the subsequent alliance life-cycle stages, it is important to consider the existence of such relationships, for they might provide an indirect path through which culture could have an impact on a particular stage. We illustrate this in Figure 24.1, where we provide a model showing that the different alliance life-cycle stages are related and that culture might affect a particular stage in a direct and indirect way. For example, this figure shows that cultural distance might influence alliance negotiations directly, but also indirectly through having an impact on partner selection, which has been shown to have an impact on subsequent negotiations.

Yet, in our review we observed that very few studies sufficiently integrate these related stages; indeed, most studies fail to consider the potential indirect paths through which

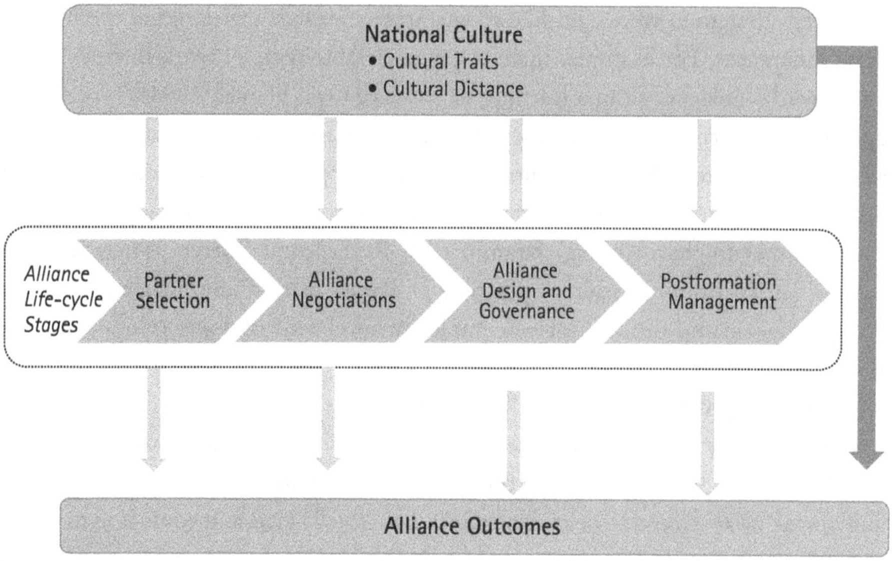

Figure 24.1. A basic model of culture and the alliance life cycle.

culture might have an impact. This is problematic as it may lead to endogeneity issues and selection bias. For example, firms make partner selection choices considering cultural factors, and subsequently firms are likely to consider both cultural factors and other partner-specific characteristics when deciding on how to structure and manage the alliances. However, studies on the structure and management of alliances typically do not consider any selection that might have happened in the preceding stage(s). This indicates a lack of integration and a tendency for studies to implicitly assume that the different stages of the alliance life cycle are independent of each other. Hence, the conclusions drawn from these studies might be inaccurate or even incorrect in the presence of self-selection. Therefore, whenever data availability allows, we recommend future research to empirically integrate the different stages in the life cycle of alliances by having a research design that allows for this unique feature of alliances. In practice, this might require researchers to use two-stage selection models or structural equation modeling. This lack of integration is not only an empirical concern, but it also signals that theoretical opportunities may arise from the integration of these different stages. Relatively few studies have taken a process approach; doing so may yield new theoretical insights into the role of culture.

Moving beyond Cultural Traits and Cultural Distance

In our review, we focused on the literature that has examined cultural distance and cultural traits. However, we noticed that several culture-related concepts that are well studied in the broader literature on culture are rarely mentioned in the cross-border alliance literature. While there are a few studies on cultural sensitivity (e.g., Johnson et al., 1996) and cultural intelligence (e.g., Pesch & Bouncken, 2018), their impact on alliances has not been systematically studied. Similarly, the effects of cultural agility and of having partners from culturally tight versus loose cultures have not been explored. Using cultural tightness–looseness as an example highlights how these concepts might be relevant in the context of alliances. In brief, cultural tightness–looseness relates to the strength of social norms in society and the associated level of sanctioning that occurs when individuals deviate from these norms (Gelfand et al., 2006, 2011). Thus, a firm originating from a culturally tight country may be less tolerant of, and more likely to sanction, the behavior of their foreign partners in cross-border alliances than a firm originating from a loose culture would be. Hence, it would be interesting to explore how these culture-related concepts affect the various stages of the alliance life cycle.

Key Insights and Implications for Practice

While we have focused on reviewing the academic literature on the impact of national culture on cross-border alliances, it is imperative that we also highlight some implications of our review for practitioners. Although few researchers in this area of research explicitly translate their findings to practical implications and actionable recommendations, we believe that we can derive five key insights from our review that are relevant for practitioners.

First, our review (also see Figure 24.1) indicates that cultural traits and cultural distance affect each of the related life-cycle stages of an alliance. Therefore, it is imperative that managers take a holistic approach and consider the influence of culture on all stages of the alliance, starting from when the idea to collaborate emerges. Failing to recognize that it is critical to take culture into account from the start and during all of the subsequent stages is likely to have a whiplash effect across the entire life cycle of the alliance and to have a significant negative impact on the alliance.

Second, akin to the relatively strong emphasis on cultural distance compared to cultural traits in alliance research, it is likely more intuitive for managers to focus on cultural differences between them and their partners than on the impact of their own cultural traits. However, we urge managers to also consider their own cultural traits and how these traits affect alliance-related decisions and collaboration, both in cross-border alliances and in domestic alliances. Specifically, it is important for managers to consider their own cultural values, tendencies, and biases when making their alliance-related decisions. Doing so is likely to lead to better informed decisions and more successful alliances.

Third, we observed a growing body of work that highlights the importance of building competences, such as cultural intelligence and cultural gap-bridging abilities (e.g., Ang et al., 2007; Backmann et al., 2020). Such competences may substantially impact the way managers handle the alliance process. Managers who possess or develop such competences should be better able to deal with the challenges associated with cultural distance. Furthermore, the literature is also increasingly recognizing cultural differences as a potential source of enrichment and provides guidelines on how to capitalize on them (e.g., Reus

& Lamont, 2009). Practitioners who encourage the development of cultural awareness and cultural intelligence in their organizations may be in a better position to capitalize on the positive aspects of cultural differences and consequently, will be more likely to form and manage cross-border alliances successfully. Hence, we would recommend that practitioners make the development of competences, such as cultural intelligence and cultural gap-bridging abilities, an inherent part of the alliance process.

Fourth, while objective cultural differences can be observed, these may not always be aligned with perceived differences. As Reus and Rottig (2009) showed, findings of the effect of culture on JV performance vary depending on whether an objective or subjective, that is, perceptual measure, is used. For practitioners it is important to be aware of differences and asymmetries in perceptions of cultural distance (e.g., Håkanson et al., 2016). While in the context of alliances these asymmetries have been left relatively unexplored, we know from the acquisition literature that they have an important impact on the outcome of strategic actions (Lim et al., 2016). Hence, practitioners would benefit from trying to determine their partner's perception of distance, which would likely prove to be particularly helpful in negotiations and in postformation alliance management.

Finally, alliances seem to be becoming more complex and increasingly include more than two partners, and some even resemble multipartner networks (e.g., Contractor & Reuer, 2019). As firms collaborate in a more complex context or with multiple partners from different cultures, it becomes all the more important for managers to pay extra attention to culture in general, as well as to the cultural dynamics that play out in such alliances. For example, in such complex multicultural collaborations, it may be particularly important to establish a "third culture" early on in order to reduce the sources of potential friction. Furthermore, it has become common for firms to maintain multiple cross-border alliances simultaneously, presenting them not only with the challenges of managing alliance portfolios with partners from a variety of cultures, but also with the opportunities to learn from this diversity. This learning may be particularly valuable in future alliances that are complex and involve multiple partners.

Conclusion

The literature on culture and cross-border alliances is vast, and numerous scholars have provided valuable insights. Our review, which we structured around each of the key stages in the life cycle of an alliance, clearly highlights the idea that cultural distance between the partners' home countries and the cultural traits of the partners are important factors that affect most aspects of cross-border alliances. Despite the many advances that have been made in the literature over the last decades, we see plenty of uncharted territory left for future research. We believe that the avenues for future research we proposed throughout this chapter clearly illustrate this, and we hope that our review and the paths we have laid out will spur future research that will benefit both academics and practitioners.

References

Ahuja, G., Polidoro, F., Jr., & Mitchell, W. (2009). Structural homophily or social asymmetry? The formation of alliances by poorly embedded firms. *Strategic Management Journal, 30*(9), 941–958.

Ang, S., Van Dyne, L., Koh, C., Ng, K. Y., Templer, K. J., Tay, C., & Chandrasekar, N. A. (2007). Cultural intelligence: Its measurement and effects on cultural judgement and decision making, cultural adaptation and task performance. *Management and Organization Review, 3*(3), 335–371.

Ariño, A. (2003). Measures of strategic alliance performance: An analysis of construct validity. *Journal of International Business Studies, 34*(1), 66–79.

Ariño, A., & Reuer, J. J. (2006). Introduction: governance and contracts in strategic alliances. In A. Ariño & J. J. Reuer (Eds.), *Strategic alliances: Governance and contracts.* London: Palgrave.

Ariño, A., Reuer, J. J., Mayer, K. J., & Jané, J. (2014). Contracts, negotiation, and learning: An examination of termination provisions. *Journal of Management Studies, 51*(3), 379–405.

Aycan, Z., Kanungo, R., Mendonca, M., Yu, K., Deller, J., Stahl, G., & Kurshid, A. (2000). Impact of culture on human resource management practices: A 10-country comparison. *Applied Psychology, 49*(1), 192–221.

Backmann, J., Kanitz, R., Tian, A. W., Hoffmann, P., & Hoegl, M. (2020). Cultural gap bridging in multinational teams. *Journal of International Business Studies, 51,* 1283–1311.

Baird, I. S., Lyles, M. A., & Wharton, R. (1990). Attitudinal differences between American and Chinese managers regarding joint venture management. *Management International Review, 30,* 53.

Barkema, H. G., & Vermeulen, F. (1997). What differences in the cultural backgrounds of partners are detrimental for international joint ventures? *Journal of International Business Studies, 28*(4), 845–864.

Beamish, P. W., & Lupton, N. C. (2009). Managing joint ventures. *Academy of Management Perspectives, 23*(2), 75–94.

Belderbos, R., Gilsing, V., & Lokshin, B. (2012). Persistence of, and interrelation between, horizontal and vertical technology alliances. *Journal of Management, 38*(6), 1812–1834.

Berry, H., Guillén, M. F., & Zhou, N. (2010). An institutional approach to cross-national distance. *Journal of International Business Studies, 41*(9), 1460–1480.

Beugelsdijk, S., Kostova, T., Kunst, V. E., Spadafora, E., & Van Essen, M. (2018). Cultural distance and firm internationalization: A meta-analytical review and theoretical implications. *Journal of Management, 44*(1), 89–130.

Beugelsdijk, S., Kostova, T., & Roth, K. (2017). An overview of Hofstede-inspired country-level culture research in international business since 2006. *Journal of International Business Studies, 48*(1), 30–47.

Boyacigiller, N. (1990). The role of expatriates in the management of interdependence complexity and risk in multinational corporations. *Journal of International Business Studies, 21*(3), 357–381.

Brandenburger, A. M., & Nalebuff, B. J. (2011). *Co-opetition.* New York: Doubleday.

Brown, L. T., Rugman, A. M., & Verbeke, A. (1989). Japanese joint ventures with western multinationals: Synthesising the economic and cultural explanations of failure. *Asia Pacific Journal of Management, 6*(2), 225–242.

Buckley, P. J., Glaister, K. W., & Husan, R. (2002). International joint ventures: Partnering skills and cross-cultural issues. *Long Range Planning, 35*(2), 113–134.

Byrne, D. E. (1971). *The attraction paradigm* (Vol. 462). New York: Academic Press.

Casmir, F. L. (1993). Third culture building: a paradigm shift for international and intercultural communication. *Communication Yearbook, 16,* 407–428.

Choi, J., & Contractor, F. J. (2016). Choosing an appropriate alliance governance mode: The role of institutional, cultural and geographical distance in international research & development (R&D) collaborations. *Journal of International Business Studies, 47*(2), 210–232.

Choudhury, P., Allen, R. T., & Endres, M. G. (2021). Machine learning for pattern discovery in management research. *Strategic Management Journal, 42*(1), 30–57.

Christoffersen, J. (2013). A review of antecedents of international strategic alliance performance: Synthesized evidence and new directions for core constructs. *International Journal of Management Reviews, 15*(1), 66–85.

Christoffersen, J., Globerman, S., & Nielsen, B. B. (2013). Cultural distance and the performance of international joint ventures: A critical assessment of model specifications and variable measurement. *International Journal of Strategic Business Alliances, 3*(1), 93–119.

Contractor, F. J., & Reuer, J. J. (2014). Structuring and governing alliances: New directions for research. *Global Strategy Journal, 4*(4), 241–256.

Contractor, F. J., & Reuer, J. J. (2019). *Frontiers of alliance research*. Cambridge, MA: Cambridge University Press.

Cuypers, I. R., Ertug, G., Heugens, P. P., Kogut, B., & Zou, T. (2018). The making of a construct: Lessons from 30 years of the Kogut and Singh cultural distance index. *Journal of International Business Studies, 49*(9), 1138–1153.

Cuypers, I. R., Ertug, G., Reuer, J. J., & Bensaou, B. (2017). Board representation in international joint ventures. *Strategic Management Journal, 38*(4), 920–938.

Cuypers, I. R., Hennart, J. F., Silverman, B. S., & Ertug, G. (2021). Transaction cost theory: Past progress, current challenges, and suggestions for the future. *Academy of Management Annals, 15*(1), 111–150.

Cuypers, I. R., & Martin, X. (2010). What makes and what does not make a real option? A study of equity shares in international joint ventures. *Journal of International Business Studies, 41*(1), 47–69.

Dasí-Rodríguez, S., & Pardo-del-Val, M. (2015). Seeking partners in international alliances: The influence of cultural factors. *Journal of Business Research, 68*(7), 1522–1526.

Delerue, H., & Sicotte, H. (2019). Formal international contracts in the presence of cultural distance: An empirical analysis of biopharmaceutical alliances. *Thunderbird International Business Review, 61*(4), 595–607.

Delerue, H., & Simon, E. (2009). National cultural values and the perceived relational risks in biotechnology alliance relationships. *International Business Review, 18*(1), 14–25.

Dikova, D., & Sahib, P. R. (2013). Is cultural distance a bane or a boon for cross-border acquisition performance? *Journal of World Business, 48*(1), 77–86.

Dikova, D., Sahib, P. R., & Van Witteloostuijn, A. (2010). Cross-border acquisition abandonment and completion: The effect of institutional differences and organizational learning in the international business service industry, 1981–2001. *Journal of International Business Studies, 41*(2), 223–245.

Dixon, P. R. (1962). Joint ventures: What is their impact on competition. *Antitrust Bulletin, 7*, 397–410.

Dussauge, P., Garrette, B., & Mitchell, W. (2000). Learning from competing partners: Outcomes and durations of scale and link alliances in Europe, North America and Asia. *Strategic Management Journal, 21*(2), 99–126.

Dwyer, F. R., & Walker, O. C., Jr. (1981). Bargaining in an asymmetrical power structure. *Journal of Marketing, 45*(1), 104–115.

Erramilli, M. K. (1996). Nationality and subsidiary ownership patterns in multinational corporations. *Journal of International Business Studies, 27*(2), 225–248.

Ertug, G., Cuypers, I. R., Noorderhaven, N. G., & Bensaou, B. M. (2013). Trust between international joint venture partners: Effects of home countries. *Journal of International Business Studies, 44*(3), 263–282.

Ertug, G., Gargiulo, M., Galunic, C., & Zou, T. 2018. Homophily and individual performance. *Organization Science, 29*(5), 912–930.

Ferrin, D. L., & Gillespie, N. (2010). Trust differences across national-societal cultures: Much to do, or much ado about nothing? In M. Saunders, D. Skinner, G. Dietz, N. Gillespie, & R. J. Lewicki (Eds.), *Organizational trust: A cultural perspective* (pp. 42–86). Cambridge, UK: Cambridge University Press.

Friedmann, W. G., & Kalmanoff, G. (1961). Joint international business ventures. *Thunderbird International Business Review, 3*(3), 1–4.

Gatignon, H., & Anderson, E. (1988). The multinational corporation's degree of control over foreign subsidiaries: An empirical test of a transaction cost explanation. *Journal of Law, Economics, & Organization, 4*(2), 305–336.

Gelfand, M. J., Brett, J., Gunia, B. C., Imai, L., Huang, T. J., & Hsu, B. F. (2013a). Toward a culture-by-context perspective on negotiation: Negotiating teams in the United States and Taiwan. *Journal of Applied Psychology, 98*(3), 504.

Gelfand, M. J., Nishii, L. H., & Raver, J. L. (2006). On the nature and importance of cultural tightness-looseness. *Journal of Applied Psychology, 91*(6), 1225–1244.

Gelfand, M., Raver, J., Nishii, L., Leslie, L., Lun, J., Lim, B., et al. (2011). Differences between tight and loose cultures: a 33-nation study. *Science (New York, N.Y.), 332*(6033), 1100–1104.

Gelfand, M. J., & Realo, A. (1999). Individualism-collectivism and accountability in intergroup negotiations. *Journal of Applied Psychology, 84*(5), 721.

Gelfand, M. J., Severance, L., Fulmer, C. A., & Al Dabbagh, M. (2013b). Explaining and predicting cultural differences in negotiations. In G. E. Bolton & R. Croson (Eds.), *The Oxford handbook of economic conflict resolution* (pp. 332–358). New York: Oxford Press.

Geringer, J. M. (1991). Strategic determinants of partner selection criteria in international joint ventures. *Journal of International Business Studies, 22*(1), 41–62.
Geringer, J. M., & Hebert, L. (1991). Measuring performance of international joint ventures. *Journal of International Business Studies, 22*(2), 249–263.
Gill, J., & Butler, R. J. (2003). Managing instability in cross-cultural alliances. *Long range Planning, 36*(6), 543–563.
Globerman, S., & Nielsen, B. B. (2007). Equity versus non-equity international strategic alliances involving Danish firms: An empirical investigation of the relative importance of partner and host country determinants. *Journal of International Management, 13*(4), 449–471.
Gulati, R. (1998). Alliances and networks. *Strategic Management Journal, 19*(4), 293–317.
Håkanson, L., Ambos, B., Schuster, A., & Leicht-Deobald, U. (2016). The psychology of psychic distance: Antecedents of asymmetric perceptions. *Journal of World Business, 51*(2), 308–318.
Hamel, G. (1991). Competition for competence and interpartner learning within international strategic alliances. *Strategic Management Journal, 12*(S1), 83–103.
Harzing, A. W., & Pudelko, M. (2016). Do we need to distance ourselves from the distance concept? Why home and host country context might matter more than (cultural) distance. *Management International Review, 56*(1), 1–34.
Hennart, J. F., & Zeng, M. (2002). Cross-cultural differences and joint venture longevity. *Journal of International Business Studies, 33*(4), 699–716.
Hoetker, G., & Mellewigt, T. (2009). Choice and performance of governance mechanisms: matching alliance governance to asset type. *Strategic Management Journal, 30*(10), 1025–1044.
Hofstede, G. (1980). *Culture's consequences: International differences in work-related values.* Thousand Oaks, CA: SAGE.
Hofstede, G. (1985). The interaction between national and organizational value systems. *Journal of Management Studies, 22*(4), 347–357.
House, R. J., Hanges, P. J., Javidan, M., Dorfman, P. W., & Gupta, V. (Eds.). (2004). *Culture, leadership, and organizations: The GLOBE study of 62 societies.* Thousand Oaks, CA: SAGE.
Huff, L., & Kelley, L. (2003). Levels of organizational trust in individualist versus collectivist societies: A seven-nation study. *Organization Science, 14*(1), 81–90.
Inglehart, R., & Welzel, C. (2005). *Modernization, cultural change, and democracy: The human development sequence.* Cambridge, UK: Cambridge University Press.
Jean, R. J. B., Sinkovics, R. R., & Kim, D. (2010). Drivers and performance outcomes of relationship learning for suppliers in cross-border customer–supplier relationships: The role of communication culture. *Journal of International Marketing, 18*(1), 63–85.
Johnson, J. L., Cullen, J. B., Sakano, T., & Bronson, J. W. (2001). Drivers and outcomes of parent company intervention in IJV management: A cross-cultural comparison. *Journal of Business Research, 52*(1), 35–49.
Johnson, J. L., Cullen, J. B., Sakano, T., & Takenouchi, H. (1996). Setting the stage for trust and strategic integration in Japanese-US cooperative alliances. *Journal of International Business Studies, 27*(5), 981–1004.
Joshi, A. M., & Lahiri, N. (2015). Language friction and partner selection in cross-border R&D alliance formation. *Journal of International Business Studies, 46*(2), 123–152.
Kale, P., Dyer, J. H., & Singh, H. (2002). Alliance capability, stock market response, and long-term alliance success: The role of the alliance function. *Strategic Management Journal, 23*(8), 747–767.
Kale, P., & Singh, H. (2009). Managing strategic alliances: What do we know now, and where do we go from here? *Academy of Management Perspectives, 23*(3), 45–62.
Kang, S., Im, S., & Park, H. (2018). Moderating roles of national culture for alliance relationship advantages and performance in Asia. *Journal of Business-to-Business Marketing, 25*(3), 233–249.
Killing, J. P. (1983) *Strategies for joint venture success.* New York: Praeger.
Kirkman, B. L., & Shapiro, D. L. (2001). The impact of cultural values on job satisfaction and organizational commitment in self-managing work teams: The mediating role of employee resistance. *Academy of Management Journal, 44*(3), 557–569.
Kogut, B., & Singh, H. (1988). The effect of national culture on the choice of entry mode. *Journal of International Business Studies, 19*(3), 411–432.
Kraaijenbrink, J., Spender, J. C., & Groen, A. J. (2010). The resource-based view: a review and assessment of its critiques. *Journal of Management, 36*(1), 349–372.

Krammer, S. M. (2018). A double-edged sword? The antipodal effects of institutional distance on partner selection in cross-border alliances. *Journal of World Business, 53*(6), 930–943.
Kumar, R., & Patriotta, G. (2011). Culture and international alliance negotiations: A sensemaking perspective. *International Negotiation, 16*(3), 511–533.
Lavie, D., Lechner, C., & Singh, H. (2007). The performance implications of timing of entry and involvement in multipartner alliances. *Academy of Management Journal, 50*(3), 578–604.
Lawrence, B. S., & N. Shah. (2020). Homophily: Measures and meaning. *Academy of Management Annals, 14(2),* 513–597.
Lee, K. H., Yang, G., & Graham, J. L. (2006). Tension and trust in international business negotiations: American executives negotiating with Chinese executives. *Journal of International Business Studies, 37*(5), 623–641.
Leiblein, M. J. (2003). The choice of organizational governance form and performance: Predictions from transaction cost, resource-based, and real options theories. *Journal of Management, 29*(6), 937–961.
Li, D., Eden, L., & Josefy, M. (2017). Agent and task complexity in multilateral alliances: The safeguarding role of equity governance. *Journal of International Management, 23*(3), 227–241.
Lim, J., Makhija, A. K., & Shenkar, O. (2016). The asymmetric relationship between national cultural distance and target premiums in cross-border M&A. *Journal of Corporate Finance, 41*, 542–571.
Lin, X., & Germain, R. (1998). Sustaining satisfactory joint venture relationships: The role of conflict resolution strategy. *Journal of International Business Studies, 29*(1), 179–196.
Lin, X., & Miller, S. J. (2003). Negotiation approaches: Direct and indirect effect of national culture. *International Marketing Review, 20*(3), 286–303.
Luo, Y. (1999). Toward a conceptual framework of international joint venture negotiations. *Journal of International Management, 5*(2), 141–165.
Luo, Y., & Shenkar, O. (2002). An empirical inquiry of negotiation effects in cross-cultural joint ventures. *Journal of International Management, 8*(2), 141–162.
Magnusson, P., Peterson, R., & Westjohn, S. A. (2014). The influence of national cultural values on the use of rewards alignment to improve sales collaboration. *International Marketing Review, 31*(1), 30–50.
Majocchi, A., Mayrhofer, U., & Camps, J. (2013). Joint ventures or non-equity alliances? Evidence from Italian firms. *Management Decision, 51*(2), 380–395.
Makino, S., Chan, C. M., Isobe, T., & Beamish, P. W. (2007). Intended and unintended termination of international joint ventures. *Strategic Management Journal, 28*(11), 1113–1132.
Martin, X., & Salomon, R. 2003. Knowledge transfer capacity and Its implications for the theory of the multinational corporation. *Journal of International Business Studies*, 34(4), 356–373.
Maseland, R., Dow, D., & Steel, P. (2018). The Kogut and Singh national cultural distance index: Time to start using it as a springboard rather than a crutch. *Journal of International Business Studies, 49*(9), 1154–1166.
Merchant, H., & Schendel, D. (2000). How do international joint ventures create shareholder value? *Strategic Management Journal, 21*(7), 723–737.
Meschi, P. X. (1997). Longevity and cultural differences of international joint ventures: Toward time-based cultural management. *Human Relations, 50*(2), 211–228.
Morris, M. W., & Gelfand, M. J. (2004). Culture and cognitive dynamics in negotiation. In M. Gelfand & J. Brett (Eds.), *The handbook of negotiation and culture* (pp. 45–70). Palo Alto, CA: Stanford University Press.
Morschett, D., Schramm-Klein, H., & Swoboda, B. (2010). Decades of research on market entry modes: What do we really know about external antecedents of entry mode choice?. *Journal of International Management, 16*(1), 60–77.
Muethel, M., & Hoegl, M. (2012). The influence of social institutions on managers' concept of trust: Implications for trust-building in Sino-German relationships. *Journal of World Business, 47*(3), 420–434.
Nguyen, H., & Larimo, J. (2011). Determinants of conflict management strategies in international joint ventures: An integrative theoretical framework. *Journal of Transnational Management, 16*(2), 116–132.
Nippa, M., & Reuer, J. J. (2019). On the future of international joint venture research. *Journal of International Business Studies, 50*(4), 555–597.
Pan, Y. (1996). Influences on foreign equity ownership level in joint ventures in China. *Journal of International Business Studies, 27*(1), 1–26.
Pan, Y. (2002). Equity ownership in international joint ventures: The impact of source country factors. *Journal of International Business Studies, 33*(2), 375–384.

Park, S. H., & Ungson, G. R. (1997). The effect of national culture, organizational complementarity, and economic motivation on joint venture dissolution. *Academy of Management Journal, 40*(2), 279–307.

Parkhe, A. (1991). Interfirm diversity, organizational learning, and longevity in global strategic alliances. *Journal of International Business Studies, 22*(4), 579–601.

Pesch, R., & Bouncken, R. B. (2017). The double-edged sword of cultural distance in international alliances: How perceived cultural distance influences trust and task discourse to drive new product development performance. *Cross Cultural and Strategic Management, 24*(1), 33–54.

Pesch, R., & Bouncken, R. B. (2018). How to achieve benefits from diversity in international alliances: Mechanisms and cultural intelligence. *Global Strategy Journal, 8*(2), 275–300.

Peterson, R. B., & Shimada, J. Y. (1978). Sources of management problems in Japanese-American joint ventures. *Academy of Management Review, 3*(4), 796–804.

Pfeffer, J., & Nowak, P. (1976). Patterns of joint venture activity: implications for antitrust policy. *Antitrust Bulletin, 21*, 315.

Piaskowska, D. (2017). When distance is good: An upper-echelons perspective on the role of distance in internationalization. In A. Verbeke, J. Puck, & R. J. M. van Tulder (Eds.), *Distance in international business: Concept, cost and value* (pp. 403–423). Bingley: Emerald Publishing.

Piaskowska, D., & Trojanowski, G. (2014). Twice as smart? The importance of managers' formative-years' international experience for their international orientation and foreign acquisition decisions. *British Journal of Management, 25*(1), 40–57.

Pothukuchi, V., Damanpour, F., Choi, J., Chen, C. C., & Park, S. H. (2002). National and organizational culture differences and international joint venture performance. *Journal of International Business Studies, 33*(2), 243–265.

Puranam, P., Shrestha, Y. R., He, V. F., & von Krogh, G. (2018). Algorithmic induction through machine learning: Opportunities for management and organization research. Available at SSRN: https://papers.ssrn.com/sol3/papers.cfm?abstract_id=3140617.

Rao, A., & Schmidt, S. M. (1998). A behavioral perspective on negotiating international alliance. *Journal of International Business Studies, 29*(4), 665–694.

Reuer, J. J. (2000). Parent firm performance across international joint venture life-cycle stages. *Journal of International Business Studies, 31*(1), 1–20.

Reuer, J. J., & Devarakonda, S. V. (2016). Mechanisms of hybrid governance: Administrative committees in non-equity alliances. *Academy of Management Journal, 59*(2), 510–533.

Reuer, J. J., Klijn, E., & Lioukas, C. S. (2014). Board involvement in international joint ventures. *Strategic Management Journal, 35*(11), 1626–1644.

Reus, T. H., & Lamont, B. T. (2009). The double-edged sword of cultural distance in international acquisitions. *Journal of International Business Studies, 40*(8), 1298–1316.

Reus, T. H., & Rottig, D. (2009). Meta-analyses of international joint venture performance determinants. *Management International Review, 49*(5), 607.

Ribbink, D., & Grimm, C. M. (2014). The impact of cultural differences on buyer–supplier negotiations: An experimental study. *Journal of Operations Management, 32*(3), 114–126.

Richards, M., & Yang, Y. (2007). Determinants of foreign ownership in international R&D joint ventures: Transaction costs and national culture. *Journal of International Management, 13*(2), 110–130.

Ring, P. S., & Van de Ven, A. H. (1994). Developmental processes of cooperative interorganizational relationships. *Academy of Management Review, 19*(1), 90–118.

Robson, M. J., Leonidou, L. C., & Katsikeas, C. S. (2002). Factors influencing international joint venture performance: Theoretical perspectives, assessment, and future directions. *MIR: Management International Review 42*(4), 385–418.

Rodríguez, C. M. (2005). Emergence of a third culture: Shared leadership in international strategic alliances. *International Marketing Review, 22*(1), 67–95.

Ronen, S., & Shenkar, O. (1985). Clustering countries on attitudinal dimensions: A review and synthesis. *Academy of management Review, 10*(3), 435–454.

Schuler, R. S., & Tarique, I. (2012). International joint venture system complexity and human resource management. In I. Bjorkman & G. K. Stahl (Eds.), *Handbook of research in international human resource management* (2nd ed.). Northampton, MA: Edward Elgar Publishing.

Schwartz, S. H. (1994). Are there universal aspects in the structure and contents of human values? *Journal of Social Issues, 50*(4): 19–45.

Shenkar, O., & Zeira, Y. (1992). Role conflict and role ambiguity of chief executive officers in international joint ventures. *Journal of International Business Studies, 23*(1), 55–75.

Stahl, G. K., & Tung, R. L. (2015). Towards a more balanced treatment of culture in international business studies: The need for positive cross-cultural scholarship. *Journal of International Business Studies, 46*(4), 391–414.

Steensma, H. K., Marino, L., & Weaver, K. M. (2000). Attitudes toward cooperative strategies: A cross-cultural analysis of entrepreneurs. *Journal of International Business Studies, 31*(4), 591–609.

Steensma, H. K., Marino, L., Weaver, K. M., & Dickson, P. H. (2000). The influence of national culture on the formation of technology alliances by entrepreneurial firms. *Academy of Management Journal, 43*(5), 951–973.

Taras, V., Steel, P., & Kirkman, B. L. (2011). Three decades of research on national culture in the workplace: Do the differences still make a difference. *Organizational Dynamics, 40*(3), 189–198.

Taylor, C. R., Zou, S., & Osland, G. E. (1998). A transaction cost perspective on foreign market entry strategies of US and Japanese firms. *Thunderbird International Business Review, 40*(4), 389–412.

Teegen, H. J., & Doh, J. P. (2002). US–Mexican alliance negotiations: Impact of culture on authority, trust, and performance. *Thunderbird International Business Review, 44*(6), 749–775.

Tidhar, R., & Eisenhardt, K. M. (2020). Get rich or die trying . . . finding revenue model fit using machine learning and multiple cases. *Strategic Management Journal, 41*(7), 1245–1273.

Tihanyi, L., Griffith, D. A., & Russell, C. J. (2005). The effect of cultural distance on entry mode choice, international diversification, and MNE performance: A meta-analysis. *Journal of International Business Studies, 36*(3), 270–283.

Trąpczyński, P., Halaszovich, T. F., & Piaskowska, D. (2020). The role of perceived institutional distance in foreign ownership level decisions of new MNEs. *Journal of Business Research, 108*, 435–449.

Trigeorgis, L., & Reuer, J. J. (2017). Real options theory in strategic management. *Strategic Management Journal, 38*(1), 42–63.

Tsang, E. W. (2005). Influences on foreign ownership level and entry mode choice in Vietnam. *International Business Review, 14*(4), 441–463.

Varma, S., Awasthy, R., Narain, K., & Nayyar, R. (2015). Cultural determinants of alliance management capability–an analysis of Japanese MNCs in India. *Asia Pacific Business Review, 21*(3), 424–448.

Wang, C. L., Lin, X., Chan, A. K., & Shi, Y. (2005). Conflict handling styles in international joint ventures: A cross-cultural and cross-national comparison. *Management International Review, 45*(1), 3–22.

Wolfe, R. J., & McGinn, K. L. (2005). Perceived relative power and its influence on negotiations. *Group Decision and Negotiation, 14*(1), 3–20.

Xia, M., Zhao, K., & Mahoney, J. T. (2012). Enhancing value via cooperation: firms' process benefits from participation in a standard consortium. *Industrial and Corporate Change, 21*(3), 699–729.

Yamin, M., & Golesorkhi, S. (2010). Cultural distance and the pattern of equity ownership structure in international joint ventures. *International Business Review, 19*(5), 457–467.

Zaheer, S., & Zaheer, A. (2006). Trust across borders. *Journal of International Business Studies, 37*(1), 21–29.

Zeira, Y., Newburry, W., & Yeheskel, O. (1997). Factors affecting the effectiveness of equity international joint ventures (EIJVs) in Hungary. *MIR: Management International Review 37*(3), 259–279.

Zhao, H., Luo, Y., & Suh, T. (2004). Transaction cost determinants and ownership-based entry mode choice: A meta-analytical review. *Journal of International Business Studies, 35*(6), 524–544.

CHAPTER

25 Multinational Enterprises and Global Human Resource Management

Wayne F. Cascio *and* David G. Collings

Abstract

This chapter considers global or international human resource management (IHRM) and its role in multinational enterprises (MNEs). We begin by providing a brief history of international business and global HRM. We then introduce the role of strategy in IHRM, emphasizing the crucial role of competitive strategy in formulating an HR strategy. We consider the critical question of how MNEs balance standardization and localization of HR policies and practices in their global operations. We highlight a number of controversies in global HRM research, including the backlash against globalization; convergence versus divergence of HR practices; evolving structures in MNEs; job aid for spouses of overseas executives; and low retention rates among repatriates. We conclude by identifying key boundary conditions on the effects of global HRM, including HR practices as cultural variables, the effects of tight versus loose cultures, individualistic versus collectivistic cultures on HR practices, and the practical implications of these influences.

Key Words: international HRM, global HRM, standardization, localization, expatriation, repatriation, strategy, culture

Introduction

A multinational enterprise (MNE) produces goods or delivers services in more than one country. In addition to private-sector organizations, MNEs also include government and nongovernment organizations (e.g., the Red Cross, the World Health Organization, the Organization for Economic Cooperation and Development). Success in conducting business across international borders requires managerial, operational, and cross-cultural competence. In addition to factors such as a viable business model, adequate capital to fund overseas expansion, well-functioning supply chains and distribution networks to get products to customers, and creative marketing strategies to encourage them to buy a company's products or services, companies need talent. That talent, whether local or multinational, comprises the intellectual capital of an organization, that is, the aggregate knowledge, skills, abilities, and personal characteristics that can be used to solve problems that customers think are important. It is talent that allows MNEs to synthesize all of the ingredients listed above for a successful international business.

This chapter focuses on global or international human resource management (IHRM)[1] and its role in MNEs. IHRM is the study and application of all HR management activities as they impact the process of managing people in enterprises in the global environment (Tarique et al., 2016). The first part of the chapter includes a brief history of international business and global HRM. We then consider the importance of strategy in IHRM, emphasizing the crucial role of competitive strategy in formulating an HR strategy. We also reflect on the critical question of how MNEs balance standardization and localization of HR policies and practices in their global operations. The chapter then highlights a series of controversies in global HRM research. These controversies include the backlash against globalization, convergence versus divergence of HR practices, evolving structures in MNEs, job aid for spouses of overseas executives, and low retention rates among repatriates. At the same time, we also identify key boundary conditions on the effects of global HRM, including HR practices as cultural variables, the effects of tight versus loose cultures, and individualistic versus collectivistic cultures, on HR practices, and the practical implications of these influences. The chapter concludes by identifying new research directions in five major areas. We also present five key theoretical principles along with five practical implications.

A Brief History of International Business and Global HRM

Since antiquity, people have left their native lands to live in foreign countries, whether as diplomats, merchants, or missionaries. The numbers of such travelers grew markedly after the fifteenth century, with the dawn of the European colonial period. In the nineteenth and early twentieth centuries, with the advent of steamships and trains, travel became easier. People could more readily choose to live for several years in a foreign country, or be sent there by employers (Wikipedia, 2020). For example, in 1911 Henry Ford opened his company's first overseas production plant in Manchester, England. By the end of the 1920s, Ford had more than 20 overseas assembly plants in Europe, Latin America, Canada, Asia, South Africa, and Australia (Gregersen, 2020). It was not until the 1950s, however, that international travel really began to flourish. By then, commercial flights on jet airliners further increased the speed of international travel. To be sure, the post-World War II era was full of promise and prosperity, as Courtney C. Brown, Editor of the *Columbia Journal of World Business*, wrote in 1966.

> A new role for business is beginning to take shape as a consequence of far-reaching changes in the structure of world commerce . . . at a far faster pace than is sometimes realized, great

[1] We use the terms *global* and *international HRM* interchangeably in this chapter.

trading companies, with home offices in many advanced nations, are becoming what has come to be known as multinational organizations. . . . This is a powerful unifying influence in the affairs of mankind that has not yet been fully recognized, but which must inevitably make itself more felt in the years to come. . . . The multinational company thereby becomes a major vehicle to carry the have-nots toward "takeoff" and the haves into frontier fields. (pp. 5, 6)

Economists since Adam Smith have argued that trade makes countries richer. It creates larger markets, which allows for greater specialization, lower costs, and higher incomes. Now fast forward to the current business environment. The nature of trade has changed, largely due to the rise of the internet and the growth in globalization—the ability of any individual or company to compete, connect, exchange, or collaborate globally (Friedman, 2016).

Trade was once largely confined to advanced economies and their large, multinational companies. Today, a more digital form of globalization has opened the door to developing countries, to small companies and startups, and to billions of individuals. Millions of small and midsize enterprises worldwide have turned themselves into exporters by joining e-commerce marketplaces such as Alibaba, Amazon, eBay, and Flipkart. Approximately 18% of the global goods trade is now conducted via international e-commerce, up from 10% just since 2017. This percentage has increased further as a result of the global COVID-19 pandemic, with widespread agreement that global lockdowns have accelerated the shift to e-commerce. Thus, in 2019, retail e-commerce sales worldwide amounted to $3.53 trillion (U.S.), and they are projected to grow to $6.54 trillion (U.S.) by 2023 (Sabanoglu, 2020). This is globalization 3.0, or digital globalization. Today, even the smallest firms can compete with the largest multinationals. Using digital platforms and tools, they can sell into fast-growing markets (Free Exchange, 2016; Lipsman, 2019; McKinsey Global Institute, 2016). Yet, multinational corporations still dominate world trade, with their global supply chains and vast distribution networks.

The Global Corporation: A Fact of Organizational Life

Today's global flows of information and knowledge are interlacing markets, media, central banks, companies, schools, communities, and individuals more tightly together than ever before. To begin to appreciate the magnitude of this trend, consider a snapshot of the 2019 *Fortune* Global 500 (the largest 500 firms in the world). Their aggregate revenues were $32.7 trillion, with profits of $2.15 trillion, and they provided jobs for 69.3 million of the world's people. We noted earlier that a fundamental building block in the evolution of a successful international business is global competence—managerial, cultural, and operational. Global competence is embedded in organizational talent and the systems and leadership that organize and deploy it, and it is empowered by technologies, platforms, and connectedness that could hardly be dreamt of in the 1960s (Cascio & Boudreau, 2016). Let's begin by identifying what makes IHRM/global HR different.

What Makes IHRM Different?

Two factors make IHRM different from human resource management in the domestic context: scope and risk exposure (Dowling et al., 2017; Khilji & Schuler, 2017). In terms of *scope,* there are at least four important differences between domestic and international operations. International operations have

1. More HR activities, such as taxation, foreign work visas, coordination of dependents, international relocation, and coordination of salaries in multiple currencies.
2. More involvement in employees' personal lives, such as housing, health, education, and recreation.
3. Management of a much wider mix of employees, coupled with complex equity issues, as the workforce mix of expatriates and locals varies.
4. Broader external influences, such as multiple governments, country laws, cultures, and languages.

Heightened *risk exposure* is a second distinguishing characteristic of IHRM. This includes legal-compliance issues in individual countries, economic risk, political risk, and the HR risk of early return of international assignees. For example, the direct cost of an early return of a family of four with two school-aged children within the first year of an international assignment averages $400,000 U.S. dollars (Chipman, 2016). On top of that, terrorism is now an ever-present risk for executives overseas, and it clearly affects how they assess international assignments (Reiche, 2014). To recognize this new reality, the U.S. State Department has now added a "k" to its travel advisories to indicate a risk of being kidnapped or held hostage (NBC News, 2019). More recently, the COVID-19 crisis has highlighted the significant risk of health emergencies for MNEs. As national borders shut down in the first quarter of 2020, MNEs were faced with complex decisions around whether and how to repatriate international assignees to their home countries and with myriad challenges concerning health and safety, family, and quarantine arrangements, in addition to tax and pay (Boccagni, 2020; Collings & Sheeran, 2020).

Our next section addresses a fundamental question, namely, the decisions, processes, and choices that MNEs make as they consider how to manage their people. This is HR strategy (Cascio & Boudreau, 2012). We focus specifically on HR strategy at the global level.

MNEs and Strategic IHRM

Strategic IHRM is a theme that has been growing in significance in recent decades as MNEs increasingly align their IHRM strategies with their competitive business strategies (Cascio & Boudreau, 2016; Schuler et al., 1993; Minbaeva & DeCieri, 2015). Thus, one way in which MNEs compete with local firms in foreign markets is through internalizing ownership-specific advantages (Rugman, 1980) by replicating in foreign subsidiaries employment practices that they perceive to be advantageous in the HQ organization. However, HRM has been viewed as one of the most nationalized of management practices, reflecting the requirements to adapt to local cultural and institutional traditions (Rosenzweig & Nohria, 1994). This means that compared to other management practices, HR practices often face the greatest pressures for local adaptation to reflect local cultural and institutional norms. Such adaptation is required to acquire legitimacy from government, the law, and other key actors in the host environment (Gooderham et al., 1999). This creates significant tension for IHRM. Indeed, the management of inter-unit linkages is considered core to the idea of strategic IHRM (Barteltt & Ghoshal, 1998), and balancing the demands for coordination, control, and autonomy is core to MNE success (Schuler et al., 1993).

One way to understand how MNEs manage their global operations is through considering the transfer of IHRM practices from HQ to subsidiary operations. In parallel to the development of the broader strategy literature that initially focused on extrapolating and exporting successful home-country systems, we now recognize the importance of a balance between global reach and local roots in IHRM strategy (Cascio & Boudreau, 2016). A key theme in IHRM has been the transfer, replication, and implementation of HR practices developed in the home country in foreign subsidiaries (Bjorkman & Lervik, 2007; Collings & Conroy, 2020). This research emphasizes the identification of exogenous factors that impact the successful transfer of these practices, particularly how MNEs navigate the institutional duality between home and host contexts (Edwards et al., 2007; Pache & Santos, 2010).

Theoretically, incompatible institutional frameworks in home and host countries are key sources of tension and are conceptualized as institutional duality (Kostova & Roth, 2002). Managing this institutional duality is an effort to balance legitimacy in the home and host countries with efficiency (Kostova & Zaheer, 1999). Conflicting institutional demands in the HQ and subsidiary contexts challenge the implementation of global HR policies and practices in local subsidiaries. For example, local norms around wage bargaining and compensation constrain the implementation of more individually oriented pay practices. Scholars explore the transfer of such individually oriented practices preferred by a parent multinational operating to countries with more collectivist traditions around collective bargaining. In so doing, they highlight the challenges of implementation in those hosts (Farndale et al., 2017; Schotter et al., 2021). Illustratively, the challenges faced by nonunion companies in establishing nonunion operations in more collectivist cultures such as Germany have long been documented. Tony Royle's research program on McDonald's attempts to manage subsidiaries outside of the United States on a nonunion basis is a good example of this tension (Royle, 2004).

At the same time, higher levels of embeddedness in both contexts result in higher pressures to conform to home and host country institutional norms. As a simplified example, while a subsidiary may depend on its HQ for resources, the subsidiary may depend on the host country for access to employees. Considerable evidence demonstrates how local managers may mobilize local resources such as employment norms or legislation to justify the adaptation of practices being pushed by HQ (Ferner et al., 2005; Walker et al., 2018). Subsidiary managers must therefore employ institutional as well as corporate resources in order to establish both internal and external legitimacy (Kostova et al., 2008).

In considering how MNEs address these challenges, four key influences (Edwards & Ferner, 2002; Ferner et al., 2013) affect the transfer of employment practices across borders. These include country-of-origin effects, host-country effects, the relative economic dominance of each country, and international integration. We provide a brief overview of each of these influences.

Country-of-Origin Effects

An MNE's country of origin has a distinctive effect on the management style and the configuration of employment practices within the firm. This reflects the embeddedness of a MNE in its home business system (Almond, 2011; Ferner, 1997). There is a rich body of literature that emphasizes the impact of a MNE's country of origin on its management practices (Edwards et al., 2020; Edwards et al., 2013). This impact is evident in the concentration of assets, core employees, and even sales in a MNE's home country. Generally, key positions in the executive team are also often largely filled by parent-country nationals (PCNs).

Consider differences in terms of how nationality affects MNE management. The impact of country of origin on management practices has been extensively researched by Anthony Ferner and colleagues in a number of countries. Initially, they conducted a series of qualitative case studies of large U.S. MNEs in four European countries Germany, Ireland, Spain. and the UK (Almond & Ferner, 2006). This study held the host country constant and explored subsidiaries in four very different host economies. They subsequently led a major international survey that compared indigenous and foreign-owned MNEs in a number of countries, including Canada, Denmark, Ireland, Spain, and the UK (Edwards et al., 2013, 2016). This research consistently demonstrated that MNEs from the U.S. display higher levels of centralization, standardization, and formalization in their approaches to HR than MNEs headquartered in other countries (Ferner et al., 2013). U.S. MNEs also tend to avoid organized labor, such as trade unions, in their global workforces to a greater degree than MNEs from other countries (Ferner et al., 2013). The country of origin does not impose a straitjacket on management, forcing all MNEs from a particular country to act in a certain way. Rather, many other factors, such as ownership structure and sector, contribute to heterogeneity among firms emanating from the same country (Hayden & Edwards, 2001).

Host-Country Effects

Host-country effects refer to features of the host location that can limit MNEs in the diffusion of HR management practices to subsidiaries. The standardization of HR practices across MNEs is clearly impacted by the institutional and cultural constraints in the host country. This reflects the idea of dual embeddedness introduced above. The higher the level of institutional constraints in the host environment, the more difficult it will be for an MNE to implement standardized practices there (cf. Gunnigle et al., 2002). Basic HRM issues are often subject to significant legal or institutional constraints in that environment (Ferner & Quintanilla, 1998). On balance, the wider literature points to the significant and interminable effects of national systems of employment regulation in constraining HR practices in subsidiary locations (Doellgast & Marsden, 2019). Farndale and colleagues' (2017) work cited earlier is a good example of research explicating the impact of host traditions with regard to collective bargaining in constraining reward practices. However, such effects are not totally constraining, and MNEs are able to create sufficient flexibility to preserve elements of their home style, even in highly regulated institutional contexts (Ferner et al., 2013).

Dominance effects

So-called dominance effects also influence the transfer of HRM policies and practices. According to Smith and Meiksins (1995), dominance effects are based on the assumption that a hierarchy of economies exists within the international capitalist system at any point in time. Countries in dominant positions are viewed as having developed methods of structuring production or division of labor, which, in turn, draw emulation and interest. Dominance effects highlight the competitive pressures at play at the international level in determining what is valued and considered legitimate. This, of course, resonates with some of the tenets of neo-institutionalism. Gunnigle et al. (2002) identified dominance effects as a key variable in explaining higher levels of standardization in U.S. MNCs in Europe at the turn of the present century. Enabled by the hegemonic position that the U.S. economy had reached at that time, U.S. firms could more credibly impose standardized management practices on their foreign subsidiaries than could their European counterparts. Hierarchies of economies do evolve over time, however (Edwards & Ferner, 2002). For example, the U.S. economy emerged as a dominant global player in the mid-part of the twentieth century. However, the emergence of Japanese firms in the 1970s and 1980s shifted the balance, and Japan overtook the U.S. position during those time periods. A key implication of dominance effects is that MNEs from dominant countries can influence the adoption of more standardized HR systems in subsidiaries (Edwards et al., 2013).

International Integration

International integration is focused on generating inter-unit linkages across borders (Edwards & Ferner, 2002). Advances in telecommunications and transportation, combined with the reduction in international barriers to trade, enable MNEs to leverage the synergistic benefits of integration of operations across national borders. However, sector (Harzing & Sorge, 2003) and nationality (Edwards et al., 2020) can have significant impacts on international integration in MNEs. We can point to two key means of integration, namely, segmentation of operations across countries and standardization across countries. The segmentation of operations, also termed *vertical integration* (Shenkar & Luo, 2004), prioritizes exploiting location advantages offered by various host locations in producing parts of a final product in various locales. The apparel or footwear industries provide key examples. Here, the production advantages of low-cost locations such as Bangladesh are reflected in production being concentrated in those locales. Design and marketing expertise are concentrated in higher-cost locales, and hence they tend to locate there.

Alternatively, international integration may be driven by standardization across different countries. This process is often facilitated by the development and production of homogeneous products or services. Standardization also facilitates MNE headquarters in coercive comparisons by generating internal competition between sites or offices and thus pressuring management and worker representatives to adopt practices favored by headquarters due to fears over production location and investment decisions (Edwards et al., 1999).

Having considered the broader strategic context of IHRM, we now turn briefly to the key question of staffing in the context of the MNE.

From IHRM to Global Talent Management

In a 50-year content analysis and review of published research in the field of IHRM, and more recently, talent management, Cascio and Boudreau (2016) noted that since the 1970s there has been prominent recognition that the use of expatriates was significant. Since the 1970s, writers have viewed parent-country national (PCN) expatriates as key to exporting home country practices or redefining them to fit new cultures, as a key issue for the definition of performance for expatriates, and thus the talent management and human resource practices supporting them. Yet, it was not until the mid-1990s that such research became widespread, and it has remained a focus well into the twenty-first century.

Notwithstanding the key focus on PCN expatriates, the literature has long since recognized a number of core roles played by expatriates in the MNE. Edstrom and Gailbraith's (1977) seminal study identifies three key drivers of expatriation. First, expatriates may fill positions when MNEs perceive that there is an insufficient supply of suitably qualified host-country nationals (HCNs) in the host country. Second, expatriation is a core means of management development for high-potential managers. A third driver of expatriation is knowledge-transfer processes within MNEs. Such roles often focus on efforts to modify and sustain organizational structure and decision processes. In reality the literature for many decades positioned the decision to use an expatriate as binary: either send a PCN expatriate or employ an HCN or local manager. However, we increasingly recognize the potential value of third-country nationals (TCNs), individuals who are a national of neither the home nor host country as a viable staffing option.

Indeed, the landscape of global staffing is now recognized as far more complex than that portrayed in earlier research. A 2007 article in the *Journal of World Business* by Collings, Scullion, and Morley called attention to the emergence of a portfolio of alternatives to the traditional international assignment. These alternatives include short-term assignments, commuter assignments, international business travel, and virtual assignments. Collings et al. (2007) argued that a standardized approach to international assignments is untenable and that it is essential to develop HR policies and procedures that reflect differences in the various forms of emerging alternative international assignments and their associated complexities. There is a need for greater attention, not simply to managing expatriates but to creating an optimal mix of expatriates, home-country nationals, third-country nationals, and the talent–management systems to enable and support such a mix.

This theoretical orientation led to the rise of "talent management" and to a precipitous drop in published articles about expatriates in leading international business journals after 2009 (Cascio & Boudreau, 2016). Indeed, the *Journal of World Business* alone published 21 articles on talent management from 2010 to 2014, including two special issues (Al Ariss et al., 2014; Scullion et al., 2010). The range of topics that have been explored in the TM literature include, *inter alia*, identifying the talent required for international business operations (Tarique & Schuler, 2010); managing top-management talent (Joyce & Slocum, 2012); linking the strategic management of business operations and TM practices (Collings et al., 2019); linking global mobility and global TM (Collings, 2014) and understanding TM in the context of organizational linkage mechanisms, such as mergers and acquisitions (Cascio & Boudreau, 2016).

More broadly, these trends reflect an expanded emphasis in the global HRM literature and a greater focus on strategic international HRM. More recently, the COVID-19 crisis placed expatriation squarely in the spotlight and raised significant questions for the future of global mobility (Collings & Sheeran, 2020; Jooss et al., 2020). By one estimate, two out of three firms permitted the return of expatriate employees to their home countries during the pandemic, and only 44% of respondents predicted returning to the same volume of moves in the future (PWC, 2020). As we outline next, there are significant challenges to global mobility that raise important questions for future study of this important area.

Controversies in Global HRM Research

The Backlash against Globalization

Open borders have allowed new ideas and technology to flow freely around the globe, accelerating productivity growth and allowing companies to be more competitive than they have been in decades. Yet there is a growing fear that globalization benefits big companies instead of average citizens, as stagnating wages and growing job insecurity in developed countries create rising disenchantment (Cascio, 2019). In theory, less-developed countries win from globalization because they get jobs making low-cost products for rich countries. Rich countries win because, in addition to being able to buy inexpensive imports, they also can sell more sophisticated products, like financial services, to emerging economies (Autor et al., 2016). The problem, according to many experts, is that workers in the West are not equipped for today's pace of change, in which jobs come and go and skills can quickly become redundant (Brynjolfsson & McAfee, 2014; McKinsey Global Institute, 2016).

The coronavirus pandemic highlighted the downsides of extensive international integration. Large multinationals suddenly realized the risks of relying on complex global supply chains. At the same time, governments of all stripes rushed to impose travel bans, additional visa requirements, and export restrictions, thereby escalating nationalism and protectionism. The pandemic is likely to have a lasting impact, although the exact extent is currently unknown. It may deal a blow to fragmented international supply chains, reduce the hypermobility of global business travelers, and encourage nationalists who favor greater protectionism and immigration controls (Legrain, 2020; Schlesinger, 2020).

Localization requirements are also part of the backlash against globalization. Since 2008, governments have imposed nearly 350 regulations worldwide requiring local sourcing, hiring, or operations. Government-backed development banks require projects to buy or build domestically in exchange for inexpensive financing (Mann & Spegele, 2017). As then EU trade commissioner, Phil Hogan, noted, "If more countries pursue the track of self-sufficiency, it will increase competition for scarce resources, drive up prices, and deepen international hostilities" (Schlesinger, 2020, p. A10).

Convergence versus Divergence of HRM Practices

A natural extension of the discussion on the standardization of HR practices is the extent to which management practices are converging worldwide. Viewed through a neo-institutional lens, the convergence of management practices was considered inevitable as advances in technology and communications have created a less differentiated world order. Differences in talent–management practices, which were historically perpetuated by the geographic isolation of businesses, were superseded by the logic of technology (Kidger, 1991). This is reflected in the tendency of organizations to copy what is perceived as effective in an attempt to gain legitimacy or the support of external agencies within a society (Strauss & Hanson, 1997).

These are mimetic institutional pressures (DiMaggio & Powell, 1983; 1991; Scott, 2013). In order to ensure their survival, organizations are obliged to respond to rationalized and institutionalized expectations or norms emanating from their environments, and to adopt expected management practices and organizational structures (Meyer & Rowan, 1977). Conformity to institutional norms creates structural similarities, or isomorphism, across organizations. Organizations within the same population facing the same set of environmental constraints will tend to be isomorphic to one another and to their environment because they face similar conditions (Dacin, 1997; DiMaggio & Powell, 1983). Such mimetic isomorphism suggests a convergence in management practices.

MNEs are considered key drivers of the convergence process (Edwards et al., 2016). While there is evidence of some convergence of HR practices globally, undoubtedly differences remain too. Cascio and Collings's (2019) review of 50 years of research in six areas of IHRM (recruitment and selection, development and training, performance management, retention, compensation and rewards, and talent review) is instructive on this question. They concluded that while there is some evidence for convergence or standardization of IHRM practices, it would be wrong to conclude that there is a set of best practices that is likely to be effective regardless of organizational context. They argue that research on the convergence of IHRM practices rarely considers their effectiveness. Rather, authors often limit their discussion to the extent to which the practices look similar. This is a key limitation, for as Sumelius et al. (2014) found in the context of performance management, employees attached less value to it when it was highly standardized, as they perceived it to be less relevant to their work. Cascio and Collings (2019) point to a number of other examples of research that highlight the importance of local cultural norms in how HR practices are perceived in local markets. For example, research on compensation clearly points to the importance of understanding national cultural norms and societal values (Sun et al., 2010; Zhang et al., 2015) on perceptions of compensation policies.

Similarly, research on recruitment points to important differences in applicant reactions to selection practices that, in turn, affect motivation, anxiety, organizational attractiveness, intention to pursue a job, and ultimately accept a job offer (McCarthy et al., 2017). Their review also highlights the impact of national culture on recruitment practices more broadly. For example, countries that score higher in uncertainty avoidance tend to use more test types and to use them more extensively in selection, to conduct more interviews, and to audit them to a greater degree (Ryan et al., 1999). Relatedly, research on perceptions of training and development practices emphasizes the importance of national culture on individual preferences for how they engage in training (empowered versus limited) and preferences for continuous learning (Luo, 2007).

Cascio and Collings (2019) question whether it is reasonable to ask whether similar practices truly represent home-country effects or whether they simply reflect Anglo-Saxon hegemony in global talent management (GTM) practice. For example, Mellahi et al.'s (2016) research on Brazilian MNEs highlights the key role of global consultancy firms in influencing performance management practices, reflective of U.S. norms in those firms. They found that rather than being influenced by their Brazilian roots, Brazilian MNEs were more concerned about legitimizing their status as global firms by replicating what they considered global best practices with regard to performance management. This strongly influenced their engagement with global consultancy firms and the adoption of global "best practices." Indeed, one recent analysis points to a hybrid effect, where HR practices in foreign-owned MNE subsidiaries are different from indigenous firms, but they also need to fit in locally, reflecting some localization effects and continued divergence (Farndale et al., 2017). They argue that in deciding which approach to pursue in different locations, MNEs weigh the potential challenges they are likely to face in implementing standardized HR approaches. This involves evaluating the degree to which the institutional constraints in the host would impact particular HRM practices, and recognizing the potential for variation across the parent and host locations. They conclude that such analyses facilitate strategy implementation, with the potential for more efficient operations and higher returns (Farndale et al., 2017).

This is certainly an area where the opportunity for future research abounds.

Evolving Structures in MNEs

The internal structure of an MNE significantly affects how MNEs organize and manage HR activities; the configuration of those activities and practices is key to MNE performance (Collings et al., 2019; Lazarova et al., 2017). Indeed, much of our understanding of the management of HRM in MNEs is based on the concept of a centralized hierarchical structure where power and control are concentrated at the MNE HQ. However, there is increasing use of more decentralized network structures in MNEs reflected in more autonomous foreign subsidiary units (Andersson et al., 2007). MNEs are evolving from traditional dyadic hierarchical structures to more complex, networked architectures with associated multilevel intra- and interorganizational linkages. This is reflected in increasingly fragmented MNE structures and the greater influence of intermediary HQ entities, such as divisional and regional HQs (Nell et al., 2017).

The emergence of these more network-based MNE structures leads to a number of tensions. At a fundamental level, there is a constant tension between corporate HQ's assertion of control over foreign subsidiaries, at a time when subsidiaries are pushing for greater levels of autonomy and influence (Conroy et al., 2019). Clearly, the level of autonomy granted by the HQ to subsidiaries impacts their freedom to make independent decisions regarding HR policies and practices (Lazarova et al., 2017). At the same time, corporate HQ can draw on a number of different mechanisms, such as formal control and social capital, in influencing the transfer of these practices (Ahlvik & Bjorkman, 2015). The implementation of standardized HR practices in the subsidiary is thus influenced by the perceived level of internal integration or fit of that practice with other subsidiary HR practices or national cultural and institutional norms (Bjorkman et al., 2011). However, a major limitation of current research in this area is that it continues to frame MNE architecture as a dyadic relationship between the corporate HQ in the home country (global) and foreign subsidiaries located in diverse host countries (local) (Collings & Conroy, 2020). To address that issue, Minbaeva and DeCieri (2015) argued for an "integrative strategy process" in navigating the global-regional-local HR model. Integrative processes, such as global HR policy bodies, or integrated global HR architectures, are deployed to manage the trade-offs between centralized hierarchies and decentralized networks. They provide managers across hierarchical levels with the platform they need to create and develop independent initiatives that are aligned to overarching corporate strategy. The development of an HR architecture to formally collect insights about these new, decentralized initiatives that might, in turn, inspire strategy discussions at the top is an important part of the process. The establishment of such processes should facilitate reverse knowledge transfer in gathering dispersed individual experiences and provide corporate leaders with the opportunity to develop new insights from autonomous initiatives. However, the tension of allowing enough scope for subsidiary managers to adapt top-down directives in ways that are responsive to local idiosyncrasies remains a key challenge (Minbaeva & De Cieri, 2015). This is another significant opportunity to explore the impact of the evolving governance of MNEs for IHRM.

We now turn to two controversies related to global mobility and staffing.

Job Aid for Spouses of Overseas Executives

Spouses accompany 73% of expatriates on long-term assignment, and 47% take their children with them (Brookfield Global Relocation Services, 2016). In many parts of the world, however, spouses of expatriates face difficult obstacles to finding jobs. While job aid for the so-called trailing spouse is a popular benefit for domestic transfers, it is less common for international transferees. Thus, interviews with 100 trailing spouses indicated that their greatest needs were for networking information to assist in their job search and for a go-to person for practical settling-in assistance (KPMG International, 2019; Mohn, 2011).

To fill their international needs, more firms are turning to short-term assignments (3 to 12 months) or "commuter assignments," in which spouses may remain at home or move to adjoining countries or regions (Collings et al., 2007). Another option is intercompany networking in which one multinational employer (MNE) attempts to place an expatriate's spouse in a suitable job with another MNE in the same city or country. Sometimes this takes the form of a reciprocal arrangement, such as "You find my expatriate's spouse a job and work visa and I will do the same for you" (Dowling et al., 2017).

Despite company efforts, it is often very difficult to place spouses abroad. Where there are language barriers or barriers due to labor laws, tradition, or underemployment, it can be almost impossible. Moreover, an international assignment can slow a spouse's professional progress and sometimes stir resentment. Perhaps this is why only 16% of spouses were employed both before the overseas assignment and also during it (Brookfield Global Relocation Services, 2016). Because 91% of married female expatriates (and 50% of married male expatriates) are in dual-career marriages, it is not surprising that spousal income loss is a key factor that determines an executive's decision to accept or reject an overseas position (Onley, 2014).

Low Retention Rates among Repatriates

Consider some sobering statistics about repatriation (Brookfield Global Relocation Services, 2016; Gerhart & Newman, 2020; KPMG International, 2019):

- Only 12% of companies have a strategy for advance, proactive repatriation planning.
- Fifty percent of companies have first discussions about repatriation within 6 months of assignment completion. Only 8% discuss repatriation before the assignment starts.
- Sixty percent rely on informal networking or the originating department to identify positions for repatriates.
- In terms of the impact on employees' careers, 43% of companies say repatriates are more likely to be future leaders, and 23% report they will receive more rapid or frequent promotions.
- Seventy-seven percent of repatriates have less disposable income when they return home.

The results are unmet expectations, feelings of being undervalued, and concerns about one's future career. Furthermore, having become accustomed to foreign ways, upon reentry expatriates often find home-country customs strange and, at the extreme, annoying. Such *reverse culture shock* may be more challenging than the culture shock experienced when going overseas (Gregersen, 1992; Schumpeter, 2015). Not surprisingly, therefore, turnover among repatriates may be 30% or more within the first year back in their home countries, and 50% within 2 years, compared with about 13% for all turnover (Kraimer et al., 2012; Lazarova, 2015). These figures appear stubbornly consistent over time and across countries. Here are three actions companies can take: (1) have champions back home who look after the interests of expatriates, (2) pay as much attention to "reboarding" repatriates as they do to "onboarding" new employees, and (3) find ways to help repatriates use what they have learned abroad (Schumpeter, 2015).

Our next section addresses some important boundary conditions that affect the actual implementation of international HR practices. These include cultural norms, as well as the effects of tight versus loose cultures and individualistic versus collectivistic cultures on HR practices.

Boundary Conditions on IHRM Practices

Cultural Norms

Culture refers to characteristic ways of doing things and behaving that people in a given country or region have developed over time (Cascio, 2019). It determines the uniqueness of a human group in the same way that personality determines the uniqueness of an individual (Ronen & Shenkar, 2017). Culture helps people to make sense of their part of the world and provides them with an identity. Cross-cultural variability can be captured at the state, ethnic/racial, religious, or socioeconomic levels (Gelfand et al., 2017). Rooted in fundamental values and beliefs, here are 10 dimensions of culture that illustrate the enormous variation and diversity in human behavior around the world (Abramson & Moran, 2018).

• Sense of self and space	• Relationships.
• Dress and appearance	• Values and norms
• Food and eating habits	• Beliefs and attitudes
• Communication and language	• Work motivation and practices
• Time and time consciousness	• Mental processes and learning

These are by no means the only ways to look at culture. Our next sections present two other useful perspectives: tight versus loose cultures and individualistic versus collectivistic cultures.

Tight Versus Loose Cultures

A different approach to classifying cultures is in terms of the strength of ***social norms***—socially agreed-upon standards of behavior that form the building blocks of social order (Gelfand, 2018). In ***tight cultures***, such norms are clear and pervasive, and they often entail strong punishments for people who don't follow them. In ***loose cultures***, social norms are less clear and fewer in number; people follow them less often, and they are punished less for deviance. Tightness–looseness is a continuum, with extreme cases at either end and varying degrees in between. The tightest cultures are Pakistan, Malaysia, India, Singapore, South Korea, Norway, Turkey, Japan, and China. The loosest are Spain, the United States, Australia, New Zealand, Greece, Venezuela, Brazil, the Netherlands, and Israel. These countries do not share any obvious qualities in common, such as language, location, religion, or traditions. Yet they do share some common features.

Tight societies focus on social order and self-regulation. Loose societies emphasize tolerance, creativity, and openness to change. There is no direct relationship between nations' scores on tightness–looseness and their economic development. This approach also differs from previous ways that scholars have compared cultures, such as whether they are collectivist or individualist. In short, the tightness–looseness lens is a new way of viewing cultures on the global map (Gelfand, 2018). It raises a tantalizing question, namely, to what extent is there convergence or standardization of specific HR or talent management practices in tight versus loose cultures? The answer is important for MNEs as they seek to develop global talent-management strategies.

Individualistic Versus Collectivistic Cultures

Triandis (1998) is best known for his lifelong work on individualism versus collectivism. He notes that vertical cultures accept hierarchy as a given, whereas horizontal cultures accept equality as a given. Individualistic cultures emerge in societies that are complex (many subgroups with different attitudes and beliefs) and loose (relatively few rules and norms about what is correct behavior in different types of situations). Collectivism emerges in societies that are simple (individuals agree on beliefs and attitudes) and tight (there are many rules and norms about what is correct behavior in different types of situations).

Triandis argues that these shared patterns of attitudes, beliefs, norms, and values (which he calls syndromes) constitute the parameters of any general theory about the way culture influences people. Crossing the cultural syndromes of individualism and collectivism with the cultural syndromes of vertical and horizontal relationships yields a typology of four kinds of cultures. According to Triandis, the following four may be the universal dimensions of these constructs:

1. **Definition of the self**—autonomous and independent from groups (individualists) versus interdependent with others (collectivists).
2. **Structure of goals**—priority given to personal goals (individualists) versus priority given to ingroup goals (collectivists).
3. **Emphasis on norms versus attitudes**—attitudes, personal needs, perceived rights, and contracts as determinants of social behavior (individualists) versus norms, duties, and obligations as determinants of social behavior (collectivists).
4. **Emphasis on relatedness versus rationality**—collectivists emphasize relatedness (giving priority to relationships and taking into account the needs of others), whereas individualists emphasize rationality (carefully computing the costs and benefits of relationships).

There are many implications and patterns of variation of these important differences with respect to organizational issues and globalization (Cascio & Aguinis, 2019). Two of these patterns are goal-setting and reward systems (individual versus team- or organization-wide) and communications (gestures, eye contact, and body language in high-context cultures versus precision with words in low-context cultures). Another is performance feedback, where the characteristics of the culture (vertical/horizontal or individual/collectivist) interact with the objectives, style, frequency, and inherent assumptions of the performance–feedback process (Cascio, 2012; Varma et al., 2015; Varela & Premaux, 2008). Finally, there are implications for training and development. These include, for example, language training for expatriates, along with training to avoid the culture shock that results from repeated disorientation experienced by individuals in a foreign land whose customs and culture differ from one's own (Cascio, 1998; Abramson & Moran, 2018). In short, culture affects the ways we think, feel, and act.

These boundary conditions on the implementation of HR practices in international contexts suggest three important implications (Cascio, 2019). (1) Do not export home country bias. HR practices that work well in the home country might be totally out of step in another country. Managers who bear responsibility for international operations need to understand the cultural differences inherent in the management systems of the countries in which their firms do business. (2) Think in global terms. To survive and grow, the wise allocation of physical and human resources across international boundaries is essential. (3) Recognize that no country has all the answers. Effective multinational managers must not only think in global terms but also be able to synthesize the best management approaches to deal with complex problems.

Research on the Effects of Culture on MNEs and Global HRM

Culture has an enormous impact on MNEs as well as on global HRM practices. Indeed, managing cultural differences across geographically dispersed locations is one of the central challenges for international business research and practice (Caprar et al., 2015). For MNEs, challenges arise from differences in cultural values between managers with different national backgrounds and from the strength of location-specific cultural norms within host countries (Leung et al., 2005). Here is just a brief sampling of some topics that researchers have examined.

Consider diversity across functions in top management teams (TMT). Milliken and Martins (1996) described it as a double-edged sword that has positive implications in some contexts and negative ones in others. Gil et al. (2019) sought to identify contextual factors that can explain the conditions under which TMT functional heterogeneity is advantageous or detrimental to firm performance and that can accelerate or hamper some of the beneficial aspects of TMT diversity. Based on a sample of TMTs from MNEs headquartered in 25 different countries, they found that increased functional diversity in highly individualistic national cultures is associated with decreased firm performance. Individualism is a social pattern that involves loosely linked individuals who perceive themselves as independent of groups; their own needs, preferences, rights, and contracts motivate them (Hofstede, 1980). Higher levels of MNE headquarters' national individualism appear to magnify the heterogeneity of the group and adversely affect firm performance. To counter these effects, highly heterogeneous management teams need to improve the quality and quantity of information exchange, collaborative behavior, and joint decision making.

Cultural distance, the magnitude of differences in sets of cultural values between countries (Kogut & Singh, 1988), is a second important contextual factor. In a study of 8,538 subsidiaries of Japanese MNEs in 28 countries, Shin et al. (2017) examined the effects of culture on the proportion of expatriate parent-country nationals in MNEs. Their analysis reveals that the relationship between cultural distance and the proportion of expatriate PCNs is convex. Below the inflection point, the relationship is negative; above the inflection point, it is significantly positive. Shin et al. (2017) also show that cultural distance alone does not account for all the effects of culture on the proportion of expatriate PCNs in foreign subsidiaries. Instead, the effects of local norms or countries' tightness–looseness moderate this relationship (Gelfand et al., 2011). Therefore, to facilitate expatriate adjustment, MNEs should consider offering scenario-based predeparture training that includes realistic social situations that incorporate expert opinions on the most appropriate behavior for each situation (Morris & Robie, 2001).

Cultural distance is an important, subtle phenomenon that affects a variety of important decisions and outcomes in MNEs. Thus, Tihanyi et al. (2005) examined the relationship of cultural distance to the choice of entry mode (acquisitions or greenfield investments vs. exporting or licensing), international diversification, and MNE performance. The results of their meta-analysis provided no evidence of a systematic, direct effect of cultural distance. However, moderator variables such as the type of measurement instrument used, MNE origin, industry type, country of investment, and sample time frame did explain the impact of cultural distance. This suggests that researchers should consider carefully alternative theoretical explanations and methodological choices when studying the effect of cultural distance on international strategies and MNE performance.

A third example of the effects of culture is on planning in MNEs. At a high level, planning includes analyzing competitors and industry dynamics, analyzing past performance, finding new markets, determining the means to achieve certain ends, and setting up controls against which to evaluate future performance. Brock et al. (2000) examined the effects of culture in the context of HQ–subsidiary relations, where subsidiaries may have varying degrees of autonomy in their choice of planning systems. MNE strategy adds another layer of complexity to this process, as MNEs may pursue global, multidomestic, or transnational strategies (Collings et al., 2019). Brock et al.'s theoretical model emphasizes that the number of different cultures that interact with the MNE, their cultural distance, and their relationship to each other will also have an influence. As one example, linguistic differences might not only help identify who gets to create corporate plans, but also how they are created and who ends up following them. Culture is just one of many factors that influence planning processes in MNEs. From a global HR perspective, however, it is important to ensure that subsidiary managers are informed and competent with respect to planning. Trying to do that through top-down pressures may be ineffective.

As a final example of the effects of culture on MNEs and global HRM, Zeng et al. (2013) examined the conditions under which an MNE's foreign direct investment (FDI) experience may actually harm the performance of subsequent subsidiaries. Using data from a sample of FDIs by South Korean MNEs between 1990 and 2006, they found that MNEs may draw incorrect inferences and learn incorrectly from their earlier expansions when new to a dissimilar culture because their learning abilities are limited by cultural differences. Those incorrect inferences by MNEs will misguide subsequent investments. By itself, therefore, FDI experience may not always be beneficial. However, that effect can be overcome if MNEs learn how to learn and accumulate host-culture experience. Expanding at a fast pace aggravates the detrimental effect of the host-culture experience. Therefore, while expanding into a variety of cultures helps an MNE to develop the skills of learning in foreign cultures, it must do so at a manageable pace in order to absorb each FDI expansion effectively. Table 25.1 offers five key theoretical and practical insights from our discussion so far.

New Research Directions

This is an exciting time in the field of global HRM, and in the sections below we identify some key directions that we believe researchers should focus on.

As we noted earlier, global talent management has become a key focus for management practice and academic research. While our understanding of GTM theory has advanced considerably over that time (see Collings et al., 2019), the empirical base that links theory to practice remains underdeveloped. Thus, a key focus for future study should be on empirically exploring the relationship between GTM and organizational performance. Studies should explore how national institutional and cultural contexts influence the impact of GTM on subsidiaries at national or regional levels. Specifically, as governance structures in MNEs continue to evolve, what are the effects of integrated HR architectures in subsidiaries located in tight (loose) and individual (collectivist) cultures? Are country-of-origin effects stronger (weaker) if HQ and subsidiaries represent tight (loose) cultures? Do tight or collectivist cultures show less tolerance for institutional pluralism? To what extent do these features of the institutional and cultural context affect subsidiary performance?

The answers to these questions will help to identify key boundary conditions on relationships with performance. Do those relationships vary by industry? It is also important to explore the differences between HQ's intended strategy when transferring GTM to subsidiaries and actual GTM implementation. Theoretically, the level of alignment between HQ intentions and a subsidiary's understanding and internalization of HQ practices has been proposed as a key variable in explaining the divergence between the two (Collings et al., 2019), but this issue merits empirical study.

Table 25.1 Five key theoretical and practical insights
Key Theoretical Insights
1. One way that MNEs compete with local firms in foreign markets is through leveraging ownership-specific advantages (Rugman, 1981). They do so by replicating in foreign subsidiaries employment practices that they perceive to be advantageous in the HQ organization. These may include HRM practices.
2. Neo-institutional theory predicts the convergence of management practices across the globe. In order to ensure their survival, organizations must respond to institutionalized expectations or norms emanating from their environments and to adopt expected management practices and organizational structures (Meyer & Rowan, 1977; Scott, 2013). Conformity to institutional norms creates structural similarities, or isomorphism, across organizations. Such mimetic isomorphism suggests a convergence in management practices (Dacin, 1997; DiMaggio & Powell, 1983). However, the empirical evidence of such convergence is limited.
3. Conflicting institutional demands in the HQ and subsidiary contexts challenge the implementation of global HR policies and practices in local subsidiaries. Theoretically, the institutional duality deriving from contradictory logics in the home and host country are key sources of tension (Kostova & Roth, 2002).
4. Culture is a key variable that affects how leaders and employees implement and interpret global HRM policies and practices. Our review highlighted the signal impact that tight versus loose cultures (Gelfand, 2018) and individualistic versus collectivistic cultures (Triandis, 1998) have on the enactment of HRM policies and practices.
5. In theory, less-developed countries win from globalization because they get jobs making low-cost products for rich countries. Rich countries win because, in addition to being able to buy inexpensive imports, they also can sell more sophisticated products to emerging economies (Autor et al., 2016). However, factors such as growing nationalism, protectionism, the increasing pace of change, and the infirmities of global supply chains exposed by the global pandemic pose serious challenges to continued globalization.
Key Implications for Practice
1. Global HRM policies and practices cannot be developed in isolation and should be linked closely with organizational strategy. Consider carefully which elements of global HRM can be implemented in a standardized manner and which elements require local adaptation.
2. Managers should be cautious in generalizing research findings on IHRM. Much of our knowledge about core aspects of Global HRM policy and practice is based on single-country and mainly Western empirical samples.
3. Global mobility is exceptionally difficult to execute effectively. Extensive research has identified the challenges of repatriation, for example. Organizations need to develop consistent and aligned HR policies to support international assignees, as well as their families, during and after their international moves.
4. The COVID pandemic is likely to pose significant challenges to traditional approaches to global mobility. Organizational leaders should carefully consider what role global mobility plays in executing their strategy and whether some strategic objectives can be achieved virtually or with local employees.
5. Culture affects the ways we think, feel, and act. It is likely to have major effects on the ways that HR processes such as staffing, communications, work motivation, training, performance management, reward systems, and conflict resolution are implemented in practice.

The failure to develop truly global talent pools that reflect the international footprints of MNEs has been identified as a failure of global talent management (Mellahi & Collings, 2010). As just one indicator of the lack of diversity, key positions in executive teams are often largely filled by PCNs. Insights from bounded rationality and agency theories help to frame the challenges of developing globally diverse talent pools. Research that identifies how MNEs can transcend these challenges and how such diversity contributes to key performance metrics at subsidiary and broader MNE levels would be welcome. Related research (Caligiuri et al., 2020; Mellahi & Collings, 2010) highlights the role of social and geographical distances in hindering the development and progression of subsidiary employees to senior corporate roles. In one empirical study, Makela et al. (2010) identify a two-stage decision process in the selection of employees to corporate talent pools—the first step in progressing through the corporate hierarchy. In step one, experience-based performance evaluations are used as inputs into step two, mainly cognition-based managerial decision-making. This means that talent-pool inclusion is not solely determined by performance evaluation, but by a more complex decision-making process. They identify three key factors that influence these decisions: (1) cultural and institutional distance between the employee under consideration and the decision makers; (2) homophily between the individual and the decision makers; and (3) the network position of the person in question. Research that demonstrates the value of social networks among host- and third-country nationals who do make it to the ranks of corporate elites and the role that such networks played in their careers would be valuable.

Indeed, the role of networks is a theme that is considered in the literature on emerging structures in MNEs. Extant research identifies the role of subsidiary actors as boundary spanners—high-level intermediaries who balance global and local power and tensions (Conroy et al., 2019). Research at the micro level could provide some very useful insights into the skills and capabilities required by these boundary spanners to navigate emerging HQ–subsidiary relationships. At a macro level, there is considerable potential for research to further illuminate the role of the HR function in managing these emerging MNE structures. In particular, how MNEs balance autonomy and control in managing subsidiary units is a key question that researchers should address.

As with any consideration of global HRM, context is a key consideration. There is little doubt that the COVID-19 pandemic is likely to have a lasting impact on global HRM practice (Caligiuri et al., 2020; Lazarova et al., 2023). One area that is likely to be particularly impacted is global mobility. As noted above, 44% of respondents to one survey predicted that MNEs will return to the same volume of moves in the future (PWC, 2020). This prediction seems optimistic, at least in the short-to-medium term, as the COVID pandemic is still unfolding at the time of writing. There is little doubt that MNEs will reevaluate the assumptions underpinning their global staffing decisions and their assumptions around the supports required for individuals in these roles. Key questions include: what work can be done as effectively remotely versus work that requires co-location and travel? What competencies will global workers require to be effective in the increasingly uncertain global work environment? How can organizations reimagine global leadership development to account for the increasing challenges around global mobility? What kinds of support mechanisms are most effective in enabling the global workforce in a post-COVID world?

Finally, the COVID pandemic has also resulted in a step-change in the extent and reach of virtual work arrangements. In the global context, there is limited understanding of the operation and effectiveness of global teams (Santistevan & Josserand, 2019). Yet during the COVID-19 pandemic, virtual work and virtual team structures, including global virtual teams, became the dominant means of operating and collaborating in many organizations. This large-scale deployment of virtual work arrangements offers considerable opportunity for future study. For example, do the principles of static and bounded conceptualizations of global work, which reflected relatively fixed membership and clear team boundaries, apply in a more dynamic context where virtual collaboration is the norm? What are the implications of the lack of supports that would have been available through physical connection and co-location when virtual interaction becomes the sole means of connection and collaboration?

Summary and Conclusions

This chapter focuses on international human resource management and its role in multinational enterprises. We began with a brief history of international business and IHRM, emphasizing what makes IHRM different from domestic HRM. We then considered the importance of competitive strategy—the decisions, process, and choices firms make in deciding how to compete—emphasizing the crucial role of business strategy in formulating an HR strategy. This includes the critical question of how MNEs balance standardization and localization of HR policies and practices in their global operations. More specifically, we examined four important influences that affect the transfer of employment practices across borders. These include country-of-origin effects, host-country effects, the relative economic dominance of each country, and international integration. The chapter then highlighted five controversies in global HRM research: the backlash against globalization, convergence versus divergence of HR practices, evolving structures in MNEs, job aid for spouses of overseas executives, and low retention rates among repatriates. At the same time, we also identified key boundary conditions that shape the implementation of HR practices: cultural norms, the effects of tight versus loose cultures and individualistic versus collectivistic cultures, along with the practical implications of these influences. We then cited examples of research on the effects of culture on MNEs and global HR practices, and we concluded the chapter by identifying five theoretical principles and five practical implications (see Table 25.1), as well as new research directions in major areas of IHRM.

References

Abramson, N. R., & Moran, R. T. (2018). *Managing cultural differences: Global leadership for the 21st century* (10th ed.). New York: Routledge.

Ahlvik, C., & Björkman, I. (2015). Towards explaining subsidiary implementation, integration, and internalization of MNC headquarters HRM practices. *International Business Review, 24*(3), 497–505.

Al Ariss, A., Cascio, W. F., & Paauwe, J. (2014). Talent management: Current theories and future research directions. *Journal of World Business, 49*(2), 173–179.

Almond, P. (2011). Re-visiting "country of origin" effects on HRM in multinational corporations. *Human Resource Management Journal, 21*(3), 258–271.

Almond, P. & Ferner, A. (Eds.). (2006). *American multinationals in Europe*. Oxford: Oxford University Press.

Andersson, U., Forsgren, M., & Holm, U. (2007). *Balancing subsidiary influence in the federative MNC: A business network view. Journal of International Business Studies, 38*(5), 802–818.

Autor, D. H., Dorn, D., & Hanson, G. H. (2016). The China shock: Learning from labor-market adjustment to large changes in trade. *Annual Review of Economics, 8*, 205–240.

Bartlett, C., & Ghoshal, S. (1998). *Managing across borders: The transnational solution*. Boston: HBS Press.

Björkman, I., Ehrnrooth, M., Smale, A., & John, S. (2011). The determinants of line management internalisation of HRM practices in MNC subsidiaries. *The International Journal of Human Resource Management, 22*(8), 1654–1671.

Bjorkman, I., & Lervik, J. E. (2007). Transferring HR practices within multinational corporations. *Human Resource Management Journal. 17*(4), 320–335.

Boccagni, E. (2020). What to consider when repatriating during the COVID-19 pandemic. https://www.thehrdirector.com/features/relocation/should-you-repatriate-during-the-covid-19-pandemic

Brock, D. M., Barry, D., & Thomas, D. C. (2000). "Your forward is our reverse, your right, our wrong": Rethinking multinational planning processes in light of national culture. *International Business Review, 9*(6), 687–701.

Brookfield GRS. (2016). *2016 global mobility trend survey*. Retrieved from https://www.bgrs.com/insights-articles/2016-global-mobility-trends-survey/ on July 4, 2017.

Brynjolfsson, E., & McAfee, D. (2014). *The second machine age: Work, progress, and prosperity in a time of brilliant technologies*. New York: W. W. Norton.

Caligiuri, P., De Cieri, H., Minbaeva, D., Verbeke, A., & Zimmermann, A. (2020). International HRM insights for navigating the COVID-19 pandemic: Implications for future research and practice. *Journal of International Business Studies, 51*, 697–713.

Caprar, D. V., Devinney, T. M., Kirkman, B. L., & Caligiuri, P. (2015). Conceptualizing and measuring culture in international business and management: From challenges to potential solutions. *Journal of International Business Studies, 46*, 1011–1027.

Cascio, W. F. (1998). The theory of vertical and horizontal individualism and collectivism: Implications for international human resource management. *Advances in International Comparative Management, 12*, 37–44.

Cascio, W. F. (2012). Global performance management systems. In I. Bjorkman, G. Stahl, & S. Morris (Eds.), *Handbook of research in international human resource management* (2nd ed., pp. 183–204). London: Edward Elgar Ltd.

Cascio, W. F. (2019). *Managing human resources: Productivity, quality of work life, profits* (11'h ed.). New York: McGraw-Hill.

Cascio, W. F., & Aguinis, H. (2019). *Applied psychology in talent management* (8th ed.). Thousand Oaks, CA: SAGE.

Cascio, W. F., & Boudreau, J. W. (2012). *Short introduction to strategic human resource management*. Cambridge: Cambridge University Press.

Cascio, W. F., & Boudreau, J. W. (2016). The search for global competence: From international HR to talent management. *Journal of World Business, 51*(1), 103–114.

Cascio, W. F., & Collings, D. G. (2019). Fifty years of research in international HRM and global talent management: How research is shaping practice. Paper presented in W. Cascio (Chair), Talent management. Symposium at the Academy of Management, 3rd HR Division International Conference, Dublin, January 2019.

Chipman, R. (2016, June 16). The real cost of expatriate assignment failure. *FIDI*. www.fidi.org/blog/real-cost-expatriate-assignment-failure

Collings, D. G. (2014). Integrating global mobility and global talent management: Exploring the challenges and strategic opportunities. *Journal of World Business, 49*(2), 253–261.

Collings, D. G., & Conroy, K. M. (2020). International HRM. In A. Wilkinson, N., Bacon, S. Snell, & D. Lepak (Eds.), *The Sage handbook of human resource management* (pp. 82–98). London: SAGE.

Collings, D. G., Mellahi, K., & Cascio, W. F. (2019). Global talent management and performance in multinational enterprises: A multilevel perspective. *Journal of Management, 45*(2), 540–566.

Collings, D. G., Scullion, H., & Morley, M. J. (2007). Changing patterns of global staffing in the multinational enterprise: Challenges to the conventional expatriate assignment and emerging alternatives. *Journal of World Business, 42*(2), 198–213.

Collings, D. G., & Sheeran, R. (2020). Global mobility in a post-Covid world. *Irish Journal of Management, 39*(2), 77–84.

Conroy, K. M., Collings, D. G., & Fahy, J. (2019). Sowing the seeds of subsidiary influence: Social navigating and political maneuvering of subsidiary actors. *Global Strategy Journal, 9*(4), 502–526.

Dacin, T. M. (1997). Isomorphism in context: The power and prescription of institutional norms. *Academy of Management Journal, 40*, 46–81.

DiMaggio, P., & Powell, W. (1983). The iron cage revisited: Institutional isomorphism and collective rationality in organizational fields. *American Sociological Review, 48*, 147–160.

DiMaggio, P. J., & Powell, W. W. (1991). Introduction. In W. W. Powell & P. J. DiMaggio (Eds.), *The new institutionalism in organizational analysis* (pp. 1–38). Chicago: University of Chicago Press.

Doellgast, V., & Marsden, D. (2019). Institutions as constraints and resources: Explaining cross-national divergence in performance management. *Human Resource Management Journal, 29*(2), 199–216. https://doi.org/10.1111/1748-8583.12214

Dowling, P. J., Festing, M., & Engle, A. D., Sr. (2017). *International human resource management* (7th ed.). Boston: Cengage Learning.

Edström, A., & Galbraith, J. R. (1977). Transfer of managers as a coordination and control strategy in multinational organizations. *Administrative Science Quarterly, 22*(2), 248–263.

Edwards, T., Colling, T., & Ferner, A. (2007). Conceptual approaches to the transfer of employment practices in multinational companies: An integrated approach. *Human Resource Management Journal, 17*(3). 201–217.

Edwards, T., & Ferner, A. (2002). The renewed "American challenge": A review of employment practices in U.S. multinationals, *Industrial Relations Journal, 33*, 94–111.

Edwards, T., Marginson, P., & Ferner, A. (2013). Multinational companies in cross-national context: Integration, differentiation, and the interactions between MNCS and nation states: Introduction to a special issue of the *ILR Review*. *ILR Review, 66*(3), 547–587.

Edwards, T., Rees, C., & Coller, X. (1999). Structure, politics and the diffusion of employment practices in multinationals. *European Journal of Industrial Relations, 5*(3), 286–306.

Edwards, T., Sánchez-Mangas, R., Jalette, P., Lavelle, J., & Minbaeva, D. (2016). Global standardization or national differentiation of HRM practices in multinational companies? A comparison of multinationals in five countries. *Journal of International Business Studies, 47*(8), 997–1021.

Edwards, T., Tregaskis, O., Collings, D., Jalette, P., & Susaeta, L. (2013). Control over employment practice in multinationals: Subsidiary functions, corporate structures, and national systems. *ILR Review, 66*(3), 670–695.

Edwards, T., Tregaskis, O., & McDonnell, A. (2020). Towards an understanding of configurational and national influences on international integration in the HR function in MNCs. *The International Journal of Human Resource Management, 33*(7), 1463–1488. doi: 10.1080/09585192.2020.1771399

Farndale, E., Brewster, C., Ligthart, P., & Poutsma, E. (2017). The effects of market economy type and foreign MNE subsidiaries on the convergence and divergence of HRM. *Journal of International Business Studies, 48*(9), 1065–1086.

Ferner, A. (1997). Country-of-origin effects and human resource management in multinational companies, *Human Resource Management Journal, 7*(1), 19–36.

Ferner, A., Almond, P., & Collings, T. (2005). Institutional theory and the cross-national transfer of employment policy: The case of "workforce diversity" in U.S. multinationals. *Journal of International Business Studies, 36*(3), 304–321.

Ferner, A., Bélanger, J., Tregaskis, O., Morley, M., & Quintanilla, J. (2013). US multinationals and the control of subsidiary employment policies. *ILR Review, 66*(3), 645–669.

Ferner, A., & Quintanilla, J. (1998). Multinationals, national business systems and HRM: the enduring influence of national identity or a process of "Anglo-Saxonization." *International Journal of Human Resource Management, 9*(4), 710–731.

Free Exchange. (2016, February 6). Trade in the balance. *The Economist*, p. 69.

Friedman, T. L. (2016). *Thank you for being late: An optimist's guide to thriving in the age of accelerations.* New York: Farrar, Straus & Giroux.

Gelfand, M. J., et al. (2011). Differences between tight and loose cultures: A 33-nation study. *Science, 332*, 1100–1104.

Gelfand, M. J. (2018). *Rule makers, rule breakers: How tight and loose cultures wire our world.* New York: Scribner.

Gelfand, M. J., Aycan, Z., Erez, M., & Leung, K. (2017). Cross-cultural industrial organizational psychology and organizational behavior: A hundred-year journey. *Journal of Applied Psychology, 102*, 514–529.

Gerhart, B., & Newman, J. M. (2020). *Compensation* (13th ed.). New York: McGraw-Hill.

Gil, A., Brouthers, L. E., & Keig, D. L. (2019). Top management team diversity, individualism–collectivism, and MNE performance. *International Journal of Cross-Cultural Management, 19*(3), 273–290.

Gooderham, P. N., Nordhaug, O., & Ringdal, K. (1999). Institutional and rational determinants of organizational practices: Human resource management in European firms. *Administrative Science Quarterly, 44*(3), 507–531.

Gregersen, E. (2020). Ford Motor Company. *Encyclopedia Britannica.* www.britannica.com/topic/Ford-Motor-Company.

Gregersen, H. B. (1992). Commitments to a parent company and a local work unit during repatriation. *Personnel Psychology 45*, 29–54.

Gunnnigle, P., Murphy, K. M., Cleveland, J., Heraty, N., & Morley, M. (2002). Localisation in human resource management: Comparing American and European multinational corporations, *Advances in International Management, 14*, 259–84.

Harzing, A. W., & Sorge, A. (2003). The relative impact of country of origin and universal contingencies on internationalization strategies and corporate control in multinational enterprises: Worldwide and European perspectives. *Organization Studies, 24*(2), 187–214.

Hayden, A., & Edwards, T. (2001). The erosion of the country of origin effect: A case study of a Swedish multinational company. *Relations Industrielles/Industrial Relations, 56*(1), 116–140.

Hofstede, G. (1980). *Culture's consequences: International differences in work-related values.* Thousand Oaks, CA: SAGE.

Jooss, S., McDonnell, A., & Conroy, K. (2020). Flexible global working arrangements: An integrative review and future research agenda. *Human Resource Management Review.* doi: 10.1016/j.hrmr.2020.100780

Joyce, W. F., & Slocum, J. W. (2012). Top management talent, strategic capabilities, and firm performance. *Organizational Dynamics, 41*(3), 183–193.

Khilji, S. E., & Schuler, R. S. (2017). Talent management in the global context. In D. G. Collings, K. Mellahi, & W. F. Cascio (Eds.), *The Oxford handbook of talent management* (pp. 399–419). Oxford: Oxford University Press.

Kidger, P. J. (1991). The emergence of international human resource management. *International Journal of Human Resource Management, 2*(2), 149–163.

Kogut, B., & Singh, H. (1988). The effect of national culture on the choice of entry mode. *Journal of International Business Studies, 19*, 411–432.

Kostova, T., & Roth, K. (2002). Adoption of an organizational practice by subsidiaries of multinational corporations: Institutional and relational effects. *Academy of Management Journal, 45*(1), 215–233.

Kostova, T., Roth, K., & Dacin, M. T. (2008). Institutional theory in the study of multinational corporations: A critique and new directions. *Academy of Management Review, 33*(4), 994–1006.

Kostova, T., & Zaheer, S. (1999). Organizational legitimacy under conditions of complexity: The case of the multinational enterprise. *Academy of Management Review, 24*(1), 64–81.

KPMG International. (2019). *2019 Global Assignment and Practices Survey.* https://assets.kpmg/content/dam/kpmg/xx/pdf/2019/10/2019-gapp-survey-report-web.pdf

Kraimer, M. L., Shaffer, M. A., Harrison, D. A., & Ren, H. (2012). No place like home? An identity strain perspective on repatriate turnover. *Academy of Management Journal 55*: 399–420.

Lazarova, M. (2015). Taking stock of repatriate research. In D. G. Collings, G. T. Wood, & P. M. Caligiuri (Eds.), *The Routledge companion to international human resource management* (pp. 378–398). New York: Routledge.

Lazarova, M., Caligiuri, P., Collings, D. G., & De Cieri, H. (2023). Global work in a rapidly changing world: Implications for MNEs and individuals. *Journal of World Business, 58*(1), 101365.

Lazarova, M., Peretz, H., & Fried, Y. (2017). Locals know best? Subsidiary HR autonomy and subsidiary performance. *Journal of World Business, 52*(1), 83–96.

Legrain, P. (2020, March 12). The coronavirus is killing globalization as we know it. *Foreign Policy*. https://foreignpolicy.com/2020/03/12/coronavirus-killing-globalization-nationalism-protectionism-trump/

Leung, K., Bhagat, R. S., Buchan, N. R., Erez, M., & Gibson, C. B. (2005). Culture and international business: Recent advances and their implications for future research. *Journal of International Business Studies, 36*, 357–378.

Lipsman, A. (2019, June 27). *Global e-commerce*. https://www.emarketer.com/content/global-ecommerce-2019

Luo, X. (2007). Continuous learning: The influence of national institutional logics on training attitudes. *Organization Science, 18*(2), 280–296.

Mäkelä, K., Björkman, I., & Ehrnrooth, M. (2010). How do MNCs establish their talent pools? Influences on individuals' likelihood of being labeled as talent. *Journal of World Business, 45*(2), 134–142.

McCarthy, J. M., Bauer, T. N., Truxillo, D. M., Anderson, N. R., Costa, A. C., & Ahmed, S. M. (2017). Applicant perspectives during selection: A review addressing "What's new?" "So what?" and "Where to next?" *Journal of Management, 43*, 1693–1725.

McKinsey Global Institute. (2016, February). *Digital globalization: The new era of global flows*. http://www.mckinsey.com/business-functions/digital-mckinsey/our-insights/digital-globalization-the-new-era-of-global-flows

Mann, T., & Spegele, A. B. (2017, June 30). Why GE builds more factories overseas. *The Wall Street Journal*, pp. A1, A9.

Mellahi, K., & Collings, D. G. (2010). The barriers to effective global talent management: The example of corporate elites in MNEs. *Journal of World Business, 45*(2), 143–149.

Mellahi, K., Frynas, J. G., & Collings, D. G. (2016). Performance management practices within emerging market multinational enterprises: The case of Brazilian multinationals. *The International Journal of Human Resource Management, 27*(8), 876–905.

Meyer, J. W., & Rowan, B. (1977). Institutionalized organizations: Formal structure as myth and ceremony. *American Journal of Sociology, 83*(2), 340–363.

Milliken, F. J., & Martins, L. L. (1996). Searching for common threads: Understanding the multiple effects of diversity in organizational groups. *Academy of Management Review 21*(2), 402–433.

Minbaeva, D. B., & DeCieri, H. (2015). Strategy and IHRM. In D. G. Collings, G. T. Wood, & P. M. Caligiuri (Eds.), *The Routledge handbook of international human resource management* (pp. 13–28). New York: Routledge.

Mohn, T. (2011, June 20). Plight of the expat spouse. *The New York Times*. www.nytimes.com/2011/06/21/business/21expats.html?pagewanted=all&_r=0.

Morris, M. A., & Robie, C. (2001). A meta-analysis of the effects of cross-cultural training on expatriate performance and adjustment. *International Journal of Training and Development, 5*, 112–125.

NBC News. (2019, April 13). These are the 35 countries with the U.S. State Department's new travel warning for kidnapping risk. www.nbcnewyork.com/news/local/us-travel-warning-kidnapping-risk-abroad-which-countries/1777585.

Nell, P. C., Kappen, P., & Laamanen, T. (2017). Reconceptualising hierarchies: The disaggregation and dispersion of headquarters in multinational corporations. *Journal of Management Studies, 54*(8), 1121–1143.

Onley, D. S. (2014, March 13). Avert assignment failure: Support spouses in overseas relocations. *SHRM Online*. https://www.shrm.org/resourcesandtools/hr-topics/global-hr/pages/spouses-overseas-relocations.aspx

Pache, A. C., & Santos, F. (2010). When worlds collide: The internal dynamics of organizational responses to conflicting institutional demands. *Academy of Management Review, 35*(3), 455–476.

PWC (2020). COVID-19: The implications for global mobility and the mobile workforce. https://www.pwc.com/gx/en/legal/assets/covid-19-pulse-survey-results.pdf on June 26, 2020.

Reiche, S. (2014, July 7). Latest research: How does terrorism influence expats? http://blog.iese.edu/expatriatus/2014/07/24/latest-research-how-does-terrorism-influence-expats/

Ronen, S., & Shenkar, O. (2017). *Navigating global business: A cultural compass.* Cambridge: Cambridge University Press.

Rosenzweig, P. M., & Nohria, N. (1994). Influences on human resource management practices in multinational corporations. *Journal of International Business Studies, 25*(2), 229–251.

Royle, T. (2004). *Working for McDonald's in Europe: The unequal struggle.* London: Routledge.

Rugman, A. M. (1980). A new theory of the multinational-enterprise-internationalization versus internalization. *Columbia Journal of World Business, 15*(1), 23–29.

Ryan, A. M., McFarland, L., Baron, H., & Page, R. (1999). An international look at selection practices: Nation and culture as explanations for variability in practice. *Personnel Psychology, 52,* 359–391.

Sabanoglu, T. (2020, November 30). Global retail e-commerce sales 2014–2023. https://www.statista.com/statistics/379046/worldwide-retail-e-commerce-sales/

Santistevan, D., & Josserand, E. (2019). Meta-teams: Getting global work done in MNEs. *Journal of Management, 45*(2), 510–539.

Schlesinger, J. M. (2020, June 20). Coronavirus reshapes world trade. *The Wall Street Journal,* pp. A1, A10.

Schuler, R. S., Dowling, P. J., & De Cieri, H. (1993). An integrative framework of strategic international human resource management. *Journal of Management, 19*(2), 419–459.

Schumpeter. (2015, Nov. 7). Not-so-happy returns: Big businesses fail to make the most of employees with foreign experience. *The Economist,* p. 62.

Scott, W. R. (2013). *Institutions and organizations,* 4th ed. Thousand Oaks, CA: SAGE.

Scullion, H., Collings, D. G., & Caligiuri, P. (2010). Global talent management. *Journal of World Business, 45*(2), 105–108.

Shenkar, O., & Luo, Y. (2004). *International business.* Danvers, MA: John Wiley.

Shin, D., Hasse, V. C., & Schotter, A. P. (2017). Multinational enterprises within cultural space and place: Integrating cultural distance and tightness–looseness. *Academy of Management Journal, 60*(3), 904–921.

Smith, C., & Meiskins, P. (1995). System, society and dominance effects in cross national organisational analysis, *Work, Employment and Society, 9,* 241–268.

Strauss, G., & Hanson, M. (1997) Book Review: American anti-management theories of organization: A critique of paradigm proliferation. *Human Relations, 50*(9), 1177–1190.

Sumelius, J., Björkman, I., Ehrnrooth, M., Mäkelä, K., & Smale, A. (2014). What determines employee perceptions of HRM process features? The case of performance appraisal in MNC subsidiaries. *Human Resource Management, 53*(4), 569–592.

Sun, S. L., Zhao, X., & Yang, H. (2010). Executive compensation in Asia: A critical review and outlook. *Asia Pacific Journal of Management, 27*(4), 775–802.

Tarique, I., Briscoe, D. R., & Schuler, R. S. (2016). *International human resource management* (5th ed.). New York: Routledge.

Tarique, I., & Schuler, R. S. (2010). Global talent management: Literature review, integrative framework, and suggestions for further research. *Journal of World Business, 45*(2), 122–133.

Tihanyi, L., Griffith, D. A., & Russell, C. J. (2005). The effect of cultural distance on entry-mode choice, international diversification, and MNE performance: A meta-analysis. *Journal of International Business Studies, 36*(3), 270–283.

Triandis, H. C. (1998). Vertical and horizontal individualism and collectivism: Theory and research implications for international comparative management. In J. L. Cheng & R. B. Peterson (Eds.), *Advances in international and comparative management* (pp. 7–35). Greenwich, CT: JAI Pres.

Varela, O. E., & Premeaux, S. F. (2008). Do cross-cultural values affect multisource feedback dynamics? The case of high power distance and collectivism in two Latin American countries. *International Journal of Selection and Assessment, 16*(2), 134–142.

Varma, A., Budhwar, P., & McCusker, C. (2015). Performance management in the global organization. In D. Collins, G. Wood, & P. Caligiuri (Eds.), *The Routledge companion to international human resource management* (pp. 172–189). London: Routledge Publishing.

Walker, J., Wood, G., Brewster, C., & Beleska-Spasova, E. (2018). Context, market economies and MNEs: The example of financial incentivization. *International Business Review, 27*(1), 21–33.

Wikipedia. (2020). Expatriate. https://en.wikipedia.org/wiki/Expatriate

Zeng, Y., Shenkar, O., Lee, S. H., & Song, S. (2013). Cultural differences, MNE learning abilities, and the effect of experience on subsidiary mortality in a dissimilar culture: Evidence from Korean MNEs. *Journal of International Business Studies*, *44*(1), 42–65.

Zhang, Y., Long, L., Wu, T., & Huang, X. 2015. When is pay for performance related to employee creativity in the Chinese context? The role of guanxi HRM practice, trust in management, and intrinsic motivation. *Journal of Organizational Behavior*, *36*(5), 698–719.

CHAPTER

26

Cultural Intelligence and Global Identity: Complementarity in Global Leadership

Soon Ang, Thomas Rockstuhl, *and* Miriam Erez

Abstract

Global leaders navigate complex intercultural interfaces. Cultural intelligence (CQ) and global identity are two major constructs that explain why some leaders are more effective in bridging cultural divides than others. Despite addressing the same question, CQ and global identity stem from very different theoretical bases. In this chapter, we review research on CQ and global identity, and we offer future research directions to integrate them more systematically. We begin with a review of the theoretical origins and conceptualizations of both constructs. We delineate their conceptual distinctiveness vis-à-vis intercultural competence and other cultural identities; and we also highlight key empirical findings. We then offer ideas to extend existing CQ and global identity research to the firm level. Specifically, we suggest that CQ and global identity complement each other in important ways to help global leaders (1) internationalize local firms; (2) sustain competitive advantage through building cosmopolitan human capital; and (3) resolve global–local tensions.

Key Words: cultural intelligence, global identity, global leadership, multinational organizations, identity theory, social identity theory, cultural competence, local-global

Introduction

Managing culture at the organizational interface is a hallmark of global leaders. Organizational interfaces are the "purposive contact points where the separate worlds of actors intersect and are central to facilitating the transfer of influence, information, and resources" (Simsek et al., 2018, p. 3). For the global leader, many of these interfaces span cultures where values and norms can vary significantly (Hofstede, 2001; House et al., 2004). The challenge of navigating complex intercultural interfaces and resolving cross-cultural tensions raises the question—who can thrive as a global leader?

In this chapter, we focus on two constructs that were developed to address the challenge of managing intercultural interfaces. They are cultural intelligence (Earley & Ang, 2003) and global identity (Erez & Gati, 2004). Cultural intelligence (CQ) refers to a person's capability to function effectively in intercultural contexts. Global identity refers to an individual's sense of belonging to teams operating in the global work environment.

Both constructs were developed at the turn of the millennium to understand why some individuals thrive more than others in multicultural work environments. Despite sharing a similar research question, both constructs originate from very different theoretical bases. As such, we believe that CQ and global identity complement each other to deepen our understanding of why some leaders are more effective in managing culture at organizational interfaces.

We have organized our chapter into three sections. In the first two sections, we review the literature on CQ and global identity, respectively. Here, we discuss their definitions and highlight key findings that shed important light on the nature of the two constructs. In the third section, we extend the extant literature on CQ and global identity from an individual-level construct to a firm-level construct to stimulate new research directions. Specifically, we discuss how firm-level CQ and the global identity of senior leaders complement each other in (1) propelling a local firm to go global; (2) sustaining global firms' competitive advantage through developing cosmopolitan human capital; and (3) enabling firms to resolve global–local tensions.

Cultural Intelligence

Origins and Conceptualization

Earley and Ang (2003) first introduced the concept of cultural intelligence (CQ) in their book published by Stanford University Press. CQ was conceived at the turn of the 21st century, when the world was experiencing unprecedented globalization and interconnectedness. International trade and advanced communication and transportation technologies have made intercultural interactions a ubiquitous part of work and life. Research on culture, however, had mostly adopted a comparative paradigm with a focus on understanding *cross-cultural* differences in organizational behaviors. Little, however, was understood about how to manage the *intercultural* interfaces. CQ, defined as an individual's capability to function effectively across cultures (Earley & Ang, 2003; Ang & Van Dyne, 2008), therefore marks a paradigm shift from a focus on explaining cross-cultural differences to bridging intercultural interfaces.

Earley and Ang (2003) drew on Sternberg's (1986) "multiple loci" of intelligence argument to conceptualize CQ as a multidimensional construct. Sternberg argued that intelligence resides in different loci within a person—metacognition, cognition, motivation, and behavior—and that a more complete understanding of intelligence requires consideration of all loci. Accordingly, Ang and colleagues defined CQ as an aggregate multidimensional construct comprising four capabilities: (1) metacognitive CQ—the mental capability to acquire and understand cultural knowledge; (2) cognitive CQ—knowledge about cultural similarities and differences; (3) motivational CQ—the capability to direct and sustain effort toward functioning in intercultural situations; and (4) behavioral CQ—the capability for behavioral flexibility in intercultural interactions (Ang & Van Dyne, 2008; Ang et al., 2007).

Over time, various scholars refined and expanded the conceptualization of the four-factor CQ. First, Van Dyne et al. (2012) advanced subdimensions to each CQ factor for more precise theorizing (Gelfand et al., 2008). Specifically, metacognitive CQ comprises subdimensions of planning, awareness, and checking. Cognitive CQ includes both culture-general and culture-specific knowledge. Motivational CQ includes intrinsic interest, extrinsic interest, and self-efficacy for intercultural encounters. Behavioral CQ includes subdimensions for repertoires of verbal behavior, nonverbal behavior, and speech acts.

An alternative conceptualization by Thomas et al. (2008, 2015) similarly proposed CQ to include cognitive, metacognitive, and behavioral dimensions. Unlike Ang et al.'s (2007) conceptualization, however, they did not view motivation as a dimension of CQ and proposed CQ to be a reflective rather than an aggregate multidimensional construct. Future research is needed to support the reflective structure and theoretically implied interchangeability of CQ dimensions as indicators of overall CQ.

In addition to individual-level CQ, Ang and Inkpen (2008) proposed a firm-level CQ construct based on resource-based theory (e.g., Wernerfelt, 1984; Barney, 1991). Resources and capabilities are defined as "the tangible and intangible assets a firm uses to choose and implement its strategies" (Barney, 2001, p. 54). These assets are assumed to be (1) heterogeneous among firms because firms combine them in different ways; and (2) often unique to a firm, making them difficult to transfer across firms. Integrating research on CQ and the resource-based theory, Ang and Inkpen (2008) conceptualized CQ at the firm level as comprising three dimensions—managerial CQ, structural CQ, and competitive CQ. Managerial CQ refers to the CQ of the top management team, whereas structural CQ refers to organizational processes and routines for managing and integrating resources within and outside the organization. Competitive CQ refers to a firm's ability to create and sustain "the type of resources necessary to compete and . . . [evaluate] the competitive risks associated with strategic decisions" (Ang & Inkpen, 2008, p. 346).

Cultural Intelligence: Conceptual Distinctiveness vis-à-vis Intercultural Competence

How different is CQ from existing cultural competence? This is an important question concerning the construct validity of CQ. In a review of cultural competence, Leung et al. (2014) observed that a number of cultural competence frameworks contain a mix of intercultural traits, attitudes, and capabilities, reflecting what Gelfand et al. (2008) termed the "jingle and jangle" of constructs in the literature. This lack of precision could be due to the inductive methodology used to develop most competency frameworks. CQ, on the other hand, is deductively grounded in the multiple loci of intelligence framework (Sternberg, 1986) and can be distinguished from intercultural traits (e.g., Multicultural Personality by van der Zee & van Oudenhoven, 2000) and intercultural attitudes (e.g., the Development Model of Intercultural Sensitivity by Bennett, 2004).

Within the domain of intercultural capabilities, existing cultural competency frameworks have tended to focus on cultural knowledge and skills (Ang et al., 2020). As a form of intelligence, CQ goes beyond knowledge and skills to include metacognitive and motivational capabilities (Bücker & Poutsma, 2010; Gelfand et al., 2008). As such, CQ shifts attention away from traditional notions of cultural competence to a more "purposive, motive-oriented and strategic" set of intercultural capabilities that emphasize personal agency and dynamism. For instance, while mirroring others' cultural behaviors (e.g., Chartrand & Bargh, 1999) may be effective and hence reflect cultural competence, it is not necessarily culturally intelligent because it lacks motivated processing of information and intentional enactment of behavior.

Finally, whereas competence refers to demonstrated behaviors, intelligence connotes a person's potential for effective behavior. Intercultural competence models sometimes include outcomes (i.e., behaving *effectively*), a mix that is symptomatic of "construct creep" in the literature (Ang et al., 2020). The clear emphasis in cultural intelligence on a person's potential to function effectively in intercultural contexts avoids this construct creep.

Cultural Intelligence: Measurement and Empirical Research

Empirical research on individual-level CQ has flourished since the validation of the 20-item Cultural Intelligence Scale (CQS, Ang et al., 2007). Research on the nomological network of CQ has examined its antecedents, intelligence correlates, and outcomes.

In terms of CQ antecedents, research shows that CQ, which is a state-like and malleable capability, is distinct from but related to both personality (i.e., trait-like individual differences) and international experience (for reviews, see Ang et al., 2020; Van Dyne et al., 2019). For example, the Big Five personality traits are distinct from, but related to, CQ (Ang, Van Dyne, & Koh, 2006). CQ also mediates the effects of personality traits, such as openness to experience, on job performance (Sri Ramalu et al., 2012). Research also supports a positive relationship between international experience and CQ (Rockstuhl & Van Dyne, 2018); even though not all individuals benefit equally from international experiences (see Chao et al., 2017; Li et al., 2013).

As a type of intelligence, CQ is related to other intelligences, such as cognitive ability (IQ)—the capability to learn (Schmidt & Hunter, 1998)—and emotional intelligence (EQ)—the capability to deal with personal emotions (Mayer & Salovey, 1993). CQ is similar to other intelligences because it deals with a set of capabilities. CQ differs, however, from IQ and EQ in that it focuses specifically on functioning in culturally diverse contexts. By contrast, IQ is not specific to certain contexts, and EQ tends to be culture-bound because emotional cues are socially constructed within a culture (Earley & Ang, 2003). Empirical research supports the conceptual distinctiveness of CQ from IQ (e.g., Klafehn et al., 2013; Rockstuhl et al., 2011) and EQ (e.g., Groves et al., 2015; Şahin et al., 2013).

In addition, empirical evidence suggests that CQ has incremental predictive validity over IQ and EQ in predicting cross-border leadership effectiveness (Rockstuhl et al., 2011) and negotiation effectiveness (Groves et al., 2015; Imai & Gelfand, 2010). For example, Imai and Gelfand (2010) found that CQ of American-East Asian dyads predicted behavioral sequences of cooperation during negotiations and, in turn, joint profits over and above IQ, EQ, and personality traits of extraversion and openness to experience.

In terms of outcomes, much empirical research has supported the importance of CQ in functioning effectively in intercultural contexts. In a review of cross-cultural competency measures, Matsumoto and Hwang (2013) concluded that "there is considerable evidence for the concurrent and predictive ecological validity of the CQS with samples from multiple cultures" (p. 856). More recently, Rockstuhl and Van Dyne (2018) conducted a meta-analysis based on 199 independent samples ($N = 44{,}155$), attesting to the rich body of empirical research on CQ.

Results of the meta-analysis highlight two key findings. First, there is strong empirical support for positive relationships of a latent construct of CQ and the four factors of CQ with intercultural effectiveness outcomes such as psychological well-being, sociocultural adjustment, intercultural judgment and decision making, observer-rated job performance (including task, citizenship, adaptive performance), and observer-rated leadership performance. Second, the four CQ factors show differential relationships with different intercultural effectiveness outcomes, thus validating the four-factor conceptualization of CQ. Specifically, whereas motivational CQ uniquely predicted sociocultural adjustment and psychological well-being, metacognitive CQ and cognitive CQ uniquely predicted intercultural judgment and decision making. In predicting observer-reported intercultural performance outcomes, only metacognitive CQ and behavioral CQ were positively related to task performance, whereas motivational CQ and behavioral CQ were positively related to citizenship performance. The latent factor of CQ was positively related to all intercultural effectiveness outcomes.

Compared to individual-level CQ, empirical research on firm-level CQ is at a relatively nascent stage. In their conceptual paper, Ang and Inkpen (2008) proposed a measure of firm-level CQ comprising managerial CQ, competitive CQ, and structural CQ. Example items are "Top Management Team members (TMT) are confident they can work with business partners from different cultures" (managerial CQ), "Our firm knows how to develop culturally appropriate norms and standard operating procedures with our international business partners" (structural CQ), or "Our firm has a process in place to evaluate the competitive risks of offshoring" (competitive CQ) (Ang & Inkpen, 2008, pp. 356–358).

Empirical studies subsequently focused on firms' managerial CQ and firm outcomes for international alliances (Pesch & Bouncken, 2017; Yitmen, 2013), multinational organizations (MNOs) (Elenkov & Manev, 2009), exporting firms (Gölgeci et al., 2017; Magnusson et al., 2013), and small businesses (Charoensukmongkol, 2016).

For instance, Elenkov and Manev (2009) found that senior executives' CQ accentuated the positive relationship between transformational leadership behaviors and innovation in multinational firms operating in multiple European countries. In another study, Gölgeci et al. (2017) showed that leaders' metacognitive CQ strengthens the positive effect of firm absorptive capacity on firm innovativeness.

Global Identity

Origins and Conceptualization

Identity Theories. The intellectual origins of global identity trace back to identity theory (Burke, 1980; Stryker, 1968) and social identity theory (Hogg & Abrams, 1988; Tajfel & Turner, 1979). Both theories offer "two perspectives on the social basis of the self-concept and on the nature of normative behavior" (Hogg et al., 1995, p. 255). Identity theorists define identity as "parts of a self [that is] composed of the meanings that persons attach to the multiple roles they typically play in highly differentiated contemporary societies" (Stryker & Burke, 2000, p. 284). "Meanings" refers to a set of expectations associated with a particular role—such as empowering subordinates and structuring tasks as part of a leader role. Similarly, Stets and Burke (2000, p. 226) suggest that "having a particular role identity means acting to fulfill the expectations of the role, coordinating and negotiating interaction with role partners, and manipulating the environment to control the resources for which the role has responsibility."

Social identity theorists define identity as "that part of an individual's self-concept which derives from his knowledge of his membership of a social group (or groups) together with the emotional significance attached to that membership" (Tajfel, 1974, p. 69). Similarly, Hogg et al. (1995, p. 259) remark that "the basic idea is that a social category (e.g., nationality, political affiliation, sports team) into which one falls, *and to which one feels one belongs*, provides a definition of who one is" (emphasis added). Hence, while identity theory emphasizes the expected behaviors of a role or position, social identity theory emphasizes the emotional attachment associated with belonging to a social category (e.g., female vs. male).

In reality, roles and social categories overlap. A global leader is both a role that comes with behavioral expectations and a social category with which one can feel an emotional attachment. Both are important; as Stets and Burke (2000) note: "when we identify with the social categories that structure society, and when we behave according to the expectations tied to our identification, we are acting in the context of referring to, and reaffirming social structure" (p. 232). Integrating the essence of identity theory and social identity theory, we propose the following definition:

> *Identity refers to the emotional significance and behavioral expectations that persons attach to the roles they occupy in the social structure or the groups and social categories to which they belong.*

Global Identity. The construct of global identity became important as people grappled with the psychological consequences of globalization. Specifically, global identity addresses fundamental questions such as "Who am I?", "Where do I belong?", and "How do I fit in?" amidst globalization (Arnett, 2002; Shokef & Erez, 2006). Arnett (2002) proposed that globalization transforms people's identities—"how they think about themselves in relation to the social environment" (p. 777). He defined global identity as individuals' "sense of belonging to a worldwide culture and includes an awareness of the events, practices, styles, and information that are part of the global culture;" and contrasted it with a local identity "based on the local circumstances, local environment, and local traditions of the place where they grew up" (p. 777).

In the context of global corporations, Erez and Gati (2004) defined global identity as "an individual's sense of belonging to, and identification with multicultural teams operating in the global work context of multinational organizations" (Shokef & Erez, 2006, p. 326). Thus, employees working in the global work context may come to adopt global values espoused by the organization. By examining one's sense of belonging to the global work environment, the construct of global identity shifts attention from competing national identities to the development of a superordinate identity that transcends national boundaries.

Drawing on typologies of organizational culture, Erez and colleagues proposed 11 core values underlying global work culture. They are competitive performance orientation, quality, customer orientation, innovation, openness to change, learning orientation, interdependence, openness to cultural diversity, trust and ethical behavior, and organizational social responsibility (Erez & Gati, 2004; Erez & Shokef, 2008; Shokef & Erez, 2006). We note, however, that these values could be "imposed etic" reflective of dominant Western MNCs. The content of global work values could evolve over time, particularly as the "global economic system . . . is now being disrupted and undergoing significant structural reshaping" (Petricevic & Teece, 2019, p. 1487). The rising threats of strategic interventions by nation-states and the growing dominance of non-Western MNOs are potential forces that could alter the content of global work culture values.

Global and local identities are not opposite ends of a single continuum. Instead, they reflect two independent identity dimensions. That is, global and local identities form a two by two matrix of identity configurations, a point we will elaborate later in this chapter.

Global Identity: Conceptual Distinctiveness vis-à-vis Other Cultural Identities.

To recapitulate, our review highlighted two key elements of identity—an emotional attachment to a referent group and a set of role expectations associated with the membership. We now compare the various conceptualizations of global identity based on these foundational elements of identity.

Consistent with our definition, Arnett's (2002) definition of global identity consists of both emotional attachment (i.e., sense of belonging) and behavioral expectations (i.e., awareness of events, practices, styles, and information that are part of the global culture). Shokef and Erez's (2006) formal definition focuses primarily on the sense of belonging to multicultural teams. However, they also suggest that once employees develop a global identity, they will "learn what is expected of them as part of their role as employees in this environment" (Shokef & Erez, 2006, p. 337).

A closely related construct to global identity is cosmopolitanism. Individuals with a cosmopolitan identity see themselves as world citizens and are aware of and concerned for universal human rights and global social movements (Pichler, 2011). Other behavioral expectations of cosmopolitans include more travel and contact with people from other cultures and more purchases abroad or consumption of foreign goods (Braun et al., 2018). These attributes of the cosmopolitan identity reflect both the emotional attachment to and behavioral expectations of belonging to the world.

What distinguishes these different conceptualizations of global identity lies more with differences in the meaning of "global" rather than "identity." Arnett's (2002) research on global identity and the cosmopolitan identity addressed the forces of globalization more broadly, with an interest in how people, in general, are being socialized into a world culture. Shokef and Erez (2006), on the other hand, examined global identity in the context of global corporations and multicultural teams more specifically. Hence, our review shows that there are different referent groups when we consider global identity. One may think of global *citizen* identity as an emotional attachment to all human beings with behavioral expectations tied to a concern for humanity (e.g., McFarland et al., 2012). Alternatively, one may consider a more specific group of entities (e.g., global corporations) within the global environment. Regardless, we suggest that scholars should make explicit the referent group of interest when examining the construct of global identity.

Global identity is distinct from related constructs such as bicultural and multicultural identities, as well as multiculturalism and polyculturalism. Bicultural and multicultural identities refer to the simultaneous identification with two or more cultures. For example, multicultural identity is variously defined as "psychological attachment to multiple cultures" (Pekerti & Thomas, 2016, p. 108) or "the condition of having attachments with and loyalties toward these different cultures" (Benet-Martínez 2012, p. 3). Global identity differs from bicultural and multicultural identities in that it concerns a single culture, such as the culture of a global corporation.

Global identity is also distinct from multiculturalism and polyculturalism (e.g., Bernardo & Presbitero, 2017). Multiculturalism is the belief that cultural groups have distinct traditions and values and should be allowed to express and uphold their cultural practices (Rosenthal & Levy, 2010). Polyculturalism, on the other hand, is the belief that "cultural traditions are not independent, sui generis lineages but rather interacting systems" (Morris et al., 2015, p. 631). Rather than addressing the question of whether cultural groups should keep their distinct traditions and practices, global identity focuses more on the sense of emotional attachment to and behavioral expectations associated with a global entity, such as a global corporation.

For the remainder of this chapter, we will focus on the construct of global identity as espoused by Erez and colleagues in the context of global corporations.

Global Identity: Measurement and Empirical Research

Erez and colleagues developed a five-item scale to measure global identity and a five-item scale to measure local identity (Erez & Gati, 2004; Shokef & Erez, 2006, 2008). Since then, several studies have examined how global identity affects outcomes, including multicultural team effectiveness and global leadership effectiveness.

To date, empirical research supports the importance of global identity on multicultural team outcomes (Shokef & Erez, 2006). Scholars have looked at team global identity from the perspective of both the team leader (Lisak et al., 2016) and the average team member (Glikson & Erez, 2013; Harush et al., 2018; Shokef & Erez, 2006). Regardless of how researchers have operationalized team global identity, results show that team global identity enhances team processes and improves team performance. For example, Shokef and Erez (2006) provided initial evidence that team global identity relates positively to team outcomes such as task performance and member satisfaction with the team. Focusing on team processes, Harush et al. (2018) showed that team global identity reduces relational conflict within multicultural teams via greater perceived proximity of team members. Glikson and Erez (2013) also showed that groups with higher global identity exhibit greater agreement regarding emotion display norms in multicultural teams than groups with lower global identity. Finally, Lisak et al. (2016) demonstrated that team leaders with a stronger global identity fostered shared innovation goals and more inclusive communication among team members, which increased teams' innovation performance.

Empirical evidence to date has shown more mixed support for the relationship between global identity and global leadership effectiveness. Studies by Lisak and Erez (2015) and Lisak et al. (2016) show a positive relationship, whereas Lee et al. (2018) found that the effect of global identity is contingent on culture-specific identities, namely, home country and host country identity.

Lisak and Erez (2015) examined the characteristics of emergent leaders in a group of MBA students working in self-managing virtual teams. The authors found that students with a stronger global identity and higher CQ are more likely to emerge as leaders than other team members. Lisak et al. (2016) examined leaders of multicultural teams in a Chinese branch of a large German MNO. They showed that leaders with a stronger global identity are more likely to foster shared innovation goals within their teams, make team communication more inclusive, and ultimately enhance team innovation. Notably, the positive effects of global identity became more pronounced as team diversity increased.

On the other hand, Lee et al.'s (2018) study of MBA students in self-managing teams showed that the effect of global identity on observers' perceptions of whether one is a good leader depends on the configuration of home country identity and host country identity. When global identity is low, those with a more balanced home country and host country identity (i.e., high-high or low-low) are perceived as better leaders, compared to those with unbalanced home country and host country identity (i.e., high-low or low-high). However, when global identity is high, members are perceived as good leaders regardless of their configuration of home and host country identities. Lee and colleagues thus concluded that the effects of global identity may be better understood by considering configurations of global and local identities.

Mixed findings such as these suggest that the relationship between global identity and global leadership effectiveness could be subject to further boundary conditions. For example, leaders may need to adapt how they express global identity-related behaviors according to the specific intercultural context. Thus, similar to how Elenkov and Manev (2009) showed that CQ strengthens the positive effects of transformational leadership behaviors in global contexts, CQ may moderate the appropriate expression and communication of leaders' global identity.

In the next section, we offer ideas to extend existing literature on CQ and global identity in two ways. First, we offer a more systematic integration of the two constructs, and we explain how they complement each other. Second, we extend the levels of analysis, from a primarily individual level to a firm level, to examine firm performance. We believe that venturing into these two relatively unchartered waters will help shed light on how leaders manage culture at the organizational interface.

Firm-Level CQ and Global Identity

How do CQ and global identity affect global firms and their performance? In this section, we examine the complementary roles of firm-level CQ and global identity in affecting how firms (1) internationalize (go from local to global); (2) sustain their global competitiveness; and (3) resolve global–local conflict and dilemmas.

We define a firm's global identity as the extent to which the firm sees itself as belonging to the category of multinational firms (as opposed to domestic firms) and embraces the demands that come with operating across national boundaries (as opposed to meeting the demands of one market alone). As a firm-level construct, global identity could reside in the CEO and top management team based on the upper echelons theory (Hambrick, 2007). It could also reside at the organizational level, where employees collectively possess a shared sense of operating in a global environment versus local environment (Albert & Whetten, 1985; Fiol, 2001). In this chapter, we focus on the upper echelons perspective as research shows the preponderant effect of CEOs and top management teams (TMTs) on firms' internationalization behaviors and outcomes (e.g., Carpenter & Frederickson, 2001; Hermann & Datta, 2002).

From Local to Global

Venturing overseas is the first step that CEOs take to bring their businesses global. Given the myriad risks (Eduardsen & Marinova, 2020) involved in operating a business in a different country, International Business (IB) scholars have sought to examine why and how firms go from national to international successfully (Papanastassiou et al., 2020). Research on the initial internationalization of firms suggests four crucial factors: (1) global vision; (2) discovery of local opportunities; (3) deployment of resources to exploit opportunities; and (4) engagement with international competitors (Matthews & Zander, 2007; Oviatt & McDougall, 1995).

We build on this work and propose that firms with a global identity and firm-level CQ capabilities are more likely to venture overseas successfully. We elaborate on our arguments below.

Leader Global Identity. "Probably the most important characteristic associated with success is that the founders of a global start-up loosen the ties that bind their business thinking to a single country or culture. . . . To be global one must first think globally" (Oviatt & McDougall, 1995, pp. 34–35). Similarly, Cavusgil and Knight (2015) found that firms that go global are often driven by leaders who possess "an entrepreneurial orientation and mental models that seem to 'discount' the risk of going international" and who are "motivated by a worldwide clientele for their offerings" (Cavusgil & Knight, 2015, p. 10).

We argue that leaders with a stronger global identity are more likely to internationalize because they are more energized by the opportunities of globalization. In the research on entrepreneurship, Cardon et al. (2009) argue that entrepreneurs' identity triggers entrepreneurial passion, which in turn mobilizes self-regulation processes directed toward the pursuit of the entrepreneurial goal, such as opportunity recognition. Similarly, we argue that leaders with a global identity are more likely to engage in self-regulation processes to pursue their goal of going global, and stay committed to their goal (Cardon et al., 2009).

Firm-Level Cultural Intelligence. Having a global identity however, is not sufficient for internationalization. We propose that the firm's CQ refers to the critical capabilities it needs to achieve its goal of internationalization, for three reasons.

First, internationalization requires the firm to discover opportunities to conduct exchange of goods or services with new partners in foreign markets (Ellis, 2011). Studies have shown that the leader's social networks offer conduits of information to detect new opportunities (Aldrich & Zimmer, 1986; Mort & Weerawardena, 2006). We propose that firms with greater managerial CQ are more likely to develop high-quality social networks globally, thus enabling them to discover new opportunities. For instance, Chua et al. (2012) showed that CQ increases affect-based trust among culturally different members of multicultural professional networks, which in turn fosters the exchange and cross pollination of ideas. In another study of German firms, Pesch and Bouncken (2017) found that firms with high managerial CQ are more likely to share, question, and challenge foreign partners' perspectives, thus enabling them to make better sense of divergent and culture-specific perspectives.

Second, firms will have to act upon the discovered opportunity (Matthews & Zander, 2007). Exploiting the opportunity requires the firm to coordinate between its internal and external resources and activities. Here, we propose that a firm's structural CQ plays an important role. A particularly important aspect of structural CQ is the firm's ability to govern its interorganizational interface that takes into consideration cultural faultlines (Ang & Inkpen, 2008). One example is that of interorganizational teamwork and partnership. Cultures differ in their meaning of teamwork. Task-oriented cultures like that of the United States tend to place more value on performance efficiency, while relationship-oriented cultures like Japan tend to emphasize cohesion and solidarity (Griffith & Myers, 2005). A culturally intelligent firm recognizes these cultural differences and creates culturally appropriate norms and processes that not only dampen cultural faultlines, but importantly, enable effective knowledge sharing and teamwork across cultures.

Third, firms that go global are confronted with international competition (Matthews & Zander, 2007). Competition could take the form of preventing imitation by other firms or attacking incumbent firms. To deal with competition, firms establish competitive advantage by, for instance, actively creating resource position barriers (e.g., machine capacity, customer loyalty, production experience) to prevent other firms from catching up (Wernerfelt, 1984), and to overcome the liability of foreignness (Zaheer, 1995). We propose that the firm's competitive CQ offers a critical capability to anticipate and deal with such competitive risks. Firms with competitive CQ create processes to assess and evaluate competitive risks associated with objective culture elements such as economic, legal, institutional, technological, and human capital factors. These firms also put in place processes to assess and monitor the financial and nonfinancial performance of their international venture. Importantly, they create contingency plans and processes to manage risks, including having an exit strategy with minimal disruption and loss.

Sustain Global Competitiveness through Cosmopolitan Human Capital

Firms that have already established their presence globally must sustain their global competitiveness. One important source of global firms' competitive advantage is their cosmopolitan human capital—the "experience and skills that individuals possess that enable them to work effectively in many different cultures" (Ng et al., p. 97). We propose that firms with greater global identity and firm-level CQ are more likely to promote values and establish routines that encourage employees to enhance their cosmopolitan human capital.

Global Identity. Senior leaders exert a powerful impact on the norms and values of organizations. Schein (1985, p. 2) remarked that "the only thing of real importance that leaders do is to create and manage culture." The question that is less examined in research is, "Where do leaders' desired behaviors originate from?" O'Reilly et al. (2014)

proposed and found that an important source is the CEO's personality. For instance, the CEO's openness to experience is associated with a culture of adaptability; the CEO's conscientiousness is related to a culture of detail orientation; and the CEO's agreeableness is inversely related to a culture of performance orientation.

In our context, we propose that leaders' global identity is a source of leaders' desired behaviors for its employees, which in turn affect the development of cosmopolitan human capital. Leaders who have a global identity embrace their role as that of working with people from diverse cultures. Their sense of belonging to a multinational firm (as opposed to a local firm) comes with a set of role expectations to seek and to respect cultural diversity. As such, we expect leaders with a global identity to promote a culture that espouses values of trust, respect, and openness toward cultural diversity (Shokef & Erez, 2006). For instance, Lisak et al. (2016) showed that leaders with a global identity are more likely to foster shared goals in multicultural teams and to motivate team members to adopt communication inclusion.

By fostering a culture of inclusive diversity (e.g., Pless & Maak, 2004), leaders promote ambient cultural harmony that encourages members from different cultures to collaborate effectively (cf. Chua, 2013). Such positive intercultural contact not only increases employees' international experiences, but also affords them opportunities to develop their global identity (Erez et al., 2013) and CQ through experiential learning (Li et al., 2013).

Firm-Level Cultural Intelligence. While leaders' global identity signals the desired behaviors for cross-cultural collaboration, we propose that firm-level CQ helps to create appropriate organizational routines to nurture cosmopolitan human capital. Organizational routines are repetitive, recognizable sets of interdependent actions involving multiple actors through which work is done (Cyert & March, 1963; Feldman & Pentland, 2003). Routines are important in that they guide organizational activity and create stability, but they can also be a source of change (Feldman & Pentland, 2003).

We propose that firms with greater CQ capabilities are more likely to develop routines to strengthen their cosmopolitan human capital. Structural CQ, as it relates to the firm's processes and routines to deploy, develop, and reward employees, is particularly relevant here (Ng et al., 2011). For example, effective manpower deployment in a global firm not only helps to promote knowledge transfer across its subsidiaries (Bartlett & Ghoshal, 1991) but also enables employees to accumulate useful international experiences and develop their CQ (Ng et al., 2009). Culturally intelligent firms create systems and processes to identify the most suitable employees to deploy. This requires firms to design a strategic data warehouse that collects and integrates data regarding their workforce worldwide, as well as develop the analytical capabilities to translate data into insights to support decision making for talent acquisition and development (e.g., McIver et al., 2018).

Culturally intelligent firms also have routines to help employees translate their international experiences to cultural intelligence (Ng et al., 2011). This could include structuring international assignments to have meaningful interdependence with people from different cultures, inculcating the habit of reflection and sharing of cross-cultural insights, and providing opportunities for employees to apply and experiment with their learning insights.

Firms with structural CQ are more likely to design culturally informed norms and processes when motivating their employees to develop cosmopolitan human capital. This could include having a flexible rather than a one-size-fits-all approach to incentivizing employees to complete and learn from international assignments. Importantly, incentives should foster cross-cultural collaboration and knowledge sharing across subsidiaries. For example, headquarters could formulate performance criteria that encourage knowledge sharing across subsidiaries and consider an appropriate mix of the individual subsidiary's performance and the group's performance.

Resolve Global–Local Tension

"MNCs are not only internationally (or in some cases even globally) active organizations, but are also nationally and regionally embedded ones" (Heidenreich, 2012, p. 550). Inherent in the global firm's operating context is a dilemma between national responsiveness and global integration (Bartlett & Ghoshal, 1991). The recent case of 3M in the wake of the COVID-19 pandemic exemplifies the immensity of the global–local dilemma. When the coronavirus hit in 2020, 3M doubled its global production of N95 respirator masks and supplied them to health care workers in Canada and Latin America, markets where 3M was a critical supplier. 3M's action, however, drew the ire of the American public. To ensure that local needs were placed above global needs, U.S. President Donald Trump invoked the Defense Production Act to mandate 3M to prioritize orders for respirator masks from the U.S. government. How should 3M have dealt with this quandary? Below, we discuss how firms' global identity and CQ affect their effectiveness in resolving the global–local dilemma, particularly when resources are limited.

Global Identity. Social identity influences how people cooperate in social dilemmas—situations that pose a conflict between individual and collective interests (Orbell & Dawes, 1981). Research consistently shows that people tend to cooperate more with ingroup than outgroup members (Balliet et al., 2014). Similarly, role identity theory suggests that enacting behaviors consistent with one's role confirms and validates that person's status as a role member (Callero, 1985).

Drawing on social and role identity theories, we propose that leaders' global identity versus local identity will affect how much they seek to contribute to global versus local interests. Leaders with a global identity have a stronger emotional attachment to becoming a citizen of the world. With this comes a deep sense of responsibility to meet global stakeholders' and humanitarian needs, as exemplified by 3M CEO Mike Roman. Conversely, leaders with a local identity will focus more on the needs of the home country. With rising negative sentiments toward globalization and a surge in nationalism, global firms are increasingly being held "at bay" by political interventions of nation-states (Petricevic &

Teece, 2019). Against this backdrop, it is possible that leaders of global firms may adopt a more local identity, prioritizing national interests over global interests.

Rather than emphasizing either global or local interests, leaders with a "glocal" identity seek to fulfill one's responsibilities toward global and local constituents. We define glocal identity as possession of an emotional attachment and a felt sense of obligation to both the local and global communities. Scholars have similarly argued for the coexistence of both a local and global identity. For instance, Arnett (2002) extended the concept of bicultural identity in immigrants to describe people who simultaneously develop a sense of belonging to the worldwide culture while retaining local practices and traditions. Similarly, in a study of global–local identity beliefs in the context of consumer brands, Strizhakova et al. (2012) found that people belonged to one of three groups: (1) local identity (embracing local brands only); (2) global identity (embracing global brands only); and (3) glocal identity (embracing both global and local brands).

We propose that leaders who embrace a glocal identity will likely be the most adaptive since global firms are inherently embedded in both national and international contexts. Compared to leaders with a global or local identity, those with a glocal identity are more likely to seek a balance in pursuing global and local interests. They constantly pay attention to the potentially conflicting needs of global and local stakeholders. In the example of the respirator masks, a glocal leader is motivated to find solutions that will satisfy demands in the global and local markets. However, whether the firm can resolve the global–local tension and with what degree of effectiveness will depend on its CQ capabilities.

Firm-Level CQ. Research on organizational tension contrasts two views of equilibrium: static and dynamic. Static equilibrium denotes a system at rest. When disequilibrium occurs, the system responds in order to rebalance opposing forces. Dynamic equilibrium, on the other hand, assumes constant motion across opposing forces. The system maintains equilibrium by adapting to a continuous pull in opposing directions (Smith & Lewis, 2011). Given that global firms are open and complex systems operating in a dynamic environment, we adopt the dynamic equilibrium model. Below, we propose that firms with greater managerial CQ, competitive CQ, and structural CQ will likely be more effective in managing global–local tension.

Firms' managerial CQ embodies the cognitive resources of the firm to interpret, make judgments and decisions, and resolve global–local tensions (Ang & Inkpen, 2008). When TMTs possess greater CQ, they are more likely to understand and detect deep cultural issues and assumptions; more motivated to learn and adjust to different cultural perspectives; and more adept in displaying appropriate behaviors to build trust and respect. Importantly, we argue that managerial CQ enables firms to exert social influence in its diverse network of stakeholders. Social influence "represents a convergence in attitudes and values among groups of actors . . . within a network" (Cannizzaro, 2019, p. 832). Leaders with greater CQ are more likely to build ties of trust with their diverse stakeholders (e.g., Chua et al., 2012), thus facilitating exchange of information to create mutually acceptable solutions.

Competitive CQ enables firms to generate resources that help them sustain a competitive advantage over other firms (Ang & Inkpen, 2008). This ability is critical in helping firms to integrate or recombine their resources so that they can adeptly innovate or increase their production of goods or services, thereby meeting the demands of diverse stakeholders. Moreover, firms with competitive CQ capabilities constantly assess their risks in local and international markets. This enables firms to weigh their options better and make more informed decisions when managing global–local tensions.

Finally, firms with structural CQ create culturally appropriate norms and routines that foster the acceptance and resolution of global–local tensions (Smith & Lewis, 2011). Firms without appropriate responses to managing the global–local tension could ignore the tension, or they could reinforce their commitment to previous behaviors (whether they were actions focused on achieving global or local interests) to maintain a sense of consistency (Weick, 1993). According to Smith and Lewis (2011), establishing routines to help employees see that tensions can and should exist opens them up to mindfully explore the tension (Langer, 1989). An example of building this as an organizational habit is creating templates that require managers to consider global and local stakeholders in their proposals or project updates. Human capital routines such as training and incentives are also important to build cognitive complexity skills and to reward behaviors that focus on both global and local interests.

Conclusion and Future Research Directions

In this chapter, we review the literature on CQ and global identity and offer ideas for integrating the two constructs at the firm level of analysis. Specifically, we propose that CQ and global identity complement each other. While having a global identity directs the leader's attention to explore and exploit international opportunities, it is CQ that enables the leader and the firm to do so effectively by overcoming cultural challenges.

We conclude with three future research directions that will advance our existing knowledge of CQ and global identity. First, in light of the growing evidence on the predictive validity of the two constructs, it behooves us to understand how we can develop CQ and global identity effectively in individuals. To date, studies have shown that direct and authentic intercultural experiences such as working in multicultural teams (Erez et al., 2013), short-term overseas assignments (Wood & Peters, 2014), and study abroad programs (Chao et al., 2017) facilitate the growth of CQ and global identity. Research on CQ also shows that training interventions are effective in developing CQ in individuals (Raver & Van Dyne, 2017). Instead of assuming a static and permanent change in CQ and global identity after going through an experience or intervention, future studies could examine trajectories of CQ and global identity development over multiple time points. For instance, Wang, Heppner, Wang, and Zhu (2015) assessed students' CQ at four time periods from predeparture to the third month in the United States. Their study revealed four intriguing CQ trajectories—consistently high CQ scores, decreasing CQ scores, increasing CQ scores, or a sharp decrease in CQ scores over the first 2 months followed by a rebound. This study highlights the importance of nonlinear growth patterns and suggests the presence of boundary conditions.

Second, research on CQ and global identity has largely posited and demonstrated positive effects. Similarly, our discussion of CQ and global identity at the firm level implies that both constructs yield effective processes and positive outcomes. As Gelfand et al. (2008) cautioned against a positive halo on CQ, future research could consider the interesting question of a potential "dark side" to CQ and global identity. For instance, could there be a curvilinear relationship with specific outcomes that underlie a "too much of a good thing" effect (Pierce & Aguinis, 2013)? For instance, could too much CQ and global identity lead to a paralysis of action in one's quest to achieve win–win outcomes, which can sometimes be unrealistic? Or, could too much CQ and global identity lead to deleterious personal outcomes, such as depletion of cognitive and emotional resources in attempting to achieve the most optimal outcomes in intercultural settings?

Third, we urge future research to extend beyond the individual level of analysis and explore the rich opportunities for research at the firm level of analysis, as we have suggested in this chapter. To date, studies on CQ and global identity have examined the effects of these two constructs in the context of individuals and teams situated in culturally diverse settings. What we know very little about is whether and how CQ and global identity of founders and senior leaders of firms affect the firm's performance. Our discussion of firm-level CQ and global identity suggests that they complement each other in predicting (1) the internationalization of local firms; (2) the sustenance of the global competitive advantage through building cosmopolitan human capital; and (3) the resolution of global–local tensions.

Managing complex intercultural interfaces is an imperative of the global leader. CQ and global identity research seek to help leaders navigate these challenges, but through distinct ways. Global identity motivates leaders through instilling in them a sense of belonging to a global corporation and of fulfilling the role expectations that come with leading the corporation. CQ, on the other hand, equips leaders with the capabilities to fulfill their roles effectively. Thus, we suggest that CQ and global identity complement each other to deepen our understanding of why some leaders are more effective than others in managing culture at organizational interfaces.

Five Key Theoretical Principles of CQ and Global Identity

1. CQ and global identity are distinct constructs rooted in different theoretical bases. CQ is a multidimensional construct that comprises intercultural capabilities, whereas global identity comprises the emotional attachment to

and behavioral expectations associated with a global entity, such as a global corporation.

2. Both CQ and global identity are malleable, state-like constructs that can be developed.
3. Both CQ and global identity can be conceptualized at different levels of analysis, including individuals, teams, and firms.
4. CQ and global identity demonstrate incremental predictive validity. Further, we theorize that CQ and global identity complement each other in predicting firms' global performance.
5. CQ and global identity are uniquely relevant to intercultural interfaces. The extent of cultural diversity that individuals, teams, and firms face presents a boundary condition to the predictive validity of CQ and global identity.

Five Practical Implications of CQ and Global Identity

1. Consider firm–CQ capabilities in addition to technical capabilities when selecting international business partners.
2. Include both CQ and global identity in the selection of global leaders.
3. Design training programs to emphasize the behavioral expectations associated with the global leadership role and the development of metacognitive and behavioral capabilities, beyond just teaching cultural knowledge.
4. Translate intercultural experiences to experiential learning: help leaders develop CQ and global identity through their intercultural experiences and develop incentive systems to encourage such CQ and global identity development.
5. Create norms and routines that foster the awareness, acceptance, and resolution of global–local tensions.

Acknowledgments

We thank Kok Yee Ng and Michele Gelfand for their constructive and insightful comments on earlier drafts of this chapter.

References

Albert, S., & Whetten, D. A. (1985). Organizational identity. In L. L Cummings & B. M. Staw (Eds.), *Research in organizational behavior* (pp. 263–295). Greenwich, CT: JAI Press.

Aldrich, H. E., & Zimmer, C. (1986). Entrepreneurship through social networks. In D. Sexton & R. Smilor (Eds.), *The art and science of entrepreneurship* (pp. 3–23). Cambridge, MA: Ballinger.

Ang, S., & Inkpen, A. C. (2008). Cultural intelligence and offshore outsourcing success: A framework of firm-level intercultural capability. *Decision Sciences, 39*, 337–358.

Ang. S., Ng, K. Y., & Rockstuhl, T. (2020). Cultural competence. In I. Johnsrude (Ed.), *Oxford research encyclopedia of psychology* (pp. 1–29). New York: Oxford University Press. doi: 10.1093/acrefore/9780190236557.013.567

Ang, S., Rockstuhl, T., & Ng, K. Y. (2020). Cultural intelligence. In R. J. Sternberg & S. B. Kaufman (Eds.), *The Cambridge handbook of intelligence* (2nd ed., pp. 820–845). Cambridge: Cambridge University Press.

Ang, S., & Van Dyne, L. (2008). Conceptualization of cultural intelligence: Definition, distinctiveness, and nomological network. In S. Ang & L. Van Dyne (Eds.), *Handbook of cultural intelligence* (pp. 3–15). Armonk, NY: M. E. Sharpe.

Ang, S., Van Dyne, L., & Koh, C. (2006). Personality correlates of the four-factor model of cultural intelligence. *Group and Organization Management, 31,* 100–123.

Ang, S., Van Dyne, L., Koh, C., Ng, K. Y., Templer, K. J., Tay, C., & Chandrasekar, N. A. (2007). Cultural intelligence: Its measurement and effects on cultural judgment and decision making, cultural adaptation and task performance. *Management and Organization Review, 3,* 335–371.

Arnett, J. J. (2002). The psychology of globalization. *American Psychologist, 57,* 774–783.

Balliet, D., Wu, J., & De Dreu, C. K. W. (2014). Ingroup favoritism in cooperation: A meta-analysis. *Psychological Bulletin, 140,* 1556–1581.

Barney, J. (1991). Firm resources and sustained competitive advantage. *Journal of Management, 17,* 99–120.

Barney, J. (2001). *Gaining and sustaining competitive advantage* (2nd ed.). Upper Saddle River, NJ: Prentice-Hall.

Bartlett, C. A., & Ghoshal, S. (1991). Managing across borders: The transnational solution. Boston: Harvard Business School Press.

Benet-Martínez, V. (2012). Multiculturalism: Cultural, social, and personality processes. In K. Deaux & M. Snyder (Eds.) *The Oxford handbook of personality and social psychology,* 623–648. Online publication.

Bennett, M. J. (2004). Becoming interculturally competent. In J. Wurzel (Ed.), *Toward multiculturalism: A reader in multicultural education* (2nd ed., pp. 62–77). Newton, MA: Intercultural Resource.

Bernardo, A. B., & Presbitero, A. (2017). Belief in polyculturalism and cultural intelligence: Individual-and country-level differences. *Personality and Individual Differences, 119,* 307–310.

Braun, M., Behr, D., & Medrano, J. D. (2018). What do respondents mean when they report to be "citizens of the world"? Using probing questions to elucidate international differences in cosmopolitanism. *Quality and Quantity, 52,* 1121–1135.

Bücker, J., & Poutsma, E. (2010). How to assess global management competencies: An investigation of existing instruments. *Management Revue, 21*(3), 263–291.

Burke, P. J. (1980). The self: Measurement requirements from an interactionist perspective. *Social Psychology Quarterly, 43,* 18–29.

Callero, P. L. (1985). Role-identity salience. *Social Psychology Quarterly, 48,* 203–215.

Cannizzaro, A. P. (2019). Social influence and MNE strategic response to political risk: A global network approach. *Journal of International Business Studies, 51,* 829–850.

Cardon, M. S., Wincent, J., Singh, J., & Drnovsek, M. (2009). The nature and experience of entrepreneurial passion. *Academy of Management Review, 34,* 511–532.

Carpenter, M. A., & Fredrickson, J. W. (2001). Top management teams, global strategic posture, and the moderating role of uncertainty. *Academy of Management Journal, 44,* 533–546.

Cavusgil, S. T., & Knight, G. (2015). The born global firm: An entrepreneurial and capabilities perspective on early and rapid internationalization. *Journal of International Business Studies, 46,* 3–16.

Chao, M. M., Takeuchi, R., & Farh, J. L. (2017). Enhancing cultural intelligence: The roles of implicit culture beliefs and adjustment. *Personnel Psychology, 70,* 257–292.

Charoensukmongkol, P. (2016). Cultural intelligence and export performance of small and medium enterprises in Thailand: Mediating roles of organizational capabilities. *International Small Business Journal, 34,* 105–122.

Chartrand, T. L., & Bargh, J. A. (1999). The chameleon effect: The perception–behavior link and social interaction. *Journal of Personality and Social Psychology, 76,* 893–910.

Chua, R. Y. (2013). The costs of ambient cultural disharmony: Indirect intercultural conflicts in social environment undermine creativity. *Academy of Management Journal, 56,* 1545–1577.

Chua, R. Y. J., Morris, M. W., & Mor, S. (2012). Collaborating across cultures: Cultural metacognition and affect-based trust in creative collaboration. *Organizational Behavior and Human Decision Processes, 118,* 116–131.

Cyert, R., & March, J. (1963). *A behavioral theory of the firm.* Englewood Cliffs, NJ: Prentice-Hall.

Earley, P. C., & Ang, S. (2003). *Cultural intelligence: Individual interactions across cultures.* Palo Alto, CA: Stanford University Press.

Eduardsen, J., & Marinova, S. (2020). Internationalisation and risk: Literature review, integrative framework and research agenda. *International Business Review, 29*(3), 101688.

Elenkov, D. S., & Manev, I. M. (2009). Senior expatriate leadership's effects on innovation and the role of cultural intelligence. *Journal of World Business, 44*, 357–369.

Ellis, P. D. (2011). Social ties and international entrepreneurship: Opportunities and constraints affecting firm internationalization. *Journal of International Business Studies, 42*, 99–127.

Erez, M., & Gati, E. (2004). A dynamic, multi-level model of culture: From the micro level of the individual to the macro level of a global culture. *Applied Psychology, 53*, 583–598.

Erez, M., Lisak, A., Harush, R., Glikson, E., Nouri, R., & Shokef, E. (2013). Going global: Developing management students' cultural intelligence and global identity in culturally diverse virtual teams. *Academy of Management Learning and Education, 12*, 330–355.

Erez, M., & Shokef, E. (2008). The culture of global organizations. In P. Smith, M. Peterson, & D. Thomas (Eds.), *Handbook of cross-cultural management* (pp. 285–300). Thousand Oaks, CA: SAGE.

Feldman, M. S., & Pentland, B. T. (2003). Reconceptualizing organizational routines as a source of flexibility and change. *Administrative Science Quarterly, 48*, 94–118.

Fiol, C. M. (2001). Revisiting an identity-based view of sustainable competitive advantage. *Journal of Management, 27*, 691–699.

Gelfand, M. J., Imai, L., & Fehr, R. (2008). Thinking intelligently about cultural intelligence. In S. Ang, & L. Van Dyne (Eds.), *Handbook of cultural intelligence* (pp. 375–388). Armonk, NY: M. E. Sharpe.

Glikson, E., & Erez, M. (2013). Emotion display norms in virtual teams. *Journal of Personnel Psychology, 12*, 22–32.

Gölgeci, I., Swiatowiec-Szczepanska, J., & Raczkowski, K. (2017). How does cultural intelligence influence the relationships between potential and realised absorptive capacity and innovativeness? Evidence from Poland. *Technology Analysis and Strategic Management, 29*, 857–871.

Griffith, D. A., & Myers, M. B. (2005). The performance implications of strategic fit of relational norm governance strategies in global supply chain relationships. *Journal of International Business Studies, 36*, 254–269.

Groves, K. S., Feyerherm, A., & Gu, M. (2015). Examining cultural intelligence and cross-cultural negotiation effectiveness. *Journal of Management Education, 39*, 209–243.

Hambrick, D. C. (2007). Upper echelons theory: An update. *Academy of Management Review, 32*, 334–343.

Harush, R., Lisak, A., & Glikson, E. (2018). The bright side of social categorization: The role of global identity in reducing relational conflict in multicultural distributed teams. *Cross Cultural and Strategic Management, 25*, 134–156.

Heidenreich, M. (2012). The social embeddedness of multinational companies: A literature review. *Socio-Economic Review, 10*, 549–579.

Herrmann, P., & Datta, D. K. (2002). CEO successor characteristics and the choice of foreign market entry mode: An empirical study. *Journal of International Business Studies, 33*, 551–569.

Hofstede, G. (2001). Culture's consequences: Comparing values, behaviors, institutions and organizations across nations (2nd ed.). Thousand Oaks, CA: SAGE.

Hogg, M. A., & Abrams, D. (1988). *Social identifications: A social psychology of intergroup relations and group processes*. London: Routledge.

Hogg, M. A., Terry, D. J., & White, K. M. (1995). A tale of two theories: A critical comparison of identity theory with social identity theory. *Social Psychology Quarterly, 58*, 255–269.

House, R. J., Hanges, P. J., Javidan, M., Dorfman, P. W., & Gupta, V. (2004). *Culture, leadership, and organizations: The GLOBE study of 62 societies*. Palo Alto, CA: SAGE.

Imai, L., & Gelfand, M. J. (2010). The culturally intelligent negotiator: The impact of cultural intelligence (CQ) on negotiation sequences and outcomes. *Organizational Behavior and Human Decision Processes, 112*(2), 83–98.

Klafehn, J., Li, C., & Chiu, C. Y. (2013). To know or not to know, is that the question? Exploring the role and assessment of metacognition in cross-cultural contexts. *Journal of Cross-Cultural Psychology, 44*, 963–991.

Langer, E. J. (1989). *Mindfulness*. Reading, MA: Addison-Wesley/Addison Wesley Longman.

Lee, Y. T., Masuda, A. D., Fu, X., & Reiche, B. S. (2018). Navigating between home, host, and global: Consequences of multicultural team members' identity configurations. *Academy of Management Discoveries, 4*, 180–201.

Leung, K., Ang, S., & Tan, M. L. (2014). Intercultural competence. *Annual Review of Organizational Psychology and Organizational Behavior, 1*, 489–519.

Li, M., Mobley, W. H., & Kelly, A. (2013). When do global leaders learn best to develop cultural intelligence? An investigation of the moderating role of experiential learning style. *Academy of Management Learning & Education, 12*, 32–50.

Lisak, A., & Erez, M. (2015). Leadership emergence in multicultural teams: The power of global characteristics. *Journal of World Business, 50*, 3–14.

Lisak, A., Erez, M., Sui, Y., & Lee, C. (2016). The positive role of global leaders in enhancing multicultural team innovation. *Journal of International Business Studies, 47*, 655–673.

McFarland, S., Webb, M., & Brown, D. (2012). All humanity is my ingroup: A measure and studies of identification with all humanity. *Journal of Personality and Social Psychology, 103*, 830–853.

Magnusson, P., Westjohn, S. A., Semenov, A. V., Randrianasolo, A. A., & Zdravkovic S. (2013). The role of cultural intelligence in marketing adaptation and export performance. *Journal of International Marketing, 21*(4), 44–61.

Matsumoto, D., & Hwang, H. C. (2013). Assessing cross-cultural competence: A review of available tests. *Journal of Cross-Cultural Psychology, 44*, 849–873.

Matthews, J. A., & Zander, I. (2007). The international entrepreneurial dynamics of accelerated internationalization. *Journal of International Business Studies, 38*, 387–403.

Mayer, J. D., & Salovey, P. (1993). The intelligence of emotional intelligence. *Intelligence, 17*, 433–442.

McIver, D., Lengnick-Hall, M. L., & Lengnick-Hall, C. A. (2018). A strategic approach to workforce analytics: Integrating science and agility. *Business Horizons, 61*, 397–407.

Morris, M. W., Chiu, C. Y., & Liu, Z. (2015). Polycultural psychology. *Annual Review of Psychology, 66*, 631–659.

Mort, G. S., & Weerawardena, J. (2006). Networking capability and international entrepreneurship: How networks function in Australian born global firms. *International Marketing Review, 23*, 549–572.

Ng, K. Y., Tan, M. L., & Ang, S. (2011). Global culture capital and cosmopolitan human capital: The effects of global mindset and organizational routines on cultural intelligence and international experience. In A. Burton & J. C. Spender (Eds.), *The Oxford handbook of human capital* (pp. 96–119), New York: Oxford University Press.

Ng, K. Y., Van Dyne, L., & Ang, S. (2009). From experience to experiential learning: Cultural intelligence as a learning capability for global leader development. *Academy of Management Learning and Education, 8*, 511–526.

Orbell, J., & Dawes, R. (1981). Social dilemmas. *Progress in Applied Social Psychology, 1*, 37–66.

O'Reilly, C. A., III., Caldwell, D. F., Chatman, J. A., & Doerr, B. (2014). The promise and problems of organizational culture: CEO personality, culture, and firm performance. *Group and Organization Management, 39*, 595–625.

Oviatt, B. M., & McDougall, P. P. (1995). Global start-ups: Entrepreneurs on a worldwide stage. *Academy of Management Executive, 9(2)*, 30–43.

Papanastassiou, M., Pearce, R., & Zanfei, A. (2020). Changing perspectives on the internationalization of R&D and innovation by multinational enterprises: A review of the literature. *Journal of International Business Studies, 51*, 623–664.

Pekerti, A. A., & Thomas, D. C. (2016). n-Culturals: Modeling the multicultural identity. *Cross Cultural and Strategic Management, 23*, 101–127.

Pesch, R., & Bouncken, R. B. (2017). How to achieve benefits from diversity in international alliances: Mechanisms and cultural intelligence. *Global Strategy Journal, 8*, 275–300.

Petricevic, O., & Teece, D. J. (2019). The structural reshaping of globalization: Implications for strategic sectors, profiting from innovation, and the multinational enterprise. *Journal of International Business Studies, 50*, 1487–1512.

Pichler, F. (2011). Cosmopolitanism in a global perspective: An international comparison of open-minded orientations and identity in relation to globalization. *International Sociology, 27*, 21–50.

Pierce, J. R., & Aguinis, H. (2013). The too-much-of-a-good-thing effect in management. *Journal of Management, 39*, 313–338.

Pless, N. M., & Maak, T. (2004). Building an inclusive diversity culture: Principles, processes and practice. *Journal of Business Ethics, 54*, 129–147.

Raver, J. L., & Van Dyne, L. (2017). Developing cultural intelligence. In K. G. Brown (Ed.), *The Cambridge handbook of workplace training and employee development* (pp. 407–440). Cambridge: Cambridge University Press.

Rockstuhl, T., Seiler, S., Ang, S., Van Dyne, L., & Annen, H. (2011). Beyond general intelligence (IQ) and emotional intelligence (EQ): The role of cultural intelligence (CQ) on cross-border leadership effectiveness in a globalized world. *Journal of Social Issues, 67*, 825–840.

Rockstuhl, T., & Van Dyne, L. (2018). A bi-factor theory of the four-factor model of cultural intelligence: Meta-analysis and theoretical extensions. *Organizational Behavior and Human Decision Processes, 148*, 124–144.

Rosenthal, L., & Levy, S. R. (2010). The colorblind, multicultural, and polycultural ideological approaches to improving intergroup attitudes and relations. *Social Issues and Policy Review, 4*, 215–246.

Şahin, F., Gürbüz, S., Köksal, O., & Ercan, Ü. (2013). Measuring cultural intelligence in the Turkish context. *International Journal of Selection and Assessment, 21*, 135–144.

Schein, E. (1985). *Organizational culture and leadership*. San Francisco: Jossey-Bass.

Schmidt, F. L., & Hunter, J. E. (1998). The validity and utility of selection methods in personnel psychology: Practical and theoretical implications of 85 years of research findings. *Psychological Bulletin, 124*, 262–274.

Shokef, E., & Erez, M. (2006). Global work culture and global identity, as a platform for a shared understanding in multicultural teams. In E. Salas (Ed.), *Research on managing groups and teams* (Vol. 9, pp. 325–352). Amsterdam: Emerald.

Shokef, E., & Erez, M. (2008). Cultural intelligence and global identity in multicultural teams. In S. Ang & L. Van-Dyne (Eds.), *Handbook of cultural intelligence. Theory, measurement and applications* (pp. 177–191). Armonk, NY: M. E. Sharpe.

Simsek, Z., Heavey, C., & Fox, B. C. (2018). Interfaces of strategic leaders: A conceptual framework, review, and research agenda. *Journal of Management, 44*, 280–324.

Smith, W, K., & Lewis, M. W. (2011). Toward a theory of paradox: A dynamic equilibrium model of organizing. *Academy of Management Review, 36*, 381–403.

Sri Ramalu, S., Shamsudin, F. M., & Subramaniam, C. (2012). The mediating effect of cultural intelligence on the relationship between openness personality and job performance among expatriates on international assignments. *International Business Management, 6*, 601–610.

Sternberg, R. J. (1986). A framework for understanding conceptions of intelligence. In R. J. Sternberg & D. K. Detterman (Eds.), *What is intelligence? Contemporary viewpoints on its nature and definition* (pp. 3–15). Norwood, NJ: Ablex.

Stets, J. E., & Burke, P. J. (2000). Identity theory and social identity theory. *Social Psychology Quarterly, 63*, 224–237.

Strizhakova, Y., Coulter, R. A., & Price, L. L. (2012). The young adult cohort in emerging markets: Assessing their glocal cultural identity in a global marketplace. *International Journal of Research in Marketing, 29*, 43–54.

Stryker, S. (1968). Identity salience and role performance: The relevance of symbolic interaction theory for family research. *Journal of Marriage and the Family, 4*, 558–564.

Stryker, S., & Burke, P. J. (2000). The past, present, and future of an identity theory. *Social Psychology Quarterly, 63*, 284–297.

Tajfel, H. (1974). Social identity and intergroup behaviour. *Social Science Information, 13*, 65–93.

Tajfel, H., & Turner, J. C. (1979). An integrative theory of intergroup conflict. In W. G. Austin & S. Worchel (Eds.), *The social psychology of intergroup relations* (pp. 33–47). Monterey, CA: Brooks-Cole.

Thomas, D. C., Elron, E., Stahl, G., Ekelund, B. Z., Ravlin, E. C., Cerdin, J. L., Poelmans, S., Brislin, R., Pekerti, A., Aycan, Z., Maznevski, M., Au, K., & Lazarova, M. B. (2008). Cultural intelligence: Domain and assessment. *International Journal of Cross Cultural Management, 8*, 123–143.

Thomas, D. C., Liao, Y., Aycan, Z., Cerdin, J. L., Pekerti, A. A., Ravlin, E. C., Stahl, G. K., Lazarova, M. B., Fock, H., Arli, D., Moeller, M., Okimoto, T. G., & van de Vijver, F. (2015). Cultural intelligence: A theory-based, short form measure. *Journal of International Business Studies, 46*, 1099–1118.

Van Der Zee, K. I., & Van Oudenhoven, J. P. (2000). The Multicultural Personality Questionnaire: A multidimensional instrument of multicultural effectiveness. *European Journal of Personality, 14*, 291–309.

Van Dyne, L., Ang, S., Ng, K. Y., Rockstuhl, T., Tan, M. L., & Koh, C. (2012). Sub-dimensions of the four factor model of cultural intelligence: Expanding the conceptualization and measurement of cultural intelligence. *Social and Personality Psychology Compass, 6*, 295–313.

Van Dyne, L., Ang, S., & Tan, M. L. (2019). Cultural intelligence. In R. Griffin (Ed.), *Oxford bibliographies in management* (pp. 1–26). New York: Oxford University Press.

Wang, K. T., Heppner, P. P., Wang, L., & Zhu, F. (2015). Cultural intelligence trajectories in new international students: Implications for the development of cross-cultural competence. *International Perspectives in Psychology: Research, Practice, Consultation, 4*, 51–65.

Weick, K. E. (1993). The collapse of sensemaking in organizations: The Mann Gulch disaster. *Administrative Science Quarterly, 38*, 628–652.

Wernerfelt, B. (1984). A resource-based view of the firm. *Strategic Management Journal, 5*, 171–180.

Wood, E. D., & St. Peters, H. Y. (2014). Short-term cross-cultural study tours: Impact on cultural intelligence. *The International Journal of Human Resource Management, 25*, 558–570.

Yitmen, I. (2013). Organizational cultural intelligence: A competitive capability for strategic alliances in the international construction industry. *Project Management Journal, 44*(4), 5–25.

Zaheer, S. (1995). Overcoming the liability of foreignness. *Academy of Management Journal, 38*, 341–363.

CHAPTER

27 Culture and Corporate Social Responsibility and Sustainability

Günter K. Stahl, Mary Sully de Luque, *and* Christof Miska

Abstract

The cultural context in which organizations and their members are embedded is increasingly being seen as a major factor influencing corporate social responsibility and sustainability (CSR/CS) strategies and practices, as well as organizational members' propensities to engage in responsible and sustainable behaviors. Despite the potentially critical role of culture in CSR/CS, we know surprisingly little about how cultural values and practices influence the adoption of CSR/CS practices at both individual and organizational levels. In this chapter, we review existing research that has explored the linkage between culture and CSR/CS and "map" this body of research by juxtaposing two perspectives: (1) the extent to which the emphasis is on "doing good" (i.e., the factors promoting the adoption of socially responsible and sustainable practices) or on "avoiding harm" (i.e., the drivers of irresponsible and unsustainable practices); and (2) the extent to which the culture–CSR/CS link is analyzed from a comparative perspective (looking at differences in CSR/CS across cultures) or an intercultural perspective (focusing on the CSR/CS-related challenges facing organizations operating in different cultural contexts). We discuss the implications for research and show how work at the intersection of culture and CSR/CS might advance further.

Key Words: corporate social responsibility, responsible leadership, sustainability, culture, cross-cultural difference

The cultural context in which organizations are embedded and in which individuals act and make decisions is increasingly being seen as a major factor influencing corporate social responsibility and corporate sustainability (CSR/CS) strategies and practices, in addition to organizational members' propensities to engage in responsible and sustainable behaviors. Because organizations and their members operate in different cultural and institutional environments, they experience different degrees of internal and external pressures to engage in CSR/CS (Aguilera et al., 2007; Matten & Crane, 2005) to embrace various societal values related to CSR/CS (Waldman et al., 2016); and face diverse constraints on the types of behavior that are endorsed and considered acceptable in a society (Jackson et al., 2019; Martin et al., 2009).

Despite the potentially critical role of culture in CSR/CS, we know surprisingly little about how national cultural orientations influence the adoption of CSR/CS practices at both individual and organizational levels. The literature on societal or country-level influences on CSR/CS has emphasized the role of formal institutions, such as political, legal, and regulatory arrangements, in shaping CSR/CS practices (e.g., Matten & Crane, 2005; Williams & Aguilera, 2008; Witt & Redding, 2012), with considerably less attention paid to informal institutions such as cultural norms and values. Aguinis and Glavas (2012), in their comprehensive review of the CSR literature, observed that the relationship between predictors at the macro level of analysis, such as national cultural orientations, and CSR outcomes remains very much a "black box." This is consistent with Ralston et al.'s (2015, p. 168) conclusion that "we still have much to learn to fully understand the dynamics of the triple-bottom-line of CR [corporate responsibility] across cultures".

In this chapter, we review existing research on the role of culture in CSR/CS, looking at both the bright side of CSR/CS (the cultural factors that promote the adoption of socially responsible and sustainable practices) and the dark side (the drivers of irresponsible and unsustainable practices). Further, we analyze the culture–CSR/CS link from both a comparative perspective, looking at differences in CSR/CS across cultures, and an intercultural perspective, focusing on the challenges that organizations encounter when they implement CSR/CS strategies in different cultural contexts. As culture is a multifaceted construct, operating at different levels (Erez & Gati, 2004; Schein, 2004), there are multiple cultural spheres (e.g., societal, industry, organization, profession, function) that interact in complex ways to exert their influence on business practices and organizational behavior, including CSR/CS activities (Schneider et al., 2014). Although the focus of this chapter is primarily on national culture—the set of shared norms, values, assumptions, traditions, and practices that exist within a society (Kroeber & Kluckhohn, 1952)—we recognize that these other cultural spheres (e.g., differences in professional or organizational cultures) may have a powerful impact on the design, adoption, and implementation of CSR/CS practices.

Role of Culture in CSR/CS

Before we consider the role of culture in CSR/CS, we start with a definition of the two key concepts of this chapter. CSR can be defined as a "firm's consideration of, and response to, issues beyond the narrow economic, technical, and legal requirements of the firm" (Davis, 1973, p. 312). CSR thus is discretionary, encompassing activities that go beyond what is required by the letter and spirit of the law and the fulfillment of minimum ethical standards. These responsibilities are either "expected" (ethical responsibilities) or "desired" (philanthropic responsibilities) by societal members (Carroll & Shabana, 2010). While there is little disagreement regarding what constitutes the economic and legal responsibilities of business organizations, the corporation's ethical and philanthropic obligations toward society are ill-defined and continuously debated as to their legitimacy (e.g., Freeman et al., 2004; Waldman & Siegel, 2008).

Like CSR, CS has been defined in many ways. The most widely used definition is from the Brundtland Report of the World Commission on Environment and Development (WCED): "Sustainable development is development that meets the needs of the present without compromising the ability of future generations to meet their own needs" (WCED, 1987, p. 43). This broad understanding is commonly specified in terms of the environmental, economic, and social dimensions (Bansal, 2005; Gladwin et al., 1995). In addition, scholars often adopt a systems perspective that views businesses as nested in much larger macroeconomic, ecological, political, and societal systems (Bansal & Song, 2017). The United Nations Sustainable Development Goals (SDGs) are one of the most recent approaches toward capturing not only the environmental, economic, and social dimensions but also applying a systems perspective on sustainable development. The 17 goals and 169 subtargets cover numerous domains such as gender equality, poverty, clean energy, justice and strong institutions, sustainable growth, or life below water.

While the concepts of CSR and CS emerged from different paradigms and origins, the two fields have since converged in terms of construct definitions, ontological assumptions, nomological networks, and measurement approaches (Bansal & Song, 2017). Both share a common interest in business–society relationships; both challenge the assumption that the main corporate objective is to maximize profits; and both often argue that a "business case" can be made for good economic, social, and environmental practices. Each equally acknowledges the limitations of such an instrumental approach to underscore firms' broader responsibilities to society (in the case of CSR) or the singular pursuit of profits that will ultimately disrupt the system in which corporations are embedded (in the case of CS). Thus, each concept considers organizations' interdependencies with broader organizational, societal, and environmental systems, respectively.

In this chapter, we draw on both perspectives but acknowledge the distinctiveness of CSR and CS, highlighting how they can complement each other in developing a better understanding of the drivers of CSR/CS, with a particular focus on culture. Assessing the role of culture regarding these concepts is important for two reasons. First, numerous calls have been made for contextualization of management research in general and research on CSR/CS in particular (e.g., Bamberger, 2008; Filatotchev et al., 2022; Rousseau & Fried, 2001; Stahl et al., 2023). Advancing our understanding of how culture may influence CSR/CS will not only lead to novel insights into how the macro-level environment shapes CSR/CS strategies and outcomes, but it can also inform the design and implementation of CSR/CS practices and guide managerial decision making in this area. This could provide answers to frequently asked questions. For example, are commonly used approaches to measure corporate social performance (CSP) universally applicable or culturally dependent? Second, from an institutional perspective, culture is commonly considered an informal element (as opposed to formal institutions, such as laws and regulations), involving normative and cultural-cognitive pressures (DiMaggio & Powell, 1983; Scott, 2001). This underlines the need to account for culture in institutional processes (Suddaby et al., 2010), relative to formal institutions. Therefore, in the context of CSR/CS, the role of culture needs to be examined with other institutional influences, which may reveal various interdependencies (Caprar & Neville, 2012).

Comparative and Intercultural/Multicultural Perspectives on "Doing Good" and "Avoiding Harm"

As noted at the outset of this chapter, despite the potentially critical role that culture plays in the adoption of CSR/CS practices, research on the culture–CSR/CS link is still in its nascent stages. In this section, we introduce a conceptual framework that will help us to systematically capture the diversified body of work on culture and CSR/CS, provide a coherent conceptual structuring for our analyses, and shed light on novel perspectives and findings. Unlike the case for a mature field of research, the purpose of this review is not to offer a comprehensive overview and synthesis of this literature; rather, we will highlight key theoretical perspectives and findings, present existing research gaps and open questions, and outline directions for future research.

Mapping the Literature on Culture and CSR/CS: A Conceptual Framework

We map the existing body of work on culture and CSR/CS by juxtaposing two dimensions, which in combination provide a useful conceptual framework for organizing this review. Our framework examines the extent to which (1) the research emphasis is on the "bright side" or on the "dark side" of the culture–CSR/CS relationship (i.e., whether the focus is on culture as a driver of responsible and sustainable practices or on its adoption of irresponsible and unsustainable practices); and (2) the research perspective is comparative or intercultural/multicultural (i.e., whether the focus is on differences in CSR/CS practices across cultures or on the implementation barriers for CSR/CS facing companies and managers in different cultural contexts).

The "Doing Good" and "Avoiding Harm" Dimensions of CSR/CS. In discussing the role of culture in CSR/CS, it is important to distinguish between responsible (or sustainable) and irresponsible (or unsustainable) practices and behaviors. There is evidence that corporate responsibility and corporate irresponsibility are distinct, orthogonal concepts that represent different dimensions, rather than reflecting opposite ends of the same dimension (Stahl & Sully de Luque, 2014; Waldman & Balven, 2014). Some authors (e.g., Greenwood, 2007) argue that corporate responsibility varies along a continuum anchored at one end by firms that actively engage with and act in the interest of a range of stakeholders, and anchored at the other end by firms that neglect their obligations to various stakeholders within society. Others (e.g., Waldman et al., 2020) suggest that corporate responsibility and irresponsibility are conceptually distinct and represent two separate dimensions. The latter view implies that corporations and their managers might engage in responsible and irresponsible activities simultaneously. For example, from a stakeholder perspective, an executive might act responsibly toward one stakeholder group (e.g., investors or consumers) but neglectful or even damaging to another (e.g., workers in the global supply chain).

There are both theoretical grounds and common-sense reasons why corporations and their executives engage in these seemingly contradictory and antagonistic activities. Research on "moral self-licensing" (Merritt et al., 2010; Ormiston & Wong, 2013) suggests that good deeds, like philanthropic activities, can liberate individuals to engage in behaviors that are irresponsible, unsustainable, or unethical. For example, managers may express strong disagreement with racist statements and ensure that their minority employees are not discriminated against racially. Concurrently, these managers may unconsciously discriminate against other minorities because they feel secure about their own "nonprejudiced" self-image, therefore paying less attention to the possible biases each of them might have. Another relevant stream of research suggests that individuals tend to show greater empathy for stakeholders who are psychologically, culturally, or otherwise close, as opposed to those to whom they feel more distant (e.g., workers in the global supply chain), which may lead them to engage in responsible or irresponsible behavior toward that particular stakeholder group (Noval et al., 2018).

Another reason why it is important to distinguish between responsible (or sustainable) and irresponsible (or unsustainable) practices and behaviors is that the two likely have different predictive antecedents. Based on the distinction between prescriptive ethics ("what to do") and proscriptive ethics ("what not to do"; Janoff-Bulman et al., 2009; Noval & Stahl, 2017), Stahl and Sully de Luque (2014) distinguished between two types of responsible/sustainable behaviors: "Doing good" (i.e., decisions and actions taken to meet the legitimate demands of stakeholders) and "avoiding harm" (actions to avoid harmful consequences for stakeholders). They show that "doing good" and "avoiding harm" represent conceptually distinct categories or types of behaviors, with different motivational bases. The "avoiding harm" dimension of CSR/CS overlaps to some degree with legal responsibilities, implying that corporations or executives may be motivated to refrain from irresponsible or unsustainable practices (e.g., harmful environmental practices) in order to reduce legal, reputational, and financial risks. By contrast, activities that fall into the "doing good" category (e.g., engagement in philanthropy) are discretionary and not mandated by the law. An executive may engage in these activities for a variety of reasons, such as the complementarity with the company's business strategy or the consistency with the executives' own moral values. Stahl and Sully de Luque's (2014) analyses suggest that cultural factors are more likely to explain a propensity to engage in "doing good" activities, whereas the tendency to refrain from activities that put others in harm's way is more likely influenced by aspects of the institutional, legal, and regulatory environment. In this chapter, we focus on antecedents of both the "doing good" and the "avoiding harm" dimensions of CSR/CS.

Comparative and Intercultural/Multicultural Perspectives on CSR/CS. Comparative and cross-cultural management scholars tend to embrace assumptions and conceptualizations representing various schools of thought, along with their respective paradigms, ontological and epistemological positions, and approaches related to culture. Essentially, three distinct, generic perspectives are relevant when one is studying culture in CSR/CS, each of which emerges from focused research domains characterized by diverse political, social, economic, and intellectual backdrops: the comparative, the intercultural, and the multicultural/dynamic perspectives (cf. Sackmann & Phillips, 2004). Viewed within the comparative perspective, the intangible concept of culture is typically traced and analyzed through dimensional comparison, traditionally across nation-states (Tung & Stahl, 2018). Comparativist researchers attempt to describe differences across cultures in terms of universal, external standards. This stream includes dimensional frameworks of national culture such as the ones developed by Hofstede, Schwartz, and the GLOBE researchers. The intercultural perspective focuses on the emergence of culture and the management of cultural differences amidst the context of intercultural interactions. The most nascent of the three viewpoints, the multicultural/dynamic perspective, acknowledges that individuals may hold simultaneous memberships in several cultural groups, and that organizational and group membership and salience may change dynamically. For the purpose of this chapter, we combined the latter two perspectives into one (intercultural/multicultural approaches to CSR/CS).

Based on the conceptual framing provided by juxtaposing the "doing good" and "avoiding harm" dimensions of CSR/CS with the comparative and intercultural/multicultural perspectives on culture, we now review and critically analyze literature on the culture–CSR/CS link.

Comparative Perspectives

Influenced by the early work of Kluckhohn and Strodtbeck (1961), values orientation theory has prompted much cross-cultural research in management sciences (Hofstede, 2001; Schwartz, 1999; Trompenaars, 1993; Triandis & Gelfand, 1998). Commonly examined in CSR/CS research, cultural values originate from the Hofstede Values Framework (Hofstede, 2001), Schwartz Values Orientation (1999), the World Values Surveys (Inglehart & Baker, 2000), and the GLOBE Project (House et al., 2004) among others.

Studies employing the Hofstede model (2001) have assessed CSR/CS through various theoretical perspectives, including stakeholder theory (Gallego-Álvarez & Ortas, 2017), institutional theory (Haxhi & van Ees, 2010), and varieties of capitalism (Hartmann, & Uhlenbruck, 2015). Overall, two cultural value dimensions, Individualism (IDV) and the Power Distance Index (PDI) (Hofstede, 2001), are frequently assessed across CSR/CS research, uncovering both consistent and disparate findings. Societies characterized as higher on IDV show greater orientation toward the self and independence from the broader group, whereas lower IDV cultures prioritize the group over the individual. Higher PDI societies exhibit unequal power distribution within their cultures, whereas lower PDI societies expect power to be distributed more equally. Societies higher on PDI showed a negative association with studies assessing corporate social performance (Cai et al., 2016), corporate environmental sustainability reporting (Gallego-Álvarez & Ortas, 2017; Gallego-Álvarez & Pucheta-Martínez, 2020), and charitable behavior (Winterich & Zhang, 2014). PDI was found to be negatively related to the level of corporate environmental sustainability reporting (Gallego-Álvareza & Ortas, 2017), supporting the notion that stakeholders from societies portrayed as lower in power distance seek to influence companies to participate in CSR/CS activities (Husted, 2005; Park et al., 2007). These studies indicate that individualistic societies will show more affinity toward CSR/CS-related activities, while societies having greater power differential have less concern for these activities. Yet, when viewed through an institutional theoretical perspective (e.g., Hartmann & Uhlenbruck, 2015; Scholtens & Dam, 2007; Vachon, 2010), relationships between IDV or PDI with CSR/CS-related outcomes are rather mixed (Ho et al., 2012; Park et al., 2007; Ringov & Zollo, 2007; Thanetsunthorn, 2015).

Asserting that culture is both aspirational values and their manifestations of behavior, the GLOBE project assessed culture by exploring both the desired values and the current practices within a society (Javidan et al., 2006b). As Caprar and Neville (2012) noted, valuing sustainability and corporate social responsibility may not always translate into its practice. Therefore, the values-practices distinction advanced by GLOBE is important for CSR/CS research. For example, the widely used distinction between "symbolic CSR" and "substantive CSR" suggests that companies often do not walk the talk when it comes to CSR/CS but instead will engage in "window-dressing" or "green-washing." GLOBE values scores may thus be more closely associated with a company's espoused values regarding CSR/CS, whereas GLOBE practices scores may be more closely related to a company's actual engagement in CSR/CS.

Two GLOBE culture dimensions receive extensive research evaluation: institutional collectivism (ISC) and power distance (PD). Research using the Hofstede framework has widely examined IDV; however, this construct—defined as ingroup or family collectivism—is different from the GLOBE ISC construct (Gelfand et al., 2004). The ISC cultural dimension exemplifies societies in which people identify with the larger collective, support institutional distribution of resources and collective action, and share a reciprocal concern for a broader collective (Gelfand et al., 2004). It is positively related to sustainability initiatives, CSR decision making, and responsible leadership (Parboteeah et al., 2012; Waldman et al., 2006; Witt & Stahl, 2016). Much like the Hofstede PDI construct, the GLOBE PD dimension describes how power is accepted in societies, with higher PD depicting more accepting societies and lower PD depicting those less accepting of power differential. PD has been negatively related to ethics, CSR, corporate social and environmental performance, and sustainability initiatives (Ringov & Zollo,

2007; Waldman et al., 2006). In a study examining CSR decision-making orientations, Waldman and colleagues (2006) found that societies displaying high ISC and low PD cultural values exhibited greater concern for stakeholders, shareholders, and overall community/state welfare. Notably, societies exhibiting higher ISC cultural dimension values promote managerial decision making related to a larger range of stakeholders and the broader society, while societies exhibiting higher PD culture dimension values had managers displaying less interest in, or concern for, stakeholders such as employees, customers, and the environment.

Overall, despite the large body of comparative research into CSR/CS and related constructs, consensus on how culture influences CSR/CS is scarce. While some general tendencies of accordance, such as PDI (Hofstede) and PD (GLOBE) are observable, careful consideration of both the various conceptualizations of culture and the multifaceted nature of CSR/CS are paramount for future comparative research (Miska et al., 2018). Therefore, in the following we see considerable value in reviewing extant comparative research in terms of "doing good" and "avoiding harm."

Comparative Perspectives on "Doing Good"

Several themes surface from research that examines comparative perspectives on "doing good." Our investigation of culture and its effects on "doing good" reveal studies exploring topics such as corporate social performance (Ho et al., 2012; Ringov & Zollo, 2007) or firms' CSR commitment (Peng et al., 2014). Several of those studies examine multiple dependent variables in aggregated form, some of which correspond to "doing good," while others relate to CSR/CS more generally. Moreover, the four original Hofstede dimensions PDI, IDV, masculinity (MAS), and uncertainty avoidance (UAE) tend to be adopted with some regularity. Thanetsunthorn (2015), for instance, examined the Hofstede dimensions in relation to CSR focused on employees, communities, and the environment. For community CSR performance, which aligns closest with "doing good" specifically, negative effects were consistently identified for PDI, IDV, and MAS. A similar pattern applied in the case of employee performance, which may likewise be interpreted as "doing good."

The prescriptive nature of "doing good" makes it pertinent for investigations involving PDI (and the corresponding GLOBE PD dimension). As such, power differences in societies may or may not make the legitimate needs of stakeholders more salient. Correspondingly, extant research reveals that the effects of PDI are rather mixed, likely in part because of the varied conceptualizations of CSR/CS discussed above. Ioannou and Serafeim (2012) argue that higher PDI may generate a sense of noble obligation on the part of those in power, whereas other research demonstrates a relationship between power distance practices and self-protective behaviors (Carl et al., 2004). Winterich and Zhang (2014) studied why people in some societies are more inclined to donate both money and time, and others are less inclined to do so. They propose and confirm that societies characterized by higher PDI engender a diluted sense of responsibility to support others, resulting in less charitable behavior.

Other GLOBE dimensions, specifically humane orientation (HOR), indicate linkages with "doing good." The HOR culture dimension characterizes societies in which individuals value fairness, generosity, altruism, and thoughtfulness toward others in social interactions (House et al., 2004; Javidan et al., 2006a; Kabasakal & Bodur, 2004). In societies exhibiting lower HOR, people are less interested in social equality and solidarity, less altruistic, and less concerned about others' needs. Conversely, societies displaying greater HOR are more likely to consider the interests of others, thus embracing norms and responsibilities that protect the well-being of others (Witt & Stahl, 2016). While few studies have thus far studied HOR in relation to CSR/CS generally, and "doing good" components particularly, positive effects are likely. To illustrate, Parboteeah et al. (2012) found a positive linkage between HOR practices and individuals' propensity to support sustainability initiatives.

The GLOBE framework offers further opportunity for research involving "doing good" components of CSR/CS specifically by leveraging its values–practices distinction. In her research, Alas (2006) divided the GLOBE cultural practices into *desired* categories—ISC, HOR, future orientation (FUT), gender egalitarianism (GEN), uncertainty avoidance (UNA)—and *undesired* categories—PD, assertiveness orientation (ASV), performance orientation (POR), and ingroup collectivism (ING). Alas argued that ethics is a means to achieve a desired state in society, which aligns with the prescriptive nature of "doing good." Thus, consideration of desired versus undesired practices or, alternatively, the discrepancies between a society's cultural values and practices (e.g., Taras et al., 2010), holds unexplored potential explanatory mechanisms regarding how culture influences "doing good" aspects of CSR/CS.

Comparative Perspectives on "Avoiding Harm"

When looking at comparative research with a focus on "avoiding harm," we identify two broad thematic areas that align with CSR/CS: environmental concerns and corruption and bribery. In contrast to the "doing good" studies, this research appears less scattered across various domains of CSR/CS. Another noteworthy aspect of the avoidance of harm literature concerns its linkages to formal institutions, such as codified laws, regulations, and legislation. This means that the proscriptive nature of "avoiding harm" could help establish better conceptualizations of the norming and conforming effects (Caprar & Neville, 2012) of culture on CSR/CS outcomes related to formal institutions.

To better understand governance issues from a cross-national perspective, several studies have examined the relationship between national culture dimensions and the nature of corruption (e.g., Boateng et al., 2020; Jain & Jain, 2018; Pillay & Dorasamy, 2010; Scholl & Schermuly, 2020). These studies highlight the importance of both national differences and social institutions when considering cross-national variances.

Seleim and Bontis (2009) investigated the association between national cultural dimensions and corruption, quantified using the Corruption Perception Index (CPI). Applying the GLOBE cultural framework, through both values and practices, their findings show the impact of UNA values, HOR practices, ING practices, and ISC practices on the level of corruption in a society. Further investigating the role culture plays in shaping the corruption levels of societies, Achim (2016) employed the Hofstede model to examine the CPI. The results indicate that societies higher on PDI exhibit elevated levels of corruption; societies lower on IDV (more collectivistic) display greater degrees of corruption; and societies lower on LTO (more short-term oriented) demonstrate higher corruption levels. Together, these findings reveal that national culture accounts for nearly half of the reported level of corruption across societies. Power imbalances, as well as individualism versus collectivism, appear to be the cultural features that are most frequently linked to corruption and bribery. Lewellyn and Bao (2017) argue that the culture dimensions of PD and ISC, which are associated with how societal members perceive themselves in relation to others, could serve as a proxy for informal institutional influences impacting earnings management. Across a sample of firms from 26 countries, these researchers examined corruption from the perspective of an informal institution. Their findings revealed that corruption plays prominently in describing cross-national variability through both the direct and collaborative effect of informal facets of the institutional environment.

Beyond corruption and bribery concerns, several studies adopt a comparative perspective to investigate how culture relates to environmental concerns. Differences in the conceptualization of these concerns yield an array of construct descriptions. To illustrate these environmental descriptor nuances, Hartmann and Uhlenbruck (2015) suggest emission reduction/resource reduction; Husted (2005) proposes environmental sustainability; and Vachon (2010) advocates green corporatism. Together, these studies tend to share the common theme of avoidance of ecological harm. Equally, the majority of these studies tend to use the original Hofstede scores which are shown to produce mixed findings. In addition to variation in conceptualizing environmental concerns, key differences in these studies are their theoretical underpinnings. For example, Hartmann and Uhlenbruck (2015) draw from varieties of capitalism, which confirms the relevance of including formal and informal (i.e., culture) institutions when assessing the "avoiding harm" aspects of CSR/CS.

Among several facets of sustainability, Roy and Goll (2014) examined the influence of culture on environmental performance, based on the Yale Center for Environmental Law & Policy's Environmental Performance Index. Aggregate measures were formed from GLOBE culture practice dimensions composed of performance-based culture (PBC), socially supportive culture (SCC), and gender egalitarianism culture (GEC). Results indicate that PBC and GEC positively impact environmental performance. Regarding formal institutions, aggregating cultural measures, as opposed to accumulation of CSR/CS variables, might thus provide a novel way of addressing the complexity associated with studying the culture–institutions–CSR/CS nexus.

Intercultural/Multicultural Perspectives

From an intercultural/multicultural perspective, culture can be relevant to CSR/CS in multifold ways. The studies reviewed below suggest that culture affects how managers address CSR/CS issues, how stakeholders perceive CSR/CS initiatives, and even to what extent stakeholders view CSR/CS activities as being "responsible" or "sustainable," suggesting that the very notions of corporate responsibility and sustainability may be subject to culturally contingent interpretations (Crilly et al., 2016; Witt & Stahl, 2016). It is therefore surprising that relatively little research has investigated the cross-cultural mechanisms associated with "doing good" and "avoiding harm," when identified under the nomenclature of CSR/CS.

As we have noted, comparative perspectives on culture and CSR/CS hold that stakeholders' expectations about company engagement in social responsibility and sustainability may vary across countries (Kumar et al., 2019; Witt & Stahl, 2016). This may be explained by culture, in conjunction with institutional arrangements. For example, Chakrabarty (2009) found that national culture has a strong influence on organizational practices in a context of "institutional voids" (i.e., deficient institutions), but that the influence of culture weakens when a country is characterized by effective institutional, regulatory, and legal frameworks. Thus, MNCs that aim to fill institutional voids as part of their "doing good" initiatives, by engaging in political CSR (i.e., the provision of public goods; see Scherer & Palazzo, 2007), need to understand the local cultural contexts in the countries where they operate.

Intercultural/Multicultural Perspectives on "Doing Good"

Intercultural/multicultural perspectives on "doing good" focus on the adoption and implementation of CSR/CS practices in different cultural contexts: specifically, the cultural factors that may promote or hinder the adoption of socially responsible and sustainable practices. Building on Bartlett and Ghoshal's (1998) seminal study of the transnational corporation, companies operating across national or cultural boundaries need to carefully balance local and global demands when confronted with CSR/CS issues (e.g., Filatotchev & Stahl, 2015; Husted & Allen, 2006). Within the framework of "transnational CSR" (Arthaud-Day, 2005; Miska et al., 2013; Stahl et al., 2018), three prototypical approaches to CSR/CS in the global arena have been identified, as illustrated in Figure 27.1. In the following, we primarily emphasize the "doing good" dimensions of CSR/CS. While many of the same considerations apply to "avoiding harm," a fundamental difference between the two dimensions is the more discretionary nature of "doing good" that enables companies to choose the extent to which they engage in CSR/CS activities. In contrast,

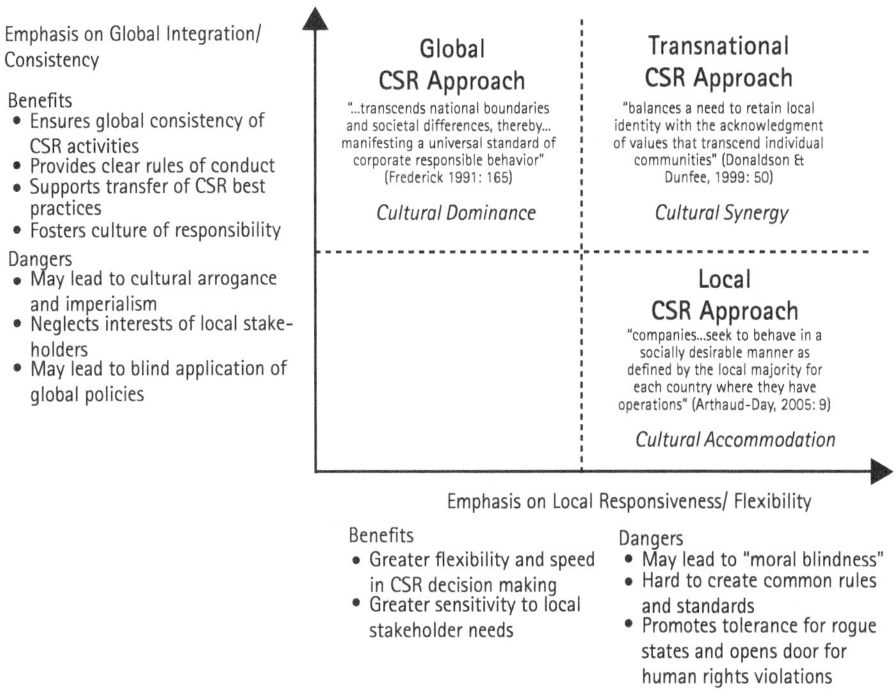

Figure 27.1. Three prototypical approaches to CSR in cross-border contexts Adapted from Stahl et al. (2018).

"avoiding harm" activities (e.g., organizational policies and practices designed to prevent employment discrimination) may be mandated by societal laws and regulations.

Figure 27.1 provides an overview of the three approaches and highlights the tensions and possible trade-offs between globally integrated and locally adapted CSR/CS strategies. From an intercultural perspective, the global CSR approach roughly corresponds to a "cultural dominance" perspective (i.e., home country-based cultural norms and values determine managerial decision making); the local CSR perspective that resembles the "cultural accommodation" approach (i.e., managers adopt the local practices in the host country and attempt to blend into the local culture and "go native"); and the transnational CSR perspective that is consistent with a "cultural synergy" strategy (i.e., managers attempt to develop new solutions to problems that leverage the cultural differences among all cultures involved while respecting each culture's uniqueness and distinctiveness), as described by Adler (2008, pp. 117–121).

Global CSR/CS Approach—"Cultural Dominance." The globally standardized CSR/CS approach implies global consistency and standardization regardless of the country in which a company operates. Companies following this approach tend to establish universal guidelines, policies, and codes of conduct and apply them to business in every cultural context. The viability of this approach rests on the assumption that universal norms and standards of responsible behavior—akin to Donaldson and Dunfee's (1999) "hypernorms"—exist that transcend the norms and values of specific societies (see Figure 27.1). Universal standards include examples such as the UN Guiding Principles on Business and Human Rights (UNGPs), the UN Global Compact, and the UN SDGs (Wettstein et al., 2019), but also corporate core values, as codified in mission statements, codes of ethics, and so on. The global approach to CSR/CS establishes clear rules of behavior, helps firms to prevent and manage reputational risks, fosters a unified culture across the organization, and ensures global consistency in managerial decision making and behavior. However, the global CSR/CS approach can lead to neglect of the needs and expectations of local stakeholders, as managers are encouraged to act everywhere in the same way as "things are done at headquarters."

Only scant research has been done on the role of culture in enacting a global CSR/CS strategy. Perhaps because of its very nature, the globally standardized CSR/CS approach implies a neglect of local stakeholder interests. We believe this is a serious research gap, since intercultural/multicultural studies could provide both an important foundation for better understanding the nature of hypernorms and deeper insight into how they might support a global approach to CSR/CS. Given that hypernorms are deemed to be cross-cultural meta-norms (Scholz et al., 2019), they raise the issue of cultural universals—cultural patterns or traits that are common to all societies—and how they can shape global standards for CSR/CS.

Local CSR/CS Approach—"Cultural Accommodation." The locally adapted CSR/CS approach is, in some ways, the mirror opposite of the globally standardized approach. It emphasizes the need for responsiveness to local circumstances and sensitivity to the needs of stakeholders in the countries where the company operates. Executives of companies implementing this approach attempt to behave in a socially acceptable manner, as defined by the local majority in each society. The locally adapted approach to CSR/CS thus requires that subsidiary managers work as cooperatively as possible with local stakeholders and take local cultural norms and sensitivities into account when making CSR/CS-related decisions. The main benefit of this approach is its greater flexibility and responsiveness to the needs and interests of stakeholders in the host country. However, this elevated responsiveness comes at a price, as practicing this approach makes it very difficult to create or apply any universally accepted norms and standards or to determine what is "responsible" conduct in a particular context.

Research on the role of culture in the enactment of a locally adapted CSR/CS strategy has largely centered on the cultural universalism versus relativism debate (e.g., Semati, 2017) and the alleged superiority of an idealistic, as opposed to a relativistic, approach to CSR/CS. Recently, however, scholars have begun to emphasize the value of culturally relativistic perspectives and approaches to CSR/CS. For example, Pratiwi (2020) argues that cultural relativism can contribute to tolerance and protection of communal rights, and can reduce discrimination against marginalized groups, helping to maintain harmony in plural societies.

Transnational CSR/CS Approach—"Cultural Synergy." The transnational CSR/CS approach can be seen as a hybrid strategy seeking to balance global and local demands. In many cases, economic needs, political pressures, and stakeholder expectations demand that companies respond to both global imperatives and local concerns simultaneously, thereby acknowledging that diverse environments and multiple stakeholder interests require complex CSR/CS strategies to produce synergistic solutions. A transnational approach requires that companies develop a global "template" for their CSR/CS activities to guide managerial decision making and ensure consistency, and transfer of best practices across the organization, while allowing subsidiary managers to adapt that template to local needs and circumstances. Global policies, norms, and codes of conduct may thus be enacted in different ways, depending on local stakeholder demands and the cultural norms of the host country.

The three approaches have far-reaching implications for the design and implementation of global CSR/CS strategies, as well as managerial decision making, since they define the space for managers to maneuver through and engage in opportunities of "doing good." Furthermore, the three perspectives require specific know-how and competencies to support their approaches, at both the individual and organizational levels. There is some evidence that the transnational approach is the most demanding, as it requires that global managers balance multiple, often contradictory expectations on the part of stakeholders, creating synergistic solutions that meet the needs of a diverse set of constituents dispersed globally. This balancing act requires high levels of cultural competence on the part of managers. Miska and colleagues (2013) conducted a multi-stakeholder simulation study that found that the transnational CSR/CS approach (determined by stakeholder opinion scores representing both global and local orientations) required a broader repertoire of intercultural competencies, compared to the global and local approaches (defined through stakeholder opinion scores representing either global or local orientations). This was particularly relevant in the domains of relationship management (e.g., initiating and maintaining relationships with people from other cultures) and self-management (e.g., identity strength and ability to manage emotions and stress). Competence-focused intercultural research has the potential to develop better understanding of how managers operating in a multicultural, multistakeholder environment may enact CSR/CS approaches that yield symbiotic benefits for a diverse set of stakeholders.

In addition, research on bi-/multicultural identity (e.g., Fitzsimmons et al., 2013; Tadmor et al., 2012) and global identity orientations (e.g., Harush et al., 2016; Shokef & Erez, 2006) can provide significant insights. Expressly relevant is research analyzing multicultural identity types that experience dissociation and/or conflict between their cultural identities. For example, Fitzsimmons et al. (2013) sought to demystify the myth about "marginals"—bicultural individuals who have been socialized in more than one culture but lack identification with any—by emphasizing their potentially positive contribution to organizations. Given their dual status as both insiders with deep cultural understanding and outsiders who can make decisions unconstrained by cultural inclinations or disinclinations, marginals may be best able to reconcile global-local dilemmas in CSR/CS-related decision making. The same may be true for individuals characterized by balanced culture-specific identities (e.g., high home, high host) (Shokef & Erez, 2006). As noted by Lee et al. (2018, p. 192), "not identifying with any particular culture offers individuals the flexibility to not completely accept the demands and norms of either culture, and to navigate more freely among the norms of different cultures."

Intercultural/Multicultural Perspectives on "Avoiding Harm"

Intercultural/multicultural perspectives on "avoiding harm" focus on a range of challenges that global corporations and their managers may face when designing and implementing CSR/CS strategies across diverse cultural contexts. Stahl et al. (2017), grouped these challenges into four categories (diversity and inclusion, ethics, sustainability, and human rights), as illustrated by Table 27.1. Effectively addressing these challenges requires an

Table 27.1 Challenges facing global corporations in the area of CSR/CS and examples of intercultural/multicultural research addressing the "avoiding harm" aspects

Challenge	Description	Example of intercultural/ multicultural research
Diversity and inclusion	The need to address the legitimate claims, rights, and expectations of a diverse set of stakeholders, spread across the globe	Reade and Lee (2020) offer a conceptual framework that highlights the critical role that leader *cosmopolitanism*, defined as an expansive identity horizon that transcends conventional social and cultural boundaries, may play in tackling social dilemmas that arise in diverse organizations characterized by polarization of political, ideological, religious, and/or cultural identities.
Ethics	The need to ensure principle-driven, legally sound, and ethically acceptable behavior	Helin and Sandström (2008) analyze the cross-cultural aspects associated with the implementation of a U.S. company's code of ethics in its Swedish subsidiary and find that employees did not react critically to its contents but to how it was implemented, stressing the importance of careful implementation of codes of ethics across cultures.
Sustainability	The need to contribute to protecting, preserving, and restoring the resources of the environment while improving human well-being and social equity	Minbaeva et al. (2018) hypothesize that failure of foreign subsidiary managers to act in accordance with espoused values such as sustainability, diversity, and inclusion, will have a more adverse effect on employee commitment in cultures that embrace behavior consistent with these values. Results of a survey of 1,760 work groups in foreign subsidiaries largely support the hypotheses.
Human rights	The need to recognize, understand, and effectively address human rights issues in the countries where the firm operates	Puffer et al. (2020), based on company case studies, develop a typology of firm responses to increased pressure for corporate responsibility with respect to human rights issues in global supply chains. The most negative archetype, the "neglecter," exhibits a disregard for global standards of CSR and employs a "when in Rome do as the Romans do" approach, as illustrated by numerous instances of human rights abuses in global supply chains.

in-depth understanding of the political, institutional, and cultural contexts in which the firm operates, as well as an understanding of the rights and legitimate demands of relevant stakeholder groups. Although there are various interdependencies between these four areas (e.g., issues related to human rights raise multiple ethical questions), for the purpose of this chapter we examine each of them separately, identifying relevant literature streams, research gaps, and directions for future research.

Diversity and Inclusion. Understanding the range of stakeholder groups with whom the firm engages, along with their diverse needs, claims, and interests, is a first step toward minimizing the potential for risk or harm to these groups. Responding effectively to the needs of diverse constituencies requires broad knowledge about the various stakeholder groups, willingness to include different voices into decision-making processes, and capacity to balance diverse and often conflicting interests (Jonsen et al., 2020). It also requires careful balancing of global versus local considerations.

As described in the previous section, globally operating companies have developed specific strategies for dealing with global–local dilemmas in the areas of CSR/CS, but anecdotal and case study evidence suggests that lack of proper understanding or handling of cross-cultural issues can have disastrous consequences for stakeholders. To illustrate, in the Chinese baby milk scandal, the New Zealand dairy company Fonterra, which owned a 49% stake in the Chinese company that had sold contaminated milk powder, failed to actively address the malfeasance because management wanted to avoid embarrassing their Chinese partners (Filatotchev & Stahl, 2015), thereby risking the health of thousands of babies. The Fonterra case demonstrates that attempts to act in a locally sensitive and culturally appropriate manner may lead to decisions that put stakeholders in harm's way. More specifically relevant to diversity and inclusion, another example of an organization facing challenges with a culturally diverse set of stakeholders is the case of IKEA Saudi Arabia. In 2012, when IKEA digitally erased all images of women from catalogues for their Saudi market, it encountered a firestorm of criticism, finding itself at the center of a global human rights controversy. While seemingly complying with local cultural norms, IKEA took action against its own corporate values, such as a belief in equality, gender egalitarianism, and diversity/inclusion (Miska & Pleskova, 2016).

Although a large body of research exists on cultural diversity in various organizational settings (see Barak, 2016; Özbilgin & Tatli, 2008; Stahl & Maznevski, 2021), apart from case study evidence like that provided above, little work has been done at the intersection of CSR/CS and cultural diversity. Highly relevant to this research area is the concept of "hypernorms," which were discussed earlier. Hypernorms represent "norms by which all others are to be judged" (Donaldson & Dunfee, 2002, p. 1858). They are so fundamental (e.g., the dignity of each human being) that they are considered a basis for evaluating and critiquing norms generated by local communities. For research at the intersection of cross-cultural studies and diversity and inclusion, hypernorms may function as central core values that help identify culturally determined divergences from these fundamental principles. From the aforementioned IKEA example, consideration of hypernorms may have reinforced the espoused corporate values and supported their enactment in the Saudi context, despite local cultural norms that might suggest the opposite.

An important aspect associated with diversity management in cross-cultural settings is the need for contextualization (Nishii & Özbilgin, 2007) representing various tensions (e.g., globalization versus localization) involving diversity management across different cultural and institutional settings (see Table 27.1). In future research, this will be a crucial direction for examining the intersection of CSR/CS and cultural diversity. As noted by Romani and Holgersson (2020), the diversity and cross-cultural management fields share several commonalities that may foster dialogue and advance research.

Ethics. Executives of global corporations face complex ethical dilemmas that prove challenging to resolve: often stemming from different corruption norms, nepotism, worker rights, consumer protection, and others (see Table 27.1). This includes deciding the right course of action for managing various legitimate competing demands within difficult gray-area situations. These situations resemble those that Badaracco (1992, p. 65) described as "conflicts of right versus right," as opposed to conflicts of right versus wrong. "Right versus right" dilemmas are common in culturally diverse environments, such as MNC subsidiaries, cross-border alliances, or transnational nongovernmental organizations (NGOs), where global policies formulated at the headquarters level (e.g., no nepotism policies) often clash with local norms and customs (e.g., employment of family members in particularistic cultures).

It is beyond the scope of this chapter to provide a broad review of research that intersects cross-cultural management and ethics. The research link with CSR/CS, however, is notable. Szőcs and Miska (2020) have observed that ethics and cross-cultural research increasingly interconnect, although further integration will be necessary to reconcile emic and etic as well as universalist and relativist approaches to ethics. Discrepancies in ethics across cultures have often been clarified through the integrative social contracts theory (ISCT) (see Table 27.2), which offers a layered systematic study of social contracts, combining cultural sensitivity with transcultural hypernorms (Donaldson & Dunfee, 1994). Interpreting the culture–ethics nexus in the context of CSR/CS, however, may obligate novel and innovative directions. This is not necessarily because of the recurring criticisms regarding ISCT (Dunfee, 2006), such as problems justifying hypernorms. Instead, the specificities of CSR/CS, including the CSR/CS "avoiding harm" dimension, overlap to some degree with the legal responsibilities of corporations requiring adherence to local laws and regulations.

Sustainability. The imperative of sustainable development emerges from the discussion on environmental management, which is closely related to the discourse on global warming and climate change (Gore, 2006; Stern, 2008). This underscores the need for executives to safeguard sustainable development for current and future generations by

Table 27.2 Review of the literature on culture and CSR/CS: Key theoretical principles and practical implications

Key theoretical principles	Key practical implications
Stakeholder theory Stakeholder theory considers the various constituencies affected by businesses. It enquires about the purpose of the firm and asks what the responsibilities of managers toward stakeholders are (Freeman et al., 2004). In this sense, stakeholder theory is descriptive/empirical, normative, and instrumental (Donaldson & Preston, 1995).	Through the lens of stakeholder theory, managers are encouraged to consider whom their businesses impact. This helps them to derive a better understanding of the value they generate and how they aim to do business. In addition, a stakeholder perspective encourages managers to build good relationships with stakeholders to support them in generating value.
Integrative social contracts theory (ISCT) ISCT links "the normative perspective of traditional philosophical social contract methodology with the specificity of moral understandings among participants in economic, social, and political organizations" (Dunfee & Donaldson, 2015, p. 1). It aims to integrate both empirical and normative theory, as well as general ethical theory and local moral rules (Scherer, 2015).	ISCT provides a framework for managers, helping them to take decisions where there might be discrepancies between universal global standards and local communities' generally accepted norms. In these constellations, managers need to identify those universal norms (hypernorms) that serve as a common denominator to determine the boundaries of adequate behavior.
Open systems perspective The open systems perspective in management theory recognizes that the appropriateness of organizational practices depends on a wider set of firm-related actors and institutional settings (e.g., Scott, 2003; Thompson, 1967), thereby shifting attention from efficiency arguments (i.e., narrow definitions of organizational performance) toward a broader understanding of effectiveness in terms of goal attainment in relation to the multiple objectives of different constituent groups (Filatotchev et al., 2022).	An open systems perspective on CSR/CS suggests that views about the purpose of the firm, the legitimacy of stakeholder groups, and the meaning of corporate responsibility (e.g., shareholder primacy vs. a broader stakeholder orientation) may vary across different constituent groups and cultural and institutional contexts.
Transnational CSR/CS framework The transnational CSR/CS framework suggests three prototypical approaches for balancing local and global demands when confronted with CSR/CS issues in different national environments (e.g., Filatotchev & Stahl, 2015; Husted & Allen, 2006)	A transnational approach requires that companies develop a global "template" for their CSR/CS activities to ensure consistency across the organization, while allowing subsidiary managers to adapt that template according to local needs and circumstances. Global policies, norms, and codes of conduct may thus be enacted in different ways, depending on local cultural norms and stakeholder demands.
Polycontextual approach *Polycontextualization* refers to the process of incorporating multiple contexts (e.g., cultural, institutional, economical, historical) for a holistic understanding of phenomena such as the impact of the macro-level environment on CSR/CS (Shapiro et al., Xiao, 2007; Tsui et al., 2007).	One of the implications of a polycontextual approach to culture and CSR/CS is that companies need to take cultural, institutional, political, economic, historical, and other factors into account when designing, adopting, or implementing CSR/CS practices in other national contexts.

contributing to sustainable economic, environmental, and social value (see Table 27.1). It also raises a question about the responsibility corporations and their leaders have to the future members of a society (Pruzan & Miller, 2007). Consequently, addressing sustainability issues requires a triple-bottom-line logic that reconciles people, profit, and planet (Elkington, 1997). It also necessitates adoption of a systems lens and long-term perspective on the part of executives to understand any direct and indirect effects their decisions and actions might have (Bansal & Song, 2017).

Research into the cross-cultural challenges associated with sustainability remains inadequate (Parboteeah et al., 2012; Tata & Prasad, 2015). As discussed earlier, comparative insights have been advanced based on the GLOBE, Hofstede, and other frameworks (Miska et al., 2018), but what remains underexplored are the cultural factors promoting or hindering the adoption of sustainable practices in different cultural contexts. Since the range of sustainability issues facing global organizations is vast and complex, each of the UN SDGs should be studied. To illustrate, when exploring SDG #17, "Partnerships for the Goals," cultural differences are likely to play a major role in cross-sector partnerships where governments, private-sector corporations, and nonprofit organizations from across the globe collaborate to safeguard more sustainable ways of operating. Nonetheless, research on the cross-cultural challenges associated with attaining SDG #17 is largely lacking. Attributable to multiple interdependencies between the SDGs, research on the role of culture in advancing the SDGs needs to explore this complexity, and the interdisciplinary resulting questions, to capture the systemic nature of the underlining issues.

Human Rights: As noted previously, companies are experiencing increased pressure from regulators, stakeholders, and the general public to help address "grand societal challenges" (Buckley et al., 2017) or "wicked problems" (Dentoni et al., 2018), such as those codified in the SDGs. Private-sector corporations—especially large MNCs, which account for almost one-third of world GDP and about one-fourth of employment (OECD, 2019)—are still seen by many as the primary source of problems, such as growing income inequality, resource depletion, and climate change, rather than as the solution to these problems. The expectation that global corporations assume co-responsibility for tackling these pressing global problems also applies to thorny issues related to human rights and their protection (Wettstein et al., 2019). The latter may include engaging in "political CSR" (Scherer et al., 2013), or the provision of public goods (e.g., education, health care, infrastructure) in emerging economies characterized by "institutional voids" (Khanna & Palepu, 2000), where institutions are deficient and the state is unable or unwilling to oblige. In these settings, MNCs often face the paradoxical challenge of operating in an environment in which human rights abuses are common, with the attendant risk of being seen as complicit in a government's corrupt practices, while at the same time filling the institutional voids that local governments are unable to address through their CSR activities (e.g., providing employment, preserving the natural environment).

Considering the frequent scandals involving MNCs engaged in human rights violations (Wettstein et al., 2019)—the "dark side"—as well as the role of MNCs as a force for good in countries characterized by deficient institutions—the "bright side"—there is a need for research on the role of culture in human rights protection and related transnational issues (see Table 27.1). For example, drawing on hermeneutico-dialogical principles, Healy (2006) proposed an approach to advance the global implementation of human rights while preserving culture-specific differences. Relevant here is the body of research on universalistic versus culturally relativistic perspectives (e.g., Semati, 2017). In cross-cultural contexts, cultural relativism, defined as "the ability to understand a culture on its own terms and not to make judgments using the standards of one's own culture" (Miller, 2007, p. 317), often serves as justification that "harming" is appropriate or justified. This occurs, for instance, with respect to the human rights obligations or the ecological elements of CSR/CS. Concerning the human rights obligations, transnational agreements and charters such as the United Nations Declaration of Human Rights provide a mode of universal standard; as regards the ecological elements, concepts such as the "safe operating space" (Rockström et al., 2009) provide a type of accounting-based foundation for the natural ecological limitations of our planet. Cross-cultural research can provide insight into both how these standards are enacted across cultures and what factors hinder their universal implementation.

Research on Culture and CSR/CS: Open Questions and Future Directions

In this chapter, we provide an overview of how existing research has approached the linkage between culture and CSR/CS. In particular, we map the existing body of work on culture and CSR/CS by juxtaposing two perspectives, which in combination offers a useful framework for organizing our review and assessing the existing research in this area. The two perspectives we examine are: (1) the extent to which the emphasis is on "doing good" or on "avoiding harm"; and (2) the extent to which the culture–CSR/CS link is analyzed from a comparative or intercultural/multicultural perspective. Based on this overview, we derive implications for research and directions on how work at the intersection of culture and CSR/CS might advance further.

As noted at the outset of this chapter, despite the critical role that culture plays in the adoption of CSR/CS practices, research on the culture–CSR/CS link is still in its infancy, and important research gaps and open questions remain. In particular, more research is needed to shed light on the linkage between cultural practices and values, such as those identified by the GLOBE project (House et al., 2004; Javidan et al., 2006b), and corporate approaches to CSR/CS. Since cultural values do not always translate into practices and behavior (Caprar & Neville, 2012), a better distinction between values, practices, and behavior would be exceedingly instructive. Also, future research should expand beyond the cultural dimensions offered by the Hofstede and GLOBE frameworks and examine dimensions that are more closely linked to CSR/CS. For example, *cultural tightness–looseness*, defined as the strength of social norms and degree of sanctioning within societies (Gelfand et al., 2006, 2011), is likely to explain a propensity to engage in socially responsible conduct and to refrain from behaviors that put societal welfare at risk or harm. Culturally tight societies promote narrow socialization, emphasizing rule compliance and punishment of deviance. They are characterized by higher monitoring and a greater level of felt accountability at both the individual and organizational levels. Gelfand and colleagues (2011) found that people in culturally tight societies considered morally charged behavior (e.g., cheating, lying) less justifiable. Thus, culture seems to have both a "norming effect," facilitating or hindering the emergence of institutional pressures for CSR/CS in a particular societal context, and a "conforming effect." The latter reflects the culturally defined propensity to adhere to social norms ("tight" cultures), whereas the former signifies more tolerance of deviant behavior and social norm violations ("loose" cultures; Caprar & Neville, 2012; Elster & Gelfand, 2021).

These findings suggest that we need a better understanding of *how* and *why* culture matters in the design, implementation, and adoption of CSR/CS practices, along with managers' CSR/CS-related choices. Answering the how and why questions will require greater attention to process and context by exploring mediating mechanisms in the culture–CSR/CS link and explicating under what conditions culture matters most in shaping CSR/CS practices and outcomes.

These questions need to be examined through both the "doing good" (i.e., how to promote corporate responsibility) and the "avoiding harm" (i.e., how to prevent corporate irresponsibility) dimensions of CSR/CS. With regard to the latter, past research has found significant cultural differences in managers' willingness to accept bribery as the price of business, as well as a willingness to engage in other forms of unethical, irresponsible and unsustainable practices (e.g., Jing & Graham, 2008; Martin et al., 2007). However, as culture is often correlated with other socio-economic influences such as GDP and institutions, it is difficult to determine which country-level factors are driving irresponsible behavior. The evidence to date fails to show the degree to which some cultures are more or less ethical than others (O'Fallon & Butterfield, 2005).

Thus, there is a need for research that will clarify the relationship between formal institutions (e.g., legal and regulatory frameworks) and informal institutions (culture) and how they affect CSR/CS. Recently, Filatotchev et al. (2022) applied an open systems approach to CSR (see Table 27.2) to analyze the interdependencies of various aspects of the external environment in the contextualization of theory and research in CSR/CS. An open-system perspective on comparative CSR/CS suggests that different social, cultural, political, economic, and historic factors may lead to the institutionalization of very different views about CSR/CS (also see Aguilera & Jackson, 2010; Filatotchev & Nakajima, 2014; Witt & Redding, 2012). This is contrary to the universalistic claims of principal-agency theory, normative stakeholder theory (see Table 27.2), and other relevant theoretical perspectives emanating from Western contexts generally and North American contexts specifically.

Across the literature examining culture and CSR/CS, demand exists for a more in-depth understanding of how aspects of context combine and interact to shape CSR/CS policies and practices. Tsui et al. (2007) have called for a polycontextual approach to comparative studies (see Table 27.2) and have raised important questions about the relationship between culture, institutions, and other national differentiators, including aspects of the political, historical, and social context. Shapiro, Von Glinow, and Xiao (2007) introduced the term *polycontextualization* to describe the process of incorporating multiple contexts (e.g., cultural, institutional, *and* historical) for a holistic and valid understanding of any phenomenon in it. A polycontextual approach to CSR/CS research is challenging because it requires comparative and cross-cultural management scholars to draw not only on cultural theories but also on theories from institutional sociology, psychology, political science, and other fields and disciplines, to help understand CSR/CS-related phenomena in a particular setting. However, this approach holds promise for offering unique and holistic insights into the drivers of CSR/CS in different cultural contexts. Based on our multifaceted overview and discussion of culture and CSR/CS, we seek to foster future research embracing many perspectives.

References

Achim, M. (2016). Cultural dimension of corruption: A cross-country survey. *International Advancement of Economic Research, 22*, 333–345.

Adler, N. (2008). *International dimensions of organizational behavior* (5th ed.). Independence, MO: Thomson/South-Western.

Aguilera, R. V., & Jackson, G. (2010). Comparative and international corporate governance. *Academy of Management Annals, 4*(1), 485–556.

Aguilera, R. V., Rupp, D. E., Williams, C. A., & Ganapathi, J. (2007). Putting the S back in corporate social responsibility: A multilevel theory of social change in organizations. *Academy of Management Review, 32*(3), 836–863.

Aguinis, H., & Glavas, A. (2012). What we know and don't know about corporate social responsibility: A review and research agenda. *Journal of Management, 38*(4), 932–968.

Alas, R. (2006). Ethics in countries with different cultural dimensions. *Journal of Business Ethics, 69*, 237–247.

Arthaud-Day, M. L. (2005). Transnational corporate social responsibility: A tri-dimensional approach to international CSR research. *Business Ethics Quarterly, 15*(1), 1–22.

Badaracco, J. L. 1992. Business ethics: four spheres of executive responsibility. *California Management Review, 34*, 64–79.

Bamberger, P. (2008). From the editors beyond contextualization: Using context theories to narrow the micro-macro gap in management research. *Academy of Management Journal, 51*(5), 839–846.

Bansal, P. (2005). Evolving sustainably: A longitudinal study of corporate sustainable development. *Strategic Management Journal, 26*(3), 197–218.

Bansal, P., & Song, H.-C. (2017). Similar but not the same: Differentiating corporate sustainability from corporate responsibility. *Academy of Management Annals, 11*(1), 105–149.

Barak, M. E. M. (2016). *Managing diversity: Toward a globally inclusive workplace.* Thousand Oaks, CA: SAGE.

Bartlett, C. A., & Ghoshal, S. (1998). *Managing across borders: The transnational solution*, 2nd Edition (2nd Revised edition). Cambridge, MA: Harvard Business School Press.

Boateng, A., Wang, Y., Ntim, C., & Glaister, K. (2020). National culture, corporate governance and corruption: A cross-country analysis. *International Journal of Financial Economics, 26*(3), 3852–3874.

Buckley, P. J., Doh, J. P., & Benischke, M. H. (2017). Towards a renaissance in international business research? Big questions, grand challenges, and the future of IB scholarship. *Journal of International Business Studies, 48*(9), 1045–1064.

Cai, Y., Pan, C., & Statman, M. (2016) Why do countries matter so much in corporate social performance? *Journal of Corporate Finance, 41*, 591–609.

Caprar, D. V., & Neville, B. A. (2012). "Norming" and "conforming": Integrating cultural and institutional explanations for sustainability adoption in business. *Journal of Business Ethics, 110*(2), 231–245.

Carl, D., Gupta, V., & Javidan, M. (2004). Power distance. In R. J. House, P. J. Hanges, M. Javidan, P. W. Dorfman, & V. Gupta (Eds.). *Culture, leadership, and organizations: The GLOBE study of 62 societies* (pp. 513–563). Thousand Oaks, CA: SAGE.

Carroll, A. B., & Shabana, K. M. (2010). The business case for corporate social responsibility: A review of concepts, research and practice. *International Journal of Management Reviews, 12*(1), 85–105.

Chakrabarty, S. (2009). The influence of national culture and institutional voids on family ownership of large firms: A country level empirical study. *Journal of International Management, 15*, 32–45.

Crilly, D., Ni, N., & Jiang, Y. (2016). Do-no-harm versus do-good social responsibility: Attributional thinking and the liability of foreignness. *Strategic Management Journal, 37*(7), 1316–1329.

Davis, K. (1973). The case for and against business assumption of social responsibilities. *The Academy of Management Journal, 16*(2), 312–322.

Dentoni, D., Bitzer, V., & Schouten, G. (2018). Harnessing wicked problems in multi-stakeholder partnerships. *Journal of Business Ethics, 150*(2), 333–356.

DiMaggio, P. J., & Powell, W. W. (1983). The iron cage revisited: Institutional isomorphism and collective rationality in organizational fields. *American Sociological Review, 48*(2), 147–160.

Donaldson, T., & Dunfee, T. W. (1994). Toward a unified conception of business ethics: Integrative social contracts theory. *Academy of Management Review, 19*(2), 252–284.

Donaldson, T., & Dunfee, T. W. (1999). Ties that bind: A social contracts approach to business ethics. Boston, MA: Harvard Business Review Press.

Donaldson, T., & Dunfee, T. W. (2002). Ties that bind in business ethics: Social contracts and why they matter. *Journal of Banking & Finance, 26*(9), 1853–1865.

Donaldson, T., & Preston, L. E. (1995). The stakeholder theory of the corporation: Concepts, evidence, and implications. *Academy of Management Review, 20*(1), 65–91.

Dunfee, T. W. (2006). A critical perspective of integrative social contracts theory: recurring criticisms and next generation research topics. *Journal of Business Ethics, 68*(3), 303–328.

Dunfee, T. W., & Donaldson, T. J. (2015). Integrative social contracts theory. In C. L. Cooper. (Ed.), *Wiley encyclopedia of management* (Vol. 2, pp. 1–5). Chichester, UK: John Wiley & Sons.

Elkington, J. (1997). *Cannibals with forks: The triple bottom line of 21st-century business.* Oxford, UK: Capstone.

Elster, A., & Gelfand, M. J. (2021). When guiding principles do not guide: The moderating effects of cultural tightness on value-behavior links. *Journal of Personality, 89*(2), 325–337.

Erez, M., & Gati, E. (2004). A dynamic, multi-level model of culture: from the micro level of the individual to the macro level of a global culture. *Applied Psychology*, 53(4): 583–598.

Filatotchev, I., Ireland, R. D., & Stahl, G. K. (2022). Contextualizing management research: An open systems perspective. *Journal of Management Studies, 59*(4), 1036–1056.

Filatotchev, I., & Nakajima, C. (2014). Corporate governance, responsible managerial behavior, and corporate social responsibility: Organizational efficiency versus organizational legitimacy? *Academy of Management Perspectives, 28*(3), 289–306.

Filatotchev, I., & Stahl, G. K. (2015). Towards transnational CSR. Corporate social responsibility approaches and governance solutions for multinational corporations. *Organizational Dynamics, 44*(2), 121–129.

Fitzsimmons, S. R., Lee, Y. T., & Brannen, M. Y. (2013). Demystifying the myth about marginals: Implications for global leadership. *European Journal of International Management, 7*, 587–603.

Freeman, R. E. A. C., Wicks, A. C., & Parmar, B. (2004). Stakeholder theory and the corporate objective revisited. *Organization Science, 15*(3), 364–369.

Gallego-Álvarez, P., & Ortas, P. (2017). Corporate environmental sustainability reporting in the context of national cultures: A quantile regression approach. *International Business Review, 26*(2), 337–353.

Gallego-Álvarez, M., & Pucheta-Martínez, I. (2020). Corporate social responsibility reporting and corporate governance mechanisms: An international outlook from emerging countries. *Business Strategy and Development, 3*(1), 77–97.

Gelfand, M., Bhawuk, D., Nishii, L., & Bechtold, D. (2004). Individualism and collectivism. In R. J. P. M. Hanges, M. Javidan, P. Dorfman, & V. Gupta (Eds.), *Culture, leadership, and organization GLOBE study of 62 societies* (pp. 437–512). Thousand Oaks, CA: SAGE.

Gelfand, M. J., Nishii, L. H., & Raver, J. L. (2006). On the nature and importance of cultural tightn looseness. *Journal of Applied Psychology, 91*(6), 1225–1244.

Gelfand, M. J., Raver, J. L., Nishii, L. H., Leslie, L. M., Lun, J., Lim, B. C., Duan, L., Almaliach, A., Ang S. Amadottir, J., Aycan, Z., Boenke, K., Boski, P., Cabecinhas, R., Chan, D., Chhokar, J., D'Amato, A., Ferrer, M., Fischlmayr, I. C., & Yamaguchi, S. (2011). Differences between tight and loose cultures: A 33-nation study. *Science, 332*(6033), 1100–1104.

Gladwin, T. N., Kennelly, J. J., & Krause, T. S. (1995). Shifting paradigms for sustainable development: Implications for management theory and research. *Academy of Management Review, 20*(4), 874–907.

Gore, A. (2006). *An inconvenient truth: The planetary emergency of global warming and what we can do about it.* New York: Rodale Books.

Greenwood, M. (2007). Stakeholder engagement: Beyond the myth of corporate responsibility. *Journal of Business Ethics, 74*(4), 315–327.

Hartmann, J., & Uhlenbruck, K. (2015). National institutional antecedents to corporate environmental performance. *Journal of World Business, 50*(4), 729–741.

Harush, R., Lisak, A., & Erez, M. (2016). Extending the global acculturation model to untangle the culture mixing puzzle. *Journal of Cross-Cultural Psychology, 47*(10), 1395–1408.

Haxhi, I., & van Ees, H. (2010). Explaining diversity in the worldwide diffusion of codes of good governance. *Journal of International Business Studies, 41*, 710–726.

Healy, P. (2006). Human rights and intercultural relations: A hermeneutico-dialogical approach. *Philosophy & Social Criticism, 32*(4), 513–541.

Helin, S., & Sandström, J. (2008). Codes, ethics and cross-cultural differences: Stories from the implementation of a corporate code of ethics in a MNC subsidiary. *Journal of Business Ethics, 82*(2), 281–291.

Ho, F. N., Wang, H. M. D., & Vitell, S. J. (2012). A global analysis of corporate social performance: the effects of cultural and geographic environments. *Journal of Business Ethics, 107*, 423–433.

Hofstede, G. H. (2001). *Culture's consequences: Comparing values, behaviors, institutions, and organizations across nations* (2nd Ed.). Thousand Oaks, CA: SAGE.

House, R. J., Hanges, P. J., Javidan, M., Dorfman, P. W., & Gupta, V. (2004). *Culture, leadership, and organizations: The GLOBE study of 62 societies.* Thousand Oaks, CA: SAGE.

Husted, B. W. (2005). Culture and ecology: A cross-national study of the determinants of environmental sustainability. *MIR: Management International Review, 45*(3), 349–371.

Husted, B. W., & Allen, D. B. (2006). Corporate social responsibility in the multinational enterprise: Strategic and institutional approaches. *Journal of International Business Studies, 37*, 838–849.

Inglehart, R., & Baker, W. (2000). Modernization, cultural change, and the persistence of traditional values. *American Sociological Review, 65*(1), 19–51.

Ioannou, I., & Serafeim, G. (2012). What drives corporate social performance? The role of nation-level institutions. *Journal of International Business Studies, 43*, 834–864.

Jackson, J. C., Gelfand, M., De, S., & Fox, A. (2019). The loosening of American culture over 200 years is associated with a creativity–order trade-off. *Nature Human Behavior, 3*, 759.

Jain, S., & Jain, S. (2018). Power distance belief and preference for transparency. *Journal of Business Research, 89*, 135–142, https://www.sciencedirect.com/science/article/pii/S0148296318301929

Janoff-Bulman, R., Sheikh, S., & Hepp, S. (2009). Proscriptive versus prescriptive morality: Two faces of moral regulation. *Journal of Personality and Social Psychology, 96*(3), 521–537.

Javidan, M., Dorfman, P., Sully de Luque, M., & House, R. J. (2006a). In the eye of the beholder: Cross cultural lessons in leadership from Project GLOBE. *Academy of Management Perspective, 20*(1), 67–90.

Javidan, M., House, R. J., Dorfman, P. W., Hanges, P. J., & Sully de Luque, M. S. (2006b). Conceptualizing and measuring cultures and their consequences: A comparative review of GLOBE's and Hofstede's approaches. *Journal of International Business Studies, 37*(6): 897–914.

Jing, R., & Graham, J. L. (2008). Values versus regulations: How culture plays its role. *Journal of Business Ethics, 80*(4), 791–806.

Jonsen, K., Levy, O., Toegel, I., & Van Zanten, J. (2020). The role of inclusion in responsible global leadership. In M. E. Mendenhall, M. Zilinskaite, G. K. Stahl, & R. Clapp-Smith (Eds.), *Responsible global leadership: dilemmas, paradoxes, and opportunities* (pp. 120–136). New York: Routledge.

Kabasakal, H., & Bodur, M. (2004). Humane orientation in societies, organizations, and leader attributes. In R. J. House, P. J. Hanges, M. Javidan, P. W., Dorfman, & V. Gupta, V. (Eds.), *Culture, leadership, and organizations: The GLOBE study of 62 societies* (pp. 564–601). Thousand Oaks, CA: SAGE.

Khanna, T., & Palepu, K. (2000). Is group affiliation profitable in emerging markets? An analysis of diversified Indian business groups. *The Journal of Finance, 55*(2), 867–891.

Kluckhohn, F., & Strodtbeck, F. (1961). *Variations in value orientations*. Evanston, IL: Row, Peterson.

Kroeber, A. L., & Kluckhohn, C. (1952). Culture: A critical review of concepts and definitions. *Papers. Peabody Museum of Archaeology & Ethnology, Harvard University, 47*(1), viii, 223.

Kumar, K., Boesso, G., Batra, R., & Yao, J. (2019). Explicit and implicit corporate social responsibility: Differences in the approach to stakeholder engagement activities of U.S. and Japanese companies. *Business Strategy and the Environment, 28*(6), 1121–1130.

Lee, Y. T., Masuda, A. D., Fu, X., & Reiche, B. S. (2018). Navigating between home, host, and global: Consequences of multicultural team members' identity configurations. *Academy of Management Discoveries, 4*(2), 180–201.

Lewellyn, K., & Bao, S. R. (2017). The role of national culture and corruption on managing earning around the world. *Journal of World Business, 52*, 798–808.

Martin, G. S., Resick, C. J., Keating, M. A., & Dickson, M. W. (2009). Ethical leadership across cultures: a comparative analysis of German and US perspectives. *Business Ethics: A European Review, 18*(2), 127–144.

Martin, K. D., Cullen, J. B., Johnson, J. L., & Parboteeah, P. K. (2007). Deciding to bribe: A cross-level analysis of firm and home country influences on bribery activity. *Academy of Management Journal, 50*(6), 1401–1422.

Matten, D., & Crane, A. (2005). Corporate citizenship: Toward an extended theoretical conceptualization. *Academy of Management Review, 30*(1), 166–179.

Merritt, A. C., Effron, D. A., & Monin, B. (2010). Moral self-licensing: When being good frees us to be bad. *Social and Personality Psychology Compass, 4*(5), 344–357.

Miller, B. (2007). *Cultural anthropology* (4th ed.). Boston: Pearson Education.

Minbaeva, D., Rabbiosi, L., & Stahl, G. K. (2018). Not walking the talk? How host country cultural orientations may buffer the damage of corporate values' misalignment in multinational enterprises. *Journal of World Business, 53*, 880–895.

Miska, C., & Pleskova, M. (2016). IKEA's ethical controversies in Saudi Arabia. In C. Barmeyer & P. Franklin (Eds.), *Intercultural management: A case-based approach to achieving complementarity and synergy* (pp. 120–133). London: Palgrave Macmillan.

Miska, C., Stahl, G. K., & Mendenhall, M. E. (2013). Intercultural competencies as antecedents of responsible global leadership. *European Journal of International Management, 7*(5), 550–569.

Miska, C., Szőcs, I., & Schiffinger, M. (2018). Culture's effects on corporate sustainability practices: a multi-domain and multi-level view. *Journal of World Business, 53*(2), 263–279.

Nishii, L. H., & Özbilgin, M. F. (2007). Global diversity management: Towards a conceptual framework. *The International Journal of Human Resource Management, 18*(11), 1883–1894.

Noval, L. J., & Stahl, G. K. (2017). Accounting for proscriptive and prescriptive morality in the workplace: The double-edged sword effect of mood on managerial ethical decision making. *Journal of Business Ethics, 142*(3), 589–602.

Noval, L. J., Stahl, G. K., & Molinsky, A. (2018). Motivated dissimilarity construal and self-serving behavior: How we distance ourselves from those we harm. *Organizational Behavior and Human Decision Processes, 148*, 145–158.

OECD. (2019 April 25). *OECD employment outlook 2019: The future of work*. Paris: Organisation for Economic Co-operation and Development. https://www.oecd.org/employment-outlook/2019/

O'Fallon, M. J., & Butterfield, K. D. (2005). A review of the empirical ethical decision-making literature: 1996–2003. *Journal of Business Ethics, 59*, 375–413.

Ormiston, M. E., & Wong, E. M. (2013). License to ill: The effects of corporate social responsibility and CEO moral identity on corporate social irresponsibility. *Personnel Psychology, 66*, 861–893.

Ozbilgin, M., & Tatli, A. (2008). Global diversity management: An evidence based approach. New York: Macmillan International Higher Education.

Parboteeah, K. P., Addae, H. M., & Cullen, J. B. (2012). Propensity to support sustainability initiatives: A cross-national model. *Journal of Business Ethics, 105*(3), 403–413.

Park, H., Russell, C., & Lee, J. (2007). National culture and environmental sustainability: A cross-national analysis. *Journal of Economics and Finance, 31*, 104–121.
Peng, Y. S., Dashdeleg, A. U., & Chih, H. L. (2014). National culture and firm's CSR engagement: A cross-nation study. *Journal of Marketing and Management, 5*(1), 38–49.
Pillay, S., & Dorasamy, N. (2010). Linking cultural dimensions with the nature of corruption: An institutional theory perspective. *International Journal of Cross Cultural Management, 10*, 363–378.
Pratiwi, C. S. (2020). Bridging the gap between cultural relativism and universality of human rights: Indonesia attitudes. *JILS, 5*, 449.
Pruzan, P., & Miller, W. C. (2007). Spirituality as the basis of responsible leaders and the responsible companies. In T. Maak & N. M. Pless (Eds.), *Responsible leadership* (pp. 68–92). New York: Routledge.
Puffer, S. M., Wesley, D., Dau, L. A., & Moore, E. M. (2020). Responsible global leadership in downstream and upstream supply chains: A typology of archetypes of strategic responses to CSR Pressures. In M. E. Mendenhall, M. Žilinskaitė, G. K. Stahl, & R. Clapp-Smith (Eds.), *Responsible global leadership* (pp. 80–100). New York: Routledge.
Ralston, D. A., Egri, C. P., Karam, C. M., Naoumova, I., Srinivasan, N., Casado, T., Li, Y., & Alas, R. (2015). The triple-bottom-line of corporate responsibility: Assessing the attitudes of present and future business professionals across the BRICs. *Asia Pacific Journal of Management, 32*(1), 145–179.
Reade, C., & Lee, H. J. (2020). Geopolitics, social polarization, and the bridging role of cosmopolitan leaders. In M. E. Mendenhall, M. Žilinskaitė, G. K. Stahl, & R. Clapp-Smith (Eds.), *Responsible global leadership* (pp. 29–44). New York: Routledge.
Ringov, D., & Zollo, M. (2007). The impact of national culture on corporate social performance. *Corporate Governance: The International Journal of Business in Society, 7*(4), 476–485.
Rockström, J., Steffen, W., Noone, K., Persson, Å., Chapin, F. S., Lambin, E. F., Lenton, T. M., Scheffer, M., Folke, C., Schellnhuber, H. J., Nykvist, B., de Wit, C. A., Hughes, T., van der Leeuw, S., Rodhe, H., Sorlin, S., Snyder, P. K., Costanza, R., Svedin, U., . . . & Foley, J. A. (2009). A safe operating space for humanity. *Nature, 461*(7263), 472–475.
Romani, L., & Holgersson, C. (2020). Global diversity management: When diversity and cross-cultural management meet. In B. Szkudlarek, J. Osland, D. Caprar, and L. Romani (Eds.), *The Sage handbook of contemporary cross-cultural management* (pp. 255–269). London: SAGE.
Rousseau, D. M., & Fried, Y. (2001). Location, location, location: Contextualizing organizational research. *Journal of Organizational Behavior, 22*(1), 1–13.
Roy, A., & Goll, I. (2014). Predictors of various facets of sustainability of nations: The role of cultural and economic factors. *International Business Review, 23*(5), 849–861.
Sackmann, S. A., & Phillips, M. E. (2004). Contextual influences on culture research: Shifting assumptions for new workplace realities. *International Journal of Cross Cultural Management, 4*(3), 370–390.
Schein, E. H. (2004). *Organizational culture and leadership* (3rd ed.). San Francisco: Jossey-Bass.
Scherer, A. (2015). Can hypernorms be justified? Insights from a discourse–ethical perspective. *Business Ethics Quarterly, 25*(4), 489–516.
Scherer, A. G., & Palazzo, G. (2007). Toward a political conception of corporate responsibility: business and society seen from a Habermasian perspective. *The Academy of Management Review, 32*(4), 1096–1120.
Scherer, A. G., Palazzo, G., & Seidl, D. (2013). Managing legitimacy in complex and heterogeneous environments: Sustainable development in a globalized world. *Journal of Management Studies, 50*(2), 259–284.
Schneider, S., Barsoux, J.-L., & Stahl, G. K. (2014). *Managing across cultures*. London: Prentice-Hall.
Scholl, W., & Schermuly, C. (2020). The impact of culture on corruption, gross domestic product, and human development. *Journal of Business Ethics, 162*, 171–189.
Scholtens, B., & Dam, L. (2007). Cultural values and international differences in business ethics. *Journal of Business Ethics, 75*, 273–284.
Scholz, M., de los Reyes, G., & Smith, N. C. (2019). The enduring potential of justified hypernorms. *Business Ethics Quarterly, 29*(3), 317–342.
Schwartz, S. H. (1999). A theory of cultural values and some implications for work. *Applied Psychology: An International Review, 48*, 23–48.
Scott, W. R. (2001). *Institutions and organizations* (2nd ed.). Thousand Oaks, CA: SAGE.
Scott, W. R. (2003). *Organizations: Rational, natural, and open systems*. New York: Prentice-Hall.
Seleim, A., & Bontis, N. (2009). The relationship between culture and corruption: A cross-national study. *Journal of Intellectual Capital, 10*(1), 165–184.

Semati, M. (2017). Beyond the binary of universalism and relativism. In H. Tumber & S. Waisbord (Eds.), *The Routledge companion to media and human rights* (pp. 158–168). New York: Routledge.
Shapiro, D. L., Von Glinow, M. A., & Xiao, Z. (2007). Toward polycontextually sensitive research methods. *Management and Organization Review, 3*(1), 129–152.
Shokef, E., & Erez, M. (2006). Global work culture and global identity, as a platform for a shared understanding in multicultural teams. In E. Salas (Ed.), *Research on managing groups and teams* (Vol. 9: 325–352). Amsterdam: Emerald.
Stahl, G. K., Filatotchev, I., Ireland, R. D., & Miska, C. (2023). Five decades of research on the role of context in management: From universalism toward contingent, multilevel and polycontextual perspectives. *Academy of Management Collections, 2*(1), 1–18.
Stahl, G. K., & Maznevski, M. (2021). Unraveling the effects of cultural diversity in teams: A retrospective of research on multicultural work groups and an agenda for future research. *Journal of International Business Studies, 52*(1), 4–22.
Stahl, G. K., Pless, N. M., Maak, T., & Miska, C. (2017). Responsible global leadership. In M. E. Mendenhall, J. Osland, A. Bird, G. R. Oddou, M. J. Stevens, M. L. Maznevski, & G. K. Stahl (Eds.), *Global leadership: Research, practice, and development* (3rd ed., pp. 363–388). New York: Routledge.
Stahl, G. K., & Sully de Luque, M. (2014). Antecedents of responsible leader behavior: A research synthesis, conceptual framework, and agenda for future research. *Academy of Management Perspectives, 28*(3), 235–254.
Stern, N. (2008). The economics of climate change. *The American Economic Review, 98*(2), 1–37.
Suddaby, R., Elsbach, K. D., Greenwood, R., Meyer, J. W., & Zilber, T. B. (2010). Organizations and their institutional environments—Bringing meaning, values, and culture back in: Introduction to the special research forum. *Academy of Management Journal, 53*(6), 1234–1240.
Szőcs, I., & Miska, C. (2020). Ethics in the context of cross-cultural management. In B. Szkudlarek, L. Romani, D. V. Caprar, & J. S. Osland (Eds.). *The SAGE handbook of contemporary cross-cultural management* (pp. 227–238). Thousand Oaks, CA: SAGE.
Tadmor, C. T., Galinsky, A. D., & Maddux, W. W. (2012). Getting the most out of living abroad: biculturalism and integrative complexity as key drivers of creative and professional success. *Journal of Personality and Social Psychology, 103*(3), 520.
Taras, V., Steel, P., & Kirkman, B. L. (2010). Negative practice–value correlations in the GLOBE data: Unexpected findings, questionnaire limitations and research directions. *Journal of International Business Studies, 41*(8), 1330–1338.
Tata, J., & Prasad, S. (2015). National cultural values, sustainability beliefs, and organizational initiatives. *Cross Cultural Management: An International Journal, 22*(2), 278–296.
Thanetsunthorn, N. (2015). The impact of national culture on corporate social responsibility: Evidence from cross-regional comparison. *Asian Journal of Business Ethics, 4*(1), 35–56.
Thompson, J. D. (1967). *Organizations in action: social science bases of administration theory.* New York: McGraw-Hill.
Triandis, H., & Gelfand, M. (1998). Converging measurement of horizontal and vertical individualism and collectivism. *Journal of Personality and Social Psychology, 74*(1), 118–128.
Trompenaars, F. (1993). *Riding the waves of culture: Understanding cultural diversity in business.* London: Economist Books.
Tsui, A. S., Nifadkar, S. S., & Ou, A. Y. (2007). Cross-national, cross-cultural organizational behavior research: Advances, gaps, and recommendations. *Journal of Management, 33*(3), 426–478.
Tung, R. L., & Stahl, G. K. (2018). The tortuous evolution of the role of culture in IB research: What we know, what we don't know, and where we are headed. *Journal of International Business Studies, 49*(9), 1167–1189.
Vachon, S. (2010). International operations and sustainable development: Should national culture matter? *Sustainable Development, 18*(6), 350–361.
Waldman, D. A., & Balven, R. M. (2014). Responsible leadership: Theoretical issues and research directions. *Academy of Management Perspectives, 28*(3), 224–234.
Waldman, D. A., de Luque, M. S., Washburn, N., House, R. J., Adetoun, B., Barrasa, A., Bobina, M., Bodur, M., Chen, Y. J., Debbarma, S., Dorfman, P., Dzuvichu, R. R., Evcimen, I., Fu, P., Grachev, M., Gonzalez Duarte, R., Gupta, V., Den Hartog, D. N., De Hoogh, A. H. B., . . . & Wilderom, C. P. M. (2006). Cultural and leadership predictors of corporate social responsibility values of top management: A GLOBE study of 15 countries. *Journal of International Business Studies, 37*(6), 823–837.

Waldman, D. A., & Siegel, D. (2008). Defining the socially responsible leader. *The Leadership Quarterly, 19*(1), 117–131.
Waldman, D. A., Siegel, D., & Stahl, G. K. (2020). Defining the socially responsible leader: revisiting issues in responsible leadership. *Journal of Leadership and Organizational Studies, 27*(1), 5–20.
WCED. (1987). *Our common future*. Oxford: Oxford University Press.
Wettstein, F., Santangelo, G. D, Giuliani, E., & Stahl, G. K. (2019). International business and human rights: A research agenda. *Journal of World Business, 53*(1), 54–65.
Williams, C., & Aguilera, R. V. (2008). Corporate social responsibility in a comparative perspective. In A. Crane, D. Matten, A. McWilliams, J. Moon, & D. S. Siegel (Eds.), *Oxford handbook of corporate social responsibility* (pp. 452–472). Oxford: Oxford University Press.
Winterich, K. P., & Zhang, Y. (2014). Accepting inequality deters responsibility: How power distance decreases charitable behavior. *Journal of Consumer Research, 41*(2), 274–293.
Witt, M. A., & Redding, G. (2012). The spirits of corporate social responsibility: Senior executive perceptions of the role of the firm in society in Germany, Hong Kong, Japan, South Korea and the USA. *Socio-Economic Review, 10*, 109–134.
Witt, M. A., & Stahl, G. K. (2016). Foundations of responsible leadership: Asian versus Western executive responsibility orientations toward key stakeholders. *Journal of Business Ethics, 136*(3), 623–638.

CHAPTER

28

The Research-Practice Gap in Cross-Cultural Organizational Psychology and Behavior: Practitioners' Perspectives

Lise Saari

Abstract

Today's organizational psychology practitioners need to have cross-cultural expertise to effectively carry out their work for global organizations. This requires a deep understanding of cross-cultural research and theories. However, there are research-practice gaps. This chapter describes relevant cross-cultural theories and constructs for practitioners, such as Power Distance, Harmony, and Cultural Distance. Areas in need of additional research for practitioners where there are gaps are also described. The chapter then summarizes some of the challenges faced by practitioners and the practical solutions used by practitioners to carry out their global work. The chapter closes with key takeaways, including the point that although current cross-cultural theories may not be comprehensive for all practitioners' needs, they are important as one set of information for working successfully across cultures.

Key Words: cross-cultural, global, research-practice, Power Distance, Cultural Distance

Organizations have become increasingly multinational, with expansions into new markets, global operations, cross-country mergers, and the network economy making working across the globe easier than ever. The work environment has become technologically linked across the globe. As a result, organizational psychology practitioners working within global organizations are facing cross-cultural issues as a daily part of their work. These practitioners regularly encounter cross-cultural differences and need to anticipate and overcome potential issues.

Another trend related to cross-cultural differences is that of multinational companies becoming more consistent across the globe. Specifically, these companies desire a focused company strategy and consistency for scaling and cost savings—whether it is a human resources program, an information technology system, or manufacturing operations. However, these strategy alignment and consistency efforts inevitably lead to cases where one size does not fit all, and cross-cultural issues must be understood and addressed.

So then, the cross-cultural questions that arise are where is consistency feasible and where are any adjustments needed? To answer these questions again requires deep understanding of cultural differences and the use of approaches that listen to, and balance across, cultures. Organizational psychology practitioners must therefore navigate between designing strategically aligned, scaled programs while ensuring approaches are effective and, where needed, customizing programs across cultures.

A deep understanding of cross-cultural differences is very relevant for organizational psychology practitioners. This cross-cultural understanding pertains to the full range of organizational psychology topics. For example, leadership styles may be more or less effective depending on the culture, employee survey data may need to be interpreted in light of country norms, selection questions may not operate the same way across cultures, and change initiatives may or may not work, depending on country culture.

There have been ongoing debates as to whether globalization will continue into the future. In recent years, there has been some movement toward what has been termed deglobalization or relocalization (Battista & DiLoreto, 2010); that is, use is made of local resources, particularly as they are related to sustainability efforts, rather than global supply chains. Whether this change will reverse globalization in organizations is yet to be seen, but we can reasonably assume that the world of work will continue to encompass the world.

Organizational Psychology Practitioners Working Cross Culturally

This chapter is based on a review of the cross-cultural literature, with a special emphasis on practitioner-oriented publications. In addition, I conducted interviews with approximately 30 organizational psychologists from countries within every major continent, all of whom have deep expertise and years of experience working with international companies. The interviews, conducted both formally and informally, provided additional insights for this chapter based on the real-world experiences of practitioners working cross culturally.

The interview questions included the following: Have any cross-cultural theories or concepts helped you in your work? What have you done differently in your projects due to potential or observed cross-cultural differences? What types of cross-cultural research or theoretical advancements would be helpful for practitioners involved with international work?

The interviews yielded a number of useful theories and concepts for cross-cultural work. Practitioners use many concepts and approaches to navigate across cultures. In addition, they used so-called practical solutions that were not necessarily theory-based, but rather were either shared by other practitioners or arrived at through their own trial and error.

This chapter reviews the cross-cultural theoretical concepts that are most relevant to practitioners and help in applied cross-cultural work. In addition, some practical solutions identified in the interviews and the literature are summarized. The chapter closes with recommendations for new cross-cultural research and theory; there are unanswered questions from the practitioner's perspective as well as research-practice gaps.

Major Cross-Cultural Theories and Concepts: From the Practitioner-Related Literature and Practitioner Interviews

A variety of cross-cultural readings and resources can assist organizational psychology practitioners working in global contexts, whether publications on specific theories or general writings introducing cross-cultural topics (e.g., Aycan & Gelfand, 2012; Early & Erez, 1997; Triandis, 1994a). Various publications have also addressed the practical implications of globalization for the work of organizational psychology professionals, such as Lundby and Jolton (2010) and Ronen and Shenkar (2017).

The cross-cultural research literature provides a range of theories and dimensions that potentially differ across cultures. The dimensions most often mentioned in the interviews and in practitioner publications are described here. However, the interviews and the practitioner literature revealed that there is not widespread and deep knowledge of some other useful cross-cultural concepts. These other useful concepts are also described.

Hofstede's Cross-Cultural Typology

The most predominant theory mentioned in the practitioner literature is Hofstede's cross-cultural typology, which has been the most discussed cross-cultural typology from the time it was first published. Hofstede's theory was also the most mentioned theory in the interviews conducted for this chapter. This may be due to its long history as one of the earliest cross-cultural organizational psychology theories. It could also be because some of the concepts ring true to practitioners in their global work. The theory was originally aimed at practitioners and is based on employee data.

Hofstede's theory was initially proposed in 1980 with four major dimensions of culture: Individualism–Collectivism, Power Distance, Masculinity–Femininity, and Uncertainty Avoidance (Hofstede, 2001). The foundation of his typology was based on employee survey data collected between 1967 and 1973 on IBM employees in 40 countries. Hofstede's 2001 analysis added 10 more countries and long-term orientation as another cultural dimension (Hofstede, 2001).

Hofstede's data source, items used, and methodology have been critiqued throughout the years. Even so, his theory and many of its constructs are frequently referred to in the work of organizational cross-cultural practitioners, as discussed next.

Individualism–Collectivism. The dimension of Individualism–Collectivism is one of the most often mentioned cross-cultural concepts in both scholarly literature and general publications. It has an extensive history of research, including work by Hofstede in the 1970s and it has been followed by many others (e.g., Gelfand et al., 2004; Minkov, 2007). Although the definition of this dimension continues to be debated, it is related to whether there is an emphasis on personal versus group goals. It is generally assumed that Individualism is a preference to do one's own thing and to go it alone, whereas Collectivism is described as a willingness to follow others, cooperate, and work in teams. For the practitioner, this has potential implications ranging from how teams interact to performance-based rewards and pay systems.

Individualism–Collectivism was a frequently mentioned cross-cultural concept by the interviewees. However, it was also mentioned that this dimension may not be as important as it once was. With many decades of strong emphasis on teaming in organizations (a counterbalance to Individualism) and globally consistent performance management programs (a counterbalance to Collectivism), this may be displayed less in today's work settings. Interviewees shared that they have seen more individualistic behaviors in countries labeled Collectivistic, such as an employee engaging in office politics that undermines a colleague or an employee questioning why their pay raise was not larger than what others received.

Also, according to Hofstede, as a country's wealth increases, it moves toward more Individualism, which may result in changes to many countries that have had economic growth in recent decades. Furthermore, a debate is ongoing regarding the meaning of the construct of Collectivism (e.g., Talhelm, 2019). The practitioner interviews also pointed out that the assumption that countries labeled Collectivistic team better than countries labeled Individualistic does not hold up, as they have observed plenty of instances of ineffective teaming (e.g., undermining a colleague, not providing needed feedback to a colleague) in countries labeled Collectivistic.

Power Distance. Power Distance (PD) refers to the extent to which members of a culture perceive much distance between those with power, such as managers and those with less power, such as line workers. The premise of the PD dimension is that leader–follower relationships are more authoritarian in high-PD cultures than low-PD cultures. At its extreme, it is displayed as rigid hierarchies and submissive subordinates. A subordinate challenging a decision of their supervisor would be seen as very inappropriate in a very high-PD culture.

The published literature mentions the concept of Power Distance extensively. It was also one of the most mentioned cultural dimensions in the interviews. Practitioners described PD as affecting a range of organizational psychology initiatives such as selection methods, survey feedback approaches, 360s, leadership models, and management development programs. Examples were given of managers from low-PD countries faltering when having employees from high-PD countries by expecting participation from employees and it was not forthcoming. The reverse was also described whereby high-PD managers were seen as too authoritarian by employees from low-PD countries. One interviewee described the issues PD country differences caused in a company acquisition as part of an M&A that ultimately failed; they now use power distance measures to help the organization decide which companies to acquire.

PD is especially relevant for leaders, manager development, and management of cross-cultural teams. Managers who work across national boundaries may face different behavior and reactions from subordinates, from an unwillingness to speak up (subordinates in a high-PD culture with a low-PD manger) to what a manager from a high-PD culture sees as inappropriate questioning by subordinates from a low-PD culture. For example, Latin America's high-PD cultures may result in participative management not being as successful as in low-PD cultures. As managers increase work across the globe and manage cross-cultural teams, and as teams increasingly become cross-cultural, PD is seen as having important implications for team and manager dynamics.

PD may also affect how candidates answer selection questions related to handling a leadership issue. For instance, some global organizations make a point of not having interview questions that include a supervisor as part of the selection item, as it can especially affect responses in high-PD cultures. A selection item about willingness to question a manager may not be acceptable in some cultures. However, practitioners also cautioned about only using "universal" selection items or removing all items that operate differently across cultures. For example, an item about speaking up about a safety issue may work differently across cultures, but a company may deem it to be an important enough behavior to assess, regardless of culture.

PD can also impact how to carry out a survey feedback session or to determine whether it is even appropriate to hold such a participation-based session. PD has been shown to affect how well goal setting works (Erez & Early, 1987), with assigned and participative goals being differentially effective depending on the PD of a culture (i.e., assigned goals are less effective in low-PD cultures). Therefore, PD can also have implications for motivation-related programs such as performance management.

Uncertainty Avoidance. The dimension of Uncertainty Avoidance (UA) in Hofstede's typology refers to the ways cultures respond to ambiguity and change. This dimension proposes that low-UA cultures are less open to change, which may also result in less innovation and possibly less openness to diversity. The concept of UA is particularly important to practitioners during change initiatives and mergers or acquisitions. This concept was not frequently mentioned in the interviews but was mentioned in the practitioner literature as potentially related to organizational change efforts. Some interviewees mentioned that for every major company change it seemed certain that countries consistently resisted and blocked change. They suggested that cultural factors, especially Uncertainty Avoidance, played a role.

Masculinity–Femininity (Gender Equality). The Hofstede construct of Masculinity–Femininity pertains to how much a society differentiates by gender, and it was originally conceptualized as an indicator of achievement and assertiveness ("High Masculinity"). Later descriptions of this construct focused on the amount of gender equality in a culture, where "High Femininity" equates to a culture with more gender equality (Hofstede, 2001). This more recent conceptualization aligns with other cross-cultural typologies such as GLOBE (House, Hanges, Javidan, Dorfman, & Gupta, 2004), which includes Gender Egalitarianism.

From the practitioners' perspective, interest in this dimension is mainly in terms of its impact on gender role job differentiation, discrimination, and gender equality. However, in practical terms, other indicators of gender equality can be relied on by practitioners—such as whether there are local laws prohibiting discrimination, employee survey questions that ask about fairness in the workplace, and adverse impact analyses of performance management, promotion, and other employment-related decisions. In addition, the United Nations has excellent up-to-date gender measures, by country, that are publicly available. These include regular measures of the percentages of a country's population that have 0, 1, or at least 2 gender biases (United Nations Development Programme, 2020). These other gender equality indicators are more recent and likely more valid measurements than a cross-cultural classification based on data from decades past.

Long-Term Orientation. Hofstede added Long-Term Orientation to his typology in later years in response to the Chinese Culture Connection (1987) study. This concept was not specifically mentioned much in the interviews, although it could apply to cultural differences around time or deadlines. Several interviewees mentioned that differences in time urgency, such as being concerned about and adhering to deadlines or differences in punctuality for meetings, caused significant cross-cultural conflict in their organizations. Interviewees mentioned setting up important global meetings with key participants where participants from some countries would repeatedly show up about 30 minutes after meeting start time with no explanation.

Although some of Hofstede's dimensions are widely cited by practitioners, his theory is not without its critics. Among the concerns with Hofstede's typology are the fact that it was based on only one company's employees, using data from more than 50 years ago, and its lack of consistent replication. For example, internal research at IBM conducted 25 years after his original research using the same survey items found only partial support for Hofstede's typology (Saari & Schneider, 2001). Of the four dimensions, Individualism–Collectivism and Uncertainty Avoidance found some support, but there was little support for the other dimensions. In fact, Type of Job explained more variance than country/culture, implying that a person's job can capture an individual's characteristics more than cultural values. Another study, using a different dataset and also conducted 25 years after the Hofstede classification, also did not find support for Hofstede's country classifications (Fernandez et al., 1997). However, it could be argued that the findings of these more recent studies could be due to cultural shifts that occurred, not to flaws with Hofstede's theory. Regardless, Hofstede's typology is still the most often cited and is referred to by organizational psychology publications and practitioners working in cross-cultural settings; having some typology, even if it is not perfect, is helpful when navigating across cultures.

GLOBE Leadership Dimensions

Another line of cross-cultural research that impacts the work of organizational psychology practitioners, especially in leadership areas, is the Global Leadership and Organizational Behavior Effectiveness (GLOBE) typology by House and colleagues (House et al., 2004). As with Hofstede's cross-cultural typology, the relative strengths and weaknesses of the GLOBE project have been debated in the literature (e.g., McCrae et al., 2008; Smith, 2006).

The GLOBE project was a large-scale, multiyear research project conducted in the 1990s in over 60 countries that focused on leadership dimensions and cultural constructs. The GLOBE dimensions were designed to help understand management practices in a country/culture (Bobina & Sabotinova, 2017). As such, the project identified some universal positive and negative leadership attributes that cross cultures, including being charismatic, value based, and not self-protective or autocratic. These universals have been helpful for organizational psychology practitioners in management development functions as they work to develop effective global leaders, such as including these attributes in leadership competency models.

As a result of the GLOBE research, nine dimensions of culture were also identified. The GLOBE project identified uncertainty avoidance and power distance (just like Hofstede), two types of Collectivism, Gender Egalitarianism, and Future Orientation (all somewhat like Hofstede), and additionally identified Performance Orientation, Assertiveness, and Humane Orientation. Thus, some of these dimensions overlap with the Hofstede dimensions, others were similar to or expanded dimensions, and some were added.

The GLOBE studies are especially relevant to organizational psychology leadership topics, such as the development and assessment of global leaders, leadership expatriate rotations, and training managers of global teams.

Other Cross-Cultural Theories and Concepts

The following cross-cultural concepts were also described in some of the interviews, although they were not explicitly named. Although these cross-cultural concepts may be less well known to practitioners, they could have important implications for work in global organizations.

Harmony/Face. Many interviewees described how cross-cultural misunderstandings can result from differences in how cultures handle conflict or differing points of view—or whether opposing viewpoints should even be expressed. The concepts of Harmony and Face were indirectly described in the interviews, with the observation that in many Asian cultures it is important to say or do something in a way that maintains harmony and/or does not cause someone to be embarrassed, that is, to lose Face. An example of these concepts included a global team working on a manufacturing problem and different levels of comfort around being direct about discussing what the causes of the problem could be. Another example is from the author: several survey feedback approaches were developed for a global company to accommodate this concept whereby managers could hold a formal feedback meeting with all their employees or have less formal one-on-one conversations with employees to gain more feedback.

While not specifically mentioned by name by the interviewees, the cross-cultural construct of Harmony (Leung et al., 2011) seems very relevant to cross-cultural work settings. Harmony is viewed as a response to conflict and is based on the notion that the handling of disputes is subject to cultural differences. According to this theory, certain cultures, especially in East Asia, are more likely to approach disagreements with interpersonal harmony and conflict avoidance as guiding principles. For example, studies have found that China exhibits more concern for disputes than is shown in the United States for disputes; the general perception in China is that a direct approach will harm a relationship (Friedman, Chi, & Liu, 2006).

The concept of Harmony is potentially important for teams and for how disagreements and conflicts that arise in organizations are handled, including the design of training programs to address conflict in the workplace. The cultural concepts of Harmony and Face may also relate to cultural norms around communication style. Researchers have investigated how teams in China communicate, and they have identified the communication style of Constructive Controversy (which may help maintain a sense of Harmony and save Face) as important for effective team functioning and innovation (Tjosvold & Yu, 2007).

Cultural Distance. The practitioner interviews also indicated that knowing *how* different two countries/cultures are in terms of cultural dimensions is helpful to ensure effective working relationships and prepare individuals for potential issues that may arise. This is especially important in cross-country mergers and acquisitions (M&As) where a high-failure rate is often attributed to cultural differences (Uhlenbruck, 2004). Several interviewees in consulting roles for M&As specifically mentioned advising clients regarding which M&As would likely be successful based on their culture distance scores. While no interviewees mentioned the use of a specific cultural distance measure, several said that comparing Hofstede's dimensions across countries helped them in their work. In the research literature, several methods for determining cultural distance have been described based on various computations. Kogut and Singh's (1988) cultural distance measure uses Hofstede dimensions to calculate average squared distances, whereas others have proposed variance-based measures of cultural distance (Beugelsdijk et al., 2015). This lack of agreement has led practitioners to rely on their own expertise or the well-known Hofstede dimensions.

Other cultural distance measures have been proposed in more recent years (e.g., Hendricks et al., 2018; Hutzschenreuter et al., 2016; Muthukrishna et al., 2020). Muthukrishna et al. (2020) have useful tables for practitioners that allow for easy country comparisons on Cultural Distance. However, researchers disagree over the best way to measure cultural distance. A coherent, agreed-upon measure of culture distance would be especially helpful for practitioners addressing mergers and acquisitions, joint ventures, and perhaps for creating cross-cultural project teams.

Tightness–Looseness. While not specifically mentioned in the interviews by name, the concept of cultural Tightness–Looseness (Gelfand et al., 2006) was also indirectly mentioned. This was described as countries where employee behaviors were more predictable ("Tight") versus not as predictable ("Loose"). Tightness–Looseness is the concept that some cultures have set norms that people follow (Tight), whereas other cultures have high variability around the norms (Loose). In Tight cultures (e.g., Austria, China, Germany, Japan, and Turkey) cultural norms are more dominant and are especially important. Conversely, in Loose cultures (e.g., Argentina, Israel, the Netherlands, Spain, the United States) variability in behavior is more culturally appropriate.

Tightness–Looseness may also relate to the amount of regional cultural variation *within* a nation's culture. Patterns in Individualism–Collectivism have been investigated within the United States, showing more Collectivism in the South and more Individualism in the West (Vandello & Cohen, 1999). Regional variations within countries have also been found for the construct of Tightness–Looseness (Chua et al., 2019; Harrington & Gelfand, 2014).

There have also been cross-cultural studies and contributions by other researchers not discussed in this chapter, such as by Ingelhart, Schwartz, and Trompenaars. This is partly due to space constraints and additionally due to these theories not being mentioned in the interviews or the practitioner literature to any great extent. This result could be attributed to less applicability of their concepts to practitioners or a lack of practitioners' awareness of these cross-cultural theories.

Other Practical Solutions Mentioned by Practitioners for Global Program Design and Implementation

A review of the practitioner literature (e.g., Lundy & Jolton, 2010) and the interviews also uncovered practical solutions used by practitioners to navigate working across the globe. Many of these topics are not addressed extensively in the research literature but are helpful to organizational psychology practitioners in global work settings.

Global Design and Implementation Teams. Organizational psychology practitioners working globally are well aware of the immense complexities across cultures. Therefore, practitioners often cite the importance of global teams for the design and implementation of projects to ensure acceptance and effectiveness across cultures. An example is a global team to help develop and deploy a company survey. The global team can be instrumental in survey item design, ensuring that all questions are culturally appropriate and translated correctly, as well as working with local management to answer questions and gain local support for addressing issues identified by the survey.

Working closely with global colleagues in planning and decision making invariably leads to better outcomes. Global colleagues can help ensure effective implementation by identifying potential barriers and solutions ahead of time. They can also help pilot new programs and help gain local support. Finally, should any issues arise, global colleagues are a link to company headquarters to get the issues addressed. In short, a global team has local experts who can help ensure program success. Building a network of colleagues across the globe is beneficial in many ways.

Employment-Related Laws. Differing labor laws, privacy laws, and work council regulations across the globe have direct impact on the cross-cultural work of organizational psychology professionals. Many practitioners described how local labor laws defined differences that had to be addressed to ensure program effectiveness, even more so than cross-cultural differences. For example, 360 feedback, where employees rate their manager, can be difficult to get approved by German works councils, and even employee surveys may need approval. Employee privacy laws differ across the globe, with the strictest laws in the European Union and the least strict laws in much of Asia. These laws can prohibit an employee survey in the EU that retains a confidential identifier on employees and at the same time be appropriate for other countries and even lead to problems of an HR manager inappropriately revealing who wrote a specific comment. Having a resource for up-to-date information on relevant laws and regulations is seen as important for practitioners working globally.

Equivalence of Meaning/Ratings. It cannot be assumed that translations maintain the important nuances and meaning of the original text, which can undermine the effectiveness of a global approach, whether a selection question, a management assessment, or a survey item. Practitioners have learned the importance of thorough translations, such as to always backtranslate, ideally by in-country colleagues who understand the business to ensure the original meaning. In addition, statistical techniques like factor analysis and item response theory analysis are also used by practitioners to ensure item equivalence and equivalence of measurement. A number of real-life examples can be shared in this regard, ranging from a U.S. automobile company using the same U.S. name, Nova, for a car in Mexico, where it means "doesn't go," to the English phrase "execute for the customer" initially translated into "kill for the customer."

Another caution by practitioners is the need for carefulness whenever comparing ratings across cultures. For those who conduct employee surveys internationally, it is well known that comparisons across countries can be problematic. Normative data (e.g., Mayflower Group, the IT survey group) shows country patterns that remain consistent across time and across companies. Similar issues exist with the use of assessments, for example, ratings of managers by employees on 360s tend to be uniformly high in high-Power Distance cultures; this was shown in a global company that wanted to highlight the best manager as identified with their 360 and every year it came up as a Brazilian manager (a very high-Power Distance culture). Therefore, practitioners are careful to interpret and present country data in the context of industry norms for each country, rather than simply making cross-country comparisons.

The above themes relate to some challenges and practical approaches used by practitioners to address cross-cultural differences. Some of the interviews also pointed out that their companies have defined some topics where cross-cultural differences may not be taken into account and where differences in cross-cultural values and norms may be viewed as non-negotiable. Examples include ensuring no discrimination based on gender (even in a culture that is low on Gender Egalitarianism) or requiring employees to immediately point out unsafe behaviors even in a culture where harmony and saving face are important.

Research-Practice Gaps

The practitioner literature and the interviews highlighted a number of areas showing gaps in knowledge related to cross-cultural organizational psychology and areas where more research is needed.

Can a unifying theory be developed? Currently, there is no unifying cross-cultural organizational psychology theory with agreed upon constructs. There is a "proliferation of cultural frameworks with overlapping dimensions and inconsistent measurement" (Tsui et al., 2007, p. 460). For example, Hofstede and GLOBE overlap on a few constructs, have other similar constructs, and differ on other constructs (Venaik et al., 2013). The disparities across theories leads to confusion and lack of clarity regarding what is important to focus on in cross-cultural situations. It has been proposed that the various cross-cultural theories should be combined (e.g., Beugelsdijk & Welzel, 2018), and some efforts have been made to integrate, consolidate, and make sense of the diverse results across theories (e.g., Ronen & Shenkar, 2017). Also, basic underlying assumptions, such as culture being based on values, have been called into question (Schwartz, 2014). A unifying cross-cultural theory to help guide practitioners and researchers would be beneficial.

Do earlier rankings and country lists still hold true? Several of the major cross-cultural theories and the measurements they are based on are now decades old. Hofstede's research is now over 50 years old, and not surprisingly, much has happened since these rankings were developed. For example, even Hofstede reported significant changes in Individualism–Collectivism over a relatively short 5-year period.

What cross-cultural concepts are appropriate to use at a multicountry level versus a country level? There are close to 200 countries in the world, and large global companies typically operate in around 150 countries. Because of cost and scale, modifications are often too difficult at the unit of every country. Therefore, from a practical standpoint, practitioners often have to operate at multicountry regional levels with regional representatives. Cultural clustering of countries has been carried out by various researchers (e.g., House et al., 2004; Muthukrishna et al., 2020; Ronen & Shenkar, 2017). These clusterings may be helpful, especially as practitioners try to balance global consistency with local culture. Knowing which cross-cultural concepts apply at a multicountry regional level, rather than only at a country level, would be useful for practitioners.

For which organizational approaches are cross-cultural differences most likely to be an issue? This question relates to the issue regarding which organizational programs or situations are more culture-free (if any) and which are more culture-bound, and if culture is not addressed there will be problems. Based on the interviews and the literature, culture appears to be more pronounced in areas such as performance appraisal, compensation, feedback, conflict, participation, leadership styles, and teaming dynamics. Culture may be less pronounced, or potentially problematic, with training and employee surveys Greater understanding is needed regarding how culture should be taken into account in these contexts. In addition, what approaches can be designed to be more culture-free without having a differential impact across cultures in terms of effectiveness—what constructs are universals (etic), and what constructs are culturally specific (emic)? The GLOBE project attempted to answer this question with their leadership attributes.

Can "culture-free" organizational psychology approaches be developed? Some of the interviewees expressed concern about typical competency-based selection methods that ask interviewees to speak about their own accomplishments or career programs that require asserting advancement desires. For instance, employees from highly collectivistic cultures fare more poorly in such contexts because they do not tout their individual accomplishments as much. There are likely cross-cultural impacts across the full range of organizational topics from selection to organizational change methods. Are some approaches more culture-free than others?

How can cultural awareness and responsiveness be balanced with the potential for stereotyping? There is a need to balance cross-cultural understanding and responsiveness with the potential for stereotyping. The stereotype may be considered negative and will therefore harm the person, or it may simply be wrong about an individual when assuming there are no individual differences, such as assuming everyone from the UK will be worse at teaming than everyone from Japan due to country differences in Individualism/Collectivism. In fact, Fisher and Schwartz (2011) found that value ratings vary much more *between* individuals than *between* countries. This finding indicates that country culture information should be used carefully; if we treat everyone according to a cultural stereotype, we will be wrong much of the time.

What do we know about unrepresented and underrepresented countries, including ones that are becoming increasingly important to organizations? Although the cross-cultural research is getting better with more countries examined with time, some sectors of the globe remain absent or mostly absent from cross-cultural research. Almost all African nations are missing, and many Eastern European nations and some Asian nations are missing. Research has now been conducted on some of these countries, such as a study on Bulgaria (Bobina & Sabotinova, 2017), but more research is needed. This issue also relates to the critique of cross-cultural research, and psychological research in general, being dominated by WEIRD—Western, Educated, Industrialized, Rich,

Democratic—countries and whether Western-centric cross-cultural models apply to these other cultures (Muthukrishna et al., 2020).

Are there generational, manager-nonmanager, or other group variations in the extent of cross-cultural differences? Much has been said in the popular press about the effects of global social media on tamping down culture. Does this mean younger members within an organization's global workforce will exhibit less cultural differences? Definitive scientific evidence on generational differences is lacking in general, and even more so within the context of cross-cultural differences. Several interviewees mentioned that they believe leaders in organizations (who are often required to speak the language of corporate headquarters and are more likely to travel across countries for their work) are less culturally bound than non-management employees. It was even mentioned that perhaps certain personality types, such as those high on openness, will be more adept at working cross-culturally.

What is the best cross-cultural training? Cross-cultural training has gone beyond expatriate training for a single manager to the realization that everyone needs to be prepared to work effectively across cultures. This includes training to increase intercultural competence on topics such as cross-cultural awareness (Littrell & Salas, 2005) and perspective taking (Fiske & Taylor, 1984). It also includes team training as global teams become more common. Cultural differences have potential implications for teams in areas such as communications, decision making (Kirchmeyer & Cohen, 1992), and team performance (Gelfand et al., 2007).

As if with foresight, decades ago Triandis (1994b) proposed the need for *cultural-generic* training. Even more so today, with the dynamic nature of work and the potential to interact with multiple cultures, transferable competencies may be more useful than culture-specific training. Employees need skills and competencies that generalize to a variety of different cultural settings.

Several interviewees also suggested that cross-cultural training and diversity training are conceptually similar. There have been proposals that the fields of diversity in organizations and cross-cultural work psychology should be connected and collaborating to advance theory, research, and practice (Ferdman & Sagiv, 2012; Lopez & Finkleman, 2012). Concepts such as cultural sensitivity and working with people from different backgrounds apply to both diversity training and cross-cultural training. This is another area in need of further investigation.

Can we select cross-culturally competent employees? Related to training organizational members to work effectively with each other across cultures, should future hiring include assessments that select people who are most effective at working with others cross-culturally? For example, attempts have been made to develop assessments of cross-cultural skills (e.g., Ang et al., 2007; Dolwet & Reichard, 2014). Ang and colleagues (2007) have developed questionnaires that measure constructs related to "cultural intelligence." Dolwet and Reichard (2014) propose that psychological resources such as building relationships, coping with stress, and adapting to novel situations are important for cross-cultural interactions, so these could presumably be used in selection. It also is possible that personality measures such as the Big 5 concepts of openness, agreeableness, and neuroticism may also relate to the ability to work effectively with other cultures. Erez and colleagues (Erez et al., 2013) have also described the construct of "global identity," which also relates to the concept of cross-cultural competence. This is an area that, again, seems to overlap with diversity. Presumably, someone who works well with people of all races, gender, age, religion, and ethnic backgrounds would also work well with people of all cultures. However, such assessment measures have not yet been developed for use by practitioners.

Does it make sense to use country as the unit of analysis and understanding? Country is an easily used unit for research purposes and is a common unit within organizations. However, is it the best unit of analysis for cross-cultural understanding and action? As some researchers (Taras et al., 2016) have noted, country may not be the best or the only appropriate unit of analysis; indeed, variability across employee groups can be captured in other important ways such as by job, profession, religion, race, or multicountry regions.

How does corporate culture relate to country culture? An added challenge for practitioners is that organizations themselves have cultures that may or may not be aligned with local cultures. Although it is generally assumed that corporate culture cannot erase national culture (e.g., Adler, 1997; Hofstede, 2001), practitioners pointed out that it could have impact. Therefore, measuring and understanding a company's unique *organizational* culture (e.g., highly participative with very direct communication and risk taking) and how it may align or clash (e.g., high-Power Distance, high harmony, high uncertainty avoidance) with *local* culture is also important for practitioners. In these cases, balancing across a globally aligned/integrated company culture and being responsiveness to local cultures may be needed.

Five Key Takeaways for Theory/Research

1. No one theory or typology explains the complexities of today's global organizations; continued, unifying research and theory building are needed.
2. Some of the most relied on theories and typologies are outdated and need to be based on more current research from today's global workforces.
3. Additional research-practice gaps need to be addressed, such as what organizational psychology approaches are more culture-free; when are cultural differences most likely to be an issue; what do we know about developing countries that are underrepresented in the current research; and can a valid/reliable assessment for cross-cultural competence be developed?
4. Cross-cultural researchers should work with diversity researchers as there is much overlap, and there is the potential for more research progress, stronger theory building, and application in organizations.

5. Research and theory on more contemporary, and likely more useful, topics for practitioners has not made its way into the practitioner nomenclature; broader dissemination of cross-cultural research and theory to practitioners would be helpful.

Five Key Takeaways for Practice

1. Although current cross-cultural theories may not be comprehensive for all practitioners' needs, they are one set of important information for working successfully across cultures.
2. Cross-cultural concepts that have been helpful for organizational psychology practitioners in global contexts include power distance, harmony, cultural tightness–looseness, and cultural distance.
3. Organizational psychologists working in global companies often rely on practical methods for addressing cross-cultural differences including using global design and implementation teams and ensuring equivalence of meaning for translated materials used in programs.
4. While cross-cultural theories and typologies can be useful, it is important that practitioners not assume that all individuals from a particular culture are essentially the same—or even that a cultural concept holds true for any company employee in a specific country.
5. The more informed an organizational psychology practitioner is when working globally, the better. With a solid understanding of, and appreciation for, cultural differences, practitioners can be effective in designing and implementing successful global programs (Saari & Schneider, 2001). As organizations become more global, understanding and appreciating culture and its complexities will become even more important. At the same time, it is important to have a deep understanding of human behavior, in general, and to recognize that there is individual variation within all cultures, and across all people.

Acknowledgments

A very special thanks to all the organizational psychology practitioners working in complex, global contexts for their expertise and cross-cultural insights that contributed formally and informally to this chapter. I would like to especially thank Victoria Berger-Gross, Samantha Boo, Anton Botha, Leila Regina El-Hage, Omar Imran, Mathian Osicki, Aarti Shyamsunder, and Xian Xu for their added contributions.

References

Adler, N. J. (1997). *International dimensions of organizational behavior.* Cincinnati, OH: Southwestern.

Ang, S., Van Dyne, L., Koh, C., Ng, K. Y., Templer, K. J., Tay, C., & Chandrasekar, N. A. (2007). Cultural intelligence: Its measurement and effects on cultural judgment and decision making, cultural adaptation and task performance. *Management and Organization Review, 3*(3), 335–371.

Aycan, Z., & Gelfand, M. J. (2012). Cross-cultural organizational psychology. *The Oxford handbook of organizational psychology, 2*, 1103–1160.

Battista, M., & DiLoreto, M. (2010). In K. Lundy & J. Jolton. (Eds.). *Going global: Practical applications and recommendations for HR and OD professional in the global workplace.* San Francisco: Jossey-Bass.

Beugelsdijk, S., Maseland, R., Onrust, M., Van Hoorn, A., & Slangen, A. (2015). Cultural distance in international business and management: From mean-based to variance-based measures. *The International Journal of Human Resource Management, 26*(2), 165–191.

Beugelsdijk, S., & Welzel, C. (2018). Dimensions and dynamics of national culture: Synthesizing Hofstede with Inglehart. *Journal of Cross-Cultural Psychology, 49*(10), 1469–1505.

Bobina, M., & Sabotinova, D. (2017). Bulgarian management in a cross-cultural space. *Journal of East European Management Studies, 22*(1), 105–127.

Chinese Culture Connection. (1987). Chinese values and the search for culture-free dimensions of culture. *Journal of Cross-Cultural Psychology, 18*(2), 143–164.

Chua, R., Huang, K., & Jin, M. (2019). Mapping cultural tightness and its links to innovation, urbanization, and happiness across 31 provinces in China. *Proceedings of the National Academy of Sciences of the United States of America, 116*, 6720–6725.

Dollwet, M., & Reichard, R. (2014). Assessing cross-cultural skills: Validation of a new measure of cross-cultural psychological capital. *The International Journal of Human Resource Management, 25*(12), 1669–1696.

Earley, C. P., & Erez, M. (1997). *New perspectives on international industrial/organizational psychology.* San Francisco: Jossey-Bass.

Erez, M., & Earley, P. C. (1987). Comparative analysis of goal-setting strategies across cultures. *Journal of Applied Psychology, 72*(4), 658.

Erez, M., Lisak, A., Harush, R., Glikson, E., Nouri, R., & Shokef, E. (2013). Going global: Developing management students' cultural intelligence and global identity in culturally diverse virtual teams. *Academy of Management Learning and Education, 12*(3), 330–355.

Ferdman, B. M., & Sagiv, L. (2012). Diversity in organizations and cross-cultural work psychology: What if they were more connected? *Industrial and Organizational Psychology, 5*(3), 323–345.

Fernandez, D. R., Carlson, D. S., Stepina, L. P., & Nicholson, J. D. (1997). Hofstede's country classification 25 years later, *The Journal of Social Psychology, 137*(1), 43–54.

Fischer, R., & Schwartz, S. (2011). Whence differences in value priorities? Individual, cultural, or artifactual sources. *Journal of Cross-Cultural Psychology, 42*(7), 1127–1144.

Fiske, S. T., & Taylor, S. E. (1984). *Social cognition.* New York: Random House.

Friedman, R., Chi, S. C., & Liu, L. A. (2006). An expectancy model of Chinese American differences in conflict-avoiding. *Journal of International Business Studies, 37*(1), 76–91.

Gelfand, M. J., Bhawuk, D. P., Nishii, L. H., & Bechtold, D. J. (2004). Individualism and collectivism. *Culture, Leadership, and Organizations: The GLOBE Study of 62 Societies*, 437–512.

Gelfand, M. J., Erez, M., & Aycan, Z. (2007). Cross-cultural organizational behavior. *Annual Review of Psychology, 58*, 479–514.

Gelfand, M. J., Nishii, L. H., & Raver, J. L. (2006). On the nature and importance of cultural tightness-looseness. *Journal of Applied Psychology, 91*(6), 1225.

Harrington, J. R., & Gelfand, M. J. (2014). Tightness-looseness across the 50 united states. *Proceedings of the National Academy of Sciences of the United States of America, 111*(22), 7990–7995.

Hofstede, G. (2001). *Culture's consequences: International differences in work-related values.* Thousand Oaks, CA: SAGE.

House, R. J. Hanges, P. J., Javidan, M., Dorfman, P., & Gupta, V. (2004). *Culture, leadership and organizations: The GLOBE Study of 62 societies.* Thousand Oaks, CA: SAGE.

Hutzschenreuter, T., Kleindienst, I., & Lange, S. (2016). The concept of distance in international business research: A review and research agenda. *International Journal of Management Reviews, 18*(2), 160–179.

Kirchmeyer, C., & Cohen, A. (1992). Multicultural groups: Their performance and reactions with constructive conflict. *Groups and Organization Studies, 17*(2), 153–170.

Kogut, B., & Singh, H. (1988). The effect of national culture on the choice of entry mode. *Journal of International Business Studies, 19*(3), 411–432.

Leung, K., Brew, F. P., Zhang, Z. X., & Zhang, Y. (2011). Harmony and conflict: A cross-cultural investigation in China and Australia. *Journal of Cross-Cultural Psychology, 42*(5), 795–816.

Littrell, I. N., & Salas, E. (2005). A review of cross-cultural training: Best practices, guidelines, and research needs. *Human Resource Development Review, 4*, 305–35.

Lopez, P. D. J., & Finkelman, J. M. (2012). A distinction without a difference? Why synergies between diversity and cross-cultural psychology benefit global organizations. *Industrial and Organizational Psychology, 5*(3), 349–351.

Lundy, K., & Jolton, J. (2010). *Going global: Practical applications and recommendations for HR and OD professional in the global workplace.* San Francisco: Jossey-Bass.

McCrae, R. R., Terracciano, A., Realo, A., & Allik, J. (2008). Interpreting GLOBE societal practices scales. *Journal of Cross-Cultural Psychology, 39*(6), 805–810.

Minkov, M. (2007). *What makes us different and similar: A new interpretation of the World Values Survey and other cross-cultural data.* Sofia, Bulgaria: Klasika i Stil Publishing House.

Muthukrishna, M., Bell, A.V., Henrich, J., Curtin, C. M., Gedranvich, A., McInerney, J., & Thue, B. (2020). Beyond Western, educated, industrial, rich, and democratic (WEIRD) psychology: Measuring and mapping scales of cultural and psychological distance. *Psychological Science, 31*(6), 678–701.

Ronen, S., & Shenkar, O. (2017). *Navigating global business: A cultural compass.* New York: Cambridge University Press.

Saari, L. M., & Schneider, B. (2001). *Going global: Surveys and beyond.* Workshop presented at the Society for Industrial Organizational Psychology Annual Conference, San Diego.

Schwartz, S. H. (2014). Rethinking the concept and measurement of societal culture in light of empirical findings. *Journal of Cross-Cultural Psychology, 45*(1), 5–13.

Smith, P. B. (2006). When elephants fight, the grass gets trampled: The GLOBE and Hofstede projects. *Journal of International Business Studies, 37*(6), 915–921.

Talhelm, T. (2019). Why your understanding of collectivism is probably wrong. *Association for Psychological Science, 32* (9), 23–25.

Taras, V., Steel, P., & Kirkman, B. L. (2016). Does country equate with culture? Beyond geography in the search for cultural boundaries. *Management International Review, 56*(4), 455–487.

Tjosvold, D., & Yu, Z. (2007). Group risk taking: The constructive role of controversy in China. *Group and Organization Management, 32*(6), 653–674.

Triandis, H. C. (1994a). Cross-cultural industrial and organizational psychology. In H. C. Traindis, M. D. Dunnette, and L. M. Hough (Eds.), *Handbook of industrial and organizational psychology* (Vol. 4, pp. 103–172). Palo Alto, CA: Consulting Psychologists Press.

Triandis, H. C. (1994b). *Culture and social behavior.* New York: McGraw-Hill.

Tsui, A. S., Nifadkar, S. S., & Ou, A. Y. (2007). Cross-national, cross-cultural organizational behavior research: Advances, gaps, and recommendations. *Journal of Management, 33*(3), 426–478.

Uhlenbruck, K. (2004). Developing acquired foreign subsidiaries: The experience of MNE S in transition economies. *Journal of International Business Studies, 35*(2), 109–123.

United Nations Development Programme (2020). Human Development Report 2020. The Next Frontier: Human Development and the Anthropocene. Posted December 15, 2020. https://hdr.undp.org/content/human-development-report-2020

Vandello, J. A., & Cohen, D. (1999). Patterns of Individualism and collectivism across the United States. *Journal of Personality and Social Psychology. 77*(2), 279–292.

Venaik, S., Zhu, Y., & Brewer, P. (2013). Looking into the future: Hofstede long term orientation versus GLOBE future orientation. *Cross Cultural Management: An International Journal, 20*(3), 361–385.

INDEX

For the benefit of digital users, indexed terms that span two pages (e.g., 52–53) may, on occasion, appear on only one of those pages

Tables and figures are indicated by *t* and *f* following the page number. Numbers followed by n indicate footnotes.

B

C

H

I

J

Q

R

U

V

X

Y